SOCIAL RIGHTS JURISPRUDENCE

In the space of two decades, social rights have emerged from the shadows and margins of human rights jurisprudence. The authors in this book provide a critical analysis of almost two thousand judgments and decisions from twenty-nine national and international jurisdictions. The breadth of the decisions is vast, from the prevention of forced evictions to the regulation of private medical plans to the development of state programs to address poverty and illiteracy. The jurisprudence not only implicates our understanding of economic, social, and cultural rights but also challenges the philosophical debates that question whether these rights can and should be justiciable.

Malcolm Langford is Research Fellow and Director of the Human Rights and Development Research Group at the Norwegian Centre on Human Rights at the University of Oslo. The author of many articles and books on human rights, economics, and law, he also advises a wide range of UN agencies on human rights and development issues and has drafted a number of key international standards in the field of economic, social, and cultural rights. He previously worked at the Geneva-based Centre on Housing Rights and Eviction (COHRE), where he founded an international litigation program, and he continues to act as an advisor in domestic and international litigation.

Social Rights Jurisprudence

Emerging Trends in International and Comparative Law

Edited by

MALCOLM LANGFORD

University of Oslo

CAMBRIDGE
UNIVERSITY PRESS

CAMBRIDGE UNIVERSITY PRESS
Cambridge, New York, Melbourne, Madrid, Cape Town, Singapore,
São Paulo, Delhi, Dubai, Tokyo, Mexico City

Cambridge University Press
The Edinburgh Building, Cambridge CB2 8RU, UK

Published in the United States of America by Cambridge University Press, New York

www.cambridge.org
Information on this title: www.cambridge.org/9780521860949

First published 2008

A catalogue record for this publication is available from the British Library

Library of Congress Cataloguing in Publication Data

Social rights jurisprudence : emerging trends in international and comparative law / edited by
Malcolm Langford.
    p.   cm.
Includes bibliographical references and index.
ISBN 978-0-521-86094-9 (hardback) – ISBN 978-0-521-67805-6 (pbk.)
1. Sociological jurisprudence.   I. Langford,Malcolm.   II. Title.
K370.S648   2009
340'.115 – dc22   2008012858

ISBN 978-0-521-86094-9 Hardback
ISBN 978-0-521-67805-6 Paperback

There is growing acceptance all over the world that certain core fundamental values of a universal character should penetrate and suffuse all governmental activity, including the furnishing of the basic conditions for a dignified life for all.

I believe that 21st-century jurisprudence will focus increasingly on socio-economic rights.

Justice Albie Sachs
Constitutional Court of South Africa*

* Albie Sachs, *Social and Economic Rights: Can They Be Made Justiciable?* (Southern Methodist University School of Law, 1999) p. 18.

Contents

Foreword

Philip Alston[*]

This book provides eloquent testimony to the fact that the debate about the justiciability of social rights has come of age. For many years the debate was dramatically stuck in the mire of what might be termed a name-calling phase, in which opponents contented themselves with proclaiming that social rights were simply not susceptible to judicial review and implementation. This argument was pursued with particular vigour by those who clung to the old certitudes that social rights were by their very nature 'positive' and thus not amenable to judicial consideration. In contrast, civil and political rights were said to be inherently 'negative' and were thus eminently well suited to being litigated in courts. Indeed, despite a literature which is by now extensive, and which very effectively debunks this simplistic dichotomy,[1] such arguments are still made by some participants in the international human rights debate.[2] By and large, however, the growing number of social rights cases decided by judicial and quasi-judicial institutions, the range of issues they deal with, the diversity of jurisdictions in which they have occurred, and a thriving scholarly literature have combined to make such debates largely irrelevant in practice.

After the name-calling phase, the second phase in the international debate over justiciability was largely devoted to enthusiastic discussions of the jurisprudence emerging from the South African Constitutional Court in its application of the provisions of the South African Constitution. To a significant extent that constitution reflected the approach adopted in the International Covenant on Economic, Social and Cultural Rights (ICESCR). Rarely have developments in the field of comparative constitutional law been so dominated by the jurisprudence not only of a single country but in this case of a single court. Many legal sceptics and even some of those with philosophical reservations were won over by the combination of conceptual experimentalism with nuance and caution with which the Constitutional Court approached its challenging task. But the extent to which this debate focused so heavily on the approach adopted by a single country also had its downside.

The only other country which was attracting attention was India, where the Supreme Court approached public interest litigation with a spirit of adventure. This jurisprudence, however, actually had a much less significant impact on the emergence of an international constituency favouring the development of social rights justiciability than was the case with the South African experiment. The reason was partly because of the almost serendipitous nature of the Indian Court's 'epistolary jurisdiction', which meant that a case could be launched and standing secured merely as a result of the Supreme Court agreeing to take up a case on the basis of a letter of complaint. In addition, the Indian developments were often not underpinned by clear constitutional provisions but depended rather heavily on progressive and creative interpretations of the right to life. Nor were all of the judgments as systematically grounded as was the case in South Africa. These problems are critically canvassed in detail by several of the contributions to this volume.

In the third and current phase of the justiciability debate, comparative constitutional lawyers have begun to transcend their fixation on the South African and Indian courts. In part this is because the

---

[*] John Norton Pomeroy Professor of Law, New York University School of Law.

[1] For a cross-section of such analyses see H. Shue, *Basic Rights: Subsistence, Affluence, and U.S. Foreign Policy*, 2nd ed. (Princeton: Princeton University Press, 1996); S. Holmes and C. Sunstein, *The Cost of Rights: Why Liberty Depends on Taxes* (New York: W. W. Norton, 1999); D. Beetham, 'What Future for Economic and Social Rights?', *Political Studies*, vol. 43 (1995) pp. 41–60.

[2] E.g., Aryeh Neier, 'Social and Economic Rights: A Critique', *Hum. Rts. Brief*, vol. 13, no. 2 (2006) pp. 1–3.

former court has produced too few relevant judgments to keep the debate focused upon itself. In part it is because of an increasingly critical literature drawing attention to the limitations of some of those judgments from various perspectives, including in terms of their impact on the situation on the ground and the Court's lack of success in fashioning procedural remedies designed to provide adequate follow-up. This is not to say that the Court's jurisprudence has not produced important achievements, as Liebenberg has noted in this volume. But the transition to the third phase is by no means premised on disillusionment with the South African experiment. On the contrary, the insights provided in the first few cases decided by that Court have provided the foundations upon which comparable developments have been able to take on a life of their own in other jurisdictions and triggered an interest in uncovering case law from elsewhere.

Thus, today, as this book shows par excellence, the debate has moved into a more mature and diverse phase with a wide range of national courts, particularly in Latin America, South Asia, and some Western countries, adopting positions in relation to social rights and an increasingly expansive array of international instances generating social rights 'jurisprudence'. Another of the volume's achievements is to give a sense of the way in which these two developments have complemented one another. Neither at the domestic nor the international level did the relevant developments occur in isolation or in ignorance of what was being done elsewhere. In this regard it is instructive to recall briefly the contribution of the United Nations Committee on Economic, Social and Cultural Rights in the justiciability debate.

Although the ICESCR was adopted in 1966 and entered into force in 1976, it was not until 1987 that a specialised expert committee, the ESCR Committee, was created to monitor State parties' compliance with their obligations. In the years immediately following the adoption of the Covenant, the question of a role for the courts in the implementation of social rights was raised but subsequently dropped rather rapidly. The International Conference on Human Rights, held in Teheran in 1968, called upon 'all Governments to focus their attention . . . on developing and perfecting legal procedures for prevention of violations and defence of economic, social and cultural rights'.[3] In response, the UN Secretary-General undertook a detailed 'preliminary study of issues relating to the realization of economic and social rights.'[4] In terms of national-level measures to promote respect for social rights, the study noted the desirability of both constitutional and legislative measures. But it also asserted that article 8 of the Universal Declaration (recognizing 'the right to an effective remedy by the competent national tribunals for acts violating the fundamental rights granted him by the constitution or by law') applied 'of course, also to economic, social and cultural rights'.[5] The study went on to note that many of those rights were capable of being protected at the national level 'by the ordinary courts' and that, in many respects, that was already the situation in various States.[6]

But these suggestions essentially fell victim to the emphasis upon international obligations on the part of the developing countries which promoted the social rights agenda most actively within the UN setting. Thus, the Secretary-General's report led to the commissioning of a major study prepared under the auspices of an official in the Government of the Shah of Iran, Manouchehr Ganji.[7] His very lengthy study ignored 'national norms and standards governing the realization of economic, social and cultural rights' on the grounds that such an endeavour would have 'vastly exceeded the scope and space allotted to the study'.[8] Instead, in a preview of many of the later debates over the content of the right to development, the study focused almost exclusively on the problems faced by developing countries in overcoming poverty. It did, however, note in passing that a study on the national dimensions of social rights, presumably including the role of the courts, 'should be undertaken in the future'.[9] But the matter would not be taken up again within the UN until after the creation of the Committee on Economic, Social and Cultural Rights.

---

[3] *Final Act of the International Conference on Human Rights* (United Nations publication, Sales No. E.68.SIV.2), resolution XXI, para. 6).

[4] E/CN.4/988.

[5] Ibid. para. 157.

[6] Ibid. para. 159.

[7] *The Realization of Economic, Social and Cultural Rights: Problems, Policies, Progress* (United Nations publication, Sales No. E.75.XIV.2.).

[8] Ibid. Part Six, para. 151.

[9] Ibid.

The evolution of thinking within the Committee proved to be both a barometer of, and in some cases a stimulus to, the evolution of thinking at the national level. This evolution was reflected on several different fronts during the Committee's first twelve years, a period in which I served as its Rapporteur for four years and Chairperson for eight years. During these formative years, issues of justiciability arose in three principal contexts: (i) the examination of States' parties reports, (ii) the drafting of General Comments, and (iii) the consideration of an international complaints procedure for social rights. In the first of these involving the examination of government reports, the Committee was not infrequently informed either that the Covenant enjoyed the status of the 'supreme law of the land' and thus had to be applied by the courts of the country concerned, or that whereas the judges were not necessarily obligated to apply its provisions, they were in fact well disposed to doing so. But such claims rarely survived intact following questions put by Committee members to government representatives requesting examples of actual judgments which might substantiate the claims. Although, as this book points out, social rights jurisprudence had begun to emerge in a number of the countries, not all were party to the Covenant. This did not stop the Committee from recommending that consideration be given in various countries to making at least some social rights justiciable.

The second context in which justiciability was considered was in the adoption of General Comments. In particular, two drafts which I prepared for the Committee, the first in 1990 and the second in 1998, addressed the potential role of the courts. The first was the framework-setting General Comment No. 3, which sought to spell out the nature of States parties obligations. In it, the Committee adopted a strategy which was at once bold and cautious. It was bold in the sense that there were relatively few national level precedents upon which to draw upon at the time. Another bold step was to specify a number of specific provisions which the Committee asserted 'would seem to be capable of immediate application by judicial and other organs in many national legal systems'. The rights specified were wide ranging and included those relating to equal rights of men and women (Art. 3 of the ESCR Covenant); equal pay for equal work (Art. 7(a)(i)); the right to form and join trade unions and the right to strike (Art. 8); the right of children to special protection (Art. 10(3)); the right to free, compulsory, primary education (Art. 13(2)(a)); the liberty to choose a non-public school (Art. 13(3)); the liberty to establish schools (Art. 13(4)); and the freedom for scientific research and creative activity (Art. 15(3)).

The Committee combined this bold approach with a relatively cautious analysis in which it deferred to the national legal system rather than insisting that all jurisdictions could and should move to such an approach to justiciability. It also relied upon the fact that litigation over issues of discrimination, which is widely pursued in most jurisdiction, also constitutes an important part of any strategy for the protection of social rights.

Reaction on the part of governments and other actors to this dimension of the Committee's analysis was muted. But there was another dimension of this General Comment No. 3 which was to prove much more significant in terms of facilitating advances in the debate over justiciability. The General Comment separated the key State obligations into a duty to take steps to progressively realise the Covenant rights and a 'minimum core obligation to ensure the satisfaction of, at the very least, minimum essential levels of each of the rights'. In relation to the latter, the Committee asserted that 'a State party in which any significant number of individuals is deprived of essential foodstuffs, of essential primary health care, of basic shelter and housing, or of the most basic forms of education is, *prima facie*, failing to discharge its obligations under the Covenant.' It justified this position by arguing that 'if the Covenant were to be read in such a way as not to establish such a minimum core obligation, it would be largely deprived of its *raison d'être*.' The Committee concluded by addressing the all-important resources dimension:

> In order for a State party to be able to attribute its failure to meet at least its minimum core obligations to a lack of available resources it must demonstrate that every effort has been made to use all resources that are at its disposition in an effort to satisfy, as a matter of priority, those minimum obligations.

As this volume demonstrates, some courts such as the Colombian Constitutional Court have embraced, in their own particular way, both approaches. In South Africa, only the former approach has proved decisive, although the argument concerning the minimum core proved central to the initial efforts by the South African Constitutional Court to give substance and procedural effectiveness to constitutional guarantees of social rights. This is not the place to explore the complex issue of how best to interpret and apply the minimum core concept, or whether it is likely to play a significant part in the future jurisprudence of the Constitutional Court.[10] Suffice it to say that the concept was central in the early moves by the Court, a fact that served to underscore the interplay between the national and international forums dealing with these issues. Moreover, the paradox is that a minimum core or threshold obligation has been derived by a number of other national and regional courts largely from civil and political rights, although the extent to which this truly represents an economic and social right obligation greatly varies, as the authors point out.

The Committee was more emboldened in 1998 on the subject of justiciability when it issued General Comment No. 9, declaring, 'While the general approach of each legal system needs to be taken into account, there is no Covenant right which could not, in the great majority of systems, be considered to possess at least some significant justiciable dimensions.' In this General Comment, we emphasised that cases involving financial implications were not necessarily off-limits to the courts. While acknowledging the principle of the separation of powers of the various branches of government, we pointed out that courts are already 'involved in a considerable range of matters which have important resource implications'.

The third context in which the Committee promoted the concept of justiciability was through its championing of an international procedure providing for the consideration of complaints alleging the violation of Covenant-protected social rights. In 1990, the same year that General Comment No. 3 was considered and adopted, I put forward a proposal that the Committee should undertake a preliminary study of the feasibility of such a procedure. The Committee agreed and requested me to submit a discussion note outlining the principal issues that would arise if such a procedure were established in relation to 'some or all of the rights recognized in the Covenant'.[11] In 1991, after considering my report,[12] the Committee placed on record its support for the proposal and asked for an additional analysis to be drawn up.[13] A year later, a report by Danilo Türk, then the Special Rapporteur on the realization of economic, social, and cultural rights of the UN Sub-Commission on Prevention of Discrimination and Protection of Minorities, endorsed the proposal.[14] The process of further refinement of the various analytical papers that I was asked to produce culminated in my being asked to draft a text of an Optional Protocol.[15] As revised by the Committee that text subsequently became the basis upon which a working group, first of the Commission on Human Rights and then of the Human Rights Council, put forward a final draft for consideration in 2008. As of this writing the drafting process, in its many permutations, has taken a mere 18 years.

In retrospect, one of the Committee's most important contributions consisted of simply breaking through the received wisdom of the day that an optional protocol was inappropriate in relation to social rights. That breakthrough, which came initially in 1990, helped to pave the way for a similar procedure to be adopted much more quickly in relation to the Convention on the Elimination of All Forms of Discrimination against Women.

This brief survey is designed to illustrate one of the points that emerges most clearly from this excellent collection of essays. It is that international developments, including those within the United Nations context, interacted in important ways with developments at the national level in terms of building support

---

[10] See R. Dixon, 'Creating dialogue about socioeconomic rights: Strong-form versus weak-form judicial review revisited', *Int J Constitutional Law*, vol. 5 (2007) pp. 391–418; and K. G. Young, 'The Minimum Core of Economic and Social Rights: A Concept in Search of Content,' *Yale Journal of International Law* vol. 33 (2008) pp. 113–175. Note the recent judgment in *Mazibuko and Ors v. City of Johannesburg & Ors*, High court of South Africa (Witswatersrand Local Division), unreported 30 April 2008, in which Tsoka J. argues that the Constitutional Court had only ruled it out in certain circumstances.

[11] U.N. Doc. E/1991/23, para. 285.

[12] U.N. Doc. E/C.12/1991/WP.2.

[13] U.N. Doc. E/1992/23, para. 362.

[14] U.N. Doc. E/CN.4/Sub.2/1992/16, para. 211.

[15] For a detailed review of the different phases and debates see P. Alston, 'Establishing a Right to Petition Under the Covenant on Economic, Social and Cultural Rights', *Collected Courses of the Academy of European Law*, vol 4, Book 2 (1995) pp. 107–152.

for, and understanding of the modalities of, approaches to making social rights justiciable. I should end, however, on a note of caution which Malcolm Langford also stresses in his introduction to the volume. Although the debate has come a very long way in the course of a couple of decades, it is premature to assume that social rights have come fully of age in terms of justiciability. There is still a long way to go and a great many challenges to be overcome before we can conclude that social rights enjoy a status in any way comparable to that of civil and political rights in terms of the ability and preparedness of judges to adjudicate upon them.

Preface

Economic, social, and cultural rights case law deserves its place as a body of comparative and international law. The rapidly growing jurisprudence and the often untapped knowledge of scholars, advocates, and judges triggered this attempt to provide a systematic, scholarly, and critical treatment of the emerging trends, and their implications for philosophical debates over the justiciability and legal nature of social rights. However, as a body of law, it also deserves scrutiny, both in the legitimacy of the legal methods and its underlying promise to achieve social change.

The origins of this book lie in research that first commenced at the European University Institute and was significantly deepened during my tenure at the Centre on Housing Rights and Evictions (COHRE) in Geneva. The Norwegian Centre of Human Rights at the University of Oslo provided a stimulating and supportive environment in which to bring this book to completion. I am grateful to the Lionel Murphy Foundation, the Government of Netherlands, and the Government of Norway, who, respectively, provided background support during each of these stages.

The authors for this volume were selected on the basis of their familiarity with relevant jurisdictions. I am particularly thankful to them for their painstaking expositions and those who peeled back new layers of unknown case law and examined to what extent it had affected poverty and discrimination. Their patience during the long process in bringing this book to fruition is much appreciated.

I am indebted to Professors Sandra Liebenberg and Philip Alston, who assisted in the early design of the book. Matthew Craven, Asbjørn Eide, Andreas Føllesdal, Wojciech Sadurski, Wouter Vandenhole, Sandra Liebenberg, Thorsten Kiefer, Jeff King, Aoife Nolan, Danie Brand, Padraic Kenna, Carolina Fairstein, and Morten Kinander kindly independently reviewed various chapters, and I am grateful to those reviewers who commented on chapters at the request of authors.

The book would not have been possible without the committed and thoughtful editorial and technical assistance of Thorsten Kiefer, Tara Smith, Khulekani Moyo, and Tiffany Henderson, and I am thankful to the Human Rights and Development Research Group at the University of Oslo for facilitating this support. Rob Zimmermann also provided valuable assistance in editing a number of chapters.

John Berger at Cambridge University Press has been patient beyond measure, encouraged the project from its inception, and helped it expand beyond its humble beginnings. Mary Cadette at Aptara, Inc., has graciously steered the unwieldy volume through the strictures of the production process. My wife, Eirinn Larsen, has also made many incisive and thoughtful suggestions throughout the book's journey.

Social rights jurisprudence would not exist without the efforts of individuals and communities who embarked on litigation as a means to address their exclusion and poverty. Behind them are often organisations, movements, and lawyers who donate much of their time. Sometimes their names are reflected in the public record; sometimes they remain invisible. Sometimes they achieve concrete justice; sometimes they don't. Sometimes they deserve justice; perhaps sometimes they don't. For scholars who ply their trade in analysing the fruits of their efforts, this fundamental contribution is acknowledged.

The cut-off date for jurisprudence in this book is March 2007, unless otherwise noted by an author.

M.L.
Oslo, 4 June 2008

PART ONE

Overview

The Justiciability of Social Rights: From Practice to Theory

Malcolm Langford[*]

1. INTRODUCTION

In the space of two decades, social rights[1] have emerged from the shadows and margins of human rights discourse and jurisprudence to claim an increasingly central place. In a significant number of jurisdictions, adjudicatory bodies have intervened to protect a wide range of social rights from intrusion and inaction by the State, and increasingly by non-State actors. The breadth of the decisions is vast. Courts have ordered the reconnection of water supplies, the halting of forced evictions, the provision of medical treatments, the reinstatement of social security benefits, the enrolment of poor children and minorities in schools, and the development and improvement of State programmes to address homelessness, endemic diseases and starvation. These are just a few examples of the almost two thousand judicial and quasi-judicial decisions from twenty-nine national and international jurisdictions which are described and critically analysed in this book.[2]

What is novel is not the adjudication of social interests. Domestic legislation in many countries provides a measure of judicially enforceable labour and social rights.[3] What is significant is that the more durable human rights dimensions of these social values or interests, whether captured in constitutions or international law, are being adjudicated. This is not to downplay the role of legislation from either a principled or pragmatic perspective. It is often more precise and contextualised and has the direct authoritative and democratic imprimatur of the legislature. But legislative rights are not always sufficient to protect human rights, and they are subject to amendment by a simple majority of the population.

The result is that we are now in a position to trace a pattern of judgments and decisions on social rights across the world. While social rights jurisprudence[4] is nascent, it cuts across common and civil law systems, developed and developing countries and regional groupings. The decisions

---

[*] Research Fellow, Norwegian Centre on Human Rights, University of Oslo. He would like to thank Andreas Føllesdal, Jeff A. King and Thorsten Kiefer for comments on this chapter.

[1] The term 'social rights' is principally used in this book since the overall focus is on human rights such as social security, health, education, housing, water and food. In some Chapters, authors analyse economic (i.e., labour rights) as well as cultural rights. Terminology also varies between the authors, where phrases such as socio-economic rights, social welfare rights or economic, social and cultural rights are sometimes preferred, particularly where this is the prevalent or relevant usage in the jurisdiction.

[2] The book is certainly not the first to deal with the area but is perhaps the most comprehensive. See also F. Coomans and F. van Hoof (eds.), *The Right to Complain about Economic, Social and Cultural Rights: Proceedings of the Expert Meeting on the Adoption of an Optional Protocol to the International Covenant on Economic, Social and Cultural Rights*, (25–28 January 1995, Utrecht, SIM Special No. 18, Utrecht); F. Coomans (ed.), *Justiciability of Economic and Social Rights: Experiences from Domestic Systems* (Antwerpen: Intersentia and Maastrict Centre for Human Rights, 2006); and R. Gargarella, P. Domingo and T. Roux (eds.); *Courts and Social Transformation in New Democracies: An Institutional Voice for the Poor?* (Aldershot/Burlington: Ashgate, 2006). The incomplete nature of scholarship is perhaps most marked in N. Jayawickrama, *The Judicial Application of Human Rights Law: National, Regional and International Jurisprudence* (Cambridge University Press, 2002). While purporting to cover all human rights, a mere fraction of the publication is devoted to economic, social and cultural rights and major cases are absent from the discussion.

[3] Jeff King in his chapter on United Kingdom analyzes in some detail the case law emanating from legislative rights noting both strengths and weaknesses.

[4] For the purposes of this book, the phrase 'social rights jurisprudence' means jurisprudence that draws on human rights in international treaties or constitutions for the protection of social rights. In some cases, adjudication bodies have invoked civil or political rights but a social right also covers the interest protected.

have been made under the umbrella of both express social rights as well as 'traditional' civil and political rights. As an example of the latter, the European Court of Human Rights has determined that the civil right to respect for family life obliges governments to guarantee protection from industrial pollution,[5] prohibitively expensive divorce proceedings[6] and, in certain instances, homelessness.[7] Even a veteran civil and political right, the prohibition on cruel and degrading treatment, was read by the UN Committee Against Torture to proscribe the demolition of housing[8] and by a US court to prohibit arrest of homeless men for sleeping in public places.[9]

This burgeoning case law provides an opportunity for determining the progress (and quality) of the jurisprudence and the potential for future development and application of the law. The case law also has consequences for the long-standing philosophical debates over economic, social and cultural rights. It is arguable that one debate has been resolved, namely whether economic, social and cultural rights can be denied the status of human rights on the basis that they are not judicially enforceable[10] – there is now too much evidence to the contrary. Equally importantly, they provide some answer to the critique that adjudicatory bodies lack the democratic legitimacy and institutional capacity to enforce such rights. As we shall see, the cases indicate that a significant number of adjudicatory bodies have been able to craft legal principles and develop legal tools that navigate the contours of philosophical concerns, such as pronouncing on the allocation of budgetary resources or making direct 'policy'.

The focus in this book is on a large but not exhaustive bundle of social rights, particularly social security, housing, health care, education, food and water – whether generally or as relevant to women or a particular excluded group. However, the number of cases on right to food and water is comparatively less, which is partly explainable by the fact that food-related cases tend to be litigated under social security, land and labour rights while the right to water is comparatively new in recognition. A significant number of authors also address labour rights although fewer discuss cultural rights. Many of the chapters address emerging issues such as direct human rights obligations of private actors and access to legal aid for social rights as well as the influence of international law on the jurisprudence. The impact of the case law on poverty and discrimination and the challenges in using litigation as a tool to address social rights violations are also taken up.

The principal criterion for the selection of the jurisdictions was that a reasonably mature jurisprudence must exist. In some of the sixteen national jurisdictions, the judgments were not predominantly 'progressive' – apex courts in United States, France and Ireland have frequently been hostile to social rights. Obviously, more jurisdictions could have been added, particularly from Europe (e.g., Poland, Russia and Germany) and South-East Asia (the Philippines and Indonesia), but it was particularly difficult to include African jurisdictions beyond South Africa using the criteria for selection. Scattered decisions can be found on housing, land, education, health and labour rights in different African countries,[11] but a mature jurisprudence is some time away as the appropriate conditions for successful and sustained social

---

[5] *López Ostra v. Spain* (1995) 20 EHHR 277.

[6] *Airey v. Ireland* (1979) 2 EHRR 305.

[7] *Botta v. Italy* (1998) 26 EHRR 241.

[8] See UN Committee Against Torture, *Hijirizi et al v. Yugoslavia*, Communication No.161 (2000) and the following cases of the European Court of Human Rights: *Mentes and Others v. Turkey*, 58/1996/677/867 and *Selcuk and Asker v. Turkey*, 12/1997/796/998-999. The Court had earlier stated that the prohibition on torture, inhuman or degrading treatment or punishment included 'the infliction of mental suffering by creating a state of anguish and stress by means other than bodily assault': see *Ireland v. United Kingdom*, Report of 5 November 1969, Yearbook XII.

[9] *Pottinger & Ors v. City of Miami*, 810 F. Supp. 1551 (1992) (United States District Court for the Southern District of Florida).

[10] See generally on economic, social and cultural rights: P. Alston and G. Quinn, 'The Nature and Scope of State Parties' Obligations under the International Covenant on Economic, Social and Cultural Rights', *Human Rights Quarterly*, Vol. 9 (1987), pp. 156–229; M. Craven, *The International Covenant on Economic, Social and Cultural Rights: A Perspective on its Development* (Oxford: Oxford University Press, 1995); M. Sepúlveda, *The Nature of the Obligations under the International Covenant on Economic, Social and Cultural Rights* (Antwerpen: Intersentia, 2002); and A. Eide, C. Krause and A. Rosas (eds.), *Economic, Social and Cultural Rights: A Textbook* (The Hague, Martinus Nijhoff, 1995).

[11] See for example, International Commission of Jurists, Kenyan and Swedish Sections, *Human Rights Litigation and the Domestication of Human Rights Standards in Sub Saharan Africa*, Vol. 1 (Nairobi: AHRAJ Case Book

rights litigation (discussed in the next Section) are only beginning to emerge in a number of African countries.

Adopting the same criteria, thirteen regional and international mechanisms were included which covers ten human rights courts and committees as well as the European Court of Justice, International Labour Organisation and World Bank Panel. The analysis covers individual and collective complaints as well as softer, but often influential jurisprudence, such as general comments and concluding observations on periodic State reports.[12] This jurisdictional analysis is complemented by specific chapters on cross-cutting topics, namely remedies, the right to legal aid in social rights litigation and multinational corporations.

This opening essay is devoted to four questions which seek to investigate the practice from historical, legal, philosophical and sociological perspectives. How do we explain the rapid and sudden increase in 'social rights jurisprudence'? What are the trends in the jurisprudence and are common judicial approaches emerging across jurisdictions? What are the consequences of the case law for the more philosophical debate on the justiciability of social rights and to what extent has it settled the debate or opened up new lines of inquiry? Lastly, do these cases indicate that litigation has the potential to concretely ensure the achievement of social rights? After addressing these questions in Sections 2–5, the Chapter concludes by drawing together the common themes and briefly analyses some of the opportunities and challenges in social rights litigation.

2. THE EVOLUTION OF THE SOCIAL RIGHTS ADJUDICATION

The rapid trajectory of social rights jurisprudence is surprising given its scattered antecedents for most of the twentieth Century. Such instances include the International Labour Organisation (ILO)'s Committee of Experts, established in 1927 to review the implementation of the initial labour conventions by member States.[13] This was followed in 1951 by the creation of a more judicial-like mechanism, the Committee on Freedom of Association which was empowered to address breaches of ILO conventions concerning freedom of association and the right to organise and bargain collectively. Fenwick notes in this book that the Committee has been remarkable for its workload, with over 2300 cases to date, and the development of considerable jurisprudence, including in the area of the right to strike.[14] Since the 1970s, greater use has also been made by worker's organisations of the constitutional complaint procedure where a State has failed to observe one of the many ILO conventions.

Early international cases on discrimination also spoke to the social arena. The founding document of the League of Nations included minority rights and, in 1935, its Permanent Court of International Justice brushed aside Albania's claim that the closure of Greek-speaking schools was consistent with the right to equality for minorities. According to the Court, equality must not only exist in law but in fact, and it went on to articulate the essentialist role of education for minorities declaring that 'there may be no true equality between a majority and a minority if the latter were deprived of its institutions (schools in our case) and were consequently compelled to renounce what constitutes the very essence of it being a minority'.[15]

In the United States, the US Supreme Court struck down separate schooling for African Americans as 'inherently unequal' in the well-known case

---

Series, 2007); O. Odindo, 'Litigation and Housing Rights in Kenya', in J. Squires, M. Langford, and B. Thiele (eds.), *Road to a Remedy: Current Issues in Litigation of Economic, Social and Cultural Rights* (Sydney, Australian Human Rights Centre and University of NSW Press, 2005), pp. 155–166; J. Mubangizi, 'The Constitutional Protection of Socio-Economic Rights in Selected African Countries: A Comparative Evaluation', *African Journal of Legal Studies*, Vol. 2, No. 1 (2006), pp. 1–19.

[12] Indeed, a significant amount of jurisprudence has emanated from bodies which do not possess full judicial status (that is, the authority to make and enforce binding judgments) but are cloaked with various other attributes of legal adjudication, for example the right to hear individual complaints, entertain evidence and make decisions by applying law to fact. This is particularly true at the international level.

[13] At that time, this covered hours of work in industry, unemployment, maternity protection, night work for women, minimum age and night work for young persons in industry. See *ILO History*, available at <http://www.ilo.org/public/english/about/history.htm>.

[14] See Chapter 28, Sections 2.3 and 3.1.

[15] *Minority Schools in Albania*, PCIJ Reports 1935, Series A/B, No. 64.

of *Brown v. Board of Education.*[16] In seeking to move beyond earlier and formalistic constructions of the constitutional right to equal protection of the law (the doctrine of 'separate but equal')[17], the Warren Court similarly recognised the fundamental value of education in contemporary America, finding that any racial bias in the manner of its delivery would frustrate the attainment of optimal educational outcomes.[18] The 1960s subsequently witnessed a growing movement to enforce social rights through the constitutional bill of rights. In this volume, Albisa and Schultz describe the nascent pro-poor jurisprudence of the US Supreme Court, which held that indigent defendants were constitutionally entitled to free legal representation on their first appeal,[19] a California law was unconstitutional for requiring new residents from other states to wait six months before receiving welfare benefits,[20] and 'property' interests covered under the US Constitution's due process clause included welfare payments.[21] However, these progressive developments were abruptly halted in 1972 by a re-constituted Court under President Nixon. The Court ruled that the Government had no obligation to provide minimum sustenance and that the right to housing, at least of a certain quality, was not protected by the Constitution, although it did order the improvement of prison conditions.[22]

Efforts were slightly more successful elsewhere. In 1972, the German Federal Constitutional Court held that the right to free choice of occupation obliged universities to demonstrate they had effectively deployed all available resources to maximise the number of places available.[23] From 1978, the Indian Supreme Court, and some state courts, went further and embarked on a process of deriving a broad range of social rights from the right to life in light of the directive principles in the Con-

stitution.[24] This stance was justified on the basis that the right to life was the 'most precious human right' and 'must therefore be interpreted in a broad and expansive spirit so as to invest it with significance and vitality which may... enhance the dignity of the individual and the worth of the human person'.[25] In its first clear social rights case in 1980, the Indian Supreme Court ordered a municipality to fulfil its statutory duties to provide water, sanitation and drainage systems.[26] The Court also relaxed rules of standing and remedies in order to facilitate both the filing of petitions and flexible remedial orders. However, Muralidhar argues in this volume that the practice of Indian courts is not as consistent or progressive as is frequently imagined. Courtis also illustrates also that labour, and to a lesser extent, social security rights have a long history of constitutional litigation in Argentina, although most early cases drew on statute law or arose in intra-federal constitutional disputes.[27]

At the regional level, the European Commission on Human Rights initially declined to offer expansive interpretations of civil rights. In 1972, it stated that it 'is true that Article 8(1) provides that the state shall respect an individual's home and not interfere with this right. However, the Commission considers that Article 8 in no way imposes on a State a positive obligation to provide a home'.[28] Five years later, the European Court of Human Rights cautiously opened the door to a different approach in its seminal case of *Airey v. Ireland* saying, 'the mere fact that an interpretation of the Convention may extend into the sphere of social and economic rights should not be a decisive factor against such an interpretation; there is no water-tight division separating that sphere from the field covered by the Convention'.[29] The Court has subsequently applied the Convention in the field of social rights but has been rather cautious about doing so as Clements and Simmons point out in Chapter 20. Since 1965, States parties to the European Social

---

[16] *Brown v. Board of Education*, 347 U.S. 483 (1954).

[17] Separate schools were justified as long as both sets of schools had substantially equal facilities: *Plessy v. Ferguson*, 163 U.S. 537 (1896).

[18] Racial segregation of schools generated a 'feeling of inferiority' depriving 'children of the minority group of equal educational opportunities': *Brown v. Board of Education*, 347 U.S. 483 (1954) at 493–494.

[19] *Douglas v. California*, 372 U.S. 353, 357–58 (1963).

[20] *Shapiro v. Thompson*, 394 U.S. 618 (1969).

[21] *Goldberg v. Kelly*, 397 U.S. 254, 264 (1970).

[22] See respectively *Lindsey v. Normet* 405 U.S. 56, 74 (1972); *Estelle v. Gamble*, 429 U.S. 97 (1976).

[23] *Numerus Clausus I Case* (1972), 33 BverfGE 303.

[24] *Sunil Batra v. Delhi Administration case*, 1978 SC 1675.

[25] See *Bandhua Mukti Morcha v. Union of India*, AIR 1984 SC 802. This included rights to 'adequate nutrition, clothing and shelter and facilities for reading, writing and expressing oneself in diverse forms, freely moving about, mixing and co-mingling with fellow human beings'.

[26] *Municipal Council Ratlam v. Vardhichand and ors*, AIR 1980 SC 1622.

[27] See Courtis, Chapter 8, Sections 4.1 and 4.2.

[28] Case 4560/70. See also Case 5727/72.

[29] *Airey v. Ireland* (1979) 2 EHRR 305.

Charter have also been required to present periodic reports on performance.[30] In their Chapter, Khalfan and Churchill draw out the development of the rich content of jurisprudence that has developed from this procedure.

From the late 1980s, the volume of social rights jurisprudence has mushroomed. This activity is particularly discernible in the countries that witnessed democratic revolutions at this time (Latin America, Eastern Europe and South Africa) as well as countries that became directly influenced by the Indian experience, particularly other South Asian countries. A number of Western countries – Canada, United Kingdom and Hungary – have witnessed a stream of somewhat mixed jurisprudence, though for different reasons. Inter-American, African, European and UN human rights treaty committees and even the International Court of Justice have now adjudicated cases concerning social rights.[31]

Pointing out the trajectory of the jurisprudence is one thing, explaining its rise is quite another. On one hand, it is undeniable that the space for the judicialisation of social rights has been significantly enlarged. The post-World War II human rights architecture gave short shrift to the enforcement of social rights. The Universal Declaration of Human Rights (UDHR) contained an almost exhaustive catalogue of human rights[32] but indi-

vidual complaints could only be made concerning violations of the rights in the International Covenant on Civil and Political Rights.[33] Its sister treaty, the International Covenant on Economic, Social and Cultural Rights (ICESCR) remains deprived of such a mechanism,[34] although the Human Rights Council is close to addressing this historical imbalance.[35]

This same division between the two sets of human rights was mirrored in Western European constitutions, a number of Latin American constitutions and many post-colonial constitutions in Africa and Asia. If included, social rights were often relegated to directive principles. Similarly, at the European level, the committee overseeing the European Social Charter lacked the judicial powers of the European Court of Human Rights. In many countries though, human rights litigation was largely impossible because of colonial or one-party rule, although it was successful in some instances in publicly highlighting injustices.[36]

---

just and favourable conditions of work; form and join trade unions; rest and leisure; adequate standard of living for health; education; and participation in cultural life (Articles 3–27).

[33] An individual complaints procedure under the First Optional Protocol to the International Covenant on Civil and Political Rights, 999 U.N.T.S. 302, *entered into force* March 23, 1976, was opened for signature on the same day as the substantive treaty.

[34] It should be noted that the so-called '1503 procedure' was set up by the UN Human Rights Commission in 1970 to hear complaints about massive violations of all rights in the Universal Declaration of Human Rights. However, the procedure is confidential and it is therefore difficult to assess the claims that have been determined in relation to social rights.

[35] See discussion in Chapter 23, Section 6. Craven, amongst others, partly attributes the differences in the treaties to apprehensions by some States around the justiciability of social rights. It was the 'primary justification both for allowing States to implement the [ESC] rights in a progressive manner and for having a reporting [as opposed to a petitions] system as the means of supervision' under the ICESCR: see Craven, *The International Covenant on Economic, Social and Cultural Rights* (n. 10 above), p.136. However, it is important not to oversimplify the causes behind the lack of a complaints mechanism for the ICESCR. Socialist states, namely China and USSR, were hostile to any form of international supervision for human rights and even blocked attempts by Italy and USA to create an expert committee to oversee the ICESCR.

[36] For example, residents of the province of Bougainville in the Australian colony of Papua New Guinea challenged, in Australian courts, the colonial government's decision to proceed with copper mining and disregard the property and land claims of indigenous landowners. The case was unsuccessful but drew some attention to the plight of

---

[30] See *European Social Charter: Collected Texts* (Council of Europe Publishing, 200, 2nd Edition) at chapter IX.

[31] In the *Legal Consequences of the Construction of a Wall in the Israeli Occupied Territories* (2004) ICJ Reports 136, the majority of the International Court of Justice opined on various activities of Israel that were said to impede and restrict the rights of Palestinian persons under the International Covenant on Economic, Social and Cultural Rights, concluding that construction of the fence and its associated regime 'impede the exercise by the persons concerned of the right to work, to health, to education and to an adequate standard of living as proclaimed in the International Covenant on Economic, Social and Cultural Rights and in the United Nations Convention on the Rights of the Child'. (p. 192.) However, the lingering misunderstandings of social rights can be witnessed in the separate concurring opinion of Rosalyn Higgins (p. 213).

[32] The UDHR includes the following rights: life; freedom from slavery; freedom from torture; recognition before the law; non-discrimination; right to an effective remedy; freedom from arbitrary arrest or exile; fair trial; presumption of innocence in criminal trials; freedom of movement and residence; asylum; a nationality; marriage; own property; freedom of conscience and religion; freedom of opinion; peaceful assembly and association; take part in government and vote; social security; work;

To some extent, this division reflected the schismatic understanding of human rights amongst scholars at the time. Human rights were frequently allocated between the two categories of negative and positive liberties as set out in the philosopher Isaiah Berlin's lecture of 1958.[37] As Sy Rubin put it, '[W]hen one discusses civil and political rights, one is generally talking about *restraints* on governmental action, not *prescriptions* for such action ... [It] is easier to tell governments that they shall not throw persons in jail without a fair trial than they shall guarantee even a minimal but sufficient standard of living'.[38] The 1960s were also partly characterised by the economic doctrines of Keynesianism in the West and centralised socialism in the East that assumed that benign policy intervention would cure a range of social ills.

However, the post-Cold War wave of democratisation and constitutionalisation took a different direction and led to the cataloguing of many justiciable economic, social and cultural rights in many constitutions.[39] In some jurisdictions, the right to bring *collective* actions (for example, with a public interest organisation acting as claimant) clearly assisted the initial development of the jurisprudence (for example, in South Africa, Argentina and Venezuela) while in Brazil, Piovesan notes that a strategic decision was made in HIV/AIDS litigation not to use this option.[40] Some of the landmark decisions include the *Grootboom* decision in South Africa, where the Court ruled that the gov-

ernment's housing policy breached the constitutional obligation to progressively realise the right to housing due to inattention to emergency relief; the *Campodónico de Beviacqua* case[41] where the Argentine Supreme Court ordered the State to continue provision of medication to a child with a disability in accordance with the right to health; and the *Eldridge* decision in Canada where the right to equality was interpreted to include the right of deaf patients to receive interpretive assistance in a province's health care facilities.[42]

Simultaneously, the number of avenues for social rights litigation at the regional and international level expanded with the newly established Inter-American Court on Human Rights (1987) and the African Commission on Human and Peoples' Rights (1987) while the European Committee on Social Rights was able to entertain collective complaints from 1999. The UN Committee on Elimination of Racial Discrimination addressed racial discrimination in the workplace in its 1988 decision *A. YlimazDogman v The Netherlands*,[43] while in 1987 the Human Rights Committee struck down social security legislation that discriminated on the basis of sex and marital status.[44] In 1987, the UN Committee on Economic, Social and Cultural Rights ('CESCR Committee') was established to monitor and guide the interpretation of ICESCR, and this gave significant impetus to efforts to move forward a coherent legal vision of economic, social and cultural rights[45] – an increasing number of judgments refer to its general comments.

This is not to overstate the case. A comparative and international patchwork of laws and legal remedies for economic, social and cultural rights remains. But the more corpulent space for social rights has allowed claimants and adjudicators to overcome one of the key hurdles raised by opponents of the justiciability of social rights. In 1975, for example, Vierdag argued that social rights were

---

the customary landowners: see M. Langford, *Bougainville and the Right to Self-Determination* (Unpublished Bachelor of Laws Thesis, University of New South Wales, 1995).

[37] I. Berlin, *Two Concepts of Liberty: Inaugural Lecture as Chichele Professor of Social and Political Theory* (Oxford: Clarendon Press, 1958).

[38] S. Rubin, *Economic and Social Rights and the New International Economic Order*, Address Before the American Society of International Law (on file with the American University International Law and Policy) quoted in H. Schwarz, 'Do Economic and Social Rights Belong in a Constitution?' *American University Journal of International Law and Policy*, Vol. 10, Summer (1995) pp. 1233–1244, at 1233 (emphasis in original).

[39] To take just a few examples of countries who inserted a full range, see the constitutions of Brazil (1988), articles 6 and 193–232, Bulgaria 1991, Burkina Faso (1991) articles 47–55; Congo (1992), articles 30–55; Colombia (1991), articles 42–82; Estonia (1992), articles 28–39, 32, 37–9, Hungary (as amended) articles 70/B-70/K; Macedonia (1991), articles 30–49; Poland (1992), articles 67–81; South Africa (1994), articles 23–31; Turkey (1987), articles 41–64. For a full list, see Jayawickrama, (n. 2 above), p. 117.

[40] See Chapter 0, Section 5.

[41] *Campodónico de Beviacqua, Ana Carina v. Ministerio de Salud y Banco de Drogas Neoplásicas*, Supreme Court of Argentina, 24 October 2000.

[42] *Eldridge v. British Columbia (Attorney General)* [1997] 3 S.C.R.

[43] Communication No. 1/1984

[44] *Zwaan-de Vries v. the Netherlands*, Communication No. 182/1984, (9 April 1987).

[45] See P. Alston, 'The Committee on Economic, Social and Cultural Rights' in P. Alston (ed.), *The United Nations and Human Rights* (Oxford: Oxford University Press, 1992), pp. 473–508.

not imbued with legal content because they were not inherently justiciable on the basis that 'implementation of these provisions [in the ICESCR] is a political matter, not a matter of law' since a Court must engage in prioritisation of resources by 'putting a person either in or out of a job, a house or school'.[46] The South African Constitutional Court, amongst others for instance, dismissed this traditional, and somewhat circular, notion stating that 'Socio-economic rights are expressly included in the Bill of Rights' and the 'question is therefore not whether socio-economic rights are justiciable under our Constitution, but how to enforce them in a given case'.[47] This reasoning directly accords with the counter-arguments of many scholars who had argued that suppositions over the justiciability of a particular right are irrelevant for determining its legal authority. Van Hoof argued in his response to Vierdag that if a social right is included in a legal instrument, whether treaty law or constitution, it is by definition legally binding and potentially capable of enforcement.[48]

On the other hand, this explanation for the evolution of social rights adjudication is not entirely satisfactory. How do we understand the large differences in judicial outcomes in countries with almost identical constitutional and justiciable protections of social rights? What explains the insipid judgments of many Eastern European judiciaries with the vanguard judgments of South Africa and Latin America? Why have some courts greatly extended the reach of civil and political rights to protect social interests, such as in India and the Inter-American human rights system, while others have displayed more caution, such as in Canada, or been quite hostile at

times, such as in Ireland and the US Supreme Court.[49]

Therefore, the prominence and authority of social rights in any legal jurisdiction must be tied to an intricate interplay of factors.[50] We can point to at least four. The first concerns the level and nature of social organisation. A clear driver of the litigation has been human rights advocates, social movements and lawyers but their potency, focus and willingness to use litigation strategies varies from jurisdiction to jurisdiction. The last decade has witnessed the rise of a broad but distinctive movement for economic, social and cultural rights which has not only sought to use courts but been active in sharing information on comparative experiences.[51] This movement has augmented the traditional trade union movement, which has been more focused on labour rights. In the case of Latin America, Couso argues that these new social rights movements are the result of the

---

[46] E.W. Vierdag, 'The legal nature of the rights granted by the international Covenant on Economic, Social and Cultural Rights', *Netherlands Yearbook of International Law*, Vol. IX (1978), pp. 69–105, at 103.

[47] *Government of the Republic of South Africa v. Grootboom and Others* 2000 (11) BCLR 1169 (CC).

[48] "While it cannot be denied that the international law-making process is extremely cumbersome and that it's outcome is often characterized by uncertainties, it is at the same time generally accepted that treaties, because of their formalized nature, constitute the most unambiguous and reliable source of international law." G.J.H. van Hoof, 'The Legal Nature of Economic, Social and Cultural Rights: a Rebuttal of Some Traditional Views', in P. Alston and K. Tomasevski (eds.), *The Right to Food* (The Hague, Martinnus Nijhoff, 1984), pp. 97–100, at 99.

[49] A number of US States have incorporated social rights within their constitutions leading to some significant judicial interventions. See Albisa and Schultz, Chapter 12, in this volume.

[50] Similarly, Alston concludes that the creation of the United Nations human rights regime in the post-World War II period was largely driven by political pragmatism and not principle: '[I]ts expansion has depended upon the effective exploitation of the opportunities which have arisen in any given situation from the prevailing mix of public pressures, the cohesiveness or disarray of the key geopolitical blocks, the power and number of the offending states and the international standing of their governments, and a variety of other, often rather specific and ephemeral, factors'. P. Alston, 'Critical Appraisal of the UN Human Rights Regime, in P. Alston (ed.) *The United Nations and Human Rights: A Critical Appraisal* (Oxford: Clarendon Press, 1992), pp. 1–21, at p. 2. The causal complexity is also manifest in the inter-war period. The birth of the International Labour Organisation (ILO) in the aftermath of the first World War is largely attributable to the founding States' fear of the successes of Bolshevism and socialism. A response that sought to address the aspirations and struggles of workers was therefore necessary. But the ostensible idealism of the States was partially nipped in the bud when the ILO began to denounce their own labour practices. See Virginia Leary, 'Lessons from the Experience of the International Labour Organisation' in Alston, *The United Nations and Human Rights*, ibid. pp. 580–619.

[51] For instance, advocates that had laboured in Canada with social rights claims under equality rights norms, participated in the debate over including socio-economic rights in the South African constitution and the formulation of the arguments in the key *Grootboom* case (n. 47 above), a case which is well known among many Latin American organisations despite the barriers of language and legal system.

political left accepting the 'stark reality of failed socialist states' and moving towards more reformist rights-based models, which saw law as a vehicle for social change.[52] This explanation carries some weight, but leftist critique of litigation continues (see Section 5 below). Moreover, a movement from the other direction is equally discernible. Mainstream human rights organisations have increasingly embraced social rights and quite a number of the leading cases were in fact brought by organisations that had traditionally focused on civil and political rights.[53]

The second is the degree of the political achievement of social rights. Judicial receptivity to social rights claims is usually conditioned by clear evidence of State or private failure. Inhumane suffering in the face of the State unwillingness to fulfil its own legislation and policy has sparked much of the groundbreaking jurisprudence from South Africa to the United States to India to Colombia. As Gauri and Brinks note, 'courts remain pro-majoritarian actors. Their actions narrow the gap between widely shared social belief and incomplete or inchoate policy preferences on the part of government, or between the behaviour of private firms and expressed political commitments'.[54]

The third is the judicial culture itself and the degree of judicialisation of human rights. The establishment of a culture of litigation for human rights within a jurisdiction makes the induction of 'newer' rights much easier. Social rights jurisprudence is almost always significant in those jurisdictions that have developed robust judicial or quasi-judicial review for civil and political rights. This creates both the underlying conditions for social rights litigation (in terms of effective court processes, freedom of expression, relative enforcement of remedies), and the acceptability of human rights legal reasoning. It is no great leap to go from assessing the proportionality of restrictions on the rights of dissidents or media proprietors to free speech to evaluating forcible evictions or denial of access by non-nationals to social security schemes. Some courts have increasingly spelt out the positive obligations surrounding civil and political rights, providing them with a new terminology that helps them overcome traditional classifications of human rights, which squirrel away civil and political rights as 'negative rights' and ESC rights as 'positive rights'. As will be discussed in Section 3, the degree of judicial openness to comparative and international law is also positively correlated with more progressive decisions.

Beyond law, social/legal movements, and judicial practice, there is perhaps a deeper keel that aids or obstructs attempts to introduce social rights within human rights practice. It is the way in which human rights are understood, valued and embedded within a particular society, a factor we might describe as culture. The permeation of human rights ideals into a particular context is closely associated with societal repulsion at, or experience of, particular manifestations of human indignity.[55] It is perhaps no different for adjudicatory bodies. The graphic presentation of forced evictions to the UN Committee on Economic, Social and Cultural Rights in 1991 helped pave the way for more vigorous concluding observations by the Committee.[56] The growing number of court orders concerning lack of state provision of HIV/AIDS medicines[57] is partly attributable to the 'shock value' that these bodies experience when confronted with clear

---

[52] See R. Gargarella, P. Domingo and T. Roux (eds.), *Courts and Social Transformation in New Democracies: An Institutional Voice for the Poor?* (Aldershot: Ashgate, 2006), p. 255.

[53] For example, cases taken by CELS in Argentina: see interview with Victor Abramovich in M. Langford, *Litigating Economic, Social and Cultural Rights: Achievements, Challenges and Strategies* (Geneva: Centre on Housing Rights & Evictions, 2003), pp. 60–65. In some cases, this movement has been bottom-up with demands from victims while in other cases it has been propelled by calls for human rights organisations to apply the indivisibility of human rights in practice.

[54] V. Gauri and D. Brinks. (ed.). *Courting Social Justice: Judicial Enforcement of Social and Economic Rights in the Developing World* (New York: Cambridge University Press, 2008)

[55] The horrors and deprivations of the Second World War helped propel the drafting of the Universal Declaration of Human Rights; agitation by urban labour, social and liberal movements in nineteenth Century ignited a measure of public and official recognition of social rights; the European revolutions of 1848 included demands for bills of rights, that included social rights, but this was only successful in one German state, although a number of countries later included social rights in their constitutions in the early twentieth Century; and the injustices of colonialism led to the rapid drafting of the International Convention on the Elimination of All Forms of Racial Discrimination.

[56] See interview with Scott Leckie in Langford, *Litigating Economic, Social and Cultural Rights* (n. 53 above) at p.157.

[57] See, for example, *TAC v. Ministers of Health*, 2002 (10) BCLR 1033 (CC).

evidence of governmental complicity or appalling apathy. This is not to say that such a practice is principled: many worthy cases go unnoticed for years. It is rather a sociological phenomenon demonstrating the manner in which human rights violations capture official attention. Indeed, social rights advocates advise initially presenting cases that show serious violations of social rights and are not significantly dissimilar with traditional civil and political rights cases.[58]

This understanding of culture works in the other direction too. Some cultures, including judicial culture, may be more resistant to social rights claims. Cass Sunstein sets out this argument in the case of the United States, noting the supposed value base of the United States, which strongly favours individual enterprise over government intervention, and a concern that increased social rights would mostly benefit racial minorities.[59] This cultural bias has perhaps effectively inhibited what he calls 'socialist movements' (essentially European social democratic movements) taking forward claims, ensuring passage of more progressive legislation and recognition of constitutional social rights. But Sunstein ultimately pours cold water on the thesis since it assumes cultures are 'static or homogeneous'.[60] He points to the radical changes in cultural mores on gender, race and homosexuality concluding that there is nothing in America that irrevocably inhibits a 'second bill of rights' containing social rights.

The adaptability of cultures to new values and rights is certainly undeniable but culture plays perhaps a different role than Sunstein suggests. A comparative review of jurisprudence indicates the crucial role of history, in particular the national and international mythologies surrounding the adoption of constitutional documents at a particular point in time. Although Sunstein later distinguishes between the US and South African Constitutions on the basis that the latter was clearly transformative (p. 216–17). Advocates seeking to advance the recognition and enforcement of social rights seem to fare better in countries whose con-

stitutional and democratic revolutions were partly aimed at overcoming social injustice (e.g. Latin America, South Africa and India) as opposed to those revolutions that were more focused on civil and political freedoms (e.g. United States and Eastern Europe). The current attempt at constitutional reform in United Kingdom may be a pertinent example of the latter. The current focus is not on asking what human rights need to be recognised today but what has been recognised in the twelfth century Magna Carta, seventeenth century English Bill of Rights and some timid advances in common law. The result at the time of writing is the meagre proposal that 'no person shall be *denied* the right to education'[61] and that 'no person shall be *denied* the right to a minimum standard of healthcare and subsistence *as set out in statutory provisions* to be enacted from time to time' (emphasis added).[62] In other instances, economic, social and cultural rights were made justiciable almost accidentally (constitutions were copied from other jurisdictions[63]) or international treaties were incorporated in the constitutional order with no public pressure.[64]

3. ASSESSING THE JURISPRUDENCE

As there is no one reason for explaining the rise of social rights jurisprudence, it is neither possible to develop any grand or universal theory from the existing jurisprudence. Indeed, it is questionable whether one should. Mark Tushnet cautions on the use of comparative law to universalise on the ideal legal doctrine lest it lead to excessive abstraction:[65]

> [C]onstitutional law is deeply embedded in the institutional, doctrinal, social and cultural

---

[58] See particular interview with Geoff Budlender in Langford, *Litigating Economic, Social and Cultural Rights* (n. 53 above), pp. 96–99.

[59] C. Sunstein, *The Second Bill of Rights: FDR's Unfinished Revolution and Why We Need It More Than Ever* (New York, Basic Books, 2004), pp. 127–138.

[60] Ibid. p. 137.

[61] The State is also to respect in education systems the 'religious and philosophical convictions' of parents.

[62] See The Smith Institute, *The constitution of the UK as of 1 January 2007*, printed in C. Bryant (ed.), *Towards a new constitutional settlement* (London: Smith Institute, 2007), appendix.

[63] Jayawickrama, *The Judicial Application of Human Rights Law* (n. 2 above).

[64] J. Levit, 'The Constitutionalisation of Human Rights in Argentina: Problem or Promise?', *Colombia Journal of Transnational Law*, Vol. 37.

[65] See M. Tushnet, *Weak Courts, Strong Rights: Judicial Review and Social Welfare Rights in Comparative Constitutional Law* (Princeton: Princeton University Press, 2007), p. 9.

contexts of each nation, and...we are likely
to go wrong if we try to think about any specific doctrine or institution without appreci-
ating the way it is tightly linked to all the contexts within which it exists.[66]

Some social rights advocates themselves have cau-
tioned against a general attempt to 'search for universal, transcendental components' of economic,
social and cultural rights.[67] According to Porter,
the legitimate 'quest for ahistorical universals and
absolutes' does not automatically require creating
a universalist *legal* framework'.[68] In his view, the
development of social rights jurisprudence should
follow the 'grounded' path of civil and political
rights, which he argues have been 'adjudicated in
historical contexts and must incorporate understanding of the subjective component of the dignity related interests'.[69]

These cautionary perspectives conform with our
attempt above to explain differences between
jurisprudence in similar-situated jurisdictions.
Different historical and cultural conditions play a
significant role. But a comparative and international analysis of the jurisprudence can still be
useful. From a positivist standpoint, it is important to understand the current trends in adjudication of social rights, to identify the common
and divergent threads, the manner of legal reasoning, and the extent to which international and
comparative law is shaping or not shaping the
developments. Taking a more normative standpoint, it is arguable that opening up the domestic window to comparative experience allows one,
whether judge or advocate, government or scholar,
to better reflect on whether the prevailing views
in a particular jurisdiction may be appropriate.
In this field, such transnational perspective and
normative reflection is sorely needed. Entrenched
assumptions about the nature of economic, social
and cultural rights have often prevailed despite
contrary comparative evidence. Indeed, cross-
jurisdictional learning has been one of the key
drivers of successful social rights litigation. Scott
and Alston have also called for greater transna-

tional 'judicial dialogue' that would lead towards
clearer consensus, particularly the interpretation
of international human rights.[70]

Of course, the extent to which judges and others can, and wish to, draw on comparative and
international jurisprudence greatly varies. The
South African Constitutional Court and Colombian Courts exhibit a fair degree of comparative
curiosity;[71] the Philippine Constitutional Court
looks primarily to the US Supreme Court; while the
European Court of Human Rights was in uproar
over the citation of *Brown v Board of Education*
from the very same US Supreme Court.[72] International law and jurisprudence is equally relevant and some jurisdictions have taken seriously
both international human rights law and jurisprudence particularly Argentina, South Africa, Nepal,
Bangladesh, Colombia and the Inter-American
and African human rights systems.

For ease of convenience, the analysis of the cases
in this Section is divided according to the taxonomy of obligations developed by the UN Committee on Economic, Social and Cultural Rights[73]
namely the obligations to *respect*, *protect* and
fulfil human rights as well as obligations stemming from equality rights. Discussion of the direct
social rights obligations of private actors will also
be made in the sub-section dealing with obligation to protect. A final sub-section then briefly

---

[66] Ibid. p. 10.
[67] B. Porter, 'The Crisis of ESC Rights and Strategies for
Addressing It', in Squires, Langford, and Thiele, *Road to
a Remedy* (n. 11 above), pp. 48–55, at 48.
[68] Ibid.
[69] Ibid. p. 50.

[70] C. Scott and P. Alston, 'Adjudicating Constitutional Priorities in a Transnational Context: A Comment on *Soobramoney*'s Legacy and *Grootboom*'s Promise', *South African
Journal on Human Rights*, Vol. 16 (2000), pp. 206–268. See
also A. M. Slaughter, 'A Typology of Transjudicial Communication', *University of Richmond Law Review*, Vol. 29, No.
1 (1994–5), pp. 99–137.
[71] Perhaps the most notable example is the Constitutional
Court of South Africa's citing of precedents from 109 different countries in a case on the death penalty: see *The
State v. Makwanyane* 1995 (3) SALR 391 (CC).
[72] Personal communication from Andi Dobrushi concerning the hearing of *D.H. and Others v. the Czech Republic*
by the Grand Chamber of the European Court of Human
Rights.
[73] See Committee on Economic, Social and Cultural Rights,
General Comment No. 12, Right to adequate food (Twentieth session, 1999), U.N. Doc. E/C.12/1999/5 (1999), para.
15. It was endorsed by the African Commission on Human
and Peoples' Rights in *SERAC v. Nigeria*, Communication
No. 155/96, Ref ACHPR/COMM/A044/1 (27 May 2002),
paras. 44–47 and also included in the South African Constitution.

examines conflicts between human rights in the socio-economic arena.

This is not to endorse this particular taxonomy as the authoritative understanding of obligations. In Chapter 23, King and myself critically ask whether this categorical approach appropriately captures the concrete nature of State duties in practice and does it really take us that much further than the traditional divide of negative and positive obligations? Indeed, like Ida Koch,[74] I suspect that our internationalist and comparative understanding of State obligations will continually develop as cased-based jurisprudence develops, which may open up new types of categories or common principles. The cases in this book demonstrate that different jurisdictions provide some signs of the way ahead. But for present purposes, this taxonomy provides a useful way of arranging the discussion but comments are made on how the jurisprudence is pointing towards more concrete principles.

There is insufficient space, however, to examine the consequences of the jurisprudence upon our understanding of the 'normative content' of each particular social right. However, many of the authors divide their review according to the different rights or bundles of rights and some efforts have been made elsewhere to commence that process of reflection.[75] It is instructive to note that adjudicatory bodies vary in the way they approach the content of the right. In some instances, they develop, quite explicitly, different tests for different social rights. In Colombia, the test on positive obligations for immediate access to social benefits is slightly stricter than it is for HIV/AIDS medicines.[76] Other courts have so far declined to pronounce on the normative content of the rights (e.g. South Africa) while others have been willing to go into some detail. The Supreme Court of Kentucky in *Rose v Council for Better Education* is an example of the latter, specifying that the duty to provide an efficient system of education means

providing each and every child with at least the seven particular capacities.[77]

The Committee on Economic, Social and Cultural Rights has attempted to develop some form of template for understanding the normative content of the rights but wide variances remain between their General Comments on different rights. Such unevenness is arguably a good thing since each right does vary in conception and possible forms of implementation. However, it is clear from the Committee that each right carries bundles of claims relating to:

- *accessibility* (e.g., in the case of housing, accessibility includes security of tenure, physical accessibility, affordability and appropriate location, or, in the case of social security, coverage, fair eligibility requirements etc),
- *availability* of either the subject of the right (e.g., food, education) or the requisite facilities or systems (e.g. hospitals or social security system); and
- some level of *adequacy, quality or cultural appropriateness* whether it be the safety of the water, the level of social benefits or the cultural dimensions of education.

Cases discussed in this book can obviously be placed in many of these categories. However, more

---

[74] I.E. Koch, 'Dichotomies, Trichotomies or Waves of Duties?', *Human Rights Law Review*, Vol. 5, (2005), pp. 81–103.

[75] See, for example, M. Langford and A. Nolan, *Litigating Economic, Social and Cultural Rights: Legal Practitioners Dossier* (Geneva: COHRE, 2006) and B. Toebes, 'The Right to Health as a Human Right in International Law' (Amsterdam: Hart/Intersentia, 1999).

[76] See discussion in Section 4.3 below.

[77] Those include:

(1) sufficient oral and written communication skills to enable students to function in a complex and rapidly changing civilization;

(2) sufficient knowledge of economic, social and political systems to enable the student to make informed choices;

(3) sufficient understanding of governmental processes to enable the student to understand the issues that affect his or her community, state and nation;

(4) sufficient self-knowledge and knowledge of his or her mental and physical wellness;

(5) sufficient grounding in the arts to enable each student to appreciate his or her cultural and historical heritage;

(6) sufficient training or preparation for advancing training in either academic or vocational fields so as to enable each child to choose and pursue life work intelligently; and

(7) sufficient levels of academic or vocational skills to enable public school students to compete favourably with their counterparts in surrounding states, in academics and the job market.

790 S.W.2d 186 (Ky. 1989), at 212–13. See discussion by Albisa and Schultz in Chapter 12, Section 4.1.

cases can be found in the first category which is possibly because existing legislation tends to focus more on the latter issues, particularly the element of quality. A significant number of cases also cross these categories. For example, in *Viceconte*, the claim was for *access* to a medicine to treat a peculiar Argentina disease that required the Government to make *available* the drug by constructing the production facilities but the process was partly delayed on account of testing the drug to ensure *quality*. It might therefore be said that large-scale or systematic violations simultaneously raise many elements of the right since they require a significant State response to gross inaction or action. Nonetheless, while the Committee's jurisprudence was partly developed in response to case law (e.g. General Comment Nos. 4 and 19), it may be useful to test their developing understanding of the rights against the jurisprudence.

3.1 Obligations to Respect

The obligation to respect in the three-fold taxonomy generally refers to State duty to abstain from interference with human rights. (Although, in the case of European Court of Human Rights the obligation to respect is interpreted much more broadly to include positive obligations). Since the 1980s, many commentators have been anxious to point out that the realisation of economic, social and cultural rights, like many aspects of civil and political rights, requires not only action but restraint by the Government.[78] Such violations by States are frequently the subject of reports by non-governmental organisations and some predict that they will from the majority of cases under the proposed complaints procedure for the International Covenant on Economic, Social and Cultural Rights.

The authors in this volume detail a significant number of such cases that could be ascribed to this category. In Argentina, Courtis describes a long arc of constitutional jurisprudence on labour rights, such as unfair dismissal, the right to strike and worker's compensation. For example, in the landmark *Aquino* case in 2004, the Supreme Court struck down a 1995 law which severely circumscribed worker's compensation on the basis that it would violate a wide range of international standards, including the International Covenant on Economic, Social and Cultural Rights.[79] Watson notes how the European Court of Justice has imbued the rather civil right to free movement of persons within the European Union with socio-economic character, striking down restrictions on access to social goods and services of non-nationals from EU member states, particularly in the area of education.[80] Byrne and Hossain describe how the Supreme Court of Bangladesh has gradually developed jurisprudence on evictions beginning with slum dwellers and more recently sex workers finding that '[T]he forcible taking away of sex workers and putting them into the ... vagrant home ... have been done without any lawful authority in derogation of their right to life or livelihood and contrary to the dignity or worth of the human person'.[81]

What is noticeable across these cases is the slow convergence of criteria that adjudicatory bodies apply in determining if an interference with a social right (or interest) by the State amounts to a human rights violation. Let us take the case of forced evictions. The criteria were explicitly set out in General Comment No. 7 on Forced Evictions by the UN Committee on Economic, Social and Cultural Rights, and can be summarised as follows:

- Any interference with a person's home requires both substantive justification, regardless of the legality of the occupation.
- Due process must be observed, which the committee described as including consultation on alternatives to eviction, adequate notice, information and access to legal remedies (including legal aid)

---

[78] See generally A. Eide, 'The Right to an Adequate Standard of Living Including the Right to Food' in A. Eide, C. Krause, A. Rosas (eds.), *Economic, Social and Cultural Rights: A Textbook* (Martinus Nijhoff, 1995), pp. 89–105 and P. Alston, 'International Law and the Human Right to Food' in P. Alston and K. Tomaševski (eds.), *The Right to Food* (The Hague, Martinus Nijhoff, 1984), pp. 9–68.

[79] *Aquino, Isacio v. Cargo Servicios Industriales S. A. s/accidentes ley 9688*, 21 September 2004. See discussion in Chapter 8, Section 4.1.
[80] See, for example, *Chen* Case C-200/02 [2004] ECR I-9925 and *Baumbast* Case C-413/99 (2002) ECJ – 17 Sep 2002.
[81] *Bangladesh Society for the Enforcement of Human Rights and Ors v. Government of Bangladesh and Ors* 53 DLR 1 later affirmed by the Appellate Division.

- At a minimum no one is rendered homeless, adequate compensation is paid for losses and that adequate and alternative accommodation is provided within the maximum available resources of the State.
- There must be no discrimination on prohibited grounds in the substantive and procedural aspects of the eviction process.

Some adjudicatory bodies have explicitly adopted or referred to this general comment, including the African Commission on Human and People's Rights[82] and courts in Argentina[83] as well as the political bodies of the Council of Europe.[84] Others have taken similar approaches. The South African Constitutional Court and the European Committee on Social Rights have found that evictions will contravene the right to housing if there is lack of justification and an absence of adequate alternatives.[85] The European Court of Human Rights in *Connors v United Kingdom* ruled that the eviction of a Gypsy family from a local authority site violated the civil right to respect of home, family and privacy on the basis that it 'was not attended by the requisite procedural safeguards, namely the requirement to establish proper justification for the serious interference with [the complainants] rights and consequently cannot be regarded as justified by a "pressing social need" or proportionate to the legitimate aim being pursued'.[86] Com-

pensation of 14,000 euros was awarded for emotional distress.[87] The Human Rights Committee almost echoes the CESCR Committee in its concluding observations on Kenya concerning the civil right to respect for the home: 'The State party should develop transparent policies and procedures for dealing with evictions and ensure that evictions from settlements do not occur unless those affected have been consulted and appropriate resettlement arrangements have been made'.[88]

But a certain unevenness in these eviction cases remains. In India, Muralidhar describes the failure of the Supreme Court to order or properly supervise mass resettlement schemes in eviction of pavement or other informal dwellers, for example in the well-known *Olga Tellis* case and more recent decisions. Clements and Simmons criticise the stance of the European Court of Human Rights for its refusal to protect Gypsies from the application of certain planning standards to the location of caravans on land they had purchased. One might posture that the reason for this unevenness is that both courts lack an explicit mandate to protect social rights and must initially invoke civil and political rights. But in Venezuela where the right to adequate housing is also enshrined in the constitution, Gonzalez notes that there is no consistency on the principle of alternative resettlement. This suggests that an element of chance is involved or that it can take time to build up precedents or judicial consensus in the area. In South Africa, the cases indicate the advantage of having explicit constitutional mention of the issues and specific legislation. After quoting provision of the constitution that prohibits evictions without a court order, the South African Constitutional Court goes on to say that 'a court should be reluctant to grant an eviction against relatively settled occupiers unless it is satisfied that a reasonable alternative is available, even if only as an interim measure pending ultimate access to housing in the formal housing programme'.[89]

---

[82] See Chirwa, Chapter 17 in this volume, Section 4.5

[83] Buenos Aires Supreme Court, *Comisión Municipal de la Vivienda v. Saavedra, Felisa Alicia y otros s/Desalojo s/Recurso de Inconstitucionalidad Concedido*, 7 October 2002. See Courtis, Chapter 8, Section 4.4.

[84] See Recommendation Rec(2004)14 of the Committee of Ministers to member states on the movement and encampment of Travellers in Europe (Adopted by the Committee of Ministers on 1 December 2004, at the 907th meeting of the Ministers' Deputies) and Recommendation Rec(2005)4 of the Committee of Ministers to member states on improving the housing conditions of Roma and Travellers in Europe (Adopted by the Committee of Ministers on 23 February 2005 at the 916th meeting of the Ministers' Deputies).

[85] See Liebenberg (Chapter 4) on *Port Elizabeth Municipality v. Various Occupiers* 2004 (12) BCLR 1268 (CC) and Khaliq and Churchill (Chapter 21) on Complaint No. 15/2003, *European Roma Rights Center v. Greece*. In the latter case, the legislation was also criticised by the adjudicatory body.

[86] *Connors v. United Kingdom*, (European Court of Human Rights, Application no. 66746/01, 27 May 2004), para. 95. See discussion of case in Clements and Simmons, Chapter 20, Section 4.1

[87] The Court has also been somewhat consistently concerned with the existence and quality of alternative accommodation in the case of eviction. See *Marzari v. Italy* (1999) 28 EHRR CD 175 where the Court attached particular importance to the local authority's efforts in this regard.

[88] *Concluding Observations of the Human Rights Committee: Kenya*, 28 March 2005, CCPR/CO/83/KEN.

[89] *Port Elizabeth Municipality* (n. 85 above), para. 28.

We should, however, disentangle what we mean by interference of the State. This concept has developed in the context of philosophical theory but its application in modern and developing welfare states requires deeper thought. State 'action' can be grouped into four categories:

- Interference with *self-organising efforts* or *key resources* of individuals or associations, for example, restrictions on trade unions, eviction of customary or informal occupiers, closure of private or religious schools or health care services or pollution of natural resources.
- Denial of access by an *individual* to an *existing government programme or employment opportunity*, whether on the general grounds of arbitrariness or unreasonableness or on prohibited grounds of discrimination. For example, in *Goldberg v Kelly*, the US Supreme Court found that the denial of a welfare benefit to an individual violated the right to due process.[90] In Colombia, the Court granted protection in the case of a poor elderly man who had not received a State subsidy because he had acquired erroneous information from the relevant administrative entity on the procedures necessary to obtain the subsidy.[91]
- The removal of *legislative protections* that require the Government to respect social rights. In *Dunmore v Ontario*, agricultural workers in Canada successfully challenged the repeal of legislation that contained certain guarantees for freedom of association.[92]
- The removal of a *government programme* that enables individuals or groups to realise their social rights. In Portugal, government decisions to remove the National Health Service and increase the qualifying age of a minimum income benefit were found to be retrogressive steps violating the right to health and social security respectively.[93] With regard to Slovakia,

Prouvez describes the decision in *L. R. et al v. Slovakia*,[94] where the UN Committee on the Elimination of Racial Discrimination found that a council resolution annulling an earlier resolution providing for low-cost housing for Roma constituted racial discrimination.

This continuum of State interference has been differently understood by scholars and adjudicatory bodies, and there is an inconsistency on this even within the CESCR Committee's practice. The latter two categories are often not theoretically included within the obligation to respect and instead placed under deliberate retrogressive measures violating the more positive duties of protect and fulfil, since it ostensibly involves the weakening of *former* and *collective* action. But conceptually separating the violations in practice is obviously more difficult.

On one hand, trying to separate them is partly justified as the resource implications of the latter are possibly more profound. The Committee explicitly qualifies the prohibition on deliberately retrogressive measures: any such measure must be 'fully justified by reference to the totality of the rights provided for in the Covenant and in the context of the full use of the maximum available resources'.[95] This concern over restricting a Government's ability to reconfigure and reduce the levels of social rights protections, particularly in the context of an economic crisis, has meant that the number of cases on this topic is not overly significant. Some Courts, for example the Hungarian Constitutional Court, relied on civil and political rights in justifying their striking down cuts to social security and other government benefits.[96]

On the other hand, there is a growing convergence in how adjudicatory bodies will adjudicate all forms of State action that interfere with the enjoyment of social rights. In the case of retrogressive measures, the Committee's language is beginning to mirror its requirements on forced evictions. It has become concerned with not only justification for such steps, but due process in terms of participation, the absence of non-discrimination, ensuring that the minimum essential levels of the rights are not reduced and that the measure is temporal

---

[90] 397 U.S. 254, 264 (1970).

[91] T-149/02. The Court ordered the relevant authority to re-examine the case and to provide the man with assistance throughout the proceeding.

[92] *Dunmore v. Ontario (Attorney General)*, [2001] 3 SCR 1016.

[93] See Portuguese Constitutional Tribunal (Tribunal Constitucional), Decision (Acórdão) N°39/84, April 11, 1984 And Portuguese Constitutional Tribunal, Decision (Acórdão) N° 509/2002, December 19, 2002 quoted in International Commission of Jurists, *Global Report on Justiciability of Economic, Social and Cultural Rights* (Forthcoming).

[94] Communication No. 31/2003, *L.R. v. Slovakia.*

[95] *General Comment 3, The nature of State parties obligations* (Art. 2, para.1 of the Covenant) (1991).

[96] For a critique of the courts failure to use social rights and international jurisprudence, see Chapter 13.

as far as possible.[97] From a human rights perspective, such convergence is important. The decision to evict 7000 individuals, remove planning permissions or reduce rental subsidies can have precisely the same impact in practice on the right to housing. Indeed, Matthew Craven raises the concern that the division of economic, social and cultural rights into obligations to respect and fulfil results in favouring the victims of the former over the latter and notes that the South African jurisprudence has veered in this direction with stronger rights to housing for victims of forced eviction than homeless persons.[98] This does not necessarily imply that the protections against forced evictions should be weakened, and we have already noted the patchiness in protection. Rather, such guarantees against forced eviction provide a strong disincentive for the State to create further homelessness and one might need to revisit the judicial review of positive obligations such as fulfilment.

3.2 Obligation to Protect and Horizontal Obligations of Private Actors

The genesis of the contemporary movement for economic, social and cultural rights is partly rooted in the concern over the enhanced role of private actors in social rights violations. The concerns have ranged from the commodification of what were formerly public goods and services, to pollution and interference with access to natural resources to the actions by international institutions such as the World Bank and IMF. Translating these concerns into a human rights and legal framework differs according to the issue but there is a noticeable increase in the number of cases that can be categorised either under the State *obligation to protect* individuals and communities from violations of their social rights *or* the direct *horizontal obligation* of such actors to, at a minimum, respect the social rights of others.

OBLIGATION TO PROTECT

The UN Committee on Economic, Social and Cultural Rights conceptualises the obligation to protect as 'measures by the State to ensure that enterprises or individuals do not deprive individuals of their access' to the relevant right.[99] The Inter-American Court of Human Rights has adopted wording which is more influenced by civil and political rights, but arguably more precise. In her chapter on the Court, Melish notes that they speak of pro-active State duties to prevent, sanction, investigate, repair violations by both government and private actors as well as fulfil human rights.[100]

There is a significant number of cases in this volume where governments have been faulted for inaction or lack of due diligence in effectively regulating the behaviour of private actors. The African Commission found that Nigeria had failed to ensure that the Shell oil company in the Delta region refrained from polluting natural resources, such as water, air and land that were used to realise various social rights.[101] Latin American courts have strongly monitored the arbitrary or discriminatory denial of access to social benefits or health care.[102] The UN Human Rights Committee has closely reviewed logging and mining activity in Sami land (with respect to the Sami's cultural rights as a minority under the ICCPR)[103] while the Inter-American Commission found Belize had violated the rights of Maya people by granting logging and mining concessions without their consent and any consultation process (under their rights to equality and property).[104] Restrictions on labour rights such as unfair dismissal from private workplaces and restrictions on collective action

[97] See for example, *An evaluation of the obligation to take steps to the 'maximum of available resources' under an Optional Protocol*, Statement, UN Doc. E/C.12/2007/1 (2007) and *General Comment 20: The Right to Social Security (Article 9)*, (Thirty-sixth session, 2006), E/C. 12/GC/20/CRP. 1, 16 February 2006, para. 31.

[98] See M. Craven 'Assessment of the Progress on Adjudication of Economic, Social and Cultural Rights', in Squires, Langford and Thiele (eds.), *The Road to a Remedy* (n. 11 above), pp. 27–42, at 30–36

[99] See *General Comment No. 12* (n. 73 above), para. 15.

[100] *Velásquez Rodríguez Case*, Judgment of July 29, 1988, Inter-Am. Ct. H.R. (Ser. C) No. 4, para. 175.

[101] *SERAC v. Nigeria* (n. 73 above).

[102] See discussion in Chapters 7 to 10. In some cases, they have ordered treatments be included in health insurance plans but private provider were then able to get a state refund.

[103] For example, see discussion by Martin Scheinin in Chapter 25, Section 2.9, of Sami cases such as *Länsman v. Finland (No. 2)* (Communication No. 671/1995) and *Ilmari Länsman et al. v. Finland* (Communication No. 511/1992), Views of 26 October 1994.

[104] *Maya Indigenous Communities of the Toledo District v. Belize*, Report No. 40/04, Case 12.053, OEA/Ser.L/ V/II.122, doc. 5 rev 1 (2005).

dismissal are also addressed by some authors in their book.[105] In *Vishaka v State of Rajasthan*, a case concerning sexual harassment at the work place, the Indian judiciary drew on the Convention on the Elimination of All Forms of Discrimination Against Women (CEDAW) to develop binding guidelines which would remain in force till such time the Parliament enacted an appropriate law.[106]

Farha notes that the first complaint decided by the Committee on Elimination of Discrimination Against Women (*A.T. v Hungary*, 2/2003) concerned 'economic and social rights violations that occurred in the private realm (the home)'.[107] The Committee found that the legal and social protections available to the complainant, a victim of domestic violence, were grossly inadequate and took a particularly wide view of the steps expected from the State. It repeated its concerns over entrenched stereotypes concerning men and women, earlier expressed in concluding observations, and instructed the State party to ensure that women would be free from all forms of domestic violence, which included that the complainant be given a safe home in which to live with her children, child support, legal assistance and reparations for the violations of her rights. The remedy was also to include the introduction of a specific law on the subject, which prohibited domestic violence, provided for protection and exclusion orders and support services and shelters.

The link between domestic violence and the need for corresponding civil *and* social rights protections, such as shelter, support services and education campaigns, has not generated as much litigation as perhaps might be expected. This may be partly a legal issue. In the Americas, Melish notes that only Article 7 of the Convention on Violence Against Women is justiciable before the Inter-American Commission on Human Rights and it is mostly concerned with civil and political rights of women facing violence. In *Maria da Penha v Brazil*,[108] which concerned a woman whose husband attempted to murder her but was never prosecuted, the Commission's recommendations are mostly focused on the State's failure to guarantee civil rights and only briefly notes that provision of shelters and education campaigns are also required under Article 7. The relative silence on the issue may also stem from the fact that domestic violence is not seen or classified as a social rights issue and indicates that we may have some way to go in understanding the indivisibility of human rights, particularly when rooted in the experiences of women.

What is also noticeable in this volume is the absence of a large number of cases directly concerned with the process of privatising social services. (The term privatisation is subject to many definitions and I take it in its broadest sense of giving the private sector a greater role in provision of social goods and services, which would include management contracts and public-private partnerships). Privatisation of public services has been the subject of, and the driving energy behind, many advocacy campaigns and the UN Committee on Economic, Social and Cultural Rights has regularly been concerned in its concluding observations on the impacts of such processes on the poor.[109] Yet, while privatisation processes have been particularly widespread in Latin America and Eastern European where the advice and conditions of the World Bank have been most influential,[110] both regions have well entrenched social rights.

Part of the answer perhaps lies in the generally accepted non-ideological nature of social rights and the reticence of Courts to pronounce on specific policy choices.[111] As early as 1991,

---

[105] See for example Chapters 7, 8, 10 and 8 of this volume.
[106] (1997) 6 SCC 241.
[107] See Chapter 26, Section 2.5.
[108] *Maria da Penha v. Brazil*, Case 12.051, Report No. 54/01, Inter-Am. Comm.H.R., OEA/Ser.L/V/II.111 Doc. 20 rev at 704 (2000).

[109] See Section 4 of Chapter 23 of this volume.
[110] For an excellent overview of this origins and impact of this trend with regard to social security, see Katharina Müller, *Privatising Old-Age Security: Latin America and Eastern Europe Compared* (Edward Elgar Publishing, 2003).
[111] One interesting exception is the early ILO standards on social security, which require mandatory government contributions to social insurance and that social security entities were not-for-profit. Chile was a still a member of these ILO standards after privatising its social security system and trade unions successfully obtained decisions from the ILO CEACR Committee that Chile was in breach. See ILO, *Report of the Committee set up to examine the representation submitted by the National Trade Union Co-ordinating Council (CNS) of Chile under Article 24 of the ILO Constitution, alleging non-observance by Chile of International Labour Conventions Nos. 1, 2, 24,*

the Committee on Economic, Social and Cultural Rights noted that the:

> [U]ndertaking [in Article 2(1) of ICCPR] "to take steps … by all appropriate means including particularly the adoption of legislative measures" neither requires nor precludes any particular form of government or economic system being used as the vehicle for the steps in question, provided only that it is democratic and that all human rights are thereby respected.

Indeed, the drafters of a clause to place the right to water in the Uruguayan constitution, successfully passed in a 2004 referendum, were careful to add a proviso that water services were to be in public hands. It will obviously provide more explicit grounds for such litigation.

However, litigation has occasionally focused on the processes associated with privatisation. The Philippines case of *Tatad v Secretary of the Department of Energy* is an example where the loosening of regulation of three oil companies was challenged on the basis of social rights.[112] The Supreme Court struck down a deregulation law that would have permitted the three major oil companies to avoid seeking permission of the regulator to increase prices. Citing the right to electricity, the Court warned that higher oil prices threaten to 'multiply the number of our people with bent backs and begging bowls'. The Court declared that it could not 'shirk its duty of striking down a law that offends the constitution' despite the law constituting an 'economic decision of Congress'.[113] In *Nkonkobe Municipality v Water Services South Africa (PTY) Ltd & Ors*,[114] the focus was on the lack of participation. A municipality was successful in nullifying a 6 year-old water privatisation contract, not because they claimed they could no longer afford the high management fees of R400000 per month being charged by the private contractor, but because the municipality itself had not earlier complied with the necessary consultation and public participation requirements, though in this case it was a matter of legislation.

However, as evidence grows of the problems of privatisation in particular contexts, it is not unlikely that courts will intervene at an earlier stage if they foresee particular dangers to social rights to which they feel the Government has paid insufficient attention. In the main, however, it appears that privatisation processes will be challenged on human rights grounds in three more indirect ways. First, *ante facto*, where the regime established for privatisation essentially allows the private actor to essentially lower the quality of the service in order to make the venture profitable. For example, in the *Aquino* case, the workers compensation legislation, which established a system for private provision of worker's compensation, was successfully challenged on the basis that it removed the option of worker's seeking full compensation through the courts and they were subsequently restricted to a no-fault, tabulated compensation regime, with a lower standard of proof as the only option.[115] There may also be challenges to the procedural rights in the process, for example, a lack of information or faulty consultation procedures, as was done in the *Nkonkobe Municipality* case.

Second, *post facto*, when private providers have failed to provide social services in accordance with social rights standards. The difficult question is of course who bears the responsibility. In some cases, the Government may be challenged for failing to regulate.[116] In other jurisdictions, the actions and omissions of private actors can be directly challenged if they are assuming the *responsibilities of a public authority*. In the United Kingdom for example, King notes that actions under the Human Rights Act can only be taken against a 'public authority' but the courts will examine whether the function 'is an exercise of statutory powers, takes the place of a central or local government function, or provides a public service'.[117] In one case, a housing association was deemed

---

112 *29, 30, 35, 37, 38 and 111* (Geneva: ILO, 1988) and discussion by Fenwick in Chapter 28, Section 5.2.

112 G. R. No. 124360 (5 November 1997).

113 Ibid. pp. 37–38. Cookie Diakno explains though that the Court also explained how the decision could be amended to allow more free floating prices, which was what eventually happened. See interview with her in Langford, *Litigating Economic, Social and Cultural Rights* (n. 53 above), pp. 48–50.

114 Case No. 1277/2001 (unreported)

115 *Aquino, Isacio v. Cargo Servicios Industriales S. A. s/accidentes ley 9688*, 21 September 2004. See discussion in Chapter 8, Section 4.1.

116 See, for example, *Tatad case* (n. 112 above).

117 King in Chapter 15, Section 4.1.

to be a public authority after taking over council apartments while in another a private association was not, despite the fact that it had taken over, and then closed, homes with long-term patients who had been placed there by the local authority.[118] In the Canadian case of *Eldridge*, the Court found that hospitals, although non – governmental, were providing publicly funded healthcare services and delivering a comprehensive healthcare program on behalf of the Government, and were thus constrained by equality rights set out in the Canadian Charter.[119] In other cases, and as will be discussed in more detail below, private entities can be directly challenged as such. In Colombia, for example, the Constitutional Court has 'ensured that private entities guarantee equal treatment to persons with disabilities'.[120]

HORIZONTAL APPLICATION

Some of the jurisprudence concerns cases brought by private actors directly against other private actors. In a number of domestic jurisdictions such action is facilitated by the constitution as well as anti-discrimination and tort laws. In Colombia, the Constitutional Court found that the constitutional right to work was violated by an employer who dismissed an employee after being tested HIV-positive.[121] The private institution was ordered to pay the applicant compensation for the damage caused. The Court also referred to the wider State obligations to protect persons with HIV, and reaffirmed the prohibition against obliging potential or current employees to take a HIV test in order to gain or maintain employment. In the *Slaight Communications* case in Canada, the Supreme Court held that the decision of a private labour arbitrator must be in conformity with the Charter which is to be interpreted as far as possible with the right to work in the ICESCR.[122] In Ireland in *Meskell v. CIE*, an employee was successful in defending their constitutional right to asso-

ciation against an employer in a case where the employer had contractually required the employee to join a trade union.[123] Liebenberg notes that the South African Bill of Rights explicitly applies both vertically and horizontally, and the South African Constitutional Court has clearly stated, for example, that the obligation to abstain from forced evictions falls on both State and non-State actors.[124]

At the international level, Clark describes the functioning of the World Bank Inspection Panel, which allows persons directly affected by Bank projects to make complaints about the compliance of the Bank with its operational procedures. The Panel has made a significant number of decisions in the area of evictions, environmental harm and indigenous peoples. But Clark is critical of the lack of explicit human rights standards in the Panel's mandates and effective enforcement powers as many decisions go unimplemented. Litigating against corporations is more difficult at the international level.

Joseph points to the stalled negotiations over the UN Norms on the Responsibilities of Transnational Corporations and other Business Enterprises with regard to Human Rights. Complaints can and have been made though under the earlier declaration, the OECD Guidelines on Multinational Enterprises. While National Contact Points, which receive complaints, have no power to enforce these Guidelines, there is the capacity for NGOs to use the proceedings 'to publicise and mobilise campaigns against companies, to enter into meaningful dialogue with companies, and to conciliate settlements with companies'.[125] Human rights have also been raised more defensively in international investment tribunals cases where, for example, the ICSID tribunal accepted amicus submissions from NGOs in the *Suez/Vivendi case*

---

[118] See *Poplar Housing and Regeneration Community Association Ltd. v. Donoghue*, [2002] QB 48 (CA). R *(H) v. Leonard Cheschire Foundation (A Charity)* [2002] EWCA Civ 266.

[119] *Eldridge* (n. 42 above). See discussion by Jackman and Porter in Chapter 11, Section 2.3.

[120] See Chapter 7, Section 5.1.

[121] SU-256/96. See discussion in Chapter 7 by Sepúlveda.

[122] *Slaight Communications Inc. v. Davidson*, [1989] 1 SCR 1038. See discussion in Chapter 11, Section 3 of this volume.

[123] [1973] IR 121. See discussion in Chapter 16, Section 2.2.

[124] *Grootboom* (n. 47 above). In *Port Elizabeth* (n. 83 above) it stated that the Bill of Rights 'counterposes to the normal ownership rights of possession, use and occupation, a new and equally relevant right not arbitrarily to be deprived of a home'.

[125] See for example, the Adidas case where The India Committee of the Netherlands lodged a complaint with the Dutch NCP claiming that Adidas had failed to ensure that its suppliers were in compliance with the OECD Guidelines on Multinational Enterprises, particularly in relation to minimum wages, unionization and child labour. A public settlement was reached in July 2003 whereby the parties agreed on common labour standards and the need for external monitoring.

on the basis that the case raised human rights issues concerning water.[126]

Joseph also charts the many attempts to use laws in national jurisdictions for the same purpose, such as tort law or the US Alien Torts Claim Act. She concludes that 'While plaintiffs have had to withstand a barrage of preliminary challenges in the salient transnational cases, some cases have been settled leading to the delivery of a measure of redress to victims, and other cases are ongoing, with possibilities for further redress and vindication'.[127]

This of course raises the question whether there is a clear State obligation to ensure that social rights can be horizontally applied, regardless of whether this right is included under a national Constitution.[128] Most UN human rights treaty bodes have focused on emphasising the State obligation to *protect* as well as *provide* adequate remedies for violations without necessarily specifying that this should allow victims to litigate against non-State actors. However, the Committee on the Elimination on Racial Discrimination seems to imply this when it notified States parties:

> [T]hat, in its opinion, the right to seek just and adequate reparation or satisfaction for any damage suffered as a result of such discrimination, which is embodied in article 6 of the Convention, is not necessarily secured solely by the punishment of the perpetrator of the discrimination; at the same time, the courts and other competent authorities should consider awarding financial compensation for damage, material or moral, suffered by a victim, whenever appropriate.[129]

At the national level there are some more clear and interesting trends. Jackman and Porter note that in *Vriend*,[130] the Canadian Supreme Court held that a failure to include sexual orientation as a prohibited ground of discrimination under provincial human rights legislation governing the actions of private employers, service and housing providers, violated Charter equality rights.[131]

3.3 Obligations to Fulfil

The idea that courts could involve themselves in questions concerning the fulfilment of social rights has been the most controversial question from a philosophical standpoint, a point taken up in Section 4 of this Chapter. These concerns feature in a number of judgments, where Courts have addressed doctrines of separation of powers when dismissing cases, explaining an order or defining the boundaries of their powers.

In some jurisdictions, these concerns have been rather fatal for the jurisprudence. Nolan notes in her chapter how the Irish Supreme Court has sought to ground itself in 'Aristotelian distinction between commutative and distributive justice [which] marks out the dividing line between the judicial and legislative spheres of operation'.[132] In the *O'Reilly* case, later approved by the Supreme Court, Justice Costello stated courts can only purportedly deal with the former while the distribution of public resources:

> [C]an only be made by reference to the common good and by those charged with furthering the common good (the Government); [distribution of public resources] cannot be made by any individual who may claim a share in the common stock and no independent arbitrator, such as a court, can adjudicate on a claim by an individual that he has been deprived of what is his due.[133]

Other adjudicators have moved forward differently (and Nolan notes that Justice Costello himself later recanted his view).[134] They have carved out for themselves a role in adjudicating the more positive obligations. No one uniform approach emerges, which can be mostly ascribed to differing legal regimes, the socio-cultural factors discussed in Section 1 above and to the developing nature of this field.

---

126 Chapter 29, Section 2.3.
127 Chapter 29, Section 4.
128 For a good overview of the general issues in this area, see A. Clapham, *Human Rights Obligations of Non-State Actors* (Oxford: Oxford University Press, 2006).
129 *General Recommendation 26, The right to seek just and adequate reparation or satisfaction* (Fifty-sixth session, 2000), U.N. Doc. A/55/18, annex V at 153 (2000).
130 *Vriend v. Alberta*, [1998] 1 SCR 493.
131 Ibid. paras. 65–66.
132 Chapter 16, Section 3.
133 *O'Reilly* [1989] I.L.R.M. 181, p. 194.
134 See Chapter 16, Section 4.1, particularly discussion in footnote 81.

In broad-brush terms, many adjudicators tend to enforce one or both of the two key State obligations identified by the Committee on Economic, Social and Cultural Rights: First, the explicit duty to take adequate steps towards the progressive realisation of the rights within available resources and, secondly, the implicit obligation to immediately achieve a minimum level of realisation. (The positive obligations to guarantee non-discrimination and equality will be discussed in the next sub-section). The articulation of these two obligations, 'taking steps' and 'minimum core', is essentially a response to the concern that adequate resources may not be available to meet social rights. States are thus expected to achieve some sort of minimum and plan for and move towards the progressive realisation for the full realisation of the rights.

The seeming logic of this approach has driven both the European Committee on Social Rights and African Commission on Human Rights to imply the defence of lack of resources into their constituent instruments – the State obligations were largely unqualified in this regard.[135] However, it should be strongly emphasised that many cases concerning positive obligations are not monetary in orientation. For example, the Inter-American Court of Human Rights found that the State responsible, Nicaragua, had failed to legislate and ensure that the lands of Indigenous peoples were demarcated and titled.[136]

Colombia is an example of a jurisdiction that has adopted and enforced both approaches. The Constitutional Court recognises that obligations concerning economic, social and cultural rights are progressive in character[137] but has drawn on General Comment No. 3 to stress that, at a minimum, the State 'must devise and adopt a plan of action for the implementation of the rights'.[138] It has

intervened to immediately enforce such rights by broadly interpreting the right to life, dignity and security and enforcing a 'minimum conditions for dignified life' (borrowing directly from the German jurisprudence on *Existenzminimum*) although it has a fairly enlarged vision of the minimum core. It has gone further and developed another arm of jurisprudence in circumstances where it finds an 'unconstitutional state of affairs'. This requires systematic and widespread violations of a number of constitutional rights which cannot be attributed to only one State authority and the Court has stepped in to make wide-ranging orders affecting policies and programs.

In some other jurisdictions one can also find a mix of cases in both categories. In Finland, local authorities have been faulted for failing to take *sufficient steps* to secure employment for a job seeker and immediatly secure child-care for a family.[139] Albisa and Schultz note that US state courts in Texas, Kentucky and New York have struck school financing systems on the grounds of failing to provide adequate or efficient education while the New York court has found 'a positive duty upon the state' to provide welfare payments to anyone considered indigent under the state's 'need standard', even if the individual could not present papers proving that he or she received no support from relatives.[140]

The South African Constitutional Court has opted for only the former approach, rejecting for the moment the idea of immediate enforcement of a minimum core obligation. In *Grootboom*, the Court found that the government authorities had failed to develop an adequate housing programme which was directed towards providing emergency relief for those without access to basic shelter.[141] This violated its duty to take reasonable legislative and other measures, within its available resources,

---

[135] See *Purohit and Moore v. The Gambia*, African Commission on Human and Peoples' Rights, Comm. No. 241/2001 (2003) and Complaint No. 13/2002, *Autism-Europe v. France*, Decision on the Merits.

[136] *The Mayagna (Sumo) Indigenous Community of Awas Tinga v. Nicaragua*, Judgment of 31 Aug. 2001, Inter-Am.Ct.H.R. (Ser.C) No.79. See also *Dunmore v. Ontario (Attorney General)*, [2001] 3 SCR 1016 and European Committee on Social Rights, *ICJ v. Portugal*, Decision No. 1/1999.

[137] See, e.g., SU-111/97.

[138] See discussion in Chapter 7, Section 3, by Sepúlveda and cases T-595/02 and T-025/04

[139] See respectively KKO 1997: 141 (Employment Act Case) Yearbook of the Supreme Court 1997 No. 141 (Supreme Court of Finland), Case No. S 98/225 (Child-Care Services Case) Helsinki Court of Appeals 28 October 199; Case. No. 3118 (Medical Aids Case) Supreme Administrative Court, 27 November 2000, No. 3118. For English summaries of a wide range of cases see <www.nordichumanrights.net/tema/tema3/caselaw/>. The different approaches in Finland are partly related to the State obligations, particularly the more graduated obligation in the case of the constitutional right to work.

[140] *Tucker v. Toia*, 43 N.Y.2d 1, 7 (1977).

[141] *Grootboom* (n. 17 above).

to achieve the progressive realisation of the constitutional right to access adequate housing.[142] In language not dissimilar to General Comment No. 3, the Court expressed the obligation in the following terms:

> The measures [by government] must establish a coherent public housing program directed towards the progressive realisation of the right of access to adequate housing within the State's available means. The program must be capable of facilitating the realisation of the right. The precise contours and content of the measures to be adopted are primarily a matter for the Legislature and the Executive. They must, however, ensure that the measures they adopt are reasonable.[143]

Liebenberg notes that the Court has introduced numerous criteria for determining such reasonableness. These include whether the programme is 'comprehensive, coherent, coordinate, with appropriate allocation of 'financial and human resources', is 'balanced and flexible' with provision for 'short, medium and long-term needs', 'reasonably conceived and implemented', 'transparent' and made 'known effectively to the public'.[144]

The South African Constitutional Court rejected the minimum core obligation on the basis that in the case of the right to housing it could not determine the minimum due to the diversity of the needs and groups[145] and raised concerns about whether the minimum could be realised immediately in the South African context. This decision is certainly not without critique. Sandra Liebenberg argues that the Court's reasonableness test, which it applies to the progressive realisation of the right, could also be adapted to cover 'survival interests'. There could be a presumption that government programs do not meet the test of reasonableness if certain minimums are not met.[146]

The Constitutional Court of Hungary takes the reverse position of its South African counterpart. It has consistently declined any role in examining whether the Government has sufficiently taken steps to realise constitutional social rights – it merely requires that such a law or programme exist.[147] Instead it turned to the German idea of *Existenzminimum*, requiring that social benefits, for example, may not be 'reduced below a minimal level'. Although in practice, the Court has been somewhat reluctant to review whether social security or housing schemes meet the minimum requirements.[148] As I argue in Chapter 13, this approach to only enforcing the minimum level is partly explainable by the Court's use of jurisprudence from jurisdictions where social rights are derived from civil and political rights and are thus more limited in scope. It may also be attributable to the possible middle class bias of the Court (it was more willing to strike down cuts in social insurance benefits than examine the adequacy of minimum safety net) and the defensive nature of the post-Communist constitutional transition. Social rights were seemingly retained and developed in the Constitutions to appease the populace frightened of market reforms rather than being part of the broader transformative democratic package as they were in Latin America and South Africa.

Melish is similarly critical of the Inter-American Court of Human Rights for only enforcing minimum (though rather enlarged) social rights protections under civil and political rights.[149] This is despite explicit obligations concerning economic, social and cultural rights being set out in Article 26 of the American Convention on Human Rights. They declined to do so on the basis that judging the level coverage of these rights 'over the entire population'[150] under article 26 conflicts with the standing requirements that an *individualised* impairment in the enjoyment or exercise of rights must be shown. Melish argues instead that the conduct-oriented duties to take steps to ensure these rights can be suitably raised

---

[142] S.26(2) of the Constitution of the Republic of South Africa.
[143] *Grootboom* (n. 47 above), para. 41.
[144] Liebenberg, Chapter 4, Section 3.1.
[145] *Grootboom* (n. 47 above), para. 33.
[146] See Sandra Liebenberg, 'Enforcing Positive Social and Economic Rights Claims: The South African Model of Reasonableness Review', in Squires, Langford and Thiele, *Road to a Remedy* (n. 11 above), pp. 73–88. Note also recent judgment in *Mazibuko & Ors v. City of Johannesburg & Ors* (Unreported, 30 April 2008) where the High Court argues the constitutional court had not categorically ruled at minimum core approach.

[147] See Constitutional Court of Hungary, Decision 772/B/1990/AB: ABH 1991, 519 at 520.
[148] See Decision 32/1998 (VI.25) AB and Decision No. 42/2000 and discussion by myself in Chapter 13, Sections 4.2 and 4.3.
[149] See *Five Pensioners' Case v. Peru*, Judgment of Feb. 28, 2003, Inter-Am. Ct. H.R. (Ser. C) No. 98 (2003).
[150] Ibid. para. 147.

by individuals who can show the appropriate damage.

This minimum core approach is particularly evident in jurisdictions where social interests are judicially protected through civil rights. For example, the Swiss Federal Court derived an implied constitutional right to basic necessities and said that while it lacked the competence to determine resource allocation, that it would set aside legislation if the outcome failed to meet the minimum claim required by constitutional rights.[151] The European Court of Human Rights and courts in the United Kingdom have been willing to enforce access to housing or social benefits for vulnerable groups in severe and very exceptional situations under civil rights to protection from cruel and degrading treatment and right to home, family life and privacy. The South Asian courts, however, have felt less restricted. They broadly interpret the right to life to include a range of social rights. However, they are somewhat selective in their degree of enforcement (strong deterence to the state shown with rights to housing and work) and in some cases the invocation of constitutional rights appears to represent a means to enforce unimplemented legislation.

However, the distinction between the more conduct-oriented duty to *take steps* and the result-oriented duty to *immediately realise* some aspect of the right is not always apparent in practice. This is particularly so when it is clear that sufficient resources are available or adjudicators believe that the State has had sufficient time to address the problem. In *Purohit v Moore*, the African Commission on Human and Peoples' Rights ordered Gambia to provide certain treatments to detained mentally ill patients once it had ascertained resources were available. In *TAC*, The South African courts ordered the Government to provide the fairly cheap drug neviropane for prevention of mother-to-child transmission of HIV. In *Autism-Europe v France* the European Committee on Social Rights stated:

[N]otwithstanding a national debate going back more than twenty years about the number of persons concerned and the relevant strategies required, and even after the enactment of the Disabled Persons Policy Act of 30 June 1975, France has failed to achieve sufficient progress in advancing the provision of education of persons with autism.[152]

3.4   Equality Rights

In quite a number of cases, both the State's negative and positive obligations towards social rights have been addressed through the judicial application of equality norms in relation to the needs of disadvantaged groups. These cases concern some of the more traditionally recognised prohibited grounds of discrimination, but they also increasingly reveal a host of other arbitrary classifications that adjudicatory bodies have viewed suspiciously.

The question of whether equality rights or guarantees possess substantive character and contain positive obligations to eliminate discrimination has exercised the attention of a number of adjudicatory bodies. In the case of Pakistan, the Supreme Court has enunciated the principle quite boldly during a flowering of public interest litigation. In *Fazal Jan v Roshua Din*, they held that the constitutional right to equality imposed positive obligations on all State organs to take active measures to safeguard the interests of women and children.[153]

In the case of the UN Human rights committee, they have moved ahead cautiously. In *Zwaan-de Vries v the Netherlands*, they construed equality rights to essentially prevent discriminatory backsliding. According to the Committee, the prohibition on discrimination in Article 26 of the International Covenant on Civil and Political Rights does not require a State to 'enact legislation to provide for social security'; only that social security legislation, once enacted, does not discriminate.[154] However, it seemingly later expanded this position in a General Comment by stating that 'the principle of equality sometimes

---

[151] *V v. Einwohrnergemeine X und Regierunsgrat des Kantons Bern* (BGE/ATF 121 I 367, Federal Court of Switzerland, of 27 October 1995). See also Constitutional Court of Hungary, Case No. 42/2000 (XI.8); BverfGE 40, 121 (133) (Federal Constitutional Court of Germany).

[152] Ibid. para. 54.
[153] PLD 1990 SC 661.
[154] *Zwaan-de Vries v. the Netherlands*, (Communication No. 182/1984), views of 9 April 1987, para. 12.4.

requires States parties to take affirmative action in order to diminish or eliminate conditions which cause or help to perpetuate discrimination prohibited by the Covenant'.[155] This may mean that a State might have to justify the absence of action to provide social security if it impinged on equality.

In Canada, this broader position was clearly articulated in the *Eldridge* case, in which the Supreme Court dismissed the British Columbian provincial government's arguments that the right to equality did not require governments to allocate resources in healthcare in order to address pre-existing disadvantage of particular groups such as the deaf and hard of hearing.[156] The Court rejected this 'thin and impoverished vision of equality' and held that the government's failure to fund or provide sign language services in the provision of healthcare to the deaf was discriminatory. However, Porter and Jackman note a certain retreat by the Court in some recent cases: in *Auton (Guardian ad litem of) v British Columbia (Attorney General)*, for instance, the Court declined to require the funding of treatment of a new treatment for autism.[157]

The Committee on Economic, Social and Cultural Rights has explicitly encouraged a more progressive approach stating that "Guarantees of equality and non-discrimination should be interpreted, to the greatest extent possible, in ways which facilitate the full protection of economic, social and cultural rights'.[158] Farha notes the substantive vision of equality of the Committee on Elimination of Discrimination Against Women, which has recognised 'that inequality exists when … differential disadvantage of women is not addressed by laws, policies, or practices'.[159] For example, the Committee urged Cuba to introduce temporary special measures to address the high levels of unemployment found amongst women,[160] and Romania to 'improve the availability, acceptability, and use of modern means of birth control to avoid the use of abortion as a method of family planning' including provision of 'sex education systematically in schools'.[161] Conventions on the right of children, migrants and persons with disabilities also demonstrate an emphasis on their substantive social rights which may also require differential modes of realisation.

The positive dimension of State obligations is particularly influential at the remedial stage. It may prevent an adjudicatory body 'equalising down' in order to achieve equality in respect of the social interest or right. In Canada, the Supreme Court has issued many positive remedial orders (extending or increasing parental, social assistance and pension benefits and extending legislative protections under security of tenure and human rights legislation). Nonetheless, it has not ruled out the possibility that it can equalise down.[162] In *Khosa v Minister of Social Development*,[163] the Constitutional Court of South Africa clearly adopted a formula of equalising up. After finding that the legislative exclusion of 'permanent residents' from a social assistance scheme violated the constitutional prohibition on unfair discrimination, the remedial order was to 'read into' the relevant legislation, the rights of permanent residents to receive the social benefits.[164] However, the Court did note that the right to social security of residents was a key factor in considering the reasonableness of the exclusion of permanent residents, and outweighed any competing financial and immigration considerations of the State.

Indirect discrimination is also raised in some cases. In *Kearney v. Bramlea Ltd*, use of income criteria to assess tenant applicants was found to be unjustified (on the basis that it took no account

---

[155] Human Rights Committee, *General Comment No. 18: Non-discrimination* (1989), para. 10.

[156] *Eldridge (n. 42 above)*, para. 87.

[157] [2004] 3 S.C.R. 657.

[158] *General Comment No. 9, The domestic application of the Covenant* (Nineteenth session, 1998), U.N. Doc. E/C.12/1998/24 (1998), para 15.

[159] Section 2.3, Chapter 26. The Convention on Elimination of Discrimination Against Women expressly obliges States to take steps to eliminate discrimination against women and permits temporary special measures to accelerate de facto equality.

[160] *CEDAW Committee, Concluding Comments on Cuba*, UN Doc. Supplement No. A/55/38, para. 270. (2000).

[161] *CEDAW Committee, Concluding Comments on Romania*, UN Doc. Supplement No. A/55/38, para. 315, (2000).

[162] See discussion by Jackman and Porter in Chapter 10, Section 6.

[163] *Khosa v. Minister of Social Development; Mahlaule v. Minister of Social Development*, 2004 (6) BCLR 569 (CC).

[164] See Chapter 4, Section 3.3. The Court also found that the legislation violated the right to social security but the judgment does not appear to suggest that a different outcome would be reached had the right to social security not also been violated.

of a person's real willingness and ability to pay) and constituted discrimination on a number of grounds, including race, sex, marital status, age and receipt of public assistance since it disproportionately affect those groups.[165] In *Rupert Althammer et al v Austria*, the Human Rights Committee found that a violation of Article 26 of the ICCPR can 'result from the discriminatory effect of a rule or measure that is neutral at face value or without intent to discriminate' but declined in that case to find that the removal of a household benefits in favour of better benefits for children with employees was indirect discrimnation.[166] This was on the basis that active employees without chilren would also be negatively affected and that Austria had provided reasonable and objective justification for the decision. However, in *Derksen and Bakker v The Netherlands* they found that legislation which failed to retroactively grant survivor's benefits to children of unmarried parents was indirectly discriminatory.[167]

Adjudicatory bodies have addressed many of the express grounds of prohibited grounds in International Covenant on Economic, Social and Cultural Rights, namely race and colour,[168] sex,[169] language,[170] religion,[171] national or social origin,[172]

property and birth.[173] However, both national and international adjudicators have regularly found other suspect classifications in the field of human rights (including social rights), whether under the prohibited ground of 'other status', general and non-specific non-discrimination provisions or by expanding the definition of the express grounds. The Committee on Economic, Social and Cultural Rights is an example of the former[174] although it is yet to provide any 'all-embracing rationale'.[175] The Human Rights Committee also seems to hint that the underlying rationale is not so much the search for specific suspect grounds but rather the arbitrariness of the classification. In the case of *Des Fours Wald erode*, which concerned a law that with retroactive effect frustrated ongoing restitution proceedings, the Committee said: 'This raises an issue of arbitrariness and, consequently, of a breach of the right to equality before the law, equal protection of the law and non-discrimination under article 26 of the Covenant'.[176]

One can thus find cases where the prohibited grounds of non-discrimination include disability,[177] age,[178] marital status,[179] sexual

---

[165] (1998) 34 CHRR D/1 and upheld in *Shelter Corporation* v *Ontario Human Rights Commission* (2001) 143 OAC 54. See B. Porter, "Homelessness, Human Rights, Litigation and Law Reform: A View from Canada", in P. Lynch and D. Otto (eds.), Homelessness and Human Rights, *Australian Journal for Human Rights*, Vol. 10, No. 2 (2004) available at <http://www.austlii.edu.au/au/journals/AJHR/2004/7.html>.

[166] (Communication No. 998/2001), Views of 8 August 2003. See discussion by Scheinin in Chapter 25, Section 2.1.

[167] (Communication No. 976/2001), Views of 1 April 2004.

[168] See particularly cases discussed in Chapter 24 on the Committee on Elimination of Racial Discrimination. Other cases concerning race and colour can be traced through the index to this book.

[169] See for example discussion of Colombian cases concerning moment right to work, social security and food on pages 149 or 156–157, and South Asian cases from pages 131–133 of this book.

[170] *Belgian Linguistics Case (No 2)* 1 EHRR 252; Application nos. 1474/62; 1677/62; 1769/63; 1994/63; 2126/64 (French speaking children were prevented, solely on the basis of the residence of their parents from having access to French language')

[171] *Jehovah's Witnesses v. Argentina*, Case No. 2137, Inter-Am. Comm. H.R., OEA/Ser.L/V/II.47, doc. 13 rev 1 (1979).

[172] See *Yean and Bosico v. Dominican Republic*, Judgment of Sept. 8, 2005, Inter-Am. Ct. H.R. (Ser. C) No. 130 (2005).

(State's refusal to register the births of children of Haitian descent, which denied them access to schooling.)

[173] See for example discussion of CERD's treatment and concluding observations on descent-based discrimination in Chapter 24.

[174] See discussion in Chapter 23, Section 3.4.

[175] Craven, *The International Covenant on Economic, Social and Cultural Rights* (n. 10 above), p. 169.

[176] *Karel Des Fours Walderode v the Czech Republic* (Communication No. 747/1997), Views of 30 October 2001, paragraph 8.3. See discussion of this and other cases in Chapter 25, Section 2.8.

[177] *Purohit and Moore v. The Gambia*, African Commission on Human and Peoples' Rights, Communication No. 241/2001 (2003).

[178] The Court of Appeal of Versailles, France, annulled a provision of a collective agreement between labour and management on the grounds that it prohibited the recruitment of people after the age of thirty five: CA Versailles, March 11, 1985, *Recueil Dalloz* (1985), 421. Cf. *Gosselin v. Quebec (Attorney General)*, [2002] 4 SCR 429, where a slender majority of the Canadian Supreme Court found that a Quebec social assistance regulation that reduced by two-thirds the amount paid to single employable persons under the age of thirty not enrolled in a workfare program was not discriminatory.

[179] *Sparks v. Dartmouth/Halifax County Regional Housing Authority*, (1993) 119 NSR (2d) 91 (NS CA). (A Black single mother of two children challenged security of tenure provisions that excluded public housing tenants'.)

orientation,[180] social status/condition,[181] receipt of public assistance,[182] nationality,[183] and refugee or migrant status.[184] Increasingly, some of these grounds are being expressly included in legal instruments, particularly disability,[185] sexual orientation[186] and 'receipt of public assistance' and 'social condition'.[187]

Van Beuren also raises the challenging question as to whether children as beneficiaries of social rights may also have greater or immediate demands on resources in comparison to adults on the basis of the principle of the best interests of the child. Article 3(1) of the UN Convention on the Rights of the Child as, 'in all actions concerning children...the best interests of the child shall be a primary consideration'. She notes that its implications beyond civil rights have not been properly explored. However, in the case of the Brazil, Piovesan describes

how the this principle was applied by the Courts and the logic would lead to some startling consequences:

> The constitutional right to the absolute priority of children and adolescents in the exercise of the right to health is established by constitutional norm which is emphasised by articles 7 and 11 from Statute of Children and Adolescents.... To submit a child or adolescent in a waiting list in order to attend others is the same as to legalise the most violent aggression of the principle of equality, essential in a democratic society provided by the Constitution, putting also into risk the clause in defense of human dignity. (Resp 577836)

3.5   Conflicts Between Rights

One particular under-treated area in the field of economic, social and cultural rights is potential and actual conflicts between the various rights in practice. The constitutional court in Hungary came to a different conclusion on legislation allowing summary eviction, finding the best interests of child was not paramount in their case.[188] Obviously, there can be direct clashes between civil and political rights and economic, social and cultural rights. It is interesting to note that France and Bangladesh were willing to sacrifice freedom of expression to permit a law on tobacco advertising while Canada was not[189] although in a more recent case, restrictions on tobacco advertising passed constitutional muster.[190] But of particular interest is where there is a clash within the social arena, which can occur in a number of ways.

The first is where social interests derived from civil and political rights may clash with express economic, social and cultural rights. For instance, in the *Chaoulli* case[191] claimants successfully challenged a ban on private health insurance and funding in Quebec because it otherwise made private health services uneconomical and forced

[180] See discussion in Chapter 25 of Human Rights Committee, *Edward Young v. Australia* (Communication No. 941/2000), Views of 6 August 2003 although the Committee places 'sexual orientation' under the ground of 'sex'. The Committee on Economic, Social and Cultural Rights, *General Comment No. 12, Right to adequate food* (Twentieth session, 1999), U.N. Doc. E/C.12/1999/5 (1999), para. 18. See also *Vriend v. Alberta* (n. 130 above) imalier it under other state.

[181] Quebec *Commission des droits de la personne v. Gauthier* (1993) 19 CHRR D/312. (Complainant refused social assistance by the respondent on the alleged grounds of the latter assuming that the complainant, a welfare recipient, would be incapable of paying rent.) Note that 'social condition' is expressly included as prohibited ground in Quebec legislation.

[182] *Kearney v Bramlea Ltd* (n. 248 below).

[183] See Human Rights Committee in *Gueye et al. v. France* (Communication No. 196/1985), Views of 3 April 1989. ("There has been a differentiation by reference to nationality acquired upon independence. In the Committee's opinion, this falls within the reference to "other status" in the second sentence of Article 26....A subsequent change in nationality cannot by itself be considered as a sufficient justification for different treatment, since the basis for the grant of the pension was the same service which both they and the soldiers who remained French had provided'. (Para 9.5).

[184] See *Khosa v. Minister of Social Development* (n. 163 above) – residency as prohibited ground.

[185] Canada was the first among constitutional democracies to include disability as a constitutionally prohibited ground of discrimination. See now the newly adopted UN Convention on the Rights of Persons with Disabilities as well as African Charter and Revised European Social Charter.

[186] See, for example, Article 23 of Constitution of Ecuador and Treaty of Amsterdam, Article 13 EC.

[187] See for example Article 14 of Spanish Constitution.

[188] See Chapter 13, page 264.

[189] See pages 136, 220 and 271 of this book.

[190] *Canada (Attorney-General) v. J.T.I. MacDonald Corp* [2007] S.C.J. No. 30.

[191] *Chaoulli v. Quebec (Attorney General)*, [2005] 1 SCR 791.

them into long waiting queues in the public system. The majority of the Court agreed that the prohibition violated rights to life and to security of the person.[192] A minority raised concerns over the use of the Charter to benefit the wealthy and agreed with the State that such a ban was necessary to protect the publicly funded system. King argues that if the right to health had been constitutionally enshrined then the Court could have perhaps better balanced the arguments.[193] Indeed, in *Kyalami Ridge*, the Constitutional Court of South Africa relied on the government's duty to fulfil the right to housing in turning down a civil rights challenge by an environmental association to making nearby land to flood victims housing.[194]

Secondly, there may be conflicts between various express economic, social and cultural rights. Muralidhar examines the way in which courts in a series of cases put greater emphasis on the right to water and environmental rights over rights to housing and settlement. In *Narmada Bachao Andolan v. Union of India*,[195] the Court acknowledged that 'conflicting rights had to be considered. If for one set of people namely those of Gujarat, there was only one solution, namely, construction of a dam, the same would have an adverse effect on another set of people whose houses and agricultural land would be submerged in water'.[196] However, the majority of the Court pleaded 'separation of powers' and deferred to the governments right to make policy decisions.[197]

The dissenting judge in *Narmada Bachao Andolan* adopted a more rigorous approach finding that there was in fact no environmental clearance for the project as required by the law and many

interim orders in the case concerning relief and rehabilitation of those evicted had not been followed.[198] In a similar case of *N.D. Jayal v Union of India*,[199] the dissenting justice articulated some principles that may help guide such balancing of rights when there is power or wealth imbalance:

> When such social conflicts arise between the poor and more needy on one side and rich or affluent or less needy on the other, prior attention has to be paid to the former group which is both financially and politically weak. Such less-advantaged group is expected to be given prior attention by a welfare state like ours which is committed and obliged by the Constitution, particularly by its provisions contained in the preamble, fundamental rights, fundamental duties and directive principles, to take care of such deprived sections of people who are likely to lose their home and source of livelihood.[200]

Clements and Simmons are similarly critical of the European Court of Human Rights decision at first instance in *Blecic v Croatia*,[201] where Croatia had terminated the tenancy/occupant rights of Serb Croat refugees who wished to return to their homes in favour of the new occupants. The Court found the termination pursued a legitimate aim and noted that where there are 'competing interests of different groups in society' in a situation of 'scarce resources,' – Croatia had argued there was a housing crisis – then the 'reasonable assessment' of which party will benefit and which will suffer is within a State's 'margin of appreciation'. Yet, in this case Mrs Blecic had occupied the home since 1953, was homeless, the dispossession was systematically tilted against Serb Croats and the Court did not consider the possibility of alternative solutions, such as allowing the present occupants temporary possession or finding alternative shelter for the refugees who were in desperate circumstances.

These dissents and critiques offer a more compelling way forward and are more consistent with some of the principles developed by judicial and quasi-judicial bodies to adjudicate economic,

---

[192] In her ruling for the four-judge majority in the case, Justice Deschamps held that the prohibition on private insurance violated the right to 'life', 'personal security' and 'inviolability' under section 1 of the Quebec Charter of Human Rights and Freedoms. The Court split 3–3 on the issue of whether the ban also violated section 7 of the Canadian Charter.

[193] 'Constitutional Rights and Social Welfare: A Comment on the Canadian Chaoulli Health Care Decision', *Modern Law Review* Vol. 69 (2006), pp. 631–643.

[194] 2001 (7) BCLR 652 (CC), para 51.

[195] (2000) 10 SCC 664. See also *T.N.Godavarman Tirumulkpad v. Union of India* (1997) 2 SCC 267 and *T.N.Godavarman Tirumulkpad v. Union of India* (2000) 6 SCC 413 concerning eviction of forest dwellers.

[196] Ibid. p. 764.

[197] Ibid.

[198] Ibid. p. 784.

[199] (2004) 9 SCC 362.

[200] Ibid. p. 418. The dissenting judge noticed that out of a total of 9239 rural affected families, cash compensation had not been paid to 1948 families.

[201] Application No.59532/00, judgment dated 29 July 2004.

social and cultural rights. This involves addressing the seriousness of the harm involved on each side of the conflict, the historical nature of the claims, the presence of discrimination of violation of a minimum core obligation and the presence of alternatives. Such principles are not unknown to civil and political rights and other fields of law.[202]

4. THE JUSTICIABILITY DEBATE REVISITED

What then of the justiciability debate? What does the emerging practice of social rights adjudication mean for the contested positions over whether economic, social and cultural rights are *legal* rights and whether courts have the *legitimacy and capacity* to adjudicate them?

The growing jurisprudence has certainly influenced the debate. One dramatic shift was that of Cass Sunstein. In 1993, in an essay 'Against Positive Rights', he argued that the inclusion of social rights in the new constitutions of post-communist European States 'was a large mistake, possibly a disaster'. For him, many social rights were 'absurd', 'Governments should not be compelled to interfere with free markets' and many 'positive rights are unenforceable by courts' since they lack the bureaucratic and policy tools'.[203] After the *Grootboom* decision in South Africa in 2000, Sunstein took a seemingly opposite view:

> The distinctive virtue of the Court's approach is that it is respectful of democratic prerogatives and of the limited nature of public resources, while also requiring special deliberative attention to those whose minimal needs are not being met. The approach of the Constitutional Court stands as a powerful rejoinder to those who have contended that socio-economic rights do not belong in a constitution.[204]

Similar movement in attitude can be seen beyond academia. The deliberations of the Human Rights Council working group, and its predecessors, on an Optional Protocol to the International Covenant on Economic, Social and Cultural Rights for complaints concerning violations of the covenant have been substantially affected by presentations on the experiences of justiciability.[205] The debate shifted from largely philosophical concerns[206] to the modalities and scope of the proposed procedure.

The sheer weight of the jurisprudence makes it difficult to argue against the *possibility* of social rights justiciability. Even Dennis and Stewart, in their clarion call to States not to adopt an Optional Protocol, acknowledge this fact, stating that they 'do not reject out of hand the notion that some social and economic rights may be domestically justiciable'.[207] But the scholarship and jurisprudence itself indicates that the philosophical debate still rumbles with a certain degree of intensity.[208] Debate is now more focused on the degree of justiciability. Should courts engage in weak and strong forms of review? What are appropriate remedies? How do you reconcile individual and collective interests, and the relationship between theories of democratic deliberation and judicial review?

The debate on judicial review is not solely confined to economic, social and cultural rights – some commentators remain hesitant about the idea of judicial review of human rights at all. It is a debate with a long pedigree. Jeremy Bentham excoriated his eighteen century contemporary Justice Mansfield for developing the English common law in defiance of 'popular assemblies' and squandering legal certainty as 'amendment from the judgment seat is confusion'.[209] Two centuries

---

[202] See also discussion of pages 36–37 below.
[203] C. Sunstein, 'Against Positive Rights: Why social and economic rights *don't* belong in the new constitutions of post-communist Europe', *East European Constitutional Review*, Vol. 2, Winter (1993), pp. 35–38.
[204] C. Sunstein, 'Social and economic rights? Lessons from South Africa', *Public Law and Legal Theory Working Paper No. 12*, University of Chicago, later published in *Designing Democracy. What Constitutions Do* (Oxford: Oxford University Press, 2001), pp. 221–37.
[205] See discussion in Chapter 23, Section 5.
[206] A typical earlier intervention was that of the Canadian government representative. She said that she accepted that if social benefits are already provided, there must be equal access, but questioned whether someone should have the right to bring a complaint for an increase in social benefits.
[207] M. Dennis and D. Stewart, 'Justiciability of Economic, Social, and Cultural Rights: Should There Be an International Complaints Mechanism to Adjudicate the Rights to Food, Water, Housing, and Health?', *American Journal of International Law*, Vol. 98, (2004), pp. 462–515, at 515.
[208] Scheinin, 'Justiciability and Indivisibility of Human Rights' (n. 211 below).
[209] *Comment on the Commentaries* (Oxford: Clarendon Press, 1928), p. 214, quoted in W. Holdsworth, *Some Makers of English Law* (Cambridge: Cambridge University Press, 1938), p.173.

later, his namesake Jeremy Waldron has levelled arguments against judicial review of human rights on both democratic and instrumentalist grounds although he hedges his argument with a number of assumptions.[210] Addressing this more foundational debate of the appropriate role of Courts is beyond the scope of this introductory reflection but many of the arguments do arise in some form as we consider the legitimacy and capacity arguments concerning social rights adjudication.

4.1 Legal Nature of Social Rights

A bundle of arguments has traditionally been used to deny the legal, and by extension, justiciable nature of economic, social and cultural rights by distinguishing them from civil and political rights. The arguments include the claims that the rights are vague, inherently of a positive nature and resource dependent. The counter-arguments are well-rehearsed and some commentators have declared the debate almost over. A former member of the Human Rights Committee, Martin Scheinin, opined that, 'the old counter-argument related to the alleged 'different nature' of these rights, as compared to more traditional human rights generally described as civil and political rights, is perhaps not yet dead and buried but nevertheless appears today as a quiet echo from the past'.[211]

As to the abstract nature of economic, social and cultural rights, they are phrased no differently than civil and political rights; the right to freedom of speech is no more concrete in expression than the right to social security. Indeed, it is arguable that 'open-textured framing' of all human rights is to be favoured: 'courts are able to respond adequately to individual circumstances and historical developments in concretising their meaning over time'.[212] Through contextual claims and counter-claims, arguments and counter-arguments, we also develop a better understanding of the content of those rights and obligations, and the voluble rise in jurisprudence is helping this process.[213] The South African Constitutional Court has precisely understood its role in this way: '

> Socio-economic rights are expressly included in the Bill of Rights; they cannot be said to exist on paper only. . . . and the courts are constitutionally bound to ensure that they are protected and fulfilled. The question is therefore not whether socio-economic rights are justiciable under our Constitution, but how to enforce them in a given case.[214]

Beyond stylistic construction, the argument that the rights are somehow substantively different has withered. Scholars have long noted that economic, social and cultural rights require not only government action, but also restraint.[215] For the right to health, protecting existing access to community health care and clean air and water can be as important as State provision of health care facilities. The nature and degree of the State obligations and financial burden to realise economic, social and cultural rights will thus vary according to context. Likewise, the assumption that civil and political rights are concerned with protection of personal freedoms from State malevolence (at no cost to the taxpayer) has been shown conceptually problematic. The right to a fair trial is largely a positive right requiring significant expenditure of state resources on courts, prison systems and legal aid. As Menéndez puts it, 'All rights, and not only social rights, are public goods rendered

---

[210] See J. Waldron, 'The core of the Case Against Judicial Review', *The Yale Law Journal*, Vol. 115 (2006), pp. 1346–1406. Responses include D. Kyritsis, 'Representation and Waldron's Objection to Judicial Review', *Oxford Journal of Legal Studies*, Vol. 26, No. 4 (2006), pp. 733–751. A. Kavanagh, 'Participation and Judicial Review: A Reply To Jeremy Waldron', *Law and Philosophy*, Vol. 22, No. 5, September (2003), pp. 451–486.

[211] M. Scheinin, 'Justiciability and Indivisibility of Human Rights', in Squires, Langford and Thiele (eds.), *The Road to a Remedy* (n. 11 above), pp. 17–26, at 17.

[212] A. Nolan, B. Porter and M. Langford, *The Justiciability of Social and Economic Rights: An Updated Appraisal*, published by Center for Human Rights and Global Justice Working Paper Series, New York University, No. 14, 2007 and the Committee on the Administration of Justice, Northern Ireland, 2007, p. 11.

[213] Defenders of social rights traditionally defended the lack of clarity of the rights on the basis 'of their exclusion from processes of adjudication' but this argumentation is not as crucial now. See this argument in S. Liebenberg, 'The International Covenant on Economic, Social and Cultural Rights and its Implications for South Africa', *South African Journal of Human Rights*, Vol. 11 (1995), pp. 359–378, at 362.

[214] *Grootboom* (n. 47 above), para. 20.

[215] See A. Eide, 'State obligations revisited' in W.B. Eide and U. Kracht (eds.) *Food and Human Rights in Development, Vol. II: Evolving issues and emerging applications* (Antwerp: Intersentia, forthcoming) pp.137–160, for a discussion.

possible by public institutions'.[216] The necessity for positive State action to realise civil and political rights has actually generated a growing jurisprudence on positive obligations within this field.[217]

The meaningless of such divisions between the two sets of rights has not escaped judicial notice. The South African Constitutional Court remarked that 'many of the civil and political rights entrenched in the text will give rise to similar budgetary implications without compromising their justiciability' and the 'fact that socio-economic rights will almost inevitably give rise to such implications does not seem to us to be a bar to their justiciability'.[218] Other courts have downplayed the general positive/negative dichotomy. In *R v Secretary of State for the Home Department, ex p Limbuela*, Lord Brown emphatically stated:

> I repeat, it seems to me generally unhelpful to attempt to analyse obligations arising under article 3 [Right not to be subjected to inhumane or degrading treatment] as negative or positive, and the state's conduct as active or passive. Time and again these are shown to be false dichotomies. The real issue in all these cases is whether the state is properly to be regarded as responsible for the harm inflicted (or threatened) upon the victim.[219]

Of course, it is possible to contend that economic, social and cultural rights require greater public investment than civil and political rights but it is a matter of degree rather than substance. We discuss below the way in which courts have handled the resource dimensions of both sets of rights. Moreover, effective social policies and investments in the short-term may mean lower governmental expenditures are needed in the long-run, 'ensuring the provision of adequate education, and training or eliminating obstacles to access to land, housing or employment may significantly reduce state expenditures related to social security, unem-

ployment, or homelessness'.[220] In some countries, public expenditures for social security are dwarfed by funds allocated to protect personal security, such as police and defence.

4.2 Legitimacy

A more persistent argument is that social rights adjudication is anti-democratic in nature; that the role of nationally elected representatives is usurped when courts pass judgment on matters of social policy and resource allocation. More specialised versions of this argument are manifest in the claim that the principle of separation of powers amongst the various branches of government is violated since in relation to law, the legislature is to make it, the executive is to implement it and the judiciary is to apply it – to interpret and particularise it. Matters of policy, whether they involve levels of social benefits or the appropriate economic policy for reducing unemployment, are the domain of the executive and the legislature. Since policy is political, it should be addressed by the more directly accountable branches of governments, by those representatives who can be easily removed by popular vote not by 'unelected' courts.

As Nolan notes in her Chapter on Ireland, this view has largely prevailed within the judiciary of that country. In *Sinnott*, Justice Hardiman declared that:

> Central to this view [of the separation of powers] is a recognition that there is a proper sphere for both elected representatives of the people and the executive elected or endorsed by them in the taking of social and economic and legislative decisions, as well as another sphere where the judiciary is solely competent[221] … [I]f judges were to become involved in such an enterprise, designing the details of policy in individual cases or in general, and ranking some areas of policy in priority to others, they would step beyond their appointed role.[222]

Reviewing the jurisprudence, one finds that courts often use this argument in order to avoid (whether reasonably or unreasonably), the 'hard' cases. For

---

[216] A. Menéndez, *New Foundations for Social Rights: A deliberative democratic approach*, ARENA Working Papers WP 02/32, University of Oslo, 2005, p. 10.

[217] See for example, A. Mowbray, *The Development of Positive Obligations under the European Convention on Human Rights by the European Court of Human Rights* (Oxford: Hart Publishing, 2004).

[218] *Ex Parte Chairperson of the Constitutional Assembly: In re Certification of the Constitution of the Republic of South Africa* 1996 (4) SA 744 (CC), para. 78.

[219] [2005] UKHL 66 para.92.

[220] Nolan, Porter and Langford, *The Justiciability of Social and Economic Rights* (n. 212 above), p. 10.

[221] [2001] 2 IR 545, para. 375.

[222] Ibid. para. 377.

example, in the Argentinean case of *Ramos*,[223] an indigent woman with eight children sought a court order for federal and local authorities to provide her with a monthly allowance to cover her family's basic needs, medical coverage to address her daughter's heart disease and a guarantee of her children's right to attend classes. The Court dismissed the case partly on the basis that the claim was not suitable for judicial review and should be directed to the government authorities since they could not exercise discretion concerning the allocation of budgetary resources. While this opinion is partly inconsistent with other decisions of the Court, Courtis notes that it may be explained by the lack of proper legal argument and that it was filed shortly after Argentina's worst economic crisis. The Court 'probably weighed the potential "snowball effect" of granting court relief in such a delicate economic and political context'.[224] It is nonetheless arguable that the Court could have rationally proceeded to such a result by examining the reasonableness of the government's response without needing to rely on the separation of powers argument.

But the argument on separation of powers is typically overstated. If courts have been constitutionally empowered to judicially review the realisation of social rights then they are simply doing their constitutional job, fulfilling the task of their branch. We have already noted judicial statements to this effect. As far back as 1970, the Constitutional Court of Germany began to cautiously indicate the conceptual problem of the distinction:

> [T]his principle does demand a strict separation of powers, but in exceptional cases permits legislative functions to be exercised by governmental and administrative bodies, or government and administration to be exercised by legislative bodies. In exceptional cases, the principle of separation of powers also permits legal protection against acts of the executive to be furnished not by courts, but by independent institutions . . . The essen-

tial point is that the rationale for separation of powers namely reciprocal restriction and control of state power, is still fulfilled.[225]

Indeed, the neat functional division between the branches of government (like between positive and negative obligations) is more an exercise in abstraction than reality in mature and modern democracies.[226] In the modern democratic state, where there is substantial law-making and adjudication by agencies, accountability in the form of tribunals, ombudspersons, legislative committees, and elaborate judicial remedies such as structural injunctions and supervisory jurisdiction,[227] the notion of a strict separation of powers is no longer tenable. The term functions more as a conclusory label for what courts feel is outside their competence than a guiding concept informing them what side of the line a particular instance of legislative or executive action falls.[228]

A second rejoinder turns on what we mean by 'democracy'. On some views, social rights are positively required by the concept of a democratic society. Judicial enforcement of social rights is thus not contrary to the will of elected representatives. The argument goes in two directions. Some argue that social rights are a prerequisite for democracy. According to Miller, 'Protective and welfare rights provide a secure basis upon which the citizen can launch into his [sic] political role'.[229] The Swiss Federal Court partly justified its derivation of a right to minimum subsistence

---

[223] Supreme Court of Argentina, *Ramos, Marta Roxana y otros v. Buenos Aires, Provincia de y otros s/amparo*, 12 March 2002. See also discussion by Piovesan of right to health cases in Chapter 9, Section 3.

[224] Courtis, Chapter 8, Section 4.3 of this volume.

[225] See *Klauss* case (30 BverfGE I, 1970).

[226] See E. Rubin, *Beyond Camelot: Rethinking Politics and Law for the Modern State* (Princeton: Princeton University Press, 2005) for an extensive critique of the separation of powers doctrine.

[227] A. Chayes, 'The Role of the Judge in Public Law Litigation', *Harvard Law Review*, Vol. 89 (1976), pp. 1281–1316 and discussion in next Chapter.

[228] The UN Committee on Economic, Social and Cultural Rights has commented that, 'While the respective competences of the various branches of government must be respected, it is appropriate to acknowledge that courts are generally already involved in a considerable range of matters which have important resource implications'. Committee on Economic, Social and Cultural Rights, *General Comment 3, The nature of State parties obligations* (Art. 2, para.1 of the Covenant) (1991).

[229] D. Miller, *Market, State and Community* (Oxford: Clarendon Press, 1989), p. 249, quoted in C. Fabre, *Social Rights under the Constitution* (Oxford: Oxford University Press, 200), p. 123.

from a range of civil and political rights on this basis:

> The guaranteeing of elementary human needs like food, clothing and shelter is the condition for human existence and development as such. It is at the same time an indispensable component of a constitutional, democratic polity.[230]

This contention may hold well with the theory of democratic deliberation where only a minimum number of substantial values are externally enforced.[231] One problem with this view is that it may prioritise the instrumental over the intrinsic importance of economic, social and cultural rights, making the key focus the idea of political participation.[232] We are also left with the result that some social rights 'may be more equal than others', and Fabre argues that we may only end up with the right to education if we take this course.[233] A bias towards the right to education and a very basic or subsistence level of health care or standard of living is discernible in countries which have a strong constitutional tilt towards civil and political rights, such as the United States[234] and United Kingdom.[235] The logic is additionally questionable since it is arguable that civil and political rights are derivable from economic, social and cultural rights since the former provides institutional protections necessary to ensure the better realisation of the latter.

Therefore, a separate path to tread is to recognise the indivisibility of human rights and accept economic, social and cultural rights in the pantheon; acknowledging that they protect fundamental interests, intrinsic to human dignity and autonomy, and that governments and majoritarian democracies do not always succeed in ensuring their protection. This 'democratic failure' may result from majoritarian democracies paying insufficient attention to minority groups. In some cases, the 'minority' might actually constitute the numerical majority – many political systems are dominated by a certain gender or political or social class, corruption and entrenched systems of political patronage. These defects of elective democracy are fairly patent. Complementary accountability mechanisms are needed to ensure that the effective exclusion from elective processes does not result in a denial of human rights. Adjudication provides an alternative and important forum in which such individuals and groups can have their voice heard.[236] Indeed, one can discern greater judicial activity in those jurisdictions where the systematic failure by State to address social disadvantage is perhaps most extreme, India, Colombia and Brazil being obvious examples.

It is arguable that judicial processes, *to the extent they are accessible*, are characterised by a high degree of 'participation,' at least at the individual or group level. Claimants are entitled to officially plead their case, information must be supplied by all parties and a systematic evaluation of the issues and evidence is undertaken. Other commentators have suggested that litigation provides an opportunity for welcome and constructive dialogue between the branches of government over effective policy-making.[237]

A final response is legal, and based on the role that courts play. The idea that courts will be 'making up' policy is very much a caricatured version of a reasonable approach of a court to these issues. Indeed, courts are perhaps the branch of government most reluctant to take the role, the so called 'least dangerous branch of government'.[238] The majority of decisions in the area of social rights have been marked by a high degree of judicial cautiousness – 'judges are not alone'[239] – and it

---

[230] V. v. Einwohnergemeinde X. und Regierungsrat des Kantons Bern (BGE/ATF 121 I 367), para. 2(b).

[231] R Gargarella ' Should Deliberative Democrats Defend the Judicial Enforcement of Social Rights?', in S. Besson, J. L. Marti and V. Seiler, *Deliberative Democracy and Its Discontents* (Aldershot: Ashgate, 2006), pp. 233–252. Nonetheless, a number of deliberative democrats tend to see basic subsistence entitlements as an essential component of the deliberative conception of democracy.

[232] This is the approach of Jurgen Habermas in *Between Facts and Norms* (MIT Press, 1996), p. 123.

[233] Fabre, *Social Rights under the Constitution* (n. 229 above).

[234] See Chapter by Albisa and Schwarz in this volume.

[235] See Chapter by King in this volume.

[236] Venezuela's constitution is also interesting in attempting to formally go further in creating a fourth branch of government with a range citizen's institutions. See Chapter 10.

[237] See further, C. Scott, 'Social Rights: Towards a Principled, Pragmatic Judicial Role', *SER Review*, Vol. 1, No. 4 (1999).

[238] See Alexander Bickel, *The Least Dangerous Branch* (Indianapolis: Bobbs-Merrill).

[239] A. Menéndez, *New Foundations for Social Rights* (n. 216 above).

has taken remarkable persistence by advocates to push courts to take a robust role in the area. The essential argument is that courts are not being asked to *make* law or policy but *review* it against a set of criteria, in this case human rights. It is at the margins that that questions arise as to whether all aspects are capable of immediate implementation or that courts will somehow tend to interfere with the separation of powers between the various branches of government.

Indeed, concerns over separation of powers tend to be manifest when courts find themselves at the borders of their powers, and it is here the debate should focus. A number of adjudicatory bodies have developed their own tests to determine the limits of their powers and these were particularly highlighted in the preceding Section on the jurisprudence. The approach has been to first apply some sort of reasonableness standard to assess a particular act or omission and/or demand some minimum level of behaviour. Secondly, remedial flexibility has been experimented with by courts as is more fully discussed in the following chapter by Roach. For example, a declaration of invalidity may be made by the Court with the government given a certain time to devise an appropriate policy response. Indeed Budlender and Roach have argued elsewhere that in the history of human rights cases, courts are most interventionist at the remedial level when governments have a demonstrable lack of *political will* or *capacity* to implement an order.[240]

What is perhaps interesting to note is that in 1953, when many scholars held rather conservative views on social rights, the philosopher W.M. Sibley essentially outlined a model for reasonableness review. Taking the hypothetical example of *A* depriving *B* of a sales commission they had jointly procured, he notes that A's behaviour might be rational but not reasonable. However, conduct can only be 'deemed reasonable by someone taking the standpoint of moral judgment' and this often requires the intervention of a third party:

> To be reasonable here is to see the matter – as we commonly put it – from the other person's point of view, to discover how each will

be affected by the possible alternative actions; and, moreover, not 'merely' to see this (for any merely prudent person would do as much) but also be prepared to be disinterestedly *influenced,* in reaching a decision, by the estimate of these possible results.[241]

The above discussion has largely concentrated on the role of adjudicatory bodies within national democracies. A similar debate arises, albeit in a different form, with regard to international adjudication of States. The objection is formally based on the idea of State sovereignty but encapsulates the idea that national democratic processes are better suited to matters of social policy etc. A response follows broadly similar lines to that enunciated above. First, States have accepted human rights obligations in international human rights treaties and customary law and submitted to the jurisdiction of such bodies. Second, some international human treaties have given States a wide degree of latitude. As Van Hoof notes, the European Court of Human Rights has given States significant margin of appreciation meaning that 'the content of given to a particular right or freedom protected by the Convention may deviate markedly from one contracting State to the other'.[242] The UN Committee of Economic, Social and Cultural Rights speaks of a 'margin of discretion' when it comes to policy choices.[243] Third, the cases in the second half of this book show that the regional and international supervisory bodies place strong emphasis on their role in examining the justification for a particular act or omission as opposed to a general deliberation on the ideal measure for such a situation. As the European Committee on Social Rights stated:

> [W]hen the achievement of one of the rights in question is exceptionally complex and particularly expensive to resolve, a State party must take measures that allows it to achieve the objectives of the Charter within a reasonable time, with measurable progress and to an extent consistent with the maximum use of available resources. States parties must be particularly mindful of the impact their choices will have for groups with heightened

---

240 K. Roach and G. Budlender, 'Mandatory Relief and Supervisory Jurisdiction: When is it Appropriate, Just and Equitable', *South African Law Journal*, Vol. 122 (2005), pp. 325–351.

241 'The Rational Versus the Reasonable', *The Philosophical Review*, Vol. 62, No. 4 (Oct. 1953), pp. 554–560.

242 Van Hoof, 'The Legal Nature of Economic, Social and Cultural Rights' (n. 48 above), p. 103.

243 See further Chapter 23.

vulnerabilities as well as for other persons affected including, especially, their families on whom falls the heaviest burden in the event of institutional shortcomings.[244]

4.3   Capacity

A third concern is whether judicial bodies are suitably situated (particularly in terms of information and expertise) to ascertain and understand the relevant facts of a case, navigate the minefield of potential competing policy choices and resource demands and craft appropriate and functional remedies. This concern has been raised in theoretical discussions but has also been subjected to some empirical testing. In a well-known 1977 major study of four human rights cases in the United States, Horowitz argued that courts struggled to obtain unbiased and sufficient evidence on the policy issues they faced and that the 'judicial process was a poor format for the weighing of alternatives and the calculation of costs'.[245] He acknowledged however that some problematic aspects of the decisions were ironed out over time and that legislators and policymakers are often subject to the same lack of capacity.[246]

Ensuring that relevant and unbiased evidence is placed before adjudicators is a major challenge, particularly in those cases that require higher levels of State action or require an understanding of complex social process in action, for example those concerning indirect discrimination.[247] Some of the major cases in this book[248] have required intensive litigation. Although the volume of evidence and time of trial pales in comparison to cases in the areas of corporations, anti-trust or property law. The challenges of obtaining evidence also varies among jurisdictions. In more adversarial common law jurisdictions, the issue may be how to ensure that the evidence and experts from opposing parties are unbiased. In jurisdictions where adjudicators play a more active role, there may be insufficient financial and temporal capacity to track down all the information and ensure it is appropriately subjected to critique.

Scott and Macklem treat this capacity issue in a positive light.[249] They contend that social rights adjudication plays a valuable function in bringing forth information into the public domain that may not be traditionally available to legislature – concrete violations of rights, particularly of marginalised groups. This confirms in many ways Roscoe Pound's old observation that:

> Judicial finding of law has a real advantage in competition with legislation in that it works with concrete cases and generalizes only after a long course of trial and error in the effort to work out a practicable principle. Legislation, when more than declaratory, when it does more than restate authoritatively what judicial experience has indicated, involves the difficulties and the perils of prophecy.[250]

Horowitz argues that the force of this argument is partly blunted by the fact that courts tended to be backward-looking as well, in terms of using precedents as existing evidence. Nevertheless, if some form of dialogical and incremental process emerges from the litigation over time (Pounds' 'trial and error') then the futuristic dimensions can be built into the judicial process – although, the same can be said for the legislative process.

Turning to expertise, can adjudicators address supposedly complex social and financial matters? The expertise needed of courts is, however, partly determined by what we ask of courts. If their role is not to decide policy and resource allocation but rather to assess whether the State (or other actors) have adequately complied with their legal obligations, then they need not be 'policy wonks'. What is required is essentially the exercise of 'traditional' judicial competences: 'hearing from the rights claimant, and other witnesses about the particular situation at issue, considering evidence

---

[244] *Autism-Europe v. France* (n. 135 above), Decision on the Merits, para. 53.

[245] D. Horowitz, *The Courts and Social Policy* (Washington, DC: The Brookings Institution, 1977).

[246] Ibid. p. 293.

[247] See Chapter by Muralidhar in this volume.

[248] See for example, *Kearney & Ors v. Bramlea Ltd & Ors*, Board of Inquiry, Ontario Human Rights Code (2001) (Canada) and *TAC v. Ministers of Health*, 2002 (10) BCLR 1033 (CC) (South Africa).

[249] C. Scott and P. Macklem, 'Constitutional Ropes of Sand or Justiciable Guarantees: Social Rights in a New South African Constitution', *University of Pennsylvania Law Review*, Vol. 141, No. 1 (1992), pp.1–148.

[250] Roscoe Pound, *The Formative Era of American Law*, at p.51, quoted in D. Horowitz, *The Courts and Social Policy* (Washington, DC: The Brookings Institution, 1977) at p.3.

from expert witnesses about the broader policy issues, hearing arguments from the parties and, finally, applying the law to the facts in a fair and impartial manner'.[251]

Of course, litigants may increasingly demand more concrete rulings, particularly where authorities have failed to develop or implement concrete plans. One can certainly discern in jurisdictions like Colombia, and to some extent India, a greater willingness to make more concretised orders in the face of government intransigence or incompetence. Of course, every area of law also benefits from greater expertise. Many courts formally or informally divide the workload amongst judges and other adjudicators according to specialty. Some courts also have the power to seek out external expertise. In India, courts have used special commissions of inquiry to examine factual or policy evidence while in the United States, courts have appointed individuals and bodies including special masters, advisory juries and court-appointed experts.[252]

But it is the 'polycentric' dilemma that, on its face, is the most difficult and the one of the most enduring arguments in the capacity debate. In his famous 1978 essay, Lon Fuller argued that the judiciary cannot and should not deal with situations in which there are complex repercussions beyond the parties and factual situation before the court.[253] Or as Vierdag puts it, how can a court make the seemingly political decision of 'putting a person either in or out of a job, a house or school'? The choice of one particular policy choice may have unforeseen consequences that the court cannot take into account; or the order to spend more on health may be detrimental for allocations on health.

But the 'polycentricity' debate is comparable to the legitimacy debate. There is an oversimplification of the problem, a devaluing of social rights and a misunderstanding of the adjudication role and potential remedies. The oversimplification comes through the caricature of social rights claims as polycentric in comparison to other areas of law. In a potent rejoinder to Lon Fuller, Jeff King argues that polycentricity is 'a pervasive feature of adjudication' which requires a refinement or rejection of the idea of polycentricity as the bright line for justiciability. He demonstrates, for example, how English courts are silent on the polycentric consequences of their mostly pro-taxpayer oriented decisions, but more willingly invoke polycentric concerns to explain away their reluctance to interfere in the allocation of resources for social welfare.[254]

This is not to deny the importance of polycentric concerns – in some cases they are particularly present, the 'elephant in the room'. But the process of social rights adjudication is not necessarily ill-equipped to address them. If we understand social rights adjudication as protecting fundamental rights, setting the processes and standards by which these rights will be measured, placing the burden on government to justify its current lack of action or realisation of the rights and using remedial discretion to find the contextually appropriate ways to enforce a duty-bearer's obligations, then polycentric concerns can be addressed.

The cases in this book demonstrate that many adjudicators are acutely aware of polycentricity and have developed legal tests in response. Let us take two examples: the allocation of budgetary resources and collective ramifications of individual complaints. In relation to the former, Sepulveda describes how the Constitutional Court of Colombia has explicitly developed a range of tests (which can vary according to the relevant right) before it orders the *immediate* minimum enforcement of a right. In the case of the right to social security, the individual must be in a situation of manifest vulnerability, having no possibility to personally remedy the problem, the State has such capacity and its inaction or omission will affect the individuals ability to enjoy 'minimum conditions of a dignified life.[255] In the case of HIV/AIDS, the Court is less concerned with the budgetary issue if the 'life and integrity' of the patient is at risk and it also applies the test to both public

---

[251] Nolan, Porter and Langford, *The Justiciability of Social and Economic Rights* (n. 212 above), p. 17.

[252] See D. Horowitz, *The Courts and Social Policy* (The Brookings Institution, 1977).

[253] L. Fuller, 'The Forms and Limits of Adjudication', *Harvard Law Review* Vol. 92 (1978–1979), pp. 353–409.

[254] 'The Pervasiveness of Polycentricity', *Public Law*, forthcoming 2008. Available at <http://papers.ssrn.com/sol3/papers.cfm?abstract‑id=1027625>.

[255] T-533/92. See discussion by Sepúlveda in Chapter 7, Section 4.2.

and private health providers.[256] This test also takes account of the fact that different medical treatments could be offered and requires that the treatment be prescribed by a physician connected to the relevant institution. The Canadian Supreme Court has similarly required government authorities to demonstrate the unavailability of resources when equality rights are being violated.[257] In a Texas Supreme Court case, the state was ordered to develop a new financing model that could ensure schools in poorer districts had adequate education (see pages 240 and 241 of book).

These tests are not dissimilar from the criteria I found in an earlier comparative survey of the judicial reasoning in human rights cases that carried budgetary implications. The review covered economic, social and cultural rights as well as many civil and political rights cases and found that the extent to which an adjudicator would make such an order was determined by four factors: (1) *seriousness* of the effects of the violation; (2) *precision* of the government duty; (3) *contribution* of the government to the violation; and (4) *manageability* of the order for the government in terms of resources.[258] This study also concluded that each of these criteria carries a large degree of subjectivity. The extent to which an adjudicator viewed, or was able to view, economic and social interests as fundamental or truly legal rights tended to affect their reasoning on all of these criteria.

A polycentric dilemma may also arise when a particular policy solution may be applicable in the case of an individual but not to a wider group. For instance, the South African Constitutional Court justified its rejection of an immediate minimum core obligation on this basis, citing in the case of the right to housing that the needs will vary widely according to different factors: e.g. 'there are those who need land; others need both land and houses; yet others need financial assistance'.[259] In

a later case on HIV/AIDS, they reiterated their position although their eventual order concentrated strongly on the design and implementation of a plan to deliver a single medicine. But these obstacles could have been addressed. While expertise or special commissions could have been ordered, procedural innovation might have been the best way forward. For example, putting the burden on the government to develop a policy on ensuring minimum entitlements for all persons. The Court could then review the reasonableness of such an entitlement package. In Colombia, the Court took a pro-active role using its test of an 'unconstitutional state of affairs' to transform individual cases into a collective case.[260] One hundred and nine separate writs of protection submitted by 1,150 IDP families were joined and the Court found that the living conditions of the IDPs constituted a massive, widespread and systematic violation of their constitutional rights.[261]

The individual or collective issue could also be addressed at the remedial stage. Kent Roach in his chapter on remedies in this book draws on the work of Abram Chayes to show that a contemporary, though certainly not new, understanding of litigation (featuring multiple parties and a more active judiciary) means that issues such as polycentricity can be incorporated within the remedial process.[262] This could involve a declaration of delayed invalidity (such as has been used by courts in Canada and Nepal) while the Government develops a plan or interim remedies that may address the emergency needs of the applicants while it takes time to develop an order for more systemic relief. The remedial orders of Venezuelan and Argentine courts sometimes allow for this.

5. IMPACT OF SOCIAL RIGHTS JURISPRUDENCE AND THE ROLE OF LITIGATION

If the philosophical debate on justiciability is the rock of Scylla (courts are, or must not be, too powerful) the question of whether litigation is an *effective* strategy is perhaps Charbydis (courts are not

---

[256] See, e.g., T-236/98, SU-480/97, T-560/98, T-505/92, T-271/95 and T-328/98 and discussion by Sepúlveda in Chapter 7, Section 5.3.

[257] In Eldridge (n. 42 above) they found the provincial government had sufficient resources while in *Newfoundland (Treasury Board) v. NAPE*, [2004] 3 SCR 381 they found that a fiscal crisis justified the delayed payment of a $14 million retroactive pay equity award.

[258] M. Langford, 'Judging Resource Availability', in Squires, Langford and Thiele (eds.), *The Road to a Remedy* (n. 11 above), pp. 89–108.

[259] *Grootboom* (n. 47 above), paras. 32–33.

[260] See section 3.3.

[261] T-025/04.

[262] See Chapter 2, Section 4.

powerful enough). The potential role of adjudication as a vehicle for social change is put into question. While this subject is not at the centre of this particular book, many of the authors take up the issue.

The critique runs that litigation strategies frequently fail to make concrete inroads in ensuring the realisation of human rights, including economic, social and cultural rights.[263] The adjudication process is often long and tortured, the eventual decision may not be favourable and, particularly, orders may not be enforced. Others add that pursuit of litigation is counter-productive. Use of legal mechanisms disempowers the poor, the marginalised and wider social movements by delegating crucial social issues to gatekeeping lawyers, conservative judges and distant international courts and committees. Litigation can distract attention and divert resources away from the development of wider social struggles and the use of policymaking forums.[264]

A particular concern is that middle classes may better capture the Courts in comparison to the poor. The *Chaoulli* decision in Canada is perhaps an example of this and one notices a greater prevalence of stronger positive orders in cases that affect the middle class. This is particularly so in the area of health and education where universal systems are more common as compared to housing, food or work. Even within such a right as housing, we can see some divergence. Cases that concern post-eviction resettlement of informal occupiers, better conditions for tenants and nomadic groups and programmes for the homeless tend to receive a more mixed responses from adjudicators. Those affecting the affordability of mortgage schemes affecting the middle class draw much stronger orders. In Argentina, the Court found that the calculation of interest for private mortgages led to a system of unserviceable

debt,[265] while in Hungary the Constitutional Court struck down an increase to 25 per cent for the subsidised mortgage interest rate after earlier permitting an increase to 15 per cent.[266] In Colombia, the Constitutional Court made extensive orders to ensure *social* housing schemes were affordable, which perhaps explains why that decision attracted comparatively more controversy.[267]

The literature on the topic is vast[268] although not always current. The debate is not necessarily confined to social rights but often covers all human rights and public interest litigation. A number of the cases discussed in this book are at the forefront of the discussion. In the United States, discussion continues on whether the well known *Brown v Board of Education* decisions of the Supreme Court were effective in addressing educational desegregation and whether the decisions were crucial for the positive progress.[269] In South Africa, relatively few dispute the effectiveness of the *TAC* decision in pushing forward a reluctant State to address the HIV/AIDS pandemic. But, as Liebenberg notes in this book, the *Grootboom* decision had less impact in addressing the needs of the homeless applicants although she notes new policy and budgetary development

---

[263] On international procedures, see Dennis and Stewart, Justiciability of Economic, Social, and Cultural Rights (n. 207 above), p. 55 and Letter from Ministry of Foreign Affairs, Sweden, to United Nations Office of the High Commissioner for Human Rights dated 28 March 2003 (copy of letter on file with author).

[264] See, for example, G. Rosenberg, *The Hollow Hope: Can Courts Bring About Social Change?* (Chicago: University of Chicago Press, 1991). For a review of the critiques from the field of critical legal studies see M. Pieterse, 'Eating Socioeconomic Rights: The Usefulness of Rights Talk in Alleviating Social Hardship Revisited,' *Human Rights Quarterly*, Vol. 29, No. 3 (2007), pp. 796–822.

[265] Supreme Tribunal of Justice, Constitutional Court, Sentence No. 85, 24 January 2002, Exp. 01–1274.

[266] Decision 66/1995 (XI. 24), ABH, 1995, 333.

[267] C-383/99, C-700/99 and C-743/99.

[268] See for example in the United States, D. Horowitz, *Courts and Social Policy* (Washington D.C.: The Brookings Institution, 1977); S. Scheingold, *The Politics of Rights: Lawyers, Public Policy and Social Change* (Ann Arbor: the University of Michigan Press, 1974); J. Handler, *Social movements and the Legal system* (New York: Academic Press, 1978); and M. McCann, *Rights at Work: Pay Equity Reform and the Politics of Mobilization* (Chicago: University of Chicago Press, 1994). In South Africa, see M. Heywood, 'Shaping, making and breaking the law in the campaign for a national HIV/Treatment Plan', in P. Jones and K. Stokke (eds.), *Democratising Development: The Politics of Socio-Economic Rights in South Africa* (Leiden: Martinus Nijhoff Publishers, 2005), pp. 181–212; T. Roux, *Understanding* Grootboom: *A Response to Cass R. Sunstein*, 12(2) *Constitutional Forum*, Vol. 12, No. 2 (2002), pp. 41-51; M. Swart, *Left Out in the Cold? Crafting Constitutional Remedies for the Poorest of the Poor*, South African Journal of Human Rights, Vol. 21, (2005), pp. 215; M. Pieterse, Eating Socioeconomic Rights: The Usefulness of Rights Talk in Alleviating Social Hardship Revisited, *Human Rights Quarterly*, Vol. 29, No. 3 (2007), pp. 796–822; K. Pillay, 'Implementation of *Grootboom*: Implications for the enforcement of socio-economic rights', *Law Democracy and Development*, Vol. 6 (2002), pp. 255–277. For the scholarly debate in Canada, see chapter 12 of this book.

[269] See Rosenberg, *The Hollow Hope* (n. 264 above).

and the confusion amongst commentators on the decision itself. Leading decisions on the right to food[270] and education[271] have had some impact in India, according to Muralidhar, but not in other areas such as the Bhopal case.[272] The reluctance of Indian courts to issue strong or binding orders in the area of housing rights has contributed to the poor implementation of their recommendations has contributed mendations for resettlement.[273]

This debate is characterised by both simplicity and nuance. Earlier critics and sometimes more recent entrants tend to conceive of litigation in the abstract and invest it with almost messianic expectations. The impact of a decision is simply measured by whether it concretely achieved a particular social right or, more rarely, had a significant wider conscious-raising effect. The objectives and context of the litigation strategy does not appear to enter the calculus. It seems pointless to expect litigation to be the magic bullet if the litigants did not have the same expectation or other avenues for social progress were unavailable. Yet, as Malcolm Feeley rightly points out, lawyers themselves may be partly to blame for this state of affairs.[274] Having trumped up the rights discourse and the value of public interest litigation, they become fair targets when the litigation fails to deliver.[275]

More recent scholarship reveals that litigation strategies often contain greater sophistication upon closer inspection. Scheingold, in the 2004 preface to the second edition of his 1974 *Politics of Rights*,[276] concludes in the US context that the:

> [O]verall message of the research on collective mobilization is that ... under the appro-

priate conditions ... rights can be deployed to promote collective political mobilization on behalf of an egalitarian agenda. By lending their discursive and institutional support, courts can make an important contribution to this process – as they did with respect to civil rights.[277]

In addition, he partially revises his findings of the role of lawyers. Evidence suggested that many were embedded in wider social movements and were strategic in their use of litigation: 'In sum, cause lawyers do not necessarily see political and legal strategies as mutually exclusive, as I originally suggested – and thus, often willingly engage in the strategic calculations that are essential to a successful politics of rights'.[278]

These reflections accord with earlier empirical research for the Centre on Housing Rights and Evictions (COHRE).[279] In interviews with social rights advocates and lawyers working in twenty-five jurisdictions, many expressed their reluctance to litigate cases that were disconnected from a community or social movement. The likelihood of obtaining and implementing an order was otherwise significantly limited. In some cases, these lessons were based on failed cases, which suggests that evaluation of the impact of social rights adjudication usually requires an adequate time span. Advocates, courts, movements and the public continually develop and refine their approaches over time.[280]

---

270 See *People's Union for Civil Liberties v. Union of India* (2001) 5 SCALE 303; *People's Union for Civil Liberties v. Union of India* (2001) 5 SCALE 303, and *People's Union for Civil Liberties v. Union of India* (2004) 8 SCALE 759.

271 *Unnikrishnan J.P. v. State of Andhra Pradesh* (1993) 1 SCC 645.

272 *Union Carbide Corporation v. Union of India* (1989) 3 SCC 38.

273 See for example, *Olga Tellis v. Bombay Municipal Corporation* (1985) 3 SCC 545 and Unreported order dated 7.5.1997 in Writ Petition No.305 of 1995 (*Bombay Environmental Action Group v. A.R. Bharati*).

274 M. Feeley, 'Hollow Hopes, Flypaper, and Metaphors, Review of 'The Hollow Hope: Can Courts Bring About Social Change? by Gerald N. Rosenberg', *Law & Social Inquiry*, Vol. 17, No. 4 (Autumn, 1992), pp. 745–760, particularly at 751.

275 Rosenberg, *The Hollow Hope* (n. 264 above).

276 S. Scheingold, *The Politics of Rights: Lawyers, Public Policy and Social Change* (Ann Arbor: the University of Michigan Press, 2004).

277 Ibid. p. xxxi.

278 Ibid. p. xxxix.

279 See Langford, *Litigating Economic, Social and Cultural Rights:* (n. 53 above).

280 Ibid. In this sense, I am in very much agreement with Pieterse (n. 268 above) (although his case review is extremely limited) when he says:

> It is therefore tempting to conclude that the inclusion of justiciable socioeconomic rights in the 1996 Constitution amounted to nothing more than the rhetorical pacification of the millions of South Africans who continue to suffer the adverse socioeconomic consequences of apartheid. But such a conclusion would not only be premature (being based, after all, on an analysis of a handful of judgments), it would also ignore the significant indirect benefits that have resulted from the Constitutional Court's socioeconomic jurisprudence. If we view the socioeconomic rights narrative as ongoing, Gabel's challenge to progressive South African lawyers, and to socioeconomic advocates globally, is to uncover these entitlements by intervening in the narrative at the stage of the rights' initial articulation and definition.

How therefore should we measure the impact of social rights litigation? There are three crucial questions that should guide such an inquiry: (i) *What is the criterion for impact?* (ii) *What is the comparator?* and (iii) *What was the cause of the success or failure?* The first two questions require a strong dosage of social scientific methodology while the latter question, if ever properly answered, certainly requires a historians' sensitivity.

5.1   Criteria

In defining the *criteria*, we must firstly ask 'whose criteria'? Is it the court's or quasi-judicial bodies' expectation as embodied in the terms of the order? Or is it the more subjective and strategic expectations of the litigants? To my mind, both are important.

Litigation is often, but not always, initiated as a part of a wider political or developmental strategy. In some case, social movements and advocates actually expect to fail in court but have developed 'the art of losing a case', as Mark Heywood puts it.[281] The mere process of litigation is used to achieve a particular goal in a wider strategy. It might be to highlight a particular injustice or gap in the law, obtain otherwise unavailable documents or commence negotiations. In the case of Nigeria where judgments take decades to be delivered, Felix Morka records that social rights litigation was used as a community mobilisation tool and a platform for making initial contact and negotiating with Government and powerful non-State actors such as multinational oil companies, who were otherwise impervious to dialogue during the authoritarian years.[282] Bruce Porter has also argued that litigation is a valid goal in and of itself. He notes that many claimants believe that the right to a hearing is as important as the remedy itself: 'When people see things and feel them and understand them as human rights issues, you claim them as rights'.[283]

However, if one develops indicators or qualitative markers to evaluate the success of such 'subjective' litigation strategies, care is needed in their selection. Malcolm Feeley rightly criticises Gerald Rosenberg for mounting his entire critique of using courts for social change on the public statements made by lawyers in those cases.[284] He points to other research which suggests that their real expectations and motivations were more strategic than their more 'naive' public utterances.

Turning to the objective criteria, evaluation methods will need to capture direct and indirect benefits. Therefore beyond direct impact on poverty and equality, we might also speak of *legal impact, policy impact, consciousness and awareness impact* and *mobilisation impact.*

In this book, authors demonstrate that many cases have had direct impact on social rights, whether the recognition of concrete legal right, improved access to a social good or prevention of retrogressive and negative social acts. In Brazil, 'judicial rulings on the free provision of medicine, coupled with well-coordinated and efficient litigation strategies have prompted changes in the law and the adoption of public policies that are considered exemplary'.[285] In Canada, a public employee's union was able to enforce a Supreme Court decision, which provided for equal pay for work of equal value when resources were available, after an improvement in the economic situation in the province of Newfoundland.[286] In France, the right to freedom of expression and property was made to yield to the right to health as restrictions on tobacco advertising were upheld by the Constitutional Council.[287] In the United States, the *Rose* case in Kentucky has led to increase resources for education or for the first time students in the State Matched or exceeded the national average in a skills assessment in 2001. In an in-depth and revealing empirical and quantitative study of five developing countries by the World Bank's Development Economics Group, Gauri and Brinks were 'impressed by what courts have been able to achieve' summarising that 'legalizing demand for

[281] See interview in Langford, *Litigating Economic, Social and Cultural Rights* (n. 53above), p. 113.

[282] Ibid. p. 113.

[283] Ibid. p. 79.

[284] M. Feeley, 'Hollow Hopes, Flypaper, and Metaphors, Review of 'The Hollow Hope: Can Courts Bring About Social Change? by Gerald N. Rosenberg', *Law & Social Inquiry*, Vol. 17, No. 4 (Autumn, 1992), pp. 745–760, particularly at 751.

[285] Piovesan in Chapter 9, Section 5.

[286] *Newfoundland (Treasury Board) v. NAPE*, [2004] 3 SCR 381. See discussion by Jackman and Porter in Chapter 11, Section 5.

[287] CC, January 8, 1191, No 99–283 DC. See discussion by Pech in Chapter 14, Section 4.

SE [socioeconomic] rights might well have averted thousands of deaths' and 'enriched the lives of millions of others'.[288]

At the regional and international level, implementation is more challenging as adjudicatory bodies usually lack effective enforcement powers. Most decisions of the African Commission have generally been poorly implemented. In the case of the European Court of Human Rights, Clements and Simmons describe the provision of compensation in a number of cases as well as 'Strasbourg-proofing' as various States reformed laws to comply with the court's rulings. Watson concludes that it 'would not be an exaggeration to state that the women of Europe are deeply indebted' to the European Court of Justice since much European legislation on gender equality has been 'case-led'.[289] The record of the European Committee on Social Rights is so far mixed – Portugal made sweeping legal and institutional changes to address child labour,[290] but Greece only partly implemented decisions on Roma by altering the wording of a discriminatory statute but denied it was legally obliged to take concrete steps to address evictions and lack of housing. In the case of international committees, the pattern is similar. Many of the concluding observations of the Committee on Economic, Social and Cultural Rights have not been observed by governments, but some have had a profound impact.[291]

Melish and Courtis make the point that impact is closely related to the nature of the remedial order. They illustrate that for the Inter-American Court of Human Rights and Argentinean courts, compensation and individual-based orders were quickly executed while wider structural and more complex orders often lagged in implementation.[292] Courtis attributes this to the institutional immaturity of the Argentinean system in dealing with more complex cases while Melish indicates that the Inter-American Court has now strengthened follow-up procedures in response to information on non-compliance. In the case of South Africa, Liebenberg notes that considerable follow-up effort through additional litigation (contempt of court proceedings and complaint to South African Human Rights Commission) and advocacy campaigns was necessary to ensure the mandatory orders for the roll-out of HIV/AIDS medicines were obeyed.[293]

Beyond direct impact, indirect indicators should be used when appropriate. McCann concludes that the indirect impact of litigation for equal pay for equal work surpassed direct effect:

My primary finding is that the political advances in many contexts matched or exceeded the wage gains. One important advance was at the level of rights consciousness. Legal rights thus became increasingly meaningful both as a general moral discourse and as a strategic resource for ongoing challenges to the status quo power relations.[294]

Examples of such *consciousness, awareness or mobilization impact* are described in the chapter by Muralidhar where litigation on rights to food and housing precipitated larger movements who monitored access to food and education. In Argentina, Abramovich noted that while the flagship case of Vicecontte has experienced significant delays in implementation, the discussion of the innovative findings amongst lawyers, judges and academics laid the ground for other cases to succeed, for example on HIV/AIDS medicines. One could also speak of *broader legal or policy impact* where a case sets a judicial precedent or instigates policy discussion and reform. The *Grootboom* case in South Africa laid much of the framework for other social and economic rights cases, from health care to forced evictions. A third category would be participatory impact where the forum is used to enable the voice of victims or achieve strategic advocacy aims. In Brazil, litigation on rights to information and health led to the granting of access to records on information on the halting of redevelopment of hospitals and suspension of medicine purchases.[295]

It may be important to consider a final category: unintended consequences. Like any other intervention, there can be unforeseen positive and

---

[288] Gauri and Brinks. *Courting Social Justice* (n. 54 above).
[289] See discussion by Watson in Chapter 22, Section 5.6.
[290] See European Committee of Social Rights, 1/1999, *ICJ v. Portugal*.
[291] See interview with Scott Leckie in Langford, *Litigating Economic, Social and Cultural Rights* (n. 53 above)
[292] See discussion by Courtis in Chapter 8, Section 5.

[293] See discussion by Liebenberg in Chapter 4, Section 8.
[294] Quoted in Scheingold, *The Politics of Rights* (n. 276 above).
[295] Superior Court of Justice, AgRg na STA 29 (2004). See discussion by Piovesan in Chapter 9, Section 3.4

negative results. Initial high profile cases in South Africa and Argentina were poorly implemented but significantly advanced the law or legal culture, which led to more successfully implemented strategies in future cases. Other results can be negative. Rosenberg points to the complacency successful court decisions can bring – implementation of judicial orders often does not materialise in a vacuum of inaction.[296] Williams and Scheingold respectively note the increasing backlash to the use of progressive rights-claiming strategies by conservative groups in the United States.[297] Such consequences need to be brought into the strategic equation even if addressing power relations should be at the core of rights-claiming strategies. It also highlights the importance of litigants and not their representatives making the key decisions in litigation strategies since it is the former who will most likely bear any fallout from the case.

5.2   What is the Alternative?

The critique of litigation as a vehicle for social change is only sustainable if there are viable alternatives or if litigation makes the situation worse in the absence of alternatives. Therefore, any critique of a decision to litigate must be placed in the strategic context. If other options such as active mobilisation, policy and law reform, negotiation, media advocacy etc were genuinely available to an individual, community or movement, then a choice to litigate should be closely scrutinised, particularly if it was the dominant and not a complementary strategy. In terms of impact and implementation, one must also look at whether a decision generated from another branch of government would be more effectively implemented.

Since this is an exercise in 'what-if,' it is of course difficult to develop significant indicators although one can engage in 'process tracing,' tracking alternatives in the absence of a controlled experiment. It is not an easy task. A senior member of the Public Union of Civil Liberties privately indicated that he thought his organisation should have turned

to mobilisation not litigation to address starvation deaths and the right to food. But the Supreme Court decision has been subsequently used to inspire a movement for monitoring the decision. The difficult question then becomes whether a grassroots-inspired movement would have succeeded more than the Court-inspired movement?

However, if litigation was the last resort, as many claim it to be, then the threshold for success should be lowered considerably. In many of the cases discussed in this book, litigation was the only available option available. Indeed, many Courts, such as those in India and Colombia, tend to rise to the role of social rights protector after clear failure to act by the executive and legislative branches.

5.3   What was the Actual Cause of the Failure or Success?

The last question is what was the actual cause of the failure or success of the case? Was it the litigation strategy or other strategies or both? Was it the use of rights-claiming strategies or other types of strategies? Was it the result of the quality of the legal system and its ability to deliver speedy, sufficiently concrete judgments with effective orders and enforcement of those orders? Was it the failure of the applicants to follow-up the order or the decision to litigate itself? Untangling the cause-and-effect is not an easy task. Some authors such as Rosenberg find that courts contributed little to the positive social reform in the United States, for example in the area of education and abortion rights despite making major judgments in the area.[298] In response, Feeley noted that the decisions were quite modest and Rosenberg misunderstood their role in the wider movement.[299]

This of course raises the question of whether we are speaking of courts or of a wider litigation strategy. Pieterse criticises the *TAC* case for being largely a failure since the litigants had to obtain further orders and mobilise for enforcement.[300] Others such as Liebenberg in this volume see *TAC* as very much a success as it contained such a comprehensive litigation strategy that focused on

[296] Rosenberg, *The Hollow Hope* (n. 264 above).
[297] Scheingold, *The Politics of Rights* (2004) (n. 276 above), pp. xxxii-xxxvii and L. Williams, 'Issues and Challenges in Addressing Poverty and Legal Rights': A Comparative United States/South African Analysis', *South African Journal of Human Rights*, Vol. 21 (2005), pp. 436–472.

[298] Rosenberg, *The Hollow Hope* (n. 264 above).
[299] Feeley, 'Hollow Hopes, Flypaper, and Metaphors' (n. 269 above).
[300] Pieterse, 'Eating Socioeconomic Rights', (n. 250 above).

follow-up and was part of a wider mobilisation effort. Court decisions viewed in isolation are thus an easy target but they do not point to the critical question: Was the choice of litigation appropriate and was an appropriate strategy crafted. Does the failure lie with the legal approach or does it lie elsewhere?

6. CONCLUSIONS

The emergence of a comparative field of social rights jurisprudence provides a welcome opportunity to examine afresh a range of legal, philosophical and practical issues. By drawing from practice, even in its contradictions, theory is both enriched and challenged. It is certainly clear that the justiciability debate has had to adjust to the reality of social rights adjudication. Theoretical concerns over the court's role in litigation cannot be reasonably seen as an axiomatic trump card but rather a factor to be contextually weighed in the decision-making process. The key issue is not whether social rights are justiciable but rather how they can be consistently adjudicated with measure of integrity, respecting the institutional nature of adjudicatory bodies and the call for justice inherent in human rights.

Drawing together the trends identified in this Chapter, we can see that the considerable expansion of justiciable human rights norms has midwifed much of the growth of social rights jurisprudence. In some cases, it has developed through the invocation of civil and political rights while in others, direct economic, social and cultural rights have facilitated litigation. This can be partly ascribed to recent constitutional reform in the democratic transition of some States and the growth of international and regional human rights mechanisms. But the presence of legal opportunities is a necessary but not sufficient condition (and in some cases, not even necessary). Given the inherent conservative nature of courts, a certain threshold of State or private failure is usually necessary to trigger a court's decision to play a more active role. Decisions of social actors to select litigation strategies vary widely between jurisdictions and sustained and progressive litigation is largely conditioned on the maturity of civil and political rights jurisprudence and the strength of rule of law institutions and even democracy itself. Con-

textual and historical understandings of human rights all form part of the calculus in determining how social rights adjudication is manifested. Yet, these factors remain constantly in flux and with movements in all these areas, Justice Albie Sach's prognostication that the '21st-century jurisprudence will focus increasingly on socio-economic rights' carries a ring of truth.[301]

The volume and diversity of jurisprudence also provides an opportunity to enrich the dialogue on our current conceptions and debates around State obligations by providing a broader source of primary, and sometimes conflicting, material. One of the interesting aspects of the jurisprudence is that it provides differing examples of how State obligations, the content of rights and the possible remedial options can be categorised. While numerous conclusions can be drawn from the case law, one clear trend can be identified that reach across and beyond traditional categories of State obligations.

It is the tendency towards the creation of a culture of justification around social rights. Mirroring the approaches of civil and political rights, administrative and to some extent tort law, one can see that the focus of judicial and quasi-judicial inquiry is upon whether a human rights duty bearer can justify their substantive or procedural action or inaction. This convergence of approach is quite explicit in the reasoning of the South African Constitutional Court where they use the reasonableness test to assess both positive and negative obligations. Similarly, the European Court has broadly construed interference with a right to include inaction in some circumstances and Clements and Simmons note that 'the effect of this approach is to place on the State the burden of justifying its failure to act'.[302] This 'justificatory' approach is manifest in the ways in which the adjudicatory bodies have implied certain obligations and defences. For example, the State defence of resources has been accepted even when not explicit in the text of a legal instrument (i.e. in the case of the African Commission on Human Rights and European Committee on Social Rights) but States are also being placed under greater scrutiny to as to whether they are meeting various

[301] Albie Sachs, *Social and Economic Rights: Can they be Made Justiciable?* (Southern Methodist University School Of Law, 1999) p. 18.
[302] See Chapter, 20, Section 4.2.

obligations. This indicates that courts are emerging as *accountability* not *policy* mechanisms.

In some ways, the jurisprudence may be moving towards the approach in equality rights. Distinctions or exclusions must be justified and issues such as resources are conceived as a defence and not an inherent part of the obligation.[303] At the same time, equality rights jurisprudence is being stretched as lawyers and social rights movement seek to apply equally protections in the social arena. This continues to raise questions about how far courts will and should go to enforce substantive equality. It also affects the specification of prohibited grounds of discrimination or identification of indirect discrimination. Discrimination in the field of economic, social and cultural rights can sometimes take different and new forms.

However, there is also a clear *divergence* between jurisdictions in relation to the justification bar that a defendant is expected to jump over. This is particularly clear in cases involving major national development or environmental projects, the provision of goods and services or remedial orders for enforcement. Some adjudicators are less demanding than others. One discernible explanatory variable is the explicit recognition of economic, social and cultural rights. The findings and orders of the Colombian and South African Courts (where this exists) are often stronger than those courts where its not, for example, South Asia. But we also see major divergences in approaches between countries with almost identical provisions (e.g. cf. Argentina and South Africa with Hungary and Ireland). The latter courts justify their conservative stance on traditional philosophical objections to economic, social and cultural rights.

A second divergence is the manner in which the courts address fulfilment obligations. This is perhaps not a surprising conclusion since it is a partly unresolved debate amongst social rights advocates. Some courts such as the Colombian Constitutional Court have developed a remarkably comprehensive approach to the issue, which should

provoke further and in-depth reflection. The Court has been willing to grant immediate *tutela orders* in individual cases where a minimum obligation has been raised while also addressing the broader reasonableness of policies and programs. Moreover, it has fused, at least in theory, the civil law preference for individual remedies and the collective impact of judgments in common law. It is not the only court with such power: it is possible in Hungary and South Africa for example. This is not to advocate the approach of one court. Context differs and there is a concern that applying 'minimum obligations' in wealthier countries can result in simply ensuring survivalism but not necessarily human dignity. But even the Colombian court appears to move beyond that reductionist position.

While the question of direct fulfilment or provision will continue to dominate scholarly pages, the majority of judicial pages will probably not. A large number of cases in this book involve State and private actions. One discernible trend is the growth in social rights claims against private agencies which might have traditionally been attempted only under contract or consumer law. Likewise, some courts are increasingly comfortable with policing the State's protective and regulatory role.

However, fewer cases have arisen in two particular areas and perhaps the most controversial areas of social welfare politics, namely the actual process of privatisation and cutbacks in social welfare. This is not to say that cases don't exist. Courts in the Philippines and Argentina have placed restrictions on privatisation in electricity and worker's compensation; Portugal and Hungary have struck down certain retrogressive rollbacks in social security and health care. Where these issues have been limited in focus (e.g., a single group of pensioners belonging to a pension fund), courts appear more willing to intervene. But when the issue assumes national importance, cases are much fewer. This may be because political strategies are preferred, the timeframe for such actions being extremely short. Or it may be that courts feel that their judicial role is being unduly stretched and that pure policy issues are beginning to intervene. Nonetheless, it remains to be seen whether courts will carve out a greater role in this area, imposing some

---

[303] For further discussion on this possibility, see M. Langford and B. Thiele, 'Introduction', in Squires, Langford and Thiele, *Road to a Remedy* (n. 11 above).

minimum standards on privatisation and roll-backs or whether this will be largely relegated to international supervision.

These conclusions obviously return us to the debate over the proper role of courts and quasi-judicial bodies in a democracy or international system. While this chapter has engaged the traditional debate over legitimacy and institutional capacity, it has sought to show that the actual practice forces a reconfiguration. Many of the adjudicatory bodies discussed in this book appear acutely aware of the constraints necessitated by their role but have fashioned a judicial role in reviewing but not leading the actual implementation of economic, social and cultural rights. As discussed, and taken up in greater detail in the following chapter, appropriate and flexible remedies may be the best means to meet these concerns but also ensure justice is done in the case.

Lastly, this book and others provide some answer to the commonly asked question of whether social rights adjudication will have impact. The answer is clearly, 'Yes, but'. *Yes*, there is evidence of cases exhibiting both direct impact on poverty and discrimination as well as indirect impact in the areas of policy, law, mobilisation and consciousness raising. *But* the impact is not even and appears to be highly dependent on a number of factors, including the nature of the order, the political and organisational power of the claimants and the institutional strength of the State. In some States, these factors are more absent. In South Asia, far-reaching decisions are often complemented by narrow orders and weak and truculent States. In Latin America and European states, implementation appears far more likely while South Africa represents perhaps a mixed case. Therefore, we can see that social rights adjudication is not without impact but should not be invested with either messianic expectations or carefree cynicism.

However, successful litigation and implementation in practices is a significant challenge. Practitioners regularly cite the burdens of lack of adequate standing provisions and procedural innovation, conservative judiciaries and powerful opponents, the lack of financial and legal resources and the challenges of trying to effectively connect claimant communities, social movements, and legal-oriented human rights advocates, and ensure decisions are implemented.[304] The financial barrier is particularly perennial and in her Chapter, Durbach sets out both the arguments for the right to legal aid in the field of socio-economic rights and some judicial recognition of such a right in both the developed and developing world. If the poor are able to have some form of financial equality of arms before adjudicators, it would certainly be likely that some of the negative dimensions of social rights adjudication could be ameliorated.

[304] See Langford, *Litigating Economic, Social and Cultural Rights* (n. 53 above), pp. 20–22 and discussion by Piovesan in Chapter 9, Section 5.

2

The Challenges of Crafting Remedies for Violations of Socio-economic Rights

Kent Roach*

1. INTRODUCTION

A common objection to the full recognition of social, economic and cultural (socio-economic) rights is the difficulty of crafting meaningful remedies. A received remedial tradition suggests that political and civil rights can be fairly easily enforced by backwards looking compensatory remedies, such as damages for aggrieved individuals. Such remedies lie within the core jurisdiction of domestic courts and often mimic the remedial process and aims of private law. In contrast, socio-economic rights may require more complex remedies such as declarations or injunctions that invite or require positive governmental action. They also raise difficult tensions between achieving corrective justice for the individuals before the court as opposed to distributive justice for larger groups not before the court. In addition, there are also tensions between ordering compensation for past violations and ensuring compliance in the future, with related tensions between achieving instant remedies that correct discrete violations as opposed to the commencement of a much more drawn out and uncertain process of systemic reform. The complex and uncertain enforcement process that is posited for socio-economic rights seems to be a better fit for the more political enforcement processes of international than domestic law. International law relies on persuasion and dialogue while domestic law employs a monological and coercive process to enforce rights, especially with negative civil and political rights.

In the first part of this chapter, I outline in greater detail the above dichotomies between a received remedial tradition that focuses on the correction of past violations suffered by individuals and a more complex remedial process with distributive and dialogic implications. In the second part, I argue that the dichotomies between simple correction of violations of political and civil rights and the admittedly difficult process of obtaining compliance with socio-economic rights dramatically underestimate the remedial complexities that are already present in the enforcement of political and civil rights. The distributional implications of traditional remedies are also underlined by the fact that some socio-economic rights can be enforced by traditional remedies such as damages, restitution and declarations of invalidity. A stark dichotomy between simple remedies required for civil and political rights and more complex remedies for socio-economic rights also ignores the increasing interdependency between domestic and international law and the dialogic turn in domestic constitutional law in many countries including Canada, India, New Zealand, South Africa, the United Kingdom and the United States. The received remedial tradition of corrective justice is inadequate for the enforcement of many civil and political rights. Recognition of a more complex, contingent and dialogical remedial process narrows the gap between traditional political and civil rights and socio-economic rights and between domestic and international enforcement of rights.

The last part of this chapter outlines the range of remedies available to enforce socio-economic rights in domestic, regional and international law. Traditional corrective remedies such as damages, restitution and immediate declarations of constitutional invalidity can play a role in enforcing socio-economic rights, but I suggest that more prospective and dialogic remedies such as declarations and delayed declarations of invalidity can also play a role. At the same time, I argue that

* Professor of Law and Prichard-Wilson Chair in Law and Public Policy, University of Toronto.

not all remedies for socio-economic rights will be soft and prospective and that injunctions, including the exercise of supervisory jurisdiction by the courts, should be available to ensure meaningful and effective remedies for socio-economic rights in cases where it is clear that governments are either unwilling or unable to respect such rights. Finally, I suggest that some of the gap between achieving justice for individual litigants in desperate conditions and achieving broader systemic reform for larger groups not before the court can be bridged by two-track remedial strategies in which courts order interim and immediate remedies to repair and prevent irreparable harm while at the same time pursuing a longer process of achieving systemic reforms.

I am not the first to argue that the received remedial tradition is inadequate. Harvard law professor Abram Chayes first recognised the inadequacy of the idealised vision of remedies in his seminal 1976 article entitled 'The Role of the Judge in Public Law Litigation'.[1] Professor Chayes argued that in the wake of *Brown v. Board of Education II*[2] American courts were ordering more complex and ongoing remedies in order to reform public institutions and assist disadvantaged groups. He contrasted a 'received tradition' based on bi-polar, retrospective, self-contained and party-controlled litigation with an emerging public law style of litigation which featured multiple parties and an active judiciary concerned more with the development of public policy than the settlement of disputes. Under the received tradition, the remedy was 'derived more or less logically from the substantive violation under the general theory that the plaintiff will get compensation measured by the harm caused by the defendant's breach of duty – in contract by giving plaintiff the money he would have had absent the breach; in tort by paying the value of the damage caused'. In contrast, in public law litigation 'relief is not conceived as compensation for past wrong in a form logically derived from the substantive liability and confined in its impact to the immediate parties; instead, it is forward looking, fashioned *ad hoc* on flexible and broadly remedial lines, often having important consequences for many persons including absen-

tees'.[3] Such complex public law remedies were often the process of negotiation and persuasion as opposed to coercive correction.

The important work of the late Professor Chayes is also a testament to the increasing interdependency of domestic and international law. He carried many of the insights of his 1976 article into subsequent work on the operation of international law and international institutions.[4] In both fields, he suggested that law was actualised more by an ongoing process of persuasion than by coercion and retrospective corrections of harms. Professor Chayes never applied his theory of remedies to the enforcement of socio-economic rights, but it provides an important intellectual foundation for greater acceptance of the concept that such rights can be enforced by both domestic courts and international bodies. In other words, rejection of the received remedial tradition opens up the prospect of domestic courts and international bodies engaging governments in an ongoing process of continued dialogue and persuasion about the importance and possibility of achieving greater compliance with socio-economic rights.

2. RECEIVED REMEDIAL DICHOTOMIES

2.1   Corrective Justice versus Distributive Justice

Aristotle identified corrective justice as 'that which plays a rectifying part in transactions between man and man' and opposed it to distributive justice 'which is manifested in distributions of honour or money or other things that fall to be divided among those who have a share in the constitution'.[5] Many theorists have argued that courts are best suited to achieving corrective justice between the two parties to a private dispute and that distributive justice among citizens should be left to legislatures.[6]

Most traditional descriptions of the remedial functions of courts proceed on corrective assumptions, which assume a close connection between

---

[1] A. Chayes, 'The Role of the Judge in Public Law Litigation', *Harvard Law Review*, Vol. 89 (1976), pp. 1281–1316.
[2] 349 U.S. 294 (1955).

[3] Chayes, 'The Role of the Judge' (n.1 above), at 1305–1306.
[4] A. Chayes and Antonia Chayes, *The New Sovereignty* (Cambridge: Harvard University Press, 1993).
[5] Aristotle, *The Nicomachean Ethics*, Book 5, Chapters 2–4.
[6] E. Weinrib, *The Idea of Private Law* (Cambridge: Harvard University Press, 1995).

the violation of a right and the crafting of a remedy to repair the harm caused by the rights violation. For example, William Blackstone appealed to a theory of corrective justice when he famously wrote that it was 'a settled and invariable principle in the laws of England that every right when withheld must have a remedy and every injury its proper redress'.[7] Blackstone's understanding of remedies informed the decision of *Marbury v. Madison*, which asserted powers of judicial review in part on the basis that an individual is entitled 'to claim the protection of the laws, whenever he receives an injury'.[8] A similar theme is found in the work of Albert Venn Dicey, who insisted that private law-making methodology should inform constitutional law and, in particular, the provision of remedies for violations of constitutional rights. He wrote that the process of providing 'remedies for the enforcement of particular rights' was the 'averting of definite wrongs'. This was the foundation for Dicey's famous statement that 'there runs through the English constitution that inseparable connection between the means of enforcing a right and the right to be enforced ... The saw ubu jus ibi remedium (where there is a right, there is a remedy) becomes from this point of view something much more important than a mere tautologous proposition'.[9] All of the above commentators applied private law methodologies to public law. It is possible to see remedies such as the exclusion of improperly obtained evidence or the provision of constitutional damages for aggrieved individuals as a form of corrective justice, while seeing more complex remedies that benefit groups as a form of distributive justice best left to the legislative and administrative process.

2.2. Individual versus Systemic Relief

There are several important corollaries for understanding remedies as an act of corrective justice. One is that the task of remedies is to provide relief for discrete harms suffered by an individual and not to engage in systemic relief aimed either at reforming large public bureaucracies or producing new legislation or governmental programs. The corrective theory of remedies assumes that justice can only be done for the individuals before the court and not for larger groups that may not be before the court or who are imperfectly represented by mechanisms such as class actions.

2.3   Immediate versus Delayed Remedies

Another corollary of a corrective understanding of remedies is that the remedy can be immediate once the court finds that the government has violated a right and the extent of the harm caused by the violation has been established. Damages are a preferred remedy because they allow for a single act of rectification or correction with no continuing involvement by the court. Declarations and injunctions are not preferred remedies in part because they require governments to take steps in the future to implement their dictates. Immediate remedies are also the norm in constitutional law. Since *Marbury v. Madison*, courts have struck down laws to the extent of their inconsistency with the constitution with immediate effect, based on the assumption that such negative and immediate remedies will achieve compliance with the constitution.

2.4   Common Law versus Equity

Another dichotomy that has affected thinking about remedies is the assumption that damages are a preferred remedy to equitable remedies in which courts require defendants to engage in certain activities in order to achieve compliance. Injunctions are problematic because they purport to compel the government to act and because they may require continued judicial involvement. Damages for individuals or remedies that resemble damages in their focus on compensation are the preferred remedies in the received remedial tradition.

2.5   Monologue versus Dialogue

Although the received remedial tradition views injunctions as an extraordinary remedy, it does accept the idea that remedies are part of a coercive and authoritative process through which the

---

[7] W. Blackstone, *Commentaries on the Laws of England*, Book 3, Ch. 7.

[8] *Marbury v. Madison* 5 U.S. 1 (1 Cranch) 137 at 163 (1803).

[9] A. Dicey, *An Introduction to the Study of the Law of the Constitution*, 10th ed. (London: Macmillan, 1959), p. 199.

court enforces the law. The remedial process is a coercive monologue in which judges lay down the law and settle disputes. The idea that a judge would engage in an ongoing re-iterative and dialogic process would be seen in the received remedial tradition as a sign that the judge had abandoned the law and descended into politics with its consequent use of negotiation and bargaining as opposed to authoritative adjudication.

2.6 Domestic Law versus International Law

The received remedial tradition of corrective justice pre-dates the emergence of international and regional law and conceives of domestic courts as the exclusive source of both authoritative adjudication and remedies. The 'hierarchical processes of adjudication or enforcement'[10] and the coercive process of ensuring that where there is a right, there is a remedy at domestic law can be contrasted to international law, which most commonly works through drawn out processes of requiring states to report back on steps that they have taken to comply with the law. The received tradition reflects a dualist approach that emphasises the separateness of domestic and international law. More specifically, it suggests that international law is less law-like than domestic law because it cannot deliver on the corrective promise of rights being enforced by one-shot coercive remedies.

3. CHALLENGING THE REMEDIAL DICHOTOMIES

3.1 The Distributive Implications of Civil and Political Rights

Corrective justice ignores the role of corrective remedies in enforcing pre-existing distributions of resources and traditional property rights. The corrective remedial goal of restoring the status quo ante will benefit economically advantaged people by attempting to return them to the position they occupied before the injury. Corrective justice

assumes the justness of the pre-existing distributions of resources and property rights in society.

The received remedial tradition underestimates the distributive and systemic effects of one-shot corrective remedies on modern bureaucratic government. For example, a standard remedy in domestic constitutional law is a stay of proceedings as a remedy to correct the violation of an accused person's right to a trial in a reasonable time or a damage award to repair the violation of a prisoner's right to humane treatment. At one level, the remedy is designed to achieve corrective justice for the individual by placing that individual in the same position that he or she would have occupied had the State not violated his or her rights. Although the remedy is conceived as an individual remedy, it occurs in the bureaucratic context of modern government and as such will have complex repercussions. A stay of proceedings to enforce a constitutional right to a trial in a speedy time can indirectly require the state to spend more funds to improve the efficiency of trials throughout the criminal justice system to ensure that similarly situated individuals do not receive stays of proceedings in the future. Likewise a damage award or a grant of habeas corpus arising from unconstitutional conditions of confinement may in substance require the state to devote more resources to prisons or mental institutions. The fact in both cases that the remedies are understood as individual and retrospective may in fact make the court less sensitive to the complex distributional and regulatory implications of the nominally individual remedy.

3.2 Systemic Claims Raised by Individuals

Although remedial claims for violations of political and civil rights are often understood as claims of individual rights, they often implicate larger groups. The nature of modern government means that justice for an individual will often require systemic measures that will deliver justice to much larger groups. In the above example, providing individuals with a trial in a reasonable time or humane conditions of confinement will of necessity require the government to reform large bureaucracies so that larger groups also receive better treatment. The conditions of modern bureaucracies often break down the distinction

---

[10] J. Brunnee and S. Toope, 'A Hesitant Embrace: The Application of International Law by Canadian Courts', *Canadian Yearbook of International Law*, Vol. 3 (2002), pp. 3–60, at 55.

between individual and systemic relief, even in the administration of traditional political and civil rights that aim to protect individuals from unjust treatment.

3.3 The Management of Delay

The received remedial tradition posits a process in which remedies can be achieved immediately by the order of damages or other remedies that restore the status quo ante. Delays either in litigating or receiving the actual remedy may often be underestimated. Many jurisdictions are now recognising that delay is sometimes inevitable. The turning point was probably the United States Supreme Court's decision in *Brown v. Board of Education II* that school desegregation could not be achieved instantaneously, but would involve a complex process in which school boards proposed desegregation plans that were then reviewed by trial courts. This 'all deliberate speed' process is notorious because of the extensive delay and resistance it caused. At the same time, however, the plan submission and review process used in school desegregation cases have become standard in many other cases, in both domestic and international law. Incremental and reiterative remedial processes take place regardless of whether the underlying rights being vindicated are traditional political and civil rights, such as the right against cruel and unusual punishment, or more positive rights, such as the right to health care or housing. The complexities of modern bureaucracies challenge the traditional model of immediate remedies because even the most immediate remedies involving bureaucracy may require the management of delay.

Traditional understandings of judicial review since *Marbury v. Madison* have been based on an understanding that courts can and should strike down laws to the extent of their inconsistency with the constitution. Such an immediate remedy serves the corrective task of having the court's remedy match and track its understanding of the substantive right in question. At the same time, a number of devices have developed in international and domestic law that contemplate a more drawn out, complex and contingent remedial process. Various rights adjudication bodies established under international and regional law often do not invalidate non-compliant legislation but rather ask states to report back to them on steps taken to ensure future compliance with the relevant rights. Such a remedial process often presumes that there is more than one way for the State to achieve compliance with the relevant right.

New ways to manage delay have also emerged in domestic constitutional law. In Canada, the courts have invented a new remedy, the 'suspended or delayed declaration of invalidity'. This remedy allows courts to declare that a law is unconstitutional but will remain in force for a period of six to eighteen months in order to allow the relevant government to enact a new law that is consistent with the constitution. This remedy assumes that there is more than one way for governments to comply with the relevant right. It was first used in a case involving minority language rights and has also proven useful in cases involving positive rights to parental leave, rights to interpreters for deaf patients and health care. The Supreme Court of Canada has warned that striking down unconstitutionally under-inclusive benefit schemes could result in an unhealthy form of 'equality with a vengeance'[11] and has recognised that a delayed declaration of invalidity allows the legislature time to extend and/or modify the impugned benefits. Those on the Supreme Court of Canada who found that social assistance rates violated rights standards would not have crafted their own remedy with revised rates, but rather would have delayed a declaration that existing benefits were inadequate for an eighteen-month period in order to give the legislature an opportunity to respond to the complexities of reforming a social assistance program.[12]

Canada is not alone in the use of a delayed declaration of invalidity. Section 172 of the South African Constitution formally recognises this remedy by providing that courts can suspend declarations of invalidity on whatever terms they consider appropriate and just. Section 4 of the United Kingdom's Human Rights Act, 1998 also allows courts to invite the legislature to enact remedial legislation. Judicial bodies that attempt to enforce positive rights may find themselves in a position somewhat closer to many international bodies than traditional domestic courts that are able to achieve

---

[11] *Schachter v. Canada* (1992) 2 S.C.R. 679, at p. 702.
[12] *Gosselin v. Quebec* (2002) 4 S.C.R. 429, at para. 296–297, per Bastarache J. in dissent.

corrective justice between the two parties to the dispute.[13]

3.4 The Rise of Equity

As discussed above, a preference for the common law remedy of damages as opposed to equitable remedies such as declarations or injunctions is part of the received remedial tradition. At the same time, courts have in many jurisdictions made much greater use of equitable remedies in public law since the 1930s. Declarations of rights were first used in civilian systems but have become accepted as a public law remedy in many common law systems. Edwin Borchard argued that declaratory relief would allow courts to become 'an instrument not merely of curative but also preventive justice'. In contrast to theories of corrective justice which were based on the commission of definite wrongs, 'no "injury" or "wrong" need have been actually committed or threatened in order to enable the plaintiff to invoke the judicial process; he need merely show that some legal interest or right of his has been placed in jeopardy or grave uncertainty'.[14]

In the 1970s, Abram Chayes developed his theory of public law litigation to explain the activism of American trial judges in crafting detailed orders to desegregate public schools and reform conditions in custodial institutions.[15] American courts, stressing their traditional equitable powers, issued detailed injunctions and retained jurisdiction in order to desegregate school systems through busing and other remedies and to reform prison conditions. They stressed that 'remedial judicial authority does not put judges automatically in the shoes of school authorities...judicial authority enters only when local authority defaults'.[16] American courts often retained jurisdiction over many

years. The Supreme Court of India has embraced a similar approach and explained: 'As the relief is positive and implies affirmative action, the decisions are not 'one-shot' determinations but have on-going implications'.[17] The courts in both countries required specific reports on compliance to be given to the court or to a court-appointed assistant. The reiterative process of equity is better suited to managing the complexities of modern bureaucratic government than the one shot process of damage awards. Judges administering equitable remedies can use declarations when appropriate, but they can also engage in stronger injunctive forms of relief when appropriate. Damage awards, whether awarded against individuals or governments, can often be easily paid from general tax revenues and may not result in the appropriate internalisation of the costs of rights infringement or in systemic reforms to ensure that similar violations do not occur again in the future.[18]

3.5 The Dialogic Turn in Domestic Constitutional Law

The received remedial tradition is premised on a monologic process in which courts enforce constitutional rights in a coercive manner on governments. Governments in turn have few responses to judicial constitutional remedies. They may disobey court orders as sometimes occurred in American controversies over desegregation or they can attempt to limit the jurisdiction of the courts or amend the constitution.

Much of the post–Second World War experience with rights, however, revolves around the development of a more dialogic approach to judicial review.[19] Post-war international rights protection instruments such as the European Convention on Human Rights and the International Covenant on Civil and Political Rights contemplated dialogue between adjudicators and legislatures by allowing legislative limits and

---

[13] C. Scott and P. Macklem, 'Constitutional Ropes of Sand or Justiciable Guarantees: Social Rights in a New South African Constitution', *University of Pennsylvania Law Review*, Vol. 141, No. 1 (1992), pp. 1–148; J. Nedelsky and C. Scott, 'Constitutional Dialogue' in Joel Bakan and David Schneiderman (eds.), *Social Justice and the Constitution: Perspectives on a Social Union for Canada* (Ottawa: Carlton University Press, 1992).

[14] E. Borchard, *Declaratory Judgments*, 2nd ed. (Cleveland: Banks-Baldwin Law Publishing, 1941), at xiv, 27.

[15] Chayes, 'The Role of the Judge' (n.1 above).

[16] *Swann v. Charlotte-Mecklenberg Board of Education* 402 US (1971) 1, at p. 16.

[17] *Sheela Barse v. Union of India* (1988) AIR 2211 at 2215 (S.C.).

[18] On the difficulties of appropriate cost internalisation, see P. Schuck, *Suing Government* (New Haven: Yale University Press, 1983).

[19] K. Roach, *The Supreme Court on Trial: Judicial Activism or Democratic Dialogue* (Toronto: Irwin Law, 2001).

derogations to be placed on rights. This structure is also found in many domestic bills of rights, including those found in Canada, New Zealand, Israel, South Africa and the United Kingdom. Bills of rights, which contemplate back-and-forth interactions between courts and governments over the treatment of rights through limitations and derogation clauses, may lead to increased acceptance of more complex and dialogic remedial processes that require the government to propose remedial plans that achieve compliance with the constitution.[20]

3.6 The Interdependence of Domestic and International Law

The received remedial tradition is decidedly dualist in its contrast between coercive and monological legal remedies at domestic law and more political and dialogic remedies at international law. Much recent experience with rights, however, challenges this sharp dualism and suggests increased interdependence of domestic and international law. Countries and in some cases individuals have increased access to regional and international bodies to adjudicate rights claims after they have exhausted domestic remedies. Many domestic courts voluntarily take note of international standards. Domestic derogations of rights may result in international adjudication.[21]

International and regional rights adjudicators often call on countries to take steps to comply with the rights standards and to report back on what they have done.[22] Dialogic remedies in both domestic and international law attempt to persuade governments to implement norms. They

recognise that there are a range of legitimate responses open to governments and much can be gained by allowing governments to select the most appropriate response. Dialogic remedies aim to promote healthy partnerships between courts and governments[23] and they are often concerned with producing systemic reforms to prevent violations in the future.

4. REMEDIES FOR VIOLATIONS OF ECONOMIC, SOCIAL AND CULTURAL RIGHTS

4.1 Declarations and Recommendations

Domestic courts and international bodies that are enforcing socio-economic rights will often be concerned about ensuring compliance with such norms in the future and with limits on their institutional competence in crafting remedies to provide benefits and programs. Consequently, they may often find declarations of rights and recommendations to governments to be appropriate remedies at least to start the process of compliance. Declarations and recommendations both rely on the moral suasion of the judicial body as opposed to its coercive powers and they both contemplate dialogue between the adjudicator and the government about the implementation of the right.

In *Lansman v. Finland*,[24] the United Nations Human Rights Committee warned that any future mining might violate the right of the Sami to culture under Article 27 and recommended consultation with the Aboriginal people. Courts in Canada have also recommended consultation with the affected groups as a way of avoiding violation of

---

[20] *Doucet-Boudreau v. Nova Scotia* (2003) 3 S.C.R. 3.
[21] K. Roach, 'Constitutional, Remedial and International Dialogues About Rights: The Canadian Experience', *Texas International Law Journal*, Vol. 40 (2005), pp. 537–576.
[22] The Chayeses argue that 'the dynamics of dialogue and accountability are central' to the managerial approach of international law to achieving compliance. 'States are given ample opportunity to explain and justify their conduct. The reasons advanced to excuse noncompliant conduct point to avenues for improvement and correction. The state concerned can hardly avoid undertaking to act along the indicated lines. As the review is reiterated over time, these promises of improvement contain increasingly concrete, detailed and measurable undertakings'. Chayes and Chayes, *The New Sovereignty* (n.4 above), at p. 230.

[23] Chief Justice McLachlin has also observed that the Canadian approach to remedies may have started a 'tradition of cooperation instead of conflict, which, if we can follow it, promises a more harmonious relationship between the judiciary and other branches of government than that which has historically prevailed in the United States'. Beverly McLachlin 'The Charter: A New Role for the Judiciary?', *Alberta Law Review*, Vol. 29 (1991), pp. 540–559, at 553.
[24] Communication No. 511/1992, UN. Doc CCPR/C/52D/511/1992, 8 November 1994 – See also the subsequent cases concerning Sami reindeer-herding rights: *Jouni E. Länsman v. Finland*, Communication No. 671/1995, UN. Doc. CCPR/C/58/671/1995, 30 October 1996.

Aboriginal rights.[25] In *The International Commission of Jurists v. Portugal*,[26] the European Committee of Social Rights made findings that child labour laws should be amended and the number of labour inspectors increased in order to remedy a violation of rights against child labour under the European Social Charter. In *Autism-Europe v. France*, the same committee indicated that insufficient educational places had been made available for persons with autism and stressed the importance of 'practical action to give full effect' to the rights.[27] Judicial bodies that use declarations will find themselves dependent on the legislative and executive branches of government to provide remedies for socio-economic rights.

Courts that appreciate the role of other institutions in responding to and implementing their judgments may be more inclined to rely on general and non-coercive remedies than those who see their judgments as the final act of justice. General declarations as opposed to detailed injunctions have emerged as the preferred remedy for enforcing the Canadian Charter.[28] In a 1997 case involving the equality rights of people who are deaf to receive sign language interpretation in hospitals, the Supreme Court stated that a 'declaration, as opposed to some kind of injunctive relief, is the appropriate remedy in this case because there are myriad options available to the government that may rectify the unconstitutionality of the current system. It is not this Court's role to dictate how this is to be accomplished'.[29] Declarations proceed on the assumption that governments will take prompt and good faith steps to comply with the court's declaration of constitutional entitlement in a manner not entirely different from the international law principle of good faith implementation of treaties. General declarations contemplate a need for other institutions to discuss and internalise constitutional norms.

The limits of declaratory relief have been exposed in another Canadian case involving the practice of customs officials in seizing material imported by a gay and lesbian bookstore. The majority of the Supreme Court relied upon a declaration that the authorities had breached freedom of expression and equality rights in the past by unfairly targeting imports destined for the bookstore. After the Court's declaration, the bookstore had to commence new litigation because of its continued dissatisfaction with its treatment by customs officials. Justice Iacobucci in his dissent in the first case anticipated this shortcoming of declaratory relief. He stated that 'declarations are often preferable to injunctive relief because they are more flexible, require less supervision, and are more deferential to the other branches of government'. At the same time, he added that 'declarations can suffer from vagueness, insufficient remedial specificity, an inability to monitor compliance, and an ensuing need for subsequent litigation to ensure compliance'. He stressed that declarations will be inadequate and place an unfair burden on successful litigants in cases of grave systemic problems and when administrators 'have proven themselves unworthy of trust'.[30] The new litigation that had to be started by the small gay and lesbian bookstore has now been thwarted by a decision not to award the litigant advance costs in order to finance the litigation.[31]

4.2 Injunctions and Retention of Supervisory Jurisdiction

An important backstop for declarations is the availability of injunctive relief and the retention of supervisory jurisdiction by courts. Such injunctions represent the more forceful remedial response that should be used in cases where softer declaratory relief is not appropriate, as discussed in the preceding sub-section. Declarations can work in cases in which governments have been inattentive to rights, but the stronger relief of injunctions accompanied with judicial retention of supervisory jurisdiction may be appropriate in those cases where governments are either

---

[25] *Delgamuukw v. British Columbia* (1997) 3 S.C.R 1010; *British Columbia v. Okanagan Indian Band* (2003) 3 S.C.R. 371.

[26] No. 1/1998.

[27] No. 13/2002. para. 53.

[28] K. Roach, 'Remedial Consensus and Dialogue under the Charter: General Declarations and Delayed Declarations of Invalidity', *University of British Columbia Law Review*, Vol. 39 (2002), pp. 211–269.

[29] *Eldridge v. British Columbia* (1997) 3 S.C.R. 324, at para. 96.

[30] *Little Sisters v. Canada* (2000) 2 S.C.R. 1120, at paras. 258–261.

[31] *Little Sisters v. Canada* (2007) SCC 2.

unwilling or simply incompetent to provide socio-economic rights.[32]

Courts in both India and the United States have ordered detailed injunctions in a variety of cases. In the United States, such orders have been made with respect to school desegregation and conditions of confinement in custodial institutions while in India they have been made with respect to child labour and conditions of confinement. A judge of the Supreme Court of India has explained that in such cases 'the court is not merely a passive, disinterested umpire or onlooker, but has a more dynamic and positive role with the responsibility for... moulding relief and – this is important – also supervising the implementation thereof'.[33]

After reviewing comparative and international law,[34] the South African Constitutional Court affirmed the ability of courts to order mandatory injunctions and to retain supervisory jurisdiction in order to enforce socio-economic rights in that country's constitution. It rejected the argument that courts were limited to declaratory relief on the basis that: 'Where a breach of any right has taken place, including a socio-economic right, a court is under a duty to ensure effective relief is granted.... Where necessary this may include both the issuing of a mandamus and the exercise of supervisory jurisdiction'.[35] At the same time, the Court stressed that due regard must be paid to the roles of the legislature and the executive in a democracy. Although the government must comply with the constitution and the courts must ensure that it complies, it will often be appropriate to leave the government some margin of flexibility to select the exact means to comply with the constitution. In this case, the Court declared the existing policy with respect to drugs to prevent mother

to child HIV transmission to be unconstitutional and ordered that the government, without delay, should permit and facilitate the use of such drugs, as well as testing and counselling to determine when the drug was necessary. The Court added that its orders did not 'preclude government from adapting its policy in a manner consistent with the Constitution if equally appropriate or better methods become available to it for the prevention of mother-to-child transmission of HIV'.[36] The Court did not require the government to report back to the court about the steps taken to comply with its declarations and orders, or even to announce such plans publicly. In many cases that require injunctive relief, such reporting back requirements will often be crucial in ensuring and monitoring compliance.[37]

A year after the above South African case, the Supreme Court of Canada upheld the discretion of a trial judge to order that minority language schools be built by certain times and to retain jurisdiction so that the government would report back on its progress after years of delay in complying with minority language education rights.[38] Following the experience with complex public law structural injunctions in the United States, the trial judge retained jurisdiction in part to provide a forum for the parties to negotiate out the complexities of the remedy and to respond to unanticipated circumstances. The procedure allowed for the possibility of the exercise of some moral suasion by the judge and modification of the order. The Supreme Court, however, only upheld the trial judge's remedy in a closely split 5:4 decision with the four judges in the minority basing their dissent on the corrective understanding of the judge's remedial role as discussed in the first part of this chapter. The minority rejected the idea that the judge could exercise a 'suasive' function or 'hold the government's feet to the fire' by requiring progress reports on the steps taken to comply with the court's judgment.[39] The minority operated on the assumption that judges act in an illegitimate and 'political' fashion if they engage in anything but the articulation and execution of legally enforceable commands, if need be, by

---

[32] K. Roach and G. Budlender, 'Mandatory Relief and Supervisory Jurisdiction: When is it Appropriate, Just and Equitable', *South African Law Journal*, Vol. 5 (2005), pp. 325–351.

[33] *Sheela Barse v. Union of India* (n.17 above), at p. 2215.

[34] For an affirmation of the Inter-American Court of Human Rights powers of supervisory jurisdiction see *Baena Ricardo et al. Case*, Supervisory Jurisdiction, Judgment of Nov. 28, 2003, Inter-Am.Ct.H.R. (Ser. C.) No. 104, as discussed in this volume by Tara J. Melish, 'The Inter-American Court of Human Rights: Beyond Progressivity', section 6.4.

[35] *Minister of Health and Others v. Treatment Action Campaign and Others* (1) (2002) 10 BCLR 1033 (CC), at para. 106.

[36] Ibid., para. 135.

[37] Roach and Budlender, 'Mandatory Relief' (n. 32 above), at pp. 333–334.

[38] *Doucet-Boudreau v. Nova Scotia* (2003) 3 S.C.R. 3.

[39] Ibid., paras. 127–128.

holding the government in contempt of court. They also expressed concerns that the trial judge would exceed his institutional role by descending into the administrative details of providing education. The majority of the Court, however, deferred to the trial judge's exercise of remedial discretion and stressed the need for effective remedies without undue delay.

4.3 Revisions of Laws and Suspended or Delayed Declarations of Invalidity

Courts in a number of jurisdictions have revised laws in order to make them constitutional. The German courts have been particularly active in this regard, but courts in both South Africa and Canada have also revised laws. For example, the Constitutional Court of South Africa has read in judicial supervision to ensure fairness and compliance with the constitution in the forced sale of property.[40] The Supreme Court of Canada has extended benefits by severing or striking down part of a law that restricted the benefits.[41] Even a traditional negative remedy such as striking down parts of a law can have the functional effect of extending state benefits.

The Supreme Court of Canada subsequently reasoned that the scope of the courts' remedial powers should not depend on the way that legislation is drafted and affirmed the ability of courts to revise laws by reading in words to statutes to cure constitutional defects. In part because of concerns about the separation of powers, this reading in or revision power is only used in cases where it is clear that both the purposes of the legislation and of the constitution support a relatively precise judicial revision of the law. In cases where these factors are not clear, the courts in both South Africa and Canada will use a suspended or delayed declaration of invalidity that gives the legislature an opportunity to enact new legislation before the unconstitutional legislation is struck down.[42]

A delayed or suspended declaration of invalidity might be appropriate in a case such as *Taylor*

v. The United Kingdom[43] in which the European Court of Justice found gender discrimination in the provision of winter fuel benefits. An immediate declaration that the benefits were invalid would have regressive effects. Indeed, the Supreme Court of Canada has labelled a lower court's striking out of benefits provided to single mothers on the basis of gender discrimination as 'equality with a vengeance' and expressed the view that as it is consistent with the larger purposes of rights protection, a delayed declaration of invalidity was the appropriate remedy in order to ensure that the vulnerable groups would continue to receive benefits from the state.[44] Such a remedy is not without its risks, however, as the legislature responded to the courts decision both by extending the period of parental leave to men but also by reducing the weeks of paid leave available. Delayed declarations of invalidity whether rendered by domestic courts or international bodies must be accompanied by effective lobbying and engagement with legislatures.

Although delay may be necessary in some cases and has the potential to allow for consultation with those affected by the remedy,[45] it is not without problems. Delay allows an unconstitutional state of affairs to persist. This may be justified in some cases where immediate compliance with the right is truly impossible. In such cases, it may be preferable for courts to acknowledge and manage delay than to ignore it or allow concerns about delay to contract its interpretation of the right to question. Tolerating and managing delay may be a better alternative than simply refusing to recognise a right because of judicial concerns about enforcement.

Nevertheless, there is a danger that courts could become too willing to accept delay and incrementalism, particularly in the context of socio-economic rights. In all cases, courts should address not only whether delay is truly necessary, but also the position of those whose rights might be infringed during the period of court sanctioned delay. The court that issues a delayed remedy should retain jurisdiction to hear claims that emergency or interim remedies should be granted

---

[40] *Jafta v. Van Rooyen* CCT 74/2003 (CC), at paras. 63–64.
[41] *Tetreault-Gadoury v. Canada* (1991) 2 SCR 22.
[42] *Schachter v. Canada* (n. 11 above).

[43] Case 382.98.
[44] *Schachter v. Canada* (n. 11 above).
[45] *Corbiére v. Canada* (1999) 2 SCR 203, at paras. 116–117 per L'Heureux-Dube J.

to prevent irreparable harm during the period of the court-ordered delay. Such requests for remedies could be decided under the same tests that apply to interim relief to be discussed in the next section. A willingness to grant interim remedies could help ensure that courts do not turn a blind eye to emergencies and hardships that emerge during the period of delay.

4.4   Interim Remedies

An important issue in the litigation of socio-economic rights is the respective emphasis placed on relief for individuals and the development of policies to achieve more systemic relief. In the *Grootboom* housing rights case,[46] the South African Constitutional Court emphasised systemic relief over individual relief by stressing that a housing policy must be developed and not that any particular individual be able to obtain a court order for housing. Such a remedial approach may stimulate government to develop a comprehensive program, but it can also leave individual litigants without an immediate and tangible remedy. It may play into the remedial dichotomies discussed in the first part of this chapter and suggest that socio-economic rights will be enforced in a more contingent and political manner than more traditional negative rights.

One possible way to combine individual and systemic relief is to obtain individual relief on an interlocutory or emergency basis while seeking more systemic relief after a trial on the merits. In some eviction cases in particular, courts might be persuaded to preserve the status quo and prevent irreparable damage by stopping the eviction on an interim basis while the ultimate relief after trial might be to develop an appropriate housing program. Interim remedies may be one way the courts can enforce minimum core obligations even while not formally recognising such requirements.[47] One observer has noted that in social action litigation in India, 'relief has been offered very often by way of interim orders. As interim orders are given before any preliminary examination of the merits of the case, they have been

qualified as 'remedies without rights'. The reasons behind the frequent use of interim orders can be found in the urgent character of many cases, and in the ongoing nature of many violations of human rights'.[48] Interim remedies are also at times available from regional and international bodies.

4.5   Compensation and Restitution

The earlier discussion suggests that whether by the use of declaratory, injunctive or interim relief or through the use of delayed declarations of invalidity, the emphasis in many socio-economic cases in both domestic and international law will often be on securing compliance in the future. As suggested in the first part of this chapter, compensation plays a central role in the remedial theory of corrective justice and plays a much less significant role in newer theories of public law litigation. Nevertheless, compensation and restitution may be appropriate in some socio-economic cases and may also be a means to challenge the remedial dichotomies discussed earlier in this chapter.

In a series of cases involving prison conditions in violation of UN minimum standards, the UN Human Rights Committee urged compensation for a person was who without food for several days.[49] Interestingly, however, the Committee, consistent with public law models, also urged that steps be taken to ensure that similar violations do not occur in the future. A similar dualistic approach aimed at compensation for past violations but also steps to ensure compliance in the future was taken by the African Commission on Human Rights in *SERAC and CESR v. Nigeria*.[50] Most adjudicators that have ordered compensation in the socio-economic context have at the same time devised remedies designed to ensure compliance with such rights in the future.

In many socio-economic cases, compensation will symbolise the suffering of those individuals before the court but additional remedies will be

---

[46] *Government of the Republic of South Africa and others v. Grootboom and others* 2000 (11) BCLR 1169 (CC).

[47] See Sandra Liebenberg in this volume for further discussion of minimum core obligations.

[48] W. Vanenhole, 'Human Rights Law, Development and Social Action Litigation in India', *Asia-Pacific Journal on Human Rights and the Law*, Vol. 2 (2002), pp. 136–210, at 159.

[49] *Mukong v. Cameroon* No 458/1991; *Lantsova v. Russian Federation* No. 763/ 15 April 2002.

[50] No. 155/96.

necessary to reform governments and ensure greater compliance in the future. In one forced eviction case, the European Court of Human Rights has awarded a substantial sum of 15,000 euros for non-pecuniary damages.[51] Such awards can help make socio-economic rights meaningful and counter concerns that they are second-class rights in relation to political and civil rights. Nevertheless, redress of past wrongs is not sufficient to enforce socio-economic rights. There is a danger that governments may pay damage awards in individual cases but not engage in reforms that will prevent future violations and ensure justice for people not before the court.[52]

A combination of restitution and compensation has some potential both to redress past wrongs and to provide future compliance with socio-economic rights. The Constitutional Court of South Africa has upheld a creative use of a judicial order that the State compensate a landowner whose lands were appropriated by homeless people. The Court held that compensation in this case would be an effective remedy both for the landowner and for those homeless people who could remain on his land until the state provided alternative land.[53] Such a remedy is not incompatible with ongoing systemic reforms enforced, if need be, by injunctions and the retention of supervisory jurisdiction. In another case, the Constitutional Court stressed the need for courts to seek a just and equitable solution on the facts of each particular case in reconciling property rights with housing rights. It allowed a small number of homeless people to remain on land they had occupied for eight years in light of the failure of the State to adequately consult with the people and explore all reasonable alternatives to eviction.[54]

4.6 Two-Track Remedial Strategies

There is much to be said for two-track remedial strategies that combine more immediate relief for successful litigants with longer-term processes designed to achieve systemic reform for both the litigants and similar groups. The Inter-American Court of Human Rights has used promising two-track strategies in indigenous rights cases. In one case, it issued an immediate order that the State not infringe or allow third parties to infringe indigenous land rights while also allowing a fifteen-month period for the demarcation and titling of indigenous lands with community participation and in accordance with the customary law of the indigenous community.[55] In another case, it ordered an immediate interim remedy to ensure adequate living conditions while also issuing a longer term relocation remedy for an indigenous community.[56]

Two-track remedial strategies challenge many of the remedial dichotomies examined in this chapter. They allow immediate, individual and interim remedies to be combined with group-based and systemic remedies that often require the management of delay and may allow for participation by the affected interests. They allow a court to order corrective and preventive justice for litigants while also recognising that systemic reform requires a longer and more dialogic process of engagement with the affected interests and the retention of supervisory jurisdiction by either domestic, regional and/or international adjudicators. They combine some of the traditional approaches of domestic courts in insisting on a close connection between right and remedy in order to correct rights violations in the past with the remedial approach long taken by international adjudicators in requiring States to report back on the steps that they have taken to ensure compliance in the future. Two-track remedies combine the corrective promise of the common law of compensation and restitution with the more complex and dialogic methods of equity in ensuring future compliance with the constitution. They also underline that traditional remedies such as compensation and interim and preventive injunctions can in some cases help advance goals of a more equitable distribution of resources provided they are not the exclusive remedies employed.

---

[51] *Connors v. United Kingdom* (May 27, 2004), at paras. 114–115.

[52] See Chapter 19 in this volume, Tara J. Melish, 'The Inter-American Court of Human Rights: Beyond Progressivity', section 6.

[53] *South Africa v. Modderklipp* CCT 20/2004 (C.C.). at paras. 58–60, 68.

[54] *Port Elizabeth v. Various Occupiers*, 2004 (12) BCLR 1268 (CC).

[55] *The Mayagna (Sumo) Indigenous Community of Awas Tinga v. Nicaragua*, Judgment of 31 Aug. 2001, Inter-Am.Ct.H.R. (Ser.C) No. 79.

[56] *Yakye Axa Indigenous Community v. Paraguay*, Judgment of 17 June, 2005, Int.Am.Ct.H.R. (Ser.C) No. 125.

5. CONCLUSION

An oversimplified understanding of the remedies for civil and political rights as simple corrective remedies that have no distributive effects is a barrier to effective remedies for socio-economic rights. Many traditional political and civil rights require complex and dialogic relief with distributional implications to be effective. Once this is recognised then the remedial process that is required to enforce socio-economic rights will appear much less anomalous, albeit no less complex. The dialogic turn in remedies opens up space for a less dichotomous process for enforcing all rights and for greater integration of the processes of domestic, regional and international enforcement of rights.

Socio-economic rights both in domestic and international law will frequently be enforced by recommendations, declarations and calls by adjudicators on legislators to revise laws. A common assumption behind such dialogic remedies is that governments are able and willing to act promptly to comply with the court's rulings. Dialogic remedies create space for continued governmental and legislative policy-making without purporting to mandate either the details of the policy or the processes that will be used to formulate those policies. In many ways, these remedies are based on a faith and trust that governments will do the right thing. At the same time, there are concerns about the effectiveness of such soft forms of relief and it will be important for courts to be able to order injunctions and maintain supervisory jurisdiction in cases where declarations will not suffice.

Double standards that treat socio-economic rights as second class, even if rejected at the rights stage, could resurface in the remedial decisions of courts. The challenge is to ensure effective remedies for all rights. As stated by the United Nations Committee on Economic, Social and Cultural Rights in its ninth comment:

> The adoption of a rigid classification of economic, social and cultural rights which puts

them, by definition, beyond the reach of the courts would thus be arbitrary and incompatible with the principle that the two sets of human rights are indivisible and interdependent. It would also drastically curtail the capacity of the courts to protect the rights of the most vulnerable and disadvantaged groups in society.[57]

To the end of ensuring effective, just and equitable remedies, courts in Canada, India, South Africa and the United States have all made clear that courts can issue injunctions against governments and exercise continued supervisory jurisdiction to ensure that governments comply with the constitution. To be sure, such remedies will not always be appropriate, but it is important that they are available.

A final challenge is to strike the right balance between individual and systemic relief, remedies that attempt to repair the harms of past violations and remedies that aim to achieve compliance with the constitution in the future. This can be done by combining both systemic and individual relief; by creative combinations of protecting people from evictions while compensating property owners, and by two-track remedial strategies in which judges order interim and immediate remedies while also providing for more systemic reforms that cannot be achieved immediately. Individual litigants without food, medicines and shelter and indigenous people deprived of their land should not continue to suffer irreparable harm and immediate remedies should be ordered to prevent irreparable harm to successful litigants and to provide some measure of compensation for past violations. At the same time, however, a more incremental, dialogic and systemic remedial approach will also be required to achieve fuller compliance with basic and important social, economic and cultural rights for all persons.

---

[57] Committee on Economic, Social and Cultural Rights, General Comment No. 9, The domestic application of the Covenant (Nineteenth session, 1998), U.N. Doc. E/C.12/1998//24 (1998), para. 10.

3

The Right to Legal Aid in Social Rights Litigation

Andrea Durbach*

1. INTRODUCTION

The right to legal assistance paid for by the State has primarily received endorsement in relation to the conduct of criminal litigation, particularly where an indigent accused confronts the potential deprivation of liberty. State-sponsored provision of legal services has not attracted parallel application to indigent litigants in civil proceedings, despite a possible adverse result – a 'substantial injustice' – due to the litigant's inability, essentially financial, to negotiate the judicial process.

In many jurisdictions where legal aid has been extended to civil proceedings, significant achievements have been made in the areas of consumer protection, social security, housing, family law, minority rights, public health and environmental protection. Indeed, it has been argued that the contraction of legal aid funding for civil cases by governments in recent years may be a consequence of these advances, coupled with budgetary concerns.[1]

In a period when funding for civil legal aid has been severely cut and civil litigation by those least able to afford access to court accordingly curtailed, the emergence of economic and social rights has gained, and continues to attract, currency within a growing number of nations. However, in the absence of mechanisms to guarantee the effective protection of these rights, the promise of their actual enjoyment is diminished. The realisation of these rights, via their adjudication and enforcement, has raised the need for a legislative framework which facilitates their execution. As one commentator has written, where a system 'purports to guarantee legal rights,' '[e]ffective access to justice can thus be seen as the most basic requirement – the most basic "human right"'[2] – underpinning that system.

This chapter explores the sources of the right to legal aid in general terms, by reference to international declarations, covenants and commentaries. It will also examine the right of access to court and to legal representation contained in international constitutional provisions and judgments, with particular reference to the judicial enforcement of socio-economic rights, such as the right to health. Since the respect, protection and fulfilment of economic and social rights demands that access to redress and remedies is available when these rights are withheld or breached,[3] this chapter will argue that effective access to appropriate forums of redress requires a concomitant right to legal aid. It concludes with an investigation of appropriate criteria comprising of a general right to legal aid and an assessment of how they might be applied, particularly against a background of competing budgetary considerations.

2. THE RIGHT 'CONSERVATIVE OF ALL OTHER RIGHTS'

[T]he right of access to the courts is fundamental to our system of justice. Indeed, it

* Associate Professor and Director of the Australian Human Rights Centre, Faculty of Law, University of New South Wales, Sydney. I am grateful to Professor Paula Galowitz, New York University for her significant contribution. My thanks also to Mark Walters for his valuable research assistance.
[1] F. Gibson, 'Under attack: Civil legal aid services in the USA', *Alternative Law Journal*, Vol. 25 (2000), pp. 173–176.

[2] M. Cappelletti, quoted in M. Gomez, *In the Public Interest: Essays on Public Interest Litigation and Participatory Justice* (Colombo: Legal Aid Centre, University of Columbo, Sri Lanka, 1993), p. 14.
[3] Committee on Economic, Social and Cultural Rights, General Comment No. 9, *The domestic application of the Covenant* (Nineteenth session, 1998), U.N. Doc. E/C.12/1998/24 (1998).

is the right "conservative of all other rights." *Chambers v Baltimore & Ohio R.R.*, 207 U.S. 142, 28 S. Ct. 34, 52 L. Ed. 143 (1907)....

[M]eaningful access requires representation. Where rights and responsibilities are adjudicated in the absence of representation, the results are often unjust. If representation is absent because of a litigant's poverty, then likely so is justice, and for the same reason. *Miranda v Sims* (2000) 98 Wn. App. 898, at 909.

In June 2005, the Canadian Bar Association (CBA) filed proceedings in the Supreme Court of British Columbia which sought to establish a constitutional right to civil legal aid in Canada.[4] In a press release announcing the test case, the then CBA President, Susan McGrath, said:

Every single day in British Columbia the rights of people who cannot afford legal services fall by the wayside. They cannot access the justice system. Often their shelter, health, safety, sustenance and livelihood are at stake.... The legal problems that arise are directly related to the fact that those we are talking about just don't have money to assert their rights.[5]

The proceedings concerned the rule of law and the rights of Canadians to effective and equal access to their judicial system 'when their fundamental interests were at stake.' According to the CBA, without legal aid, 'access to justice is meaningless.'[6]

Debates about access to justice have traditionally focused on gaining access to the courts, and

reforms offering upgrades in access are often viewed as being synonymous with providing and enhancing justice. Rules in relation to standing, procedural efficiency, case management and costs[7] have been debated and adopted as potential antidotes to the growing 'divergence...between the professed democratic idea of legal equality and the profound inequalities of the legal system in practice.'[8]

While 'there is little point in opening the doors to the courts if litigants cannot afford to come in,'[9] the focus on increasing access has, however, tended to highlight that access per se is of little value unless it facilitates and secures substantive justice. The 'prevailing theme is that more is better, and (the) focus is how to achieve it.'[10] Where the panacea for attaining justice is presented as increasing accessibility to the legal system, the objective of achieving effective justice ultimately runs the risk of compromise. Addressing the Australian Law Reform Commission conference, *Managing Justice*, in 2000, the Chief Justice of Australia, His Honour Justice Murray Gleeson AC, remarked:

[If] we are setting ourselves the objective of making the process of civil litigation available to a substantially wider group of people...then, we need some understanding of how the system would cope if such wider availability were achieved. If we have no plan for this, then all we are doing is creating greater access to an increasingly inefficient system.

The Chief Justice continued: 'If we are serious about giving people more access to justice, then we need a reasonably clear understanding of the

---

[4] *The Canadian Bar Association v. Her Majesty the Queen in Right of the Province of British Columbia, The Attorney General of Canada and Legal Services Society* filed 20 June 2005. Statements of Defence were filed on October 2005 and a year later, on 5 September, 2006, the Supreme Court of British Columbia dismissed the case holding, inter alia, that the CBA lacked "public interest standing" to bring the case (required in the absence of the CBA's "direct interest in this action") and that the statement of claim failed "to disclose a reasonable claim pursuant to any of the Charter or constitutional provisions pleaded." (para 119). See http://www.canlii.org/en/bc/bcsc/doc/2006/2006bcsc1342/2006bcsc1342.html. On 3 March 2008, the Court of Appeal for British Columbia upheld the Supreme Court's decision that the claim was "not justiciable" (para 53). See: http://www.courts.gov.bc.ca/Jdb-txt/CA/08/00/2008BCCA0092err4.htm

[5] Press Release issued by Canadian Bar Association, Vancouver dated 20 June 2005.

[6] Ibid.

[7] *Managing Justice: A review of the federal civil justice system*, Australian Law Reform Commission, Report no. 89, (Sydney: Commonwealth of Australia, 1999).

[8] A. Lester, 'Legal Aid in a Democratic Society,' in *Legal Aid in South Africa* (Durban: University of Natal, 1974), pp. 1–12, at 7.

[9] Justice John Toohey in an address to the National Environmental Law Association, 1989, quoted in a speech given by Justice Peter McClellan, *Access to Justice in Environmental Law – An Australian Perspective*, Commonwealth Law Conference, London, 12 September, 2005.

[10] D. L. Rhode, 'Access to Justice,' *Fordham Law Review*, Vol. 69 (2001), pp. 1785–1819, at 1786.

kind of justice to which such access would be worth having.'[11]

Similar sentiments were expressed by the President of the Canadian Law Commission, Roderick Macdonald, whose paper to the conference addressed the question of whether there was any point in redesigning institutions of civil justice to facilitate greater access. He said:

> I ... once believed that achieving access to justice was essentially a matter of removing barriers to courts such as cost, delay and complexity. Now I no longer see the objective in purely structural terms. Rather the challenge runs much deeper. It is to rethink our attitudes about what law in a modern pluralistic society actually comprises ...[12]

As the proceedings launched by the Canadian Bar Association in British Columbia correctly assert, the right to civil legal aid goes to ensuring meaningful access to justice – particularly when fundamental interests are at stake – and the effective application of its attendant props, the rule of law, equality and fairness.

3. RETHINKING ACCESS TO JUSTICE IN CONTEMPORARY DEMOCRACY

The extent to which the state intervenes to ensure that the rights and interests of the relatively powerless are adequately represented and mediated speaks of its adherence to and implementation of democratic principles. It is universally accepted that all citizens (and in many cases, even noncitizens) of a democratic state are afforded equal protection before courts and tribunals and the right to a fair and public hearing.[13] While the right

to a fair hearing has real utility and usually takes effect *after* the point of entry to the courts, no universal right exists which affords equal protection to citizens to access courts in order to take up the invitation of a 'fair and public hearing.' And it is primarily in cases of the indigent accused in criminal proceedings, whose right to physical liberty may be at stake, where courts and governments have been compelled to ensure that access to justice, in the form of state-funded representation for the accused, is available.

3.1 Extending the Right to a Fair Hearing: Addressing the Point of Access

Effective participation in a democratic society requires the actual enjoyment of rights afforded by the State and access to mechanisms which facilitate their realisation and protection. Without the capacity to claim a right and access a remedy in the event of its breach, the promise of equal access to rights and protection before the courts rings hollow and confidence in democratic institutions, such as the judicial system, risks erosion. The right of effective access to justice and the existence of mechanisms which ensure its protection is accordingly of 'paramount importance among other new rights.'

The content of the right of effective access to justice articulated as an entitlement to legal aid has been explored and expanded in various jurisdictions via an investigation of the complementary right to a fair hearing – both where a party seeks to initiate proceedings or is brought before a court by another. As litigation in contemporary democracies has become more layered and elaborate, requiring extensive legal research, expert testimony and complex legal argument often beyond the capacity of the ordinary litigant in person, the assertion or defence of legal rights and the construction of evidence and argument in support frequently demands legal representation to ensure a party's effective participation in the proceedings and ultimately, access 'to the kind of justice ... worth having.' In cases where procedures

---

[11] Hon. Murray Gleeson AC, 'Managing Justice in the Australian Context' in *Managing Justice – the way ahead for civil disputes*, Proceedings of the Australian Law Reform Commission conference, *Managing Justice*, 18–20 May 2000, p. 8.

[12] Prof. Roderick A. Macdonald, 'Implicit Law, Explicit Access' in *Managing Justice – the way ahead for civil disputes*, ibid., p. 2.

[13] See Amendment V1 of the American Constitution (Bill of Rights) 1789; Article 10 of the Universal Declaration of Human Rights 1948; Article 6 of the European Convention on Human Rights 1950; Article 25 of the International

Covenant on Civil and Political Rights 1966; Section 11 of the Canadian Charter of Rights and Freedoms 1982; Article 47 of the Charter of Fundamental Rights of the European Union 2000.

are complex and the law convoluted, the provision of legal aid by the State offers recognition that an indigent person 'lacking the means to provide his own suit of armour, is given one with which he can, perhaps, grapple and cope with the legal system which...is complicated and...in many respects, menacing.'[14]

The 'access-based approach' developed by Deborah Perluss with specific reference to the provisions of the Washington State Constitution[15] 'requires a court to consider, as a matter of fairness and justice, the litigant's ability to navigate the system of justice in which he or she is found.'[16] The European Court of Human Rights has effectively adopted this principle and, in the case of *P, C and S v United Kingdom*,[17] which concerned care and adoption proceedings and the circumstances in which children may be taken into care, the Court queried the fairness of proceedings where an applicant appears without legal representation and 'manages to conduct his or her case in the teeth of all the difficulties' (para. 91). The Court continued: 'There is the importance of ensuring the appearance of the fair administration of justice and a party in civil proceedings must be able to participate effectively, inter alia, by being able to put forward the matters in support of his or her claims.'[18]

Twenty-two years earlier, in the Irish case of *Airey v Ireland*,[19] in which the applicant, Mrs Airey, sought a decree of judicial separation from her husband, the European Court of Human Rights similarly held that the ability to present a case 'properly and effectively' before a court was intrinsic to the right of access to court.[20] In asserting that her right to

a fair hearing included the right to state-funded legal representation, Mrs Airey relied on Article 6 of the European Convention on Human Rights, which provides that everyone, '(i)n the determination of his *civil rights and obligations* (author's emphasis) or of any criminal charge against him,' is entitled to a fair and public hearing.[21] Given the prominence in democratic societies of the right of access to court, the European Court of Human Rights held that the fulfilment of the right required deliberate State action. 'The Convention,' said the Court, 'is intended to guarantee not rights that are theoretical or illusory but rights that are practical and effective. This is particularly so of the right of access to the courts.'[22]

A party's capacity to represent him or herself effectively in the absence of 'competent and sustained representation by an experienced lawyer familiar with the case and with the law' was more recently considered by the European Court of Human Rights in libel proceedings brought against two Greenpeace campaigners by McDonald's. While the campaigners were unsuccessful in their defence to the libel claim in proceedings before the Court in 2004 alleging, inter alia, a violation by the United Kingdom of Article 6 of the European Convention,[23] Helen Steel and David Morris were awarded damages. The Court held that the denial of legal aid to the applicants had deprived them of the 'opportunity to present their case effectively before the court,'[24] denying the applicants a fair trial. The European Court of Human Rights considered that in complex litigation, such as the McDonald's libel claim,

...neither the sporadic help given by the volunteer lawyers nor the extensive judicial assistance and latitude granted to the applicants

---

[14] M. Zander, 'Legal Aid in a Democratic Society' in *Legal Aid in South Africa* (University of Natal, 1976), pp. 12–22, at 15.

[15] D. Perluss, 'Washington's Constitutional Right to Counsel in Civil Cases: Access to Justice v. Fundamental Interest,' *Seattle Journal for Social Justice*, Vol. 2 (2003–4), pp. 571–607, at 574.

[16] Ibid., p. 573.

[17] *P, C and S v. United Kingdom* (2002) 35 EHRR 31.

[18] Ibid. at para. 91. quoted in Geoff Budlender, 'Access to Courts,' *The South African Law Journal*, Vol. 121 (2004), pp. 339–358, at 341.

[19] *Airey v. Ireland* (1979) 2 EHRR 305.

[20] In an Australian family law case, *Sajdak v. Sajdak* (1993) FLC 92–348 at 79, 687, the Court considered the impact of the absence of legal representation (in addition to other factors such as inability to speak English) on a litigant's capacity to present her case effectively and held: 'In the present case...the husband is in receipt of Workcare pay-

ments and the wife social security benefits. Neither can speak English. The welfare of a child is involved. The husband was represented both at the trial and on appeal, and the wife was not. The likelihood of an injustice occurring was greatly exacerbated by her lack of representation and in fact we have found that an injustice did occur in that she was unable to properly present her case.' Quoted in Sally Kift, 'The *Dietrich* Dilemma,' *Queensland University of Technology Law Journal*, Vol. 13 (1997), pp. 205–228, at 222.

[21] Article 6 of the European Convention on Human Rights, 1950.

[22] *Airey v. Ireland* (n. 19 above), p. 314, para. 24.

[23] *Steel and Morris v. The United Kingdom* (2005) ECHR 103.

[24] Ibid., para. 59.

as litigants in person, was any substitute for competent and sustained representation by an experienced lawyer familiar with the case and with the law of libel... The very length of the proceedings is, to a certain extent, a testament to the applicants' lack of skill and experience.... Finally, the disparity between the respective levels of legal assistance enjoyed by the applicants and McDonald's... was of such a degree that it could not have failed, in this exceptionally demanding case, to have given rise to unfairness, despite the best efforts of the judges at first instance and on appeal.[25]

The extent to which a fair hearing might be implied in accordance with the 'principles of fundamental justice'[26] was explored in the Canadian case, *New Brunswick (Minister of Health and Community services) v G(J)*.[27] As in the English case of *P, C and S v United Kingdom*, *New Brunswick* considered the requisites for a fair trial in the context of a child protection hearing where the state sought temporary custody of a mother's children. By reference to section 7 of the Canadian Charter of Rights – which protects against the deprivation of 'the right to life, liberty and security of the person... except in accordance with the principles of fundamental justice' – the Canadian Supreme Court held that when a parent confronts the temporary loss of custody of a child, 'fundamental justice' demands that he or she 'must have an opportunity to present (their) case effectively. Effective parental participation at the hearing,' said Chief Justice Lamer, 'is essential for determining the best interests of the child, in circumstances where the parent seeks to maintain custody of the child'[28] and, as per *Airey v Ireland* and *Steel and Morris v the United Kingdom*, for ensuring the conduct of a fair trial. After examining particular features of the case, namely, the 'seriousness of the interests at stake, the complexity of the proceedings,

and the capacities of the appellant,' Chief Justice Lamer concluded that 'the appellant's right to a fair hearing required that she be represented by [State-funded] counsel.'[29]

In the cases discussed above, it is the lack of fairness of proceedings arising from an absence of counsel (or legal aid) – rather than their criminal or civil character[30] – which informed a decision by the court to uphold an entitlement to legal aid. These cases largely construe legal aid as a 'juridical right'[31] which guarantees individuals the right of access to the courts, a claim that has its source in the classical political right of equality before the law. The provision of state-funded legal representation in criminal cases also finds justification within the civil and political rights framework – protection against an individual's deprivation of liberty. Construing legal aid as a 'welfare' or 'social right' however, linked to 'the amelioration of a particular social situation or complex of conditions' and addressing broad social concerns rather than individual grievances,[32] has had a slow and sporadic reception by courts.

With the increasing ratification of human rights treaties and conventions by states, including the International Covenant on Economic, Social and Cultural Rights, the incorporation of socio-economic rights in domestic legislation, constitutions and Charters or Bills of Rights, and a growing appreciation by the courts of the necessary interdependence[33] of human rights (political, social and economic), the grounds for making a distinction between criminal and civil proceedings when affording legal aid, are becoming less tenable.

---

[25] Ibid., para. 69.
[26] Section 7, Canadian Charter of Rights and Freedoms 1982.
[27] (1999) 66 CRR (2nd) 267.
[28] Quoted in the Hon. Earl Johnson, Jr., 'Will Gideon's Trumpet Sound a New Melody? The Globalisation of Constitutional Values and Its Impact for a Right to Equal Justice in Civil Cases,' *Seattle Journal for Social Justice*, Vol. 2, No. 1 (2003), pp. 201–241, at 213.

[29] *New Brunswick (Minister of Health and Community Services) v. G. (J.)*, [1999] 3 S.C.R. 46, para. 75. See also *Laskowska v. Poland (Application no. 77765/01)* ECHR (Fourth Section) 13 March 2007 (Final 13/06/07).
[30] Perluss, ' Right to Counsel' (n. 15 above), pp. 578–591.
[31] J. Gordley, 'Variations on a Modern Theme,' in M. Cappelletti, J. Gordley and E. Johnson, Jr., *Towards Equal Justice: A Comparative Study of Legal Aid in Modern Societies* (Dobbs Ferry, NY: Milan, Guiffre & Oceana Publications, 1975), pp. 77–132, at 85.
[32] Ibid., p. 109.
[33] C. Scott, 'The Interdependence and Permeability of Human Rights Norms: Towards a Partial Fusion of the International Covenants on Human Rights,' *Osgoode Law Journal*, Vol. 27 (1989), pp. 769–878, at 778.

3.2 Deprivation of Liberty and Livelihood: Two Sides of the Same Coin

If we are to take human suffering seriously, we must also consider seriously the fact that the poorest and most vulnerable members of all societies suffer most from deprivations of both political and economic rights.[34]

'THE POOR MAN CHARGED WITH CRIME'

The right to legal assistance sponsored by the State has increasingly gained acceptance in the conduct of criminal litigation, particularly where an accused is indigent and confronts the possible loss of liberty. In 1963, in the landmark case of *Gideon v Wainwright*,[35] the United States Supreme Court unanimously held that the Sixth[36] and Fourteenth Amendments[37] to the American Constitution required American courts to provide lawyers to defendants in criminal proceedings where they were unable to afford their own counsel. While the tendency of the American Supreme Court had been to uphold 'the right to a lawyer as an essential safeguard of liberty,'[38] prior to 1963, the Supreme Court had held that each state[39] and the circumstances of each case[40] must ultimately determine the extent and application or otherwise of the right. In *Gideon v Wainwright*, the Supreme Court finally deemed '(t)he right of one charged with crime to counsel...fundamental and essential to fair trials' in every state, declaring:

> [R]eason and reflection require us to recognize that in our adversary system of criminal justice, any person haled into court, who is too poor to hire a lawyer, cannot be assured a fair trial unless counsel is provided for him. This seems to us to be an obvious truth....From the very beginning, our state and national

constitutions and laws have laid great emphasis on procedural and substantive safeguards designed to assure fair trials before impartial tribunals in which every defendant stands equal before the law. This noble ideal cannot be realized if the poor man charged with crime has to face his accusers without a lawyer to assist him.[41]

In the absence of a constitutional provision guaranteeing 'one charged with crime' the right to counsel, the Australian High Court was asked to consider the content of the right to a fair trial in the case of *Dietrich v The Queen*.[42] Mr Dietrich was charged with various offences relating to the importation and possession of heroin and tried in the County Court of the state of Victoria. He pleaded not guilty and was unrepresented during a trial which lasted almost forty days. His attempts to secure legal aid to fund a not guilty plea were unsuccessful and the Victorian court refused to adjourn the proceedings to allow him time to obtain representation, convicting him of a charge of importation which carries a sentence of long-term imprisonment.

On appeal, the High Court of Australia overturned the conviction and ordered a new trial. The Court's decision centred on the finding that Dietrich, an indigent accused facing a serious criminal offence, had a common law right to a fair trial. This right was effectively denied to him when his request to the state Victorian court for an adjournment of the proceedings to secure legal representation was refused. The Court, making 'it quite clear that they (were) dealing with the criminal justice system, not with the civil justice system,'[43] said that the fairness of the trial depended on the particular circumstances of the case and that such circumstances were to be of a serious criminal nature.

In South Africa, the question whether indigent accused were entitled to legal representation at public expense 'once its lack amounted to a handicap so great that to try them on their own lay beyond the pale of justice' was 'settled decisively'[44] with the implementation of section 25 (3) (e) of the

---

[34] Ibid.

[35] (1963) 372 U.S. 335.

[36] The Sixth Amendment provides: 'In all criminal prosecutions, the accused shall enjoy the right...to have the Assistance of Counsel for his defense.'

[37] Section (1) of the Fourteenth Amendment provides: 'No State shall...deprive any person of life, liberty, or property, without due process of law; nor deny to any person within its jurisdiction the equal protection of the laws.'

[38] *Gideon v. Wainwright* (n. 35 above), per Justice Black. See: caselaw.lp.findlaw.com/scripts/getcase.pl?court= US&vol=372 &invol=335.

[39] See *Powell v. Alabama* (1932) 287 U.S. 45.

[40] See *Betts v. Brandy* (1942) 316 U.S. 455.

[41] *Gideon v. Wainwright* (n. 35 above).

[42] (1992) 177 CLR 292.

[43] *Williams & Anor v. Official Trustee in Bankruptcy & Anor* (1994) 122 ALR 585, at 600.

[44] *S v. Vermaas; S v. Du Plessis* (1995) 2 SA 292 (CC), at 15, per Justice Didcott.

new South African Constitution of Act 200 of 1993. The section provides: 'Every accused person shall have the right to a fair trial, which shall include the right...to be represented by a legal practitioner of his or her choice or, where substantial injustice would otherwise result, to be provided with legal representation at state expense, and to be informed of these rights.'

While 'substantial injustice' might result from the failure to 'proceed without a lawyer for the defence' in criminal proceedings, the South African Constitutional Court, in the cases of *S v Vermaas and Du Plessis*, determined that the ramifications of the case and their complexity or simplicity, the accused's aptitude or ineptitude to fend for him/herself and the gravity of the potential consequences of a conviction, ought to be factors the court takes into account when evaluating an entitlement to legal representation at state expense.[45]

The absence of the implementation of any financial and administrative structures necessary to give effect 'to the right to legal representation at the expense of the state' provided for in section 23(3)(e) of the South African Constitution was clearly of concern to the Court. Justice Didcott concluded his judgment in *Vermaas* with words of 'public importance,' which arguably have equal application to the absence of mechanisms available for the enforcement of socio-economic rights. He said:

> We are mindful of the multifarious demands on the public purse and the machinery of government that flow from the urgent need for economic and social reform. But the Constitution does not envisage, and it will surely not brook, any undue delay in the fulfilment of any promise made by it about a fundamental right....in spite of section 25(3)(e), the situation still prevails where during every month countless thousands of South Africans are criminally tried without legal representation because they are too poor to pay for it. They are presumably informed in the beginning, as the section requires them peremptorily to be, of their right to obtain that free of charge in the circumstances which it defines. Imparting such information becomes an empty ges-

ture and makes a mockery of the Constitution, however, if it is not backed by mechanisms that are adequate for the enforcement of the right.[46]

Historically, the provision of legal aid to indigent people was founded on notions of charity and natural justice. While justice and the 'rights of man' were theoretically accessible to all, those lacking the means to access justice – 'justice might be free but not the means for its attainment'[47] – were at the mercy of the 'charitable impulses'[48] of the bar who either dispensed professional goodwill to the poor as an 'honorific duty'[49] or were assigned by the state to perform a gratuitous obligation.[50] As the 'old vision of the state as preserver of natural rights'[51] became less feasible and declined, the State was entrusted by its citizens with the power to govern in exchange for it assuming responsibility to protect and enhance their social and economic well-being.

As 'charitable impulses,' 'gratuitous obligations' and the State's responsibility to administer justice equally to rich and poor developed into international conventions,[52] comprehensive legal aid programs and laws, democratic societies predominantly honoured their commitment to the right to equal justice and a fair hearing by limiting its application to a criminal trial. State-sponsored provision of legal counsel in criminal proceedings has however not attracted broad parallel application to indigent litigants in civil proceedings, despite the 'substantial injustice'[53] or 'threat to fundamental interests'[54] which the potential deprivation of livelihood might trigger due to a litigant's inability, essentially financial, to assert or defend a right in civil proceedings, often via a complex and alien judicial process.

---

[45] Ibid., para. 15. See also Geoff Budlender, 'Access to Courts' (n. 18 above), p. 342.

[46] *S v. Vermaas; S v. Du Plessis* (1995) 2 SA 292 (CC), at 16.
[47] Cappelletti, 'The Emergence of a Modern Theme' in Mauro Cappelletti et. al. (n. 31 above), pp. 5–76, at 18.
[48] Ibid. p. 14.
[49] Ibid. p. 23.
[50] Ibid.
[51] Ibid.
[52] See for example, Article 14(3) of the International Covenant on Civil and Political Rights 1966 which provides that an accused has the right to legal assistance at state expense where a person has insufficient means and the interests of justice require representation.
[53] See *Airey v. Ireland* (n. 19 above).
[54] See Canadian Bar Association Press Release (n. 5 above).

A Parallel Right 'to Combat Social Exclusion'

Explanations for the absence of a right to legal aid in civil litigation have tended to cling to notions of legal aid priorities (often politically driven), fiscal restraint and budgetary considerations and courts have legitimately demonstrated a reticence to direct the work of the legislature in relation to resource allocations. The declaration of a social right or its breach and a direction to a State to take all reasonable measures to effect its obligations under law is, however, a very different exercise to a direction to allocate certain resources to honour the right or remedy the breach. The deprivation of liberty argument (which has underscored the provision of legal aid in criminal law proceedings) has also held moral and philosophical sway over demands for social and economic justice, despite the obvious denial of the latter leading to lives in jeopardy. As Scott Leckie has observed: '[M]ost would recoil in horror at the deprivation of the freedom of life...but display considerably more tolerance when human suffering or death stem from preventable denials of the basic necessities of life such as food, health care or a secure place to live.'[55]

Roger Smith has argued that the purpose of legal aid is to ensure that citizens can exercise their rights 'to combat social exclusion,'[56] namely the decline of effective participation in society which might take the form of physical or economic deprivation. While traditionally linked to the civil right guaranteeing physical liberty and security, legal aid is 'also linked to the modern struggle against poverty and...to contemporary "social rights" such as the rights to an adequate diet, to decent housing and to medical care.'[57] Indeed, the term 'access to justice' has been defined within the context of development as the '[a]bility of people

from disadvantaged groups to prevent and overcome human poverty by seeking and obtaining a remedy, through the justice system, for grievances in accordance with human rights principles and standards.'[58]

In a case where labour tenants and occupiers faced eviction in breach of the Bill of Rights to the South African Constitution,[59] the right to security of tenure *and* to legal aid were considered by the South African Land Claims Court. Section 25(6) of the Constitution reads:

A person or community whose tenure of land is legally insecure as a result of past racially discriminatory laws or practices is entitled, to the extent provided by an Act of Parliament, either to tenure which is legally secure or to comparable redress.

The Court found that despite the constitutional guarantee and legislation providing 'farm dwellers with procedural and substantive protection against eviction,'[60] a very large number of people for whose benefit the legislation was enacted, do not enjoy security of tenure because they were extremely poor and vulnerable. The Court continued:

When their tenure security is threatened or infringed, they do not understand the documents initiating action or the processes to follow in order to defend their rights. On the other hand they cannot afford the fees for a lawyer to represent them because of their poverty. As a result they are quite often unable to defend or enforce their rights and their entitlement under the Constitution.[61]

The Court went on to make the observation that no rationale appears to exist for maintaining a distinction between civil and criminal matters given the 'equally complex' issues that arise in

---

[55] S. Leckie, 'Another Step towards Indivisibility: Identifying the Key Features of Violations of Economic, Social and Cultural Rights,' *Human Rights Quarterly*, Vol. 20 (1998), pp. 81–124, at 83.

[56] See R. Smith, 'Legal Aid Crisis: A Principled Approach to Change,' *Bulletin – Justice*, Winter (2004), p. 1, available at: http://www.justice.org.uk/images/pdfs/winterbulletin.pdf. This twelve-principle approach was developed by the JUSTICE organisation in response to the British Department for Constitutional Affairs proposals for cuts to legal aid.

[57] Gordley, 'Variations on a Modern Theme' (n. 31 above), p. 109.

[58] R. Sudarshan, 'Rule of Law and Access to Justice: Perspectives from UNDP Experience,' paper presented to the European Commission Expert Seminar on The Rule of Law and the Administration of Justice as part of Good Governance, Brussels, 3–4 July 2003, p. 6. See also UNDP Practice Note 9/3/2004.

[59] *Nkuzi Development Association v. Government of the Republic of South Africa and The Legal Aid Board*, LCC 10/01, decided 6 July 2001 (see also (2002) 2 SA 733 (LCC)).

[60] Budlender, 'Access to Courts' (n. 18 above), p. 340.

[61] Per Acting Judge Moloto in *Nkuzi Development Association* (n. 59 above).

civil litigation and the difficulty with fully comprehending the relevant laws and procedures. 'Failure by a judicial officer to inform these (civil) litigants of their rights, how to exercise them and where to obtain assistance,' said the Constitutional Court, 'may result in a miscarriage of justice.'[62]

The Court ordered that 'the persons who have a right to security of tenure…and whose security of tenure is threatened or has been infringed, have a right to legal representation or legal aid at State expense if substantial injustice would otherwise result, and if they cannot reasonably afford the cost thereof from their own resources,' adding that '(t)he State is under a duty to provide such legal representation or legal aid through mechanisms selected by it.' The potentially severe consequences of being deprived of a home and the incapacity to readily secure suitable alternative accommodation were found to constitute 'substantial injustice.'[63]

Access to justice and the realisation of 'modern social rights' increasingly require effective legal representation where barriers to access are not solely limited to a litigant's ability to pay. Language and cultural backgrounds present major impediments to immigrant and refugee populations attempting to access effective justice within foreign legal systems.[64] People with intellectual and physical disabilities are frequently prevented from understanding legal proceedings or actively participating in their cases and require 'accommo-

dations' to access the court system. By reference to the Americans with Disabilities Act (ADA) of 1990, Lisa Brodoff and others have argued that 'the only reasonable accommodation under Title II of the ADA…for litigants with disabling conditions, is an attorney':

> Only an attorney can provide the knowledge, energy, strategy, translation, and understanding to mount a case or a defense for those whose disabilities block their capacity to do so *pro se*.[65]

While choice and competency of a legal representative have triggered debates about meeting the requirement for adequate and effective legal representation,[66] the case of *Purohit and Moore v The Gambia*[67] clearly underscores the need for free legal assistance to patients detained in psychiatric institutions in error or indefinitely. The complainants, mental health advocates, submitted a communication on behalf of patients detained in a psychiatric unit pursuant to the mental health legislation of the Republic of The Gambia. They alleged in particular that the Lunatics Detention Act (LDA) afforded no review or appeal procedures in relation to patient determinations or certifications and that no compensation or legal aid was available where the rights of patients (in psychiatric care) were breached.

The Gambia advised the African Commission on Human and Peoples' Rights that legal procedures and provisions under the nation's Constitution did exist to facilitate access to legal redress; it was apparent however that only persons charged with Capital Offences under the Poor Persons Defence (Capital Charge) Act were eligible for legal assistance. In response, the African Commission said that it could not 'help but look at the nature of people that would be detained…under the Lunatics

---

[62] Ibid.

[63] The orders made by the Land Claims Court included a provision that 'substantial injustice' could also include the potentially severe consequences that might arise if the litigant concerned is not likely to be able effectively to present his or her case unrepresented, having regard to the complexity of the case, the legal procedure, and their education, knowledge and skills.

[64] S. Shettey, 'Equal Justice under the Law: Myth or Reality for Immigrants and Refugees,' *Seattle Journal for Social Justice*, Vol. 2 (2003–4), pp. 565 569, at 567. See also A. Durbach, 'Defining Pro Bono – Challenging Definitions,' *Law Society Journal*, Vol. 38, No. 9 (2000), pp. 64–68: 'Although cost is often cited as the primary barrier to commencing litigation and accordingly, a barrier to access to justice, Her Honour Justice Catherine Branson of the Federal Court has argued, by reference in particular to the Native Title Jurisdiction of the Court, that a failure to appreciate the customs and cultural history and experience of litigants, either by their legal advisers or members of the judiciary, and not cost, presents a critical barrier to access to justice for indigenous and non-English speaking people.'

[65] L. Brodoff, Susan McClellan and Elizabeth Anderson, 'The ADA: One Avenue to Appointed Counsel before a Full Civil Gideon,' *Seattle Journal for Social Justice*, Vol. 2 (2004), pp. 609–640, at 611.

[66] S. Ellmann, 'Weighing and Implementing the Right to Counsel,' *The South African Law Journal*, Vol. 120 (2004), pp. 318–338, at 331; *Charles v. S* (2002) 3 All SA 471 (E) 475f-g; Derek O'Brien and John Arnold Epp, 'Defending the Right to Choose: Legally Aided Defendants and Choice of Legal Representative,' *E.H.R.L.R*, Vol. 4 (2001), pp. 409–420.

[67] *Purohit and Moore v. The Gambia*, African Commission on Human and Peoples' Rights, Comm. No. 241/2001 (2003).

Detention Act and ask...whether or not these patients (could) access the legal procedures available without legal aid.' Those detained under the LDA, stated the Commission 'are likely to be people picked up from the streets or people from poor backgrounds.'[68] Accordingly, even if they had access to procedures whereby they might challenge their detention, 'the avenues for redress' were only of use if affordable: the remedies are not 'realistic...in the absence of legal aid services.'[69] As such, the Commission held that The Gambia had failed to meet the equal protection of the law provisions of Article 3 of the African Charter.

In addition, the Commission found that the failure of the LDA to afford detainees held under the LDA any opportunity to challenge their detention[70] was a breach of Article 7(1) of the Charter, which guarantees 'every individual the right to have his cause heard' where his 'fundamental rights as recognised and guaranteed by conventions, laws, regulations and customs in force' have been violated. The Commission concluded that:

> The entitlement of persons with mental illness or persons being treated as such to be heard and to be represented by Counsel in determinations affecting their lives, livelihood, liberty, property or status, is particularly recognised in Principles 16, 17 and 18[71] of the UN Principles for the Protection of Persons with Mental Illness and the Improvement of Mental Care.[72]

The right 'to be heard and to be represented by Counsel in determinations affecting' life, liberty or livelihood is at the core of petitions for a right to legal aid in criminal and civil jurisdictions. 'By and large' people facing criminal charges and those seeking access to court to assert their rights to shelter and security of tenure, to the care and custody of children, to health care and social services, are 'more likely to be poorer than the population as a whole'[73] and financially and often culturally and psychologically, in need of legal representation. In both criminal and civil litigation, the right to effective legal representation provided by the State is often critical to the realisation of the right to a fair trial; perhaps more importantly, the right to legal aid can have a very significant impact on outcome, tipping the balance against the deprivation of liberty or livelihood.[74]

4. DOING JUSTICE TO THE MOST 'BASIC HUMAN RIGHT': GUARANTEEING THE ENJOYMENT OF SOCIO-ECONOMIC RIGHTS

> [R]ights without remedies are of little value. To possess a right of free speech or movement is of little value if you lack the legal means to vindicate it when others obstruct it; and legal means include both access to the courts and skilled representation in court. (Lord Justice Stephen Sedley[75])

In the past decade, there has been an increasing incorporation of elements of economic, social and cultural rights into the constitutions and national legislation of nearly all countries.[76] Where the laws or constitution of a nation 'purport to guarantee legal rights,' 'effective access to justice can...be seen as the most basic requirement – the most basic "human right"'[77] – 'underpinning...all other rights.'[78]

Article 2(1) of the International Covenant on Economic, Social and Cultural Rights (CESCR) provides that each State party take steps 'to the maximum of its available resources' towards 'achieving progressively the full realization of the rights' contained in the Covenant 'by all appropriate means, including particularly the adoption of legislative measures.' In addition to the implementation of legislation to effect the progressive

---

68 Ibid., para. 53.
69 Ibid., paras. 36 and 37.
70 Ibid., para. 69.
71 Principle 18, Procedural safeguards (adopted 17 December 1991), provides: 'The patient shall be entitled to choose and appoint a counsel to represent the patient as such, including representation in any complaint procedure or appeal. If the patient does not secure such services, a counsel shall be made available without payment by the patient to the extent that the patient lacks sufficient means to pay.'
72 *Purohit and Moore* (n. 67 above), para. 72.

73 Brodoff et al., 'The ADA' (n. 65 above), p. 612.
74 The Hon. Robert W. Sweet quoted in Brodoff et al., 'The ADA,' p. 617: 'As every trial judge knows, the task of determining the correct legal outcome is rendered almost impossible without effective counsel. Courts have neither the time not the capacity to be both the litigant and the impartial judges on any issue of genuine complexity.'
75 Quoted in Budlender, 'Access to Courts' (n. 18 above), p. 345.
76 See Leckie, 'Another Step' (n. 55 above), pp. 84–85.
77 Cappelletti quoted in Mario Gomez (n. 2 above), p. 14.
78 Budlender, 'Access to Courts' (n. 18 above), p. 345.

realisation of economic, social and cultural rights, General Comment 3 on Article 2 (1) of the CESCR indicates that 'judicial and other effective remedies' may be appropriate to consider with respect to rights considered justiciable within particular legal systems.[79] That economic, social and cultural rights are increasingly justiciable in many democratic nations is an important step towards their realisation.[80] However in the absence of mechanisms to guarantee justiciability, the promise of their actual enjoyment is diminished.

Perhaps the most significant barrier to the application of a right to legal aid in civil litigation by states supportive of socio-economic rights and their realisation, is the cost of sustaining a comprehensive legal aid program and effectively managing competing demands for state resources. There are obvious benefits to ensuring effective representation in complex litigation affecting 'fundamental interests,'[81] particularly where the claimant of a right is unable to appreciate the full implications of a right under threat, fails to understand the legal issues and processes at play and is unable to articulate a clear position, including the presentation of evidence and legal argument. Providing counsel for indigent civil litigants can reduce litigation and eliminate delays in *pro se* representation, saving 'society money in the long run.'[82] Lisa Brodoff points out that 'additional societal benefits, perhaps worth more than the costs, could accrue, with the primary benefit being restored

confidence in the justice system' which may have delivered flawed, inappropriate and unworkable outcomes 'because of the inadequacies in the presentation of the case.'[83]

In the case of the *State of Punjab v Ram Lubhaya Bagga*,[84] the Indian Supreme Court held that, '(n)o State or country can have unlimited resources to spend on any of its projects.' Article 39A of the Indian Constitution of 1949 provides that 'the State shall...provide free legal aid...to ensure that opportunities for securing justice are not denied to any citizen by reason of economic or other disabilities.' The obligation on the Indian State is however moderated by the proviso that it give effect to rights 'within the limits of its economic capacity and development.'[85] Similarly, while the South African Constitution provides that a legal representative is to be appointed at state expense 'if substantial injustice would otherwise result,'[86] the South African Legal Aid Guide of 2004 makes it clear that 'the many claimant demands on the public purse' of a developing country will limit the funding of legal aid 'for the foreseeable future.'[87] Accordingly, the Legal Aid Board has prioritised in theory certain areas of service delivery to include: the rights to legal aid enshrined in the Constitution; vulnerable groups (including children, women, the aged, AIDS orphans, domestic workers, farm workers, refugees); the landless; victims of racial attacks; personal injury cases; and the poor who have suffered material loss due to mistreatment or neglect by servants of the State, provisional government or local authorities.

The provision of legal representation at state expense, as with the provision of health care services, housing and education, carries inevitable and extensive budgetary implications for any nation committed to the realisation of economic, social and cultural rights as the critical course towards democratic development. Stephen Ellmann argues that despite the cost of rights, their adjudication – which may be informed by

---

[79] Committee on Economic, Social and Cultural Rights, General Comment No. 3, The nature of States parties' obligations (Fifth session, 1990), U.N. Doc. E/1991/23, annex III at 86 (1990), para. 5. See also UN Committee on Economic, Social and Cultural Rights, 'The Limburg Principles on the Implementation of the International Covenant on Economic, Social and Cultural Rights,' UN Doc. E/CN.4/1987/17, annex, reprinted in *Human Rights Quarterly*, Vol. 9 (1987), pp. 122–135.

[80] See generally, Leckie, 'Another Step' (n. 55 above); Scott, 'Interdependence and Permeability' (n. 33 above); S. Liebenberg, 'The Courts and Socio-Economic Rights: Carving out a Role' *ESR Review*, Vol. 3, No. 1 (2002), available at http://www.communitylawcentre.org.za/ser/esr2002/2002july_courts.php.

[81] See para. 2 in Statement of Claim in the *Canadian Bar Association v. Her Majesty the Queen in the Rights of the Province of British Columbia and others*. 'Fundamental interests' are defined as: (a) life; (b) liberty; (c) livelihood; (d) equality; (e) health; (f) housing; (g) safety; (h) security; and (i) sustenance. See http://www.cba.org/CBA/News/2005_Releases/2005-06-20_legalaid.aspx.

[82] S. Bidran and Pedram Ben-Cohen quoted in Brodoff et al., 'The ADA' (n. 65 above), p. 621.

[83] Statement of Claim in *Canadian Bar Association* (n. 81 above), at paras. 47, 55, 65.

[84] (1998) 4 SCC 117, at p. 130, para. 29.

[85] See Directive Principles of State Policy contained in Part IV of the Indian Constitution 1949.

[86] Section 35(3)(g).

[87] Chapter 3, 'Legal aid priorities, inclusions and exclusions,' *South African Legal Aid Guide* 2004 (11th edition).

'prevailing resource constraints'[88] – 'need not lead to the conclusion that judges should measure the dimension of those rights in the light of their costs.'[89] However, where the execution of one right (to legal representation) – the:

> most basic "human right" – is clearly bound up with the 'practical and effective' (as opposed to 'theoretical or illusory')[90] realisation or enjoyment of others (in this case, social rights), what constitutes a fair hearing, equality before the law and 'substantial injustice' cannot appropriately be determined by reference to 'what the nation can afford.'

Tied to the question of cost is a reticence by courts 'to pronounce on matters involving state action or budgetary and policy implications'[91] for an apparent lack of competency or legitimacy.[92] The growing acknowledgment of the interdependency of human rights as 'mutually reinforcing or mutually dependent, but distinct,'[93] that, for example, 'the realisation of social and economic rights is integral to the full enjoyment of the right to life,'[94] has considerably eroded the argument that courts offend the separation of powers doctrine when making determinations in relation to social rights. It is uncontroversial that the adjudication of social rights 'may result in courts making orders which have direct implications for budgetary matters.'[95] Indeed, in the South African Constitutional Court's certification of the 1996 Constitution hearing, the Court noted that 'such implications' would arise 'even where a court enforces civil and political rights such as equality, freedom of speech and the right to a fair trial.'[96]

A demonstration of indigence, financial hardship and compliance with a 'means test' have served as the traditional bases or criteria for eligibility for legal representation provided at state expense. In criminal proceedings, the additional feature of potential deprivation of liberty, has served as the rationale for affording legal aid to the accused, particularly those defending serious offences. The principle focus of this chapter has been to portray the evolution of evidence and legal argument in support of extending the right to legal aid in the context of socio-economic litigation, where the deprivation of livelihood and potentially life, is often the consequence of an obstruction or breach of a socio-economic right. The realisation of socio-economic rights – and a corresponding or enabling right to civil legal aid – appropriately calls for a legislative framework which facilitates the adjudication and enforcement of these rights by an 'independent and impartial judiciary, accessible by all.'[97]

Recognising that fashioning a broad right to legal aid will trigger concerns about public policy and budgetary implications, it may be 'wise public policy'[98] to guide the judicial process in the determination of the right to civil legal aid by signalling some additional criteria, 'regardless of means'[99] on which to found the right. These might include circumstances where the absence of legal counsel would impede the 'effective presentation of the case'[100] or the achievement of a fair trial[101] give rise to 'substantial injustice'[102] or prejudice the vindication of fundamental interests.

In addition, where legal proceedings which raise a significant public interest or systemic practices or failures affecting a broad class of people (as is often the case with socio-economic rights litigation) cannot be determined for want of legal representation at state expense, the interests of justice and public policy may dictate that legal aid, as of right, be provided. The provision of state funding for litigation, which addresses 'broad social concerns rather than individual grievances,'[103] can offer the state many benefits, such as clarification of the law, economies of scale (where, with limited allocation of resources, legal

---

[88] M. Pieterse, 'Possibilities and Pitfalls in the Domestic Enforcement of Social Rights: Contemplating the South African Experience,' *Human Rights Quarterly*, Vol. 26 (2004), pp. 882–905, at 892.
[89] Ellmann, 'Right to Counsel' (n. 66 above), p. 328.
[90] *Airey v. Ireland* (n. 19 above).
[91] Pieterse, 'Possibilities and Pitfalls' (n. 88 above), p. 886.
[92] Budlender, 'Access to Courts' (n. 18 above), p. 352.
[93] Pieterse, 'Possibilities and Pitfalls' (n. 88 above), p. 891, fn. 42.
[94] Ibid. p. 891.
[95] *Ex Parte Chairperson of the Constitutional Assembly: In re Certification of the Constitution of the Republic of South Africa* 1996 (4) SA 744 (CC), quoted in Pieterse, 'Possibilities and Pitfalls' (n. 88 above), p. 886.
[96] Ibid.

[97] Leckie, 'Another Step' (n. 55 above), p. 105.
[98] *Lassiter v. Department of Social Services* (1981) 452 US 18.
[99] Canadian Bar Association Press release (n. 5 above).
[100] *Airey v. Ireland* (n. 19 above).
[101] *Steel and Morris v. United Kingdom* (n. 23 above).
[102] *Nkuzi Development Association v. Government of the Republic of South Africa* (n. 59 above).
[103] Goidley 'Variations on a Modern Theme' (n. 31 above).

proceedings yield effective outcomes for a large section of the community experiencing common difficulties), and impetus for reform and structural change.[104]

The extent to which rights can be asserted and enforced and remedies accessed when breaches occur is a significant measure of the viability of a democratic society.[105] The right to legal aid is a critical precursor to the effective enjoyment of socio-economic rights. This right, 'conservative of every other right,'[106] is fundamentally linked to the amelioration of social and economic deprivation. To profess adherence to the 'democratic idea of legal equality' while maintaining an exclusion from such equality when 'people with low incomes...are denied legal aid in cases where...they are unjustly evicted or threatened about the custody of their children'[107] or denied access to appropriate mental health care, is acutely at odds with a nation's commitment to the economic, social and cultural health and development of its citizens. Without the legal means to vindicate rights in civil law matters, these rights are accorded a differential standard of protection 'in disregard of the international human rights law principle that all rights are indivisible and inter-

dependent.'[108] The indivisibility of human rights in relation to legal aid was boldly recognised by the Committee of Ministers of the Council of Europe almost fifteen years ago with the adoption of Recommendation 93(1) on effective access to the law and justice for the very poor[109] . The Recommendation provides that particularly vulnerable individuals ('the very poor')[110] who lack the means to ensure the protection of their legal rights, should have effective access to legal aid, irrespective of the character of the right infringed (i.e. civil, political, economic, social or cultural). The Committee went further, recommending that legal aid should be extended to all types of legal disputes and judicial proceedings, whether criminal, civil or administrative. Modern democracies could do well to replicate the provision of state legal aid without discrimination to 'the very poor' and so facilitate 'the proper dispensation of justice and the effective functioning of a modern rule of law.'[111]

---

[104] A. Durbach, 'Aid in the Public Interest" *Reform* (Australian Law Reform Commission), Vol. 73 (1998), pp. 16–20, at 16.

[105] See Council of Europe Committee of Ministers Resolution 78(8) on Legal Aid and Advice adopted 2 March, 1978.

[106] *Miranda v. Sims* (2000) 98 Wn. App. 898, at 909.

[107] Press release issued by the Canadian Bar Association, Ottawa, dated 5 October 2006.

[108] Statement of Claim in the *Canadian Bar Association v. Her Majesty the Queen in the Rights of the Province of British Columbia and others*, (n.81 above), para. 90(e).

[109] Adopted on 8 January 1993.

[110] 'Persons who are particularly deprived, marginalised or excluded from society both in economic and in social and cultural terms.' See 'International standards on legal aid: relevant texts and summaries of documents,' Open Society Justice Initiative, available at <http://www.justiceinitiative.org/db/resource2?res_id= 102807>.

[111] 'The Institution of Legal Aid,' Report and Proposals of the Hellenic Republic National Commission for Human Rights, Proposal (d), dated 25 June 2001, at http://www.nchr.gr/category.php?category'id=92.

PART TWO

Select National Jurisdictions

4

South Africa

Adjudicating Social Rights Under a Transformative Constitution

Sandra Liebenberg*

1. INTRODUCTION

The 1996 South African Constitution[1] is renowned internationally for its holistic, inclusive Bill of Rights. In addition to traditional civil and political rights, the Bill of Rights includes a comprehensive set of social, economic and cultural rights. All these rights are enforceable by the courts[2], and the courts have a wide discretion to grant 'just and equitable' remedies.[3]

This chapter discusses the history and background of the inclusion of socio-economic rights in the 1996 Constitution, and the evolving jurisprudence on the enforcement of these rights. This jurisprudence illustrates how the South African courts are developing a principled and pragmatic model for the judicial review of socio-economic rights, which supports the transformative goals of the Constitution. Some of the main critiques of certain aspects of the courts' jurisprudence are also discussed.

* Sandra Liebenberg is Professor, H.F. Oppenheimer Chair in Human Rights Law, Department of Public Law, Stellenbosch University. This chapter is based upon work supported by the South African National Research Foundation. Any opinion, findings and conclusions or recommendations expressed in this material are those of the author and therefore the NRF does not accept any liability in regard thereto.
1 The Constitution of the Republic of South Africa Act, 1996 ('the Constitution').
2 See section 38 of the Constitution.
3 Under section 172 of the Constitution, a court must declare invalid law or conduct that is inconsistent with the Constitution to the extent of its inconsistency, and may make 'any order that is just and equitable.'

2. INCLUDING SOCIO-ECONOMIC RIGHTS AS JUSTICIABLE CONSTITUTIONAL RIGHTS

The inclusion of socio-economic rights as fully justiciable rights in the Bill of Rights was the subject of extensive academic and public debate and contestation. This debate must be viewed in the context of the transition from a system of parliamentary sovereignty through which the *apartheid* system was enacted to a constitutional democracy.[4] A critical objective of the Constitution is that it facilitates the transformation of South

4 The multi-party negotiations for a political settlement in South Africa led firstly to the adoption of the 'interim' Constitution Act 200 of 1993 ['the interim Constitution'] by the pre-democratic Tricameral Parliament. South Africa's first democratic elections in April 1994 were held in terms of this transitional Constitution, which also contained a set of thirty-four Constitutional Principles (agreed on during the 1991–1993 political negotiations) to which the 'final' Constitution had to conform. The 1996 Constitution was drafted and adopted by the Constitutional Assembly consisting of the two houses of the democratically elected Parliament sitting jointly. The Constitutional Court was required to certify that the draft final constitutional text conformed to the aforementioned Constitutional Principles (referred to as 'the certification process.'). The Constitutional Court refused to certify the first draft of the Constitution: see *Ex parte Chairperson of the Constitutional Assembly: In re Certification of the Constitution of the Republic of South Africa 1996* (10) BCLR 1253, 1996 (4) SA 744 (CC) ['*First Certification* judgment']. The Constitutional Assembly reconvened and amended the text of the Constitution, which was re-submitted to the Court on 11 October 1996. This amended text was certified by the Court as being in compliance with the Constitutional Principles: *Certification of the Amended Text of the Constitution of the Republic of South Africa, 1996* 1997 (2) SA 97 (CC) ['*Second Certification* judgment']. The 1996 Constitution entered into force on 4 February 1997.

African society. Key elements of this transformation include the dismantling of a plethora of racist
and sexist laws and institutions, redressing their
legacy, healing the divisions of the past and building a new society committed to social justice and
the improvement in the quality of people's lives.[5]
As Budlender AJ wrote in *Rates Action Group v City
of Cape Town*:[6]

> Ours is a transformative constitution....
> Whatever the position may be in the USA or
> other countries, that is not the purpose of
> our Constitution. Our Constitution provides
> a mandate, a framework and to some extent
> a blueprint for the transformation of our
> society from its racist and unequal past to a
> society in which all can live with dignity.[7]

Much of the debate concerning whether socio-
economic rights should be included in the South
African Constitution centred on whether and in
what form these rights could best contribute to
achieving the transformative aspirations of the
new constitutional order.[8] The various draft proposals of the African National Congress (ANC) for
a Bill of Rights supported the inclusion of socio-
economic rights in some form.[9] Socio-economic

rights were viewed as facilitating social transformation and deepening civic equality and democratic participation.[10] Women's rights advocates
also supported the constitutional protection of
socio-economic rights on the basis that it would
advance substantial gender equality in South
Africa.[11]

The interim Constitution contained a small, but
significant core of socio-economic rights in chapter 3 relating to 'fundamental rights'. These were
children's rights (section 30), labour rights (sections 12 and 27), the right to an environment that
is not detrimental to health (section 29), and educational rights (section 32). In addition, the right
to property (section 28) and free economic activity (section 26) were entrenched as fundamental
rights.

During the negotiations on the drafting of the
1996 Constitution, most political parties supported the entrenchment of at least some socio-
economic rights in the Bill of Rights. There was
also a vigorous campaign by a range of civil society organisations (including trade unions, church
groups, women's groups, human rights NGOs, and
developmental NGOs) supporting the inclusion of
socio-economic rights as fully justiciable rights.
These organisations argued that socio-economic
rights were essential to the reconstruction and
development of a democratic South Africa, and
protected the interests of the most disadvantaged
members of society.[12] A major concern related to
the impact of a constitutional guarantee of property rights on the imperative to achieve a more
equitable distribution of wealth to redress the
legacy of colonial and apartheid rule.[13] In this

---

[5] See the postamble of the interim Constitution, the preamble and s.1 of the 1996 Constitution. The foundational values of the Constitution are human dignity, equality and
freedom: see sections 1, 7(1) and 36 of the Constitution.
[6] 2004 (12) BCLR 1328 (C). On the transformative goals of
the Constitution, see further *Bato Star Fishing (Pty) Ltd v.
Minister of Environmental Affairs and Tourism and Others*
2004 (7) BCLR 687 (CC), para. 73.
[7] Ibid. para. 100.
[8] For some of the early debates on the question of the
inclusion of socio-economic rights in the Constitution,
see: E. Mureinik, 'Beyond a Charter of Luxuries: Economic Rights in the Constitution', *South African Journal
on Human Rights*, Vol. 8 (1992), pp. 464–474; N. Haysom,
'Constitutionalism, majoritarian democracy and socio-
economic rights', *South African Journal on Human Rights*,
Vol. 8 (1992), pp. 451–463; D. Davis 'The case against the
inclusion of socio-economic demands in a Bill of Rights
except as directive principles', *South African Journal on
Human Rights*, Vol. 8 (1992), pp. 475–490.
[9] For a discussion of the ANC's proposals regarding the
entrenchment of socio-economic rights in a future South
African Bill of Rights, see N. Haysom, 'Democracy, Constitutionalism and the ANC's Bill of Rights for a New South
Africa', *South African Journal on Human Rights*, Vol. 7
(1991), pp. 102–109, at 106–107. See also Albie Sachs,
'Towards a Bill of Rights in a Democratic South Africa',
South African Journal on Human Rights, Vol. 6 (1990),
pp. 1–24. Socio-economic rights have a strong resonance
with the Freedom Charter adopted by the Congress of the
People on 26 June 1955, which contains various provisions relating to the socio-economic needs of people, and

the active role of the State in achieving a redistribution of
resources in South African society.
[10] Ibid.
[11] S. Liebenberg, 'Social and Economic Rights: A Critical
Challenge' in S. Liebenberg (ed.), *The Constitution of
South Africa from a Gender Perspective* (Cape Town: The
Community Law Centre in association with David Philip,
1995), pp. 79–96.
[12] *Petition of the Ad Hoc Committee for the Campaign
on Socio-Economic Rights* presented to the Constitutional Assembly (19 July 1995), extracts published in Sandra Liebenberg and Karisha Pillay (eds.), *Socio-economic
Rights in South Africa: A Resource Book* (Cape Town: Community Law Centre, University of the Western Cape – The
Socio-Economic Rights Project, 2000), pp. 19–20.
[13] See S. Terreblanche, *A History of Inequality in South
Africa 1652–2002* (Pietermaritzburg: University of Natal
Press and KMM Review Publishing, 2002). The property clause (s. 25) was drafted to emphasise 'the nation's

context, the entrenchment of socio-economic rights in the Bill of Rights was viewed as providing constitutional support for positive, redistributive state measures to ensure equitable access to resources and social services.

The Constitutional Assembly ultimately included a comprehensive set of socio-economic rights as justiciable rights in Chapter 2 (Bill of Rights). During the Certification process, objections were raised against the inclusion of socio-economic rights in the Bill of Rights.[14] The main thrust of these objections was that socio-economic rights breached the separation of powers doctrine in that they authorised judicial intrusion in the budgetary and policy-making spheres of the legislature and executive. In addition, it was argued that socio-economic rights were not justiciable. The Court responded to the separation of powers objection as follows:

> It is true that the inclusion of socio-economic rights may result in courts making orders which have direct implications for budgetary matters. However, even when a court enforces civil and political rights such as equality, freedom of speech and the right to a fair trial, the order it makes will often have such implications. A court may require the provision of legal aid, or the extension of state benefits to a class of people who formerly were not beneficiaries of such benefits. In our view it cannot be said that by including socio-economic rights within a bill of rights, a task is conferred upon the courts so different from that ordinarily conferred upon them by a bill of rights that it results in a breach of the separation of powers.[15]

Regarding the 'justiciability' objection, the Court held that socio-economic rights 'are, at least to some extent, justiciable....At the very minimum, socio-economic rights can be negatively protected from improper invasion.'[16] In fact, the Court's jurisprudence has developed considerably beyond this minimalist model of 'negative' protection, and significant protection is also accorded to the positive duties imposed by socio-economic rights.

3. SOCIO-ECONOMIC RIGHTS IN THE CONTEXT OF THE BILL OF RIGHTS

3.1 The Relevant Provisions

The Constitution places an overarching obligation on the State to 'respect, protect, promote and fulfil the rights in the Bill of Rights'.[17] This establishes that all the rights in the Bill of Rights impose a combination of negative and positive duties on the State, thus countering the predominantly defensive metaphors traditionally associated with human rights.[18] However, slotting claims into one or more of these categories of duties should not be determinative of the appropriate

---

commitment to land reform, and to bring about equitable access to all South Africa's natural resources' (see s. 25(4)(a) and s. 25(8)). In addition, the property clause contains provisions mandating positive state measures to achieve equitable access to land (s. 25(5)), tenure reform (s. 26(6)), and land restitution (s. 25(7)). On South Africa's constitutional property jurisprudence, see A. J. van der Walt, *Constitutional Property Law* (Cape Town: Juta & Co, 2005).

[14] The *First Certification judgment* (n. 4 above), paras. 76–78. The main objectors were the SA Institute of Race Relations, the Free Market Foundation and the Gauteng Association of Chambers of Commerce and Industry. Other civil society organisations argued in favour of the inclusion of socio-economic rights at the Certification hearings.

[15] Ibid. para 77.

[16] Ibid. para 78.

[17] Section 7(2). This typology is partly based on the analysis by Henry Shue of the obligations imposed on states by human rights: *Basic Rights: Subsistence, Affluence and US Foreign Policy* (Princeton, New Jersey: Princeton University Press, 1980), p. 5. See Memorandum by Technical Committee to Theme Committee 4 (Bill of Rights) of the Constitutional Assembly (8 March 1996). It is also used by the UN Committee on Economic, Social and Cultural Rights (CESCR) to analyse the duties imposed by various rights in the International Covenant on Economic, Social and Cultural Rights: e.g., General Comment No. 12 (Twentieth session, 1999), *The right to adequate food (art. 11 of the Covenant)* UN doc. E/2000/22, para. 15; General Comment No. 14 (Twenty-second session, 2000), *The right to the highest attainable standard of health (art. 12 of the Covenant)* UN doc. E/C.12/2000/4, paras. 33–37; General Comment No. 15 (Twenty-ninth session, 2002), *The right to water (arts. 11 and 12 of the Covenant)* UN doc E/C 12/2002/11, paras. 20–29. For an exposition of these duties in the context of the African regional human rights system, see *The Social and Economic Rights Action Center and the Center for Economic and Social Rights v. Nigeria*, Comm. No. 155/96, October 2001, African Commission on Human and Peoples' Rights.

[18] Justice Kriegler observed in *Du Plessis v. De Klerk* 1996 (5) BCLR 658 (CC): 'We do not operate under a Constitution in which the avowed purpose of the drafters was to place limits on governmental control. Our constitution aims at establishing freedom and equality in a grossly disparate society' (para. 147).

interpretative approach in any particular case.[19] The adjudication of socio-economic rights claims should always be a contextual inquiry guided by the nature of the interests and values at stake, the history and facts of the case, and the cogency of the justifications that are offered by the respondent for taking or failing to take particular steps.

A set of important socio-economic rights are protected in sections 26 and 27 of the Constitution. Section 26(1) entrenches the right of everyone 'to have access to adequate housing', and s. 27(1) the right of everyone 'to have access to (a) health care services, including reproductive health care; (b) sufficient food and water; and (c) social security, including, if they are unable to support themselves and their dependants, appropriate social assistance.' These first sections are qualified by a second subsection, which reads, 'The state must take reasonable legislative and other measures, within its available resources, to achieve the progressive realisation of each of these rights.'[20] Section 26(3) provides for protection against arbitrary evictions and demolitions of people's homes, and section 27(3) provides that 'No one may be refused emergency medical treatment.'

In addition to these provisions, the Constitution also entrenches further socio-economic rights consisting of children's socio-economic rights,[21] educational rights,[22] and the socio-economic rights of detained persons, including sentenced prisoners.[23] The property clause of the Bill of Rights includes a set of provisions placing an obligation on the State to foster equitable access to land, land restitution and tenure security.[24] Finally, the Bill of Rights provides for the protection of labour rights,[25] environmental rights,[26] and language and cultural rights.[27] Like all the other rights in the Bill of Rights, the socio-economic rights are subject to the 'general limitations clause' in section 36.[28]

3.2 Horizontal Application

The South African Bill of Rights is also remarkable for its express provisions providing for both the vertical and horizontal application of the Bill of Rights.[29] Section 8(1) states that the Bill of Rights 'applies to all law, and binds the legislature, the executive, the judiciary and all organs of state.' Section 8(2) specifies that a provision in the Bill of Rights 'binds a natural and juristic person if, and to the extent that, it is applicable, taking into account the nature of the right and the nature of any duty imposed by the right.' In order to give effect to the horizontal application of a right in the Bill of Rights, a court 'must apply, or if necessary develop, the common law to the extent that legislation does not give effect to that right.'[30] Another significant provision is section 39(2), which enjoins a court, tribunal or forum when interpreting any legislation, and when developing the common law or customary law 'to promote the spirit, purport and objects of the Bill of Rights.'

These provisions create the possibility for socio-economic rights to apply in legal relations between

---

[19] For insightful critiques of the limitations of this typology, see M. Craven, 'Assessment of the Progress on Adjudication of Economic, Social and Cultural Rights in J. Squires, M. Langford and B. Thiele (eds.), *The Road to a Remedy: Current Issues in the Litigation of Economic, Social and Cultural Rights* (Australian Human Rights Centre, The University of New South Wales with Centre on Housing Rights and Eviction, Distributed by UNSW Press, 2005), pp. 27–42, at 30–36; and Bruce Porter, 'The Crisis of ESC Rights and Strategies for Addressing It' in Squires, Langford, and Thiele, pp. 43–69, at 55–58.

[20] The influence of Article 2 of the International Covenant on Economic, Social and Cultural Rights is evident in the drafting of this provision.

[21] Section 28(1)(c) gives every child the right to 'basic nutrition, shelter, basic health care services and social services'. A child is defined in section 28(3) as a person under the age of 18 years.

[22] Section 29. This includes the right of everyone to 'a basic education, including adult basic education' (s. 29(1)(a)).

[23] Section 35 (2)(e) confers the right 'to conditions of detention that are consistent with human dignity, including at least exercise and the provision, at state expense, of adequate accommodation, nutrition, reading material and medical treatment.'

[24] See note 13 above.

[25] Section 23.

[26] Section 24.

[27] Sections 30–31.

[28] Section 36 provides that the rights in the Bill of Rights 'may be limited only in terms of law of general application to the extent that the limitation is reasonable and justifiable in an open and democratic society based on human dignity, equality and freedom....' In determining whether a limitation is 'reasonable and justifiable', a number of factors must be taken into account (see section 36(1)(a)–(e)). Essentially a court will inquire into whether there is a sufficiently important purpose for limiting a right, and whether the limitation is proportional.

[29] Vertical application refers to the applicability of the Bill of Rights to the State and its organs, whereas horizontal application refers to the applicability of the Bill of Rights in relations between private parties.

[30] Section 8(3).

private parties. The Constitutional Court has acknowledged that at least some of the duties imposed by socio-economic rights are binding on private parties. In its landmark decision of *Government of the Republic of South Africa v Grootboom and Others*[31] (*'Grootboom'*), the Constitutional Court held that section 26(1) imposes, at the very least, a negative obligation 'upon the State *and all other entities and persons* to desist from preventing or impairing the right of access to adequate housing.'[32] This negative duty 'is further spelt out in section 26(3) which prohibits arbitrary evictions.'[33] Section 26(3) has already had an impact on the common law of property.[34] In the Constitutional Court's recent decision in *Port Elizabeth Municipality v Various Occupiers*[35] (*'PE Municipality'*), Sachs J described this potentially far-reaching impact as follows:

> In sum, the Constitution imposes new obligations on the courts concerning rights relating to property not previously recognised by the common law. It counterposes to the normal ownership rights of possession, use and occupation, a new and equally relevant right not arbitrarily to be deprived of a home. The expectations that ordinarily go with title could clash head-on with the genuine despair of people in dire need of accommodation. The judicial function in these circumstances is not to establish a hierarchical arrangement between the different interests involved, privileging in an abstract and mechanical way the rights of ownership over the right not to be dispossessed of a home, or vice versa. Rather it is to balance out and reconcile the opposed claims in as just a manner as possible taking account of all the interests involved and the specific factors relevant in each particular case.[36]

The background common law rules relating to contract and property can serve to perpetuate deprivation and grossly unequal access to economic resources.[37] This is particularly acute in the South African context given our colonial and apartheid history of large scale dispossession of land and property and entrenched social inequalities. The application of socio-economic rights norms to common law norms governing access to economic resources is thus a critical challenge for ensuring that socio-economic rights fulfil their transformative potential.[38]

3.3 Legal Standing and Access to Legal Services

Of particular importance to the practical justiciability of socio-economic rights, are the generous provisions on legal standing (*'locus standi'*) contained in the Bill of Rights. Section 38 confers standing on a broad category of persons who may approach a court for appropriate relief, alleging that a right in the Bill of Rights has been infringed or threatened. This includes anyone acting on behalf of persons who cannot act in their own name,[39] class actions,[40] actions in the public interest,[41] and associations acting in the

---

[31] 2000 (11) BCLR 1169 (CC).

[32] Ibid. para. 34 [emphasis added]. See also *Minister of Health and Others v. Treatment Action Campaign and Others (1)* 2002 (10) BCLR 1033 (CC), para. 46 (*'TAC'*).

[33] Ibid.

[34] See T. Roux, 'Continuity and change in a transforming legal order: The impact of section 26(3) of the Constitution on South African law', *The South African Law Journal*, Vol. 121 (2004), pp. 466–492.

[35] 2004 (12) BCLR 1268 (CC).

[36] Ibid. para 23.

[37] For a discussion of the strategic importance for social rights advocates to engage with background common law rules protecting and distributing entitlements, see L. Williams, 'Beyond labour law's parochialism: A re-envisioning of the discourse of distribution' in J. Conaghan, M. Fischl and K. Klare, (eds.) *Labour Law in an Era of Globalization: Transformative Practices and Possibilities* (Oxford: Oxford University Press, 2002), pp. 93–114.

[38] For a general discussion on the horizontal application of the socio-economic rights provisions of the SA Constitution, see S. Liebenberg, 'The interpretation of socio-economic rights' in M. Chaskalson *et al.* (eds.), *Constitutional Law of South Africa*, Second Edition (Cape Town: Juta & Co & Centre for Human Rights, Faculty of Law, University of Pretoria, 2004), ch. 33, at pp. 57–61; D. Chirwa, 'Obligations of non-state actors in relation to economic, social and cultural rights under the South African Constitution', *Mediterranean Journal of Human Rights*, Vol. 7 (2003), pp. 29–67; D. Brand, 'Introduction to socio-economic rights in the South African Constitution' in D. Brand and C. Heyns (eds.), *Socio-Economic Rights in South Africa* (Pretoria: Pretoria University Law Press, 2005), pp. 39–42.

[39] Section 38 (b).

[40] Section 38 (c).

[41] Section 38 (d). The most famous case in this regard is *TAC* (n. 32 above), where a non-governmental organisation successfully challenged the Government's programme on the prevention of mother-to-child transmission of HIV. On the general requirements for public interest actions, see *Lawyers for Human Rights & Ano v. Minister of Home Affairs & Ano* 2004 (7) BCLR 775 (CC), para 18.

interest of their members.[42] The Courts have given a broad interpretation to the standing provisions in section 38 requiring only an allegation that, objectively speaking, a right in the Bill of Rights has been infringed or threatened, and that the party seeking relief has a sufficient interest in obtaining the remedy they seek.[43] In addition, it is possible for individuals and organisations to participate in human rights litigation through *amicus curiae* ('friend of the court') interventions. In order to be admitted as an *amici* to litigation, applicants must demonstrate that their submissions will be useful to the Court and different from those of the parties to the litigation.[44] *Amici* interventions offer an important opportunity for non-governmental organisations and others with experience and expertise in the field to contribute to the development of South Africa's social rights jurisprudence.[45]

The leading case in South Africa on class actions claims is *Permanent Secretary, Department Welfare, E Cape Provincial Government and Another v Ngxuza and Others*.[46] The case concerned an application for the reinstatement of the disability grant of tens of thousands of social grant recipients that had been unlawfully terminated by the Eastern Cape provincial government. The Supreme Court of Appeal held that the case was well suited to class action proceedings in that those affected by the arbitrary administrative action of the provincial government were a large and disparate group of claimants, all poor and 'lacking in protective and assertive armour', and each with

a small monetary claim unsuited for individual enforcement.[47]

However, a major problem in the South African context remains the problem of access to legal services for the poor. As the Supreme Court of Appeal commented in the *Ngxuza* decision, 'The law is a scarce resource in South Africa.'[48] Section 35(3) of the Constitution, which guarantees the right to a fair criminal trial, expressly guarantees the right to legal representation at state expense 'if substantial injustice would otherwise result.'[49] However, section 34, which guarantees a right of access to courts, does not expressly confer a right to legal representation. A system of State legal aid for indigent persons in criminal and civil cases is provided through the Legal Aid Board. The Board has recently shifted its emphasis from a *judicare* system (state funding for private attorneys and advocates) to the establishment of Justice Centres envisaged as 'one-stop legal aid shops.' However, this system still excludes a large proportion of the population due to the strict financial means test, lack of physical access to Justice Centres, particularly in rural areas, and the bias towards funding for criminal over civil matters. Most public interest socio-economic cases are run by non-governmental organisations such as the Legal Resources Centre, Lawyers for Human Rights, the AIDS Law Project and the Women's Legal Centre. University law clinics also play an important role in this context.[50]

Despite these initiatives, many in South Africa experience violations of socio-economic rights, which go unchallenged due to a lack of access to legal services. A concerted multi-prong strategy is needed to ensure consistent access to quality legal services for disadvantaged communities. This is a critical challenge if socio-economic rights are to

---

[42] Section 38 (e). See, for example, *Highveldridge Residents Concerned Party v. Highveldridge TLC and Others* 2003 (1) BCLR 72 (T) which concerned the disconnection by a local authority of the water supply to households in a township.

[43] *Ferreira v. Levin No* 1996 (1) BCLR 1 (CC); Iain Currie and Johan de Waal, *The Bill of Rights Handbook*, Fifth Edition, (Cape Town: Juta & Co, 2005), ch. 4.

[44] Rules of the Constitutional Court, Government Notice R1675, Government Gazette 25726, 31 October 2003, Rule 10. Similar provisions exist with regard to *amici* interventions in the High Courts and the Supreme Court of Appeal.

[45] For example, the Community Law Centre (University of the Western Cape) and the South African Human Rights Commission intervened as joint *amici curiae* in the *Grootboom* case (n. 31 above), and made an important contribution to developing the arguments in relation to section 26 of the Constitution.

[46] 2001 (4) SA 1184 (SCA) ('*Ngxuza*').

[47] Ibid. paras. 12–13.

[48] *Ngxuza* (n. 46 above), para. 1.

[49] Section 35 (3) (g).

[50] The Law Society of the Cape of Good Hope has initiated a system making it mandatory for practising attorneys in their jurisdiction to do twenty-four hours of pro bono work each year. It remains to be seen whether other Law Societies will follow suit. For a more detailed discussion of these and other proposals in South Africa (e.g. compulsory community service for law students and/or graduates), see Jason Brickhill, 'The right to a fair civil trial: The duties of lawyers and law students to act pro bono', *South African Journal on Human Rights*, Vol. 21 (2005), pp. 293–322.

play a meaningful role in facilitating transformation in South Africa.

3.4 Introducing the Leading Socio-Economic Rights Cases

It is now over ten years into our young democracy, and a burgeoning body of jurisprudence has developed on socio-economic rights in all three tiers of the court system: the High Courts, the Supreme Court of Appeal and the Constitutional Court.[51]

The landmark cases that have established the foundations of the Constitutional Court's jurisprudence on socio-economic rights are *Soobramoney v Minister of Health, KwaZulu-Natal*[52] ('*Soobramoney*'), *Grootboom*,[53] and *Minister of Health and Others v Treatment Action Campaign & Others*[54] ('*TAC*'). A brief description of these cases will assist in sketching the context for the analysis of the jurisprudence follows.

Soobramoney was the first major Constitutional Court case to consider the enforceability of socio-economic rights. The applicant, an unemployed man in the final stages of chronic renal failure, sought a positive order from the courts directing a provincial hospital to provide him with ongoing dialysis treatment, and interdicting the provincial Minister of Health from refusing him admission to the renal unit of the hospital. Without this treatment the applicant would die, as he could not afford to obtain the treatment from a private clinic. He relied primarily on section 11 (the right to life), and section 27(3) (the right to emergency medical treatment). The application was dismissed in the High Court and was taken on appeal to the Con-

stitutional Court. The Court held that the right to medical treatment should not be inferred from the right to life in the context of the express entrenchment of a right of access to health care services in section 27.[55] It furthermore held that section 27(3) was applicable only to 'sudden catastrophes', which called for immediate medical attention, and not to the ongoing treatment of chronic illnesses for the purposes of prolonging life.[56] The Court then proceeded to consider the applicability of sections 27(1) and (2) (the qualified right of access to health care services). It held that there was no breach of section 27 as the appellant had not shown that the guidelines set by the hospital authorities for admission to the dialysis programme were unreasonable nor was it suggested that they were not applied 'fairly and rationally' in the appellant's case.[57] The Court emphasised that the appellant's claim had to be evaluated within the broader context of the needs which the health services have to meet. If the same principle were to be extended to other patients requiring expensive, tertiary medical interventions, 'the health budget would have to be dramatically increased to the prejudice of other needs which the State has to meet.'[58] The Court signalled a deferential review standard in matters of social and economic policy by stating that 'a court will be slow to interfere with rational decisions taken in good faith by the political organs and medical authorities whose responsibility it is to deal with such matters.'[59] Mr. Soobramoney's appeal was accordingly dismissed.

---

[51] The High Courts and Supreme Court of Appeal all have jurisdiction in constitutional matters (for example, Bill of Rights litigation) with the exception of a limited number of constitutional matters that fall within the exclusive jurisdiction of the Constitutional Court (s. 167 (4) of the Constitution). It is a requirement that the Constitutional Court confirm any order of constitutional invalidity in respect of an Act of Parliament, a provincial Act or any conduct of the President made by the High Courts or Supreme Court of Appeal before that order has any force (s. 167 (5) read with s. 172(2)(a)).
[52] 1997 (12) BCLR 1696.
[53] *Grootboom* (n. 31 above).
[54] *TAC* (n. 32 above).

[55] For a critique of this form of 'negative textual inferentialism', see C. Scott and P. Alston, 'Adjudicating Constitutional Priorities in a Transnational Context: A Comment on *Soobramoney's* Legacy and *Grootboom's* Promise', *South African Journal on Human Rights*, Vol. 16 (2000), pp. 206–268, at 236–237; M. Pieterse, 'A Different Shade of Red: Socio-Economic Dimensions of the Right to Life in South Africa', *South African Journal of Human Rights*, Vol. 15 (1999), pp. 372–385.
[56] *Soobramoney* (n. 52 above), paras. 13, 20–22.
[57] Ibid. paras. 25, 36.
[58] Ibid. para. 28. This is the classic issue of 'polycentricity' in adjudication described by L. Fuller in 'The Forms and Limits of Adjudication', *Harvard Law Review*, Vol. 92, pp. 353–409.
[59] Ibid. para. 29. For a discussion of the standard of rationality review applied in the *Soobramoney* case see S. Liebenberg, 'The Interpretation of Socio-Economic Rights' (n. 38 above), ch. 33, pp. 32–33; Darrel Moellendorf, 'Reasoning about Resources: *Soobramoney* and the Future of Socio-Economic Rights Claims', *South African Journal on Human Rights*, Vol. 14 (1998), pp. 327–333.

Grootboom concerned a group of adults and children who had moved onto private land from an informal settlement owing to the 'appalling conditions' in which they lived.[60] They were evicted from the private land. Following the eviction, they camped on a sports field in the area. However, they could not erect adequate shelters as most of their building materials had been destroyed during the eviction. Accordingly, they found themselves in a precarious position where they had neither security of tenure, nor adequate shelter from the elements. They applied to the Cape High Court on an urgent basis for an order against all three spheres of government requiring them to provide temporary shelter or housing until they obtained permanent accommodation. The High Court held that there was no violation of section 26 (the right of everyone to have access to housing), but found a violation of section 28(1)(c) (the right of children to shelter). On appeal, the Constitutional Court declared that the State's housing programme fell short of compliance with section 26 (1) and (2) (the qualified right of everyone to have access to adequate housing), but found no violation of the right of children to shelter under section 28(1)(c).

TAC involved a challenge to the limited nature of the measures introduced by the State to prevent mother-to-child transmission (MTCT) of HIV. Firstly, it was contended that the State unreasonably prohibited the administration of the antiretroviral drug, Nevirapine, at public hospitals and clinics outside a limited number of research and training sites. This drug was of proven efficacy in reducing *intrapartum* mother-to-child transmission (MTCT) of HIV. Secondly, the state failed to produce and implement a comprehensive national programme for the prevention of MTCT of HIV. Both the High Court and the Constitutional Court (on appeal) held that the State's programme to prevent MTCT of HIV did not comply with its obligations in terms of sections 27 (1) and (2) (the qualified right of everyone to have access to health care services). The Constitutional Court made both declaratory and mandatory orders against the Government.

The reasoning of the Court in *Grootboom*, *TAC* and subsequent judgments is discussed below in the context of an analysis and evaluation of the rapidly evolving jurisprudence on socio-economic rights since the *Soobramoney* decision. First, the model of review developed by the Constitutional Court for the positive duties imposed by socio-economic rights is considered. Thereafter, we consider how the Court has approached the review of the negative duties imposed by these rights. Although the negative and positive duties are intertwined and cannot be compartmentalised into separate categories, the two types of duties will be considered separately in this chapter as there are differences in the model of review which the Court has applied to these duties.

4. ENFORCING THE POSITIVE DUTIES IMPOSED BY SOCIO-ECONOMIC RIGHTS

This section focuses on two types of cases involving positive conduct on the part of organs of State. The first entails a situation where government does not have a programme in place to cater for the socio-economic needs of a particular group. This situation is exemplified by the *Grootboom* and *TAC* cases. The second situation concerns the exclusion of a particular group from an existing legislative programme catering for socio-economic rights. This is exemplified by the decision of the Constitutional Court in *Khosa v Minister of Social Development; Mahlaule v Minister of Social Development*[61] (*'Khosa'*). Both types of cases entail an overlap between socio-economic rights and a substantive concept of equality rights. Although the Court did not explicitly decide the *TAC* and *Grootboom* cases in terms of an equality analysis, the failure to make provision for the needs of a disadvantaged group can also be understood as an equality rights violation.[62] In the *Khosa* case, the Court's decision was explicitly based on

---

[60] *Grootboom* (n. 731 above), para. 3.

[61] 2004 (6) BCLR 569 (CC).

[62] P. de Vos, '*Grootboom*, The Right of Access to Housing and Substantive Equality as Contextual Fairness', *South African Journal on Human Rights*, Vol. 17 (2001), pp. 258–276; see also the analysis by T. Roux, 'Legitimating Transformation: Political Resource Allocation in the South African Constitutional Court', *Democratization*, vol. 10 (2003), pp. 92–111, at 97.

the intersection between equality rights and the right to social security.

4.1 The Model of Reasonableness Review

In *Soobramoney*, *Grootboom* and *TAC* the Court was squarely confronted with the challenge of developing a model for the enforcement of the positive duties imposed by sections 26 and 27. The Court rejected the notion that these provisions impose a direct, unqualified obligation on the State to provide social goods and services to people on demand. It did so in the context of arguments raised by the *amici curiae* ('friend of the court') interventions in the *Grootboom* and *TAC* cases. The *amici* sought to persuade the Court to adopt the notion of minimum core obligations as developed by the United Nations Committee on Economic, Social and Cultural Rights.[63] It held that socio-economic rights did not 'give rise to a self-standing and independent positive right enforceable irrespective of the considerations mentioned in section 27(2).'[64] The latter, it will be recalled, refers to the qualifications relating to reasonable measures, progressive realisation and the availability of resources.

The Court voiced a number of concerns regarding the concept of minimum core obligations. First, the Court identified the problem of defining 'the minimum core' given the fact that groups are differently situated and have varying social needs.[65] Second, the Court was of the view that minimum core obligations impose unrealistic duties on the State in that it is 'impossible to give everyone access even to a 'core' service immediately.[66] Finally, the Court held that the minimum core was incompatible with the institutional competencies and role of the courts.[67] However, it did indicate that the evidence in a particular case may show that there is a minimum core of a particular service that should be taken into account in determining whether the measures adopted by the State are reasonable.[68]

The Court proceeded to develop a model of 'reasonableness review' for adjudicating positive claims to the provision of social services and resources. In reviewing the positive duties imposed by the socio-economic rights provisions on the State, the central question that the Court asks is whether the means chosen are reasonably capable of facilitating the realisation of the socio-economic rights in question.[69] However, the Court

---

[63] In its General Comment No. 3, the Committee stated that it 'is of the view that a minimum core obligation to ensure the satisfaction of at the very least, minimum essential levels of each of the rights is incumbent upon every State Party. Thus, for example, a State Party in which any significant number of individuals is deprived of essential foodstuffs, of essential primary health care, of basic shelter and housing, or of the most basic forms of education is, *prima facie*, failing to discharge its obligations under the Covenant.... In order for a State Party to be able to attribute its failure to meet at least its minimum core obligations to a lack of available resources it must demonstrate that every effort has been made to use all resources at its disposition in an effort to satisfy, as a matter of priority, those minimum obligations.' See General Comment No. 3 (Fifth session, 1990), *The Nature of States' Parties Obligations (article 2(1) of the Covenant)*, UN doc. E/1991/23, para. 10. For an application of this concept in the context of the specific rights protected in the Covenant, see General Comment No. 12 (n. 17 above), para. 17; General Comment No. 14 (n. 17 above), paras. 43, 47; General Comment No. 15 (n. 17 above), paras. 37–38.

[64] *TAC* (n. 32 above), para. 39.

[65] *Grootboom* (n. 31 above), paras. 32–33. Thus in the context of the right to have access to adequate housing, the Court highlighted the fact that the needs were diverse: 'there are those who need land; others need both land and houses; yet others need financial assistance' (para. 33).

[66] *TAC* (n. 32 above), para. 35.

[67] Thus it held that 'courts are not institutionally equipped to make the wide-ranging factual and political enquiries necessary for determining what the minimum core standards' should be (*TAC*, ibid. para. 37). And further: 'Courts are ill-suited to adjudicate upon issues where court orders could have multiple social and economic consequences for the community. The Constitution contemplates rather a restrained and focused role for the courts' (para. 38).

[68] *Grootboom* (n. 31 above) para. 33; *TAC*, ibid. para. 34.

[69] See *Grootboom*, ibid. para. 41. This constitutes a means-end justificatory model in which the Court asks itself the basic question whether a particular policy or programme can be justified. It will be justified if 'it is reasonably related to the constitutionally prescribed goal of providing access to the relevant socio-economic rights.' See D. Brand, 'The Proceduralisation of South African Socio-Economic Rights Jurisprudence, or "What Are Socio-Economic Rights For?"' in H. Botha, A. van der Walt and J. van der Walt (eds.), *Rights and Democracy in a Transformative Constitution* (Sun Press, 2004), 33, at 39–43. Reasonableness review also has synergies with the UN Committee on Economic, Social and Cultural Rights' views that States parties to the Covenant are under an obligation to take steps that are 'deliberate, concrete and targeted as clearly as possible towards meeting the obligation recognized in the Covenant,' General Comment No. 3 (n. 63 above), para. 2. It also approximates the description of 'obligations of conduct' imposed by economic, social and cultural rights according to The Maastricht

emphasised that it would not prescribe particular policy choices to government:

> A Court considering reasonableness will not enquire whether other more desirable or favourable measures could have been adopted, or whether public money could have been better spent. The question would be whether the measures that have been adopted are reasonable. It is necessary to recognise that a wide range of possible measures could be adopted by the State to meet its obligations. Many of these would meet the requirement of reasonableness. Once it is shown that the measures do so, this requirement is met. (para. 41)

However, as we shall see, the Court has been prepared in certain cases to apply a fairly stringent standard of scrutiny to the Government's policy choices and to be prescriptive regarding the provision of a particular service to the beneficiaries. This has generally occurred in cases where there cannot be reasonable democratic disagreement about the type of service required to give effect to the socio-economic right in question, and where the impact of the denial of the service in question on the beneficiary group is severe.[70] In cases, where there has been a failure to make provision for a particular group, but there exists a range of possible policy solutions, the Court has formulated a remedy that allows the State a degree of latitude in designing an appropriate policy solution.[71]

The assessment of the reasonableness of government programmes is influenced by two further factors. The internal limitations of section 26(2) require that the rights may be 'progressively realised'[72] and that the availability of resources is

'an important factor in determining what is reasonable.'[73] This is a consequence of the Court's interpretation that the positive duties imposed by the socio-economic rights provisions are both defined and limited by the second subsection of sections 26 and 27.[74] While both concepts provide the State with a potential justification for failing to ensure access to socio-economic rights, it is important to recognise that this can also support a finding of unreasonable acts or omissions by the State. Thus claimants could rely on the interpretation of 'progressive realisation' by the Court and the UN Committee on Economic, Social and Cultural Rights to argue that the State has not taken any steps or made sufficient progress in dismantling obstacles that impede access to the rights. The Court's endorsement of the UN Committee's on Economic, Social and Cultural Rights views that 'retrogressive measures' require particular justification[75] creates the basis for challenging cutbacks in social programmes. Similarly, if the evidence establishes that the State does have adequate resources, a failure to provide for the satisfaction of basic needs or to spend its resources efficiently may support a finding of unreasonableness.

The Court has indicated that it will assess the reasonableness of the State's conduct in the light of the social, economic and historical context, and consideration will be given to the capacity of institutions responsible for implementing the programme.[76]

Initially, it appeared that the Court would adopt a thin standard of rationality review in socio-economic rights cases.[77] However, in its subsequent jurisprudence the Court has clarified that its standard of scrutiny in socio-economic rights

---

Guidelines on Violations of Economic, Social and Cultural Rights. Thus an obligation of conduct 'requires action reasonably calculated to realize the enjoyment of a particular right.' An obligation of result, on the other hand, 'requires States to achieve specific targets to satisfy a detailed substantive standard.' The Maastricht Guidelines on Violations of Economic, Social and Cultural Rights, *Human Rights Quarterly*, Vol. 20 (1998), pp. 691–705, para. 7.

[70] For example, the *TAC* & *Khosa* cases (discussed further in sections 4.2 and 4.3 below).

[71] For example, the *Grootboom* case (discussed further below in this section and in section 8 below).

[72] Thus the Court in *Grootboom* (n. 31 above) held as follows: 'The term "progressive realisation" shows that it was contemplated that the right could not be realised immediately. But the goal of the Constitution is that the basic needs of all in our society be effectively met and

the requirement of progressive realisation means that the State must take steps to achieve this goal. It means that accessibility should be progressively facilitated: legal, administrative, operational and financial hurdles should be examined and, where possible, lowered over time. Housing must be made more accessible not only to a larger number of people but to a wider range of people as time progresses' (para. 45).

[73] *Grootboom*, ibid. para. 46.

[74] *Soobramoney* (n. 52 above), paras. 11, 28; *Grootboom*, ibid. para. 38; *TAC* (n. 32 above), para. 39.

[75] *Grootboom*, ibid. para 45, citing General Comment No. 63, para. 9.

[76] *Soobramoney*, (n. 52 above), para. 16; *Grootboom*, ibid. para. 43; *Khosa*, (n. 61 above), para. 49.

[77] See the discussion of *Soobramoney* in section 3.4 above.

cases is more substantive than simply enquiring whether the policy was rationally conceived and applied in good faith.[78] In the *Grootboom* and the *TAC* cases, the Court developed the following criteria for assessing the reasonableness of government programmes impacting on socio-economic rights:

- The programme must be comprehensive, coherent, coordinated;[79]
- Appropriate financial and human resources must be made available for the programme;[80]
- It must be balanced and flexible and make appropriate provision for short, medium and long-term needs;[81]
- It must be reasonably conceived and implemented;[82] and
- It must be transparent, and its contents must be made known effectively to the public.[83]

The element of the reasonableness test that comes closest to a threshold requirement is that a reasonable government programme must cater for those in urgent need:

> To be reasonable, measures cannot leave out of account, the degree and extent of the denial of the right they endeavour to realise. Those whose needs are most urgent and whose ability to enjoy all rights is therefore most in peril, must not be ignored by the measures aimed at achieving realisation of the right. It may not be sufficient to meet the test of reasonableness to show that the measures are capable of achieving a statistical advance in the realisation of the right. Furthermore, the Constitution requires that everyone be treated with care and concern. If the measures, though statistically successful, fail to respond to the needs of those most desperate, they may not pass the test.[84]

This requirement of the reasonableness test is justified particularly in terms of the value of human dignity.[85]

In *Grootboom*, the Court found that the Government's housing programme (though in other respects rational and comprehensive) was inconsistent with section 26 of the Constitution in that it failed 'to provide relief for people who have no access to land, no roof over their heads, and who are living in intolerable conditions or crisis situations.'[86] The Court did not specify what form this relief should take, but simply made a declaratory order to the effect that the State's housing programme should include 'reasonable measures' to provide relief for this group of housing beneficiaries.[87] However, it did indicate in its judgment that these measures should be similar, 'but not necessarily limited to those contemplated in the Accelerated Managed Land Settlement Programme'.[88] This programme had been drafted by the local authority, but was not in force when the case commenced.[89]

In *TAC*, the Government had defended its restrictive policy on mother-to-child transmission by raising a range of concerns, from the efficacy and safety of Nevirapine to a lack of resources and capacity to roll-out a comprehensive programme to prevent MTCT of HIV throughout the public health sector. The Court closely scrutinised and ultimately rejected all of these justifications. It held that the failure to take measures without delay to permit and facilitate the use of the anti-retroviral drug, Nevirapine, throughout public health care facilities in South Africa for the purpose of preventing MTCT of HIV was unreasonable. These omissions violated the right of access to health care services entrenched in section 27.

With regard to the first leg of the challenge (the restriction placed on doctors from prescribing Nevirapine in facilities where testing and counselling facilities already exist), the Court held that 'this aspect of the claim and the orders made will not attract any significant additional costs.'[90] With

---

[78] *Bel Porto School Governing Body and Others v. Premier, Western Cape and Another* 2002 (9) BCLR 891 (CC), para. 46; *Khosa* (n. 61 above), para. 67.
[79] *Grootboom* (n. 31 above), paras. 39 and 40.
[80] Ibid., para. 39.
[81] Ibid., para. 43.
[82] Ibid., paras. 40–43.
[83] *TAC* (n. 32 above), para. 123.
[84] *Grootboom* (n. 31 above), para. 44.
[85] Thus in *Grootboom*, ibid., the Court held: 'It is fundamental to an evaluation of the reasonableness of State action that account be taken of the inherent dignity of human

beings....In short, I emphasise that human beings are required to be treated as human beings' (at para. 83). See Sandra Liebenberg, 'The value of human dignity in interpreting socio-economic rights', *South African Journal on Human Rights*, Vol. 21 (2005), p. 1–31.
[86] *Grootboom*, ibid., para. 99.
[87] Ibid. para. 2(b) of the Order.
[88] Ibid.
[89] Ibid. para. 60.
[90] *TAC* (n. 32 above), para. 71. The administration of the drug is a relatively simple procedure, and the manufacturers had made a free offer of the drug to the South

regard to the second leg (the extension of testing, counselling and treatment facilities to clinics that currently lack these facilities), the Court noted that government had committed 'substantial additional funds' for the treatment of HIV, including the reduction of MTCT.[91] As far as the capacity arguments of the Government were concerned, particularly in relation to training for counselling on the use of Nevirapine, the Court found that this was 'not a complex task and it should not be difficult to equip existing counsellors with the necessary additional knowledge.'[92] Thus the costs and capacity arguments did not have sufficient cogency to outweigh the impact on a particularly vulnerable group of the denial of a basic life-saving medical intervention. The Court was prepared to grant mandatory orders relating to the provision of Nevirapine for the purpose of reducing the risk of mother-to-child transmission of HIV in public hospitals and clinics where medically indicated, and to extend testing and counselling facilities throughout the public health sector 'to facilitate and expedite' the use of Nevirapine.[93]

In this case the Court was prepared to be specific regarding the nature of the service to be provided, namely an antiretroviral drug to reduce mother-to-child transmission of HIV and the attendant testing and counselling facilitating. The Court even specified the particular drug, Nevirapine,[94] while making provision in its order for the Government to adapt its policy 'if equally appropriate or better methods become available to it for the prevention of mother-to-child transmission of HIV.'[95] Key factors in accounting for the Court's boldness in this case was the lack of other alternatives for achieving a substantial reduction in mother-to-child transmission of HIV, the severe impact on poor mothers and children of the denial of antiretroviral treatment, and the nature of the expert and other evidence the Treat-

ment Action Campaign placed before the Court. This evidence enabled it to analyse and deal with the financial and capacity implications of its intervention.[96]

4.2   Interpreting Children's Socio-Economic Rights

In both *Grootboom* and *TAC*, the Court also had to deal with the arguments that the rights of children to shelter and basic health care services respectively had been breached. The 'basic' socio-economic rights of children entrenched in section 28(1)(c) of the Constitution are not qualified as are the socio-economic rights in sections 26 and 27.[97] The question which arises is whether these provisions impose direct obligations on the State to ensure the provision of a basic level of socio-economic rights to children, without the qualifications relating to reasonable measures, progressive realisation and resource constraints. In *Grootboom*, the Court held that the 'carefully constructed constitutional scheme for the progressive realisation of socio-economic rights would make little sense if it could be trumped in every case by the rights of children to get shelter from the State on demand.'[98] It held that section 28(1)(b) and (c) must be read together. While the former provision defines those responsible for giving care, the latter 'lists various aspects of the care entitlement.'[99] It concluded that the primary duty to fulfil a child's socio-economic rights rests on that child's parents or family where the child is being cared for in the family.[100]

Concerns were voiced over the implications of this reasoning for children who live with parents or other caregivers who are too poor to provide them with the basic necessities of life.[101] In *TAC*, the

---

African government for 5 years (para. 19). As the Court observed: 'Where counselling and testing facilities exist, the administration of Nevirapine is well within the available resources of the State and, in such circumstances, the provision of a single dose of Nevirapine to mother and child where medically indicated is a simple, cheap and potentially lifesaving medical intervention.' (para. 73).

[91] *TAC*, ibid. paras 118–120.

[92] Ibid. para. 95.

[93] Ibid. para. 135.

[94] Nevirapine was already the government's drug of choice in its pilot sites.

[95] Ibid. para. 4 of the Order. The remedy awarded in *TAC* is discussed further in section 8 below.

[96] See, for example, TAC, ibid., para. 90 on the nature of the expert evidence before the Court in relation to the extension of testing and counselling facilities throughout the public health sector.

[97] Section 28(1) reads in part: 'Every child has the right ... (b) to family care or parental care, or to appropriate alternative care when removed from the family environment; (c) to basic nutrition, shelter, basic health care services and social services;'

[98] *Grooboom* (n. 31 above), para. 71.

[99] Ibid. para. 76.

[100] Ibid. para. 77.

[101] See, for example, J. Sloth-Nielsen, 'The child's right to social services, the right to social security, and primary prevention of child abuse: Some conclusions in the

Court clarified that the State's duty to provide children's socio-economic rights were not only triggered when children were physically separated from their families. Thus children are entitled to the protection contemplated by section 28 'when the implementation of the right to parental or family care is lacking.'[102] In *TAC*, the Court was dealing with children born to mothers who were too poor to afford private medical care and who were, as a result, dependent on State health care facilities.[103] However, the Court did not conclude that these children enjoyed an unqualified, direct claim to the provision of health care services. Instead, the Court relied on the denial of the right of children to basic health care services to support its finding that the Government's rigid policy on Nevirapine was unreasonable because the policy excluded and harmed a particularly vulnerable group.

This illustrates that the Court is more comfortable applying a model of reasonableness review to the positive obligations imposed by the socio-economic rights provisions in the Constitution. However, there are indications that the jurisprudence on children's direct entitlement to socio-economic provisioning may develop further, particularly in contexts where children lack family care.[104] A critical area where the State's obligations to provide social grants and services to children remains to be tested is in relation to child-headed households, a phenomenon fuelled by the HIV/AIDS epidemic ravaging South Africa.[105]

4.3 The Intersection between Equality Rights and Socio-Economic Rights

The decision of the Constitutional Court in *Khosa* is significant in that it illustrates how equality

rights and socio-economic rights can mutually reinforce each other to support a finding that a government programme unreasonably or unfairly excludes a particular group. The effect of such a finding is that the programme must be expanded to include the excluded group.

This case concerned the exclusion of destitute permanent residents in South Africa from various social grants payable to citizens in terms of the Social Assistance Act 59 of 1992 and in amendments to this Act.[106] The Court held that this legislative exclusion violated both the prohibition on unfair discrimination in the Constitution (section 9(3)) and the right of everyone to have access to social assistance (section 27(1)(c) read with (2)). To remedy the breach, the Court read the category of permanent residents into the provisions of the statute governing eligibility for social grants (a 'reading in' remedy).[107]

The Court first proceeded to consider the reasonableness of the exclusion of permanent residents from the Social Assistance Act in terms of the qualified right of access to social security in section 27 of the Constitution. It identified the following factors as relevant to the assessment of the reasonableness of the exclusion: '...the purpose served by social security, the impact of the exclusion on permanent residents and the relevance of the citizenship requirement to that purpose.'[108] Furthermore, the assessment of the reasonableness of the exclusion must have regard to 'the impact that this has on other intersecting rights', for example, the equality rights entrenched in section 9 of the Constitution.[109]

According to the Court, the purpose of the right of access to social assistance for those unable to support themselves and their dependants is to ensure that the basic necessities of life are accessible to all. It is an expression of our constitutional commitment to the values of human dignity, freedom and equality.[110]

---

aftermath of *Grootboom*', *South African Journal on Human Rights*, Vol. 17 (2001), pp. 210–231.

[102] *TAC*, (n. 32 above), para. 79.

[103] Ibid.

[104] See for example, *Centre for Child Law & Ano v. Minister of Home Affairs and Others* 2005 (6) SA 50, para. 17. The case concerned the rights, including the socio-economic rights, of unaccompanied foreign children in South Africa.

[105] B. Goldblatt and S. Liebenberg, 'Giving money to children: The state's constitutional obligations to provide child support grants to child headed households', *South African Journal on Human Rights*, Vol. 20 (2004), pp. 151–164; S. Liebenberg, 'Taking stock: The jurisprudence on children's socio-economic rights and its implications for government policy', *ESR Review*, Vol. 5 (2004) pp. 2–6.

[106] These grants, which include disability grants, grants to the aged and child support grants, are payable to persons who pass a means test and fulfil the other eligibility criteria prescribed in the Act and regulations. The amendments, which were not in force at the time of the litigation, were in terms of the Welfare Laws Amendment Act 106 of 1997.

[107] Ibid. paras. 86–98.

[108] Ibid., para. 49.

[109] Ibid. See also para. 45.

[110] Ibid. para. 52.

The Court noted that the Constitution confers the right of access to social security on 'everyone.'[111] It proceeded to consider whether financial considerations could constitute a valid ground for limiting access to the benefits only to citizens.[112] The State had argued that the extension of social grants to permanent residents would impose 'an impermissibly high financial burden on the state.'[113] In assessing the validity of this argument, the Court was confronted with a lack of evidence as to 'the numbers of persons who hold permanent resident status, or who would qualify for social assistance if the citizenship barrier were to be removed.'[114] The State estimated that the additional annual cost of including permanent residents in the relevant grants 'could range between R243 million and R672 million' ($30,100 000–$86,000 000). The possible range of the increase indicated the speculative nature of the calculations. Even so the Court deduced that the cost of including permanent residents in the system would be only a small proportion of the total cost of social grants.[115] Thus the State was unable to produce convincing evidence to support its argument that the costs of extending social grants to permanent residents would impose an excessively high financial burden on it.

The State further argued that the exclusion of permanent residents from social grants was reasonable in that it furthered the immigration policy of the State, which seeks to exclude persons who may become a burden on the state and thereby to encourage self-sufficiency among foreign nationals. The Court accepted that limiting the cost of social welfare was a legitimate government concern, and that it was also permissible to control applications for permanent residence by excluding those who may become a burden on the State. However, once a person is admitted as a permanent resident and later becomes 'a burden' to the

State, it is not justifiable to exclude them from access to social assistance. The Court held that this 'may be a cost we have to pay for the constitutional commitment to developing a caring society, and granting access to socio-economic rights to all who make their homes here.'[116]

Examining the claim through the lens of equality rights, the Court inquired whether the exclusion of permanent residents from social grants amounted to 'unfair discrimination' in terms of section 9 (3) of the equality clause.[117] The test for unfair discrimination involves the consideration of a number of factors, particularly its impact on the group discriminated against.[118] As citizenship is not a listed prohibited ground of discrimination, the burden is on the applicants to prove that it is unfair.[119] The Court noted that non-citizens were

---

[111] Section 27(1). See *Khosa*, ibid. paras. 53–57.

[112] Ibid. paras. 45, 58–67.

[113] Ibid. para. 60.

[114] Ibid. para. 61–62.

[115] Approximately one fifth of the projected expenditure on social grants for permanent residents is in respect of child grants. The unconstitutionality of the citizenship requirement in respect of the child support grant was already conceded by the State. The remainder 'reflects an increase of less than 2% on the present cost of social grants (currently R26.2 billion) even on the higher estimate.' Ibid. para 62.

[116] *Khosa* (n. 61 above), para. 65.

[117] Section 9 of the equality clause prohibits direct or indirect unfair discrimination on a range of listed grounds (including race, sex, gender, sexual orientation, age, disability etc.). These do not represent a closed list. Other unlisted grounds (e.g. citizenship, HIV-status etc) may be recognized as analogous grounds of differentiation if they have an adverse effect on the dignity of the individual, or some other comparable effect: *Harksen v. Lane NO and Others* 1997 (11) BCLR 1489 (CC), para. 46 ('*Harksen*'). See, for example, *Hoffmann v. South African Airways* 2000 (11) BCLR 1211 (CC) (HIV-positive status recognised as an analogous ground of discrimination). Section 9(2) also provides expressly that restitutionary measures (affirmative action) may be taken '[t]o promote the achievement of equality.'

[118] In the case of *Harksen*, ibid., the Court summarised the relevant considerations to be:

'(a) the position of the complainants in society and whether they have suffered in the past from patterns of disadvantage, whether the discrimination in the case under consideration is on a specified ground or not;
(b) the nature of the provision or power and the purpose sought to be achieved by it. If its purpose is manifestly not directed, in the first instance, at impairing the complainants in the manner indicated above, but is aimed at achieving a worthy and important societal goal, such as, for example, the furthering of equality for all, this purpose may, depending on the facts of the particular case, have a significant bearing on the question whether complainants have in fact suffered the impairment in question;
(c) with due regard to (a) and (b) above, and any other relevant factors, the extent to which the discrimination has affected the rights or interests of the complainants and whether it has led to an impairment of their fundamental human dignity or constitutes an impairment of a comparably serious nature.' (para. 51).

[119] Section 9(5) creates a rebuttable presumption that discrimination is unfair if it is based on one of the grounds listed in section 9(3).

a vulnerable group in society.[120] Their exclusion from important statutory benefits has 'a strong stigmatising effect.'[121] Like citizens, permanent residents contribute to the welfare system through the payment of taxes. Consequently, 'the lack of congruence between benefits and burdens created by a law that denies benefits to permanent residents almost inevitably creates the impression that permanent residents are in some way inferior to citizens and less worthy of social assistance.'[122] Analysing the impact of the exclusion, the Court held that it not only places an undue burden on the families, friends and communities of the permanent residents, but 'is likely to have a serious impact on the dignity of the permanent residents concerned who are cast in the role of supplicants.'[123] The Court concluded that the total denial of access to a constitutionally protected socio-economic right also constituted unfair discrimination in terms of section 9(3). It relegated them 'to the margins of society' and deprived them 'of what may be essential to enable them to enjoy other rights vested in them under the Constitution.'[124]

The Court's assessment of the reasonableness of the exclusion of permanent residents in *Khosa* incorporates a proportionality analysis. There were other less drastic methods for reducing the risk of permanent residents becoming 'a burden' to the State than excluding them from gaining access to social assistance.[125] Ultimately, the impact of the exclusion from social assistance on the life and dignity of permanent residents outweighed the financial and immigration considerations on which the State relied.[126] The stringent standard of review applied in this case should be understood in the context of the denial of a basic social benefit to a vulnerable group, and the intersecting breaches of a socio-economic right and the right against unfair discrimination.

The intersection of equality rights and socio-economic rights offers much untapped potential to challenge inequalities in access to resources and services that are based on, for example, gender, sexual orientation, and HIV-status.[127]

4.4 Evaluating 'Reasonable Review'

This model of reasonableness review gives the Court a flexible and context-sensitive tool for adjudicating socio-economic rights claims. It allows government the space to design and formulate appropriate policies to meet its socio-economic rights obligations. At the same time, it subjects government's choices to the requirements of reasonableness, inclusiveness and particularly the threshold requirement that all programmes must provide short-term measures of relief for those whose circumstances are urgent and intolerable. Government has the latitude to demonstrate that the measures it has adopted are reasonable in the light of its resource and capacity constraints and the overall claims on its resources. The Court has made clear that although its orders in enforcing socio-economic rights claims may have budgetary implications, they are not 'in themselves directed at rearranging budgets.'[128]

Reasonableness review enables the Court to adjust the stringency of its review standard informed by factors such as the position of the claimant group in society,[129] the nature of the resource or service claimed,[130] and the impact of the denial of access to the service or resource in question on

---

[120] Firstly, foreign citizens are a minority in all countries and have little political muscle. Secondly, citizenship is a personal attribute which is difficult to change (para. 71).
[121] *Khosa* (n. 61 above), para. 74.
[122] Ibid.
[123] Ibid. para. 76.
[124] Ibid. paras. 77, 81.
[125] Ibid. paras. 64–65.
[126] Ibid. para. 82.

[127] A key piece of legislation enacted to give effect to the guarantee against unfair discrimination in section. 9 of the Constitution is the Promotion of Equality and Prevention of Unfair Discrimination Act 4 of 2000. This legislation prohibits unfair discrimination by the State and private parties in a range of social sectors based on listed and analogous grounds. The legislation make provision for the recognition of additional grounds of prohibited discrimination, specifically HIV-status, nationality, socio-economic status, and family responsibility and status (s. 34). On the implications of this legislation for women's socio-economic equality, see Sandra Liebenberg and Michelle O'Sullivan, 'South Africa's new equality legislation: A tool for advancing women's socio-economic equality?', *Acta Juridica* (2001), pp. 70–103.
[128] *TAC* (n. 32 above), para. 38.
[129] In *Grootboom, TAC* and *Khosa*, the Court emphasised the fact that the affected group were disadvantaged.
[130] In *Soobramoney*, a more tertiary and expensive form of medical treatment was claimed and the Court applied a deferential standard of review based on rationality. In contrast, in *Grootboom, TAC* and *Khosa* the review standard was stricter and involved a more searching scrutiny

the claimant group.[131] The Court's jurisprudence suggests that the government's justifications will be subject to more stringent scrutiny when a disadvantaged sector of society is deprived of access to essential services and resources. In this regard, the Court has acknowledged the poor as a vulnerable group in society, whose needs require special attention.[132] Requiring government to justify its socio-economic priority-setting promotes 'a culture of justification,'[133] one of the underlying purposes of constitutional review and an important element of South Africa's project of transformative constitutionalism.

However, the Court's jurisprudence, particularly its rejection of minimum core obligations, has attracted a fair deal of criticism.[134] It has been questioned whether the Court's jurisprudence sufficiently protects vulnerable groups who face an absolute deprivation of minimum essential levels of basic socio-economic goods and services. This category of claimants is in danger of suffering irreparable harm to their lives, health and sense of human dignity if they do not receive urgent assistance. In addition, if their basic needs are not met, they will not benefit from the progressive improvement in living standards.[135] One of the unresolved questions in this context is whether the socio-economic rights provisions allow individuals to claim direct access to social goods and services, as opposed to only a right to a reasonable government programme. There are some indications that the Court prefers not to grant direct individual relief in cases where individuals and groups claim access to a particular socio-economic service or resource.[136] The Court's preference for systemic programmatic and legislative remedies probably has its origin in the prevalent difficulty in adjudication of ensuring that the relief given to particular litigants is not inequitable to other social groups or results in unforeseeable distortions in social and economic planning.[137] On the other hand, as cases such as *TAC* and *Khosa*, indicate, where the deprivations are urgent and deprive people of what they need to survive with human dignity, more robust remedies will be given.

It has also been argued 'reasonableness review' amounts essentially to an administrative law model, and that insufficient attention is paid to the substantive standards that should guide the determination as to whether the State has met its obligations in relation to socio-economic rights. Thus Marius Pieterse argues:

> [G]iven the relatively abstract and open-ended nature of the reasonableness inquiry, doubts may nevertheless be expressed about its suitability in developing a socio-economic rights jurisprudence resonating with international law and with the transformative aims of the constitutional order. This is so especially where a reasonableness analysis is undertaken separately from an understanding of the content of various socio-economic rights and the obligations they impose.[138]

On the other hand, there have also been academic commentators who have argued that the notion

---

of government's justifications for denying the applicants access to a basic level of service provision.

[131] In *Grootboom, TAC* and *Khosa*, the Court emphasised the severe impact on the claimants of the deprivation in question.

[132] See *Grootboom* (n. 31 above), para. 36; *TAC* (n. 32 above), para. 79.

[133] This phrase was coined by a South African constitutional lawyer, Etienne Mureinik: 'A Bridge to Where? Introducing the Interim Bill of Rights', *South African Journal on Human Rights*, Vol. 10 (1994), pp. 31–48 at 31–32.

[134] See, for example, David Bilchitz, 'Giving Socio-Economic Rights Teeth: The Minimum Core and Its Importance', *South African Law Journal*, vol. 118 (2002), pp. 484–501; David Bilchitz, 'Towards a Reasonable Approach to the Minimum Core: Laying the Foundations for Future Socio-Economic Rights Jurisprudence', *South African Journal of Human Rights*, Vol. 19 (2003), pp. 1–26; Sandra Liebenberg, 'South Africa's Evolving Jurisprudence on Socio-Economic Rights: An Effective Tool in Challenging Poverty', *Law, Democracy & Development*, Vol. 6 (2002), pp. 159–191.

[135] See particularly Bilchitz, 'Giving Socio-Economic Rights Teeth', ibid. p.491.

[136] Thus in *Grootboom* (n. 31 above), the Court held that neither section 26 nor s. 28 (right of children to shelter) 'entitles the respondents 'to claim shelter or housing immediately on demand.' (para 95). In *TAC* the Court stated (in response to the *amici's* arguments): 'We therefore conclude that section 27(1) of the Constitution does not give rise to a self-standing and independent positive right enforceable irrespective of the considerations mentioned in section 27(2)' (para. 39).

[137] This is related to the polycentricity problem described by Fuller (n. 58 above).

[138] M. Pieterse, 'Coming to terms with the judicial enforcement of socio-economic rights', *South African Journal of Human Rights*, Vol. 20 (2004), pp. 383–465, at 410–411. See also Bilchitz, 'Towards a Reasonable Approach to the Minimum Core', (n. 134 above); and D. Brand, 'The proceduralisation of South African socio-economic rights jurisprudence', (n. 09 above), p. 33.

of minimum core obligations is not appropriate to the judicial review of positive socio-economic rights claims.[139] Thus Wesson argues that it is unrealistic and, in certain circumstances, unconscionable to argue that core needs should always take precedence over non-core needs. He further argues that the minimum core has the potential to be counterproductive in that they divert state resources to temporary, emergency-type measures that do not constitute long-term investments.[140] Such measures do not constitute an efficient allocation of scarce resources.[141]

However, the Court has recognised that government programmes that do not cater for the situation of those experiencing urgent deprivation and intolerable living conditions do not comply with the constitutional standard of reasonableness. Thus the Court has in effect affirmed that responsiveness to people's basic needs is an integral part of rights-conscious social policy-making and implementation.

Securing social benefits can help empower beneficiaries to pursue organisational and other strategies aimed at a more fundamental transformation of unjust political, social and economic arrangements.[142] However, if social rights claims are to perform this role, they must provide meaningful and effective measures of relief to those living in poverty. This can only be accomplished if the model of reasonableness review is substantively interpreted and applied by the courts. A substantive interpretation of reasonableness requires a careful analysis of the impact of socio-economic deprivations on the ability of disadvantaged groups to participate as equals in all spheres of South African society. It also requires that the state be placed under a stringent bur-

den to justify its failure to plan for, adopt and implement programmes enabling disadvantaged groups to gain access to basic social services and resources.[143] This would include placing the burden of proving the reasonableness of its lack of provisioning on the State, and incorporating a proportionality analysis.[144] The latter would require the State to show that it had exhausted all reasonable alternatives to ensure that disadvantaged groups do not experience a total denial of access to basic needs, including the adoption of mitigating measures.[145]

5. ENFORCING THE NEGATIVE DUTIES IMPOSED BY SOCIO-ECONOMIC RIGHTS

Another set of socio-economic rights cases dealt with by the courts has involved situations where individuals or groups have been deprived of the existing access that they enjoy to social rights. The Constitutional Court has characterised these situations as violations of the *negative* duties imposed by social rights.[146] They have mostly arisen in the context of the eviction of people from their homes,

---

[139] A. Sachs, 'The judicial enforcement of socio-economic rights: The *Grootboom* case', *Current Legal Problems*, Vol. 56 (2003), pp. 579–601; M. Wesson, '*Grootboom* and beyond: Reassessing the socio-economic rights jurisprudence of the South African Constitutional Court', *South African Journal of Human Rights*, Vol. 20 (2004), pp. 284–308.

[140] Ibid. pp. 303–305.

[141] Ibid. p. 304.

[142] I explore the relation between basic needs claims and transformative strategies in the context of Nancy Fraser's theories of social justice in: S. Liebenberg, 'Needs, Rights and Transformation: Adjudicating Social Rights in South Africa', *Stellenbosch Law Review*, Vol. 17 (2006), pp. 5–36,. on-line at <http://www.nyuhr.org/research`publications.html>.

[143] For an argument that a stringent standard of review in this context is required by the value of human dignity, see S. Liebenberg (n. 85 above).

[144] This heightened standard of reasonableness review is discussed in more detail in S. Liebenberg, 'Enforcing Positive Socio-Economic Rights Claims: The South African Model of Reasonableness Review' in Squires, Langford and Thiele, *Road to a Remedy* (n. 19 above), pp. 73–88.

[145] General Comment No. 3 (n. 63 above) of the UN Committee on Economic, Social and Cultural Rights can be read to support such a proportionality analysis: 'The Committee wishes to emphasise, however, that even where the available resources are demonstrably inadequate, the obligation remains for a State party to strive to ensure the widest possible enjoyment of the relevant rights under the prevailing circumstances' (para. 11). And: 'Similarly, the Committee underlines the fact that even in times of severe resource constraints whether caused by a process of adjustment, of economic recession, or by other factors the vulnerable members of society can and indeed must be protected by the adoption of relatively low-cost targeted programmes' (para. 12).

[146] *Grootboom* (n. 31 above), para 34; *TAC* (n. 32 above) para 46. An example, of the enforcement of this negative duty in the context of the right of access to water occurred in *Residents of Bon Vista Mansions v. Southern Metropolitan Local Council* 2002 (6) BCLR 625 (W). In this case, the High Court held that the disconnection by a local authority of the water supply to the residents constituted a *prima facie* breach of the applicants' constitutional right to have their existing access to water respected (s. 27(1)(b)). In the absence of justification for this

reinforced by the explicit guarantee in section 26(3).[147] Much of the jurisprudence has evolved in the context of the interpretation of key pieces of legislation enacted to give effect to section 26(3), particularly the Prevention of Illegal Eviction from and Unlawful Occupation of Land Act 19 of 1998 ('PIE').[148]

The leading decision on the interpretation of PIE is that of the Constitutional Court in *Port Elizabeth Municipality v Various Occupiers* ('*PE Municipality*').[149] The judgment illuminates how PIE must be interpreted to promote the purposes and values behind section 26(3). The case concerned an eviction application by the Port Elizabeth Municipality against some sixty-eight people who were occupying shacks erected on privately owned land within the jurisdiction of the Municipality. Most had come to the undeveloped land after being evicted from other land. The Municipality was responding to a neighbourhood petition in launching the application. The Court observed that section 26(3) acknowledges that the 'eviction of people living in informal settlements may take place, even if it results in loss of a home.'[150] However, it went on to affirm that generally 'a court should be reluctant to grant an eviction against relatively settled occupiers unless it is satisfied that a reasonable alternative is available, even if only as an interim measure pending ultimate access to housing in the formal housing programme.'[151] Thus, in order to satisfy a court that it is 'just and equitable' to evict people from their homes, organs of State will have to show that serious consideration was given to the possibility of providing alternative accommodation to the occupiers.[152] The Court also indicated that, in the absence of special circumstances, 'it would

not ordinarily be just and equitable to order eviction if proper discussions, and where appropriate, mediation, have not been attempted.'[153] The critical point that Justice Sachs makes in his judgment is that in the clash between property rights and 'the genuine despair of people in dire need of accommodation', the courts should not automatically privilege property rights.[154] Their role instead is to find a just and equitable solution in the context of the specific factors relevant in each particular case.

The recent decision of *President of the Republic of South Africa and Another v Modderklip Boerdery (Pty) Ltd* ('*Modderklip*')[155] concerned the interpretation of the State's duties in the context of a private landowner's unsuccessful efforts to execute an eviction order granted in terms of PIE against a community occupying his land. At the time of the landowner's attempted execution of order, it was estimated that the community numbered approximately 40000, of whom roughly a third were alleged to be illegal immigrants.[156] The owner was confronted by a demand from the sheriff of the High Court for a deposit of R1, 8 million ($230000) to secure the costs of the eviction, an amount exceeding the value of the land. After attempts to get various organs of State to assist him in enforcing the eviction order failed, he applied to the Court for an order obliging the State to assist him in vindicating his property rights in terms of the Constitution. The Constitutional Court did not consider it necessary to resolve the case on the basis of the landowner's property rights (in terms of section 25) or the housing rights of the occupiers (section 26).[157] Instead it held that the State's failure to take reasonable steps to assist the landowner to vindicate his property and at

---

disconnection, the applicants were entitled to have their supply reconnected.

[147] Section 26(3) reads: 'No one may be evicted from their homes or have their homes demolished without an order of Court made after considering all relevant circumstances. No legislation may permit arbitrary evictions.'

[148] PIE repealed the old Prevention of Illegal Squatting Act 52 of 1951 referred to above. Another key piece of legislation giving effect to s. 26(3) is The Extension of Security of Tenure Act 62 of 1997 (ESTA).

[149] *Port Elizabeth Municipalityv Various Occupiers* (n. 35 above).

[150] Ibid. para. 21.

[151] Ibid. para. 28.

[152] Ibid.: The existence of a housing programme 'designed to house the maximum number of homeless people over the shortest period of time in the most cost effective way' is not enough to determine 'whether and under what con-

ditions an actual eviction order should be made in a particular case' (para 29).

[153] Ibid. paras. 39–47, para. 43.

[154] Ibid. para. 23.

[155] *President of RSA and Another v. Modderklip Boerdery (Pty) Ltd and Others* 2005 (8) BCLR 786 (CC).

[156] Ibid. para. 9

[157] Ibid. para. 26. This contrasts with the Supreme Court of Appeal's direct reliance on the property rights (section 25) of the owner and the housing rights (section 26) of the community in their judgment in the case: *President of the Republic of the Republic of South Africa and Others v. Modderklip Boerdery (Pty) Ltd* 2004 (8) BCLR 821. In addition, the Supreme Court of Appeal held that the equality provisions in terms of section 9(1) and (2) of the Constitution had also been infringed.

the same time avoid the large-scale social disruption caused by the eviction of a large community with nowhere to go, was a violation of the principle of the rule of law in section 1(c) as well as the right of access to courts or other independent forums in section 34 of the Constitution.[158] The Court held that the progressive realisation of the right of access to housing or land for the homeless requires 'careful planning', 'fair procedures' and 'orderly and predictable processes'.[159] Land invasions should always be discouraged.[160] At the same time, these measures will not be deemed reasonable if they are 'unduly hamstrung so as to exclude all possible adaptation to evolving circumstances. If social reality fails to conform to the best laid plans, reasonable and appropriate responses may be necessary.'[161]

The novel remedy granted by the Court was to require the State to compensate the landowner for the occupation of its property. This compensation is to be calculated in terms of section 12(1) of the Expropriation Act 63 of 1975.[162] Significantly, the order expressly declared 'that the residents are entitled to occupy the land until alternative land has been made available to them by the state or the provincial or local authority.'[163] Thus the effect of the order in the *Modderklip* case was to prevent the eviction of the community from the land until some form of alternative accommodation was provided and to require the State to compensate the private landowner for bearing the public duty of accommodating the community in the interim.

The Court's decision in *Jaftha v Schoeman and Others; Van Rooyen v Stoltz and Others* ('*Jaftha*')[164] represents a significant development in the Court's approach to the review of the obligations imposed by social rights. This case involved a challenge to the constitutionality of provisions of the Magistrates' Court Act that permitted the sale in execution of people's homes in order to satisfy (sometimes trifling) debts. The two applicants, both women of meagre means, owned homes that had been acquired through the assistance of state subsidies. When they fell in arrears in respect of very minor debts (e.g. the purchase of vegetables), a judgment was obtained against them and their homes were ultimately sold in execution. The effect of such sales-in-execution would be the eviction of people from their homes. It was also common cause that, if the applicants were evicted, they would have no suitable alternative accommodation.[165]

The Constitutional Court characterised the provisions of the Act as authorising a negative violation of section 26(1) in that it permitted 'a person to be deprived of existing access to adequate housing.'[166] This negative duty is not subject to the qualifications in subsection (2) relating to resource constraints and progressive realisation. Where people are deprived of existing access to housing (and by implication, other socioeconomic rights), this constitutes a limitation of their rights which falls to be justified in terms of the stringent requirements of the general limitations clause (section 36), including the requirement of law of general application.[167] The Court expressly did not elaborate on the circumstances which would constitute a violation of the negative duties imposed by the Constitution.[168]

The Court found no justification for the overly broad provisions of the Magistrate's Court Act in terms of the general limitations clause.[169] By way of remedy it 'read in' provisions to the Act

---

158 *Modderklip* (n. 155 above), paras. 43–51 See A. van der Walt, 'The State's duty to protect property owners v. The State's duty to provide housing: Thoughts on the *Modderklip* Case', *South African Journal on Human Rights*, Vol. 21 (2005), pp. 144–161.
159 Ibid. para. 49.
160 Ibid.
161 Ibid.
162 Section 12(1) provides that in respect of the expropriation of property or the taking of a right to use property, compensation must not exceed the amount which the property would have realised if sold in the open market by a willing seller to a willing buyer; and an amount to make good any actual financial loss caused by the expropriation or the taking of the right.
163 Ibid. para. 68, Order, para. 3(c).
164 2005 (1) BCLR 78 (CC).

165 Ibid. para. 12.
166 Ibid. paras. 31–34.
167 On the requirements of the general limitations clause, see note 28 above. The requirement of 'law of general application' requires limitations to be authorised by law thus excluding limitations through mere policies or practices. Furthermore, such law must be clear, accessible and precise, it must apply impersonally, and not be arbitrary in its application. See: *Dawood v. Min of Home Affairs* 2000 (3) SA 936 (CC) para. 47 and the discussion in Currie and de Waal (eds.), *The Bill of Rights Handbook*, (n. 43 above), at 168–174.
168 Ibid. para. 34.
169 Ibid. paras. 35–51.

requiring judicial oversight of executions against the immovable property of debtors taking into consideration 'all relevant circumstances'.[170] Among the guiding factors relevant to the exercise of this judicial oversight is whether an order authorising the sale-in-execution would be 'grossly disproportionate':

> This would be so if the interests of the judgment creditor in obtaining payment are significantly less than the interests of the judgment debtor in security of tenure in his or her home, particularly if the sale of the home is likely to render the judgment debtor and his or her family completely homeless.[171]

Another consideration is the finding of 'creative alternatives' allowing for debt recovery but which use the sale-in-execution of the debtor's home 'only as a last resort.'[172] Thus, the fact that a person might be rendered homeless is a weighty consideration in judicial oversight over sales-in-execution.

Finally, the High Court (Witwatersrand Local Division) held in a recent case[173] that legislation[174] which permits local authorities to evict occupiers of buildings which are considered unsafe, a fire risk or hazardous to health must be interpreted in the light of the constitutional right of access to adequate housing in section 26 of the Constitution as well as the human dignity. The establishment by the Municipality of the occupation of unhealthy or unsafe buildings does not automatically require a court to make an eviction order, but merely triggers the court's discretion.[175] Factors the court will consider in exercising its discretion are the degree of emergency and desperation of the people living in these buildings, the period that they have been occupying the buildings and the requirement of non-arbitrariness and due process in section 26(3) of the Constitution.[176] The City of Johannesburg had sought to evict a number of occupiers

from various properties as part of its Johannesburg Inner City Regeneration Strategy. The Court found that the City had no programme in place as required by the *Grootboom* judgment to provide temporary accommodation for persons such as the respondents, who would face homelessness if evicted as they were too poor to secure alternative accommodation.[177] If evicted, the applicants would be far worse off than their current unsafe accommodation.[178] The suggestion by the applicants that the occupiers relocate to one of the informal settlements far away from the City centre was rejected by the Court as being inconsistent with the African philosophical concept of *ubuntu* which pervades the Constitution and emphasises the interconnectedness of individual and communal welfare, and 'the responsibility to each that flows from our connection.'[179] The eviction of the applicants would deprive them of their livelihood as many of them eke out an existence in informal economic activities (such as refuse recycling) closely linked to the city centre. Interestingly, the Court referred to the right to work (which is not expressly included in the text of the South African Constitution) as 'one of the most precious liberties that an individual possesses'; 'An individual has as much right to work as the individual has to live, to be free and to own property. To work means to eat and consequently to live. This constitutes an encompassing view of humanity.'[180]

The City was interdicted from evicting the occupiers until a comprehensive and co-ordinated programme was adopted to deal with the housing crisis of the poor people in the inner city of Johannesburg, alternatively, until such time as suitable alternative accommodation is provided to them. The City's appeal to the Supreme Court of Appeal against the High Court's refusal of the eviction order was, however, upheld in *The City of Johannesburg v Rand Properties and Others* (2007 (6) BCLR 643 (SCA)). However, the Supreme Court of Appeal required the City to provide temporary accommodation to those residents who are evicted and are in desperate need of housing assistance. Such temporary accommodation is to consist at least of a place where those evicted can live secure against eviction, a structure that is

---

170 Ibid. paras. 52–67.
171 Ibid. para. 56.
172 Ibid. para. 59.
173 *The City of Johannesburg v. Rand Properties and others (Pty) Ltd*, 2006 (6) BCLR 728 (W).
174 The relevant legislation is the National Building Regulations and Building Standards Act 103 of 1977, the Health Act 63 of 1977 as well as the City of Johannesburg's fire by-laws.
175 *The City of Johannesburg*, (n. 173 above) para. 29.
176 Ibid. para. 29 read with para. 36.

177 Ibid. paras. 22, 47.
178 Ibid. para. 57.
179 Ibid. para. 63.
180 Ibid. para. 64.

waterproof and secure against the elements, and the provision of basic sanitation, water and refuse services. The Court justified this finding on the basis of the requirement in *Grootboom* that organs of state have a special duty towards persons experiencing housing crises or living in intolerable conditions.

On 19 February 2008, the Constitutional Court handed down judgment in the appeal from the judgment of the Supreme Court of Appeal in *Occupiers of 51 Olivia Road v City of Jhb*.[181] The Court endorsed the settlement agreement which had been reached between the occupiers (who had initiatied the litigation) and the City in response to an order made by the Court after argument in the matter for the parties to 'engage meaningfully' with each other. The purpose of such engagement was to attempt to resolve the issues in the application and making conditions in the relevant buildings 'as safe and conducive to health as is reasonably practicable.'[182] In its judgment, the Constitutional Court affirmed the basic principle that in situations where people face homelessness due to an eviction, public authorities should generally engage seriously and in good faith with the affected occupiers with a view to finding humane and pragmatic solutions to their dilemma. The Court stated that the objectives of such engagement are to ascertain what the consequences of an eviction might be, whether the city could help in alleviating those dire consequences, whether it is possible to render the buildings concerned relatively safe and conducive to health for an interim period, whether the city had any obligations to the occupiers in the prevailing circumstances; and when and how the city could or would fulfil these obligations.[183]

A second major feature of the judgment is that it affirms that local authorities are obliged to consider the availability of suitable alternative accommodation or land in deciding whether to proceed with an eviction in terms of National Building Regulations and Standards Act, 1977. This aspect of the judgment is particularly significant as the Supreme Court of Appeal had held that this was not a relevant factor for the City to consider in deciding whether it was neces-

sary to order people to vacate their homes. The Court held said that local authorities must function in a systemic, integrated manner. The relevant departments of a municipality cannot function in isolation from each other with 'one department making a decision on whether someone should be evicted and some other department in the bureaucratic maze determining whether housing should be provided.'[184] The Constitutional Court thus affirmed that section 26 of the Constitution which protects housing rights is relevant to all eviction decisions, including those taken pursuant to health and safety legislation.

The final aspect of the judgment concerns the provision in the Act that a failure to comply with a notice to vacate makes an occupier liable on conviction to criminal penalties. The Court held that this provision of the legislation violates section 26(3) of the Constitution which provides that no-one may be evicted from their home without an order of court made after considering all relevant circumstances.[185] In order to cure this constitutional defect, the Court read appropriate wording into the section to provide for judicial oversight of evictions in terms of the legislation.

These housing cases illustrate the stringent standard of review the courts apply to laws or conduct that deprive people of existing access to socio-economic rights. They also illustrate how negative and positive duties are frequently intertwined in socio-economic rights cases. Thus, for example, while there is no automatic right to alternative accommodation when people are evicted from their homes, the lack of such alternative accommodation is certainly a weighty factor for a court in considering whether it is just and equitable to issue an eviction order.[186]

6. DEFENDING PROGRAMMES GIVING EFFECT TO SOCIO-ECONOMIC RIGHTS

Socio-economic rights can also serve to assist the State in defending pro-poor legislation and programmes against attack by powerful private

---

[181] 2008 (5) BCLR 475 (CC).
[182] Ibid., para. 5–6; 9–30.
[183] Ibid., para. 14.

[184] Ibid., para. 44.
[185] Ibid., paras. 47–51.
[186] See S. Liebenberg, 'Towards a Right to Alternative Accommodation? South Africa's Constitutional Jurisprudence on Evictions', *Housing and EC Rights Quarterly*, Vol. 2, No. 3 (2005), pp. 1–5.

interests in society. This is illustrated by the case of *Minister of Public Works v Kyalami Ridge Environmental Association* ('*Kyalami Ridge*').[187] In this case, the Ministry of Public Works relied on its constitutional obligation to assist people in crisis situations[188] to defend its decision to establish a transit camp on the grounds of a prison owned by it in order to temporarily house destitute flood victims. This decision was challenged by a neighbouring residents' association on the grounds that there was no legislation authorising the Government to establish the transit camp and that the decision was unlawful in that it contravened the town planning scheme and environmental legislation.

The Constitutional Court held that none of the laws relied on by the association excluded or limited the government's common law power to make its land available to flood victims pursuant to its constitutional duty to provide them with access to housing.[189] Furthermore, procedural fairness did not require government to do more in the circumstances than it had undertaken to do, namely to consult with the Kyalami residents in an endeavour to meet any legitimate concerns they might have as to the manner in which the development will take place. The Court observed in this regard:

> To require more would in effect inhibit the government from taking a decision that had to be taken urgently. It would also impede the government from using its own land for a constitutionally mandated purpose, in circumstances where legislation designed to regulate land use places no such restriction on it.[190]

Such legislative and executive conduct will be liable to challenge, however, if there is a breach of other provisions of the Bill of Rights (e.g., the right to just administrative action) despite its pro-poor objectives.[191]

7. OTHER RIGHTS

The cases discussed have been the most significant thus far in the development of South Africa's jurisprudence on socio-economic rights. They have primarily concerned rights to land and housing, health care services, and social security. However, it is important to note that a range of social rights cases are litigated every day in the Magistrate's Courts, the High Courts, the Supreme Court of Appeal and specialised courts such as the Labour Courts and the Land Claims Court.[192]

There have been a number of High Court decisions enforcing the socio-economic rights of prisoners protected in section 35(2)(e) of the Constitution.[193] In *B & Others v Minister of Correctional Services & Others*,[194] the Cape High Court directed the respondents to supply two HIV-positive applicants with antiretroviral medication which had been prescribed for them in fulfilment of their right to be provided with 'adequate medical treatment' at state expense. The Court found that the Ministry had failed to make out a case that it could not afford the relevant treatment.[195]

In the field of social security rights, the High Courts have relied extensively on the right to administrative justice to enforce people's rights of access

---

[187] 2001 (7) BCLR 652 (CC).

[188] See the decision in *Grootboom* (n. 31 above).

[189] *Kyalami Ridge* (n. 187 above), para. 51.

[190] Ibid., para. 109.

[191] A recent example of such as a case concerned regulations promulgated under the Medicines and Related Substances Act 101 of 1965 which sought to establish a pricing system for medicines in order to make them more transparent and affordable for consumers. Various aspects of these regulations were set aside by the Constitutional Court primarily for non-compliance with the principles

of administrative justice. *Minister of Health and Another v. New Clicks SA (Pty) Ltd and Others* 2006 (1) BCLR 1 (CC).

[192] See, for example, *Ntshangase v. The Trustees of the Terblanche Gesin Familie Trust* [2003] JOL 10996 (LCC) (the obstruction by an owner of an occupier from accessing grazing lands and a watering hole on his property that the occupier previously used for cattle, constitutes an eviction in terms of the Extension of Security of Tenure Act); *Zulu v. Van Rensburg* 1996 (4) SA 1236 (LCC) (the impounding of the cattle of an occupier constitutes an eviction which must comply with the requirements of the Extension of Security of Tenure Act). For a critical appraisal of the performance of the Land Claims Court established in 1996 under the Restitution of Land Rights Act 22 of 1994, see T. Roux, 'Pro-Poor Court, Anti-Poor Outcomes: Explaining the Performance of the South African Land Claims Court', *South African Journal on Human Rights*, Vol. 20 (2004), pp. 511–543.

[193] Section 35(2)(e) guarantees to everyone who is detained, including every sentenced prisoners the right 'to conditions of detention that are consistent with human dignity, including at least exercise and the provision, at state expense, of adequate accommodation, nutrition, reading material and medical treatment.'

[194] 1997 (6) BCLR 789 (C).

[195] Ibid., paras. 56, 60. See also *Strydom v. Minister of Correctional Services & Others* 1999 (3) BCLR 342 (W).

to social assistance grants as well as their right not to have these grants unjustly suspended or terminated.[196] Administrative justice rights are an important vehicle for protecting a range of socio-economic rights, including access to basic services such as electricity and water supply.[197]

Although there has not to date been a major test case on the right to education protected in section 29 of the Constitution, the Constitutional Court has held in respect of the right to basic education in section 32(a) of the interim Constitution, 1993, that this provision 'creates a positive right that basic education be provided for every person and not merely a negative right that such a person should not be obstructed in pursuing his or her basic education.'[198] Access to existing educational institutions has been protected through the right against unfair discrimination.[199] Jurispru-

dence also exists on the interpretation of the right of learners to receive instruction in the language of their choice in public educational institutions, as set forth in section 29(2) of the Constitution.[200]

8. REMEDIES AND IMPLEMENTATION OF THE JUDGMENTS

The courts have wide remedial powers to grant effective remedies in social rights cases. A court deciding a constitutional matter within its power must declare that any law or conduct that is inconsistent with the Constitution is invalid to the extent of its inconsistency.[201] In addition, the court can make any order that is 'just and equitable', including an order limiting the retrospective effect of the declaration of invalidity, and an order suspending the order of invalidity for any period and on any conditions, to allow the competent authority to correct the defect.[202]

The Constitutional Court has emphasised the critical importance of developing effective, and, if need be, innovative remedies to vindicate constitutional rights:

> Particularly in a country where so few have the means to enforce their rights through the courts, it is essential that on those occasions when the legal process does establish that an infringement of an entrenched right has occurred, it be effectively vindicated. The courts have a particular responsibility in this regard and are obliged to 'forge new tools' and shape innovative remedies, if need be, to achieve this goal.[203]

This is particularly relevant in socio-economic rights cases, where the poor often lack access to legal services, and cannot afford to engage in on-going litigation to secure an effective remedy.

The South African courts have dealt with the circumstances under which they should grant

---

[196] See, for example, *Bushula & Others v. Permanent Secretary, Department of Welfare, Eastern Cape Provincial Government* 2000 (7) BCLR 728 (E); *Mahambehlala v. MEC for Welfare, Eastern Cape and another* 2002 (1) SA 342 (SE); *Vumazonke v. Member of the Executive Council for Social Development, Eastern Cape and Three Similar Cases* 2005 (6) SA 229. For a discussion of these developments, see: Sandra Liebenberg, 'The Judicial Enforcement of Social Security Rights in South Africa: Enhancing Accountability for the Basic Needs of the Poor' in Eibe Riedel (ed.), *Social Security as a Human Right: Drafting a General Comment on Article 9 ICESCR – Some Challenges* (Berlin: Springer–Verlag, 2007), pp. 69–90.

[197] Administrative justice rights are protected through the common law and the Promotion of Administrative Justice Act 3 of 2000, which was enacted to give effect to the right to just administrative action in s. 33 of the Constitution.

[198] *Ex parte Gauteng Provincial Legislature: In re Dispute Concerning the Constitutionality of Certain Provisions of the Gaunteng School Education Bill of 1995* 1996 (4) BCLR 537 (CC) at para. 9. However, the main issue in this case was whether the State was under a positive duty to assist in the establishment of educational institutions based on a common culture, language or religion to give effect to s. 32 (c) of the interim Constitution. The Court held that there was no such positive duty on the State.

[199] *Matukane & Others v. Laerskool Potgietersrus* 1996 (3) SA 223 (WLD). The school concerned had rejected black learners' application to a dual medium school on the basis that it would detrimentally affect the Afrikaans culture and ethos of the school. The Court found that this policy unlawfully discriminated against pupils on the basis of their race. A more complex question concerns the economic accessibility of schooling in a system which permits the charging of school fees subject to exemptions for those parents who cannot afford the fees. For a discussion of this issue, see F. Veriava and F. Coomans, 'The right to education' in D. Brand and Christof Heyns (eds.), *Socio-Economic Rights in South Africa* (Cape Town: Pretoria University Law Press, 2005), pp. 57–83, at 68–71.

[200] The leading decision is *Western Cape Minister of Education v. Governing Body of Mikro Primary School* 2005 (10) BCLR 973 (SCA).

[201] Section 172 (1)(a).

[202] Section 172(1)(b).

[203] *Fose v. Minister of Safety and Security* 1997 (3) SA 786 (CC) at para. 69 (footnotes omitted); Mia Swart, 'Left out in the cold? Crafting constitutional remedies for the poorest of the poor', *South African Journal on Human Rights*, Vol. 21 (2005), pp. 215–240.

mandatory relief to enforce the positive duties imposed by socio-economic rights, particularly the remedy of assuming a supervisory jurisdiction over the implementation of the order. In terms of such an order, the State will usually be ordered to devise and present to court a plan of action to remedy the violation, and to report back to the court on its implementation at regular intervals. At both the stages of the approval and implementation of the plan, the applicant and other interested parties (including a possible independent 'court monitor') will be given an opportunity to comment. The court will thereupon give directions concerning further steps to be taken to achieve the vindication of the constitutional right at issue (this type of an order is also referred to as a 'structural interdict'). Wim Trengove argues that these orders are particularly suited to cases that seek to redress systemic violations of socio-economic rights, requiring far-reaching institutional and structural reforms over a period of time.[204] They cannot be remedied by a single court order made once and for all. Such orders should strive to preserve the choice of means of the legislative and executive as to the precise manner in which to remedy the situation while not abdicating the court's responsibility to ensure that constitutional objectives are fulfilled. The court thus retains jurisdiction over the enforcement of the order.

In *Grootboom*, the Constitution Court confined itself to making a declaratory order.[205] Later, in *TAC*, the Court confirmed its wide remedial powers, including the granting of mandatory relief with or without the exercise of some form of supervisory jurisdiction.[206] The Courts should be guided

by '[t]he nature of the right infringed and the nature of the infringement as to the appropriate relief in a particular case.'[207] The critical consideration is what would constitute an *effective* remedy in the circumstances of the case.[208]

Although the Court in *TAC* made both declaratory and mandatory orders against the State, it declined to exercise a supervisory jurisdiction as it was invited to do by the applicants. It held that there were no grounds for believing that the Government would not respect and execute the orders of the Court.[209] The High Courts have generally granted supervisory orders more readily.[210] The most recent example is the decision of the Cape High Court in *City of Cape Town v Rudolph*.[211] The Court in this case handed down a structural

---

[204] W. Trengove, 'Judicial remedies for violations of socio-economic rights', *ESR Review*, Vol. 1 No. 4 (1999), pp. 8–11, at 9. See also chapter 2 in this volume.

[205] *Grootboom* (n. 31 above), para 99. This order has attracted criticism: see Kameshni Pillay, 'Implementation of *Grootboom*: Implications for the enforcement of socio-economic rights', *Law Democracy and Development*, Vol. 6 (2002), pp. 255–277.

[206] *TAC* (n. 32 above), paras. 104–106. In this respect, the Court rejected the State's contention that the Court's power in the present case was confined to issuing a declaratory order. The State argued that the doctrine of separation of powers precluded the courts from making orders 'that have the effect of requiring the executive to pursue a particular policy' (at para. 97). The power of the Court to make 'supervisory orders' was specifically recognised in *Pretoria City Council v. Walker* 1998 (2) SA 363 (CC), 1998 (3) BCLR 257 (CC), para. 96. An order of this nature was made by the Constitutional Court in *August*

and Another v. Electoral Commission and Others 1999 (4) BCLR 363 (CC) (requiring the Independent Electoral Commission to make all the necessary and reasonable arrangements for prisoners to exercise their right to vote coupled with an order to submit a detailed plan to the Court on its implementation). See also *Sibiya and Others v. DPP: Johannesburg High Court and Others* 2005 (8) BCLR 812 (CC) (requiring the respondents to take all necessary steps to set aside and replace by an appropriate alternative sentence all death sentences imposed before 5 June 1995 in terms of the applicable legislation, and ordering them to report back to court by affidavit on the steps taken).

[207] *TAC* (n. 32 above), para. 106.

[208] Ibid. para. 102 (citing Ackermann J in *Fose* (n. 203 above), para. 106, and paras. 112–113.

[209] Ibid. para. 129. In this regard the Court indicated that supervisory orders should not be made unless they are necessary to secure compliance with a court order.

[210] In *Grootboom v. Oostenberg Municipalityand Others* 2000 (3) BCLR 277 (C), the High Court found a violation of section 28(1)(c) of the Constitution. In the first part of its order, the Court declared in broad terms that the appropriate organ or department of State is obliged to provide the applicant children, and their accompanying parents, with shelter until such time as the parents are able to shelter their own children. The second part of the order directs the respondent to present, under oath, reports to the Court on the implementation of the order within a period of three months from the date of the order. The applicants are given an opportunity to deliver their commentary on these reports (at 293 H - J – 294 A – C). See also the supervisory order in the *TAC* High Court decision: *Treatment Action Campaign and Others v. Minister of Health and* Others 2002 (4) BCLR 356 (T), 386 I–387 H. See also, *Strydom v. Minister of Correctional Services and Others* 1993 (3) BCLR 342 (W) (ordering the Ministry of Correctional Services to report to court setting out a timetable within which the electrical upgrading of the maximum security section of Johannesburg Prison would be commenced and completed).

[211] 2003 (11) BCLR 1236 (C).

interdict ordering the City of Cape Town to report back to the Court on the steps it was taking to comply with the *Grootboom* judgment, particularly the implementation of an emergency housing programme for those in desperate need.

The relatively tardy implementation by the State of the *Grootboom* order has been attributed to the rather weak, declaratory remedy made by the Court. A widely misunderstood feature of the case is the fact that the position of the actual *Grootboom* community was settled and the settlement agreement made an order of Court (dated 21 September 2000). In terms of this settlement agreement, the *Grootboom* community were permitted to continue residing on the periphery of the Wallacedene sportsfield on a temporary basis until housing became available to them under one of the State's housing programmes for the broader Wallacedene. Provision was also made for funding to purchase building material required to waterproof the community's existing accommodation as well as basic sanitation, water and refuse services. Thus, the reported judgement of the Constitutional Court in the *Grootboom* case dealt only with the general obligations of the State in terms of section 26 of the constitution It is in this context that the order was made declaring that a reasonable programme in terms of section 26 must incorporate a programme 'to provide relief for people who have no access to land, no roof over their heads, and who were living in intolerable conditions or crisis situations.'[212] There was a considerable delay in implementing such a programme. Only in August 2003 did the national and provincial ministers of housing approve a new programme entitled '*Housing Assistance in Emergency Circumstances.*' This programme was incorporated in the National Housing Code in 2004.[213] It remains to be tested whether this programme fulfils the constitutional obligations in terms of section 26 as elaborated in the *Grootboom* judgment.[214] The position of the Grootboom community itself is also by all accounts unsatisfactory. Their accommodation on the sportsfield was intended to be temporary,

and yet 5 years after the judgment they are still located in crowded, unsanitary conditions on the periphery of the sportsfield with highly inadequate services.[215]

In the case of *City of Cape Town v Rudolph,*[216] the Cape High Court found that the City of Cape Town had not complied with its obligation in terms of *Grootboom* to develop and implement a housing programme for those in desperate need. A similar finding was made by the Witwatersrand Local Division of the High Court in the *City of Johannesburg* case[217] discussed above. In the latter case, the Court noted that the national Emergency Housing Programme requires municipalities to investigate and assess the emergency housing need in their areas of jurisdiction and to therefore '*plan proactively*'.[218] Once emergency needs are identified, municipalities must apply to the provincial departments of housing for funding in terms of this programme. However, the City of Johannesburg had failed to take proactive steps in terms of this programme to improve the condition of the relevant buildings and to forestall the imminent eviction. Nor had they engaged in 'any form of constructive consultation with any of the Respondents.'[219]

As noted above, in the *TAC* case the Court made a range of mandatory orders against the State while declining to exercise a supervisory jurisdiction over the implementation of these orders. In the immediate aftermath of the judgment, there was a lack of urgency in implementing the Court's rulings at both national level and in relation to some of the provinces. The TAC was compelled to undertake a range of actions in an effort to ensure the proper implementation of the orders. These included correspondence, meetings, a complaint to the South African Human Rights Commission, and during December 2002 contempt of court proceedings were launched against the national

---

[212] *Grootboom* (n. 31 above), para. 99.

[213] It is incorporated as Chapter 12 of the National Housing Code.

[214] For a detailed study of the implementation of the *Grootboom* judgment, see Pillay, Implementation of *Grootboom* (n. 205 above).

[215] B. Schoonakker, 'Treated with contempt: Squatters' precedent-setting victory has gained them only stinking latrines', *Sunday Times*, 21 March 2004; Pillay, ibid.

[216] *Rudolph* (n. 211) above.

[217] *City of Johannesburg* (n. 173) above.

[218] Ibid. para. 45.

[219] Ibid. para. 47. The Supreme Court of Appeal also found that the City had not pursued with sufficient vigour an application under Chapter 12 of the National Housing Code to provide housing to persons evicted from unsafe inner-city buildings.

Minister of Health and the Member of the Executive Committee ('MEC') for Health of the Mpumalanga province.[220] Although not perfect, a national programme for the prevention of MTCT of HIV has been adopted by the Government in response to the *TAC* judgment. There can be little doubt that lives have been saved as a result of the litigation and surrounding mobilisation. This is largely due to the organising capabilities and dedication of the TAC. In addition, the *TAC* judgment and its aftermath had a significant impact in the ultimate adoption of a national antiretroviral treatment plan for all those living with HIV/AIDS.[221]

In conclusion, the Court should overcome its reluctance to grant supervisory remedies in order to facilitate the long-term structural reforms required to realise socio-economic rights.[222] Supervisory orders have a rich potential not only for the courts to monitor the implementation of such orders, but also to enhance the participation of both civil society and the state institutions supporting constitutional democracy (such as the SA Human Rights Commission and the Commission for Gender Equality) in the implementation of socio-economic rights judgments.[223]

Courts can also give forms of tangible relief to those experiencing immediate deprivations to avoid irreparable threats to life, health and future

development. The nature and extent of this relief will depend on the context, but must reflect the conviction expressed in *Grootboom* that a society 'must seek to ensure that the basic necessities of life are provided to all if it is to be a society based on human dignity, freedom and equality.'[224] In the *Khosa* and *Jaftha* decisions, the Court has been willing to grant remedies, reading into legislation the excluded group or provisions to ensure consistency with the provisions of the Constitution (the 'reading in' remedy). This is generally considered to be quite an intrusive remedy. However, it is justifiable in these cases given the fact that these were disadvantaged claimants exposed to a serious deprivation of social benefits and resources by the relevant legislation. Striking down the legislation would not have been an appropriate remedy, as it would have deprived many others of important rights and benefits. Another innovative remedy was handed down in the *Modderklip* case in which the Court ordered the State to pay compensation to a landowner for the illegal occupation of his land while permitting the community to remain on the land until alternative accommodation was made available.

9. CONCLUSION

What are the results thus far from South Africa's bold experiment with the entrenchment of socio-economic rights as justiciable rights? In the first place, the caution of sceptics that social rights adjudication would cast the courts in an inappropriate and unmanageable role has proven to be unfounded. The courts have proved themselves quite capable of developing a sophisticated and nuanced model of review for adjudicating social rights claims. This has enabled the courts to respect the institutional competencies and roles of the other branches of government while playing a meaningful role in enforcing constitutionally guaranteed socio-economic rights.

The second predication was that justiciable socio-economic rights would amount to a dead letter as the courts would be unwilling and unable to enforce them. This would result in discrediting

---

[220] M. Heywood, 'Contempt or compliance? The *TAC* case after the Constitutional Court judgment', *ESR Review*, Vol. 4, No. 4 (2003), pp. 7–10; Swart, 'Left out in the cold?' (n. 208 above), p. 215, pp. 223–224.

[221] For an excellent account of the use by the TAC of legal and mobilisation strategies, see Mark Heywood, 'Shaping, making and breaking the law in the campaign for a national HIV/Treatment Plan', in Peris Jones and Kristian Stokke (eds.), *Democratising Development: The Politics of Socio-Economic Rights in South Africa* (Martinus Nijhoff Publishers, 2005), pp. 181–212. See also the TAC website: <http://www.tac.org.za>.

[222] For criticisms of the Court's reticence to grant supervisory orders, see David Bilchitz (note 134 above) at 23–24; Pillay (note 205 above), pp. 275–276; Marius Pieterse (note 138 above), pp. 415–417.

[223] On the roles of the Human Rights Commission and Commission for Gender Equality in relation to socio-economic rights, see Liebenberg, 'The Interpretation of Socio-Economic Rights' (n. 38 above), pp. 64–66; D. G. Newman, 'Institutional monitoring of social and economic rights: A South African case study and a new research agenda', *South African Journal on Human Rights*, Vol. 19 (2003), pp. 189–216.

[224] *Grootboom* (n. 31 above), para. 44.

the Bill of Rights in the eyes of the public. This prediction has also not materialised. There is a burgeoning jurisprudence on these rights, which has made a tangible contribution in many cases to improving the quality of life of disadvantaged groups. One need only reflect on the provision of anti-retroviral treatment for people living with HIV/AIDS, the winning of social security benefits for non-citizens, and the significant procedural and substantive protections for people facing evictions from their homes.

However, to assist in facilitating a transformation in unjust social and economic relations in South Africa, socio-economic rights jurisprudence and litigation strategies must continue to develop in the various areas identified in this chapter. This includes extending legal services to the poor, ensuring that reasonableness review provides robust and substantive protection to those lacking access to critical social services and resources, and developing effective remedies and implementation strategies in socio-economic rights litigation. Finally, without a strong civil society movement capable of using socio-economic rights litigation strategically in pursuit of a broader transformative programme, the potential of these rights will remain unrealised. As Chaskalson P (as he then was) observed in *Soobramoney*:

> We live in a society in which there are great disparities in wealth. Millions of people are living in deplorable conditions and in great poverty. There is a high level of unemployment, inadequate social security, and many do not have access to clean water or to adequate health services. These conditions already existed when the Constitution was adopted and a commitment to address them, and to transform our society into one in which there will be human dignity, freedom and equality, lies at the heart of our new constitutional order. For as long as these conditions continue to exist that aspiration will have a hollow ring.[225]

Postscript:

On 30 April 2008, the Witwatersrand Division of the High Court handed down a landmark judgment in *Mazibuko and Others v The City of Cape Town* Case No. 06/13865 (W)(judgment unreported at the date of writing). The Court ruled that the City of Johannesburg's practice of forced installation of prepayment water meters in Phiri, Soweto, violated the rights to be unconstitutional and unlawful. The Court also ordered the City to provide residents of Phiri with 50 litres of free basic water per person per day, setting aside the City's decision to limit free water to 25 litres per person per day. The City was also directed to provide residents of Phiri with the option of a metered water supply. The decision was based on the rights to just administrative action and the right of everyone to have access to sufficient water in terms of section 27 of the Constitution. The City has given notice of its intention to appeal against the judgment.

[225] *Soobramoney* (n. 52 above), para. 8.

5

India

The Expectations and Challenges of Judicial Enforcement of Social Rights

S. Muralidhar*

1. INTRODUCTION

A discussion on the Indian jurisprudence in the area of economic and social rights has to begin with the Constitution. The Indian legal system is complex: Inherited from the colonial and common law model,[1] the formal legal system is based on a written constitution, in effect since 1950. The Constitution delineates the enforceable fundamental rights and the non-enforceable Directive Principles of State Policy (DPSP) as well as the powers and obligations of the State. A significant feature of the Constitution of India is the principle of checks and balances by which every organ of state is controlled by and is accountable to the Constitution and the rule of law. The validity of the decisions of the Government can be challenged in the Supreme Court or the High Courts and writs of mandamus are available to enforce the State's obligations. Also, the laws made by the legislature can be struck down by these courts, if found contrary to the provisions of the Constitution. In addition, there are a number of statutes, both at the federal and provincial (state) levels that touch upon various aspects of economic, social and cultural rights.

These broad powers of constitutional review, combined with far-reaching legislation, have proved critical in the judicial enforcement of economic, social and cultural rights, which has produced a

vast body of case law in the Supreme Court and the High Courts. This piece cannot traverse the entire gamut of these sources for want of space and so is confined to discussing the broad contours of the law and some of the significant decisions handed down by the Courts seeking to enforce economic and social rights in India.

The first part of this article sets out the position of socio-economic rights in the Indian Constitution. This is followed by an overview of the position in relation to access to legal services, the growth of judicial activism and public interest litigation. The judicial decisions in areas of specific rights, including the rights to housing, health care, food, work and education are thereafter discussed. The penultimate section seeks to review the impact of judicial intervention. The conclusion is an assessment of the Indian experience in judicial enforcement and protection of economic, social and cultural rights.

2. SOCIO-ECONOMIC RIGHTS WITHIN THE CONTEXT OF THE CONSTITUTION

The Constitution of India, in its Preamble, reflects the resolve to secure to all its citizens 'justice, social, economic and political; liberty of thought, expression, belief, faith and worship and equality of status and of opportunity'[2]. Among the fundamental rights guaranteed to all persons under

---

* LL.M., Ph.D., Judge, High Court of Delhi and formerly Advocate, Supreme Court of India. The views expressed here are the author's own.
[1] C. J. Dias, 'The Impact of Social Activism and Movements for Legal Reform', in Sara Hossain *et al.* (eds.), *Public Interest Litigation in South Asia: Rights in Search of Remedies* (Dhaka, The University Press Ltd., 1997), pp. 14 at 5: 'Most countries of South Asia, upon attaining independence, inherited the legacy of a colonial system ... (they) have found that their 'received' legal systems are both alien and alienating'.

[2] The Preamble, an integral part of the Constitution, can be a useful interpretative tool. The Supreme Court of India in *D.S. Nakara v. Union of India* (1983) 1 SCC 305 observed (at 327): 'while interpreting or examining the constitutional validity of legislative/administrative action, the touchstone of the Directive Principles of State Policy in the light of the Preamble will provide a reliable yardstick to hold one way or the other'.

Part III of the Constitution are the right to life (Article 21) and the right to equality (Article 14). Freedom of speech and expression, the freedom to assemble peaceably, the freedom to form associations, the freedom of movement and residence, and the freedom to practise any profession and to carry on any occupation, trade or business[3] are also part of the chapter on fundamental rights (see Article 19). These are subject to reasonable restrictions on the grounds of sovereignty and integrity of the country, security of the State, public order, decency or morality.[4] The right to equality under article 14, the right against double jeopardy and self-incrimination under Article 20, the right to life under Article 21 and the right to be informed of the grounds of arrest and the right to consult and be defended by a legal practitioner of one's choice under article 22 are available to all persons,[5] while the freedoms enumerated under Article 19 are available for enforcement only by citizens.

The remedy provided in the Constitution for violation of rights and against unlawful legislative and executive acts is to approach the High Courts under article 226 and the Supreme Court under article 32 of the Constitution. Judicial review of executive action, legislation and judicial and quasi-judicial orders is recognised as part of the 'basic structure' of the Constitution.[6] The power of judicial review cannot be taken away even by an amendment to the Constitution.[7] The Supreme Court has the final word on the interpretation of the Constitution. The law declared by the Supreme Court is binding and enforceable by all authorities – executive, legislative and judicial.[8]

Part IV of the Constitution lists out the Directive Principles of State Policy (DPSP). Many of the provisions in Part IV correspond to the provisions of the International Covenant on Economic Social and Cultural Rights (ICESCR). For instance article 43 provides that the State shall endeavour to secure, by suitable legislation or economic organisation or in any other way, to all workers, agricultural, industrial or otherwise, work, a living wage, conditions of work that ensure a decent standard of life and full enjoyment of leisure and social and cultural opportunities, and in particular the State shall endeavour to promote cottage industries on an individual or co-operative basis in rural areas. This corresponds more or less to Articles 11 and 15 of ICESCR.[9] However some of the rights in the ICESCR, for instance the right to health (Article 12 of the ICESCR) and a plethora of other economic, social and cultural rights, have been interpreted by the Indian Supreme Court to form part of the right to life under article 21 of the Constitution thus making it directly enforceable and justiciable.[10] As India is a party to the ICESCR, the Indian legislature has enacted laws giving effect to some of its treaty obligations and these laws are in turn enforceable in and by the courts.[11]

At the time of drafting of the Constitution, it was initially felt that all of the rights in the DPSP should be made justiciable. However, a compromise had to be struck between those who felt that the DPSPs

---

[3] The right to property, which was earlier provided in Article 19(1)(f) as a fundamental right, was omitted by the Constitution (44th Amendment) Act, 1978, and correspondingly recognised as a constitutional right under article 300 A. This change made unavailable a challenge to the validity of a statute on the ground that it violated the fundamental right to property and was therefore liable to be declared unconstitutional under Article 13.

[4] Articles 19(2) to 19(6) of the Constitution.

[5] Under Article 22(3), the right to be informed of the grounds of arrest and to be defended by a lawyer of one's choice is not available for any person who is an enemy alien or to a person who is preventively detained.

[6] *L. Chandrakumar v. Union of India* (1997) 3 SCC 261. The High Courts and the Supreme Court can declare a statute made either by Parliament or a state legislature to be inconsistent with or in derogation of the fundamental rights (in terms of Article 13 of the Constitution) or to be ultra vires or beyond the competence of the legislature.

[7] *Keshavananda Bharati v. State of Kerala* (1973) 4 SCC 225 ['Fundamental Rights Case'].

[8] *Union of India v. Raghubir Singh* (1989) 2 SCC 754 at 766 para. 7; Article 142 of the Constitution declares that any order of the Supreme Court is enforceable throughout the territory of India and Article 144 mandates that all civil and judicial authorities shall act in aid of the Supreme Court.

[9] Illustratively, the rights to education and health are contained in Articles 45 and 47, respectively, which read thus: 'The State shall endeavour to provide early childhood care and education for all children until they complete the age of six years'. And '[t]he State shall regard the raising of the level of nutrition and the standard of living of its people and the improvement of public health as among its primary duties and, in particular, the State shall endeavour to bring about prohibition of the consumption except for medicinal purposes of intoxicating drinks and drugs which are injurious to health'.

[10] *Paschim Banga Khet Majoor Samity v. State of West Bengal* (1996) 4 SCC 37.

[11] Appendix I sets out a table of laws that are related to specific fundamental rights and DPSPs enumerated in the Constitution.

could not possibly be enforced as rights and those who insisted that the Constitution should reflect a strong social agenda.[12] Consequently, article 37 of the Constitution declares that the DPSP 'shall not be enforceable by any court, but the principles therein laid down are nevertheless fundamental in the governance of the country and it shall be the duty of the state to apply these principles in making laws'.

The subsequent amendments to the Constitution have emphasised the need to give priority to the DPSPs over the fundamental rights. In the context of land reforms, the 25th Amendment to the Constitution in 1971 inserted Article 31C[13] which insulated from judicial challenge a law giving effect to the DPSPs in article 39 (b)[14] and 39 (c)[15] of the Constitution. The statement of objects and reasons in the Bill that introduced this amendment made it explicit that the intention was to give priority to the directive principles over the fundamental rights.[16]

---

[12] G. Austin, *The Indian Constitution: Cornerstone of a Nation* (Oxford: Clarendon Press, 1966), pp. 77–83. It requires to be mentioned that when the Indian Constituent Assembly drafted the Constitution, it probably had for reference the Universal Declaration of Human Rights, 1948 [UDHR], which emphasises the universality and indivisibility of the civil and political rights on the one hand and economic, social and cultural rights on the other. The two major covenants came much later in 1966, and India did not ratify them until April 1979.

[13] Article 31C reads thus: 'Notwithstanding anything contained in Article 13, no law giving effect to the policy of the State towards securing *all or any of the principles laid down in Part IV* shall be deemed to be void on the ground that it is inconsistent with, or takes away or abridges any of the rights conferred by Article 14 or Article 19 *and no law containing a declaration that it is for giving effect to such policy shall be called in question in any Court on the ground that it does not give effect to such policy*'. The italicised portions were respectively struck down by the Supreme Court of India as being invalid in *Minerva Mills v. Union of India*, (1980) 2 SCC 591 and *Keshavananda Bharti v. The State of Kerala* (1973) Supp. SCC 1.

[14] Article 39(b) reads: 'The State shall, in particular, direct its policy towards securing . . . that the ownership and control of the material resources of the community are so distributed as best to subserve the common good'.

[15] Article 39(c) reads: 'The State shall, in particular, direct its policy towards securing . . . [t]hat the operation of the economic system does not result in the concentration of wealth and means of production to the common detriment'.

[16] The attempt in 1976, to further amend Article 31C, to insulate the challenge to laws that gave effect to all or any of DPSPs, through the 42nd Amendment to the Constitution was struck down in *Minerva Mills v Union of India* (1980) 3 SCC 625.

2.1 Coverage of Disadvantaged Groups and Non-Nationals

The recognition in the Indian Constitution of the need for affirmative action provisions for socially and educationally disadvantaged groups is significant. In India, certain classes of citizens have historically and socially suffered discriminatory treatment, including those officially known as Scheduled Castes (SC) and Scheduled Tribes (ST). Article 15(4), which prohibits discrimination on the grounds of religion, race, caste, sex or place of work, nevertheless contains a provision that permits the State to make 'any special provision for the advancement of any socially and educationally backward classes of citizens or for the SCs and STs'.[17] In matters of public employment also, the State can make special reservation in favour of 'any backward class of citizens, which, in the opinion of the State, is not adequately represented in the services under the State'.[18] The traditions and customs that are followed by the tribal communities in different parts of India have been allowed to continue even after the making of the Constitution and Article 244, read with Schedule V to the Constitution, ensures the preservation and protection of the tribal culture, customs and traditions.[19]

The Indian Constitution recognises religious minorities as well as linguistic minorities. There are specific provisions in the chapter on fundamental rights that recognises the right of 'every religious denomination or any section thereof' to have the right to establish and maintain institutions for religious and charitable purposes and to manage their own affairs in matters of religion.[20] An educational institution for a religious minority that is not financially supported by the State is free to devise its own admission procedures subject to regulation by the State.[21]

---

[17] Article 15(3) likewise permits the State to make special provisions for women and children, which may involve positive discrimination.

[18] Article 16(4) of the Constitution of India.

[19] There are special laws that ensure that transfer of land in tribal areas is permissible only between tribals. In other words, there is a bar on the transfer of land in tribal areas from a tribal to a non-tribal, and this could include the State as well. In the context of the law applicable in the State of Andhra Pradesh in India, see *Samatha v. State of A.P.* (1997) 8 SCC 191.

[20] Article 26 of the Constitution of India.

[21] See Article 30 which recognises that 'all minorities whether based on religion or language, shall have the

2.2 Horizontal Application

The specific wording of the different provisions of the Constitution indicates whether it is enforceable only against the State or also against individuals and non-state entities. For instance, article 14 requires that 'the State shall not deny to any person equality before the law or equal protection of the law within the territory of India'. Article 15 (1) also requires that 'the State shall not discriminate against any citizen on the grounds only of religion, race, caste, sex, place of birth or any of them'.[22] On the other hand, article 15 (2) which guarantees that 'no citizen shall, on grounds only of religion, race, caste, sex, place of birth or any of them be subject to any disability, liability, restrictions or condition with regard to' access to shops, public restaurants, use of wells, tanks, bathing places, roads, is enforceable even against other persons, including associations, firms or corporations.[23] Article 17, which abolishes untouchability, and article 23, which prohibits the trafficking of human beings and degrading forms of forced labour, are likewise enforceable even against individuals and non-state entities. The prohibition in article 24 against employment of children below the age of 14 years in any factory or mine or in any other hazardous employment is also enforceable not only against the State, but against corporations as well.

Part IV A of the Constitution, which was inserted by the 42nd Amendment in 1976, sets out, in article 51A, fundamental duties which, among others, require every citizen of India 'to promote harmony and spirit of common brotherhood amongst all the people of India transcending religious, linguistic and regional or sectional diversities; to renounce practices derogatory to the dignity of women'[24]

and a citizen who is a parent or guardian 'to provide opportunities for education to his child or as the case may be ward between the age of 6 and 14 years'.[25]

Thus, there are various provisions in the Constitution that are reflective of the horizontal application of rights in the context of the universal characteristic of non-discrimination as well as the unique characteristic of the particular right.

2.3 International Law and the Constitution

Article 51(c) of the DPSP requires the State to 'foster respect for international law and treaty obligations in the dealings of organised people with one another'. Under article 253 of the Constitution, the Parliament has the power to make any law 'for implementing any treaty, agreement or convention with any other country or countries or any decision made at any international conference, association or other body'. For instance, the Immoral Traffic (Prevention) Act, 1956, was enacted following the ratification by the Government of India of the International Convention for the Suppression of the Traffic in Persons and of the Exploitation of the Prostitution of Others. Similarly, the Persons with Disabilities (Equal Opportunities, Protection of Rights and Full Participation) Act, 1995, was enacted pursuant to India becoming a signatory to the Proclamation on the Full Participation and Equality of People with Disabilities in the Asian and Pacific Region.

The Indian Judiciary has in the recent past drawn on international human rights law to redress the grievance of women facing sexual harassment at the workplace. In *Vishaka v. State of Rajasthan*[26] it was declared that the provisions of the Convention on the Elimination of All Forms of Discrimination Against Women (CEDAW), to which India was a State party, were binding and enforceable as such in India. The Court proceeded to adapt several of the standards and norms contained in the CEDAW provisions while formulating binding guidelines which would remain in force till such time the Parliament enacted an appropriate law.[27]

---

right to establish and administer educational institutions of their choice'. For the law in this regard, see the decisions of the Supreme Court of India in *P.A. Inamdar v. State of Karnataka* (2005) 6 SCC 537.

[22] Similarly, Article 16 which guarantees equality of opportunity in matters of public employment, Article 21 which guarantees the right to life and Article 22 which guarantees protection against arrest and detention in certain cases are enforceable only against the State.

[23] In *M.C. Mehta v. Union of India* (1987) 1 SCC 395, the principle of absolute liability of a corporation to compensate for the loss and injury caused on account of its hazardous activity was recognised. The legal position was explained with reference to the constitutional framework of Article 21, in its expanded connotation.

[24] Article 51A (e) of the Constitution of India.

[25] Article 51A (k) inserted by the 86th Amendment to the Constitution in 2002.

[26] (1997) 6 SCC 241.

[27] More recently, in *Pratap Singh v. State of Jharkhand* (2005) 3 SCC 551, the Court was called upon to interpret the

2.4 Legal Standing and Access to Legal Services

The challenge of providing equal and effective access to justice has been daunting for successive governments, legislatures and the judiciary. Although the Constitution in article 39 A, a directive principle of State policy, requires the State to secure that 'the operation of the legal system promotes justice' and that it ought to provide free legal aid by suitable legislations or schemes, much remains to be done to deliver the constitutional promise. One response to the problem has been the judicial innovation of 'Public Interest Litigation' (PIL), which has enabled issues concerning the underprivileged sections of society to be brought before the courts. A precursor to this was the Supreme Court invoking its powers of judicial review, and in assertion of its predominant role as the interpreter of the Constitution, to expand the scope and content of the right to life under article 21 of the Constitution and introduce the notion of substantive due process. This is discussed in the Section that immediately follows.

2.5 Substantive Due Process

In the initial phase the Indian Supreme Court was reluctant to recognise any of the directive principles as being enforceable in the courts of law. In fact, it was held that 'the directive principles have to conform to and run subsidiary to the chapter on fundamental rights'.[28] In the *Fundamental Rights*

case,[29] the majority opinions of the Supreme Court of India reflected the view that what is fundamental in the governance of the country cannot be less significant than what is significant in the life of the individual. One of the judges constituting the majority in that case said: 'In building up a just social order it is sometimes imperative that the fundamental rights should be subordinated to directive principles'.[30] This view that both the fundamental rights and DPSP are complementary, 'neither part being superior to the other', has held the field since.[31] However, even here the Court has retained its power of judicial review to examine if in fact the legislation under examination is intended to achieve the objective of articles 39(b) and (c), and where the legislation is an amendment to the Constitution, whether it violates the basic structure of the Constitution.[32] Likewise, courts have used DPSP to uphold the constitutional validity of statutes that apparently impose restrictions on the fundamental rights under article 19 (freedoms of speech, expression, association, residence, travel and to carry on business, trade or profession) as long as they are stated to achieve the objective of the DPSP.[33] The DPSPs are seen as aids to interpret the Constitution and more specifically to provide the basis, scope and extent of the content of a fundamental right.[34]

The recognition that the fundamental rights chapter (Chapter III of the Constitution) implicitly acknowledges the right of substantive due process had to wait for nearly three decades after the

---

provisions of the Juvenile Justice (Care and Protection of Children) Act, 2000, and whether the date for determining the age of the juvenile offender would be the date of the offence or the date on which the juvenile is produced before the court or competent authority. In that process, it was noticed that the predecessor legislation, the Juvenile Justice Act, 1986 was enacted to bring the legal regime in India consistent with the United Nations Standard Minimum Rules for the Administration of Juvenile Justice. It was observed that the 'Constitution of India and the juvenile justice legislations must necessarily be understood in the context of the present day scenario and having regard to International Treaties and Conventions' and that the legislation of 2000 'has not only to be read in terms of the Rules but also the Universal Declaration of Human Rights and the United Nations Standard Minimum Rules for the Protection of Juveniles'.

[28] *State of Madras v. Champakam Dorairajan* (1951) SCR 525.

[29] See n. 7 above.

[30] Mathew, J. in the *Fundamental Rights Case*, ibid. para. 1707, p. 879.

[31] V.R. Krishna Iyer, J. in *State of Kerala v. N.M. Thomas* (1976) 2 SCC 310, para. 134, p. 367.

[32] *Minerva Mills v. Union of India* (1980) 3 SCC 625; *Waman Rao v. Union of India* (1981) 2 SCC 362.

[33] For instance Article 43 dealing with living wages and conditions of work has been relied upon to sustain the reasonableness of the restriction imposed by the Minimum Wages Act, 1948: *Chandra Bhavan v. State of Mysore* (1970) 2 SCR 600.

[34] To quote Mathew, J. in the *Fundamental Rights Case* (n. 7 above), para. 1714, p. 881: 'Fundamental rights have themselves no fixed content; most of them are empty vessels into which each generation must pour its content in the light of its experience. Restrictions, abridgement, curtailment and even abrogation of these rights in circumstances not visualised by the constitution makers might become necessary; their claim to supremacy or priority is liable to be overborne at particular stages in the history of the nation by the moral claims embodied in Part IV'.

commencement of the Constitution. In 1950 in *A.K. Gopalan v. State of Madras*,[35] the Court felt constrained to adopt a legalistic and literal interpretation of article 21 as excluding any element of substantive due process. It was held that as long as there was a law that was validly enacted, the Court could not examine its fairness or reasonableness. This view underwent a change in 1978, soon after the internal emergency during which there were large-scale violations of basic liberties and political rights.[36] This was done through a series of cases of which *Maneka Gandhi v. Union of India*[37] was a landmark. The case involved the refusal by the Government to grant a passport to the petitioner, which thus restrained her liberty to travel. In answering the question whether this denial could be sustained without a pre-decisional hearing, the Court proceeded to explain the scope and content of the right to life and liberty. The question posed and the answer given now was: 'Is the prescription of some sort of procedure enough or must the procedure comply with any particular requirements? Obviously the procedure cannot be arbitrary, unfair or unreasonable'.[38] Once the scope of article 21 had thus been explained, the door was open to its expansive interpretation to include various facets of life. In 1981, in *Francis Coralie Mullin v. The Administrator*,[39] the Supreme Court declared:

> The right to life includes the right to live with human dignity and all that goes with it, namely, the bare necessaries of life such as adequate nutrition, clothing and shelter and facilities for reading, writing and expressing oneself in diverse forms, freely moving about and mixing and commingling with fellow human beings. The magnitude and components of this right would depend upon the extent of economic development of the country, but it must, in any view of the matter, include the bare necessities of life and also the right to carry on such functions and activities as constitute the bare minimum expression of the human self.

2.6 Right to Legal Aid

In 1987, the Indian Parliament enacted the Legal Services Authorities Act (LSAA) which gives an expansive meaning to 'legal services' to include legal advice apart from legal representation in cases. Section 12 of the LSAA lists out the categories of persons automatically entitled to legal aid without having to satisfy a means test. This includes a member of the historically and socially disadvantaged groups (Scheduled Caste or Scheduled Tribe);[40] a victim of trafficking in human beings or forced labour; a person with disabilities and 'a person under circumstances of underserved want such as being a victim of a mass disaster, ethnic violence, caste atrocity, flood, drought, earthquake or industrial disaster'.[41] The LSAA set up a network of legal aid institutions at the village,[42] district,[43] and state level[44] and the National Legal Services Authority (NALSA).[45] These authorities usually comprise members of the judiciary and the executive at the local level.

The functions of NALSA under section 4 of the LSAA include organising 'legal aid camps, especially in rural areas, slums or labour colonies with the dual purpose of educating the weaker sections of the society as to their rights as well as encouraging the settlement of disputes through *lok adalats*'[46] and 'taking necessary steps by way of social justice litigation with regard to consumer protection, environmental protection or any other matter of special concern to the weaker sections,

---

[35] (1950) SCR 88.
[36] See generally G. Austin, *Working a Democratic Constitution: The Indian Experience* (New Delhi: Oxford University Press, 2000).
[37] (1978) 1 SCC 248.
[38] Ibid. p. 281.
[39] (1981) 2 SCR 516.

[40] In the Indian Constitution there is an implicit recognition of certain recognised castes and tribes that have suffered disproportionately due to their social, educational and economic disadvantage and the need for affirmative action by the State to protect their interests (Article 15 (3) of the Constitution).
[41] Section.12 (e), LSAA. These categories of persons have nevertheless to cross the threshold of a prima facie case to prosecute or to defend (s.13 (1) LSAA).
[42] The Taluk Legal Services Committee under s.11 A LSAA.
[43] The District Legal Services Authority under s.9 LSAA.
[44] The State Legal Services Authority under s.6 LSAA.
[45] Section 3, LSAA. Apart from these authorities, there is the Supreme Court Legal Services Committee under section 3A, LSAA and a High Court Legal Services Committee at the level of each High Court under section 8A LSAA.
[46] Section 4 (e) LSAA. *Lok Adalat*, an Urdu expression, in its literal translation means 'people's court'. However, it usually denotes an informal dispute settlement mechanism presided over by a judicial officer and consisting of lay members. The *lok adalat* usually attempts bringing about settlement of pending cases in courts.

of the society and for this purpose, give training to social workers in legal skills'.[47] Although the LSAA envisages a proactive role for judges, its core area of activity has centered around the organising of *lok adalats* since it is seen as a useful case management device. They are held periodically, on court holidays, within the court premises and the 'benches' comprise a judge, a lawyer and a social worker. Pending claims in courts for land acquisition compensation, motor accident compensation, insurance claims and claims by banks against defaulters are the most common categories of cases sent to the *lok adalat*. A reference to the *lok adalat* can be made by any one of the parties to the litigation. There are no appeals from the decisions of the *lok adalat* that record a compromise.[48] Encouraged by the 'settlement' of a large number of cases,[49] the LSAA was amended in 2002 to enable the setting up of 'permanent' *lok adalats* which can dispose of disputes involving certain public utilities[50] even if no settlement is reached.[51]

The organisation of *lok adalats* and legal aid camps has not necessarily been a success.[52] More importantly, they underscore the failures of the formal legal system. The reasons offered for persuading the litigant to participate in the *lok adalat* are usually that the pending dispute in court would entail unforeseeable delays, prohibitive costs and uncertain results.[53]

Also relevant in the context of economic and social rights is the fact that legal aid is still seen as a welfare measure to which the recipient has no 'right'. It therefore does not come as a surprise that the legal services that are presently available are poorly utilised.[54] The reasons could be general lack of awareness of the availability of legal aid, the belief that a person who gets help for 'free' is disabled from demanding quality service and, thirdly the disinterestedness of lawyers and legal aid administrators in providing competent legal assistance.

These factors explain in large measure why civil society groups continue to approach the High Courts and the Supreme Courts in PIL cases for the redress of many of the grievances of the citizens in the area of economic and social rights. As the ensuing discussion on the specific areas of these rights show, the remedies under the statutes concerning them are hardly enforced. This could be attributed to both a lack of awareness of their provisions or plain indifference of those charged with the responsibility of their enforcement.

2.7 Judicial Activism and Public Interest Litigation

A reference has already been made to the internal emergency that was in force between 1975 and 1977 and its aftermath and this contributed significantly to the change in the judiciary's perception of its role in the working of the Constitution. On the political front the new formation that emerged at the end of the internal emergency

---

[47] Section 4 (d) LSAA.

[48] The number of all *lok adalats* held in the country up to March 31, 2005 was 457,566: *Nyaya Deep* (the official journal of NALSA), Vol. VI Issue 2, 194.

[49] Ibid. The figures in relation to motor accident *lok adalats* according to the NALSA as on March 31, 2005 are that 854,529 cases have been settled and over Rs. 525 billion have been distributed as compensation.

[50] For e.g., municipal bodies or entities established for the supply of water, electricity or providing public transport.

[51] Sections 22 A to 22 E of LSAA.

[52] See S. Singh, *Legal Aid: Human Right to Equality*, 312 (New Delhi: Deep and Deep, 1998) where the author states, after a survey of the functioning of the scheme in Punjab, 'An all-round dissatisfaction with functioning of the scheme has been recorded. 75.4 percent beneficiaries are discontented with inexperienced advocates and the other 24.6 percent express disinterested counsels as the cause of their dissatisfaction' and further '76.7 percent of the legal aid counsels are with less than 10 years of standing and 63.3 percent of them join for monetary considerations and only 20 percent accept this service with a missionary zeal. The remaining 16.7 percent are legal aid counsels only by the diktats of the judicial officers'. Also see, N.R. Madhava Menon, 'Legal Services Act and Justice to the Poor' *Indian Bar Review*, vol. 14 No. 3 (1987), pp. i–vii at v: 'If a court finds on application by parties indicating their intention to compromise why should it not get the matter settled then and there instead of transferring it to the Lok Adalat?'.

[53] For a critique of the provisions of the LSAA see S. Muralidhar, *Law, Poverty and Legal Aid: Access to Criminal Justice*, (New Delhi: LexisNexis Butterworths, 2004), ch. 3.

[54] A substantial portion of the funding of the state legal services authorities is by grants made by NALSA. For the legal services authorities of 33 states and union territories including the Supreme Court Legal Services Committee, NALSA made an aggregate grant of Rs.2.35 million in 1995–96 (1 USD=45 Indian Rupees approx). This rose to Rs.5.99 million in 1997–98 and Rs.20.54 million in 1999–2000. In 2000–2001, NALSA made an aggregate grant of Rs.30.32 million for only 13 of the 33 states and union territories and the Supreme Court Legal Services Committee, which indicated that only these many authorities had been able to spend the grants made in the previous year.

was unstable. It was already collapsing by 1978/ 1979, which was when the judiciary initiated PIL, an entirely judge-led and judge-dominated movement.[55] The judges who were responsible for this innovation had earlier submitted reports, as part of expert committees, to address the issue of providing effective legal aid.[56] The recommendations in these reports, which envisioned PIL as a tool for delivering legal services, were however not acted upon by the executive government of the day. The development of the jurisprudence of economic, social and cultural (ESC) rights is also inextricably linked to this significant development.

What made PIL unique was that it acknowledged that a majority of the population, on account of their social, economic and other disabilities, were unable to access the justice system. The insurmountable walls of procedure were dismantled and suddenly the doors of the Supreme Court were open for issues that had never reached there before. By relaxing the rules of standing and procedure where even a postcard would be treated as a writ petition, the judiciary ushered in a new phase of activism where litigants were freed from the stranglehold of formal law and lawyering.[57]

The past two decades have witnessed range of PIL cases on diverse issues – human rights, environment, public accountability, judicial accountability, education, to name but a few. In the earliest of the PIL cases, *Hussainara Khatoon v. State of Bihar*[58] the Supreme Court recommended release of the indigent prisoner on personal recognizance bonds, rather than on unaffordable monetary bail bonds. Another instance of creative judicial activism was in moulding reliefs for rickshaw pullers from Punjab facing problems of obtaining finances to purchase rickshaws.[59]

3. NATURE OF ORDERS AND TECHNIQUES OF ENFORCEMENT

In the sphere of economic, social and cultural rights, PIL orders invariably have two distinct parts – the *declaratory* part and the *mandatory* part. Declaratory orders and judgments, without consequential directions to the state authorities, require acceptance by the State as to their binding nature under articles 141 and 144 of the Constitution before implementation can follow. The judgment in *Unnikrishnan J.P. v. State of Andhra Pradesh*[60] is an instance of a declaration: the 'right to education is implicit in and flows from the right to life guaranteed under Article 21'[61] and that 'a child (citizen) has a fundamental right to *free education* up to the age of fourteen years'.[62] The State responded to this declaration nine years later by inserting, through an amendment to the Constitution, article 21-A, which provides for the fundamental right to education for children between the ages of 6 and 14. Mandatory orders, on the other hand, are specific time bound directions to the errant administrative or state authority requiring it to take specific steps. For instance, the PIL that sought strict implementation of the Pre-Natal Diagnostic Techniques (Regulation and Prevention of Misuse) Act, 1994, aimed at preventing the malaise of female foeticide, has witnessed the Supreme Court making periodic orders for time bound compliance.[63] The Court has explained this technique to be that of a 'continuing mandamus' where the Court keeps the case on board over a length of time for ensuring the implementation of its directions.[64]

---

[55] For an analytical account see Upendra Baxi, 'Taking Suffering Seriously: Social Action Litigation in the Supreme Court of India', in Jagga Kapur (ed.), *Supreme Court on Public Interest Litigation*', Vol. I (New Delhi: LIPS Publications, 1998) p. A-91.

[56] The first was a report titled 'Processual Justice to the People' submitted in May 1973 by an expert committee chaired by Justice V. R. Krishna Iyer, which made a strong pitch for reforming the institutions comprising the legal systems as well as the procedures. The second, submitted in 1977 by a committee comprising Justice P. N. Bhagwati and Justice V. R. Krishna Iyer, was titled 'Report on National Juridicare: Equal Justice – Social Justice'. The latter Report drew up a draft legislation institutionalising the legal aid delivery system. Neither report was acted upon.

[57] See generally A. Desai and S. Muralidhar, 'Public Interest Litigation: Potential and Problems' in B.N. Kirpal *et al.* (ed.), *Supreme But Not Infallible: Essays in Honour of the Supreme Court of India* (New Delhi: Oxford University Press, 2000), pp. 159–192.

[58] (1980) 1 SCC 81.

[59] *Azad Rickshaw Pullers' Union v. State of Punjab* (1980) Suppl. SCC 601.

[60] (1993) 1 SCC 645. The case concerned the challenge to the validity of certain provincial state laws regulating the charging of fees by private educational institutions and prohibiting the charging of 'capitation' fees from students seeking admission.

[61] Ibid. p. 730.

[62] Ibid. p. 735. Emphasis added.

[63] *CEHAT v Union of India* (2001) 7 SCALE 477 and (2001) 8 SCALE 325.

[64] *Vineet Narain v. Union of India* (1998) 1 SCC 226.

The Court has been required to be innovative in its PIL jurisdiction and has thereby been able to overcome the apparent difficulties posed by these cases. First, the Court usually is concerned with the importance of the cause and will persist with the case even where it finds that the petitioner is not acting bona fide or where the petitioner does not wish to pursue the case further. In either case, the Court can continue with the petition, even without the presence of the petitioner, by appointing an *amicus curiae* instead.[65] Since the Court does not insist on formal pleadings and petitions in PIL, it usually appoints a senior counsel as *amicus curiae* to assist it in addressing the issue in legal terms, sifting out the relevant facts from the documents and pleadings and in helping sharpen the focus of discussion, conscious of the contingencies of judicial functioning.[66] This however can result in the petitioner losing control of the case, giving rise to understandable misgivings.

Secondly, while deciding disputed facts, the Court will in the first instance call for a response from the Government, local authority and any other opposing party. Where the objectivity or veracity of the response is in doubt, or where there is no response at all, the Court will appoint commissioners to verify the facts and submit a report to the Court.[67] The same device can be adopted at the stage of implementation of the Court's orders.[68] Where technical questions that do not admit of judicially manageable standards are involved, the Court can take the help of commissioners or expert bodies. In environmental matters, the Court usually requests an expert or specialist body, like the National Environment Engineering Research Institute, to ascertain the facts and submit a report to the Court

together with recommendations on possible corrective measures.[69] The Court will hear objections to the report before deciding to either accept[70] or reject it.[71]

The Court usually builds into its directions a forewarning of the consequences of disobedience or non-implementation. Thus, while laying down a detailed schedule for conversion of the mode of motor vehicles plying on Delhi roads to clean fuels, the Court warned that violation of the order would invite action for contempt of court.[72] In the post-judgment phase, too, the Court has often retained the case on board for monitoring the implementation of its directions. Thus the PIL case, in which detailed guidelines concerning arrests were laid down, has been listed with fair regularity and the directions monitored till the present, six years after the main judgment.[73]

4. ANALYSIS OF SPECIFIC RIGHTS

4.1 Right to Work

The right to work is expressed in the Indian Constitution as a directive principle of State policy, which is not enforceable in the courts. Article 41 provides that 'the State shall within the limits of its economic capacity and development, make effective provision for securing the right to work, to education and to public assistance in cases of unemployment, old age, sickness and disablement, and in other cases of undeserved want'.[74] As regards the rights in work, two of the provisions in Chapter III of the Constitution contain enforceable fundamental rights: non-discrimination (article 14) and equality of opportunity in matters of public employment (article 16). There are other DPSP provisions that recognise the rights in work.

---

[65] *Sheela Barse v. Union of India* (1988) 4 SCC 226. See also, *S.P. Anand v. H.D. Deve Gowda* (1996) 6 SCC 734.

[66] A senior advocate has been assisting the Supreme Court as *amicus curiae* in the PIL concerning the protection of forest cover: *T.N. Godavarman Tirmulapad v. Union of India* (1997) 2 SCC 267.

[67] In *M.C. Mehta v. Union of India* (2002) 5 SCALE 8, a lawyer was requested to verify the facts concerning the threat posed to the Taj Mahal by polluting units in the vicinity.

[68] In *Sheela Barse v. Union of India* (1994) 4 SCALE 493, a senior advocate was given the mandate of ensuring the implementation of the judgment of the court in *Sheela Barse v. Union of India* (1993) 4 SCC 204, which had declared the jailing of the mentally ill to be unconstitutional. In the PIL concerning the protection of forest cover, a High Powered Committee appointed by the court has been charged with overseeing the implementation of the court's directions.

[69] In Re: *Bhavani River-Shakti Sugars Ltd.* (1998) 6 SCC 335 and *Indian Council for Enviro-Legal Action v. Union of India* (1996) 3 SCC 212.

[70] In *A.P. Pollution Control Board (II) v. Prof. M.V. Nayudu* (2001) 2 SCC 62, the Court relied on reports of three expert bodies, which concurred in their findings against the grant of exemption to the industrial unit.

[71] *Goa Foundation v. Diksha Holdings* (2001) 2 SCC 97.

[72] *M.C. Mehta v. Union of India* (1998) 6 SCC 63.

[73] *D.K. Basu v. State of West Bengal* (1997) 1 SCC 416 (main judgment). For a sampling of subsequent orders, see those reported in (1999) 7 SCALE 222, (2000) 5 SCALE 353 and (2001) 7 SCALE 487.

[74] This corresponds to Article 6 ICESCR.

Article 42 enjoins the State to make 'provisions for securing just and humane conditions of work and for maternity relief'. Article 43 provides that the State shall endeavour to secure a living wage and a decent standard of life for all workers. There are number of laws, as enumerated in Appendix I of this chapter, that seek to give effect to these DPSPs. The most recent is the National Rural Employment Guarantee Act, 2005, which is an acknowledgement of the minimum core content of the right and requires the State to not only identify a 'poor household' but also provide one able bodied member of such household one hundred days of work to tide over the severe problem of rural unemployment during non-agricultural seasons.

As far as the experience in cases before the courts, the results have not been encouraging. In one of the early cases the enforceability of the right to work was tested. The context was the large-scale abolition of posts of village officers in the State of Tamil Nadu in the south of the country. The Court disagreed with the contention that such abolition of posts would fall foul of the DPSP, stating:

> It would certainly be an ideal state of affairs if work could be found for all the able bodied men and women and everybody is guaranteed the right to participate in the production of national wealth and to enjoy the fruits thereof. But we are today far away from that goal. The question whether a person who ceases to be a government servant according to law should be rehabilitated by giving an alternative employment is, as the law stands today, a matter of policy on which the court has no voice.[75]

A possible approach the Court could have adopted was to keep the case on board and require the Government to formulate a scheme for alternative employment to the workmen. The issue of non-implementation of the law abolishing the pernicious practice of bonded labour came for consideration in *Bandhua Mukti Morcha v. Union of India*.[76] This was a PIL case in the Supreme Court brought by an NGO highlighting the deplorable condition of bonded labourers in a quarry in Haryana, not very far from the Supreme Court. The Court drew on the DPSPs while giving extensive

directions to the state government to enable it to discharge its constitutional obligation towards the bonded labourers:[77]

> The right to live with human dignity enshrined in Article 21 derives its life breath from the Directive Principles of State Policy and particularly clauses (e) and (f) of Article 39 and Article 41 and 42 and at the least, therefore, it must include protection of the health and strength of workers, men and women, and of the tender of age of children against abuse, opportunities and facilities for children to develop in a healthy manner and in conditions of freedom and dignity, educational facilities, just and humane conditions of work and maternity relief. These are the minimum requirements which must exist in order to enable a person to live with human dignity and no State has the right to take any action which will deprive a person of the enjoyment of these essentials.…where legislation is already enacted by the State providing these basic requirements to the workmen and thus investing their right to live with basic human dignity, with concrete reality and content, the State can certainly be obligated to ensure observance of such legislation for inaction on the part of the State in securing implementation of such legislation would amount to denial of the right to live with human dignity enshrined in Article 21.[78]

To overcome the hurdle on account of the non-enforceability of the DPSP provisions, the Court drew on article 21 and in effect recognised the rights in work as being enforceable.[79] But this trend has seen a slow but sure reversal, particularly in the context of the rights in work. For instance, in 1988 in a case concerning the regularisation of the services of a large number of casual

---

[77] Ibid. p. 183, para. 10. In *Central Inland Water Transport Corporation v. Brojo Nath Ganguly* (1986) 3 SCC 227, the Supreme Court held a hire-and-fire policy of a government corporation to be untenable as it would be inconsistent with the DPSP.

[78] Article 42 provides for just and humane conditions of work and maternity relief. Article 39(e) asks the State to direct its policy towards securing that citizens are not by economic necessity forced into avocations unsuited to their age and strength.

[79] It is another matter that the directions given in the *Bandhua Mukti Morcha* case are yet to be fully implemented and the case continues on the Court's list of business for monitoring: see *Bandhua Mukti Morcha v. Union of India* (2002) 6 SCALE 175.

---

[75] *K. Rajendran v. State of Tamil Nadu* (1982) 2 SCC 273, at p. 294, para. 34.

[76] (1984) 3 SCC 161.

(non-permanent) workers in the posts and tele-graphs department of the Government, the Court was prepared to invoke the DPSP and recognise the lack of choice of the disadvantaged worker. It said:

> The Government cannot take advantage of its dominant position, and compel any worker to work even as a casual labourer on starvation wages. It may be that the casual labourer has agreed to work on such low wages. That he has done because he has no other choice. It is poverty that has driven him to that state. The Government should be a model employer. We are of the view that on the facts and in the circumstances of this case the classification of employees into regularly recruited employees and casual employees for the purpose of paying less than the minimum pay payable to employees in the corresponding regular cadres particularly in the lowest rungs of the department where the pay scales are the lowest is not tenable.[80]

However, in October 2005 the question whether this decision requires reversal was considered by the present Supreme Court in a case involving the question of regularising the services of casual workers who had been working for the state government in Karnataka for periods ranging between ten and twenty years.[81]

This trend can also be attributed to the impact of the economic policies that have accompanied liberalisation. In 1983, the Court was prepared to recognise the right of workmen of a company to be heard at the stage of the winding up of such company. The Court invoked article 43A, a constitutional directive principle, which required the State to take suitable steps to secure participation of workers In management.[82] However, in 2001,

in a challenge by workmen to the decision of the Government to divest its shareholding in a public sector undertaking in favour of a private party, the Court refused to recognise any right in the workmen to be consulted.[83] The Supreme Court has also declined to read into the law concerning abolition of contract labour any obligation on the employer to re-employ such labour on a regular basis in the establishment.[84]

In the context of both the right to work and rights in work, the trend of judicial decisions has witnessed a moving away from recognition and enforcement of such rights and towards deferring to executive policy that has progressively denuded those rights.

4.2 Right to Shelter

There is no express recognition of the right to shelter under the Indian Constitution. The judiciary has nevertheless stepped in to recognise this right as forming part of article 21 itself.[85] However, the Court has never really acknowledged a positive obligation on the State to provide housing to the homeless. Even in the much cited decision in *Olga Tellis v. Bombay Municipal Corporation*,[86] where the Court held that the right to life included

---

[80] *Daily Rated Casual Labour Employed under P & T Department v. Union of India* (1988) 1 SCC 122 at paras. 7 and 9; similar orders were made in *Dharwad P.W.D. Employees Association v. State of Karnataka* (1990) 2 SCC 396; *Jacob M. Puthuparambil v. Kerala Water Authority* (1991) 1 SCC 28; *Air India Statutory Corporation v. United Labour Union* (1997) 9 SCC 425.

[81] *Secretary, State of Karnataka v. Umadevi* Order dated (2006) 4 SCC 1. The judgments have been reversed holding that even if the employees had served for a number of years, they could not claim a right to regularisation since tier initial appointment was illegal.

[82] *National Textile Workers Union v. P.R. Ramakrishnan* (1983) 1 SCC 249.

[83] In *BALCO Employees' Union v. Union of India* (2002) 2 SCC 333, the Supreme Court held that there was no requirement of 'prior notice and hearing to persons who are generally affected as a class by an economic policy decision of the government ... the dis-investment policy cannot be faulted if as a result thereof the employees lose their rights or protection under Articles 14 or 16'.

[84] In *Steel Authority of India Ltd. v. National Union Waterfront Workers* (2001) 7 SCC 1, it was contended that when the employment of contract labour is abolished in any establishment, the workers so employed would be left without any remedy and that therefore there must be a corresponding obligation on the employer who violated the law to re-employ them. Negating this argument, the Court said that the principle that a beneficial law required liberal interpretation 'does not extend to reading in the provisions of the Act what the legislature has not provided whether expressly or by necessary implication, or substituting remedy or benefits for that provided by the legislature'. With this, the Court reversed the earlier decision in *Air India Statutory Corporation v. United Labour Union* (1997) 9 SCC 377.

[85] *Shanti Star Builders v. Narayan K. Totame* (1990) 1 SCC 520: 'The right to life ... would take within its sweep the right to food ... and a reasonable accommodation'. In *Bandhua Mukti Morcha v. Union of India* (1991) 4 SCC 177, the Court recognised the right of rescued bonded labour to accommodation as part of their rehabilitation.

[86] (1985) 3 SCC 545.

the right to livelihood, it disagreed with the contention of the pavement dwellers that since they would be deprived of their livelihood if they were evicted from their slum and pavement dwellings, their eviction would be tantamount to deprivation of their life and hence be unconstitutional.[87] This trend has continued ever since. In *Municipal Corporation of Delhi v. Gurnam Kaur*,[88] the Court held that the Municipal Corporation of Delhi had no legal obligation to provide pavement squatters alternative shops for rehabilitation, as the squatters had no legal enforceable right. In *Sodan Singh v. NDMC*,[89] the Supreme Court reiterated that the question whether there can at all be a fundamental right of a citizen to occupy a particular place on the pavement where he can squat and engage in trade must be answered in the negative. In a case concerning slum dwellers in Ahmedabad, despite the Court making observations about the DPSPs creating positive obligations on the State 'to distribute its largesse to the weaker sections of the society envisaged in Article 46 to make socio-economic justice a reality',[90] no actual relief was granted to the slum dwellers.

As in the area of the right to work, there has been a marked regression in the area of the right to shelter, compounded by the bringing of PIL cases to the courts by other classes of residents seeking eviction of slum dwellers as part of the protection and enforcement of the former's rights to a clean and healthy environment as demonstrated by the following case.

FORCED EVICTIONS: A CASE STUDY IN MUMBAI

The PIL case brought by the Bombay Environmental Action Group (BEAG)[91] in the Bombay High Court in February 1995 contended that the Sanjay Gandhi National Park had been encroached upon in a large scale by slum dwellers who had put up unauthorised structures and that the authorities were indifferent to the resultant threat to the park. On the basis of the recommendations of a committee appointed by it to examine the problem, the High Court on May 7, 1997 passed a detailed order in regard to removal of encroachments and eviction of unauthorised occupants. The High Court at this stage did not give any notice or hearing to the slum dwellers. A cut-off date of January 1, 1995 was fixed; those slum dwellers who did not figure in the electoral rolls for the area by that date would be ineligible for any rehabilitation and could be forcibly evicted.[92] The provincial state government was required, within eighteen months, to relocate those eligible to a place outside the boundaries of the National Park and thereafter demolish the structures occupied by them. Until such time electricity and water supply to the structure could be continued.

By the time the case was heard next on July 17, 1999, 20,000 structures had already been demolished, but the rehabilitation of those eligible was yet to be completed. The Government informed the Court that at the alternate sites, which were at a considerable distance, each eligible dweller would be allotted pitches of 15 ft. by 10 ft., for which they each had to pay Rs.7,000 in four instalments. When the slum dwellers complained of arbitrariness in the preparation of lists of eligible persons, the High Court appointed a grievance redressal committee comprising two retired judicial officers and a bureaucrat and mandated that the committee's decision would be final and not be called into question in any court or tribunal. It directed that the map prepared and the survey carried out by the forest department and submitted to the court was to be treated as final.[93]

In a further order passed on March 13, 2000 the High Court expedited the demolitions and decried the attempts by the association of slum dwellers to ask for resettlement on the periphery of the park. The Court said: 'There is no question of this aspect being considered either by the committee appointed by this court or by the petitioners and

---

[87] Ibid. p. 579: 'No one has the right to make use of a public property for a private purpose without the requisite authorisation and, therefore, it is erroneous to contend that the pavement dwellers have the right to encroach upon pavements by constructing dwellings thereon....If a person puts up a dwelling on the pavement, whatever may be economic compulsions behind such an act, his use of the pavement would become unauthorised'.

[88] (1989) 1 SCC 101.

[89] (1989) 4 SCC 155.

[90] *Ahmedabad Municipal Corporation v. Nawab Khan Gulab Khan* (1997) 11 SCC 123.

[91] Writ Petition No. 305/95 (*Bombay Environmental Action Group v. A.R. Bharati*).

[92] Unreported order dated 7.5.1997 in Writ Petition No. 305 of 1995 (*Bombay Environmental Action Group v. A.R. Bharati*).

[93] Order dated 17.7.1999 in W.P. No. 305 of 1995 (*BEAG v. A.R. Bharati*).

for that matter even by the court'.[94] The demolitions soon gained momentum and were carried
out at the rate of 1,000 structures a day with the
alternate sites either not being made available or
not being equipped for any form of resettlement.
Only about 4,000 families could find resources
to pay the amount stipulated. The rest found it
plainly unaffordable. This led to protests that were
brutally put down. The High Court on 17 April,
2000, passed a further order prohibiting demon-
strations and agitations within 1 km of the periphery of the national park. Having no alternative, the
slum dwellers on April 26, 2000, moved an application before the High Court seeking to be joined
in the BEAG's writ petition and be given a hearing. The High Court refused to pass orders and
adjourned the hearing on the application to a date
beyond the summer recess of the court.[95] By then
the demolitions were complete.

A telling feature of the above case is that at no
stage did the BEAG or the Government or even the
Court think it necessary to solicit the views of the
slum dwellers who were in fact the ones directly
affected. None of the orders reflect their point of
view. To compound this, no attempt was made to
find out whether the plan of the park submitted
by the forest department or the list prepared by
it of the eligible encroachers was in fact correct
or not. The device of having the aggrieved slum
dwellers approach a grievance redressal committee and preventing them from approaching
any other court or even the High Court directly,
meant that they would be denied access to justice
and would not have any judicial remedy against
an adverse order made without hearing them.
Inequitably, the burden was on the slum dweller
to show that he was wrongly categorised as being

ineligible for an alternate site. Considering the difficulty for a person to have her name included in
an electoral roll, the choice of the electoral roll
as the qualifying requirement meant that a larger
number of persons would be rendered ineligible
and faced the prospect of immediate demolition of
their hutments and consequent eviction. Preservation of the national park appears to have been
prioritised over the bundle of survival rights – to
shelter, health and education, to name a few – of
the slum dwellers.

4.3   Right to Health

This has been perhaps the least difficult area in
terms of justiciability for the Supreme Court, but
not in terms of enforceability. Article 47 of DPSP
provides for the duty of the State to improve public
health. However, the Court has always recognised
the right to health as being an integral part of the
right to life.[96] The principle was tested in a case of
an agricultural labourer whose condition, after a
fall from a running train, worsened considerably
when as many as seven government hospitals in
Calcutta refused to admit him as they did not have
beds vacant. The Supreme Court did not stop at
declaring the right to health to be a fundamental
right and asked the Government of West Bengal to
pay him compensation for the loss suffered. It also
directed the Government to formulate a blueprint
for primary health care with particular reference to
treatment of patients during an emergency.[97]

In *Consumer Education and Research Centre v.
Union of India*[98] the Supreme Court, in a PIL
case, tackled the problem of health of workers in
the asbestos industry. Noticing that long years of
exposure to the harmful substance could result in

---

[94] Unreported order dated 13.3.2000 of the Bombay High
Court in W.P.305/95 (*BEAG v. A.R. Bharati*). The slum
dwellers found that besides the alternate site at Kalyan
being inaccessible and under-serviced, it was unaffordable for many of them. They had little choice, for if they
did not exercise the option to shift, their present dwelling
would be demolished anyway.

[95] S.L.P.(C) No. Nil/2000 in the Supreme Court (*Nivara Hakk
Welfare Centre v. Bombay Environmental Action Group*).
The adjournment of the application to June 2000 ensured
that a majority of the demolitions took place without hin-
drance. The fact that this was the peak monsoon period in
Mumbai made the situation even more poignant for the
slum dwellers. The Special Leave Petition in the Supreme
Court of India challenging the orders of the High Court
dated 17.7.1999 and 13.3.2000 was dismissed *in limine*.

[96] See *Francis Coralie Mullin* (n. 39 above); *Paramanand
Katara v. Union of India* (1989) 4 SCC 286.

[97] *Paschim Banga Khet Majoor Samity v. State of West Bengal*
(1996) 4 SCC 37.

[98] (1995) 3 SCC 42. A note of caution was struck when government employees protested against the reduction of
their entitlements to medical care. The Court said: 'No
State or country can have unlimited resources to spend
on any of its projects. That is why it only approves its
projects to the extent it is feasible. The same holds good
for providing medical facilities to its citizens including
its employees. Provision of facilities cannot be unlimited.... The principles of fixation of rate and scale under
the new policy is justified and cannot be held to be violative of Article 21 or Article 47 or the Constitution': *State of
Punjab v. Ram Lubhaya Bagga* (1998) 4 SCC 117 at 130.

debilitating asbestosis, the Court mandated the provision of compulsory health insurance for every worker as enforcement of the worker's fundamental right to health. Other health-related issues that have been considered in PILs include the quality of drugs and medicines being marketed in the country,[99] the rights of the mentally ill,[100] and the minimum standards of care to be observed in mental hospitals.[101]

In the area of the right to health, the conceptual framework has not been difficult to evolve with the Court readily recognising it as part of the enforceable right to life.[102] Secondly, the identification of emergency medical care as a core right has been a useful yardstick to evaluate the extent of State obligations. It should be possible to contend that the health policy priorities of the State will have to be tailored to meet these specific minimum obligations.

4.4   Right to Education

The insertion of article 21-A in Part III of the Indian Constitution in the year 2002,[103] which provided for the fundamental right of education to all chil-

---

[99] *Vincent Pannikulangura v. Union of India* (1987) 2 SCC 165; *Drug Action Forum v. Union of India* (1997) 6 SCC 609; *All India Democratic Women Association v. Union of India* (1998) 2 SCALE 360.

[100] *Sheela Barse v. Union of India* (1993) 4 SCC 204.

[101] *Rakesh Chandra Narayan v. Union of India*, 1991 Supp. (2) 626, 1989 Supp (1) SCC 644, 1994 Supp. (3) SCC 478; *Supreme Court Legal Aid Committee v. State of Madhya Pradesh* (1994) 5 SCC 27; 1994 Supp. (3) SCC 489.

[102] In *Paschim Banga* (n. 97 above), the Court said: 'Article 21 imposes an obligation on the State to safeguard the right to life of every person. Preservation of human life is thus of paramount importance. The government hospitals run by the state and the medical officers employed therein are duty bound to extend medical assistance to preserving human life. Failure on the part of the government hospital to provide timely medical treatment to a person in need of such treatment results in the violation of his right to life guaranteed under Article 21'.

[103] Earlier, the right to education was to be found in article 45 of the DPSP, which corresponds to Article 13 (1) ICESCR, and which stated 'the State shall endeavour to provide, within a period of ten years from the commencement of this Constitution, for free and compulsory education for all children until they complete the age of fourteen years'. Thus, while the right of a child not to be employed in hazardous industries was, by virtue of Article 24, recognised to be a fundamental right, the child's right to education was put into Part IV for a period of ten years. Correspondingly Article 45 has also undergone a change (see n. 9 above for present text).

dren between the ages of 6 and 14, occurred at the end of a process that was triggered off by the judgment of the Supreme Court of India in *Unnikrishnan J.P. v. State of Andhra Pradesh*.[104] The occasion was the challenge brought by private medical and engineering colleges to provincial state laws regulating the charging of 'capitation' fees from students seeking admission. The college managements were seeking enforcement of their right to do business. The Court expressly negated this claim and proceeded to examine the nature of the right to education. The Court refused to accept the non-enforceability of the DPSP and the margin of appreciation claimed by the State for its progressive realisation. The Court asked:

> It is noteworthy that among the several articles in Part IV, only Article 45 speaks of a time-limit; no other article does. Has it no significance? Is it a mere pious wish, even after 44 years of the Constitution? Can the State flout the said direction even after 44 years on the ground that the article merely calls upon it to endeavour to provide the same and on the further ground that the said article is not enforceable by virtue of the declaration in Article 37. Does not the passage of 44 years – more than four times the period stipulated in Article 45 – convert the obligation created by the article into an enforceable right? In this context, we feel constrained to say that allocation of available funds to different sectors of education in India discloses an inversion of priorities indicated by the Constitution. The Constitution contemplated a crash programme being undertaken by the State to achieve the goal set out in Article 45. It is relevant to notice that Article 45 does not speak of the "limits of its economic capacity and development" as does Article 41, which inter alia speaks of right to education. What has actually happened is – more money is spent and more attention is directed to higher education than to – and at the cost of – primary education. (By primary education, we mean the education, which a normal child receives by the time he completes 14 years of age). Neglected more so are the rural sectors, and the weaker sections of the society referred to in Article 46. We clarify, we are not seeking to lay down the priorities for the Government – we are only emphasising the constitutional policy as disclosed

---

[104] See n. 60 above.

by Articles 45, 46 and 41. Surely the wisdom of these constitutional provisions is beyond question...[105]

The Court then proceeded to examine how and to what extent this right would be enforceable.[106] The decision in *Unnikrishnan* has been applied by the Court subsequently in formulating broad parameters for compliance by the Government in the matter of eradication of child labour:

Now, strictly speaking a strong case exists to invoke the aid of Article 41 of the Constitution regarding the right to work and to give meaning to what has been provided in Article 47 relating to raising of standard of living of the population, and Articles 39 (e) and (f) as to non-abuse of tender age of children and giving opportunities and facilities to them to develop in a healthy manner, for asking the State to see that an adult member of the family, whose child is in employment in a factory or a mine or in other hazardous work, gets a job anywhere, in lieu of the child. This would also see the fulfillment of the wish contained in Article 41 after about half of a century of its being in the paramount parchment, like primary education desired by Article 45, having been given the status of fundamental right by the decision in *Unnikrishnan*.[107]

The significance of *Unnikrishnan* has been the identification of primary education as a minimum core of the right to education, and this was implicit in the wording of article 45 which set an outer time limit for the 'progressive realisation' of this right. Secondly, it prompted a constitutional amendment that formally acknowledged the transformation of this right from a DPSP to an enforceable fundamental right. The importance of the case also lies in its impact on judicial decision-making where creativity and innovation are key determinants to effective intervention.

4.5 Right to Food

The issue of recurrent famines in some of the drought-prone regions of India has received a mixed reaction in courts. When a PIL case concerning starvation deaths in some of the poorest districts in the state of Orissa was taken up for consideration, the reaction of the Supreme Court in 1989 was to defer to the subjective opinion of the executive Government that the situation was being tackled effectively.[108] In the early 1990s, the National Human Rights Commission (NHRC) was approached by civil society groups to take action, but its intervention also had only limited success.[109] The Indian Supreme Court's current engagement, again in a PIL case, which confronted the paradox of food scarcity while the State's silos overflowed with food grains in the midst of starvation, has been a contrast to the earlier response.

In April 2001, the People's Union for Civil Liberties approached the Court for relief after several states in the country faced their second or third successive year of drought and, despite having 50 million tonnes of food stocks, failed to make available the minimum food requirements to the vast drought-stricken population. To begin with, the Court identified the area of immediate concern, ordering governments 'to see that food is provided to the aged, infirm, disabled, destitute women, destitute

---

[105] Ibid. p. 733, paras. 172, 181 and 183.

[106] Ibid. paras. 181 and 182, the Court explained: 'The right to education further means that a citizen has a right to call upon the State to provide educational facilities to him within the limits of its economic capacity and development. By saying so, we are not transferring Article 41 from Part IV to Part III – we are merely relying upon Article 41 to illustrate the content of the right to education flowing from Article 21. We cannot believe that any State would say that it need not provide education to its people even within the limits of its economic capacity and development. It goes without saying that the limits of economic capacity are, ordinarily speaking, matters within the subjective satisfaction of the State'.

[107] This it did in a PIL, *M.C. Mehta v. State of Tamil Nadu* (1996) 6 SCC 772. Further in para. 31 it said: 'We are, however, not asking the State at this stage to ensure alternative employment in every case covered by Article 24, as Article 41 speaks about right to work "within the limits of the economic capacity and development of the State." The very large number of child labour in the aforesaid occupations would require giving of job to a very large number of adults, if we were to ask the appropriate Government to assure alternative employment in every case, which would strain the resources of the State, in case it would not have been able to secure job for an adult in a private sector establishment or, for that matter, in a public sector organisation. We are not issuing any direction to do so presently. Instead, we leave the matter to be sorted

out by the appropriate Government. In those cases where it would not be possible to provide job as above mentioned, the appropriate Government would, as its contribution/grant, deposit in the aforesaid Fund a sum of Rs.5,000/- for each child employed in a factory or mine or in any other hazardous employment'.

[108] *Kishen Pattanayak v. State of Orissa* (1989) Supp. (1) SCC 258.

[109] Annual Report of the NHRC for the year 1995–1996.

men who are in danger of starvation, pregnant and lactating women and destitute children, especially in cases where they or members of their family do not have sufficient funds to provide food for them'.[110] The states were directed to ensure that all the Public Distribution System (PDS) shops were reopened and made functional. Thereafter the states were asked to identify the below poverty line (BPL) families in a time-bound schedule and information was sought on the implementation of various Government schemes that were meant to help people cope with the crisis.[111]

This was followed by identification by the Court of the most vulnerable states where hunger and starvation were widespread. On November 28, 2001, the Court made a detailed order containing three major components:[112]

- The benefits available under eight nutrition-related schemes of the Government were recognised as entitlements.
- All state governments were asked to provide cooked midday meals for all children in government and government-assisted schools.
- Governments were asked to adopt specific measures for ensuring public awareness and transparency of the programmes.

Acting on the information provided to it, the Court was able to specify the minimum quantities of food and nutrition that had to be made available: each child up to the age of six years was to receive 300 calories and 8–10 grams of protein; each adolescent girl 500 calories and 20–25 grams of protein; each malnourished child 600 calories and 16–20 grams of protein. Following up on this, the Supreme Court in May 2002 gave further directions empowering village administrative bodies (gram sabhas) to oversee the distribution of food supplies under the schemes and setting up grievance redressal mechanisms.

The right to food petition has been instrumental in ensuring the extension of the mid-day meal programme to most of the states in the country. Civil

society groups have used the Court's orders as a useful campaign tool and to seek accountability and information from ration shops under the public distribution system. The Court on its part has persisted with the monitoring of its directions and the supervision of the effectiveness of the steps taking in compliance with its directions.[113]

5. IMPACT OF JUDICIAL INTERVENTION

The intervention by the Court in a wide range of issues, including those involving economic, social and cultural rights, has generated a debate about the competence and legitimacy of the judiciary in entering areas which have for long been perceived as belonging properly within the domain of the other organs of state.[114] But that by itself may not explain the necessity for the Court's intervention in the larger perspective of the development of the law and of healthy democratic practices that reinforce public accountability. To place the debate in its perspective, it may be necessary to briefly recapitulate the implications of judicial intervention through PIL in the area of ESC rights.

The positive implications include:

- Finding a space for an issue that would otherwise not have invited sufficient attention. The decision in *Vishaka*,[115] for instance, has brought into public discourse the issue of sexual harassment of women in the workplace, which had otherwise been ignored by the executive and the legislature. It becomes immediately useful, as a law declared by the Supreme Court, to demand recognition and enforcement of the right to access judicial redress against the injury caused to women at the workplace.
- Catalysing changes in law and policy in the area of ESC rights. Many of the recent changes in law and policy relating to education in general, and primary education in particular, are owed to the decision in *Unnikrishnan*.[116]
- Devising benchmarks and indicators in several key areas concerning ESC rights. For instance, the decision in *Paschim Banga*[117] delineates the

---

[110] *People's Union for Civil Liberties v. Union of India* (2001) 5 SCALE 303.

[111] *People's Union for Civil Liberties v. Union of India* (2001) 7 SCALE 484.

[112] Order dated November 28, 2001, in W.P.(C) No. 196/2001 (*People's Union for Civil Liberties v. Union of India*). The website <http://www.righttofoodindia.org/> contains the complete text of all orders as well as the petition.

[113] *People's Union for Civil Liberties v. Union of India* (2004) 8 SCALE 759.

[114] See generally, Desai and Muralidhar (n. 57 above).

[115] See n. 26 above.

[116] See n. 60 above.

[117] See n. 10 above.

right to emergency medical care for accident victims as forming a core minimum of the right to health and the orders in *PUCL v. Union of India*[118] underscore the right of access for those below the poverty line to food supplies as forming the bare non-derogable minimum that is essential to preserve human dignity.

• Development of a jurisprudence of human rights that comports with the development of international law. PIL cases concerning environmental issues have enabled the Court to develop and apply the 'polluter pays principle',[119] the precautionary principle,[120] and the principle of restitution.[121]

There are a host of other issues that arise in the context of the Court's intervention through PIL and to some of these we now turn.

5.1 Court as Arbiter of the Conflict of Public Interests

The PIL case brought before the Supreme Court in 1994 by the Narmada Bachao Andolan (NBA), a mass-based organisation representing those affected by the large-scale project involving the construction of over 3,000 large and small dams across the Narmada river flowing through Madhya Pradesh, Maharashtra and Gujarat, provided the site for a contest of what the Court perceived as competing public interests: the right of the inhabitants of the water-starved regions of Gujarat and Rajasthan to water for drinking and irrigation on the one hand and the rights to shelter and livelihood of over 41,000 families comprising tribals, small farmers, and fishing communities facing displacement on the other. In its decision in 2000, the Court was unanimous that the Sardar Sarovar Project (SSP) did not require re-examination either on the ground of its cost-effectiveness or in regard to the aspect of seismic activity. The area of justiciability was confined to the rehabilitation of those displaced by the SSP.[122] By a majority of two to

one,[123] the Court struck out the plea that the SSP had violated the fundamental rights of the tribals because it expected that: 'At the rehabilitation sites they will have more, and better, amenities than those enjoyed in their tribal hamlets. The gradual assimilation in the mainstream of society will lead to betterment and progress'.[124] The Court acknowledged that in deciding to construct the dam 'conflicting rights had to be considered. If for one set of people namely those of Gujarat, there was only one solution, namely, construction of a dam, the same would have an adverse effect on another set of people whose houses and agricultural land would be submerged in water'.[125] However, 'when a decision is taken by the government after due consideration and full application of mind, the court is not to sit in appeal over such decision'.[126] Even while it was aware that displacement of the tribal population 'would undoubtedly disconnect them from the past, culture, custom and traditions', the Court explained it away on the utilitarian logic that such displacement 'becomes necessary to harvest a river for the larger good'.[127]

5.2 Legitimacy and Competence

The majority opinion in the Narmada case further highlighted the two principal concerns of the justiciability debate – legitimacy and competence. It declared that 'if a considered policy decision has been taken, which is not in conflict with any law or is not malafides, it will not be in public interest to require the court to go into and investigate those areas which are the functions of the executive'.[128] Further, 'whether to have an infrastructural [sic] project or not and what is the type of project to be undertaken and how it is to be

---

[118] See notes 110 to 113 above.
[119] *S. Jagannath v. Union of India* (1997) 2 SCC 87.
[120] *Vellore Citizens' Welfare Forum v. Union of India* (1996) 5 SCC 647.
[121] *In Re: Bhavani River-Shakti Sugars Ltd.* (1998) 6 SCC 335.
[122] *Narmada Bachao Andolan v. Union of India* (2000) 10 SCC 664 at 696: '[I]t was only the concern of this court for the protection of the fundamental rights of the oustees under

Article 21 of the Constitution of India which led to the entertaining of this petition'.
[123] Kirpal J. wrote the majority opinion for himself and Anand CJ, ibid., while Bharucha J. dissented on the question of environmental clearance, which he found to be mandatory and non-existent and further on the consequent issue of *pari passu* rehabilitation of the oustees, which again he found to be wholly unsatisfactory. While the majority opinion permitted the raising of the height of the dam, the dissenting opinion would have injuncted further construction till the grant of environment clearance and prior satisfactory rehabilitation of the oustees.
[124] Ibid. pp. 702–03.
[125] Ibid. p. 764.
[126] Ibid.
[127] Ibid. p. 765.
[128] Ibid. p. 703.

executed, are part of policy-making process and the courts are ill-equipped to adjudicate on a policy decision so undertaken'.[129] The dissenting opinion, however, found that there was in fact no environmental clearance for the project as required by the law and it directed that till such clearance was accorded 'further construction work on the dam shall cease'.[130] The majority's concerns about lack of competence to adjudicate on the issues raised was answered in the dissent thus: 'The many interim orders that this court made in the years in which this writ petition was pending show how very little had been done in regard to the relief and rehabilitation of those ousted. It is by reason of the interim orders, and, in fairness, the cooperation and assistance of learned counsel who appeared for the states, that much that was wrong has now been redressed'.[131]

The issue of displacement of large sections of the population on account of the construction of a multi-purpose dam and the question of their right to rehabilitation again came up for consideration in *N.D. Jayal v. Union of India*.[132] This was a PIL questioning the decision taken to construct the Tehri Dam at the confluence of the Bhagirathi and Bhilangana rivers in the Garhwal region of the Himalayas in the State of Uttaranchal. The petitioners contended that the structure of the dam and its location in a seismically active zone rendered it unsafe with the potential for irreversible harm to human life as well as the environment. The other issue concerned the rehabilitation of those in the villages that would be either fully or partially affected by the dam.[133] It was contended that the environment clearance was conditional upon *pari passu* implementation of the rehabilitation and environmental plans and that in the

absence of the rehabilitation of those affected, the construction of the dam ought not to be permitted. Two of the three judges constituting the bench that heard the case declined to examine the safety aspects of the dam, following the dictum in the *Narmada* decision holding that:

> [W]hen the government or the authorities concerned after due consideration of all view points and full application of mind took a decision, then it is not appropriate for the court to interfere. Such matters must be left to the mature wisdom of the Government or the implementing agency. It is their forte.... The consideration in such cases is in the process of decision and not in its merits.[134]

In regards to the rehabilitation issue, the Court accepted the version of the Government that there was 'substantial compliance with all the conditions'[135] and that the monitoring of the fulfilment of the conditions for environment clearance would be done by the High Court of Uttaranchal.

The dissenting judge differed on both aspects of safety as well as rehabilitation. Applying the precautionary principle based in international environmental law, but which had also become part of domestic law, it was held that 'it is only after 3-D non-linear analysis of the dam is completed and the opinion of the experts on the safety aspects is again sought that further impoundment of the dam should be allowed'.[136] For the first time perhaps, it was thus acknowledged that:

> [T]here are economic costs as well as social costs and environmental costs involved in a project of construction of a large dam. The social cost is also too heavy. It results in widespread displacement of local people from their ancestral habitat and loss of their traditional occupations. The displacement of

---

[129] Ibid. p. 762. The majority opinion envisioned the role of the court thus: 'the central government had taken a decision to construct a dam as that was the only solution available to it for providing water to the water-scarce areas. It was known at that time that people will be displaced and will have to be rehabilitated. There is no material to enable this court to come to the conclusion that the decision was mala fide. A hard decision need not necessarily be a bad decision'.

[130] Ibid. p. 783.

[131] Ibid. p. 784.

[132] (2004) 9 SCC 362.

[133] It was noticed in the judgment (p. 394 SCC) that the project would fully affect 37 villages, 88 villages partially and the entire Tehri town, which would get submerged as a result of the dam.

[134] Ibid., p. 380. The majority reiterated an earlier judgment by the Supreme Court in *Tehri Bandh Virodhi Sangarsh Samiti v. State of U.P.* (1992) Supp. 1 SCC 44 where the Court had declined to go into the safety aspects of the Tehri Dam. However, after the dismissal of that petition, on October 21, 1991, an earthquake measuring 6.1 on the Richter scale hit the Garhwal region, killing 2,000 people and causing massive damage to the villages, the Tehri town and to the constructions made for the dam. This prompted the second petition filed on December 7, 1991 by N.D. Jayal and other human rights and environment activists in the Supreme Court.

[135] Ibid. p. 402.

[136] Ibid. p. 415.

economically weaker sections of the society and tribals is the most serious aspect of displacement from the point of view of uprooting them from their natural surroundings. Absence of these surroundings in the new settlement colonies shatters their social, cultural and physical links.[137]

The conflict of rights in the context of dams and power projects was also noticed:

> When such social conflicts arise between the poor and more needy on one side and rich or affluent or less needy on the other, prior attention has to be paid to the former group which is both financially and politically weak. Such less-advantaged group is expected to be given prior attention by a welfare state like ours which is committed and obliged by the Constitution, particularly by its provisions contained in the preamble, fundamental rights, fundamental duties and directive principles, to take care of such deprived sections of people who are likely to lose their home and source of livelihood.[138]

The purported major premise of the *Narmada* and *Tehri* decisions that it would neither be legitimate nor competent for courts to enter into the arena of policy decisions of the State concerning ESC rights is of course also belied in the decisions in certain other PIL cases that suggest otherwise.

5.3 Environment v. Livelihood: An Avoidable Problem

There are other contexts in which the Court's decisions exacerbate the conflicts between competing sets of rights and interests. In a PIL case concerning protection of the country's forest cover, the Supreme Court has, with a view to ensuring strict implementation of the various statutes concerning forests, given wide-ranging directions, including the complete ban on the felling of trees all over the country, directing that governments will permit cutting of trees only after obtaining prior permission of the Court on a case by case basis[139] and setting up of a High Powered Committee to take over the functions of the state administration in regard to granting of licences for felling timber and imposing penalties for violations.[140] The directions have had the effect of not only unilaterally and severely restricting the rights of forest dwellers to remain in and access the forests for fuel and other produce for their basic survival, but have also questioned the very legality of their status.[141] This has, however, not been accounted for by the Court and the attempts by the affected persons to access the courts for redress have been either denied or severely curtailed.[142]

A PIL case brought forth seeking clearing of solid waste/garbage in the major metropolises in the country, witnessed a concerted attempt by the Court, inter alia, to strictly enforce municipal laws that penalise littering of streets,[143] to explore the possibility of privatising the work of clearing garbage[144] and exempting the workforce from the protective cover of labour welfare legislation.[145] Of equal concern was the Court's perception that slum clearance was interrelated with garbage disposal since, according to the Court, 'slums generated a great deal of solid waste'.[146] Likening slum dwellers on public land to 'pickpockets', the Court called for an explanation as to why large chunks of land acquired by the land development agency

---

[137] Ibid. p. 409. The dissent noticed an earlier order of the Supreme Court passed in *Karjan Jalasay Yojana Assargrasth Sahkar Ane Sangarsh Samiti v. State of Gujarat* 1986 Supp. SCC 350, where in the context of acquisition of land for the construction of a dam, the Supreme Court mandated that while taking possession of the land the Government would simultaneously 'provide alternative dwelling to the person who is dispossessed, so that the person dispossessed should not be without roof over his head even for a single day'. If alternative land or alternative employment was not arranged by the Government it would 'pay to the head of the family at the latter's place of residence compensation equivalent to minimum wage every fortnight during the period alternative land or employment is not provided'.

[138] Ibid. p. 418. The dissenting judge noticed that out of a total of 9,239 rural affected families, cash compensation had not been paid to 1,948 families.

[139] *T.N. Godavarman Tirumulkpad v. Union of India* (1997) 2 SCC 267.

[140] *T.N. Godavarman Tirumulkpad v. Union of India* (2000) 6 SCC 413.

[141] Other PILs by environmentalists which have not adequately accounted for the concerns of forest dwellers include *Pradeep Kishen v. Union of India* (1996) 8 SCC 599 and *Animal & Environmental Legal Defense Fund v. Union of India* (1997) 3 SCC 549.

[142] For e.g., see *T.N. Godavarman Tirumulkpad v. Union of India* (2000) 10 SCC 494.

[143] *Almitra H. Patel v. Union of India* (2000) 1 SCALE 568.

[144] *Almitra H. Patel v. Union of India* (2000) 8 SCC 19.

[145] *Almitra H. Patel v. Union of India* (2000) 2 SCC 166.

[146] *Almitra H. Patel v. Union of India* (2000) 8 SCC 19.

were occupied by slums.[147] This was done without affording the slum dwellers an opportunity of being heard and oblivious to the direct conflict of two competing public interests: the right of one set of urban dwellers to a clean environment and that of the slum dwellers to shelter.[148]

5.4 Mass Disasters, Mass Torts

The failures of the formal legal system in India, in the context of mass disasters, are best exemplified by the litigation arising out of the Bhopal Disaster as the following case study demonstrates.

THE BHOPAL GAS LEAK DISASTER: CASE STUDY

When the lethal MIC gas leaked from the factory of Union Carbide India Limited (now Eveready Industries India Limited) on the night of December 23, 1984, it triggered off not just one mass disaster, but several of them. Twenty years after the event, we have voluminous data that reveals a mind-boggling myriad of multiple disasters on several fronts.

Soon after the event, the Indian Parliament in 1985 enacted the Bhopal Gas Leak Disaster (Processing of Claims) Act, 1985, by which the Union of India would be the sole plaintiff representing all the victims of the disaster who would be potential claimants for compensation in a court of law. This, it was believed, would ensure effective access to justice for the Bhopal gas victims. Armed with this Act, the Union of India filed a suit for compensation against Union Carbide Corporation (UCC) before Judge Keenan of the Southern District Court, New York. UCC erected a preliminary defence: it sought to demonstrate that the proper forum for adjudication of this suit was not the court in New York, but the one in India. UCC's expert witness in those proceedings, Nani

Palkhivala, glibly asserted on affidavit: 'There is no doubt that the Indian judicial system can fairly and satisfactorily handle the Bhopal litigation'.[149] Accepting Palkhivala's description of the Indian legal system, Judge Keenan dismissed the suit subject to UCC submitting to the jurisdiction of Indian courts. Thereafter, in September 1986, the Union of India filed its suit against the UCC in the District Court in Bhopal. In February 1989, the Supreme Court of India approved a settlement whereby UCC would pay the victims $US 470 million in full and final settlement of all civil and criminal claims, in the present and in the future. There was a huge public outcry that the settlement was a 'sell-out'. Review petitions were filed challenging it. The Supreme Court justified its acceptance of the settlement on February 14, 1989 on the ground that 'this court, considered it a compelling duty, both judicial and humane, to secure immediate relief to the victims'.[150]

Twenty years after the settlement, the relief to the victims has been neither adequate nor immediate. The presumptions on which the settlement was worked out, 3,000 dead and 100,000 injured, underestimated the extent of the figures by a factor of five. In March 2003, the official figures of the awarded death claims stood at 15,180 persons and awarded injury claims at 553,015 persons. The range of compensation which was assumed would be paid in the settlement order was Rs. 100,000 to 300,000 for a death claim, Rs. 25,000 to 100,000 for temporary disablement and Rs. 50,000 to 200,000 for permanent disablement. However, each death claim has resulted in an award of not more than Rs. 100,000 and overwhelmingly an injury claim has been settled for as little as Rs. 25,000.

The astounding and inexplicable feature of the 'settlement' was that UCC was absolved of any liability for future claims. The defenceless population in Bhopal have been left to fend for themselves

---

[147] *Almitra H. Patel v. Union of India* (2000) 1 SCALE 568 at 570.

[148] Similarly, the Court's directions to relocate the pollution-causing industries in Delhi to the neighbouring states has resulted in severe dislocation and loss of livelihoods to thousands of workmen. The main order for closure is reported as *M.C. Mehta v. Union of India* (1996) 4 SCC 750. The subsequent orders highlighting the plight of the affected workmen are reported under the same description in (1999) 2 SCC 91; (2000) 5 SCC 525 and (2000) 8 SCC 535.

[149] Affidavit dated December 18, 1985, of Nani Ardeshir Palkhivala in support of defendant UCC's motion for dismissal on Forum Non Conveniens Grounds – reproduced in Upendra Baxi and Thomas Paul (eds), *Mass Disasters and Multinational Liability: The Bhopal Case* (New Delhi: N.M. Tripathi, 1986), pp. 222–227, at 225.

[150] *Union Carbide Corporation v. Union of India* (1989) 3 SCC 38 at 43. In the judgment in the review petitions (*Union Carbide Corporation v. Union of India* (1991) 4 SCC 584) the Supreme Court upheld the settlement as regards the civil liability but reopened the criminal cases against the UCC, its Indian counterpart and directors and employees.

with no protocol for treatment being available to date. The report of the Gas Relief Department of the Government of Madhya Pradesh dated December 3, 1997 indicated that 22.8 per cent of the affected population suffered from general ailments, 62.46 per cent from throat disorders, 3.32 per cent from eye disorders, 5 per cent from potential disorders and 4.61 per cent from mental disorders. A study conducted in 1990 of 522 patients at two government hospitals meant for the gas victims revealed that over 35 per cent of the patients had been prescribed irrational, banned or unnecessary medicines; and 72 per cent had been given medicines that had no effect at all. A study undertaken by the International Medical Commission on Bhopal (IMCB) confirmed that the victims received at best only temporary symptomatic relief. Further, 'the inadequacies of the government's health care system has led to a flourishing business situation for private medical practitioners. In the severely affected areas nearly 70 per cent of the private doctors are not even professionally qualified, yet they form the mainstay of medical care in Bhopal'.[151] The petition also pointed out the findings of the Comptroller and Auditor General that there were numerous financial irregularities in the utilisation of the grants already made. Another serious issue pointed out was that '70% of the equipment in the hospitals and clinics under the department of gas relief are dysfunctional'[152] and that there was a severe shortage of medicines and availability of medical facilities in Bhopal.[153] This necessitated another PIL case by the victims in which the Supreme Court has issued directions appointing expert committees to monitor the medical relief and rehabilitation aspects.[154]

The continuing suffering of the Bhopal gas victims has been compounded by the inability of the legal system to provide meaningful and effective redress. The disaster answers the prognosis of Marc Galanter that 'at its best, the Indian legal system's treatment of civil claims is slow and cumbrous'.[155]

6. ASSESSMENT OF INDIAN EXPERIENCE

The discussion in this piece has largely concentrated upon the decisions of the Indian Supreme Court. The decades of the 1970s and 1980s witnessed a concerted move by the Court to transcend its earlier conservative phase and give a positive direction to the Court's intervention in issues concerning the poor and the disadvantaged. It did this through a creative interpretation of constitutional provisions and a welcome assertion of its powers. The judicial innovation of PIL as a tool to enable access to justice defined a new chapter in the evolution of the Supreme Court as a central player in people's lives.

There has been a discernible shift in the approach of the Court over the past two decades to issues concerning economic and social rights. The explicit adaptation of international law standards has been sporadic although one instance is the case concerning the sexual harassment of women in the workplace.[156] However, there are a number of cases where the orders passed are perfectly consistent with those norms. For instance, the directions issued in the cases concerning emergency medical care, compulsory free primary education and the right to food recognise the State obligation to provide the minimum core of the social right. However, as the decisions in the areas of the right to work and the right to shelter reveal, the judiciary appears to have unquestioningly deferred to executive policy that has progressively denuded these rights. The policy decision to continue with large dams and projects that result in the displacement of millions of people, many of them already socially and economically disadvantaged, has resulted in weakening the ability of such populations to find meaningful livelihood consistent with their right to human dignity. It results in depriving them of a host of other economic and social rights as well. The fact that many of these policies are in a draft form and are inconsistent with state obligations under constitutional and international law only adds to the difficulty.

The courts when approached with petitions seeking enforcement of economic and social rights are

[151] W.P.(C) No. 50 of 1998 (*Bhopal Gas Peedit Mahila Udyog Sanghatan v. Union of India*) in the Supreme Court of India, para. 12.
[152] Ibid. para. 16.
[153] Ibid. paras. 24.1 and 2.
[154] *Bhopal Gas Peedit Mahila Udyog Sanghatan v. Union of India* (2004) 8 SCALE 128 and 129.
[155] Affidavit dated December 5, 1985 of Marc Selig Galanter in support of Union of India's Claim, reproduced in Upen-

dra Baxi and Thomas Paul, *Mass Disasters and Multinational Liability: The Bhopal Case* (New Delhi: N.M. Tripathi, 1986) pp. 161–180 at p. 178.
[156] *Vishaka* (n. 26 above).

often required to contend with barriers erected by the law and policy divide, the legitimacy and competence conundrum and the conflict of rights and public interests, to name a few. The discussion in this piece shows how their efforts at overcoming these barriers are not consistent and at times ineffective. The need for the intervention of the Court is nevertheless underscored by whatever positive impact it has had thus far on policy and law making in the sphere of economic and social rights. It has also helped to establish judicial standards for testing the reasonableness of executive and legislative action. Also, till the objective of providing effective access to justice through an institutionalised model of legal services delivery is achieved, the use of PIL as a legal aid tool will have to be persisted with.

The unfinished agenda is a long one indeed. The Bhopal Gas disaster continues to be a grim reminder of the inability of the legal system to cope with the challenges posed by such calamities.[157] It also serves to highlight the pervasive influence of transnational corporations in both law and policy making. The increasing instances of the State withdrawing from its welfare role and resorting to privatisation of the control and distribution of basic community resources like water and electricity and for providing health care and education are a cause for concern for those wishing to assert the obligation of the State in the spheres of economic and social rights. The withdrawal of the State in these areas results in a prominent role for the corporate sector in the control of common resources of the community. While on the one hand this transition requires to be contested on the political and judicial fronts, there is a need for the law to clearly demarcate the liability of the corporate sector for the violation of economic and social rights. The international law standards, as much as domestic law, have to be shaped to meet this challenge. The Indian legal system is faced with the challenge of having to learn from the past and order its future. The Indian people have much hope and expectation of it.

---

[157] Further, the costs and losses arising out of the Bhopal gas leak disaster have had to be borne by the victim. As pointed out by a legal scholar: 'There is considerable neglect of the costs that are generated in an accident or disaster which, therefore, remains beyond the reckoning that is undertaken in determining compensation. The externalizing of losses and costs, apart from making of compensation an inadequate guide to understanding the cost of the accident or disaster, also reveals the law's expectation that a victim bear a part of the cost. The consequent impoverishment that results is not, it would appear, within the law's ken'. Usha Ramanathan, 'A Critical Analysis of the Laws Relating to Compensation for Personal Injury', Thesis submitted for the Degree of Doctor of Philosophy, Delhi University, September 2001, p. 356.

Appendix I

Table showing illustrative list of statutes corresponding to particular economic, social and cultural (ESC) rights in provisions in the Indian Constitution.

Provision of the Indian Constitution	Corresponding Law Enacted by the Indian Parliament
Article 14 – Equality before the law and equal protection of laws Article 39(d) – Equal pay for equal work	Equal Remuneration Act, 1976
Article 15(3) – Affirmative action provision for women and children Article 39(f) – Right of children against exploitation	Protection of Women in Domestic Violence Act, 2005 Juvenile Justice (Care and Protection of Children) Act, 2000 The Child Labour (Prohibition and Regulation) Act, 1986
Article 17 – Prohibition of untouchability	Protection of Civil Rights Act, 1955 Scheduled Castes and Scheduled Tribes (Prevention of Atrocities) Act, 1986 The Employment of Manual Scavengers and Construction of Dry Latrines (Prohibition) Act, 1993
Article 23 – Prohibition of traffic in human beings and forced labour	The Immoral Traffic (Prevention) Act, 1956 The Bonded Labour System (Abolition) Act, 1976 The Contract Labour (Regulation and Abolition) Act, 1970
Article 24 – Prohibition of employment of children below 14 years in hazardous occupation	Factories Act, 1948 The Child Labour (Prohibition and Regulation) Act, 1986
Article 39 A – Equal justice and free legal aid	The Legal Services Authorities Act, 1987
Article 41 – Right to work	The National Rural Employment Guarantee Act, 2005
Article 42 – Just and humane conditions of work Article 43 – Living wage for workers	Minimum Wages Act, 1948 Payment of Wages Act, 1936 The Employees State Insurance Act, 1948 Maternity Benefit Act, 1961 The Beedi and Cigar Workers (Conditions of Employment) Act, 1966 The Plantations Labour Act, 1951
Article 46 – Promotion of interests of SCs, STs and weaker sections	Scheduled Castes and Scheduled Tribes (Prevention of Atrocities) Act, 1988
Article 47 – Right to minimum standard of living and public health	Mental Health Act, 1987
Article 51(c) – Respect for international law and treaty obligations	The Protection of Human Rights Act, 1993 The Persons with Disabilities (Equal Opportunities, Protection of Rights and Full Participation) Act, 1995

Note: This is only an illustrative and not an exhaustive list; the statutes enacted by the legislatures of each of the states are not included.

6

South Asia

Economic and Social Rights Case Law of Bangladesh, Nepal, Pakistan and Sri Lanka

Iain Byrne* and Sara Hossain**

1. INTRODUCTION

This chapter sets out a non-exhaustive survey[1] of four key South Asian jurisdictions – Bangladesh, Nepal, Pakistan and Sri Lanka.[2] In doing so, it reveals the development by courts in each country of a rich and fertile seam of law that has contributed over two decades to advancing the recognition of economic and social rights (ESRs) not merely in the region, but globally.

While many working on ESRs both inside and outside the region are increasingly familiar with the decisions of the Indian Supreme Court, they appear less so with the judgments handed down by courts in the other countries within South Asia, which are largely based on each country's particular constitutional and statutory arrangements and socio-economic and cultural contexts.

With the exception of Bhutan and Nepal, all of the South Asian countries were colonised by the British Empire (subsequently becoming members of the Commonwealth) and adopted the common law system with some variations (especially Sri Lanka). All the countries apply personal status laws based on religion, which vary depending on the community concerned, to determine rights within the family. All have similar court systems, with superior courts adjudicating on fundamental rights claims and with the Supreme Court hearing constitutional writ petitions directly (India, Nepal, Sri Lanka) or on appeal from High Courts (Bangladesh, Pakistan), which have original jurisdiction to do so.[3]

The constitutions of Bangladesh, Nepal, Pakistan and Sri Lanka are very much products of their time reflecting the socialist vision of post-colonial states in the second half of the twentieth century and pledging a fundamental commitment to democracy and to norms of equality and non-discrimination. All offer varying levels of protection to economic and social rights, mainly but not exclusively through Directive or Fundamental Principles of State Policy, as in the case of India. Although considered non-justiciable, they have been increasingly invoked to give meaning

* Iain Byrne is Senior Lawyer for the Commonwealth and Economic and Social Rights Programme at INTERIGHTS and a Fellow of the Human Rights Centre, Essex University. The authors would like to acknowledge the research assistance of Najrana Imaan, and the contributions of Sapana Malla and Rup Narayan Shrestha with the Nepal references in the preparation of this chapter.
** Sara Hossain is an Advocate of the Supreme Court of Bangladesh, and a former Senior Lawyer for the South Asia Programme at INTERIGHTS.

[1] The focus of this chapter is on writ petitions involving the direct application of fundamental rights. In addition, the scope of this chapter means that we cannot hope to cover extensively all of the different economic and social rights that come before South Asian courts in depth, e.g., there is jurisprudence on employment and property rights law which is not featured here but which has been extensively covered in other publications on those particular disciplines.

[2] In this chapter, we refer to South Asia as comprising the countries which form part of the South Asian Association for Regional Cooperation (SAARC), namely Afghanistan, Bangladesh, Bhutan, India, Maldives, Nepal and Sri Lanka. See <http://saarc-sec.org>.

[3] In Bangladesh, the Appellate Division of the Supreme Court hears appeals from writ petitions regarding, among others, enforcement of fundamental rights, while the High Court Division has original jurisdiction over such writ petitions; in India, the Supreme Court directly hears such petitions, and may also hear appeals from original petitions before the various High Courts; in Nepal, the Supreme Court adjudicates directly on fundamental rights claims; in Pakistan, the Supreme Court hears appeals from the various High Courts which have original jurisdiction over writ petitions, and in Sri Lanka, the Supreme Court hears fundamental rights petitions directly.

to the contours of the fundamental right to life. The commitment of each State to UN standards on economic and social rights (in a part of the world where no regional mechanism exists) is high, at least in terms of ratification.

This chapter begins in Section 2 by outlining the nature of constitutional and judicial protection of economic and social rights in each of the four countries. Consideration is given to issues of standing, the use of international instruments and horizontal application of rights. In section 3, the relationship of economic and social rights jurisprudence to gender issues is examined, followed by a comprehensive examination of various substantive rights in Section 4.

2. NATURE OF CONSTITUTIONAL AND JUDICIAL PROTECTION OF ECONOMIC AND SOCIAL RIGHTS IN EACH COUNTRY

None of the South Asian constitutions contain a comprehensive set of justiciable fundamental economic and social rights. Instead, such guarantees are mostly contained in a set of Directive or Fundamental Principles of State Policy[4] which, as in India, are intended to act as a guide to the executive in governing the country but do not have the same status as enforceable rights. Many of the provisions are similar in nature and provide a detailed and extremely progressive set of policy aims. The courts in each country have taken varying positions with regard to the extent to which they interpret these Principles as imposing any binding obligations on the state.

All four countries have a good record of having acceded to the four main UN economic, social and cultural rights treaties. Bangladesh, Nepal and Sri Lanka have ratified the International Covenant on Economic, Social and Cultural Rights (ICE-SCR) (Pakistan has signed it) and all countries have ratified the Convention on the Rights of the Child (CRC), the Convention on the Elimination of All Forms of Race Discrimination (CERD) and the Convention on the Elimination of All Forms

of Discrimination against Women (CEDAW). In addition, Courts across the region have on a few, although relatively rare, occasions referred to relevant international standards, including both treaties and soft law.

The development of public interest litigation (PIL), based initially upon Indian precedents and practice, now includes relaxed standing requirements designed to promote access to justice, as well as innovative remedies, and is well-established in the South Asian courts.

2.1   Bangladesh

Bangladesh became independent in 1971, following a war with Pakistan. Whilst many laws from the Pakistan era have remained in force, subsequent legal developments have been distinct, with a constitution adopted on the 4 November 1972. Article 11 of the Constitution states that the 'Republic shall be a democracy in which fundamental human rights and freedoms and respect for the dignity and worth of the human person shall be guaranteed'.[5]

Reflecting the socialist vision of the country's founders, Part II of Bangladesh's Constitution contains an elaborate set of Fundamental Principles of State Policy (FPSPs). These include exhortations to the State to ensure the participation of women in national life; the emancipation of peasants and workers from all forms of exploitation; the need for the State, through planned economic growth, to achieve a steady improvement in the material and cultural standard of living with a view to securing basic necessities such as food, clothing, shelter, education and medical care, together with the right to work for a reasonable wage having regard to the quantity and quality of work; the right to reasonable rest, recreation and leisure and the right to social security arising from unemployment, illness or disability. Other provisions cover rural development, including in education, public health and standard of living; free and compulsory education for all children as may be determined by law;

---

[4] The Irish Constitution of 1922 was the first to elaborate a set of Directive Principles of Social Policy and this model has been adopted in many post-colonial jurisdictions in Africa and Asia.

[5] The case of *A.T. Mridha v. State* 25 DLR 335 (see paras. 10 and 53) {1973} is the earliest reported decision to mention the Bangladesh Constitution vis-à-vis human progress and happiness.

improving public health and nutrition; work as a right and as a duty and the preservation of national culture and heritage. Article 8(2) makes clear that although the principles are fundamental to the country's governance and shall be applied by the State in the making of laws and a guide to interpretation to the Constitution and other laws, they shall not be judicially enforceable.

The Supreme Court had initially emphasised that the FPSPs, whilst they must be applied by the State in the making of appropriate laws, are not justiciable by the courts[6] (for the 'obvious reason,' according to the Court, that they are directed towards socio-economic development which can only be achieved gradually by the State according to available resources and technical knowledge)[7] and that where they are in conflict with fundamental rights, the latter must prevail.[8] However, the Court has since recognised that the FPSPs are 'fundamental to the Governance of the country,' and guide the interpretation of Constitutional provisions.[9] The Court has also observed that the article 8(2) provisions are compulsory and binding through the use of the word 'shall' and that non-justiciability does not mean that the State can continue to ignore the FPSPs indefinitely.[10] This approach appears to reflect that of the UN Committee on Economic, Social and Cultural Rights in its views on the implementation of State obligations.[11]

Relevant fundamental rights in Part III include equality before the law (article 27), the prohibition of discrimination on grounds of race, religion, sex, caste and place of birth, and of discrimination by the State between men and women 'in the state and public life,' as well as affirmative action provisions for women, children and 'backward sec-

tions' (article 28), equality of opportunity in public employment (article 29), prohibition of forced labour (article 34), freedom of association (article 38), freedom of profession or occupation (article 40) and the right to property (article 42).

The judiciary is organised at two levels, with subordinate courts below and a Supreme Court comprising of the Appellate and High Court Divisions. The Family Courts are the courts of first instance, open to all religious communities, each of which is governed by its own personal status laws (Buddhist, Christian, Hindu or Muslim as applicable).[12] The jurisdiction and functions of these courts are governed by the Family Courts Act 1985.

The Supreme Court has held that: 'National Courts should not straightway ignore the international obligations which a country undertakes. If the domestic laws are not clear enough or there is nothing therein, the national courts should draw upon the principles incorporated in the international instruments'.[13] The Court has also on occasion made specific reference to relevant international standards in finding violations of economic and social rights.[14]

---

[6] *Sheikh Abdus Sabur v. Returning Officer and Others* 9 BLD (AD) 25, at paras. 11, 38 See also *Bangladesh v. Winifred Rubie* 1982 BLD (AD), at paras. 34, 37.

[7] *Kudrat-e-Elahi Panir v. Bangladesh* 44 DLR (1992) (AD) 319. According to the Court, whether all these prerequisites for peaceful socio-economic revolution exist is for the State to decide (paras. 22–26).

[8] *Hamidul Huq Chowdhury v. Bangladesh* 34 DLR (1982) 190, at paras 10 and 12.

[9] A. *Wahab v. Secretary, Ministry of Land and others* 1 MLR (HC) (1996) 338.

[10] *Masdar Hossain (Md.) and Others v. Bangladesh* 2 BLC 444, at para. 37.

[11] *General Comment No. 3, The nature of States parties' obligations* (Fifth session, 1990), U.N. Doc. E/1991/23, annex III at 86 (1991), para. 9.

[12] The Family Courts currently do not operate in the three districts comprising the Chittagong Hill Tracts, where various indigenous communities apply their own distinct laws, side by side with the religion based personal status laws.

[13] Per Bimalendu Bikash Roy Chowdhury, J. in *Hussein Mohammed Ershad v. Bangladesh & Ors* 21 BLD (AD) (2001) 69, at para. 2. The Courts will also of course give direct effect to binding norms of customary international law (*Bangladesh v. Unimarine SA Panama* 29 DLR (1977) 252), except where there is clear domestic legislation on the issue (*Bangladesh and Others v. Sombon Ashavon*, 32 DLR (1980) 198): for further discussion see M. Shah Alam, *Enforcement of International Human Rights Law in Domestic Courts* (Dhaka: New Warsi Book Corporation, 2007) at 100 ff.

[14] In *Ain O Salish Kendra (ASK) and Others v. Government of Bangladesh and others* (1999) 19 BLD (HCD) 488, the Supreme Court found the wholesale eviction of slum dwellers not only to be contrary to domestic law, but also to the UN resolution of the 1976 UN Habit Conference on Human Settlements (A/Res./31/109) preventing discrimination against minorities in terms of constituting a gross violation of the right to adequate housing (see para. 1). In *Rabia Bhuiyan v. Ministry of LGRD and others* 59 DLR (AD) (2007) 176, the Court referred to the relevant General Comments of the Committee on Economic, Social and Cultural Rights in laying down guidelines for the state to ensure the provision of safe drinking water to the people, in the context of widespread arsenic contamination of groundwater.

The Supreme Court, when asked to consider the potential impact of a flood action project, funded with foreign donations, on the lives, property and environmental security of over a million people, overruled the High Court which had held that the petitioner, an environmental lawyers' organisation, lacked standing within the meaning of article 102 of the Constitution to bring the action. The Court defined an aggrieved person as 'not only any person who is personally aggrieved but also one whose heart bleeds for his less fortunate fellow beings for a wrong done by the government or a local authority in not fulfilling its constitutional or statutory obligations'.[15] In subsequent decisions resulting from PIL, the courts have provided expanded interpretations of the right to life to address issues concerning, among others, gender equality, workplace safety, shelter and freedom from forced eviction and access to safe and potable water.

While increasing recourse is taken to PIL to address economic and social rights, the implementation of the courts' judgments and orders in such cases faces increasing difficulty, partly due to their court's own massive backlogs and consequent incapacity to ensure timely hearing of cases.[16]

2.2   Nepal

Nepal's current Constitution dates from 1990 when the country embraced democracy. The Directive Principles and Policies of the State (DPPS) contained in Part 4 of the Nepal Constitution have been described as 'legal rights in the making' whilst at the same time being necessary for the stability of democracy and civil liberties.[17]

As in Bangladesh, the courts have made clear that although they can indicate to the State where it has exceeded its powers in relation to the DPPS, they

cannot implement and enforce the DPPS.[18] However, in accordance with article 24(2) of the Constitution, the DPPS are 'fundamental to the activities and governance of the State and shall be implemented in stages through laws within the limits of the resources and the means available in the country'. Moreover, a number of the DPPS overlap significantly with or replicate the country's international commitments, and where this is the case, the Supreme Court has ruled that the government may be required to give effect to them.[19] This has happened despite the express stipulation in article 24(1) of the Constitution that the DPPS are not enforceable in any court.[20]

Detailed DPPS provisions are found in article 25, where the State is enjoined to promote conditions of welfare, ensure the equitable distribution of economic gains on the basis of social justice and to prevent economic exploitation and eliminate all types of economic and social inequalities, and article 26, where a comprehensive plan of action is laid out. Article 26(1) requires the State to pursue a policy of raising the standard of living of the general public through the development of education, health, housing and employment and equitable distribution of resources. Other provisions discuss protection of the environment (article 26(4)), participation of the labour force in securing the right to work (article 26(6)), enhancing female participation by making special provision for their education, health and employment (article 26(7)), safeguarding the rights and interests of children to ensure they are not exploited (article 26(8)), promoting education, health, employment and social security provision for 'socially backward' groups and the elderly and disabled (article 26(9) and (10))

[15] Dr. Mohiuddin Farooque v. Bangladesh 49 DLR (AD) (1997) 1.
[16] In 2003, the then Law Minister was quoted as saying that a total of ten million (9,683,305) cases were pending in different courts, with about 4,946 in the Appellate Division and 127,244 in the High Court Division: see MM Yousuff, Administration of Judicial System in Bangladesh at <www.rghr.net/mainfile.php/0503/455/>.
[17] S.P.S. Dhungel, B. Adhikari, B.P. Bhandari and C. Murgatroyd, Commentary on the Nepalese Constitution (Kathmandu: DeLF, 1998), p. 199.

[18] Yogi Naraharinath et al. v. Hon'ble Girija Prasad Koirala & Ors NKP 2053, Vol. 1, p. 33, Decision No. 6127 (case dealing with protection of environmental heritage); see also Yogi Narhari Nath v. Prime Minister 5 S.Ct.Bull.5 Bhadra 1–15, 2053 at Dhungel, Adhikari, Bhandari and Murgatroyd, Commentary on the Nepalese Constitution, ibid., pp. 124 and 203.
[19] See the Bonded Labour case or Kumar Pyakurel v. HMG Nepal 6 S.Ct.Bull. 11 (Kartik 1–15, 2054), decision date B.S. 2054/4/10 (25/07/1997) and the Rani Pokhari case or Prakash Mani Sharma v. HMG Nepal NKP 2054 V.6, p.312, decision no. 6391; 6 S.Ct.Bull. 5 (Asoj 16–30, 2054)
[20] The Supreme Court has gone on to hold that it has the power under article 24 to identify those actions of the government contravening the directive principles (see Yogi Naraharinath case, n. 19 above)

and the provision of free legal aid for the poor (article 26(14)). This in turn has spawned numerous statutes and programmes of action.[21] It was only with the restoration of democracy in 1990 that any kind of concerted state action took place to implement these provisions and programmes, and even now it would be true to say (as with the other countries in the region) that Nepal still has far to go in achieving the aspirations of articles 25 and 26.

In terms of relevant 'fundamental rights,' article 20 protects individuals against exploitation through trafficking or forced labour. Article 11 provides that 'special provisions may be made by law for the protection and advancement of the interests of ... those who belong to a class which is economically, socially or educationally backward'.

A Supreme Court with jurisdiction over fundamental rights is established under article 88. This Article is reinforced by article 23, in Part III, which addresses individual rights. Article 88 gives the Court extraordinary powers to protect fundamental rights, and also to provide remedies where existing remedies appear to be ineffective. The Nepal Supreme Court has held that a basic feature of any competent judicial system is to ensure justice through the provision of legal aid to everyone, including the poor and disabled.[22]

The Supreme Court, in ruling that the right to equality must be enjoyed equally by both men and women, noted that Nepal had ratified CEDAW and the two Covenants, namely the ICCPR and the ICESCR, and was also subject to the Universal Declaration on Human Rights (UDHR).[23] In another case, it also noted that cruelty against children in the context of child labour was criminalised by both domestic law and the CRC.[24]

In terms of horizontal application, the Nepal Supreme Court has defined a state agency against which fundamental rights may be enforced as being any agent through which the State exercises its powers, including those of both national and local government. Conversely, a family planning association that is a voluntary organisation with no state support could not be held liable for breach of fundamental rights.[25]

2.3 Pakistan

Pakistan's Constitution, dating from 1973, guarantees a number of socio-economic fundamental rights (Part 2), including the outlawing of slavery, forced labour, trafficking and employment of children under 14 in hazardous industries (article 11); freedom of association (article 17); the right to enter any lawful profession or occupation and to conduct a trade or business (article 18); the right to refuse to receive religious instruction at educational institutions (article 22); the right to property (Arts. 23 and 24); and the rights to protection of 'the marriage, the family, the mother and the child' as well as public employment (Arts. 25 and 27 respectively).

The Principles of Policy, also contained in Part 2 but in a separate chapter, comprise two core Articles which elaborate a number of guarantees. Article 37 provides that the State shall promote the educational and economic interests of backward classes or areas; remove illiteracy and provide free and compulsory secondary education within a minimum possible period; make technical and professional education generally available and higher education equally accessible to all on the basis of merit; ensure inexpensive and expeditious justice; secure just and humane conditions of work with suitable employment for women and children, with maternity benefits, and enable full participation in all national activities, including public service, through education and training. Article 38 enjoins the State to secure the well-being of all by raising their standard of living through equitable distribution of wealth and adjustment of rights between employers, employees and landlords and tenants and to provide work facilities

---

[21] See Dhungel, Adhikari, Bhandari and Murgatroyd, *Commentary on the Nepalese* Constitution (n. 18 above), pp. 209–225.

[22] *Adv. Lilamani Poudel v. HMG et al.*, NKP 2060 (regulation excluding serious crimes, such as trafficking, rape, corruption etc., from legal aid inconsistent with values and norms of Legal Aid Act, which required that the decision on determination of eligibility for legal aid should not be based on seriousness of offence).

[23] *Rina Bajracharya et al. v. HMG, Secretariat of Minister Council et al.* NKP 2057, Vol. V, p. 376 Decision No. 6898 or S.C. Bull Vol. 11, Issue 5 (2000), at p. 13.

[24] *Tarak Dhital on behalf of Dhiraj KC v. Chief District Officer Kathmandu, et al.* Supreme Court publication, Human Right Related Decision, NKP, 2059 (Decision Date: 2058/2/28).

[25] *Som Pudasaini v. Family Planning Association of Nepal* 4: 16 S. Ct. Bull. 1 (2052)

and an adequate livelihood for all balanced with reasonable rest and leisure; social security through compulsory insurance or other means; basic necessities of life such as food, clothing, housing, education and medical relief for all those permanently or temporarily unable to earn their livelihood through infirmity, sickness or unemployment; and to reduce income disparity. There is no explicit provision in the Constitution that the Principles of Policy are not judicially enforceable.

Examples of reference to international instruments include judgments from the Lahore High Court recognising the protection afforded to the right to choice regarding marriage by Article 16 of CEDAW,[26] a decision from the Supreme Court promoting access to justice that lists the relevant provisions of the UDHR,[27] and citation of the 1972 Stockholm Declaration in an environmental protection case.[28]

The Supreme Court began to expand access to justice through PIL in the early 1990s when it stated that every citizen had the right to obtain justice and this could be facilitated through PIL, allowing simple and direct petitions to the Supreme Court as well as potentially widening the scope of justiciable rights.[29]

2.4 Sri Lanka

The Sri Lankan legal system is based on a complex mixture of English common law combined with Roman-Dutch, Sinhalese, Muslim[30] and customary law. The current Constitution was adopted on 16 August 1978. Relevant fundamental rights provisions include equality (article 12) and freedom of association (article 14(1) (c)). Notably, the Sri Lankan Constitution contains no express guarantee of the right to life.

The Directive Principles of State Policy (DPSP) are provided for in article 27. Thus, in article 27(2)(b), the State is required to promote public welfare by establishing a social order in which social, economic and political justice guides all national institutions. In addition, the State is under an obligation to establish a democratic socialist society, the aims of which include realisation by all of an adequate standard of living for themselves and their families, including adequate food, clothing and housing; the continuous improvement of living conditions and full enjoyment of leisure and social and cultural opportunities; economic development through both public and private activity; equitable distribution of material resources for the common good; establishment of a just social order in which the means of production, distribution and exchange are not concentrated in the hands of the State or a privileged few, but dispersed among the people; raising moral and cultural standards; the complete eradication of illiteracy and guarantee of the right to universal and equal access to education at all levels; the elimination of discrimination and prejudice through education; ensuring equal opportunity; elimination of economic and social privilege and disparity and exploitation; ensuring social security and welfare; development of culture and language; protection and preservation of the environment.

---

[26] *Mst. Saima & 4 others v. The State* PLD 2003 Lah 747 (complaint filed by mother challenging the validity of her daughter's marriage on grounds of the kazi's incompetence was rejected by the Lahore High Court, which recognised the protection to the institution of marriage under both Article 35 of the Constitution and Article 16 of CEDAW). See also *Mst. Humaira Mehmood v. The State and Others* PLD 1999 Lah 494, where the High Court ruled that under Muslim law, an adult woman may not be forced into marriage, and that a marriage without her consent is not valid. The Court also referred to Articles 5 and 6 of the Cairo Declaration of Human Rights in Islam.

[27] *Al-Jehad Trust v. The Federation of Pakistan* 1999 SCMR 1379 (recommendations made to the government to introduce laws which would ensure that the people of the Northern Areas enjoyed fundamental rights with special reference to access to justice).

[28] *SIUT v. Nestle Milkpak Limited* 2005 CLC 424.

[29] *Darshan Masih v. The State* PLD 1990 SC 513 and *Akbar Ali v. Secretary, Ministry of Defence* 1991 SCMR 2114.

[30] Dutch colonial administrators codified the rules of inheritance, marriage and divorce in order to facilitate the application of Muslim family law. This Code was preserved and adapted by the British after their defeat of the Dutch in 1799. The British later enacted the Registration of Muslim Marriages Ordinance 1896, repealing parts of the earlier Anglo-Dutch Code. The other major piece of legislation relating to Islamic family law is the Muslim Intestate Succession Ordinance 1931 still in force today. The 1896 Ordinance was in turn repealed by the post-independence Muslim Marriage and Divorce Act 1951, which essentially reinforces the principle that, in matters of personal status, the rights and duties of the parties involved are to be determined by the school of law to which the parties belong.

The DPSPs are not judicially enforceable.[31] The Supreme Court, while clearly identifying their constitutional importance, has noted that they project the aims and aspirations of a democratic government, and as such are required to be implemented through legislation.[32] In relation to the interrelationship of fundamental rights and DPSPs, the Supreme Court has noted in *Seneviratne v. University Grants Commission*,[33] referring to Indian decisions, that 'the provisions are part and parcel of the Constitution and the Court must take due recognition of these and make proper allowance for their operation and function'.

The Courts have adjudicated on relatively few economic and social rights claims, and where they have done so, they have invoked fundamental rights, such as the right to equality. Similarly there have been only a few references to international standards. In one such case on the environment, the Sri Lankan Supreme Court noted that: 'As a member of the United Nations, Sri Lanka can hardly ignore the Declaration of the United Nations Conference on the Human Environment (1972) and the Rio Declaration on Environment and Development (1992), even though they are not legally binding'.[34]

3. GENDER ISSUES

The focus of economic and social rights jurisprudence addressing gender issues has mainly con-

cerned rights relating to marriage, as well as property and inheritance rights and employment rights, with some courts adopting somewhat conservative approaches as they attempt to balance the advancement of women's rights with perceived entrenched public support for traditional practices.

The Nepal Supreme Court's approach may perhaps be best summarised by the following dicta that tackle discrimination, but not at the cost of social instability:

> Equality shall not be absolute [but] rather... relative. There [is a natural]...difference between man and woman...[which] naturally [exists in] Nepalese society as well... Existing law and [the] constitution have been recognized in [accordance with] the culture, tradition, values and norms of the society throughout [our] long history. If such laws [are] changed randomly, the structure and system of society may [be disrupted].[35]

This approach may be seen in two cases where the Court has affirmed the right to equality of women whilst seeking to reconcile it with traditional practices 'in the interests of stability'. In *Mira Dhungana v. Ministry of Law, Justice and Parliamentary Affairs*[36] the Court, whilst falling short of declaring as unconstitutional a legislative provision which gave a son but not a daughter (at least until she was 35 and remained unmarried) a share of his father's property from birth, nevertheless required the State within one year to review the legislation after consulting widely amongst interested parties, including women's groups. The Court, in so doing, held that a declaration of unconstitutionality was not the correct approach in dealing with a provision that was undoubtedly discriminatory but also a part of the country's historic traditions and social fabric. Similarly, in *Sapana Pradhan Malla v. Ministry of Law, Justice and Parliamentary Affairs*,[37] the Court refrained from striking down a law prohibiting a daughter or daughter-in-law from inheriting the tenancy rights of her father after his death. At the same time, it should be noted that in these judgments the Court has

---

[31] See article 29, Constitution of Sri Lanka 1978. Also note that the Select Committee on the revision of the 1972 Constitution did state that the Draft Constitution as presented did not permit restrictions on fundamental rights by reference to DPSPs: see J. Wickramaratne, *Fundamental Rights in Sri Lanka* (Stamford Lake: Colombo, 2006) at p. 45, fn. 42.

[32] *Re the Thirteenth Amendment to the Constitution Bill* [1987] 2 Sri. LR 312.

[33] [1979-79-80] 1 Sri. LR 182, where the Supreme Court accepted a 55 per cent distribution of places in university admissions district-wise on basis of population made by the UGC on the ground that it was required to conform to national policy, citing in aid DPSPs on 'protecting a social order in which justice...shall guide all institutions; and the right to education.

[34] *Bulankulama & Ors v. The Secretary, Ministry of Industrial Development & Ors* ('Eppawala case'), S.C. Application No. 884/99 (F/R), available at: <http://www.elaw.org/resources/text.asp?ID=1883> (last visited 15/11/2006), reprinted in *South Asian Environmental Reporter*, Vol. 7, No. 2 (2000).

[35] *Chanda Bajracharya v. Secretariat of Parliament, Singh Durbar, Kathmandu* et al., NKP 2053, Vol. 7, p. 537, Supreme Court. Edited for English.

[36] 4 S.Ct. Bull 1 (Fagun 1–15, 2052).

[37] 5 S.Ct. Bull. 1 (Asoj 16–30, 2053).

also taken cognizance of the fact that Nepal has ratified CEDAW and other international standards and must act in accord with them.[38]

In *Fazal Jan v. Roshua Din*,[39] the Supreme Court of Pakistan held that the fundamental constitutional right to equality required the State to make special provision for the protection of women and children and imposed a positive obligation on all State organs to take active measures to safeguard their interests.[40] The Court has also supported affirmative action to counter gender discrimination, such as upholding a quota system for women's admission to a medical college.[41]

Many Pakistani cases deal with the application of Muslim inheritance laws. Courts have been prepared to protect women's rights in the absence of action by the legislature,[42] or have recognised the absence of social organisations for women in rural areas and recommended the establishment of such advocacy groups, particularly in relation to inheritance rights.[43] Other examples of positive decisions include: upholding the right of a Muslim woman to enter into a valid marriage without the consent of her guardian;[44] invoking a FPSP on the protection of marriage to hold that prolonged cohabitation gives rise to a presumption of marriage with a sex worker; and finding unfair discrimination in the case of a female applicant who had

not been considered for a job on the basis of her gender.[45]

In Bangladesh, the High Court has directly considered the right to gender equality in the context of employment and rights within the family (including with respect to divorce, maintenance and custody), and through its decisions on the right to life impacted on women's rights to livelihood and to health. For example, the Court has struck down regulations of the state airline providing a lower retirement age for female employees[46] and a government circular restricting the functions of local government representatives elected to seats reserved for women.[47] It has also found unconstitutional the forcible eviction of sex-workers and of (among others, women) slum dwellers as a threat to their livelihood[48] and has made observations regarding how available remedies such as 'restitution for conjugal rights' are inconsistent with the constitutional prohibition on gender discrimination.[49]

In a number of decisions, the High Court has accepted the notion that the interpretation of constitutional rights may be affected by changing social norms, and has sought to interpret such rights consistently with a progressive interpretation of religious or customary traditions, with one of the most potentially far-reaching decisions involving the declaration of 'fatwas' by unauthorised persons to be without any lawful authority.[50] However, in general such decisions have either been set aside on appeal, or been stayed pending further consideration by the apex Court.[51]

---

[38] *Rina Bajracharya et al. HMG, Secretariat of Minister Council et al.* NKP, 2057, Vol. V, p. 376 (right to equality shall have to be accessible for both men and women equally. Different treatment of men and women flight attendants declared void in light of international commitments and constitutional prohibition on discrimination); *Prakash Mani Sharma et al. v. HMG, Woman Child and Social Welfare Ministry et al.* NKP 2060, Vol. 9/10, p. 726 (given inconsistent maternity leave provisions under various laws, appropriate standards should be determined for women workers by taking into account international standards).

[39] PLD 1990 SC 661.

[40] Miscarriage of justice where woman did not have adequate representation in inheritance case.

[41] *Shirin Munir v. Government of Punjab PLD* 1990 SC 295.

[42] *Ghulam Ali v. Ghulam Sarwar Naqvi PLD* 1990 SC 1; *Ghulam Haider v. Niaz Muhammad PLD* 1995 SC 620; *Inayat Bibi v. Issac Nazir Ullah PLD* 1992 SC 385 (inheritance rights of Christian women); *Shahro v. Fatima PLD 1998 SC 1512* (inheritance rights of women and girls under Muhammadan law). See also *Irshad Ahmad v. Pakistan* PLD 1993 SC 464 (since polygamy is permitted by law for Muslims, the State is obliged to provide medical benefits to both wives).

[43] *Mst. Nasreen v. Fayyaz Khan PLD* 1991 SC 412.

[44] *Hafiz Abdul Waheed v. Mrs. Asma Jehangir & another PLD 1997 Lah 301; PLD 2004 SC 219.*

[45] *Mrs. Naseem Firdous v. Punjab Small Industries Corporation M.D.* PLD 1995 Lah 584.

[46] *Dalia Parveen v. Bangladesh Biman Corporation & Another 48 DLR (1996) (HCD) 132; Bangladesh Biman Corporation v. Rabia Bashri Irene and another* 55 DLR (AD) (2003) 132 (upholding 52 DLR (2000) 308).

[47] *Shamima Sultana Seema vs. Bangladesh* 57 DLR 201.

[48] *Bangladesh Society for the Enforcement of Human Rights and Others v. Bangladesh* 53 DLR (2001) 1.

[49] *Nelly Zaman v. Ghiyasuddin* 34 DLR (1982) 221 and more recently *Khodeja Begum v. Sadeq Sarkar* 50 DLR (1998) 181 (which found this 'remedy' to be a violation of social justice, the right to equal protection of the law, the right to non-discrimination and the rights to life and liberty) (but see, contra, *Chan Mia v. Rupnahar* 51 DLR (1999) 292).

[50] See for example *Md. Hefzur Rahman v. Shamsun Nahar Begum and another* 15 BLD (1995) 34 (holding that on divorce a Muslim man must maintain his wife at a reasonable level till she remarries).

[51] *Hefzur Rahman (Md) v. Shamsun Nahar Begum and another* 51 DLR (AD) 172 reversing 15 BLD (1995) 34. The

Significantly, the High Court has accepted that affirmative action provisions are required to ensure substantive equality, holding that in giving a literal interpretation of the concept of equality by maintaining similar standards towards men and women, the concept of gender equality while being followed in form, would not follow the spirit of the Constitution.[52] It has also found that the State has positive obligations to prevent violence against women in the form of illegal corporal punishments imposed by village tribunals, purporting to issue 'fatwas' for violation of perceived community norms,[53] and to prevent forced evictions and assaults of sex-workers.[54]

4. SUBSTANTIVE RIGHTS

4.1 Health and Environment – Expansive Definitions of the Right to Life

These four South Asian Courts, reflecting the approach taken in India, have adopted an expansive definition of their respective constitutional provisions on the right to life to indirectly protect some economic and social rights, most notably in relation to health and environmental rights.

ENVIRONMENT

Responding to the serious problems faced by both urban and rural dwellers (although in varying degrees), South Asian courts have been in the forefront of environmental protection, frequently handing down detailed orders for the authorities

to take more concerted action, particularly in relation to the right to ensure that all those affected are fully consulted and able to participate in decisions regarding the environment.

The Supreme Court of Nepal has held that the right to a decent environment is part of the right to life[55] and that all industries are under an obligation to protect the ecological balance.[56] The Court has also held that the right to environmental protection places the government under a special duty to regulate pollution levels,[57] and accordingly has issued detailed directions in relation to establishing a national mechanism for regulating vehicle pollution.[58] A number of cases have also dealt with protection of Nepal's valuable archaeological and cultural heritage.[59]

Pakistani courts have heard a wide variety of cases concerned with environmental and health protection. In *Shehla Zia v. WAPDA*,[60] the Supreme Court was required to consider a petition from a group of local residents seeking to halt the construction of an electricity grid station based on potential health hazards of electromagnetic transmissions.

Appellate Division did not accept arguments that given the changed social milieu and a perspective of securing women's rights, post-divorce maintenance should be provided for Muslim women, observing that this issue could only be addressed through legislation.

[52] *Shamima Sultana Seema v. Bangladesh* 57 DLR 201 at paras. 30 and 37 (holding that commissioners directly elected to reserved seats on city corporations should have the same rights, functions and responsibilities as those elected to general seats). However, later challenges by women's groups to provisions for indirect election of women to seats reserved in the National Parliament (on the grounds that these would not further substantive equality, or enable effective representation of women's interests) failed in both Divisions of the Supreme Court (*Farida Akhter v. Bangladesh* WP No. 3975 of 2004).

[53] *Hanufa* case (2001/01/02). Subsequently, the Appellate Court stayed the High Court's ruling.

[54] *Bangladesh Society for the Enforcement of Human Rights and Others v. Bangladesh* 53 DLR (2001) 1.

[55] *Leaders Inc. v. Godavari Marble Industries* 4 S.Ct. Bull. 1 (Magh 16–29, 2052), or *Surya P. Dhungel v. Godavar Marble Industries*, NKP 2052, Golden Jubilee Celebration of His Majesty, Special Vol., p. 169.

[56] *Surendra Bhandari v. Shree Distillery Pvt. Ltd. B.S.* 2053, Writ No. 3259.

[57] *Advocate Bhojraj v. Ministry of Population and Environment et al.* Supreme Court Writ 4193, B.S. 2056 (Government given one fiscal year to determine appropriate levels in accordance with the Environment Protection Act).

[58] *Advocate Prakash Mani Sharma v. Hon'ble Prime Minister Girija Prasad Koirala* Supreme Court Writ No. 25, B.S. 2058. See also *Advocate Bharat Mani Gautam v. HMG Secretariat of Ministerial Council et al., Singh Darbar, Kathmandu* et al. Supreme Court Human Rights, 2056, p. 365 (use of particular polluting vehicles controlled subject to certain exceptions required for economic reasons, such as tractors etc.).

[59] *Yogi Naraharinath* (n.19 above) (prime duty and liability of government is to protect and conserve archaeologically important items and the natural environment otherwise we forget our ancient cultural and civilization); *Machchhendra Lal Kayastha v. Hon'ble Health Minister, HMG, Ministry of Health* 2057, Vol. 4, p. 303 (the Supreme Court issued directive order to government that if any archaeologically important building is repaired, the work should not disrupt the real structure of building and its art); *Bijay Kumar Basnet et al. v. Kathmandu Metro Polition City Major, Keshav Sthapit et al.* 2059, Vol. 1, 2, p. 37 (local authority could not permit retail building in contravention of statutory duty to conserve certain areas due to their historical archaeology and cultural importance as well as their containing national resources).

[60] PLD 1994 SC 693.

Referring to Indian jurisprudence, the Court, holding that the right to live in a clean environment is based on the constitutional right to life and dignity, applied the 'precautionary principle' set out in the 1992 Rio Declaration which it found, although not binding, to be of 'persuasive value and commands respect'. The Court went on to hold that although it lacked the expertise to adjudicate on the different scientific and policy arguments at stake, this did not prevent it from ordering the authorities to initiate a public consultation process for all such projects, including establishing a Scientific Commission to examine the health risks.[61] Hence the Court, as with the approach of the South African Constitutional Court, by recognising its limitations on adjudicating on substance and focusing instead on process and whether, in effect, the state had done all it could reasonably do in the circumstances, was able to offer protection.

In other cases, the Pakistani courts have laid down guidelines for a municipal authority for minimising city pollution. In Lahore,[62] the High Court issued directives to both governmental and non-governmental organisations to check and penalize vehicles responsible for excessive city pollution in Karachi;[63] prohibiting the dumping of industrial and nuclear waste in a coastal area following a newspaper report that land had been allocated for that purpose;[64] ordering a local authority to take all necessary measures to maintain and preserve a children's park based on the fact that it was the fundamental right of the citizens to enjoy recreational facilities such as green belts;[65] and, restraining a multi-national company from building a factory to produce bottled water in 'Education City' on the grounds that that it would both be detrimental to the environment and would affect the interests of the plaintiff medical and educational institutions.[66]

Bangladeshi courts have also been active in environmental protection, often utilising the 1995 Environmental Conservation Act in response to PIL claims brought by activist NGOs and lawyers. In perhaps the most far-reaching of the cases brought by the Bangladesh Environmental Lawyers Association (BELA),[67] and which saw the first formal recognition of public interest litigation, the Supreme Court gave directions that the State could only proceed with a mega-development project, the 'Flood Action Plan' (FAP), subject to compensation and rehabilitation of persons displaced, and to adherence to the relevant statutory procedures.[68] Relevant constitutional rights upheld included property and livelihood[69] (since the local fishing industry would be adversely affected).[70] However, although the Court held that the FAP was clearly in breach of the mandatory statutory scheme it did not require it to be completely halted since it had already been significantly progressed.

In *Dr. Mohiuddin Farooque & others v. Govt. of Bangladesh,*[71] the Supreme Court allowed a PIL petition brought by the BELA under articles 18, 21, 31 and 32 of the Constitution read with section 4 of the 1995 Act. It requested that industrial units and factories adopt adequate and sufficient

---

[61] For further commentary on the case see M. Lau, 'Islam and judicial activism: Public interest litigation and environmental protection in the Islamic Republic of Pakistan,' in A. Boyle and M. Anderson (eds.), *Human Rights Approaches to Environmental Protection* (Oxford: Clarendon, 1996), pp. 285–302 at 296–299.

[62] *Mrs. Anjum Irfan v. Lahore Development Authority* PLD 2002 Lah 555, also reported at PLJ 2002 Lahore 2014.

[63] *In re: Pollution of Environment Caused by Smoke Emitting Vehicles* 1996 SCMR 543.

[64] *In re Human Rights Case (Environment Pollution in Balochistan)* PLD 1994 Supreme Court 102.

[65] *Manzoor Bhatti v. Executive Officer, Cantonment Board Multan and another* PLD 2002 Lahore 412.

[66] *SIUT v. Nestle Milkpak Limited* 2005 CLC 424.

[67] *Dr. Mohiuddin Farooque and another v. Bangladesh & Ors* 49 DLR (AD) 1 and 50 DLR (1998) 84.

[68] Ibid. at paras. 45 and 81. Although the Court held that it could not enforce the Guiding Principles on the Flood Action Plan encouraging popular participation since they did not have the force of law (para. 31) it did also find that there had been a failure to follow legislation which required making compensation and rehousing (para. 45). It also refused to adjudicate the claims regarding non-consultation and non-participation of the people in the Plan process on the grounds that these were disputed questions of fact.

[69] Ibid. at para. 73: *Dr Mohiuddin Farooque v. Bangladesh & Ors,* 48 DLR (1997) 438 was followed, where it was recognized (at para. 17) that the right to life includes the right to a livelihood.

[70] The Court (para. 65) also ordered the Government to take action under Article 24 of the Constitution (requiring the adoption of measures to protect monuments, objects or places of special artistic or historical importance or interest) to protect two special mosques from damage caused by the project.

[71] 55 DLR (2003) 69.

measures to control pollution within a stipulated time and report on compliance, and the Court stated that:

> Articles 31 & 32 guarantee a right to life. This expression life does not mean merely an elementary life or sub-human life but connotes the life of the greatest creation of the Lord who has at least a right to a decent and healthy way of life in a hygienic condition. It also means a qualitative life among others, free from environmental hazards (para. 53.)

In another case brought by BELA,[72] the Supreme Court responded with urgent preventive measures to reduce the high pollution levels of the capital Dhaka ('one of the worst in the world' according to the Court) by issuing detailed interim orders.[73]

The Court has also on several occasions tackled the illegal conversion of inner city open spaces in the capital into residential plots instead of parks and leisure facilities as originally designated. In *RAJUK v. Mohsinul Islam*,[74] the Court considered the scope of the term 'improvement' under the town planning legislation. In *Md Saleemullah v. State*,[75] the Court found that in converting the open space meant for being transformed into a park, the respondents had acted without any lawful authority and violated fundamental rights, and caused detriment to the health and well-being of the people of the area. The Court approved the decision in the case of *Dr. Mohiuddin Farooque v. Bangladesh and others*,[76] noting that 'in that case it was observed that the State is bound to protect the health and longevity of the people living in the country as right to life guaranteed under articles 31 and 32 of the Constitution includes protection of health and normal longevity of a man [*sic*] free from threats of man-made hazards unless that threat is justified by law'. It was further observed that 'the right to life under the aforesaid Articles of the Constitution being a fundamental right it can be enforced by this Court to remove any unjustified threat to the health and longevity of the people as the same are included in the right to life'.[77] More recently, the apex Court held that the conversion into a shopping mall of an area allocated for a multi-story car park in the Metropolitan Development Plan was a clear violation of Article 32, which did not contemplate a statutory body charged with environment protection acting instead as an instrument of exploitation.[78]

In a significant case, *Bulankulama & Ors v. The Secretary, Ministry of Industrial Development & Ors*,[79] the Sri Lankan Supreme Court found breaches of local residents'[80] rights to equality before the law, to carry on any profession or trade and to freedom of movement, in a case where the implementation of a phosphate mining exploration contract would have resulted in considerable environmental damage to an area of great historical and archaeological importance as well as the forcible resettlement of thousands of people. Referring to the requirement under both the Environmental Act 1980 and Principle 17 of the Rio Declaration on Environment and Development to carry out an environmental impact assessment to ensure any proposed development was both environmentally sound and sustainable, the Court ordered a comprehensive study on the location, quantity and quality of phosphate minerals to be carried out prior to any contract being entered into, noting that 'publicity, transparency and fairness are essential [*if the goal of*] sustainable

---

[72] *Dr. Mohiuddin Farooque & others v. Bangladesh* 55 DLR (2003) 613.

[73] These included enforcing restrictions against the use of hydraulic horns; implementing decision of ensuring that all imported motor vehicles are fitted with catalytic converters; ensuring reduction and removal of toxic and hazardous constituents from petroleum; and phasing out existing two-stroke engines on three wheelers by December 2002 (see para. 14).

[74] *Rajdhani Unnayan Kortripokkho (RAJUK) and another v. Mohshinul Islam and another* 53 DLR (2001) (AD) 79 (para 9). See also *Giasuddin vs. Dhaka Municipal Corporation* 1997 BLD 577 where it was observed that a public park is necessary for protecting the health and hygiene of the inhabitants of the area by providing open space and gardens (para. 6).

[75] *M. Saleem Ullah v. Bangladesh & Others* (2003) 55 DLR 1 at para 12.

[76] 48 DLR 438.

[77] No. 76 at para. 10.

[78] *Sharif Nurul Ambia v. Dhaka City Corporation* 58 DLR (AD) (2006) 253.

[79] Also known as the *Eppawela Case*, reported at (2000) 3 Sri LR 243 [p12] at 316.

[80] The Court overruled the respondents' objections that the petitioners lacked *locus standi* on the basis that the fundamental rights involved were shared with the people of the country and, as a collective personality, they were entitled to expect that the government would act according to the law. The fact that the petitioners' rights were linked to the communal rights of others did not affect their standing before the court.

development is to be achieved'. The Court also noted that sustainable development has been accepted as part of customary international law as well as the environmental law of Sri Lanka.[81] In addition, the government's environmental agency was ordered to implement the 'precautionary principle' and the 'polluter pays principle' by adopting measures to prevent environmental degradation in the project area and assessing the compensation to be recovered from the polluters as the cost of reversing the damaged environment. Given the area's extreme historical importance and archaeological value, any development activity was also required to be accompanied by proper studies and proposals for mitigating any adverse impact on the country's unrenewable cultural heritage.

HEALTH

In relation to health, both the Nepal and Pakistan Supreme Courts have upheld the right to clean water, the former noting that the provision of clean water is an integral part of public health[82] and the latter interpreting the right to life as entailing the fundamental right of every person to have clean, unpolluted and drinkable water.[83] In a similar vein, the Appellate Division of the Bangladesh Supreme Court in *Rabia Bhuiyan v. Ministry of Local Government, Rural Development* has held the government responsible for violation of the right to life, due to its failure to comply with statutory duties to provide access to safe and potable water, in the context of widespread arsenic-contamination of groundwater.[84]

Other health rights cases addressed by Pakistani courts include the mislabeling of food;[85] halting the sale of infected betel nuts;[86] ordering the relo-

cation of a hazardous leather hide market;[87] and, upholding a petition challenging the legality of cigarette adverts on radio and TV as being detrimental to the right to life by encouraging smoking particularly amongst the young.[88]

Tobacco advertising has also been addressed by the High Court in Bangladesh in *Professor Nurul Islam and others v. Government of the People's Republic of Bangladesh & Others*.[89] The Court, in considering PIL challenging tobacco advertising under articles 11, 18, 31 and 32 of the Constitution, laid down detailed rules which went as far as not only stopping advertising but also halting tobacco production, prohibiting importation for a set period and banning smoking in public places.[90]

In another PIL case brought by BELA claiming violations of articles 31 and 32,[91] the Court had to consider government inaction regarding the import of powdered milk contaminated with potentially high levels of radiation following the nuclear disaster at Chernobyl. Although the Court could not decide the case on the merits, ordering more evidence to be gathered, it did direct the government to implement effective testing, noting that:

> It is the primary obligation of the State to raise the level of nutrition and the improvement of public health by preventing use of contaminated food, drink, etc. Though that obligation under Article 18(1) of the Constitution cannot be enforced, [the] State is bound to protect the health and longevity of the people living in the country as right to life guaranteed under Article 31 and 32 of the Constitution [that] includes protection of health and normal longevity free from threats of man

---

81 Dicta of Weeramantry J. in *Hungary v. Slovakia* (International Court of Justice, 1997 General List Nos. 92, 25 September 1997) applied.
82 *Nimimaya Maharjan v. His Majesty of Government* NKP, 2053, Vol. 8, p. 627 SC.
83 *General Secretary West Pakistan Salt Miners Labour Union, Khewra, Jhelum v. the Director Industries and Mineral Development, Punjab Lahore* 1994 SCMR 2061.
84 59 DLR (2007) (AD) 176.
85 *Karachi Metropolitan Corporation v. Qarshi Industries Ltd* 2002 Sup Ct 439 – includes the requirements for proving the violation.
86 *Adeel-ur-Rahman & Others v. The Federation of Pakistan and Others* 2005 PTD 172 (State is under a duty to protect a person's right to life from those elements which may harm him including impure food items).

87 *Anjuman Tajran Charam v. The Commissioner Faislabad Division, Faislabad* 1997 CLC 1281 (in order to enforce fundamental rights courts can require public functionaries to do something which they are not normally required to do under any other specific law).
88 *Pakistan Chest Foundation & Others v. The Govt. of Pakistan* 1997 CLC 1379.
89 (2000) 52 DLR 413.
90 Government to stop production of tobacco leaves step by step; restrict issuance of license for setting up Tobacco or Bidi companies; prohibit importation of tobacco for some time and in the meantime to impose heavy duties on importation; no advertising or promotion by relevant ministries, any other concern, authority or agencies; Government to give direction to appropriate authorities to prohibit smoking in public places (at para. 34).
91 *Dr. Mohiuddin Farooque v. Bangladesh* 48 DLR (1996) 438.

made hazards unless the threat is justified by law...Right to life under Articles 31 & 32 of the Constitution not only means protection of life & limbs necessary for full enjoyment of life but also includes, amongst others, protection of health & normal longevity of an ordinary human being...Right to life under the aforesaid Articles being a fundamental right, it can be enforced by this court to remove any unjustified threat to the health & longevity of the people as the same are included in the right to life.[92]

Arguably the most significant health case[93] considered by the Sri Lankan Supreme Court to date was a challenge in 2003 to various provisions of an Intellectual Property Bill designed to secure compliance with the TRIPS Agreement[94] and therefore allowing foreign patent holders of any product or process, including medicinal drugs and the processes for their manufacture, to control the supply and price of such drugs in the Sri Lankan market. The Court agreed with the petitioners that, in the absence of the mitigating measures incorporated into TRIPs, this would result in the increase of the prices of such medicine in the market as the aforementioned provisions would have the effect of removing the power of the Sri Lankan authorities or a Sri Lankan citizen from obtaining medicines for the 'people of Sri Lanka' at the cheapest available price and from a source of their choice and would as such breach the right to equal protection under the law under Art 12(1) of the Constitution.[95] As such the Bill could only become law

if passed by a special majority as required by Article 84(2) of the Constitution:

> The provisions in Article 12(1) guarantee equal rights as well as equal protection and the provision of the TRIPS Agreement cannot be applicable to developed and developing countries equally without attributing due consideration to such rights with particular reference to the mitigatory provisions in the Agreement...Producers of patented products and processes and their agents in developed nations and consumers of such products in developing countries such as Sri Lanka cannot be taken as parties that are similarly circumstanced. There is ample justification to treat them differently as they cannot be put on equal footing. If they are to be treated equally such decision should be justified by relevant criteria...The learned Additional Solicitor-General has showed no such justification by a relevant differentiation between the aforementioned parties. Nor has he given any indication as to why the mitigatory provisions suggested by the TRIPS Agreement could not be considered in the enactment of the Bill.

4.2 Livelihood and Forced or Bonded Labour/Workers' Rights

South Asian jurisdictions have adopted an expansive definition of the right to life to protect the right to livelihood. Referring to the interpretation of the right to life in the Indian case of *Olga Tellis v. Bombay Municipal Corporation*, the Bangladesh Supreme Court in *Bangladesh Society for the Enforcement of Human Rights and Ors v. Government of Bangladesh and Ors*,[96] stated that sex workers have a guaranteed right to life and livelihood and that the latter is an important facet of the former; thus the easiest way of depriving a person of a right to life is to deny him/her of the means of livelihood.[97] In relation to the application of Muslim Law, the Court noted that:

> The preamble of our Constitution pledges high ideals of trust and faith in the Almighty Allah and that the State religion is Islam but we are not subjected to Shariat Law making

---

[92] Ibid., paras. 20–21.

[93] *Re: A Bill bearing the title 'Intellectual Property,' in the matter of petitions under Article 121(1) of the Constitution* (SC Special Determination 14/2003).

[94] Under the Trade Related Intellectual Property Rights (TRIPS) Agreement, domestic governments are not able to accord to their own citizens or corporate entities any protection or privileges which are not granted to foreign persons or corporate entities subject to certain mitigating measures not included in the Sri Lankan Bill such as the Doha Declaration, which makes provision for compulsory licensing and parallel importing of pharmaceutical drugs to meet national health emergencies. This includes granting of compulsory licenses in respect of pharmaceutical products with regard to public health crises including those related to HIV/AIDS, tuberculosis, malaria and other epidemics.

[95] In reaching its decision the Court drew on a World Health Organization (WHO) Report on 'TRIPS and Health Section in the South-East Asia Region,' published by WHO, which sets out the consequences of adherence to the

TRIPS agreement on the health of people in the South and East Asian countries including Sri Lanka.

[96] 53 DLR (2001) 1.

[97] AIR 1986 SC 180 at para. 12.

sexual intercourse even with consent between men and women, other than husband and wife, a heinous offence of jina [*sic*]/fornication punishable even with stoning to death but the same is not the law of the land to be enforced in the Courts of Law. However, though certain Shariat laws have found place in our personal laws and those are part of our laws enforceable in the Court of Law. (Para 10.)

The Pakistan Supreme Court has held that the right to livelihood is guaranteed under the laws of Pakistan and Islam.[98] With regard to forced or bonded labour, Pakistan, like India and Nepal, has enacted specific legislation, the Bonded Labour System (Abolition) Act in 1992, to tackle the problem by effectively extinguishing bonded debts.[99] The Supreme Court gave its first and landmark judgment on bonded labour in a PIL that preceded the Act by two years. *In Darshan Masih v. State*,[100] the Supreme Court on the basis of a letter sent by bonded labourers in the brick kiln industry gave *suo motu* recommendations as to the laws and rules that ought to be formulated for regulating the relationship between employers and employees. The results were swift and dramatic but not necessarily long lasting. Within months of the Supreme Court's judgment, tens of thousands of labourers in the kilns had left their work and it seemed that all those reportedly held in debt bondage in the country would soon be free. However, an assessment conducted a decade after the judgment concluded that 'debt bondage remains both widespread and virtually unchallenged by the Government of Pakistan. Indeed, it is both remarkable and tragic how little government officials have been willing to do to enforce the country's laws and to bring an end to debt bondage, and how willingly they appear to tolerate its persistence'.[101] The practice still continues to occur in the brick kilns – the subject of the original case – despite a number of subsequent decisions outlawing the practice and requiring the release of victims.[102] Given

the scale of the problem in Pakistan (as in several other countries in the region bar Sri Lanka), real change will only occur with effective monitoring and enforcement, including providing appropriate welfare schemes.

In Nepal the courts, prompted by civil society, have been active in tackling bonded and child labour. In one of its earliest judgments,[103] given by the Supreme Court under the new Constitution, the Informal Sector Service Centre (INSEC), a national NGO, successfully obtained an order of mandamus under article 20 of the Constitution directing the government to eradicate the traditional practice of Kamaiya (forced labour practices) in the West of the country, to initiate alternative welfare and rehabilitation measures as soon as possible and to pass legislation in compliance with Nepal's ratification of international instruments against bonded labour in particular, and human rights breaches in general. In another case, the Court considered child labour, noting that cruel behaviour towards and torture of children was outlawed by both domestic law and the CRC.[104]

In Bangladesh, although the issue of bonded labour has not been addressed directly, the Court has intervened in PIL cases in relation to the conditions of work of those employed in hazardous industries. For example, in *Salma Sobhan, Executive Director, Ain o Salish Kendra (ASK) v. Government of Bangladesh and others*,[105] the Bangladesh High Court examined a PIL petition

---

[98] *Shaukat Ali v. Govt. of Pakistan* PLD 1997 Supreme Court 342.

[99] The Implementation Rules were issued three years later.

[100] PLD 1990 SC 513.

[101] Submission by Anti-Slavery International to UN Human Rights Commission, *Bonded Labour in Pakistan* (June 1999) at <http://www.antislavery.org/archive/submission/submission1999–08Pakistan.htm>.

[102] Almost without exception, however, these cases have been brought to court only after local government offi-

cials refused to take action or failed to do so when cases were brought to their attention. In late 1998, for example, a court ordered the release of fourteen bonded labourers held at a brick kiln in Rawalpindi District (owned by Altaf: HR Petition No. 110/4/1998). The fourteen consisted of seven adults (four men and three women) and seven children, all considered by the court to be in bondage. The owner of the kiln claimed that they owed him 73,000 Rupees (about US$1,400). The local police refused to carry out the 'recovery notice' which the court issued, calling for the release of fourteen detainees. The court eventually dispatched its bailiff to carry out nighttime releases.

[103] *Sushil Raj Pyakurel v. His Majesty of Government, Secretariat of Ministerial Council, et al.* NKP 2059.

[104] *Tarak Dhital on behalf of Dhiraj KC v. Chief District Officer Kathmandu*, et al. NKP 2059

[105] Writ Petition No. 6070 of 1997 (31 May, 2001). There are pending writ petitions regarding the collapse of two buildings, following allegations of non-compliance with statutory duties, in particular regarding the construction industry, which resulted in the deaths of workers.

regarding the safety of workers in the garment industry, following reports of a significant number of fire related deaths due to non-compliance with the Factories Act 1965 and Fire Services Ordinance 1959. The judgment is significant given that the Court did not merely limit its findings to the obligations of the particular public and private respondents, but also gave directions for the establishment of a suitable national monitoring mechanism, with tripartite involvement of the Government, employers and trade unions, to ensure the implementation of national standards.

In addition to livelihood and forced labour, there is of course a considerable body of employment rights jurisprudence in each of the jurisdictions underpinned by a statutory regulatory framework. While a detailed exploration of this case law is beyond the scope of this chapter, some notable examples may be mentioned. A few of the employment rights issues that have been addressed by South Asian Courts include:

- differences in retirement ages for men and women are gender-discriminatory (Bangladesh);[106]
- the right to form an association does not include the right to strike (Bangladesh);[107]
- protecting minimum wages for unskilled workers (Pakistan);[108]
- the unfair reduction of wages is unlawful under Islamic law (Pakistan);[109]
- employers have obligations to provide adequate insurance for employees (Pakistan);[110]
- sufficient notice must be given to an employee dismissed prior to reaching retirement age (Pakistan);[111]
- an unlawfully dismissed employee has the right to adequate compensation but not reinstatement (Pakistan);[112]

- State directed to consider fixing maternity leave by taking into consideration the provision of international instruments (Nepal);[113]
- freedom of association includes the right to form trade unions which was violated by a requirement of resigning from trade union membership for promotion[114] and that this right encompassed not only joining but also continuing membership of a trade union[115] but did not extend to the freedom to strike[116] (Sri Lanka).

While the South Asian courts have all developed extensive jurisprudence on issues of discrimination or equality of opportunity in relation to appointments, promotions and benefits related to employment in public service, these cannot be considered in depth here.[117]

4.3 Livelihood/Forced Eviction/Housing

The Courts have been relatively vigilant in relation to housing rights, particularly with respect to forced evictions of slum dwellers. In Bangladesh, the High Court has given several important judgments in writ petitions by way of PIL, challenging forced eviction of slum dwellers without sufficient notice and alternative arrangements being made for their rehabilitation. For example, in the *ASK, Modhumala, Kalam* and *Bangladesh Legal Aid Services Trust* cases (see below), the Court has laid down guidelines for the rehabilitation of slum dwellers and stated that forced eviction without any alternative accommodation and rehabilitation was unlawful. However, it must be recognised that successive administrations have failed to implement these decisions, continuing instead

---

106 *Bangladesh Biman Corporation v. Rabia Bashri Irene* 55 DLR (AD) (2003) 132.
107 *Abu Hossain v. Registrar*, Trade Unions, 45 DLR 192.
108 *Annoor Textile Mills v. Federation of Pakistan* PLD 1994 SC 568.
109 *Govt. of NWFP v. Sherwani* 1994 SC 72.
110 *Muhammad Habib Khan v. Pakistan Tobacco Limited* PLD 1991 SC 183.
111 *Muhammad Janan v. General Manager, Pakistan Mineral Development Corp., Islamabad* PLD 2003 SC 156.
112 *Raziuddin v. Chairman, Pakistan Int'l Airlines* PLD 1992 SC 531.

113 *Prakash Mani Sharma et al v. HMG, Woman Child and Social Welfare Ministry et al.* NKP 2060, Vol. 9/10, p. 726.
114 *Ariyapala Gunaratne v. People's Bank* (1986) 1 Sri. LR 338.
115 *De Alwis v. Gunawardene* SC (FR) 7/87, SCM 23.03.1988.
116 *Yasapala v. Wickremasinghe* FRD (1) 143.
117 See, for example, the landmark decision of the Bangladesh Supreme Court in *Dr. Nurul Islam v. Bangladesh (1981) 33 DLR AD 201* finding the 'public interest' retirement of a senior government official to be without lawful authority being discriminatory and arbitrary; that qualification tests for public employment should not be arbitrary and should have a rational relationship with the suitability of the candidate for public office and be consistent with the doctrine of equality of opportunity (*Gazi Jashimuddin v. Bangladesh* 50 DLR (1998) 31).

to carry out sporadic evictions without undertaking any resettlement plan, and also failing to follow through systematically with designing and implementing such plans where they have at least been initiated.[118]

In the first landmark decision on this issue, the High Court in its 1999 judgment of *ASK v. Government of Bangladesh*[119] considered a petition by two slum dwellers and three NGOs working in the area, following mass forced evictions and house demolitions in informal settlements in Dhaka carried out wholly without notice. Referring to the well-known Indian judgment in *Olga Tellis v. BMC*,[120] the High Court concluded that although the rights to livelihood and shelter, which had been severely impacted, were not judicially enforceable they could be derived from the fundamental rights to life, dignity and equal protection under the law: 'Our Constitution both in the Directive State Policy and in the preservation of the fundamental rights provided that the State shall direct its policy towards securing that the citizens have the right to life, living and livelihood'. (Para 9.)

Hence the Court was able to lay down guidelines for the rehabilitation of slum dwellers to be carried out in phases and to direct that the Government could only carry out eviction of slum dwellers when alternate arrangements could be made for their abode, rather than carrying out wholesale demolition of slums.[121]

Subsequent decisions by the Court have reaffirmed this approach, holding that even those trespassing on land should not be evicted forcibly without notice – the affected occupiers have the right to the opportunity to leave of their own free will.[122] Due process required compliance with existing legislation, which provided for a mandatory and minimum notice period of seven days.[123]

In *Kalam and Others v. Bangladesh and Others*,[124] the High Court, citing its earlier decision in *ASK*, gave orders in a petition from a large number of families who had been living in shanty houses in a Dhaka slum for more than thirty years, allowing them to continue residing there by stopping a forced eviction which was threatened to be carried out by the Government without prior notice. The petitioners did not claim any proprietary right over the land but only permission to continue living there. The Court noted that all persons enjoyed the same set of constitutional rights based on social justice, fairness and dignity, irrespective of whether they were poor or marginalised.[125] However it refrained from making any directions, following an assurance given on behalf of the government that the petitioners and other slum dwellers would not be evicted without rehabilitation.[126]

Protection has also been extended to the right to freedom from eviction of sex workers in the landmark case of *Bangladesh Society for the Enforcement of Human Rights and Ors v. Government of Bangladesh and Ors.*[127] The Court drew upon earlier decisions on eviction of slum dwellers and ruled that the forced eviction of a large number of sex workers and their children[128] violated their right to life, which included the right to livelihood

---

[118] Decisions taken at various times for rehabilitation of evicted slum dwellers, for example in 2007 to form a seven-member rehabilitation committee to prepare a plan for immediate and long-term rehabilitation of slum dwellers in Dhaka, with government to provide the land for this project and NGOs to provide the funds for the construction of the shelter homes, are yet to be implemented. See news report dated 19 February, on the website for Bangladesh Sangbad Sangstha: <http://www.bssnews.net/index.php?genID=BSS-04-2007-02-19&id=7>.

[119] 19 BLD (1999) 488.

[120] AIR 1986 SC 180.

[121] Ibid. para. 17.

[122] *Aleya Begum v. Bangladesh & Others* 53 DLR (2001) 63, para. 37.

[123] *Modhumala v. Bangladesh* 53 DLR (2001) 540, paras. 8 and 15.

[124] 21 BLD 446.

[125] *Kalam and Others v. Bangladesh and Others* 21 BLD 446, para. 7.

[126] Ibid. para. 7. See also the judgment of the High Court on 15.11.2007 in *Bangladesh Legal Aid and Services Trust (BLAST) and Others v. Bangladesh* in Writ Petition No. 5915 of 2005 (not available at time of going to press) directing the Government to allow slum dwellers to remain in possession for two years while plans are made for their rehabilitation and resettlement prior to eviction.

[127] 53 DLR (2001) 1, judgment dated 14 March 2000; later affirmed by the Appellate Division.

[128] The workers and their children were amongst 2,667 permanent and 300 casual residents of the Nimtali and Tanbazar areas in Narayanganj who were forcibly and violently evicted by the police during the night/early morning of 23–24 July 1999. Of those arrested, 155 were then forcibly detained in a vagrant home and allegedly subjected to mental and physical torture and denied visits from their families. The petitioners alleged that such detention violated the sex-workers rights to legal protection against harmful and unlawful action to their life and liberty contrary to articles 31 and 32 including right to livelihood.

(see above), and also their right to be protected against forcible search and seizure of their home. The Court further noted its dissatisfaction with the passive role played by the police and the district administration in allowing local house owners and 'hoodlums' 'to carry out the evictions. In so holding, the Court made the following observations on the requirements for any effective rehabilitation scheme, and on the acquiescence of the local authorities, particularly the police, in the violations:

[T]he forcible taking away of sex workers and putting them into the…vagrant home…have been done without any lawful authority in derogation of their right to life or livelihood and contrary to the dignity or worth of the human person, as they do not come squarely within the mischief of the definition of Vagrant under the Vagrancy Act, and no proceeding in accordance with law or any finding was arrived at as to their vagrant nature…Although their consent had been taken for improvement of their conditions upon rehabilitation but the rehabilitation scheme must not be compatible with the dignity and worth of human person but designed to uplift personal morals and family life and provision for jobs giving them option to be rehabilitated or to be with their relations and providing facilities for better education, family connection and economic opportunities in order to do so much to minimize the way as has been done in respects of the sex-workers of Nimtali and Tanbazar. The respondents must co-ordinate their efforts with the UNDP or other appropriate organisations formulating and adopting a durable pilot scheme for the purpose of the sex-workers of the country with a sense of security.…

However, where such evictions are carried out by private parties, no constitutional remedy is available since such guarantees cannot be applied horizontally,[129] although this does not preclude the victims seeking compensation though an ordinary civil action.

In the Nepali case of *Rajan Manandhar v. His Majesty of Government, Kathmandu Valley, Municipal Development Plan Implementation Committee*,[130] the Supreme Court declared void a municipal development scheme which would have resulted in the forced eviction of the petitioner and the destruction of his house without providing the chance for sufficient clarification.

Other housing cases considered by Nepal and Pakistani courts include the protection of right to access to basic shelter for a landless peasant where ownership was called into question due to the failure to pay the necessary taxes since it was state policy to provide such land;[131] ordering that existing residents should not be displaced as a result of housing laws directing that no residences should be in industrial locations;[132] and the process of housing allocation in respect of an employee housing foundation.[133]

4.4 Property and Land

Courts across the region, in interpreting the relevant constitutional provisions, have recognised that the right to property is not absolute but can sometimes be acquired in the public interest. In the case of *Ad. Mithiles Kumar Singh v. Hon'ble Prime Minister, Office of Prime Minister, Singh Durbar, Kathmandu et al.*,[134] the Supreme Court of Nepal, whilst recognising that to acquire, own, sell and otherwise dispose of property is a legal and indeed constitutional right under article 17,[135] nevertheless held that it did not enjoy absolute status. It went on to hold in *Nanda Kumari Rawal v. HMG, Ministry of Industry et al.*,[136] that while the right to property may not be considered

---

[129] *Sultana Nahar, Advocate v. Bangladesh & Ors* 18 BLD (HCD) (1998) 363. Although the manner of the evictions was condemned by the Court, it could not reinstate the workers in the property as it was owned by private individuals and the eviction was not carried out by a government agency.

[130] Supreme Court Publication, Human Right Related Decisions, Special Vol., 2059 p. 317 (Nepal).
[131] *Hirasingh Roka v. Municipal Development Committee Dhangadhi et al.* (Unreported judgment) (Nepal).
[132] *Umar Din v. Muhammad Abdul Aziz Sharqi* PLD 1985 SC 265 (Pakistan).
[133] *Federal Govt. Employee's Housing Foundation v. Muhammad Akram Alizai, Deputy Controller, PCB, Islamabad* PLD 2002 SC 1079 (Pakistan).
[134] Supreme Court Publication, Special Vol. 2059, p. 203 (Nepal).
[135] See also *Purna Bahadur Thapa v. Land Reform Office* 2050, Vol. 2, p. 88 SC (property right does not only mean ownership right over physical thing but also includes the right to possess, control and acquire benefit from such property).
[136] NKP 2050, Vol. 4, pg. 180.

as inviolable under article 17(2) of the Constitution,[137] property may be acquired in the public interest provided this is done in accordance with the law and not arbitrarily.[138] Further, the owner of the property has a right to a fair hearing and information prior to any acquisition being carried out[139] and must be adequately compensated.[140]

Similarly, in Bangladesh and Pakistan, the superior courts have upheld acquisitions of property for the public purpose, but have reviewed acquisition decisions where they were taken arbitrarily or with non-application of mind.[141] In one case (later reversed) the Bangladesh High Court found the acquisition of property for a private school to be void, referring to the Fundamental Principles of State Policy in articles 14, 17 and 19 and holding that the school did not conform to the national education policy.[142]

4.5 Education

Several South Asian education cases are concerned with the legality of affirmative action measures designed to promote access for certain disadvantaged groups by establishing a quota system of reserved places – reflecting many similar cases in India. For example, in the case of *Ajaya Kumar Jha/Pradhos Chhetri et al. v. Executive Board of Tribhuvan University et Al.*,[143] the Nepali

Supreme Court held that any quota system based on reserved places had to be grounded in law and, in the absence of this, a University's decision to adopt such a system to benefit women, Dalits and other groups breached the right to equality under article 11.

In two other judgments, the Nepali Courts asserted the need for free education at the primary level (which is mandatory under articles 13(2) (a) and 14 of the ICESCR and article 28 of the CRC) as compared to secondary. In *Mohan Kumar Karna v. Education and Support Ministry et al.*,[144] the Supreme Court affirmed that whilst there was a statutory duty to provide free education at the secondary level for certain disadvantaged groups – including women and Dalits – this did not extend to a general duty for all since there was no constitutional bar on requesting fees. Every democratic state should be able to determine its own education policy based on its level of economic development. However, this limited position regarding the State's obligations to enable access to education at the secondary level may be contrasted with its duty to provide universal free education at the primary level, as *Ekaraj Bastola v. Bhabasagar Shrestha* made clear based on article 26 of the Constitution.[145]

In Pakistan, the Courts have applied fundamental rights in determining issues concerning education, by striking down a government policy which allowed free migration from one medical college to another on the ground that it violated the education rights of students at an over-crowded college;[146] upholding the reservation of seats in educational institutions on grounds of disability or for persons from 'backward areas';[147] allowing equal treatment for a school compared to other evicted tenants even if this meant hardship for the pupils[148] and affirming the right to education of a student who was allowed to continue his studies.[149] The Bangladesh High Court has also addressed the issue of education, holding for

---

[137] Article 17(2) provides that the State shall not, except in the public interest, requisition, acquire or create any encumbrances on the property of any person.

[138] See also *Sita Bista Chhetri v. HMG, Ministry of Home et al.* 2051, Vol. 11, p. 552.

[139] *Rajendra Prasad Rijal vs. HMG et al.* Supreme Court Human Rights Special Volume, 2059, p. 286; see also *Jhamak Bahadur Niraula v. HMG Secretariat* 2055, Vol. 1, p. 17 (notification through NTV, Radio Nepal Gazette etc. not sufficient and reasonable to notify concerned person).

[140] *Indra Kumari Gautam v. Secretariat Ministerial Council* NKP 2058, Vol. 1, 2, p. 21 SC; see also Pakistan case *Land Acquisition Collector & another v. Abdul Wahid Chaudhry & others* 2004 DLR 608 (right of compensation and list of factors to be used in accurately evaluating price of a piece of land or property).

[141] *East Pakistan v. Lodh 11 DLR (SC) 411*; and see also *Sankar Gopal Chatterjee v. The Additional Commissioner 41 DLR (1989) 326*, and *Ali Jan Khan v. Bangladesh 37 DLR (AD) (1985) 161*.

[142] *Winifred Rubie v. Bangladesh* 1981 BLD 30 reversed by the Appellate Division in 1982 BLD (AD) 34; see also discussion by M. Islam, *Constitutional Law of Bangladesh* (Dhaka: Mullick Brothers, 2003), p. 56–57.

[143] (Unpublished).

[144] NKP, 2060, Vol. 7/8, p. 551.

[145] NKP, 2054, Vol. 5, p. 267.

[146] *Aneel Kumar v.. University of Karachi* PLD 1997 SC 377.

[147] *Abdul Baqi v. Muhammad Akram* PLD 2003 SC 163; *Mstt Attiya Bibi v. Federation of Pakistan* 2001 SCMR 1161 and *Shireen Raza v. Federation of Pakistan* 2002 SCMR 1218.

[148] *Province of Punjab v. Muhammad Tufail* PLD 1985 SC 360.

[149] *Shah Alam Khan v. Vice-Chancellor, Agriculture University* PLD 1993 Supreme Court 297.

example that the disqualification on grounds of age of a candidate from obtaining an admit card to take part in an examination amounted to discrimination.[150]

5. CONCLUSION

During the last three decades, South Asian courts have provided a rich and most varied of economic and social rights jurisprudence. In some areas, they have been in the forefront of advancing jurisprudence on economic, social and cultural rights not just regionally but globally. Such advances have largely been achieved through timely and opportune judicial activism combined

---

[150] *Dr. Manzoor Rasheed Chowdhury v. The Principal, Dhaka Medical College and Others* 22 BLD (HCD) (2002) 6.

with the creativity and persistence of lawyers and activists. Notable judicial victories might appear to be a drop in the ocean in the face of the continuing widespread and systemic denial of economic, social and cultural rights across the region. Yet such decisions can provide important lessons and perhaps even inspiration for those seeking to hold to account violators of such rights.

At the same time, the challenge of responding to such lessons, and translating inspiration into action remains an overwhelming one. Many significant judicial decisions are not implemented fully or even in part. Advances in jurisprudence urgently need to be matched by action on the ground to ensure compliance of all concerned authorities with the judgments and orders of national courts, to ensure effective enforcement and enjoyment of economic and social rights.

7

Colombia

The Constitutional Court's Role in Addressing Social Injustice

Magdalena Sepúlveda*

1. INTRODUCTION

In 1991, Colombia adopted a remarkably progressive Constitution, and the Constitutional Court established therein has emerged as a leading actor in the affairs of the country. The Court is the highest judicial body and is entrusted with the 'safeguarding of the integrity and supremacy of the Constitution' (article 241). This has prompted a profound change in the legal culture of the country, including considerable attention to the judicial enforcement of economic, social and cultural rights. Composed of nine judges elected by the Senate for a period of eight years with no re-election,[1] the Constitutional Court has taken extraordinary steps towards making the protection of economic, social and cultural rights effective in the country. This protection has been achieved through the abstract constitutional review of legislation, as well as through decisions adopted in individual cases.

According to article 1 of the new Constitution, Colombia is a 'social state' (estado social),[2] 'based on respect of human dignity, on the work and the solidarity of the individuals who belong to it, and the predominance of the general interest'. These principles, considered the pillars of the Colombian State, combined with specific constitutional rights, have provided the basis for the Constitutional Court's decisions regarding the protection of economic, social and cultural rights ('ESC rights').

The main mechanism for the judicial protection of these rights is the writ of protection of fundamental rights (acción de tutela or tutela action), which is one of the most important instruments envisaged in the Constitution to guarantee respect for human rights.[3] Article 86 of the Constitution recognises the right of every person to file a writ of protection before any court or tribunal for the immediate protection of her or his 'fundamental constitutional rights'. All decisions by ordinary judges on a writ of protection are sent to the Constitutional Court and are susceptible to review. This process of review has enabled the Court to develop an important body of jurisprudence on the protection of ESC rights.

While the Constitutional Court has also contributed significantly to the protection of ESC rights by reviewing the constitutionality of legislation,[4] this chapter focuses on the case law

* Research director of the International Council on Human Rights Policy (Geneva). The author wishes to thank Rodolfo Arango and Mark Manly for their comments on an earlier draft. The research for this paper was conducted in 2005 and reflects developments up to 31 March 2006.

[1] The judges are elected from lists presented to the Senate by the president of the Republic, the Supreme Court of Justice and the Council of State (article 239).

[2] The concept of 'estado social' is equivalent to the 'Sozialer Rechtsstaat' of the German Constitution (Grundgesetz). According to the Constitutional Court, the welfare state (estado de bienestar) and the social state (estado social) are not equivalent concepts. See C-1064/01 and T-533/92. This article follows the references employed by the Court. The letter refers to the type of judgment: 'C' judgments (Constitutional Review judgments, see note 16), 'T' judgments (tutela judgments) and 'SU', (Unification judg-

ments, see note 17) and is followed by the registration number and the year.

[3] The Constitution also envisages other mechanisms for the protection of the rights enshrined in the Constitution, such as constitutional judicial review (article 241.3) and actio popularis for the protection of collective rights (article 88). However, the judicial protection of economic, social and cultural rights has been governed by the writ of protection.

[4] For example, judgment C-776/03, in which the extension of a value added tax to some basic staples was

generated by the Court's practice of reviewing writs of protection for fundamental rights. The focus on the Constitutional Court's jurisprudence on such writs is justified by the fact that a review judgment of a lower court decision by the Constitutional Court implies, in practice, the delivery of a new judgment. Additionally, the review judgments of the Constitutional Court bind ordinary judges, whose decisions in *tutela* actions are reversed if they are contrary to the Court's case law.[5]

2. OVERVIEW OF RELEVANT PROVISIONS IN THE 1991 CONSTITUTION

The Colombian Constitution divides protected rights into three groups: fundamental rights, social, economic and cultural rights, and collective and environmental rights.[6] The first group (articles 11–41) comprises classic civil and political rights, including some negative duties relating to ESC rights. The second group (articles 42–77) is concerned mainly with ESC rights, while the third group (articles 78–82) is mainly devoted to the protection of consumer rights and the right to a healthy environment. Despite these headings, the Court has noted that the Constitution does not exhaustively establish which fundamental constitutional rights can be enforced through a writ of protection.[7] It therefore falls to the presiding judge to determine if the rights claimed are immediately enforceable or not.

2.1 ESC Rights in the Constitution

The list of ESC rights provisions enshrined in the Constitution is extensive and includes, *inter alia*, the right to work and the right to enjoyment of just and favourable conditions of work (article 25), the freedom of choice of occupation, work, or other gainful activities (article 26), the freedom to form and join trade unions (article 39), the freedom

of education, the freedom to undertake scientific research and academic freedom (article 27), the protection of the family (article 42), the right to social security (article 48), the right to health end environmental protection (article 49), the right to adequate housing (article 51), the right to leisure (article 52), the right to work and rights related to work (article 53), the right to technical and vocational guidance (article 54), the right to collective bargaining (article 55), the right to strike (article 56), the right to property, including intellectual property (article 58), the right to education (article 67), the right to establish educational institutions (article 68), the right to have access to university education and the protection of the autonomy of universities (article 69), the right to equal access to culture (article 70) and freedom in the search for knowledge and artistic expression (article 71). In addition, the Constitution includes several provisions aimed at the protection of vulnerable and disadvantaged groups within society,[8] as well as special protective measures for women, children, adolescents, older people and persons with disabilities (articles 46–47). All of these provisions are viewed as the expression of the principle of the social state.[9]

The Constitution also envisages that international human rights treaties ratified by Colombia take precedence over domestic law (article 93). The rights recognised in, for example, the International Covenant on Economic, Social and Cultural Rights ('ICESCR') and the Additional Protocol to the American Convention in the Area of Economic, Social and Cultural Rights should, therefore, also be taken into account since Colombia is a party to both treaties. International labour treaties ratified by Colombia are part of domestic legislation (article 53) as well. It is not rare in this regard to find that the Constitutional Court has expressly

---

declared unconstitutional, C-383/99, C-700/99 and C-747/99, which declared unconstitutional the system for financing social housing because the Court considered that the system made the right to housing unattainable (see section 4.3).
[5] See section 2.2.
[6] Title II, chapters 1, 2 and 3.
[7] See section 2.2.

[8] For example, the Constitution recognises the duty to provide special protection to groups that are discriminated against or marginalised and to those individuals who, on account of their economic, physical, or mental condition, are in a situation of manifest vulnerability (*debilidad manifiesta*) (article 13), the duty to give support to unemployed persons and to ensure that disabled persons have access to work appropriate to their conditions (article 54) and the duty to take special measures to promote access to basic goods and services for low-income individuals (article 334).
[9] See, e.g., judgment C-1064/01.

found violations, in some judgments, of international human rights and humanitarian law treaties ratified by Colombia.[10]

2.2   The Writ of Protection

The writ of protection *(acción de tutela)* enshrined in article 86 of the Colombian Constitution was established to ensure respect of constitutional rights and freedoms. It was an innovative contribution of the 1991 Constitution and has emerged as the most significant tool for the judicial protection of ESC rights. This writ may be filed by any person whose 'fundamental constitutional rights' are threatened or violated by an action or omission of any public authority, and its effect is to request immediate protection. The writ may also be filed against private individuals if they are entrusted with providing a public service, if their conduct may affect seriously and directly the collective interest or in respect of whom the applicant may find himself or herself in a state of subordination or vulnerability (article 86).

According to the Constitution, the writ requires a summary proceeding, and the trial judge has a time period of ten days between the filing of the writ of protection and its resolution. This writ is only obtainable if no other means of judicial defence are available to the affected party, unless the writ is used as a temporary device to avoid irreversible harm. The writ should be submitted to a judge in the area where the incident(s) in question have taken place[11] and by the affected party or a person acting on her or his behalf. There is no formal requirement for a lawyer or formal legal petition. In some cases, the ombudsperson *(defensor del pueblo)* may lodge the petition on behalf of the affected party.

The *tutela* decisions have no specific remedy. According to article 86 of the Constitution, the protection afforded consists of an order issued by a judge enjoining others to act or refrain from acting. Thus, judges have the discretion to determine the measures that they consider necessary to preserve constitutional rights. The decision, which

must be complied with immediately,[12] may be challenged before a superior court judge.[13]

As noted, all decisions by ordinary judges on the protection of fundamental rights are sent to the Constitutional Court for eventual review (article 241.9). The Constitutional Court selects for review those judgments that it considers necessary to modify or pertinent for the development of its own case law.[14] The review of the judgment by the Constitutional Court implies, in practice, a new judgment.[15] Upon reviewing lower court judgments, the Constitutional Court tends to unify the standards developed by the judges of the first and second instance, who are obliged to follow the decisions of the Constitutional Court.[16]

3. THE ROLE AND INTERPRETIVE FRAMEWORK OF THE CONSTITUTIONAL COURT

It is important to keep in mind from the outset that, in general, the Court recognises that ESC rights are progressive in nature.[17] However, in line with international human rights law,[18] the

---

[10] See, e.g., judgments T-341/94, T-323/94, SU-1150/00 and T-025/04.

[11] Legislative Decree 1382 (2000) has further regulated the competence of courts to receive *tutelas*.

[12] If the respective authority does not comply with the decision, it is possible to file a contempt motion *(incidente de desacato)* in order to request compliance with the judgment. Through this procedure, the judge may order the arrest or other sanctions against the respective public official and his/her superior until they comply with the *tutela* judgment (Article 27 Decree 2591 (1991)). This provision has been applied by the Constitutional Court several times and has proved to be an effective way to ensure compliance with *tutela* judgments.

[13] The appeal must be filed within three days following the judgment. A judgment on the appeal must be delivered within twenty days.

[14] The Court reviews approximately 1 per cent of the thousands of decisions of ordinary courts on the protection of constitutional rights. The Constitutional Court has one month to select, at its discretion, the judgments it will review and three months to hand down the final judgments (articles 31 and 32, Legislative Decree 2591 of 1991).

[15] The review judgments are decided by review chambers *(salas de revisión)*, which are composed of three magistrates.

[16] Sometimes, the Court directly issues judgments aimed at unifying criteria developed in the case law on a given matter. These are called 'unification judgments' *(sentencias de unificación de criterios jurisprudenciales)*. These decisions are adopted by the full Chamber *(sala plena)*.

[17] See, e.g., SU-111/97.

[18] See, in this regard, Committee on Economic, Social and Cultural Rights ('CESCR'), *General Comment No. 3, The nature of States parties' obligations*, (Fifth session, 1990), U.N. Doc. E/1991/23, annex III at 86 (1991).

Court has noted that the progressive realisation of these rights should not be interpreted as depriving the State's obligations of all meaningful content. Rather, it has stressed that the constitutional recognition of these rights requires that the State, at a minimum, must devise and adopt a plan of action for the implementation of the rights. According to the Court, the lack of such planning would be contrary to the Constitution.[19] Additionally, it has noted that the progressive nature of a right cannot justify the failure to take any action and that retrogressive measures in the enjoyment of ESC rights (or in the allocation of resources for their satisfaction) are, *prima facie*, inconsistent with the Constitution.[20]

Nonetheless, what is notable about the Court's case law is that it has gone beyond the mere recognition of these general duties. Indeed, the Court has stressed that, in certain circumstances, ESC rights are susceptible to direct application by the courts through *tutela* actions. In order to reach this conclusion, the Court has undertaken a systematic and teleological interpretation of the Constitution, placing the values enshrined in article 1 of the Constitution, such as the protection of individual dignity and the principle of the 'social state', as the guiding principles of its work.[21]

The immediate applicability of ESC rights has been developed by the Court principally through three interpretive practices: (a) a broad interpretation of 'fundamental rights', such as the right to life, dignity and physical integrity; (b) the concept of 'minimum conditions for a dignified life' (*mínimo vital*); and (c) the concept of 'unconstitutional state of affairs' (*estado de cosas inconstitucional*). The following Section briefly examines these concepts as they have been developed by the Court, and, in addition, section 4 includes examples of how the Court has applied these concepts in the protection of specific ESC rights. It is important to note that, due to the high number of *tutela* decisions,[22] the Court's judgments are not always

as consistent as one might expect. The following examination therefore tries to simplify the issues by referring to major trends.

3.1 Broad Interpretation of 'Fundamental Rights'

According to article 86 of the Constitution, the writ of protection is established for the protection of 'fundamental constitutional rights'. Nonetheless, the Constitutional Court has rejected a formalistic interpretation of the Constitution,[23] considering that the writ of protection extends to rights that, 'by nature', are fundamental; this has created the possibility for the judicial protection of ESC rights in certain circumstances.[24]

One of the principal means the Court has used judicially to protect ESC rights has been the development of the concept of 'related fundamental right' or 'fundamental right by connection' (*derecho fundamental por conexidad*).[25] This concept refers to situations in which ESC rights are so intertwined with fundamental rights that lack of immediate protection would violate or threaten enjoyment of the latter. As shown in section 4, the writ of protection is granted for the protection of ESC rights as fundamental rights by connection only in exceptional circumstances, when, for example, their immediate protection is required in order to respect the life, dignity, or physical integrity of the individual.[26]

3.2 The Concept of the Minimum Conditions for a Dignified Life

Following the case law of the administrative courts in Germany, the Colombian Constitutional Court has developed the concept of *mínimo vital* (*Existenzminimum*),[27] which refers to the right of every

---

[19] See, e.g., T-595/02 and T-025/04.
[20] See, e.g., T-602/03. In that judgment, the Court notes that retrogressive measures in public policies would be in violation of Article 2(1) ICESCR. In the same vein, in T-025/04, the Court explicitly refers to General Comments Nos. 3 and 14 issued by the CESCR.
[21] See, e.g., T-533/92.
[22] According to the latest information available, In 1992, the Court decided 182 *tutela* cases; in the year 2004, this number increased to 1,133. See www.constitutional.gov.co.

[23] As mentioned, under the heading 'fundamental rights' (articles 11–41), the Constitution includes mainly civil and political rights. See section 2.
[24] See also article 2, Legislative Decree 2591 (1991).
[25] See, e.g., T-406/92, T-571/92 and T-116/93.
[26] See, e.g., T-002/92 and T-406/92.
[27] See R. Arango and J. Lemaitre (eds.), *Jurisprudencia constitucional sobre el derecho al mínimo vital* [Constitutional Case Law on the Minimum Conditions for a Dignified Life] (Bogotá: Ediciones Uniandes, 2002), p. 7.

person to 'minimum conditions for a dignified life'.[28] Although the Court recognises that this right is not enumerated in the Constitution, it considers that it may be constructed from the right to life, right to health and the right to work and social security.[29]

According to the Court, in cases of extreme urgency in which the basic subsistence of the individual and her family is in jeopardy, it is possible to file a writ of protection as a fast-track emergency measure for the enforcement of ESC rights. The Court's reasoning has been that, if an individual were in an extremely vulnerable situation and without immediate protection, her conditions of subsistence would fall below an accepted minimum, thus violating her inherent human dignity. Therefore, immediate judicial protection is called for. Generally, as we see in the examples below, the Court has referred to this concept when an individual's pension, salary, or maternity benefits are denied and such benefits are the only source of income for that individual and her family. Although *tutela* protection generally would not be available in this type of circumstance (as the affected individual has the possibility of recourse to other means of judicial redress such as labour or administrative tribunals),[30] the Court has generally immediately enforced the rights claimed in order not to delay a remedy to the already precarious situation of the petitioner.[31] It would be fair to say that, by providing immediate protection to ESC rights in this type of case, the Court applies the Latin maxim '*justitia dilata est justitia negata*' (justice delayed is justice denied).

3.3 The Concept of the 'Unconstitutional State of Affairs'

Another tool developed by the Court to determine the direct applicability of ESC rights is the concept of the 'unconstitutional state of affairs' (*estado de cosas inconstitucional*). As this concept is not envisaged in the Constitution and it goes against the *inter partes* effects of the *tutela* proceedings, its development is a clear demonstration of judicial creativity. When considering individual cases, the Court has found that there is an unconstitutional state of affairs if: (a) there are systematic and widespread violations of several constitutional rights that affect a significant number of people and (b) the violations of these rights cannot be attributed to only one State authority, but are due to structural deficiencies.

If the Court finds that the situation constitutes an unconstitutional state of affairs, it does not wait until more petitions are submitted claiming the violation of the same rights due to the same circumstances, but requests the adoption of remedies that are aimed at protecting not only those who filed the writ of protection, but all individuals in the same circumstances. Additionally, the Court has generally ordered a range of State authorities to undertake coordinated efforts to remedy the situation and often requires that a plan of action be designed and implemented to deal with the situation.

The judgments in which the Court has found an unconstitutional state of affairs constitutes recognition of the fact that individuals who are in a vulnerable and marginalised situation are often unable to seek judicial redress. So, by examining the circumstances of those who, for a variety of reasons, are in a position to submit a claim, the Court's ruling seeks redress for everybody in the same circumstances. The application of this concept has proven to be an effective 'checks and balances' mechanism, requiring the authorities to comply with the basic rights and principles established in the Constitution. It has also encouraged collaboration among different authorities to resolve the unconstitutional 'state of affairs'.

The Court has made use of this concept in a limited number of cases, but, in all instances, these are situations with significant impact on Colombian society. As we will see, the Court has

---

[28] See, e.g., T-207/95, T-254/93, T-539/94 and T-431/94.

[29] However, the Court has not been consistent in its case law and has given different meanings to this concept. Sometimes, it refers to the 'right to minimum conditions for a dignified life' as an implicit fundamental right (e.g., T-236/98, T-307/98, T-260/98 and T-841/04). On other occasions, it has employed this concept as the test to determine if a violation of an ESC right is so closely related to a fundamental right ('fundamental right by connection') that it requires immediate protection. For a comprehensive analysis of the different meanings that the Court has used in regard to the *minimo vital*, see Arango and Lemaitre, *Jurisprudencia constitucional* (n. 28 above), pp. 3–129. In any case, it is worth stressing that, from the Court's case law, the *minimo vital* is, beyond doubt, not synonymous with 'minimum salary' (see, e.g., SU-995/99).

[30] See section 2.2.

[31] SU-995/99.

applied this concept, *inter alia*, to protect internally displaced persons (IDPs)[32] and detainees facing inhumane prison conditions.[33]

4. SELECTED ECONOMIC, SOCIAL AND CULTURAL RIGHTS

The Court has developed an impressive body of case law regarding the protection of ESC rights through the three concepts mentioned above. Due to the overwhelming number of cases, it is not possible to provide a comprehensive overview. Thus, this analysis is limited to some key judgments of the Constitutional Court in *tutela* proceedings.[34] The selection of the cases has been guided by the aim of demonstrating that ESC rights can be and, indeed, are subject to judicial supervision. The selected case law also reflects the main trends in the area. In some of the cases, the Court has exercised a certain degree of judicial activism to ensure that the plaintiffs, who generally belong to marginalised groups in society, secure effective enjoyment of their ESC rights.

4.1 The Right to Work

The right to work (article 25) and the freedom to choose a profession or occupation (article 26) are fundamental rights explicitly enforceable through the writ of protection. However, the Constitutional Court has stated that the right to work does not mean that the State has an obligation to provide work. According to the Court, the legal remedy provided by the *tutela* does not protect the aspiration actually to obtain public or private employment.[35]

Nonetheless, the Court has demonstrated the justiciability of the right to work in a variety of other ways, particularly in the area of the right to equal treatment. For example, in the case of a woman who was denied admission to the Naval Academy on the basis of a policy of not admitting women cadets, the Court protected the right of a woman freely to choose her occupation. The Naval Academy contended that it did not have adequate facilities to receive women cadets, but the Court rejected this argument and ordered the Academy to admit the applicant, notwithstanding that it would need to assume a cost for making its facilities available to women.[36]

In another case, the right to equal access to employment was protected when the Court found that the right to work had been violated because a man was dismissed from his job as a janitor in a public institution. The employer allegedly considered that janitorial duties should be performed by women. In this case, the Court found that the difference in treatment between men and women was not reasonable and objective, and it therefore ordered the reinstatement of the petitioner.[37] Similarly, the Court has considered it unconstitutional to forbid women to work night shifts.[38]

In a landmark case in which the applicant was dismissed after being tested HIV-positive, the Court found that the worker's dismissal was a violation of his right to work and constituted an attack on his reputation. Consequently, the Court ordered the private institution concerned to pay the applicant compensation for the damage caused. In its judgment, the Court stressed that the State must ensure protection to HIV-positive persons, and it reaffirmed the prohibition against obliging potential or current employees to take a HIV test in order to gain or maintain employment.[39]

In a number of decisions, the Court has stressed the importance of the prohibition of discrimination among workers, particularly in the case of trade union workers. For example, the Court has noted that there should be no difference in salary between workers who belong to a trade union and those who do not.[40] In this regard, the Court has found that these rights are violated when there is a salary increase only for workers who do not belong to the trade union or when trade union workers are excluded from working extra hours.[41]

---

[32] See section 5.6
[33] See section 5.5.
[34] The cases examined here refer mainly to the direct protection of ESC rights. However, it is important to keep in mind that the Court has also protected these rights through the right of equality and the prohibition of discrimination (articles 5 and 13) and through *actio popularis* for the protection of collective rights (article 88).
[35] T-008/92.

[36] T-624/95.
[37] T-026/96.
[38] C-622/97.
[39] SU-256/96.
[40] T-061/97. See also SU-342/95 and SU-510/95.
[41] See, e.g., T-230/94, T-079/95, T-143/95, SU-342/95 and SU-510/95.

The Court has also stressed that neither public, nor private employers can discriminate against an employee or determine the salary scale in an arbitrary manner. According to the Court, salaries must be commensurate with the training, experience and knowledge of the employee.[42]

The Court has also protected workers by limiting the so-called *ius variandi*, the discretional power of employers to change the conditions, place and time of work. According to the Court, the right to safe and healthy working conditions limits this discretional power, and this right is violated if an employer changes the worker's place of work without taking into account the worker's state of health.[43] The Court has ruled that workers can therefore demand the immediate protection of their right to work when travel to a work site or the workplace itself causes pain or excessive discomfort or endangers the basic health of the worker, even if the effects do not necessarily lead to death.[44] For example, in the case of a teacher whose delicate state of health had been worsened by the need to travel a long distance to her workplace, the Court ordered the State authorities to transfer her to another workplace. Additionally, it stated that, in the event there were no vacancies, she must be given priority in future openings.[45] In the same vein, in the case of a teacher who suffered from depression and was assigned to a locality with a high level of violence, the Court ordered the Ministry of Education to transfer the applicant to a more stable area as soon as vacancies were available there.[46]

In a more debatable line of decisions, petitioners have successfully used the *tutela* to request the immediate payment of back wages. Although the Court has consistently stated that, as a general rule, the *tutela* is not the appropriate judicial mechanism to seek redress in cases concerning non-compliance with labour contracts (as these cases should be decided by labour tribunals), it has granted the writ in situations in which the absence of the wages owed has demonstrably threatened fundamental rights to life, health, minimum conditions for a dignified life and human dignity.[47] Generally, this occurs when the salary is the only source of income of the worker and her family. The Court has indicated that when the payment of salaries is interrupted indefinitely, there is a presumption that the worker's right to minimum conditions for a dignified life have been violated.[48] Thus, while individuals have other means of redress, the Court has allowed them to invoke the preferential and summary proceedings of the writ of protection since time-consuming administrative or labour proceedings would not provide the urgent protection that employees require.

Finally, it is worth stressing that, according to the Court's case law, wages should provide all workers and their families not only with the satisfaction of the basic biological needs of individuals and families, but must also be sufficient to cover the satisfaction of, inter alia, clothing, health, education, housing and social security needs.[49]

4.2 The Right to Social Security

The Constitution recognises the right to social security as an inalienable right of all individuals (article 48), but does not specify that it is immediately enforceable. Nonetheless, according to the case law of the Constitutional Court, the right assumes, in particular circumstances, a fundamental character because of its relevance in ensuring other fundamental rights ('fundamental right by connection') or in ensuring minimum conditions for a dignified life. This is the case when individuals are in a position of manifest vulnerability (*debilidad manifiesta*) in which the immediate protection of their rights is required to prevent jeopardy to their dignified subsistence.

In 1992, a landmark decision was reached in regard to social security. A 63-year-old man living in absolute poverty, without contact with his family, requested, through a writ of protection, that the State provide him with economic assistance so that he could undergo an eye operation that would enable him to recover his sight. In its judgment (a good example of judicial activism), the Court

---

[42] SU-519/97. See also T-061/97.

[43] See, e.g., T-483/93.

[44] See, e.g., T-694/98.

[45] See T-704/01. Similar issues were decided in, inter alia, T-670/99, T-485/98, T-208/98, T-516/97, T-455/97 and T-002/97.

[46] T-026/02.

[47] See, e.g., T-049/03, T-1097/02, T-175/03, T-601/03 and T-346/04.

[48] See, e.g., T-308/99, T-387/99 and T-346/04.

[49] See, e.g., T-011/98. See also T-192/03.

recognised that the scope and content of social benefits should be determined by law. However, it found that the legislature had not complied with its duty to adopt a law to address the situation of persons in the plaintiff's condition, and such a gap in the social security scheme justified the Court's protection. Therefore, the Court granted the *tutela* and ordered the social security system (*Instituto Colombiano de Seguros Sociales*) to provide the treatment.

The test developed by the Court in this case has been applied in several subsequent judgments. Thus, the Court has held that, in exceptional circumstances, the right to social security is not a programmatic right, but, rather, is immediately applicable. The test developed by the Court to assess when this right will become immediately applicable is as follows: (a) the individual is in a situation of manifest vulnerability (*debilidad manifiesta*) because of his economic, physical, or mental situation; (b) there is no possibility for the individual or his family to take action to remedy the situation; (c) the State has the possibility to remedy or mitigate his condition; and (d) the State's inaction or omission will affect the individual's ability to enjoy minimum conditions of a dignified life.[50]

If these conditions are met, the Court orders the State to comply immediately with its duty to *fulfil* (provide) social assistance. The State has thus been obliged, inter alia, to provide medical treatment,[51] to receive free of charge an indigent mentally ill woman in a public institution for people with mental illness[52] and to provide a poor elderly man with a dignified place to end his days (i.e., a retirement home).[53]

In regard to the enjoyment of the right to social security, the Court has also supervised the fairness of the administrative procedures involved in the provision of social benefits. Any welfare programme, according to the Court, should comply with due process principles, such as the duties: (a) to take special care of vulnerable or disadvantaged people, including elderly people and physically or mentally disabled persons, so as to avoid social exclusion and discrimination; (b) to allow participation of beneficiaries in hearings and com-

mittees that decide on their situation; and (c) to provide timely, pertinent, correct and comprehensive information on the procedures required to obtain the relevant subsidy.[54] Thus, for example, the Court granted *tutela* protection in the case of a poor elderly man who had not received a State subsidy because he had acquired erroneous information from the relevant administrative entity on the procedures necessary to obtain the subsidy.[55]

Although the writ of protection is not the appropriate path for achieving the payment of unpaid social security benefits (because there are other legal means available), the Court has stated that, if the lack of payment implies a violation of the fundamental rights of the petitioners, it is possible to enforce this right through such a writ. For example, while an order for the payment of maternity benefits is outside the scope of the *tutela*, if the minimum conditions for a dignified life of the mother and the newborn depend on the payment of maternity benefits, this right becomes a fundamental right that is immediately enforceable by a writ of protection.[56]

It is worth noting that the right to social security through a *tutela* procedure is not justiciable for everybody. Such protection will be granted only in exceptional circumstances wherein individuals find themselves in a state of dire need that requires immediate judicial protection. Therefore, not all elderly persons, unemployed persons, mothers, or other persons in need of social security can effectively invoke their right to social security though a writ of protection, but only those individuals whose minimum subsistence depends on such benefits.

4.3   The Right to Adequate Housing

The Colombian Constitution incorporates the right to adequate housing, but, in contrast to other constitutionally protected ESC rights, this right only extends to Colombian citizens and not to

---

[50] See, e.g., T-533/92.
[51] T-533/92.
[52] T-046/97.
[53] T-1330/01.

[54] See, e.g., T-149/02 and T-499/95.
[55] T-149/02. The Court ordered the relevant authority to reexamine the case and to provide the man with assistance throughout the proceeding.
[56] See T-568/96, T-270/97, T-567/97, T-662/97, T-175/99, T-362/99, T-496/99, T-104/99, T-139/99, T-210/99, T-365/99, T-458/99, T-258/00, T-467/00, T-1168/00, T-736/01, T-1002/01, T-497/02, T-664/02 and T-707/02.

everybody. The Constitution places a duty upon the State to establish the conditions necessary to give effect to this right and to promote plans for public housing, appropriate systems of long-term financing and community plans for the execution of these housing programmes (article 51).

The most far-reaching cases involving the protection of the right to adequate housing have emerged during judicial review of the constitutionality of the legal provisions that established the system for financing social housing.[57] In its decisions, the Court considered the system existing at that time for financing social housing unconstitutional because it was held that the provisions in force made dignified housing unattainable.[58] These decisions generated an enormous public debate and provoked strong criticism from economists and financial institutions.[59] Nonetheless, overall, the Court's decisions stressed that the State cannot ignore the need for adequate housing and that this right must be progressively developed through an adequate financing system.[60]

As in the case of other ESC rights, the Court has applied the concept of 'fundamental right by connection'. In other words, the Court considers the right to adequate housing as a progressive right not directly applicable by the courts, except when its violation also entails a violation of fundamental rights such as the right to life, dignity and equality.[61]

The Court has protected some important components of the right to housing. For example, the Court found a violation of the right to adequate housing and the right to minimum conditions for a dignified life in the case of a 73-year-old internally displaced woman who, having requested housing subsidies from the entity in charge of the implementation of IDP policies, did not receive an adequate response to her requests. The institution had merely informed her that she needed to go to another public institution in charge of housing benefits. Taking into account the vulnerability of the woman, the Court declared her right to adequate housing immediately enforceable. In the judgment, the Court noted that the protection of the right to housing imposes on the competent authorities the duty to provide adequate information and assistance on the procedures and requirements necessary to have effective access to housing subsidies.[62] This ruling is in line with several other judgments in which the Court stresses that public institutions have a duty to act rationally and in good faith for the protection of the rights of individuals.[63]

4.4 The Right to Health

Although the Constitution does not explicitly use the term 'right to health', scholars and the Constitutional Court have adopted this expression to refer to the content of article 49.[64] This provision states that 'public health and environmental protection are public services for which the State is

---

[57] See, e.g., C-383/99, C-700/99 and C-743/99.

[58] To understand these complex judgments, I would briefly note that, in 1998, there was a crisis in the financial system as a consequence of a drastic increase in interest rates and an unprecedented decrease in real estate prices. At that time, the system for financing social housing relied on a monetary unit (*unidad de poder adquisitivo constante*) that increased in line with the consumer price index (*índice de precios al consumidor*). According to the Court, the use of this system added to the cost of debt obligations in favour of financial institutions and to the detriment of debtors. Although the Court considered that the establishment of mechanisms to index the value of mortgage debt to inflation was constitutional, it found that the existing system was unconstitutional because the system led to what qualifies as usury under Colombian law.

[59] S. Kalmanovitz, 'Los efectos económicos de la Corte Constitucional' [The Economic Effects of the Constitutional Court) (1998), available at <www.banrep.org/junta/publicaciones/salomon/K-EfectosCorte.pdf>; S. Clavijo, 'Fallos y fallas económicas de las altas cortes: El caso de Colombia 1991–2000' [Judgments and Economic Defects of the High Courts: the case of Colombia 1991–2000] (Hispanic American Centre for Economic Research, 2001), available at: <www.hacer.org/pdf/clavijo.pdf>; M. M. Cuellar, 'La prueba de razonabilidad y la estabilidad de las reglas del juego' [The Reasonableness Test and Stability of the Rules of the Game], *Revista de economía institucional*, Vol. 7, No. 12 (June 2005), pp. 13–42 (last visited July 2008).

[60] For a more detailed examination of these judgments, see M. J. Cepeda, 'Judicial Activism in a Violent Context: The Origin, Role and Impact of the Colombian Constitutional Court', *Washington University Global Studies Law Review*, Vol. 3 (2004), pp. 643–645.

[61] See, e.g., T-569/95.

[62] T-602/03.

[63] See, e.g., note 56.

[64] See M. Arbelaez, 'Diez años de la protección constitucional del derecho a la salud: La jurisprudencia de la Corte Constitucional Colombiana (1991–2001)' [Ten Years of Constitutional Protection of the Right to Health: the case law of the Colombian Constitutional Court (1991–2001)] (2002). Available at: <http://www.cajpe.org.pe/rij/bases/juris-nac/arbelaez.pdf> (last visited July 2008).

responsible. All individuals are guaranteed access to services that promote, protect, and rehabilitate public health'. Generally, this right is considered progressive in nature, except when there is a nexus with a fundamental right. Nonetheless, it is worth noting that, according to the Constitution, the right to health of children is a fundamental right *per se*, subject to immediate application by the courts (article 44).

The Court has demonstrated an important level of judicial activism in several crucial cases of immediate application of the right to health of children.[65] In a landmark case, 418 parents from one of the poorest districts in Bogotá filed a writ of protection alleging the violation of their children's right to health and requested that the Court order the State authorities to institute a free vaccination programme for their children. The parents argued that their children were in a high-risk situation and that they (the parents) did not have the resources to cover the cost of the vaccines. The Court ordered the relevant municipal authorities to institute a free infant vaccination programme for the poor.[66] Recognising that its judgment could be considered to affect the principle of separation of powers and determine the allocation of public resources, the Court stressed that the lack of a vaccination plan to cover these children violated the core content of their right to health, perpetuating the disadvantages from which they already suffered.

In another case, the petitioner, a 10-year-old boy who had been deaf from birth, requested the Court to order a private health provider to supply an ear implant. This treatment was excluded from the compulsory health plan (*plan obligatorio de salud*), the content of which is determined by a law and formed part of the contract between the father of the boy and the private health provider. Although the Court noted that neither the life, nor the physical integrity of the boy would be threatened if the treatment were not provided, the Court, referring to the notion of 'minimum conditions for a dignified life', stated that denying the boy the possibility to hear would certainly violate his dignity. Therefore, the Court ordered the private company to provide the treatment.[67]

Some of the most far-reaching judgments referring to the immediate enforceability of the right of children to health are the so-called overseas treatments. These judgments refer to cases in which the Court orders health care providers (public or private institutions) to cover the expenses involved in undertaking treatment outside Colombia when no national treatment is available. In 1995, in a landmark case of a girl who suffered leukaemia and needed a complex transplant that could not be undertaken in Colombia, the Court ordered the social security system to pay for the girl's treatment in a specialised clinic in the United States.[68] In a similar case in which national treatment was not available, but the affected boy was affiliated with a private health company, the Court ordered the company to pay for the cost of the treatment abroad.[69]

According to the Court, overseas treatment can be ordered when the following requirements are met: (a) there are circumstances of extreme gravity that affect the life of the patient; (b) the required medical treatment cannot be undertaken in Colombia; (c) there is medical certification that the treatment would be effective in the particular circumstances of the patient and that the treatment is not experimental; and (d) the individual is unable to cover the cost, but the State has the resources available to do so.[70]

These cases indicate that the right to health care services implies, at least in the case of children, the right to obtain access to expensive, specialist health care services when life or dignified living are in danger. In these cases, it is up to the State to allocate the resources to cover the costs.[71] As

---

[65] See, e.g., T-117/99, SU-043/95, SU-111/97, SU-039/98, T-236/98, T-093/00 and T-421/01.

[66] SU-225/98.

[67] T-236/98.

[68] T-165/95. In addition to the payment for the treatment, the Court also ordered the public institution to cover the flight tickets of the girl and one of her parents and to provide them with US$125,000 as advance payment of expenses. To put this into perspective, one should take into account that Colombia ranked 75th in the 2007/2008 Human Development Index and has a GDP per capita of 7,256 USD. See Human Development Report, 2007/2008, p. 230.

[69] The estimated cost of the treatment was approximately US$371,740, plus medication and travel expenses.

[70] SU-819/99.

[71] It is interesting to compare the reasoning of these rulings of the Colombian Constitutional Court with the more restrictive approach of the South African Constitutional Court in *Soobramoney v. Minister of Health (KwaZulu-Natal)*, 1977(12) BCCR 1969 (CC). It is clear that, for the Colombian Constitutional Court, when life is in danger,

has been noted, the decisions of the Court in cases involving the protection of the right of children to health, rather than reflecting judicial activism, are more properly evidence of effective enforcement of very progressive constitutional norms, particularly as these concern children.[72]

In general, except in the case of children, the justiciability of the right to health in *tutela* actions depends on the circumstances of the case. So, it falls to the judge to decide in the case of an adult if the right to health is directly applicable or not. The Court has mostly considered this right immediately applicable only when it is connected to a fundamental right such as the right to life, personal integrity, dignity and the minimum conditions for the dignified life of the petitioner.[73] If these rights are at stake, the Court requests the State or private entities to provide to the plaintiffs the requested medication or medical treatment necessary for the immediate protection of their right to health.

Of particular interest are those cases in which the Court orders the provision of treatments or medicines that are excluded by law from the catalogue of available treatments (in the compulsory health plan).[74] In such cases, the Court has found that strict compliance with the compulsory health plan would entail a violation of fundamental rights. The Court has thus *de facto* amended the law and the rules of procedure of health care institutions. As we will see, this type of protection has been particularly important in HIV/AIDS cases.[75]

However, while the Court has tended to deny relief to adults when the nexus between the right to health and one of the fundamental rights has not been proven,[76] it has not always been consistent. For example, it has denied the request for the

payment of fertilization[77] and sterilization treatments,[78] considering that these treatments are not linked to a woman's right to life, personal integrity, or human dignity; yet, curiously, it has ordered the provision of Viagra, considering that a man's sexual function is so vital that it forms part of his dignified life.[79]

In regard to private entities, particularly health care providers, the Court has not limited its approach to ordering them to provide treatment or medicine, but has also retained the power to supervise the provision of their services so as to prevent the entities from violating the rights of individuals. For example, the Court has expressed concern when medical treatment is delayed because of inefficiencies in the responses of private health providers. According to the Court, the State has a duty to ensure that medical services are supplied efficiently and with continuity, even when the services are provided by private entities (raising the *obligation to protect*).[80] It is nonetheless worth noting that, when the Court orders private health providers to cover the costs of an overseas treatment or the payment of medication or treatment excluded from the compulsory health plan, private health providers are able to request the reimbursement of the costs from the State.[81]

In conclusion, in the implementation of the right to health, the Court has shown the highest level of judicial activism by requiring the State to comply with its *duty to fulfil* (provide). Although, oftentimes, these judgements have significant budgetary implications, the Court makes an effort not to fall into a utilitarian calculus, but rather to place the protection of individual dignity at the centre of its decisions. From the Court's standpoint, utilitarian considerations carry less weight than the Constitutional commitment to protect human dignity. Additionally, it is important to

---

the right to health is justiciable, notwithstanding the budgetary issues that enforcement of the right may raise.

[72] See M. García Villegas, 'Derechos sociales y necesidades políticas: La eficacia judicial de los derechos sociales en el constitucionalismo colombiano' [Social Rights and Political Necessities: The Judicial Effectiveness of Social Rights in Colombian Constitutional Law], in S. Boaventura de Sousa and M. García Villegas (eds.), *El caleidoscopio de las justicias en Colombia* [The Kaleidoscope of Justice in Colombia] (Bogota: Siglo del Hombre Editores, 2001), p. 467.

[73] See, e.g., T-067/94, T-192/94, T-328/98, T-177/99, T-027/99 and T-636/01.

[74] See, e.g., SU-043/95 and SU-819/99.

[75] See section 5.3.

[76] See, e.g., T-576/94, T-409/95 and T-1036/00.

[77] The Court has stated that infertile women have the option of adoption to become mothers. See, e.g., T-1104/00, T-689/01, T-946/02, T-512/03 and T-901/04.

[78] T-348/97.

[79] T-926/99.

[80] See, e.g., T-227/01, T-428/98, T-030/94, T-059/97, T-088/98, T-428/98 and T-018/03.

[81] This type of expense is covered by a special solidarity fund (*Fondo de Solidaridad y Garantía del Sistema General de Seguros y Salud*) established by law. See Law 100 (1993) and Legislative Decree 1203 (1990).

note that, by granting *tutela* protection against private health providers, the Court has stressed the State's *duty to protect* individuals in the context of the privatisation of public services. Although the law establishes and regulates the responsibilities of private health care providers, the State is ultimately responsible for the protection of the individual.

4.5   The Right to Education

The Constitution recognises the right to education as a fundamental right immediately enforceable by courts through the writ of protection even when private individuals are entrusted with the provision of education (article 27).[82] According to the Constitution, education is compulsory and free of charge in State institutions for children between the ages of 5 and 15 years who cannot afford to pay (article 67). In addition, in the case of children, the right to education must be considered in conjunction with the constitutional provision that establishes special protective measures for children (article 44). This provision recognises that children enjoy the rights set out in international treaties ratified by Colombia.

The Constitutional Court has stressed this last point: that constitutional protection must also take into account the broader scope of the right to education envisaged at the international level, particularly that contained in the Convention on the Rights of the Child. Thus, for example, despite the fact that the Constitution establishes a specific age limit for free education (15 years of age), the Court has determined that this provision must be read in conjunction with the Convention on the Rights of the Child, under which a child is any person below the age of 18. Therefore, those children who are between the ages of 15 and 18 and who have not finished the nine years of basic instruction, have, as in the case of any child below 15, the immediate right to education, free of charge, from the State.[83]

The Court has developed extensive case law in regard to the right to education, with a particular focus on the State's duty to ensure access to educational institutions. Therefore, the Court has found that there is a violation of the right to education when public or private schools deny access to children without adequate justification.[84]

The Court has noted that the right to education also implies duties for students. Thus, if a student does not comply with academic or disciplinary requirements, sanctions can be enacted.[85] Nonetheless, the Court has noted that mandatory regulations on personal appearance (e.g., maximum hair length, dress code and prohibition of make-up) must be proportionate, reasonable and not contrary to human dignity.[86] The Court has considered, for example, that it is unreasonable to deny the right to education to students who contravene regulations on hair length,[87] or for a school to expel pregnant students.[88]

Several cases have dealt with the right to education in private schools. The Court has found that the right to education has been violated if a private school abruptly suspends a minor because their parents or those responsible for the child have not paid the tuition.[89] The right to equal access to education has also been found to have been violated when a private school refused to continue providing education to a 6-year-old child with attention deficit disorder. After considering the limited availability of special education programmes, the widespread nature of this phenomenon and the grave consequences for children and society if these children become marginalised, the Court ordered that all schools must provide education to children with attention deficit disorder even if the schools are not specialised in this type of education.[90]

---

[84] It is considered unjustified to expel a student due to lack of payment, non-compliance with strict dress regulations, or the activities of parents in the school parent associations. See, e.g., T-402/92 and T-450/92.

[85] T-519/92 and T-323/94.

[86] See, e.g., SU-642/98, T-366/97, T-633/97 and T-124/98. According to the Court, in academic institutions, individuals have a right to determine how they appear.

[87] See, e.g., T-065/93.

[88] See, e.g., T-393/97 and T-377/95.

[89] See SU-624/99. Similarly, private schools cannot hold back grading certificates even if tuition has not been paid by the guardians of a student.

[90] See T-255/01.

[82] Although article 27 literally refers only to the 'freedoms' of the right to education, such as the freedom of education, the freedom to undertake scientific research and academic freedom, the Court has interpreted this provision to include all aspects of the right to education; see, e.g., T-534/97.

[83] See T-323/94 and T-236/ 94.

5. THE ESC RIGHTS OF VULNERABLE GROUPS

The Constitution expressly provides for the protection of specific groups such as women, children, adolescents, older persons, disabled persons and indigenous peoples. Additionally, the Constitution envisages a duty to protect 'those individuals who, on account of their economic, physical, or mental conditions, are in obviously vulnerable circumstances' (article 13). All these provisions are viewed by the Constitutional Court as concrete manifestations of the principle of the 'social state'.[91] The following section examines the protection of some particularly important groups.

5.1   Persons with Disabilities

The Constitution provides for special protection for persons with disabilities (article 47) and, in particular, for disabled children (article 23). The Court has interpreted these provisions as requiring that the State not only abstain from measures that might have a negative impact on persons with disabilities, but also take affirmative action to reduce structural disadvantages.[92]

In several cases, the Court has stressed that there is a right of access by persons with disabilities to any place intended for use by the general public. The Court has noted that State authorities, as well as private entities, must ensure persons with disabilities with access to public places. It has also found that there had been discrimination against disabled persons, inter alia, when the construction by private entities of a stadium did not provide for adequate access for wheelchairs,[93] when there was a failure to provide people with disabilities with access to a privately run public transportation system,[94] and when parking barriers built on sidewalks indirectly obstructed the path of visually impaired persons.[95] By ensuring that disabled persons have access to public places and to transportation, the Court has removed major obstacles to the realisation of most of their ESC rights. At the same time, given the increasing tendency for the

privatisation of public service provision, the Court has ensured that private entities guarantee equal treatment to persons with disabilities.

The duty to take positive action for the protection of persons with disabilities has also been supported by the Court in regard to other rights such as the right to education (e.g., stating that educational institutions have a duty to provide access to disabled persons, even if this results in additional burdens for these institutions)[96] and the right to work (e.g., requiring public school authorities to take affirmative action for the protection of a blind teacher).[97]

In the case of children, the Court has held that the State must provide assistance, free of charge, to a disabled child when the economic situation of his parents or guardians so dictates.[98] Moreover, it has argued that medical assistance for disabled children should cover not only the costs of seeking a cure, but also the costs of the improvement of the quality of life when a cure is not possible. According to the Court, if such treatment were denied, this would entail a violation of the fundamental rights of the children as children and as persons with disabilities.[99]

5.2   Pregnant Women and Newborns

The Court has noted that, in accordance with the Constitution, as well as international treaties ratified by Colombia, the State has positive obligations in regard to pregnant women and newborn children. According to the Court, these rights are so fundamental that, in certain circumstances, they are immediately enforceable through the constitutional protection of *tutela* even if this requires the compliance of a State duty to *fulfil* (provide).

For the protection of pregnant women, the Court has generally applied the concept of the minimum conditions for a dignified life.[100] Thus, it has granted women immediate protection of their claims when they have been arbitrarily fired

[91] C-1064/01.
[92] See, e.g., T-427/92.
[93] T-288/95.
[94] T-595/02.
[95] T-024/00.

[96] See, e.g., T-1134/00 and T-150/02.
[97] T-100/94.
[98] See, e.g., T-159/95, T-640/97, T-556/98, T-338/99 and T-179/00.
[99] See, e.g., T-920/00.
[100] See section 3.2.

from their jobs for being pregnant,[101] when their salaries or maternity benefits are not paid on time,[102] or when they require food subsidies because they have been abandoned or are unemployed.[103] In these cases, for the immediate enforcement of their rights through a writ of protection, the pregnant woman or the mother must find herself in an extremely vulnerable situation and the salary or the benefits in question must be her only source of income.

5.3 Persons with HIV/AIDS

According to the Court, the State must take special measures to protect the dignity and human rights of people living with HIV/AIDS. For the Court, the link between the right to health and the right to life is clear in HIV/AIDS cases, and the former can thus be protected through *tutela* proceedings ('fundamental right by connection').

The Court has adjudicated several cases in which social security entities and private health providers have refused to make retroviral or medical examinations available to HIV/AIDS patients on the grounds that these treatments are excluded by law from the compulsory health plan. In such cases in which the patient cannot finance his own treatment, the Court has ordered the provision of the medicines and the necessary treatments notwithstanding that these are not provided for in the catalogue of available treatments under the compulsory health plan. According to the Court, the State has a special duty to protect HIV/AIDS patients; thus, legal norms that exclude a necessary treatment or medicine denying them integral assistance are unconstitutional.[104]

The Court has developed a test to establish when social security entities and private health companies are obliged to provide benefits that are explicitly excluded from the compulsory health plan. The protection is provided by the Court when: (a) the lack of medicine or treatment threatens the right to life or the integrity of the patient; (b) the medicine and the treatment cannot be replaced by

one of the treatments included in the health plan or, when a replacement exists, it does not have the same effect; (c) the patient cannot afford the cost of the medicine or the treatment; and (d) the medicine or the treatment has been prescribed by a physician who belongs to the requested institution (private health care provider or social security entity). If these requirements are met, the Court requires State institutions or private health companies to provide the treatments or the medicines that were initially excluded.[105]

By the same token, in cases in which a private health company requires that an individual be affiliated with the company for a minimum period before becoming entitled to treatment or medicines, the Court has found that, if the treatments or medicines are essential for the life or physical integrity of the individual and the individual cannot afford the payment, the company must provide the treatments even if the patient has not met the contractual criteria for receiving the medicines.[106]

In other cases, several individuals filed a *tutela* alleging that they had acquired AIDS because of blood transfusions in a particular hospital. They asked the Court to order the institution permanently to provide them with all required medical assistance and treatments. Although the institution alleged that its responsibility had not been judicially proven, the Court, considering the direct link between the right to health and the right to life in HIV/AIDS cases, ordered the institution to provide the petitioners the necessary medical assistance while the ultimate responsibility of the institution was being examined in ordinary court proceedings.[107]

It is worth noting that, according to the Court, persons infected with HIV/AIDS are entitled to special protection, but they must also behave with extreme caution in situations in which there is a health-related risk for other people. According to the Court, because of the risk of contagion, people living with HIV/AIDS must comply in a more rigorous manner with the constitutional duties to respect the rights of others and not to abuse one's

---

[101] See, e.g., T-606/95, T-739/98, T-1002/99, T-1620/00, T-0255A/01 and T-167/03.
[102] See, e.g., T-270/97, T-576/97 and T-365/99.
[103] See, e.g., C-470/97, T-694/96, T-373/98 and T-792/98.
[104] See, e.g., T-505/92, T-271/95, SU-480/97, T-185/00 and T-376/03.

[105] See, e.g., T-236/98, SU-480/97, T-560/98, T-505/92, T-271/95 and T-328/98.
[106] See, e.g., T-150/00, T-1204/00, T-284/01, T-755/01, T-699/02 and T-448/03.
[107] SU-645/97.

own rights (article 95). From the Court's point of view, this provision entails a duty to undertake the necessary precautions to avoid transmitting the disease to other people (such as by using contraceptives during sexual relations and avoiding the donation of organs and blood). Following this line of argument, the Court has held that a person who has knowingly infected another with HIV may be obliged to pay the cost of treatment.[108]

5.4   Indigenous Peoples

Several constitutional provisions refer to the rights of indigenous peoples, including, for example, pluralistic democracy (article 1), recognition of the ethnic and cultural diversity of the Colombian nation (article 7), the protection of different cultures (article 8), recognition of various languages (article 10), the principle of equality among all cultures (article 70) and the right to education in their own culture, as well as the right to cultural identity (article 68).

In regard to the enjoyment of ESC rights by indigenous peoples, the Court has made an effort to apply these principles, taking special care in supervising the right of indigenous peoples to enjoy their culture. Thus, the Court has noted that the exploitation of natural resources in indigenous territories must be in line with the State obligation to protect traditional ways of life.[109] The Court has held that any authorisation to exploit natural resources in indigenous territory requires the participation of the indigenous community, which has a 'fundamental right to be consulted' when a project for resource exploitation is proposed in its territories.[110]

Although the right to be consulted is included at the international and national levels,[111] the Court has not limited itself simply to declaring this right, but it has enunciated some of the essential elements of this right. According to the Court,

the mere physical participation of the indigenous community in consultations is not sufficient; rather, it is necessary to comply with a set of requirements, including that the community: (a) be informed of the overall project and of the procedures and activities for the implementation of the project; (b) be informed of the effects that the project might have on its way of life, economy and culture; (c) have the opportunity, freely and without any interference, to convene its members or representatives to evaluate the advantages and disadvantages of the project on the community and its members; and (d) have the opportunity to make itself heard in relation to its concerns and opinions on the feasibility of the project. In addition, the State authorities have an obligation to submit to the community alternatives for a settlement or an agreement.[112]

According to the Court, without these requirements, there would be no active and effective participation of the community. When the Court has found that these requirements have not been met in a concrete case, it has ordered compliance.[113] A number of additional issues have been dealt with in cases brought by or on behalf of indigenous peoples.[114] In a case in which the construction of a dam was affecting the hunting and fishing activities of an indigenous community, forcing it to change its traditional economy, the Court ordered the State to take the specific measures necessary to enable the community to improve its economy under the new circumstances.[115] In a landmark decision, the Court has also ordered the suspension of an oil exploitation project in indigenous territories because the consultation requirements had not been met.[116]

It is worth noting that, in taking into account the special relationship between indigenous communities and their land, the Court has recognised the right of indigenous peoples to hold their ancestral territories as collective property (articles 329–331) as a fundamental right immediately enforceable by the courts. This is a higher degree of protection than that given to the right to individual property, which can only be invoked directly when a

---

[108] T-488/98. In this case, the Court ordered the petitioner's husband to pay the cost of the medical treatment for HIV as it had been proved that he had infected her.

[109] See, e.g., T-380/93.

[110] See, e.g., SU-383/97.

[111] See the International Labour Organisation Convention (No. 169) concerning Indigenous and Tribal Peoples in Independent Countries (which has been ratified by Colombia), article 330 of the Constitution and Law 99 (1993).

[112] SU-039/97.

[113] Ibid.

[114] See, e.g., T-007/95, T-342/94 and T-380/93.

[115] T-652/98.

[116] SU-039/97.

violation is linked to a violation of a fundamental right such as the right to life or dignity.[117]

Interestingly, the Court has also recognised that the right of indigenous peoples to health includes recognition of the importance of traditional healing practices and medicines. In a case concerning an indigenous prisoner who had refused a conventional medical treatment for cancer, the Court recognised his right to be transferred to a jail in his own region so he could receive the traditional medical treatment he required.[118]

5.5 Prisoners and Detained Persons

Detained persons have filed numerous *tutela* claims against prison administrators because of inhumane conditions such as overcrowding and lack of adequate food, medical care and security. The precarious nature of prison conditions has led the Court to apply the concept of 'unconstitutional state of affairs' in this area.[119] According to the Court, inhumane conditions in prisons constitute widespread and systematic violations of a variety of detainees' rights, and several State authorities have been found responsible for the situation. Consequently, the Court has ordered that all relevant entities undertake coordinated steps to improve the prison system and satisfy the basic needs of detainees. To this end, the Court has ordered the entities to design and implement a plan of action.[120]

In its case law, the Court has stressed the State's obligation *to fulfil* (provide) the ESC rights of detainees. From the Court's point of view, detainees are unable to realise these rights by themselves not only because they are in jail, but also because, in the great majority of cases, they lack economic resources.[121] The Court has noted, for example, that the right to adequate food in prisons means that food must be hygienic, satisfy dietary needs and be of the quantity and quality necessary for the development of a healthy individual.[122] It has also stressed the duty of the State

to provide all detainees access to preventive, curative and rehabilitative health services.[123] In this regard, the Court has considered that denial of a medical examination (X-ray) to a detainee represented a failure of the medical personnel and prison authorities and a violation of the individual's right to health and personal integrity. Consequently, the Court ordered the prison authorities to provide, within a period of 48 hours, medical assistance to the petitioner and all the medicines that the treatment required.[124]

5.6 Internally Displaced Persons

Internal armed conflict in Colombia has led to the forced displacement of over two million individuals, who, because of the violence, are unable to return to their homes.[125] Most IDPs are forced to migrate to the main cities, where they suffer from severe deprivation and extreme poverty. This humanitarian crisis led to several Court judgments according to which the State had to take urgent measures immediately to satisfy the most pressing needs of the IDPs and to take more long-term measures to ensure the rights of these individuals.[126] The vulnerability of IDPs clearly shows the indivisibility and interdependency of all human rights because IDPs endure violations of numerous human rights throughout the displacement circle, a fact that has been recognised by the Court. As the Court has noted, the massive forced displacement of Colombians gives rise to 'multiple, massive and continuous violations'.[127]

The approach taken by the Court in IDP cases has been in line with international law. In fact, the Court has noted that forced displacement also violates international human rights treaties and humanitarian law treaties ratified by Colombia such as the International Covenant on Civil and Political Rights, the International Covenant

---

[117] See, e.g., T-567/92, T-188/93, T-652/98, T-257/93, SU-510/93, T-652/98, T-405/93 and SU-039/97.
[118] T-214/97.
[119] See section 3.3.
[120] See T-153/98, T-606/98 and T-607/98.
[121] See T-535/98 and T-583/98.
[122] See T-208/99. See also T-714/96.

[123] See, e.g., T-545/03.
[124] T-606/98.
[125] Colombia has the world's second largest IDP population after Sudan. See, e.g., *The State of the World's Refugees. Human Displacement in the New Millennium*, Oxford University Press, 2006, p. 170.
[126] See, e.g., T-025/04, T-098/02 and T-606/03. In regard to the protection of the right of an IDP woman to adequate housing, see section 4.3.
[127] SU-1150/00.

on Economic, Social and Cultural Rights, the Convention on the Rights of the Child, the Convention on the Elimination of All Forms of Discrimination against Women, the American Convention on Human Rights, and Article 3 common to the four Geneva Conventions, as well as Protocol II of the Geneva Conventions.[128] It is worth noting that the Court has stated that the Guiding Principles on Internal Displacement (1998) are binding in Colombia.[129]

As indicated above, the Court has exercised creativity in the protection of IDPs by considering that their situation constitutes an 'unconstitutional state of affairs'.[130] In a landmark case that involved the joinder of 109 separate writs of protection submitted by 1,150 IDP families, the Court found that the living conditions of the IDPs constituted a massive, widespread and systematic violation of their constitutional rights.[131] In this judgment, the Court attributed responsibility to a wide range of State agencies, determining that, in essence, there had been a system-wide failure to respect, protect and fulfil the rights of internally displaced Colombians and Colombians at risk of displacement. In particular, the Court found that State authorities had not complied with their constitutional obligations when formulating and implementing public policies relating to the protection of IDPs. It also found that the allocation of resources for the protection of IDPs was not sufficient to ensure effective protection because there was a disparity between the resources allocated and the magnitude of the crisis. Consequently, the Court ordered the executive and legislative branches of the State to fulfil their obligations towards the internally displaced population by allocating sufficient financial resources to ensure the effective enjoyment of basic rights.

Obviously, the implementation of this judgment has had direct financial and budgetary implications. Nonetheless, the Court stressed that it is specifically empowered to decide whether or not the legislative and the executive branches of the State have failed to comply with their constitutional duty to protect human dignity and respect

Constitutional values such as the principles of the social state and solidarity.[132]

6. OBSTACLES AND CRITICISM OF THE COURT

The 1991 Constitution entrusted the Constitutional Court with the difficult task of preserving the integrity and supremacy of a Constitution that provides a relatively high level of protection for ESC rights. One of the tools that the Court has used to comply with this mandate is the writ of protection, through which the Court has – under certain circumstances – directly applied the ESC rights enshrined in the Constitution.

Despite the notable contribution of the Constitutional Court in ensuring the application of constitutional principles to the cases submitted to it, its judicial activism has not been free of criticism.[133] It has been argued that the Constitutional Court has violated the principle of separation of powers by ordering the realisation of public policies and allocation of resources. On the contrary, others have argued that the Court has wisely assumed its role as the 'guardian of the Constitution', making effective the protection of fundamental rights such as the right to life, dignity, and personal integrity and the values of Colombian society envisaged in article 1 of the Constitution.

Furthermore, it has been argued that the Court has acted more with judicial self-restraint than with activism. According to this view, in the great majority of cases related to the protection of ESC rights, instead of protecting the least well off in society, the Court has protected those individuals who are in a weak position because the State (and, in some cases, private institutions) have not fulfilled a contractual relationship (e.g., in the case

---

[128] SU-1150/00.
[129] See, e.g., T-327/01, T-268/03, T-419/03 and SU-1150/00.
[130] See section 3.3.
[131] T-025/04.

[132] To ensure full compliance with T-025/04, the Court has filed several contempt motions (see n. 13 above) against high-ranking public officials (see Judicial Orders 333, 334 and 335 of 2006).
[133] The strongest controversy generated by the Court has not revolved around its decisions regarding the protection of ESC rights through writs of protection, but rather because of the exercise of its other functions. In this regard, one might argue that the greatest political impact of the Court has arisen from its abstract constitutional review judgments when it has been called to decide on complex and sensitive legislation relating to the most pressing national problems.

of workers or pensioners claiming immediate payment of their rights and benefits). From this standpoint, the Court has not intervened in the allocation of resources. Rather, it has ordered the payment of benefits that should have been paid. Nonetheless, even in such situations, it is recognised that by giving access to the immediate protection of ESC rights in these cases, the Court has protected individuals from the detrimental consequences that would arise for these individuals and their families if salaries or social benefits were not paid.[134]

Regardless of these different approaches to the ESC rights case law of the Court, there seems to be many more followers than opponents to the approach taken by the Court to ESC rights protection. It seems beyond doubt that the Court, within the sphere of its competencies, has responded to the challenges posed to the judicial system by the complexities of life in Colombia.[135] In a society with high levels of social exclusion, the Court has tried to ensure equality of opportunity and to protect those who are in a disadvantaged or vulnerable position.

Indeed, the application of the *tutela* to the protection of ESC rights has filled gaps in the protection of the most vulnerable and the most disadvantaged groups within society that legislators and politicians have neglected or otherwise failed to fill.[136] Moreover, it has been argued that the role played by the Court by protecting rights through the *tutela* has been an instrument against violence. According to this view, the *tutela* has enabled groups traditionally under-represented in the political system to promote their interests through institutional channels, as opposed to violent means.[137] It has also been argued that the pro-

tection of ESC rights through the writ of protection has contributed to a change in legal culture, encouraging decision-makers to take these rights seriously and to prioritise them politically.[138] In addition, *tutela* protection has changed the relationships between the individual and the public administration for the better by forcing the latter to comply with its duties in accordance with due process.[139]

The examination of the case law shows us that the Court has not ignored the importance of the principle of separation of powers and the need to respect expenditure priorities adopted through the national budget process. However, it has considered that, in exceptional circumstances, when an individual is in a situation of extreme necessity, the only way for the Court to uphold its Constitutional mandate to safeguard the life, personal integrity and human dignity of the individual is to order the relevant authorities to undertake the required expenditure. Therefore, in such cases, the Court has made an effort not to undertake utilitarian calculus, but rather to place the protection of individual dignity at the centre of its decisions.

7. CONCLUDING OBSERVATIONS

The writ of protection has been a key device for the protection of economic, social and cultural rights in Colombia. The Constitutional Court has been entrusted by the Constitution with the safeguarding of its 'integrity and supremacy' and in certain circumstances, the protection of ESC rights has been necessitated, in the eyes of the Court, by the need to protect human dignity and ensure compliance with the constitutional principles of the 'social state' and 'solidarity'. A literal interpretation of the Colombian Constitution principally suggests that recourse to the courts alleging the immediate protection of a right that has

---

[134] See M. García Villegas, 'Derechos sociales' (n. 73 above), pp. 455–546.

[135] Indeed, Colombia has been embroiled in an internal armed conflict for more than forty years, and, although the country is rich in natural resources, it has an extremely high level of inequality; the poorest 10 per cent of the population account for only 0.7 per cent of consumption, and the wealthiest 10 per cent are responsible for 46.9 per cent of all consumer spending. See Human Development Report, 2007/2008, p. 282.

[136] As one commentator notes, 'the Court has modified the balance of social and political power, inter alia, granting more power to weak, vulnerable, marginal and disorganised persons with constitutional rights'. See Cepeda, 'Judicial Activism' (n. 61 above), p. 650.

[137] Ibid., p. 667.

[138] R. Arango, 'La jurisdiccion social de la tutela' [The Social Jurisdiction of Tutela Protection] in C. M. Molina Betancour (ed.), *Corte Constitucional 10 años: Balance y perspectivas* [Ten Years of the Constitutional Court: Assessment and Perspectives] (Bogotá: Universidad del Rosario, 2003), pp. 116–117.

[139] R. Uprimny, 'Las transformaciones de la administración de justicia en Colombia' [The Transformation of the Administration of Justice in Colombia] in Boaventura de Sousa and Villegas, *El caleidoscopio* (n. 73 above), pp. 261–316.

been violated or that is about to be violated is only established for traditional civil and political rights.[140] However, the teleological interpretation by the Constitutional Court has permitted such protection to be available also for ESC rights when the violations of these rights will affect fundamental rights such as the right to life, personal integrity or dignity, when the violations interfere with the minimum conditions for a dignified life, or when there is an unconstitutional state of affairs.

The judicial creativity exercised by the Constitutional Court has developed an important and sometimes ambitious case law in the area of ESC rights. The present overview of the case law of the Constitutional Court provides us with a variety of examples of how the judicial protection of these rights is possible through the enforcement not only of the negative duties imposed by socio-economic rights, but also of positive duties sometimes requiring the allocation of significant resources by the State. The Colombian Constitution also offers the opportunity for holding private actors accountable for human rights violations, in particular when they are carrying out the functions of the State. In numerous cases, the writ of protection has been used against private individuals who have been responsible for violating or restricting the enjoyment of ESC rights. Likewise, the jurisprudence has provided good examples of judicial protection against bureaucratic failures and unfair administrative methods that have hindered the enjoyment of ESC rights. Despite the textual limitation of article 86, there is no doubt that the Court sometimes provides constitutional protection when individuals have other means of redress available. Nonetheless, as the Court has explained, it is reasonable to provide immediate relief through the writ of protection when the individual's situation would otherwise worsen. It should also be mentioned that many of the cases examined show that the Court's approach has drawn upon international law. The Court has not hesitated to invoke the provisions of various human rights instruments ratified by Colombia, including soft-law instruments such as the

Guiding Principles on Internal Displacement. The Court has, moreover, not limited the judicial protection of ESC rights to individual plaintiffs, but, in several judgments, has ordered the State to undertake coordinated measures to eliminate situations of wide-spread violation, thereby expanding the protection to individuals who were not directly involved in the corresponding proceedings.

The Court has therefore played a key role in protecting individuals against violations of ESC rights by supervising the design and implementation of public policies in order to ensure that vulnerable groups have the chance to avail themselves of the available remedies and can enjoy their rights.

Litigation, though, is not the only way to advance ESC rights, and it is not always the most effective strategy. Thus, in a country with enormous inequalities, the Court's task, while necessary, is obviously only limited; the effective protection of ESC rights should be a holistic enterprise. The Court is perfectly aware of this.[141] Stressing that the Constitution binds not only the judiciary, but also the executive and legislative branches of the State and that the Court is the body entrusted with interpreting the Constitution and upholding rights and principles, the Court supervises actions by all branches of the State so as to ensure compliance with the principle of the social state. According to the Court, respect for this principle imposes on all authorities the duty to take steps to address social inequalities, to facilitate the inclusion and participation of the population in the economic and social life of the nation and to stimulate the progressive improvement of the material conditions of existence of marginalised sectors of society.[142] Although there is still much room for improvement, it is difficult to deny that the Colombian Constitutional Court has played a leading and illuminating role in the judicial protection of ESC rights.

---

[140] See text accompanying note 7 above.

[141] See, e.g., T-111/97. In the judgment, the Court notes that the enforcement of ESC rights generally requires legislation that develops the rights. However, it adds, in exceptional circumstances, these rights must be given effect even without a relevant law.

[142] See, e.g., T-165/95, T-505/92 and T-025/04

8

Argentina

Some Promising Signs
Christian Courtis*

* Legal officer for Economic, Social and Cultural Rights, International Commission of Jurists, Geneva. Law professor, University of Buenos Aires Law School, Argentina; Visiting Professor, ITAM Law School, Mexico. Specialised in Human Rights Law, Constitutional Law and Legal Theory. The jurisprudence in this chapter is updated as to July 2006.

INTRODUCTION

1. INTRODUCTION: JUDICIAL REVIEW IN ARGENTINA

The judicial system in Argentina is a combination of a U.S.–inspired constitutional framework and a civil law–inspired institutional framework, a model not uncommon in Latin America. The Argentine constitution, passed in 1853, was strongly influenced by the U.S. constitution, with the adoption of federalism and a tripartite partition of government, comprised of an independent executive, legislature and judiciary.[1] Since its inception, the Supreme Court of Argentina has often considered legal precedents handed down by its U.S. counterpart, especially in matters where both constitutions are alike. For example, the Argentine Supreme Court resorted to the *Marbury v Madison* decision as part of its declaration of its powers of judicial review. Federal judicial review also follows the diffuse system of the United States whereby any judge can interpret the Constitution within the limits of a concrete case, but a declaration of unconstitutionality has effects only for the case where it is pronounced, the Supreme Court being the ultimate interpreter of the federal Constitution.

On the other hand, Argentina drew on the European legal tradition in at least three important aspects. First, the organisation of the judiciary and the offices of the attorney general,[2] public prosecutor and public defender, follow the shape of a permanent and professional continental bureaucracy.[3] Second, procedures are mostly conducted in writing, together with generous possibilities for appeal and the review of previous decisions. No discretion is formally granted for public prosecutors to dismiss cases (although there are, of course, informal ways of dismissal), the 'legality principle' rule.[4] Third, Argentina inherited the continental law tradition of codification. Unlike the U.S. federal system, substantive codes are passed by the Federal Congress and are binding for the entire country, although provincial courts enforce them. Procedural codes are provincial, and both substantive and procedural codes exhibit the influence of European law, particularly that of France, Germany, Italy and Spain.

The federal system permits provincial governments to make laws, depending on the matters entrusted to the federal government or reserved by the provinces in the Federal Constitution. Provinces also have their own constitutions, and provincial courts therefore apply federal and provincial constitutional law and common codified law. While provincial constitutions largely adopt a U.S.-like judicial review system, some provinces have created different systems,

---

[1] See J. Miller, María A. Gelli and S. Cayuso, *Constitución y poder político* [Constitution and political power] (Buenos Aires: Astrea, 1991). In 1994, a number of changes regarding the appointment and removal of lower judges were introduced in a constitutional amendment, but neither the structure nor the jurisdiction of the judiciary changed significantly.

[2] The attorney general represents the 'objective interest of the law' before the Supreme Court and is independent of the political branches. He briefs the Supreme Court on admissibility and on the merits of cases of public relevance.

[3] See E. Raúl Zaffaroni, *Estructuras judiciales* [Judicial Structures] (Buenos Aires: Ediar, 1994).

[4] See Julio B. J. Maier, *Derecho Procesal Penal* [Criminal Procedure Law], Vol. I: *Principios*, 2nd edition (Buenos Aires: Editores del Puerto, 1999).

merging features of the diffuse judicial review tradition of the United States with features of the continental concentrated judicial review tradition.[5]

2. SOCIAL AND ECONOMIC RIGHTS WITHIN THE CONSTITUTIONAL AND LEGAL SYSTEM

The origin of a mature model of social and welfare legislation in Argentina dates from the 1940s. Some incipient legislative measures can be traced to earlier decades, particularly in the field of the limitation of working hours and workers compensation for occupational injury or disease. The first recognition of social and economic rights at the constitutional level was in the 1949 Constitution, a document abrogated shortly thereafter with the overthrow of Peron, the president of Argentina, by a *coup d'état* in 1955. In 1957, a constitutional amendment incorporated social and economic rights into the text of the original 1853 Constitution. In both cases, the recognition of social and economic rights followed the lines of the 'industrial democracy' model. Rights were assigned primarily to the worker in the formal market.[6] Thus, the list of recognised constitutional social and economic rights focuses principally on individual and collective workers' rights and social insurance, with a minor mention of family protection. Section 14 bis of the Argentine Constitution provides that:

1. Labour in its several forms shall be protected by law, which shall ensure to workers: dignified and equitable working conditions; limited working hours; paid rest and vacations; fair remuneration; minimum vital and adjustable wages; equal pay for equal work; participation in the profits of enter-

prises, with control of production and collaboration in management; protection against arbitrary dismissal; stability of the civil servant; free and democratic labour union organisations recognised by the mere registration in a special record.

2. Trade unions are hereby guaranteed: the right to enter into collective labour bargaining; to resort to conciliation and arbitration; the right to strike. Union representatives shall have the guarantees necessary for carrying out their union tasks and those related to the stability of their employment.

3. The State shall grant the benefits of social security, which shall be of an integral nature and may not be waived. In particular, the laws shall establish: compulsory social insurance, which shall be in charge of national or provincial entities with financial and economic autonomy, administered by the interested parties with State participation, with no overlapping of contributions; adjustable retirements and pensions; full family protection; protection of homestead; family allowances and access to decent housing.

While educational policies were universal and partially departed from this approach, the assignment of other social and economic rights heavily depended on the inclusion of the breadwinner worker in the formal labour market. This applied to social security and health insurance, credit for housing and retirement pensions, family allowances and other income transfer schemes. It was assumed that women, children and dependents received benefits through the male breadwinner's position. This legal framework suffered no serious challenge as Argentina's economy rapidly grew between the 1940s and the mid-1970s, and an almost full and stable employment rate explains the lack of an unemployment insurance scheme and relatively successful social integration.

The mid-1970s witnessed a deep political and economic crisis. A harsh military regime took power in 1976. High inflation, ballooning external debt and a deep financial deficit in the social security system accompanied massive violations of human rights. While democracy was regained in 1983, the economic and social situation continued to stagnate. Unemployment steadily rose;

---

[5] The European or continental concentrated judicial review tradition, inspired by Hans Kelsen and originally enshrined in the 1920 Austrian constitution, grants a constitutional court (separated from the ordinary judiciary) the monopoly of constitutional review, as opposed to the U.S. system, where any judge can declare a statute unconstitutional. Moreover, the European tradition allows for the 'abstract' declaration of unconstitutionality, that is, the possibility of declaring a statute unconstitutional without requiring proof of direct grievance by the plaintiff and without reference to a concrete application.

[6] See, generally, E. Isuani, Rubén Lo Vuolo and Emilio Tenti Fanfani, *El Estado Benefactor: Un paradigma en crisis* [The Welfare State: A paradigm in crisis] (Buenos Aires: CIEPP/Miño y Dávila, 1991).

the federal government failed to pass necessary, but slight parametric reforms to the social security system; and the country suffered two major bouts of hyperinflation, in 1987 and 1989. In 1989, President Menem took charge and carried out far-reaching market reforms, including the partial privatisation of the social security system, decentralisation of the health and educational systems, privatisation of the labour compensation scheme, the establishment of greater flexibility in employment relations and the weakening of the bargaining power of trade unions. Broader economic changes included the deregulation of various sectors, the liberalisation of external tariffs and trade barriers, the privatisation of public enterprises and assets, etc. Inflation was controlled and some signs of economic recovery were reflected in growth figures, but unemployment and inequality rose dramatically.[7]

Shortly before the expiry of President Menem's term in 1994, the two major political parties agreed to amend the Constitution, granting the president the opportunity to seek a new term. As a part of the political agreement on amendment, new social rights were added to the Constitution. Consumer rights, environmental rights, collective injunctions,[8] equality of opportunities, affirmative action and indigenous peoples' rights were included. More importantly, a number of international human rights treaties and instruments were incorporated in the Constitution and given superior status within the constitutional hierarchy. These treaties and instruments include the Universal Declaration of Human Rights, the International Covenant on Economic, Social and Cultural Rights, the Convention on the Rights of the Child and the Convention for the Elimination

of All Forms of Discrimination against Women. The social and economic rights enshrined in these instruments now form part of the Bill of Rights, supplementing the rights that were already included in the 1853 Constitution and the above-quoted amendments in 1957.

In terms of the federal distribution of powers, legislation covering economic and social rights is shared between the federal and the provincial spheres. Labour codes and laws are passed by the Federal Congress[9] and applied by provincial courts. Health, social security and education regulations are complex. While there is a general trend to fix a minimum common baseline through federal legislation, there are many exceptions to this approach. An attempt has been made to unify the health system, but disparities still exist. The health system consists of three parts: a private sector, principally organised through a scheme of public health insurance corporations, a scheme run by trade unions for workers in the formal sector (essentially funded by contributions from employees and employers) and a residual public system (principally funded by public finances and run by provincial and municipal governments). The Federal Congress has tried to establish a mandatory minimum common health plan for every component of the system. The social security system is characterised by dualism, with a federal, public 'pay-as-you-go' system and a privately run individual capitalisation system. But many exceptions and particular regimes remain in place. Regarding education, the Federal Congress is empowered to fix a common policy with minimum standards through a Federal Educational Act, but implementation is carried out at a provincial level, although the public universities are autonomous. Housing policies, as well as social assistance and poverty reduction programmes, are both federal and provincial.

---

[7] See A. Barbeito and Rubén Lo Vuolo, *La nueva oscuridad de la política social: Del estado populista al neoconservador* [The New Darkness of Social Policy: From the Populist to the Neoconservative State], 2nd edition (Buenos Aires: Miño y Dávila-CIEPP, 1998).

[8] A great number of socio-economic rights cases were filed under the rules of a collective injunction, the so-called collective *amparo*. The amparo is a traditional constitutional injunction granting the plaintiff injunctive relief when a constitutional right is threatened. While the 'classical *amparo*' limited *locus standi* to an individual grievance, the inclusion of a 'collective *amparo*' enlarged *locus standi*, allowing a member of the aggrieved class, NGOs and the ombudsman to bring cases before courts when massive infringement of constitutional rights occurred.

3. LEGAL THEORY AND PRACTICE

While part of the Argentine academic and legal orthodoxy maintains a traditional approach in relation to social and economic rights, the 1994 constitutional amendments have fostered new strategies on the enforceability of those rights,

[9] Except for public employment laws, which are provincial.

including activism in the judicial field. Surprisingly, the impetus for change has mostly come through court decisions, while constitutional legal doctrine still repeats the traditional canon. Two important normative developments have led to this evolution:

a) The inclusion of a broader span of social and economic rights in the Constitution. Several provinces have also adopted constitutional amendments or simply passed new constitutions. In most of these cases, the new constitutional texts include social and economic rights such as workers rights, the right to social security, the right to education, the right to health care, the right to housing and, in some cases, rights regarding the situation of vulnerable groups or minorities, such as women, children, indigenous people, persons with disabilities, and so forth.

b) The ratification of international human rights treaties – both regional and universal – as mentioned in section 2. This process led to the establishment of a privileged status for international instruments in the legal hierarchy with respect to domestic statutes and, in the case of the instruments mentioned in section 75, paragraph 22 of the Constitution, rendered them equal relative to the Constitution.[10] The Argentine legal tradition regarding international law has been monist; thus, international treaties ratified by countries are considered part of domestic law and are directly applicable by domestic courts.[11]

These two factors have generated new debates on the nature and scope of social and economic rights in both legal doctrine and litigation before courts. The first problem raised by this new normative panorama is the classical question one finds in the field of social and economic rights: Are we speaking of proper human rights or are we faced with some other kind of legal norms? Can the rights be directly invoked before the judiciary or should they be characterised as institutional guarantees, principles, directives, or legal goals or standards purported to guide the action of the political branches of government? The responsive approach to these questions should properly focus on the relevant legal texts. The construction of legal arguments needs, at a minimum, to respect the form chosen by the drafters of a country's constitution. In the case of Argentina, some constitutional norms are not drafted in the language of rights, but are phrased as goals, principles, or directives. For example, the mention of access to housing in section 14 bis of the Argentine Constitution looks primarily as if it is setting a general policy goal, rather than establishing a right ('In particular, the laws shall establish... access to decent housing'). However, some constitutional social and economic clauses, as well as the clauses contained in international human rights instruments, are crafted in terms of rights, such as the right to health care, the right to education or the right to adequate housing. As will be shown hereafter, judges have gradually recognised this fact.

A second debate is centred on the controversy over the concept of social and economic rights even when these are framed as rights (see chapters 1 and 2 for an in-depth discussion of this debate). Leaving aside workers rights and social security rights, which have rarely been contested as to their enforceable nature, social and economic rights have traditionally been treated in constitutional law doctrine as 'programmatic' rights, that is, as mere indicative goals for the political branches of government, but not as judicially enforceable individual or collective entitlements. The renewed recognition and expansion of social and economic rights in the Argentine Constitution, together with the influence of the jurisprudence of international treaty-monitoring bodies such as the UN Committee on Economic, Social and Cultural Rights, have led to a widening discussion on the extent and possibilities of the judicial enforcement of these rights. In the same vein, concrete judicial experiences have challenged the idea that social and economic rights are not judicially enforceable, and in some fields, there is growing case law

---

[10] The full list contains the Universal Declaration of Human Rights, the American Declaration of the Rights and Duties of Man, the American Convention on Human Rights, the International Covenant on Civil and Political Rights, the International Covenant on Economic, Social and Cultural Rights, the Convention against Genocide, the Convention against Torture, the Convention on the Elimination of All Forms of Racial Discrimination, the Convention on the Elimination of All Forms of Discrimination against Women, the Convention on the Rights of the Child, the Optional Protocol to the International Covenant on Civil and Political Rights and the Inter-American Convention on Forced Disappearance of Persons.

[11] See, generally, M. Abregú and C. Courtis (eds.), *La aplicación de los tratados sobre derechos humanos por los tribunales locales* [The application of human rights treaties by local courts] (Buenos Aires: Editores del Puerto, 1997).

showing exactly the opposite trend. Generally speaking, there is, in Argentina, increasing acceptance of the possibility of invoking social and economic rights before courts both by the judiciary and scholars.[12]

4. JUDICIAL ENFORCEMENT OF SPECIFIC RIGHTS

4.1 Labour Rights

Since the 1940s, there has been a longstanding tradition of judicial enforcement of both individual and collective labour rights through ordinary and specialist labour courts. Litigation has mostly emerged from collective bargaining processes involving employers, trade unions and the State[13] and the individual dimensions of the employment relationship. The fact that labour rights are considered to be judicially enforceable and that labour courts exist for this purpose does not indicate an absence of problems with enforceability. Labour courts are overwhelmed with cases, and procedures for labour law are favourable to the lodging of appeals, thereby making the entire adjudication process slow and cumbersome and creating incentives for workers to settle instead of waiting for full, but belated compensation. High unemployment, underemployment and informal employment also pose difficult problems for litigation strategies on behalf of workers.

The judicial enforcement of labour rights draws mainly on statutory law; constitutional rights are mostly reflected in legislation and regulations. There is, however, some space left for constitutional litigation, although few cases have so far drawn on international instruments. Since offer-

ing a whole account of Argentine labour case law would require more space than is available here,[14] a number of developments will now be indicated that may help provide a depiction of the evolution of labour law adjudication in the last fifteen years.

Jurisprudential debate has been particularly heated over individual labour rights and the level of deference the courts should pay to workers. Courts have discussed the realm of the *pro operaris* (pro-worker) principle, which has arisen in cases concerning the acceptability of workers renouncing some of their rights,[15] abuse of the employers managerial powers,[16] the extent of protection against unfair dismissal, including work stability and the basis to fix compensation for unjust dismissal,[17] the balance between introducing wage bonuses and incentives and the principle of equality and the prohibition on discrimination.[18] Argentine courts have also adjudicated on the parameters of collective rights, including the prevalence of collective labour agreements that involve amelioration of workers rights *vis-à-vis*

---

[12] See V. Abramovich and C. Courtis, 'Hacia la exigibilidad de los derechos económicos, sociales y culturales: Estándares internacionales y criterios de aplicación ante los tribunales locales' [Towards the enforcement of economic, social and cultural rights: international standards and applicability criteria before local courts] in Abregú and Courtis, *La aplicación de los tratados* (n. 11 above), pp. 283–350; Víctor Abramovich and Christian Courtis, *Los derechos sociales como derechos exigibles* [Social rights as enforceable rights] (Madrid: Trotta, 2001), chapter III.

[13] See, generally, E. Isuani, Rubén Lo Vuolo and E. Tenti Fanfani, *El Estado Benefactor: Un paradigma en crisis* [The Welfare State: A paradigm in crisis] (Buenos Aires: Miño y Dávila-CIEPP, 1999) and Barbeito and Lo Vuolo, *La nueva oscuridad de la política social* (n. 7 above), pp. 24–47.

[14] See, generally, M. Eduardo Ackerman (ed.), *Colección de análisis jurisprudencial: Derecho del Trabajo y de la Seguridad Social* [Labour Law and Social Security Law: a case law analyses reader] (Buenos Aires: La Ley, 2004).

[15] See, for example, *Padín Capella, Jorge D. v. Litho Formas S. A.*, Supreme Court of Argentina, 12 March 1987; *Bariain, Narciso T. v. Mercedes Benz Argentina S. A.*, 14 May 1985, *Reggiardo de Henri, Irma v. EFA*, National Labour Court of Appeals, Chamber VI, 14 August 1985; National Labour Court of Appeals, Chamber III, *Casteñán, Gustavo A. v. Raña Veloso, Raúl y otros*, 30 August 1985.

[16] See *Prinetti, Jorge M. v. Bagley, S. A.*, National Labour Court of Appeals, Chamber III, 27 October 1999.

[17] See *De Luca, José E. y otro v. Banco Francés del Río de la Plata*, Supreme Court of Argentina, 25 February 1969; *Figueroa, Oscar F. y otro v. Loma Negra C.I.A.S.A.*, Supreme Court of Argentina, 4 September 1984; *Pelaia, Aurelio P. v. Sadaic*, Supreme Court of Argentina, 30 June 1992; *Vega, Humberto A. v. Consorcio de Propietarios del Edificio Loma Verde y otro s/accidente ley 9688*, Supreme Court of Argentina, 16 December 1993; *Vega, Leonardo M. y otros v. D'Angiola Arcucci*, Supreme Court of Argentina, 25 June 1996; *Villarreal, Adolfo v. Roemmers*, Supreme Court of Argentina, 12 October 1997; *Mastroiani, Ricardo A. v. Establecimiento Modelo Terrabusi S. A.*, Supreme Court of Argentina, 27 May 1999.

[18] See *Ratto, Sixto y otro v. Productos Stani S. A.*, Supreme Court of Argentina, 26 August 1966; *Segundo, Daniel v. Siemens S. A.*, Supreme Court of Argentina, 26 June 1986; *Fernández, Estrella v. Sanatorio Güemes, S. A.*, Supreme Court of Argentina, 23 August 1988; *Jáuregui, Manuela Yolanda v. Unión Obreros y Empleados del Plástico*, Supreme Court of Argentina, 7 August 1984; *Martinelli, Oscar Héctor Cirilo y otros v. Coplinco Compañía Platense de la Industria y Comercio S. A.*, Supreme Court of Argentina, 12 December 1993.

statutory clauses,[19] the freedom to form and join trade unions[20] and the right to strike.[21]

These rights came under serious attack in the early 1990s during the Menem administration. The number of justices of the Supreme Court was extended from five to nine, and partisan judges were appointed to fill the vacant positions. Laws aiming to liberalise labour conditions, displace or limit the application of collective labour agreements on the basis of economic emergencies,[22] limit workers' compensation for injury and disease and privatise the coverage of workers' compensation[23] were upheld by the Supreme Court on the basis of due deference to the powers of Congress.[24] The Supreme Court also took a restrictive view on the extent of solidarity of the labour duties amongst subcontracting or outsourcing parties.[25]

After the 2001 crisis, the composition of the Supreme Court changed again, and new case law overturned previous precedents and aligned itself in a pro-worker trend.[26] There are some signs of greater consideration of international instruments by the Supreme Court. The *Aquino* case, decided in 2004, is a good example of this development.[27] *Aquino*[28] involved a constitutional challenge of a statutory change in the area of workers' injury and occupational disease benefits. The system had previously provided workers that claimed to be victims of occupational injuries or diseases with an option: They either chose a no-fault, tabulated compensation regime, with a lower standard of proof, or a full compensation tort regime, where the plaintiff had to prove negligence or lack of control of dangerous installations by the employer. In September 1995, the Congress approved an act to replace the whole workers' compensation system. The court-based workers' compensation scheme was abolished and a new insurance scheme

[19] See *Romano, Adolfo R. y otros v. Usina Popular y Municipal de Tandil*, S. E. M., Supreme Court of Argentina, 31 July 1979; *Nordensthol, Gustavo J. C. v. Subterráneos de Buenos Aires*, Supreme Court of Argentina, 12 April 1985; *Soria, Silverio F. v. D.N.V.*, Supreme Court of Argentina, 12 April 1985; *Bismarck, Almirón y otro v. Cooperativa Eléctrica Ltda. de Pergamino*, Supreme Court of Argentina, 12 February 1987.

[20] Supreme Court of Argentina, *Outon, Carlos J. y otros*, 29 March 1967; Supreme Court of Argentina, *Asociación de Trabajadores del Estado v. Provincia de Corrientes*, 14 July 1999.

[21] Supreme Court of Argentina, *Beneduce, Carmen J. y otras v. Casa Augusto*, 18 December 1967; Supreme Court of Argentina, *Riobo, Alberto v. La Prensa, S. A.*, 16 February 1993; Buenos Aires Supreme Court, *Leiva, Horacio y otros v. Swift Armour S. A.*, 6 July 1984. See, generally, J. Rizzone, 'Acerca del derecho de huelga en la doctrina de la Corte Suprema de la Nación Argentina' [On the right to strike in the doctrine of the Supreme Court of Argentina], *Revista de la Sociedad Argentina de Derecho Laboral*, Vol. III, No. 9 (March–April 2001), pp. 39–44.

[22] Supreme Court of Argentina, *Soengas, Héctor R. y otros v. Ferrocarriles Argentinos*, 7 August 1990, *Cocchia, Jorge D. C. Estado nacional y otro*, 2 December 1993.

[23] Supreme Court of Argentina, *Gorosito v. Riva S. A. s/daños y perjuicios*, 1 February 2001.

[24] For a general comment, see G. Gianibelli and O. Zas, 'Estado social en Argentina: modelo constitucional y divergencias infraconstitucionales' [Welfare State in Argentina: constitutional model and subconstitutional departures], *Revista Contextos*, No. 1, Buenos Aires (1997), pp. 159–231.

[25] Supreme Court of Argentina, *Rodríguez, Juan R. v. Compañía Embotelladora Argentina S. A. y otro*, 15 April 1993; Supreme Court of Argentina, *Luna, Antonio R. v. Agencia Marítima Rigel S. A. y otros*, 2 July 1993, Supreme Court of Argentina, *Escudero, Segundo R. y otros v. Nueve A. S. A. y otro*, 14 September 2000.

[26] See, for example, Supreme Court of Argentina, *Castillo, Angel Santos v. Cerámica Alberdi S. A.*, 7 September 2004 (concerning the unconstitutionality of establishing federal jurisdiction on workers injury claims) and decisions quoted in the next footnotes.

[27] In the same sense, see Supreme Court of Argentina, *Vizzoti, Carlos Alberto v. Amsa S. A. s/despido*, 14 July 2004, which concerns the unconstitutionality of a reduction of the base to fix compensation for illegal dismissal. The Court draws on constitutional clauses and on Articles 23 and 25 of the Universal Declaration of Human Rights, Article XIV of the American Declaration of the Rights and Duties of Man, Articles 6 and 7 of the International Covenant on Economic, Social and Cultural Rights, Article 11 of the Convention on the Elimination of All Forms of Discrimination against Women, Article 32 of the Convention on the Rights of Children and Article 5 of the Convention on the Elimination of All Forms of Racial Discrimination). See also Supreme Court of Argentina, *Milone, Juan Antonio v. Asociart S. A. Aseguradora de Riesgos del Trabajo s/accidente ley 9688*, 26 October 2004. The case involved the unconstitutionality of periodical payment of workers' injury compensation without option for a single payment. Quoting constitutional clauses and Article 5 of International Labour Organisation Convention 17, Article 7 and 12 of the International Covenant on Economic, Social and Cultural Rights, Articles 6 and 7 of the Protocol of San Salvador, Additional Protocol to the American Convention on Human Rights in the area of Economic, Social and Cultural Rights; the Supreme Court stressed, in this case, the duty of the progressive realisation of economic, social and cultural rights (Article 2(1) of the International Covenant on Economic, Social and Cultural Rights) in connection with the duty of continuous improvement of the living conditions (Article 11(1) of the International Covenant on Economic, Social and Cultural Rights).

[28] *Aquino, Isacio v. Cargo Servicios Industriales S. A. s/accidentes ley 9688*, 21 September 2004.

managed by private entities was established. *Aquino* challenged the limitation of the full compensation tort option in favour of the worker on constitutional grounds. The new legislation eliminated the full compensation option. In 2004, the newly composed Supreme Court reversed a previous decision and held that the regime was unconstitutional. The Court not only based its opinion on constitutional grounds (the right of the worker to dignified and equitable working conditions and the integral character of social security and compensations), but also drew on international human rights standards. The judgment mentions the applicability of Articles 7(a)(ii), 7(b), 12(2)(b) and 12(2)(c) of the International Covenant on Economic, Social and Cultural Rights, Articles 11(1)(f) and 11(2)(d) of the Convention for the Elimination of All Forms of Discrimination against Women, Article 32 of the Convention on the Rights of the Child and Article 19 of the American Convention on Human Rights. References to the International Covenant on Economic, Social and Cultural Rights underline the linkages between full compensation for work injury and disease and the right to just and favourable conditions of work. The Court mentions several General Comments of, and the concluding observations on, periodic reports by States parties issued by the Committee on Economic, Social and Cultural Rights, which oversees the first-mentioned covenant. The Court considered that the new Act violates the prohibition of retrogression by adopting a measure that deliberately restricts the right to full compensation.

4.2 Social Security Rights

The doctrinal debate on the judicial enforcement of social security rights is similarly circumscribed. Litigation in the field of social security has been an established practice for more than forty years.

The basis of the social security system follows the sketch of what some scholars have called a conservative or corporate welfare state. It is largely based on an ongoing economic and political bargaining process amongst employers, trade unions and the State. It has also maintained clear differentiated status levels and a traditional sexual division of labour, whereby men are incorporated in the formal workforce and women are dedicated mainly to reproductive work.[29] While the first social security schemes originated in the second decade of the twentieth century, the existence of an institutional arrangement that can be properly called a social security system dates from the last half of the 1940s. Previous schemes were fragmentary and self-managed and only covered a small section of the working population. In 1952, the first moves towards the unification and centralisation of the system were taken. A national social security agency was created, and a pay-as-you-go arrangement took the place of the capitalisation principle that had been predominant during the previous period. The system was co-funded by payroll taxes levied on both employers and workers. Economic and demographic changes, which included the formation of an industrial workforce, migration from rural to urban areas and incoming migration from Europe and neighbouring countries, created a favourable environment for the establishment of the new model. Coverage grew dramatically, – from 420,000 persons in 1944 to an impressive 2,300,000 persons in 1949.

The judicial enforceability of social security rights emerged in the 1960s, beginning with claims regarding the determination of pension payments. Most claims were based on statutory challenges and were decided by courts in favour of claimants. In the 1980s and 1990s, social security legal suits claims exploded in number. Claims were directed at challenging the denial of pensions and the readjustment of pension benefits through statutory levelling criteria.[30] Again, claimants won most of these cases.

In 1993, an important statutory change introduced a parallel system. Workers could choose between remaining in the state-run pay-as-you-go system, or move to the privately run individual accounts system.[31] The State also modified the

---

[29] See G. Esping-Andersen, *The Three Worlds of Welfare Capitalism* (Princeton, NJ: Princeton University Press, 1990), chapter 1; Gøsta Esping-Andersen, *Social Foundations of Postindustrial Economies* (Oxford: Oxford University Press, 1999), chapter 5; Barbeito and Lo Vuolo, *La nueva oscuridad de la política social* (n. 7 above), pp. 24–47.

[30] Pension levelling means the regular adjustment of pension payments in order to offset losses in the purchasing power of the local currency. See Supreme Court of Argentina, *Rolón Zappa, Víctor Francisco*, 30 October 1986.

[31] See *Guillermo V. Alonso, Política y Seguridad Social en la Argentina de los 90* [Social Policy and Social Security in

requirements and conditions of the pay-as-you-go system, including severing the link between pensions and past wage levels, in order to encourage a shift to the private system. Specialist social security courts were created for channelling litigation, and laws were passed to block suits or lessen their chance of success before lower courts. For instance, a right to ordinary review of appellate decisions before the Supreme Court that basically favoured the State, the losing part in the vast majority of cases in this area, was included in the law, and the Government was granted the right to oppose claims by stating that it lacked funding for payments. These procedural changes were aimed at allowing the Government to challenge or delay payments ordered by appellate decisions. In turn, the laws that modified the criteria for the determination of pension levels and those that established procedural obstacles to recover pension payments were constitutionally challenged. A number of cases were won before appellate courts,[32] but the Menem-appointed Supreme Court overturned some of these decisions.[33] As was the case with

labour rights, the post-Menem Supreme Court overturned some of the previous case law on constitutional grounds and expanded its interpretation of social security rights on the basis of international human rights standards. Two examples illustrate this trend.

In *Sánchez*,[34] the Supreme Court overturned its *Chocobar* precedent and held that the prohibition on indexing benefits to inflation was not applicable to the pension system. They ordered the Government to readjust lagged pension levels according to the official wage index variations. The majority decision of the Court stresses the links between pension levels and the rights to food, housing, education and health or the right to an adequate standard of living for retired workers. The Supreme Court drew on constitutional principles – the right to pension levelling (that is, the right to have pension payments readjusted, as explained elsewhere above), the duty of Congress to adopt positive actions to ensure the rights of elderly persons – and also on international human rights instruments. They quoted Article 22 of the Universal Declaration of Human Rights and Articles 26 and 29 of the American Convention on Human Rights, underlining the progressive development of human rights, and the fact that the availability of resources cannot be employed as an argument to deny or restrict recognised rights.

In *Itzcovich*,[35] the Supreme Court declared that a clause of the so-called Social Security Solidarity Act, which subjected appellate decisions on social security matters to an ordinary appeal to the Supreme Court, was unconstitutional. The majority of the Court stated that the Government had unreasonably enacted this legal measure to delay social security payments and that principles of due process applied to social security, thereby requiring that litigants be assured a speedy trial, certainty and foreseeability. The decision draws on constitutional principles and on Article 25 of the American Convention on Human Rights (the right to judicial protection) and quotes the

the Argentina of the 1990s] (Buenos Aires: Miño y Dávila-FLACSO, 2000); Christian Courtis, 'Social Rights and Privatisation: Lessons from the Argentine Experience', in Koen De Feyter and Felipe Gómez Isa (eds.), *Privatisation and Human Rights in the Age of Globalisation* (Antwerp-Oxford: Intersentia, 2004), pp. 175–205.

[32] See National Social Security Court of Appeals, Chamber II, *Ciampagna, Rodolfo N. v. ANSeS*, 11 April 1997 (unconstitutionality of lack of funds defence); National Social Security Court of Appeals, Chamber II, *González, Herminia del Carmen v. ANSeS*, 20 November 1998 (unconstitutionality of mandatory character of Supreme Court decisions on social security for lower courts).

[33] See Supreme Court of Argentina, *Chocobar, Sixto Celestino v. Caja de Previsión para el Personal del Estado y Servicios Públicos*, 27 December 1996. The Court upheld legislation that forbade any automatic adjustment of prices following changes in price-level indexes in order to prevent the administrative or judicial readjustment of pay-as-you-go system pensions, while quoting, paradoxically, the Universal Declaration of Human Rights and the American Convention on Human Rights. See also Supreme Court of Argentina, *González, Herminia v. ANSeS*, 21 March 2000 (upholding the mandatory character of Supreme Court decisions on social security for lower courts); Supreme Court of Argentina, *Aguiar López, Eduardo v. INPS – Caja Nacional de Previsión para Trabajadores Autónomos*, 17 March 1998; Supreme Court of Argentina, *Heit Rupp, Clementina v. ANSeS*, 16 September 1999; *Adamini, Juan Carlos v. Poder Ejecutivo Nacional s/amparo*, 14 September 2000. But see Supreme Court of Argentina, *Barry, María Elena v. ANSeS s/reajustes por movilidad* and *Hussar, Otto v. ANSeS s/reajustes por movilidad*, 10 October 1996 (procedural changes that

force social security plaintiffs to reinitiate their claims violate the right to due process).

[34] *Sánchez, María del Carmen v. ANSeS s/reajustes varios*, Supreme Court of Argentina, 17 May 2005, reaffirmed on 28 July 2005.

[35] *Itzcovich, Mabel v. ANSeS s/reajustes varios*, Supreme Court of Argentina, 29 April 2005.

Las Palmeras case decided by the Inter-American Court of Human Rights.[36]

4.3 Health Rights

While labour and social security rights were already well-established fields of litigation, the judicial enforcement of health rights dramatically expanded in the 1990s. Because of the social and economic crisis of the 1980s and 1990s, courts were being asked to rule on inclusion in medical plans, the extension of health care coverage, access to medication and the forced termination of health coverage. Legal regulations gradually imposed a mandatory minimum health coverage on all health providers, that is, private entities, trade unions and the public sector. As soon as litigation was perceived as a successful means to ensure health rights, the span and variety of cases broadened remarkably.

The right to health was not included directly in the 1957 constitutional amendments, which incorporated labour and social security rights into the Constitution. The 1994 amendments included a brief mention on the protection of the health of consumers. The full recognition of a constitutional right to health was realised through the constitutional priority accorded to the International Covenant on Economic, Social and Cultural Rights and the Convention on the Rights of the Child (many cases concern access to health care for children), and courts recognised this constitutional hierarchy. While international human rights law played an important role in identifying a constitutionally protected right to health, most of the cases (with important exceptions) were decided on a statutory basis. By 2005, a fairly mature body of case law from the Supreme Court and lower courts had emerged. Important trends set by this case law are summarised below, and some of the main cases are then described.[37]

The Supreme Court has also held that the right to health creates not only negative, but also positive obligations for the State. Courts have entertained individual and collective claims regarding positive obligations; for example access to treatment and medication, and negative obligations, such as protection against termination of coverage. Importantly, the federal government has been considered the ultimate guardian of the health system, regardless of the existence of the duties of other parties, but both public and private defendants have been sued. Furthermore, the courts have imbued the right to health with a right to judicial review. Legislation passed by Federal Congress is considered one of the measures adopted by the State to comply with international obligations regarding the right to health. Therefore, failure by the government to comply with statutory regulations requiring access to health care creates a ground for individual and collective victims to make a judicial claim for the enforcement of the regulations.

Courts have also held that, in compliance with international obligations, the State is permitted to impose health coverage duties on non-state actors, such as private health insurance companies and health entities run by trade unions. Courts have likewise determined that private health care providers are obligated, as a constituent part of the right to health, to carry out special duties with respect to the care of their health care recipients that go beyond the wording of private contractual arrangements. Attention has also been paid by courts to the duties that all actors, public and private, must perform to protect the health of children and persons with disabilities.

However, some issues remain unresolved. Among these is the problem of the core content of the right to health and the mandatory content of the rights that cannot be postponed or altered by statutory law, as articulated by the Committee on Economic, Social and Cultural Rights. As most of the case law is decided on the basis of statutes and regulations, there is little commentary on this topic.

---

[36] Inter-American Court of Human Rights, *Las Palmeras v. Colombia*, 6 December 2001, Inter-Am. Ct. H.R. (Ser. C) No. 90.

[37] For a complete account, see Christian Courtis, 'La aplicación de tratados e instrumentos internacionales sobre derechos humanos y la protección jurisdiccional del derecho a la salud: apuntes críticos' [The application of international human rights treaties and instruments and the judicial protection of the right to health: critical

appraisals], in V. Abramovich, A. Bovino and C. Courtis (eds.), *La aplicación de los tratados de derechos humanos en el ámbito local: La experiencia de una década (1994–2005)* [The local application of human rights treaties: the experience of a decade (1994–2005)] (Buenos Aires: Ed. del Puerto, 2007).

Some doubts also remain on the weight of the positive obligations of the State to provide health care, particularly for indigent people who cannot afford health services. Also, references to the relevant General Comments issued by the Committee on Economic, Social and Cultural Rights have been erratic, and there are no clear criteria regarding their normative value.

An important Supreme Court precedent involved a claim for individual coverage regarding children with disabilities. In *Campodónico de Beviacqua*,[38] the Court upheld an appellate court decision ordering the Government to continue providing medication to a child with a disability. The Government had previously delivered the medication, but interrupted the provision with a notice that the previous delivery had been based on 'humanitarian reasons' and the interruption therefore did not constitute a breach of a legal duty. The Supreme Court confirmed the appellate court decision, stating that:

- The right to health is a constitutionally protected right: the right is included in international human rights treaties granted constitutional hierarchy.
- Public authorities have an immediate duty to guarantee this right with positive actions, regardless of other duties imposed on different actors.
- International human right treaties specifically protect children's life and health.
- [Article 12 of the] International Covenant on Economic, Social and Cultural Rights recognises the right of everyone to the enjoyment of the highest attainable standard of physical and mental health and includes State duties to satisfy this right. Among the measures to be adopted to satisfy this right, the State shall adopt a plan to reduce child mortality, to guarantee children a healthy development and to provide assistance and medical services in case of illness.
- States parties to the International Covenant on Economic, Social and Cultural Rights undertook to take steps to the maximum of its available resources, with a view to achieving progressively the full realisation of the rights recog-

nised in the Covenant (quoting Article 2.1 of the International Covenant on Economic, Social and Cultural Rights).
- In States parties with a federal structure, it is the legal responsibility of the federal government to ensure the implementation of the Covenant, regardless of constitutional duties established by domestic law to other political entities such as provinces.[39]
- The Convention on the Rights of the Child includes the obligation to guarantee effective access to health and rehabilitation services to children with disabilities (quoting Articles 23, 24 and 26 of the Convention on the Rights of the Child).

The Supreme Court summarised its doctrine in the following paragraph:

The Government has assumed explicit international duties to promote and facilitate health treatment required by children, and cannot validly refuse to comply with those duties with the excuse of the inactivity of other public or private entities, especially when all of them participate in the same health system and when the best interests of the child are at stake: these interests shall be protected beyond other considerations by all branches of government (art. 3, Convention on the Rights of the Child).

Similar cases have involved individual claims for coverage by indigent children with disabilities[40] and HIV-positive patients[41] and preliminary measures to ensure access to medication and treatment,[42] as well as a series of claims for medical

---

[38] *Campodónico de Beviacqua, Ana Carina v. Ministerio de Salud y Banco de Drogas Neoplásicas*, Supreme Court of Argentina, 24 October 2000.

[39] The Supreme Court quotes the concluding observations made by the conclusions and recommendations of CESCR: Switzerland, U.N. Doc. E/C.12/1/Add.30 (1998), and Articles 28(1) and 28(2) of the American Convention on Human Rights.

[40] *Monteserin, Marcelino v. Estado Nacional – Ministerio de Salud y Acción Social – Comisión Nacional Asesora para la Integración de Personas Discapacitadas – Servicio Nacional de Rehabilitación y Promoción de la Persona con Discapacidad*, Supreme Court of Argentina, 16 October 2001.

[41] *A., C. B. C. Ministerio de Salud y Acción Social s/amparo ley 16.986*, Supreme Court of Argentina. See attorney general's brief of 19 March 1999 and court decision of 1 June 2000.

[42] See, for example, Supreme Court of Argentina, *Alvarez, Oscar Juan v. Buenos Aires, Provincia de y otro s/acción de amparo*, 12 July 2001; Supreme Court of Argentina, *Orlando, Susana Beatriz v. Buenos Aires, Provincia de y otros s/amparo*, 4 April 2002; Supreme Court of Argentina,

coverage by individuals against for-profit health insurance companies, entities run by trade unions and state-run social entities.[43] Lower courts have also decided successful cases.[44]

The Supreme Court also adjudicated a collective case regarding compliance with the statutory-mandated provision of HIV-related medication.

> *Díaz, Brígida v. Buenos Aires, Provincia de y otro (Estado Nacional – Ministerio de Salud y Acción Social de la Nación) s/amparo*, 25 March 2003; Supreme Court of Argentina, *Benítez, Victoria Lidia y otro v. Buenos Aires, Provincia de y otros s/acción de amparo*, 24 April 2003; Supreme Court of Argentina, *Mendoza, Aníbal v. Estado Nacional s/amparo*, 8 September 2003; Supreme Court of Argentina, *Rogers, Silvia Elena v. Buenos Aires, Provincia de y otros (Estado Nacional) s/acción de amparo*, 8 September 2003; Supreme Court of Argentina, *Sánchez, Enzo Gabriel v. Buenos Aires, Provincia de y otro (Estado Nacional) s/acción de amparo*, 18 December 2003; Supreme Court of Argentina, *Laudicina, Angela Francisca v. Buenos Aires, Provincia de y otro s/acción de amparo*, 9 March 2004; Supreme Court of Argentina, *Sánchez, Norma Rosa c/Estado Nacional y otro s/acción de amparo*, 11 May 2004. The Court declared itself incompetent, but, notwithstanding, ordered preliminary injunctive relief in *Diéguez, Verónica Sandra y otro v. Buenos Aires, Provincia de s/acción de amparo*, 27 December 2002; Supreme Court of Argentina, *Kastrup Phillips, Marta Nélida v. Buenos Aires, Provincia de y otros s/acción de amparo*, 11 November 2003; Supreme Court of Argentina, *Podestá, Leila Grisel v. Buenos Aires, Provincia de y otro s/acción de amparo*, 18 December 2003. Cases were dealt with under the original jurisdiction of the Supreme Court because plaintiffs sued both the federal State and a province.

[43] Supreme Court of Argentina, *N., L. M. y otra v. Swiss Medical Group S. A.*, attorney general's brief of 11 June 2003 and Court decision of 21 August 2003; Supreme Court of Argentina, *Martín, Sergio Gustavo y otros v. Fuerza Aérea Argentina – Dirección General Bienestar Pers. Fuerza Aérea s/amparo*, attorney general's brief of 31 October 2002, Court decision of 8 June 2004; *M., S. A. s/materia: previsional s/recurso de amparo*, Supreme Court of Argentina, 23 November 2004. In the same vein, see *R., R. S. v. Ministerio de Salud y Acción Social y otro s/amparo*, Federal Administrative Court of Appeal, Chamber II, 21 October 1997; *T., J. M. v. Nubial S. A.*, National Civil Court of Appeals, Chamber C, 14 October 1997.

[44] See, amongst many others, Bahia Blanca Civil and Commercial Court of Appeals, Chamber II, *C. y otros v. Ministerio de Salud y Acción Social de la Provincia de Buenos Aires*, 2 September 1997 (forcing a public hospital to provide treatment); Tucumán Administrative Court of Appeals, Chamber II, *González, Amanda Esther v. Instituto de Previsión y Seguridad Social de Tucumán y otro s/amparo*, 15 July 2002 (forcing a public social entity to provide treatment); Buenos Aires Administrative Court of Appeals, Chamber II, *Sociedad Italiana de Beneficencia en Buenos Aires v. GCBA s/otras causas*, 7 October 2004; Buenos Aires Administrative Court of Appeals, Chamber I, *Centro de Educ. Médica e Invest. Clínicas Norberto Quirno v. GCBA s/otras causas*, 22 June 2004 (backing the legal imposition of coverage duties on private providers); Buenos Aires Administrative Court of Appeals, Chamber II, *Trigo, Manuel Alberto v. GCBA y otros s/Medida Cautelar*, 12 May 2002; Buenos Aires Administrative Court of Appeals, Chamber I, *Rodríguez Miguel Orlando v. GCBA s/otros procesos incidentales*, 22 December 2004; Buenos Aires Administrative Court of Appeals, Chamber I, *Defensoría del Pueblo de la Ciudad de Buenos Aires (Denuncia incumplimiento respecto a la afiliada Brenda Nicole Deghi) v. GCBA s/otros procesos incidentales*, 10 February 2005 (providing treatment through preliminary measures); Buenos Aires Administrative Court of Appeals, Chamber I, *Zárate, Raúl Eduardo v. GCBA s/Daños y Perjuicios*, 21 August 2002; Buenos Aires Administrative Court of Appeals, Chamber II, *Villalba de Gómez, Leticia Lilian v. GCBA (Hospital General de Agudos Franciso Santojani) y otros s/Daños y Perjuicios*, 8 April 2003; Buenos Aires Administrative Court of Appeals, Chamber II, *Echavarría, Adriana Graciela v. GCBA y otros s/Daños y Perjuicios*, 22 April 2003; Buenos Aires Administrative Court of Appeals, Chamber I, *B. L. E. y otros v. OSBA s/Daños y Perjuicios*, 27 August 2004 (awarding compensation for damages caused by denial of or inadequate treatment); Buenos Aires Administrative Court of Appeals, Chamber I, *Roccatagliata de Bangueses, Mercedes Lucía v. OSBA s/otros procesos incidentales*, 10 June 2002; Buenos Aires Administrative Court of Appeals, Chamber I, *Urtasun, Teodoro Alberto v. Instituto Municipal de Obra Social s/Cobro de Pesos*, 22 April 2004 (imposing treatment on public social entities).

[45] Supreme Court of Argentina, *Asociación Benghalensis y otros v. Ministerio de Salud y Acción Social – Estado Nacional s/amparo ley 16.688*, attorney general's brief of 22 February 1999, Court decision of 1 June 2000.

In *Asociación Benghalensis*,[45] a coalition of NGOs filed an amparo (collective action) action against the national government that demanded full adherence by the government to a federal statute that guaranteed the provision of HIV-related medication to public hospitals. The appellate court granted injunctive relief to the plaintiffs. On appeal, the Supreme Court upheld the judgment in accordance with the brief provided by the attorney general. The attorney general pointed out that the right to health is recognised in international human rights treaties (quoting Article 12(c) of the International Covenant on Economic, Social and Cultural Rights, Articles 4(1) and 5 of the American Convention on Human Rights and Article 6 of the International Covenant on Civil and Political Rights). According to the attorney general, 'the State not only has to abstain from interfering in the exercise of individual rights, but also has the duty to perform positive actions, without which the exercise of rights would be illusory'. On this basis, 'the State has a duty to provide the reagents and medication necessary for the diagnosis and treatment of the illness'. The majority of the Court followed the attorney general's brief, and two judges concurred in separate judgments.

Another recurrent issue in litigation is the exclusion from and termination of health coverage, particularly by private health insurance companies and social entities run by trade unions. Some of these cases involve discrimination, while in others the issue at stake is the role of unemployment. Coverage by social entities is predicated upon the holding of a formal job in a particular economic sector, and unemployment breaks this legal link, thereby resulting in the cessation of coverage. In *Etcheverry v Omint*,[46] the Supreme Court decided that refusal to maintain membership in a private health insurance fund, when the plaintiff was detected as being HIV-positive, amounted to a breach of consumer rights and the right to health. The plaintiff was a previous customer of the health plan through an agreement with his employer. When he became unemployed, he requested the maintenance of coverage, offering to pay for the service. After the plaintiff had tested HIV-positive, the health insurance company refused to maintain him in the health plan. The Supreme Court, following the attorney general's opinion, stated that private health insurance companies had special duties regarding their customers that extend beyond a mere commercial deal. The attorney general stressed that, according to the law, health insurance companies carry duties related to the protection of the right to health, as provided by international human rights treaties. Thus, they bear 'a social pledge to their users'. The Court ordered the health insurance company to keep the plaintiff as its client. Similar cases were decided by the Supreme Court[47] and by lower courts.

Other cases are related to the constitutional validity of regulations issued by public authorities. In *Asociación de Esclerosis Múltiple de Salta*,[48] the Court upheld an appellate court decision that nullified a regulation issued by the Ministry of Health that excluded some treatments related to multiple sclerosis from the mandatory minimum health coverage plan. The Court followed the opinion of the attorney general, who considered that the challenged regulation was unreasonable and that it impinged upon the right to health as contained in international human rights treaties. While the attorney general does not refer explicitly to the prohibition of retrogression, the reasonableness standard he employs comes close to it. It is also important to point out that despite the traditional relative effect of declarations of unconstitutionality in the Argentine legal tradition, whereby judicial declarations of unconstitutionality only affect the case in which they are pronounced, the fact that an NGO filed the case as an amparo action representing a group of persons with multiple sclerosis in the province meant that the decision positively benefited the entire group of affected persons.

In some cases, private health care providers challenged the imposition of legal duties, for example, the inclusion of HIV treatment in health plans, by statutory regulations. The basis for the constitutional challenge was a violation of freedom of contract and property rights and the unreasonableness of the regulations. In *Hospital Británico*,[49] the Supreme Court dismissed the petitions and considered that the imposition of regulations on private health care providers was a valid way for the government to comply with international obligations with regard to the right to health. In another case, *Policlínica Privada*,[50] the Court decided that a local government could not force a private hospital to keep a patient after the coverage period had expired, but that the government had the duty to admit the patient into a public facility.

Lower courts have also adjudicated a series of fascinating cases concerning the right to health. *Viceconte*[51] was decided by the Federal Administrative

---

[46] Supreme Court of Argentina, *Etcheverry, Roberto E. v. Omint Sociedad Anónima y Servicios*, attorney general's brief of 17 December 1999, Court decision of 13 March 2001.

[47] Supreme Court of Argentina, *V., W. J. v. Obra Social de Empleados de Comercio y Actividades Civiles s/sumarísimo*, 2 December 2004.

[48] Supreme Court of Argentina, *Asociación de Esclerosis Múltiple de Salta v. Ministerio de Salud – Estado Nacional s/acción de amparo-medida cautelar*, attorney general's brief of 4 August 2003, Court decision of 18 December 2003.

[49] Supreme Court of Argentina, *Hospital Británico de Buenos Aires v. Estado Nacional – Ministerio de Salud y Acción Social s/amparo*, Attorney-General's brief of 29 February 2000, Court decision of 13 March 2001.

[50] Supreme Court of Argentina, *Policlínica Privada de Medicina y Cirugía S. A. v. Municipalidad de la Ciudad de Buenos Aires*, 11 June 1998.

[51] Federal Administrative Court, Chamber IV, *Viceconte, Mariela v. Estado nacional – Ministerio de Salud y Acción Social s/amparo ley 16.986*, 2 June 1998.

Appellate Court, and the case has attracted significant scholarly attention. A collective injunction challenged the interruption of the production of a vaccine designed to eradicate an endemic disease peculiar to Argentina. The plaintiff represented a population of about 3,500,000 people who were potentially exposed to the disease. While the Government had previously funded the research, validated the vaccine, ordered the production of a significant number of experimental doses in a foreign laboratory and carried out an initial vaccination of the population, which was successful in terms of the prevention of the disease, political and administrative changes led to a halt in the building of the facilities to produce the vaccine in Argentina. When the foreign laboratory exhausted its supply of doses, access to the vaccine came to an end. The plaintiff argued that the interruption of the production of the vaccine by the Government violated the duty to prevent, treat and control epidemic and endemic diseases that is enshrined in Article 12(2)(c) of the International Covenant on Economic, Social and Cultural Rights. The appellate court agreed and ordered the Government to provide funding and adopt the measures necessary to ensure the production of the vaccine.

Some other Supreme Court cases, even if not directly dealing with the right to health, touched on matters closely connected to a human rights approach to health. For example, in *Benítez*,[52] the Court had the opportunity to decide on the issue of a compulsory HIV test of a police officer by the Federal Police Department. The department carried out the test secretly, without obtaining informed consent from the plaintiff. When the officer tested positive, he was dismissed from the force. While the Supreme Court ruled, with two justices dissenting, that it was not illegal for the police department to carry out health tests on its employees without securing consent, the Court declared that the dismissal was unjustified and amounted to discrimination on the basis of health and ordered the restoration of his position. The Court invoked anti-discrimination standards set out in the American Convention on Human Rights.

There are, however, some borderline cases where the Supreme Court demonstrated a reluctance to find violations. Perhaps the most representa-

tive of such cases is *Ramos*,[53] in which an indigent woman with eight children claimed relief on the grounds that she was unemployed, that her children could not go to school due to her lack of resources, that one of her daughters suffered from a heart disease and required medical assistance and that she had no one from whom she could claim alimony. She maintained that her situation and that of her children amounted to a violation of social and economic rights enshrined in the Constitution and in international human rights treaties ratified by Argentina. She requested that the Court order federal and local authorities to provide her with assistance in order to respect her and her children's right to food, health, education and housing, which meant the provision of a monthly allowance to cover her family's basic needs. She also claimed medical coverage to address her daughter's heart disease, a guarantee of her children's right to attend classes and a declaration of unconstitutionality and invalidity of the behaviour of the State's authorities.

The Court dismissed the case, finding that: (a) there was a failure by the plaintiff to prove manifest illegal and arbitrary conduct by State authorities since the Government had not directly denied access to education or medical treatment; and (b) the claim was not suitable for discussion before courts, but should be instead directed to the relevant government administration. In *obiter dicta*, the Supreme Court stated that it could not assess general opinions about situations beyond the court's jurisdiction or use discretion concerning the allocation of budgetary resources. While this opinion is partly inconsistent with previous and later decisions of the Court, two factors may explain it. On the technical side, the claim was vague: no statutory clauses were mentioned, the plaintiff juxtaposed various positions in the same suit without narrowing them properly, and no clear criteria was advanced on how to specify the content of the different rights that were invoked. On the political side, the lawsuit was filed shortly after the outburst of the devastating social, political and economic crisis of December 2001, the worst crisis in Argentina's history. The number of Argentines living under the poverty line rocketed from 15–17 per cent of the population to

---

[52] Supreme Court of Argentina, *Benítez, Ricardo Ernesto v. Policía Federal s/amparo*, 17 December 1996.

[53] Supreme Court of Argentina, *Ramos, Marta Roxana y otros v. Buenos Aires, Provincia de y otros s/amparo*, 12 March 2002.

45–50 per cent. The Court probably weighed the potential 'snowball effect' of granting court relief in such a delicate economic and political context in terms of both interference with the political branches of government and of attracting an insurmountable burden of cases.

4.4   Housing Rights

While the original mention of housing in the 1957 constitutional amendment was rather limited, the inclusion of international human rights treaties and declarations in the Constitution have strengthened litigation in the field of housing rights. The last five years have witnessed an unprecedented flow of housing rights cases, particularly before local courts. Courts have heard both negative and positive rights – based claims, and most of the decisions have been in favour of claimants.[54]

Some cases related to the links between due process and forced evictions. In a number of judgments, courts in the city of Buenos Aires declared that a provision of the local administrative procedural code that granted the city administration the power to summarily evict tenants from state-owned housing was unconstitutional, breaching the right to due process.[55] Explicit connections were made between the right to due process, the right to challenge eviction orders legally and the right to housing, and, in *Saavedra*,[56] specific reference was made to General Comments 4 and 7 of the Committee on Economic, Social and Cultural Rights. Lower courts have often concurred. In *Gianelli*,[57] a local trial court declared that if tenants with children were threatened with forced

eviction, the government authority must assure alternative housing. The judge drew explicitly on the right to housing as enshrined in the Constitution and the right of children to social protection.

Criminal courts have also declined to prosecute irregular occupants of state-owned lands. In *Bermejo*,[58] a criminal court decided that sixty indigent families living on publicly owned lands could not by indicted for usurpation: criminal prosecution would amount to the criminalisation of poverty. The Court requested that the city administration take measures to tackle the problem, invoking the right to adequate housing in international human rights, and national and local constitutional law.

In some other cases though, the Supreme Court has been more reluctant to protect interference with housing. While the Cordoba Supreme Court considered that statutory provisions protecting family housing against seizure were in line with the provincial constitution, the Federal Supreme Court decided that the constitution had gone beyond its legal capacity, affecting the power of the Federal Congress to pass the Civil Code.[59]

The right to inclusion in a housing plan has been the subject of a number of cases. The Buenos Aires Administrative Appellate Court confirmed the decisions and preliminary injunctions ordered by lower courts that required the city administration to refrain from excluding plaintiffs from housing plans and to guarantee them the right to adequate housing.[60] A Neuquén Appellate Court

---

[54] See, generally, S. Tedeschi, 'El derecho a la vivienda a diez años de la reforma de la Constitución' [The right to housing ten years after the constitutional amendment], in Abramovich, Bovino and Courtis, *La aplicación de los tratados* (n. 37 above).

[55] Buenos Aires Supreme Court, *Comisión Municipal de la Vivienda v. Saavedra, Felisa Alicia y otros s/Desalojo s/Recurso de Inconstitucionalidad Concedido*, 7 October 2002, and *Comisión Municipal de la Vivienda v. Tambo Ricardo s/desalojo*, 16 October 2002.

[56] Buenos Aires Supreme Court, *Comisión Municipal de la Vivienda v. Saavedra, Felisa Alicia y otros s/Desalojo s/Recurso de Inconstitucionalidad Concedido*, 7 October 2002.

[57] Buenos Aires Administrative Trial Court No. 3, *Comisión Municipal de la Vivienda v. Gianelli, Alberto Luis y otros s/Desalojo*, 12 September 2002.

[58] Buenos Aires Federal Criminal Court No. 11, *Bermejo*, 26 April 2004.

[59] See Supreme Court of Argentina, *Banco del Suquía S. A. v. Juan Carlos Tomassini s/Ejecutivo*, 19 March 2002.

[60] See Buenos Aires Administrative Court of Appeals, Chamber I, *Benítez, María Romilda y otros v. GCBA s/medida cautelar*, 16 November 2001; Buenos Aires Administrative Court of Appeals, Chamber I, *Tarantino, Héctor Osvaldo y otros v. GCBA s/amparo (artículo 14 CCABA)*, 28 December 2001; Buenos Aires Administrative Court of Appeals, Chamber II, *Fernández, Silvia Graciela y otros v. GCBA s/amparo (art. 14 CCABA) Incidente de Apelación Medida Cautelar*, 7 September 2001 (preliminary measure); Buenos Aires Administrative Court of Appeals, Chamber II, *Fernández, Silvia Graciela y otros v. GCBA s/amparo*, 28 December 2001 (final decision); Buenos Aires Administrative Court of Appeals, Chamber II, *Ríos Alvarez, Gualberto Felipe v. GCBA s/amparo (art. 14 CCABA)*, 11 March 2002; *Arrua, Juana y otros v. GCBA s/amparo (art. 14 CCABA)*, 11 March 2002; Buenos Aires Administrative Court of Appeals, Chamber II, *Morón Jorge Luis v. GCBA s/amparo*, 8 October 2003 (most of

ordered the provincial government to adopt measures to provide health treatment to a child and housing to her family, taking into consideration her precarious health condition and the possibilities of aggravation due to the lack of habitability of their dwelling.[61]

Court action has also forced the Buenos Aires city administration to adopt measures to cope with collective housing problems. In *Agüero*,[62] a collective injunction involved the situation of eighty-six families living in irregular conditions on State-owned land. The suit was settled, and the administration agreed to design a specific housing plan for the families. The administration's failure to comply led to a new injunction and to a court-ordered seizure of public monies to secure funding for the promised plan. A new and more specific agreement was struck, and international human rights standards on housing played an important role in the bargaining process. The administration adopted a three-stage plan to build ninety-one dwellings, giving priority in the legal tender to enterprises offering jobs to residents. Affordability issues were also considered: the administration was to offer residents access to a special line of credit and the repayments were not to exceed 20 percent of the monthly income of the families.

The implementation of housing plans has also been reviewed. In *Pérez*,[63] a Buenos Aires Administrative Appellate Court considered that a public refuge for the homeless did not meet adequate habitability conditions and ordered the gov-

ernment to relocate the dwellers. In *Delfino*,[64] a Buenos Aires Administrative Appellate court considered that the conditions of government-funded private hostels, where housing plan beneficiaries lived, did not meet habitability conditions and ordered the city administration to adopt measures to provide the dwellers with adequate housing. Courts also imposed fines on public officials for failing to comply with a court agreement that involved ensuring adequate housing conditions to a number of families included in an emergency housing plan.[65]

4.5 Educational Rights

The right to education was not explicitly included in the 1853/1860 Constitution. References to education were limited to an obligation on the provinces to ensure elementary education (article 5) and the recognition of the freedom 'to teach and learn' (article 14). The 1994 amendments gave new shape to the right. They added new powers of Congress regarding education. The Federal Congress is now empowered to 'enact laws referring to the organisation and basis of education' (article 75(19)). The provision provides that State responsibility cannot be delegated and that there must be family and society participation, the fostering of democratic values and equal opportunities with no discrimination and the guarantee of free and equitable State public education, as well as the autonomy and self-sufficiency of national universities. Article 75(17) also provides that the State must 'guarantee respect for the identity and the right to bilingual and intercultural education' of indigenous peoples (article 75(17)). Moreover, the right to education is included in a number of international human right declarations and treaties incorporated in the Constitution.[66]

---

these quoted General Comments issued by the Committee on Economic, Social and Cultural Rights, including the prohibition of retrogression standard); Buenos Aires Administrative Trial Court No. 9, *Paéz, Hugo y otros v. GCBA s/amparo*, 17 May 2004; Buenos Aires Administrative Trial Court No. 5, *Rosito Alejandra v. GCBA s/amparo*, 3 May 2004; Buenos Aires Administrative Trial Court No. 6, *Romero Liliana v. GCBA s/amparo*, 7 May 2005; Buenos Aires Administrative Court of Appeals, Chamber II, *Silva, Mora Griselda v. GCBA s/amparo (art. 14 CCABA)*, 24 February 2003 (making clear that the order to the government to satisfy the right to access to decent housing shall include the plaintiff and her family group).

[61] See Neuquén Civil Court of Appeals, Defensor de Derechos del Niño y del Adolescente c/Provincia de Neuquén, 18 October 2002.

[62] Buenos Aires Administrative Trial Court No. 5, *Agüero, Aurelio E. v. GCBA s/amparo*, friendly settlement, December 2003.

[63] See Buenos Aires Administrative Court of Appeals, Chamber I, *Pérez, Víctor Gustavo y otros v. GIBA s/amparo*, 26 January 2001.

[64] See Buenos Aires Administrative Court of Appeals, Chamber I, *Delfino, Jorge Alberto y otros v. GCBA s/amparo*, 11 June 2004.

[65] See Buenos Aires Administrative Appellate Court, Chamber II, *Ramallo, Beatriz v. Ciudad de Buenos Aires*, 30 September 2004.

[66] See Article 26, Universal Declaration of Human Rights; Article 13, International Covenant on Economic, Social and Cultural Rights; Articles 28 and 29, Convention on the Rights of the Child; Article 10, Convention on the Elimination of All Forms of Discrimination against Women; Article 5, Convention on the Elimination of All Forms of Racial Discrimination and Article XII of the American Declaration of the Rights and Duties of Man.

Courts have considered comparatively fewer cases on the right to education, although there are a number of Supreme Court and provincial court decisions on the matter. In a recent case, the Supreme Court had the opportunity to decide a collective claim involving failure of a province to comply with the regulations of the Federal Educational Act.[67] This Act seeks the achievement of equality in education and purports to assure minimum common rules and standards in education throughout the country regardless of the jurisdiction. The province of Tucumán had decided not to apply the Act and maintained the previous educational scheme. Parents filed an injunction, arguing constitutional and statutory violations, in particular a violation against equality of opportunities in education, because diplomas issued in the province would lack nationwide validity. The Court decided in favour of the plaintiffs, invalidating the provincial decision to avoid compliance with the Federal Educational Act. The Court resorted to the American Convention on Human Rights and the International Covenant on Economic, Social and Cultural Rights, stating that maintaining the previous educational scheme would amount to affecting the children's right to undertake further studies in other provinces and put them at a disadvantage regarding access to certain jobs.

The *Lifschitz*[68] case involved a claim by a low-income family who had a child with a disability. The child's mother claimed that the child was denied access to a public special education institution, purportedly for lack of vacant places. She also complained about the general absence of accessible public transportation to the school, which also affected her son. She sought to force the government authorities to provide the family with a subsidy to cover attendance at a private special school and private transportation for the child to attend the school. The Supreme Court agreed, basing its decision on statutory provisions and the consideration of the child's best interests, as set out in the Convention on the Rights of the Child, and ordered the Federal Government to provide the child with the subsidy. In

another case concerning children with disabilities, *R.C.S*,[69] a Tucumán appellate court ordered the government to provide the plaintiff – an elementary school student with cerebral palsy – with an integrative teacher to ensure full integration in his school class. The decision was based on provincial constitutional and statutory law.

In *Painefilu*,[70] a Neuquén civil trial court granted collective injunctive relief to a Mapuche indigenous group and ordered the provincial government to adopt measures to provide bilingual education to the children in the community. The administration had previously ignored petitions in this regard. The judge ordered the government to appoint a bilingual teacher and granted the community the right to participate in the selection of the teacher.

Reference can also be made to a range of decisions that affected different aspects of the right to education. In *Asesoría Tutelar Justicia Contencioso Administrativo y Tributario de la C.A.B.A. v GCBA*,[71] a statute passed by the Buenos Aires city legislature ordered the construction of a school within a certain period, but the relevant government department had not commenced with the works. The case was brought to the court by a public defender on behalf of the group of working class children who would have benefited from the school. The court quoted the International Covenant on Economic, Social and Cultural Rights and the Convention on the Rights of the Child to back its decision. In *Santoro*,[72] an appellate court considered that the government's refusal to allow a student to transfer from one school to another was arbitrary and revoked it. The decision quotes the Convention on the Rights of the Child. In *Vanzini*,[73] an appellate court granted injunctive

[67] Supreme Court of Argentina, *Ferrer de Leonard, Josefina y otros v. Superior Gobierno de la Pcia. de Tucumán s/amparo*, 12 August 2003.
[68] Supreme Court of Argentina, *Lifschitz, Graciela v. Estado Nacional s/sumarísimo*, 15 June 2004.
[69] Tucumán Administrative Court of Appeals, Chamber I, *R. C. S. y otro v. I.P.S.S.T. y otro s/ amparo*, 25 March 2005.
[70] Junin de los Andes (Neuquén) Civil Trial Court, *Painefilu, Mariano y otros v. Consejo de Educación de Neuquén*, February 2000.
[71] Buenos Aires Court of Appeals, Chamber I, *Asesoría Tutelar Justicia Contencioso Administrativo y Tributario de la CABA v. GCBA s/amparo*, 1 June 2001.
[72] Buenos Aires Administrative Court of Appeals, Chamber I, *Santoro, Francisco Roberto y otro v. GCBA s/amparo (art. 14 CCABA)*, 14 May 2002.
[73] Buenos Aires Administrative Court of Appeals, Chamber I, *Vanzini Oscar Alberto v. Colegio Liceo No. 1 Figueroa Alcorta s/amparo (art. 14 CCABA)*, 12 May 2004.

relief to the plaintiff, an elementary school student with a particular health condition who had requested the annulment of an examination and the provision of a new date to sit for the test. Courts have also awarded damages for injuries suffered by students on school premises.[74]

4.6 The Right to Food

Cases regarding the right to food were unheard of before the economic crisis of December 2001. There is no constitutional mention of a right to food, and its textual basis lies exclusively in Article 11 of the International Covenant on Economic, Social and Cultural Rights and Articles 24(2)(c) and 27(3) of the Convention on the Rights of the Child. After the onset of the 2001 economic crisis and after poverty levels had dramatically risen, a number of right-to-food cases were brought before courts. The courts of the city of Buenos Aires granted injunctions directing the city administration to include a plaintiff and her family in a food plan designed to provide access to food to low-income groups[75] and to include a patient undergoing a cancer treatment in a food plan and provide the patient with adequate food.[76] Similar cases were registered in local courts of the provinces of Entre Rios[77] and Tucumán.[78]

4.7 The Right to Water

A number of provincial cases have dealt with water rights. Legal strategies have varied. In some cases, water pollution has been framed as a violation of the right to health, of environmental rights and even of property rights;[79] in other cases, the aim

has been to require the provision of a mandatory minimum amount of water, regardless of the payment capacity of plaintiffs.[80] A few cases have referred to the 'right to water' and include quotes taken from General Comment No. 15 issued by the Committee on Economic, Social and Cultural Rights.[81]

---

otros s/amparo, 9 June 1998 (considering the pollution of underground waters illegal and requiring the municipal government to provide safe drinking water to neighbours); Neuquén Civil Court of Appeals, Second Chamber, *Menores Comunidad Paynemil s/acción de amparo*, 19 May 1997 (considering water pollution by an oil company illegal and forcing the provincial state to provide safe drinking water to the indigenous community involved); Neuquén Supreme Court, *Defensoría de Menores No. 3 c/ Poder Ejecutivo Municipal s/acción de amparo*, 2 March 1999 (similar to the case previously quoted); La Plata (Buenos Aires province) Federal Court of Appeals, Chamber II, *Asociación para la Protección del Medio Ambiente y Educación Ecológica '18 de Octubre' c/ Aguas Argentinas S. A. y otros s/amparo*, 8 July 2003 (interim measure ordering the province, the municipality and the water company to stop behaviour affecting the balance among strata of underground water and to take measures to reestablish the balance).

80 Mendoza Supreme Court, Second Chamber, *Villavechia de Pérez Lasala, Teresa c/ Obras Sanitarias de Mendoza S. E. s/acción de inconstitucionalidad*, 5 February 1990 (considering that water provision and sewage are essential social services and that powers to cut the service should be read restrictively); Mar del Plata (Buenos Aires province) Civil and Commercial Court of Appeal, Second Chamber, *ACIDECON c/ OSSE M. D. P. s/amparo*, 27 April 1998 (considering that an immediate cut-off of water services for lack of payment is abusive); Bahia Blanca (Buenos Aires province) Civil and Commercial Court of Appeals, Chamber II, *Ambientalista del Sur c/ Azurix S. A.*, 3 May 2000 (interim measure requiring a privately run water company to provide safe drinking water to users); Moreno (Buenos Aires province) Civil Trial Court, *Usuarios y consumidores en defensa de sus derechos c/ Aguas del Gran Buenos Aires s/amparo*, 21 August 2002 (declaring unconstitutional the power to cut off home water services for lack of payment and ordering the water company to avoid cutting water services and to reconnect services to users subjected to such a cut-off); Cordoba Civil and Commercial Trial Court No. 51 (substitute judge), *Quevedo, Miguel Angel, Márquez, Ramón Héctor, Boursiac, Ana María, Pedernera, Luis Oscar y otros c/ Aguas Cordobesas S. A. s/amparo*, 8 April 2002 (considering that a privately run water company had a statutory duty to provide a minimum amount of safe drinking water to plaintiffs, regardless of the existence of unpaid bills).

81 See, for example, Cordoba Civil and Commercial Trial Court No. 8, *Marchisio, José Bautista y otros s/amparo*, 16 October 2004 (requiring that the municipality take measures to minimise the impact of water pollution in a river crossing the city and that the provincial state provide an amount of safe drinking water to plaintiffs).

---

74 See, for example, Buenos Aires Administrative Court of Appeals, Chamber I, *Raimondo Inés Beatriz c/ GCBA s/Daños y Perjuicios*, 26 March 2004.

75 Buenos Aires Administrative Trial Court No. 3, *C., M. D. y otros v. GCBA s/amparo*, 11 March 2003.

76 See Buenos Aires Administrative Court No. 4, *González Rayco, Artidoro v. GCBA s/amparo*, 19 May 2005.

77 Parana (Entre Rios) Family and Juvenile Court No. 2, *Defensor del Superior Tribunal de Justicia v. Estado Provincial – Acción de amparo*, 28 June 2002.

78 Tucumán Administrative Court of Appeals, Chamber I, Rodríguez, José Angel y otra v. Sistema Provincial de Salud y otro s/amparo s/medida cautelar, 12 October 2003.

79 San Isidro (Buenos Aires province) Civil and Commercial Court of Appeals, First Chamber, *Fundación Pro Tigre y Cuenca del Plata c/ Municipalidad de Tigre y*

4.8 Indigenous Peoples' Rights

A growing number of decisions refer to indigenous peoples' rights. No mention was made of the rights of indigenous peoples in the 1853/1860 Constitution. The 1994 amendments added a specific clause, empowering Congress to:

> Recognise the ethnic and cultural pre-existence of indigenous peoples of Argentina. To guarantee respect for the identity and the right to bilingual and intercultural education; to recognise the legal capacity of their communities, and the community possession and ownership of the lands they traditionally occupy; and to regulate the granting of other lands adequate and sufficient for human development; none of them shall be sold, transmitted or subject to liens or attachments. To guarantee their participation in issues related to their natural resources and in other interests affecting them. The provinces may jointly exercise these powers. (art. 75(17))

In July 2000, Argentina ratified International Labour Organisation Convention 169 concerning Indigenous and Tribal Peoples in Independent Countries. While not granted primacy in the constitutional hierarchy, general treaties are placed below the Constitution, but above federal statutes and local constitutions and statutes.

In *Wichi Hoktek T'Oi*,[82] the Supreme Court granted injunctive relief to an indigenous community seeking annulment of two provincial decrees that authorised the indiscriminate exploitation of forests in claimed historical lands. No consultation with the community had been carried out before the decrees were issued. The provincial supreme court had denied injunctive relief, considering that further proof was needed to adjudicate the case, but the Supreme Court reversed the decision and remanded the case to the provincial supreme court, which proceeded to grant injunctive relief to the indigenous community on the basis of the constitutional clause (article 75(17) noted above) and Convention 169. The Supreme Court found that the decrees violated the collective property rights of the communities over their ancestral lands and that they were issued in viola-

tion of the right of the communities to consultation.

The *Lhaka Honhat*[83] case involved an indigenous community's claim against a provincial plan to subdivide and allocate to third parties ancestral lands the indigenous title to which was in the process of being recognised. The case involved an ongoing petition before the Inter-American Commission on Human Rights. While the federal government had agreed to seek a friendly solution with the indigenous community, the province continued to allocate land to third parties. The community filed an injunction before a provincial court, which, again, considered that additional proof was necessary in order to adjudicated the case. The petition was finally decided by the Supreme Court, which reversed the provincial court decision and ordered the provincial government to halt the apportionment of land to third parties and to provide the community with a title for the claimed lands.

Provincial courts have decided a number of other cases concerning indigenous peoples, including adjudications in historical land conflicts[84] and the recognition of cultural differences and historical claims as defences in criminal proceedings.[85]

5. REMEDIES

Cases vary a great deal, and the courts have resorted to an array of remedies to confront violations of socio-economic rights: declaring the unconstitutionality of laws, upholding the

---

[82] Supreme Court of Argentina, *Comunidad Indígena Hoktek T'Oi Pueblo Wichi v. Secretaría de Medio Ambiente y Desarrollo Sustentable s/amparo*, 8 September 2003.

[83] Supreme Court of Argentina, *Asociación de Comunidades Aborígenes Lhaka Honhat v. Poder Ejecutivo de la Provincia de Salta*, 15 June 2004.

[84] See, for example, Pico Truncado (Santa Cruz) Civil, Commercial and Mining Trial Court, *Paisman, Ruben Alejandro v. Consejo Agrario Provincial S/Acción de Amparo*, 24 March 2000; Jujuy Civil and Commercial Court of Appeals, Chamber I, *Comunidad Aborigen de Quera y Aguas Calientes – Pueblo Cochinota v. Provincia de Jujuy*, 4 September 2001; Rio Negro III Circuit, Civil, Commercial and Mining Trial Court No. 5, *Sede, Alfredo y otros v. Vila, Herminia y otros s/Desalojo*, 12 August 2004; Rio Negro Supreme Court, *CO. DE. C. I. de la Provincia de Río Negro s/acción de amparo*, 16 August 2005.

[85] See, for example, Neuquén Supreme Court, *Puel, Raúl s/daño*, 12 March 1999; Bariloche (Rio Negro) Investigative Criminal Court No. II, *Fernández, Edgardo R. s/usurpación*, 21 April 2004; Bariloche (Rio Negro) Investigative Criminal Court No. II, *Guarda Fidel psa. Usurpación*, 11 November 2004.

constitutionality of government powers to impose duties on private parties in order to protect socio-economic rights, imposing both positive and negative duties in individual claims (in cases both against the government and against private parties), imposing positive and negative duties in collective cases, awarding damages for breach of duties stemming from socio-economic rights, and so on.

There is some variation in the extent of positive duties imposed on the government in collective cases. In some cases, courts have described the exact measure to be taken by the government, while, in others, the judicial decision states the violation and requires the government to take adequate measures and to report back to the court within a specified time frame. While remedies have mostly been effective in individual cases, some problems have arisen in the implementation of judicial orders requiring complex measures, for example, to take the necessary steps to produce a vaccine or to provide safe drinking water to an indigenous group that has suffered because of water pollution. There is not a significant tradition of 'complex' or 'structural reform' litigation before Argentine courts; complex socio-economic rights cases have led to the acknowledgement of some implementation problems in the remedial phase.

6. CLOSING REMARKS

It is evident that there is a growing trend to grant social and economic rights – at least *prima facie* – legal value and to confront challenges that have prevented these rights from becoming operative before courts. The possibilities for additional judicial enforcement of economic, social and cultural rights are considerable in Argentina, although a number of barriers remain, whether doctrinal, procedural, or cultural. Most of these obstacles are based on the notion that the courts should principally concern themselves with the settlement of property disputes between individual private parties and that the State should be granted wide discretion in matters involving the design and implementation of social policies. However, these

arguments, once influential in Argentine legal culture, are gradually losing their grip, and the number of cases in the areas of health, housing and educational rights is undoubtedly significant.

But the judicial enforcement of social and economic rights, as with any set of rights, requires the development of standards and criteria and a new litigation culture and practice, without which any application of abstract legal concepts is impossible. While the recent Argentine experience has contributed towards this end through an increase in judicial reasoning based on constitutional and international human rights norms and international jurisprudence, adjudication is still largely based on statutory grounds. There have, of course, been important exceptions, as this chapter has demonstrated.

It is also worthwhile analysing some of the underlying factors that have rendered cases more successful. A large number of claimants, whether individuals or representatives of a collective, have requested injunctions and preliminary measures, which suggests that the judiciary is more sensitive to economic, social and cultural rights when claimants face urgent situations. Another remarkable feature is the propensity of judges to accept claims based on social rights and impose positive obligations on governments and private parties where children are involved.

Moreover, it is important to underscore that, despite the predominant theory among scholars, judges have progressively assumed an active role in guaranteeing socio-economic rights without much hesitation. When the government has brought out arguments revolving around a lack of jurisdiction or argued its exclusive powers regarding policy issues or the assignment of funding, many courts have simply rejected such arguments, reaffirming their jurisdiction by citing their role as guardians of the application of the law, be it the Constitution, international human rights treaties, or statutory law. Additionally, the difference between positive and negative duties has not played an important role in judicial decisions; judges have enforced both positive and negative duties, as some of the reviewed cases show.

9

Brazil

Impact and Challenges of Social Rights in the Courts

Flavia Piovesan*

1. INTRODUCTION

The adoption of the new Constitution in Brazil in 1988 ushered in a new era of social rights protections and a nascent jurisprudence on the topic. Supported by a broad-ranging recognition of social rights, the Brazilian judiciary has issued a number of seminal decisions that have positively affected the realisation of these rights, particularly the right to health. This chapter examines the protection of social rights in the Brazilian Constitution of 1988, emphasising the innovations and advances the Constitution has produced by identifying these rights, for the first time, as fundamental rights. From this constitutional analysis, the chapter moves on to examine the justiciability of social rights in Brazilian courts, analysing cases relating to the right to health and education and evaluating the response of Brazilian courts to the interpretation and implementation of social rights. Finally, the chapter draws some conclusions on the impact of social rights judgments in Brazil and offers thoughts on ways to address the challenges of ensuring a fuller use of the justiciable possibilities.

2. SOCIAL RIGHTS IN THE 1988 CONSTITUTION

The Brazilian Constitution of 1988 represents a legal landmark in the country's democratic transition and in the movement towards the institu-tionalisation of human rights. Reflecting the 'post-dictatorship' democratic consensus, this consti-tutional text marks the break with the era of the authoritarian military regimes that had held power since 1964. Following on twenty-one years of authoritarian rule, the Constitution was designed to restore the rule of law, the separation of powers, federalism, democracy and fundamental rights in accordance with the principle of human dignity. In article 1(III) of the Constitution, human dignity is established as the centrepiece and interpretive conscience of the country's legal framework. Because of the high levels of public participation in the preparation of the Constitution, the document possesses considerable popular legitimacy.

The Constitution is remarkable for its consolidation of fundamental rights and guarantees in Brazil; indeed, it is the most advanced, wide-ranging and detailed document on the subject in the country's constitutional history. It is the first Brazilian Constitution to commence with chapters dedicated to rights and guarantees, carving them in 'stone clauses' (the so-called untouchable part of the Constitution), thereby rendering the rights immune to amendment (article 60, paragraph 4). The Constitution makes provision for new constitutional rights and recognises the inherently collective nature of seemingly individual human rights, noting, for example, the prerogative of unions, guilds and professional associations to defend human rights. International human rights treaties are incorporated as constitutional provisions,[1] and Brazil's international

* Professor of Constitutional Law and Human Rights at the Catholic University of São Paulo and professor of Human Rights in the Postgraduate Programmes of the Catholic University of São Paulo and the Catholic University of Paraná. A special acknowledgement is due to Akemi Kamimura for her assistance with the research for this chapter.

[1] Article 5, paragraph 3 states that, if international human rights treaties are approved by each house of the national Congress by a three-fifths majority over two terms, then they will be equivalent to constitutional amendments. Furthermore, according to article 5, paragraph 2, the rights and guarantees enshrined in the Constitution do not exclude others derived from the constitutional regime or principles or from international treaties ratified by

relations are to be governed by the principles of human rights.

2.1 Social Rights Protections

The indivisibility of human rights is recognised, and economic, social and cultural rights are positioned in the same section of the Constitution as fundamental rights. Previous constitutions have incorporated these rights (dating back to 1934) in a separate chapter. The 1988 Constitution asserts that social rights are fundamental rights and have immediate application. In doing this, the Constitution not only sets out the basic social rights in article 6 (education, health, work, housing, leisure, security, social security, protection of motherhood and childhood, and assistance for the destitute), it also sets out a series of rules to govern the programmes, guidelines and goals to be pursued by the State and by society. Foremost among the examples of this approach are the provisions that establish the relevant rights, as well as the corresponding duties of the State, such as health (article 196), education (article 205) and the practice of sports (article 217). Under the terms of article 196, health is the right of everyone and a duty of the State; it is to be guaranteed as far as possible by means of social and economic policies aimed at reducing the risk of illness and other hazards and by universal and equal access to treatment and services for its promotion, protection and recovery.[2] In the field of education, according to the Constitution, access to compulsory and free edu-

cation is a subjective public right, and the Constitution adds that the competent authority, the Government, shall be held liable for the failure of the government to provide compulsory education or the failure to provide it sufficiently.

With respect to the rights to health and education, the Constitution regulates the specific budgetary allocations that are to be made in these domains. For example, article 212 of the Constitution provides that:

> The Union shall apply, annually, never less than eighteen per cent, and the states, the Federal District, and the municipalities, at least twenty-five per cent of the tax revenues, including those resulting from transfers, in the maintenance and development of education.[3]

The federal government is also permitted to intervene in states that do not apply the mandatory minimum of state tax revenues towards the maintenance and development of education and towards public health services (article 34, VII, e).

The Constitution of 1988 has therefore initiated an expansion in the State's duties by incorporating socio-economic responsibilities that are judicially enforceable (see Section 2.2). Politics is no longer conceived as a legally free domain. There are not only constitutional limits, but also obligations imposed by a binding document, together with a distinctive framework for the regulation of political activity. As Canotilho notes: 'The task of any Constitution is always reality: the major challenge is whether to constitutionally judicialise this task or abandon it to politics. All Constitutions are intended, implicitly or explicitly, to make politics conform'.[4]

It is notable that social rights are included amongst the 'stone clauses'. Bonavides states in this regard, 'social rights are not only justiciable, they are enshrined in the constitutional system that guarantees the supreme unshakeable nature of

---

Brazil. See F. Piovesan, *Direitos Humanos e o Direito Constitucional Internacional* [Human Rights and International Constitutional Law], 7th edition (São Paulo: Saraiva, 2006), pp. 51–91.

[2] On this subject, Varun Gauri observes:

A review conducted for this paper assessed constitutional rights to education and health care in 187 countries. Of the 165 countries with available written constitutions, 116 made reference to a right to education and 73 to a right to health care. Ninety-five, moreover, stipulated free education and 29 free health care for at least some population subgroups and services. Brazil offers a compelling example of the force of human rights language. The Brazilian Constitution of 1988 guarantees each citizen the right to free health care. Although the constitutional guarantee has not eliminated shortages and inequalities in the sector, that provision had real "bite" in 1996, when a national law initiated a program of universal access to highly active anti-retroviral therapy (HAART) for AIDS patients, free of charge.

V. Gauri, 'Social Rights and Economics: claims to health care and education in developing countries', *World Development*, Vol. 32, No. 3 (2004), pp. 465–477.

[3] Regarding the right to health, budget funds are to be made available in keeping with the criteria established in article 198 of the Constitution.

[4] J. Joaquim Gomes Canotilho, *Direito Constitucional e Teoria da Constituição* [Constitutional Law and Theory of the Constitution] (Coimbra, Brazil: Livraria Almedina, 1998).

paragraph 4 of article 60'.[5] Social rights are therefore untouchable, so much so that any statutory law or amendment to the Constitution that alters, abolishes or revokes social rights automatically falls under the shadow of unconstitutionality.

To these human rights have been added those in international human rights treaties. Since the beginning of democratisation and, more specifically, the adoption of the 1988 Constitution, Brazil has ratified key international treaties protecting human rights,[6] including those in the field of social rights, which includes the International Covenant on Economic, Social and Cultural Rights and the Protocol of San Salvador in the area of economic, social and cultural rights. The post-1988 era has also seen a major surge in human rights legislation, and many of the laws have been directly inspired by the new Constitution.

2.2   Judicial Enforceability

In addition to these advances, the 1988 Constitution significantly enriched the catalogue of enforceable constitutional guarantees. Prior to 1998, there were three petition mechanisms to

address violations of human rights: (a) habeas corpus; (b) the writ of mandamus (to protect 'clear legal' rights); and (c) people's action (to protect public property). These constitutional instruments were based on a liberal model focusing on curbing arbitrary State action. The 'interpretation to block', which is designed to prevent governmental excesses, can be applied to these guarantees (constitutional hermeneutics in a liberal context). The 1988 Constitution brought in new remedial rights, namely, a writ of injunction (to assure the immediate exercise of constitutional rights should a regulatory provision be lacking) and direct action for unconstitutionality on the basis of omission (to assure the effectiveness of constitutional provisions in the case of inaction by the State).[7] Furthermore, the Constitution significantly broadened the scope of the 'people's action' from protection of public property to the areas of environment and public administration.[8]

These new constitutional instruments are grounded on a social model that focuses attention on an action or a duty of the State. Strikingly, this means that a failure by the State to implement constitutional dictates, particularly those related to social rights, can be considered an unconstitutional act and subject to judicial review. Moreover, as noted by Tércio Sampaio Ferraz Jr,[9] the courts are more fully empowered to adopt a teleological or substantive approach to interpretation – constitutional hermeneutics in the social context – in order to achieve the social values in the Constitution.

The 1988 Constitution is therefore both a commendable milestone in Brazil's history and a significant reinvention of Brazil's legal framework

[5] P. Bonavides, *Curso de Direito Constitucional* [Course of Constitutional Law] (São Paulo: Malheiros, 2000).

[6] Foremost amongst them are the: Inter-American Convention to Prevent and Punish Torture (ratified on 20 July 1989); the Convention against Torture and Other Cruel, Inhuman or Degrading Treatment or Punishment (ratified on 28 September 1989); the Convention on the Rights of the Child (ratified on 24 September 1990); the International Covenant on Civil and Political Rights (ratified on 24 January 1992); the International Covenant on Economic, Social and Cultural Rights (ratified on 24 January 1992); the American Convention on Human Rights (ratified on 25 September 1992); the Inter-American Convention to Prevent, Punish and Eradicate Violence against Women (ratified on 17 November 1995; the Protocol to the American Convention regarding the Abolition of the Death Penalty (ratified on 13 August 1996); the Protocol to the American Convention in the Area of Economic, Social and Cultural Rights (the 'Protocol of San Salvador') (ratified on 21 August 1996); the Rome Statute, which created the International Criminal Court (ratified on 20 June 2002); the Optional Protocol to the Convention on the Elimination of All Forms of Discrimination against Women (ratified on 28 June 2002); and the two Optional Protocols to the Convention on the Rights of the Child, regarding children's involvement in armed conflicts and regarding the sale of children, child prostitution and pornography (ratified on 24 January 2004). In addition to these advances, one might add Brazil's recognition, in December 1998, of the jurisdiction of the Inter-American Court of Human Rights.

[7] On this subject, see articles 5, LXXI and 103, paragraph 2 of the Constitution of 1988, which, respectively, provide for the writ of injunction and the action of unconstitutionality due to omission. For more on these instruments, see Flávia Piovesan, *Proteção Judicial contra Omissões Legislativas: ação direta de inconstitucionalidade por omissão e mandado de injunção* [Judicial Protection against Legislative Omissions: direct action of unconstitutionality due to omission and writ of injunction], 2nd edition (São Paulo: RT, 2003).

[8] See articles 5, LXXIII and 129, III of the Constitution, which deal, respectively, with people's action and public civil action. Note that public civil action was already provided for in Law 7,347 of 24 July 1985.

[9] T. Sampaio Ferraz Jr, *Interpretação e Estudos da Constituição de 1988* [Interpretation and Studies of the Constitution of 1988] (São Paulo: Atlas, 1990).

through the protection of human rights, notably, social rights. Considering the scope of the constitutional protections for socio-economic rights, it is important to evaluate the degree of justiciability of these rights in Brazilian courts. The following two sections concentrate on cases relating to the rights to health and education as adjudicated by higher courts, namely, the Federal Supreme Court, the highest court in the country, and the Superior Court of Justice, which adjudicates federal law.[10]

3. RIGHT TO HEALTH CARE

Judicial rulings have affirmed that the right to health is an inalienable and indispensable constitutional prerogative stemming from the right to life. In practice, this has led to rulings holding that the State has a duty to formulate and implement policies designed to guarantee universal and equal access to pharmaceutical, medical and hospital services and assistance for all persons, including people living with HIV/AIDS. The judgments illustrate a clear preference for the respect for life as an inalienable subjective right ensured by the Constitution itself rather than for the financial or other secondary interests of the State. The intention is to ensure the availability of the most suitable and effective health care treatments that are capable of protecting the dignity of patients and limiting the amount of suffering to the greatest extent. In this sense, there is a jurisprudential tendency to downplay formalistic, procedural approaches to law in favour of an emphasis on the importance of the right to life.

Judgments have also authorised differential treatment for national health service patients wishing to upgrade the 'class' of their hospital treatment, provided the balance is paid in full by the patient. But it is the generational factor that is by far the most explicit and prevalent when it comes to positive differentiation among groups: courts have repeatedly stressed the absolute priority of children and adolescents in access to health care.

The majority of rulings have enforced the right to health, but not all rulings have followed this trend. Drawing on the classical liberal approach, these decisions dismissed the justiciability of the right to health on the basis of the doctrine of separation of powers, the government's discretionary powers in budgetary allocations and the principle of 'possible reserve', which postulates that the budget is limited, finite and insufficient to guarantee full economic support for all public policies. In these cases, the judiciary has indicated its lack of authority to control the criteria and plans of the government in seeking to satisfy the population's health demands.

Meanwhile, a significant number of rulings have concerned the scope of the coverage of private health insurance plans, but rulings have been based not on human rights, but consumer rights, as set out in Brazil's Consumer Defence Code. Therefore, in the field of the right to health, one can discern that jurisprudence oscillates between ensuring access to health through the provision of medicine and health services as an inviolable constitutional right and treating health as a relationship between consumer and supplier, the former being more vulnerable and therefore deserving of more legal protection. In the case of constitutional jurisprudence, the focus of the judicial inquiry is not necessarily the quality of the health services provided, but the access to these services, their scope and their coverage.

3.1 Access to Medicine and Medical Treatment

In a series of rulings from the early 1990s, the Supreme Court has established the precedent that the right to health derives from the right to life, thereby recognising a right to medicine among the underprivileged, HIV virus carriers and people with other severe illnesses.

An illustrative case is RE 271286 AgR/RS, brought by an indigent woman with HIV/AIDS, in which the Court held that the right to health was 'a constitutional consequence inalienable from the right

[10] In Brazil, the Federal Supreme Court is the highest court in the judicial branch of the government. It is responsible, essentially, for constitutional matters. It consists of eleven justices appointed by the president of the Republic. These justices must be confirmed by an absolute majority in the Senate. The Superior Court of Justice, meanwhile, is Brazil's highest court for upholding federal laws, although its decisions can be appealed to the Supreme Court if there is a constitutional question. It consists of thirty-three justices, one-third of whom are judges in federal and state courts and one-third are, in equal numbers, lawyers and staff of the public prosecution service.

to life'.[11] The judgment specified that the 'subjective public right to health represents an inalienable legal prerogative' and that the State is responsible for formulating and implementing policies aimed at guaranteeing universal and equal access for all persons, including HIV virus carriers, to pharmaceutical, medical and hospital assistance. It stressed that the Government cannot transform a constitutional rule into an empty constitutional promise. Accordingly, the free distribution of medicine would:

> [L]end effectiveness to these constitutional precepts, representing a reverent gesture of solidarity for the life and health of people, particularly those who have nothing and own nothing other than a perception of their own humanity and their essential dignity.[12]

The Supreme Court added that:

> [T]he fundamental nature of the right to health – that represents, in the context of the historical evolution of the basic rights of the human person, one of the most important expressions of real or concrete liberties – imposes upon the government a positive duty to provide that will only be fulfilled by government bodies when they adopt measures designed to promote, in full, the effective compliance with the determinations contained in the constitutional text.

Similarly, in another case, the same Court asserted:

> [G]iven the choice between protecting the inviolability of the right to life, which qualifies as an inalienable subjective right guaranteed by the Constitution of the Republic (article 5, main clause), or allowing, contrary to

this express fundamental prerogative, a financial, secondary interest of the State to prevail, ethical and legal reasoning allows the judge only one possible option: the indeclinable respect for life.[13]

In the same vein, the Superior Court of Justice has established the right to health in several decisions to be a duty of the State, which 'must ensure those in need not just any form of treatment, but the most suitable and effective treatment, capable of providing the patient the greatest dignity and least amount of suffering'. Consequently, the medicine that is most effective and suitable for treatment must always be assured, even though it may not be provided for in any policy or ordinance of the Ministry of Health.[14]

The Superior Court of Justice has shifted away from a procedural and formalistic approach. One other example is a judicial ruling in a public civil action to protect the right to life and health of a child suffering from a serious disease. Overruling the decision of a state court, which had dismissed the case without a judgment on the merits on the grounds that the public prosecution service lacked the legitimacy to litigate an inalienable individual interest, the Court emphasised the importance of the judiciary in seeking to establish jurisdiction in such cases in order to protect fundamental rights so that 'citizens have their role in society facilitated with the contribution of the judiciary, whether in legal relations of private law, or in those of public law'.[15] In another judgment, the Court ruled in favour of a special appeal on the grounds that health is the duty of the State, finding that the lack

---

[11] *Diná Rosa Vieira v Município de Porto Alegre*, RE-271286 AgR/RS-Rio Grande do Sul (2000).

[12] Similarly, prominent rulings have been handed down by the Supreme Court in the following cases: RE 232335 (2000), AI 232469 (1998), RE 236200 (1999), RE 236644 (1999), AI 238328-AgR (1999), RE 242859 (1999), RE 247900 (1999), RE 264269 (2000), RE 267612 (2000), RE 273042 (2001), RE 273834 (2001), RE 255627-AgR/RS (2000), AI 238328-AgR/RS (1999), SS 702-AgR/DF (1994) and AI 486816-AgR/RJ (2005), among others. In case RE-195192/RS (2000), a writ of mandamus was made for the purchase and supply of medicine for a rare disease involving children or adolescents; the Supreme Court instructed the Government to find ways to ensure health, and it stressed the linear responsibility of the federal, state and municipal governments for Brazil's national health service.

[13] Federal Supreme Court, DJ, Section 1, of 13 February 1997, No. 29, p. 1830.

[14] See RMS 17903 (2004). In the same light, see other key rulings determining the provision of medicine as a duty of the State: Resp 684646 (2005), Resp 658323 (2005), AgRg na STA (suspension of a preliminary injunction) 59 (2005), AgRg na SS 1408 (2004), AgRg na STA 83 (2004), RMS 17425 (2004), Resp 625329 (2004), Resp 507205 (2003), Resp 430526 (2002), RMS 13452 (2002), RMS 11129 (2002), Resp 212346 (2002), Resp 325337 (2001), RMS 5986 (2002), RMS 11183 (2000), Resp 57608 (1996). In case Resp 658323 (2005), the Superior Court of Justice asserted: 'The national health service targets the full application of healthcare, whether individual or collective, and it should provide healthcare treatment for those who need it, regardless of the degree of complexity'. In case Resp 656979 (2005), the Court recognised that the free provision of medicine is the common responsibility of the federal, state and municipal governments.

[15] Superior Court of Justice, Resp 662033 (2004).

of medicine could cause the premature death of a child with a serious illness (spinal muscular atrophy).[16] Similarly, the Court has repeatedly authorised the use of money contained in government severance indemnity funds to pay for the treatment of serious illnesses, even though this is not provided for in law.[17]

Nonetheless, there are also a number of judgments that exhibit a manifestly classical liberal approach to the separation of powers whereby the justiciability of the right to health has been dismissed by the courts. One such instance is the ruling handed down in case RE 259508 AgR/RS (2000), which concerned the law in the state of Rio Grande do Sul that made provision for the free distribution of medicine to the poor and to HIV/AIDS carriers by means of an agreement between the state government and the municipality of Porto Alegre. The Supreme Court ruled that it had no authority to examine the effectiveness of the right to health *vis-à-vis* this agreement, just as it has no authority to supervise the Government's political criteria of 'convenience' and 'opportunity' in satisfying the population's health demands, since this would contravene the principle of the separation of powers.

The justiciability of social rights has also been denied in the context of insufficient budgetary resources. For example, in case RMS 6.564/RS (1996), the Superior Court of Justice asserted that in the Brazilian legal and constitutional system, 'no agency or authority can take on expenses without proper budget forecasting. Government agencies are bound by the allocation assigned in the budget for expenditure, whatever the nature, under penalty of committing misappropriation'.[18]

3.2 Differential Treatment

On constitutional grounds, the Supreme Court has permitted patients covered by the national health service to upgrade the 'class' of their hospital treat-ment, on condition that the balance be paid in full by the patient.[19] The justification for this is that the Constitution establishes the right to health and the universal and equal access to services and treatment that promote, protect and provide for the recovery of health. Consequently, there should be no obstacles erected by government authorities to reduce or inhibit this access. The decision does not strictly contravene the principles of equity or equality, as it does not establish unequal treatment for people in the same situation; rather, it authorises differential treatment in differential situations, with no added burden on the public system.

Rulings have been delivered by both the Supreme Court and the Superior Court of Justice stressing the absolute priority of children and adolescents in the exercise of the right to health[20] and guaranteeing differential hospital admittance and treatment for children and adolescents in the national health system.[21] According to the Superior Court of Justice,

> The constitutional right to the absolute priority of children and adolescents in the exercise of the right to health is established by constitutional norm which is emphasised by articles 7 and 11 from Statute of Children and Adolescents.... To submit a child or adolescent in a waiting list in order to attend others is the same as to legalise the most violent aggression of the principle of equality, essential in a democratic society provided by the Constitution, putting also into risk the clause in defense of human dignity. (Resp 577836)

The Superior Court of Justice has also addressed the right to health of prisoners.[22] In one case, the Court authorised home detention as opposed to imprisonment on the grounds of the sentenced individual's critical state of health (a serious, postoperative illness and the need for chemotherapy and strong drugs) and the prison service's inability to cope with such a situation.

---

[16] Superior Court of Justice, MC 7240 (2004).

[17] Foremost among other rulings are Superior Court of Justice, Resp 644557 (2004) and Superior Court of Justice, Resp 686500 (2005).

[18] On this topic, see A. G. Bontempo, *Direitos Sociais: Eficácia e acionabilidade à luz da Constituição de 1988* [Social Rights: Efficacy and actionability in the light of the 1988 Constitution] (Curitiba, Brazil: Juruá, 2005), p. 274.

[19] See Federal Supreme Court, RE 226835/RS (1999) and RE 261268/RS (2001).

[20] See the discussion by van Bueren in chapter 27 of this volume on the theoretical and legal justifications for prioritising children.

[21] On this subject, see Superior Court of Justice, Resp 577836 (2005), Resp 95168 (2001), Resp 128909 (2001) and Resp 89612 (1997).

[22] Superior Court of Justice, HC 19913/SP (2004).

3.3 The Scope of Health Insurance Contracts and Liability for Health Damage

Meanwhile, the scope of coverage of private health insurance plans has been subject to significant judicial scrutiny, albeit not based on the human rights approach, but based on consumer rights as enunciated in Brazil's Consumer Defence Code. The predominant jurisprudential tendency is to reject the limitation clauses in health insurance contracts. Some rulings have admitted claims for moral damages in cases where health insurance companies have refused to pay for the treatment of fully paid-up insured customers suspected of having cancer.[23] Other judgments have recognised the abusiveness of clauses in health insurance plans that deny treatment for infectious and contagious diseases requiring special notification, such as AIDS.[24] These decisions are based on the principle that interpretations should protect consumers given the unequal and asymmetric relationship between consumers and providers.

Compensation has been granted by the Superior Court of Justice, under the civil law of torts, for a failure to provide proper and appropriate medical services. In one case, the patient lost a kidney as a result of the non-provision of medicine, and the Court held that the 'omission to supply medicine undoubtedly represents an unmistakable liability apt to produce the duty to compensate'.[25] Other rulings have awarded compensation for physical

disablement that has resulted after mothers took thalidomide during pregnancy.[26]

3.4 Right to Information and Right to Health

Finally, the Superior Court of Justice has linked the right to information and the right to health, holding that the withholding of information from the public on the halting of hospital redevelopment and the suspension of medicine purchases by the administration amounted to a patent public health risk.[27]

4. RIGHT TO EDUCATION

Judicial activity in the domain of the right to education has principally concerned the right to elementary schooling (pre-school education and childcare). This constitutional right has been derived from the duty of the State with respect to education, and courts have stressed the importance of verifying unrestricted compliance with constitutional dictates and not shying away from them on the pretence of deficient funding. Not unlike the situation in the field of health, a number of fundamental claims have also been made not on the grounds of a human rights approach, but a consumer relations approach. These include claims focusing on registration at universities and monthly education fees.

4.1 Pre-School Education and Childcare

In a series of rulings, courts have determined that the right to pre-school education is of absolute importance. In a leading case, the Supreme Court asserted:

> In accordance with the dictates of article 208, item IV of the Federal Constitution, comprising the duty of the State in the area of education to guarantee assistance for children of zero to six years of age in day-care centres and pre-schools, the State – the federal government, the states themselves, that is, federal units, and municipalities – should equip itself for unrestricted compliance with the

---

[23] Superior Court of Justice, AgRg no AG 520390 (2004).

[24] Superior Court of Justice, AgRg no RESP 265872 (2003), AgRg no Resp 251722 (2001), Resp 255064 (2001), Resp 311509 (2001), Resp 244841 (2000), Resp 24097 (2003), Resp 304326 (2003), Resp 255065 (2001, in relation to cirrhosis). Similarly, clauses that govern temporary treatment and hospital admittance are also considered abusive, in accordance with rulings handed down in cases Resp 251024 (2002) and Resp 158728 (1999). However, there are a minority of cases that consider the exclusion of AIDS from insurance contracts to be valid (Resp 160307 (1999)).

[25] In this case, the Superior Court of Justice ordered the state of Rio de Janeiro to pay a patient 500 reales minimum monthly wages in moral damages and a lifelong annuity corresponding to half the wages the patient would have received if the patient had not lost the kidney: See 'Superior Court of Justice condena o Rio por não dar remédio a transplantado', *Folha de São Paulo*, 28 June 2005, p. C6 and 'Rio terá que indenizar transplantado que perdeu rim', *O Estado de São Paulo*, 28 June 2005, p. A18.

[26] Superior Court of Justice, Resp 60129 (2004).

[27] Superior Court of Justice, AgRg na STA 29 (2004).

constitutional dictates, without hiding behind excuses related to deficient funding.[28]

Similarly, other rulings reinforce the duty of the State to guarantee a vacancy in day-care centres for children up to 6 years of age, primarily following the publication of Constitutional Amendment 14, in 1996, that establishes that 'municipalities shall act on a priority basis in elementary education and in the education of children' (Constitution, article 211, paragraph 2, with wording from Constitutional Amendment No. 14/96).[29]

The Superior Court of Justice has also heard cases on the right to access to elementary education. Foremost among the examples is a decision on a public civil action guaranteeing day-care services for a child of up to 6 years of age, a judgment that was grounded on both the constitutional duty of the State and the subjective right of the child. The Court stated:

> The right to children's education cannot be relegated to anything less than a constitutional guarantee. The State has the duty to provide education in day-care centres for children from 0–6 years of age. What does not strike us as being legitimate is to delegate this duty to private institutions and leave children on a 'waiting list'.[30]

4.2   Higher Education: Registration and Fees

There are also a sizable number of cases relating to registration in universities and to the charging of monthly education fees. The majority of these rulings, which concerned students who were behind in paying their higher education fees, have determined that the payment of monthly fees in arrears cannot be viewed as a pre-condition for the renewal of course registration, thus protecting the right to registration renewal.[31] There have also been rulings in cases in which military personnel or civil servants have been transferred by the Government and the right to university registration has been denied in the new provincial states to which the individuals have been transferred, as well as the right of their children to be registered in elementary schools.

5. CONCLUSION: IMPACT, CHALLENGES AND PERSPECTIVES

When considering the justiciability of the rights to health and education before Brazil's higher courts, one is struck by the relative infrequency of legal cases calling for the judicial determination of social rights, despite the possibilities opened up by the 1988 Constitution. Nonetheless, we are able to point to an increasing trend to litigate at least the right to health, which has led, in the majority of cases, to the recognition that the State has concrete and justiciable human rights obligations. Most notable have been judicial rulings on the free provision of medicine, which, coupled with well-coordinated and efficient litigation strategies, have prompted changes in the law and the adoption of public policies that are considered exemplary.

The cases discussed are almost entirely individual claims. With respect to the claims for the provision of HIV-related medicines, the reliance on individual claims was a deliberate litigation strategy. That is, individual claims were chosen instead of class-action claims, given the risk that the latter would be rejected by the courts on account of the unfamiliarity of judges with such cases and the fears of the judiciary of the substantial implications of such a broad collective ruling. Nevertheless, individual legal victories[32] prompted a universal legislative response, and a law was passed that mandated the free provision of medicine for all people living with HIV. In other words, by virtue of the large number of court rulings instructing the government to provide free medicine for people with the HIV virus, Law No. 9,313 on the

---

[28] Federal Supreme Court, RE 411518/SP (2004).

[29] Similarly see, amongst others, RE 398722/SP (2004), REr 377957/SP (2004), RE 411332 (2004), RE 402024 (2004), AI 410646 AgR (2003), RE 411518 (2004), RE 352686/SP (2004).

[30] Resp 575280/SP (2004). On the same subject, Resp 503028 (2004) recognises the authority of the public prosecution service to claim a place for children in a day-care centre.

[31] See Superior Court of Justice rulings RESP 611394/RN (2004), Resp 311394 (2001), Resp 365771 (2004), Resp 384491 (2003), AgRg Resp 491202 (2003).

[32] See the cases on access to medicine and medical treatment examined in section 3.1. Also, on the topic, see F. Piovesan, 'A Litigância de Direitos Humanos no Brasil: desafios e perspectivas no uso dos sistemas nacional e internacional de proteção' [Human Rights Litigation in Brazil: challenges and perspectives of using national and international systems of protection] in F. Piovesan, *Temas de Direitos Humanos* [Human Rights Themes], 2nd. edition (São Paulo: Max Limonad, 2003), pp. 399–434.

free distribution of medicine for HIV carriers and AIDS patients was approved on 13 November 1996, sanctioning Brazil's national health service to supply all the necessary medicine for treatment.

Given the urgency of cases involving the AIDS epidemic, the movement in defence of the rights of people carrying the HIV virus prioritised the legal and policy dimensions of the crisis by focusing on the self-executing nature of the constitutional provisions and lobbying the executive branch through participation in various projects, councils and commissions, which permitted the relevant issues to be addressed extensively within the national health service by means of ministerial and inter-ministerial ordinances.[33] In addition to this legislation, public policy on AIDS treatment is now considered exemplary,[34] placing Brazil at the forefront of the international debate. Indeed, Brazil proposed a resolution to the United Nations Human Rights Commission, which was eventually approved, providing that access to medicine for diseases such as AIDS, malaria and tuberculosis was a fundamental human right. This, in turn, has motivated Brazil's action in breaching patents, within the framework of the World Trade Organisation, to produce AIDS medicines.[35]

However, the judicial cases addressed here whether in the area of health, or in the area of education, do not mention international human rights treaties or the General Comments of the relevant United Nations committees. This silence on the available international legal corpus for protection highlights both the Brazilian judiciary's unfamiliarity with the subject and its refractory attitude towards international law, as well as the failure of litigators to exploit international human rights instruments.

The degree to which the Brazilian judiciary is called upon to settle cases involving the protection of socio-economic rights also reveals the somewhat timid approach by civil society towards economic, social and cultural rights as true legal, claimable and justiciable rights. As Asbjørn Eide and Allan Rosas note:

> Taking economic, social and cultural rights seriously implies a simultaneous commitment to social integration, solidarity and equality, including the issue of income distribution. Social, economic and cultural rights include protection for vulnerable groups as a central concern....Fundamental needs must not be made contingent on charity from state programs and policies, but must be defined as rights.[36]

Moreover, access to higher levels of justice is limited. Only 30 percent of the people involved in disputes in Brazil appeal to state courts.[37] As Maria Teresa Sadek explains:

> [T]he reasons for this are numerous, ranging from distrust of the law and its institutions to the trivialisation of violence....On the other hand, albeit to a lesser degree than in the past, the population is relatively unaware of both their rights and of the institutional channels available to settle their disputes.

---

[33] The collection of the resulting rules through publication by the Ministry of Health, Health Policy Secretariat, National Sexually Transmitted Infections and AIDS Coordination, organised by Miriam Ventura, of *Legislação sobre DST e AIDS no Brasil* [Legislation on Sexually Transmitted Infections and AIDS in Brazil], 2nd. edition (Brasília: Fundação MacArthur do Brasil, October, 2000).

[34] Varun Gauri, in analysing the impact of Law 9,313 of 13 November 1996, notes: 'Partly as a result, in major Brazilian cities, AIDS deaths have dropped sharply, falling over 40% during 1997–2002'. 'Social Rights and Economics' (n. 2 above), p. 465.

[35] On 24 June 2005, the Brazilian government announced that it would breach the patent on the drug Kaletra, made by the US company Abbott and used to treat AIDS virus carriers: 'Governo dá dez dias para quebrar patente', *Folha de São Paulo*, 25 June 2005, p. C1; 'Costa assume UNAIDS e reforça pressão por quebra de patentes', *O Estado de São Paulo*, 28 June 2005, p. A18.

[36] A. Eide and A. Rosas, 'Economic, Social and Cultural Rights: a universal challenge' in A. Eide, C. Krause and Allan Rosas, *Economic, Social and Cultural Rights: a textbook* (Dordrecht, the Netherlands: Martinus Nijhoff Publishers, 1995), pp. 17–18. Paul Farmer writes:

> The concept of human rights may at times be brandished as an all-purpose and universal tonic, but it was developed to protect the vulnerable. The true value of human rights movement's central documents is revealed only when they serve to protect the rights of those who are most likely to have their rights violated. The proper beneficiaries of the Universal Declaration of Human Rights...are the poor and otherwise disempowered.

Paul Farmer, *Pathologies of Power* (Berkeley, CA: University of California Press, 2003), p. 212.

[37] M. Tereza Sadek, F. Dias de Lima and J. Renato de Campos Araújo, 'O Judiciário e a Prestação da Justiça' [The Judiciary and Judicial Protection] in Maria Teresa Sadek (ed.), *Acesso à Justiça* [Access to Justice] (São Paulo: Fundação Konrad Adenauer, 2001), p. 7.

There is also a clear relationship between human development indices and litigation, whereby the judiciary is used far more in regions that show higher human development indices.[38]

The low number of cases involving the protection of socio-economic rights in Brazil also reflects what might be termed a 'reciprocal aversion' between the population and the judiciary. Both sides indicate that this aversion is one of the major obstacles to judicial efficiency. According to research conducted by the Instituto Universitário de Pesquisas do Rio de Janeiro-Associação Brasileira das Mantenedoras do Ensino Superior, 79.5 percent of judges recognise that one of the crucial problems of the courts is that they are beyond the reach of the majority of the population. Likewise, research carried out not only in Brazil, but also in Argentina, Ecuador and Peru, show that 55 to 75 percent of the population are concerned about the inaccessibility of the judiciary.[39]

In order to develop a human rights jurisprudence and consolidate the judiciary as a 'locus' for safeguarding these rights, it is therefore essential that civil society, through its multiple organisations and movements, submits cases to the courts with more frequency, maximising the emancipatory and transformational potential of the law. Litigation strategies should be scaled up to the national level in order to maximise the potential for the justiciability and enforceability of socio-economic rights as true subjective public rights[40] in conjunction with the empowerment of civil society so that it can play its active and creative role of social protagonist. This is the only way to ensure greater transparency and accountability concerning the duties of the State to guarantee the rights to health and education.[41]

---

[38] Tereza Sadek, ibid. pp. 20–21, notes:

> With reference to these regions, the HDI [Human Development Index] illustrates that the North and Northeast display the lowest socio-economic indicators in Brazil. In contrast, the South and Centre-West present the best conditions with respect to the HDI. It is interesting that the higher the HDI, the better the relation between the number of lawsuits filed and the population. In other words, the judiciary is used far more in regions that have higher human development indices.

[39] See A. M. Garro, 'Access to Justice for the Poor in Latin America' in Juan E. Méndez, Guillermo O'Donnel and Paulo Sérgio Pinheiro (eds.), *The (Un)rule of Law and the Underprivileged in Latin America* (South Bend, IN: University of Notre Dame Press, 1999), p. 293. See also Flavia Piovesan, 'A Litigância de Direitos Humanos no Brasil' (n. 33 above), p. 410.

[40] Note that, in virtue of the indivisibility of human rights, the violation of economic, social and cultural rights entails the violation of civil and political rights, which explains why socio-economic vulnerability leads to greater precariousness in the realisation of civil and political rights. Amartya Sen writes:

> The negation of economic liberty, in the form of extreme poverty, makes individuals vulnerable to violations of other forms of liberty. . . . The negation of economic liberty implies the negation of social and political liberty.

Amartya Sen, *Development as Freedom* (New York: Alfred A. Knopf, 1999), p. 8.

[41] Varun Gauri (n. 3 above) notes: 'From the perspective of social rights, participation, empowerment, transparency, and accountability in service delivery are important for ensuring health care and education quality' (p. 470).

10

Venezuela

A Distinct Path Towards Social Justice
Enrique Gonzalez*

1. INTRODUCTION: PARTICIPATORY DEMOCRACY AND A SOCIAL-ORIENTED ECONOMY

In the late 1980s and throughout the 1990s, a longstanding economic crisis led to the adoption of neo-liberal policies, which included the ongoing privatisation of public services.[1] In 1999, new political forces were elected into government, which triggered a process for the drafting of a new Constitution. In reaction to neo-liberal policies, the 1999 Constitution of the Bolivarian Republic of Venezuela promotes a distinct path for the country in which the concept of social justice plays a central role.[2]

The new Republic is based on the development of a democratic 'Social State of Law and Justice'. Proclaiming justice, equity and human rights among its superior values (article 2), the Constitution sets the respect of human dignity and the fulfilment of constitutional rights and duties among its purposes (article 3). The extensive rights charter includes comprehensive recognition of human rights and several guarantees for their real-

isation, including the establishment of institutions for ensuring due process and the constitutional recognition of international human rights law.[3] The Constitution develops a comprehensive regime for the protection and promotion of human rights by the State, but it also establishes the principles of social cooperation, solidarity and co-responsibility of all members of society and the State in the fulfilment of constitutional purposes (article 4).

One of the most outstanding features of the new Constitution is the redesign of the structure of public powers. The new Republic includes the traditional executive, legislative and judicial branches, but it also creates two new independent branches: the electoral branch, which is in charge of the administration of the public electoral process, and the citizen branch, which is in charge of control powers.[4] The citizen branch is made up of the Public Attorney's Office, the Public Audit Office, and the new Office of the Ombudsperson, the State body that defends human rights before the administration. The heads of these three institutions sit on the Moral Council, which has the power to oversee the performance of authorities in the other public branches, including the justices of the Supreme Tribunal of Justice.[5] However,

---

* Over the last decade, Enrique Gonzalez has worked with several Venezuelan non-governmental organisations and public institutions in the field of economic, social and cultural rights. He is the author of several articles and manuals on human rights.

[1] In paragraph 8 of its Concluding Observations on Venezuela's Country Report, the UN Committee on Economic, Social and Cultural Rights ('CESCR') noted 'that the recent economic recession and the adverse effects of structural adjustment programmes undergone by Venezuela in the past ten years have restricted the ability of the State party to comply with its obligations under the Covenant'. Committee on Economic, Social and Cultural Rights, Concluding Observations of the CESCR: Venezuela, U.N. Doc. E/C.12/1/Add.56 (2001).

[2] The new Constitution was passed on 31 December 1999 following a drafting process in the National Assembly and approval through a universal referendum. Official Gazette No. 36.860, 30 December 1999.

[3] The State has the duty to respect and ensure human rights as set under national and international law and according to the principles of progressiveness, 'non-renounceability' and interdependence (article 19). International human rights treaties have constitutional status and are 'directly and immediately' applicable by the courts (article 23). Everyone is entitled to seek the protection of international human rights bodies, while the State has the duty to comply with the decisions issued by the latter (article 31).

[4] See Article 136.

[5] The model was proposed for the first time by the Liberator Simon Bolivar, the Venezuelan hero of Latin American wars of independence against the Spanish empire,

it can only establish moral sanctions that must be checked by the National Assembly, which may eventually lead to legal action.

The Constitution creates an alternative model to representative democracy, setting out what has been called participatory democracy. It includes classical institutions for the exercise of political rights under representative democracy, but it also creates multiple institutions for local and communitarian participation (articles 62 to 70). Political rights are advanced through a complex system of referenda, which can be instigated by citizen initiative. Referenda can call for the impeachment of all democratically elected officials, but they cannot lead to the abrogation of amnesty and human rights–related laws (articles 71 to 74). The appointment of the justices of the Supreme Tribunal and the leadership of the electoral and citizen branches are to include civil society participation. Also, constitutional duties include the duty to participate in public life and to promote and protect human rights as the foundation of democratic coexistence and social peace (article 132).

With respect to the economic dimension, the Constitution endorses a 'social-oriented economy': an economy that recognises economic rights and liberties and makes their exercise conditional, to a certain degree, upon the fulfilment of their social function (articles 112 to 118). Social justice and the redistribution of wealth are established as constitutional principles, and the State is variously bound to regulate economic relations (articles 299 to 310), promote all forms of collective association for a productive economy (articles 70 and 118) and protect workers in traditional economic sectors, such as fishermen and artisans (articles 305 and 309), and small companies and family enterprises (article 308).

2. ECONOMIC, SOCIAL AND CULTURAL RIGHTS IN THE CONSTITUTION

Over fifty articles recognise, quite extensively, economic, social and cultural rights ('ESC rights').

which took place in the first half of the nineteenth century. Bolivar's thinking is the main source of inspiration for the new Republic. He proposed the creation of a fourth branch of power, which would help keep in check the traditional powers.

They include both justiciable guarantees and obligations concerning policy formulations. For example, several provisions put the duty upon the State to guarantee the availability of financial resources for the adoption of positive measures to realise ESC rights. At the same time, the Constitution includes participatory mechanisms aimed at promoting the active involvement of citizens in the design and co-management of public social services and policies as part of participatory democracy. The Constitution also recognises the right of everyone to act before the courts in defence of collective and diffuse interests. This has profound implications for the justiciability of collective rights, as it allows for the extension of constitutional judgments to persons who do not participate in the relevant case.

Turning to specific rights, the right to social security includes the State's obligation to create and maintain a social security system, which must provide protection to all the population, regardless of their ability to contribute to the system's fund (article 86). The right to health, which is considered part of the right to life, includes the State's obligation to ensure universal access to public health services through a public health system (articles 83 to 85). The right to adequate housing is the responsibility of both the State and the community, but the State has the obligation to adopt measures to ensure that families without resources can enjoy the right (article 82).

Family rights include the State's obligation to protect families (articles 75 to 77). The rights of children (article 78), young persons (article 79), elderly persons (article 80) and people with disabilities (article 81) are also recognised. The Constitution recognises the equal rights of women both before the law (article 21) and in labour relations (articles 88 and 89). It sets equal rights and duties in marriage and recognises the right to salary and social security of domestic workers and home workers (article 88). The right to the protection of motherhood and parenthood includes the State's obligation to provide family planning services (article 76). In one of its most characteristic features, the Constitution includes gender-sensitive language throughout the text.

Education is considered both a human right and a public service that must be ensured by the State. Duties of the State encompass equal opportunities and free access, including to higher education, and the respect of academic and related economic freedoms (articles 102 to 109). Cultural rights include freedom of cultural and scientific creation and the recognition of national cultural values; the State is obliged to protect and promote national cultures (articles 98 to 101 and article 110). The Constitution also recognises the right to sports and leisure (article 111).

The right and duty to work includes the State's obligation to adopt measures to protect labour and to ensure that everyone may have access to a decent job. Labour guarantees include equal rights of men and women, the right to a sufficient salary, a prohibition on regressive bargaining of labour rights and benefits, and nullity of employers' acts that collide with the Constitution. Union rights include freedom of workers to associate, democratic union freedom, the right to strike and collective bargaining (articles 87 to 97).

The Constitution declares Venezuela a multicultural and multiethnic society and, for the first time in the country's history, recognises the rights of indigenous peoples,[6] including rights to ancestral territories, intercultural bilingual education and participation, together with an extensive recognition of cultural rights, among which is the right to the rule of indigenous customary law and the use of traditional medicine (articles 119 to 126). Several provisions also afford for the protection of collective and individual rights through a safe, clean and ecologically balanced environment (articles 127 to 129).

The right to food can be derived from the right to food security, which is defined as the adequate and permanent availability of food and access to food for all (article 305). The State has the obligation to promote agrarian reform and sustainable agrarian development, while peasants and small farmers are entitled to the right to property and ownership of the land (articles 306 and 307). Finally, the Constitution includes the right to public services of sufficient quality, as well as the right to the protection of consumer rights (article 117).

The Inter-American Commission on Human Rights considers that the Constitution includes reforms that represent 'an important advance in the protection of human rights in the country'.[7] However, it considers that there is also 'some loss of ground…which may pose problems for the rule of law'.[8] In reporting on Venezuela, several United Nations human rights committees have pointed to the positive aspects of the new Constitution, without making this criticism. In its 2001 Concluding Observations on Venezuela, the Committee on Economic, Social and Cultural Rights was positive towards the Constitution:

> The Committee welcomes the adoption of the new 1999 Constitution, which incorporates a wide range of human rights, including a number of the economic, social and cultural rights enshrined in the Covenant, and the fact that article 23 of the Constitutional accords international human rights instruments, to which Venezuela is a party.[9]

The Committee on the Elimination of Racial Discrimination, the Human Rights Committee and the Committee against Torture have also expressed their satisfaction with the rights and principles contained in the Constitution,[10] although the Human Rights Committee expressed its concern about the principle of progressiveness, as set out in article 19.[11]

---

[6] Previously, indigenous people endured a so-called special regime, which was oriented towards their assimilation in national society. See article 77 of the 1961 Constitution.

[7] Inter-American Commission on Human Rights, *Report on the Situation of Human Rights in Venezuela*, 29 December 2003, OAS/Ser.L/V/II.118. doc. 4 rev. 2, para. 51.

[8] Ibid. para. 55. The Commission points to the following factors: pre-trial on the merits prior to the investigation of crimes involving senior officials of the armed forces; participation of the National Electoral Council in union elections; lack of clear limits on the exercise of the legislative power by the executive and the qualification of the right to '*objective and veracious*' information. The report does not consider the status of social rights under the new Constitution.

[9] Committee on Economic, Social and Cultural Rights, *Concluding Observations of the Committee on Economic, Social and Cultural Rights: Venezuela*, 21 May 2001, E/C.12/1/Add.56, para. 3.

[10] Committee on the Elimination of Racial Discrimination, *Concluding Observations: Venezuela*, 19 August 2005, CERD/C/VEN/CO/18, para. 4; Human Rights Committee, *Concluding Observations: Venezuela*, 26 April 2001, CCPR/CO/71/VEN. paras. 3 and 4; Committee against Torture, *Conclusions and Recommendations: Venezuela*, 23 December 2002, CAT/C/CR/29/2, paras. 6 and 7.

[11] Ibid. para 5. The concern expressed by the Human Rights Committee does not seem to take into account the international doctrine on ESC rights, which is centred around the principle of progressiveness (see article 2.1 of the International Covenant on Economic, Social and Cultural Rights ('ICESCR'))

3. JURISPRUDENCE: GENERAL REVIEW

3.1 The Judiciary

Under the 1999 Constitution, the Supreme Tribunal of Justice is divided into six courts: the Criminal Law Court, the Administrative Law Court, the Civil Law Court, the Electoral Court, the Social Court and the Constitutional Court. The Social Court is in charge of the labour, agrarian and child's rights jurisdictions, while the Constitutional Court is responsible for constitutional matters, including the repeal of national and state laws and appeals to judgments of the other Supreme Tribunal courts. In recent years, the decisions issued by both courts, which are new to the Venezuelan judiciary, have been the most significant for the justiciability of ESC rights.

The plenary of the National Assembly is responsible for the appointment of justices of the Supreme Tribunal of Justice, and the pre-selection of candidates involves the participation of civil society, universities, the citizen branch and a special commission of the National Assembly. As for lower court judges, their appointment and ongoing evaluation are a function of the judiciary's administrative body, which reports to the Supreme Tribunal.

In 2004, the National Assembly adopted a law that developed this constitutional design. Even though the new law excludes any direct participation of the executive in the process of appointing justices, several human rights organisations considered that it was aimed at guaranteeing government control of the Supreme Tribunal[12] because it allows for their appointment through a simple majority of members of Parliament when a qualified majority cannot reach agreement. In fact, this approach, which is not dissimilar to that established in other countries of the region,[13] would

avoid obstruction in judicial appointments by giving the majority the final say.

Critics also pointed to other factors that would affect the independence of the judiciary, such as the high percentage of judges with a lack of permanent tenure or political interference in the decisions of the Supreme Tribunal of Justice. This criticism is not new to the Venezuelan judiciary. In a 1996 report, the Lawyers Committee for Human Rights, a non-governmental organization ('NGO'), identified political interference, corruption, institutional neglect and the failure to provide access to justice by the vast part of the population as the roots of 'the extraordinary corrosion of the judicial function'.[14]

According to the new government, these structural aspects of the judiciary are being tackled, whereas critics of the government consider that political interference in the judiciary has worsened. As this chapter shows, the Supreme Tribunal of Justice has issued decisions that back governmental policies and also decisions that contest them. In any case, the political tensions that have followed the adoption of the new Constitution can hardly be expected to have left the judiciary completely intact.[15]

As for the status of judges, the Inter-American Commission on Human Rights takes note in its latest report of a process by which, by the end of 2005, the Supreme Tribunal had granted 60 per cent of judges with secure tenure. It also acknowledged actions taken in recent years to promote access to

---

[12] Human Rights Watch, *Rigging the Rule of Law: Judicial Independence under Siege in Venezuela* (New York, 2004), Vol. 16, No. 3 (B).

[13] A brief comparative study of the process for the appointment of justices throughout the region leads to the impression that the campaign against the law was not devoid of political motivations. Actually, in many jurisdictions, the executive plays a major, even constitutional role in the process. In the United States, justices are appointed by the president, and the Senate confirms by a simple majority. In Mexico, a lack of accord in the Senate leads to the appointment of justices by the president. In Chile, the president appoints justices according

to a list of nominees presented by the Supreme Court. In Nicaragua, the Senate appoints the nominees of the president by a six-tenths majority. In Panama, the government appoints justices, and the National Assembly may confirm by a simple majority. In Paraguay, the appointment by the Senate must meet with the approval of the executive. In the Dominican Republic, the president is chair of the body that appoints justices.

[14] Lawyers Committee for Human Rights, *Halfway to Reform: The World Bank and the Venezuelan Justice System* (August 1996), available at <http://www.humanrightsfirst.org/pubs/descriptions/halfway.htm>.

[15] The political crisis of recent years included a failed coup d'état in April 2002, which was condemned worldwide. However, a few months later, the Supreme Tribunal declared that there had not been a breach of the Constitution, but a 'power void', due to the temporary absence of the president of the Republic. This controversial decision, which was passed by a slim majority of justices, allowed for the perception that the Court had backed an illegal attempt at changing the Constitution. The judgment was later revised and revoked by the Constitutional Court.

justice in different regions of the country and to increase the number of decisions issued by judicial instances. However, it highlights several cases of judges who were removed that 'might have legitimate grounds, such as corrupt or illegal practices', but which point to the need to strengthen the judicial career service.[16]

3.2 Jurisprudence Under the 1961 Constitution

Under the 1961 Constitution, ESC rights were deemed programmatic guidelines and not readily enforceable rights.[17] The Supreme Court of Justice considered that court actions aimed at the protection of constitutional rights did not allow for mandatory orders to be issued, nor for collective remedies that benefited persons other than the petitioners. For decades, almost all such actions were either dismissed or ruled out on technical or formal grounds, thereby impeding the justiciability of ESC rights. However, in the late 1990s, before the adoption of the new Constitution, the courts increasingly accepted that ESC rights were subject to the protection of the courts.[18]

3.3 Jurisprudence Under the 1999 Constitution

Under the new Constitution, the status of justiciability of ESC rights has been significantly advanced, although the jurisprudence is yet to

reach a point of maturity and is contradictory at times. However, the new Supreme Tribunal of Justice has consistently stated that constitutional rights possess a normative nature and are therefore immediately enforceable by the courts. Even if the courts frequently decide cases on traditional and overly technical grounds, there is a general trend to recognise the claims of rights holders. The judiciary has extensively developed the content of social rights and the nature of State duties, as these relate to constitutional rights and are a consequence of the 'Social State of Law' clause. It has issued significant orders for compliance by both public and private institutions and recognised the collective dimensions of constitutional actions, frequently extending the reach of judgments to non-litigants, as a consequence of the constitutional right to the protection of collective and diffuse interests.

3.4 Types of Actions

The *amparo constitucional* is the most effective constitutional action for the protection of human rights; it can also be introduced against private actors. Hearings on *amparo* actions have prevalence over any other legal action and must be treated with urgency by the courts. In all cases, an *amparo* claim must contain evidence of a violation or threat of violation to a constitutional right or guarantee, but an *amparo* judgment cannot generate new rights or establish public duties involving constitutional rights if the duties are not directly related to the prevention or restitution of the reported threat or violation. Furthermore, an *amparo* action may be ruled out if the judges find that there is room for other legal recourse that may lead to effective remedy or if the violation or menace has ceased when the hearing takes place.

The *amparo* may be filed as a single action or it may be part of a demand for the revocation of a legal or administrative act. It may also be accompanied by a petition for temporary measures while the substance of the case is decided. Such measures may be aimed at demanding the suspension or reversal of an action by public or private actors.

There are two legal routes for the revocation of administrative acts or laws that are considered unconstitutional. The first revolves around the ability to seek annulment of an administrative act that has individual consequences; the annulment can

---

[16] Inter-American Commission on Human Rights, *Annual Report 2005*, 27 February 2006, OEA/Ser.L/V/II.124, chapter 4, paras. 286–303.

[17] Luz Mejia, 'Venezuela' in Inter-American Institute of Human Rights, *Los Derechos Economicos, Sociales y Culturales: Un Desafío Impostergable* [Economic, Social and Cultural Rights: An unavoidable challenge] (San José, Costa Rica: IIHR, 1999), pp. 309–311. This article includes a thorough review of ESC rights jurisprudence under the 1961 Constitution.

[18] The most relevant cases led to the recognition of a right to access to treatment by HIV-positive people living in poverty (1997). The Supreme Court of Justice also commanded the Social Security Agency to provide immediate neurosurgery to ten insured patients and honour longstanding debts with several private entities that provided psychiatric services to insured patients. One case struck down legislation that had levied compulsory monthly fees at a public university, and another one protected the right to a fair pension of ex-employees of a public electricity company. As for labour rights, most actions were invariably dismissed on formal grounds.

only be obtained after all other available administrative remedies have been exhausted. The other option is the annulment of acts with a general impact (e.g., rules of procedure, administrative decrees, or resolutions) and acts of national, regional, or local legislatures.[19] If the court finds that the petition is legitimate, it may annul the act, the legal disposition, or the entire law. But neither action is particularly swift, so such claims are frequently accompanied by an *amparo* action or a petition for temporary measures.

Ordinarily, remedies ordered by courts in all jurisdictions can be revised on appeal, but *amparo* sentences can only be revised by the Constitutional Court, which is part of the Supreme Tribunal. The Constitutional Court can also revise the orders of the other Courts of the Supreme Tribunal if a clear violation of proceedings can be demonstrated.

There is a consistent and solid jurisprudence on the State's responsibility in relation to acts licit and illicit, although it has not yet settled the relationship between the right to compensation of victims of human rights violation and the State's 'patrimonial' responsibility. The most outstanding development is a decision, on appeal of the Constitutional Court, which revoked a previous ruling that the murder of a citizen by a police officer on leave was not the State's direct responsibility. The Court found that the State's patrimonial responsibility represents a basic guarantee of the 'State of Law' and that it should be interpreted progressively and always in favour of a victim. This is particularly so when viewed in light of the content of article 30 of the Constitution, which sets out the State's obligation to provide adequate compensation to the victims of human rights violations.[20]

3.5 Collective and Diffuse Interests

'Collective interests' are those interests held by a given group of people that may not be quantifiable, but can be identified at a given time and space as belonging to a specific sector of the population. Diffuse interests are those that affect the community as a whole, without the possibility of identifying a given nexus among them. In the case of contractual relations, collective or diffuse interests only apply to public services. This is because contracts can only bind the parties, whereas the conditions under which contractual public services are provided may affect the quality of life of 'all the population, or a huge segment of it, as an undetermined service provision that must be provided by the contractor'.[21]

Constitutional actions for the protection of collective or diffuse interests must be introduced before the Constitutional Court of the Supreme Tribunal of Justice, and the petitioner(s) must have a direct relation with the portion of society affected by the situation that originates the action. Frequently, actions have been dismissed because the courts considered that the petitioners could not prove their direct relation with the collective. However, the Office of the Ombudsperson is entitled to act in all circumstances on behalf of collective or diffuse interests. In fact, in every action that may have collective dimensions, the Constitutional Court must seek the opinion of this office in order to guarantee that the interests of the collective are represented before the law.

In several cases, the Court has extended, at its own initiative, the reach of its judgments to persons who did not take part in the action. In one of its rulings, the Constitutional Court considered that 'it would be absurd that someone may obtain a favourable ruling that ceases or avoids a damage in a collective situation, but, in spite of the ruling, the rest of the people pertaining to the collective should keep on facing the same damage or menace of damage'.[22]

3.6 Contesting the Supremacy of International Law

In complying with their duties, Venezuelan courts are more inclined to draw from national jurisprudence and national precedents than from international human rights law. This is due partly to an often formal approach to jurisprudence and partly to a rich constitutional tradition wherein

---

[19] These claims must be introduced before the Supreme Tribunal of Justice, and the challenged acts must be in direct violation of constitutional dispositions.

[20] Supreme Tribunal of Justice, Constitutional Court, Sentence No. 2818, 19 April 2002, Exp. 01–1532. All the judgments cited in this chapter are available at <http://www.tsj.gov.ve>; the translations have been made by the author.

[21] Ibid.

[22] Supreme Tribunal of Justice, Constitutional Court, Sentence No. 676, 30 June 2000, Exp. 00–1728.

constitutional rights prevail over international human rights. Several decisions have, all the same, underpinned the importance of respecting international treaties, and they are increasingly being referred to as a secondary or, in some cases, primary source. However, in at least two decisions reviewed in this chapter, the Court has made decisions that contradicted the recommendations or decisions of international bodies.[23]

Furthermore, as a consequence of a heated public debate that followed a judgment on freedom of expression in 2001, the Supreme Tribunal of Justice issued a resolution defending this decision and the jurisdiction of the Court. This resolution was considered regressive with respect to the constitutional status of international law since the Court stated that its judgments were not subject to the interpretation of international bodies. Even if it recognised the constitutional status of international law, it stated that, according to the Constitution, the Court is the ultimate body for the protection of the law of the country.[24] Nevertheless, international law is playing an increasingly relevant role in national human rights jurisprudence even in the wake of this resolution.

3.7   Contents of Rights versus Public Policy

In one of its more controversial decisions concerning ESC rights, the Court explicitly recognised the justiciability of these rights, while, at the same time, striking down the action. In 2002, the National Medical Guild filed an *amparo* action before the Supreme Tribunal Court asking that it order the Ministry of Health and the Social Security Agency to guarantee the provision of sufficient resources in order to combat the ongoing crisis in hospitals. After reviewing the nature of civil and political rights and ESC rights under international law, the Court stated that the normative value of ESC rights under the new Constitution makes them automatically justiciable before the courts. Otherwise, they could not be considered

'as right(s) but as moral aspiration(s)'. However, the courts can only control the juridical acts of the administration that affect the individual or the collective, but not political decisions, which are subject to the will of the government. Since public spending is an element of policy decisions and not part of the content of the rights, the Court ruled that public finances could not be governed by the judicial arm of the State.[25]

Several NGOs have argued that this decision undermines the justiciability of these rights,[26] although an analysis of the decision under international doctrine is not necessarily conclusive. Initially, in General Comment No. 3, the Committee on Economic, Social and Cultural Rights did not identify the availability of resources as one of the standards that should be open to review before the courts.[27] On the other hand, the later General Comment No. 9 states that courts should be allowed to decide on issues related to the allocation of resources. While the 'respective competencies of the various branches of government must be respected', the Committee called for an ample interpretation of the nature of ESC rights in order to avoid the protection of these rights being curtailed.[28] Finally, General Comment No. 14 states that 'insufficient expenditure... of public resources which results in the non-enjoyment of the right to health by individuals or groups'[29] constitutes a violation of the right, but it also considers that the Covenant 'acknowledges the constraints due to the limits of available resources'.[30] Additionally, it states that all victims of a violation of the right to health should be entitled to adequate

---

[23] See below. One is a decision on women's political rights that contradicts doctrine on positive action (gender perspective), and another, related to trade union elections, dismissed a recommendation issued by the Committee on Freedom of Association (labour rights) of the International Labour Organisation.

[24] Supreme Tribunal of Justice, Resolution of the Court, 25 July 2001.

[25] Supreme Tribunal of Justice, Constitutional Court, Sentence No. 1002, 26 May 2004, Exp. 02–2167.

[26] Venezuelan Programme for Education and Action in Human Rights (Provea), 'Derecho a la justicia' [Right to Justice], in *Informe Anual 2003–2004*; Citizen's Action against AIDS (ACCSI), *Criterio de ACCSI* [Criteria of ACCSI], Provea, *Servicio informativo*, No. 137, April 2004, available at <http://derechos.org.ve>.

[27] Committee on Economic, Social and Cultural Rights, *General Comment No. 3: The nature of States parties obligations (article 2, paragraph 1)*, 14 December 1990 (Fifth session, 1990), para. 5.

[28] Committee on Economic, Social and Cultural Rights, *General Comment No. 9: The domestic application of the Covenant*, 9 December 1998 (Nineteenth session, 1998), para. 10.

[29] Committee on Economic, Social and Cultural Rights, *General Comment No. 14: The right to the highest attainable standard of health (article 12)*, 11 August 2000 (Twenty-second session, 2000), para. 52.

[30] Ibid. para. 90.

reparation, 'which may take the form of restitution, compensation, satisfaction or guarantees of non-repetition'.[31]

In its decision, the Court ordered the Office of the Ombudsperson and the health authorities to find the best way to secure the needed resources. Thus, the key would lie in determining if this mandate of the Court amounts to an 'adequate' means of reparation under General Comment No. 14. Also, it must be asked whether the recognition of the justiciability of ESC rights is, by itself, significant progress in the enforcement of these rights through the courts or if this progressive case law is actually undermined by the decision. In any case, jurisprudence on these rights shows a general trend to recognise their justiciability whenever a violation is duly identified.

This decision would also seem to contradict an earlier 2001 judgment, whereby the Constitutional Court ordered the Social Security Agency to guarantee access to HIV treatment for insured patients, stating that it could not accept the argument of a lack of resources as a cause for denying the treatment (see Section 4.4 below). However, the Social Security Agency's budget is a contributory fund, aimed at covering health-related contingencies of insured workers. Thus, the judgment did not set the agency's budget policy priorities, but pointed to specific legal duties the fund must assume as a result of its juridical relationship with insured workers. In fact, the later decision cites the HIV treatment judgment as an example of a case in which the administrative body's omission affects the juridical relationship.

3.8   Gender Perspective

While there are no court decisions specifically touching on the socio-economic aspects of women's rights, one decision was regressive in relation to affirmative action and the political rights of women. On the eve of the 2000 general elections, an action was launched against a resolution of the Electoral Council, which temporarily ruled against a 1995 legal provision that set the obligation of political parties to guarantee a 30 per cent quota for women candidates. The Elec-

toral Court of the Supreme Tribunal of Justice considered that this rule was relevant under the previous Constitution because it aimed to lessen the unequal status of women *at that time*. However, the Court found that the provision had been automatically derogated 'due to the fact that it is not in correspondence with what the Constitution establishes in relation to right to equal treatment before the law and non-discrimination'.

This decision is based on a somewhat anachronistic and anti-juridical belief that legal action has an immediate impact on society. Indeed, it professes to understand the social reality faced by Venezuelan women according to the constitutional status of women's rights. It is contrary to the United Nations Convention on the Elimination of All Forms of Discrimination against Women, which encourages states to adopt 'temporary special measures aimed at accelerating de facto equality between men and women' (Article 4).

4.   ANALYSIS OF SELECTED RIGHTS

4.1   Labour Rights

The most progressive and consistent jurisprudence issued by the Supreme Tribunal of Justice concerns labour rights. The Court has extensively ruled on the inherent nature of these rights and on the judiciary's duty to protect labour. It has also promoted legal reform by drafting and presenting before Parliament a proposal for a law that emphasises swift conciliation-based proceedings in labour disputes. The entry into force of the new Organic Law on the Labour Process has allowed for a dramatic reduction in the number of labour disputes brought before the courts and in the time needed for a final court resolution.[32]

In 2002, the Social Court issued jurisprudential criteria aimed at preserving the principles of proper labour relations with respect to new forms of employment that have been qualified as fraudulent. The Court was concerned with a practice whereby workers were being compelled to

---

[31] Ibid. para. 59.

[32] A year after the entry into force of the law in 2002, 95 per cent of such disputes were being resolved before reaching the courts, while the average time for final court resolutions in labour disputes had been cut from eight years to six months. See Provea, *Servicio informativo*, No. 135, March 2004, available at <http://www.derechos.org.ve>.

establish 'commercial' relationships with their employers so that employers could avoid the burden of making contributions for various social benefits required under the law. According to the Court, workers under these contracts are equally entitled to their legal labour rights, provided that the core elements of a labour relationship are in place. The Court stated that labour laws are aimed at protecting the relationship of workers before their employers, which is a 'relationship of evident economic inequity'. It also found that, 'if a worker and an employer could convene that their relationship should be judged according to civil law, the right to work would be irrelevant, because its application would depend on the sole will of the parties'.[33]

Several decisions have led to the protection and extension of the social benefits that spring from labour relations.[34] The Supreme Tribunal of Justice has ordered that, if an employer retains the worker's social benefits at the end of employment, the worker is entitled to reclaim the accumulated interest on the debt, which will have to be indexed according to currency rates at the time of the sentence. The Court considered that the lack of due payment is unlawful enrichment by the employer at the expense of the worker.[35] The Court also ruled that food tickets and other monthly monetary benefits enjoyed by workers must be added to the calculations of social benefits after the cessation of employment even if they are not part of the salary.[36] In another case, the Court established that employers must respect the right of workers to paid holidays and that the corresponding salary must be considered part of the duties of the employer and not as an arbitrary benefit.[37]

4.2   Trade Union Rights and Freedoms

In 2000, the National Electoral Council called for a national referendum in order to ask the population if they agreed to suspend temporarily the officers of the main national federation of trade unions (the Confederación de Trabajadores de Venezuela, 'CTV') so as to hold democratic elections for the union within 180 days of the suspension. If the referendum were approved, it would be the first time in the history of the CTV that its officers would be elected through direct vote of the associated workers. The CTV officers had initially agreed to the referendum, but later filed a case before the Supreme Tribunal of Justice, arguing that the referendum was in violation of International Labour Organisation (ILO) Conventions and the Venezuelan Constitution. The ILO Committee on Freedom of Association also issued a recommendation calling on the State to halt the referendum because it found that 'the reform of the trade union movement...cannot be done under violation of ILO Conventions'.[38]

The Constitutional Court ruled against the petition of the CTV officers, arguing that the consultation process was aimed at implementing the Constitution. The Court found that the referendum would not represent administrative intervention in the CTV, 'but protection of the State in order to make effective the democratic process within the trade union movement'.[39] It also stated that, under Article 8.1.a ICESCR, 'the State has not only the power, but the obligation to ensure trade union democracy and the exercise of the rights of workers'.[40]

The case involved a conflict between two different approaches to the protection of trade union rights. On the one hand, the Court understood

---

[33] Supreme Tribunal of Justice, Social Court, Sentence No. 61, 16 March 2000, Exp. 98–546.

[34] Under Venezuelan labour law, workers are entitled to social security rights and to several labour-related benefits that derive from the duties of employers, such as the provision of food tickets or food services at the workplace, paid holidays, family aid and housing funds. Also, at the end of a labour relationship, workers are entitled to a settlement benefit that is proportional to the length of the relationship.

[35] Supreme Tribunal of Justice, Social Court, Sentence No. 642, 14 November 2002, Exp. 00–449.

[36] Supreme Tribunal of Justice, Social Court, Sentence No. 489, 30 July 2003, Exp. 02–562.

[37] Supreme Tribunal of Justice, Social Court, Sentence No. 101, 21 February 2002, Exp. 01–599.

[38] ILO, CXL VII 2001–01–0116–8ES Doc, Case No. 2067, pp. 28. Cited in Provea, 'Derechos de los Trabajadores', Situación de los Derechos Humanos en Venezuela, octubre 2000-septiembre 2001 [Worker's rights, Human Rights Annual Report 2000-01], (Caracas: Provea, 2001), p. 90, available at <http://www.derechos.org.ve>.

[39] Supreme Tribunal of Justice, Constitutional Court, Sentence No. 1447, 28 November 2000, Exp. 00–3047.

[40] According to Article 8.1.a of the Covenant, the States parties undertake to ensure the right of trade unions 'to function freely subject to no limitations other than those prescribed by law and which are necessary in a democratic society in the interests of national security'.

that the State's obligation to guarantee the democratic rights of trade union associates neutralises the argument that the referendum interferes in trade union freedoms. On the other hand, the ILO Committee on Freedom of Association viewed the referendum itself as a form of intervention. In order to settle the controversy, the Court invoked norms contained in the ICESCR to make a determination against specific recommendations of the ILO Committee. A critical analysis of the decision would involve examining whether the claim of the trade union officers to maintain the *status quo* should prevail over the rights of associated workers to vote for such officers, whether the Court should consider if the State is entitled to call for the referendum in order to guarantee the democratic process within the trade union movement and whether there are any other means to comply with the State's obligation to protect workers' right to vote.

As an outcome of the case, CTV elections were held in October 2001, after which the historical leadership claimed victory. However, the results were not accepted by the other contenders nor by the government because almost half the paper ballots had disappeared before the count. In January 2005, the National Electoral Council declared the CTV elections void, a decision that was not contested before the courts, though it did lead to further complaints before the ILO.

This clash between the State and trade union leadership was brought to a head in December 2002. Opposition parties, the leadership of the national employers association and the CTV called for a 'national civic work stoppage' against the government. The observance of the strike by labour was uneven, but several industrial sectors and public services were seriously affected due to a major lockout in the private sector and in local governments held by opposition parties. A week later, most officers of the management of Petróleos de Venezuela, S.A., the huge state-owned petroleum company that accounts for the majority of Venezuela's income, joined the protest. By then, the leaders of the national protest had issued a call for civil disobedience aimed at ousting the government. The Office of the Ombudsperson and the most important human rights NGO considered the protest unlawful because the organisers had not complied with the law and were not guaranteeing

minimum services, and because they sought the intervention of the military.[41]

The Supreme Tribunal of Justice admitted a constitutional action for the protection of collective interests against the organisation that had led the protest in the oil industry and issued a temporary injunction ordering that all oil-related sectors should follow the official decrees that they should resume activities.[42] The Court stated that the suspension of these activities 'implies the violation of social and collective rights such as the right to health...because they affect the quality of life, the collective and the access to services'. A relevant proportion of managers and workers in the oil industry did not comply with the judgment after declaring that they would disobey it. In the following weeks, the company expelled thousands of managers and workers, a decision that led to further conflict.

In its decision, the Court ordered that the organisers of the protest be notified of the Court process, but did not explore the workers' right to strike. At first instance, this omission seems to represent a denial of the right to strike. However, an analysis of the conflict in the oil industry under both Venezuelan law and ILO doctrine may lead to the conclusion that a violation of trade union rights in the oil industry was not at stake. First of all, the leaders of the protest were members of the senior management of a public company, whereas the ILO Committee on Freedom of Association considers that public servants who exercise authority in the name of the State are excluded from the right to strike.[43] Second, the protest was explicitly aimed at the ousting of the government, whereas the Committee considers that 'strikes of a purely political nature...do not fall within the scope of

41 'Consecuencias Laborales de la Paralizacion de la Industria Petrolera' [Labour Consequences of Paralysis in the Petroleum Industry] in Office of the Ombudsperson, *Derechos Humanos en Venezuela, Anuario 2003* [Human Rights in Venezuela, Annual Report 2003] (Caracas: Office of the Ombudsperson, 2003), pp. 366–370; 'El Paro Petrolero' [The Oil Stoppage] in Provea, *Situacion de los Derechos Humanos en Venezuela: Informe Anual 2002–03* [The Human Rights Situation in Venezuela, Annual Report 2002–03] (Caracas: Provea, 2003), pp. 477–478.

42 Supreme Tribunal of Justice, Constitutional Court, Sentence No. 3342, 19 December 2002, Exp. 02–3157.

43 ILO, *Freedom of Association: Digest of decisions and principles of the Freedom of Association Committee of the Governing Body of the ILO*, 4th (revised) edition (Geneva: ILO, 1996), para. 534.

the principles of freedom of association'.[44] Third, the protestors did not comply with the legal procedure for calling a strike, which is another condition for the strike to be considered legitimate under international labour law.[45] Finally, the protest was aimed at the total stoppage of national oil production and distribution. The increasing lack of petrol gas throughout the country was having a huge impact on the provision of basic social services. In such a context, the ILO Committee has consistently stated that the prohibition of strikes is acceptable if essential services are interrupted and if this endangers the life, personal safety, or health of the whole or part of the population.[46] Thus, it appears that the State would have been entitled to call off the protest on the basis of ILO doctrine even if the work stoppage had been organised by workers' associations.[47]

4.3   Social Security Rights

In recent years, several decisions of the Supreme Tribunal of Justice have recognised the demands of groups of workers whose social security rights were affected by the privatisation of public companies throughout the 1990s. One case benefited around 6,000 pensioners of the public telephone company, which was privatised in 1991. After a long legal process, the Social Court ruled against the demand of a small group of petitioners. However, the Constitutional Court accepted an appeal against the judgment and ordered the Social Court to issue a new judgment recognising the claims. According to the Constitutional Court, 'the principle of social security is in the public order domain, and it cannot be modified by collective bargaining or agreements between private parties',[48] as such freedom could bring about serious damage to workers. Thus, the State has the obligation to protect labour in all contexts of society, including the private sector. Also, due to the fact that the Constitution establishes that pensions must be equivalent to the minimum wage, this protection must extend to the field of private pensions.

In its final decision, the Social Court ordered the yearly adjustment of the pensions of retired workers as of the date of retirement. It extended the judgment to all pensioners of the company and to surviving relatives of deceased pensioners in order to guarantee swift and equal justice to all.[49] The Social Court found that even if pensioners are bound by individual contracts, they all share the same juridical status in their 'labour' relation with the company. Thus, due to the fact that the 'Social State of Law' promotes the access of all people to an effective remedy, it would be unfair ('dantesque') not to extend the effects of the sentence to the collective, as they are perfectly identical, even if their contractual situations are not identical.

A similar case involved workers at Viasa, the national airline. After a long judicial process, a lower court recognised the rights of the pensioners, a decision that was later ratified by the Supreme Tribunal of Justice.[50] In other cases, the Court ruled in favour of retired public servants whose rights to pensions were affected by institutional reforms that accompanied the new Constitution. The affected workers included employees of the local government of Caracas[51] and of the National Agrarian Institute, which the newly passed Land Act closed down without establishing measures to guarantee that the retired workers would receive their benefits.[52]

The Court has also ordered Parliament to legislate to protect unemployment subsidies that were outlawed by the passage in 2002 of the new Law on the

---

[44] Ibid. para. 481. This view is shared by the ILO Committee of Experts.

[45] B. Gernigon, Alberto Odero and Horacio Guido, 'ILO principles concerning the right to strike', *International Labour Review*, Vol. 137, No. 4, where the ILO doctrine used for the interpretation of this case is cited.

[46] ILO, 'Freedom of Association' (n. 43 above), para. 492.

[47] As for the strike in other sectors, some court decisions in petitions aimed at banning the protest were delayed until the strike had ended, at the beginning of February 2003, presumably with the aim of avoiding further conflict. Several leaders of the protest have since faced criminal prosecution for promoting violent and destructive activity and trying to change the government through unconstitutional means.

[48] Supreme Tribunal of Justice, Constitutional Court, Sentence No. 03, 25 January 2005, Exp. 04–2847.

[49] Supreme Tribunal of Justice, Social Court, Sentence No. 816, 26 July 2005, Exp. 0545.

[50] Supreme Tribunal of Justice, Constitutional Court, Sentence No. 1363, 27 June 2005, Exp. 03–2521.

[51] Supreme Tribunal of Justice, Constitutional Court, Sentence No. 164, 5 February 2002, Exp. 01–2483.

[52] Supreme Tribunal of Justice, Constitutional Court, Sentence No. 2150, 3 September 2002, Exp. 02–1397.

Social Security System, which did not provide for a transitional regime. The Court found this omission in violation of social security rights and ordered Parliament to legislate in order to repair the damage. It also issued provisional measures to put an end to the damage, ruling against the provision of the new law that had revoked the subsidy and ordering the temporary enforcement of the previous regime. These remedies were ordered 'due to the urgency of the need to correct the situation and comply with the State's duties under international human rights law'.[53]

4.4 Health Rights

The right to health has been the subject of a rapidly expanding jurisprudence. In one case, a legal provision was struck down in a case brought before the Supreme Tribunal of Justice. The Constitutional Court ruled against a provision of the Law on the Value Added Tax that charged private health services with an 8 per cent tax. The Court argued that private health expenditure should not be interpreted as an investment, but as the exercise of a fundamental human right.[54]

In 2001, the newly empowered Supreme Tribunal of Justice ratified a previous decision that had granted the right to access to HIV treatment by people insured through the Social Security Agency. The Court stated that the issue went beyond simple health care for a given ill person, pointing instead 'to the ideal health care needed in order to guarantee the mental, social, and environmental integrity of all people'.[55] The Court extended the 'effects' of the decision to the entire segment of the insured population that might be infected by the virus, as the decision allowed for the 'protection of a relatively large segment of society, made up of individuals whose constitutional rights and guarantees must necessarily be reinforced'. The Court was deciding on appeal, so it was by its own initiative that it recognised the collective dimensions of the case. The Court also stated that

the Social Security Agency could not justify non-compliance with its legal duties because of a lack of resources that is a consequence of administrative inefficiency. With this decision, the right to access to HIV treatment achieved universal status under Venezuelan law.[56]

The Supreme Tribunal of Justice has also issued several decisions protecting the continuity and accessibility of health services. In one case, the Court ratified a previous decision that had ordered the Social Security Agency to reverse the closure of emergency services and of the night shift in one of its health centres.[57] In another case, the Court ordered a lower court to mediate between an NGO that provides non-profit health-care services in a poor community and the doctor that had sued them because of outstanding payment arrears. The Court argued that the necessary guarantees must be provided so that the execution of a judgment would not affect the services provided or the right to health of the community.[58]

In several cases, the Supreme Tribunal employed different methods to provide compensation for victims of health accidents. In one instance, a citizen was severely burned after being involved in the catastrophic failure of a high-tension switch belonging to the public electricity service. Revising a prior judgment on appeal, the Court stated that its fundamental mission was to protect and ensure human rights and, thus, to do all it deemed necessary to repair, as far as possible, the serious moral and physical damage caused by violations of these rights.[59] The Court ordered a monetary compensation that included the mandatory payment of a life pension. In another case, an army lieutenant suffered an injury on the elbow as a consequence of military exercises. His petition before the Ministry of Defence for due treatment and economic compensation was never heard. In 1999, he filed an action before the Supreme Tribunal,

---

[53] Supreme Tribunal of Justice, Constitutional Court, Sentence No. 91, 2 March 2005, Exp. 03–1100.

[54] Supreme Tribunal of Justice, Constitutional Court, Sentence No. 1505, 5 June 2003, Exp. 03–0124.

[55] Supreme Tribunal of Justice, Constitutional Court, Sentence No. 487, 6 April 2001, Exp. 1343.

[56] For a discussion on this process, see Enrique Gonzalez, 'Juridical action for the protection of collective rights and its legal impact: a case study', *JLME*, Vol. 30, No. 4 (2002), pp. 644–54.

[57] Supreme Tribunal of Justice, Constitutional Court, Sentence No. 1280, 12 June 2002, Exp. 00–2305.

[58] Supreme Tribunal of Justice, Constitutional Court, Sentence No. 1038, 27 May 2004, Exp. 03–2627.

[59] Supreme Tribunal of Justice, Administrative Court, Sentence No. 01386, 15 June 2000, Exp. 10.690.

which ordered the military authorities to provide treatment and economic aid to the petitioner. The Court found that the right to health 'is conceived as a positive or enforceable right, which is characterised by being teleologically oriented to the satisfaction of an obligation which, for the State, represents a duty to intervene in order to create the conditions necessary to the enjoyment of this fundamental right, as well as to the removal of the conditions that affect or impede its exercise'.[60]

4.5 Affordability of Housing Costs

One of the most relevant decisions under the present Constitution concerns economic rights and the sustainability of housing costs. It occurred as a result of a case introduced before the courts by debtors in balloon credit schemes. These credits were housing loans offered by the private banking sector throughout the 1990s in which the interest is recalculated every year not only in relation to the total amount of the debt, but also to the debt accumulated at the end of each year.[61] This makes it almost impossible for most debtors to settle the debt. The ongoing process for the implementation of the decision benefited around 90 per cent of the people who had taken out these loans.

The case developed jurisprudence in relation to the sustainability of housing costs and to the role of the State in redistributing wealth. The Court stated that financial entities authorised to act to carry out housing policies have special responsibilities regarding the fulfilment of the right to adequate housing and found that this type of loan violated the sustainability of housing costs, thus affecting the housing rights of the debtors. The decision stated that the aim of the welfare State is to protect social rights and also to ensure fair economic relations. Thus, under the 'Social State of Law', the State is entitled to restrict economic freedoms in order 'to protect people against unbalanced conduct that exploits sectors of the population'. In this context, the role of the State is to avoid the negative effects of unequal economic relations, which, if not catered to by the courts,

would 'generate a disproportionate advantage for the naturally dominant party'.[62]

The Court banned this type of credit scheme, temporarily suspended the payment of interest and annulled the clauses that allowed the lenders to recalculate the debt each year. The judgment declared that the yearly calculation of interest on unpaid interest and loan principle is to be considered usury in the banking system. It suggested a complex process for restructuring the housing loans through a common agreement between the parties and ordered Venezuela's Central Bank to establish a fair interest rate to be applied to the recalculation of the credits.

In another case, a community in which a publicly funded housing development was facing steady deterioration filed an action before a superior court arguing that the public housing authority had, for years, not met their demands for rehabilitation and maintenance. The decision, which was later ratified by the Supreme Tribunal of Justice, ordered the authorities to facilitate the provision of new housing to the petitioners whose houses had severe structural damage and to repair the damage in the remainder of the houses.[63]

Several housing rights cases are related to illegal occupations by homeless people who sought the protection of the courts against forcible eviction or asked for compensation after having been evicted. However, the subsequent jurisprudence does not explore the legal guarantees that must be in place regarding forced evictions and the orders in the two cases reviewed are not consistent. In one case, the Court ordered the authorities to provide adequate housing even if this was not part of the petitioners' plea. In the other, it dismissed a specific petition for adequate housing. This is not consistent with General Comment No. 7 on forced evictions, which states that 'evictions should not result in individuals being rendered homeless'.[64] However, in both cases, all the procedural protections that, according to the Committee, should

---

[60] Supreme Tribunal of Justice, Constitutional Court, Sentence No. 1286, 12 June 2001, Exp. 01–2832.

[61] These loans were also taken out to a lesser extent to buy vehicles.

[62] Supreme Tribunal of Justice, Constitutional Court, Sentence No. 85, 24 January 2002, Exp. 01–1274.

[63] Supreme Tribunal of Justice, Constitutional Court, Sentence No. 1494, 6 August 2004. Exp. 03–1193.

[64] Committee on Economic, Social and Cultural Rights, *General Comment No. 7: The right to adequate housing (article 11.1): forced evictions*, 20 May 1997 (Sixteenth session, 1997), para. 16.

be applied in relation to forced evictions were in place.[65]

In the first case, a group of illegal occupants, who claimed that the authorities dealing with their situation had promised them new housing, asked the Supreme Tribunal of Justice to order the fulfilment of the promise and to protect them against imminent eviction. In its decision, the Court recognised that the petitioners lacked access to adequate housing, but considered that this situation cannot lead to the violation of the right to property of third parties through the illegal practice of land occupations.[66] Furthermore, the Court considered that the occupants had put at risk their lives because there was a gas pipeline on the land and that it was the duty of the State to protect them from health hazards. Thus, it dismissed the action, but it did not provide for any means of protection, nor did it order the housing authorities to deal with housing rights.

In the second case, a group of families that had occupied a plot of land for a long period of time appealed a court decision that had dismissed their demand to revoke the act that led to the demolition of their shanty houses and to their eviction. The Supreme Tribunal of Justice ratified the superior court decision, without exploring the legal status of the administrative acts, but instead, explored the consistency of the judicial process that preceded and followed the eviction. However, in this case, it ordered the local authorities responsible for the eviction promptly to find adequate housing for the petitioners 'in accordance with their constitutional and legal duties related to the protection and guarantee of the right to adequate housing and the protection of families'.[67]

4.6 Agrarian Rights and the Right to Property

The structure of land tenure in Venezuela has been characterised since colonial times by the concentration of most arable land in the possession of a small number of proprietors. Major portions of available fertile land are idle or underdeveloped, while most State-owned land does not have agricultural potential. This has led to a critical dependence on food imports. A timid agrarian reform applied by the State in the 1960s did little to change this situation.[68] On the other hand, the legal status of land ownership is frequently dubious due both to deficiencies in official records and irregular procedures, and land occupations.

The new Land Act, which was passed in late 2001, creates a legal framework for agrarian reform and rural development. It establishes the social function of land ownership and tenure and is aimed both at promoting a fair distribution of the land and at boosting agricultural production to provide for better food security. It establishes a complex process for evaluating land tenure and the land production status of rural arable land, which allows the administration either to certify the productivity of a given parcel of land, or to order its repossession in case it is not being used for agriculture.

In 2002, the National Federation of Livestock Farmers (Fedenaga) filed a petition challenging five articles of the Land Act and arguing that these violated the right to legal defence and to due process. In its decision, the Constitutional Court found that while three of the challenged articles were constitutionally valid, two were unconstitutional, since they did not respect the necessary guarantees for the protection of the right to property. The first of the latter established that, once the National Land Institute had identified a parcel of land as non-productive, it could temporarily take over the land so that the land could be put to work, while the propriety rights case was being heard before the courts. The second established that illegal occupants of lands declared 'under recovery' had no right to compensation for their chattel. The Court stated that, 'given its social utility, the right to property is by nature subject to limitation, but limitations cannot bring about the total denial of the right... because this would mean denying the constitutional dimension'.[69]

---

[65] Ibid. para. 16.

[66] Supreme Tribunal of Justice, Constitutional Court, Sentence No. 1465, 13 August 2001, Exp. 01–1585.

[67] Supreme Tribunal of Justice, Constitutional Court, Sentence No. 3257, 16 December 2004, Exp. 03–2694.

[68] According to the 1997 agrarian census, of a total of 30 million hectares of rural land, about 2.3 million hectares were by then dedicated to agriculture. At the same time, 2 per cent of the land tenants held around 60 per cent of the arable land. See Provea, 'Derecho a la tierra' [Right to land], *Annual Report 2000–01*, p. 192.

[69] Supreme Tribunal of Justice, Constitutional Court, Sentence No. 2855, 20 November 2002. Exp. No. 02–0311.

In the first stages of implementation of the agrarian reform, the land that was distributed among small peasant farmers was State owned. However, people who claim property over the land that is subject to intervention have contested some of the most recent actions. In 2003, the National Land Institute issued a decree establishing that arable land officially declared 'under recovery' could be occupied by groups of organised peasants under its legal authority until a decision had been taken on the legal ownership of the land. This process, which is based on the National Land Institute's legal powers to establish the status of the production of land, has led to several legal actions by individuals and companies that claim they are the legal owners of occupied plots and that they have not been able to exercise their rights vis-à-vis the government administration.

In one of these cases, the petitioners appealed to the Supreme Tribunal of Justice against a lower court *amparo* judgment that petitioners had not exhausted the available administrative remedies. After reviewing the case, the Social Court stated that the constitutional balance between the rights to economic freedom and to property and the State power to intervene in agrarian reform should avoid excessive intervention of the State in the economy, while, at the same time, curtailing abuses of private economic rights. However, the National Land Institute has the obligation to notify all parties that may be affected by the procedure it applies. Therefore, the judgment ordered the authorities to evict the new occupants of the land and to restore the rights of the petitioners, while a final decision was taken on the ownership of the land.[70]

This decision protected the right to property of the alleged proprietors, but was contrary to ESC rights principles relating to forced evictions because it offered no compensation to the evicted peasants. Provea, the NGO, considered that the Court should have ordered the prohibition of further adjudications of ownership of the plot, while demanding that the process be restarted in respect of due process. According to Provea, 'in human rights terms, it is not acceptable that the peasants be prejudiced

before the final judicial decision about the ownership of the land'.[71]

In a recent case with wide dimensions, the Social Court ordered the Ministry of Agriculture to set a fair range of prices for coffee products since these had not been updated in years. The Court found that the omission had affected coffee production and could lead to massive imports that would affect the rights to food security and sustainable agrarian development. The Ministry was ordered to establish an inter-institutional commission to develop market studies, suggest economically sound coffee prices and evaluate the impact of the current prices for producers.[72]

4.7 Indigenous Peoples' Rights

In recent years, the Supreme Court of Justice has ruled on one relevant case related to indigenous peoples' rights. It concerned a petition that requested the Court to halt the development of a high-tension power line between Venezuela and Brazil until a proper socio-cultural impact study could be undertaken. The project involved vast woodland areas, sparsely inhabited by many indigenous communities, and was started in 1997 under the previous administration. Several communities and ecological organisations contested the project because of its potential impact on fragile ecosystems and on the welfare and culture of the indigenous peoples that live in the affected areas.

In 2001, the Supreme Tribunal ruled against the petition, pointing out first that, after a consultation process run by the new government, the number of indigenous leaders who had agreed on the continuation of the project was much higher than the number of those who were contesting. Thus, the petition could not be considered a legitimate claim by the indigenous communities affected by the project as a whole. Second, the Court determined that ruling in favour of the petitioners would violate the principle of non-retroactivity of the law, because the project was agreed upon under the 1961 Constitution, which did not

[70] Supreme Tribunal of Justice, Constitutional Court, Sentence No. 3052, 4 November, 2003, Exp. 03-2151.

[71] Provea, *Servicio informativo*, No. 129, 7–20 November 2003, available at <http://www.derechos.org.ve>.

[72] Supreme Tribunal of Justice, Constitutional Court, Sentence No. 602, 29 April 2005, Exp. 05-0367

establish the duty to provide for environmental impact studies, nor did it recognise indigenous peoples' rights.[73]

This latter argument is not consistent with the Court's jurisprudence, as the Constitution has been applied retroactively in various contexts. Furthermore, if this argument was applied under any and all circumstances, it would lead to a severe diminishing of the effectiveness of the Constitution, as any act agreed upon prior to its entry into force would not be subject to interpretation under the new constitutional framework. However, the Court did explore the arguments related to violation of environmental rights under the new Constitution because the letter of intent that both government administrations had initially agreed upon included the commitment to promote reasonable policies for the protection of the environment. The judgment pointed to the fact that several impact studies had been implemented throughout the years and that the environmental authorities had issued the subsequent legal permits. The Court stated that, thus, 'what is needed is to guarantee that the conditions and measures ordered by such authorities, which are aimed at reducing the environmental impact, are duly met'.

Finally, the Court stated that, according to the Constitution, the State must adopt measures to improve the basic living conditions of all citizens, including indigenous communities. It also pointed to ILO Convention 107 on indigenous and tribal populations, which establishes that economic development policies and special development projects in areas inhabited by indigenous peoples must be specifically aimed at 'the improvement of the conditions of life and work and level of education of the populations concerned' (Article 6).[74] The Court argued that, in order to fulfil these obligations, the State 'has the duty to provide sufficient electrical supply for these peoples, due to its relation with the improvement of their basic conditions of life'. However, in order to avoid the potentially negative effects

that the project could have on the environment, the Court ordered the environmental authorities to implement a special surveillance plan, in coordination with the Office of the Ombudsperson and the participation of the local indigenous communities.

When deciding that electrical supply is needed in order to provide services related to ESC rights to the indigenous populations, the Court should have taken into account whether the project was intended to protect their rights and the extent to which the works actually benefit or affect the exercise of these rights. It should also have investigated the scope and nature of the studies undertaken by the environmental authorities and the degree to which they had taken into account the indigenous peoples' rights. In any case, even if the judgment may have been conditioned by the political consequences of an eventual order to stop the project, it seems to be legitimate in so far as most indigenous leaders of the communities in the area had finally agreed to the project.

5. CONCLUSION: FIRST STEPS IN A DISTINCT PATH TOWARDS SOCIAL JUSTICE

The entry into force of the new Constitution is a positive step for the progressive realisation of ESC rights of the residents of Venezuela, particularly those that face structural poverty and social exclusion. This new law includes the thorough recognition of ESC rights as fundamental human rights, with multiple constitutional guarantees for their realisation. The constitutional framework also provides the foundation for the development of an active political society, through the establishment of several institutions for a participatory democracy, in which the people can further the exercise of political and economic rights in demand for social justice.

After the sanction of the new Constitution, the nation has faced a political conflict of high intensity, which has rendered it impossible to achieve a general democratic consensus for the progressive development of its social regime. This conflict is the expression of a global tension between two visions of a contemporary society. One model defends the primacy of individual rights and economic freedoms, denies the nature of social rights as human rights, and advocates for

---

[73] Supreme Tribunal of Justice, Constitutional Court, Sentence No. 1600, 20 December 2002, Exp. No. 00–1641.

[74] ILO Convention 107 Concerning the Protection and Integration of Indigenous and Other Tribal and Semi-Tribal Populations in Independent Countries, 2 July 1959. Ratified by Venezuela on 27 October 1982. Only on 22 May 2002 did Venezuela ratify ILO Convention 169, which, in 1989, updated ILO Convention 107.

trade liberalisation and structural reform, in order to dismantle the Social State. The other model defends the equal status of all human rights, demands the adoption of strong measures for the redistribution of wealth, and advocates for the strengthening of the role of the State in the economic and social arenas as a necessary tool to achieve social justice.

As the UN Committee on Economic, Social and Cultural Rights has stated, 'globalization risks downgrading the central place accorded to human rights' in international law – a risk which is 'especially the case in relation to economic, social and cultural rights'.[75] In the same spirit, Miloon Kothari, Special Rapporteur on adequate housing has stated that 'unfettered globalization cannot bring about the fulfilment of economic, social and cultural rights'.[76] Jean Ziegler, Special Rapporteur on the right to food, has also pointed out that international trade liberalisation and globalization have been harmful to the right to food, producing 'increased hunger and malnutrition rather than safer food security'.[77]

After several national elections, it is clear that the vast majority of Venezuelan people have decided to move away towards the second vision, and put in place a Constitution aimed at building a strong 'Social State of Law'. Due to the interests at stake, the conflict between the major political parties is unavoidable. However, six years after the adoption of the new Constitution, most political actors seem to finally agree that democratic decisions expressed through the polls must prevail, and that the search for alternatives to the will of the major-

ity should be sought for through institutional and peaceful means.

The jurisprudential developments related with the new framework for the realisation of social rights and interests have lead to significant advancements within the judicial arena. At the same time, some of the decisions reviewed in this chapter have been decided on excessively formal grounds without attention to the merits of the case, others are difficult to reconcile with each other, and there has been insufficient attention to international human rights legal doctrine. However, an overall evaluation shows a clear trend towards the recognition of the demands of individuals and collectives whose ESC rights have been affected either by public or private actors.

The judicial branch is also in need of reform, particularly in relation to rectifying some of its historical deficiencies and to guarantee swift delivery of justice, such as the implementation of judicial orders. This is particularly so in cases related with social rights, which affect strong economic interests. For instance, the decision on the right to pensions of retired workers of the public telephone company is still the subject of negotiations and controversy outside the tribunals. Also, much has yet to be done in order to guarantee fair access to the courts by the poor, and to address structural corruption in the judiciary.

In the present state of globalisation, the more fundamentalistic neo-liberal trends for the reduction of the State are being imposed on developing countries by international institutions. Under such circumstances, the legal developments that have been reviewed stand as a powerful signal for the furthering of ESC rights through administrative, legislative and judicial measures. They also allow for positive developments for the defense of ESC rights through legal action. Thus, the present situation in Venezuela can be considered as overall favorable for the justiciability of these rights, and for the positive recognition of social demands in a society that, despite its enormous resources, still faces huge social inequalities and injustice.

---

[75] 'Globalization and Economic, Social and Cultural Rights', statement by the Committee on Economic, Social and Cultural Rights, May 1998. 01/05/98.

[76] Report of the Special Rapporteur on adequate housing as a component of the right to an adequate standard of living, Mr. Miloon Kothari, 1 March 2002, E/CN.4/2002/59, para. 54.

[77] 'The right to food', Report by the Special Rapporteur on the right to food, Mr. Jean Ziegler, 10 January 2002, E/CN.4/2002/58, para. 110.

11

Canada

Socio-Economic Rights Under the Canadian Charter

Martha Jackman* and Bruce Porter**

1. INTRODUCTION

Louise Arbour, the former UN High Commissioner of Human Rights and a former Justice of the Supreme Court of Canada, has observed in commenting on the scope of constitutional rights in the Canadian Charter of Rights and Freedoms[1] ('the Charter') that 'the potential to give economic, social and cultural rights the status of constitutional entitlement represents an immense opportunity to affirm our fundamental Canadian values, giving them the force of law'.[2] Meeting this challenge is, however, at best a work in progress. The UN High Commissioner also notes that: 'The first two decades of Charter litigation testify to a certain timidity – both on the part of litigants and the courts – to tackle head on the claims emerging from the right to be free from want'.[3] As a result, the constitutional status of socio-economic rights in Canada remains, to a large extent, an open question – perhaps the most central unresolved issue in Canadian Charter jurisprudence.

The Charter, marking its twenty-fifth anniversary in 2007, contains no explicit reference to any of the guarantees in the International Covenant on Economic, Social and Cultural Rights[4] ('ICESCR'). The closest the Charter comes to recognising a socio-economic right is the section 23 right to publicly funded minority language education at the primary and secondary levels, 'where numbers warrant'. The minority language education guarantee has been interpreted by the Supreme Court as a 'novel form of legal right' which 'confers upon a group a right which places positive obligations on government to alter or develop major institutional structures.[5]

As High Commissioner Arbour explains, however, when the Charter is considered in light of the historical expectations and broader values surrounding its adoption, it is clear that the obligations of governments to maintain and develop 'major institutional structures' in support of substantive rights need not be limited to minority language rights. Of particular importance in this respect are the equality rights guarantees in section 15 of the Charter,[6] and the right to 'life, liberty and security of the person' in section 7.[7] These rights, which might otherwise be classified as 'civil and political', are best understood in the Canadian context as including both civil and political and socio-economic dimensions. When the Charter was adopted in 1982, equality rights experts and advocacy groups considered the adequacy and accessibility of publicly funded programs, such as social assistance, universal healthcare, education and unemployment insurance as implicit in these broadly framed Charter rights.[8]

* Faculty of Law, University of Ottawa.
** Director, Social Rights Advocacy Centre. The authors would like to thank Vince Calderhead and an anonymous reviewer for their comments and assistance.

[1] Canadian Charter of Rights and Freedoms, Part I of the Constitution Act, 1982, being Schedule B to the Canada Act 1982 (UK), 1982, c.11 ('Charter').
[2] L. Arbour, '"Freedom From Want" – From Charity to Entitlement', LaFontaine-Baldwin Lecture, Quebec City (2005), p. 7, available at: <www.unhchr.ch/huricane/huricane.nsf/0/58E08B5CD49476BEC1256FBD006EC8B1?opendocument>.
[3] Ibid.
[4] International Covenant on Economic, Social and Cultural Rights, 16 December 1966, 993 UNTS 3 (entered into force 3 January 1976).

[5] *Mahe v. Alberta*, [1990] 1 S.C.R. 342 at 389.
[6] Section 15 provides that: 'Every individual is equal before and under the law and has the right to the equal protection and equal benefit of the law without discrimination and, in particular, without discrimination based on race, national or ethnic origin, colour, religion, sex, age or mental or physical disability'.
[7] Section 7 provides that: 'Everyone has the right to life, liberty and security of the person and the right not to be deprived thereof except in accordance with the principles of fundamental justice'.
[8] B. Porter, 'Expectations of Equality', *Supreme Court Law Review*, Vol. 33 (2006), pp. 23–44.

2. THE CANADIAN CHARTER AS A SOURCE OF PROTECTION FOR SOCIO-ECONOMIC RIGHTS

2.1 Historical Context and Legislative History of the Charter

Canadian rights culture in the 1960s and 1970s was significantly affected by the civil rights movement in the United States. In this period, broad anti-discrimination guarantees were introduced in federal and provincial human rights legislation across Canada. Considerable attention was paid to emerging civil rights jurisprudence from the United States, but at the same time, Canadian rights culture absorbed a distinctive commitment to social rights and to an emerging system of international human rights protections in which Canada was directly engaged.[9] Prime Minister Pierre Elliot Trudeau, who presided over the initiative to adopt a constitutional charter of rights after his re-election in 1980, linked the proposal to his ideal of a 'just society'. In an article on 'Economic Rights' he wrote as a law professor in 1962, Trudeau had affirmed that: 'if this society does not evolve an entirely new set of values ... it is vain to hope that Canada will ever reach freedom from fear and freedom from want. Under such circumstances, any claim by lawyers that they have done their bit by upholding civil liberties will be dismissed as a hollow mockery'.[10]

Unlike the United States, Canada ratified the ICESCR in 1976 at the same time as the International Covenant on Civil and Political Rights ('ICCPR')[11]. In 1980–81, the Special Joint Committee of the Senate and the House of Commons on

the Constitution of Canada considered including an explicit reference to ICESCR rights under section 36 of the Constitution Act, 1982.[12] As enacted, section 36 states that federal and provincial governments 'are committed to ... providing essential public services of reasonable quality to all Canadians'.[13] However, rather than pressing for explicit inclusion of socio-economic rights under section 36 of the Charter, most human rights experts and advocacy groups emphasised the importance of framing rights, such as the right to equality, as expansively as possible. The Charter could then be applied to require governments to take positive action to address the needs of vulnerable groups, to remedy systemic inequality, and to maintain and improve social programs on which the enjoyment of equality and other Charter rights depends.[14]

Section 15 of the Charter, originally entitled 'non-discrimination rights' was renamed 'equality rights' and significantly expanded after an unprecedented lobbying campaign by women's groups, disability rights groups and others. Section 15 was reworded to guarantee both equality 'before and under' the law, and the equal 'protection and benefit' of the law. This wording (unique at that time) was intended to ensure that equality rights applied to social benefit programs, such as welfare and unemployment insurance, and that the positive obligations of governments toward disadvantaged groups were constitutionally recognised and affirmed.[15] As the Canadian Bar Association noted at the time: '[it] is an equality

---

[9] Ibid. 23–35.

[10] P. Trudeau, 'Economic Rights', *McGill Law Journal*, Vol. 8 (1961–62), pp. 122–125, at 125. Subsequently, as federal Minister of Justice, Trudeau released a discussion paper on the Liberal government's proposal for a new Charter of Rights in which he suggested that while a constitutional guarantee of economic rights was desirable and 'should be an ultimate objective of Canada' it 'might take considerable time to reach agreement on the rights to be guaranteed'. On that basis, Trudeau concluded that it was 'advisable not to attempt to include economic rights in the constitutional bill of rights at this time'. See P.E. Trudeau, *A Canadian Charter of Human Rights* (Ottawa: Queen's Printer, 1968), p. 27.

[11] International Covenant on Civil and Political Rights, 16 December 1966, 999 UNTS171 (entered into force 23 March 1976).

[12] Canada, Special Joint Committee of the Senate and the House of Commons on the Constitution of Canada, *Minutes of Proceedings and Evidence*, 32nd Parl., No. 49 (30 January 1981), pp. 65–71. Section 36 is set out in Part III of the Constitution Act, 1982.

[13] Canada has stated in its Core Document to UN treaty monitoring bodies that the provisions of Section 36: 'are particularly relevant in regard to Canada's international obligations for the protection of economic, social and cultural rights'. However, the justiciability of the governmental 'commitments' in section 36 has never really been tested; see L. Sossin, *Boundaries of Judicial Review: The Law of Justiciability in Canada* (Toronto: Carswell, 1999), pp. 184–91; A. Nader, 'Providing Essential Services: Canada's Constitutional Commitment Under Section 36' *Dalhousie Law Journal*, Vol. 19 (1996), pp. 306–372; see also *Winterhaven Stables Ltd.* v. *A.G. Canada* (1988), 53 DLR (4th) 413 (Alta. CA), at 432–4.

[14] Porter, 'Expectations of Equality' (n. 8 above), pp. 23.

[15] Ibid.

rights section, not merely an anti-discrimination section. The difference between an equality purpose and an anti-discrimination purpose is that the former is broader and more positive than the latter'.[16]

In addition, as a result of energetic lobbying by disability rights groups, Canada became the first among constitutional democracies to include disability as a constitutionally prohibited ground of discrimination.[17] This signalled the importation into Canadian constitutional law of an approach to equality that had already been accepted under provincial human rights legislation: remedial in its focus, and recognising that discrimination could include a failure to take positive measures to accommodate the unique needs of protected groups, even in the absence of discriminatory intent.[18] An 'undue hardship' test had been adopted under Canadian human rights legislation as the standard for determining whether 'reasonable steps' or 'reasonable measures' had been taken to accommodate the needs of protected groups in view of cost, health and safety and other relevant factors.[19] However, Canadian courts and tribunals adopted a significantly more rigorous standard than was applied by US courts.[20] In this sense, the type of obligations contained in Article 2 of the ICESCR, to take reasonable steps based on a maximum of available resources, had already become familiar to Canadians in their courts' approach to human rights protections. This is particularly true for Quebec, where socio-economic rights were explicitly included under the Quebec Charter of Human Rights and Freedoms.[21]

The wording of section 7 of the Charter, which guarantees the 'right to life, liberty and security of the person' and the right not to be deprived thereof 'except in accordance with principles of fundamental justice' similarly reflects historical Canadian values linked with socio-economic rights. A proposed amendment to add a right to 'the enjoyment of property' to the Charter was rejected in part because of fears that property rights would conflict with Canadians' commitment to social programs and give rise to challenges to government regulation of the private market. Provincial governments opposed Charter recognition of property rights on the grounds that constitutional entrenchment of such rights could give rise to challenges to government regulation of corporate interests and control of natural resources.[22] Similarly, the phrase 'fundamental justice' was preferred over any reference to 'due process of law' because of concerns around the use of the due process clause in the United States during the *Lochner* era as a means for propertied interests to challenge the regulation of private enterprise and the promotion of social rights.[23]

2.2 Socio-Economic Rights in Sections 7 and 15 of the Charter

In light of the Charter's wording and historical context there is significant opportunity, as High Commissioner Arbour has suggested, for Canadian courts to interpret substantive Charter obligations, particularly under sections 7 and 15, to

[16] Canada, The Sub-committee on Equality Rights of the Standing Committee on Justice and Legal Affairs, Written Submissions, Submission of the Canadian Bar Association, cited in B. Porter, 'Twenty Years of Equality Rights: Reclaiming Expectations', *Windsor Yearbook of Access to Justice*, Vol. 23 (2005), pp. 145–192, at footnote 83.

[17] See generally Y. Peters, 'From Charity to Equality: Canadians with Disabilities Take Their Rightful Place in Canada's Constitution', in D. Stienstra, A. Wight-Felske and C. Watters (eds.), *Making Equality – History of Advocacy and Persons with Disabilities in Canada* (Concord Ontario: Captus Press, 2003), pp. 119–136; M. D. Lepofsky, 'A Report Card on the Charter's Guarantee of Equality to Persons with Disabilities after 10 Years – What Progress? What Prospects?', *National Journal of Constitutional Law*, Vol. 7 (1998), pp. 263–431.

[18] *Ontario Human Rights Commission v. Simpsons-Sears*, [1985] 2 SCR 536.

[19] Ibid. paras. 20–9.

[20] *Central Okanagan School District No. 23 v. Renaud*, [1992] 2 SCR 970.

[21] Quebec Charter of Human Rights and Freedoms, R.S.Q. 1977, c. C-12. For a discussion of the socio-economic rights guarantees under the Quebec Charter, see P. Bosset, 'Les droits économiques et sociaux, parents pauvres de la Charte québécoise? Étude no. 5' [Economic and social rights, poor parents of the Quebec Charter? Study No. 5], in Commission des droits de la personne et des droits de la jeunesse du Québec, *Après 25 ans: La Charte québécoise des droits et libertés, Volume 2: Études* (Montreal: Commission des droits de la personne et des droits de la jeunesse du Québec, 2003), pp. 229–244, available at: <http://www.cdpdj.qc.ca/fr/droits-personne/bilan-charte.asp?noeud1=1&noeud2=16&cle=0>.

[22] S. Choudhry, 'The *Lochner* Era and Comparative Constitutionalism', *International Journal of Constitutional Law*, Vol. 2 (2004), pp. 17–24.

[23] Ibid.

include most, if not all, components of the rights contained in the ICESCR.[24] While the jurisprudence of the Supreme Court of Canada has not yet moved clearly in this direction, neither has it foreclosed it.

From its earliest decisions under the Charter to its most recent, the Supreme Court has been careful to leave open the possibility that the Charter may protect a range of socio-economic rights. In its 1986 decision in *Irwin Toy*,[25] the Court rejected attempts by corporate interests to situate their economic claims within the scope of section 7, finding that private property rights had been intentionally excluded from the Charter. However, the Court was careful to distinguish what it characterised as 'corporate-commercial economic rights' from 'such rights, included in various international covenants, as rights to social security, equal pay for equal work, adequate food, clothing and shelter'. The Court found that it would be 'precipitous' to exclude the latter class of rights at so early a moment in Charter interpretation.[26]

During the 1990s, most Canadian lower courts called upon to consider socio-economic rights claims rejected such challenges on the basis that economic rights were beyond both the scope of section 7 and the legitimate purview of the courts.[27] At the Supreme Court level, however,

the question about the status of ICESCR rights under section 7, which had been left unanswered in *Irwin Toy*, lay essentially dormant for seventeen years. During this period, few socio-economic rights cases reached the appellate level and no case involving poverty or social assistance was heard by the Supreme Court. In the 2003 *Gosselin* case, the Supreme Court considered a challenge to grossly inadequate levels of social assistance benefits in Quebec, paid to employable recipients not enrolled in workfare programs. In an important dissenting judgment (supported by Justice L'Heureux-Dubé), Justice Arbour found that the section 7 right to 'security of the person' places positive obligations on governments to provide those in need with an amount of social assistance adequate to cover basic necessities.[28] The majority of the Court left open the possibility of adopting this 'novel' interpretation of the right to security of the person in a future case, but found that there was insufficient evidence in this case to make such a finding. Chief Justice McLachlin stated, for the majority:

> The question therefore is not whether s. 7 has ever been – or will ever be – recognized as creating positive rights. Rather, the question is whether the present circumstances warrant a novel application of s. 7 as the basis for a positive state obligation to guarantee adequate living standards. I conclude that they do not.[29]

While its approach to section 7 has been inconclusive, in its early section 15 Charter jurisprudence, the Supreme Court of Canada played a leading role, internationally, in affirming and developing a notion of substantive equality that includes important dimensions of socio-economic rights and places positive obligations on governments to remedy disadvantage. The Supreme Court has recognised that programs such as social assistance for single mothers are 'encouraged' by section 15, and has justified positive remedies to

---

[24] For elaboration of this possibility, see M. Jackman, 'The Protection of Welfare Rights Under the Charter', *Ottawa Law Review*, Vol. 20, No. 2 (1988), pp. 257–338; B. Porter, 'Judging Poverty: Using International Human Rights Law to Refine the Scope of *Charter* Rights', *Journal of Law and Social Policy*, Vol. 15 (2000), pp. 117–162; D. Wiseman, 'The *Charter* and Poverty: Beyond Injusticiability', *University of Toronto Law Journal*, Vol. 51 (2001), pp. 425–458; R. Bahdi, 'Litigating Social and Economic Rights in Canada in Light of International Human Rights Law: What Difference Can it Make?', *Canadian Journal of Women and the Law*, Vol. 14 (2002), pp. 158–184; The Honourable C. L'Heureux-Dubé, 'A Canadian Perspective on Economic and Social Rights' in Y. Ghai and J. Cottrell (eds.), *Economic, Social And Cultural Rights In Practice: The Role of Judges in Implementing Economic, Social and Cultural Rights* (London: Interrights, 2004), pp. 42–49; M. Young, 'Section 7 and the Politics of Social Justice', *University of British Columbia Law Review*, Vol. 38 (2005), pp. 539–560.

[25] *Irwin Toy Ltd. v. Quebec (Attorney General)*, [1989] 1 SCR 927.

[26] Ibid. pp. 1003–4.

[27] See, for example, *Masse v. Ontario Ministry of Community and Social Services)* (1996), 134 DLR. (4th) 20 (Ont. SCJ), leave to appeal to Ontario Court of Appeal denied, (1996) 40 Admin. LR 87N, leave to appeal to the Supreme Court

of Canada denied, (1996) 39 CRC. (2d) 375. See generally D. Parkes, 'Baby Steps on the Way to a Grown up Charter: Reflections on 20 Years of Social and Economic Rights Claims', *University of New Brunswick Law Journal*, Vol. 52 (2003), pp. 279–298; M. Jackman, 'Poor Rights: Using the *Charter* to Support Social Welfare Claims', *Queen's Law Journal*, Vol. 19 (1993), pp. 65–95; Porter, 'Judging Poverty' (n. 24 above).

[28] *Gosselin v. Quebec (Attorney General)*, [2002] 4 SCR 429, at paras. 82–83.

[29] Ibid. para. 83.

under-inclusive benefit programs on that basis.[30] In several key cases, the Court issued positive remedial orders extending or increasing parental, social assistance and pension benefits and extending legislative protections under security of tenure and human rights legislation.[31] These decisions suggested that the Court would fulfil its constitutional mandate to ensure that governments met their substantive equality rights obligations, notwithstanding a steady stream of media and right wing criticism about the Court's excessive 'judicial activism'.[32]

However, even in its most progressive equality rights decisions, the Supreme Court has insisted on sidestepping the issue of whether, in the absence of an under-inclusive program or benefits scheme, the Charter imposes a positive obligation on governments to provide benefits or social programs necessary to address the needs of disadvantaged groups.[33] The Court has stepped back from an explicit affirmation of a key element of the notion of equality that was advanced by groups during the pre-Charter debates about the wording of section 15 and that is also at the core of Canada's international human rights obligations – the obligation of governments to protect vulnerable groups through appropriate legislative measures and to take positive action to remedy socio-economic disadvantage that is independent

of the obligation to ensure that existing legislation and benefit schemes are not under-inclusive or discriminatory.[34]

2.3 The Horizontal Application of the Charter

Section 32(1) of the Charter provides that the Charter applies to the federal parliament and provincial legislatures and to the actions and decisions of federal and provincial/territorial governments. In principle, the Charter does not therefore apply to non-governmental entities. However, as the courts' understanding of state action has evolved, it has become clear that the Charter does provide important socio-economic rights protections in the private as well as the public sphere.

First, the Supreme Court has emphasised that governments cannot contract out of their constitutional obligations.[35] Where private actors are given responsibility for the implementation of specific government policies or programs, these entities will be subject to the Charter in relation to those activities. The importance of this principle in the socio-economic rights context was evident in the Supreme Court's 1999 decision in the *Eldridge* case.[36] The applicants, who were deaf, argued that the lack of sign language interpretation services within the publicly funded healthcare system violated their section 15 equality rights. The Supreme Court found that, although hospitals were non-governmental entities not otherwise subject to the Charter, in providing publicly funded healthcare services, they were acting as the vehicles chosen by government to deliver a comprehensive healthcare program, and were therefore subject to the requirements of the Charter.[37] Thus, the Court found that hospitals' failure to provide medical interpretation services necessary

---

[30] *Schachter v. Canada*, [1992] 2 SCR 679, at para. 41.
[31] M. Buckley, '*Law v. Meiorin*: Exploring the Governmental Responsibility to Promote Equality Under Section 15 of the Charter', in F. Faraday, M. Denike and M.K. Stephenson (eds.), *Making Equality Rights Real: Securing Substantive Equality Under the Charter* (Toronto: Irwin Law, 2006), pp. 179–206 and see the discussion in Part 7, below.
[32] Porter, 'Expectations of Equality' (n. 8 above), pp. 36–38; B. Porter, 'Beyond *Andrews*: Substantive Equality and Positive Obligations After *Eldridge* and *Vriend*', *Constitutional Forum*, Vol. 9 (1998), pp. 71–82; M. Jackman, '"Giving Real Effect to Equality": *Eldridge v. B.C. (A.G.)* and *Vriend v. Alberta*', *Review of Constitutional Studies*, Vol. 4 (1998) pp. 352–371. For a discussion of the critiques of 'judicial activism' in Canada from a socio-economic rights perspective, see L. Weinrib, 'The Canadian Charter's Transformative Aspirations', in J.E. Magnet et al. (eds.), *The Canadian Charter of Rights and Freedoms: Reflections on the Charter After Twenty Years* (Toronto: LexisNexis Butterworths, 2003), pp. 17–37; M. Jackman, '*Charter* Equality at Twenty: Reflections of a Card-Carrying Member of the Court Party', *Policy Options*, Vol. 27, No. 1 (Dec. 2005 – Jan. 2006), pp. 72–77.
[33] *Vriend v. Alberta*, [1998] 1 SCR 493, at para. 64; see generally Porter, 'Reclaiming Expectations' (n. 16 above), pp. 180–185.

[34] For a discussion of substantive equality and positive obligations in Canadian and other jurisprudence, see S. Fredman, 'Providing Equality: Substantive Equality and the Positive Duty to Provide', *South African Journal on Human Rights*, Vol. 21 (2005), pp. 163–190; G. Brodsky & S. Day, 'Beyond the Social and Economic Rights Debate: Substantive Equality Speaks to Poverty', *Canadian Journal of Women and the Law*, Vol. 14 (2002), pp. 185–220.
[35] *Eldridge v. British Columbia (Attorney General)*, [1997] 3 SCR 624, at para. 40.
[36] Ibid.
[37] Ibid. paras. 40–52.

to ensure that the deaf enjoyed the equal benefit of healthcare services violated section 15.

The other important horizontal dimension of Charter-based protection for socio-economic rights is found in governments' obligation to protect vulnerable groups from violations of their rights by others, at least in so far as such an obligation can be grounded in a requirement that legislation not be under-inclusive. In the *Vriend* case,[38] the Supreme Court held that a failure to include sexual orientation as a prohibited ground of discrimination under provincial human rights legislation governing the actions of private employers, service and housing providers, violated Charter equality rights.[39] Underscoring the importance of distinguishing between private activity that is not subject to the Charter, and laws regulating private activity, that are subject to review, the Court rejected the government's argument that the discrimination at issue in the case resulted from the actions of private entities, not from those of government.[40] As Justice Cory declared: 'Even if the discrimination is experienced at the hands of private individuals, it is the state that denies protection from that discrimination'.[41]

Similarly, in the 2001 *Dunmore* case, the Supreme Court dealt with a claim that the decision of a newly elected government to revoke legislation protecting the right of agricultural workers to organize and bargain collectively violated the section 2(d) Charter guarantee of 'freedom of association'. The Court had to consider whether: '2(d) obligates the state simply to respect trade union freedoms, or additionally to protect trade union freedoms by prohibiting their infringement by private actors'.[42] Noting that the Court's understanding of 'state action' had matured since its early decisions on the application of the Charter, and that:

> [T]his Court has repeatedly held in the s. 15(1) context that the Charter may oblige the state to extend underinclusive statutes to the extent underinclusion licenses private actors to violate basic rights and freedoms', the Court concluded that 'it is not a quantum leap to suggest that a failure to include someone in

a protective regime may affirmatively permit restraints on the activity the regime is designed to protect.[43]

It should also be noted that other statutory means exist in Canada for challenging violations of socio-economic rights by non-state actors. Socio-economic rights are dealt with by a wide variety of administrative tribunals in employment, housing and other matters, as well as by the courts. In addition, human rights legislation in all provinces/territories and at the federal level protects the right to equality in the private sector. The courts' approach to positive obligations under human rights legislation has been similar to their approach to substantive equality under section 15 of the Charter. So, for example, in the area of housing rights, human rights legislation has been successfully used to challenge landlords' practice of screening prospective tenants based on income level, credit history or reference requirements – practices which were identified by the CESCR as problematic in relation to the right to adequate housing under Article 11 of the ICESCR.[44] In Quebec, as noted above, socio-economic rights are explicitly recognised under the Quebec Charter of Human Rights and Freedoms and in some cases extend to private actors.[45]

3. INTERNATIONAL HUMAN RIGHTS LAW AS A SOURCE OF PROTECTION FOR DOMESTIC SOCIO-ECONOMIC RIGHTS

3.1 The 'Interpretive Presumption'

Rights contained in international human rights treaties ratified by Canada are not directly enforceable by Canadian courts unless they are incorporated into Canadian law by parliament or

---

[38] *Vriend v. Alberta* (n. 33 above).
[39] Ibid. paras. 65–66.
[40] Ibid.
[41] Ibid. para. 103
[42] *Dunmore v. Ontario (Attorney General)*, [2001] 3 SCR 1016, at para. 13.

[43] Ibid. para. 26.
[44] *Kearney v. Bramalea Ltd* (1998), 34 CHRR D/1 (Ont. Bd. Inq.), upheld in *Shelter Corporation v. Ontario Human Rights Commission* (2001), 143 OAC 54 (Ont. Sup. Ct.); *Whittom v. Québec (Commission des droits de la personne)* (1997), 29 CHRR D/1 (Que. CA); *Ahmed v. Shelter Corporation* (Unreported, Ont. Bd. Inq., M. A. McKellar, Decision No 02–007, 2 May 2002); *Sinclair and Newby v. Morris A Hunter Investments Limited* (Unreported, Ont. Bd. Inq., M. A. McKellar, Decision No 01–024, 5 November 2001). *Conclusion and recommendations of CESCR: Canada*, UN. Doc. E/C.12/1993/5 (1993), para. 18.
[45] Quebec Charter of Human Rights and Freedoms, (n. 21 above).

provincial legislatures.[46] There has been no serious discussion of incorporating any international human rights treaties into Canadian law. Rather, the emphasis has been on ensuring that the Charter, federal and provincial human rights legislation, and other domestic laws, give effect to Canada's international human rights obligations.

The Supreme Court affirmed in its 1989 *Slaight Communications* decision, with specific reference to the ICESCR, that an 'interpretive presumption' exists according to which 'the Charter should generally be presumed to provide protection at least as great as that afforded by similar provisions in international human rights documents which Canada has ratified'.[47] This has meant, as Justice L'Heureux-Dubé stated for the majority of the Court in the 1999 *Baker* decision, that international human rights law is 'a critical influence on the interpretation of the scope of the rights included in the *Charter*'.[48] Justice L'Heureux-Dubé further elaborated on this point in a subsequent case, where she stated that:

Our *Charter* is the primary vehicle through which international human rights achieve a domestic effect (see *Slaight Communications Inc. v. Davidson*, [1989] 1 S.C.R. 1038; *R. v. Keegstra*, [1990] 3 S.C.R. 697). In particular, s. 15 (the equality provision) and s. 7 (which guarantees the right to life, security and liberty of the person) embody the notion of respect of human dignity and integrity.[49]

3.2 Review of Discretionary Decision-Making for Consistency with Socio-Economic Rights

The interpretive presumption affirmed in *Slaight Communications* has important implications not only for the scope of the Charter, but also for statutory interpretation and the exercise of conferred discretion by administrative actors. The Supreme Court has emphasised that the Charter is not the sole preserve of the judiciary. As Chief Justice McLachlin has expressed it:

The *Charter* is not some holy grail which only judicial initiates of the superior courts may touch. The *Charter* belongs to the people. All law and law-makers that touch the people must conform to it. Tribunals and commissions charged with deciding legal issues are no exception. Many more citizens have their rights determined by these tribunals than by the courts. If the *Charter* is to be meaningful to ordinary people, then it must find its expression in the decisions of these tribunals.[50]

All conferred decision-making authority must be exercised in a manner consistent with the Charter, which in turn is assumed to be consistent with the ICESCR. It is by means of this interpretive presumption that the Court was able to ensure, in *Slaight Communications*, that the decision of a private labour arbitrator was in conformity with the Charter and hence with the recognition of the right to work and the obligation to protect vulnerable workers under the ICESCR.

The interpretive effect of international human rights law on discretionary decision-making may, alternatively, be applied directly without invoking Charter rights, as affirmed by the Supreme Court in the 1999 *Baker* case.[51] Mavis Baker, a Jamaican citizen who had worked illegally in Canada as a domestic worker for a number of years and who had given birth to four children in Canada, was issued with a deportation order. She sought review of the deportation order under a provision of the federal Immigration Act allowing for humanitarian and compassionate review. The immigration officer charged with the review was asked to overturn the deportation order based on the best interests of the children, as protected under the International Convention on the Rights of the Child

---

[46] *Baker v. v. Canada (Minister of Citizenship and Immigration)*, [1999] 2 SCR 817, at paras. 69–71.

[47] *Slaight Communications Inc. v. Davidson*, [1989] 1 SCR 1038, at 1056-7; see also R. Sullivan, *Driedger on the Construction of Statutes*, 3rd edition (Toronto: Butterworths, 1994), p. 330: 'the legislature is presumed to respect the values and principles enshrined in international law, both customary and conventional. In so far as possible, therefore, interpretations that reflect these values and principles are preferred'; cited in *Baker v. Canada* (n. 46 above), para. 70 and in *R. v. Sharpe*, [2001] 1 SCR 45, at para. 175.

[48] *Baker v. Canada* (n. 46 above), para. 70.

[49] *R. v. Ewanchuk*, [1999] 1 SCR 330, at para. 73.

[50] *Nova Scotia (Workers' Compensation Board) v. Martin; Nova Scotia (Workers' Compensation Board) v. Laseur*, [2003] 2 SCR 504, at para. 29.

[51] *Baker v. Canada* (n. 46 above). For a discussion of the case see D. Dyzenhaus, ed., *The Unity of Public Law* (Oxford: Hart Publishing, 2004).

(CRC),[52] but declined to do so. No Charter claim was made on behalf of either Ms. Baker or her children and the issue in the case was whether the officer's decision, which was inconsistent with the best interests of the children as recognised under the CRC, could be overturned for that reason. The Supreme Court reversed the immigration officer's decision on the basis that it was unreasonable because of 'the failure to give serious weight and consideration to the interests of the children'.[53] On the question of the role of the CRC in assessing reasonableness, the Court held that:

> The principles of the Convention and other international instruments place special importance on protections for children and childhood, and on particular consideration of their interests, needs, and rights. They help show the values that are central in determining whether this decision was a reasonable exercise of the H[umanitarian] & C[ompassionate Review] power.[54]

The implications of the *Baker* decision are significant for the application of a reasonableness test to discretionary decisions or policies in relation to evictions into homelessness; denials of financial assistance necessary for adequate food or housing; access to healthcare, educational aids and assistance; and many other areas affecting the enjoyment of ICESCR rights in Canada.[55]

3.3   CESCR Jurisprudence Relating to the Charter

The importance of interpreting the Charter and other Canadian laws so as to give effect to ICESCR rights has become a central concern for the UN Committee on Economic, Social and Cultural Rights (CESCR) over the course of several periodic reviews of Canada's compliance with its Covenant obligations.

The Committee commented, during Canada's second periodic review in 1993, that 'the process of interpretation of the Charter is still in its early stages, but that its provisions and the interpretations adopted by the Supreme Court in early cases suggest that Canadian courts will give full consideration to the rights in the Covenant when interpreting and applying the Canadian Charter of Rights and Freedoms'.[56] However, the Committee also expressed concern that Canadian lower courts had characterised ICESCR rights 'as mere "policy objectives" of governments rather than as fundamental human rights'.[57] In its 1993 report, the Committee encouraged Canadian courts 'to continue to adopt a broad and purposive approach to the interpretation of the Charter of Rights and Freedoms and of human rights legislation so as to provide appropriate remedies against violations of social and economic rights in Canada'.[58]

Subsequent CESCR reviews manifest similar concerns. In 1998, the Committee expressed particular reservations about Canadian lower court Charter interpretations that denied remedies for violations of the right to an adequate standard of living. The Committee also questioned governments' decision to advance Charter interpretations that would deprive claimants of any remedy to the denial of basic necessities.[59] At its May 2006 review of Canada's Fourth and Fifth Period Reports, the Committee again criticised 'the practice of

---

[52] Convention on the Rights of the Child, 20 November 1989, 1577 UNTS 3 (entered into force 2 September 1990).

[53] *Baker v. Canada* (n. 46 above) at para. 65.

[54] *Ibid.* at para. 71. Two of seven judges in the *Baker* case dissented on the question of the majority's direct recourse to international human rights law. They held that giving this kind of direct interpretive effect to international human rights law would allow indirectly what is not allowed directly, giving the force of law to treaties negotiated by the executive, without parliamentary approval. However, the dissenting judgment acknowledged that the same result might have been reached by way of a *Charter* claim, based on the 'interpretive presumption' that the *Charter* would subsume the protections of rights of children under international human rights law and that the exercise of discretion must conform with the *Charter;* ibid. para. 81, per Iacobucci J.

[55] See generally: C. Scott, 'Canada's International Human Rights Obligations and Disadvantaged Members of Society: Finally Into the Spotlight?', *Constitutional Forum,* Vol. 10, No. 4 (1999), pp. 97–111; L. Sossin, 'From Neutrality to Compassion: The Place of Civil Service Values and Legal Norms in the Exercise of Administrative Discretion', *University of Toronto Law Journal,* Vol. 56 (2005), pp. 427–447; L. Sossin and L. Pottie 'Demystifying the

Boundaries of Public Law: Policy, Discretion and Social Welfare', *U.B.C. Law Review,* Vol. 38 (2005), pp. 147–87.

[56] *Concluding Observations of CESCR: Canada,* (n. 44 above), para 5.

[57] Ibid. para. 21.

[58] Ibid. para. 30.

[59] *Conclusions and recommendations of CESCR: Canada,* E/C.12/1/Add.31 (1998), paras. 14–15. For a discussion of the significance of the CESCR 1998 comments on Canada, see Scott, 'Canada's International Human Rights Obligations and Disadvantaged Members of Society' (n. 55 above).

Canadian governments to urge upon their courts an interpretation of the Canadian Charter of Rights and Freedoms denying protection of Covenant rights'.[60]

4. STANDING AND ACCESS TO LEGAL SERVICES

4.1 Standing to Pursue Charter Claims

Section 24(1) of the Charter provides that an individual whose Charter rights have been infringed has automatic standing to challenge that violation before the Canadian courts in order to obtain an 'appropriate and just' remedy.[61] The Supreme Court has also established criteria for granting public interest standing in constitutional cases, pursuant to Section 52 of the Constitution Act, 1982. In particular, individuals or groups seeking public interest standing to challenge a Charter rights violation must demonstrate: first, that a serious constitutional issue is being raised; second, that they have a genuine interest in the issue, and; third, that there is no other reasonable or effective way for the matter to come before the courts.[62]

The Supreme Court has also recognised public interest standing of affected individuals to challenge governmental failures to comply with inter-governmental agreements and legislative or administrative obligations engaging socio-economic rights, even where there is no statutory right conferred upon the individual. In the 1986 *Finlay* case,[63] the Supreme Court granted public interest standing to Jim Finlay, a social assistance recipient, to litigate the issue of alleged provincial non-compliance with the adequacy requirements of the Canada Assistance Plan Act, a cost-sharing agreement governing conditions for the

provision of social assistance programs and services.[64] The Supreme Court rejected governments' arguments that inter-governmental agreements of this nature were political in nature and could not, therefore, be challenged by individuals. The Court found that: 'the particular issues of provincial non-compliance raised by the respondent's statement of claim are questions of law and as such clearly justiciable'.[65] The Court granted Finlay standing to bring an action challenging the legality of the federal cost-sharing payments, based on the province of Manitoba's violation of the federal requirement that social assistance payments meet the 'basic requirements' of a person in need.[66]

4.2 Funding for Socio-Economic Rights Litigation

There is no explicit right to publicly funded legal aid under the Charter. The Supreme Court has, however, recognised the right to state-funded legal counsel as a component of section 7, where this is necessary to ensure that a decision affecting an individual's life, liberty and security of the person respects the principles of fundamental justice. In the 1999 *G.(J.)* case,[67] the Supreme Court held that the failure to provide publicly funded legal aid in child protection proceedings infringed a low-income parent's security of the

---

[60] *Conclusions and recommendations of CESCR: Canada*, E/C.12/CAN/CO/5 (2006), para. 11(b).

[61] See generally: K. Roach, *Constitutional Remedies in Canada* (Aurora: Canada Law Book, 1994) [looseleaf].

[62] *Canadian Council of Churches v. Canada (Minister of Employment and Immigration)*, [1992] 1 SCR 236. See generally R. J. Sharpe and K. Roach, *The Charter of Rights and Freedoms*, 3rd edition (Toronto: Irwin Law, 2005), pp. 186–189.

[63] *Finlay v. Canada (Minister of Finance)*, [1986] 2 SCR 607; for a discussion on the case, see M. Young, 'Starving in the Shadow of the Law: A Comment on *Finlay v. Canada (Minister of Finance)*', *Constitutional Forum*, Vol. 5, No. 2 (1994), pp. 31–37.

[64] *Finlay v. Canada*, ibid.

[65] Ibid. para. 33.

[66] Ibid. paras. 33–6. In its subsequent decision on the merits of the case, the Supreme Court found that the provinces were obliged to ensure 'reasonable compliance' with the adequacy requirements of the Canada Assistance Plan, but that a 5 percent reduction of benefits to recover overpayments was within the provinces' margin of discretion; see *Finlay v. Canada (Minister of Finance)*, [1993] 1 S.C.R. 1080. This important basis for challenging inadequate social assistance rates disappeared in 1996, however, when the federal government revoked the Canada Assistance Plan Act; see S. Day and G. Brodsky, *Women and the Equality Deficit: The Impact of Restructuring Canada's Social Programs* (Ottawa: Status of Women Canada, 1998); L. Lamarche and C. Girard, 'Évolution de la sécurité sociale au Canada: la mise à l'écart progressive de l'état providence canadien', *Journal of Law and Social Policy*, Vol. 13 (1998), pp. 95–124; B. Porter, 'Using Human Rights Treaty Monitoring Bodies in Domestic Social And Economic Rights Advocacy: Notes from Canada', *Economic and Social Rights Review*, Vol. 2 (1999), available at: <www.communitylawcentre.org.za/ser/esr1999/1999jul_seradvocacy.php>.

[67] *New Brunswick (Minister of Health and Community Service) v. G.(J.)*, [1999] 3 SCR 46.

person under section 7. Jeanine Godin had been threatened with loss of custody of her children based on evidence of her parental fitness contained in fifteen affidavits presented by three lawyers acting for the government, over the course of a three-day hearing. Chief Justice Lamer concluded that 'without the benefit of counsel, the appellant would not have been able to participate effectively at the hearing ... thereby threatening to violate both the appellant's and her children's section 7 right to security of the person'.[68]

While limited civil legal aid is available in all provinces/territories and is supplemented by funding for community legal clinics in some areas, many low-income claimants, especially women, are unable to secure funding for legal challenges relating to the enjoyment of their socio-economic rights.[69] The inadequacy of available legal aid funding has been identified as a concern by the Committee on Economic, Social and Cultural Rights and by the Committee on the Elimination of Discrimination Against Women and is currently being challenged by the Canadian Bar Association as a violation of sections 7 and 15 of the Charter.[70]

In its 2003 *Okanagan Indian Band* decision,[71] the Supreme Court recognised the special considerations that come into play in public interest litigation. In that case, dealing with an Aboriginal rights claim to log on Crown land, the Bands involved argued that in view of the importance of the issues raised and their lack of financial resources to fund a trial, the Court should order the provincial government to pay the Bands' legal fees and disbursements in advance, whether or not they were ultimately successful in their claim. The Supreme Court concluded that a grant of interim costs could be justified in public interest cases if the following criteria were met: first, that the party seeking such an award genuinely could not afford to pay for the litigation and no other realistic option existed for bringing the issues to trial; second, that the claim to be adjudicated was *prima facie* meritorious, and; third, that the issues raised in the case transcended the individual interests of the particular litigants, were of public importance and had not been resolved in previous cases.[72]

Aside from the possibility of legal aid funding on a case-by-case basis, or of a request for advance costs pursuant to the *Okanagan Indian Band* decision, funding for socio-economic rights claims may also be available from the Court Challenges Program of Canada ('CCPC').[73] Funded by the federal government but administered independently of it, the CCPC provides test cases litigation funding in Charter minority language rights cases and in section 15 equality cases involving the federal government or matters of federal jurisdiction. The CESCR has recognised the CCPC as an important positive measure and has recommended its extension to include challenges by equality seeking groups to provincial laws and policies.[74]

---

[68] Ibid. para. 81. For comments on the significance of the case in relation to socio-economic rights, see L'Heureux-Dubé, 'A Canadian Perspective on Economic and Social Rights' (n. 24 above), pp. 44–5; L. Addario, *Getting a Foot in the Door: Women, Civil Legal Aid and Access to Justice* (Ottawa: Status of Women Canada, 1998); H. Lessard, 'The Empire of the Lone Mother: Parental Rights, Child Welfare Law, and State Restructuring', *Osgoode Hall Law Journal*, Vol. 39 (2001) pp. 717–771.

[69] See L. Addario, *Getting a Foot in the Door: Women, Civil Legal Aid and Access to Justice* (Ottawa: Status of Women Canada, 1998); M. Buckley, *The Legal Aid Crisis: Time for Action* (Ottawa: Canadian Bar Association, 2000).

[70] *Conclusions and recommendations of CESCR: Canada*, 2006 (n. 60 above), para. 11(b); Committee on the Elimination of Discrimination Against Women, Concluding Observations on Canada, U.N. Doc. A/58/38 (2003), paras. 355–56; Canadian Bar Association, 'CBA Launches Test Case to Challenge Constitutional Right to Civil Legal Aid' Vancouver (2005), available at: <www.cba.org/CBA/News/2005_Releases/2005–06–20_legalaid.aspx>.   See also discussion of this legal challenge in Chapter 3 of this volume.

[71] *British Columbia (Minister of Forests) v. Okanagan Indian Band*, [2003] 3 SCR 371.

[72] Ibid. paras. 40–1; see C. Tollefson, D. Gilliland and J. DeMarco, 'Towards a Costs Jurisprudence in Public Interest Litigation', *Canadian Bar Review*, Vol. 83 (2004), pp. 473–514. In a more recent case, however, the Supreme Court declined to award costs, distinguishing the *Okanagon* case as being 'out of the ordinary' in that a failure to award costs in that case would have 'the effect of leaving constitutional rights unenforceable and public interest issues unresolved'. *Little Sisters Book and Art Emporium v. Canada (Commissioner of Customs and Revenue)*, 2007 SCC 2.

[73] A. Peltz and B. Gibbons, *Deep Discount Justice: The Challenge of Going to Court with a Charter Claim and No Money* (Winnipeg, Manitoba: The Court Challenges Program of Canada, 1999), available at: <www.ccppcj.ca/documents/justice-e.html>.

[74] *Conclusions and recommendations of CESCR: Canada*, (1993), (n. 44 above), paras. 6, 28; CESCR, *Conclusions and recommendations of CESCR: Canada*, (1998), (n. 59 above), paras. 8, 59; CESCR, *Conclusions and recommendations of CESCR: Canada*, (2006), (n. 60 above), para. 13. Sadly, the minority Conservative Government of Prime Minister Stephen Harper announced on September 25, 2000 that all funding for the Court Challenges Program

5. JUSTIFIABLE LIMITS AND THE BALANCING OF RIGHTS

5.1 Justifiable Limits on Socio-economic Rights

Section 1 of the Charter allows governments to argue that violations of Charter rights are 'reasonable' and 'demonstrably justified in a free and democratic society'. In its 1986 decision in the *Oakes* case,[75] the Supreme Court established a set of criteria for determining whether a rights infringement is justified under section 1. First, governments must show that the objectives they are pursuing are sufficiently important to warrant the violation of an individual Charter right. Second, they must show that the means they have adopted to achieve those objectives are proportional, that is: that they are rationally connected to their objectives; that they violate individual rights as little as possible, and; that the benefits to society resulting from the Charter violation outweigh the harm to individual Charter rights.[76]

While the Supreme Court has exercised considerable deference with respect to governments' assessment of socio-economic priorities, it has also held that the financial burden on governments of respecting Charter rights does not justify a rights violation under section 1.[77] However, in cases involving positive dimensions of socio-economic rights, the Court's approach to justification based on available resources has been refined. In the *Eldridge* case, for example, the provincial government argued that the cost of providing medical interpretation services to the deaf, and potentially to non-English-speaking patients, would divert resources from other healthcare needs and would interfere with governments' ability to choose among competing priorities in the healthcare system. The Supreme Court considered the cost of interpreter services in relation to the overall provincial healthcare budget, and concluded that the government's refusal to fund such services was not reasonable, even if some defer-

ence was granted to government decision-making in this area:

> In the present case, the government has manifestly failed to demonstrate that it had a reasonable basis for concluding that a total denial of medical interpretation services for the deaf constituted a minimum impairment of their rights. As previously noted, the estimated cost of providing sign language interpretation for the whole of British Columbia was only $150,000, or approximately 0.0025 percent of the provincial health care budget at the time.[78]

In the more recent *NAPE* case,[79] the Supreme Court considered the constitutionality of a provincial government's decision to erase a $14 million retroactive pay equity award owed to women public sector employees. This action was taken in conjunction with broad-ranging government expenditure cuts in response to a ballooning provincial deficit. The Court concluded that, in exceptional circumstances, a fiscal crisis may warrant overriding a Charter right, in this case, the right to compensation for unequal pay for work of equal value. As the Court explained:

> At some point, a financial crisis can attain a dimension that elected governments must be accorded significant scope to take remedial measures, even if the measures taken have an adverse effect on a *Charter* right, subject, of course, to the measures being proportional both to the fiscal crisis and to their impact on the affected *Charter* interests. In this case, the fiscal crisis was severe and the cost of putting into effect pay equity according to the original timetable was a large expenditure ($24 million) relative even to the size of the fiscal crisis.[80]

Following the *NAPE* decision, the financial burden on government of responding to a socio-economic rights claim has become an explicitly relevant factor in determining whether a rights violation will be considered justified by the courts under section 1 of the Charter. The standard of reasonableness applied in the *Eldridge* case is, however, more

---

will be eliminated. A major campaign has been launched for a reversal of this decision.

[75] *R. v. Oakes*, [1986] 1 SCR 103.

[76] See generally Sharpe and Roach, *The Charter of Rights and Freedoms* (n. 62 above), pp. 62–85.

[77] *Schachter v. Canada* (n. 30 above), p. 709; *Egan v. Canada*, [1995] 2 SCR 513 at para. 99; *Nova Scotia (Workers' Compensation Board) v. Martin* (n. 50 above), para. 109.

[78] *Eldridge v. British Columbia (Attorney General)* (n. 35 above), para. 87.

[79] *Newfoundland (Treasury Board) v. NAPE*, [2004] 3 SCR 381.

[80] Ibid. para. 64.

consistent with the requirement under Article 2 of the ICESCR that a government take 'steps ... to the maximum of its available resources' to realize socio-economic rights.

5.2   Section 1 as a Guarantee of Socio-economic Rights

The Supreme Court has affirmed that section 1 plays a dual role, both as a limit to rights and a guarantee of rights. The Court has also suggested that the section 1 analysis must be guided by the values underlying the Charter, which it has identified as including social justice and enhanced participation in society.[81] As Justice Arbour observed: 'We sometimes lose sight of the primary function of s. 1 – to constitutionally guarantee rights – focussed as we are on the section's limiting function'.[82]

In interpreting and applying section 1, the Supreme Court has underscored governments' obligations to protect the rights of vulnerable groups and international human rights law generally and the ICESCR in particular, in determining whether Charter rights – particularly those of more advantaged interests – may be limited in order to protect socio-economic rights. In the *Irwin Toy* case,[83] for example, restrictions on advertising aimed at children under the age of 13 were found to be a justifiable infringement of toy manufacturers' Section 2(b) rights to freedom of expression, because such restrictions were consistent with the important Charter value of protecting vulnerable groups such as children. While evidence in the case suggested that other less restrictive means were available to the government, the Court affirmed that 'This Court will not, in the name of minimal impairment [of a Charter right] ... require legislatures to choose the least ambitious means to protect vulnerable groups'.[84]

In its 1989 decision in *Slaight Communications*,[85] the Court found that an adjudicator's order requiring an employer to provide a positive letter of reference to a wrongfully dismissed employee was a justifiable infringement of the employer's right to freedom of expression because it was consistent with Canada's commitments under the ICESCR to protect the employee's right to work. Chief Justice Dickson held in this regard:

> Especially in light of Canada's ratification of the *International Covenant on Economic, Social and Cultural Rights* ... and commitment therein to protect, *inter alia*, the right to work in its various dimensions found in Article 6 of that treaty, it cannot be doubted that the objective in this case is a very important one. ... Given the dual function of s. 1 identified in *Oakes*, Canada's international human rights obligations should inform not only the interpretation of the content of the rights guaranteed by the *Charter* but also the interpretation of what can constitute pressing and substantial s. 1 objectives which may justify restrictions upon those rights.[86]

The result of the section 1 balancing in *Slaight Communications* was that the adjudicator's duty to recognise the vulnerability of workers in relation to employers, and to protect the right to work as recognised in the ICESCR, took precedence over the employer's explicitly protected right to freedom of expression under section 2(b) of the Charter.

6. POSITIVE AND NEGATIVE DUTIES IN RELATION TO SOCIO-ECONOMIC RIGHTS

The Supreme Court has affirmed that the Charter places duties on governments that may be categorised as both positive and negative. The Court has recognised, for example, that the democratic rights contained in section 3 of the Charter include positive duties: federal and provincial governments must hold regular elections to allow

---

[81] *R. v. Big M Drug Mart Ltd.*, [1985] 1 SCR 295, at p. 344; *Reference re Secession of Quebec*, [1998] 2 SCR 217, at para. 64; *R. v. Oakes* (n. 75 above), p. 136; *Irwin Toy Ltd. v. Quebec (Attorney General)*, (n. 25 above), pp. 1003–4; *Vriend v. Alberta* (n. 33 above), para. 64; *Eldridge v. British Columbia (Attorney General)* (n. 35 above), para. 73.

[82] *Gosselin v. Quebec (Attorney General)* (n. 28 above), paras. 350–4.

[83] *Irwin Toy Ltd v. Quebec (Attorney General)* (n. 25 above).

[84] Ibid. p. 993. See however *RJR-Macdonald Inc. v. Canada*, [1994] 1 SCR 311, where the Supreme Court granted a

tobacco manufacturer's section 2(b) challenge to federal tobacco advertising and marketing restrictions, notwithstanding evidence of tobacco related harm to health, and the particular vulnerability of children and youth to tobacco advertising.

[85] *Slaight Communications Inc. v. Davidson* (n. 47 above).

[86] Ibid. pp. 1056–7.

citizens to select their representatives and the failure to hold such elections would violate the Charter.[87] The potential scope of Charter duties to enhance participatory decision-making in the sphere of socio-economic rights remain largely unexplored by the courts, but this is clearly an area in which positive duties to protect democratic and other rights may equally apply.[88]

The 'fundamental freedoms' set out in section 2 of the Charter, such as freedom of expression and freedom of association, have generally been interpreted by the Court as imposing negative duties to refrain from state interference with individual rights,[89] but the Court has recognised the need to 'nuance' the distinction between positive and negative duties in this context also.[90] In the *Dunmore* case, described above, the Court imposed a duty on the government to protect agricultural workers from interference with their right to freedom of association.[91] The Court has also found that, in some circumstances, positive action may be required to protect the section 2(b) right to freedom of expression of disadvantaged groups.[92]

The right to equality, in particular, has been described as a 'hybrid' right, since it is neither purely positive nor purely negative. The Court has held that: 'In some contexts it will be proper to characterize s. 15 as providing positive rights'.[93] Section 15 not only requires governments to refrain from discriminating against protected groups, but may also require governments to adopt positive measures to ensure equality, as was found in the *Eldridge* case, or positive measures of protection from discrimination by others, as was found in *Vriend*.[94]

Similarly, section 7 of the Charter has both positive and negative dimensions. Section 7 imposes negative duties on governments to refrain from interfering with individual physical or psychological security or integrity. An illustration of this aspect of section 7 in the socio-economic rights context is found in the 1988 *Morgentaler* case,[95] dealing with women's access to reproductive health services. A provision of the federal Criminal Code requiring that abortions performed in hospitals be approved by 'Therapeutic Abortion Committees' was found by the Supreme Court to be an unlawful state interference with psychological and bodily integrity, that violated pregnant women's rights to 'life, liberty and security of the person' in a manner that was not in accordance with section 7 principles of fundamental justice or justifiable under section 1 of the Charter.[96]

An example of a positive duty associated with section 7 is the requirement that publicly funded legal aid be provided in child custody cases or other cases in which section 7 rights are at issue, as was found in the *G(J)* case described above.[97] As noted earlier, in both the *Irwin Toy* and the *Gosselin* cases, the Supreme Court left open the possibility that the State may also have a positive obligation to provide financial assistance or other measures necessary to ensure access to adequate food, housing and other necessities, in order to comply with the right to security of the person under section 7.[98]

The Supreme Court has pointed out that the distinction between government action and inaction, and between positive and negative rights or duties, is 'problematic'.[99] It has also recognised that as a

---

[87] *Haig v. Canada (Chief Electoral Officer)*, [1993] 2 SCR 995.

[88] See M. Jackman, 'The Right to Participate in Health Care and Health Resource Allocation Decisions Under Section 7 of the Canadian Charter', *Health Law Review*, Vol. 4 (1995/1996), pp. 3–11.

[89] See K. Roach and D. Schneiderman, 'Freedom of Expression in Canada' in G. A. Beaudoin and E. Mendes (eds.), *The Canadian Charter of Rights and Freedoms*, 4th edition (Markham: LexisNexis Butterworths, 2005), pp. 259–323.

[90] *Dunmore v. Ontario (Attorney General)* (n. 42 above), para. 20.

[91] For a discussion of the implications of the *Dunmore* case and freedom of association, see P. Barnacle, 'Dunmore meets Wilson and Palmer: interpretation of freedom of association in Canada and Europe', *Canadian Labour & Employment Law Journal*, Vol. 11, No. 2 (2004), pp. 205–236.

[92] *Haig v. Canada* (n. 87 above), p. 103. See however *Native Women's Association of Canada v. Canada*, [1994] 3 SCR 627.

[93] *Schachter v. Canada* (n. 30 above), p. 721.

[94] *Eldridge v. British Columbia (Attorney General)* (n. 35 above); *Vriend v. Alberta* (n. 33 above).

[95] *R. v. Morgentaler*, [1988] 1 SCR 30.

[96] See S. Rogers, 'Abortion Denied: Bearing the Limits of Law' in C. M. Flood (ed.), *Just Medicare: What's In, What's Out, How We Decide* (Toronto: University of Toronto Press, 2006), pp. 107–136, at 109–11; M. Jackman, 'Section 7 of the Charter and Health Care Spending' in G. P. Machildon, T. McIntosh and P.-G. Forest (eds.), *The Fiscal Sustainability of Health Care in Canada* (Toronto: University of Toronto Press, 2004), pp. 110–136, at 111–114.

[97] *New Brunswick (Minister of Health and Community Service) v. G.(J.)* (n. 67 above).

[98] *Irwin Toy Ltd. v. Quebec (Attorney General)* (n. 25 above); *Gosselin v. Quebec (Attorney General)* (n. 28 above).

[99] *Vriend v. Alberta* (n. 33 above), para. 53.

general pattern, '[v]ulnerable groups will claim the need for protection by the government whereas other groups and individuals will assert that the government should not intrude'.[100] The Court held in *Vriend* that the distinction between governmental action and failure to act is not a valid basis on which to determine whether or to what extent the Charter applies.[101] Rather, the Court held that since the Charter applies to all matters within the authority of the legislature, it will be engaged even if the legislature refuses to exercise its authority.[102]

At the same time, however, as discussed earlier, the Court has been unwilling to clearly affirm that the Charter imposes a positive obligation on governments to adopt measures necessary to address the needs of disadvantaged groups. Thus, in his dissenting judgment on the appropriate remedy in the *Vriend* case, Justice Major made the astonishing suggestion that the legislature should be given the option of complying with section 15 equality rights in the Charter by revoking its human rights legislation altogether, thereby remedying the discriminatory 'under-inclusion'.[103] The majority of the Court, though opting for a remedy of 'reading in' the additional ground, did not seem to rule out the possibility of this kind of draconian legislative response, insisting that it was not required to decide in that case whether governments have any obligation to provide legislative protection from discrimination.[104]

In recent section 7 and section 15 jurisprudence, there are worrying indications that this 'timidity' on the part of the Supreme Court with respect to socio-economic rights is developing into a stronger inclination to avoid imposing positive constitutional requirements on governments that correspond to the obligations to protect and to fulfill rights under the ICESCR and other international human rights treaties. In its 2005 decision in the *Auton* case, involving a section 15 challenge to a provincial government's failure to fund intensive behavioural treatment for autistic children, Chief Justice McLachlin, writing for the Court, stated that: 'this Court has repeatedly held

that the legislature is under no obligation to create a particular benefit. It is free to target the social programs it wishes to fund as a matter of public policy, provided the benefit itself is not conferred in a discriminatory manner'.[105] Similarly, in the 2005 *Chaoulli*[106] decision, involving a section 7 challenge to provincial government restrictions on private healthcare funding designed to protect the universal medicare system, the Chief Justice asserted that: 'The *Charter* does not confer a freestanding constitutional right to health care. However, where the government puts in place a scheme to provide health care, that scheme must comply with the *Charter*'.[107]

Clearly this 'truncated' notion of positive obligations under sections 7 and 15 is at odds with the 'interpretive presumption' that the Charter provides rights protections at least equivalent to those under international human rights law that is binding on Canada. Further, it results in a discriminatory approach to socio-economic rights in which the right to healthcare of those who have unique needs, such as autistic children, or of those who cannot afford or are ineligible for private healthcare insurance, are denied Charter protection, while those whose health rights can be vindicated by challenges to governmental 'interference' will be actively protected through judicial intervention. In this sense, the timidity to which the High Commissioner refers is now threatening to undermine the Court's commitment to substantive equality and has prompted widespread expressions of concern among many legal commentators in Canada.[108]

---

[100] *Irwin Toy v. Quebec (Attorney General)* (n. 25 above), pp. 993–4.

[101] *Vriend v. Alberta* (n. 33 above), para. 53.

[102] Ibid. para. 6.

[103] Ibid. paras. 196–197.

[104] Ibid. paras. 62–64. See Porter, 'Reclaiming Expectations' (n. 16 above), pp. 180–5.

[105] In support of this statement, the Chief Justice cites *Granovsky v. Canada (Minister of Employment and Immigration)*, [2000] 1 SCR 703, at para. 61; *Nova Scotia (Attorney General) v. Walsh*, [2002] 4 SCR 325, at para. 55; *Hodge v. Canada (Minister of Human Resources Development)*, [2004] 3 SCR 357, at para. 16.

[106] *Chaoulli v. Quebec (Attorney General)*, [2005] 1 SCR 791.

[107] Ibid. para. 104. For a discussion of the case see M.-C. Prémont, 'L'affaire Chaoulli et le système de santé au Québec: Cherchez l'erreur, cherchez la raison', *McGill Law Journal*, Vol. 51 (2006), pp. 167–196; M. Jackman, '"The Last Line of Defence for [Which?] Citizens": Accountability, Equality and the Right to Health in *Chaoulli*', *Osgoode Hall Law Journal*, Vol. 44 (2006), pp. 350–375; C. Flood, K. Roach and L. Sossin (eds.), *Access to Care, Access to Justice: The Legal Debate over Private Health Insurance in Canada* (Toronto: University of Toronto Press, 2005).

[108] See, for example, B. Ryder, C. Faria and E. Lawrence, 'What's *Law* Good For? An Empirical Overview of *Charter* Equality Rights Decisions', *Supreme Court Law Review*, Vol. 24 (2004), pp. 103–126; Faraday, *Making Equality*

7. PRINCIPLE AREAS OF SOCIO-ECONOMIC RIGHTS LITIGATION

7.1 Housing Rights

The 1990 *Alcohol Foundation* case[109] was an early application of Charter equality rights in the context of access to housing. A by-law of the city of Winnipeg, imposing restrictions on the establishment of group homes for persons with drug or alcohol addictions in residential neighbourhoods, was found to discriminate on the basis of disability and was struck down as violating section 15. In rendering its decision, however, the Court of Appeal noted that it might have been willing to uphold the by-law if the municipal government had introduced any evidence at all to justify it under section 1 of the Charter.

In the 1993 *Sparks* case,[110] Irma Sparks, a Black single mother of two children challenged the exclusion of public housing tenants from security of tenure provisions as a violation of equality rights, after being issued an eviction order with no reasons given and one (rather than three) months' notice to vacate. The Nova Scotia Court of Appeal found that public housing residents were disproportionately single mothers, Black and poor, and that their exclusion from provincial residential tenancies legislation constituted adverse effect discrimination on the grounds of race, sex, marital status and poverty. Significantly, the Court found that poverty was a personal characteristic analogous to those enumerated under section 15 of the Charter.[111]

7.2 Health Rights

In the *Eldridge* case, as discussed above, a non-profit provider of interpreter services informed the provincial government that it could no longer afford to offer such services without public funding.[112] At a meeting of health ministry officials, it was decided not to provide funding, in part because of concerns that this might lead to similar request from other groups. As a result, the two claimants, both of whom were born deaf, were unable to communicate effectively with their healthcare providers.[113] In arguing that the failure to fund interpretation services did not amount to adverse effects discrimination under the Charter, the province insisted that section 15 does not oblige governments to address the needs of disadvantaged groups where the disadvantage exists independently of state action. A unanimous Court responded to this argument as follows:

> [T]he respondents and their supporting interveners...assert...that governments should be entitled to provide benefits to the general population without ensuring that disadvantaged members of society have the resources to take full advantage of those benefits...In my view, this position bespeaks a thin and impoverished vision of s. 15(1). It is belied, more importantly, by the thrust of this Court's equality jurisprudence.[114]

In considering whether the failure to fund interpretation services was justified in light of competing priorities within the healthcare system, the Court considered not only the fact that the cost would be minimal relative to the overall provincial healthcare budget, but also the nature of the disadvantage experienced by the group and the fact

Rights Real (n. 31 above); S. McIntyre and S. Rogers (eds.), *Diminishing Returns: Inequality and the Canadian Charter of Rights and Freedoms*, (Markham: LexisNexis Butterworths, 2006); Flood, *Access to Care*, ibid. Some critics have claimed, however, that this jurisprudence simply validates initial critiques of the potential of *Charter* review as a mechanism for progressive social change; see, for example, A. Hutchinson, 'Condition Critical: The Constitution and Health Care', in Flood, *Access to Care*, ibid. pp. 101–15; A. Petter, 'Wealthcare: The Politics of the *Charter* Revisited', in Flood, Access to Care, ibid. pp. 116–38; J. Bakan, *Just Words: Constitutional Rights and Social Wrongs* (Toronto: University of Toronto Press, 1997).

[109] *Alcohol Foundation of Manitoba et al. v. Winnipeg (City)*, (1990) 6 W.W.R 232 (Man. CA).

[110] *Sparks v. Dartmouth/Halifax County Regional Housing Authority* (1993) 119 NSR (2d) 91 (NS CA).

[111] See M. Jackman, 'Constitutional Contact with the Disparities in the World: Poverty as a Prohibited Ground of

Discrimination Under the Canadian *Charter* and Human Rights Law', *Review of Constitutional Studies*, Vol. 2 (1994), pp. 76–122; L. Iding, 'In a Poor State: The Long Road to Human Rights Protection on the Basis of Social Condition', *Alberta Law Review*, Vol. 41 (2003), pp. 513–525.

[112] *Eldridge v. British Columbia (Attorney General)* (n. 35 above), paras. 3–4.

[113] In particular, one of the applicants, Linda Warren, had delivered twins prematurely by emergency ceasarean section without any hospital staff being able to communicate with her about the procedure or her newborns' survival or state of health.

[114] Ibid. para. 72–3.

that the government had made no effort to provide any interpreter services at all.[115]

As discussed in section 6 above, the claimants in the *Chaoulli* case[116] challenged the ban, under Quebec health and hospital insurance legislation, on private health insurance and funding. The claimants argued that the ban violated their rights to life, liberty and security under section 7, because it effectively rendered the provision of private health services uneconomical and thereby forced them to wait for services within an over-burdened public system. A four-judge majority of the Supreme Court agreed with the claimants that, in view of lengthy waiting times for treatment within the public system, the prohibition on private insurance violated rights to life and to security of the person.[117] The majority pointed to the absence of similar restrictions on private funding in other countries with public healthcare systems as proof that the ban was arbitrary and thus not in accordance with section 7 principles of fundamental justice. In rejecting the claimants' Charter arguments, the three dissenting justices referred to evidence accepted at trial that the ban on private insurance was necessary to protect the publicly funded system, upon which every-one relies. In concluding that the limits on pri-vate care were rational and justified under sec-tions 7 and 1 of the Charter, Justice Binnie warned that 'the *Canadian Charter* should not become an instrument to be used by the wealthy to "roll back" the benefits of a legislative scheme that helps the poorer members of society'.[118] The majority's decision in the *Chaoulli* case has been widely criticised by legal and health policy commen-tators.

7.3   Right to an Adequate Standard of Living and Social Security

In the 2002 *Falkiner* case,[119] the Ontario Court of Appeal struck down the province's 'spouse in the house' rule as discriminatory against single mothers and social assistance recipients. The rule treated single mothers living with a man as if they were spouses for the purposes of eligibility for social assistance. This had the effect of either reducing their benefits or disentitling them from assistance altogether, based on the income of the man with whom they were residing. The Court found that the policy denied single mothers on social assistance the ability to cohabit with men in the early stages of a relationship without becom-ing financially dependent. Having found discrimi-nation under section 15, the Court did not address the question of whether the rule also violated sec-tion 7 of the Charter.

In the *Gosselin* case,[120] described above, Louise Gosselin challenged a Quebec social assistance regulation that reduced by two-thirds the amount paid to single employable persons under the age of thirty not enrolled in a workfare program. In a split-decision, the Supreme Court found no dis-crimination under section 15. A majority of five judges concluded that the government had not treated those under the age of thirty as less worthy than older welfare recipients by making increased payments conditional on participation in workfare programs – programs that the majority concluded were designed specifically to integrate young wel-fare recipients into the workforce and to promote self-sufficiency. The four dissenting justices found, on the evidence, that it was highly improbable that young welfare recipients could actually be enrolled in workfare programs at all times in order to qualify for the higher rate of assistance. They also found that reducing the rate for young recip-ients to one-third the amount deemed necessary to meet basic living requirements clearly violated claimants' section 15 dignity interest. Seven of nine judges found no violation of the right to secu-rity of the person under section 7 of the Char-ter, but left open the possibility that a denial of

[115] Ibid. para. 93; see generally D. Greschner, 'How Will the Charter of Rights and Freedoms and Evolving Jurispru-dence Affect Health Care Costs?', in T. McIntosh et al. (eds.), *The Governance of Health Care in Canada* (Toronto: University of Toronto Press, 2004), pp. 83–124.

[116] *Chaoulli v. Quebec (Attorney General)* (n. 106 above).

[117] In her ruling for the four judge majority in the case, Justice Deschamps held that the prohibition on private insur-ance violated the right to 'life', 'personal security' and 'inviolability' under section 1 of the Quebec Charter of Human Rights and Freedoms. The Court split 3–3 on the issue of whether the ban also violated section 7 of the Canadian Charter.

[118] Ibid. para. 94.

[119] *Falkiner v. Ontario (Ministry of Community and Social Services)*, (2002) 212 DLR (4th) 633 (Ont CA).

[120] *Gosselin v. Quebec (Attorney General)* (n. 28 above).

adequate financial assistance might violate section 7 rights in some other circumstances. The majority's unwillingness to find a Charter violation on the facts of the case has been harshly criticised within and outside the anti-poverty community in Canada.[121]

7.4 Right to Work

In three early Supreme Court decisions dealing with the right to strike known as the 'labour trilogy', a majority of the Court found that the right to strike is not protected by the Charter's section 2(d) guarantee of 'freedom of association'.[122] Subsequent decisions extended these findings to deny section 2(d) protection for the right to bargain collectively and to benefit from a particular labour relations regime.[123] This jurisprudence has placed serious limits on Canadian workers' ability to claim rights protected in Article 6 of the ICESCR by way of Charter review.[124]

The Supreme Court's 2001 decision in *Dunmore*,[125] described above, suggests a somewhat more positive outlook for Charter-based labour rights claims.[126] In that case, agricultural workers in Ontario, a clearly disadvantaged group, challenged the repeal of legislation enacted by a previous government designed to bring agricultural workers into the province's labour relations regime. The workers in *Dunmore* argued that the legislative repeal infringed their right to associate under section 2(d) of the Charter and their equality rights under section 15. The Court found a violation of the right to freedom of association in the case, but did not deal with the section 15 claim. In a significant judgment in relation to the notion of 'retrogressive measures' discussed by the CESCR in its General Comment No. 3, the Court found the repeal of the previous legislation unconstitutional to the extent that it denied agricultural workers the benefits of collective bargaining laws. The Court suspended the declaration of invalidity for 18 months to give the government an opportunity to enact new legislation that would minimally protect the rights of agricultural workers to form associations. The legislation subsequently adopted by the province did not, however, restore full collective bargaining rights for agricultural workers, and has since been challenged.[127]

In the 2004 *NAPE* case,[128] described in Part 5.1 above, a public employees' union challenged a provincial decision to rescind a pay equity award pursuant to a pay equity regime and a collective bargaining agreement. While the Supreme Court declined to rule on the question of whether a regime to ensure compensation for denial of equal pay for work of equal value was itself required by section 15, it did find that insofar as such a regime had been created and the new pay equity rights had been implemented and incorporated into a collective agreement, the repeal of the award was discriminatory against women workers. However, the Court concluded that the province's fiscal crisis justified the measure under section 1 of the Charter. Since the *NAPE* decision, the economic situation in Newfoundland has improved and women have successfully lobbied for payment of the award.[129]

---

121 See for example G. Brodsky, '*Gosselin v. Quebec (Attorney General)*: Autonomy with a Vengeance', *Canadian Journal of Women and the Law*, Vol. 15 (2003), pp. 194–214; J. Keene, 'The Supreme Court, the Law Decision, and Social Programs: The Substantive Equality Deficit' in Faraday, *Making Equality Rights Real* (n. 31 above), pp. 345–370; M. Jackman, 'Sommes nous dignes? L'égalité et l'arrêt *Gosselin*', *Canadian Journal of Women and the Law*, Vol. 17 (2005), pp. 161–76.

122 Reference re Public Service Employee Relations Act (Alta.), [1987] 1 SCR 313; *PSAC v. Canada*, [1987] 1 SCR 424; *RWDSU v. Saskatchewan*, [1987] 1 SCR 460.

123 *Professional Institute of the Public Service of Canada v. Northwest Territories (Commissioner)*, [1990] 2 SCR 367; *Delisle v. Canada (Deputy Attorney General)*, [1999] 2 SCR 989.

124 See generally: D. Pothier, 'Twenty Years of Labour Law and the Charter' *Osgoode Hall Law Journal*, Vol. 40 (2002) pp. 369–400; J. Fudge, 'Labour is not a Commodity: The Supreme Court of Canada and the Freedom of Association', *Saskatchewan Law Review*, Vol. 67 (2004), pp. 425–452.

125 *Dunmore v. Ontario* (n. 42 above).

126 Barnacle, 'Dunmore Meets Wilson and Palmer' (n. 91 above); J. Fudge, 'Labour Is Not a Commodity: The Supreme Court of Canada and the Freedom of Association', *Saskatchewan Law Review*, Vol. 67, No. 2 (2004) pp. 25–52.

127 *Fraser v. Ontario (Attorney General)*, [2006] OJ. No. 45 (Ont. Sup. Ct.).

128 *Newfoundland (Treasury Board) v. NAPE* (n. 79 above).

129 J. Baker, 'Pay equity cash "addresses a wrong"', *The Telegram (St. John's)*, 24 March 2006, p. A3.

7.5   Right to Education

In dealing with French and English minority language education rights guaranteed under section 23 of the Charter, the Supreme Court recognised in its 1990 decision in *Mahe v. Alberta* that the courts have a mandate to ensure that governments meet positive obligations to allocate resources and to create necessary institutional structures for the realisation of the right.[130] In this context, the Court has been required to address the more difficult remedial issues arising from positive obligations to fulfil socio-economic rights.[131]

These issues were the focus of the Supreme Court's 2003 decision in *Doucet-Broudreau*.[132] In that case, francophone parents in New Brunswick applied for an order that French-language facilities and programs be provided at the secondary school level in five school districts. The trial judge found that the provincial government had failed to prioritise these obligations as required by section 23 of the Charter. He ordered the province to undertake its 'best efforts' to provide school facilities and programs by specific dates and he retained jurisdiction to hear reports on the status of the efforts made over time. A narrow majority of the Supreme Court upheld the trial judge's order, finding that the positive guarantees contained in section 23 and the necessity of timely governmental compliance in the minority language education setting may require courts to order prospective remedies to guarantee that rights are meaningfully and promptly implemented.

In the 1997 *Eaton* case,[133] the Supreme Court considered the application of section 15 to the rights of children with disabilities and the accommodation of their needs by the public education system. The case involved a 12-year-old student with cerebral palsy, who was unable to communicate through speech, sign language or other alternative means. The girl's parents claimed that the decision to place their daughter in a segregated special education setting, rather than integrating her into the regular school system, was a viola-

tion of her right to equality under section 15. The Court found that a presumption in favour of integrated schooling would work to the disadvantage of pupils who require special education in order to achieve equality, and that the best interests of the child should be assessed by a court without the burden of a presumption in favour of integration.[134] While the *Eaton* decision was controversial within the disability community, the Court's emphasis on positive obligations to address real educational needs, instead of only on discriminatory stereotypes, has been seen as a positive move toward informing equality rights analysis with an understanding of the 'social construction of disability'. This approach is consistent with the recognition of the section 15 equality guarantee as a positive social right to have unique needs met in the most effective way.[135]

8. REMEDIES

Section 24(1) of the Charter provides that courts can grant whatever remedy is 'appropriate and just in the circumstances' for a violation of a Charter right. Section 52(1) of the Constitution Act, 1982 states that laws are of no force and effect to the extent of their inconsistency with the Constitution. There is thus a wide range of remedies available for violations of Charter rights, and Canadian courts have made use of this remedial flexibility in dealing with socio-economic rights claims.

Upon finding a Charter violation, Canadian courts may issue an immediate declaration of invalidity or they may suspend the declaration for a set period of time to provide governments with an opportunity to determine the best remedy or to

---

130 *Mahe v. Alberta* (n. 5 above) at p. 389.
131 See M. Power and P. Foucher, 'Language Rights in Education' in M. Bastarache (ed.), *Language Rights in Canada*, 2nd edition (Cowansville: Yvon Blais, 2004), pp. 365–452.
132 *Doucet-Boudreau v. Nova Scotia (Minister of Education)*, [2003] 3 SCR 3.
133 *Eaton v. Brant County*, [1997] 1 SCR 241.

134 Ibid., paras. 78–81.
135 Y. Peters, *Twenty Years of Litigating for Disability Equality Rights: Has It Made a Difference? An Assessment by the Council of Canadians with Disabilities* (Winnipeg: Council of Canadians with Disabilities, 2004), available at Council of Canadians with Disabilities, <www.ccdonline.ca/publications/20yrs/20yrs.htm>; F. Sampson, 'Beyond Compassion and Sympathy to Respect and Equality: Gendered Disability and Equality Rights Law', in D. Pothier and R. Devlin (eds.), *Critical Disability Theory: Essays in Philosophy, Policy and Law* (Vancouver: University of British Columbia Press, 2002), pp. 257–284; E. Chadha and T. Sheldon, 'Promoting Equality: Economic and Social Rights for Persons with Disabilities', *National Journal of Constitutional Law*, Vol. 16 (2004), pp. 27–102.

put in place necessary legislation or programs.[136] In rare cases, the courts may issue a constitutional exemption to protect the interests of a party who has succeeded in having a legislative provision declared unconstitutional, where the declaration of invalidity has been suspended.[137] The courts may award damages or order governments to take positive remedial action, and their orders may be enforced against the Crown through contempt of court proceedings.[138] Where appropriate, courts may also issue supervisory orders and maintain ongoing jurisdiction over the implementation of remedies that take time to put in place, where this is deemed appropriate and just.

In assessing the proper role of the judiciary in relation to legislatures, an over-riding principle linked to the rule of law is that rights must have effective remedies. The Supreme Court has emphasised that the exercise of judicial deference vis-à-vis the role of the legislature in exercising socio-economic policy choices should not render Charter rights illusory or immunise certain areas of government authority from Charter review.[139] As Justice Binnie wrote in the *NAPE* case:

> If the "political branches" are to be the "final arbitrator" of compliance with the *Charter* of their "policy initiatives", it would seem the enactment of the *Charter* affords no real protection at all to the rightsholders the *Charter*, according to its text, was intended to benefit. *Charter* rights and freedoms, on this reading, would offer rights without a remedy by denying effective remedies.[140]

The Court has held that where appropriate, deference 'will be taken into account in deciding whether a limit is justified under s. 1 and again in determining the appropriate remedy for a *Charter* breach'.[141]

The application of deference at the remedial stage in socio-economic cases has led to a judicial preference for suspended declarations of invalidity in situations where positive remedial action is required and in which governments have various policy options available to achieve Charter compliance. A leading example of a suspended declaration is found in the *Eldridge* case. While the trial and appellate courts had concluded that section 15 ought not to be invoked to second-guess governments' choices in the allocation of scarce resources among competing healthcare priorities, the Supreme Court insisted that section 15 did apply to a failure to fund interpreter services, and that even if a deferential standard of justification under section 1 were to be adopted, the failure could not be justified.[142] It was at the remedial stage that deference to legislative policy choices was found by the Court to be appropriate. As Justice LaForest explained:

> A declaration, as opposed to some kind of injunctive relief, is the appropriate remedy in this case because there are myriad options available to the government that may rectify the unconstitutionality of the current system. It is not this Court's role to dictate how this is to be accomplished. Although it is to be assumed that the government will move swiftly to correct the unconstitutionality of the present scheme and comply with this Court's directive, it is appropriate to suspend the effectiveness of the declaration for six months to enable the government to explore its options and formulate an appropriate response.[143]

Another factor that may weigh in favour of a suspended declaration of invalidity is the importance of democratic participation and consultation with affected minorities. The Supreme Court has pointed out that the Charter may create a

---

[136] *Schachter v. Canada* (n. 30 above); see K. Roach, 'Remedial Consensus and Dialogue Under the Charter: General Declarations and Delayed Declarations of Invalidity', *University of British Columbia Law Review*, Vol. 35 (2002), pp. 211–70.

[137] Ibid., pp. 715–7; *Rodriguez v. British Columbia (Attorney General)*, [1993] 3 SCR 519 at p. 577.

[138] *Doucet-Boudreau v. Nova Scotia (Minister of Education)* (n. 132 above), para. 136; K. Roach and G. Budlender, 'Mandatory Relief and Supervisory Jurisdiction: When Is It Appropriate, Just and Equitable', *South African Law Journal*, Vol. 122 (2005), pp. 325–351; Roach, *Constitutional Remedies in Canada* (n. 60 above), pp. 13–90.

[139] *Symes v. Canada*, [1993] 4 SCR 695, at p. 753.

[140] *Newfoundland (Treasury Board) v. NAPE* (n. 74 above), para. 111.

[141] *Vriend v. Alberta* (n. 33 above), para. 54; see also D. Wiseman, 'The *Charter* and Poverty' (n. 24 above).

[142] *Eldridge v. British Columbia (Attorney General)* (n. 35 above), para. 85.

[143] Ibid. para. 96.

'dialogue' between courts and legislatures.[144] As the Court stated in its 1999 *Corbière* decision:

> The remedies granted under the *Charter* should, in appropriate cases, encourage and facilitate the inclusion in that dialogue of groups particularly affected by legislation. In determining the appropriate remedy, a court should consider the effect of its order on the democratic process, understood in a broad way, and encourage that process.[145]

In other socio-economic rights cases, however, 'reading in' has been determined to be the most appropriate remedy, insofar as this is most consistent with the nature of the right, the context of the legislation and with the purposes of the Charter. In *Vriend*, for example, the majority of the Court determined that, even in the face of evidence of a clear legislative intent to exclude sexual orientation from Alberta's human rights legislation, reading this ground of discrimination into the statute was preferable to striking the legislation down and potentially leaving other groups without protection. The majority found that the legislative intent in that case was 'inconsistent with democratic principles', making it appropriate to extend the legislative protection of the province's human rights act to gays and lesbians in order to achieve Charter compliance.[146]

In the *Doucet-Boudreau* case, where the trial judge had determined that ongoing supervision of the implementation of complex obligations to provide for French language secondary school education was required, the Supreme Court similarly agreed that a declaration of invalidity was an inadequate remedy.[147] The trial judge had established deadlines for various school districts and set dates for submitting reports to the court on progress made. On appeal, the majority of the Supreme Court found that the supervisory order issued by the trial judge was a 'just and appropriate' remedy in

the circumstances.[148] The Court emphasised that courts must be creative in considering different remedial options in order to ensure that remedies are both responsive to particular needs and contexts, and effective.[149] In the *Doucet-Boudreau* case, the Court found that maintaining supervisory jurisdiction was an appropriate response to concerns about assimilation of minority language communities and ongoing delays in governmental action.[150]

9. CONCLUSION

In light of the historical expectations of rights holders, the Charter's open-ended and expansive wording, its balancing of individual rights and collective values, the important interpretive role the ICESCR can play both in determining the scope of rights and the responsibilities of governments, and the broad range of remedies available for Charter violations, there is no reason why the Canadian courts should not play an active role in safeguarding socio-economic rights in Canada. As yet, however, the courts have largely failed to fulfill the Charter's promise in this regard. As High Commissioner Arbour has pointed out, this may be due to timidity on the part of litigants as well as the courts.[151] Few socio-economic rights cases have been brought before the courts in the first quarter century of constitutional democracy in Canada. And, as the CESCR points out, one cannot absolve Canadian governments from responsibility either. Why, the CESCR has asked, should governments not be encouraging courts to consider Canada's international human rights obligations when interpreting the Charter, rather than arguing against interpretations that would provide effective remedies for these rights?[152]

While there have been some important Charter victories for socio-economic rights claimants, there have also been very disappointing losses. Courts have sidestepped the issue, so central to

---

[144] See generally K. Roach, *The Supreme Court on Trial: Judicial Activism or Democratic Dialogue* (Toronto: Iriwin Law, 2001); for a critique of this approach, see however A. Petter, 'Twenty Years of Charter Justification: From Liberalism to Dubious Dialogue', *University of New Brunswick Law Journal*, Vol. 52 (2003), pp. 187–200.

[145] *Corbière v. Canada (Minister of Indian and Northern Affairs)*, [1999] 2 SCR 203, at para. 116.

[146] *Vriend v. Alberta* (n. 33 above), paras. 175–9.

[147] *Doucet-Boudreau v. Nova Scotia (Minister of Education)* (n. 132 above), paras. 66–87.

[148] Ibid. para. 86.
[149] Ibid. para. 59.
[150] Ibid. paras. 66–70.
[151] Arbour, 'Freedom from Want' (n. 2 above), p. 7.
[152] *Conclusions and recommendations: Canada, 2006* (n. 57 above), para. 11(b); G. Brodsky, 'The Subversion of Human Rights by Governments in Canada', in M. Young et al. (eds.), *Poverty: Rights, Social Citizenship and Legal Activism* (Vancouver: UBC Press, 2007) [forthcoming].

international human rights law in general and to socio-economic rights in particular, of whether governments do indeed have a positive constitutional duty to attend to the needs of those who are without adequate food, housing, healthcare, education or decent work, in a country with such an abundance of resources that all should enjoy these core human rights. As long as the obligation of governments to protect and promote socio-economic rights is considered ancillary to Charter compliance rather than as central to it, socio-economic rights will continue to be marginalised in Canada.

If, however, Canadian rights claimants have suffered from the disadvantage of a lack of any explicit Charter recognition of socio-economic rights, they have also benefited from the ability to frame socio-economic rights claims as fundamental issues of constitutional inclusion. This is Canada's potential contribution to the field of socio-economic rights – to enhance the understanding of these rights as central to all human rights, rather than as a separate category of rights. Given the historical expectations associated with the adoption of the Charter, those who are faced with hunger or homelessness amidst affluence see issues of constitutional interpretation as being linked to underlying issues of equal citizenship and social inclusion. In cases where Canadian courts have suggested that homelessness or poverty do not engage equality rights or the right to security of the person, or that those who can afford to buy it have a right to healthcare while those who rely on publicly funded healthcare do not, the courts have not been seen to be merely deciding the scope of particular words or provisions. Rather, such decisions are considered by rights claimants and by an increasing number of commentators as serious assaults on the very values of dignity and equal citizenship that the Charter embodies.

It is in this sense that the constitutional status of socio-economic rights in Canada is much more than a matter of the scope of particular Charter guarantees. It is, fundamentally, a question of the integrity with which the Charter will be interpreted and applied, and the values that will be conveyed to governments and citizens, as those that are deserving of constitutional status. As High Commissioner Arbour has eloquently summarised it:

> Whatever cause there may have been to question the equal status and justiciability of economic, social and cultural rights 60 years ago, one thing is clear: there is no basis for categorical disclaimers today. ... The legality of judicial review of all human rights is not open to question under the Canadian constitutional system.[153]

[153] Arbour, 'Freedom from Want' (n. 2 above), pp. 7, 9.

12

The United States

A Ragged Patchwork

Cathy Albisa* and Jessica Schultz**

1. INTRODUCTION

The United States government is infamously reticent to recognise economic and social rights on the international stage.[1] Domestically, these rights are not currently recognised by the national constitution, and their enjoyment is primarily determined by legislative fiat. With a few significant exceptions,[2] the concept of economic and social rights has not taken root in the popular imagination, making legislative assaults on social protection possible without any serious political costs.

Given the socio-economic indicators in the United States, which include the highest rate of child poverty among wealthy countries, and severe gaps in access to health care, there is a pressing need to develop stronger jurisprudence in this arena so as to buttress basic levels of protection against perpetual changes in the political winds. This article reviews avenues used by advocates to develop such jurisprudence, as well as emerging and promising long-range strategies. In particular, Section 2 outlines the history of economic and social rights in the United States, Section 3 reviews the federal constitutional framework in relation to these rights, and Section 4 explores work to date at the sub-national level in individual state constitutions.

2. HISTORY OF ECONOMIC AND SOCIAL RIGHTS IN THE UNITED STATES

It is generally agreed that the drafters of the U.S. Constitution were primarily concerned with curbing the abuse of government power. As Richard Posner, a well-known conservative appellate court judge and scholar once said: 'The men who wrote the Bill of Rights were not concerned that the federal government might do too little for the people, but that it might do too much for them'.[3]

* Cathy Albisa is the Executive Director of the National Economic and Social Rights Initiative (NESRI) and a constitutional and human rights lawyer with a background on the right to health. She would like to thank Professors Martha Davis and Rhonda Copelon for comments on different versions of sections in this article, Carol Anderson for her groundbreaking historical work, Daniel Wheelen for his extraordinary historical research as well (from whose work much of the historical section was derived), Maya Wiley for her invaluable insights and analysis on the intersection of race and economic and social issues, Jamie Brooks for her assistance with the right to health section, Maria Foscarini and Patrick Markee with their assistance on the housing section, and Mitra Ebadolahi for her wonderful editing assistance. Finally, she would like to thank Malcolm Langford for his extraordinary patience.

** Jessica Schultz is a researcher at the Chr. Michelsen Institute working on corruption and development issues. The first version of this paper was initially prepared as a project of the Adjudication Working Group of ESCR-Net, a coalition of organisations and activists from around the world dedicated to advancing economic, social and cultural rights. She would like to thank Larry Cox, Bruce Porter, and Chris Jochnick for their valuable comments and support.

[1] During the 2001 Human Rights Commission meeting, for example, U.S. delegates lobbied other government representatives to retract their support for resolutions to provide AIDS treatments to poor people and to declare a 'right to food'.

[2] One notable exception is the right to education. Access to education is universal in the United States, although there are serious questions around adequacy and equality. Additionally, there is significant support for a guaranteed pension plan for workers through the federal social security program. Recent attempts to undermine the public, and therefore guaranteed, nature of that system have met with strenuous public resistance.

[3] *Jackson v. City of Joliet*, 715 F.2d 1200 (7th Cir.), *cert. denied*, 465 U.S. 1049 (1983).

Upon its creation the U.S. Constitution did not address economic and social rights, with the exception of a negative right to property, or create any positive government obligations.[4] It is also the case, however, that the original drafters were deeply concerned with notions of equality (albeit within their particular historical vision of the concept), which requires an evolving view of government's obligations in the economic and social sphere.

The first significant U.S.-based movement to establish a social right was the common schools movement of the early nineteenth century. This movement advocated for compulsory universal education. Some commentators claim that it was in fact evangelical Christians who supported public schools to inculcate religious values that had a greater influence in their establishment. But the dominant view is that the movement stemmed from reformers in the northeast of the United States, in particular Horace Mann of Massachusetts, who had the greatest impact.[5]

Horace Mann and other reformers strongly advocated for public schools because they believed that the young republic needed an educated citizenry and an active civil society. These reformers also believed that in the nascent U.S. democracy citizens should be able to rise through the social hierarchy on the basis of merit. Finally, they seemed concerned with what they saw as a need to acculturate new immigrants to the country. Over time, the common schools movement succeeded in cementing the notion that every child should be in school until young adulthood, and that education should be a public good accessible to every child. That notion continues to be plainly reflected on the sub-national level in state constitutions, almost all of which include protections for the right to education.

The next significant legal step in the development of economic and social rights in the United States was the promulgation of labour laws in the 1930s in response to many decades of activism by the labour movement. These included the introduction of a minimum wage law and the obligation to pay increased wages for any time worked over forty hours in the week. Because the United States had also been plunged into a severe economic depression in the 1930s, other rights started gaining popularity, such as rights to social security for the elderly, widows and orphans, as well as the disabled.

During this period, major welfare programs were established to address the basic needs of these groups through cash assistance and other avenues. The popularity of economic and social rights continued to rise after the Second World War with the GI bill, which guaranteed housing and education for the returning soldiers. It is critically important to note, however, that these landmark pieces of legislation were created and implemented in a plainly racist manner. Thus, for example, support for housing was premised on living in segregated neighbourhoods.[6]

Although deeply undermined by the racist framework, the 1940s overall represented a high point for economic and social rights. In his 1941 State of the Union address, President Roosevelt emphasised freedom from want in addition to classic civil and political rights concepts:

> The basic things expected by our people of their political and economic systems are simple. They are: equality of opportunity for youth and for others; jobs for those who can work; security for those who need it; the ending of special privilege for the few; the preservation of civil liberties for all; the enjoyment of the fruits of scientific progress in a wider and constantly rising standard of living.

---

[4] As Mary Ann Glendon notes, the U.S. Constitution was written before our legislatures began to attend systematically to citizens' welfare. In most other liberal democracies, the welfare state was in place well before constitutional regimes were established. See M. A. Glendon, 'Rights in Twentieth-Century Constitutions', *University of Chicago Law Review*, Vol. 59, No. 1 (1992), p. 521. See also S. Bandes, 'The Negative Constitution: A Critique', *Michigan Law Review*, Vol. 88, No. 8 (1990), pp. 2313–2316. Bandes argues that the lack of affirmative duties in the Constitution reflects conventional Western wisdom condemning only 'active injustice' (articulated by Aristotle, Hobbes and Kant).

[5] D. Ravitch, 'American Traditions of Education', in Terry Moe (ed.), *A Primer on America's Schools* (Stanford, CA: Hoover Institution Press, 2001), pp. 1–14.

[6] *The Race to Rebuild: The Color of Opportunity and the Future of New Orleans*, publication by The Center for Social Inclusion, August 2006, at p. 5, available at <www.soros.org/resources/articles_publications/publications/racetorebuild_20060908/racetorebuild_20060908.pdf> (accessed 31 October 2006).

These are the simple, the basic things that must never be lost sight of in the turmoil and unbelievable complexity of our modern world. The inner and abiding strength of our economic and political systems is dependent upon the degree to which they fulfill these expectations.[7]

In his 1944 State of the Union address, President Roosevelt proposed a legislative agenda to protect economic and social rights. He stated that:

We have come to a clearer realization of the fact, however, that true individual freedom cannot exist without economic security and independence. "Necessitous men are not free men." People who are hungry, people who are out of a job are the stuff of which dictatorships are made.[8]

His legislative agenda, also referred to as the 'second bill of rights' included:

- The right to a useful and remunerative job in the industries or shops or farms or mines of the nation;
- The right to earn enough to provide adequate food and clothing and recreation;
- The right of farmers to raise and sell their products at a return which will give them and their families a decent living;
- The right of every business man, large and small, to trade in an atmosphere of freedom from unfair competition and domination by monopolies at home or abroad;
- The right of every family to a decent home;
- The right to adequate medical care and the opportunity to achieve and enjoy good health;
- The right to adequate protection from the economic fears of old age, and sickness, and accident, and unemployment;
- And finally, the right to a good education.[9]

Again, missing from Roosevelt's agenda was racial equality within the economic and social sphere. This, unfortunately, may be one of the reasons

his agenda received public approval, and why the GI Bill of Rights (which included education and housing) and national service (which created jobs) went forward. It is also worth noting that the ongoing war only strengthened Roosevelt's support for economic and social rights.

The historic changes in labour law and the emerging social protection programmes of the 1930s and 1940s had a significant constitutional impact. Prior to this period, Supreme Court rulings indicated that the national Congress had no authority to legislate these matters, and that such authority was reserved for the individual states. After enormous political upheaval, including a threat by President Roosevelt to 'pack the court' by increasing the number of justices from nine to fifteen, the Supreme Court ultimately found in favour of constitutional authority for Congress's actions. This historic shift in the Court's attitude, which occurred because of a change in one Justice's political position, is known as 'the switch in time that saved nine' in law schools across the nation.

These developments also unfolded on the international stage. In early 1948, the U.S. government proposed to the UN Commission on Human Rights that the Universal Declaration of Human Rights ('UDHR') protect '*Social rights*, such as the right to employment and social security and the right to enjoy minimum standards of economic, social and cultural well-being'.[10] On 10 December 1948, the UN General Assembly unanimously adopted the UDHR.

The application of the UDHR principles to the United States, however, proved to be deeply contentious. The American Bar Association ('ABA') strenuously opposed the concept of international human rights, claiming that they undermined sovereignty. Particular hostility was reserved for economic and social rights.[11] To stave off critics

---

[7] F. D. Roosevelt, 'The Four Freedoms.' Speech delivered 6 January 1941. Full text available at <www.americanrhetoric.com/speeches/fdrthefourfreedoms.htm> (accessed 31 October 2006).

[8] F. D. Roosevelt, 'State of the Union Message to Congress.' Speech delivered 11 January 1944. Full text available at <www.fdrlibrary.marist.edu/011144.html> (accessed 31 October 2006).

[9] Ibid.

[10] D. J. Whelan, 'The United States and economic and social rights: past, present ... and future?' at p. 8, available at <www.du.edu/gsis/hrhw/working/2005/26-whelan-2005.pdf> (accessed 31 October 2006).

[11] Opponents to the UN human rights covenants also took offense at the UN's definition of 'civil and political rights.' The right protecting 'freedom of movement', for example, would certainly frustrate enforcement of the Internal Security Act (or McCarran Act) of 1950, which provided for the fingerprinting and registration of 'subversives' – especially communists. Freedom of asylum would

like the ABA, Eleanor Roosevelt stated that: 'the United States Government does not consider that economic, social and cultural rights imply an obligation on governments to assure the enjoyment of these rights by direct government action' immediately after the Declaration was adopted.[12] This became the standard U.S. position, which in essence was that economic and social rights were somehow not really rights.

Still, the ABA had significant influence on policymakers and public opinion and opposition to human rights became fierce. ABA President Frank Holman was a particularly damaging critic, describing the UDHR as 'a proposal for worldwide socialism to be imposed through the United Nations on the United States and on every other member nation'.[13] Issues of race were not far below the surface throughout this controversy, and Holman and others clearly feared that the emerging civil rights movement would be legitimised through the human rights system. For example, Holman wrote that Article 16 of the Universal Declaration 'means that mixed marriages between the races are allowable without regard to state or national law or policy forbidding such marriages'.[14]

After these attacks, the United States retreated dramatically from economic and social rights. It then entered into cold war ideology where economic and social rights were associated with the 'communist threat' and were suddenly transformed into something profoundly 'un-American'.

Despite the emergence of cold war geo-politics, the influence of the civil rights, labour, welfare and women's movements was felt at both the legislative and judicial level. Even at the height of the cold war, during the 1960s and 1970s, policy victories established major social programs. President Johnson declared a 'war on poverty' and President Nixon oversaw the greatest expansion to the food program in U.S. history, calling hunger a national shame. In 1970, Congress passed the Occupational Safety and Health Act.

What was missing from these victories was an acknowledgement by political bodies that there were fundamental rights at stake that these programs were protecting. A similar approach was taken by the courts, which issued decisions during this period that were sympathetic to the interests of the poor, but never recognised economic and social rights on a constitutional level. This would later make the welfare and food program very vulnerable to attack during the 1990s, when the safety net was dismantled for the poorest families in the country.

More systematic support for the concept of economic and social rights increased slightly during the Carter years.[15] The United States finally signed the ICESCR and Presidential Directive NSC-30, which outlined the formal human rights policy of the United States, stating that 'it will also be a continuing U.S. objective to promote basic economic and social rights (e.g., adequate food, education, shelter and health)'.[16] However, this commitment was primarily externally focused and always far less emphasised than the civil and political rights agenda.

President Ronald Reagan's election in 1980 ushered in a dramatic shift in U.S. human rights policy. In October of 1981, a memo from Deputy Secretary of State William Clark and Undersecretary of Management Richard Kennedy to Secretary of State Alexander Haig advised the Administration to replace the 'human rights' language with terms like 'individual rights', 'political rights', and 'civil liberties'.[17] The next U.S. State Department

---

overturn the barring of communists from entering the United States, which was also provided for in the Act. See W. Fleming, 'Danger to America: The Draft Covenant on Human Rights (Part I),' *American Bar Association Journal*, Vol. 37, No. 10 (1951), p. 818. President Truman initially vetoed the Act, complaining that it flew in the face of civil liberties. Congress overrode the veto. The law was finally repealed in 1990 – only to be partially resurrected in the guise of the USA PATRIOT Act of 2001.

[12] Whelan, 'The U.S. and ESR' (n. 10 above), at p. 9.

[13] Ibid. p. 9.

[14] Ibid. p. 10. Holman also stated that 'it would have been better for this country, better for the world [and] better for civilization, if the South had won the civil war.' See C. Anderson, *Eyes Off the Prize: The United Nations and the African American Struggle for Human Rights* (New York: Cambridge University Press, 2003).

[15] Still, even the Carter administration had begun to speak of economic and social 'rights' as not really being rights over time. Ibid. at pp. 12–13.

[16] J. Carter, 'Human Rights.' Presidential Directive 30, 17 February 1978. Full text available at <www.jimmycarterlibrary.org/documents/pddirectives/pres_directive.phtml> (accessed 31 October 2006).

[17] Whelan, 'The U.S. and ESR', at p. 14. See also P. Alston, 'U.S. Ratification of the Covenant on Economic, Social and Cultural Rights: The Need for an Entirely New

Human Rights Report removed all mention of economic and social rights. A 1988 statement by the Deputy Assistant Secretary of State for Human Rights and Humanitarian Affairs, Paula Dobriansky, reflected an ongoing strategy of moulding human rights to fit the ideology of the U.S. government. In that statement, Dobrianksy addressed the 'myth' that economic and social rights are part of the human rights framework.[18]

The scepticism of the U.S. government has not significantly changed in the last two decades, with the judiciary reflecting similar views to the other branches of government. Legal jurisprudence has been deeply influenced by both the international and domestic political context, and as noted above U.S. courts have never fully embraced economic and social rights. On the other hand, the U.S. Supreme Court has, as described below, responded to social pressures and movements over time and addressed some of the major issues around education and social protection through existing constitutional norms. Moreover, state courts are also emerging as an important source of protection for these rights.

3. FEDERAL CONSTITUTIONAL FRAMEWORK

Economic and social rights, with the exception of the right to property, are notably absent from the U.S. Constitution. While some scholars have attempted to create theories that the U.S. Constitution's original text directly protects economic and social rights, they have had very little influence.[19] Other legal experts argue that the U.S.

Constitution may not have included such rights from the start, but can easily be, and should be, expanded to do so. During the 1950s and 1960s, a sympathetic U.S. Supreme Court did consider such claims and alluded to their potential validity. However, the Court ultimately rejected direct constitutional protections for economic and social rights.

Nonetheless, economic and social rights advocates have achieved some limited protection for these rights through other constitutional avenues. It is the poor that primarily face economic and social rights violations, and these violations are often exacerbated by a parallel failure to protect procedural or other civil and political rights recognised under U.S. law. Moreover, within the U.S. context, poverty is highly racialised and socially excluded communities are at the greatest risk of not having their rights protected.

For these reasons, legal advocates have pursued due process and equal protection legal strategies, as well as strategies focusing on the intersection between civil/political and economic/social rights, to protect the rights of the poor. Due process guarantees and guarantees of equal protection of the laws have together provided a modest legal defence against attacks on economic and social rights. The U.S. Supreme Court has also addressed, with mixed results, policies that restrict access to social support in a way that undermines the exercise of a civil or political right, as well as circumstances where poverty itself limits the ability of individuals to exercise such rights.

The U.S. Constitution requires due process of law through its Fifth and Fourteenth Amendments. Due process guarantees are triggered when a government entity infringes upon a property or liberty interest. Certain economic and social interests created by legislation have been construed to be like property and give rise to property interests. The due process clause has been invoked to protect cash benefits, shelter, and other basic necessities for the very poor.

Additionally, the Fifth and Fourteenth Amendments of the U.S. Constitution both address legal equality. The Fourteenth Amendment provides that: 'No State shall...deny to any person within its jurisdiction the equal protection of the laws'.

Strategy', *American Journal of International Law*, Vol. 84, No. 2 (1990), p. 372, and H. Hartmann, 'U.S. Human Rights Policy under Carter and Reagan, 1977–1981,' *Human Rights Quarterly*, Vol. 23, No. 2 (2001), pp. 402–430.

[18] Alston, 'U.S. Ratification of the Covenant on Economic, Social and Cultural Rights', ibid. p. 374.

[19] See generally F. I. Michelman, 'The Supreme Court, 1968 Term Foreword: On Protecting the Poor through the Fourteenth Amendment,' *Harvard Law Review*, Vol. 83, No. 1 (1969), pp. 7–282; C. L. Black, Jr., 'Further Reflections on the Constitutional Justice of Livelihood,' *Columbia Law Review*, Vol. 86, No. 6 (1986), pp. 1103–1117; and A. Amar, 'Forty Acres and a Mule: A Republican Theory of Minimum Entitlement,' *Harvard Journal of Law and Public Policy*, Vol. 13, No. 37 (1990), pp. 40–43.

The Fifth Amendment contains a similar prohibition that applies to the federal government.[20]

Equal protection guarantees are triggered when government action results in both differential treatment (i.e. intent to discriminate) and impact or effect.[21] However, every difference in treatment is not given the same level of constitutional scrutiny. Rather, there are three distinct levels:

- Strict scrutiny applies if a law or practice discriminates on the basis of race or national origin. These are considered 'suspect classifications' and the government must demonstrate a compelling state interest as well as show that the classification is 'narrowly tailored' and the 'least restrictive means' available to meet that interest. Once strict scrutiny is triggered, a government policy is rarely found to fulfil constitutional requirements.
- If the law or practice discriminates on the basis of gender or birth status on its face, an intermediate standard of review is used, and the government must demonstrate a substantial state interest.
- Finally, other 'non-suspect' classifications are generally upheld as long as the State demonstrates a 'rational basis' for making its distinction. It is virtually unheard of for a court to strike down legislation using the rational basis test, and virtually any reason put forth by the State can be deemed rational.

This approach to equality diverges from international norms in two significant ways. First, international norms prohibit discrimination where it has *either* a discriminatory purpose *or* effect, while U.S. jurisprudence requires both simultaneously.[22] Second, as reflected in Article 2 of the

ICESCR, international norms require States to protect human rights without discrimination 'of any kind as to race, colour, sex, language, religion, political or other opinion, national or social origin, property, birth *or other status*' [emphasis added].[23] Human rights treaty bodies generally require the state to provide a 'sufficient justification' for differential treatment in any relevant category, which is more vigorous than a rational basis test. However, the U.S. standard is more rigorous with regards to *de jure* racial and national origin classifications.

Finally, the U.S. Supreme Court also applies a strict scrutiny standard – requiring the government to demonstrate that a policy is narrowly tailored to serve a compelling state interest – when government action burdens the exercise of a 'fundamental right'. Fundamental rights under U.S. jurisprudence are essentially all civil and political constitutional rights. Thus, the Supreme Court has found that in areas of social and economic policy, 'a statutory classification that neither proceeds along suspect lines nor infringes fundamental [civil and political] rights must be upheld against equal protection challenge if there is any reasonably conceivable state of facts that could provide a rational basis for the classification'.[24]

3.1   U.S. Supreme Court Case Law Affecting Economic and Social Rights

The first significant constitutional decision regarding economic and social rights in the twentieth century was *National Labor Relations Board v. Jones & Laughlin Steel Corporation*, decided in 1937.[25] This case represented a fundamental change in interpretation of the federal

---

[20] In *Washington v. Davis*, the Court stated that the Fifth Amendment contains 'an equal protection component prohibiting the United States from invidiously discriminating between individuals or groups.' 426 U.S. 229, 239 (1976).

[21] In one housing case, a non-profit developer sought a zoning change from single-family residential to multi-family residential to attract more racially diverse tenants. The municipality rejected his proposal, and the Supreme Court affirmed its right to do so. Although there was clear discriminatory impact, intent was not proven. See *Village of Arlington Heights v. Metropolitan Housing Development Corp.*, 429 U.S. 252, 265 (1977).

[22] See, e.g., International Convention on the Elimination of All Forms of Racial Discrimination, adopted and opened

for signature and ratification by General Assembly resolution 2106 (XX) of 21 December 1965, *entry into force* 4 January 1969, in accordance with Article 19 at Art. 1.

[23] International Covenant on Economic, Social and Cultural Rights (New York, 16 Dec. 1966), 993 U.N.T.S. 3, *entered into force* 3 Jan. 1976.

[24] See *FCC v. Beach Communications, Inc.*, 508 U.S. 307, 313 (1993). For a compelling attack on the presumption of constitutionality as to the outcomes of democratic political processes that impact poor people, *see* S. Loffredo, 'Poverty, Democracy and Constitutional Law,' *University of Pennsylvania Law Review*, Vol. 141, No. 4 (1993), pp. 1277–1389.

[25] *National Labor Relations Board v. Jones & Laughlin Steel Corp.*, 301 U.S. 1 (1937).

government's powers. Under the U.S. Constitution, the federal government may only legislate in areas where the constitution directly provides it authority to do so. Otherwise legislative powers are reserved to the states. Prior to 1937, this was interpreted rather strictly and the Court generally took the position that the national Congress could not legislate in the arena of economic and social rights, including labour standards.

Reversing its long-standing position, however, the Court in *Jones & Laughlin* upheld the comprehensive labour reforms adopted during the Roosevelt administration. The Court reasoned that labour practices affected interstate commerce, an area that falls within Congress's constitutional power to legislate.[26] While this case did not obligate the national government to protect economic and social rights, it did open the door for protective legislation, in particular as applied to private actors. Based on 'commerce clause' reasoning, the Court later found Congress empowered to address a host of other human rights concerns through national legislation, including civil rights legislation to protect against race and sex discrimination.

Brown v. Board of Education was the first major case directly addressing an economic and social right, the right to education.[27] In this historic case, the Supreme Court found the long-standing practice of racially segregated public school systems unconstitutional. The case recognised the relationship between equality and the right to education, stressing that:

> [I]t is doubtful that any child may reasonably be expected to succeed in life if he is denied the opportunity of an education. Such an opportunity, where the state has undertaken to provide it, is a right which must be made available to all on equal terms.[28]

The Court also referred to education as a prerequisite to the meaningful exercise of other citizenship rights,[29] implicitly acknowledging the interdependence of economic, social, civil and political rights.[30]

In the 1960s, the Court began to develop more jurisprudence specifically about the poor. In *Douglas v. California*, the Court found that poor people were constitutionally entitled to free legal representation on their first appeal of a criminal conviction.[31] *Shapiro v. Thompson* struck down a California law requiring new residents to wait six months before receiving welfare benefits.[32] Although the Court's decision was technically based on the right to travel between the states of the United States, it noted that California's flawed policy denied poor people their means of subsistence. However, the Court also noted that as a matter of national Constitutional law, '[p]ublic assistance benefits are "a privilege" and not a "right",[33] laying the groundwork for more recent rulings finding that limiting the time period that public assistance benefits are available 'does not implicate a fundamental right' domestically.[34]

Nonetheless, in *Goldberg v. Kelly* the Court found the scope of 'property' interests covered under the U.S. Constitution's due process clause included welfare payments.[35] The Court explained that since a government benefit provides an eligible recipient with 'the very means by which to live', the government may not impair that recipient's interest arbitrarily and must provide a trial-like hearing prior to termination of benefits.[36] In a subsequent case involving disability benefits, *Mathews v. Eldridge*, the Court also recognised a property interest in social security, but deemed a post-termination proceeding sufficient to satisfy procedural due process, as the individuals affected were not on the margins of subsistence like the welfare recipients in *Goldberg*.[37]

Lower courts also expanded the *Goldberg* holding to other contexts, such as housing. For example, the federal appellate courts of the Second and the Fourth Circuits of the United States extended the *Goldberg* hearing requirement to public housing residents.[38] In *Joy v. Daniels*, another Fourth

---

[26] U.S. CONST. art. I, §8, cl. 3.
[27] *Brown v. Board of Education*, 347 U.S. 483 (1954).
[28] Ibid. 493.
[29] Ibid. 494.
[30] Notably, in 1993, the U.S. explicitly affirmed the interdependence of all human rights along with other UN mem-

ber nations at the World Conference on Human Rights in Vienna.
[31] 372 U.S. 353, 357–58 (1963).
[32] 394 U.S. 618 (1969).
[33] Ibid. 627, n.6.
[34] *Turner v. Glickman*, 207 F. 3d 419, 424 (7th Cir.2000).
[35] 397 U.S. 254, 264 (1970).
[36] Ibid.
[37] 424 U.S. 319, 331 (1975).
[38] *Escalera v. New York City Housing Authority*, 425 F.2d 853, 861 (2d Cir. 1970); *Caulder v. Durham Housing Authority*,

Circuit case, the court found that due process guarantees prohibited arbitrarily ejecting low-income residents from a quasi-public housing unit, and thus invalidated a lease clause that gave a landlord the ability to terminate a lease without cause.[39]

In *Williams v. Barry*, a lower federal court held that the city of Washington D.C. had to satisfy procedural protections before cutting off funds to support shelters for homeless men.[40] The judges noted that homeless people have a valid property interest in continued occupancy and use of their shelter. The Court stated that, '[i]nstead of eliminating the means for obtaining the basic necessities of life', as in *Goldberg*, 'the District of Columbia [in this case] would eliminate those very end product life support functions'.[41] Therefore, despite the absence of an independent right to housing, homeless persons were found to possess a property interest in continued occupancy and use of their shelter because the city had 'charted a course of deliberate, consistent action that solidified and expanded the homeless person program'.[42] The city was temporarily enjoined from cutting those services until procedural safeguards had been provided.[43]

The Supreme Court during this time, however, was slowly becoming more hostile to economic and social rights and the rights of poor. Judicial appointments by President Richard Nixon appeared to close the window for the development of economic and social rights. In *Dandridge*

v. Williams, the Supreme Court confirmed that the Constitution contains no affirmative state obligations to care for the poor, upholding a state statute capping federal welfare grants below the level required to sustain a large family.[44] The Court essentially stated that economic and social rights were not justiciable:

> [T]he intractable economic, social, and even philosophical problems presented by public welfare assistance programs are not the business of this Court.[45]

In *Lindsay v. Normet*, the Court rejected a challenge to a state's summary eviction procedure by tenants who refused to pay their rent on the grounds that the premises had been declared uninhabitable, thus rejecting even the negative components of economic and social rights.[46] The Court held that there is no constitutional right to adequate housing:

> We do not denigrate the importance of decent, safe, and sanitary housing. But the Constitution does not provide judicial remedies for every social and economic ill. We are unable to perceive in that document any constitutional guarantee of access to dwellings of a particular quality...Absent constitutional mandate, the assurance of adequate housing and the definition of landlord-tenant relationships are legislative, not judicial, functions.[47]

Finally, the Supreme Court rejected the incipient right to education in *San Antonio Independent School District v. Rodriguez* (1973) by upholding a property-tax-based school finance system that produced per-pupil spending disparities, finding that such systems are problematic only when they deprive students of *any* educational opportunity.[48] This decision, though bleak, did not completely extinguish the issue. The Court expressly distinguished the wealth-based inequalities in *Rodriguez* from a situation in which the educational system failed to provide each child with a sufficient level of minimum skills to enjoy the

---

433 F.2d 998, 1002–03 (4th Cir. 1970) (noting that '[t]he "privilege" or the "right" to occupy publicly subsidised low-rent housing seems to us to be no less entitled to due process protection than entitlement to welfare benefits which were the subject of decision in *Goldberg* or the other rights and privileges referred to in *Goldberg*.')

[39] 479 F.2d 1236, 1242 (4th Cir. 1973). For application of procedural due process in other ESR settings, see also *Caramico v. HUD*, 509 F. 2d 694, 700 (2d Cir. 1974) (when a plaintiff has legally resided in his/her apartment for a substantial period of time, he/she has an protected interest in continued occupancy); *Perry v. Sindermann*, 408 U.S. 593, 602–03 (1972) (if a college professor can demonstrate an 'expectancy' of re-employment, he/she must receive an opportunity for a hearing before being fired).

[40] 490 F. Supp. 941, 945–46 (D.D.C. 1980).

[41] Ibid. 946.

[42] Ibid. 946–47.

[43] Ibid. 947. On appeal, the D.C. Circuit upheld the District Court's finding that notice and an opportunity to present written comments was sufficient to satisfy any procedural protection required and did not reach the issue of whether there was a due process right at stake. See *Williams v. Barry*, 708 F.2d 789, 792 (D.C. Cir. 1983).

[44] 397 U.S. 471, 486 (1970).

[45] Ibid. 487.

[46] 405 U.S. 56, 74 (1972).

[47] Ibid. p. 74. It should be noted that the Court in *Lindsay* did not categorically reject a right to housing at all under the federal Constitution, although this case is frequently cited for that proposition.

[48] 411 U.S. 1, 54–56 (1973).

rights to speech and political participation[49] or where poor children faced an economic barrier to accessing education, such as tuition fees for primary or secondary education.[50]

Nearly a decade later, in *Plyler v. Doe*, the Court issued a schizophrenic decision striking down a Texas law that excluded undocumented immigrant children from public schools.[51] On the one hand, the Court emphasised that education was not a right guaranteed under the federal Constitution.[52] On the other, the Court stated education must be distinguished from social welfare legislation based on 'the importance of education in maintaining our basic institutions, and the lasting impact of its deprivation on the life of a child'.[53]

Moreover, although the Court did not attempt to justify its decision based on existing discrimination jurisprudence (which requires a strict scrutiny standard of analysis),[54] it nonetheless held that a state could not discriminatorily deny access to education to a class of children without fulfilling some substantial government goal.[55] This holding was in stark contrast with the likely result under a 'rational basis' standard of review, which is the standard normally applied in cases where no suspect class or fundamental right is at issue.

The Court found that none of the justifications proffered by the state of Texas in *Plyler* were sufficient to counterbalance the social costs of 'denying [undocumented children the] ability to live within the structure of our civic institutions, and foreclos[ing] any realistic possibility that they will contribute in even the smallest way to the progress of our nation'.[56] A subsequent decision, *Papsan v. Allain*, confirmed that the constitutional status of a right to a 'minimally adequate' education is still unsettled.[57]

Plyler was an analytically muddled but ultimately ethical decision consistent with human rights norms. It is unclear, however, whether even that confused decision would hold today. The Court

definitively rejected the notion of positive state obligations in *Deshaney v. Winnebago County Dept. of Social Services*, stating that the federal Constitution's Due Process Clause 'is phrased as a limitation on the State's power to act, not as a guarantee of certain minimal levels of safety and security', and thus 'cannot fairly be extended to impose an affirmative obligation on the State'.[58] Indeed, the Supreme Court stated that the 'Due Process Clauses generally confer no affirmative right to governmental aid, *even where such aid may be necessary to secure life*'.[59]

Despite the value afforded to civil and political rights in U.S. jurisprudence, the Court even rejected the principal of indivisibility and denied remedies where a failure to protect economic and social rights clearly undermined 'fundamental' civil and political rights. For example, in *Lyng v. International Union*, the Court upheld a 1981 statute that decreased or denied food stamp eligibility to households in which any member was participating in a legally protected labour strike, rejecting challenges based on the First and Fifth Amendments.[60]

From the 1990s onwards, the Supreme Court has continued to narrow legal avenues to protect the rights of the poor. For example, in *Department of Housing and Urban Development v. Rucker* (2002), the Court upheld the right of authorities running public housing units for the poor to evict residents when a household member or guest engaged in drug-related activity.[61] Under this decision, a public housing tenant may be evicted whether or not he or she knew (or even could have or should have known) about the illegal drug activity.[62] This decision led to entire families being evicted from their homes because a household member or guest, often an adolescent, engaged in nonviolent drug-related activity.

Finally, for many people even the right to property for those of modest means and little power appears to be at significant risk after the 2005 decision of *Kelo v. City of New London*,

---

[49] Ibid. 37.
[50] Ibid. 25, n.60.
[51] 457 U.S. 202, 222–25 (1982).
[52] Ibid. 221.
[53] Ibid.
[54] Indeed, the Court explicitly stated that undocumented immigrants did not constitute a suspect class deserving of close scrutiny under constitutional law. Ibid. 223.
[55] Ibid. 223–25.
[56] Ibid. 224.
[57] 478 U.S. 265, 285 (1986).

[58] 489 U.S. 189, 195 (1989).
[59] Ibid. 196. Emphasis added.
[60] 485 U.S. 360, 370–74 (1988).
[61] 535 U.S. 125 (2002).
[62] 'There are, moreover, no "serious constitutional doubts" about Congress' affording local public housing authorities the discretion to conduct no-fault evictions for drug-related crime.' Ibid. 135.

Connecticut.[63] In *Kelo*, the Supreme Court upheld a locality's eminent domain power to confiscate property from mid- and low-income residents so that private developers could further the broad goal of 'economic development'.[64] In the past, the Court had approved the use of eminent domain in the case of "public use" such as construction of a new state highway, or in cases where property was severely degraded and the failure to maintain it was creating a public hazard or loss in some significant way. Although experts on the "takings clause" of the U.S. Constitution claim that the *Kelo* case, which allowed the state to condemn well-kept homes belonging to families which – in some cases – had lived there for generations, was squarely within precedent and far from a radical departure from past jurisprudence, the case caused alarm across the nation. Given the growing power of developers and the trend in many urban centers towards allowing, and even subsidizing, developers to re-develop large tracts of cities in a way that inevitably permanently displaces primarily working class communities, there was a strong political backlash after *Kelo*. Several states passed legislation severely limiting localities' abilities to exercise eminent domain. Perhaps the most amusing response was a small campaign to persuade a small municipality to condemn the home of one of the Justices of the Supreme Court who voted with the majority in *Kelo*. The goal of the campaign was to highlight that with three out of five votes of a local town council, anyone could lose their home to the government and the interests of private developers.

Because the U.S. Supreme Court has failed to develop the Constitution into a legal instrument that affords protection for economic and social rights, legal advocates have turned toward subnational constitutions as a strategic avenue for their advocacy. This approach poses additional challenges, but because state constitutions play a different role within the U.S. legal system than the national constitution, it also presents opportunities not available at the national level.

4. DIRECT PROTECTION THROUGH STATE CONSTITUTIONAL PROVISIONS

Within the United States, there are fifty subnational constitutions. Each state within the federal union has its own constitution with a unique history. State constitutions have long played an important role in guaranteeing individuals' human rights. The Tenth Amendment of the United States Federal Constitution specifically leaves 'significant residual powers of government' to the states.[65] Indeed, states have a 'sovereign right to construe their constitutions more broadly than the federal Constitution',[66] and should 'follow an independent path as regards rights under their own constitutions'.[67] As noted by New York State's highest court, 'the [US] Supreme Court's role in construing the Federal Bill of Rights is to establish minimal standards for individual rights applicable throughout the Nation. The function of the comparable provisions of the State Constitution, if they are not to be considered purely redundant, is to supplement those rights to meet the needs and expectations of the particular State'.[68] Legal scholars have long supported this position: '[S]tate courts cannot rest when they have afforded their citizens the full protections of the federal Constitution. State constitutions, too, are a font of individual liberties, their protections often extending beyond those required by the Supreme

---

[65] R. L. Maddex, *State Constitutions of the United States*, (Washington, D.C.: Congressional Quarterly, 1998), p. xii. The 10th Amendment to the U.S. Constitution states: 'The powers not delegated to the United States by the Constitution, nor prohibited by it to the states, are reserved to the states respectively, or to the people.'

[66] National Law Center on Homelessness and Poverty, *Homelessness in the United States and the Human Right to Housing* (Washington, D.C.: National Law Center on Homelessness and Poverty, 2004), p. 43, citing A. Cohen, "After the War: Poverty Law in the 1980s: More Myths of Parity – State Court Forums and Constitutional Actions for the Right to Shelter", *Emory Law Journal*, Vol. 38, No. 3 (1989), p. 623 ('a state court is entirely free to read its own State's constitution more broadly than [the Supreme Court] reads the Federal Constitution, or to reject the mode of analysis used by [the] Court in favor of a different analysis of its corresponding constitutional guarantee.'). See also *Arcara v. Cloud Books, Inc.*, 68 N.Y.2d 553, 557 (1986) (indicating that, though the State of New York is bound by Supreme Court decisions defining and limiting Federal constitutional rights, the State nevertheless was bound to abide by its own independent judgment in determining the scope and effect of the New York State Constitution); *People v. P.J. Video, Inc.*, 68 N.Y.2d 296, 301–02 (1986) (same); and *Cooper v. California*, 386 U.S. 58, 62 (1967) (indicating that the Supreme Court's holding regarding the Fourth Amendment does not affect the State's power to impose higher standards on searches and seizures than required by the Federal Constitution, if it chooses to do so).

[67] National Law Center on Homelessness and Poverty, '*Homelessness in the US*' (n. 66 above), p. 43.

[68] *Arcara v. Cloud Books, Inc.*, 68 N.Y.2d 553, 557 (1986).

---

[63] 125 S. Ct. 2655.
[64] Ibid. 2665–66.

Court's interpretation of federal law'.[69] Particularly notable among these additional guarantees are economic and social rights protections.

Indeed, to the extent that *substantive economic and social rights* in the United States are recognised, they are found mainly in state constitutions. Only state courts at this point are likely to seriously address either positive obligations or economic and social rights. Virtually every state constitution protects the right to education, and many have provisions that may protect economic and social rights more broadly. Moreover, state constitutions are far more flexible and changeable than the national Constitution. They are amended far more often and interpreted in many cases by judges who are elected. Thus, some of the considerations that restrain the Supreme Court from breaking with past precedent at the federal level do not apply at the state level. A great deal of litigation has already been undertaken with regard to some economic and social rights, as detailed below, and creative strategies to further develop these sub-national constitutions are being discussed and written about with increasing interest.

4.1. The Right to Education

As noted above, virtually every state constitution in the United States contains an education provision, requiring the state to establish an educational system. The state's obligations and the scope of the right to education are framed in a variety of ways. Over half of the education provisions contain some description of the requisite quality of education to be offered.[70] And the constitutions of at least ten states mandate non-discrimination and/or expressly provide that education should be provided to all children in the state.[71] State courts'

interpretations of the right to education have varied based on the different educational provisions as well as the local and national context.

Between 1971 and 1973, advocates relied upon the federal Equal Protection Clause to argue that education was a 'fundamental right' and that policies which resulted in per-pupil spending disparities impinged upon that right. Such policies were therefore subject to strict scrutiny under an equal protection analysis.[72] In 1973, however, the Supreme Court closed this line of cases with its decision in *San Antonio Independent School District v. Rodriguez*.[73]

Consequently, between 1973 and 1979, advocates attacked unfair school finance systems using equal protection and education clauses found in state constitutions. This strategy had mixed success, largely because it was difficult to clearly separate the impacts of disparate school spending from other variables that negatively affected educational opportunities. The strategy was finally abandoned in favour of an approach focusing on the adequacy of education rather than equity per se.[74]

Three cases in particular illustrate how the right to education has been defined over the past two decades in state courts: *Edgewood Independent School District v. Kirby*,[75] *Rose v. Council for Better Education*,[76] and *Campaign for Fiscal Equity v. The State of New York*.[77]

The *Edgewood* case, decided in 1989, was one of the first cases to use an 'adequacy' rather than 'equity' argument to challenge school finance systems. In that case, the Texas Supreme Court found that the state's property tax-based system

[69] W. J. Brennan, Jr., 'State Constitutions and the Protection of Individual Rights,' *Harvard Law Review*, Vol. 90, No. 3 (1977), p. 491.

[70] R. M. Jensen, 'Advancing Education through Education Clauses of State Constitutions,' *BYU Educ. & L.J.*, Vol. 1997, No. 1 (1997), pp. 4–5. For example, some state constitutions require that the education offered be of 'high quality.' Ill. Const. art. X, 1; Va. Const. art. VIII, 1. In other states, the educational system is required to be 'thorough and efficient.' Md. Const. art. VIII, 1; Minn. Const. art. XIII 1; N.J. Const. art. VIII, 4; Ohio Const. art. VI, 2; Pa. Const. art. III, 14; W.Va. Const. art. XII, 1.

[71] Jensen, 'Advancing Education' (n. 70 above), p. 5. *See, e.g.* Wash. Const. art. IX, 2 ('for . . . the children residing within its borders without distinction or preference on account of race, color, caste, or sex . . . free from sectarian con-

trol and open to all children in [the] state'). *See also* Ark. Const. art. XIV, 1; Alaska Const. art. VII, 1; Haw. Const. art. X, 1; Ill. Const. art. X, 1; Mass. Const. art. 61; Mich. Const. art. VIII, 2; Mont. Const. art. X, 7; N.J. Const. art. VIII, 4; N.M. Const. art. XII, 1; N.Y. Const. art. XI, 1.

[72] *See, e.g., Serrano v. Priest*, 5 Cal. 3d 584, 604–18 (1971) (holding that the right to education is a fundamental interest analogous to the right to vote and a compelling state interest would be required in order to justify wealth classifications that interfere with this right).

[73] 411 U.S. 1, 35 (1973) (holding that state-provided education, though essential, is not a 'fundamental right' worthy of strict scrutiny since education is neither explicitly nor implicitly provided for in the Constitution).

[74] *See* M. Heise, 'State Constitutions, School Finance Litigation, and the "Third Wave": From Equity to Adequacy', *Temple Law Review*, Vol. 68, No. 3 (1995), pp. 1152–1176.

[75] 777 S.W.2d 391 (Tex. 1989).

[76] 790 S.W.2d 186 (Ky. 1989).

[77] 719 N.Y.S.2d 475 (2001).

for financing public education violated the state constitution. Throughout Texas, the tax burden and money raised varied dramatically, with the wealthiest areas enjoying both disproportionately low taxes and well-resourced schools. Article VII, section 1 of the Texas state constitution declares that 'a general diffusion of knowledge' is 'essential to the preservation of the liberties and rights of the people'.[78] To that end, 'it shall be the duty of the Legislature of the State to establish and make suitable provision for the support and maintenance of an efficient system of free schools'.[79]

The Court held that 'efficient' conveys the meaning of effective or 'productive of results' as well as the economical use of resources.[80] It found that '[t]he present system … provides not for a diffusion that is general, but for one that is limited and unbalanced. The resultant inequalities are thus directly contrary to the constitutional vision of efficiency'.[81] In particular, the Court noted that efficiency does not require a per capita distribution, but that there must be direct and close correlation between a district's tax effort and the education resources available to it.[82] Rather than ordering a specific remedy or requiring the legislature to raise taxes, the court set a time limit for the legislature to develop a new financing system.[83]

The Texas legislature's first attempts to fulfill its obligations under the decision were deemed unconstitutional.[84] In 1993, a new law was passed which provided for partial recapture of revenues from districts with high property wealth for redistribution to districts with low property wealth. The constitutionality of this scheme was affirmed by the Supreme Court of Texas in *Edgewood Independent School District v. Meno*.[85]

Also in 1989, the Supreme Court of Kentucky had the opportunity to examine its own constitutional mandate to provide an 'efficient system of common schools throughout the state'. In *Rose v. Council for Better Education*, the Court went into much more explicit detail about what efficiency requires.[86] In fact, it found that '[a]n efficient system of education must have as its goal to provide each and every child with at least the seven following capacities'.[87] Those include:

(1) sufficient oral and written communication skills to enable students to function in a complex and rapidly changing civilization;

(2) sufficient knowledge of economic, social and political systems to enable the student to make informed choices;

(3) sufficient understanding of governmental processes to enable the student to understand the issues that affect his or her community, state and nation;

(4) sufficient self-knowledge and knowledge of his or her mental and physical wellness;

(5) sufficient grounding in the arts to enable each student to appreciate his or her cultural and historical heritage;

(6) sufficient training or preparation for advancing training in either academic or vocational fields so as to enable each child to choose and pursue life work intelligently; and

(7) sufficient levels of academic or vocational skills to enable public school students to compete favourably with their counterparts in surrounding states, in academics and the job market.

Like the Texas courts, the Kentucky court did not require the state legislature to enact any specific legislation, including raising taxes.[88] Its

---

[78] 777 S.W.2d 391, 394 (Tex., 1989).

[79] Ibid.

[80] Ibid. 395 ('"Efficient" conveys the meaning of effective or productive of results and connotes the use of resources so as to produce results with little waste').

[81] Ibid. 396.

[82] Ibid. 397–98.

[83] Ibid. 399 ('Although we have ruled the school financing system to be unconstitutional, we do not now instruct the legislature as to the specifics of the legislation it should enact; nor do we order it to raise taxes. The legislature has primary responsibility to decide how best to achieve an efficient system. We decide only the nature of the constitutional mandate and whether that mandate has been met.').

[84] See *Edgewood Independent School District v. Kirby*, 804 S.W. 2d 491, 492–93 (1991) and *Carrollton Farmers Branch Independent School District v. Edgewood Independent School District*, 826 S.W.2d 489, 493–94 (1992).

[85] 917 S.W. 2d 717 (1995).

[86] 790 S.W.2d 186 (Ky. 1989) (finding that Kentucky's entire system of common schools is unconstitutional).

[87] Ibid. 212–13.

[88] Ibid. 215–16 ('Since we have, by this decision, declared the system of common schools in Kentucky to be unconstitutional, Section 183 [of the Kentucky state constitution] places an absolute duty on the General Assembly to re-create, re-establish a new system of common schools in the Commonwealth.').

instructions were nevertheless quite onerous to the General Assembly, which was directed to 'recreate and re-establish a system of common schools'.[89] The Assembly quickly passed the Kentucky Education Reform Act of 1990, which resulted in tax legislation that increased revenues by more than one billion dollars. Revenues for all school districts increased by at least eight per cent and, in some districts, up to twenty-five per cent. To some observers, the *Rose* decision 'constitutes one of the most comprehensive interventions by a state judiciary into the realm of legislative policy-making for education'.[90]

Since *Rose*, Kentucky schools have steadily improved. For the first time, Kentucky students in all three grades tested in 2001 matched or exceeded the national average on a basic skills assessment. The relative success of school reform in Kentucky, as opposed to other states, is due in large part to effective citizen advocacy groups that not only laid the groundwork for reform but also monitored implementation in the succeeding years.[91]

More than a decade after these initial adequacy decisions came down in Texas, Kentucky and elsewhere, education reform advocates won a major victory in New York. The first success actually occurred in 1995, when the highest court of that state – known as the Court of Appeals – found that New York's Constitution guaranteed every child a sound basic education which consists at least of the 'basic literacy, calculating, and verbal skills necessary to enable children to eventually function productively as civic participants capable of voting and serving on a jury'.[92] The Court explicitly stated that achieving this required minimally adequate physical facilities, access to instrumentalities of learning (such as desks, chairs, and reasonably current textbooks), and being taught reasonably up-to-date curricula by adequately trained teachers.[93]

The case was sent back to the lower court to determine whether New York was violating this standard in New York City. In a detailed decision, the court found that New York was in violation of the standard and that both educational inputs and outputs where inadequate.[94] The State of New York argued that the low educational outputs were a result of the low socio-economic status of many New York City students, and disavowed responsibility to address these students' needs. Disturbingly, the mid-level appellate court agreed with the State's arguments, reversing the trial court's decision and explicitly finding that an eighth grade education (which was the level most poor students were afforded) was adequate to meet constitutional guarantees.[95]

The New York Court of Appeals then took up the case once more and reversed the mid-level appellate court, holding that New York state was indeed in breach of its constitutional duties and that all students, regardless of their economic situation, were entitled to a high school level education.[96] In 2003, the Court of Appeals ordered a three-part remedy: (1) the State must ascertain the 'actual cost of providing a sound basic education in New York City'; (2) the State must reform the funding

[89] Ibid.

[90] *See* K. Alexander, 'The Common School Ideal and the Limits of Legislative Authority: The Kentucky Case,' *Harvard Journal on Legislation*, Vol. 28, No. 2 (1991), pp. 341–42.

[91] For more information, contact the Prichard Committee for Academic Excellence: <http://www.prichardcommittee.org>. (The Prichard Committee is a statewide education advocacy committee in Kentucky) (website last accessed 18 November 2006.)

[92] *Campaign for Fiscal Equity v. State of New York*, 86 N.Y.2d 307, 316 (1995).

[93] Ibid. 317.

[94] *Campaign for Fiscal Equity v. State of New York*, 719 N.Y.S.2d 475, 491–92 (2001). In fact, the Court found that approximately 30 per cent of all students who entered 9th grade in New York dropped out before graduation. Ibid. 515–16. In his decision, Judge DeGrasse outlined seven resources essential to a sound basic education: (1) sufficient numbers of qualified teachers, administrators and other personnel; (2) appropriate class sizes; (3) adequate and accessible school buildings with sufficient space for classes and curriculum; (4) sufficient and up-to-date books, supplies, libraries and educational technology and laboratories; (5) suitable curricula, including an expanded platform of programs to help at-risk students by giving them 'more time on task'; (6) adequate resources for students with extraordinary needs; and (7) a safe and orderly environment. Ibid. 550.

[95] *Campaign for Fiscal Equity v. State of New York*, 295 A.D.2d 1 (2002). Specifically, the court emphasised that 'the proper standard is that the State must offer all children the opportunity of a sound basic education, not ensure that they actually receive it,' and that students who willingly dropped-out did not necessarily prove that the State had failed to fulfil its constitutional duty to provide a 'sound basic education' for its students. Ibid. 15.

[96] *Campaign for Fiscal Equity v. State of New York*, 100 N.Y.2d 893, 914 (2003) (holding that the constitutional requirement of a 'sound basic education' included 'a meaningful high school education' and that according to this standard 'it may, as a practical matter, be presumed that a [high school] dropout has not received a sound basic education.').

system to ensure that 'every school in New York City would have the resources necessary for providing the opportunity for a sound basic education'; and (3) the State must put in place a system of accountability that will ensure that the reforms actually provide this opportunity.[97] The remedy involved 1.93 billion additional dollars of funding for New York City schools.

In the area of education, these cases demonstrate a willingness by courts to develop detailed indicators to assess a State's compliance with constitutional rights. The standards they prescribe exceed the 'core minimum' content required under international law. Articles 13 and 14 of the ICESCR stipulate that primary education shall be compulsory and available free to all,[98] and secondary education 'shall be made generally available and accessible to all by every appropriate means'.[99] In addition, the 'material condition of teaching staff' must also continuously improve.[100] The *Rose* and *CFE* decisions demand even more by enumerating specific skills students need to pursue economically productive and politically engaged lives. This is, however, in line with emerging international standards such as the definition of 'basic learning needs' adopted by the World Declaration on Education.[101]

4.2 The Right to Housing and Welfare Assistance

While many state courts have struggled to delineate the right to education under state constitutional law, other social and economic rights have received far less extensive treatment. One reason is that advocates must locate those rights in vague constitutional language. Still, the following cases illustrate the promise of using such provisions, especially with respect to welfare assistance and housing. In *Tucker v. Toia* for example, the New York Court of Appeals was asked to

interpret article XVII of the New York Constitution: 'the aid, care and support of the needy are public concerns and shall be provided by the state and by such of its subdivisions … as the legislature may … determine'.[102] The Court found that the language imposed 'a positive duty upon the state' to provide welfare payments to anyone considered indigent under the state's 'need standard', even if the individual could not present papers proving that he or she received no support from relatives.[103]

Another well-known New York case, *Callahan v. Carey*, relied on article XVII to challenge the city's inadequate emergency shelter system.[104] In *Callahan*, the National Coalition for the Homeless filed a class-action suit on behalf of homeless men in Manhattan, requesting that the city provide shelter to any man who asked for it in accordance with the New York constitution and other state and municipal laws.[105]

After difficult negotiations spanning two years, plaintiffs and defendants ultimately entered into a consent decree in 1981 which required New York City to furnish sufficient beds to meet the needs of every homeless man applying for shelter provided that '(a) the man meets the need standard to qualify for the home relief program established in New York State; or (b) the man by reason of physical, mental or social dysfunction is in need of temporary shelter'.[106] Among other things, the *Callahan* consent decree mandated a minimum of three feet between beds and one toilet for every six residents.[107] These standards

---

97 Ibid. 930.
98 International Covenant on Economic, Social and Cultural Rights (New York, 16 Dec. 1966) 993 U.N.T.S. 3, *entered into force* 3 Jan. 1976.
99 Ibid. Art. 13(2)(b).
100 Ibid. Art. 13(2)(e).
101 UNESCO, World Declaration of Education for All, 9 March 1990. Full text available at <http://portal.unesco.org/education/en/ev.php-URL_ID=18693&URL_DO=DO_TOPIC&URL_SECTION=201.html> (accessed 18 November 2006).

102 43 N.Y.2d 1, 7 (1977).
103 Ibid. 8–9.
104 See Coalition for the Homeless, <www.coalitionforthehomeless.org>, for more on *Callahan*. The full text of the 1979 *Callahan v. Carey* decision is available at <http://www.coalitionforthehomeless.org/downloads/callahanfirstdecision121979.pdf> (accessed 18 November 2006). A useful History of Modern Homelessness in New York City is also available at <www.coalitionforthehomeless.org/downloads/NYCHomelessnessHistory.pdf> (accessed 18 November 2006).
105 *Callahan v. Carey*, New York County Supreme Court, Index No. 42582/79.
106 'The *Callahan* Consent Decree: Establishing a Legal Right to Shelter for Homeless Individuals in New York City,' p. 2. August 1981. Full text available at <http://www.coalitionforthehomeless.org/downloads/callahanconsentdecree.pdf> (accessed 18 November 2006).
107 Ibid. p. 2–3. In addition, City defendants were obligated to provide other specific goods and services, like a sturdy bed at least 30 inches wide, clean linens, a lockable

demonstrate the capacity of state courts in the United States to fashion remedies addressing complicated social issues. However, monitoring and enforcing the decree proved difficult, and several more cases were brought to extend the right to shelter to other groups of homeless people.

In *Eldredge v. Koch*, the New York Supreme Court upheld the constitutional right of homeless single women to shelter equal to that provided for homeless men.[108] The city resisted enforcing that decision and was reprimanded by the court in a follow-up case three years later.[109] In *McCain v. Koch*, the Court ruled that homeless families with children were also entitled to emergency shelter, and that, once the city had undertaken to provide such shelter, it was obliged to furnish shelters meeting minimum standards.[110] The judge cited prior precedent, which had held that 'in a civilized society, a "shelter" which does not meet minimum standards of cleanliness, warmth, space and rudimentary conveniences is no shelter at all'.[111]

Other courts have recognised a right to shelter based on 'general welfare' provisions of their state constitutions as well as state and local statutes.[112]

In 1975, the New Jersey Supreme Court held that a zoning ordinance in Mount Laurel township violated the constitutional requirement that the state's police power promote 'public health, safety, morals or the general welfare'.[113] Because the land use controls excluded low- and moderate-income families from the municipality, they were deemed invalid.[114] 'There cannot be the slightest doubt that shelter, along with food, are the most basic human needs', the Court wrote.[115] 'It is plain beyond dispute that proper provision for adequate housing of all categories of people is certainly an absolute essential in promotion of the general welfare required in all local land use regulation'.[116] The Court imposed an obligation on every 'developing municipality' to provide a realistic opportunity for 'decent and adequate low and moderate income housing'.[117] This opportunity extended to 'the municipality's *fair share* of the present and prospective regional need therefore'.[118] Unfortunately, the Court failed to provide any guidance about how the township was to fulfil this mandate. Instead, it granted the township 90 days to reform its land use regulations.[119] For five years thereafter, Mount Laurel and the other municipalities affected did virtually nothing to comply with the judgment.

In 1980, six cases stemming from this New Jersey Supreme Court decision were consolidated into 'Mount Laurel II'.[120] In his 1983 opinion, Chief Justice Wiletz declared that without more forceful judicial intervention, 'Mount Laurel will not result in housing, but in paper, process, witnesses, trials and appeals'. It was time, he wrote, to 'put some steel into the doctrine'.[121] The Court replaced the standard of 'developing municipality' with the 'growth area' designation already used in the State Development Guide Plan.[122] The 'fair share'

---

storage unit, laundry facilities, and a staff attendant-to-resident ratio of at least 2 per cent.

108 *Eldredge v. Koch*, 98 A.D.2d 675 (1983) (decided on equal protection grounds with reference to both federal and state constitutions).

109 *Gerald v. Koch*, Index No. 8978–86 (N.Y. Sup. Ct. May 9, 1986).

110 *McCain v. Koch*, 70 N.Y.2d 109, 113–14 (1987).

111 Ibid. 119–20. In 1986, however, the Appellate Division, while upholding the *McCain v. Koch* injunction, found that plaintiffs were *not* entitled to any standard of adequacy. *McCain v. Koch*, 117 A.D.2d 198, 218 (1986) (holding that homeless plaintiffs did not have a due process right to be housed in any particular neighborhood or type of housing). Litigation in lower courts continues, mainly in the form of motions for injunctive relief that seek to prohibit the city from housing homeless people in certain kinds of facilities. For more information, see Coalition for the Homeless, <www.right2shelter.org> (accessed 18 November 2006).

112 In *Hilton v. City of New Haven*, a Connecticut trial court interpreted a general welfare statute to find a state obligation to provide shelter for all homeless people. No. 8905–3165, 1989 Conn. Super. LEXIS 52, at *11, *24 (Conn. Super. Ct. Dec. 27, 1989) (noting historical 'tradition in Connecticut dating from the middle of the 17th Century right down to the present that the public will be responsible for all medical care and other needs of [the] poor' and declaring that 'Section 17–273 of the Connecticut General Statutes requires each town in Connecticut to provide for and support any person in the town who lacks sufficient funds for his or her support [including] the pro-

vision of emergency shelter [for homeless persons]'). See also *Hodge v. Ginsburg*, 172 W. Va. 17, 22–23 (W. Va. 1983).

113 *Southern Burlington County N.A.A.C.P. v. Township of Mount Laurel*, 67 N.J. 151, 175–80 (1975). The zoning ordinance was also held to be a violation of both the equal protection and due process clauses of the New Jersey constitution.

114 Ibid. 165–71, 173–74.

115 Ibid. 178.

116 Ibid. 179.

117 Ibid. 188.

118 Ibid.

119 Ibid. 191.

120 *Southern Burlington County N.A.A.C.P. v. Township of Mount Laurel*, 92 N.J. 205 (1983).

121 Ibid. 199.

122 Ibid. 215.

obligations of these areas would be determined by a panel of three judges.[123]

The Court's standard of providing a 'realistic opportunity' for the production of low and moderate income housing would clearly require more than eliminating exclusionary zoning regulations. Thus, each municipality was obliged to prove, by a preponderance of the evidence, 'a likelihood – to the extent economic conditions allow – that the lower income housing will actually be constructed'.[124]

Faced with tremendous pressure to respond to this ruling, the New Jersey legislature passed the Fair Housing Act in 1985. This Act codified the Mount Laurel I doctrine but replaced the judicial framework established in Mount Laurel II. It created a Council on Affordable Housing to monitor 'fair share' compliance.[125] Through rezoning, the Mount Laurel decisions also allowed for construction or rehabilitation of 54,000 low- and moderate-income housing units in the suburbs that would have been impossible beforehand.[126]

Extending these rulings to other state courts is not an easy task. State constitutional provisions vary dramatically, and few states have constitutional language as specific that found in New York's Constitution, or courts as progressive as those in New Jersey. Often state courts adopt a very deferential standard of review towards legislative choices on these issues,[127] leaving little role for judicial oversight for the protection of economic and social rights.

4.3 The Right to Health Care

Unlike education, health care is rarely addressed in the context of state constitutions. Health care legal advocates, however, are using creative strategies to develop a right to health jurisprudence.

With regard to the state constitutional 'landscape', only eight state constitutions – Alaska, Hawaii, Michigan, Mississippi, North Carolina, New York, South Carolina, and Wyoming – directly allocate responsibility for promoting or protecting health, or assisting the indigent sick, to the state. Of these, six states – Alaska, Hawaii, Michigan, North Carolina, New York, and Wyoming – have constitutional provisions requiring the legislature to promote and protect the public health.

None of these states, however, has interpreted such provisions to mean that the state must expand access to health care for the uninsured or underinsured. These health promotion/ protection provisions, presumably, authorise state legislatures to protect the public health generally by mandating vaccines, and regulating the environment, food, safety, etc. Nevertheless, since a population with inadequate health insurance may pose a public health problem, an advocate could use these constitutional provisions to argue for increasing funding for state health insurance programs. Unfortunately, even if successful, this strategy would have limited application since only these six states have adopted such provisions.

Other explicit state constitutional provisions require the legislature to fund health-related activities or target a specific population for health care benefits. For example, Mississippi, Hawaii, and Arkansas require the legislature to pass laws for the treatment and care of the mentally ill. However, both Mississippi's and Hawaii's provisions merely permit, but do not mandate, laws for the care of the indigent sick in state hospitals.

Thus, an advocate has little explicit state constitutional language to rely on in attempting to expand individual rights to health care. An alternative strategy, however, would be to look for implicit constitutional language such as welfare or similar assistance provisions aimed at benefiting the poor generally. There are many state constitutional provisions that could be used indirectly to support increased access to health care. These provisions do not mention promoting or protecting health, or providing health care services per se, but they do contain language that may be used to support increasing access to health care for those who cannot afford it. For

---

[123] Ibid. 215–16.
[124] Ibid. 221–22.
[125] *See* C. M. Harr, *Suburbs Under Siege: Race, Space and Audacious Judges* (Princeton, NJ: Princeton University Press, 1996). Other commentators express a much more critical view of Mount Laurel's legacy. See B. K. Ham, 'Exclusionary Zoning and Racial Segregation: A Reconsideration of the Mount Laurel Doctrine,' *Seton Hall Constitutional Law Journal*, Vol. 7 (Winter 1997), pp. 577–616.
[126] Har, *Suburbs Under Siege* (n. 125 above), at 132.
[127] *State ex rel. K.M. v. West Virginia Dept. of Health and Human Services*, 212 W.Va. 783, 575 S.E.2d 393 (W.Va.2002).

example, the courts in North Carolina have consistently found that it is an obligation of the state to care for the indigent sick.[128] Moreover, Alabama's constitutional provision requiring counties of the state 'to make adequate provisions for the maintenance of the poor' has been interpreted to support the constitutionality of the Alabama Health Care Responsibility Act, which, *inter alia*, imposes financial responsibility for the medical care of county indigents upon the county itself.[129]

Given that almost half the states have some form of constitutional provision for assisting the poor, this strategy offers more potential than relying on explicit health-related state constitutional provisions. Unfortunately, only four of the twenty-three state provisions contain mandatory language. Moreover, as noted above, many state courts limit the effectiveness of these poverty provisions because they apply a very deferential rational basis review when adjudicating claims of welfare assistance under these provisions.[130] Thus, state legislatures are given a great deal of latitude in designing the nature and scope of their assistance programs.

As in the federal context, equal protection approaches can also afford modest protections. In two states, New York and Maryland, courts have applied a strict scrutiny standard in cases where the state has denied public medical benefits to legal immigrants. In these two cases, the courts struck down the exclusion of legal immigrants from public health insurance programs.[131] There have also many state level constitutional cases that have established protection for abortion and contraception, including funding for indigent women.[132]

5. CHILDREN AND ECONOMIC AND SOCIAL RIGHTS

Children are amongst the most vulnerable populations for economic and social rights violations in the United States. While there are many legislative policies addressing children, they are clearly inadequate as the rate of child poverty and other indicators reflect. Although U.S. law and policy, consistent with international law, incorporates a 'best interests of the child' standard in most areas of social policy, its fierce resistance to providing social support to families makes it virtually impossible to actually protect the best interest of children Indeed, there are welfare policies that literally penalize children for being born into poor families. For example, in many states if a child is born into a family receiving cash assistance through the welfare program, she or he is not eligible for welfare benefits. This policy's stated goal is to deter women from having children while receiving benefits. But the state 'punishes' and 'deters' the mother by denying newborn children subsistence benefits. This policy has been upheld at both the state and federal constitutional level.[133]

---

[128] *Craven County Hosp. Corp. v. Lenoir County* 75 N.C.App. 453, 459 331 S.E.2d 690, 694 (N. Carolina 1985):

> [I]t has been uniformly held in this State that the care of the indigent sick and afflicted poor is a proper function of the Government of this State, and that the General Assembly may by statute require the counties of the State to perform this function at least within their territorial limits. Citing *Martin v. Comrs. of Wake, 208 N.C. 354, 365, 180 S.E. 777, 783 (1935).* In the absence of a delegation by the State to the counties of the obligation to pay the cost of medical care of the indigent sick, such obligation is that of the State. Citing *Board of Managers v. Wilmington,* 237 N.C. 179, 74 S.E.2d 749 (1953).

[129] *Board of Com'rs of Wilcox County v. Board of Trustees of the University of Alabama,* 483 So.2d 1365 (Alabama 1985).

[130] See n. 127 above.

[131] *Ehrlich v. Perez,* 394 Md. 691, 908 A.2d 1220 (Maryland 2006); *Aliessa ex rel. Fayad v. Novello,* 96 N.Y.2d 418, 730 N.Y.S.2d 1 (N.Y. 2001).

[132] See e.g. *Alaska v. Planned Parenthood,* 28 P.3d 904 (Alaska 2001); *Simat Corp. v. Ariz. Health Care Cost Containment Sys.,* 203 Ariz. 454 (2002); *Committee to Defend Reprod. Rights v. Myers,* 625 P.2d 779 (Cal. 1981); *Doe v. Maher,* 515 A.2d 134 (Conn. Super. Ct. 1986); *Doe v. Wright,* No. 91 CH 1958 (Ill. Cir. Ct. Dec. 2, 1994); *Humphreys v. Clinic for Women, Inc.,* 796 N.E.2d 247, 260 (Ind. 2003); *Moe v. Sec'y of Admin. & Fin.,* 417 N.E.2d 387 (Mass. 1981); *Women of Minn. v. Gomez,* 542 N.W.2d 17 (Minn. 1995); *Jeannette R. v. Ellery,* No. BDV-94–811 (Mont. Dist. Ct. May 22, 1995); *Right to Choose v. Byrne,* 450 A.2d 925 (N.J. 1982); *New Mexico Right to Choose/NARAL v. Johnson,* 975 P.2d 841 (N.M. 1998); *Planned Parenthood Ass'n v. Dep't of Human Resources,* 663 P.2d 1247 (Or. Ct. App. 1983), aff'd on statutory grounds, 687 P.2d 785 (Or. 1984); *Doe v. Celani,* No. S81–84CnC (Vt. Super. Ct. May 26, 1986); *Women's Health Ctr. v. Panepinto,* 446 S.E.2d 658 (W. Va. 1993).

[133] *Sojourner v. Dep't of Human Services,* 177 N.J. 318 (2003); *C.K. v. New Jersey Dept. of Health and Human Services,* 92 F.3d 171 (3rd Cir. 1996).

Children living in poverty are also at risk of being taken from their families for economic reasons. In several states, children are taken into what is known as 'foster care', i.e., become wards of the state, simply because their parents cannot afford adequate housing. In such cases, it would actually require fewer resources to house the entire family. Courts confronted with challenges under sub-national state constitutions to such irrational policies have declined to take action. For example, in *Tilden v. Hayward*, the court noted that '[i]t has been shown time and again that it is more economical to house an intact family than to provide child protective services for a single child'.[134] Nonetheless, the court concluded it was not within the court's authority to order housing assistance for the families at issue.

Thus, under U.S. law children are supposed to be protected by 'neglect' and 'abuse' statutes that guarantee that states will take guardianship over children if they are not cared for appropriately and provided with their basic needs. But in reality, the failure to ensure social protection for families combined with zealous use of these statutes only results in the painful separation of families due to poverty and children being put into an overburdened foster care system that rarely guarantees a safe and healthy environment for its wards. It is important to note that when children are removed from families they are often in unacceptable situations. However, the question remains whether the State has met its obligation to enable the families to properly care for their children. This is an obligation that is not adequately recognised anywhere in U.S. law or policy.

6. CONCLUSION: COMPARATIVE AND HUMAN RIGHTS LAW STRATEGIES

Despite efforts by the U.S. government to restrict the recognition of economic and social rights, advocates have advanced successful claims using a range of tools, from non-discrimination statutes to specific constitutional language. The decisions described above demonstrate that economic and social rights are, in fact, justiciable. They affirm a court's capacity to assess the availability of

resources, to balance competing demands on those resources, and to monitor the adequacy of complex social policies. However, they also reveal areas that, as noted with respect to housing and the Fourteenth Amendment, fall short of human rights standards. As networking among economic and social rights practitioners increases, we can better redress such discrepancies by drawing upon strategies and solutions from different domestic contexts.

Currently, the development of economic and social rights jurisprudence in the United States faces several obstacles including:

- An inherently decentralised effort in the various states;
- Limited positive jurisprudential precedent;
- Flawed federal models that may influence state courts; and
- A lack of awareness about alternative legal systems that can offer compelling analyses to support economic and social rights.

Introducing state courts to the international human rights framework, most likely through comparative law analysis, can provide conceptual cohesion and criteria on economic and social issues that address some of these obstacles. In particular:

- Turning to human rights law as an **interpretive tool for state constitutions** can mitigate the decentralised nature of state work by offering a coherent conceptual basis to link efforts (although, resources and strategies must still be developed and tailored for multiples sites).
- The human rights framework offers a wide range of **jurisprudential precedent and models** to evaluate, and brings state court jurisprudence into the world community where state courts can learn from and participate in global debate.
- State court development of international principles provides fertile territory for **creating a dialogue** between the national and state level that enables more thoughtful legal development in this arena.

A human rights approach to state level legal work holds enormous promise in the long run. Early signs include judges, such as Justice Margaret Marshall, Chief Justice of the Supreme Judicial Court of Massachusetts, speaking out about the value

---

[134] *Tilden v. Hayward* 1990 WL 131162 Del.Ch.,1990. Sep 10, 1990 at p. 17

of using comparative law to interpret state law and constitutions.[135] More over, legal advocates and scholars have begun to engage in a strategic conversation regarding the use of international human rights standards as a tool to develop subnational constitutions in the United States.

For example, in the *Spirit of Our Times*, Professor Martha Davis notes that international law is relevant to state constitutional jurisprudence for at least three separate reasons.[136] First, the federal government has bound itself to human rights obligations and expressed its expectation that those obligations would be met by the States. Second, the federal government has bound itself to human rights obligations that are more appropriately implemented, or can only be implemented, at the state level due to the nature of U.S. federalism. Third, human rights law provides a rich source of comparative law to fully develop state

constitutional jurisprudence. Professor Davis also notes that specific state constitutions were influenced by the international legal and political context in which they were drafted, developed and adopted.

Only state courts at this point are likely to address either positive obligations or economic and social rights. State courts have an opportunity and duty to take leadership in the development of economic and social rights jurisprudence, and are well positioned to do so with regards to both positive obligations and economic and social rights. Moreover, state courts are no strangers to the use of human rights law. There are numerous examples of state court decisions that have relied upon or cited these standards to interpret domestic law.[137]

---

[135] Marshall, Chief Justice of the Supreme Judicial Court of Massachusetts, noted that 'in many ways, state judges are uniquely positioned to take advantage of the significant potential of comparative constitutional law.' M. H. Marshall, '"Wise Parents Do Not Hesitate to Learn From Their Children": Interpreting State Constitutions in An Age of Global Jurisprudence,' *New York University Law Review*, Vol. 79, No. 5 (Nov. 2004) (speech), p. 1641. She posits three reasons for this. First, she notes that:

> As a state court judge, I have frequent occasion to look to the constitutional law of fifty other American jurisdictions, even though other states' interpretations of their constitutions have no precedential weight for Massachusetts. They do, however, provide guidance, perspective, inspiration, reassurance, or cautionary tales. How odd, then, when one stops to think of it: A novel issue of constitutional law will send us, our clerks, and counsel to the library to uncover any possible United States source of authority – including the note of a second-year law student. But in our search for a useful legal framework, we ignore the opinion of a prominent constitutional jurist abroad that may be directly on point.

She goes on to say that: 'Second, state court judges work actively in the open tradition of the common law. *Erie Railroad Co. v. Tompkins*, 304 U.S. 64 (1938), removed much of the traditional common-law role from the federal courts, but what Holmes described as expounding from experience is the quintessential role of a state court judge.' She quotes Oliver Wendell Holmes, Jr., *The Common Law 1* (Boston: Little, Brown & Co., 1990) (1881) with 'The life of the law has not been logic; it has been experience.' Finally, she recognises that '[a]s charters of "positive liberty," some state constitutions may bear close affinity to the new constitutions of other democracies.'
[136] *The Spirit of Our Times: State Constitutions and International Human*, Professor Martha Davis, 30 N.Y.U. Rev. L. & Soc. Change 359 (2006).

[137] *See, e.g., New Hampshire v. Robert H.*, 118 N.H. 713, 716 (1978) (citing International Covenants on Civil and Political Rights and on Economic, Social and Cultural Rights to support notion that parental rights are natural and inherent under State Constitution in action to terminate parental rights); *Pauley v. Kelly*, 162 W. Va. 672, 679, n.5 (1979) (court interprets State Constitution more broadly than the Federal Constitution on the right to education and cites the Universal Declaration of Human Rights for the proposition that education is a fundamental right); *In re Julie Anne*, 121 Ohio Misc.2d 20, 36 (Ohio Com. Pl., 2002) (noting that the 1989 UN Convention on the Rights of the Child (CRC) requires the 'best interests of the child' to be a primary consideration); *Batista v. Batista*, 1992 WL 156171 at 6–7 (Conn. Super. Ct. 1992) (finding it an 'embarrassment' that the U.S. at that time had not signed the CRC, and holding in accordance with the CRC that the child's wishes should be taken into account in a custody proceeding); *Commonwealth v. Edward Sadler*, 3 Phila. 316, 330 (Pa. Com. Pl. 1979) (citing the Universal Declaration of Human Rights to support the holding that the state had an obligation to educate juveniles in custody); *Boehm v. Superior Court*, 178 Cal. App. 3d 494, 501–02 (1986) (citing the Universal Declaration of Human Rights for the proposition that it was inhumane for California to exempt allowances for clothing, transportation or medical care from its calculation of payment rates for General Relief); *Moore v. Ganim*, 233 Conn. 557, 637–38 (1995) (Berdon, J., dissenting) (citing the Universal Declaration of Human Rights to support the proposition that the State Constitution included a right to welfare). *See also, American National Ins. Co. v. Fair Employment & Housing Com.*, 32 Cal. 3d 603, 608 n.4 (1982) (noting the Universal Declaration of Human Rights' relevance to a discrimination claim based on disability); *Sterling v. Cupp*, 290 Ore. 611, 622 n.21 (1981) (citing, *inter alia*, the Universal Declaration of Human Rights as persuasive authority supporting a prohibition on female correctional officers from performing searches or pat-downs of male inmates' genital regions except under circumstances of necessity); *City of Santa Barbara v. Adamson*, 27 Cal. 3d 123, 130 n.2 (1980) (citing language from the Universal Declaration of Human Rights in discussion of California's

Finally, state court judges are already familiar with the process of using comparative law, and human rights approaches used internationally as well as in other countries, may mirror state constitutional protections in a manner that makes them extremely relevant. Indeed, the broad scope of rights addressed by the international system, including economic and social rights, in many cases is a closer analogue to the issues presented on the state level. Accordingly state courts may well find that they have more to learn from writ-

ings on international human rights than they do from federal jurisprudence.

As Professor Davis notes, human rights law serves the same purpose, and is in fact part of comparative law for purposes of constitutional interpretation. Given the current resistance to acknowledging that economic and social rights norms are binding on the United States, at this point in time, the most relevant and practical approach for state courts is the comparative law approach.

constitutional amendment recognizing a right to privacy in one's family as well as in one's home); *Bixby v. Pierno*, 4 Cal. 3d 130, 143 n.9 (1971) (citing the Universal Declaration of Human Rights in support of the obligation to protect the fundamental right to practice one's trade); *In Re White*, 97 Cal. App. 3d 141, 148, n. 4 (1979) (in striking down a term of probation prohibiting a former prostitute from entering certain neighborhoods, the court cited, *inter alia*, the Universal Declaration of Human Rights' provision on freedom of movement within a state); *Wilson v. Hacker*, 101 N.Y.S.2d 461, 473 (Sup. 1950), (citing the Universal Declaration of Human Rights for the principal of non-discrimination based on sex); *Cramer v. Tyars*, 23 Cal. 3d 131, 151 n. 1 (1979) (Newman, J. dissenting) (citing the Universal Declaration of Human Rights to support his conclusion that the questioning of a mentally retarded person by the prosecution in a hearing regarding his committal was 'cruel and degrading'). *But see, People v. Barnes*, 2002 WL 53230 at *7 (Cal. Ct. App. 2002) (rejecting CRC provision banning life imprisonment or execution of minors); *People v. Brazile*, 2001 WL 1423739 at *21-*22 (Cal. Ct. App. 2001) (same), *Wynn v. State*, 804 So. 2d 1122, 1148 (Ala. Crim. App. 2000) (same). These cases are distinguishable, however, as the U.S. specifically placed a reservation on the juvenile death penalty provision in the ICCPR.

13

Hungary

Social Rights or Market Redivivus?
Malcolm Langford*

1. INTRODUCTION

The fall of the Berlin Wall and the concurrent demise of many communist governments ushered in a period of frenzied constitution-making in Eastern Europe and, for the first time, the opportunity for the constitutional judicial review of human rights. While the Eastern European constitutions of the communist period had included social rights, they were rarely subject to judicial scrutiny.

The extent to which these new constitutions recognise social rights varies between the States that were formally under the influence or direct rule of the Soviet Union. As Sadurski notes, of twenty post-communist states in Eastern and Central Europe, eleven have fully-fledged catalogues of economic, social and cultural rights with the remainder recognising a more limited number of rights, and two possessing virtually none at all.[1] Equally, the degree of justiciability varies, with fourteen constitutions making no distinction between the enforceability of civil and political rights and economic, social and cultural rights.[2]

The case of Hungary represents perhaps a midway course. The Hungarian Constitution provides recognition of a number of social rights and over the past decade the Constitutional Court has attempted to develop a systematic approach to

their interpretation, although not without controversy. The Court has been seen as caught between encouraging the post-communist impulse of providing the legal foundations for a market economy and paying heed to a relatively strong public consensus for continuing some version of the communist welfare state.[3] Although, the repeated characterisation of social rights as a product of communist memory in related scholarly literature rings strange in the international context where social rights are often normatively and empirically viewed as universal 'givens' and are critiqued by left and right. Its response has been largely to follow the example of the German Federal Constitutional Court, which has adopted a seemingly robust but rather circumscribed approach to social rights, except in some instances where the Court has sought to use property rights to guarantee social protections.

This chapter will briefly outline the constitutional framework for judicial protection of social rights in Hungary, the general interpretive approach adopted by the Court and its application of the constitutional rights concerning to work, social security, housing and education. The Court's application of the rights is placed in the wider economic and political context.

2. THE CONSTITUTIONAL PROTECTION OF SOCIAL RIGHTS

Social rights first appeared in the Hungarian Constitution passed by the National Assembly in 1949, drafted by the then Hungarian Workers' Party. However, following the logic and approach of

---

* Research Fellow, Norwegian Centre on Human Rights, University of Oslo. He would like to thank Wojciech Sadurski, Morten Kinander and Claude Cahn for reviewing the chapter.

[1] W. Sadurski, *Rights before Courts: A Study of Constitutional Courts in Postcommunist States of Central and Eastern Europe* (Dordrecht: Springer, 2005), p. 177.

[2] Ibid., p. 179. For example, in 1997, Latvia amended its constitution to include a wide range of economic, social and cultural rights and the provisions of international human rights treaties, and has subsequently witnessed an incipient jurisprudence.

[3] See B. Gero, *The Role of the Hungarian Constitutional Court*, Working Paper, Institute on East Central Europe, March, 1997; and Sadurski, *Rights before Courts* (n. 1 above), p. 171.

the 1936 Fundamental Law of the Soviet Union, power was strongly vested in the presidency and ministers, with the legislature and judicial bodies possessing extremely limited influence. The 1972 constitutional reforms during the 'Kádár era' slightly ameliorated this situation with a movement from totalitarianism to authoritarian dictatorship, a clearer delineation of the various branches of government and some notion of the rule of law.[4] In April 1984, a Constitutional Committee was established for the purpose of parliamentary vetting of the constitutionality of legislation, but the system was strongly criticised, not least because it denied the right of individual petition. To a certain degree, social rights were protected under the relatively socialist model of economic governance though some have argued that the measures to realise social rights were also used as tools of oppression: 'the right to work not only guaranteed employment but also allowed the regime to enforce compulsory employment for all adult males and all single females because the regime could best exercise power over the populace while they were at work'.[5]

From May 1988, a new era of constitutionalism emerged with the triumph of reformist leadership in the Hungarian Socialist Workers' Party, who called for socialist pluralism, although not political pluralism, and a program of constitutional change.[6] This was quickly followed in February 1989 with a renunciation of political monopoly by the party and, after pressure from emergent opposition parties, the holding of a national roundtable with major political stakeholders. The result was an adaptation of the old Constitution – characterised by some as a 'patchwork'[7] – and the expectation that a new constitution would be developed once a democratically elected parliament was formed. The latter expectation never materialised although further amendments to the constitution were approved by the new Parliament in 1990.

The revised constitution contains many social rights, namely the right to work, rights to trade union and other associations, including the right to strike, the right to highest attainable standard of physical and mental health, the right to social security, the right to education and rights to cultural and scientific freedoms,[8] and protection of children,[9] with the language largely reflecting that of international human rights instruments, though with some differences as will be discussed below. The constitutional chapter on human rights is headed by an article on the right to life and to human dignity, the later concept playing a very important role in Hungarian constitutional interpretation.[10] Likewise protections on equality and discrimination have played a significant role in constitutional jurisprudence; the Constitution possessing guarantees for equality between men and women in respect of all rights and the prohibition of discrimination with respect to human rights on a range of prohibited grounds.[11] The Government is also obliged to strictly penalise in law any kind of discrimination and promote 'equality of rights for everyone through measures aimed at eliminating the inequality in opportunity'.[12]

The Constitution and related statutes enable residents, public interest organisations and elected representatives to bring a wide variety of legal actions to challenge violations of social rights embedded in the Constitution. In a chapter preceding the establishment of the Government, the Constitution creates a powerful Constitutional Court with powers to review the constitutionality of laws[13] and receive constitutional complaints from *any person*.[14] While the German precedent largely influenced the creation of a supreme constitutionally focused judicial body, the nature

---

[4] See G. Brunner, 'Structure and Proceedings of the Hungarian Constitutional Judiciary', in L. Sólyom and G. Brunner (eds.), *Constitutional Judiciary in a New Democracy: The Hungarian Constitutional Court* (Ann Arbor: University of Michigan Press, 2000), pp. 65–102, at 67.

[5] Hungary, Country Guide, available at <http://reference.allrefer.com/country-guide-study/hungary/>.

[6] Brunner, 'Hungarian Constitutional Judiciary' (n. 4 above).

[7] For an insightful analysis, see Morten Kinander, 'The accountability function of courts in Eastern central Europe: The case of Hungary and Poland (on file with author).

[8] Articles 70/B-70/G.

[9] Article 67.

[10] Article 54. See generally, C. Dupré, *Importing the Law in Post-Communist Transitions: The Hungarian Constitutional Court and the Right to Human Dignity* (Oxford: Hart, 2003).

[11] Namely, 'race, colour, gender, language, religion, political or other opinion, national or social origins, financial situation, birth or any other grounds': Article 70/A(1).

[12] Article 70/A(2) and (3).

[13] Article 32/A(1).

[14] Article 32/A(2).

of the complaint system differs. The Hungarian Court is empowered by statute to hear complaints from any person concerned with the constitutionality of *any legal or administrative norm* without the petitioner needing to demonstrate a violation or interference with a fundamental right or other interest. This right to 'posterior review of legal norms' through popular action has spawned the largest number of cases in the Court's docket, leading the Constitutional Court and others to call for more stricter admissibility requirements in the empowering statute. Interestingly, a petitioner may also claim that there has been an unconstitutional omission to legislate by a State authority if the Constitution, statute, delegated legislation, or the annulment of a law, explicitly, or implicitly, creates a mandate for legislation.

A more circumscribed 'constitutional complaint' is also permitted, whereby other domestic remedies must be exhausted and injury demonstrated, but its usage is dwarfed by the popular actions. Brunner points out that this 'constitutional complaint' is useful in circumstances where the law or administrative norm in question has been repealed but still exerts an effect, a situation that cannot be addressed through the popular 'posterior review of legal norms'.[15] In addition, the Parliament, the President or Government may call for preventive constitutional review in certain circumstances.[16] The Parliament may request the Court to review draft Acts or parliamentary rules of procedures, with parliamentary standing committees or fifty legislators having the right to instigate the former action. The President may also demand that the Court review Acts before their promulgation and, together with the Government, ask for the constitutional assessment of international treaties before their confirmation by Parliament.

Beyond the apex court, a system of courts headed by the Supreme Court is established by the Constitution for the general administration of justice. Such courts are required to 'protect and guarantee the constitutional order, as well as the rights and lawful interests of citizens'[17] and if in a proceeding a judge is of the view that a legal provision is unconstitutional the matter must be referred to the Constitutional Court.[18]

The Constitutional Court is also required to ensure 'harmony' between Hungarian domestic and international legal obligations 'assumed' by the country. This monist-dualist hybrid creates the potential for strong synergies between the interpretations by international bodies such as the UN Committee on Economic, Social and Cultural Rights and the Court's development of Hungarian jurisprudence. But the Court has rarely looked to the international sphere for inspiration, unlike their Latvian counterparts for example,[19] tending to content themselves with comparative lessons from Europe, particularly Germany, and the United States.

3. THE APPROACH OF THE HUNGARIAN CONSTITUTIONAL COURT

While the Hungarian Constitutional Court has been eulogised or demonised as 'activist', a closer reading of its judgments reveals an inherent conservatism or minimalism in its interpretive approach to express constitutional social rights. The Court's constitutional vision of social rights is perhaps best summed up in remarks it made during a case on the right to environmental health:

> Social rights are implemented both by the formation of adequate institutions and by the rights of the individual to have access to them, which rights are to be specified by the legislature. In a few exceptional cases, however, certain social rights to be found in the Constitution have an element of subjective (justiciable) right.[20]

Social rights therefore compel the State to create the necessary legislation and structures but the Court will not inquire as to the effectiveness or reasonableness of those mechanisms or measures except in very limited cases. This includes situations in which it is questionable whether the State has ensured a minimum level of the social right, whether there has been unequal or discriminatory

---

[15] Brunner, 'Hungarian Constitutional Judiciary' (n. 4 above), p. 84.

[16] Ibid., pp. 78–79.

[17] Article 50(1) Constitution.

[18] Section 38(1) Constitutional Court Act. See Brunner, 'Hungarian Constitutional Judiciary' (n. 4 above), p. 82.

[19] Cf. Case No. 2000–08-0109 of the Constitutional Court of Latvia (n. 1 above).

[20] Decision 28/1994, para. 29(b).

treatment in the exercise of the right, or whether disproportionate restrictions have been placed on the right. These justiciable 'exceptions' correspond, to a certain degree, with civil and political rights, namely the right to life, right to non-discrimination and right to freedom from arbitrary action.

When faced with pressing social rights claims, the Court has instead turned to property rights (both express and implied) to protest social interests. For example, it relied on the principle of legal certainty and proprietary interest in contributions to protect changes to social insurance schemes. While this has led to close scrutiny of retrogressive measures, the Court has left itself open to the charge that it is more concerned with protecting the social rights entitlements of the middle class than the poor,[21] since the use of property rights largely favours those with greater power in the market. This is a charge it might have avoided had it been willing to use less deference in cases concerning the minimal entitlements of the poor.[22]

4. SELECTED RIGHTS

4.1 Labour Rights

In the early 1990s, the Court was offered the opportunity to outline its views on the broadly worded article 70/B that states that, 'everyone has the right to work and to freely choose his job and profession'. In a series of cases concerning restrictions on various occupations, the Court offered its views on both parts of the right with a marked preference for enforcement of the second limb.

In the case of *Freedom of Enterprise on the Licensing of Taxis*,[23] the Court was confronted with the legality of a decision by Budapest's local authority to restrict the number of taxi drivers. The decision was made in accordance with traffic and roads legislation and the Budapest authority argued that an oversupply of taxis had paradoxically not

led to a competitive pricing but instead to over-charging and exploitative practices.[24] The Court struck down the provision due to its interference with the right to work. Declining to find the restriction unconstitutional on the basis of the general constitutional principles of a 'market economy' or 'freedom of competition', the Court considered that the *numerus clausus* or quota system for taxi licences interfered with the right to freely choose one's occupation. In an earlier decision the Court had already expressly found that 'The right to enterprise is one aspect of the constitutional fundamental right to choose freely one's occupation... The State may not prevent or make impossible the launching of an entrepreneurship'.[25]

The Court found that the measure lacked objective justification. Restrictions on entry into a certain profession would be permitted as long as they applied equally to everyone: for example, the passing of an exam or the completion of a certain course of study. Moreover, the absoluteness of the measure was considered by the Court to be extremely serious as it weighed competing policy considerations: 'In evaluating the objective restrictions, attention must also be paid to the fact that since this restriction involves the total negation of a fundamental right such an instrument must not be applied to regulate competition'.[26] The Court pointed the way to constitutionally resolving the exploitative practices within the taxi market through the use of administrative measures such as the requirement for receipts and the use of meters. Interestingly, the Court notes that the Government does not have the option of selecting a regulatory instrument with a lower cost if constitutional rights were infringed.[27]

In a later decision, the Court took a similar approach to the powers of the Hungarian Medical

---

[21] See A. Sajó, 'Social Rights as Middle-Class Entitlements in Hungary: The Role of the Constitutional Court' in R. Gargarella, P. Domingo and T. Roux (eds.) *Courts and Social Transformation in New Democracies: An Institutional Voice for the Poor?* (Aldershot/Burlington: Ashgate, 2006), pp. 83–106.

[22] See discussion in sections 4.2 and 4.3 below.

[23] Decision 21/1994 (16 April 1994).

[24] See Gero, *The Role of the Hungarian Constitutional Court* (n. 3 above), p. 6 and footnote 39. The national legislation permitting such restrictions stated the reasons for the need for local government action: 'The undesired expansion of supply, the deterioration of the quality of the service, the unduly high price level for the service, the ensuing economic hardship for a large number of the entrepreneurs, the non-payment of taxes and service charges': see Decision 21/1994 (16 April 1994), V(5).

[25] Decision 54/1993 (X. 13) AB (Mk 1993/147), p. 8802.

[26] Ibid. IV(3).

[27] 'Public administration may not lighten its burdens at the expense of such a restriction of fundamental rights': ibid. V(5).

Association (HMA), striking down its power to reject properly qualified foreign doctors from registering their names in the Medical Practitioner's National Register and, together with the Minister, its unfettered discretion over their applications to join the HMA, on the basis that it interfered with the free choice of occupation. In strong language on the working rights of non-citizens, the Court stated:

> According to the Hungarian Constitution, the right to free choice of job and profession is a human right, that is, contrary to some foreign constitutions, not a citizen's right.... According to the practice of the Constitutional Court, the right to work...is violated in the most serious way if the person cannot choose a profession; those provisions which exclude the ability to choose because of objective reasons must be examined in the strictest way.[28]

The Court in Decision 32/1998, declined to find, however, certain eligibility criteria for social security benefits in violation of the right to work. Section 37/C(1) of the Welfare Act permitted local municipalities to require beneficiaries to participate in designated programmes (e.g., family support service or other institutions) corresponding to their social and mental health situation.[29] In particular, the organisations challenged the requirement that persons in need of care, who had rights under section 93 to 'personal care on a voluntary basis', were required to participate in a mental health programme. The Court demurred though that this 'cooperation obligation' could be justified on the basis that its aim was to help persons 'manage the living difficulties and mental problems that result from constant unemployment'.[30]

During the course of its seminal decision on taxi licensing, discussed above, the Court also offered some comment on the wider notion of the right to work: 'The right to work as a subjective right

[justiciable right] must be distinguished from the right to work as a social right, especially the latter's institutional aspect, namely, the State's duty to engage in an appropriate employment and job-creation policy'.[31] This statement carries a clear implication that the State's duty with respect to fulfilling the right to work does not extend to a guarantee of job, but rather is an obligation of conduct by the State to take steps towards that end. As Justice Sólyom, who wrote the decision, later argued in a scholarly article, addressing both the right to employment as well as the right to equal pay (Article 70/B(2)):[32]

> With the right to work there emerged relatively few problems. The Constitutional Court soon turned the treatment of persons with equal dignity into the test of the equality principles (thus, the results oriented claims to equal payment and other issues failed) and equated the right to work with free enterprise. *It also stated on the negative side that the right to work secured no subjective right to obtain a given job.*[33]

The Court's statement also clearly suggests that this duty to create the conditions for employment may not be justiciable: a distinction is made between the subjective justiciable right and the 'social' or collective non-justiciable aspects of the right, seemingly placing positive obligations in the latter category. As will be seen below, this interpretation is largely consistent with rulings by the court on other social rights. However, the failure by the State to take positive steps towards the provision of employment or equal pay can be construed in subjective or individual terms. As the UN Committee on Economic, Social and Cultural Rights has commented, the failure to adopt a national employment policy or implement technical and vocational training programmes can have a direct impact on an individual and their right to work,[34]

---

[28] Decision 39/1997, para. 6.2. The judgment also places great emphasis on the lack of administrative fairness, 'Because of the unlimited discretionary power the HMA has, the judicial remedy in the case of a refusal of the request is pointless: none of the legal rules contains any aspect or measure according to which the court can review the legality of the decision'.

[29] Decision 32/1998 (VI. 25) AB.

[30] Ibid., Para. 2.

[31] Decision 21/1994 (n. 23 above), para. 3.

[32] See L. Sólyom, 'Introduction to the Decisions of the Constitutional Court', in L. Sólyom and G. Brunner (eds.), *Constitutional Judiciary in a New Democracy: The Hungarian Constitutional Court* (Ann Arbor: University of Michigan Press, 2000), pp. 1–64, at 35.

[33] Decision 54/1993 (X. 13) AB (Mk 1993/147). Emphasis added.

[34] The Committee has stated:

> Violations of the obligation to fulfil occur through the failure of States parties to take all necessary steps to ensure the realization of the right to work.

and these issues could easily and imaginably be the subject of litigation. In Hungary, such a likelihood for justiciability is only enhanced by the availability of popular actions for abstract review and the justiciable obligation of the State to constitutionally legislate for those mandates within the Constitution. The question of the obligation to take positive measures to protect persons from interference with their right to work by private actors is also ignored in the Court's binary conception of social rights.

The Court's reticence to enlarge on the justiciable scope of the right to work is perhaps not only attributable to a need to distinguish the new market economy from the older socialist economy,[35] but is possibly also a product of German constitutional influence. The German constitution protects the right to freely choose an occupation – but not the more general right to work. The Federal Constitutional Court of Germany has strongly defended the protection of the former in a decision concerning women's entry into certain occupations, and in a *numerus clausus* case concerning restrictions on places for the study of medicine in universities. In language not dissimilar from the Hungarian taxis case, the German Court stated:

> An absolute restriction on admission to the university, however, leads to the glaring inequality that one class of applicants receives everything and the other receives nothing.... Because of these effects, absolute admission

restrictions are undisputedly on the edge of constitutional acceptability.[36]

However, it is arguable that the Hungarian Court's comments on the wider aspects of the right to work have perhaps overlooked some of the more progressive elements of the German jurisprudence, where it has examined the positive obligations that flow from civil and political rights and its willingness to intervene to ensure that the government has taken sufficient steps where rights are manifestly violated. For example, in the *Numerus Clausus* cases it initially considered that adequate steps had been taken to provide sufficient places of study for medicine but in later cases, where more precise evidence was provided, it found that the universities had excess capacity.[37]

In addition to the right to work, issues of trade union rights have been raised before the Court. In these cases, the key issue has been the extent to which individuals are bound by the rules and decisions of the union. In Decision 8/1990, the Court struck down a provision of the Labour Code, which permitted a trade union to represent employees without representation. The petitioner raised the constitutional question in the immediate aftermath of the collapse of the communist state, arguing that the authority of the trade unions was weakened by the need for greater pluralism and representation. The Court declined to examine whether the substance of the constitutional provisions concerning trade unions – namely the duty of unions to represent employee interests[38] and their right to form organisations[39] – affected the manner in which trade unions could represent their employees. Instead, the Court examined the question from the perspective of the right to human dignity of an individual who may have a decision made on his behalf without his authorisation: 'This potential infringement upon the right to self-determination may not be

---

Examples include the failure to adopt or implement a national employment policy designed to ensure the right to work for everyone; insufficient expenditure or misallocation of public funds which results in the non-enjoyment of the right to work by individuals or groups, particularly the disadvantaged and marginalized; the failure to monitor the realization of the right to work at the national level, for example, by identifying right-to-work indicators and benchmarks; and the failure to implement technical and vocational training programmes.

See General Comment No. 18, Article 6: the equal right of men and women to the enjoyment of all economic, social and cultural rights (Thirty-fifth session, 2006), U.N. Doc. E/C.12/GC/18 (2006), para. 36.

[35] Note the following strong language with respect to the taxi licences: 'The application of a numerus clausus is particularly impermissible for the planning of needs, for such a licensing mechanism is the hallmark of central planning and not the market economy': Decision 21/1994 (16 April 1994), IV(3).

[36] *Numerus Clausus I* case (33 BVerfGE 303).
[37] Ibid.
[38] 'Trade unions and other representative organisations shall protect and represent the interests of employees, members of co-operatives and entrepreneurs' (article 4).
[39] 'Everyone has the right to establish or join organisations together with others to protect his economic or social interests' (article 70/C(1)); and 'The right to strike may be exercised within the framework of the statute regulating such right' (article 70/C(1) A two-thirds majority of Parliament is necessary for the passage of any statute concerning the right to strike: Article 70/C(3).

eliminated even by the fact that a representation without authorisation must take into account the employee's interest, since the interests of the individual employee are only presumed by the trade union'.[40]

4.2 Social Security Rights

The Court's intervention in social security reforms in the mid-1990s is perhaps the most well-known and discussed instance of its application of constitutional rights in the socio-economic arena.

Initially, in 1990, a one-person majority of the Court signalled that it would take a fairly relaxed attitude to changes to the social security system. With premonitions of its later reasoning on the right to work, the Court demonstrated scepticism towards any results-based approach to social security opining that 'social security means neither guaranteed income, nor that the achieved living standard could deteriorate as a result of the unfavourable development of economic conditions'.[41] The Court declined to view the right to social security as containing any justiciable or 'subjective' substance, thereby reducing Article 70/E to a social goal or objective. This constitutional right nonetheless required some action, namely the organisation and operation of a 'social insurance scheme and system of welfare benefits for those not insured', but the means by which 'this goal was to be reached was not a constitutional question'.[42]

But the issue remained potent in the immediate aftermath of the early transition period, as inflation rose rapidly, eroding the value of fixed incomes such as pensions, and many pensioners fell below the poverty line. This was brought to a head in a 1993 case concerning a cap on pension levels,[43] which primarily affected those on higher pensions. The Court declined to find the measures discriminatory or otherwise unconstitutional since the primary duty on the State was simply to provide social security services (in this case

pensions) and the level of pensions was always connected to the health of the economy and social security institutions.[44]

The Court's principal concern, as later expanded upon in some detail in the mid-1990s, was not so much the realisation of the right to social security but rather the guarantee of legal certainty and the protection of property rights, whether acquired through market, social security or other system.[45] But since the pension systems inherited from the socialist times were largely public-financed Pay-As-You-Go systems with weak links between contributions and benefits,[46] a majority of the Court found that no rights to legal certainty of protection of social property rights had been created through the existing pension system.[47] Moreover, the Court found that the State was not burdened with any duty to keep pensions in line with the cost of living.[48]

This interpretive approach to social security matured in the 1995 *Social Benefits* case and related decisions, even though the judgments went partly, and controversially, against the Government. While a number of institutional reforms to the social security system were introduced in the early 1990s,[49] the Government sought more radical changes in the mid-1990s on the basis that poor economic growth, high public debt, and budget and current account deficits prevented the sustenance of a system that the country had largely inherited from socialist times. The International Monetary Fund also threatened to quit the

---

[40] Decision 8/1990, Part III.

[41] 772/B/1990/AB:ABH 1990, p. 520 and also Decision 26/1993(IV.29)AB:ABH 1993, 196; MK 5651/1993.

[42] L. Sólyom, 'Introduction to the Decisions of the Constitutional Court' (n. 32 above), p. 36.

[43] Decision 26/1993 (IV. 29).

[44] Gero, *The Role of the Hungarian Constitutional Court* (n. 3 above), pp. 10–11.

[45] Sajó, 'Social Rights as Middle-Class Entitlements in Hungary' (n. 21 above).

[46] See K. Müller, *Privatising Old-Age Security: Latin America and Eastern Europe Compared* (Cheltenham: Edward Elgar Publishing, 2003), pp. 72–73.

[47] The Polish Tribunal took the opposite view although under slightly different circumstances: see Sajó, 'Social Rights as Middle-Class Entitlements in Hungary' (n. 21 above), p. 88 and footnote 16.

[48] Ibid.

[49] Müller notes in relation to pensions that 'Early reforms introduced some changes to the organisation, financing and eligibility of the existing retirement scheme. Pension finances were separated from the state budget and from the health fund. Social insurance was granted autonomy and, and self-government was restored' although attempts to increase the retirement age were resisted until the mid-1990s: Müller, *Privatising Old-Age Security* (n. 46 above), p. 73.

country if social benefits were not cut.[50] Finance Minister Bokros introduced a tranche of reforms to Parliament, that included tax increases,[51] a shift to a needs-based system for a range of social benefits (family allowances, maternity benefits, sickness benefits, health care), payment of university fees and an increase in the subsidised mortgage rate.[52] While most commentators see the reforms as emerging from the financial crisis,[53] Katharina Müller notes the strong ideological influence of the international financial institutions, particularly in the area of pensions, and their desire to create an Eastern European precedent for privatised social security.[54]

The introduction of the Economic Stabilisation Act[55] into Parliament, which contained the above reform measures, prompted a wave of petitions to the Court. In its seminal decision, which concerned the conversion of the previous package of universal family allowances and maternity benefits into a needs-based system,[56] the Court repeated its earlier views on the right to social security and then proceeded to fully articulate its approach, namely the principles of legal certainty and property rights. Dealing with the first element, the decision states: 'The Constitutional Court declares that the principle of legal certainty as the most substantial conceptual element of the rule of law and theoretical basis of the protection of acquired rights is of particular significance from the viewpoint of the stability of welfare systems'.[57] Any interference with legal certainty was to be evaluated according to its impact on fundamental rights, irrespective of whether a beneficiary had made contributions.[58] The Court did not examine though the impact of the retrogressive measure on the right to social security, but rather examined their implications for the implied right to legitimate expectations or acquired social benefits:

> Changing a benefit without transition or 'degrading' it from an insurance to a form of assistance also brings about an essential change in the legal position in the sense that the person concerned falls into a weaker category of protection of legitimate expectations (the protection of property ceases), and this amounts to an intervention in fundamental rights.

The Court secondly articulated that where there is an 'insurance' element in the welfare system, any change must be evaluated in the context of the right to property:

> Property is afforded a constitutional protection in its capacity as the traditional means of securing an economic basis for the autonomy of individuals. The constitutional protection must track the changing social role of property so as to fulfil the same task.... [T]he constitutional protection extends to rights with an economic value which today perform this former role of ownership, including public

---

[50] See K. Lane Scheppele, 'Democracy by Judiciary. Or, Why Courts Can Be More Democratic than Parliaments', in A. Czarnote, Martin Krygier and Wojciech Sadurski (eds.), *Rethinking the Rule of Law after Communism* (Budapest: CEU Press, 2005), pp. 25–60, at 46.

[51] See further Gero, *The Role of the Hungarian Constitutional Court* (n. 3 above), p. 9.

[52] For discussion of the Court's judgment on interest rates for subsidised mortgages, see section 4. 3.

[53] See Gero, *The Role of the Hungarian Constitutional Court* (n. 3 above), p. 9.

[54] Müller, *Privatising Old-Age Security* (n. 46 above) outlines the World Bank's role as follows:

> While it's early advice had been limited to reforms within the existing PAYG scheme, the Bank's campaign for pension privatisation in the region started at a seminar in late 1993, where most Hungarian experts rejected the plan. After the release of the Bank's 1994 report, its pension reform recommendations to the Hungarian turned more explicit. It advocated a 'systemic change, involving splitting the current single public scheme into two mandatory pillars – a flat citizen's pension and a...full funded [private] second tier. It was argued that the existing public PAYG scheme was financially unviable and 'could explode' in the next decade. At the request of the Ministry of Finance, the Bank's Budapest office became directly involved in the Hungarian pension reform around 1995. World Bank experts were careful not to take an active role in public discussion.... Clearly, the Bank aimed at creating a precedent: 'Passage of the Hungarian pension reform by Parliament has demonstrated the political and economic feasibility of this type of reform in Central Europe'. (pp. 80–81)

[55] The full name of the law was Act XLVIII/1995 on the Amendment of Certain Laws to Promote Economic Stabilisation.

[56] This included the family allowance, the child care benefit, the child care fee, the pregnancy allowance, the maternity benefit and the child care allowance.

[57] Decision 43/1995: 30 June 1995, para. 1.

[58] Ibid. section II.

law entitlements (for instance, to entitlement from the social insurance).[59]

This approach was partially justified on the grounds that individuals invest their income in a collective, as opposed to a private or asset-based, system, in order to allay future risks and contingencies. However, the Court acknowledged that the traditional approach to the justiciability of property rights could not be strictly applied since there was not an exact matching between contributions and benefits. The system contained no individual accounts or capitalisation; there was some element of redistribution across beneficiaries and contributors accepted some long-term risks as to payment of the benefits. The Court's answer to this dilemma was to simply focus on the proportionality analysis and determine whether the changes were justified in the public interest, but the Court noted that 'the protection of expectations and benefits is stronger depending on whether or not they are provided on the basis of financial contribution'.[60]

In accordance with the right to social security, the Court did note that social benefits may not be 'reduced below a minimal level' required for the right to social security. This appears to create a subjective or justiciable right under article 70/E, and Sadurski contends that this doctrine is contradictory since this enforceable minimum conflicts with the generally soft 'goal' approach of the Court.[61] In the context of Hungary, where social rights are expressly provided for in the Constitution, this charge is correct, but partially explainable by the Court's use of jurisprudence from countries where constitutional social rights are not explicit, and are instead derived from civil and political rights and therefore cautiously applied.

In determining whether the impact on acquired and property rights was proportional, the Court noted the difficulties the Government was facing in terms of the financing of the system, both through lack of government finances and employer contributions. Yet the Court faulted the law for failing for its non-temporal character – no transitional period was allowed. This was particularly pertinent in the case of family and maternal benefits since they 'play an important role in the long-term decisions pertaining to the livelihood of the family, as regards whether to have a child or children and their schooling and education' (part II). This reasoning was buttressed by reference to the constitutional directive principles requiring the State to support marriage and the family (articles 15 and 16), the right of mothers to receive support and protection before and after the birth of a child (article 66(2)) and the right of children to protection (article 67(1)), although the Court is quick to affirm that there is no subjective right to a family allowance of a specific type or amount.[62] The Court also recalled its decision on abortion and that 'positive counter-measures' such as social benefits were necessary in order to encourage and enable women to have children – thereby protecting both the mother's right to self-determination and the right of the foetus to life.

The result was that the Court struck down the measure as unconstitutional for lack of proportionality, although its remedy was both temporary and limited. The acquired rights were to accrue to children already born or who would be born within 300 days of the date of promulgation of the Act, of 15 June 1995. By implication, the Government was permitted to re-introduce reforms for children born later. Anticipating the charge that the burden of providing the existing system of benefits, even for a smaller-defined group of children and families, would be onerous, the Court distinguished between short- and long-term benefits. The family and maternity allowances were of a short-term nature since the existing system would quickly expire once the children identified by the Court had reached an age that no longer triggered the provision of the benefits.

This decision paved the way for a finding of unconstitutionality in relation to a range of other measures. Decision 56/1995 concerned the partial shifting of the burden of insurance for sickness benefits to the insured and employers. In particular, employers were now required to pay for significantly more days of sick leave before the social fund intervened with financial support. The Court noted that the immediate introduction of the

---

[59] Decision 64/1993 (XII.22): MK 1993/184 at 11078 quoted in Decision 43/1995, ibid.
[60] Decision 43/1995: 30 June 1995, section II.
[61] Sadurski, *Rights Before Courts* (n. 1 above), p. 181.

[62] '[t]he maternity benefit, the pregnancy allowance and other benefits or even the concrete regulation or extent of the family allowance cannot be directly derived from the provisions of the Constitution'. Ibid. section III.

system amounted to unwarranted interference with the legal certainty and that it violated the acquired rights of employers who had made past contributions to the fund. Decisions were also handed down on subsidised interest rates and higher education fees, which will be analysed in the following Sections of the Chapter.

Though the decision was overwhelmingly supported by the public,[63] the Hungarian Government reacted with some hostility to the decision and commentators such as András Sajó lambasted the Court, accusing it of returning to a communist vision of the welfare state and hobbling Hungary's shift to a market economy and balanced budget. In his 1996 paper, Sajó criticises the Court for going beyond the minimalist approach, outlined by the German Federal Constitutional Court, and attempting to protect all social security entitlements without regard for their level or need of residents: 'The Court's reasoning implies that, wherever there is a constitutional task for the state, legislation cannot deprive rights-holding beneficiaries of what was once promised by law'.[64] Turning to the Court's construction of social property rights, he mourns the departure from the US Court's approach of simply requiring due process in relation to the termination of benefits and the requirement that compensation be granted for interference with social benefits. The finding that the change to sickness benefits also failed to take account of the fact that the employers contribution covered other benefits, not only sick leave, and the decision on arbitrariness lacked justification according to Sajó.

But this critique involves a certain misreading of the judgment since the Court's strong emphasis was on the short-term impact of the reform, and essentially the lack of due process. The Court was particularly reticent about protecting benefits of a long-term nature and specifically declined to order that compensation be provided for interference with social property rights. (It should also be noted that the European Court of Human Rights has protected social insurance contributions as property rights and the Hungarian Court's deci-

sions in this regard are not particularly innovative or new).[65] This more nuanced reading is borne out by the fact that in the two years following the judgment, the social security reforms were largely implemented, with even more radical changes than originally anticipated, and in 2006, Sajó acknowledged that his earlier fears of a return to communism through the courtroom were not realised.[66] Indeed, Sajó now focuses more sharply on the failure of the Court to protect the minimum levels of social security at a time when Hungary has been experiencing growing levels of poverty. He fingers the Court for supporting the political elites in paying more attention to the social rights of the middle class and not the poor. This can be particularly seen in the Court's decision to refrain from enforcing the minimum level for the protection of the right to housing in the social welfare system (see Section 4.2 below).

But the deeper and fundamental problem of the Hungarian Constitutional Court is its decision to impose an unjustified theory of justiciability on express social rights and seek to protect them in a backhanded way through implied rights and property rights. This approach can be particularly seen in a decision three years later on pension rights where the Court refused to strike down legislation that reduced the rate by which pensions were to rise *vis-à-vis* inflation on the basis that the pensioners had no vested rights in the rate of increase.[67] In a manner similar to the Inter-American Court of Human Rights,[68] the Hungarian Court, when confronted with claims of violations of the positive dimensions of social rights turns to largely civil rights (property, legal certainty) or simply dismisses the claims. When the decisions of the Court are read together, they bear out Sajó's later claim that the Courts are protecting the middle class at the expense of the poor.

Instead, the Court would do well to revisit its early decisions, declare the right to social security and other social rights justiciable and seek to build

---

[63] See Scheppelle, 'Democracy by Judiciary' (n. 50 above), p. 49.

[64] András Sajó, 'How the Rule of Law Killed Hungarian Welfare Reform', *East European Constitutional Review*, Winter (1996), pp. 31–41, at 39.

[65] See Chapter 20 by Clements and Simmons in this book.

[66] See Sajó, *Social Rights as Middle-Class Entitlements in Hungary* (n. 21 above), p. 105 (fn. 47).

[67] Summarised in 'Constitution Watch: Hungary', *East European Constitutional Review*, Vol. 9, Nos. 1–2 (Winter/Spring 2000), pp. 18–21, at 20–21, discussed in Sadurski, *Rights before Courts* (n. 1 above), p. 181.

[68] See Chapter 19 on Inter-American Court of Human Rights by Melish in this book.

a more coherent interpretive framework such as that developed by the UN Committee on Economic, Social and Cultural Rights. This approach, more flexible and nuanced than the communist scarecrow versions of social rights imagined by some Hungarian judges, contains four key elements with respect to positive obligations to fulfil the right: the duty to plan and take steps to establish a reasonably designed scheme, the immediate protection of the minimum level, the duty to progressively improve realisation of the right (in the case of social security, extending the levels and types of benefits) and strong justification for any deliberately retrogressive measures. Protection of acquired social insurance rights could be considered under property rights, but deliberations over the reasonableness in changes to benefits could be better analysed in the context of considering the justifications for retrogression. This does not necessarily mean a pure and strict 'ratchet' theory that prevents any reform[69] – for example the approach that was debated and rejected in Polish cases on social security reform – but a more contextual approach based on a range of reasonableness factors.[70]

Under such a framework, it is likely that the 1995 reforms would have been strongly scrutinised for similar reasons, but that the results may have been partially different. The Government may have been given more flexibility in moving to a needs-based system, but warned that progressive improvement was required as resources improved, the need to protect the minimum levels and ensure the shift to a more privatised scheme of pensions was properly regulated and did not violate the right to social security. Indeed, the claim by the Court to protect human dignity rings rather hollow.

Three years later, the Court had an opportunity to test the strength of its resolve concerning its jurisprudence that the Government must ensure a minimum level of social security. In Decision 32/1998, the petitioning organisations challenged the adequacy of unemployment benefits in the Welfare Act, which were set at a minimum of 70 per cent of the old age pension, though total income, which included all benefits, must reach 80 per cent.[71] After repeating its findings in earlier cases, the Court suspended it proceedings so that a study could be undertaken to determine whether this 80 per cent threshold could 'secure the minimum livelihood necessary for the realisation of the right to human dignity in line with the constitutional requirement specified in the holdings'.

4.3 Housing Rights

In the last two decades, the challenge of providing adequate housing has come under serious pressure. Claude Cahn writes:

> [S]ince the collapse of Communism, Hungarian authorities have significantly eroded rights associated with the right to adequate housing and policies aimed at securing adequate housing for all. For example, Hungary already has among the lowest public housing stocks in Europe and as a result of diminishing resources, local authorities have since the early 1990s been selling off what public housing stocks do exist – a fact which national lawmakers have done nothing to check. At the same time, Hungarian lawmakers have knocked out previously existing protections against forced evictions; since 2000, the notary (an assistant to the mayor) may order eviction, against which no appeals are suspensive. Previously only a court could do so and the eviction could only be implemented following final ruling. Police must implement notary-ordered evictions within eight days. Although there is a requirement to re-house evicted furniture, there is no requirement to re-house evicted persons!

---

[69] See Sadurski, *Rights before Courts* (n. 1 above), pp. 182–3.

[70] The judgments of the Polish Tribunal, the apex court, are perhaps interesting in this respect. Their decision to strike down legislation which restricted the pension rights of persons with disabilities is quite justifiable on traditional human and social rights grounds. The Tribunal noted the objectionability of such deprivation being borne by a particular group, and that is directly conflicted with the obligation for 'even fuller implementation' of the right to social security. Decision K. 1/88, quoted in Sadurski. On the other hand, the Tribunal was loathe to go further and develop a more principled approach to retrogression and merely stated that this obligation for progressive improvement can generally only be viewed over a long period of time: it would take several consecutive laws to violate the right. But this obviously largely removes the subject from the realm of justiciability given the difficulty of such long-range litigation.

[71] Decision 32/1998 (VI.25) AB.

These developments, combined with rising prices in Hungary, have resulted in new armies of homeless. The Hungarian Ministry of Social Affairs estimates the homeless population to be approximately 30,000.... There are clear indications that practices of forced evictions and related homelessness are disproportionately falling against Hungary's Romani community.[72]

The initial foray of the Court into the area of housing concerned competing rights over 'local government apartments' or 'social tenancies'. A 1991 Act had transferred ownership of 'state-owned residential apartments' to local municipalities and the Real Estate Act established the right of tenants to purchase their apartment within a period of five years whereby the price of the apartment was not to exceed 50 per cent of market value. This provision was challenged by local municipalities who

alleged that it was an unconstitutional encumbrance on their property rights. Drawing on the principles in its earlier decision on the property of cooperatives,[73] and hewing somewhat closely the position of the European Court of Human Rights, the Court noted that restrictions on property rights could be justified in the public interest, and noted the public benefits of measures for 'town planning, land reform, rent control and security of tenure'. However, the interference with the right to property had to be proportional, meaning that it should not be of an unspecified duration, there should be equal treatment and compensation may need to accompany the relevant restriction.

One might imagine that the circumstances of the case would have led to a survival of the impugned Act. Local municipalities had been given the property without payment, the Government had originally indicated that there would be an encumbrance, and the tenants were more akin to owners. 'The tenants had often lived for most of their lives in the apartments, and, as in many other formerly socialist Eastern European countries, they could not be removed from the property, they were entitled to bequeath it and rents were significantly lower than the market rate'.[74] The Court, however, considered the measure 'grave', even if anticipated by legislation, finding that municipalities were burdened by an excessive period for the right to purchase (five years) and that the loss in market value of the property must be compensated for by the State. The Court left open the possibility that tenants could be required to pay the difference, although it noted that it is not 'required that the full amount of compensation shall be paid by the tenants entitled to purchase'. Nevertheless, the resulting compensation vouchers provided to local municipalities were below the market value and the Court in Decision 28/1991 refused to condemn it, noting that the municipalities must accept the burdens that come with freely given property. The controversies over the sale of such apartments continues though and Cahn notes that:

> Due to pressure on public housing stocks, increasingly bizarre responses to this crisis are reported, such as the adoption in some

---

[72] C. Cahn, 'Roma rights, racial discrimination and ESC rights', *Human Rights Tribune*, Vol. 11, No. 3 (2005), available at <http://www.hri.ca/tribune/onlineissue/V11–3-2005/Roma_Rights.html>. See also the European Commission against Racism and Intolerance, *Third Report on Hungary* (Strasbourg: Council of Europe, 2004):

> As concerns housing, it seems that Roma are still disproportionately subject to forced evictions throughout Hungary. Since May of 2000, notaries of local governments are entitled to order the eviction of unlawful tenants, and any appeals launched against such orders are not suspensive. ECRI's attention has been drawn to the fact that this procedure has a particularly adverse impact upon Roma, as many of them are in a difficult social and economic situation.... Moreover, ECRI is very concerned at reports from several sources according to which illegal forced evictions of Roma families have been taking place, sometimes followed by immediate demolition of houses. It is also worrying to learn that in some cases when Roma wish to settle in a neighbourhood or village, they encounter fierce resistance from local authorities, often under the pressure of the local population....

> A more general problem which affects the situation of Roma is the lack of housing allocated on a social basis in Hungary. ECRI understands that public housing is a matter for local authorities and it seems that there is an urgent need for a comprehensive national policy in social housing. ECRI is pleased to learn that the government has launched programmes to raise the number of social housing in Hungary.

> Roma in Hungary are in some cases confined to segregated settlements which lack the basic amenities for a decent life, with serious consequences for their health and their capacity to improve their situation in other areas.

[73] Decision 21/1990 (X. 4).

[74] See Gero, *The Role of the Hungarian Constitutional Court* (n. 3 above), p. 5.

municipalities of auctioning off social housing to the highest bidder, to name only one example. In early 2005, the Hungarian Constitutional Court declared a number of local practices in this area unconstitutional and a review of all related local practices has been ordered, as yet without significant impact.[75]

The Court was perhaps more lenient to home owners when it could construe housing rights as property rights.[76] In its first case concerning subsidised mortgage interest rates, the Court was prepared to allow an increase in the effective interest rate from 3 to 15 per cent in light of the country's financial crisis.[77] This provided an 'exceptional circumstance' for the interference with a private contract. However, when this figure was pushed up to 25 per cent in the 1995 social reforms package, the Court baulked at this rise.[78] The Court firstly noted that the economic circumstances of the country had much improved since 1991. Some commentators criticised the Court for simply basing its judgment on the rate of inflation,[79] while Sajó notes that the interest service burden had effectively doubled due to the increase in inflation from (an admittedly low rate in) 1993 to 1995. Secondly, the Court found that the new measure was discriminatory because of the nature of the earlier 1991 reforms. These reforms had presented mortgage payers with two options: pay half of the loan immediately or submit to the new rate of 15 per cent. Those who accepted the former option were not subject to the new rate increase, while the latter group could not have reasonably expected that the rate would not change to their disadvantage.

In Decision 42/2000, the Court was directly confronted with the question of whether the right to housing, or the 'right to have a shelter', was a constitutional right. The petitioners in the case, the Ombudsmen for Civil Rights and the Ombudsmen for the Rights of National and Ethnic Minorities, argued that it formed an independent right within the broader right to social security in article 70/E and other constitutional provisions concerning protection for the family, young persons and persons in need (articles 15–17). They also asked the Court to rule on the ensuing State obligations and whether there was an unconstitutional omission by the State to legislate, on account of its failure to create an adequate regulatory and institutional system to ensure sufficient access to housing. In particular they pointed to the asymmetric legislative design of housing programmes: local municipalities were tasked with managing social housing, for example, but resources were not evenly or adequately distributed to them.

In response, the Court dismissed the claim concerning the existence of a right to housing in the Constitution. After reciting its earlier jurisprudence on the right to social security, that the State need only organise and operate a system of social security and benefits, the Court affirmed its earlier judgment that '[i]t does not follow from this provision of the Constitution that citizens would have a subjective right to state support in acquiring a flat, nor is the State obliged to secure a specific form and system of support for housing'.[80] The Court also baulked at establishing what it called 'partial rights', noting the dangers of adding 'more and more new elements of social benefits as constitutional rights'.[81] It was particularly concerned that it might reduce the liberty of the legislature to define the tools in guaranteeing social security and might violate the principle that social benefits can only be realised in accordance with 'the capacity of the national economy', since the State would be compelled to 'secure certain forms of support on a constant basis'.

The Court did affirm though, in particularly strong language, the importance of securing the minimum level of the right to social security that would guarantee human dignity. Over the objections of two judges, it opined that, in the case of homelessness, 'the State obligation to provide support shall include the provision of shelter when an emergency situation directly threatens human life'.[82] The Court quickly qualified this statement

---

[75] Cahn, 'Roma rights, racial discrimination and ESC rights' (n. 72 above).

[76] Indeed, in its decision on social tenancies, the Court again gave property rights a social flavour holding that the justification for protection of the right to property stemmed from its 'capacity as the traditional means of securing an economic basis for the autonomy of individual action'. This gave the Court the power to imbue other forms of social entitlements with the character of property rights. See Decision 21/1990 (X. 4), para. 1.

[77] Ibid. p. 8.

[78] Decision 66/1995 (XI. 24), ABH, 1995, 333.

[79] See Gero, *The Role of the Hungarian Constitutional Court* (n. 3 above), p. 17, f. 10.

[80] ABH 1995, 801, 803, in Decision 42/2000, Part IV.

[81] Decision 42/2000, Part V, para. 2.

[82] Ibid. Part IV.

nonetheless by noting that this was an 'extreme situation'. The Court then moved to reject the second demand of the petitioners, that there was an unconstitutional omission to legislate, seemingly on the basis that the right to housing was not a constitutional character. However, the Court briefly examined whether the current legislative framework met the general demands of article 70/E and articles 15–17. After examining the Social and Administration and Social Benefits Act and the Protection of Children and Administration of Guardianship Act, which include provision for homeless persons, social housing and some housing support for children and families, the Court simply exhorted the Government to 'endeavour to increase the level of support and to expand the scope of social benefits in line with the capacity of society' or what it also referred to as the 'prevailing capabilities of the economy'.

The decision exhibits the same problematic features of earlier decisions discussed above, and has been much criticised, even by those who lamented the Court's earlier social activism.[83] The Court shies from delving into international jurisprudence to determine the content of social right. While the Court adds a 'coda' to its decision, listing the relevant international covenants, it fails to note that an independent right to housing has been repeatedly recognised at the international level in legal treaties and declarations,[84] and derived by from meta-rights such as the right to an adequate standard of living. A 1987 UN General Assembly resolution states:

The General Assembly reiterates the need to take, at the national and international levels,

measures to promote the right of all persons to an adequate standard of living for themselves and their families, including adequate housing; and calls upon all States and international organisations concerned to pay special attention to the realization of the right to adequate housing ...[85]

The UN Committee on Economic, Social and Cultural Rights has similarly derived the right to housing, water and food, from the right to an adequate standard of living and indicated the limits for adding any additional rights,[86] thereby allaying fears about an ever-expanding list.

The Court also fails to develop a more robust jurisprudence for evaluating whether the Government is meetings its constitutional obligations, besides simply meeting the demand of the minimum level. The Court's traditional understanding of economic and social rights comes to the fore, and it even opens with a discussion of the difference between first- and second-generation rights, and the need to allow the State adequate discretion with social rights. It fails to look to the substantial comparative and international jurisprudence that has developed more sophisticated and flexible measures to determine whether the State is reasonably taking the appropriate steps towards the progressive realisation of the right. Yet even when the Court consider the minimum level, as in this case, it refrains from actually interrogating the Government's institutional response with any degree of rigour or authority, leaving it open to the charge that it is more concerned with the rights of the middle class, not of the poor.

---

[83] See Sajó, 'Social Rights as Middle-Class Entitlements in Hungary' (n. 21 above), p. 105 (fn. 47).

[84] See, for example, International Convention on the Elimination of All Forms of Racial Discrimination (1965), United Nations General Assembly resolution 42/146, 'The Realization of the Right to Adequate Housing', adopted on 7 December 1987; UN Commission on Human Settlements, Resolution 16/7, 'The realization of the human right to adequate housing', adopted on 7 May 1997, Para. 4; UN Commission on Human Settlements, resolution 14/6, 'The Human Right to Adequate Housing', adopted on 5 May 1993; Vancouver Declaration on Human Settlements (1976), adopted by the UN Conference on Human Settlements in 1976, section iii(8). For further international standards, see COHRE, *Legal Resources for Housing Rights: International and national standards* (Geneva: COHRE, 2000), available at <http://www.cohre.org/view_page.php?page>.

[85] United Nations General Assembly resolution 42/146, 'The Realization of the Right to Adequate Housing', adopted on 7 December 1987.

[86] See Committee on Economic, Social and Cultural Rights, *General Comment No. 4, The right to adequate housing*, (Sixth session, 1991), U.N. Doc. E/1992/23, annex III at 114 (1991), Committee on Economic, Social and Cultural Rights, *General Comment No. 12, Right to adequate food* (Twentieth session, 1999), U.N. Doc. E/C.12/1999/5 (1999); Committee on Economic, Social and Cultural Rights, *General Comment No. 15, The right to water* (Twenty-ninth session, 2002), U.N. Doc. E/C.12/2002/11 (2003). For a debate on the potential for additional rights, see Malcolm Langford, 'Ambition that overleaps itself? A Response to Stephen Tully's 'Critique' of the General Comment on the Right to Water', *Netherlands Quarterly of Human Rights*, Vol. 26, No. 3 (2006), pp. 433–459, and the following replies and responses.

A fourth cluster of housing cases concern the conditions imposed by local authorities on applicants for social housing, although in these cases the Court has so far ruled on the basis of administrative law principles and not constitutional rights. In Decision 47/1996, the Court struck down a decree issued by the city of Békés that required social housing applicants to pay a deposit with their application and to have worked or resided in the city for ten years. The Court found that the decree of the municipality had exceeded its constitutional competence by going beyond the bounds of housing legislation, imposing irrelevant and unreasonable conditions, particularly since the decree 'exclude[d] the unemployed from the circle of persons who can be taken into account on the basis of social need, together with contract workers and sole traders'.[87] In Decision 20/2000, the Court found that the Municipality of Ferencváros had similarly erred by stipulating conditions that had no bearing on applicant's 'social, income and financial' situation, as required by the Housing Act.

In subsequent actions brought by the European Roma Rights Centre (ERRC) and Foundation for Romani Civil Rights, six municipalities were challenged for imposing arbitrary conditions for social housing applicants. In its submissions, the ERRC likewise cited the municipality's lack of legal competence but also claimed the rules were retroactive, vague, indirectly discriminatory towards Roma and violated the minimum level of the right to social security since it would threaten Roma and others with homelessness. Evidence was submitted on the relationship between wider discriminatory attitudes and practices, the cuts in social housing and resulting adverse impact on Roma applicants. In Decision, 4/2005, the Court considered the particular claim against the Third District of Budapest, whose decree excluded applicants that had illegally occupied a dwelling in the previous five years, or were subject to court proceedings concerning the non-payment of rent or utility costs and so forth. However, after striking down the decree on the basis that it did not relate to the applicant's 'social, income and financial' situation, it declined

to examine the wider claims, in particular that the decree violated the constitutional right to equal treatment.[88] Three of the cases against the remaining municipalities are pending[89] but the law was amended in 2006 to specify that municipal rules concerning the allocation of social housing must be social in nature.[90]

Lastly, it is worth pointing to an evictions case that, even though it was not argued on constitutional rights grounds, clearly evinces the preference of the Court for property over social rights.[91] The Hungarian Human Rights Information and Documentation Centre (INDOC) requested the Court answer the question as to whether the Protection of Children Act (which largely domesticated the Convention on the Rights of the Child) prevailed over legislation permitting notary-ordered evictions without appeal. In particular, INDOK raised the issue of children who would be automatically remanded into state care if their families were evicted and made homeless. The Court, however, ruled that the requirement to evict prevailed over the best interests of the child.

4.4 Education Rights

The right to education was considered, somewhat tangentially, in the context of a challenge to the restitution of church schools.[92] The petitioners partially attacked Act XXXIII/1991 on the Settlement of Ownership of Real Estate Formerly Owned by Churches on the basis that it did not guarantee a religiously neutral and non-ideological school in each locality. This result would lead to a violation of the constitutional right to 'freedom of thought, conscience and religion' and the principle of the separation of church and State as laid down in Article 60.

The Court commenced its decision by laying down general markers on the State's responsibilities in the field of religion. The principle of separation of

---

[87] Quoted in European Roma Rights Centre, Motion to the Constitutional Court.

[88] Decision 4/2005, Part III, para. 2.
[89] See ERRC, *Hungarian Constitutional Court Strikes Down Discriminatory Housing Decree: Ruling Reverses Local Rules Precluding Roma from Access to Social Housing*, available at <http://www.errc.org/cikk.php?cikk=2157>.
[90] Personal communication from Claude Cahn.
[91] I am indebted to Claude Cahn for pointing out this case to me.
[92] Decision 4/1993.

church and State required the State to be neutral – remaining unattached to any church, not taking a stance on religious issues and treating all churches equally and so on – but the right to freedom of conscience and religion – 'part of human quality'[93] – required additional negative and positive duties, even if they were at times contradictory. The State must not only prevent discrimination on the basis of religion but it must 'guarantee the conditions that are necessary for the freedom of religion to prevail'.[94] Likewise the State must protect and facilitate the broader right to freedom of conscience. In the event of conflict, a compromise must be found.

In the specific context of education, the Court noted that legislation implementing article 60 of the Constitution permitted parents or guardians the right to decide on a child's moral and religious education, while article 60/F requires the State to provide 'free and compulsory' primary education, as part of the wider right to education. Applying the earlier enunciated principles, the Court held that the State must not only ensure that public schools are neutral with respect to religion but must ensure that they are available in order to enable those attending to make a 'free and well-founded' choice about matters of conviction and conscience. At the same time, the State must provide sufficient, but necessarily full support, to those parents who wished their child to have a religious education in a 'committed' school.

These two doctrines resulted in a potential clash in the context of church property restitution. Local authorities could be deprived of their institutional capacity to provide neutral schooling. The Court refused however to impugn the legislation on this basis since it specified that its provisions were not to infringe upon the responsibilities of local authorities and local authorities had the right to receive a substitute piece of land from the central Government. The inevitable question was whether the new neutral school would be an adequate substitute – issues of distance and quality come to mind. The Court indicated that attendance at a neutral school should not represent an 'undue burden' for those choosing this option but noted that resolution of this issue was best left to the

merits of a particular case. Although it did note that the local government was under an obligation to provide neutral schooling 'even if the number of children is low'.[95]

5. CONCLUDING REMARKS

The Hungarian Constitutional Court has been characterised as an activist court – 'the most powerful high court in the world' – both in its treatment of civil and political rights and economic, social and cultural rights,[96] though its 'activism' has clearly faded with the government's appointment of new, mostly sympathetic, judges in 1998 and a reportedly increased centralisation of power in the Office of the Prime Minister.[97] Its willingness to intervene to protect pensioners, families, students and mortgagees amongst others from the harsher aspects of social reforms in the 1990s is indicative. Despite the criticism of some commentators that the Court was engaged in 'socialism redivivus', there is some justification for the Court's intervention, particularly as unnecessary short-term harm would be caused due to the legitimate expectations that had been created by the existence of various social programs. It is also questionable whether Hungary needed to be the World Bank 'pilot project' for the region.

A closer look at the jurisprudence reveals though a much more complex picture and one that is representative of the region.[98] Sadurski accurately

---

[93] Ibid. Part I, para 1(a).
[94] Ibid. Part I, para 2(b).

[95] Ibid., Part I, para. 2(c).
[96] A. Örkény and K. Lane Scheppele, 'Rule of Law: The Complexity of Legality in Hungary', in M. Krygier and A. Czarnota (eds.), *The Rule of Law after Communism: Problems and Prospects in East-Central Europe* (Aldershot: Ashgate, 1999), pp. 55–77 at 59, quoted in M. Kinander, 'The accountability function of courts in Eastern central Europe: The case of Hungary and Poland' (on file with author).
[97] See Scheppelle, 'Democracy by Judiciary' (n. 50 above), p. 53.
[98] G. Halmai also notes that this 'activism' should also be seen in the context of the Court' limited jurisdiction, it's very limited power to review and annul court decisions and consider concrete cases: 'The Hungarian Approach to Constitutional Review: The End of Activism? The First Decade of the Hungarian constitutional Court' in Wojciech Sadurski (ed.), *Constitutional Justice, East and West: Democratic Legitimacy and Constitutional Courts in Post-Communist Europe in a Comparative Perspective* (The Hague: Kluwer Law International, 2002), p. 209.

summarises the approach of the Court's in the region when he says:

> [I]t is significant that, when constitutional courts in the regions have had a choice between striking down a law under a general constitutional clause such as 'social justice' or 'equality' on the one hand, or under a specific social welfare right on the other, they have usually opted for the former solution. This is a symptom of a certain malaise over the direct enforcement of socio-economic rights.[99]

This preference for the use of property rights could be characterised as a form of 'market redivivus', where the Court was only prepared to protect social interests when a market rationale could be found. But the result is that the judicial social protection favours only those with strong market interests, and Andras Sajó is correct to question whether the Court has failed to give impetus to transformative welfare policies that would protect the poor.

Understanding the Court's approach is difficult. The motivation, on one hand, may be pragmatic. Civil and property rights permitted a safe way out of the conflicting social demands of the populace and the principle of judicial restraint.[100] But it is arguable that the interpretive method is indicative of a deeper misunderstanding or even distrust of social rights themselves. This is apparent in the use of comparative jurisprudence by the Court, with a strong preference for the seminal developments in German constitutional jurisprudence of the 1970s. One possible explanation for this preference for property rights, making social rights a mere derivative of other rights, is the nature of the

Hungarian transition in 1989. While social rights were part of the democratic revolutions in Latin America and South Africa, and Courts have been increasingly open to applying them judicially, the reverse was perhaps the case in Hungary's transition to democracy. Protecting social rights was a defensive gesture (ensuring that the population didn't nostalgically long for the past) as opposed to a key demand amongst the reformists.

While Sadurski suggests that the fault might lie in the social rights themselves, and that it may be preferable and logically consistent to reshape the constitutional framework and place social rights in the 'category of constitutional "targets"', the opposite conclusion should be drawn in the case of Hungary. The Court should move away from its interpretation of social rights as essentially constituting targets and instead embrace a model of reasonableness review for all the dimensions of social rights, as is increasingly being adopted by both common law and civil law countries.[101] This would require the State to justify the absence of social policy and programmes to protect the social rights of individuals and groups whose human dignity has been demeaned by their social conditions. While the result is that sometimes the right becomes simply a 'right to have a reasonable policy', a situation which Sadurski dismisses as outside the framework of human rights, the use of such an approach in practice can lead to concrete judgments and influence in the lives of individuals in both the short and long run.[102]

---

[99] Sadurski, *Rights Before Courts* (n. 1 above), pp. 184–5.
[100] Ibid. p. 191.

[101] See chapter 1 of this book.
[102] See S. Liebenberg, 'Enforcing Positive Socio-Economic Rights Claims: The South African Model of Reasonableness Review' in J. Squires, M. Langford and B. Thiele (eds.), *The Road to a Remedy: Current Issues in the Litigation of Economic, Social and Cultural Rights* (Australian Human Rights Centre, The University of New South Wales with Centre on Housing Rights and Eviction, Distributed by UNSW Press, 2005), pp. 73–88.

14

France

Rethinking 'Droits-Créances'

Laurent Pech*

1. INTRODUCTION

In the field of human rights, or to use a more recent term, some would say a more 'fashionable' one, fundamental rights,[1] it is common to distinguish between individual rights and collective rights as well as between '*droits-libertés*' and '*droits-créances*'. Social rights can come within each of these categories.[2] However, it is the latter notion that is by far the most widely debated in France. Indeed, any discussion on social rights as constitutional '*droits-créances*', that is, rights to claim a benefit or access to a service from public authorities, often tends to polemic. Also labelled '*droits à...*' [rights to] (as opposed to '*droits de...*' [rights of]), numerous academics have denied their justiciability and regretted the fact that their programmatic nature undermines the concept of subjective rights.[3] These social rights as positive constitutional rights (*droits-créances*) will be the focus of this Section. A brief overview of the historical context surrounding their constitutional recognition (Section 2) as well as an understanding of the legal changes brought by the progressive emergence of the *Conseil constitutionnel* [Constitutional Council] as an effective constitutional judge (Section 3) appear imperative in order to fully appreciate the legal impact of the on-going 'constitutionalisation' of this particular category of fundamental rights (Section 4).

2. THE CONSTITUTIONAL RECOGNITION OF SOCIAL RIGHTS

Any overview of the constitutional recognition of social rights by the Preamble to the Constitution of 27 October 1946 ('1946 Preamble') should be preceded by a succinct presentation of the main characteristics of the founding text of French political modernity, the Declaration of Human and Civic Rights of 26 August 1789 ('1789 Declaration'). The celebrated Declaration is often described as a 'liberal' text insofar as it protects individual rights with no reference to any collective structure of socialisation such as the family or associations. The famous '*Loi le Chapelier*' [Le Chapelier Law] issued in 1791 actually went even further by *de facto* prohibiting any possibility of collective

---

* *Jean Monnet* Lecturer in EU Law, National University of Ireland, Galway. The author would like to dedicate the present study on France to the memory of Professor Louis Favoreu, former Dean of the Faculty of Law of Aix-en-Provence.

[1] The number of academic references has been deliberately limited in this study of France. For further references as well as a substantial introduction to the constitutional protection of fundamental rights in the French legal order, see generally L. Favoreu *et al.*, *Droit des libertés fondamentales* [Fundamental liberty rights], 3rd edition (Paris: Dalloz, 2004); B. Mathieu and M. Verpeaux, *Contentieux constitutionnel des droits fondamentaux* [The constitutional procedural law of fundamental rights] (Paris: LGDJ, 2002). It is also important to point out that the concept of 'fundamental rights', i.e. in simple terms, human rights of constitutional value, is not without its strident critics in France. See in particular the brilliant and incisive presentation of Etienne Picard, 'Droits fondamentaux' [Fundamental rights] in D. Alland and S. Rials (eds.), *Dictionnaire de la culture juridique* [Dictionary of legal culture] (Paris: Lamy-PUF, 2003), p. 544. For a concise and stimulating introduction in English, see G. Scoffoni, 'The Protection of Human Rights in France. A Comparative Perspective' in R. P. Peerenboom (ed.), *Human Rights in Asia. A Comparative Legal Study of Twelve Asian Jurisdictions, France and the United States* (London: Routledge, 2006).

[2] Social rights are themselves classically distinguished from civil and political rights as well as the so-called 'rights of the third generation', for example, the right to a clean environment.

[3] See, e.g., the highly critical synthesis by D. Cohen, 'Le droit à...' [The right to...] in *L'Avenir du droit. Mélanges en hommage à François Terré* [The future of law. Writings in honor of François Terré] (Paris: Dalloz-PUF-Jurisclasseur, 1999), p. 393.

representation for workers, hence demonstrating the revolutionaries' suspicion towards intermediary bodies.

The individual rights protected by the 1789 Declaration are usually labelled '*droits-libertés*', that is, rights implying a (political or civic) freedom to act, as well as the idea of inherent limits on state power. Since then, it is typical to argue that the primary function of fundamental rights is to protect the *status negativus* of the citizen. In other words, in the sphere of liberty protected by the constitution, the individual is protected from undue intervention by public authorities. The rights protected by the 1789 Declaration are also said to exemplify the decisive legal notion of subjective rights. For instance, the right to freedom of expression, as a subjective right, confers on a legal person an individual prerogative that can be enforced (legal notion of 'opposability' in French law) on a third party and in particular, on public authorities. The most important legal point is that the judicial enforcement of a subjective right is theoretically not dependent upon prior legislative concretisation.[4]

The increased influence of socialist thought and Marxist criticism progressively added to the political imperative to give constitutional recognition to a new generation of human rights, the so-called social rights. Even though numerous social rights benefited from legislative advances in the second half of the nineteenth-century, constitutional recognition was the fruit of exceptional circumstances, principally the cessation of the Second World War and the willingness of the major political forces at the time to define a new social contract. It would be wrong, however, to assume that the idea of '*droits-créances*' is an invention of the twentieth century.

The revolutionaries who ruled in 1793 were the first to conceptualise the idea that individuals possess a (constitutional) right to claim minimal assistance as well as education from the State.[5] For instance, the 1793 Bill of Rights declared that 'society owes maintenance to unfortunate citizens either through procuring work for them, or assur-ing means of existence to those who are unable to work' (Article 21). The 1793 Declaration embodies the idea of a society bestowed with an active responsibility or duty towards its citizens. Half a century later, the French Constitution of 1848 stipulates that the Republic must assume the responsibility to put at the disposal of all the education indispensable to all men.

In light of these constitutional developments, the 1946 Preamble may be better understood with its constant emphasis on the nation, or the collectivity, as the new 'debtor' of the rights guaranteed by paragraph 5 and paragraphs 10 to 13. It is stipulated that 'Each person has the duty to work and the right to employment' (para. 5) and that the State 'shall provide the individual and the family with the conditions necessary to their development' (para. 10). The right to health and social security, particularly in the form of social assistance, is protected in paragraph 11[6] while paragraph 12 articulates the more generalised rights to social security and equality in times of disaster: 'The Nation proclaims the solidarity and equality of all French people in bearing the burden resulting from national calamities'. Finally, paragraph 13 concerns the right to education by invoking the idea of a State duty: 'The Nation guarantees equal access for children and adults to instruction, vocational training and culture. The provision of free, public and secular education at all levels is a duty of the State'.

It is also important to point out that as soon as the 1946 Constitution with its Preamble entered into force, paragraphs 5 and 10 to 13 were understood as embodying social rights belonging to the '*droits-créances*' category, meaning rights that imply, as a matter of principle, *positive* action from public authorities. This view is still the dominant one today. However, this view often fails to reflect the more nuanced and contemporary understanding of social rights. While social rights can be labelled collective rights and in most cases, they also take generally the form of '*droits-créances*', they can nonetheless resemble '*droits-libertés*'.

---

[4] See, e.g., D. Rousseau, *Droit du contentieux constitutionnel* [Constitutional procedural law], 6th edition, (Paris: Montchrestien, 2001), p. 121.

[5] For a brief introduction, M. Borgetto, 'Droits sociaux' [Social Rights] in Alland and Rials (n. 1 above), p. 555.

[6] Paragraph 11 guarantees 'to all, notably to children, mothers and elderly workers, protection of their health, material security, rest and leisure. All people who, by virtue of their age, physical or mental condition, or economic situation, are incapable of working, shall have the right to receive suitable means of existence from society'.

That is the case, for instance, for rights associated to the worker's status such as the right to strike or the right to join a union. On the other hand, social rights are not the sole rights that can be labelled '*droits-créances*'. Civil and political rights as well as rights of the so-called third generation can also belong to this category and generate positive obligations through the use of the concept 'objective of constitutional value'. Regarding rights of the third generation, a recent and good example is offered by the constitutionalisation in 2005 of 'the right to live in a balanced and healthy environment'.[7] Most French professors of law have already labelled it a '*droit-créance*' and widely debated the question whether or not it is a genuine subjective right, that is, a justiciable right.[8]

Before exploring further the constitutionalisation of positive social rights in France, several caveats must be articulated. First, several French scholars are inclined to automatically associate '*droits-créances*' with constitutional objectives or principles, therefore denying their justiciable character, this latter concept being itself the subject of diverse and confused understandings.[9] This is not our view. A '*droit-créance*' does not exclude *per se* the quality of subjective right. Second, the relative imprecision of the concept of '*droit-créance*' should also be noted, and its definition likely to vary with each scholar.[10] The notion is understood here as a right conferring on the individual a legal prerogative to demand from public authorities access to certain benefits or services.[11] The underlying idea is that each individual has the power to demand positive action from public authorities. The heart of the problem is whether or not the '*droits-créances*' are directly enforceable against the state ('*opposables à l'État*'). For Jean Rivero, an eminent law professor, without legislative concretisation, '*droits-créances*' remain 'virtual' law.[12] We do not share this opinion. At the very least, it must be qualified in the light of the 1971 landmark ruling by the Constitutional Council, which held that the legally binding character of social rights guaranteed by the 1946 Preamble cannot be denied.

Several distinguished authors have sought to deny the legal character of the positive social rights spelt out by the 1946 Preamble. Their operational nature was contested and they were even suspected of weakening the concept of human rights itself.[13] Interestingly, an identical debate surrounded the illustrious 1789 Declaration. In his classic work, professor Carré de Malberg argued that it was not, strictly speaking, a declaration of rights but a declaration of principles, since the 1789 Declaration does not formulate legal rules which may be applied in practice by the judge.[14]

---

[7] Article 1 of the Environment Charter annexed to the French Constitution. See *Loi constitutionnelle* No 2005–205 of the 1st of March 2005.

[8] The review of the French Constitutional Council offers a good set of studies on this issue. See *Cahiers du Conseil Constitutionnel* 15 (2003). The review is available online at: <http://www.conseil-constitutionnel.fr/cahiers>

[9] A particularly striking example is given by the presentations made by three law professors before the French National Assembly on the legal impact of the Environment Charter following its 'constitutionalisation'. Faced with the issue of justiciability of some of its provisions, no common ground emerges from the 'audition' and moreover, each professor relies on different terms to analyse the problem. See Assemblée Nationale, Commission des Lois Constitutionnelles, Audition sur le projet de loi constitutionnelle relatif à la Charte de l'environnement (No. 992): MM. Guy Carcassonne (Paris X-Nanterre), Dominique Chagnollaud (Paris II-Assas), Bertrand Mathieu (Paris I-Panthéon-Sorbonne), Compte rendu No 10 [National Assembly, Constitutional Law Committee, Hearing on the constitutional bill regarding the Environment Charter (no. 992)...report no. 10], December 3, 2003 (available at: <http://www.assembleenationale.com/12/cr-cloi/03–04/liste.asp>).

[10] To our knowledge, the most exhaustive work on the constitutional concept of '*droits-créances*' is due to L. Gay, *La notion de 'droits-créances à l'épreuve du contrôle de constitutionnalité* [The notion of *droits-créances* under the test of constitutionality], Ph.D. thesis, Faculty of Law of Aix-en-Provence, 2001. A summary of her work is available at: <www.conseil-constitutionnel.fr/cahiers/ccc16/univl.htm>.

[11] See e.g. R. Pelloux, 'Vrais et faux droits de l'homme, problèmes de définition et de classification' [True and false human rights, problems of definition and classification], *Revue du Droit public* (1981), 54.

[12] J. Rivero, *Les libertés publiques. Les droits de l'homme* [The public liberties. The human rights] (Paris: PUF, 1995), Vol. 1, p. 100.

[13] J. Rivero, 'Déclarations parallèles et nouveaux droits de l'homme' [Parallel declarations and new human rights], *Revue Trimestrielle des droits de l'homme*, No. 2 (1990), 323.

[14] R. Carré de Malberg, *Contribution générale à la théorie de l'Etat* [General contribution to theory of the State], new edition, Vol. 2 (Paris: CNRS, 1962), p. 581. For a brief and interesting exposé of the opinions of two other major figures, Léon Duguit and Maurice Hauriou, see Christophe de la Mardière, 'Retour sur la valeur juridique de la Déclaration de 1789' [Study concerning the legal force of the Declaration of 1789], *Revue francaise de droit constitutionnel*, No. 38 (1999), 235.

These attempts to deny the legal nature of the principles enunciated by the 1789 Declaration and the 1946 Preamble have been rendered vain by the Constitutional Council's jurisprudence. Since its 1971 ruling, all these principles have constitutional value and are legally binding on all public authorities. Moreover, it is also unmistakable from the case law that there is simply no legal hierarchy between the 1789 Declaration and the 1946 Preamble despite several scholarly attempts to argue otherwise. Civil and political rights cannot claim any legal precedence, as a matter of principle, over the socio-economic rights recognised by the *pouvoir constituant* [constituent power] in 1946. It is now well established that all constitutional norms, including the fundamental rights recognised by the constitutional text and protected by the constitutional judge, are all situated at the same level in the hierarchy of norms.

3. THE EMPOWERMENT OF THE CONSTITUTIONAL JUDGE

Since 1958, and the entry into force of the Constitution of the Fifth Republic, significant developments have taken place, especially the rise of authentic judicial review of statutory law by the Constitutional Council, which has significantly elevated the status and importance of the Constitution and constitutionally-based decision-making in the political life of France.[15] It is worth recalling that before 1958, the *Conseil d'Etat*, on the basis of its general jurisdiction in litigation involving the administration, used the 1789 Declaration and 1946 Preamble as 'sources' from which it derived the so-called 'general principles of law', that is, unwritten principles protecting citizens against arbitrary or illegal acts of the executive, but the two texts were deemed to be without normative or legal value.

The situation was dramatically altered by a 1971 ruling, '*Liberté d'Association*',[16] France's equiva-

lent of *Marbury v. Madison*. In this decision, the Constitutional Council refused to allow the promulgation of a law enacted by Parliament on the ground that it was substantively unconstitutional. More precisely, the Constitutional Council voided the statute on the basis of the fundamental rights provisions contained in the 1789 Declaration and in the 1946 Preamble. With this decision, the Constitutional Council qualified these two texts as legally binding. Its reasoning was based on the fact that the Constitution's Preamble – which provides, '[t]he French people hereby solemnly proclaim their attachment to the Rights of Man and the principles of national sovereignty as defined by the Declaration of 1789, reaffirmed and complemented by the Preamble of the Constitution of 1946' – is *itself* legally binding. Therefore, in one short sentence ('Considering the Constitution and its Preamble…'), the Constitutional Council created a vast body of substantive constitutional law, with all the human rights and principles contained in the 1789 Declaration and the 1946 Preamble. In other words, since 1971, these two texts have constitutional value and any violation of their provisions would cause a statute to be invalidated.

The positive socio-economic rights guaranteed by the 1946 Preamble are hence legally binding on all public authorities. In practice, however, the impact of such a 'constitutionalisation' is somewhat limited. Indeed, even though the legally binding character (it has become fashionable to speak of '*juridicité*') of socio-economic rights is now indisputable under French constitutional law, their 'justiciability' is still understood differently when compared to civil and political rights.

4. THE ONGOING CONSTITUTIONALISATION OF POSITIVE SOCIAL RIGHTS: SELECTED EXAMPLES

The Constitutional Court's ruling of 1971 provided that social rights were legal binding norms, yet in practice the case law appears to introduce a 'radical distinction' between the '*droits-libertés*' and

[15] For further references, see L. Pech, 'Rule of Law in France' in R. Peerenboom (ed.), *Asian Discourses of Rule of Law. Theories and Implementation of Rule of Law in Twelve Asian Countries, France and the US* (London: Routledge, 2004), p. 79. For its clarity and accuracy, the work of John Bell should also be singled out. See in particular *French Legal Cultures* (London: Butterworths, 2001).

[16] CC, July 16, 1971, No 71–44DC. For the text of major decisions (also freely available at: <www.conseil-

constitutionnel.fr>) and extensive commentaries and references, see the classic work of Louis Favoreu and Loïc Philip, *Les grandes décisions du Conseil constitutionnel* [The important decisions of the Constitutional Council], 13th edition (Paris: Dalloz, 2005).

the '*droits-créances*'.[17] The argument, an accurate one, runs that while the Constitutional Council strictly scrutinises any law involving the first category of rights, it affords the Parliament and the Government a wide margin of appreciation when a social right is concerned. The existence of different degrees of judicial scrutiny is not a French peculiarity, but a recurrent feature under comparative constitutional law.[18] Two situations may be distinguished to appreciate the limited scope of judicial review when positive social rights are concerned. In the first, positive social rights can be mentioned to justify legislative action. In the second, they may serve as constitutional arguments to invalidate laws whenever their scope appears to be restricted.

The right to employment provides a good example of a '*droit-créance*' that a political majority may rely upon to advance its legislative agenda. In 1983, the Constitutional Council explicitly recognised its constitutional value and declared that the legislature can define rules with a view to increase access to employment, for instance, by imposing compulsory age limits or by taking measures to improve the employment of particular categories of workers.[19] In a highly charged political context, the Council also ruled in 2000 that the legislature, by reducing the legal length of the workweek to thirty-five hours, merely implemented paragraphs 5 and 11 of the 1946 Preamble.[20] To survive constitutional review, however, the social rights guaranteed by the 1946 Preamble, as implemented by the Parliament, should not disproportionately undermine other fundamental rights. A balancing act is thus required and it is left to the Constitutional Council to scrutinise legislation on a case-by-case basis. In the 2000 decision, the Council ruled that the legislature struck a fair balance between the relevant social rights and freedom of enterprise (*liberté d'entreprendre*).

The right to health also offers an interesting example. In 1991, the Constitutional Council declared that measures prohibiting or restricting advertisement in favour of tobacco and alcohol are aimed at guaranteeing for all the protection of health in conformity with paragraph 11 of the 1946 Preamble.[21] Once again, the right to property and freedom of enterprise had to yield.

It is hence manifestly clear that the 1946 Preamble can be relied upon by the legislature to constitutionally validate public policies in the social field even though in so doing it may restrict the exercise of other competing fundamental rights. It is nonetheless important to stress that the Constitutional Council does not allow for these limitations to *substantially* affect their exercise. This was the case in the situation where a new legislative definition of the notion of redundancy for economic reasons, i.e. when redundancy is motivated by the economic difficulties of the employer or by technological mutations,[22] was put forward. For the Council, the legislative proposal excessively affected freedom of enterprise.[23]

It is useful to distinguish the above from a second scenario where positive socio-economic rights serve as constitutional arguments to invalidate legislation. In such a situation, the constitutional judge's attitude is generally one of self-restraint. Accordingly, it is common for the Constitutional Council to declare that the relevant law does not deprive the pertinent social right of sufficient 'legal guarantees'.[24] The latter expression remains somewhat obscure, but appears to exclude measures that would annihilate the effectiveness of the relevant fundamental right. What is clear, by way of contrast, is that the Constitutional Council has so far avoided to define the minimum content of social rights. In the end, the case law indicates that the Parliament is bestowed with a wide margin of appreciation regarding the extent to which it undermine or denature the relevant social fundamental rights. On the other hand, the existing services of general interest (the notorious *services publics*) that can be linked to a constitutional

---

[17] X. Prétot, 'Les bases constitutionnelles du droit social' [Constitutional bases of social law], *Droit social*, No. 3 (1991), 194.

[18] Some constitutional texts actually formalise the existence of different degrees of judicial scrutiny. See, e.g., Article 53 of the Spanish Constitution of 1978. The so-called principles of economic and social policy cannot be the subject of an individual appeal for protection (*recurso de amparo*) to the Constitutional Court. This procedure is only applicable with regard to the more 'classic' fundamental rights and liberties recognised by the constitutional text.

[19] CC, May 28, 1983, No 83–156 DC.

[20] CC, January 13, 2000, No 99–423 DC.

[21] CC, January 8, 1991, No 90–283 DC, para. 8.

[22] See Art. L311–1 of the French Labour Code for an exhaustive definition.

[23] CC, January 12, 2002, No 2001–455 DC, para. 50.

[24] CC, August 14, 2003, No 2003–483 DC, para. 8.

obligation appear to be entirely protected from any political desire to suppress them.

This brief overview of the constitutional jurisprudence does not offer, however, any clear conclusion on the question of the justiciability of social rights.[25] To put it succinctly, the dominant legal school of thought supports the view that positive social rights are not justiciable in the traditional meaning of the term in France, that is, they do not embody 'subjective rights' and therefore private parties cannot *directly* rely on them before an ordinary judge to claim access to/creation of a particular benefit or service from public authorities.[26] Without legislative concretisation, positive

social rights do not have direct effect. Yet, for Guy Braibant, the eminent jurist and the French representative to the European Convention in charge of drafting the EU Charter of Fundamental Rights, positive social rights have nonetheless a 'normative justiciability', meaning that judges can set aside or nullify norms that undermine their implementation.[27]

On the issue of justiciability, the 'right' to decent housing offers a particularly interesting case. A certain number of associations have been very active with litigation on the judicial front with the goal of convincing courts to make the right directly enforceable against reluctant public authorities or private parties. The legal situation is relatively complex since, strictly speaking, the Constitutional Council, in a 1995 ruling, did not consider the possibility for everyone to have decent housing to be a 'fundamental right', but rather recognised it as 'an objective of constitutional value'.[28] The French debate on the 'right' to decent housing is also likely to confuse the external observer since several pieces of legislation have labelled it a 'fundamental right'.[29] To make matters worse, some legal scholars assimilate – wrongly, dare we say – '*droits-créances*' and the so-called objectives of constitutional value.

In simple terms, one may argue that constitutional objectives, as defined by the Constitutional Council, are neither fundamental rights nor justiciable, but rather constitutional 'goals' used to balance the exercise of fundamental rights with competing public interests.[30] The maintenance of public order, the respect of the rights of others and the preservation of socio-cultural pluralism were the first objectives of constitutional value formally recognised by the Council in 1982.[31] In

---

[25] Space precludes analysis of the case law dealing with the justiciability of social rights guaranteed by international instruments. To briefly understand, however, how French courts may admit the justiciability of human rights guaranteed by international instruments, one may note the recent and important judgment delivered by the *Cour de cassation* in May 2005 regarding the Convention on the Rights of the Child of 26 January 1990. For the first time, the Court has recognised the 'direct applicability' of Art. 3–1 ('In all actions concerning children, whether undertaken by public or private social welfare institutions, courts of law, administrative authorities or legislative bodies, the best interests of the child shall be a primary consideration') and Article 12.2 ('For this purpose, the child shall in particular be provided the opportunity to be heard in any judicial and administrative proceedings affecting the child, either directly, or through a representative or an appropriate body, in a manner consistent with the procedural rules of national law') of the Convention. See Cass. 1er civ., 18 May 2005, Bull. No. 212, reaffirmed in Cass. 1er civ, 14 June 2005, Bull. No. 245. These provisions were previously denied justiciability on the ground that they were deemed to exclusively confer an obligation on the State. Thanks to this recent judgment, the case law of the *Cour de cassation* is now in now finally line with the position adopted by the *Conseil d'Etat* which has first accepted the justiciability (the French administrative supreme court speaks more accurately of 'direct effect' rather than 'direct applicability', but the meaning is the same) of certain provisions of the Convention. For a concise, but instructive introduction to this problem, see R. Abraham, 'La notion d'effet direct des traités internationaux devant le Conseil d'Etat (à propos de la convention de New York sur les droits de l'enfant)' [The notion of direct effect of international treaties before the Council of State (regarding the New York Convention on the Rights of the Child], *Recueil Le Dalloz*, No. 2 (1998), 15.

[26] By comparison with other constitutional texts, the French Constitution can be said to lack clarity. The explanation for this is straightforward: the founding fathers simply did not envisage that the Constitutional Council would effectively protect fundamental rights against the will of the legislature. Accordingly, one cannot find any details on the issue of justiciability. This is in striking contrast with the Spanish Constitution, for example, which expressly

stipulates that principles of economic and social policy may only be invoked in the ordinary courts in the context of the legal provisions by which they are developed (Article 53.3).

[27] *La Charte des droits fondamentaux de l'Union européenne* [Charter of fundamental rights of the European Union] (Paris: Seuil, 2001), p. 46.

[28] CC, January 15, 1995, No 94–359 DC, para. 7.

[29] See, e.g., Loi No. 89–462, July 6, 1989: '*le droit au logement est un droit fondamental* [the right to housing is a fundamental right]'.

[30] See, e.g., B. Faure, 'Les objectifs de valeur constitutionnelle: une nouvelle catégorie juridique', [The constitutional objectives: a new legal category], *Revue française de droit constitutionnel*, No. 21 (1995), 63.

[31] CC, January 27, 1982, No 82–141 DC, para. 5.

some instances, these constitutional objectives can also be considered as constitutional norms likely to strengthen the effective exercise of some fundamental rights. The preservation of pluralism may limit freedom of enterprise by requiring transparency and prohibiting excessive market power. Yet, on the other hand, it allows a more effective exercise of the freedom of the press and preserves the right of readers to receive pluralist information.[32]

In any case, the main use of decent housing as an objective of constitutional value is to channel legislative action.[33] Whenever the legislature is willing to pursue this objective, the Constitutional Council is likely to find the legislative proposal in conformity with the Constitution. Such was the case in 1998 when a new tax on unoccupied housing was instituted[34] and in 2000 when the Parliament created a new obligation for any lessor to provide tenants with decent housing.[35] This is not to say that the 'right' to decent housing can justify substantial limitations on competing fundamental rights such as the freedom to contract (liberté contractuelle).

An interesting general argument has been made regarding the likely legal obstacles any 'neoliberal' political majority would face if tempted to shrink the French welfare state. According to Guy Braibant, the constitutional protection of social rights, whether in the form of positive fundamental rights or through the notion of constitutional objectives, would exclude any 'retrogressive' legislation that would suppress housing benefits for low-income families, social security, family welfare benefits or the right to free education.[36] This analysis is controversial. Indeed, the case law of the Constitutional Council is rather ambiguous.

In 1984, the Council expressly forbade the Parliament from diminishing the level of protection previously accorded to a fundamental right.[37] And in 1995, a ruling appeared to extend the application of the so-called effet cliquet doctrine to social rights.[38] In a recent speech, however, the president of the Constitutional Council (until March 2007), Pierre Mazeaud, went as far as to declare that such a doctrine was abandoned in 1986.[39] One may therefore conclude that no government is precluded from diminishing the level of protection accorded to social rights.

Irrespective of the effet cliquet doctrine, it is clear that public authorities are not under any sort of constitutional obligation to positively act in order to provide a benefit or service that does not yet exist. Similarly, positive socio-economic rights do not give the right to claim before a court the deliverance of a service or access to a benefit. As previously mentioned, without legislative concretisation of the 'droits-créances', their justiciability is severely limited and positive action from public authorities cannot be judicially commanded.

It should also be mentioned that constitutional social rights have also been invoked in individual public law cases, the above cases by the Constitutional Council being concerned with the constitutionality of legislation. It is important to stress that there is no legal obstacle for a private party to directly invoke before a court negative as well as positive social rights guaranteed by the Constitution, even in the (rare) situation where no legislation further develops them. The French legal debate is often confused since constitutional scholars do not clearly distinguish between justiciability (notion of direct effect) and invocability (notion of indirect effect). For example, regarding the 'right to health', the Preamble of 1946 speaks of protection of health rather than of a right – and the Council of State did not exclude the possibility of ruling on the conformity of some administrative acts limiting health-related public spending

[32] CC, October 10–11, 1984, No 84–181 DC.

[33] As a constitutional objective, rather than a fundamental right, the Council of State ruled that it lacks direct effect. See, e.g., CE, ord. réf., May 3, 2002, 'Association de réinsertion sociale du Limousin', Actualité juridique du droit administratif (2002), 818. It is important, however, to note that several first-instance courts have ruled otherwise. For this author, these courts erred in their interpretation of the law.

[34] CC, July 29, 1998, No 98–403 DC.

[35] CC, December 7, 2000, No 00–436 DC, para. 56.

[36] See G. Braibant, 'L'environnement dans la Charte des droits fondamentaux de l'Union européenne' [The environment in the Charter of fundamental rights of the European Union], Cahiers du Conseil constitutionnel, No. 15 (2003).

[37] CC, October 10–11, 1984, No 84–181 DC, para. 37.

[38] CC, January 19, 1995, No 94–359 DC.

[39] P. Mazeaud, 'L'erreur en droit constitutionnel' [The error in constitutional law], speech at the Institut de France, October, 25–26, 2006, p. 8 (speech available at: <http://www.conseil-constitutionnel.fr/divers/documents/erreur.pdf>).

with this 'droit-créance'.[40] The Council of State also agreed to nullify any administrative act that would run counter to the principle of material security; a principle that Paragraph 11 of the 1946 Preamble guarantees.[41]

In a more revolutionary development, by express reference to the case law of the Constitutional Council, and again on the basis of this Paragraph 11, the Court of Appeal of Riom set aside a private body's implementation of a legislative measure excluding foreigners from the ambit of a welfare benefit aimed at disabled people.[42] As for the right to education, on several occasions, the Council of State expressly mentioned Paragraph 13 of the 1946 Preamble to remind the administration of its duty to fully take it into account[43] or to justify the implementation of certain administrative measures.[44] On the basis of this case law, the Administrative Tribunal of Bordeaux sanctioned a mayor's discriminatory refusal to register children of immigrant families.[45] To end this brief overview, the right to employment also offers examples where courts directly rely on it to interpret and strike down conflicting legal provisions. For instance, on the basis of Paragraph 5 of the 1946 Preamble, in 1985, the Court of Appeal of Versailles annulled a provision of a collective agreement between labour and management on the grounds that it prohibited the recruitment of people after the age of thirty-five.[46]

5. CONCLUDING REMARKS

To summarise, positive social rights of constitutional value can be invoked either to guide the judge's interpretation of any legal provision or to

argue before the competent jurisdiction that an administrative regulation or an act of private law (by reason of the so-called 'horizontal effect' of fundamental rights[47]) should be struck down for violating them. Incidentally, it should be noted that for peculiar and complex procedural reasons, 'ordinary' courts are prohibited from ruling on the constitutionality of statutory laws.[48] It does not mean, however, that constitutional social rights cannot be relied upon before ordinary courts to challenge the legality of administrative acts or of acts of private law. The most important point, however, as far as justiciability is concerned, is that only constitutional subjective rights can give rise to legal claims demanding *positive action* from public authorities or private parties. The problem with positive social rights is that legal scholars as well as the 'supreme' courts of the French legal order (*Conseil d'Etat, Cour de cassation*) are reluctant to consider them as subjective rights. In other words, without legislative concretisation, courts of last resort are generally unwilling to recognise that these rights *directly* create legal obligations enforceable against public authorities or private parties.

In the end, the dominant legal approach in France offers a line of reasoning that one may find duplicated *grosso modo* in the EU Charter of Fundamental Rights. According to one of its most influential drafters previously quoted, Guy Braibant, the Charter's social rights are not generally deemed to be of a 'subjective' nature, therefore directly justiciable, but can be assimilated to

---

[40] CE, April 30, 1997, '*Association nationale pour l'éthique de la médecine libérale*', *Revue française de droit administratif* (1997), 480. See also CE, April 27, 1998, '*Confédération des syndicats médicaux français*, *Revue française de droit administratif* (1998), 973.

[41] CE, June 6, 1986, '*Fédération des fonctionnaires, agents et ouvriers de la fonction publique et sieur Goyeta*', Recueil, 158.

[42] CA Riom, January 29, 1996, *Droit social* (1996), 987.

[43] CE, February 6, 1980, '*Confédération syndicale des familles*', *Actualité juridique du droit administratif* (1980), 366.

[44] CE, October 16, 1987, '*Genessaux*', *Revue française de droit administratif* (1989), 154.

[45] TA Bordeaux, 14 juin 1988, '*El Aouani*'.

[46] CA Versailles, March 11, 1985, *Recueil Dalloz* (1985), 121.

[47] Contrary to the situation in Germany or Spain, the question of the horizontal applicability of fundamental rights does not preoccupy French legal scholars and the issue has yet to be explicitly addressed by the constitutional judge. To our knowledge, the first exhaustive study on the subject is due to D. Ribes, *L'effet horizontal des droits fondamentaux*, Ph.D. thesis, Faculty of Law of Aix-en-Provence, 2005 (publication forthcoming).

[48] Contrary to the situation of the United States Supreme Court or that of other constitutional courts in Europe, French constitutional review is essentially an *ex ante* review. The problem is that in the present system, once a law is in fact promulgated, it is no longer subject to constitutional challenge, even though serious constitutional questions may arise in its application. Indeed, neither citizens nor courts can refer cases to the Constitutional Council *a posteriori*. It is highly problematic insofar as laws not submitted to the Constitutional Council for review cannot be challenged once promulgated even if they contain unconstitutional provisions. For further explanations, see Laurent Pech, 'Rule of Law in France' (n. 16 above).

'principles' (in Eurospeak) that courts can rely on to set aside or nullify infra-constitutional norms because of their 'normative justiciability'.[49] Such is the legal regime, for instance, of the constitutional right to work or the 'right' to decent housing (as a constitutional objective) in French law. Interestingly, Guy Braibant recalls the conflicts he encountered with the German, Spanish and, in particular, the British representatives, when he suggested to include a set of social rights in the EU Charter. These representatives allegedly had a much more restrictive vision of the notion of justiciability and fought hard not to give the name of 'right' to what French lawyers commonly call '*droits-créances*', and therefore the use of the term 'principle' as a solution of compromise.[50] Unsatisfied, the British Government pushed later for additional amendments to dilute the potential scope of the Charter once it becomes legally binding.[51]

Thanks to this watering down, the opponents to the ratification of the EU Constitution in France have presented the EU Charter of Fundamental Rights as a legal retreat when compared with the protection offered by French constitutional law and the European Convention on Human Rights. Even though the legal arguments raised against the EU Charter have often plainly demonstrated the legal ignorance or intellectual duplicity of those advancing them,[52] the willingness of some national governments to deprive socio-economic 'principles' of any justiciable effect has damaged the popularity of European integration and given great weight to the accusations of its allegedly 'neo-liberal' nature. In doing so, however, French critics of the EU Constitution revealed their deficient constitutional knowledge. Contrary to many affirmations to the contrary, freedom of enterprise is constitutionally protected by the Constitutional Council and more importantly, the justiciability of positive social rights under French constitutional law is also severely limited.

---

[49] *La Charte des droits fondamentaux de l'Union européenne*, (n. 27 above), p. 85.

[50] Ibid. p. 46.

[51] The French press widely presented the addition of a set of amendments to the EU Charter as a British 'victory'. In particular, the 'new' paragraph 5 attached to Article II-112 has been severely criticised: 'The provisions of this Charter which contain principles may be implemented by legislative and executive acts taken by institutions, bodies, offices and agencies of the Union, and by acts of Member States when they are implementing Union law, in the exercise of their respective powers.

They shall be *judicially cognisable only* [our emphasis] in the interpretation of such acts and in the ruling on their legality'.

[52] See the sad example given by Serge Regourd, professor of public law at the University of Toulouse-I, interview with the communist newspaper *L'Humanité* on the EU Charter, 'Une conception des droits purement libérale' [An idea of purely liberal rights], October 25, 2004.

15

United Kingdom

Asserting Social Rights in a Multi-layered System

Jeff A. King*

1. INTRODUCTION

The United Kingdom's constitution is for the most part unwritten. Early protections of rights, such as the Magna Carta 1215 and 1297, and the Bill of Rights 1689, were assertions of the power of barons and later Parliament against the overreaching monarchy, yet were not entirely without benefit to the common person. Human rights were also given some but rather limited protection under the common law.[1] The infringement of certain liberty or property interests has for some time given rise to a principle of statutory interpretation whereby ambiguities were construed against the government.[2] To a more limited extent, courts would on occasion take notice of international human rights law when required to interpret ambiguous statutory terms.[3]

Against such a background, the adoption of the Human Rights Act 1998 ('HRA 1998') was a watershed in the United Kingdom's constitutional history. Coming into force in 2000, the Act led to a profound shift in the role of the judiciary as a guardian of rights. However, it would be wrong to think that the HRA 1998 provides the departure point for the United Kingdom on the judicial protection of social welfare rights. Judicial controls on the abuse of power and protection of statutory entitlements in the welfare state were developed largely in the context of administrative law, and also to a great degree through the proliferation of statutory tribunals and non-adjudicative complaints mechanisms. The role of courts in protecting social rights in the United Kingdom can only be understood against this background.

This chapter briefly surveys how social rights have been protected both judicially and by quasi-judicial or informal complaints mechanisms.[4] In Section 2, the statutory tribunals and non-judicial complaints panels are examined while in Section 3, I canvass the main developments in administrative law. Section 4 reviews the youthful, but occasionally promising development of a jurisprudence on welfare interests under the HRA 1998. By way of conclusion, I note some recent developments in the advocacy of a bill of social rights, and the quite serious attention given to that proposal by an important government committee.

2. NON-JUDICIAL AND QUASI-JUDICIAL COMPLAINTS MECHANISMS

Left-leaning progressives in Britain have not looked first to courts to defend welfare interests.[5] J. A. G. Griffith's *The Politics of the Judiciary* provides a catalogue of instances where the courts

* Fellow and Tutor in Law, Ballid College, University of Oxford. The author would like to thank Professor Sandra Fredman, Graham Gee, John Stanton-Ife and Malcolm Langford for helpful comments. The chapter's length often necessitated brief treatment of complex issues. This chapter uses neutral case citation format where possible (i.e., EWHC, EWCA and UKHL). All such decisions are available for free in full-text form at <www.bailii.org>. The author remains responsible for any errors.
1 P. Craig, *Administrative Law*, 5th edition (London: Sweet & Maxwell, 2003), pp. 562–568.
2 F. A. R. Bennion, *Statutory Interpretation*, 4th edition (London: Butterworths, 2002), pp. 705–735.
3 M. Hunt, *Using Human Rights Law in English Courts* (Oxford: Hart, 1997), ch. 8; Shaheed Fatima, *Using International Law in Domestic Courts* (Oxford: Hart, 2006).

4 For other in-depth and critical surveys, see E. Palmer, *Judicial Review, Socio-economic Rights and the Human Rights Act* (Oxford: Hart, 2007), and S. Fredman, 'Social, Economic, and Cultural Rights' in D. Feldman (ed.), *English Public Law* (Oxford: Oxford University Press, 2004), pp. 529–579.
5 For an early critique, see H. J. Laski, 'Judicial Review of Social Policy in England', *Harvard Law Review*, Vol. 39, No. 7 (1925–26), pp. 832–848.

have decided cases on what is viewed as typically conservative views of the underlying social questions.[6] Carol Harlow and Richard Rawlings review the advantages and drawbacks of judicialising the welfare state, and are ambivalent about the success or desirability of such a process.[7]

Due to the high costs for both government and claimants of resolving disputes over statutory entitlements in courts, the Franks Report in 1957 recommended the expansion and reform of statutory tribunals. The ongoing importance of administrative tribunals in the welfare state was affirmed in the JUSTICE/All Souls Report, which made comprehensive recommendations for improving administrative justice.[8] The tribunals have for some time been regarded as playing the leading role in securing administrative justice in the welfare state.[9] There are a range of tribunals dealing with grievances against decisions made in the context of social security allocation, housing benefits, access to schooling, and issues of discrimination and unfair dismissal in employment.[10]

Tribunals are tailored to the needs of each subject-matter.[11] The social security appeals tribunals provide an illustrative example. Under the Social Security Act 1998, a person may first complain to the relevant agency through a two-step internal process. Thereafter, an appeal lies to the Social Security and Child Support Appeal Tribunal. The tribunal consists of one to three persons, usually a legally trained chairperson who may or may not be flanked by two laypersons having relevant expertise in the subject-matter (e.g., health, disability). From this tribunal, an appeal lies to the Social Security and Child Support Commissioners, and from there on points of law to the Court of Appeal. Empirical studies of the social security tribunals found that they had made substantial improvements in the quality and objectivity of administrative decision-making regarding social benefits.[12] The existence of the tribunal structure has been offered as the reason for which there has been so little judicial review in the area of social security.[13]

A white paper produced by the Department of Constitutional Affairs proposed major reform, rationalisation, and increased judicialisation of the tribunal system, and has ultimately led to the introduction of a bill to reform and rationalise the tribunal system,[14] much of which was ultimately incorporated into the Tribunals, Courts and Enforcement Act 2007. The Act provides for a more independent 'tribunal judiciary', provides a unified structure of appeal and review within a Lower Tribunal, Upper Tribunal, with appeals to the Court of Appeal, and attends to many other miscellaneous matters. Time will tell whether it improves access to justice.

Many social services in Britain are administered by local authorities. A complaints mechanism relating to the delivery of services is provided under a 1990 amendment the Local Authority

---

[6] J. Griffith, *The Politics of the Judiciary*, 5th edition (London: Fontana Press, 1997). See also John Griffith, 'The Political Constitution', *Modern Law Review*, Vol. 42, No. 1 (1979), pp. 1–21; Craig, *Administrative Law* (n. 1 above), p. 65. See A. Tomkins, *Our Republican Constitution* (Oxford: Hart, 2005) for a more recent attack on looking to courts for positive social change. For a nuanced view of law and welfare administration generally, see R. Cranston, *Legal Foundations of the Welfare State* (London: Butterworths, 1985).

[7] C. Harlow and R. Rawlings, *Law and Administration*, 2nd edition (London: Butterworths, 1997), pp. 472–494.

[8] P. Neill, *Administrative Justice: Some Necessary Reforms (A Report of the Committee of the JUSTICE-All Souls Review of Administrative Law in the United Kingdom)* (Oxford: Clarendon Press, 1988), ch. 9.

[9] H. Street, *Justice in the Welfare State*, 2nd edition (London: Steven and Sons, 1975).

[10] Some tribunals relating to social rights presently include: the Social Security and Child Support Commissioners (social security, council tax, child support and housing benefits claims), the Special Educational Needs and Disability Tribunal, School Admission and Exclusion Appeals Panels, Care Standards Tribunal (complaints against independent residential care and nursing homes, registered children's homes), Gender Recognition Panel (considering applications from transsexuals for full legal recognition of their gender), Employment Tribunals and Employment Appeal Tribunals (unfair dismissal, racial and sex discrimination among others). For an overview of some but not all of the various tribunals, see the websites of the Tribunals Service (<www.tribunals.gov.uk>) and the Administrative Justice and Tribunals Council (<www.ajtc.gov.uk>).

[11] Craig, *Administrative Law* (n. 1 above), p. 259. The summary that follows is indebted to Craig's treatment at pp. 259–265.

[12] See generally J. Baldwin, N. Wikeley and R. Young, *Judging Social Security: The Adjudication of Claims for Benefit in Britain* (Oxford: Clarendon Press, 1992).

[13] P. Robson, 'Judicial Review and Social Security' in T. Buck (ed.), *Judicial Review and Social Welfare* (London: Pinter, 1998), pp. 90–113, at p. 100.

[14] Department of Constitutional Affairs, *Transforming Public Services: Complaints, Redress, and Tribunals* (London: HMSO, 2004).

Social Services Act (LASSA) 1970.[15] Luke Clements describes the procedure as consisting of three parts: (1) an optional informal (often oral) stage; (2) a formal stage adjudicating written complaints; and (3) a review of this decision before a panel comprised of an independent chairperson and two others. Each stage is normally completed within twenty-eight days.[16] At the formal stage, the local authority is required to investigate the complaint and if appropriate may appoint an independent person to oversee the investigation. The local authority is mandated to seek expert advice where needed. At the review stage, a formally independent chairperson sits with two wing members having relevant experience.[17] Complainants are not allowed legal representation at the hearings (though non-legal representation is allowed), and neither is the local authority. The review panel is required to provide clear reasons and its findings are amenable to judicial review, but not appeal. Its recommendations are non-binding, but the local authority is legally required to provide reasons for disregarding them.[18] There is a similar procedure for complaints about the administration of the National Health Service.

The advantages of these procedures are that they are inexpensive, the duty to establish facts (including on matters of expert opinion) is placed on the public authority and not the claimant, and the public authority is required to assist the claimant in formulating his or her complaint where needed. Furthermore, the 'floodgates' concern of establishing a precedent is highly diminished. On the other hand, the procedures raise concerns about the independence of the various adjudicators from the initial decision-maker. There are also acute concerns about the extent to which an unrepresented party can properly advance a claim.[19]

Furthermore, matters of broader social policy, to say nothing of primary legislation, are what such mechanisms (as well as the tribunals) are unwilling to question.[20] Finally, the overt aim of efficiency produces compromise in an area that the idea of social rights as human rights would deem to be one of principle. As a leading text on administrative law puts the matter:

> [In courts of law] the public wants the best possible article, and is prepared to pay for it. But in administering social services the aim is different. The object is not the best article at any price but the best article that is consistent with efficient administration....The whole system is based on compromise, and it is from the dilemma of weighing quality against convenience that many of its problems arise.[21]

Thus one can see that despite legitimate concerns regarding efficiency in the allocation of resources, there is potentially a different standard of justice operating in the functioning of the tribunal and less formal complaints systems.

There has been a considerable amount of interest expressed of late in the promise of the various ombudsmen in protecting against maladministration.[22] Ombudsmen have powers to investigate individual grievances against the administrative state, and issue a report specifying recommended remedies that often include compensation.[23] Yet they also can and do make non-binding recommendations concerning policy.[24] There is a Local Government Ombudsman in England, a Parliamentary and Health Service Ombudsman for the United Kingdom (health

---

[15] The amendment being section 50 of the National Health Service and Community Care Act 1990. A detailed summary of the procedure is outlined in L. Clements, *Community Care and the Law*, 3rd edition (London: LAG, 2004), pp. 497–517.

[16] Ibid. p. 503.

[17] Ibid. p. 505.

[18] *R. v. Wigan MBC, Ex p Tammadge* (1997–98) 1 CCLR 581 (QBD) (once the panel's findings are accepted, the authority cannot refuse to carry out duty due to financial constraints); *R v. Avon County Council, ex p M* [1994] 2 FLR 1006 (QBD).

[19] H. Genn and Y. Genn, *The Effectiveness of Representation at Tribunals* (London: Lord Chancellor's Department, 1989), p. 107 (finding that due to representation appel-

lants' rates of success increased from 30–48 per cent in social security appeals, 20–38 per cent before immigration adjudicators, and from 20–35 per cent in mental health review tribunal hearings). See also H. Genn, B. Lever and L. Gray, *Tribunals for Diverse Users* (London: Department of Constitutional Affairs, 2006), in particular for data disaggregated by ethnicity.

[20] Clements, *Community Care and the Law* (n. 15 above), p. 511.

[21] W. Wade and C. Forsyth, *Administrative Law*, 5th Ed, (Cambridge: Cambridge University Press, 2004), p. 908.

[22] See generally M. Seneviratne, *Ombudsmen: Public Services and Administrative Justice* (London: Butterworths, 2002).

[23] Ibid. pp. 215–217.

[24] R. Kirkham, 'Auditing by Stealth? Special Reports and the Ombudsman', *Public Law* [2005], pp. 740–748, at 747–748; Seneviratne, *Ombudsmen* (n. 22 above), pp. 10–21.

service in England only), and a range of others addressing various matters in Northern Ireland, Wales and Scotland.[25] In addition to investigating the conduct of administrative officials, they may also review the conduct of the various informal review panels. Most agree that ombudsmen play a very important role in providing access to justice in the welfare state. However, the remit of such ombudsmen is 'maladministration', which, though the scope of the term is notoriously ambiguous,[26] in practice concerns chiefly the manner and not the substance of the decisions made.[27] This is a considerably smaller range of matters than what would be reviewable under a bill of social rights, and both commentators and the JUSTICE/All Souls Committee have recommended that judicial review and the role of ombudsmen should be seen as complementary and not mutually exclusive.[28]

Quite notably, statutory complaints mechanisms examined above are absent in the area of decision-making concerning homelessness, which comprises the legal obligations of local authorities to accommodate the homeless. Until relatively recently, aggrieved persons have been limited to the procedures of internal review[29] and judicial review. There is thus comparatively more judicial review in the field of homelessness,[30] some of which is examined below. Section 204 of the Housing Act 1996 allowed appeals on points of law to the County Court from internal review decisions, and section 11 of the Homelessness Act 2002 gave the County Court jurisdiction to order that the local authority provide interim accommodation pending the outcome of an appeal under the 1996 Act.

A variety of disputes relating to private and social housing are dealt with by various tribunals and courts, but there has been criticism of the complex and diffuse approach and with the pervasive presumption of equal bargaining power between landlord and tenant. Many have proposed the creation of a housing tribunal. The Law Commission has undertaken a wide-ranging consultation process on the reform of housing and homelessness adjudication, and adopted a final report advocating better provision of information, encouragement of non-formal dispute resolution, and a rebalancing of jurisdictions as between courts and the new tribunal system.[31] This may well pave the way for a new and likely fairer approach to housing rights adjudication.

3. THE PROTECTION OF WELFARE RIGHTS IN ADMINISTRATIVE LAW

By contrast with the mostly positive reception of the informal and quasi-judicial complaints mechanisms discussed above, many lament the scant protection given to welfare interests by the courts.[32] However, some noteworthy developments have taken place in the last decade.

3.1 Standing and Access to Justice

To have standing for judicial review, an applicant must have 'sufficient interest' in the matter to which the application relates.[33] In a series of cases since 1982, the 'sufficient interest' test has been expansively applied, including allowing public interest standing whereby concerned organisations can apply for review of a decision.[34] In the

---

[25] These include the Scottish Legal Services Ombudsman, Scottish Public Services Ombudsman, Northern Ireland Ombudsman, Public Services Ombudsman for Wales.

[26] Seneviratne, *Ombudsmen* (n. 22 above), pp. 40–48.

[27] *R v. Commissioner for Local Administration, Ex p Eastleigh BC* [1988] QB 855 (CA).

[28] Seneviratne, *Ombudsmen* (n. 22 above), p. 63; Neill, *Administrative Justice* (n. 8 above), p. 86.

[29] D. Cowan and S. Halliday, *The Appeal of Internal Review: Law, Administrative Justice and the (non) emergence of disputes* (Oxford: Hart, 2003).

[30] D. Pollard, 'Judicial Review and Homelessness' in Buck, *Judicial Review and Social Welfare* (n. 13 above), pp. 158–181.

[31] The Law Commission, *Housing: Proportionate Dispute Resolution: The Role of Tribunals* (London: Law Commission, 2008) (Law Comm No. 309).

[32] E. Palmer, 'Resource Allocation, Welfare Rights – Mapping the Boundaries of Judicial Control in Public Administrative Law', *Oxford Journal of Legal Studies*, Vol. 20, No. 1 (2000), pp. 63–88; K. D. Ewing, 'Social Rights and Constitutional Law', *Public Law* [1999], pp. 104–123; K. D. Ewing, 'The Case for Social Rights' in Tom Campbell, Jeffrey Goldsworthy and Adrienne Stone, *Protecting Human Rights Instruments and Institutions* (Oxford: Oxford University Press, 2003), pp. 323–337; Fredman, 'Social, Economic and Cultural Rights' (n. 4 above), p. 529; Martin Chamberlain, 'Democracy and Deference in Resource Allocation Cases: A Riposte to Lord Hoffmann', *Judicial Review*, Vol. 8, No. 1 [2003], pp. 12–20.

[33] Order 53 r.3(5) Rules of Court, later incorporated into section 31(3) Supreme Court Act 1981.

[34] *R v. Inland Revenue Commissioners, ex p National Federation of Self-Employed and Small Businesses* [1982] AC 617

Ex p Child Action Poverty Group case, Justice Woolf (as he then was) found that the organisation had sufficient interest as a body designed to represent the interests of unidentified claimants that were being denied social security payments.[35] In *Ex p Help the Aged and Blanchard*, Lord Woolf (as he had then become) held that the applicant organisation had standing and quashed the local authority's decision to take account of financial constraints in deciding whether to meet its duty to provide for the assessed needs of the elderly under section 21 of the National Assistance Act 1948.[36]

The Civil Procedure Rules (1999) provide that any person may apply for permission to file evidence or make representations at a hearing for judicial review.[37] Interventions are increasingly common under the HRA 1998.[38]

In an important case concerning access to justice, before the adoption of the HRA 1998, the High Court held that even in Britain's unwritten constitution there were some common law constitutional rights which could only be abrogated by a clear provision of a statute.[39] The Lord Chancellor had issued an Order under the vague provisions of s.130 of the Supreme Court Act 1981 which created the effect that litigants in person (i.e. those not assisted by counsel) who received income support were no longer exempt from the payment of court fees. The Court found that such an Order would 'totally preclude the poor from access to the courts'[40] and they had no hesitation in declaring the Order unlawful due to its absence of unequivocal statutory authorisation.

3.2 *Wednesbury* Review and the Non-Justiciability Doctrine

Under the traditional heads of judicial review of administrative discretion,[41] courts frequently claimed that an authority's allocation of scarce resources raises non-justiciable issues.[42] However, this claim is too broad. A more nuanced understanding is that courts regard challenges to discretionary allocative decision-making on grounds of *Wednesbury* unreasonableness as raising non-justiciable issues. In the *Wednesbury* case, the court held that a decision will be set aside if it is so unreasonable that no reasonable person could have made it.[43] *Wednesbury* unreasonableness is regarded by courts and commentators alike to be a highly deferential standard,[44] and provides for considerably less judicial scrutiny than the South African concept of *Grootboom* reasonableness.[45]

The non-justiciability doctrine under this head of review was made clear in the two leading cases on legal challenges to the central government's controls on local authority taxing and spending, *Nottinghamshire CC v. Secretary of State for the Environment and another appeal*[46] and *R v. Secretary of*

(HL). Leading developments in the law on public interest standing came in *R v. Inspectorate for Pollution, ex p Greenpeace (No.2)* [1994] 4 All ER 329 (QBD); *R v. Secretary of State for Foreign Affairs, ex p World Development Movement* [1995] 1 WLR 386 (QBD). See also Wade and Forsyth, *Administrative Law* (n. 21 above), pp. 691–92.

[35] *R v. Secretary of State for Social Services, ex p Child Action Poverty Group* [1990] 2 QB 540 (QBD).

[36] *R v. Sefton BC, ex p Help the Aged and Blanchard* [1997] 4 All ER 532 (CA); see also *R v. Lord Chancellor, ex p Child Action Poverty Group* [1998] 2 All ER 755 (CA).

[37] CPR 54.177.

[38] *R (on the application of Northern Ireland Human Rights Commission) v. Greater Belfast Coroner* [2002] UKHL 25 (NI); see also comment, L. Blom-Cooper, 'Third Party Intervention and Judicial Dissent', *Public Law* [2002], pp. 602–605; S. Hannett, 'Third Party Intervention: In the Public Interest?', *Public Law* [2003], pp. 128–150.

[39] *R v. Lord Chancellor, ex p Witham* [1999].

[40] Ibid. p. 578.

[41] The grounds of relief were summarised in a classic though not exhaustive statement by Lord Diplock in *Council of Civil Service Unions v. Minister for the Civil Service* [1985] 1 AC 374 (HL) (the *GCHQ* case), p. 410ff, as power to set aside decisions on grounds of (1) illegality (e.g., in bad faith, for improper purposes, or taking account of irrelevant considerations), (2) irrationality, and (3) procedural impropriety.

[42] For statements in obiter to this effect, see *Rowling v. Takaro Properties Ltd* [1978] AC 728 (HL), p. 754; *Barrett v. Enfield LBC* [1998] 3 WLR 79 (HL), p. 97 (Lord Slynn) and p. 111 (Lord Hutton); *X (Minors) v. Bedfordshire County Council* [1995] 2 AC 633 (HL), p. 737; *Lonrho Plc v. Tebbit* [1991] 4 All ER 973 (CA), p. 981. For critical analysis, see J. A. King, 'The Justiciability of Resource Allocation', *Modern Law Review*, Vol. 70 (2007), pp. 197–224.

[43] *Associated Picture Houses Ltd. v. Wednesbury Corporation* [1948] 1 KB 223 (CA), pp. 233–234 (Lord Greene MR); see also the *GCHQ* case , ibid., at p. 410 (Lord Diplock): 'a decision which is so outrageous in its defiance of logic or of accepted moral standards that no sensible person who had applied his mind to the question could have arrived at it'.

[44] *R v. Chief Constable of Sussex Ex p. International Trader's Ferry Ltd.* [1999] 2 AC 418 (HL), p. 452; *R. v. Secretary of for the Home Department Ex p Daly* [2001] 2 AC 532 (HL), p. 549.

[45] M. Wesson, '*Grootboom* and Beyond: Reassessing the Socio-Economic Jurisprudence of the South African Constitutional Court', *South African Journal on Human Rights*, Vol. 20, No. 2 (2004) pp. 284–308.

[46] [1986] 1 All ER 199 (HL).

State for the Environment, Ex p Hammersmith and Fulham LBC.[47] In *Nottinghamshire CC,* Lord Scarman held that 'the levels of public expenditure and the incidence and distribution of taxation are matters for Parliament'.[48]

However, the leading authority is *R v. Cambridge Health Authority, Ex p B.*[49] The case concerned a local health authority's decision to deny funding for potentially life-saving medical treatment to a ten year old child afflicted with acute leukaemia. The request concerned treatment that was of an experimental nature, and was denied for reasons of resource constraints among others. The trial judge insisted that in denying life saving treatment, the local authority must do more than 'toll the bell of tight resources'. The Court of Appeal rejected this reasoning in a widely quoted speech of Sir Thomas Bingham MR:

> Difficult and agonising judgments have to be made as to how a limited budget is best allocated to the maximum advantage of the maximum number of patients. That is not a judgment which the court can make. In my judgment, it is not something that a health authority such as this authority can be fairly criticised for not advancing before the court.[50]

This statement has been endorsed more than once in the House of Lords[51] and the Court of Appeal.[52]

It has also been the subject of considerable academic commentary, often critical.[53] In practical terms, it means that under this deferential head of review, legal challenges to public resource allocation decisions are bound to remain difficult.

This thesis was tested in *R (on the application of Ann Marie Rogers) v. Swindon NHS Primary Care Trust, Secretary of State for Health.*[54] The case involved a challenge to a local health authority's policy for funding the provision of an unlicensed breast cancer drug called Herceptin. At the time the challenge arose, the drug was pending regulatory approval by European and United Kingdom agencies. Some local authorities began funding treatment prior to such approval, but the funding policies varied in different regions. Some authorities funded the drug upon clinical recommendation, while others applied a policy of 'exceptionality', meaning that a patient had to demonstrate exceptional need. This led to arguments that access to the life-saving drug essentially depended on a 'post-code lottery'.[55] The Swindon Primary Care Trust (PCT) had a policy of refusing to fund treatment, except for in undefined exceptional circumstances. Rogers challenged the rationality of the policy, as well as its compliance with her rights under the European Convention on Human Rights. The trial court dismissed the claim, but the Court of Appeal allowed her appeal. The Court found that a policy of exceptionality was not *per se* irrational, but could only be regarded as rational if 'it is possible to envisage, and the decision-maker does envisage, what such exceptional circumstances may be'.[56] The Court held that once the health authority found that available resources were irrelevant, as it had in that case, then there could be no rational reason to refuse funding due to personal characteristics, and in fact there was no rational reason to refuse for clinical characteristics.[57] It quashed the policy for

---

[47] [1991] 1 AC 521 (HL).

[48] Ibid. p. 204. Compare with *Bromley v. Greater London Council* [1983] 1 AC 768 (HL) (the Fare's Fair case). The Law Lords quashed the GLC's decision implementing the Labour party election manifesto commitment to cut London transport fares by 25 per cent. Though admitting the powers conferred by statute were wide and discretionary, a majority of the House of Lords held nonetheless that among other things the council was obliged to run the London Transport Executive on 'ordinary business principles'.

[49] [1995] 2 All ER 129 (CA).

[50] Ibid. p. 137.

[51] *R v. East Sussex County Council, Ex p Tandy* [1998] 2 All ER 769 (HL), p. 777; *R v. Chief Constable of Sussex, ex p International Trader's Ferry Ltd.* [1999] 2 AC 418 (HL), p. 430 (rejecting the legal challenge to a police authority's decision to limit policing of animal rights protestors due to its financial constraints).

[52] *R v. Secretary of State for Health, Ex p Pfizer* [2002] EWCA Civ 1566, paras. 8–9 (rejecting drug company's challenge to the Secretary of State's classification of the drug Viagra such that it was only funded by the NHS for limited classes of patients). See also, K. Syrett, 'Impotence or Importance? Judicial Review in an Era of Explicit NHS Rationing', *Modern Law Review,* Vol. 67, No. 2 (2004), pp. 289–304.

[53] E. Palmer and M. Sunkin, 'Needs: Resources and Abhorrent Choices', *Modern Law Review,* Vol. 61, No. 3 (1998), pp. 401–414; B. Lee, 'Judicial Review and Access to Health Care', in Buck, *Judicial Review and Social Welfare* (n. 13 above), pp. 39–54, esp. at pp. 47ff.

[54] [2006] EWCA Civ 392.

[55] See generally K. Syrett 'Opening eyes to the reality of scarce health care resources? R (on the application of Rogers) v. Swindon NHS Primary Care Trust and Secretary of State for Health', *Public Law* [2006], pp.664–673.

[56] *Rogers* (n. 54 above).

[57] Ibid. paras. 79–82.

being irrational, though it refused to order funding of treatment in that case.[58] Although the case suggested a more interventionist judicial role to some, the Court distinguished *Ex p B* because the PCT explicitly disavowed the relevance of cost in the *Rogers* case. The Court was emphatic that, had financial constraints been a relevant aspect of the decision, it would be 'very difficult, if not impossible, to say that such a policy was arbitrary or irrational'.[59] It has thus affirmed *Ex p B* but clarified that it applies to decisions in which the cost of the allocation is an explicit and legally relevant part of the decision.[60] The decision thus recognised a suitably narrow application of the *Ex p B* case.

3.3 Illegality and the Enforcement of Statutory Duties

A decision is regarded as 'illegal' under administrative law if it is taken in bad faith, for improper purposes, in reliance on an irrelevant consideration, or fails to take account of a relevant consideration.[61] Traditionally, the courts have been slow to quash decisions interpreting the scope of statutory duties to provide resource-intensive welfare benefits. However, more recently they have provided greater protection.

Such a shift can be seen in the divergence between the holdings of the House of Lords in *R v. Gloucestershire County Council, Ex p Barry*[62] and the following year in *Ex p Tandy*.[63] In the former case, Lord Nicholls found that the local authority was entitled to have regard to its financial resources when it determined the 'needs' of persons under the Chronically Sick and Disabled Persons Act 1970 (which provided that local authorities were under a duty to provide for a person's needs). Only a year later, in *Ex parte Tandy*, their Lordships held that section 298 of the Education Act 1991 requires the education authority to determine the meaning of the terms 'suitable education' *without* regard to its financial resources. Beth Tandy

was a child suffering from a medical condition that prevented her from attending school. She received home tuition from the local education authority for five hours a week between 1992 until 1996, at which time the authority told her parents that they must cut the tuition to three hours per week for purely financial reasons. The House of Lords quashed the decision for taking account of an irrelevant consideration. There were acute public policy concerns at stake. Elizabeth Palmer observes that after *Ex p Barry*, local authorities across the country began to refuse to meet what appeared to be mandatory statutory obligations under the National Assistance Act (NAA) (1948) for residential care of the elderly.[64] The authorities evidently began to regard mandatory duties as permissive powers, a view corrected by legal challenges and ultimately the decision of the House of Lords in *Ex p Tandy*.

In giving effect to statutory duties implicating resource allocation, the courts will give varying relief depending on how precise the statutory obligation is. One way in which vague statutory duties have been given legally binding effect is when a vague duty 'crystallizes' upon a particular assessment. There is a line of cases in which a local authority had already assessed the needs of the elderly, disabled and homeless, but then refused to carry out its duty for lack of resources. The Court quashed the decisions in such cases, finding that having already determined a need to exist, the statute imposed a duty on the authorities to provide the services.[65]

The opposite tendency can be seen in the judicial development of the concept of 'target duties'.[66] The term 'target duty' was employed by Lord Woolf LJ in *R v. Inner London Education Authority, Ex*

---

[58] Ibid. para. 83.
[59] Ibid. para. 58 [emphasis added]. See also paras. 77–79. The Court finds at para. 57 that the case was not about the allocation of resources.
[60] Syrett (n. 55 above), pp. 667ff.
[61] See A. Le Seur and M. Sunkin, *Public Law* (London: Longman, 1997), ch. 23.
[62] [1997] 2 All ER 1 (HL).
[63] *Ex p Tandy* (n. 49 above).

[64] Palmer, 'Resource Allocation, Welfare Rights' (n. 32), p. 82.
[65] *R v. Sefton Metropolitan Borough Council, ex p Help the Aged* [1997] 4 All ER 532 (CA) (duties to shelter the aged under the National Assistance Act 1948); *R v. Birmingham City Council, ex p Mohammed* [1998] 3 All ER 788 (CA) (duty to provide facilities grant for the disabled under the Housing Grants, Construction and Regeneration Act of 1996); *R v. Kensington and Chelsea Royal LBC, ex p Kujtim* [1999] 4 All ER 161 (CA) (duty to provide housing under the National Assistance Act 1948); *R (on the application of Batantu) v. Islington LBC* (2001) 4 CCLR 445 (QB) (duty to provide accommodation under section 47(1)(a) National Heath Service and Community Care Act 1990).
[66] C. Callaghan, 'What is a "Target Duty"?', *Judicial Review*, Vol. 5, No. 3 [2000], pp. 104–107.

p Ali,[67] when categorising the nature of the duty contained in section 8 Education Act 1944. Lord Woolf found section 8 to be a target duty that was under the circumstances unenforceable by individuals. In *R (G) v. Barnet LBC*,[68] the House of Lords considered the effect of section 17 of the Children Act 1989, which provides that local authorities are under a duty to 'safeguard and promote the welfare of children within their area who are in need'. Lord Hope held that 's17(1) is concerned with general principles and is not designed to confer absolute rights on individuals'.[69] It is noteworthy that the idea of target duties is a judge-made concept and has been criticised.[70] In reading down the literal thrust of the statute, it may be argued that judges emasculate it rather than reading ambiguities consistently with the UK's international social rights commitments.

Courts can also control unlawful administrative action by declaring the adoption of certain delegated legislation *ultra vires* the enabling statute. In *Ex p Joint Council for the Welfare of Immigrants*, the Secretary of State adopted regulations that denied benefits to asylum seekers who did not claim asylum immediately.[71] The object was to discourage economic migrants. The Court of Appeal found that the effect of the regulations was to put legitimate asylum seekers in an intolerable situation of having either to abandon their asylum claims and return to face persecution, or to stay and maintain the claims in an utter state of destitution. Lord Justice Simon Brown found this to be an interference with basic human rights, and that 'so basic are the rights here at issue that it cannot be necessary to resort to the European Convention on Human Rights to take note of their violation'.[72] He referred to English authority from 1803, which held that in respect of the rights of certain poor foreigners in Britain, 'the law of humanity, which is anterior to all positive laws, obliges us to afford them relief, to save them from starving'.[73] The Court found that only primary legislation could achieve such a draconian result, though whether primary legislation could achieve the end is now also in doubt.[74]

3.4 Procedural Propriety and Substantive Legitimate Expectations

Courts may enforce a legitimate expectation of the receipt of a substantive benefit (e.g., welfare benefit or housing) when an authority goes back on a promise to continue performing a statutory function in a particular way.[75] In the leading authority, *Ex p Coughlan*, the Court of Appeal quashed the decision of a local health authority that breached its promise to Mrs Coughlan that she would have a home for life in the housing unit into which she was induced to move by the promise at issue. The authority sought to close the house and move the residents in order to save money. The Court of Appeal found that when the promise induces a legitimate expectation of a substantive benefit, it would hold the authority to that promise if not to do so would permit an 'abuse of power'.[76] After the legitimacy of the expectation has been established, the court undertakes to weigh 'the requirements of fairness against any overriding interest relied upon for the change of the policy'.[77] Naturally, arguments concerning resource constraints were and will continue to be raised at this stage of the analysis. In this regard, courts will engage explicitly in balancing competing interests. In *Ex p Coughlan*, the savings generated by closing the house were found by the court to be insufficient to override the promise to Mrs Coughlan of a home for life.[78]

---

67 *R v. Inner London Education Authority, ex p Ali* (1992) Admin LR 822 (CA). Section 8 reads 'it shall be the duty of every local education authority to secure that there shall be available for their area sufficient schools – (a) for primary education...'

68 *R (on the application of G) v. Barnet LBC; R (on the application of A) v. Lambeth LBC; R (on the application of W) v. Lambeth LBC* [2003] UKHL 57.

69 Ibid. para. 80. There was an impassioned dissent by Lord Nicholls, to which Lord Steyn subscribed.

70 L. Clements, 'The Collapsing Duty: A Sideways Look at Community Care and Public Law', *Judicial Review*, Vol. 2, No. 3 [1997], pp. 162–165.

71 *R v. Secretary of State for Social Security, ex p Joint Council for the Welfare of Immigrants* [1997] 1 WLR 275 (CA).

72 Ibid. p. 292.

73 Ibid. quoting Chief Justice Lord Ellenborough in *Reg. v. Inhabitants of Eastbourne* (1803) 4 East 103, p. 107.

74 Ibid. p. 293. The doubt arises from the HRA 1998 case of *Ex p Adam|, Limbuela, and Tesema*, discussed below at n. 106 and accompanying text.

75 *R v. North East Devon on Health Authority, ex parte Coughlan* [2001] QB 213 (CA), para. 55; see also Craig, *Administrative Law* (n. 1 above), ch.19 for extensive discussion.

76 Ibid. para. 57.

77 Ibid. para. 57.

78 Ibid. paras. 88–89.

Another case dealt instructively with the acute difficulty raised in resource allocation cases: the problem of there being more legitimate claims than available resources. In *Ex p Bibi and Al-Nashed*, the Court of Appeal found that the applicant had a legitimate expectation of receiving council housing, but that so did others on the list,[79] and there were a number of similar cases at issue.[80] However, rather than denying relief altogether, the Court remanded the case back to the authority for reconsideration in light of its finding of a legitimate expectation. It also suggested that monetary compensation would be appropriate in that case.[81]

The doctrine of substantive legitimate expectations may be a welcome addition to the range of legal controls on abuse of power in the welfare state.[82] Unfortunately, however, its effect is limited to the relatively few cases where the authority has made a specific promise. The courts have been careful in pointing out that such promises are by their nature likely to be made to one or a small number of persons.[83]

3.5 Conclusions about the Role of Administrative Law

Administrative law will remain an important and likely primary judicial recourse for protecting social rights. It is essential in preventing the abuse of power by administrative decision-makers who decide the welfare entitlements of Britain's most vulnerable people. However, in most cases courts are limited to scrutinising the manner and not the substance of the decisions, as the non-justiciability doctrine demonstrates. Challenges to broader questions of social policy and primary legislation, of direct concern in human rights adjudication, remain for the most part beyond the reach of British courts in their exercise of judicial review.

4. THE HUMAN RIGHTS ACT 1998

It was hoped that the coming into force in 2000 of the HRA 1998 would herald greater protection for welfare rights in the UK, despite the European Convention on Human Rights' ('ECHR') somewhat scant overt protection of social rights.[84] The Act incorporated most of the ECHR and made consideration of the jurisprudence of the Strasbourg-based European Court of Human Rights ('ECtHR') obligatory in UK courts, though its conclusions are not binding. Therefore, the Strasbourg jurisprudence on positive obligations and welfare rights is highly persuasive authority. At the same time, the UK has not incorporated the European Social Charter into its law, nor has it taken the less ambitious step of ratifying the Protocol providing for a system of collective complaints under the European Social Charter.

4.1 Standing and Accountability

Under sections 7(1) and 7(3) of the HRA 1998, only a victim of a violation of a Convention right can seek relief from the Court,[85] which is in contrast to the approach under administrative law. Courts are empowered by section 6 to review the conduct of 'public authorities' or of any persons performing 'functions of a public nature'. What constitutes a function of a public nature is of acute concern in connection with welfare rights. Many services provided to the sick, disabled and elderly have been contracted out.[86] Such was the case in *Poplar Housing and Regeneration Community Association Ltd. v. Donoghue*, where a tenant facing eviction sought to assert her right to respect for family life under Article 8 ECHR against the housing association.[87] The local authority had transferred the council flat at issue to the association. Lord Woolf found that the association was a 'public

---

[79] *R (on the application of Bibi) v. London Borough of Newham; R (on the application of Al-Nashed) v. London Borough of Newham* [2001] EWCA Civ 607, paras. 40–44.

[80] Ibid. para. 58.

[81] Ibid. para. 54.

[82] For a critical appraisal, see Fredman, 'Social, Economic, and Cultural Rights' (n. 4 above), pp. 570–572.

[83] *Ex p Coughlan* (n. 75 above), para. 59. '[M]ost cases of an enforceable expectation of a substantive benefit ... are likely in the nature of things to be cases where the expectation is confined to one person or a few people'.

[84] E. Palmer, 'Courts, Resources and the HRA: Reading section 17 of the Children Act 1989 Compatibly with Article 8 ECHR', *European Human Rights Law Review*, Vol. 8, No. 3 (2003), pp. 308–324. For a review of the European court's jurisprudence on social rights, see chapter 20 in this book.

[85] *Director General of Fair Trading v. Proprietary Association of Great Britain* [2002] 1 WLR 269 (CA).

[86] Paul Craig, 'Contracting Out, the Human Rights Act and the Scope of Judicial Review', *Law Quarterly Review*, Vol. 118 (2002), pp. 551–568.

[87] [2002] QB 48 (CA).

authority', but nevertheless claimed deference was owed on whether the section of the Act at issue was legitimate and proportionate. In *R(H) v. Leonard Cheschire Foundation (A Charity)*,[88] the appellants challenged the decision of a private foundation to close a home in which they resided as long-term patients. The majority had been placed there by local authorities. The relevant legislation allowed the local authorities to give care either themselves or to contract out.[89] In this case, the Court of Appeal found that public funding alone was not enough to sustain the argument that the body was a 'public authority' and the appeal was dismissed.[90] The House of Lords in *Aston Cantlow PCC v. Wallbank* held that courts must inquire whether the body challenged is either a 'core' public authority, or a 'hybrid' public authority.[91] A core public authority, though it is 'not capable of being defined precisely',[92] is 'a body whose nature is governmental'.[93] This may be contrasted with 'hybrid' authorities, which include private organisations that exercise public functions. The public function test is not applied generally or in the abstract, but is a question asked in relation to the particular power being exercised in the case at issue. Lord Hope held that courts must give a generously wide scope to the expression of public function. Relevant factors include whether the relevant function is publicly funded, is an exercise of statutory powers, takes the place of a central or local government function, or provides a public service.[94]

When reviewing primary legislation for compatibility with Convention rights, section 3 of the HRA 1998 requires courts first to read the statutory provision so far as possible to comply with Convention rights (even if this comports a strained construction). Where it is impossible to do so, they must issue a declaration of incompatibility under section 4. The political effect of such a declaration is considered profound. To date the government has not failed to change a provision in accordance with such a declaration. Nonetheless, a declaration of incompatibility formally has no effect on the validity of a law.

4.2 From Non-Justiciability to Judicial Deference

The nature of what is justiciable in the United Kingdom has changed in line with the expanded mandate for the review of discretion and in particular primary legislation. O'Sullivan referred to this idea when he argued that the non-justiciability doctrine in *Ex p B* ought to be replaced with the more flexible doctrine of the margin of appreciation, which would allow review of exceptional cases.[95] Scholars and judges have both maintained that the margin of appreciation doctrine should not be applied in Britain, because the doctrine is justified on the basis that the Strasbourg court is distant from and unfamiliar with local circumstances, a problem not faced by national authorities such as courts.[96] Yet as in Strasbourg, English courts have developed the margin of discretion or 'discretionary area of judgment' doctrine such that it often precludes questions of economic and social policy from review.[97] A leading case in this regard is *Donoghue*, in which Lord Woolf CJ held that '[t]he economic and other implications of any policy in this area [i.e. public

---

[88] [2002] EWCA Civ 266.

[89] Section 26 of the National Assistance Act 1948.

[90] See Craig, 'Contracting Out' (n. 86 above), for criticism.

[91] [2003] UKHL 37.

[92] Ibid. para. 47 (Lord Hope).

[93] Ibid. para. 7 (Lord Nicholls).

[94] Ibid. para. 12 (Lord Nicholls); see also paras. 63–64 (Lord Hope). For a highly contentious application of this authority, see *YL (by her Litigation Friend the Official Solicitor) v. Birmingham City Council and others* [2007] UKHL 27 (a majority of the House of Lords declaring that a particular private, for-profit home caring for a significant portion of publicly funded residents was not discharging functions of a public nature). See S. Palmer, 'Public, Private and the Human Rights Act 1998: An Ideological Divide,' *Cambridge Law Journal*, Vol. 66 No. 3 (2007), pp. 559–573.

[95] D. O'Sullivan, 'The Allocation of Scarce Resources and the Right to Life Under the European Convention on Human Rights', *Public Law* [1998], pp. 389–395. See generally, King, 'Justiciability of Resource Allocation' (n. 42 above); see also Palmer, 'Courts, Resources and the HRA'. (n. 32 above).

[96] J. Laws, 'The Limitations of Human Rights', *Public Law* [1998], pp. 254–265; Craig, *Administrative Law* (n. 1 above), p. 583; *R v. Department of Public Prosecutions, Ex p Kebilene* [2000] 2 AC 326.

[97] *R (Hooper) v. Secretary of State for Pensions* [2005] UKHL 29, para. 36; *Marcic v. Thames Water Utilities Ltd.* [2004] UKHL 66, paras. 68, 71; *Ex p Kebilene*, ibid, p. 381; see also comments *in obiter*, *A and others, X and others v. Secretary of State for the Home Department* [2004] UKHL 56, paras. 38–39; *R (on the application of Pro Life Alliance) v. BBC* [2003] UKHL 23, para. 76; D. Pannick, 'Principles of Interpretation of Convention rights under the Human Rights Act and the Discretionary Area of Judgment', *Public Law* [1998], pp. 545–551, at 550.

housing allocation] are extremely complex and far-reaching. This is an area where, in our judgment, the courts must treat the decisions of Parliament as to what is in the public interest with particular deference'.[98]

One recent unfortunate example is the case of *R (Douglas) v. (1) North Tyneside Metropolitan Borough Council and (2) Secretary of State for Education and Skills*.[99] Mr. Douglas challenged without success a regulation that denied student loans to those over the age of 55. The court accepted as valid justification for the restriction that people over 55 were less likely to repay the outstanding sum. Lord Justice Scott Baker held:

> The courts in my judgment have to be careful when considering an issue of justification such as would arise in the present case...not to trespass into the discretionary area of resource allocation. That is an area that is not justiciable.[100]

As noted above and as will be seen below, such a statement no longer appears supportable. The issue is better regarded as one of whether the courts should, in the circumstances of the narrower issues raised, show deference to the findings of another branch of government. Such has been the approach in some cases where the courts have declined relief but have not invoked the concept of justiciability by name.[101] The development of this more nuanced approach is a sound interpretation of Lord Hoffmann's judgment in *Begum v. Tower Hamlets LBC*.[102] He held that where review of administrative practices in the welfare state is concerned, the principles of democratic accountability, efficiency, and the sovereignty of Parliament should guide the court's judgment.[103] Such principles were not explicitly offered as a test, and have not since served to guide the courts' approach. While guidance is still wanting, it is nevertheless clear that courts will enforce positive obligations and Convention rights that impact upon public resource allocation, whether discretionary or legislative. The issue under the HRA 1998 is now one of deference rather than justiciability.

4.3 HRA 1998 Jurisprudence Involving Welfare Interests

There are a number of recent cases where courts have applied careful scrutiny of statutory provisions and administrative action implicating resource allocation. A representative but not exhaustive treatment follows.

4.3.1. Right not to be Subjected to Inhumane or Degrading Treatment (Article 3 ECHR)

Two representative cases show the way in which the concept of degrading treatment has been used to protect the rights of destitute asylum seekers. In *R (on the application of Q) v. Secretary of State for the Home Department*,[104] the issue was whether regulations prohibiting the Secretary of State from providing aid to asylum-seekers who did not apply for asylum 'as soon as reasonably possible' were contrary to Article 3. The asylum seekers were restricted from any work, paid or unpaid. The Court of Appeal held that the designation of persons as not having filed as soon as practicable was 'treatment' within the meaning of Article 3, and furthermore that the system used had unsatisfactory features and was thus unfair to applicants.[105]

The *Q* decision was affirmed in the unanimous decision of the House of Lords in *Ex p Adam, Limbuela and Tesema*.[106] The three conjoined appeals presented similar facts. Each applicant was an asylum-seeker (two eventually granted refugee status) who had not presented his application as soon as reasonably practicable to the Secretary of State's satisfaction. They were denied support. While Mr Limbuela and Mr Adam were required to sleep on the street, Mr Tesema avoided this only by means of an interim injunction. Each had

---

[98] *Donoghue* (n. 87 above), p. 71.
[99] [2003] EWCA Civ 1847.
[100] Ibid. para. 62.
[101] *Donoghue* (n. 87 above), p. 69; *International Transport Roth GmbH v. Secretary of State for the Home Department* [2002] EWCA Civ 158.
[102] [2003] 2 AC 430 (HL), para. 42ff.
[103] Ibid. para. 43.
[104] [2003] EWCA Civ 364.
[105] Compare with *R (on the application of T et al.) v. Secretary of State for the Home Department* [2003] EWCA. Civ. 1285 (loss of dignity and emotional distress not severe enough for article 3 threshold).
[106] *R v. Secretary of State for the Home Department ex p Adam; R v. Secretary or State for the Home Department ex p Limbuela; R v. Secretary of State for the Home Department ex p Tesema* [2005] UKHL 00, para. 0 (Lord Bingham).

exhausted all means of charitable support and was faced with sleeping outside and begging for food. The issue at the House of Lords was whether the Secretary of State's position amounted to inhuman and degrading treatment and was thus contrary to Article 3. The Law Lords held that the treatment must amount to a very high threshold of severity, but that such a threshold had been surpassed in this case. Lord Bingham (the same judge who gave the leading opinion in *Ex p B*), found that '[t]reatment is inhuman or degrading if, to a seriously detrimental extent, it denies the most basic needs of any human being'.[107] Thus, the Secretary of State's duty to avoid a breach of Article 3 arises whenever it appears on a fair and objective assessment of all relevant facts and circumstances that an applicant faces 'an imminent prospect of serious suffering caused or materially aggravated by denial of shelter, food, or the most basic necessities of life'.[108] He continued to find that factors such as age, gender, mental and physical health, existing means of support, weather and degree of suffering already experienced should influence the decision about whether an imminent prospect exists. In particular, there was substantial agreement that prolonged sleeping out in the open in a country such as the United Kingdom could amount to degrading treatment.[109] The case can be viewed as a substantial development in the recognition of positive duties in the United Kingdom.[110]

Article 3 has also been employed to protect an inmate's right to food.[111] Justice Lightman quashed the decision of a prison governor to limit an inmate's intake to one meal a day as punishment for refusal to wear prison clothes. He found that such an objective cannot 'excuse the governor from performance of the obligation to provide food to that prisoner or can detract from the fundamental right of the prisoner to adequate food'.[112]

4.3.2. Right to a Fair Trial (Article 6 ECHR)

Claimants have been less successful in their attempts to obtain rights to trial for the adjudication of welfare benefits claims. In *R (P, C and T) v. Alperton*, the High Court held that educational rights provided by statute are not 'civil' rights within the meaning of Article 6(1) of the Convention.[113] However, in *Begum v. Tower Hamlets*, a majority of the House of Lords was prepared to accept for the sake of argument that certain rights in respect of duties to accommodate the homeless were civil rights within the meaning of Article 6(1).[114] The more difficult issue was whether Article 6(1) required a full, judicial trial in cases where a person contests a local authority's findings as to his or her rights under the statutory regime allocating public housing. Runa Begum had refused the authority's offer of accommodation, claiming the area was rife with drug use, racism and that the building was located near her estranged, potentially dangerous husband. The Court of Appeal agreed that Runa Begum was entitled under Article 6(1) to more than internal review of the decision and held that the local authority could comply by engaging an independent fact-finder.[115] However, the House of Lords held that rights of this type are of a different nature and called for a different form of protection. In the leading speech, Lord Hoffmann found that following the decision of the ECtHR in *Bryan v. United Kingdom*,[116] an independent and impartial determination would be satisfied by a composite procedure consisting of an administrative decision and the availability of judicial review. The procedure must allow for full 'jurisdiction to deal with the case as the nature of the decision requires'.[117]

Some progressive scholars agree that the judicialisation of such rights would impede access to justice and Parliament's clearly expressed view that factual determinations remain with the local authority.[118] Whether true or not, the decision may

107 Ibid. para. 7.
108 Ibid. para. 8.
109 Ibid. paras. 9 (Lord Bingham) and 60 (Lord Hope).
110 For a more in-depth analysis, see S. Fredman, 'Positive Rights Transformed: Positive Duties and Positive Rights', *Public Law* [2006], pp. 498–520; see also S. Palmer, 'A Wrong Turning: Article 3 ECHR and Proportionality', *Cambridge Law Journal*, Vol. 65, No. 2 (2006), pp. 438–451.
111 *R v. Governor of HMP Franland ex p Russell and Wharrie* (2000) 1 WLR 2027 (QBD).
112 Ibid. p. 2037.

113 [2001] EWHC Admin 229. The Court of Appeal arguably put the finality of this finding in doubt by deciding the case on the assumption that education rights were civil rights.
114 [2003] UKHL 5.
115 [2002] 1 WLR 2491 (CA).
116 (1996) 21 EHRR 342.
117 *Begum* (n. 114 above), para.37.
118 I. Loveland, 'Does Homelessness Decision-Making Engage Article 6(1) of the European Convention on

be more fairly criticised for Lord Hoffmann's statements about the role of rights in protecting welfare entitlements. For instance, he claims that judicial determinations of private rights are necessary, cannot be compromised, and are part of the rule of law. By contrast, 'utilitarian considerations have their place when it comes to setting up, for example, schemes of regulation or social welfare'.[119] On the one hand, such a position denies the existence of balancing of different needs under civil rights adjudication. On the other, it suggests that social rights are not rights in the sense of serving as constraints on competing interests such as economic growth and efficiency.

4.3.3. RESPECT FOR PRIVACY, FAMILY LIFE AND HOME (ARTICLE 8 ECHR)

In *R (on the application of Razgar) v. Secretary of State for the Home Department*, the House of Lords found that Article 8 may be contravened where the threat of deportation would have foreseeable and 'extreme' consequences for the health of an individual.[120] In that case, it was found that the applicant's deportation to Germany could have sufficiently serious effects on his mental health that Article 8 could be engaged. Notably, however, the treatment faced would not have to meet the Article 3 threshold.

The availability of this type of remedy was tested in a case in which the person challenged her deportation to Uganda on grounds that the withdrawal of National Health Service funded treatment of her AIDS condition would constitute a grave threat to her health.[121] The House of Lords rejected her claim with regret, finding that it did not fall into the category of 'very exceptional circumstances' as provided by the ECtHR standard in HIV deportation cases set in *D v. United Kingdom*.[122]

There have been a number of challenges under Article 8 to decisions affecting housing rights. It has often been held that it is not necessary to have

a legal right of possession to the housing at issue in order to engage Article 8.[123] In the *Anufrijeva* case, the Court of Appeal held that Article 8 was capable of imposing a positive obligation on the State to provide accommodation where otherwise family life was to be serious inhibited or the welfare of children threatened.[124] The local authorities in that case had misinterpreted their public law duties to provide support to the claimants and also caused substantial delay. In one of the claims, the local authority had failed to discharge its duty to provide accommodation suitably adapted to the claimant's special needs. In the two other claims, the mishandling of asylum applications led to a denial of adequate shelter in one case and a substantial delay in admitting the refugee's family in the other. The case provides an illuminating discussion of the jurisprudence regarding positive obligations to provide welfare support, both at the ECtHR and in the UK.[125] It found, however, that such an obligation could only be imposed in extreme circumstances. The Court found it 'hard to conceive' of a case where Article 8 obliges the government to provide welfare support where the claimant's 'predicament is not sufficiently severe to engage article 3'.[126] This raises the question of whether this is a stricter approach than the one announced in the *Marzari v. Italy* decision of the ECtHR. Under similar circumstances in that case, the European Court held that 'a refusal of the authorities to provide assistance... to an individual suffering from a severe disease might in certain circumstances raise an issue under article 8 of the Convention because of the impact of such refusal on the private life of the individual'.[127] The *Marzari* case demonstrates a willingness

---

Human Rights', *European Human Rights Law Review*, Vol. 2, No. 2 (2003), pp. 177–204. See also I. Loveland, *Housing Homeless Persons* (Oxford: Clarendon Press, 1995).

[119] *Begum* (n. 14 above), para. 43.

[120] [2004] UKHL 27, para. 10 (Lord Bingham).

[121] *N v. Secretary of State for the Home Department* [2005] UKHL 31.

[122] (1997) 24 EHRR 425, para. 49ff.

[123] *Michalak v. Wandsworth LBC* [2002] HLR 721; *Royal Borough of Kensington and Chelsea v. O'Sullivan* [2003] EWCA 371; *R (on the application of Gangera) v. Hounslow London Borough* [2003] EWHC Admin. 794, para. 29 ('Article 8 protects respect for the rights of a trespasser to a home as much as one who is lawfully resident.'); see also, *Kay and others v. Lambeth LBC; Leeds CC v. Price and others* [2006] UKHL 10, para. 150 (Lord Scott) which resolved a dispute in the House of Lords on this issue.

[124] *Anufrijeva and Another v. Southwark London Borough Council; R (N) v. Secretary of State for the Home Department; R (M) v. Secretary of State for the Home Department* [2003] EWCA Civ 1406; see also *R. (on the application of T et al.) v. Secretary of State for the Home* [2003] EWCA Civ 1285, para. 11.

[125] *Anufrijeva*, ibid. paras. 14–43.

[126] *Anufrijeva*, ibid. para. 43.

[127] (1999) 28 EHRR CD 175, pp. 179–180.

to place emphasis on the vulnerabilities of the claimant as a crucial deciding factor, and made no mention of an Article 3 threshold. The Court of Appeal discussed *Marzari* in its judgment, but did not address whether the finding in that case was consistent with its own views on the use of Article 3. Ultimately, all three claims examined in the *Anufrijeva* case were denied for failure to be sufficiently exceptional.[128]

Article 3 was not used as such a threshold in the High Court decision of *R (Bernard) v. Enfield London Borough Council*, approved in *Anufrijeva*, and in which Justice Sullivan found that a severely disabled woman's Article 8 rights had been violated by the council's failure to provide her with housing suited to her disability.[129] It was accepted by the council that it had breached its duty to her under the National Assistance Act 1948. The flat failed to provide the claimant with wheelchair-access to a lavatory, and as a result she constantly soiled herself. She could not look after her children adequately. She had no privacy, and was confined to an extremely small area. While Justice Sullivan held that it was not a breach of Article 3, he accepted that it did contravene Article 8 because it made it virtually impossible for her to have any meaningful private or family life for the purposes of Article 8. The judge placed emphasis on the fact that disabled people are a 'particularly vulnerable group'.[130]

In both *Anufrijeva* and *Bernard,* as with *Razgar* and *N*, there is a clear attempt to fashion the category of potential claimants in a narrow manner, and to be cautious about preventing an expansion of the category. A similar position is taken in *Royal Borough of Kensington and Chelsea v. O'Sullivan*, in which the judge rejected the claimant's attempt to remain in her council flat after her husband, the grantee of the flat, died.[131] The judge referred to the courts' desire to avoid becoming engaged in 'macro level' housing allocation issues. The claimant's case was not sufficiently exceptional to warrant doing precisely this.[132]

The concern again came sharply into focus in the *Kay and others v. London Borough of Lambeth and*

others case.[133] Of these two conjoined appeals, the *Leeds* case involved a number of traveller families (also referred to in the judgment as 'gypsies') who had occupied council land for a period of two days and sought to contest the council's order for possession as a violation of their Article 8 rights. They claimed that, following the *Connors* decision of the Strasbourg court,[134] the local authority had failed to implement its obligations under statutory scheme for the protection of traveller families, and had failed to give adequate weight to the exceptional circumstances of their family.[135] Their claims were unanimously rejected by the House of Lords, but an important split in the judgment signals a difference of opinion that may be appealed to Strasbourg. The main issue was whether the claimants could raise an Article 8 defence in proceedings against them in County Court for possession of property where the domestic law of property afforded no defence. All of their Lordships agreed that a legal challenge to the compatibility of primary housing legislation could be mounted (itself an important shift from the position taken in the earlier case of *Quazi*),[136] but that this must be raised in the High Court and not the County Court.[137] The majority and minority split on the important question of whether a claimant ought to be allowed to raise an Article 8 defence in County Court proceedings that would take account of his or her exceptional individual circumstances. Lord Bingham (Lords Nicholls and Walker concurring) found that the County Court should consider 'highly exceptional cases' of this sort. The majority rather found that under no circumstances whatsoever could a claimant raise a successful Article 8 defence that does not go the validity of the controlling law but rather seeks to curtail the exercise of powers under such law.[138] In the course of giving this judgment, very little

---

[128] *Anufrijeva* (n.124 above) para. 43.

[129] [2002] EWHC 2282.

[130] Ibid, para. 32.

[131] *O'Sullivan* (n. 123 above), para. 82.

[132] Ibid. para. 82.

[133] *Kay and others v. Lambeth London Borough Council; Leeds County Council v. Price and others* [2006] UKHL 10.

[134] *Connors v. United Kingdom* (2004) 40 EHRR 189 (finding, at para. 84, that 'special consideration should be given to their needs and their different lifestyle both in the relevant regulatory framework and in reaching decisions in particular cases').

[135] *Kay and others* (n. 133 above), para. 7.

[136] *Harrow London Borough Council v. Quazi* [2004] 1 AC 983 (HL).

[137] *Kay and others* (n. 133 above), para. 39 (Lord Bingham, for Lords Hope and Walker concurring) and para. 110 (Lord Hope, Lords Scott and Brown, Baroness Hale concurring).

[138] Ibid. para. 110 (Lord Hope). Lord Scott endorses the finding at para. 174.

emphasis was placed on the vulnerability of the group at issue, and some rather sweeping statements were made. For instance, Baroness Hale took pains to say that Article 8, while it comprises positive obligations, 'does not confer any right to health or welfare benefits or to housing. The extent to which any member state assumes responsibility for supplying these is very much a matter for that member state'.[139] The claim was not joined by any other Law Lord, and is likely inconsistent with the otherwise undisturbed findings in the cases discussed above, as well as with the findings of the Strasbourg court in the *Connors* case. More generally, the *Connors* judgment, which specifically requires judges to consider whether special attention has been given to the needs of UK travellers 'in reaching decisions in specific cases', would appear to contradict the findings of the majority in this case. It can only be hoped that if the case is heard at the Strasbourg court, the opportunity to clarify the situation will be taken.

A more receptive approach to Article 8 claims from traveller and gypsy claimants may be found in the *South Bucks District Council v. Porter* case.[140] In three conjoined cases, the claimants had acquired land for the purposes of establishing caravan sites but were subsequently denied planning permission for that use of the land. The claimants remained on site, and the Council applied under planning legislation to have them evicted. The planning legislation conferred a discretion on the judge to decide whether to issue an injunction upon application, non-compliance with which could result in imprisonment. An important issue on appeal was the degree to which the court ought to take account of human rights considerations under Article 8 when exercising such judicial discretion on whether to grant injunctive relief. The House of Lords found that the Court of Appeal's guidance on the issue was correct, and that when a court considers whether to issue an injunction and thus interfere with a person's Article 8 interest in a home and private life, the decision must be proportionate in the Convention rights sense. As explained by the Court of Appeal:

> Proportionality requires not only that the injunction be appropriate and necessary for the attainment of the public interest objective

sought – here the safeguarding of the environment – but also that it does not impose an excessive burden on the individual whose private interests – here the gypsy's private life and home and the retention of his ethnic identity – are at stake.[141]

Thus although the court is not to review each planning decision strictly on its merits, neither is it to exercise a more lenient, merely supervisory jurisdiction.[142] In the exercise of the statutorily conferred judicial discretion, the judge must engage in a proportionate balancing process that takes account of article 8 interests.

4.3.4. FREEDOM OF ASSEMBLY AND ASSOCIATION (ARTICLE 11 ECHR)

There have been comparatively few complaints under this Article.[143] In *National Union of Rail, Maritime and Transport Workers v. London Underground*, the Court of Appeal upheld the finding of the Strasbourg court that Article 11 does not guarantee the right to strike in and of itself.[144] It also does not require an employer to engage in collective bargaining.

4.3.5. PROHIBITION OF DISCRIMINATION (ARTICLE 14 ECHR)

Courts are in some cases more willing to provide relief even for resource intensive rights when the Article 14 right to enjoy Convention rights 'without discrimination' is at issue. In *Ghaidan v. Godin-Mendoza*, the House of Lords held that the Convention required that the survivors of homosexual partners enjoy the same statutory tenancy rights as do the surviving spouses/partners of married couples (or unmarried couples who lived as husband and wife).[145] It was common ground that Godin-Mendoza's Article 8 right to a home was engaged for the purposes of an Article 14 analysis. Lord Nicholls also held that 'arguments based on the extent of the discretionary area of judgment

---

[139] Ibid., para. 190.
[140] [2003] UKHL 26.
[141] [2001] EWCA Civ 1549, para. 41, repeated in Lord Bingham's judgment, ibid., para. 20.
[142] *South Bucks* (n. 140 above), paras. 20, 27, and 38 (Lord Bingham).
[143] J. Wadham, H. Mountfield and A. Edmundson, *Blackstone's Guide to the Human Rights Act 1998*, 3rd edition (Oxford: Oxford University Press, 2003), p. 117.
[144] [2001] EWCA Civ 211.
[145] [2004] UKHL 30.

accorded to the legislature lead nowhere in this case'.[146] Similarly, the Court of Appeal declared certain provisions of housing legislation invalid in *R (Morris) v. Westminster CC*[147] because the provision required the housing authority, when determining whether someone is in 'priority need' for housing, to disregard whether such a person had certain persons as dependents who were from abroad. The Court of Appeal found that the provision: (1) fell within the ambit of Article 8, (2) discriminated on grounds of national origin, and (3) was not proportionate to the legitimate objective of discouraging benefits tourism. The case was a bold step, involving complex housing and immigration legislation. The case straddles the fault line between macro-level housing policy and seemingly plain discrimination.

The House of Lords was less receptive to discrimination arguments in access to public benefits in *R (Carson) v. Secretary of State for Works and Pensions*[148] and *R (Hooper) v. Secretary of State for Pensions*.[149] In *Carson*, one claimant challenged the lower pension rate she received as a result of living in South Africa, while the other claimant challenged the rule that those under twenty-five years of age received a lower jobseeker's allowance. Both claims were dismissed. In *Hooper*, certain widowers challenged benefits provisions that provided less generous support than what was provided to widows. In fact, Parliament had legislatively equalised the payments (by levelling down what was paid to women) and the claimants attacked the period prior to the legislative action. The House of Lords rejected the claims, with Lord Hoffmann finding that whether or not social circumstances were such that a continued policy of giving more support to widows than widowers, and when such circumstances had changed and Parliamentary response was needed, were, due to their indeterminate nature, quintessentially matters for 'legislative judgment'.[150] It is not clear that *Carson* or *Hooper* would have a chilling effect on social rights litigation under the HRA 1998, as the outcome in the two cases could be equally plausible under a bill of social rights.

4.3.6. THE NON-DENIAL OF THE RIGHT TO EDUCATION (PROTOCOL 1 TO THE ECHR, ARTICLE 2)

In *Holub and another v. Secretary of State for the Home Department*, the court applied the Strasbourg court's leading *Belgian Linguistics Case*.[151] The Court of Appeal found that everyone is entitled to be educated to a minimum standard, but also found that right to an effective education was not to the most effective education possible.[152] In another case, the Court of Appeal held that the meaning of 'education' did not include vocational training.[153] As noted above, the *Douglas* case rejected the claim of discrimination in access to education on the basis of age for reasons of justiciability.[154]

The leading case on the non-denial of the right to education is now *Ali v. Lord Grey School*.[155] In one of two leading opinions, Lord Bingham set out what he referred to as a 'highly pragmatic' test to be applied to the specific facts of the case: 'have the authorities of the state acted so as to deny to a pupil effective access to…educational facilities?'[156] Lord Hoffmann, in the concurring leading opinion, held that the right does not guarantee access to any particular educational institution.[157] In addition to agreeing with Lord Bingham, he agreed with the trial judge that the existence of alternative, suitable and adequate education that the student or parents chose not to use will preclude a finding that Article 2 of the protocol has been violated.[158] He also found that '[e]veryone is no doubt entitled to be educated to a minimum standard'.[159] Despite the potential these words present for future cases, subsequent cases have emphasised the restrictive nature of Lord Hoffman's holding.[160]

The facts of *Ali* involved three boys excluded from school pending the outcome of a criminal

---

[146] Ibid. para. 19.
[147] [2005] EWCA Civ 1184.
[148] [2005] UKHL 37.
[149] [2005] UKHL 29.
[150] Ibid. para. 37 (Lord Hoffmann).

[151] *Belgian Linguistics Case (No.2)* (1968) 1 EHRR 252.
[152] [2001] 1 WLR 1359, p. 1367.
[153] *R (Jacob Youngson) v. Birmingham City Council* [2001] LGR 218.
[154] N. 99 above.
[155] [2006] UKHL 14.
[156] Ibid. para. 24.
[157] Ibid. para. 55.
[158] Ibid. paras. 50, 62.
[159] Ibid. para. 56.
[160] *A v. Essex County Council* [2008] EWCA Civ 364; *S. v. Chapman* [2008] EWCA Civ 800.

investigation into a fire they were alleged to have started on school premises. After discontinuation of prosecution for want of evidence, the school invited the student and his parents to a meeting to discuss reinstating him. The student's parents decided not to attend, and another pupil who did attend was in fact reinstated. This finding, together with the offer of alternative education in the interim, was fatal to Ali's claim in that case. Baroness Hale dissented, finding that the proposed meeting, and peremptory permanent exclusion after their absence, was not sufficiently accompanied by the usual procedural safeguards for exclusion and that the student should not be held responsible for his family's failure to respond to the offers.[161]

In *Begum v. Denbigh High School*, a girl was excluded from school for insisting on wearing a *jilbab*, a form of Muslim dress that obscures the contours of the body, instead of the school uniform.[162] She argued that her freedom of expression and right to the non-denial of education were infringed. The Law Lords referred to the *Ali* case for the relevant law on the education claim, and found in her case that (1) she chose not to comply with a rule to which the school was entitled to adhere, and (2) she failed to secure prompt admission to another school where her religious convictions could be accommodated.[163] Considerable weight was placed on two distinct facts. First, the school was run by a head teacher who was a woman of Bengali Muslim origin. She had arranged rather painstakingly for the design of a school uniform in consultation with Muslim parents, Muslim members of the board of governors, and Chairman of the local Council of Mosques. The second fact was that more than one other school in the area was willing to accept the student. However, it was unclear whether those schools were as high performing.[164] This aspect is not of minor concern in light of the importance laid upon the existence of alternative educational facilities, both in this case and in *Ali*. Baroness Hale (the first and only female Law Lord), Lord Nicholls concurring in her result, dissented on the claim of whether the right was infringed but found that the infringement was justified. She found that while keeping Shabina

Begum away from the school for reasons of political disagreement would not be justified, the actual reason in this case of protecting other girls from peer and male pressure to conform to more conservative practices was justified.[165] She accepted the 'pressure' claim offered by the school without calling for any further evidence of its existence. The case invites comparison with approaches in other multi-cultural countries.[166]

4.3.7. CONCLUSION ON HRA 1998

It is clear that courts will in some cases provide protection to welfare interests and enforce positive obligations where public resource allocation is implicated. Nonetheless, the replacement of the non-justiciability doctrine with a strong variant of judicial deference means that courts will continue to draw a line between cases of an extreme or exceptional nature, typically involving highly vulnerable groups, and those that raise the spectre of weighty demands on state finances. Until Britain adopts or incorporates social rights, courts will feel restrained in reviewing resource allocation decisions for lack of a clear constitutional mandate.

5. A BILL OF SOCIAL RIGHTS FOR BRITAIN?

As noted above,[167] there has for some time been advocacy of a more direct and robust protection of social rights as human rights in the UK constitutional order. Northern Ireland is presently contemplating the adoption of a bill of rights that contains the right to healthcare, to protection against destitution, to shelter, to work and to protection against a dangerous environment. The draft bill has been prepared by the Northern Ireland Human Rights Commission.[168] At the time of writing, three options are under consideration: (1) a set

---

[161] Ibid. paras. 78, 83.
[162] [2006] UKHL 15.
[163] Ibid. para. 36 (Lord Bingham).
[104] Ibid. para. 97 (Baroness Hale) and para. 41 (Lord Nicholls).

[165] Ibid. para. 98.
[166] An interesting comparison, despite important differences, can be made with the decision of the Supreme Court of Canada about the right of a Sikh student to carry a *kirpan* (ceremonial dagger) in his turban: *Multani v. Commission scolaire Marguerite-Bourgeoys* [2006] 1 SCR 256.
[167] Ibid.
[168] The NIRC is mandated under the Belfast (Good Friday) Agreement 1998 to draft the bill consistently with circumstances in Northern Ireland and to draw as appropriate on international instruments and experience. Section 69(7) of the Northern Ireland Act 1998 directs the Commission to 'advise' the Secretary of State for Northern

of rights phrased in unconditional terms, whose enforceability shall be determined by the courts; (2) a broader set of rights that are to be progressively realised, based largely on the South African model; and (3) a combination of both approaches with two sets of rights.[169]

Geraldine van Bueren has argued in favour of incorporating the International Covenant on Economic, Social and Cultural Rights (ICESCR) into UK law, using in part the model provided by the HRA 1998.[170] Quite importantly, a similar (though more qualified) conclusion was reached in a report by the Joint Committee on Human Rights, a multiparty body representing members of the House of Commons and the House of Lords. The Committee found that:

> Providing the Covenant rights with legal status in UK law would broaden and strengthen the developing culture of respect for human rights in the UK, and make clear that human rights address essential human needs, and help to ensure that provision is made for the most vulnerable people in our society.[171]

The Joint Committee critically examined the troublesome relationship between social rights and (1) legal indeterminacy, (2) democracy, and (3) resource allocation. It found that in no case was the wholesale exclusion of justiciable social rights justified.[172] It thus recommended that Parliament consider the idea of incorporation. Whether Parliament would adopt such a bill may be a different story. As part of a larger package of constitutional renewal, the Labour government has proposed to conduct a wide consultation on the adoption of a new British bill of rights. In a Green Paper, the government poured cold water on the idea of social rights in any new bill of rights even before launch-

ing any serious discussion on the matter.[173] Popular support among mainstream academics and institutions has been more sanguine, and the topic is sure to arise once more over the course of the national discussion on a bill of rights formally launched by the Labour government in March 2008. The shockingly cool attitude of the United Kingdom towards justiciable social rights is evident in its being, along with Poland, the only European country to have signed a special opt-out protocol to the Treaty of Lisbon that prevents Title IV of the European Union Charter of Fundamental Rights, which contains the Charter's social rights and solidarity provisions, from having any application in the United Kingdom.[174] Notwithstanding this attitude (even under a Labour Government), more mainstream views, both popular and academic, have remained more optimistic (if not entirely unequivocal) on the desirability and feasibility of putting social rights in a UK bill of rights.[175]

6. CONCLUSION

This chapter has attempted to show the main ways in which a person who feels that her or his social rights have been denied in the United Kingdom can go about seeking relief. There are various components in the multi-layered regime of protection. A patchwork of statutory tribunals and informal complaints mechanisms allow persons to contest assessments and challenge the abuse of power in the administration of welfare programmes. The

---

Ireland on the appropriate content of a bill of rights. It is expected to do so by the end of 2008.

[169] Northern Ireland Human Rights Commission, *Progressing a Bill of Rights for Northern Ireland: An Update* (2004), pp. 71–76. See how Bill of Rights Forum Final Report: Recommendations to the Northern Ireland Human Rights Commission on a Bill of Rights for Northern Ireland (31 March 2008).

[170] G. van Bueren, 'Including the Excluded: The Case for an Economic, Social and Cultural Human Rights Act', *Public Law* [2002], pp. 456–472.

[171] *Report of the Joint Committee on Human Rights of the House of Lords and House of Commons: The International Covenant on Economic, Social and Cultural Rights, Twenty First Report of Session 2003–2004* (20 October 2004), para. 73.

[172] Ibid. paras. 59–72.

[173] See Ministry of Justice, *The Governance of Britain*, (London: HMSO, 2007), para. 204.

[174] See Protocol on the Application of the Charter of Fundamental Rights of the European Union to Poland and to the United Kingdom, Art. 1(2), appended to the Treaty of Lisbon amending the Treaty on European Union and the Treaty establishing the European Community (3 December 2007).

[175] See the report of a panel of distinguished public law scholars, Report of the JUSTICE Constitution Committee, *A British Bill of Rights: Informing the Debate* (London: Justice, 2007), paras. 90–111 (esp. para. 95, noting 89 percent popular support for a constitutional right to health care). A draft bill of rights produced by academics and students in a seminar run by Oxford University Professors Vernon Bogdanor and Stefan Vogenauer included draft articles on the rights to health, subsistence and education. See V. Bogdanor, T. Khaitan and S. Vogenauer, 'Should Britain Have a Written Constitution?', *The Political Quarterly* (2007), Vol.78, No.4, pp. 499–517, esp. at p. 516

advantages of speed and efficiency, as well as a more inquisitorial role for the adjudicators, have presented substantial benefits to claimants. The jurisdictions of the various ombudsmen have been exercised in a way that has expanded the scope and nature of remedies one can claim against public-decisionmakers in the administrative state. However, the coverage provided by such quasi-adjudicative and non-adjudicative institutions is not complete. Certain questions of policy, in some cases including more controversial interpretations of statutory provisions, present difficult issues that such institutions are often unwilling to resolve. To resolve such disputes, persons may turn to the courts. Yet in the exercise of judicial review, courts typically view challenges to discretionary resource allocation decisions on grounds of reasonableness to be non-justiciable. Despite this, when local authorities or central government disregard their statutory duties, courts will enforce them even when resources are heavily implicated. Yet under neither statutory tribunal mechanisms nor judicial review is the important issue of whether certain broader policies and primary legislation are themselves contrary to a reasonable conception of what social and other human rights are. Such questions are more familiar in claims arising under the HRA 1998. While the judgments of the appeal courts find in a number of cases that a strong form of judicial deference to government or Parliament when they allocate public resources is desirable, a number of recent cases demonstrate a more nuanced position. The courts have rather done what the common law has always commended. They have inched forward, one case at a time, building upon rational principles laid down in the United Kingdom, Strasbourg and elsewhere.

It is thus small wonder that the developments internationally and in particular in South Africa have emboldened the Joint Committee on Human Rights to suggest that incorporation of a bill of social rights should be given serious consideration. On the one hand, protection of social rights as human rights will remain incomplete in the United Kingdom until such a time arrives. On the other, there are more hopeful signs of progress towards that goal than at any other time in nearly eight hundred years of constitutional government.

16

Ireland

The Separation of Powers Doctrine vs. Socio-economic Rights?

Aoife Nolan*

1. INTRODUCTION

The Irish Constitution is the oldest in Europe and predates the international human rights discourses, including those regarding socio-economic rights. Its framers expressly included only one socio-economic right (the right to education) in the document, preferring instead to set out 'the principles for the State to apply towards the promotion of the people as a whole in the socio-economic field'[1] in the form of non-justiciable 'principles of social policy'. In the words of one commentator, while Eamon de Valera,[2] the leading figure in the drafting of the constitution, cleverly genuflected before socio-economic rights, he made sure to insert them in a part of the constitution that is *prima facie* unenforceable.[3]

Despite the lack of provision for a comprehensive range of socio-economic rights under the Irish Constitution, a number of judges have handed down decisions resulting in the direct or indirect protection of socio-economic rights. However, concerns about the implications of adjudication of socio-economic rights for the separation of powers and the involvement of the courts in what have been deemed issues of 'distributive justice' has, in more recent times, resulted in a general reluctance on the part of courts to recognise and give proper effect to such rights.[4]

2. PROTECTION OF SOCIAL RIGHTS UNDER THE IRISH CONSTITUTION

2.1 Overview of Relevant Provisions

The Constitution contains a wide range of socio-economic, rights-related provisions of both a justiciable and non-justiciable nature. Article 42 provides that:

4. The State shall provide for free primary education and shall endeavour to supplement and give reasonable aid to private and corporate educational initiative, and, when the public good requires it, provide other educational facilities or institutions with due regard, however, for the rights of parents, especially in the matter of religious and moral formation.

5. In exceptional cases, where the parents for physical or moral reasons fail in their duty

---

* Aoife Nolan is Assistant Director of the Human Rights Centre and Law Lecturer at Queen's University, Belfast. The author would like to thank Professor Gerry Whyte and Claire McHugh for helpful comments on earlier drafts. The input of Ciarán O'Kelly, Rory O'Connell and Úna Breatnach is also gratefully acknowledged.

1 Constitution Review Group, *Report of the Constitution Review Group* (Dublin: Stationery Office, 1996), p. 391 ('CRG').

2 The Constitution was primarily the work of Eamon de Valera, President of the Executive Council of the Irish Free State, who oversaw, and was heavily involved in, its drafting.

3 G. Quinn, 'Rethinking the Nature of Economic, Social and Cultural Rights in the Irish Legal Order', in C. Costello (ed.), *Fundamental Social Rights: Current European Legal Protection and the Challenge of the EU Charter on Fundamental Rights* (Dublin: Trinity College, 2001), pp. 35–54, at 49.

4 There is also a range of statutory socio-economic rights provided for under Irish law. However, this chapter focuses primarily on those socio-economic rights that arise under the Constitution. Furthermore, while there is no doubt that the supremacy of EU law over constitutional law may have future implications for Irish constitutional law on socio-economic rights, the (thus far negligible) impact of EU law on constitutional socio-economic rights jurisprudence is not dealt with in this chapter.

towards their children, the State as guardian of the common good, by appropriate means shall endeavour to supply the place of the parents, but always with due regard for the natural and imprescriptible rights of the child.

The duty set out in the latter sub-section necessarily has a corresponding right, which can be used as the basis of a claim against the State.

Many of the socio-economic rights accorded under the Irish constitution are 'unenumerated' personal rights, which are primarily guaranteed under article 40.3.1° of the Constitution. This provision states that: '[t]he State guarantees in its laws to respect, and, as far as practicable by its laws to defend and *vindicate* the personal rights of the citizen' [emphasis added]. It is clear that this article imposes a duty on the State to take positive action in appropriate circumstances.[5] In *Ryan* v. *The Attorney General*, Justice Kenny in the High Court held that the 'personal rights' mentioned in article 40.3.1° are not exhausted by the rights to 'life, person, good name and property rights' expressly enumerated in the following section 40.3.2°,[6] a position confirmed by the Supreme Court in the same case.[7] Court-identified, unenumerated (i.e. unwritten) socio-economic rights under article 40.3.1° include various rights of the child,[8] the right to bodily integrity,[9] including the right not to have health endangered by the State,[10] and the right to work or to earn a livelihood.[11] The Irish Courts have therefore been prepared to recognise that the Constitution protects unenumerated socio-economic rights, although only the first two of the rights just mentioned have been held to give rise to a positive obligation on the State.

In addition, civil and political rights have the potential to serve as sources of socio-economic rights under the Constitution or to be applied in such a way as to protect socio-economic rights.[12]

Article 45 of the Irish Constitution provides that:

The principles of social policy set forth in this Article are intended for the general guidance of the Oireachtas. The application of those principles in the making of laws shall be the care of the Oireachtas exclusively and *shall not be cognisable by any Court* under any of the provisions of this Constitution. [Emphasis added][13]

These principles have clear implications for the enjoyment of socio-economic rights. For example, article 45.2(ii) requires the State to direct its policy towards securing that the ownership and control of the material resources of the community may be so distributed amongst private individuals and the various classes as best to subserve the common good. Meanwhile, in article 45(4)(i), the State pledges itself to safeguard with especial care the economic interests of the weaker sections of the community, and where necessary, to contribute to the support of the infirm, the widow, the orphan, and the aged.

I will not discuss these directive principles in any detail, since the primary focus of this chapter is justiciable socio-economic rights under the Irish Constitution.[14] It should be noted, however, that article 45 has been used by the Irish courts as an interpretive instrument with regard to, amongst other things, the identification of unenumerated personal rights under article 40.3 of the Constitution. One example is the case of *Murtagh Properties* v. *Cleary*,[15] in which Justice Kenny in the High Court referred to the directive principle in article 45.2(i) that '[t]he State shall, in particular, direct its policy towards securing (i) That the citizens (all of whom, men and women equally, have the right to an adequate means of livelihood) may through their occupations find the means of making reasonable provision for their domestic needs'. He held that the parenthesis recognises the right to

---

[5] G. Whyte, *Social Inclusion and the Legal System – Public Interest Law in Ireland* (Dublin: Institute of Public Administration, 2002), p. 19.

[6] [1965] IR 294, at 312–3 ('*Ryan* v. *Attorney General*').

[7] Ibid. p. 344.

[8] See section 4.5 below.

[9] See *Ryan* v. *Attorney General* (n. 6 above), p. 313.

[10] See *The State (C)* v. *Frawley* [1976] IR 365, as discussed in section 4.1. below.

[11] See section 4.2 below.

[12] See section 4.1 below.

[13] The Houses of the Oireachtas - Dáil Éireann and Seanad Éireann – are the Irish houses of parliament.

[14] For more on the content and judicial treatment of Article 45, see G. Whyte and G. Hogan (eds.), *J.M. Kelly: the Irish Constitution*, 4th edition (Dublin: Butterworths, 2003), pp. 2077–86; and G. Hogan, 'Directive Principles, Socio-Economic Rights and the Constitution', *Irish Jurist*, Vol. 36 (2001), pp. 174–98, at 179–81. For more on the evolution of the directive principles, see Whyte and Hogan, *J.M. Kelly*, ibid. pp. 175–9.

[15] [1972] IR 330 ('*Murtagh Properties*').

an adequate means of livelihood and, while this is not enforceable against the State, its existence logically entails that each citizen has the right to earn a livelihood. He continued to state that the phrase 'all of whom, men and women equally' shows that the right is one conferred equally on men and women. Justice Kenny commented that the statement in article 45 on non-cognisability means that the courts have no jurisdiction to consider the application of the principles in article 45 in the making of laws. However, this does not mean that the courts may not take article 45 into consideration when deciding whether a claimed constitutional right exists.[16]

Hogan and Whyte have observed that there has been a progressive minimisation of the effect of the exclusion in article 45 but that this has not yet been considered by the Supreme Court.[17] The reluctance displayed by Irish courts towards addressing or employing directive principles in their decisions contrasts sharply with the approach adopted by courts in other jurisdictions, such as India.

2.2   Horizontal Application

While the wording of articles 40.3.1°,[18] 42.4 and 42.5 refer expressly to the duties of the State to give effect to constitutional rights, the Irish Supreme Court has made it clear that constitutional rights (including socio-economic rights) may have direct horizontal effect and are not binding on the State alone.

The most significant case dealing with this issue is that of *Meskell* v. *CIE*.[19] Here the defendant employers agreed with trade unions to terminate the contracts of employment of all their employees and to offer each employee immediate re-employment upon the same general terms as prior to the termination if he agreed, as a special and additional condition of his employment, to be 'at all times' a member of one of the four trade unions. Pursuant to that agreement, the plaintiff's contract of employment was terminated by the defendants. The plaintiff was not re-employed by the defendants as he refused to accept the special condition.

The Supreme Court held that the right of citizens to form associations and unions, guaranteed by article 40.6.10° of the Constitution, necessarily recognised a correlative right to abstain from joining associations and unions. In this case, the plaintiff was entitled to damages because, amongst other things, he had suffered loss caused by the defendant employers' conduct in violating a right guaranteed to him by the Constitution. The Court stated, *per* Justice Walsh, that:

> It has been said on a number of occasions in this Court...that a right guaranteed by the Constitution or granted by the Constitution can be protected by action or enforced by action even though such action may not fit into any of the ordinary forms of action in either common law or equity and that the constitutional right carries within it its own right to a remedy or for the enforcement of it. Therefore, if a person has suffered damage by virtue of a breach of a constitutional right or the infringement of a constitutional right, that person is entitled to seek redress against the person or persons who have infringed that right.[20]

The Court expressly agreed with the statements of Justice Budd in *Educational Company of Ireland Ltd* v. *Fitzpatrick (No. 2)*,[21] that 'if one citizen has a right under the Constitution there exists a correlative duty on the part of *other citizens* to respect that right and not to interfere with it'.[22] It has been observed that the defendant in *Meskell* was a semi-state nationalised corporation – and hence not an entirely private entity.[23] In subsequent cases, however, Irish courts have held that constitutional rights can apply horizontally to purely private bodies.[24]

---

[16] See also *Minister for Posts and Telegraphs* v. *Paperlink* [1984] ILRM 373.

[17] Whyte and Hogan, *J.M. Kelly* (n. 14 above), p. 2083.

[18] See p. 296 above.

[19] [1973] IR 121 ('*Meskell*').

[20] Ibid., p. 133.

[21] (1961) IR 345, p. 368 [emphasis added].

[22] *Meskell* (n. 19 above), p. 133. See also, Justice Costello's statements in *Hosford* v. *Murphy & Sons Ltd* [1988] ILRM 300, at 304.

[23] C. O'Cinneide, 'Grasping the Nettle: Irish Constitutional Law and Direct Effect' in J. Fedtke and D. Oliver (eds.), *Human Rights in the Private Sphere* (London: Cavendish, 2007), 213, p. 220.

[24] See, e.g., *Glover* v. *BLN Limited* [1973] IR 388, where the defendants were the board of directors of a private company. Here, the Supreme Court stated that 'public policy

There is very limited socio-economic rights-specific case law dealing with the issue of horizontal application and most of those cases that do exist involve the right to earn a livelihood or the right to education.[25]

2.3 The Potential of International Law

Ireland has ratified many of the international instruments that have been invoked by advocates bringing socio-economic rights litigation before courts and other decision-making bodies. These include the International Covenant on Economic Social and Cultural Rights ('ICESCR'), the Convention on the Rights of the Child ('CRC'), the International Covenant on Civil and Political Rights ('ICCPR'), the International Convention on the Elimination of All Forms of Racial Discrimination

('CERD') and the Convention on the Elimination of All Forms of Discrimination Against Women ('CEDAW'). Ireland's dualist system requires that its international obligations be expressly incorporated into domestic law in order for them to be enforceable before the national courts.[26] This has not occurred in relation to any of the UN human rights instruments that Ireland has ratified and, hence, their provisions (socio-economic or otherwise) are not directly enforceable by the national courts. The Supreme Court has stated that, in the absence of such incorporation, the principles of international treaty law do not prevail over domestic legislation.[27] Furthermore, the Supreme Court has held that, under article 29 of the Constitution, international law confers no rights capable of being invoked by individuals.[28] This finding does

and the dictates of constitutional justice require that statutes, regulations or agreements setting up machinery for taking decisions which may affect rights or impose liabilities should be construed as providing for fair procedures'

[25] See, e.g., *Murtagh Properties* (n. 15 above) in which Kenny J stated that 'It follows that a policy or general rule under which *anyone* seeks to prevent an employer from employing men or women on the ground of sex only is prohibited by the Constitution' (p. 336) [emphasis added]. See also *Lovett* v. *Gogan* [1995] 1 I.L.R.M. 12, which involved the right to livelihood. See also, *Crowley* v. *Ireland* [1980] IR 102 and *Conway* v. *Irish National Teachers Organisation* [1991] ILRM 497, which centered on the right to primary education. A further socio-economic, rights-related example is *Hosford* v. *Murphy & Sons Ltd* (n. 22 above). This case concerned an action taken against factory owners by children whose father had suffered a severe electric shock and permanent brain damage whilst working for the defendants in their factory premises. Amongst other things, the decision focused on article 42(1), according to which the State is obliged 'to respect the inalienable right and duty of parents to provide, according to their means, for the religious and moral, intellectual, physical and social education of their children'. Costello J in the High Court opined that the rights which Mr Hosford enjoyed under article 42.1 did not include an ancillary right not to be injured by a negligent act which interfered with his ability to exercise his rights vis-à-vis his children. Hence, his children would not enjoy any implied ancillary right that their father would not be negligently injured and the defendants' negligent act did not infringe any of their article 42 rights. It is important to note that, while denying the existence of the constitutional rights asserted by the plaintiffs, the Court stated that if the plaintiffs could have established that the defendants were guilty of a breach of a constitutionally imposed duty which inflicted harm on the plaintiffs then damages would have been recoverable even though at common law an award in respect of such harm could not be made.

[26] Article 29(6) of the Constitution states that: 'No international agreement shall be part of the domestic law of the State save as may be determined by Parliament'. For more on the impact of this provision, see, amongst others, the statements made by the Supreme Court in the following decisions: *Re Ó Láigléis* [1960] I.R. 93; *Application of Woods* [1970] IR 154; *Kavanagh* v. *Governor of Mountjoy Prison* [2002] 3 I.R. 97; *Norris* v. *Att. Gen* [1984] IR 3, and *Crotty* v. *An Taoiseach* [1987] I.R. 713.

[27] See *Sumers Jennings* v. *Furlong* [1966] IR 183. However, the same is not necessarily true of customary international law, which may have a more forceful effect in Irish municipal law. There have been several cases in which the courts have taken the view that principles of customary international law form part of domestic law by virtue of article 29(3), see Whyte and Hogan, *J.M. Kelly* (n. 14 above), p. 492. For a discussion of the incorporation of customary international law into Irish law and the relationship of customary international law and Irish municipal law, see C. R. Symmons, 'The Incorporation of Customary International Law into Irish Law' in G. Biehler (ed.), *International Law in Practice: An Irish Perspective* (Dublin: Thompson Roundhall, 2005), pp. 111–183. However, principles of customary international law may only be regarded as incorporated into Irish domestic law where they are not contrary to the provisions of the Constitution, statute law or common law. In *Horgan* v. *Taoiseach* [2003] 2 I.L.R.M. 357, the High Court stated that, where a conflict arises between a principle of international law and domestic constitutional, statutory or other judge-made law, 'the rule of international law must in every case yield to domestic law' (at 393). For an exhaustive treatment of the interaction of international law and domestic law in the Irish context, see Whyte and Hogan, *J.M. Kelly* (n. 14 above), pp. 492–500.

[28] Section 29(3) states that 'Ireland accepts the generally recognised principles of international law as its rule of conduct in its relations with other States'. According to Fennelly J in *Kavanagh* v. *Governor of Mountjoy Prison* (n. 26 above): 'The obligation of Ireland to respect the invoked principles is expressed only in the sense that it is to be' its rule of conduct in its relations with other States. 'No single word in the section even

not auger well for those seeking to place reliance on international instruments in an attempt to secure rights being denied by the domestic legal order.[29]

Several judges have, however, been willing to recognise that while not binding on courts, international agreements may have a persuasive value, and have used such instruments as an aid to the interpretation of national rules.[30] For instance, in the case of O'Donoghue v. The Minister for Health,[31] discussed below, Justice O'Hanlon in the High Court referred to education-related provisions of the Universal Declaration of Human Rights and various articles of the CRC. The European Convention for the Protection of Human Rights and Fundamental Freedoms ('ECHR'), in particular, has been called on in aid by various Irish judges to justify the 'discovery' of unenumerated rights, although not in the socio-economic area.[32]

Overall, however, Irish courts have not proved receptive to arguments based on international law – including instruments providing for socio-economic rights. Indeed, the reluctance of the Irish courts to take international law, including the ICESCR, into account arguably amounts to a violation of the State's obligations under the ICESCR, in light of, amongst other things, the UN Committee on Economic, Social and Cultural Rights' statements in its General Comment No. 9 on the Domestic Application of the Covenant.[33]

2.4   Right to Civil Legal Aid for Socio-Economic Rights Litigation

Despite the fact that Ireland was a party in possibly the most celebrated case involving a regional human rights body recognising the right to civil legal aid, Airey v. Ireland,[34] the Irish courts have traditionally been highly reluctant to recognise a constitutional right to civil legal aid.[35] Recently, there has been a move towards judicial recognition of an unenumerated constitutional right under article 40.3.1° to civil legal aid in certain circumstances. In O'Donoghue v. Legal Aid Board,[36] the plaintiff was seeking a divorce and maintenance. She had experienced a delay of twenty-five months between contacting the Legal Aid Board for legal aid and ultimately obtaining a legal aid certificate. In the High Court, Justice Kelly held that the plaintiff had a constitutional right to civil legal aid derived from her constitutional right of access to the courts and her constitutional right to

arguably expresses an intention to confer rights capable of being invoked by individuals' (p. 126). This statement was quoted approvingly by Justice Kearns in the High Court in Horgan v. An Taoiseach [2003] 2 IR 468.

[29] G. Biehler, 'International Law Procedures', in G. Biehler, (ed.), International Law in Practice: An Irish Perspective (Dublin: Thompson Roundhall, 2005), pp. 184–240, at 197–8. A more positive aspect of the Kavanagh and Horgan decisions is that, in both cases, the plaintiffs were allowed to bring their claims based on international law before the courts and obtained a decision on the merits (ibid. pp. 198–9). Biehler points out that there have been numerous instances of international law-based arguments being fully heard by Irish courts, notwithstanding that those arguments have ultimately been rejected (ibid. pp. 200).

[30] F. Ryan, Constitutional Law (Dublin: Round Hall, 2001), p. 55. It has also been suggested that unincorporated international agreements may also have indirect legal effect through the operation of a presumption of compatibility of domestic legislation with international obligations, see Whyte and Hogan, J.M. Kelly (n.14 above), p. 553.

[31] [1996] 2 IR 20. Hereinafter, 'O'Donoghue' or the 'O'Donoghue case'.

[32] Law Society of Ireland, Human Rights Law (2004), p. 37. See, e.g., Heaney v. Ireland [1994] 3 IR 593, in which Costello J in the High Court invoked Article 14(3)(g) of the ICCPR, as well as the European Court of Human Rights' interpretation of Article 6 of the ECHR, to support his identification of the right to silence as a latent constitutional guarantee (ibid.).

[33] UN Doc. E/C.12/1998/24. The Committee stated that 'it is generally accepted that domestic law should be interpreted as far as possible in a way in which conforms to a State's international legal obligations. Thus, when a domestic decision maker is faced with a choice between an interpretation of domestic law that would place the state in breach of the Covenant and one that would enable the State to comply with the Covenant, international law requires the choice of the latter'. (At para. 15).

[34] (1980) 2 EHRR 305.

[35] An exception to this are two decisions of Lardner J in the early 1990s in the cases of Stevenson v. Landy and others, unreported, High Court, 10 February 1993, and Kirwan v. Minister for Justice [1994] 1 ILRM 444. In these cases, a right to civil legal aid was recognised in the context of wardship proceedings and the executive review of the detention of an individual found guilty but insane, respectively. Rather than focussing on the existence of a constitutional right to civil legal aid, these decisions centred on the need for civil legal aid in the particular cases in order to ensure the constitutional requirements of fair procedures, and that the courts should administer justice with fairness, be given effect to. Lardner J's approach was not followed by other judges, however. For more on this, see Whyte, 'Social Inclusion' (n. 5 above), pp. 246–254.

[36] [2004] IEHC 413.

fair procedures. Justice Kelly referred to previous High Court decisions in which it was held that legal aid was constitutionally mandated[37] and stated that 'it seems to me that the unfortunate circumstances of the plaintiff in the present case are such that access to the courts and fair procedures under the Constitution would require that she be provided with legal aid'. He found that the Board should have adhered to its own target of two to four months between a person first making contact with the Board and having a consultation with a solicitor.

This decision was confirmed in *Magee* v. *Minister for Justice, Equality and Law Reform*.[38] Justice Gilligan in the High Court quoted Justice Kelly's decision approvingly, holding that in this case the plaintiff was constitutionally entitled to be provided with legal aid for the purpose of being adequately represented at the inquest into her son's death while in garda (police) custody. It remains to be seen whether or not the approach of the High Court in these cases will be confirmed by the Supreme Court. Whyte observes that the reluctance of other judges to recognise a constitutional right to civil legal aid, taken together with the opposition expressed by leading members of the Supreme Court in *Sinnott* v. *Minister for Education*[39] and *TD* v. *Minister for Education*[40] (see below) to the judicial recognition of socio-economic rights, might give rise to grounds for pessimism on this point. This is despite the fact that Justice Kelly's decision in *O'Donoghue* brings the constitutional position on civil legal aid more into line with that of the European Convention on Human Rights as stated in *Airey*.[41]

In Ireland, civil legal aid is primarily provided for under legislation. Ireland has had a state-funded legal aid scheme since 1979.[42] Its current design is based on the provisions of the Civil Legal Aid Act 1995 ('1995 Act'), which aims 'to make provision for the grant by the State of legal aid and advice to persons of insufficient means in civil cases'.[43]

The 1995 Act provides for the establishment of a Legal Aid Board whose primary functions include the provision of legal aid and advice in civil cases to persons who satisfy the requirements of the Act.[44]

In terms of the 1995 Act, legal aid[45] and advice will not be granted by the Legal Aid Board in respect of a number of matters. For the purposes of socio-economic rights litigation, it is important to note that these include representative actions and class actions.[46] This has clear implications for those seeking to bring collective socio-economic rights claims. That said, the Act provides that an application for a legal aid certificate shall not be refused 'by reason only of the fact that a successful outcome to the proceedings for the applicant would benefit persons other than the applicant'.[47] The Act also expressly states that legal aid will not be granted in relation to 'test cases'.[48] Furthermore, the fact that the Legal Aid Board is not permitted to provide representation before administrative tribunals (with the exception of the Refugee Appeals tribunal)[49] means that legal aid is unavailable to those seeking to enforce their socio-economic rights-related entitlements before bodies such as the Social Welfare Appeals Office, the Equality Tribunal or the Employment Appeals Tribunal. Finally, under the Act there is a blanket exclusion of housing matters with some very limited exceptions, which has very serious implications for those of limited means threatened with losing their homes.[50]

---

[37] See the *Stevenson* and *Kirwan* cases (n. 35 above).

[38] Unreported, High Court, 26 October 2006, pp. 11–13.

[39] [2001] IESC 63 ('*Sinnott*').

[40] [2001] IESC 101 ('*TD*').

[41] In discussion with G. Whyte (1 June 2006).

[42] Free Legal Advice Centres, *Access to Justice: A Right or a Privilege?* (Dublin: FLAC, 2005), p. 7.

[43] Civil Legal Aid Act 1995. Cited in Free Legal Advice Centres, *Access to Justice* (n. 42 above), p. 7.

[44] 1995 Act, Section 5(1).

[45] Legal aid is defined in Section 27(1) of the 1995 Act as: 'representation by a solicitor of the Board, or a solicitor or barrister engaged by the Board under Section 11, in any civil proceedings to which this section applies and includes all such assistance as is usually given by a solicitor and, where appropriate, barrister in contemplation of, ancillary to or in connection with, such proceedings, whether for the purposes of arriving at or giving effect to any settlement in the proceedings or otherwise'.

[46] Section 28(9)(a)(vii), (ix).

[47] Section 28(9)(d).

[48] Section 28(9)(a)(viii).

[49] In 1991, the Legal Aid scheme was extended to apply to proceedings before the Refugee Appeals Tribunal by Ministerial Order.

[50] For instance, the 1995 Act fails to cover proceedings brought under the Housing Act 1966 ('1966 Act'), including proceedings seeking recovery of possession of dwellings from occupants of local authority accommodation under Section 62 of the 1966 Act. The High Court has found on two occasions that there is no right to legal aid under the constitutions in relation to defending eviction

The Legal Aid Board has been criticised for prioritising family law and child care over any other kind of law. The Free Legal Advice Centre ('FLAC') points out that there is significant demand for assistance in the areas of debt, employment, housing and social welfare law (all of which have clear implications for socio-economic rights) that are not being met by the current civil legal aid scheme.[51] In addition, FLAC has argued that the merits test provided for under the 1995 Act is problematic,[52] highlighting that the criteria establishing whether applicants 'merit' legal aid include no provision that civil legal aid should be available to a person who needs it in order to access justice. This is despite the fact that the right to legal aid is based on that need.[53] In the past, the financial eligibility requirements set out under section 29 of the 1995 Act were criticised as too harsh.[54] However, in September 2006, these were reformed by means of ministerial regulation.

Finally, there are major problems in relation to how the scheme operates in practice. There have been numerous complaints about the inadequate money, staff and other resources allocated to the Legal Aid Board and about resultant delays experienced by those seeking civil legal aid. This has improved since *O'Donoghue* v. *Legal Aid Board*, however, with increased resources being made available to the Board and waiting lists being reduced.

Having highlighted the shortcomings of the statutory system in terms of providing for legal aid for social rights litigation, it is important to note the role that the Irish Human Rights Commission ('Commission') may play in this context. Where an applicant does not qualify for assistance under the Civil Legal Aid Act, the Criminal Justice (Legal Aid) Act 1962 or otherwise, the Commission may

choose to provide (or arrange the provision of) legal advice, legal representation or such other assistance as the Commission deems appropriate in the circumstances.[55] Furthermore, the Commission may institute proceedings for the purpose of obtaining relief of a declaratory or other nature in respect of any matter concerning the human rights[56] of any person or class of persons.[57]

All in all, however, there is extremely limited civil legal aid available to those seeking to forward socio-economic rights claims before the Irish Courts.

3. BACKGROUND TO THE CONTEMPORARY APPROACH OF THE IRISH COURTS

The landmark High Court decision of *O'Reilly* v. *Limerick Corporation*[58] can be regarded as the origin of the contemporary and dominant approach of the Irish Supreme Court to socio-economic rights. In this case, the plaintiffs were members of the Traveller community, living in conditions of extreme deprivation. They initiated legal proceedings against the local authority, seeking a mandatory injunction requiring the authority to provide serviced halting sites under the Housing Act 1966. They also asserted that the State should pay them damages for sufferings, which they had undergone in the past. This latter claim was based on an allegation that the conditions which the plaintiffs had been required to endure amounted to a breach of their constitutional rights. They asserted that the right to be provided with a certain minimum standard of basic material conditions to foster and protect someone's dignity and freedom as a human

---

proceedings taken by local authorities in terms of Section 62(3) of the 1966 Act, due to the fact that, according to the Court, eviction proceedings taken by public authorities are straightforward and relatively simple, involving the establishment of certain straightforward proofs. (*Dublin Corporation* v. *Hamilton*, unreported, High Court, 19 June 1998; *Byrne* v. *Scally and Dublin Corporation*, unreported, High Court, 12 October 2000).

[51] Free Legal Advice Centres, *Access to Justice* (n. 42 above), p. 35.
[52] See Section 24 of the 1995 Act.
[53] Free Legal Advice Centres, *Access to Justice* (n. 42 above), p. 52.
[54] Ibid.

[55] The Human Rights Commission Act 2000, Section 10.
[56] 'Human rights' for the purposes of Section 10 means (a) constitutional rights or (b) rights guaranteed:

to persons by any agreement, treaty or convention to which the State is a party and which has been given the force of law in the State, or by a provision of any such agreement, treaty or convention which has been given such force.

[57] Similarly, where the case has strategic importance or may set a precedent, the Equality Authority, at its discretion, may provide free legal assistance to those making complaints of discrimination under the Employment Equality Act 1998 and the Equal Status Act 2000, see Free Legal Advice Centres, *Access to Justice* (n. 42 above), p. 9.
[58] [1989] I.L.R.M. 181 ('*O'Reilly*' or the '*O'Reilly* case').

person was one of the unenumerated personal rights embraced under article 40.3.2°.[59]

The presiding judge, Justice Costello, claimed not to have jurisdiction to adjudicate on the claim. He argued that, in doing so, he would be adjudicating on an allegation that the organs of government responsible for the distribution of the nation's wealth had improperly exercised their powers. According to Justice Costello, the Aristotelian distinction between commutative and distributive justice marks out the dividing line between the judicial and legislative spheres of operation.[60] The courts are limited to dealing with issues of commutative justice, while the distribution of public resources (i.e. goods held in common for the benefit of the entire community):

> [C]an only be made by reference to the common good and by those charged with furthering the common good (the Government); [distribution of public resources] cannot be made by any individual who may claim a share in the common stock and no independent arbitrator, such as a court, can adjudicate on a claim by an individual that he has been deprived of what is his due.[61]

Justice Costello continued:

> What would be involved in the exercise of the suggested jurisdiction would be the imposition by the court of its view that there has been an unfair distribution of national resources. To arrive at such a conclusion it would have to make an assessment of the validity of the many competing claims on those resources, the correct priority to be given to them and the financial implications of the plaintiff's claim. As the present case demonstrates, it may also be required to decide whether a correct allocation of physical resources available for public purposes has been made. In exercising this function the court would not be administering justice as it does when determining an issue relating to commutative justice but it would be engaged in an entirely different exercise, namely an adjudication on the fairness or otherwise of the manner in which other organs of State had administered public resources. Apart from the fact that mem-

bers of the judiciary have no special qualifications to undertake such a function, the manner in which justice is administered in the courts, that is, on a case by case basis, makes them a wholly inappropriate institution for the fulfilment of the suggested role. I cannot construe the Constitution as conferring it on them.[62]

The analysis of distributive and commutative justice employed by Justice Costello in *O'Reilly* is arguably unsuitable for application to cases in which the State has failed to vindicate a citizen's socio-economic rights. It would seem that such cases should actually be classified as commutative/rectificatory justice as they involve a wrong in the form of a breach of a constitutional right of a citizen: any remedy granted is aimed towards rectifying the wrong committed by the State.[63] Admittedly, such a remedy will usually involve, as a knock-on effect, the distribution of public resources; it is, however, merely a secondary symptom of the case, as is the distribution of public resources stemming from an award of damages in a case where a servant of the state commits a tort[64] or violates a civil and political right.

Justice Costello ultimately dismissed the claim stating that in order to comply with the Constitution, such a petition should 'be advanced in Leinster House rather than in the Four Courts'.[65] In doing so, he appeared to fail to recognise the often very limited ability of vulnerable and marginalised groups, such as the one at issue in this case, to ensure that their socio-economic rights are vindicated or forwarded through the democratic system as a result of, amongst other things, a lack of organisational ability or political clout, as well as the existence of hostility or indifference towards them by the elected branches of government and/or a majority of the electorate. Some groups that are particularly vulnerable to violations of their socio-economic rights – for instance, children and other disenfranchised groups – are effectively precluded from 'advancing their petition in Leinster House'. This is due to both their express

---

[59] Ibid. at 192.
[60] Whyte and Hogan, *J.M. Kelly*, (n. 14 above), p. 116.
[61] *O'Reilly* (n. 58 above), p. 194.
[62] Ibid. p. 195.
[63] C. O'Mahony, 'Education, Remedies and the Separation of Powers', *Dublin University Law Journal*, Vol. 24 (2002), pp. 57–95, at 76.
[64] Ibid.
[65] *O'Reilly* (n. 58 above), p. 195. Leinster House is the seat of the Irish parliament.

exclusion from the democratic decision-making processes as well as, in many instances, their inability to rely on other (enfranchised) members of society to ensure the 'virtual' or indirect representation of their interests in such processes.[66]

4. SELECTED RIGHTS

4.1 Protection of Socio-Economic Rights by Means of 'Civil and Political' Rights

There are several civil and political rights-related provisions of the constitution that could be used as a basis for indirect protection of socio-economic rights.[67] For instance, an expansive interpretation of the right to life protected by article 40.3.2° of the Constitution could give rise to socio-economic rights being protected by means of that right. Indeed, in rejecting calls for the explicit inclusion in the Irish Constitution of guarantees of socio-economic rights, the Constitution Review Group concluded that, where anyone falls below a minimum level of subsistence, the Constitution appears to offer ultimate protection through judicial vindication of fundamental personal rights such as the right to life and the right to bodily integrity.[68]

In addition to being employable to indirectly protect socio-economic rights-related interests, the right to life under the Constitution may also serve as a basis for the identification of socio-economic rights. This was clearly demonstrated by the decision in *Ryan* v. *AG*. Here, a woman challenged the fluoridation of the public water supply on the grounds that this constituted, amongst other things, a violation of her and her children's personal rights under article 40.3. In that case, Justice Kenny in the High Court held that 'water today is a necessity of life and that the Plaintiff probably has a right of access to a supply of water'.[69] On appeal to the Supreme Court, it was accepted by the Attorney General that water is one of the essentials of life, and 'that man therefore has an inherent right to it'.[70] In its judgment, the Supreme Court did not take issue with this point. These dicta would appear to indicate that the right to life under article 40.3.2° encompasses the right to water. There have, however, been no further judicial statements on this issue. Another example of the right to life being interpreted expansively to encompass socio-economic rights is the decision of *G* v. *An Bord Uchtála*.[71] Here, Justice Walsh stated that the right to life 'necessarily implies the right to be born, the right to preserve and defend (and to have preserved and defended) that life, and the right to maintain that life at a proper human standard in matters of food, clothing and habitation'.[72]

The unenumerated personal right to bodily integrity that has been judicially identified as protected by article 40.3.1° could perform a similar function. The case of *The State (C)* v. *Frawley*[73] concerned a prisoner who was suffering from a sociopathic personality disorder. According to the opinion of a clinical psychologist (which was not disputed by the State), the prisoner required expensive treatment in a highly specialised psychiatric unit, which was not available in Ireland and would only be appropriate to the needs of the prisoner and a very small number of other people. The High Court held that the right to bodily integrity operated to prevent an act or omission on the part of the Executive, which, without justification or necessity, would expose the health of a person to risk or danger.[74] The Executive is thus constitutionally obliged to protect the health of persons held in custody as well as was reasonably possible in all the circumstances of a case.[75] The Court found, however, that the failure on the

---

[66] For more on the 'virtual representation' of minority groups in majoritarian decision-making processes, see J. Ely, *Democracy & Distrust: A Theory of Judicial Review* (Cambridge, MA: Harvard University Press, 1980).

[67] By 'indirect protection' I mean where other non-socio-economic rights are applied or interpreted by the courts so as to protect socio-economic rights-related interests.

[68] CRG (n. 1 above), p. 236. The prohibition on torture, inhuman or degrading treatment or punishment set out in Article 3 of the European Convention on Human Rights (and incorporated into Irish domestic law by the ECHR Act 2003) can arguably perform a similar function. Courts in the United Kingdom have accepted that intolerable living conditions for which the State is responsible can constitute a violation of Article 3: see King's chapter on the United Kingdom in this volume for an overview of the relevant cases.

[69] [1965] IR 294, at 315.

[70] Ibid. p. 342.

[71] [1980] IR 32 ('*G* v. *ABU*').

[72] Ibid. p. 69.

[73] [1976] IR 365 ('*Frawley*').

[74] Ibid. p. 372.

[75] Ibid. See also *The State (Richardson)* v. *The Governor of Mountjoy Prison* [1980] ILRM 82.

part of the Executive to provide the prisoner with expensive treatment in a special institution of a kind that was not present in Ireland did not constitute a failure to protect his health as well as was reasonably possible in all the circumstances of the case.[76]

On a related note, there are judicial statements suggesting that there is an unenumerated right to health protected by the Constitution, independent of the right to bodily integrity. In the case of *Heeney* v. *Dublin Corporation*,[77] Justice O'Flaherty of the Supreme Court stated that, it was 'beyond debate that that there is a hierarchy of constitutional rights and at the top of the list is the right to life, followed by the right to health and with that the right to the integrity of one's dwellinghouse'.[78] However, the parameters of this judicially identified right to health are somewhat unclear, to say the least.[79]

There has been at least one instance of a court holding that the unenumerated right to bodily integrity imposes a positive obligation on the state. The case of *O'Brien* v. *Wicklow UDC*[80] concerned a claim by travellers that the State, acting thorough the local authority, had a duty to provide serviced halting sites for them. Justice Costello found that the deplorable conditions under which the plaintiffs were living infringed their constitutional right to bodily integrity.[81] Having considered the defendant local authority's statutory powers to provide serviced halting sites under the Housing Act 1988 in light of the plaintiff's constitutional right to bodily integrity, he held that the local authority was under a legal duty to provide such sites and he granted a mandatory order directing that the defendants to provide at least three serviced halting sites.[82] It should be noted however that this was only an ex tempore judgment and hence has extremely limited precedential value. The decision is also probably at odds with the later Supreme Court findings in the cases *Sinnott v. Minister for Education*[83] and *TD v. Minister for Education.*[84] Certainly, thusfar, the Supreme Court (as opposed to lower courts) has not interpreted the right to bodily integrity so as to encompass social and economic rights within it.[85]

4.2 Labour Rights

There are a large number of Irish cases dealing with labour rights. Indeed, article 40.6.1°(iii) sets out the right of the citizens to form associations and unions. In this chapter, however, I will focus in particular on the right to work/earn a livelihood. In *Tierney* v. *The Amalgamated Society of Woodworkers,*[86] Justice Budd of the High Court agreed with the assertion that the right to work and earn one's livelihood, as an unenumerated right, is just as important a personal right of the citizen as a right to property and just as much entitled to vindication under article 40 of the Constitution. He went on to conclude, however, that the failure of a trade union to submit an individual's name for membership of the union or to hold an election, even though the individual was qualified for membership in accordance with the rules of the trade union, did not amount to any infringement of the Constitution.

Subsequently, as discussed in Section 2.1 above, the right to an adequate means of livelihood was recognised in the High Court case of *Murtagh Properties.*[87] In the later case of *Murphy v. Stewart,*[88]

---

[76] *Frawley* (n. 73 above), pp. 372–3.
[77] [1998] IESC 26.
[78] Ibid. para 16. In this case, the plaintiffs had sought an injunction commanding Dublin Corporation to take certain steps in relation to the breakdown in the elevator services in the Ballymun flats complex, in the City of Dublin. In granting the injunction, O'Flaherty J stated the corollary of the constitutional guarantee of inviolability of the dwelling of every citizen must be that a person should be entitled to the freedom to come and go from his dwelling provided he keeps to the law.
[79] See the discussion of *In re Article 26 and the Health (Amendment) (No.2) Bill 2004* [2005] IESC 7 for further discussion on the existence of a right to healthcare under the Constitution. Hereinafter '*In re Article 26 and the Health (Amendment) (No.2) Bill*'.
[80] Unreported, High Court 10 June 1994.
[81] Ibid. p. 4.

[82] In doing so, Costello J withdrew from the stance he had adopted in the *O'Reilly* case. He stated that, 'I don't think it is necessary to say whether I am now expressing a different view to the one which I expressed in the case of *O'Reilly and Ors* v. *Limerick Corporation*. . . . Even, however, if the view which I am now expressing represents a change of views on my part, then I accept my views have changed . . .' (ibid. pp. 3–4).
[83] N. 39 above.
[84] N. 40 above.
[85] There is, however, evidence that they might be prepared to do so in the future. See the discussion of *In re Article 26 and the Health (Amendment) (No. 2) Bill* for more on this.
[86] [1959] IR 254.
[87] See n. 15 above.
[88] [1973] IR 97.

the Supreme Court stated that, while citizens have a constitutional right to form associations and unions under article 40.6.1°(iii), there is no constitutional right to join the union of one's choice. Referring to *Murtagh Properties*, Justice Walsh accepted that among the unspecified personal rights guaranteed by the Constitution is the right to work. He stated that if the right to work was reserved exclusively to members of a trade union which held a monopoly in this field and the trade union was abusing the monopoly in such a way as to effectively prevent the exercise of a person's constitutional right to work, the question of compelling that union to accept the person concerned into membership (or, indeed, of breaking the monopoly) would fall to be considered for the purpose of vindicating the right to work.[89]

The courts have made clear that the freedom to exercise the constitutional right to earn a livelihood is not absolute and that it may be subject to legitimate legal restraints.[90] It is also primarily a negative right: in *Shanley* v. *Galway Corporation*,[91] the High Court stated that the Constitution 'does not impose a positive duty either on the State, or on any body such as a local authority to which the State may have delegated powers, to provide a livelihood for the plaintiff'.[92] In *Greally* v. *Minister for Education (No. 2)*,[93] Justice Geoghegan in the High Court stated that 'because a person has a right to a particular livelihood it does not mean that he has a right to receive employment from any particular employer'.[94] The Courts have held, however, that statutory restrictions on the right to earn a livelihood must be clear and that such restrictions must not be disproportionate.[95]

4.3 Social Security Rights

Rights to social welfare entitlements are granted by statute, rather than under the constitution, so these will not be discussed at length. The Supreme Court has held that the right to receive benefit or retain benefit wrongly paid derives from statute and does not partake of the nature of a constitutional property right.[96] It is worth noting, however, that despite the absence of any constitutional provision setting out a right to social security, judicial application of the principles of natural and constitutional justice has significantly improved the legal position of the welfare claimant who wishes to challenge a departmental decision affecting his or her rights under the welfare code.[97] Attempts to protect social security rights–related entitlements through reliance on the constitutional guarantee to equality before the law have been generally unsuccessful,[98] largely due to the courts' employment of a highly restrictive 'invidious discrimination test'.[99] There have, however, been instances in which plaintiffs have relied successfully on article 41 (in particular article 41.3.1° obliging the State to protect the institution of marriage from attack), which enshrines the constitutional protection of the family unit, in challenging discrimination against married couples under welfare legislation.[100]

---

[89] See also *Yeates* v. *Minister for Posts and Telegraphs* [1978] ILRM 22; *Parsons* v. *Kavanagh* [1990] ILRM 560; *Lovett* v. *Gogan*, [1995] 1 I.L.R.M. 12; *Murtagh Properties* v. *Cleary* [1972] IR 330.

[90] Irish Human Rights Commission, *Making Economic, Social and Cultural Rights Effective: An IHRC Discussion Document* (Dublin: IHRC, 2005), p. 112.

[91] [1995] 1 IR 396.

[92] Irish Human Rights Commission, 'Making ESC Rights Effective' (n. 90 above), p. 112.

[93] [1999] 1 IR 1.

[94] Ibid.

[95] Irish Human Rights Commission (n. 90 above), p. 112. See, e.g., *Cox* v. *Ireland* [1992] 2 IR 503. For a detailed analysis of the right to work/earn a livelihood, see J. Casey, *Constitutional Law in Ireland* (Dublin: Roundhall, 2000), pp. 404–410.

[96] *Minister for Social, Community and Family Affairs* v. *Scanlon* [2001] IESC 1, at 17.

[97] Whyte, 'Social Inclusion' (n. 5 above), p. 124.

[98] Article 40.1 of the Constitution. See, e.g., *MhicMhathúna* v. *Attorney General* [1995] 1 IR 484; *Dennehy* v. *Minister for Social Welfare*, unreported, High Court, 26 July 1984; *Lowth* v. *Minister for Social Welfare* [1999] 1 ILRM 5.

[99] See the Supreme Court decision in *O'Brien* v. *Keogh* [1972] IR 144, at 156, in which the Court stated that '(a)rticle 40 does not require identical treatment of all persons without recognition of differences in relevant circumstances. [footnote omitted] It only forbids invidious discrimination'. See also *per* Kenny J in *Murphy* v. *Attorney General* [1982] IR 241, at 283 where he stated the court will set a legislative inequality aside as being repugnant to the Constitution if any state of facts exists which may reasonably justify it (see *Murphy* v. *The Attorney General* [1982] IR 241, at 283 and 284). The Courts have since distanced themselves from the 'invidious discrimination test', employing a 'rationality test' in a number of equality cases. The author is, however, unaware of any cases involving social security rights to which this test has been applied.

[100] *Hyland* v. *Minister for Social Welfare* [1989] IR 624; *J.H.* v. *Eastern Health Board* [1988] IR 747. Unsuccessful attempts to rely on Article 41 include *MhicMhathúna* (n. 98 above).

4.4   The Right to Education

The right to education is set out in article 42.[101] In particular, article 42.4 provides that '[t]he State shall provide for free primary education and shall endeavour to supplement and give reasonable aid to private and corporate educational initiative, and, when the public good requires it, provide other educational facilities or institutions with due regard, however, for the rights of parents, especially in the matter of religious and moral formation'. Quinn has suggested that the inclusion of the right to education in the Irish Constitution had less to do with the substantive right to education of the child *per se* and more to do with preserving the arrangement between the funders of education (the State) and the providers of education (religious bodies and parents) prevailing at the time at which the Constitution was being drafted.[102] In practice, however, the courts have begun separating out the substantive right from the tangled historical arrangements and have enforced it against the State so as to require education facilities and opportunities of a certain quantity as well as quality.[103]

It has been established that the article imposes both a duty to provide free primary education and a right to receive such education.[104] It does not necessarily place a duty on the State to provide free primary education itself, but rather enjoins it to provide *for* such education by ensuring that machinery exists under which, and in accordance with which, such education is provided (e.g. by funding private institutions which provide primary education).[105] While there is an explicit obligation on the State to provide for primary education, court decisions have been crucial in delineating the precise parameters of this duty.

In *O'Donoghue* v. *Minister for Health*,[106] the mother of a severely mentally disabled[107] eleven-year-old boy instituted legal proceedings against the Ministers for Heath and Education. She sought an order from the High Court directing the defendants to provide for free primary education for her son and also a declaration that, in failing to provide for such education, the State had deprived him of his constitutional rights under articles 40 and 42. Up until the initiation of legal proceedings, State support for the child's education had been limited and wholly inadequate and the major part of such education as he had received was the result of private funding.

The State argued, amongst other things, that (a) the applicant, by reason of being profoundly mentally and physically disabled, was ineducable, and all that could be done for him to make his life more tolerable was to attempt to train him in the basics of bodily function and movement; and (b) the education that the State was obliged to provide pursuant to article 42.4 was education of a conventional, scholastic nature, and that such training as could be provided to the plaintiff could not be regarded as 'primary education' within the meaning of that expression as used in article 42.4.

In the High Court, Justice O'Hanlon referred to the definition of education set out by the Supreme Court in the earlier case of *Ryan* v. *A.G.*, in which education was defined as 'the teaching and training of a child to make the best possible use of his inherent and potential capacities, physical, mental and moral'.[108] In light of this definition, taking into account the advances made internationally in the area of education for children who suffer from a severe or profound mental handicap, as well as the evidence (which was to the effect that the applicant had made good progress and could make further progress), he held that the applicant was not ineducable.

With regard to the second argument, the judge examined the dictionary definitions of the terms

---

[101] There are other Constitutional articles which might have a bearing on the provision of primary education in the absence of a specific articulation of that duty, (e.g. Article 40.3.1° (which provides protection for personal rights unenumerated in the Constitution), the guarantee of equality before the law contained in article 40.1 and, arguably, article 42.1. In this chapter, however, I shall focus exclusively on those provisions that expressly guarantee that right.

[102] Quinn, 'Rethinking the Nature of ESC Rights' (n. 3 above), p. 49.

[103] Ibid.

[104] See *Crowley* v. *Ireland* (n. 25 above), at 122.

[105] Ibid. p. 126.

[106] See n. 31 above.

[107] There are four categories of developmental disability (or 'handicap' which was the term employed by the Court in this case): 'mild', 'moderate', 'severe' and 'profound'.

[108] See n. 6 above, p. 350.

used in both the Irish and English versions of article 42.4.[109] He then stated that:

> There is a constitutional obligation on the State by the provision of Article 42.4 of the Constitution to provide for free basic elementary education of all children and that this involves giving each child such advice, instruction and teaching as will enable him/her to make the best possible use of his/her inherent and potential capacities, physical, mental and moral, however limited these capacities might be.[110]

He went on to say that as soon as it had been established in the 1970s that children with a severe mental handicap were educable, there arose a constitutional obligation on the part of the State to provide for free primary education for such children. He held further that education for profoundly handicapped children could correctly be described as 'primary education' within the meaning of the phrase used in article 42.4.[111]

Having considered a large volume of documentary evidence, as well as oral evidence, on the approaches adopted to the education of such children in numerous other jurisdictions, the judge stated that the evidence in the case gave rise to a strong conviction that, in order for primary education to meet the special needs of such people, a new approach from that currently available would be required in respect of the pupil-teacher ratio, the age of commencement, and continuity and duration of education. While Justice O'Hanlon did not actually prescribe a pupil-teacher ratio, he made it clear that the ratio of one-to-twelve would not discharge the State's obligations under article 42.4 to profoundly handicapped children. In relation to age of commencement, he pointed out that early intervention and assessment was of vital importance if conditions of mental and physical handicap were not to become intractable. Furthermore, with regard to duration, he stated that the process of education should ideally continue for as long as the ability for further development was discernible.[112]

The judge made an order declaring that the respondent, in failing to provide for free primary education for the child and in discriminating against him as compared with other children, deprived him of constitutional rights arising under article 42 of the Constitution. He also granted damages.[113]

This case made it clear that the State's obligation under article 42.4 covers *all* children in the State and that special measures have to be put in place for those children who, because of their disability, are unable to benefit from conventional education. However, the issue of the right to primary education of adults remained unresolved.

The right to primary education of adults was the subject of the case of *Sinnott* v. *Minister for Education*.[114] Here, the plaintiff was a severely autistic twenty-three-year-old man. Despite a campaign conducted over two decades by his mother, the State had failed to provide him with any consistent suitable training or education. In these proceedings, the applicant and his mother sought declarations as to their constitutional rights, a mandatory injunction directing the Minister to discharge the State's obligations to the plaintiff and damages for negligence and breach of both constitutional and statutory rights. The State argued, amongst other things, that the duty to provide for primary education for the plaintiff ceased when he reached eighteen years of age.

In the High Court, Justice Barr argued that there is nothing in article 42.4 that supports the contention that there is an age limitation on a citizen's right to on-going primary education provided for by the State. He pointed out that in the plaintiff's case there was a fundamental need for continuous education and training which was not age-related.

---

[109] The Constitution was drafted in two languages, Irish and English, by two different authors almost simultaneously, with each co-author borrowing from the other's work. Where the texts clash, the national language, Irish, takes precedence (Article 25(4) of the Constitution).

[110] *O'Donoghue* (n. 31 above), p. 65. O'Hanlon J's comments were subsequently expressly accepted by McGuinness J in the High in *Comerford* v. *Minister for Education* [1997] 2 ILRM 134, 144. She also accepted the applicant's lawyer's assertion that 'the right to free primary education extends to every child, although the education provided must vary in accordance with the child's abilities and needs'. (ibid. p. 143).

[111] *O'Donoghue* (n. 31 above), p. 67.

[112] Ibid. p. 70.

[113] The case was appealed by the State. On 6 February 1997, the Supreme Court made the order that the plaintiff was entitled to free primary education in accordance with article 42.4 and the High Court's order was otherwise confirmed.

[114] See n. 39 above.

He argued that, in the absence of a specific provision in the constitutional article, it would be wrong to imply any age limitation on the constitutional obligation of the State to provide for the primary education of those who suffer severe or profound mental handicap.[115] Thus, the ultimate criterion in interpreting the State's constitutional obligation was 'need' and not 'age'.[116]

The case was appealed by the State to the Supreme Court, which was required to determine two key points. First, the extent of the right to free primary education under article 42.4, and, second, the right of the High Court, having regard to the doctrine of the separation of powers, to grant a mandatory injunction formulating and directing the application of future policy in relation to educational needs. The Court's findings in relation to the latter point will be dealt with later in this chapter in Section 7.

The Court found for the State on both issues. The majority took the view that the State's duty to provide, for free, primary education applies to children only, not adults, and that the duty ceased to apply even in the case of a person with severe mental handicap once the age of eighteen was reached. The judges argued that article 42 located education in the context of the family and that the word 'child' had a clear age-related meaning in this context. While any age would be arbitrary to some extent, the age of eighteen was reasonable as the age at which society no longer treated a young person as a child. One judge went so far as to say the obligation ended when a child reached twelve – that is, the age at which an ordinary child could be taken to have finished primary school![117] Only one judge, Chief Justice Keane, agreed with Justice O'Hanlon in the High Court that the State's obligation was open-ended.

The definition of 'primary education' set out by Justice Barr in the High Court was not challenged by the State before the Supreme Court. However, all the judges, with the exception of Justice Murphy (who argued that the training required by Mr. Sinnott could not be described as education under an originalist interpretation of article 42.4), seemed satisfied that Justice Barr's definition was correct.

Thus, while the Court accepted the broad definition of the substantive content of the right to primary education set out in *O'Donoghue*, it proceeded to define the category of people entitled to assert this right in a very narrow 'age-' rather than 'need'-centred way.

The judicial reluctance to become involved in so-called distributive justice issues, as demonstrated in *O'Reilly*, had previously been reiterated in several cases and confirmed by the Supreme Court.[118] The issue arose again in *Sinnott*. Here, Justice Hardiman dealt expressly with the question of the power of the court to ensure that a person's constitutional rights (including those of a socio-economic nature) were not circumvented or denied. Having quoted Justice Costello's judgment in *O'Reilly* approvingly and at length,[119] he stated that, apart from in an extreme case where the government would ignore a constitutional imperative and defy a court declaration on a topic, the courts should refrain from exercising such a power. They should do so for several reasons. Firstly, were the courts to exercise such a power, this would offend the constitutional separation of powers.[120] Secondly, it would lead the courts into the taking of decisions in areas in which they have no special qualification or experience. Thirdly, it would permit the courts to take such decisions even though they are not, and cannot be, democratically responsible for them as the legislature and executive are. Finally, the evidence-based adversarial procedures of the court, which are excellently adapted for the administration of commutative justice, are too technical, too expensive, too focused on the individual issue to be an appropriate method for deciding on issues of policy. Justice Hardiman continued:

> Central to this view [of the separation of powers] is a recognition that there is a proper sphere for both elected representatives of the people and the executive elected or endorsed by them in the taking of social and economic and legislative decisions, as well as another sphere where the judiciary is solely competent[121] ... [I]f judges were to become involved in such an enterprise, designing the details of

---

[115] (2000) IEHC 148, para. 85.
[116] Ibid. para. 86.
[117] Per Murphy J in *Sinnott* (n. 39 above), para. 236.

[118] E.g. see *MhicMhathúna v. Attorney General* [1995] 1 IR 484 and *Frawley* (n. 73 above).
[119] *Sinnott* (n. 39 above), paras. 335–346.
[120] Ibid. para. 374.
[121] Ibid. para. 375.

policy in individual cases or in general, and ranking some areas of policy in priority to others, they would step beyond their appointed role.[122]

The rigid and conservative view of the separation of powers doctrine expressed by Justice Hardiman in this case foreshadowed the Supreme Court's holding in the *TD* case, which is discussed in Section 4.5.

A later case involving the right to education once again raised the issue of the obligation imposed by the State by article 42.4. In *O'Carolan v. Minister for Education*,[123] the parents of an autistic boy with challenging behaviour sought, inter alia, a mandatory order requiring the State to provide appropriate education for their son. The State had made a number of placement offers, none of which the applicants thought adequate in terms of being best suited to provide for their son's educational needs. The applicants wanted the State to fund placement at a Centre for Developmental Disabilities abroad. The State's most recent Dublin-based placement offer, which was at issue in the case, was, in the view of the applicants and expert witnesses, inappropriate, inadequate, and not in accordance with international best practice. With regard to the conflict of evidence, Justice MacMenamin in the High Court ultimately sided with the State's experts, finding the Irish placement to be suitable. However, the case is disturbing as the Judge's interpretation of the right to education would appear to involve a weakening of the obligation imposed on the State by article 42.4. Justice MacMenamin stated that the kernel of the case was whether the State had breached its duty, as set out under article 42 and identified by Justice O'Hanlon in the case of *O'Donoghue*. He found that the facility put forward by the State was 'objectively adequate and in compliance with the constitutional duties of the respondents'. In doing so, he stated that the test was not whether the State's offer was better than that desired by the plaintiffs or whether it was optimal. Rather, the question was whether it was 'appropriate'. O'Mahony observes that Justice MacMenamin's decision that the test was not whether an alternative placement was better or the best so long as the placement in question was appropriate to

the needs of a particular child would appear to run directly contrary to O'Hanlon's statement in *O'Donoghue* that the 'education' contemplated in article 42.4 should enable a child 'to make the best possible use of his or her inherent and potential capacities'.[124] It also contradicts Chief Justice O'Dalaigh's comments in *Ryan v. AG*.

The decision is arguably of limited jurisprudential value as, firstly, it is a High Court, rather than a Supreme Court decision, and secondly, Justice MacMenamin also failed to take into account any authorities other than *O'Donoghue* on the scope of the right to education under article 42.4.[125] Worryingly, however, a narrow conception of 'appropriateness' was also used in a subsequent High Court decision, *O'C. v. Minister for Education and Science & Ors*.[126] Here, Justice Peart held that the Minister's failure to provide an autistic child with a particular form of autism-specific education which had been demonstrated to be effective for that child did not mean that the Minister had failed to 'provide for an *appropriate* education as required by the Constitution' [emphasis added]. Notably the judge in that case did not cite the *O'Carolan* case or, indeed, any major right to education decision.

It remains to be seen what approach will be adopted by the Supreme Court. Should it choose to embrace the approach of Justice MacMenamin in *O'Carolan* in future cases, this would have a significant impact on the extent of the State's obligation under article 42.4. Indeed, it is arguable that the way in which the scope of the education right has been progressively curtailed through judicial interpretation in an era of increased resources is

---

[124] C. O'Mahony, 'The Right to Education and "Constitutionally Appropriate" Provision', *Dublin University Law Journal*, Vol. 28 (2006), p. 422.
[125] Ibid.
[126] [2007] IEHC 170. This case was a challenge brought on behalf of a child with autism. His parents claimed, amongst other things, that in failing to provide free education and health care services for the child appropriate to his needs, and in discriminating against the child with respect to provision of appropriate educational and health care facilities vis-à-vis other children, the State had deprived the child of his constitutional rights pursuant to articles 40, 41 and 42 of the constitution. The Court concluded that the model of education provided for the child by the State was appropriate. In doing so, the Court emphasised that, when it came to deciding whether the education model proposed by the State was appropriate, it was not necessary for it to evaluate the alternative model recommended by the parents, which had proved beneficial to the child.

---

[122] Ibid., para. 377.
[123] (2005) IEHC 296.

out of step with Ireland's obligation under the ICE-SCR to progressively realise economic and social rights.[127]

4.5 Children's Rights

The Constitution contains one provision which expressly furnishes children with a socio-economic right operable against persons other than the State. Article 42.1 provides that parents are obliged 'to provide, according to their means, for the religious and moral, intellectual physical and social education of their children'. The constitutional duty imposed on parents by that article imposes a corresponding right on children to seek the provision for such education from their parents where their parents fail to provide such.[128] Applying article 42.5 to article 42.1, it would appear that where parents fail in their duty to provide for the religious and moral, intellectual, physical and social education of their children, the State 'by appropriate means shall endeavour to supply the place of the parents'. It would thus seem that article 42.1 may also serve as the basis for socio-economic rights claims of children against the State. The extent and nature of such a claim as might be made presumably depends on the interpretation adopted of what is required of the State where they 'endeavour to supply the place of parents'.[129]

By far the most significant body of jurisprudence on children's socio-economic rights centres on children's unenumerated constitutional rights. The unenumerated rights of the child were first dealt with at length in *G* v. *An Bord Uchtála*.[130] Having upheld the right of a parent to the custody and control of the upbringing of a daughter, Chief Justice O'Higgins in the Supreme Court observed that:

> The child also has natural rights...Having been born, the child has the right to be fed and to live, to be reared and educated, to have the opportunity of working and of realising his/her full personality and dignity as a human being. These rights of the child (and others which I have not enumerated) must equally be protected and vindicated by the State. In exceptional cases the State, under the provisions of Article 42.5 of the Constitution, is given the duty, as guardian of the common good, to provide for a child born into a family where the parents fail in their duty towards that child for physical or moral reasons.[131]

This ruling was built on in the High Court decision of *FN* v. *Minister for Education*.[132] The '*FN* case' involved a thirteen-year-old in state care who suffered from hyperkinetic conduct disorder and required a period of time in a secure unit that could contain him safely while confronting his behaviour. Having referred to the unenumerated rights of the child mentioned by the High Court and the Supreme Court in *G* v. *ABU*, and the further elaboration of children's constitutional rights by the Supreme Court in *The Adoption (No. 2) Bill, 1987*[133] and *M.F.* v. *Superintendent Ballymun*

---

[127] In discussion with Claire McHugh (15 September 2006).

[128] For more on this, see the statements of the High Court in *A.G.* v. *Dowse & Anor* [2006] IEHC 64, where MacMenamin J stated that '[a]mongst the natural and imprescriptible rights of [the child] to which this Court must have due regard is the right to have his needs, including his religious, moral, intellectual, physical and social education provided for by the applicants [his adoptive parents] in accordance with their means'.

[129] It should be noted that the language of article 41.3.1° of the Constitution ('The State pledges itself to guard with special care the institution of marriage, on which the Family is founded...') clearly restricts constitutional recognition to families based on marriage. Thus, the rights and duties set out in article 41 and 42 of the Constitution apply to marital families and their members only. It has been stated by the courts on several occasions that the rights of children who are members of non-marital families are personal rights guaranteed by article 40.3, rather than by articles 41 and 42. For example, with regard to article 42.5, in *G* v. *An Bord Uchtála* [1980] IR 32, Justice Walsh concluded that the State owed a similar duty to protect children born outside the marital family as that prescribed by article 42.5. In his view, this obligation stemmed from article 40.3 of the Constitution. He continued to say that there was no difference between the

obligations owed by an unmarried parent to their child under article 40.3 and those owed by a married parent under article 42.5. The constitutional amendment legislation presented in February 2007 (discussed in section 4.5) sought to ensure an equitable standard of protection for all children regardless of the marital status of their parents. The Bill proposed replacing the existing article 42.5 with, amongst other things, a statement that '(i)n exceptional cases, where the parents of *any* child for physical or moral reasons fail in their duty towards such child, the State as guardian of the common good, by appropriate means shall endeavour to supply the place of the parents, but always with due regard for the natural and imprescriptible rights of the child' [emphasis added].

[130] See n. 129 above.

[131] Ibid. pp. 55–56.

[132] [1995] 1 IR 409. Hereinafter '*FN*' or the '*FN* case'

[133] [1989] I.R. 656.

Garda Station,[134] Justice Geoghegan stated that: 'I would take the view that where there is a child with very special needs which cannot be provided by the parents or guardian, there is a constitutional obligation on the State under article 42, s. 5 of the Constitution to cater for those needs in order to vindicate the constitutional rights of the child'.[135] Such secure accommodation, services and arrangements as were necessary to meet the requirements of FN were held to be not so impractical or so prohibitively expensive as to come within any notional limitation on the State's constitutional obligations.[136] Justice Geoghegan stated that he was of the view that the State was under a constitutional obligation towards the applicant to establish as soon as reasonably practicable suitable arrangements of containment with treatment for the applicant. The State did not appeal *FN* and, in the subsequent case of *DD* v. *Eastern Health Board*[137] involving a disturbed eleven-year-old boy, the Eastern Health Board did not dispute that it owed a constitutional duty to the child to meet his special needs and accepted that it was in breach of this constitutional duty.

The most important recent case focusing on children's socio-economic rights is that of *TD v. Minister for Education*.[138] The applicants in *TD* were a sample of a large group of non-offending children in the care of regional Health Boards (local authorities), whose special needs were not being met by the State. Due to a lack of treatment and secure accommodation, the court was forced to order the placement of such children in detention centres, police stations, hotels, adult prisons and even adult psychiatric hospitals.[139] In *TD*, the Supreme Court heard an appeal against a decision of Justice Kelly in the High Court granting a mandatory injunction directing the Minister to take all steps necessary to facilitate the building and opening of secure and high support units in set locations with a prescribed number of beds

and in accordance with a fixed time-scale.[140] The High Court made this decision primarily on the basis of the right/obligation identified in the *FN* case. The State's grounds of appeal chiefly centred on, amongst other things, the claim that, in making of the orders under appeal, the High Court had entered into questions of policy and usurped the executive power in violation of the principle of separation of powers.[141]

All five Supreme Court Justices in the *TD* case referred to Justice Costello statements in the *O'Reilly* case approvingly. Even Denham J, who ultimately disagreed strongly with the finding of the majority, agreed with Justice Costello's ruling in *O'Reilly* that the distribution of the nation's wealth is a matter for the executive and the legislature.[142] The heavy reliance of the majority of the Court in *TD* and *Sinnott* on the reasoning and authority of the *O'Reilly* case is open to question. This is due to the failure of the majority of the Supreme Court to recognise that while the plaintiffs in *O'Reilly* relied on a previously unidentified unenumerated constitutional right, the applicants in *TD* and *Sinnott* relied on rights expressly identified in the text of the Constitution and in previous case law. Where such rights have previously been recognised as being protected by the constitution, adjudication involving them involves no more of a transfer of power to the judiciary at the expense of other branches of government than adjudication involving 'traditional' civil and political rights with implications for public expenditure and policy. Furthermore, in *O'Reilly*, Justice Costello did not determine that there had been a breach of a constitutional right. Rather he analysed the concept of distributive justice. However, in *TD* the applicants were not making a case that the nation's wealth be justly distributed, rather their cases were

---

[134] [1991] 1 IR 189.

[135] *FN* (n. 132 above), p. 416.

[136] Per Denham J, *TD* (n. 40 above), para. 103.

[137] Unreported, High Court, Costello J, 3 May 1995.

[138] See n. 40 above.

[139] R. Dooley & M. Corbett, 'Child Care, Juvenile Justice and the Children Act 2001', *Irish Youthwork Scene: A Journal for Youth Workers*, No. 36 (2002). available at <http://www.childrensrights.ie/pubs/ChildCareJuvenileJustice.doc> (last accessed 1 May 2008)

[140] *TD* (n. 40 above), paras. 14–31. In an earlier case, *DB* v. *Minister for Justice & Ors.* [1998] IEHC 123, Kelly J had already made a mandatory order, directing the respondents to, amongst other things, take all steps necessary to complete two developments in County Dublin within the time scale specified by departmental officials in evidence before the Court, and to ensure that there was adequate secure high support accommodation available for the applicant and for others with similar needs. This decision was not, however, appealed by the State.

[141] For more details on the State's submissions, see *TD* (n. 40 above), paras. 40–49, *per* Keane J.

[142] *TD* (n. 40 above), para. 137.

brought to protect recognised and acknowledged constitutional rights.[143]

In his judgment in *TD*, Justice Hardiman reiterated his concerns about judicial involvement in areas 'more obviously within the ambit of the legislative or executive government',[144] quoting approvingly a commentator who argued that incorporating justiciable socio-economic rights into the Constitution by referendum would mean a significant transfer of power from the elected branches of government to an unelected judiciary.[145] The other judges of the Court articulated similar views. Justice Murphy expressly doubted the existence of any socio-economic constitutional right apart from the right to education set out in article 42, stating that '[w]ith the exception of the provisions dealing with education, the personal rights identified in the Constitution all lie in the civil and political rather than the economic sphere'.[146] Another member of the court expressed 'the gravest doubts as to whether the courts at any stage should assume the function of declaring what are today frequently described as 'socio-economic rights' to be unenumerated rights guaranteed by Article 40'.[147] Thus, the correctness of the rights identified in *FN* were questioned directly or indirectly,[148] while two justices also appeared to question the binding nature of the statement of the Chief Justice in *G* v. *ABU*, set out above.[149]

The questioning of the rights enunciated in *FN* by various members of the Supreme Court in *TD* was done unilaterally, as the State did not dispute the conclusions in the earlier case. Therefore, these and other comments in relation to socio-economic rights were *obiter*. One of the results of this spontaneous questioning of *FN* by the Supreme Court was that lawyers on both sides were not given the opportunity to comment on, attack or defend the ruling. It was suggested by one Irish source that part of the reason for the Supreme Court's decision to question *FN* was that the Court realised that if it accepted that *FN* was correctly

decided and, therefore, that the rights identified by Justice Geoghegan existed, it would not make sense to say that there was no way of enforcing those rights.

In the earlier decision of *North Western Health Board* v. *W. (H.)*,[150] three Supreme Court judges mentioned *FN* in the context of discussing children's unenumerated personal rights without expressly declaring a reservation about the rights declared in that case.[151] Thus, the rights recognised by the High Court in *FN* must be regarded as part of Irish constitutional law as it stands at the moment. Although the Court's comments in *TD* on the correctness of the judgment in *FN* and the appropriateness of interpreting the Constitution to include socio-economic rights were also negative, it must be recalled that they were obiter and thus do not form part of a binding precedent.

In February 2007, the Irish Government published the Twenty-eighth Amendment to the Constitution Bill 2007. The draft legislation provided for the replacement of article 42.5 of the Constitution with a provision explicitly recognising constitutional rights of the child, other than those related to primary education. Despite the recommendation of a large number of children's rights advocates that any proposed amendment should include a statement of the child's socio-economic rights, the wording put forward by the Government did not make any express reference to such rights. However, the statement set out in the proposed provision article 42A.1 that 'The State acknowledges and affirms the natural and imprescriptible rights of all children' left open the possibility for further judicial 'discovery' or confirmation of unenumerated socio-economic rights of the child. Due to the dissolution of government prior to a general election in May 2007, the Bill fell. In December 2007, the Joint Committee on the Constitutional Amendment on Children was established. This Committee has been tasked to examine the 2007 Bill and to make any recommendations to the wording of the proposed constitutional amendment provided for in the bill that seem appropriate to it. It remains to be seen what wording (if any) will ultimately be put to the electorate and it is unclear whether or not the Committee will

---

143 *Per* Denham J, *TD*, ibid. para. 137.
144 *TD*, ibid. para. 241.
145 Ibid. para. 244.
146 Ibid. para. 167.
147 Ibid. per Keane CJ, para. 66.
148 Ibid. *per* Murphy J (paras. 172–6), Hardiman J (para. 260) and Keane CJ (para. 66).
149 Ibid. *per* Murphy J (paras 173–176) and Keane CJ (para. 63–7).

150 [2001] IESC 70 (8th November, 2001).
151 Ibid. *per* Murphy J (para. 202), Keane CJ (para. 80) and Denham J (para. 160).

recommend the explicit inclusion of additional socio-economic rights of the child in the Constitution. Furthermore, it is not guaranteed that such a proposed amendment would be carried if put to the electorate by referendum.

5. THE DEATH KNELL FOR UNENUMERATED SOCIO-ECONOMIC RIGHTS?

The statements made by various members of the Supreme Court in *TD* suggest that it is unlikely that the Court, as currently constituted, will be prepared to identify further unenumerated constitutional socio-economic rights under article 40.3.1°.[152] However, the Supreme Court's approach in the case *In re Article 26 of the Constitution and the Health (Amendment)(No. 2) Bill 2004*[153] would appear to signal a slight softening in its stance. In this case, Counsel submitted that the Constitution, and specifically the right to life and the right to bodily integrity of such persons as derived from article 40.3.1° and 2°, imposes an obligation upon the State to provide at least a basic level of in-patient facilities to persons in need of care and maintenance who cannot provide for it themselves. Interestingly, rather than rejecting the existence of such a right out of hand (as might have been expected from its comments in *TD*), the Court stated that, '[i]n a discrete case in particular circumstances an issue may well arise as to the extent to which the normal discretion of the Oireachtas in the distribution or spending of public monies could be constrained by a constitutional obligation to provide shelter and maintenance for those with exceptional needs'.[154]

The Court did not consider it necessary to examine such an issue in the circumstances that arose from an examination of the Bill referred to it. Instead, the Court focused on whether, assuming there is such a constitutional right to maintenance, the

charges for which the Bill provided could be considered an impermissible restriction of any such right. The Court did not consider, however, that it could be an inherent characteristic of any right to such services that they be provided free, regardless of the means of those receiving them.

Counsel assigned by the Court argued alternatively that the charges actually provided for in the Bill would cause undue hardship to persons of limited means who have, for a range of reasons, a special need for maintenance by a Health Board in receiving in-patient services. The Court held that the real question was whether the charges were such that they would so restrict access to the services in question by persons of limited means as to constitute an infringement or denial of the constitutional rights asserted. It concluded that, on the basis of the structure of the proposed statutory scheme, they were not. One commentator has observed that the fact that the Court upheld the proposed charge for in-patient services only after satisfying itself that the statutory regime would not unduly deny access to these services would suggest, by implication, that legislation that did unduly deny access to such services might be regarded as unconstitutional.[155]

This decision is a positive (albeit limited) departure from the strident, 'anti-unenumerated socio-economic rights' views expressed by the Supreme Court in *TD*. However, as Doyle and Whyte point out, before we conclude that the Supreme Court is in the throes of undergoing a 'Pauline conversion', particularly on the matter of implied constitutional rights and socio-economic rights, it is important to put the Court's decision in context.[156] Doyle and Whyte observe that the Bill in question was designed 'to shore up a policy that was known to be legally invalid at least since 2001 and that implementation of that policy had the whiff of bad faith about it'.[157] In their view it is more likely that

---

[152] I note, however, that since *TD*, the personnel of the Supreme Court have changed significantly with two members of the majority in *TD* having retired. In addition, Geoghegan J, who decided *FN*, was appointed to the Supreme Court in 1999 (although he was not on the panel that heard the *TD* case). Consequently, despite the existence of that precedent, future efforts to litigate children's socio-economic rights or seek mandatory orders may not meet with as cold a reception as they did in the *TD* case.

[153] See n. 79 above.

[154] Ibid., *per* Murray J, para. 34.

[155] G. Whyte, 'Socio-Economic Rights in Ireland: Judicial and Non-Judicial Enforcement', paper presented at the Conference on *Economic, Social and Cultural Rights: Models of Enforcement* organised by the Irish Human Rights Commission, Dublin, Ireland, 9–10 December 2005.

[156] O. Doyle & G. Whyte, 'The Separation of Powers and Constitutional Egalitarianism after the *Health (Amendment) No. 2 Bill Reference*', in E. O'Dell (ed.), *Older People in Modern Ireland: Essays in Law and Policy* (Dublin: First-law, 2006), pp. 393–426, at 425.

[157] O'Dell, ibid., pp. 425–426. In 2001, legislation was passed that made it clear that people aged seventy and upwards

the decision simply indicates that there are limits to what even judicial conservatives will tolerate from the other branches of government, and that action taken in bad faith affecting constitutional rights will never pass muster.[158]

6. CRITIQUE OF SUPREME COURT'S APPROACH TO POSITIVE OBLIGATIONS

The restrictive approach adopted by the Irish Supreme Court to socio-economic rights issues is open to question on many grounds, including the fact that the distinction between distributive and commutative justice is hardly watertight.[159] It is also debatable whether the Constitution does erect an impenetrable barrier between the courts and issues of distributive justice, in light of provisions such as article 42.4, which would appear to give parents and children a justiciable right to insist that the State should finance primary education.[160] Furthermore, there is no reason in principle why distributive and commutative justice must be segregated in accordance with the constitutional function of the person making the decision, bearing in mind that the distinction between the two kinds of justice 'is no more than an analytical convenience, an aid to orderly consideration of problems'.[161] However, even if one accepts the conventional view that the elected branches of government are better equipped to design schemes of distributive justice, while courts are better at dealing with commutative justice, that does not necessarily justify the Court adopting such a restrictive approach to socio-economic rights issues. As mentioned previously during the discussion of the *O'Reilly* case above, it is arguable that in cases where the State has failed to vindicate a citizen's constitutional socio-economic right, the justice at issue is commutative rather than

distributive in nature. Therefore, in such cases, socio-economic rights issues will fall to be dealt with by the courts. In addition, the majority of the Supreme Court in *TD* appeared oblivious to the reality that judicial decisions in relation to civil and political rights can also have budgetary and policy implications.

Hogan and Whyte have stated that, in the absence of a subsequent decision reversing or qualifying the Court's approach in *TD*, it can be presumed that the Irish Supreme Court does not consider the resolution of socio-economic issues that have implications for public spending or policy to fall within the judicial sphere of operations.[162] However, recent developments have made it clear that this is not fully correct. In the case of *In re Article 26 of the Matter of Article 26 of the Constitution and the Health (Amendment) (No. 2) Bill 2004*,[163] the Supreme Court struck down an attempt by the government to retrospectively legalise illegal nursing home charges to medical card holders, finding that the attempt to retrospectively legalise the charges involved the abrogation of a property right protected by the Irish Constitution.[164] In doing so, the Court expressly stated that the property of persons of modest means must be deserving of particular protection, since any abridgement of the rights of such persons will normally be proportionately more severe in its effects.[165] According to government sources, repayments to former patients and their families who were illegally charged may cost the State between €500 million and €1.2 billion. This case demonstrates that the Court does not hesitate to deal with socio-economic issues that have implications for public spending or policy in situations where the constitutional rights at issue are not perceived as being 'socio-economic' in nature.

Finally, the Court's refusal to become involved in issues of policy fails to recognise the fact that sometimes a question put before a judge can be

---

were eligible for the relevant in-patient services free of charge. From then on, there was no possible room for doubt that Health Boards were not entitled to impose any charges for in-patient services on persons aged seventy or above. However, the practice continued.

[158] Ibid. p. 426. For more on judicial refusals to countenance 'bad faith' on the part of government in the context of remedies, see the statements of Murray J, below at p. 23.

[159] See Whyte, 'Social Inclusion' (n. 5 above), p. 13.

[160] Ibid.

[161] M. De Blacam, 'Children, Constitutional Rights and the Separation of Powers', *Irish Jurist*, Vol. 36 (2002), pp. 113–142, at 131, citing J. Finnis, *Natural Law and Natural Rights* (1900), at 170.

[162] Whyte and Hogan, *J.M. Kelly* (n. 14 above), p. 122.

[163] Unreported, 16 February 2005.

[164] While the right to property could be classified as a social right or used to support social rights, this does not appear to be how it is perceived by the Supreme Court and the right to property has not been subject to the same degree of judicial reluctance displayed towards the application and enforcement of more 'traditional' socio-economic rights.

[165] See n. 79 above, para. 120.

viewed as both a question of policy *and* as a question of law.[166] For instance, a case where a child has an unusual form of disability and no provision has been made by the State to meet his educational needs; meeting those needs may well entail issues of policy about the nature, delivery and cost of the service. However, at the same time, there is also a plain and simple issue about the failure of the State to meet the child's explicit constitutional entitlement under the Constitution. In such a case, to say that the issue is one of policy and is therefore not justiciable does not answer the plaintiff's case; it simply ignores it.[167] This might be viewed as an abdication of the Court's responsibility to give a decision on a constitutional question before it. Martha Minow has pointed out that judicial inaction, as well as judicial action, may impair relationships with other branches and undermine the government's overall obligation to respect persons.[168] While it is definitely important for judges to understand their relationships with other people and institutions, such understanding is quite different from ceding responsibility for what ensues. 'The courts' own responsibilities to the parties before them cannot be acquitted simply by asserting deference to other branches'.[169]

7. TD – A FLAWED BALANCING EXERCISE?

In the *TD* case, Justice Hardiman built upon his comments in the *Sinnott* case, in which he emphasised that '[the separation of powers] is not a mere administrative arrangement: it is itself a high constitutional value…It is an essential part of the democratic procedures of the State, not inferior in importance to any article of the Constitution'.[170] In *TD*, he stated that the High Court's statement that the Court has to attempt to fill the vacuum

that exists by reason of the failure of the legislature and executive to vindicate children's constitutional rights came close to 'asserting a general residual power in the courts, in the event of a (judicially determined) failure by the other branches of government to discharge some (possibly judicially identified) constitutional duty'.[171] If this were accepted, it would have the effect of attributing a paramountcy to the judicial branch of government which was contrary to his view of the Constitution, under which no branch of government is attributed with 'an overall, or residual, supervisory power over the others'.[172] He rejected the premise that 'the boundaries [between the functions of the different organs] are porous or capable of being ignored or breached because one organ rightly or wrongly considers that another organ is unwise or inadequate in the discharge of its own duties'.[173] Acknowledging the checks and balances provided by the Constitution (including that of judicial review of legislation), he further stated that the existence of such powers does not suggest that a court, or any other organ of government, can strike its own balance, in a particular case, as to how the separation of powers is to be observed.[174]

These comments are inconsistent with previous Supreme Court statements that the segregation of functions under the Irish doctrine of separation of powers is not absolute,[175] and appear to ignore the role granted to the Court as guardian of the rights and principles set out in the Constitution.[176] Justice Hardiman's remarks on the courts' inability to strike a balance are especially worthy of note. They appear to suggest that the courts – who are undoubtedly the ultimate interpreters of the Constitution – are not entitled to rule on how the separation of powers doctrine operates in a particular situation. It has been pointed out that, contrary to what Justice Hardiman suggests, a balance *does* have to be struck in such a situation

---

[166] Paraphrased from De Blacam, '*Children, Constitutional Rights'* (n. 161 above), p. 135.

[167] Ibid.

[168] She makes this assertion in the context of arguing that the separation of powers necessarily involves continuous relationships between the branches rather than confining each to entirely distinct fields of competence. M. Minow, *Making All the Difference – Inclusion, Exclusion and American Law* (London: Cornell University Press, 1990), p. 369.

[169] Ibid.

[170] *Sinnott* (n. 39 above), at para. 346. Keane CJ expressly agreed with Hardiman J's analysis of the separation of powers doctrine (para. 109).

[171] *TD* (n. 40 above), para. 353.

[172] Ibid. para. 350.

[173] Ibid. para. 357.

[174] Ibid. para. 352.

[175] See *Lynham v. Butler (No. 2)* [1933] IR 74 and *Abbey Films Limited v. Attorney General* [1981] I.R. 158.

[176] For a contrasting view of the separation of powers under the Irish Constitution and the court's role in relation to both enforcing the separation of powers and upholding constitutional rights, see Denham J's dissenting judgment in *TD*.

and that even where the courts refuse to intervene in executive action, that in itself is striking a balance.[177] It is clear that the majority in *TD* considered the Court's power to vindicate constitutional rights to be limited by the principle of the separation of powers.[178] Thus, they regarded their duty to uphold (a very rigid version) of the separation of powers doctrine as outweighing their duty to protect and vindicate the constitutional rights at issue.[179]

Finally, it is also possible to classify the courts' duty to uphold constitutional socio-economic rights as an aspect of the judicial function under the separation of powers (as opposed to being part and parcel of the principle of constitutional supremacy). According to this view, judicial inaction or deference in the face of a failure by the State to give effect to constitutional socio-economic rights may itself amount to a breach of the separation of powers.

7. REMEDIES AVAILABLE TO IRISH COURTS

In a celebrated ruling, the Supreme Court asserted that it has a broad jurisdiction to protect the constitutional rights of citizens, stating that 'no one can with impunity set these rights at nought or circumvent them, and the courts' powers in this regard are as ample as the defence of the Constitution requires'.[180] In a later case, the Court stated further that, '[w]here the people by the Constitution create rights against the State or impose duties upon the State, a remedy to enforce these must be deemed to be also available'.[181] In a judg-

ment involving the constitutional rights of a child with a serious personality disorder predating *TD*, Chief Justice Hamilton stated that '[it] is part of the courts' function to vindicate and defend the rights guaranteed by Article 40, section 3. If the courts are under an obligation to defend and vindicate the personal rights of the citizen, it inevitably follows that the courts have the jurisdiction to do all things necessary to vindicate such rights'.[182]

The Irish Supreme Court has adopted an extremely restrictive attitude towards the granting of positive orders against the State. In *Sinnott*, several of the judges' *obiter* either expressly or implicitly indicated a reluctance to grant a mandatory injunction in a constitutional context.[183] However, at least two of them acknowledged that there could be extreme circumstances in which such orders might be appropriate, but that the facts of this case were not so extreme as to warrant the granting of such an order.[184] Subsequently, the Supreme Court adopted an even harder line on the granting of mandatory orders against the state in the *TD* case.

In the High Court in *TD*, Justice Kelly had argued that, in directing the executive to adhere to its *own* policy, he was not making policy. However, a majority of the Supreme Court held that, in granting the mandatory orders under appeal, which required the executive power of the State to be implemented in a specific manner by the expenditure of money on defined objects within particular time limits, Justice Kelly had violated the constitutionally mandated separation of powers. The majority was of the view that making such orders involved the High Court effectively determining the policy which the executive is to follow in dealing with a particular social problem.[185]

---

[177] De Blacam, *'Children, Constitutional Rights'* (n. 161 above), p. 141.

[178] Murray J and Hardiman J stated this expressly, while the findings of the other judges indicate implicit agreement.

[179] It is important to note, however, the Court's later statements in *In re Article 26 and the Health (Amendment) (No. 2) Bill* where it stated *per* Murray J that, 'the separation of powers, involving as it does respect for the powers of the various organs of State and specifically the power of the Oireachtas to make decisions on the allocation of resources, cannot in itself be a justification for the failure of the State to protect or vindicate a constitutional right'.

[180] *Per* Ó Dálaigh CJ in *State (Quinn)* v. *Ryan* [1965] I.R. 70, p. 122.

[181] *Per* Walsh J in *Byrne* v. *Ireland* [1972] I.R. 241, p. 281. See further comments by Walsh J in the same case, pp. 279–80. For similar comments, see *per* Budd J in *Company of Ireland Ltd.* v. *Fitzpatrick (No. 2)* [1961] I.R. 345, at 368; *per* Walsh J in *McGee* v. *Attorney General* [1974] IR 204.

[182] *DG* v. *Eastern Health Board & Ors* 1997 3 I.R. 511, at 522. Prior to *TD*, there were other judicial statements in cases involving children's constitutional rights indicating that, where appropriate, the Court was entitled to grant injunctive relief to ensure the enforcement of children's constitutional socio-economic rights. See, e.g., *DD* v. *Eastern Health Board* at 7; *Comerford* v. *Minister for Education* [1997] 2 ILRM 134, at 147–8.

[183] Geoghegan J (para. 417), Hardiman J (paras. 333–351), Denham J (para. 156) and Keane CJ (para. 80). Murray and Fennelly JJ stated that it was not necessary to consider the issue (paras. 272 and 424 respectively). Murphy J did not refer to the issue of remedies in the course of his judgment.

[184] Denham J (para. 156) and Geoghegan J (para. 417).

[185] *Per* Keane J (para. 80). See also, Murphy J (paras. 224–5).

According to Murray J, such an order should only be granted where there has been 'a conscious and deliberate decision by [an] organ of State to act in breach of its constitutional obligations accompanied by bad faith or recklessness'.[186] In his view, a court would also have to be satisfied that the absence of good faith or the reckless disregard of rights would impinge on the observance by the State party concerned of any declaratory order made by the court.[187] Justice Hardiman agreed with Murray stating that such an order could only be granted as 'an absolutely final resort in circumstances of great crisis and for the protection of the constitutional order itself'.[188] In his view, no such circumstances that would justify the granting of such an order had occurred since the enactment of the Constitution in 1937.[189] According to both judges, even in such extreme circumstances, the mandatory order granted might direct the fulfilment of a manifest constitutional obligation, but should not specify the means or policy to be used in fulfilling the obligation.[190]

The single dissenting judge (Justice Denham) adopted a different approach, arguing that it was clear from the case law that in rare and exceptional cases (such as this one), to protect constitutional rights, a court may have a jurisdiction, and even a duty, to make a mandatory order against another branch of government.[191] She further pointed out that a decision of a court, even if it is in relation to a single individual, may affect policy: 'The expense of the case itself and its outcome may have profound and far-reaching effects. Simply because a case affects a policy of an institution does not *per se* render it unconstitutional or bring it into conflict with the principle of the separation of powers'.[192] She disagreed with the majority that in making an order such as that granted by the High Court against the executive, the court was formulating policy, stating instead

that the order merely mandated the State's own policy.[193]

The Irish Supreme Court has thus limited its ability to grant mandatory orders to such an extent that it is very unlikely that such an order will be granted against the state – particularly with regard to constitutional socio-economic rights, which raise their own especial concerns in relation to the doctrine of the separation of powers.[194] On a more constructive note, the *TD* case was positive in relation to at least one aspect of enforcing socio-economic rights. While the majority of

---

[186] *TD* (n. 40 above), para. 232.

[187] Ibid.

[188] Ibid. para. 367. It is interesting to note that Hardiman J did not consider the circumstances in the case before him as being of 'great crisis'. Nor did he appear to view the consistent disregard of declaratory orders granted in similar cases preceding *TD* by the elected branches of government as constituting a threat to the constitutional order.

[189] Ibid. para. 367.

[190] *Per* Murray J (para. 232) and *per* Hardiman J (para. 366).

[191] Ibid. 139. See also para. 16.

[192] Ibid. para. 133.

[193] Ibid. para. 134.

[194] I note, however, that dicta from various Supreme Court judges and High Court decisions suggest that advocates might have more success in obtaining mandatory orders where the socio-economic rights obligations at issue are statutory, rather than constitutional, in nature or where the services or facilities being demanded are already in existence. It is interesting to consider Hardiman J's comment in *Sinnott* that 'the enforcement of duties imposed by the legislature is obviously an exercise of a different kind from the devising or inferring of such duties without legislative intervention' (para. 379). In the *TD* case, Hardiman J discussed the possibility that relief could be afforded to the applicant under legislation (at paras. 261–2). These dicta appear to imply that it is possible that the Supreme Court would have been prepared to adopt a less restrictive approach to the granting of mandatory orders where the duties at issue were statutory rather than constitutional in nature. This is arguably borne out by the High Court decision in *Jeremiah Cronin (a minor) suing by his mother and next friend Margaret Cronin* v. *Minister for Education and Science & Ors*, Case 1144OP of 2003. In this case, Laffoy J granted a mandatory interlocutory order, ordering the Minister for Education and Science to provide twenty-nine hours home tuition a week to an autistic child, pending either the securing of an appropriate school place for the child or the outcome of his full action against the State. The complainants alleged that by failing to provide educational services appropriate to the child's needs, the defendants were in breach of their obligations under, amongst other things, the Education Act 1998. Laffoy stated that, in reaching her conclusion, she had regard to the decision of the Supreme Court in *TD* and, in particular, to the observations of (Keane CJ) at page 287 of that judgment. She said that she was 'satisfied that granting a mandatory injunction does not fall foul of that decision. The relief granted is limited to the particular needs of the Plaintiff and merely extends a programme which the First Defendant has already sanctioned'. According to O'Mahony, '[t]his analysis would suggest that the restriction imposed in *TD* on mandatory relief applies only to orders which require the implementation of whole new ranges of services or facilities and does not apply to individual plaintiffs who wish to be provided with facilities or services which are already in place. (C. O'Mahony, 'A New Slant on Educational Rights and Mandatory Injunctions?' *Dublin University Law* Journal, Vol. 27 (2005), pp. 363–367, at 365).

the Supreme Court refused to grant a mandatory order on the basis that doing so would constitute a violation of the doctrine of separation of powers, they did not base their decision on inherent judicial incapacity to grant such an order. In fact, their judgments make it clear that in some extreme circumstances the courts could grant a mandatory order. This would suggest that the Court does not regard itself as institutionally *incapable* of formulating complex mandatory orders.

8. CONCLUSION: FUTURE DEVELOPMENTS?

This final section focuses on means by which socio-economic rights may be accorded a greater level of protection within the Irish legal order in future.

One way in which the restrictive approach adopted by the Irish courts to socio-economic rights might be addressed is by amending the Irish Constitution by referendum so as to include socio-economic rights. The recent developments with regard to the possible future amendment of the constitution to afford greater protection to children's rights have already been discussed. However, recommendations that the constitution be altered so as to include socio-economic rights have not been made solely in this context. In 1996, a majority of the Constitutional Review Group (CRG) rejected arguments in favour of including in the Constitution 'a personal right to freedom from poverty or of specific personal economic rights' (i.e., socio-economic rights).[195] This was largely due to concerns that rendering such rights justiciable would lead to a distortion of democracy by according judges power in relation to policy and budgetary matters that were more appropriately left to the elected branches of government. The CRG were also of the opinion that a right to freedom from poverty would not be capable of objective determination and that the elected branches of government might be placed in a position where they would have no discretion in relation to what amount of revenue would be necessary in order to satisfy such right.[196] This was an extremely disappointing development for proponents of socio-economic rights. It served to demonstrate the

misperceptions about socio-economic rights (and what judicial adjudication of them would entail) that underlay (and continue to underlie) the attitudes of legal professionals and others in Ireland.

Another means by which the Irish judiciary might positively develop its socio-economic rights jurisprudence is through more extensive reference to, and employment of, international law in its interpretation of the rights set out in the Constitution.

In addition, the passing of the European Convention of Human Rights Act (ECHR Act) in 2003 means that there is a new, albeit statutory, source of norms to be employed to give effect either directly or indirectly to socio-economic rights claims. Section 3(1) of the Act requires every organ of the state to perform its function in a manner compatible with the State's obligation under the convention provisions. This includes those convention obligations which have implications for the enforcement of socio-economic rights. The passing of the Act has increased the extent to which the ECHR is relied on and cited in Irish courts requiring, as it does, that, in interpreting and applying any statutory provision or rule of law, courts shall, as far as is possible 'do so in a manner compatible with the State's obligations under the Convention provisions'.[197] The Act also provides that judicial notice must be taken of, *inter alia*, the Convention provisions and jurisprudence of the European Court of Human Rights (ECtHR)[198] and that, when interpreting and applying the Convention provisions, courts must take due account of the principles laid down in, amongst other things, such decisions and judgments. Amongst other things, the Act empowers the High Court and the Supreme Court to make a declaration that a statutory provision or rule of law is incompatible with the State's obligations under the Convention, where no other legal remedy is adequate or available.[199]

In the United Kingdom, courts at all levels have relied on jurisprudence of the ECtHR in

---

[195] See CRG, *Report* (n. 1 above), pp. 234–6.

[196] For more on this, see ibid.

[197] Section 2, ECHR Act 2003. For information on how the Act has operated since its introduction, see D. O'Connell, S. Cummiskey, E. Meeneghan & P. O'Connell, *ECHR Act 2003: A Preliminary Assessment of Impact* (Dublin: Law Society of Ireland/Dublin Solicitors Bar Association, 2006).

[198] Ibid. Section 4.

[199] Ibid. Section 5.

considering socio-economic rights-related claims brought under the UK Human Rights Act 1998. It was hoped that the Irish courts would adopt a similar approach when dealing with socio-economic rights-related cases arising under the ECHR Act. Initially, however, there were relatively few cases in which the legislation was cited. In the case of *Dublin City Council* v. *Fennell*,[200] the Irish Supreme Court held that the ECHR Act did not operate retrospectively, either to past events (i.e. events prior to the coming into force of the Act), actions that have already been initiated or pending litigation. This decision meant that it was some time before the Irish courts (and particularly the Supreme Court) were able to develop jurisprudence under the Act.

There is a growing body of housing rights case law developing under the Act as a result of claimants bringing complaints based on Article 8 ECHR (right to respect for private and family life, home and correspondence). There have been a number of positive decisions in which the High Court has found the State not to be in compliance with its obligations under Article 8. In one instance, this occurred where a local authority failed to provide appropriate mobile home accommodation to members of a Traveller family living with severe

physical disabilities.[201] In another case, a section of the Housing Act 1966 was found to be in breach of Article 8, which set out a summary procedure for the recovery of possession of dwellings by local authorities from their tenants but did not provide adequate procedural safeguards.[202] Unfortunately, this judicial willingness to engage progressively with the State's obligations under Article 8 does not appear to be shared by all members of the bench.[203]

All in all, these developments taken together with the recent decisions involving the right to civil legal aid, as well as the Supreme Court's failure to expressly reject the existence of further unenumerated socio-economic rights in the case of *In the Matter of re Article 26 of the Constitution and the Health (Amendment)(No. 2)*, suggest that the debate on the judicial enforceability of socio-economic rights in Ireland has not been foreclosed by the decisions in *TD* and *Sinnott*.

---

[200] [2005] IESC 33.

[201] *O'Donnell* v. *South Dublin County Council*, Record No.2006/19, 22 May 2007.

[202] See M. Carolan, 'Judge Finds Housing Codes Breaches Rights' *Irish Times*, 9 May 2008, referring to the decision of Laffoy J in *Donegan* v. *Dublin Council and the Attorney General*, High Court, 8 May 2008.

[203] See, e.g., *Doherty & Anor.* v. *South Dublin County Council* [2007] IEHC 4; *Leonard* v. *Dublin City Council* + Ors [2008] IEHC 79.

PART THREE

Regional Procedures and Jurisprudence

17

African Regional Human Rights System

The Promise of Recent Jurisprudence on Social Rights

Danwood Mzikenge Chirwa[*]

1. INTRODUCTION

The adoption of the African Charter on Human and Peoples' Rights ('African Charter') in 1981[1] marked the introduction of a third regional human rights system after the creation of the European and Inter-American systems respectively. Adopted partly due to external pressure on African governments to establish a regional human rights regime and partly as a response to the gross human rights violations committed by some African leaders, the African Charter is distinctive in its attempt to append an African 'fingerprint' on the human rights discourse.[2] Not only did its content draw on existing international and regional human rights treaties, the drafters of the African Charter were mandated to have regard to the values of African civilisation and the needs of Africa in formulating the Charter.[3]

One of the unique features of the African Charter is the recognition of economic, social and cultural rights on the same footing as civil and political rights.[4] The Charter, as will be shown below, prescribes the same enforcement mechanisms for all the rights it recognises. While much of the litigation that it has generated concerns civil and political rights, some interesting jurisprudence on socio-economic rights has begun to emerge. This chapter analyses critically the protection of socio-economic rights in the African regional system focussing mainly on the African Charter and the jurisprudence of the African Commission on Human and Peoples' Rights ('African Commission'). Some discussion will also relate to the potential contribution to the protection of these rights by the two specialised instruments, the African Charter on the Rights and Welfare of the Child ('African Children's Charter') and the Protocol to the African Charter on Human and Peoples' Rights on the Rights of Women in Africa ('Women's Protocol') adopted in 1990 and 2003 respectively, and the Protocol to the African Charter on Human and Peoples' Rights on the Establishment of an African Court on Human and Peoples' Rights ('African Court's Protocol') adopted in 1998.

2. ENTRENCHMENT OF THE INDIVISIBILITY OF ALL RIGHTS

The African Charter declares in its preamble that 'civil and political rights cannot be dissociated from economic, social and cultural rights in their conception as well as their universality' and, rather controversially, that 'the satisfaction of economic, social and cultural rights is a guarantee for the enjoyment of civil and political rights'. While this

---

[*] Associate Professor, University of Cape Town. The author would like to thank Anashri Pillay, Aifheli Shihvase and Malcolm Langford for their useful comments on an earlier version of this chapter.
[1] Adopted by the Organisation of African Unity (OAU) at the 18th Conference of Heads of State and Government on 27 June 1981, entry into force 21 October 1986.
[2] See generally M. Mutua, 'The Banjul Charter and the African fingerprint: An evaluation of the language of duties', *Virginia Journal of International Law*, Vol. 35 (1995), pp. 339–380, at 339.
[3] E. Kodjo, 'The African Charter on Human and Peoples' Rights', *Human Rights Law Journal*, Vol. 11, Nos. 3–4 (1990), pp. 271–282, at 274.
[4] El-Obaid & Appiagyei-Atua have argued that 'A truly African conception of rights would not identify civil and political rights as distinct from economic, social and cultural rights', in E. A. El-Obaid & K. Appiagyei-Atua, 'Human rights in Africa: Linking the past to the present', *McGill Law Journal*, Vol. 41 (1996), pp. 819, 846. The

African Charter also recognises third-generation rights such as the right to economic, social and cultural development, the right to national and international peace, the right to a general satisfactory environment, and the right of peoples to freely dispose of their wealth and natural resources. See articles 19–24.

declaration is an affirmation of the important notion of the interdependence and indivisibility of all human rights, some commentators have warned that it could be misconstrued to mean that the African Charter gives credence to the idea that the implementation of economic, social and cultural rights in the African context deserves priority over the protection of civil and political rights.[5] This idea, sarcastically termed the 'full-belly thesis' by Rhoda Howard, was held and propagated by many African leaders and scholars in the post-colonial period.[6]

However, the African Commission has adopted an approach to interpreting the African Charter that cogently reinforces the concept of the indivisibility of all rights. When considering communications brought before it, the Commission considers the facts in light of all relevant rights applicable. It has not adopted a contextual approach that considers only the most relevant right applicable to the facts of the case where the facts raise legal issues affecting more than one right.[7] Consequently, the Commission has in some cases found violations of rights belonging to all, or two of the three traditional categories of rights.

For example, in *The Social and Economic Rights Action Centre & the Centre for Economic and Social Rights v. Nigeria*,[8] the communication alleged that the state-owned Nigerian Petroleum Company

'NNPC' and Shell Petroleum Development Corporation 'Shell', in which the NNPC held majority shares, had committed a range of human rights violations for which Nigeria was responsible. It was alleged that the companies had exploited oil reserves in Ogoniland in Nigeria without regard for the health or environment of the local communities. No facilities were put in place to prevent the wastes from spilling into neighbouring villages. As a result, water, soil and air were polluted, causing serious short-term and long-term health complications to the local population. It was further alleged that the Nigerian government condoned these violations by failing to monitor the activities of the oil companies or enforcing domestic environmental standards. The government also facilitated the abuses, it was alleged, by allowing oil companies to use the government's security forces to carry out several military operations against members of the Ogoni people who were protesting against the activities of the oil companies. Among other things, these forces burned and destroyed several villages and homes, crops, farm animals and even killed some of the people. In 2001, the African Commission found Nigeria to be in violation of a range of rights including the right not to be discriminated against, the right to life, the right to property, the right to health, the right to family protection, the right of peoples to freely dispose of their wealth and natural resources, and the right to a general satisfactory environment. As will be shown below, this case is, thus far, the linchpin of the African Commission's decisions as far as the interpretation of socio-economic rights under the African Charter is concerned.

In some cases, the African Commission has found certain conduct, which would otherwise have been determined solely on the basis of civil and political rights, to constitute violations of certain socio-economic rights. In *Malawi African Association & Others v. Mauritania*, for example, it held that holding people in solitary confinement both before and during trial, especially where such detention is arbitrary, amounts to an infringement of the right to respect for one's life and integrity of person, as well as the right to a family life.[9]

The African Commission has also upheld the indivisibility of all rights by considering some human

---

[5] R. Gittleman, 'The African Charter on Human and Peoples Rights: A legal analysis', *Virginia Journal of International Law*, Vol. 22 (1982), pp. 667–714, at 667.

[6] R. Howard, 'The full-belly thesis: Should socio-economic rights take priority over civil and political rights? Evidence from Sub-Saharan Africa', *Human Rights Quarterly*, Vol. 5 (1983), pp. 467, 468.

[7] As a counter-illustration, the South African Constitutional Court in *Soobramoney v. Minister of Health* (1998) (1) SA 765 (CC), para. 15, refused to hold that the right to life imposes a positive obligation on the State to provide life saving treatment to a critically ill patient arguing that the right of access to health, which is expressly recognised by the South African Constitution, was more relevant to such a claim than the right to life.

[8] Communication 155/96 ('SERAC Case'), Ref. ACHPR/COMM/A044/1 (27 May 2002). For reviews of the case see D. M. Chirwa, 'Toward revitalising economic, social and cultural rights in Africa: Social and Economic Rights Action Centre and the Centre for Economic and Social Rights v. Nigeria', *Human Rights Brief*, Vol. 10, No. 1 (2002), pp. 14; F. Coomans, 'The Ogoni case before the African Commission on Human and Peoples' Rights', *International & Comparative Law Quarterly*, Vol. 52 (2003), pp. 749. See also *Free Legal Assistance Group & Others v. Zaire*, Communications 25/89, 47/90, 56/91, 100/93 (2000) AHRLR 74 (ACHPR 1996) ('*Zaire* Case').

[9] Communications 54/91, 61/91, 98/93, 164–196/97, 210/98, (2000) AHRLR 149 (ACHPR 2000), paras. 119–120 & 124 ('*Mauritanian* Case').

rights issues as posing a 'special threat to human rights', entailing violations of both civil and political rights and economic, social and cultural rights. For instance, in *Union Interafricaine des Droit de l'Homme & Others v. Angola*, it stated that mass expulsion of aliens 'calls into question a whole series of rights' recognised in the African Charter, including the right not to be discriminated against, the right to property, the right to work, the right to education, and the right to family protection.[10]

This jurisprudence demonstrably underscores the interrelatedness and indivisibility of all rights and allows for a holistic development of all Charter rights.

3. THE NATURE OF THE OBLIGATIONS UNDER THE AFRICAN CHARTER

3.1 State Obligations

The African Charter formulates socio-economic rights neither with claw-back clauses nor with such conventional internal limitations as 'progressive realisation' and 'within available resources'. It also does not have a derogation clause.[11] It may therefore be asked whether socio-economic rights obligations under the African Charter are realisable immediately or whether resource constraints could constitute a valid defence by the State for non-satisfaction of these rights.

Chidi Odinkalu, relying on some 'out-of court' statements of certain members of the African Commission, is of the view that by formulating its rights without internal modifiers, the African Charter requires States parties to implement socio-economic rights immediately.[12]

However, in recent case law the African Commission seems to have taken a contrary position. The African Commission attempted to outline the socio-economic obligations of states in greater detail for the first time in the *SERAC* Case. It stated that all rights generate the duties to respect, protect, promote and fulfil.[13] It defined the duty to respect as requiring the state to refrain from interfering with the enjoyment of all fundamental rights and to 'respect right holders, their freedoms, autonomy, resources, and liberty of their action'.[14] This duty means that the State should respect the free use of resources owned by the individual or in association with others.[15] The duty to protect, it was held, obliges the State to protect right-holders from political, economic, and social interferences by other subjects through legislation and provision of effective remedies.[16] The African Commission defined the duty to promote as requiring States parties to promote tolerance, raise awareness and build infrastructures to enable individuals to exercise their rights and freedoms.[17] Lastly, the African Commission defined the duty to fulfil as requiring the state to move its machinery towards the actual realisation of the rights and as consisting of direct provision of basic needs or resources that can be used for meeting those basic needs.[18]

It is clear that the duty to respect can easily be implemented and enforced immediately as happened in the *SERAC* Case. However, the other duties to protect, promote and fulfil may not be implemented or enforced with equal ease as issues of resource availability could come into play.

In the *SERAC* Case, the African Commission made statements suggesting that it has adopted the minimum core obligations concept developed by the UN Committee on Economic, Social and Cultural Rights ('CESCR'), which monitors the implementation of the International Covenant on Economic, Social and Cultural Rights ('ICESCR'). It stated that 'the minimum core of the right to food requires that the Nigerian government should not destroy or contaminate food sources'.[19] It stated similarly

---

[10] Communication 159/96, (2000) AHRLR 18 (ACHPR 1997), paras. 15–17. See also *Amnesty International v. Zambia* Communication 212/98, (2000) AHRLR 325 (ACHPR 1999).

[11] The Commission has insisted that Charter rights do not admit of derogation during emergency situations or special circumstances See for example, *Commission Nationale des Droit de l'Homme et des Libertes v. Chad* Communication 74/95, (2000) AHRLR 66 (ACHPR 1994), para. 21 ('*Chad* Case'); *Media Rights Agenda & Others v. Nigeria* (2000) AHRLR 200 (ACHPR 1998), para. 67 ('*Media Rights* Case').

[12] C.A. Odinkalu, 'Implementing economic, social and cultural rights under the African Charter on Human and Peoples' Rights', in M. Evans and R. Murray (eds.), *The African Charter on Human and Peoples' Rights: The system*

in practice, 1986–2000 (Cambridge: Cambridge University Press, 2002), pp. 178–218, at 196–8.

[13] *SERAC* Case (n. 8 above), para. 44.

[14] Ibid. para. 45.

[15] Ibid.

[16] Ibid. para. 46.

[17] Ibid.

[18] Ibid. para. 47.

[19] Ibid. para. 65.

that the minimum obligation embodied in the right to shelter obliged the Nigerian government 'not to destroy the houses of its citizens and not to obstruct efforts by individuals or communities to rebuild lost homes'.[20] It could therefore be argued that both the duty to respect and the minimum core obligations implicit in socio-economic rights under the African Charter are claimable immediately.

However, such a view may not be lightly inferred from the Commission's statements cited above, as they appear to reflect a misunderstanding of the concept of minimum core obligations. What the African Commission is referring to in these statements is clearly the duty to respect the relevant socio-economic rights. By contrast, the minimum core obligations concept was designed essentially to ensure that States take positive measures to satisfy minimum essential levels of each of the socio-economic right in the ICESCR.[21] Thus, since the African Commission did not identify any positive obligations that could be said to form part of the minimum core of the rights to shelter and food, and considering other statements it made (which are discussed below) in the same case, it cannot be said conclusively that the minimum core obligations concept forms part of its jurisprudence.

Other passages in the *SERAC* Case suggest that the African Commission has adopted the reasonableness test, similar to that developed by the South African Constitutional Court, as a benchmark for determining compliance by States with their positive obligations.[22] The African Commis-

sion construed the right to a healthy environment under Article 24 of the African Charter as obligating states to 'take reasonable' measures to 'prevent pollution and ecological degradation, to promote conservation, and to secure an ecologically sustainable development and use of natural resources'.[23] A State could therefore be in violation of a given socio-economic right if it can be shown that it failed to take reasonable measures to realise that right. However, the Commission did not elaborate on what constitutes 'reasonable steps'. As a result, it remains unclear as to when a State will be held to be in violation of its positive obligations in relation to socio-economic rights under the African Charter.

An opportunity to clarify this jurisprudence arose in *Purohit and Moore v. The Gambia*.[24] It was alleged in this case alleged that The Gambia violated a range of rights under the African Charter including the right to health. The complainants argued that the Lunatic Detention Act, the principal legislation governing mental health, was outdated and inadequate to provide protection to the rights of mental patients. It was argued that the Act did not provide safeguards to protect the rights of persons undergoing diagnosis for mental illness, and during their certification and detention as mental patients. It was also alleged that the Psychiatric Unit, where mental patients were detained, was overcrowded; the living conditions in the Unit were poor; and that patients were treated without giving consent. In finding The Gambia liable for violating, among other things, the right to health, the African Commission noted that it was aware that millions of people in Africa were unable to enjoy this right maximally because African countries are generally faced with the problem of

---

[20] Ibid. paras. 61 and 62.

[21] See Committee on Economic, Social and Cultural Rights, *General Comment No. 3, The nature of States parties' obligations* (Fifth session, 1990), U.N. Doc. E/1991/23, annex III at 86 (1991), para 10.

[22] The South African Constitutional Court has held that in any challenge in which it is alleged that the State has failed to meet the positive obligations in relation to socio-economic rights, the question will be whether the legislative and other measures taken by the state are reasonable. The reasonableness test entails a range of considerations. Firstly, the programme must be a comprehensive and co-ordinated one that 'clearly allocates responsibilities and tasks to the different spheres of government and ensures that appropriate financial and human resources are available'. Secondly, the measures adopted must be directed towards the progressive realisation of the right within the state's available means. Thirdly, the policies and programmes adopted must be reasonable 'both in their conception and their implementation'. Fourthly, the programme or measure must be 'balanced and flexible

and make appropriate provision for attention to housing crises and to short term, medium and long term needs'. Fifthly, the programme must respond to those 'whose needs are most urgent and whose ability to enjoy all rights therefore is most in peril'. See *Government of the Republic of South Africa and Others v. Grootboom and Others* 2000 (11) BCLR 1169 (CC). For critiques of this case, see S. Liebenberg, 'South Africa's evolving jurisprudence on socio-economic rights', *Law, Democracy and Development*, Vol. 6, No. 2 (2002), pp. 151–191, at 159. For a deeper discussion of the case and the South African jurisprudence on socio-economic rights, see S. Liebenberg's chapter in this volume.

[23] *SERAC* Case (n. 8 above), para. 52.

[24] Communication 241/2001, unpublished, ('*Purohit* Case').

poverty.[25] It therefore defined the State's obligation implicit in Article 16, which entrenches the right to enjoy the best attainable physical and mental health, as requiring States to '*take concrete and targeted steps, while taking full advantage of its available resources*, to ensure that the right to health is fully realised in its all aspects without discrimination of any kind'.[26] This case establishes that resource scarcity is a possible defence to a case alleging violations of economic, social and cultural rights under the African Charter. This interpretation makes practical sense as it is unrealistic considering the many socio-economic problems and human, infrastructural and financial resource constraints that African states face to expect them to be bound by unqualified positive obligations implicit in socio-economic rights and other rights.

However, the *Purohit* Case should have clarified the standard for holding States accountable for positive obligations in relation to socio-economic rights more clearly. For one thing, it is not clear whether 'concrete and targeted steps' should be understood in the context of the reasonableness test as defined by the South African Constitutional Court or in the context of CESCR's definition of State obligations in General Comment No. 15. This confusion is compounded by the fact that the African Commission did not relate its understanding of the socio-economic rights obligations incumbent upon The Gambia in this case to its earlier holding in the *SERAC* Case requiring States to take reasonable steps to realise these rights. Furthermore, it is not clear whether the socio-economic rights obligations are required to be discharged as a matter of priority in the context where resources are lacking. Given the fact that poverty is widespread across the continent and the fact that the African Charter does not expressly incorporate internal limitations in its socio-economic rights provisions, it is arguable that the framers of the African Charter intended that these provisions are interpreted in a manner that obligates States to give priority to meeting basic needs. Consequently, while the lack of availability of resources could constitute an acceptable ground for exempting states from liability for failing to realise socio-economic rights, States ought to shoulder the burden of showing that they have used the available resources optimally to meet the basic needs of their people as a matter of priority.[27]

3.2 Obligations of Non-State Actors

Another distinctive feature of the African Charter lies in its recognition of duties of non-state actors. The Charter avers in its preamble that 'the enjoyment of rights and freedoms also implies the performance of duties on the part of everyone'. This preambular statement is reinforced by its substantive provisions. Firstly, Article 27(2) states that: 'The rights and freedoms of each individual shall be exercised with due regard to the rights of others, collective security, morality and common interest'. Secondly, Article 28 postulates that every individual has 'the duty to respect and consider his fellow beings without discrimination, and to maintain relations aimed at promoting, safeguarding and reinforcing mutual respect and tolerance'. Article 29 then enumerates some of the traditional duties individuals owe to their parents, families, communities and state. These provisions represent an African conception of human rights, which regards rights and duties as inseparably linked.[28] They lend support to current efforts aimed at holding non-state actors responsible for human rights abuses.[29]

However, the African Charter does not expressly make provision for the enforcement of the

---

[25] Ibid. para. 84.
[26] Ibid. (emphasis added).

[27] This argument is based on paragraph 10 of CESCR's General Comment No. 3 (n. 21 above). Article 60 of the African Charter allows the African Commission to draw inspiration from international law on human and peoples' rights when interpreting provisions in the African Charter.
[28] M. Mutua, 'The Banjul Charter: The case for an African fingerprint', in A. An-Na'im (ed.), *Cultural transformation and human rights in Africa* (London: Zed Books Ltd, 2002), 68–107, at 68, 81; K. Mbaye, & B. Ndiaye, 'The Organisation of the African Unity', in K. Vasak (ed.), *The International dimensions of human rights*, Vol. 2, (Westport: Greenwood Press, 1982), pp. 583–629, at 583, 588–9.
[29] See N. Jägers, *Corporate human rights obligations: In search of accountability* (Antwerpen: Intersentia, 2002); D. Weissbrodt and M. Kruger, 'Norms on the Responsibilities of Transnational Corporations and Other Business Enterprises with regard to Human Rights', *American Journal of International Law*, Vol. 97 (2003), p. 901; International Council on Human Rights Policy, *Beyond voluntarism: Human rights and the developing international legal obligations of companies* (Versoix: International Human Rights Policy, 2002).

obligations of non-state actors through direct communications against these actors. This means that these obligations will largely be enforced indirectly by bringing communications against states. As noted above, States parties to the African Charter have the duty to protect the rights recognised in the Charter. Article 21(5) of the African Charter defines this duty very forcefully in the context of the right of peoples to freely dispose of their wealth and natural resources. It obligates States parties to 'eliminate all forms of foreign economic exploitation particularly that practiced by international monopolies so as to enable their peoples to fully benefit from the advantages derived from their natural resources'.[30] According to the African Commission, this provision is a ringing reminder of the continent's colonial past, during which human and material resources of Africa were exploited for the benefit of colonial masters, that has left Africa's resources and its people still vulnerable to foreign misappropriation.[31] By implication, multinational corporations and other business enterprises have the obligation to refrain from exploiting natural resources on the continent without sharing the benefits with the local people. Thus, in the *SERAC* Case, Nigeria was also found to be in violation of the right of the Ogoni people to freely dispose of their wealth and natural resources on the ground that the government had failed to monitor and regulate the operations of the oil companies in Nigeria, thereby allowing them to exploit oil reserves in Ogoniland in a manner that did not respect the rights of the Ogoni people and deprived these people of the material benefits from those natural resources.[32]

The African Commission in the *SERAC* Case cited the Inter-American Court of Human Rights' ('IACHR') case of *Velásquez Rodríguez v. Honduras*,[33] and the European Court of Human Rights' ('ECHR') case of *X & Y v. Netherlands*[34] in support of its finding that Nigeria had breached the duty to protect the Ogoni people from abuses committed by oil companies. It can therefore be said that the Commission has adopted the due diligence

standard developed by the IACHR (and implicitly adopted by the ECHR[35]), which posits that the State will be held responsible for human rights abuses committed by non-state actors if it is established that it failed to exercise 'due diligence' or to take 'reasonable' or 'serious' steps to prevent or react to violations of human rights committed in the private sphere.[36]

Apart from this case, the doctrine of State responsibility has hardly been invoked to hold non-state actors indirectly responsible for socio-economic rights.[37] As will be noted later, the African Commission is empowered to undertake studies and researches on African problems, formulate and lay down principles and rules relating to solving such problems, organise seminars, and disseminate information concerning human and peoples' rights. However, it has not used this mandate to promote adherence by non-state actors to human rights. In particular, out of the six special rapporteurs appointed by the African Commission, none of them has a mandate to consider the problem of non-state actors in Africa. The Guidelines for National Periodic Reports, which are quite detailed, concentrate on traditional communal obligations (which do not relate much to human rights) without asking States to report on measures taken to monitor, regulate and non-state actors to prevent human rights infringements or measures taken to react to those infringements. Furthermore, none of the many resolutions adopted by the Commission thus far relate directly to non-state actors.[38]

It can therefore be concluded that the African Charter departs from the traditional position that human rights bind states only by expressly

---

[30] Article 21(5).

[31] *SERAC* Case (n. 8 above), para. 56.

[32] Ibid. paras. 55 and 58.

[33] Inter-Am. Ct. H.R., *Velásquez Rodríguez Case*, Judgment of July 29, 1988 (Ser. C) No. 4.

[34] Application No. 8978/80, judgment dated 26 March 1985; 91 ECHR (1985) (Ser. A).

[35] See M. Scheinin, 'State responsibility, good governance and indivisible human rights' in H. Sano and G. Alfredsson (eds.), *Human rights and good governance: Building bridges* (The Hague: Martinus Nijhoff, 2002), pp. 29–45, at pp. 29, 35.

[36] See D.M. Chirwa, 'The doctrine of state responsibility as a potential means of holding private actors accountable for human rights', *Melbourne Journal of International Law* Vol. 5, No. 1 (2004), pp. 1–36, at pp. 1, 14–18.

[37] A limited number of cases have dealt with state responsibility for civil and political rights. See *Chad* Case (n. 11 above); *Amnesty International & Others v. Sudan* Communication 92/93 (2000) AHRLR pp. 296–312 (ACHPR 1995).

[38] The resolutions of the African Commission adopted up to 2001 are reprinted in C. Heyns (ed.), *Human rights law in Africa series*, Vol. 1 (Leiden: Martinus Nijhoff Publishers, 2004), pp. 506–611.

recognising that non-state actors also have human rights obligations. However, this framework has had little practical significance because the African Charter does not expressly recognise the right to bring communications against these actors and also because the available 'non-judicial' mechanisms for enforcing these obligations have not been used to ensure that these actors are held accountable for violations of human rights in general and socio-economic rights in particular.

4. GENERAL PROTECTION OF SOCIO-ECONOMIC RIGHTS IN THE AFRICAN CHARTER

The socio-economic rights expressly recognised in the African Charter include the right to property, the right to work, the right to health, and the right to education. The Commission has also implied a number of other rights, namely the rights to adequate housing and food. This part discusses the manner in which these rights are protected and the jurisprudence that has arisen from them thus far.

4.1 The Right to Property

Article 14 of the African Charter provides that '[t]he right to property shall be guaranteed'. While this right is one of the oldest rights to be recognised in comparative human rights law, its relevance in the African context has been questioned for reasons related to its alleged association with individual privileges and vested colonial and neo-colonial interests, controversies surrounding land reform and access to land for the majority of poor Africans in independent Africa, and gender insensitive traditional inheritance regimes concerning land.[39] The main concern seems to be the lack of detail regarding the principles that must govern land reform or redistribution. This concern is underscored by the 'claw-back clause' to Article 14, which provides that the right to property 'may only be encroached upon in the interest of public need or in the general interest of the community

and in accordance with the provisions of appropriate laws'. According to Chidi Odinkalu, this provision is arguably 'the most far-reaching claw-back clause in the Charter' and may permit the tramping of property rights without giving reasonable notice and compensation and respecting the right of appeal to a competent tribunal.[40]

However, the jurisprudence of the African Commission suggests that land reform policies and legislation may not be justifiable if they do not conform to international human rights standards. The Commission has interpreted claw-back clauses so restrictively that domestic laws limiting rights cannot be valid unless they are of general application,[41] proportionate, necessary and acceptable in a democratic society,[42] and do not undermine constitutional and international standards.[43] Thus, it was held in one case that the decrees passed by the Nigerian military government, which authorised the sealing of the premises of two magazines and the seizures of copies of these magazines amounted to a violation of the right to property.[44]

At a minimum, the right to property protects existing access to one's property. In the *Media Rights* Case, it was stated that the right to property includes 'a right to have access to property of one's own and the right not for one's property to be removed'.[45] It also includes the right of owners 'to have undisturbed possession, use and control of their property however they deem fit'.[46] Thus, it has been held that confiscation and looting of peoples' property and the expropriation or destruction of their land and houses amounts to

[39] J. Oloka-Onyango, 'Beyond the rhetoric: Reinvigorating the struggle for economic, social and cultural rights in Africa', *California Western International Law Journal*, Vol. 26 (1995), pp. 1–71, at pp. 1, 49–50.

[40] Odinkalu, 'Implementing economic, social and cultural rights' (n. 12 above), p. 191.

[41] *Constitutional Rights Project & Another v. Nigeria* Communication 102/93, (2000) AHRLR 191 (ACHPR 1995), paras 58–59 ('*Constitutional Rights* Case 1'); *Constitutional Rights Project & Others v. Nigeria* Communications 140/94, 141/94, 145/94, (2000) AHRLR 227 (ACHPR 1999), para 44 ('*Constitutional Rights* Case 2').

[42] *Amnesty International & Others v. Sudan* Communications 48/90, 50/91, 52/91, 83/93, (2002) AHRLR 297 (ACHPR 1999), paras 79–80; *Media Rights* Case (n. 11 above), paras. 68–9.

[43] *Amnesty International v. Zambia* Communication 212/98, (2000) AHRLR 325 (ACHPR 1999); *Constitutional Rights* Case 1 (n. 41 above), para. 58; *Constitutional Rights* Case 2 (n. 41 above), paras 40–41.

[44] *Media Rights* Case (n. 11 above), para. 77.

[45] Ibid.

[46] *Huri-Laws v. Nigeria* Communication 225/98, (2000) AHRLR 273 (ACHPR 2000), ('*Huri-Laws* Case') para. 52.

an infringement of the right to property.[47] Likewise, searching one's premises and seizing one's property without a warrant constitutes a violation of this right.[48]

The African Commission has also held that the State has a duty to take measures to protect the right to property. In the *Mauritanian* Case, where the complainants' property was looted and expropriated, it was held that Mauritania had the responsibility to ensure the freedom of its citizens, to carry out inquiries and initiate judicial action against perpetrators of human rights violations.[49]

4.2   The Right to Work

Article 15 of the African Charter provides that every individual has the 'right to work under equitable and satisfactory conditions' and to 'receive equal pay for equal work'. It is debatable whether this article obliges States to provide employment,[50] but the jurisprudence of the African Commission clearly establishes that it requires them not only to protect and respect this right but also to facilitate the realisation of this right. In *Pagnoulle (On behalf of Mazou) v. Cameroon*, the African Commission found the government of Cameroon to be in violation of the right to work by failing to reinstate a magistrate, who had been sentenced to a prison term by a military tribunal, after he was granted amnesty in accordance with the law.[51] The African Commission has stated that the right to work is necessary for ensuring an existence worthy of human dignity.[52] Thus, it has considered unremunerated work as constituting a violation of the right to respect for the dignity inherent in the human being and condemned slavery-like practices.[53] Furthermore, the initial Guidelines for National Periodic Reports 1989 produced by the African Commission require States to furnish

information regarding, among other things, laws, administrative regulations, collective agreements, court decisions and other measures aimed at both 'protecting' the right to work and 'promoting' and 'safeguarding' this right.[54] These Guidelines also require States to report on rights that may be regarded as flowing from the right to work, but are not expressly recognised by the African Charter. For example, they require States to report on the right to equal opportunity for promotion, the right to rest, leisure, limitation of working hours and holiday with pay, and trade union rights.[55] It can therefore be concluded that the African Commission views the right to work quite broadly as encompassing many other labour-related rights.

4.3   The Right to Health

Article 16(1) of the African Charter provides that every person has the right to 'enjoy the best attainable state of physical and mental health'. This provision assumes, and correctly so, that one's health is dependent on many factors including one's individual and socio-economic conditions.[56] Thus, it entitles an individual to the best state of health achievable taking into account such conditions.

The right to health as defined by the African Charter encompasses the protection of both the right to health care and the right to the underlying conditions of health.[57] The former is made more explicit in Article 16(2) of the Charter, which enjoins States parties to take necessary measures to 'ensure' that their people 'receive medical attention when they are sick'. In the *Purohit* Case, the African Commission held that the right to health includes 'the right

---

[47] *Mauritanian* Case (n. 9 above), para. 128.

[48] *Huri-Laws* Case (n. 46 above), paras. 52–3. This holding is significant considering that the African Charter does not expressly recognise the right to privacy.

[49] *Mauritanian* Case (n. 9 above), para. 134.

[50] U. Umozurike, *The African Charter on Human and Peoples' Rights* (The Hague: Martinus Nijhoff Publishers, 1997), p. 46.

[51] Communication 39/90, (2000) AHRLR 57 (ACHPR 1997), para. 29.

[52] *Mauritanian* Case (n. 9 above), para 135.

[53] Ibid.

[54] Para II.3–10. The Guidelines are reprinted in Heyns, *Human rights law in Africa series* (n. 38 above), pp. 507–24. New and very brief Guidelines, also reprinted in Heyns, *Human rights law in Africa series*, pp. 569–670, were adopted in 1998, but it is not clear whether they supersede the initial Guidelines.

[55] Initial Guidelines for National Periodic Reports 1989, paras II.8–10.

[56] D. M. Chirwa, 'The right to health in international law: Its implications for the obligations of state and non-state actors in ensuring access to essential medicine', *South African Journal on Human Rights*, Vol. 19, No. 4 (2003), pp. 541–566, at pp. 541, 546–7.

[57] Article 12 of the ICESCR has been interpreted similarly, see Committee on Economic, Social and Cultural Rights, General Comment No. 14, The right to the highest attainable standard of health (Twenty-second session, 2000), U.N. Doc. E/C.12/2000/4 (2000), para. 4.

to health facilities, access to goods and services to be guaranteed to all without discrimination of any kind'.[58] The view that Article 16 of the Charter also protects the underlying preconditions of health was affirmed in the *Zaire* Case, where the African Commission held that failure of the government of Zaire to provide basic services such as drinking water and electricity and the shortage of medicine amounted to an infringement of the right to health.[59] Similarly, in the *Mauritanian* Case, the African Commission found Mauritania to be in violation of this right by failing to provide sufficient food, adequate hygiene and blankets to prisoners.[60]

In both the *Mauritanian* Case and the *Zaire* Case, the Commission found violations of positive obligations to fulfil the right to health. However, it did not elaborate a standard for determining when the State can be said to be in violation of such obligations, presumably because the allegations were not disputed by the States concerned. Nevertheless, the African Commission has stated that the responsibility of the State in relation to the right to health is 'heightened' in cases where the individual is incarcerated.[61] It has thus held, on a number of occasions, that denying a detainee whose health is deteriorating or threatened, access to doctors or medical attention, constitutes an infringement of this right.[62] In the *Purohit* Case discussed earlier, the African Commission found The Gambian government liable for violating, among other things, the right to health for failing to amend the Lunatic Detention Act, which did not make adequate provision for therapeutic objectives and resources and programmes for the treatment of persons with mental disabilities.[63]

4.4   The Right to Education

Article 17(1) of the African Charter provides that: 'Every individual shall have the right to education'.

This article also recognises the right of individuals to take part in the cultural life of their community and obligates States parties to promote and protect morals and traditional values. Unlike Article 13 of the ICESCR, the African Charter defines the right to education so briefly that it is not clear what it actually entails. For example, it is not clear whether it obliges States to introduce compulsory and free primary education. It also does not specify what the objectives and goals of education should be in the African context.

However, the initial Guidelines National Periodic Reports 1989 suggest that this right is open to a broad interpretation. They require States to report on measures taken to, among other things, realise the right to receive compulsory and free primary education, make secondary and vocational education available, make higher education accessible to everyone, and encourage and intensify adult literacy programmes.[64] The African Commission has underlined that education should be geared to the needs of specific groups such as women, children, refugees, internally displaced persons, victims of armed conflicts and other disadvantaged groups.[65] It has also asked States parties to include the study of human and peoples' rights in the curriculum at all levels of public and private education.[66]

In the *Zaire* Case, the African Commission suggested that failure to provide access to existing institutions of learning would amount to a violation of the right to education. Zaire was found to have infringed this right because it had closed universities and secondary schools in the country for two years.[67]

4.5   Implied Rights to Housing and Food

While the African Charter deserves merit for entrenching the notion of the indivisibility of all human rights, it has been rightly criticised for not expressly recognising some of the key socio-economic rights such as the rights to social

---

[58] Para. 80.
[59] Para. 47.
[60] See para. 122.
[61] *Media Rights* Case (n. 11 above), para 91; *International Pen & Others (on behalf of Saro-Wiwa) v. Nigeria* Communications 137/94, 139/94, 154/96 & 161/97, (2000) AHRLR 212 (ACHPR 1998) ('*Saro Wiwa* Case'), para. 112; *Huri-Laws* Case (n. 46 above), para. 41.
[62] Ibid.
[63] See paras. 79–85.

[64] See paras. II.46–57.
[65] Resolution on Human and Peoples' Right Education (14th Session, 1–10 December 1993), para. 1, reprinted in Heyns, *Human rights law in Africa* (n. 38 above), pp. 531–532.
[66] Ibid. para. 3.
[67] Paras. 4 and 48.

security, adequate housing, adequate standard of living, adequate food, and social security.[68] The African Commission has responded to this criticism in a very intriguing way. In the *SERAC* Case, whose facts have already been discussed above, it found Nigeria to be in violation of the rights to housing and food although these rights are not expressly recognised in the Charter. According to the African Commission, the right to housing is implicitly entrenched in the rights to property, family protection, and to enjoy the best attainable state of mental and physical health.[69] The African Commission held similarly that the right to food is implicitly recognised by a combined reading of the provisions guaranteeing the rights to life, enjoy the best attainable state of physical and mental health, and economic, social and cultural development.[70]

Having held so, the African Commission stated, echoing CESCR's General Comment on the Right to Adequate Housing,[71] that the right to shelter goes further than the protection and provision of a roof over one's head.[72] This right, it was held, also protects 'the right to be left alone and to live in peace – whether under a roof or not', and the right not to be evicted.[73] With respect to the right to food, the African Commission stated that this right is closely linked to the dignity of human beings and therefore essential to the enjoyment of other rights.[74] It requires States to protect and improve existing food sources and food production, and to ensure access to adequate food.[75] The right also requires States not to, and not allow third parties to, destroy or contaminate food sources let alone prevent peoples' efforts to feed themselves.[76] The African Commission found that Nigeria had violated the right to housing by destroying houses, homes and villages of the Ogoni people and by harassing and obstructing those who attempted to rebuild their homes. It also held that Nigeria had violated the right to food by destroying and allow-

ing oil companies to destroy food sources, and obstructing the Ogoni people from feeding themselves.

This is a landmark decision not only because it dealt with a range of socio-economic rights issues in greater detail than any of the African Commission's previous decisions on these rights but also because it set the precedent that some rights, which are not expressly recognised in the African Charter, could be said to be implicitly recognised by a combined reading of some expressly recognised rights. Considering that Article 60 of the African Charter allows the African Commission to draw inspiration from international human rights law when interpreting the provisions of the African Charter and that Article 7 of the African Court Protocol also allows the African Court to apply the African Charter and 'any other relevant human rights instrument ratified by the States concerned', it is possible to enforce any socio-economic right that is not expressly recognised by the African Charter.[77]

5. SOCIO-ECONOMIC RIGHTS OF VULNERABLE GROUPS

Apart from protecting rights that can generally be claimed by anyone, the African Charter recognises specific rights of certain vulnerable groups such as women, children, the aged and the disabled. Article 18(3) of the African Charter enjoins States to 'ensure the elimination of every discrimination against women and also ensure the protection of the rights of the woman and the child as stipulated in international declarations and conventions'. This article can be construed to mean that States are bound to implement socio-economic rights of women and children recognised in international covenants and declarations adopted both before and after the adoption of the Charter. Thus, States parties to the Charter can be said to be bound by the socio-economic provisions contained in the 1979 UN Convention on the Elimination of All Forms of Discrimination against

---

[68] Oloka-Onyango, 'Beyond the rhetoric' (n. 39 above), p. 51.
[69] Para. 60.
[70] Para. 64.
[71] See Committee on Economic, Social and Cultural Rights, General Comment No. 4, The right to adequate housing (Sixth session, 1991), U.N. Doc. E/1992/23, annex III at 114 (1991), para. 8(b).
[72] *SERAC* Case (n. 8 above), paras. 61 & 63.
[73] Ibid.
[74] Ibid. para. 65.
[75] Ibid.
[76] Ibid.

[77] See also the comments by Professor Victor Dankwa in M. Langford, *Litigating economic, social and cultural rights: Achievements, challenges and strategies* (Geneva: COHRE, 2003), p. 119, arguing that 'There is hardly a right at the international level that cannot be subject to protection in the African system'.

Women ('CEDAW')[78] as well as the 1989 UN Convention on the Rights of the Child ('CRC').[79]

However, the African Charter has been criticised for failing to provide adequate protection of women's and children's rights mainly because the provision protecting these rights is located in Article 18, which also guarantees the right to family protection.[80] This context, it has been argued, 'reinforces outdated stereotypes about the proper place and role of women in society'[81] considering that '[t]he family unit remains the most oppressive of rights of women (and girl children) in African societies'.[82]

The Women's Protocol was adopted on 10 July 2003 by the African Heads of State and Government partly in response to this concern and partly to place CEDAW in the African context.[83] The key principle underlying the Women's Protocol is that women must be treated equally in the enjoyment of all rights. In addition, the Protocol also requires States parties to take specific positive action to realise women's rights.[84] For example, it obligates States to guarantee without discrimination, and adopt appropriate (special) measures for the enjoyment by women, the right to education and training, the right to equal opportunities in work and career advancement and other economic opportunities, the right to health including sexual and reproductive health, the right to food security, the right to adequate housing, the right to a positive cultural context, and the right to inheritance.[85] Most of these rights are not expressly recognised in the African Charter.

The Women's Protocol also recognises the rights of more vulnerable women. For example, it not only requires States to give special attention to women in rural areas but it also recognises the rights of widows,[86] who are often subjected to demeaning conduct based on some traditional practices regarding inheritance and funeral rites.[87] It also requires states to take special measures to protect the rights of elderly women, women with disabilities and women in distress.[88]

It must be noted that all rights in the Women's Protocol are subject to the same monitoring and implementation mechanisms available under the African Charter.[89] The socio-economic rights provisions in the Women's Protocol are therefore justiciable before the African Commission and the African Court on Human and Peoples' Rights.

The African Children's Charter, by contrast, was adopted barely a year after the adoption of the CRC, primarily as a rearguard action in response to the CRC, which, although it was ratified almost universally, allegedly did not adequately take into account the circumstances of the African child.[90] It prohibits all forms of exploitation of children and requires States to take measures to protect children from harmful work, ensure that refugee children receive humanitarian assistance, and provide material assistance to children living under regimes practising apartheid or in States subject

---

[78] E.g., the CEDAW enjoins states parties to take all appropriate measures to eliminate discrimination against women in order to ensure to them equal rights with men in the fields of education, employment, health care and other areas of economic and social life. See articles 10–13.

[79] E.g., the CRC recognises the rights of a child to enjoy the best attainable standard of health, to benefit from social security including social insurance, to an adequate standard of living, to education, to rest and leisure, and to protection from economic exploitation. See articles 23–32.

[80] E. Delport, 'The African regional system of human rights – Why a Protocol on the Rights of Women?', unpublished paper on file with author.

[81] C. Heyns, 'The African regional human rights system: The African Charter', *Pennsylvania State Law Review*, Vol. 108 (2004), pp. 679, 687.

[82] H. Onoria, 'Introduction to the African system of protection of human rights and the Draft Protocol', in W. Benedek, E.M. Kisaakye & G. Oberleitner (eds.), *Human rights of women: International instruments and African experiences* (New York: Zed Books, 2002), pp. 321, 233–4.

[83] See D. M. Chirwa, 'Reclaiming (Wo) Manity: The merits and limits of the African Protocol on Women's Rights', *Netherlands International Law Review*, Vol. LIII, (2006), pp. 63, 68–71; F. Banda, 'Blazing a trail the African Protocol on Women's Rights', *Journal of African Law*, Vol. 50 (2006), pp. 72–84. M. S. Nsibirwa, 'A brief analysis of the Draft Protocol to the African Charter on Human and Peoples' Rights on the Rights of Women', *Human Rights Law Journal*, Vol. 1, No. 1 (2001), pp. 40, 41–2.

[84] See e.g. Article 12(2) recognising the right to education.

[85] See Articles 12–18 & 21. Moreover, the Protocol recognises such other rights as the right to peace, the right to a healthy and sustainable development, and the right to development. See articles 10, 18 and 19.

[86] Article 20.

[87] See e.g. A. K. Wing & T. M. Smith, 'The African Union and women's rights', *Transnational Law and Contemporary Problems*, Vol. 13 (2003), pp. 32–82, at 33, 38–41.

[88] Articles 22–24.

[89] Articles 26–27 of the Protocol.

[90] See F. Viljoen, 'The African Charter on the Rights and Welfare of the Child', in C.J. Davel (ed.), *Introduction to child law in South Africa* (Lansdown: Juta Law, 2000), pp. 214–231 at 214, 218–219.

to military destabilisation.[91] These provisions are obviously significant in the African context where socio-economic hardships affecting children are often caused or exacerbated by armed conflicts, famine and natural disasters.[92] Apart from these, the key socio-economic rights the African Children's Charter recognises – the rights to education, health and family protection – are already entrenched in the African Charter. Perhaps the main contribution of the African Children's Charter to the protection of children's rights lies in the fact that it is more detailed than the African Charter in its definition of socio-economic rights such that it is much easier to pinpoint the obligations engendered by these rights than is the case with those in the African Charter.[93]

The Children's Charter, unlike the Women's Protocol, creates its own monitoring and enforcement mechanisms separate from those created by the African Charter. It entrusts the functions of promotion and protection of the children's rights to the Committee of Experts on the Rights and Welfare of the Child ('African Committee on Children's Rights'). The latter has the power to examine State reports, to receive individual and interstate communications and to conduct investigations.[94] The first African Committee on Children's Rights was inaugurated in April 2002 and is now in its early stages of operation.[95]

Article 18(4) of the African Charter also guarantees the right of the aged and disabled to 'special measures of protection in keeping with their physical or moral needs'. In the *Purohit* Case, the African Commission held that: '[P]ersons with mental illness should never be denied their right to proper

health care'.[96] It stated that because of their disability, mental patients 'should be accorded special treatment which would enable them not only attain but also sustain their optimum level of independence and performance'.[97] This holding suggests that a State shoulders a high burden to demonstrate that the failure to meet the socio-economic rights of mental patients was due to the lack of resources.

The upshot of this discussion is that the socio-economic rights of various vulnerable groups such as women, children, the aged, the disabled, and refugee children are well protected in the African regional system through the parent instrument – the African Charter – and other instruments such as the Women's Protocol and the African Children's Charter.

6. ENFORCEMENT MECHANISMS AND EFFECTIVENESS OF THE SYSTEM

6.1 The African Commission

The African Commission was officially inaugurated on 2 November 1987. It has dual powers to protect and promote human and peoples' rights.[98] The protective mandate comprises receiving and deciding communications from States,[99] individuals and non-governmental organisations ('NGOs').[100] A communication has to meet admissibility criteria before it can be considered.[101] Thus far, only one communication has been commenced by a State.[102] The rest have been brought by individuals and NGOs. The promotional mandate includes examining State reports. States parties are required to submit reports every two years.[103] NGOs are also allowed to submit

---

[91] Articles 15, 23 and 26.

[92] See D. M. Chirwa, 'The merits and demerits of the African Charter on the Rights and Welfare of the Child', *International Journal of Children's Rights*, Vol. 10 (2002), pp. 157–177, at 157, 168.

[93] E.g., the Children's Charter (Article 11) defines the right to education as encompassing free and compulsory primary education and requires States to, among other things, encourage the development of secondary schools and make higher education accessible to all.

[94] See Articles 43–45 of the African Children's Charter.

[95] See generally A. Lloyd, 'Regional developments on the rights and welfare of children in Africa: A general report on the African Charter on the Rights and Welfare of the Child and the African Committee of Experts', available at <http://www.uwe.ac.uk/law/research/acr/report.htm> (last visited: 20 March 2005).

[96] Para. 85.

[97] Ibid. para. 81.

[98] Article 45 of the African Charter.

[99] Article 47 of the African Charter.

[100] Though not expressly stated, the Commission's power to receive individual communications can be regarded as flowing from Article 55 of the Charter.

[101] For example, Article 56 of the African Charter stipulates that communications shall only be considered if they are sent after exhausting local remedies, are compatible with the African Charter, are submitted within reasonable time, and are not written in disparaging language.

[102] Heyns, '*African human rights system*' (n. 81 above), p. 693.

[103] Article 62 of the African Charter.

shadow or alternative reports.[104] As part of its promotional mandate, the African Commission has appointed six special rapporteurs to investigate human rights issues on specific themes, a move which has been described as 'innovative' because the African Charter does not make specific provision for them.[105] The Special Rapporteur on Extra-Judicial, Summary or Arbitrary Executions was the first to be appointed in 1994. The Special Rapporteur on the Rights of Women in Africa and the Special Rapporteur on Prisons and Conditions of Detention in Africa were appointed in 1999. The Special Rapporteurs on Freedom of Expression in Africa; Refugees, Asylum Seekers and Internally Displaced Persons in Africa; and Human Rights Defenders in Africa were appointed in 2004. The African Commission also adopts resolutions on human rights issues from time to time.

While the African Commission deserves credit for the work it has done in interpreting the African Charter progressively and in a manner that reinforces the indivisibility of all rights, it is probably the least effective of the three regional human rights systems in practice.[106] During the first ten years of its existence, the African Commission adhered to Article 59 of the African Charter, which articulates the principle of confidentiality regarding measures taken by it in enforcing the provisions of the African Charter.[107] This principle weakened the effectiveness of the African Commission considerably as there was no publicity about the decisions and measures taken by it.[108]

Fortunately, the African Commission decided to depart from the principle of confidentiality in 1994. Its decisions, activity reports, resolutions and other documents have since been open to the public. Many commentators have observed that the Commission's performance has improved remarkably since it became more transparent and open to the public.[109]

Another important factor that has affected the effectiveness of the African Commission relates to the powers of the Commission. The African Charter does not empower the African Commission to grant remedies to redress the violations nor to enforce its orders. The African Commission is required, after considering all the relevant information concerning the communication, to simply prepare a report stating the facts and its findings and send it to the State concerned and the Assembly of Heads of State.[110] In this report may be included such recommendations as the African Commission deems fit.[111] Decisions of the African Commission are therefore not enforceable.[112] This has prompted Nsongurua Udombana to remark that the African Commission is a 'toothless bulldog' – it can bark but not bite.[113]

The fact that the African Commission does not have enforcement powers has not been helped by the lack of political will on the part of African states to implement Charter rights. States found liable under the African Charter do not always abide by the findings of the African Commission or implement its recommendations.[114] In 1998, the African Commission itself expressed this concern, noting that 'the non-compliance by some States Parties with the Commission's recommendations affects its credibility'.[115] This situation has not improved. For example, although the African Commission in

[104] M. Evans, T. Ige and R. Murray, 'The reporting mechanism of the African Charter on Human and Peoples' Rights' in Evans and Murray (eds.), *The African Charter on Human and Peoples' Rights* (n. 12 above), pp. 36–61 at 36, 57.

[105] J. Hurrington, 'Special Rapporteurs of the African Commission on Human and Peoples' Rights', *African Human Rights Law Journal*, Vol. 1, No. 2 (2001), p. 247.

[106] According to Cees Flinterman and Catherine Henderson, 'The African Charter falls short of truly effective human rights protection'. See C. Flinterman and C. Henderson, 'The African Charter on Human and Peoples' Rights' in R. Hanski and M. Suski (eds.), *An Introduction to the International Protection of Human Rights: A textbook*, 2nd revised edition (Turku: Institute for Human Rights, 1999), pp. 387–396 at 387, 395.

[107] This Article [59(1)] provides that 'All measures taken within the provisions of the Present Charter shall remain confidential until such a time as the Assembly of Heads and Government otherwise decide'.

[108] F. Viljoen, 'Introduction to the African Commission and the regional human rights system', in C. Heyns (ed.), *Human rights law in Africa series*, Vol. 1 (Leiden: Martinus Nijhoff Publishers, 2004), 214–231 at 385, 429–30.

[109] Ibid.

[110] See Article 52 of the African Charter.

[111] See Article 53 of the African Charter.

[112] See also comments by Professor Victor Dankwa, a Member and former Chairperson of the African Commission, quoted in Langford, 'Litigating economic, social and cultural rights' (n. 77 above), p. 121.

[113] N.J. Udombana, 'Towards the African Court on Human and Peoples' Rights: Better late than never', *Yale Human Right & Development Law Journal*, Vol. 3 (2000), pp. 47–11, at pp. 45, 64.

[114] Ibid. pp. 67–9.

[115] See Eleventh Annual Activity Report of the African Commission on Human and Peoples' Rights 1997–1998, 22nd–23rd Ordinary Session, OAU Doc. DOC/OS/43 (XXIII), para. 38, available at <http://www.achpr.org/english/˷

the *SERAC* Case, decided in October 2001, recommended a range of actions to be taken by the Nigerian government to redress the human rights violations in Ogoniland, these recommendations have not yet been implemented by the State concerned.[116]

The lack of respect for the African Commission's orders has sometimes led to irreversible consequences. Two instances amply illustrate this problem. They both concerned interim injunctive orders issued by the African Commission. The first concerned the planned execution of Ken Saro Wiwa and eight others, who had been involved in activism around the exploration of oil reserves in Ogoniland. The Commission faxed a *note verbale* to Nigerian authorities indicating that it had received a communication challenging the convictions of these activists and asking that the executions be delayed until the Commission discusses the case with the Nigerian authorities.[117] Similar action was taken by the African Commission in relation to the planned executions of twenty-two Rwandees who had been found guilty of various offences related to the 1994 genocide in Rwanda.[118] In both instances, the respective governments disregarded the African Commission's injunctive orders and proceeded with the executions. Later, the Commission found that the convictions of Saro Wiwa and others contravened a range of rights in the African Charter.[119]

Like the communications procedure, the State reporting mechanism has not worked as well as it should, mainly because the level of state compliance with their reporting obligations is generally very low.[120] Furthermore, the African Com-

mission has not developed a consistent policy of making comprehensive concluding observations to States. As a result, it is not possible to follow up on progress made by States since the last report.[121]

The lack of financial support to the African Commission from States has added to the above problems.[122] Consequently, the Commission holds a maximum of two, two-week long sessions per year only, and it cannot carry out its mandate effectively.

However, it must be noted that recent developments that have taken place on the continent herald better prospects for the protection of human rights, including socio-economic rights, in Africa. As noted above, the African Commission has handed down a few important decisions, especially the *SERAC* Case and the *Purohit* Case, interpreting a range of socio-economic rights provisions in the African Charter innovatively and establishing that these rights are justiciable and enforceable at an international level. While the adoption of the African Children's Charter and the Women's Protocol, as shown above, strengthens the normative framework for the protection of socio-economic rights, the adoption of the African Court's Protocol and the establishment of the African Court of Human and Peoples' Rights can, as will be shown below, also be regarded as a positive sign that African States are beginning to take these rights seriously. These developments must also be considered in the light of Constitutive Act of the African Union, adopted in 2001, which created the African Union and replaced the OAU in 2002. This Act considers the protection of human rights in Africa as a central objective of the African Union.[123]

---

doc_target/documentation.html?../activity_reports/ activity11_en.pdf > (last visited 10 June 2005).

[116] See also comments by Felix Morka, the Director of SERAC, one of the two NGOs that brought the SERAC Case before the African Commission, as quoted in Langford, *Litigating economic, social and cultural rights* (n. 77 above), p. 122.

[117] See the facts in the *Saro Wiwa* Case (n. 61 above).

[118] Udombana, *Towards the African Court on Human and Peoples' Rights* (n. 113 above), p. 69.

[119] See the *Saro Wiwa* Case (n. 61 above).

[120] As of March 2008 fifteen States had not submitted their initial reports to the Commission and most of those that had done so had overdue reports. See 'Status on submission of state initial/periodical reports to the African Commission' available at <http://www.achpr.org/ english/_info/state_report_considered_en.html> (accessed 31 July 2008). See also M. Evans, T. Tokumbo and R. Murray, 'The reporting mechanism of the African

Charter on Human and Peoples' Rights', in Evans and Murray, 'The African Charter on Human and Peoples' Rights' (n. 12 above), pp. 36, 41; G.W. Mugwanya, 'Examination of state reports by the African Commission: A critical appraisal', *African Human Rights Law Journal*, Vol. 1, No. 2 (2001), pp. 264–284, at 268, 277.

[121] Viljoen, 'Introduction to the African Commission' (n. 108 above), pp. 475–476.

[122] Udombana, '*Towards the African Court on Human and Peoples' Rights*' (n. 113 above), p. 71.

[123] See articles 3–4. By contrast, the OAU Charter did not make express commitments to the protection of human rights as a key objective of the OAU. See also V. O. Nmehielle, 'The African Union and African renaissance: A new era for Human Rights protection in Africa?', *Singapore Journal of International and Comparative Law*, Vol. 7

6.2 The African Court on Human and Peoples' Rights

The African Court's Protocol was adopted in 1998 and came into force on 25 January 2004 after the fifteenth instrument of ratification was submitted. The Protocol vests the protective mandate of the African Commission in the African Court.[124] This provision can be construed to mean that the African Commission will continue to carry out the promotional mandate. While many have questioned the wisdom of retaining the African Commission given the limited amount of resources that African States place at the disposal of these institutions,[125] the African Court's Protocol seeks to cure the limitations of the African Charter in two principal ways.[126] Firstly, the Protocol empowers the Court to grant remedies where it finds a violation, including payment of fair compensation or reparation.[127] The Court may also take provisional measures in cases of extreme gravity or urgency.[128] Secondly, the Protocol provides that the execution of the orders of the Court shall be monitored by the Council of Ministers.[129] As noted above, the African Charter did not grant these powers to the African Commission, which undermined the effective operation of the human rights system under the African Charter. The recognition of

remedial and enforcement powers presents better prospects for the protection of socio-economic rights, in particular because court orders to ensure that violations of these rights are being redressed sometimes require positive action by the State and supervision of their implementation by an independent organ.[130] For example, in the *Purohit* Case, the African Commission recommended that the Gambian government should repeal the Lunatic and Detention Act, create an expert body to review all persons detained under this Act and make recommendations for their release or treatment, and provide medical and material care for persons suffering from mental health problems in the territory of The Gambia. In order to ensure that such an order is fully implemented, there is need for an independent body to monitor or supervise its implementation.

Eleven judges of the Court were sworn in on 2 July 2006 in Banjul in The Gambia in order to bring the Court into full operation. It must also be noted that in July 2004, the African Union took a decision to integrate the African Court on Human and Peoples' Rights and the African Court of Justice created by the African Union into one Court.[131] Although it is not yet clear what the composite court will look like, this appears to be the right decision as it is not feasible for African states to sustain the two Courts, the African Commission, the African Committee on Children's Rights, and other intergovernmental institutions established under the African Union.[132]

---

7. CONCLUSION

This chapter has demonstrated that the normative framework for the protection of socio-economic rights in the African regional system is very strong. The African Charter expressly proclaims the principle of the indivisibility of all rights by recognising a range of socio-economic rights and third-generation rights side by side with civil and

---

(2003), pp. 412–446, at 412; E. Baimu, 'The African Union: Hope for better protection of human rights in Africa', *African Human Rights Law Journal*, Vol. 1, No. 2 (2001), pp. 299–314, at 299.

[124] Article 2 of the African Court's Protocol.

[125] See, e.g., A. O'Shea, 'A critical reflection on the proposed African Court on Human and Peoples' Rights', *African Human Rights Law Journal*, Vol. 1, No. 2 (2001), pp. 285–298, at 285.

[126] On the relationship between the Court and the Commission see Udombana, '*Towards the African Court on Human and Peoples' Rights*' (n. 113 above), p. 5; J. Harrington, 'The African Court on Human and Peoples Rights', in Evans and Murray (eds.), *The African Charter on Human and Peoples' Rights* (n. 12 above), p. 305. However, one of the concerns about the Protocol is that it does not allow individuals or NGOs to approach the Court directly. According to article 5, it is only the African Commission, States and intergovernmental bodies that can bring cases before the Court. Individuals or NGOs may bring cases before the Court where a State makes a declaration accepting the competence of the Court to determine cases instituted directly by NGOs and individuals or via the Commission: Article 53 of the African Charter as read with article 34(6) of the Africa Court Protocol.

[127] Article 27 of the Protocol.

[128] Ibid.

[129] See Article 29 of the Protocol.

[130] See W. Trengove, 'Judicial remedies for violations of socio-economic rights', *ESR Review*, Vol. 1, No. 4 (1999), pp. 8–11, at 8.

[131] AU Doc Assembly/AU/Dec.45 (III), taken at the Third Ordinary Session of the Assembly of the African Union.

[132] See e.g., N.J. Udombana, 'An African Human Rights Court and an African Unions Court: A needful duality or needless duplication', *Brooklyn Journal of International Law*, Vol. 28 (2003), pp. 811–870, at 811.

political rights. The African Commission has upheld this principle in practice when determining communications. In addition, it has interpreted socio-economic rights provisions in the Charter generously to cure some of the deficiencies in the African Charter. This normative framework has been strengthened substantially by the two specialised instruments, the Women's Protocol and the African Children's Charter. The African Charter also recognises that non-state actors have human rights obligations.

Perhaps one area where the African Commission's jurisprudence could be improved relates to the nature of the positive obligations implicit in socio-economic rights. While the Commission has stated quite clearly that states have the duties to respect, protect, promote and fulfil all rights in the African Charter, it has not made it quite clear whether States have to implement positive obligations in relation to socio-economic rights immediately or progressively. Considering that African States face acute resource constraints, it is submitted that the notions of progressive realisation and available resources ought to be implied in the socio-economic provisions of the Africa Charter as internal limitations to these rights. However, bearing in mind the fact that poverty is widespread on the continent, it is vitally important that States are obligated to prioritise the realisation of minimum essential levels of socio-economic rights.

This chapter has also shown that the strength of the African Charter at the normative level has not been matched by its enforcement mechanisms. The African Charter requires the African Commission to operate in a confidential manner. It also does not entrust the African Commission with the power to grant remedies for violations of human rights or to monitor the execution of its decisions. States have also given lukewarm financial and political support to the African Commission. These factors have combined over the years to hamper the effectiveness of the Commission.

However, the African Commission no longer adheres to the confidentiality principle. Furthermore, the protective mandate of the African Commission is going to be improved considerably by the Court on Human and Peoples' Rights. The establishment of the African Union also seems to have revived the commitment by African states to respecting human rights. These developments herald better prospects for the protection of human rights generally and economic, social and cultural rights in particular on the continent.

Notwithstanding these positive developments, the adoption of norms and creation of monitoring institutions will not be enough to ensure that people exercise their socio-economic rights. The ultimate obligation to implement these rights rests with States.

18

The Inter-American Commission on Human Rights

Defending Social Rights Through Case-Based Petitions

Tara J. Melish*

1. INTRODUCTION AND BACKGROUND

The Inter-American Commission on Human Rights ('Commission') is the 'engine' of the inter-American human rights system. It is the first responder and, in most cases, final arbiter of the thousands of human rights complaints brought to the system's attention each year. Created in 1959, the Commission is an autonomous organ of the Organization of American States ('OAS'), mandated 'to promote the observance and defense of human rights' in all OAS Member States. It has been headquartered in Washington, D.C., since 1960, where it meets in ordinary and special sessions several times a year. A 'principal organ' of the OAS since 1970, the Commission has both contentious and promotional functions,[1] which, in contrast to the more limited jurisdiction of its sister organ, the Inter-American Court of Human Rights (see following Chapter in this volume), it is competent to exercise over all thirty-five OAS Member States.[2]

The Commission is composed of seven members of 'high moral character and recognised compe-

tence in the field of human rights', who serve in a personal capacity, on a part-time basis, for terms of four years and who may be re-elected once.[3] They are supported by a full-time Secretariat,[4] responsible for the receipt and processing of all petitions, correspondence and communications, as well as the preparation of draft reports, resolutions, studies and any other work entrusted to it by the Commission.[5]

The Commission's extensive case-based jurisprudence, as developed under its rule-bound contentious jurisdiction, is the subject of this chapter. Nevertheless, it is important to highlight at the outset the extensive *promotional* functions the Commission enjoys. These functions, broad and flexible in scope, allow the Commission to extend its cognisance beyond the individualised concrete 'cases' or 'disputes' that typify its more limited contentious jurisdiction, to address directly the

---

* Tara J. Melish is a human rights attorney and legal specialist in the field of comparative systems of social rights protections. J.D., Yale Law School; B.A., Brown University. The jurisprudence in this article is updated as to November 2006. The author thanks the John D. and Catherine T. MacArthur Foundation for a research and writing grant that made this work possible. All views expressed herein are those of the author alone.

[1] These functions are laid out in Articles 41 and 42 of the American Convention on Human Rights, as well as in the Commission's Statute and Rules of Procedure.

[2] Although the government of Cuba was excluded from participation in the OAS in 1962, the State of Cuba remains a de jure member of the regional body and continues to be subject to the supervisory jurisdiction of the Commission.

[3] American Convention on Human Rights, art. 62.3, Nov. 22, 1969, 1144 U.N.T.S. 123, O.A.S.T.S. No. 36, at 1, OEA/Ser.L/V/II.23 doc. rev. 2, entered into force July 18, 1978, arts. 34, 36, and 37. They are elected by secret ballot and majority vote by the OAS General Assembly from a list of candidates proposed by the Member States. None of the seven elected Commissioners may be nationals of the same state. Ibid. arts. 36 and 37.2.

[4] The Secretariat is composed of an Executive Secretary, Assistant Executive Secretary, staff attorneys, specialists, administrative staff, fellows and interns. The Executive Secretary, who must be a person of high moral character and recognised competence in the field of human rights, is appointed by the Secretary General of the OAS in consultation with the Commission.

[5] All final decisions on such matters are taken by majority vote of the seven elected Commissioners or, in urgent situations when not in session, by the Commission's President or Vice-President. See Rules of Procedure of the Inter-American Commission on Human Rights, art. 25.2, approved during Commission's 109th extraordinary period of sessions, Dec. 4–8, 2000, entered into force May 1, 2001 ['Commission Rules of Procedure'].

more generalised or structural manifestations of human rights abuse. Effective use of the inter-American system requires a clear appreciation of the distinctiveness of these dual competences and the types of abuses most appropriately dealt with under each. The generalised claims or issues not appropriate for case-based adjudication, as that term is understood by the inter-American organs, can always be brought to the Commission's attention instead under its broader, more flexible promotional mandate.

This promotional mandate includes the authority to hold general or thematic hearings, undertake onsite visits, publish special country and thematic reports, issue guidelines and general recommendations, request information on the measures States have taken to progressively realise rights, review States' periodic reports on the progress they have made in achieving the full enjoyment of human rights, and provide advisory services at the request of OAS Member States, among others.[6] Through these mechanisms, the Commission may address the larger structural, contextual or historic dimensionality of human rights abuse that would not necessarily be cognisable, on its own, through the individual petitions process.

Social rights advocates may, for example, use this competence to request general or thematic hearings before the Commission on topics of concern that affect the observance of economic, social and cultural rights in the region. Such hearings take place semi-annually during the period of every regular three-week session set aside for general and case-based hearings.[7] Over the last several years, social rights advocates have presented general hearings on such issues as justiciability standards for social rights claims, the right to adequate housing in the United States, Canada and Brazil, land reform in Mexico, the right to food in various countries of the region, labour rights in the southern cone, human trafficking and the slave trade, the condition of migrant labourers, indigenous land rights, the situation of HIV/AIDS and budgets in the region, contamination of human settlements from regional garbage dumps, the effects of extractive industries on indigenous peoples, and the human rights impacts of free trade agreements, among many others.

Especially when used in conjunction with discrete litigation initiatives involving narrower, concretised examples of the larger abuses discussed thematically in hearings, the 'general hearings' tool is of key importance for economic, social, and cultural rights advocacy. It allows advocates to raise regional awareness about issues of grave concern, stimulating media interest and organising constituencies on the ground. It also serves as an opportunity to interact directly with the members and staff of the Commission in an effort to raise their awareness about, and sensitivity to, concrete violations of economic, social, and cultural rights in the region. This, in turn, may help lay the groundwork for litigation in the social rights field, highlighting to the Commissioners the importance and gravity of the issues at stake. It may also be used to complement ongoing litigation that tackles a discrete, justiciable aspect of the broader, more structural problem addressed in the thematic hearing. In this way, the promotional and adjudicatory functions of the Commission, though jurisdictionally distinct, are dynamically linked and should be used in concurrent and complimentary fashion by advocates in support of efforts to protect economic, social, and cultural rights on the ground, where it counts, in local and national communities.

Social rights advocates may also formally request that Commissioners and Commission staff undertake onsite visits to areas where economic, social and cultural rights abuse has occurred or is occurring.[8] Such visits allow Commissioners to speak directly with victims, appreciate first-hand the actual conditions in which people live and in which violations unfold, and thereby be in a better position to resolve concrete cases involving economic, social, and cultural rights. The Commission often follows up on these visits by issuing press releases covering the nature and findings of their visits or, sometimes, by issuing a special country or thematic report that highlights the key

[6] See, e.g., American Convention (n. 3 above), art. 41.
[7] For the rules on requesting a thematic hearing, see Commission Rules of Procedure (n. 5 above), art. 64. Requests must be submitted to the Executive Secretariat at least fifty days in advance of the respective session.

[8] Since 1961, the Commission has undertaken approximately 100 onsite visits to observe first-hand the human rights situation in the countries of the region. Today, the Commission undertakes roughly four or five such visits per year, depending on resource availability.

findings of the Commission in relation to particular types of abuse.[9]

Each of the seven members of the Commission also serves as a Country and/or Thematic Rapporteur. Over the last several years the Commission has had thematic rapporteurships in some or all of the following areas: women's rights, children, indigenous peoples, persons deprived of liberty, refugees, migrant workers and their families, freedom of expression, human rights defenders, and, most recently, racial discrimination and the rights of persons of African descent. A new rapporteurship on economic, social and cultural rights has also been under consideration.[10] Each of these rapporteurships can be used strategically by advocates to focus national and international attention on distinct contours of human rights abuse at the local level and, particularly, on the special measures required to address such abuses as they affect groups in particularly vulnerable situations. This may be achieved by requesting a given rapporteur to undertake a focused onsite visit, to prepare a special report or study, to formulate general guidelines or a declaration of principles, or to spearhead the issuance of general recommendations or observations on a discrete issue within the rapporteurship's competence.

Finally, periodic State reporting mechanisms on the progressive measures taken and setbacks encountered in the realisation of economic, social, and cultural rights are envisioned under two of the region's core human rights treaties.[11] Once properly implemented,[12] these mechanisms may

be harnessed to further refine the system's understanding of how and why economic, social, and cultural rights are violated. State periodic reporting procedures thus promise useful synergistic effects in the individual petitions process, even while serving broader purposes of a political-promotional nature. Advocates must keep these jurisdictional distinctions constantly in mind, using them to their full advantage, and remembering that assessment standards appropriate to the Commission's promotional functions will not necessarily be applicable to its narrower contentious competence, where issues of justiciability and party standing take centre stage.[13]

Though still in its relative infancy, the economic, social and cultural rights jurisprudence of the Commission is beginning to mature as advocates present an ever-widening array of cases and arguments before it. These strategic advances are owed primarily to the perseverance and creativity of regional advocates, the pressing demands of poverty, violence, exclusion, exploitation and lack of rule of law in the region, and the broad jurisdiction of the regional organs over economic, social and cultural rights. Consequently, the Commission today recognises economic, social and cultural rights, together with the rule of law, as the 'foremost challenges' the regional human rights system must now confront.[14]

---

[9] See, for example, the Commission's 1997 report on the situation of human rights in Ecuador, OEA/Ser.L/V/II.96, doc. 10, rev. 1 (1997), particularly its discussion of the impact of oil development activities on the right to health of indigenous populations in the interior. The Commission's reports can be accessed on its website: <http://www.iachr.org>.

[10] Given the broad scope of this category, it would appear more advisable to consider the creation of a special rapporteur on a discrete social right, such as the right to health, the right to education, the right to housing, or the right to free labour association and just work conditions.

[11] See American Convention (n. 3 above), art. 42; Additional Protocol to the American Convention on Human Rights in the Area of Economic, Social and Cultural Rights, art. 19.1, Nov. 17, 1988, O.A.S.T.S. No. 69 (1988), 28 I.L.M. 156 (1989), entered into force Nov. 16, 1999 ('Protocol of San Salvador').

[12] Unfortunately, both mechanisms have laid effectively dormant since 1979 and 1999 when the two instruments

entered into effect. In 2005, the OAS General Assembly issued Resolution 2074 (XXXV-O/05) calling for the establishment of a Working Group under the San Salvador Protocol to monitor States parties' progressive realisation of the economic, social, and cultural rights enshrined therein. Although there are many troublesome aspects to the envisioned Working Group – such as its functioning within the Inter-American Council on Integral Development, rather than the Inter-American Commission on Human Rights – advocates will have to work tirelessly to turn this procedure into one that is useful for both monitoring and adjudicatory work in the field of economic, social, and cultural rights.

[13] See, in particular, Tara J. Melish, 'Rethinking the "Less as More" Thesis: Supranational Litigation of Economic, Social and Cultural Rights in the Americas', New York University Journal of International Law and Politics, Vol. 39 No. 2 (2006), pp. 171–343, which uses a quadrant-based matrix to distinguish conceptually between the dimensions of human rights obligations that are directly applicable in the inter-American system in adjudicatory verses promotional contexts.

[14] Address of the President of the Inter-American Commission on Human Rights, Dr. Clare K. Roberts, before the Permanent Council of the Organization of American States, Wash., D.C., 15 April 2005.

This chapter addresses the many ways the Commission has used its case-based contentious jurisdiction to develop a growing jurisprudence on economic, social and cultural rights. While a great deal of work remains ahead, significant jurisprudential developments have been achieved through the Commission's merits-based decisions, approval of friendly settlements, and issuance of precautionary measures. Before turning to these advances, each considered severally below, brief sketches are presented of the Commission's jurisdiction over economic, social and cultural rights, the legal obligations that correspond to such rights in adjudicatory contexts, and the inter-American systems' procedures for considering individual complaints.

2. SOCIAL RIGHTS OVER WHICH THE COMMISSION EXERCISES JURISDICTION

The Commission has extensive subject-matter jurisdiction over autonomous economic, social and cultural rights.[15] These rights are protected directly under the American Declaration of the Rights and Duties of Man ('American Declaration'), the American Convention on Human Rights ('American Convention'), and the Additional Protocol to the American Convention in the Area of Economic, Social and Cultural Rights ('San Salvador Protocol'). They may also be protected indirectly through other core regional instruments over which the Commission enjoys contentious jurisdiction.[16] Special mention in this regard

should be made of the Inter-American Convention to Prevent, Sanction and Eradicate Violence Against Women, whose adjudicable provisions, while not expressly enshrining individual social rights, provide important safeguards for protecting women from the institutional and private abuse that often trap them in situations of poverty, destitution, and social exclusion and impede them from accessing jobs, education, health care and other essential social rights.[17]

Significantly, the American Declaration, the American Convention, and the San Salvador Protocol all recognise, in largely parallel and autonomous terms, the rights to health, education, social security, housing, labour guarantees, and unionisation. As at least one of these instruments applies in the individual petitions process to every OAS Member State, the Commission is competent to adjudicate individual complaints of social rights violations with respect to every State in the Americas.

2.1   American Declaration[18]

The American Declaration, adopted in 1948, enshrines the full spectrum of human rights recognised by American States. Among other rights of a more classic 'civil and political' nature, these include the right to housing (Articles IX and XI), the right to health (Article XI), the right to education (Article XII), the right to culture (Article XIII), the right to work, fair remuneration, and rest (Article XIV and XV), the right to social security (Article XVI), the right to property (Article XXIII),

---

[15] A former President of the Commission has affirmed in an address before the OAS Permanent Council that 'More than any of the other great human rights instruments of the modern world, the American Convention emphasizes economic rights and economic development, as does the Charter of the Organization of American States'. OEA/Ser.L/V/II.91, Doc. 7 rev. at 275, 278, (1996). The Commission has likewise recognised that '[t]he Inter-American states have pledged in the Charter and in the Convention...or through the Declaration, to promote and protect civil and political rights, and economic, social and cultural rights'. OEA/Ser.L/V/II.85 doc. 9 rev. at 563 (1994).

[16] The other regional treaties over which the Commission enjoys full or partial contentious jurisdiction include those on torture, forced disappearance, and violence against women. See Inter-American Convention to Prevent and Punish Torture, Dec. 9, 1985, O.A.S.T.S. No. 67, entered into force Feb. 28, 1987, art. 8; Inter-American Convention on the Forced Disappearance of Persons, June 9, 1994, O.A.S. Doc. OEA/Ser.P AG/doc.3114/94

rev. 1, entered into force Mar. 29, 1996, 33 I.L.M. 1529 (1994), art. XIII; Inter-American Convention to Prevent, Sanction and Eradicate Violence against Women, Jun. 9, 1994, entered into force Mar. 5, 1995, art. 12 ['VAW Convention'].

[17] The Convention in fact defines 'violence against women' as including sexual harassment in the workplace, educational institutions, health facilities or any other place, by any person, and recognises that such violence 'prevents and nullifies' the exercise of a woman's economic, social and cultural rights. VAW Convention (n. 16 above), arts. 2 and 5. Although limited in contentious proceedings to applying Article 7 of the VAW convention, the Commission has decided an important case on domestic violence under the treaty. See *Maria da Penha v. Brazil*, Case 12.051, Report No. 54/01, Inter-Am. Comm.H.R., OEA/Ser.L/V/II.111 Doc. 20 rev. at 704 (2000).

[18] American Declaration of the Rights and Duties of Man, May 2, 1948, O.A.S. Res. XXX, Int'l Conference of Am. States, 9th Conference, OEA/Ser.L/V/I.4 Rev. XX (1948).

and the right to special protection for mothers, children and the family (Articles VI and VII). While not itself a treaty, the Declaration is considered to have binding legal effect on all OAS Member States. This owes to such 'States' common ratification of the OAS Charter, a binding treaty under which all OAS Member States commit to respect and observe human rights in the region. The Declaration, adopted contemporaneously with the Charter, defines, for its part, the human rights to which States have committed under the Charter.[19] Consistent with this view, the Commission's Statute recognises the human rights the Commission is competent to apply, under both its contentious and promotional functions, as those set forth in the American Convention in relation to States parties thereto, and the rights set forth in the American Declaration in relation to all other OAS Member States.[20]

Accordingly, each of the autonomous social rights guaranteed in the Declaration may be adjudicated by the Commission when alleged to have been violated to the detriment of individual rights-holders by any one of the eleven OAS Member States that are not party to the American Convention.[21] For the remaining twenty-four Member States, the American Declaration cannot be invoked directly in the individual petitions process, but remains applicable for purposes of interpreting the congruent, yet more or less precisely defined, norms in the American Convention. Such interpretive guidance, mandated by Article 29.d of the Convention,[22] is particularly significant for giving contour

and content to the catalogue of social rights guaranteed under Convention Article 26.[23]

2.2 American Convention

The American Convention is, by design, a binding treaty and likewise includes an extensive catalogue of economic, social and cultural rights. These include the rights to education, to unionisation, to strike, to employment, to adequate food, to health, to social security, to housing, to culture, and to just labour conditions. These rights are autonomously guaranteed under Article 26 of the Convention, the lone rights-based provision under the Chapter heading 'Economic, Social and Cultural Rights'.[24] By its terms, Article 26 protects a set of distinct rights that are textually defined as those 'derived from'[25] or 'implicit in the economic, social, educational, scientific, and cultural standards set forth in the [OAS Charter]', a regional treaty ratified by all OAS Member States. That treaty refers expressly to the 'right to education', the 'right to material well-being', the 'right to collective bargaining', the 'right to strike', and the right to work. It refers implicitly to the rights to 'adequate housing',

---

[19] See, e.g., *Interpretation of the American Declaration of the Rights and Duties of Man Within the Framework of Article 64 of the American Convention on Human Rights*, Advisory Opinion OC-10/89, July 14, 1989, Inter-Am. Ct. H.R. (Ser. A) No. 10 (1989), para. 47 ('That the Declaration is not a treaty does not, then, lead to the conclusion that it does not have legal effect'); *Roach and Pinkerton cases*, Res. 3/87, Case 9647 (U.S.), Inter-Am. Comm. H.R., para. 48, OEA/Ser.L/V/II.71 Doc. 9 rev. 1 (1987).

[20] Statute of the Inter-American Commission on Human Rights, art. 1.2, Oct. 1979, O.A.S. Res. 447 (IX-0/79), O.A.S. Off. Rec. OEA/Ser.P/IX.0.2/80, vol. 1, at 88 ['Commission Statute'].

[21] These States include Antigua and Barbuda, Bahamas, Belize, Canada, Cuba, Guyana, St. Kitts and Nevis, St. Vincent and the Grenadines, St. Lucia, Trinidad and Tobago, and the United States. As Trinidad and Tobago denounced the Convention in 1998, the Declaration is now applied to it for purposes of the Commission's supervisory jurisdiction over human rights in that country.

[22] See American Convention (n. 3 above), art. 29.d (prohibiting the interpretation of any Convention provi-

sion in a way that limits or excludes the Declaration's 'effect'); see also *Maya Indigenous Communities of the Toledo District v. Belize*, Report No. 40/04, Case 12.053, OEA/Ser.L/V/II.122, doc. 5 rev. 1 (2005), paras. 86–88 (explaining respective roles of Declaration and Convention in assisting in the interpretation of the other).

[23] See, e.g., *Jesús Manuel Naranjo Cárdenas et al. (Pensioners of the Venezuelan Aviation Company (VIASA)) v. Venezuela*, Report No. 69/04, Petition 667/01, OEA/Ser.L/V/II.122, doc. 5, rev. 1 (2005), para. 46 ('Article 26 of the American Convention contemplates in a generic way the protection of economic, social and cultural rights. The American Declaration in its Article XVI establishes in a specific way the right to social security.... [T]he Commission considers that it has competence *ratione materiae* regarding the alleged violations to the guarantee of the right to social security by virtue of Article 26 of the American Convention'.)

[24] Article 26 reads: 'The States Parties undertake to adopt measures, both internally and through international cooperation, especially those of an economic and technical nature, with a view to achieving progressively, by legislation or other appropriate means, the full realization of the rights implicit in the economic, social, educational, scientific, and cultural standards set forth in the Charter of the Organization of American States as amended by the Protocol of San Salvador'. For a brief discussion of the drafting history behind this article, see Melish, 'Rethinking the "Less as More" Thesis' (n. 13 above), pp. 225–30.

[25] 'Derived from' ('*se derivan de*') is the term used in the Spanish text, which is the official OAS text for purposes of treaty interpretation.

'proper nutrition', just labour conditions, the highest attainable standard of health, and the benefits of culture.[26] All of these rights may thus be protected in the individual petitions process through application of Convention Article 26, in conjunction with the duties in Articles 1 and 2. Essential aspects of these rights, moreover, may concurrently be protected in both their substantive and procedural dimensions through application of Articles 3 through 25 of the Convention, the provisions formally placed under the Chapter heading 'Civil and Political Rights'.[27]

The American Convention is the primary instrument that defines what human rights the Commission is competent to apply with respect to the twenty-four OAS Member States that are parties to that instrument.[28] For such States, the norms contained in the Declaration should be invoked only for interpretive purposes with respect to Convention-based norms, not as an autonomous basis for finding state responsibility in the individual petition process.[29]

2.3 Protocol of San Salvador

Finally, the Commission enjoys jurisdictional competence over the Protocol of San Salvador, a specialised regional instrument that protects, in direct terms, the rights to health, a healthy environment, food, education, work, just and equitable conditions of work, trade unionisation, social security, the benefits of culture, and special protection for the family, children, the elderly, and persons with disabilities.[30] While the Commission is competent to apply all of these rights to State parties under its promotional mandate, it is competent to apply only two under its contentious mandate: the right to unionise and the right to education, protected respectively under Protocol Articles 8.1.a and 13.[31]

Petitions alleging violations of the rights to education and unionisation to the detriment of individual rights-holders may thus be lodged with the Commission against the thirteen American States that have ratified the Protocol.[32] The extensive catalogue of other social rights guaranteed in the Protocol may be used in petitions lodged against those States only to the extent they are invoked to assist in the interpretation of the scope and content of the congruent but less precisely defined social rights consecrated in the Convention, particularly those guaranteed under Article 26.[33]

3. COMPLAINT PROCEDURES AND LEGAL STANDING

Established in 1960, the Commission did not in fact acquire its contentious competence to

---

[26] See Charter of the Organization of American States, arts. 34, 45, 49, 50.

[27] For a description of how economic, social and cultural rights can effectively be protected in the individual petitions process through the Convention's Chapter II norms, see Tara Melish, *Protecting Economic, Social and Cultural Rights in the Inter-American Human Rights System: A Manual on Presenting Claims* (Quito: Orville H. Schell, Jr. Center for International Human Rights, Yale Law School and CDES, 2002), pp. 193–332. A second edition is being prepared for 2009, given that the vast bulk of the Commission's Convention-based social rights jurisprudence has been issued post-2001.

[28] See, e.g., Commission Statute (n. 20 above), art. 1.2. These twenty-four States include: Argentina, Barbados, Bolivia, Brazil, Chile, Colombia, Costa Rica, Dominica, Dominican Republic, Ecuador, El Salvador, Grenada, Guatemala, Haiti, Honduras, Jamaica, Mexico, Nicaragua, Panama, Paraguay, Peru, Suriname, Uruguay, and Venezuela.

[29] An exception to this rule has been recognised by the Commission where the acts giving rise to 'continuing violations' occurred before the American Convention was ratified by a defendant State. See, e.g., *Romeel Eduardo Díaz Luna v. Peru*, Petition, 430/00, Report N° 85/05, Inter-Am. Comm. H.R., OEA/Ser.L/V/II.124, doc. 5 (2006), para. 24 (judicial ruling ordering payment of social benefits); *Octavio Ruben Gonzalez v. Paraguay*, Case 12.358, Report No. 83/03, Inter-Am. C.H.R., OEA/Ser.L/V/II.118 Doc. 70 rev. 2 at 405 (2003), para. 19 (forced disappearance). The Commission has at times, and inconsistently, applied a second exception where the norms in the Declaration and Convention do not wholly overlap, particularly in the area of social rights. This exception appears unjustified, however, as it conflicts with both the plain text of Article 1 of the Commission's Statute and the broad protections in Article 26 of the American Convention. It is

in the process of being abandoned in the Commission's social rights jurisprudence.

[30] See Protocol of San Salvador (n. 11 above), arts. 6–18.

[31] See ibid. art. 19.6.

[32] These include: Argentina, Brazil, Colombia, Costa Rica, Ecuador, El Salvador, Guatemala, Mexico, Panama, Paraguay, Peru, Suriname, and Uruguay.

[33] See, e.g., *Ana Victoria Villalobos et al. v. Costa Rica*, Report No. 25/04, Case 12.361, Inter-Am. Comm. H.R., OEA/Ser.L/V/II.122 Doc. 5 rev. 1 at 237 (2004), para. 70 ('The allegations raised under the Protocol of San Salvador [including claimed violation of the right to health] may be taken into account in interpreting the international obligations of the State under Article 26 of the American Convention ... but those Articles of the Protocol are not directly cognizable within the individual petition system'.).

examine individual petitions until 1966.[34] Since then, the Commission has examined tens of thousands of individual complaints of human rights violations, currently receiving approximately 1,400 per year.[35] With a staff of approximately thirty lawyers, the body is actively considering over 1,000 concrete cases at any given moment, a caseload that includes increasing numbers of social rights claims.

To present a case to the inter-American system, petitions alleging discrete human rights violations to the detriment of individual rights-holders may be faxed or mailed to the Commission's Secretariat. Formal processing will begin if the petition prima facie meets the admissibility requirements provided for in Articles 25 through 41 of the Commission's Statute. If not, the petition will be returned to the sender without processing or transmittal to the State. The following three Sections detail the jurisdictional grounds that are considered in every formal admissibility report to ensure the Commission is properly exercising its competence over a given case. Where these grounds are found to be satisfied, a formal admissibility report will be issued and the Commission will proceed to the stage of examining the merits of the case.[36] If they are not satisfied, an inadmissibility report will be issued and the case will be dismissed. Significantly, the Commission may, in its discretion, take up under its broader promotional mandate any issue found inadmissible under its more limited contentious competence.[37]

3.1 Legal Standing: Jurisdiction *Ratione Personae*

The Commission's contentious jurisdiction is limited to 'cases', defined in the classic sense of an adverse controversy between a claimed individual rights-holder and a claimed duty-holder, in which concrete injury to the former and causal responsibility of the latter may be demonstrated. This core jurisdictional requirement is reflected in the Commission's rules on legal standing, which require prima facie proof of both concrete individualised injury suffered by the alleged victim and conduct by state agents through which causal responsibility for that injury may be imputed to the State.

The Commission has permissive standing rules for who may initially lodge a contentious complaint with it alleging human rights violations by an OAS Member State: 'any person, group of persons or non-governmental organization' may do so.[38] This is true irrespective of whether they themselves are victims, have a personal interest in the controversy, have powers of attorney, or have even notified the alleged victim of the petition. By contrast, the Commission's rules with respect to the '*victim*', on whose behalf the petition is lodged, are quite restrictive. A petition will only be admissible where it is lodged on behalf of a person or persons who satisfy two requirements. First, they must be natural persons; the Commission is not competent to adjudicate alleged violations of the rights of 'juridical persons' (e.g., companies, NGOs, unions, corporations, medical

---

[34] Following authorisation by the OAS member states in 1965, OEA/Ser.C/I.13, at 32–34 (1965), the Commission amended its Statute in 1966 to include the examination of individual petitions as part of its regular competence. OEA/Ser.L/V/II.14, doc. 35, at 26–27 (1996). That competence is currently reflected in Commission Rules of Procedure (n. 5 above), arts. 49–50, and Commission Statute (n. 20 above), art. 20.

[35] The number of individual petitions lodged with the Commission has increased significantly with the years. In 1970, the first year in which its individual case figures were reported, the Commission received just 103 petitions involving concrete cases. See OEA/Ser.L/V/II.25, doc. 9 rev. (1971).

[36] In situations of urgency, the Commission may issue a merged admissibility and merits report.

[37] See, e.g., *Víctor Nicolás Sánchez et al.* ('*Operation Gatekeeper*') *v. United States*, Report No. 104/05, Petition 65/99, Inter-Am. Comm. H.R., OEA/Ser.L/V/II.124, doc. 5 (2006), para. 76 (finding complaint inadmissible but, given the gravity of the situation, deciding to 'continue to supervise the situation, in accordance with its broad mandate to promote the observance and protection of

human rights in the Hemisphere'); *Elias Santana et al. v. Venezuela*, Report No. 92/03, Case 453/01, Inter-Am. Comm. H.R., OEA/Ser.L/V/II.118, doc. 70 rev. 2 (2004), paras. 90–92 (finding inadmissible complaint involving freedom of association, but instructing the Commission's Special Rapporteur for Freedom of Expression to prepare a special report on the situation given its gravity and importance for the region); *see also Corumbiara v. Brazil*, Report No. 32/04, Case 11.556, Inter-Am. Comm. H.R., OEA/Ser.L/V/II.122, doc. 5 rev. 1 (2005), para. 124; *Statehood Solidarity Committee v. United States*, Dissenting Opinion of José Zalaquett, Report No. 98/03, Case 11.204, Inter-Am. Comm. H.R., OEA/Ser./L/V/II.114, doc. 70 rev. 2 (2003), para. 18 ('I am of the view that the type of issues dealt with in the present case can and should be dealt with by the Commission and other organs of the Organization of American States through their promotional functions rather than by deciding on a claim or communication.').

[38] See American Convention (n. 3 above), art. 44.

institutions, or banks).[39] Second, the alleged victim must be specifically identified by name or individually determinable, and must have personally suffered *concrete* (not speculative or hypothetical) injury to a protected right.[40] The Commission is not competent to adjudicate generalised harms that affect broad sectors of society on an undifferentiated basis, a competence reserved exclusively for its broader promotional mandate. In this respect, it has repeatedly warned that its case-based jurisdiction does not admit actions pursued as '*actio popularis*', 'class action suits', 'public interest actions' or other types of actions *in abstracto* presented in the name of indeterminate groups of persons, such as 'all citizens and inhabitants' of a particular country, 'all potential women voters', or 'the great majority of voters'.[41]

The Commission must also assure itself that it has proper ratione personae jurisdiction over the respondent State. For this to be true, two requirements must be satisfied. First, the respondent must be an OAS Member State. Second, prima facie evidence must be available that causal responsibility for the violation can plausibly be imputed to the State *through its conduct*.[42] Where there is no reasonable basis for finding a causal relationship, on a proximate basis, between the concrete harm experienced by the alleged victim and the acts or omissions of state agents, the Commission lacks grounds for exercising its contentious jurisdiction over the respondent State and the claim will be dismissed as beyond the Commission's case-based competence. Consequently, the core justiciability requirements of (1) concrete individualised injury and (2) imputation of causal responsibility for that injury to an OAS Member State exercising jurisdiction over the injured individual, are key to the admissibility of every case lodged under the contentious jurisdiction of the inter-American human rights organs.

3.2 Jurisdiction Ratione Materiae, Ratione Loci, and Ratione Temporis

Before exercising its contentious jurisdiction, the Commission must also assure itself that it has competence over the alleged abuse presented to it in terms of its subject matter (*ratione materiae*), location (*ratione loci*), and time frame (*ratione temporis*). To satisfy the Commission's ratione materiae jurisdiction, petitions must allege violation of only those norms over which the Commission in fact exercises jurisdiction with respect to the respondent State. Close attention must therefore be paid to both the State's ratification history vis-à-vis the region's human rights instruments and the specific jurisdictional limitations within those instruments. To satisfy the

---

[39] See ibid., art. 1.2 ('For the purposes of this Convention, "person" means every human being'.); *Banco de Lima v. Peru*, Report No. 10/91, Case 10.169, Inter-Am. Comm. H.R., OEA/Ser.L/V/II.79.rev.1, doc. 12 (1991), at 423, 425, paras. 2–3 (finding petition by bank stockholders to protect the interests of the bank inadmissible); *Mevopal, S.A. v. Argentina*, Report 39/99, Inter-Am. Comm. H.R., OEA/Ser.L/V/II.106, doc. 6 rev. (2000) (no jurisdiction over private company); *Ana Victoria Villalobos et al. v. Costa Rica* (n. 33 above) (no jurisdiction over medical fertility companies); *Metropolitan Nature Reserve v. Panama*, Case 11.533, Report No. 88/03, Inter-Am. Comm. H.R., OEA/Ser.L/V/II.118, doc. 5 rev. 2 (2003). ('[P]etition is inadmissible, further, because the environmental, civic, and scientific groups considered most harmed by the alleged violations are legal entities and not natural persons'.)

[40] See, e.g., *Elias Santana et al. v. Venezuela*, Report No. 92/03, Case 453/01, Inter-Am. Comm. H.R., OEA/Ser.L/V/II.118, doc. 70 rev. 2 (2004), paras. 45 *op. cit.* (finding complaint inadmissible given that 'petitioners have not submitted sufficient evidence to demonstrate the specific manner in which their personal situation was injured by the operative portion of the judgment'); *Metropolitan Nature Reserve v. Panama* (2003), paras. 27–31 (finding petition challenging highway authorization inadmissible because 'it is overly broad'; 'the Commission requires a petition denouncing a concrete violation with respect to a specific individual').

[41] See, e.g., *Janet Espinoza Feria et al. v. Peru*, Report No. 51/02, Case 12.404, Inter-Am. Comm. H.R., OEA/Ser.L/V/II.117, doc. 1 rev. 1 (2003); *Felix Roman Esparragoza Gonzalez and Nerio Molina Peñaloza v. Venezuela*, Report No. 48/04, Case 12.210, Inter-Am. Comm. H.R., OEA/Ser.L/V/II.122, doc. 5 rev. 1 (2005), para. 40. Despite these statements, it is not clear that the Commission's standing rules for victims in fact preclude class action suits, provided the class is sufficiently determinable and its individual members have suffered demonstrable concrete harm of a common nature and causal provenance.

[42] See, e.g., *Víctor Nicolás Sánchez et al. ('Operation Gatekeeper') v. United States*, Report No. 104/05, Petition 65/99, Inter-Am. Comm. H.R., OEA/Ser.L/V/II.124, doc. 5 (2006), Concurring Opinion of President Clare K. Roberts (concluding that the case is 'manifestly unfounded' on ground that the state is not legally responsible through its conduct for alleged harm). Many other cases are submitted to the system with this problem, although they are often returned to the petitioner without a formal admissibility decision being rendered.

Commission's *ratione loci* competence, the alleged abuse must have occurred within the respondent State's jurisdiction, either in terms of its territorial boundaries or within an extraterritorial locus over which it exercises effective 'authority and control'.[43] Finally, satisfaction of the Commission's *ratione temporis* competence requires that the alleged facts giving rise to the claimed violation must have occurred *after* the legal obligations to 'respect' and 'ensure' the protected rights at issue entered into force for the respondent State.[44]

3.3 Other Admissibility Requirements

Once the Commission is satisfied that it has proper jurisdiction over the substance of the claim, it must also assure itself that four other core admissibility requirements are satisfied. These requirements reflect the subsidiary nature of the inter-American human rights system as well as basic comity and fairness considerations in the exercise of international adjudicatory procedures. They include: (1) the prior exhaustion of effective domestic remedies,[45] (2) a six-month time limit on the presentation of complaints, running from the date on which the party alleging the violation was notified of the final judgment in the internal jurisdiction,[46] (3) the identification by name of the petitioners and, where practicable, the alleged vic-

tims, and (4) a prohibition on the presentation of the same or similar claims to multiple adjudicatory procedures at the international level.[47] Appropriate exceptions are recognised for each of these core admissibility rules,[48] although their application in a given case must generally be demonstrated as part of the petitioners' prima facie burden.

3.4 Further Processing of the Complaint

Once an admissibility report is issued, the Commission will proceed to the merits of the case. In so doing, it will consider the written briefs, observations, and other information submitted by the parties, supplemented, where appropriate, by oral presentations, witness testimony, onsite visits, and independent investigations or inquiries by the Commission. The Commission will generally put itself at the disposal of the parties to determine whether it is possible to reach a friendly settlement of the matter.[49] Where settlement is not possible, the Commission will issue a confidential report on its findings of fact and conclusions of law and, where violations are found, issue appropriate remedial recommendations. The State will then be given a period of three months from the date of transmittal of the confidential report to comply with those recommendations.[50] Where compliance is deemed satisfactory, the Commission will publish a report on the merits of the case, referencing the compliance measures duly adopted by the State. Where compliance is unsatisfactory,

---

[43] See, e.g., *Coard et al. v. United States*, Case 10.951, Report No. 109/99, Inter-Am. Comm. H.R., OEA/Ser.L/V/II.106, doc. 6 rev. (2000), para. 37 (extraterritorial application depends on 'whether, under the specific circumstances, the State observed the rights of a person subject to its authority and control').

[44] An exception is generally recognised for 'continuing violations'.

[45] The petitioner must have attempted, without success, to obtain a remedy through the courts or authorities of the country concerned *before contacting the Commission*. These remedies must have been pursued to the highest level of appeal available in the internal jurisdiction. See American Convention (n. 3 above), art. 46.a; see also Commission Rules of Procedure (n. 5 above), art. 31.1.

[46] American Convention (n. 3 above), art. 46.b; see also Commission Rules of Procedure (n. 5 above), art. 32.1. Under the Commission's Rules of Procedure, however, a victim who has *not* been able to exhaust local legal channels for one of the reasons enumerated in Article 46.2 should present her petition *within a reasonable time*. Ibid. art. 32.2. The determination of 'reasonableness' is made on a case-by-case basis. Needless to say, it is always best to present a petition as soon as possible after the occurrence of the events in question.

[47] American Convention (n. 3 above), arts. 46.c and 47.d; see also Commission Rules of Procedure (n. 5 above), arts. 33.1.a and 33.1.b. The rule is not blindly applied. Its application is determined within the context of its primary objective: to avoid the duplication of international procedures. Exceptions are provided in the Commission's Rules of Procedure (n. 5 above), art. 33.2.

[48] For a more complete analysis of these admissibility rules and their exceptions, see Melish, *Protecting Economic, Social, and Cultural Rights* (n. 27 above), chapter 2. The Court has repeatedly insisted, 'It is generally accepted that the procedural system is a means of attaining justice and that the latter cannot be sacrificed for the sake of mere formalities'. *Cayara Case, Preliminary Objections*, Judgment of Feb. 3, 1993, Inter-Am. Ct. H.R. (Ser. C) No. 14, para. 42.

[49] American Convention (n. 3 above), art. 48.f.

[50] A copy of the relevant portions of the confidential report will be sent to the petitioners, although they are not at liberty to publish or distribute it.

the Commission will vote to either refer the case to the Inter-American Court of Human Rights for final binding resolution or publish its merits report and continue to supervise compliance with its own recommendations. Since 2000, a presumption has existed that cases resolved against States that have accepted the Court's jurisdiction and that have not duly complied with the Commission's recommendations will be referred to the Court.[51]

4. CORRESPONDING LEGAL DUTIES IN THE INDIVIDUAL PETITIONS PROCESS

In the exercise of its contentious competence, the Commission has generally been consistent in applying the same legal obligations to all human rights protected in the regional instruments, regardless of subjective characterisation as civil, cultural, economic, political or social. That is, for purposes of establishing State responsibility under contentious process, it applies the general duties to 'respect' and to 'ensure', through the *adoption of appropriate, necessary or reasonable measures*, the free and full exercise of guaranteed rights to all individuals within a State's jurisdiction.[52] These obligations, set out in Chapter I of the Convention, apply equally to the rights in Chapter II and Chapter III. They are also the obligations that the Commission applies to the full panoply of rights set out in the American Declaration.

As described more fully in the following chapter, these individual-oriented, conduct-based duties[53]

are broken down into those corresponding to 'negative' duties of abstention or restraint in the exercise of state conduct and to 'positive' duties of reasonable prevention, diligent response, and appropriate provision when individuals' rights are threatened or harmed by the conduct of either state agents or private actors.[54] State responsibility for a given human rights violation is thus determined on the basis of whether or not concrete individualised harm, once established, may reasonably be imputed to the State through the unreasonable *acts* or *failures to act* of its agents. It is satisfaction of these two core justiciability requirements in the inter-American system (proof of concrete individual injury and imputed causal responsibility) that compels direct application to all rights-based contentious claims of the individual-oriented and conduct-based dimensions of human rights duties.[55]

That the corresponding obligation 'to adopt all appropriate measures to respect and ensure' the rights of individuals applies to economic, social and cultural rights as fully as it does to civil and political rights is most clearly evident in the Commission's jurisprudence under the American Declaration, an instrument that does not differentiate between 'sets' of rights. Indeed, in adjudicating concrete cases of human rights abuse under the Declaration, the Commission regularly finds concurrent State responsibility, on the basis of

---

[51] Only where 'a reasoned decision' against referral is provided by an absolute majority of the Commission's members may referral be avoided. Commission Rules of Procedure (n. 5 above), art. 44.1.

[52] See, e.g., *Maya Indigenous Communities of the Toledo District v. Belize* (n. 22 above), paras. 132, 134, 143 (finding Belize responsible for failures regarding 'the positive steps that the State must take to respect and ensure ... rights', including their failure 'to take the appropriate measures to protect the right' at issue and their failure 'to take appropriate or adequate measures' to consult affected populations).

[53] The term 'conduct-based duties' is used here to distinguish conceptually between the dimensions of human rights obligations that are geared toward assessing *what a State has in fact done* (conduct) to ensure the enjoyment of human rights to all persons within its jurisdiction, especially in the face of vulnerability, versus *the factual or statistical enjoyment* of such rights in that jurisdiction (results), irrespective of the measures undertaken by the State. Only the former provides the proper basis for

imputation of state responsibility in the inter-American system's individual complaints procedure.

[54] The Commission applies the same duty-based standards as the Court in assessing State responsibility in contentious processes. For a slightly more developed assessment, see the following Chapter in this volume as well as Tara J. Melish & Ana Aliverti, '"Positive Obligations" in the Inter-American Human Rights System', *Interights Bulletin*, Vol. 15, Issue 3 (2006), pp. 120–22.

[55] Because their counterpart 'collective-oriented' and 'result-based' dimensions do not correspond to, and are not capable of assessing, these core litigation requirements, they are inappropriate for direct application in adjudicatory procedures in the inter-American system. They are the primary reserve of the system's political, promotional, monitoring, and advisory mechanisms. A quadrant-based framework has been advanced to illustrate these distinct dimensions, with 'conduct'/'result' – based and 'individual'/'collective'-oriented dimensions arrayed in a two-by-two matrix. It is asserted that only quadrant 1 duties (representing the conduct-based, individual-oriented dimensions of human rights obligations) are properly justiciable in non-strict-liability supranational individual petitions processes. See Melish, 'Rethinking the "Less as More" Thesis' (n. 13 above).

identical facts and government conduct, for discrete violations of the rights to health, education, work, and rest, on the one hand, and the rights to life, integrity, religion, and movement, on the other.[56]

This longstanding practice under the Declaration accentuates the highly troubling nature of the Commission's recent application to social rights claims, when framed under Article 26 of the Convention, of obligations that are distinct in nature from those it applies consistently to the *same or similar* claims when invoked under the Declaration or other Convention-based norms. That is, while applying the litigation-appropriate dimensions of human rights obligations to claims framed under these latter norms, it has, at least in one disquieting 2005 admissibility decision,[57] applied the litigation-inappropriate dimensions of human rights obligations to claims framed under Article 26. The result of this improper application is to render the associated claims non-cognisable in the individual petitions process.

This inchoate practice, if extended, threatens to reverse what was, between 2001 and 2005, a growing trend in favour of the equalisation of legal standards for all human rights claims framed under the Convention. That is, despite the Commission's general neglect of Article 26 in its first two decades of case-based work under the Convention, 2001 witnessed an important jurisprudential shift in which the Commission began to recognise State responsibility under the individual complaints mechanism for breach of the discrete social rights guaranteed autonomously in Article 26 of the Convention.[58] The post-2000 decisions were significant both in their express recognition that Article 26 enshrined the autonomously enforceable rights to health, to just labour conditions, to unionisation, to social security, and to work, among other key social rights, and in their prima facie grounding of state responsibility for violation of those discrete rights in the individual-oriented, conduct-based dimensions of the duties enshrined in Articles 1 and 2 of the Convention.

It initially appeared in fact that the Commission's treatment of Article 26 would remain unaffected by the Court's brief but opaque reflections on an improperly framed, and hence properly set aside, Article 26 claim in the 2003 *Five Pensioners v. Peru* case, the first case in which the Court expressly considered an Article 26 claim.[59] That is, it appeared that the Commission recognised that the non-cognisability of the *improperly framed* Article 26 claim in that case did not speak to the adjudicability of *properly framed* Article 26 claims presented to the system's contentious jurisdiction. Indeed, in 2004, over a one-Commissioner dissent, the Commission specifically found a right-to-social-security claim framed under Article 26 admissible on facts virtually identical to the 2003 *Five Pensioners Case*,[60] insisting that it be assessed in accordance with the general litigation-appropriate duties established in Article 1.1 of the Convention.[61] In 2004 it likewise found a right-to-health claim admissible under Article 26,[62] while recognising in 2005 its competence to adjudicate alleged violations under Article 26 of the rights to work and to just conditions of work.[63]

---

[56] See, e.g., *Coulter et al. Case v. Brazil*, Res. 12/85, Case 7615, Inter-Am. Comm. H.R., OEA/Ser.L/V/II.66, doc. 10 rev. 1 (1985), at 24, 33 (violations of right to health, work, life, family and movement based on same state conduct); *Jehovah's Witnesses v. Argentina*, Case No. 2137, Inter-Am. Comm. H.R., OEA/Ser.L/V/II.47, doc. 13 rev. 1 (1979) (violation of right to education and right to religion based on same state conduct); Case 1802 (Paraguay), Inter-Am. Comm. H.R., OEA/Ser.L/V/II.43 doc. 21 corr. 1 (1978) (violation of rights to health, work, rest, family, life).

[57] See *Luis Rolando Cuscul Pivaral and Others Affected by HIV/AIDS v. Guatemala*, Petition 642/05, Report No. 32/05, Inter-Am. Comm. H.R., OEA/Ser.L/V/II.124, doc. 5 (2006), paras. 42–44.

[58] See, e.g., *Milton García Fajardo et al v. Nicaragua*, Case 11.281, Report No. 100/01, Inter-Am. Comm. H.R., OEA/Ser./L/V/II.114, doc. 5 rev. (2002) (finding State responsibility for violating labour rights protected under

Article 26 of Convention); *Jorge Odir Miranda Cortez et al v. El Salvador*, Case 12.249, Report No. 29/01, Inter-Am. C.H.R., OEA/Ser./L/V/II.111, doc. 20 rev. at 284 (2001), paras. 45–46 (finding right to health claim admissible under Article 26 of Convention for failure to reasonably provide antiretroviral medications, and finding right to life and right to integrity claims subsumed therein).

[59] For a relevant discussion, see Melish, 'Rethinking the "Less as More" Thesis' (n. 13 above), pp. 268–274.

[60] See *VIASA Pensioners v. Venezuela* (n. 23 above).

[61] See ibid. para. 63, in which Commission concluded that it had jurisdiction to examine the complaint regarding the alleged violation of Article 26 taken together with Article 1.1.

[62] *Ana Victoria Villalobos et al. v. Costa Rica* (n. 33 above), para. 52.

[63] *Laura Tena Colunga et al. v. Mexico*, Report No. 44/04, Petition 2582/02, Inter-Am. Comm. H.R., OEA/Ser.L/V/II.122, doc. 5 rev. 1 (2005). The case was, however, found inadmissible for alleging claims under a collective bargaining agreement. In each of the above cases, it was clear that the petitioner was challenging discrete instances of

In the 2005 admissibility decision of *Luis Rolando Cuscul Pivaral and Others Affected by HIV/AIDS v. Guatemala*, the Commission nonetheless appeared to temporarily retreat from its position on Article 26 in a case virtually identical to the 2001 access-to-antiretroviral-treatment case that had jumpstarted the Commission's emerging Article 26 jurisprudence.[64] Citing the Court's *Five Pensioners* dicta on Article 26, the Commission concluded that the Court's 'reflections' with respect to the right to social security and the non-cognisability of the 'collective dimensions' of 'progressive development' in the individual petitions process were equally applicable to the right to health. However, apparently on the false assumption that 'progressive development', interpreted in its collectively-oriented, result-based dimensions, was the *only* obligation relevant to the 'right to health' as an autonomous human rights guarantee, it inappropriately dismissed as inadmissible the Article 26 claim. It proceeded to suggest that contentious claims involving health rights were admissible under only two suppositions: where the right to equal protection of the law, under Article 24, was violated, and where a grave or immediate risk of loss of life of a person is demonstrated, thereby implicating Article 4 of the Convention.[65] This unjustifiably limited view, admitting but a fraction of the arbitrary forms of State conduct that commonly violate the health rights of individuals, if adopted in future decisions, would serve effectively to remove Article 26 and its autonomous protections from the Commission's contentious jurisdiction, in direct defiance of the Convention's express inclusion of all protected rights, when framed as justiciable 'cases', within that jurisdiction. It would also appear to limit the scope of Article 4's protection of 'life' to its narrowest physiological confines,[66] in conflict with the Court's broader 'life project' jurisprudence.[67]

The risks that this 180-degree turnaround, if extended to further cases, would present to the system's growing jurisprudence on economic, social and cultural rights cannot be overstated. It is imperative that the Commission confront the *Five Pensioners* dictum directly, recognising that while the standard of 'progressive development of rights' urged by petitioners in that case with respect to result-based human rights achievement over national collectivities is cognisable under the Commission's promotional and monitoring competence, it does not correspond to the jurisdictional parameters of the system's individual petitions process, a fact aptly and expressly recognised by at least one Judge on the *Five Pensioners* Court.[68] Such a course will permit the Commission to refocus, in the individual petitions process, on applying the litigation-*appropriate* dimensions of state obligations to the autonomous social rights guaranteed in Article 26,[69] just as it has long done with respect to the autonomous social rights guaranteed under the Declaration as well as those framed more broadly under Chapter II norms of the Convention. Only in this way may litigation of autonomous economic, social and cultural rights

---

[64] In that case, *Odir Miranda* (n. 58 above), the Commission held in its admissibility report that the right to health was directly adjudicable under Article 26 and that allegations regarding the right to life and right to integrity were 'secondary in nature to' and subsumed within the Article 26 claim. As such, in a case in which the Commission was asked to determine the 'international liability of the Salvadoran State for the delay in providing the proper medication and treatment to the patients', the Article 26 right-to-health claim was found admissible, while the Articles 4 and 5 life and integrity claims were not. See ibid. paras. 44–49. *Cuscul Pivaral* (n.57 above) turned this finding on its head.

[65] *Cuscul Pivaral* (n. 57 above), paras. 42–44. The implication was that the litigation-appropriate duties under Articles 1 and 2 would be applied to these Chapter II norms as the basis for determining state responsibility,

arbitrary state conduct that had caused direct harm to the named victims in their personal capacities, i.e., not to broad collectivities or as a general matter of 'non-progressive' or 'regressive' action or achievement.

[66] Ibid. para. 44.

[67] See section 5.1 of subsequent Chapter in this volume.

[68] Reasoned Opinion of Judge de Roux Rengifo, *Five Pensioners Case v. Peru*, Judgment of Feb. 28, 2003, Inter-Am. Ct. H.R. (Ser. C) No. 98 (2003). Judge Sergio García Ramírez of the Court also indicated in his own concurring opinion that future Article 26 claims may be considered where framed in their 'individual-oriented', not 'collectively-oriented', dimensions. See ibid. For a discussion, see Tara J. Melish, '*Counter-rejoinder*. Justice vs. Justiciability?: Normative Neutrality and Technical Precision, The Role of the Lawyer in Supranational Social Rights Litigation, *New York University Journal of International Law and Politics*, Vol. 39, No. 2 (2006), pp. 409–414.

[69] In many ways, the Commission prompted the Article 26 confusion in the *Five Pensioners Case* by attempting to apply litigation-inappropriate dimensions of human rights duties (such as a generalized 'prohibition on regressivity') to Article 26 claims rather than relying on the standard individual-oriented, conduct-based duties it applies to all other rights-based norms in the Convention and Declaration. See *Five Pensioners* Case (n. 68 above).

in the regional system proceed on a rational, effective, and legitimate basis.[70]

5. JURISPRUDENCE: ANALYSIS OF SPECIFIC RIGHTS

Given its comprehensive contentious jurisdiction over social rights, the Commission has developed a growing case-based jurisprudence on the rights to health, to education, to labour guarantees, to social security, to culture, and to housing and land resources, under both the American Declaration and the American Convention. This extensive jurisprudence, particularly as developed over the last six to seven years, is considered below.

5.1   Right to Health

Given the health-related focus of many regional social movements, the Commission has been particularly active in adjudicating individual complaints involving the right to health. While the first such cases were decided in the 1970s and 1980s under the American Declaration, the Commission has begun more recently to address the right to health under the American Convention. In so doing, it has fluctuated broadly in its normative reliance on the right to life, the right to integrity, and the autonomous right to health, guaranteed under Convention Articles 4, 5 and 26, respectively.[71] The right-to-health cases considered to

date by the Commission nonetheless tend to fall into four broad categories, each discussed below. These cases reflect a broad understanding of the right to health as encompassing not just medical care in a narrow sense but also the underlying determinants of health.[72]

The earliest set of right-to-health cases resolved by the Commission have involved indigenous communities. These cases have tended to arise where 'development' projects, particularly of an extractive nature, are authorised by American governments without being properly accompanied by appropriate measures to *prevent* harm to the health and well-being of surrounding populations, or to reasonably *respond* to such harm where it results from State-authorised conduct. The Commission has decided two such cases invoking the right to health under Article XI of the American Declaration. In the first, *Coulter v. Brazil*, the Brazilian government approved an extraction plan after valuable mineral deposits were discovered on the ancestral territory of the Yanomami Indigenous People. To facilitate miners' and prospectors' access to the previously isolated area, the State built a highway directly through Yanomami territory. This led, foreseeably, to the introduction of new and previously unknown diseases into the area, with grave consequences for the affected human communities: Hundreds of Yanomami died, the result of the government's failure to offer adequate preventive and responsive health and social services.[73] Accordingly, on the basis of Brazil's 'failure ... to take timely and effective measures' to protect the affected Yanomami from

---

[70] For a fuller discussion of the dangers associated with application to social rights of the litigation-inappropriate dimensions of human rights obligations in adjudicatory contexts, see Melish, 'Rethinking the "Less as More" Thesis' (n. 13 above) and T. J. Melish, 'A Pyrrhic Victory for Peru's Pensioners: Pensions, Property and the Perversion of Progressivity', *CEJIL Revista: Debates sobre Derechos Humanos y el Sistema Interamericano*, Vol. 1, No. 1 (2005), pp. 51–66.

[71] The Commission has at times found that Article 26 is the primary norm under the Convention when health issues are involved, and that it subsumes congruent claims under Articles 4 and 5. See *Odir Miranda* (n. 58 above), paras. 45–46. At others, it has found that Article 4 is the primary norm, subsuming within it claims under Articles 26 and 5. See *Cuscul Pivaral* (n. 57 above). And at still others, particularly when an Article 26 claim is not alleged, it has found that the 'right to health' is expressly protected in Articles 4 and 5 in addition to the rights to life and integrity. See, e.g., *Mendoza Prison Inmates v. Argentina*, Report N° 51/05, Petition 1231/04, Inter-Am. Comm. H.R., OEA/Ser.L/V/II.124, doc. 5 (2006); *Juan*

Hernández v. Guatemala, Report No. 28/96, Case 11.297, Inter-Am. Comm. H.R., OEA/Ser.L/V/II.95, doc. 7 rev. (1997), paras. 60–61.

[72] These include an adequate supply of safe food, nutrition, housing, access to safe and potable water and adequate sanitation, safe and healthy working conditions, a healthy environment, access to health-related education and information, including on sexual and reproductive health, and participation in health-related decision-making at the community, national and international levels. See, e.g., Committee on Economic, Social and Cultural Rights, *General Comment No. 14, The right to the highest attainable standard of health* (Twenty-second session, 2000), U.N. Doc. E/C.12/2000/4 (2000), paras. 4 and 11.

[73] In addition, the tribe was forced to abandon its traditional land, its culture and social organisation were fractured, and prostitution was introduced. The Brazilian government tried to resettle the tribe, but failed to respond with adequate social or health services.

foreseeable injury to their health, the Commission found the government internationally responsible under Declaration Article XI for violating the right to health of the affected members of the Yanomami.[74]

Similarly, the Commission found Paraguay internationally responsible for violating the right to health, under Article XI of the Declaration, of the members of the Aché Indigenous People. This resulted from Paraguay's failure to take appropriate and necessary preventive and responsive measures to protect members of the tribe from the onset of a fatal epidemic that affected their lives and health.[75] Not only was that epidemic foreseeable given the nature of state and third-party conduct in the victims' ancestral habitat, but the State was found to have actively deprived the tribal members of medical attention and medicines. Analogous claims have been made in the more recent *Sarayaku* case, albeit under the right-to-health guarantee of Article 26 of the Convention.[76]

A second set of right-to-health cases has arisen where persons in state custody require medical attention and the State fails negligently, recklessly or intentionally to provide it. Specifically, the Commission has found that failure to provide medical attention on a reasonable basis to prisoners violates both the autonomous right to health under Article XI of the Declaration[77] and the rights to life and integrity (read to encompass the right to health) under Articles 4 and 5 of the Convention.

In *Juan Hernández v. Guatemala*, for example, the Commission found violations of the Convention-based rights to life and integrity, where a detainee died in a Guatemalan prison of cholera, a common, easily preventable and easily curable disease. State responsibility arose given that prison authorities, having complete control over the victim, failed to act 'with the diligence required to protect the victim's life and health'.[78] That is, despite knowledge of the victim's easily treatable health condition, they failed to provide the victim with sufficient rehydration formula and to transfer him to a hospital facility, as was obviously the appropriate course given the severity of his condition. Consequently, the State, as guarantor of the health and life of persons in its custody, was found to have 'violated by omission its duty to guarantee the health' of the victim.[79]

The Commission has reaffirmed and expanded this legal principle with respect to mental health. In *Victor Rosario Congo v. Ecuador*,[80] a man in state custody suffering from psychosis died due to dehydration and malnutrition after being left in an isolation cell for over forty days. Despite documented head injuries and temporal and spatial disorientation, he was at no time given medical attention, removed to a health facility, or given the assistance he needed in cleaning and feeding himself, given the evident poor state of his health.

In the Commission's view, OAS member States' duties to ensure the health and integrity of persons in state custody are heightened when those persons have an intellectual, psychiatric, or psychosocial disability.[81] In the *Congo* case, the measures incumbent upon the State included not only medical care to heal the detainee's physical injuries, but also 'such vital ministrations as cleansing, food, and psychological attention' to treat his depression and the psychosis characteristic of Ganser's

---

[74] *Coulter et al. Case v. Brazil*, Res. 12/85, Case 7615, Inter-Am. Comm. H.R., OEA/Ser.L/V/II.66, doc. 10 rev. 1 (1985) The Commission also found violations of Articles I and VIII, protecting the rights to 'life, liberty, and personal security' and 'residence and movement', respectively.

[75] *Aché People v. Paraguay*, Case 1802, Inter-Am. Comm. H.R., OEA/Ser.L/V/II.43 doc. 21 corr. 1 (1978). The Commission also found the State responsible for violating the rights of the Aché to work, to rest, and to special protection of the family, under Declaration Articles XIV, XV and VI.

[76] *Kichwa Peoples of the Sarayaku Community and its Members v. Ecuador*, Report No. 64/04, Petition 167/l03, Inter-Am. Comm. H.R., OEA/Ser.L/V/II.122, doc. 5 rev. 1 (2005) (*'Sarayaku Case'*). The health of the Sarayaku community has been put at risk through government-supported oil exploration activities on the community's ancestral territory and through blockades of the river the community uses to enter and leave its territory to access health services and health-related goods.

[77] Case No. 6091 (Cuba), Res. No. 3/82, Inter-Am. Comm. H.R., OEA/Ser.L/V/II.57, doc. 6 rev.1 (1982) (failure to protect health and well-being in custody).

[78] *Juan Hernández v. Guatemala*, Case 11.297, Report No. 28/96, Inter-Am. Comm. H.R., OEA/Ser.L/V/II.95, doc. 7 rev. (1997), at 406, para. 17. Because the victim was in State custody he 'had no means to turn to his relatives and friends, to an attorney or to a private physician; the State, therefore, had complete control over his life and personal safety'.

[79] Ibid. para. 16.

[80] *Victor Rosario Congo v. Ecuador*, Report No. 63/99, Case 11.427, Inter-Am. Comm. H.R., OEA/Ser.L/V/II.102, doc. 6 rev. (1999).

[81] Ibid. para. 67.

syndrome.[82] In coming to this conclusion, the Commission cited case law from the European regional human rights system, as well as the UN Mental Health Principles and the Minimum Standards for the Treatment of Prisoners. In doing so, it concluded that applicable international standards require that 'every detention center shall possess the services of at least one qualified physician, who must possess some psychiatric knowledge'. Moreover, '[t]his physician must be responsible for the physical and mental health of the inmates and must see those with health problems every day as well as those drawn to his attention'.[83] Because the State failed to show that it took the measures incumbent on it to ensure Mr. Congo's physical and mental health, including that he was fed while in state custody, the Commission found Ecuador responsible for violating Articles 4 and 5 of the Convention.

Significantly, as a measure to ensure against future recurrence of similar abuses in detention facilities, the Commission specifically recommended that the Ecuadorean State '[p]rovide medical and psychiatric care for persons suffering from mental illness and confined in penitentiary facilities' and '[a]ssign to the health services of the penitentiary system specialists able to identify psychiatric disorders that can affect the lives and the physical, mental and moral integrity of those confined in it'.[84] A similar case, *Damião Ximenes Lopes v. Brazil*, was also recently resolved by the Commission and, in 2005, sent to the Court for final decision. In that case, a man died two days after being admitted to a state-run psychiatric facility where he was subjected to severe physical abuse and denied proper physical and mental health care.[85] In proceedings before the Court, Brazil recognised its responsibility for breach of Mr. Ximenes rights to life and integrity under the Convention. This followed from the hospital's grossly inadequate treatment of the victim as well as the State's failure to

take appropriate measures to prevent abuse in the mental health facility.

A third, closely related set of cases involves the State duty to ensure general conditions of health, hygiene and sanitation in prison or custodial facilities. In the 2002 Grenada prison cases of *Paul Lallion*[86] and *Benedict Jacob*,[87] for example, the Commission found that the inhuman conditions of detention to which the petitioners were subjected violated their rights under Article 5 of the Convention. Significantly, in coming to this conclusion, the Commission evaluated the petitioners' allegations in light of the United Nations Standard Minimum Rules for the Treatment of Prisoners.[88] Finding that the prisoners' conditions failed 'to meet several of these minimum standards of treatment of prisoners, in such areas as hygiene, exercise and medical care', the Commission concluded that the inmates' rights had been violated under the Convention. The Commission currently has several similar cases under consideration, each involving severe overcrowding, lack of sanitary facilities, insufficient food, and inadequate medical attention, having found the respective alleged violations of the 'right to health' admissible under Articles 4 and 5 of the Convention.[89]

A fourth set of cases, still in initial stages of jurisprudential development by the Commission, arises where individuals who are not in state custody need direct provision of medications, medical services or other health-related goods from the government because they are unable to provide

---

[82] Ibid. para. 74.

[83] Ibid. para. 80; see also paras. 66, 77–80, 82.

[84] Ibid. para. 98. These were in addition to the usual recommendations to investigate and sanction those responsible for the violation and to compensate the victim's family.

[85] *Damião Ximenes Lopes v. Brazil*, Case 12.237, Report No. 38/02, Inter-Am. C.H.R., OEA/Ser.L/V/II.117, doc. 1 rev. 1 (2003) (admissible as to Convention Articles 4, 5, 11 and 25). For the Court's 2006 final judgment on the case, see *Ximenes Lopes v. Brazil*, Judgment of July 4, 2006, Inter-Am. Ct. H.R. (Ser. C) No. 149.

[86] *Paul Lallion v. Grenada*, Case 11.765, Report No. 55/02, Inter-Am. C.H.R., OEA/Ser.L/V/II.117, doc. 1 rev. 1 (2003).

[87] *Benedict Jacob v. Grenada*, Case 12.158, Report No. 56/02, Inter-Am. C.H.R., OEA/Ser.L/V/II.117, doc. 1 rev. 1 (2003).

[88] These rules provide for minimum basic standards in prison contexts on medical treatment, accommodation, hygiene, sanitation, exercise, etc. They include the requirement that all accommodation meet health requirements related to air content, minimum floor space, lighting, heating and ventilation; that sanitary installations be adequate to enable every prisoner to comply with the needs of nature when necessary and in a clean and decent manner; and that a medical officer examines on a daily basis all sick prisoners, all who complain of illness, and any prisoner to whom his attention is specially directed. Ibid.

[89] See, e.g., *Mendoza Prison Inmates v. Argentina*, Report No. 51/05, Petition 1231/04, Inter-Am. Comm. H.R., Annual Report 2005, paras. 5 and 46; *Adolescents in the Custody of the Febem v. Brazil*, Case 12.328, Report No. 39/02, Inter-Am. C.H.R., OEA/Ser.L/V/II.117, doc. 1 rev. 1 (2003).

for themselves. Most of these cases, though not all,[90] have involved access to antiretroviral medications for persons living with HIV/AIDS, a set of cases that raise complicated issues. While the Commission has issued precautionary measures in a large number of these (see Section 7.4 below), it has to date issued formal admissibility decisions in only two, *Odir Miranda v. El Salvador* and *Luis Rolando Cuscul Pivaral v. Guatemala*,[91] the former under Article 26 (right to health) of the Convention, the latter under Article 4 (right to life). The issue to be resolved in both cases is whether the State breached its Convention-based legal obligations held to the alleged victims, causing them concrete harm, by unreasonably failing to provide antiretroviral drugs and testing to them.[92]

Finally, in 2003, the Commission found admissible an interesting case with respect to the right to a healthy environment. In *Marcel Claude Reyes et al. v. Chile*, the petitioners alleged that Chile violated the right to freedom of expression and free access to state-held information under Article 13 of the Convention by failing to release information about a deforestation project the petitioners wanted to evaluate in terms of its environmental impacts.[93] The Commission found that the State has a positive obligation to provide information to the public in such circumstances. The case was forwarded to the Court, which in 2006 found Chile responsible for breach of Convention Article 13.[94] The decision promises important carry-over implications for a variety of citizen initiatives aimed at ensuring that proper environmental and human impact studies are undertaken prior to state authorisation or implementation of development projects and other initiatives that may detrimentally affect surrounding human populations.

5.2   Right to Education

The Commission has likewise begun to jurisprudentially develop caselaw on the autonomous right to education. While this caselaw has to date focused on Article XII of the American Declaration and Article 13 of the Protocol of San Salvador, it is hoped that the Commission will soon extend the basis for its decisions to the autonomous guarantee of the right to education enshrined in Convention Article 26.[95] The system's first right-to-education case, *Jehovah's Witnesses v. Argentina*, was adjudicated in 1978 under the American Declaration. It stemmed from a presidential decree that prohibited all activities of the Jehovah's Witness religious order in Argentina, including in the nation's schools. Three hundred primary-school children were consequently expelled from educational establishments, denied school enrolment or prevented from taking final exams on account of their continued exercise of their religious faith.[96] Based on these state-authorised acts and the particularised education-related injuries they caused, the Commission found Argentina internationally responsible for violating the affected children's right to education under Article XII of the Declaration.

In a similar, more recent case, the Commission found the Dominican Republic internationally responsible for violating Article XII of the Declaration to the detriment of a young girl arbitrarily dismissed from school on account of her ethnic descent. The Dominican Republic in effect maintained a policy of conditioning school registration on possession of a birth certificate, while concurrently maintaining a policy of regularly denying birth certificates to persons of Haitian lineage. After failing to present a birth certificate to her school (despite repeated attempts to access one), the thirteen-year-old girl of Haitian descent was arbitrarily expelled by school staff. The only educational alternative left open to her was attendance at night literacy classes for adults, clearly inadequate for a thirteen-year-old child. This unreasonable situation was found by the Commission to constitute a violation of the young girl's right to education under Article XII of the

---

[90] See, for example, the *Yakye Axa* and *Sawhoyamaxa* cases (discussed below) in which the Commission found Paraguay responsible for failure to provide needed food and health supplies to two extremely vulnerable and impoverished indigenous communities.

[91] *Odir Miranda* (n. 58 above), *Cuscul Pivaral* (n. 57 above).

[92] The Commission has approved a final report on the merits in the *Odir Miranda* case, although it remains confidential while El Salvador is given the opportunity to comply with the Commission's merits-based recommendations.

[93] *Marcel Claude Reyes et al. v. Chile*, Case 12.108, Report No. 60/03, Inter-Am. Comm. H.R., OEA/Ser.L/V/II.118 Doc. 70 rev. 2 at 222 (2003).

[94] *Case of Claude Reyes et al. v. Chile*, Judgment of Sept. 19, 2006, Inter-Am. Ct. H.R. (Ser. C) No. 151.

[95] In this way, the binding nature of the right to education with respect to all OAS member states will be clear.

[96] *Jehovah's Witnesses v. Argentina*, Case No. 2137, Inter-Am. Comm. H.R., OEA/Ser.L/V/II.47, doc. 13 rev. 1 (1979).

Declaration, a right also guaranteed in the Dominican Constitution to all person's within the State's jurisdiction.[97]

Finally, in potentially the first case in which the Commission will rule directly on a violation of the Protocol of San Salvador, the Commission has declared admissible claims that the State of Brazil violated the right to education of adolescents held in a state prison. Petitioners allege that the children were held in isolation, under degrading and unsanitary conditions, and without access to educational programs necessary for their development.[98] The case is proceeding under Article 13 of the Protocol in this latter respect, in conjunction with other alleged violations under the American Convention.

5.3 Right to Social Security

The right to social security has also been addressed directly by the Commission in an increasing number of cases and under a variety of Convention-based guarantees. In *Five Pensioners v. Peru*,[99] the Commission found State responsibility for violation of the right to social security under Article 26 of the Convention. The violation stemmed from the effects of pension-reform legislation on five retired civil service workers, whose vested benefits were reduced by almost eighty per cent of their pre-reform worth. In addition to the Article 26 violation, the Commission concurrently found breach of the pensioners' right to property under Convention Article 21 and, given the State's failure to execute judicial orders from the nation's highest courts in the pensioners' favour, their right to judicial protection under Article 25.

Similar claims were found admissible against Peru in 2002[100] and Venezuela in 2004.[101] The latter, *Pensioners of the Venezuelan Aviation Company v. Venezuela*, was particularly significant given that the Commission expressly found that it had competence 'regarding the alleged violations to the guarantee of the right to social security by virtue of Article 26 of the American Convention'.[102] This view prevailed notwithstanding a dissent that invoked the 2003 *Five Pensioners Case*, in which the Inter-American Court declined to rule on a congruent right-to-social-security claim under Article 26.[103] The decision signalled that the Commission as a whole did not view 'progressive development of economic, social and cultural rights' as the proper justiciable standard applicable to determining violations of the discrete rights guaranteed under Article 26, such as the right to social security, and that it did not read the Court's *Five Pensioners* Case as signalling to that effect.

Unequal treatment in the distribution of pension benefits has also drawn the censure of the Commission in the individual petitions process. In the 1990 *National Vanguard Movement of Retirees and Pensioners* Case,[104] the State of Uruguay readjusted pension and retirement payments for beneficiaries within the same income category so that some were receiving more than the Average Wage Index and others receiving less. Although the case was formally found inadmissible for failure to exhaust domestic remedies, the Commission felt compelled to affirm that readjustment of pension payments to a level lower than a common index

---

[97] While the Commission's merits-based report is not published given the case's referral to the Court, the Commission's main recommendations are included in the Court record. See *Yean and Bosico v. Dominican Republic*, Judgment of Sept. 8, 2005, Inter-Am. Ct. H.R. (Ser. C) No. 130 (2005), para. 29 (noting Commission's finding that the State violated the girls' right to education under Article XII of the American Declaration).

[98] *Adolescents in the Custody of the Febem Case* (n. 89 above).

[99] *'Five Pensioners' Case* (n. 68 above). This case is more fully discussed in the following Chapter of this volume. It is contended that the Commission should not have found a violation of either Article 21 or 26, given the peculiar facts of the case and the permissibility of restrictions on rights when 'necessary in a democratic society' and 'intended to satisfy a compelling public interest'. See Melish, 'A Pyrrhic Victory' (n. 70 above).

[100] *National Association of Discharged and Retired Staff of the Office of the Comptroller General of the Republic of Peru v. Peru*, Case 12.313, Report No. 47/02, Inter-Am. Comm. H.R., Doc. 5 rev. 1 at 397 (2002).

[101] *VIASA Pensioners v. Venezuela* (n. 23 above).

[102] Ibid. para. 46.

[103] Ibid. Reasoned Vote by C. K. Roberts ('I share the decision of admissibility in the present report with the exception of the inclusion of Article 26. In my opinion, the facts do not establish a prima facie case of the violation of Article 26. My position is reinforced by the fact that in the *Five Pensioners Case*, the request to rule on the progressive development of economic, social and cultural rights in Peru on facts similar to the facts of this case was denied by the Inter-American Court').

[104] *National Vanguard Movement of Retirees and Pensioners v. Uruguay*, Report No. 90/90, Case 9893, Inter-Am. Comm. H.R., OEA/Ser.L/V/II.79 rev. 1 Doc. 12 (1991), para. 25.

violates the right to equal protection of the law under Convention Article 24.[105]

Each of the above cases dealt specifically with retirement pensions. Nonetheless, given that Article 26 of the Convention and Article XVI of the Declaration protect the 'right to social security' more broadly, the same principles apply to all forms of social assistance that protect individuals from the 'consequences of unemployment, old age, and any disabilities arising from causes beyond [an individual's] control that make it physically or mentally impossible . . . to earn a living'.[106]

5.4 Right to Housing and Related Land Resources

Important jurisprudential developments have taken place with respect to the right to adequate housing and housing-related resources, such as land, as well. These advances have been most prominent in four core areas: (1) forced evictions and removals; (2) retaliatory abuses for popular organising around land claims; (3) dilatory processing of land claims; and (4) housing and property confiscations.

The Commission has addressed the issue of forced evictions and collective expulsions in several cases. In 2004, in *Corumbiara v. Brazil*, it found violations of Convention Articles 4, 5, 8 and 25 in relation to a violent forced eviction of 500 families of extremely poor, landless rural workers. The families, without access to employment, land or credit and for whom ownership of a small parcel of land represented one of their only hopes for surviving in dignity, had invaded a small portion of a ranch to meet their immediate survival needs and to put pressure on the government to solve the land crisis in Northern Brazil. When the owner of the ranch sought their eviction, a court order was granted the same day and, in the dark of dawn, a violent eviction operation was illegally carried out by military police with the assistance of private gunmen hired by local landowners. The evictors, wearing masks and face paint, used tear-gas bombs, personal weapons, and deadly force. At least nine squatters were killed, most shot in the back or at close range, and over 100 were wounded as a result of the violent confrontation. The entire settlement, including all of the evictees' belongings, was then destroyed and set ablaze.

While the Commission held that 'it is beyond the scope of this case to examine the economic, social, historic, and other reasons that might have led the occupying workers to make the decision to invade Santa Elena ranch in July 1995 and set up a camp there', it affirmed that it would analyse the way in which the court order for eviction was carried out. The Commission held that any use of excessive force – defined as force not strictly necessary and proportionate to the situation – violates the right to humane treatment and, accordingly, any resulting death is arbitrary. It thus found Brazil internationally responsible for violating Articles 4 and 5 of the Convention to the detriment of the injured and deceased workers. It is unfortunate that the petitioners did not broaden their claims under Articles 11, 25 and 26 of the Convention, and that the Commission did not do so *sua sponte*, to address the many other ways in which the forced eviction and lack of effective mechanisms for accessing basic housing needs violated minimum international law duties of the State, such as through the wholesale destruction of the evictees' possessions, the lack of notice and consultation, the dawn timing of the eviction, and the lack of housing alternatives to address the immediate needs of the evictee families.[107]

---

[105] Ibid.

[106] See American Declaration (n. 18 above), art. XVI. Though formally found inadmissible for not being presented within a 'reasonable time', the Commission has, for example, been presented with a petition alleging violation of Convention Article 25 for failure to comply with a domestic judicial ruling ordering the payment of social benefits. *Romeel Eduardo Días Luna v. Peru*, Report No. 85/05, Petition 430/00, Inter-Am. Comm. H.R., OEA/Ser.L/V/II.124, Doc. 5 (2000).

[107] See, e.g., Committee on Economic, Social and Cultural Rights, *General Comment No. 7, Forced evictions, and the right to adequate housing* (Sixteenth session, 1997), U.N. Doc. E/1998/22, annex IV at 113 (1997), paras. 15–16; Committee on Economic, Social and Cultural Rights, *General Comment No. 4, The right to adequate housing* (Sixth session, 1991), U.N. Doc. E/1992/23, annex III at 114 (1991). Although the respective adjudicatory bodies took very different approaches to the cases, the factual similarities are striking between *Corumbiara v. Brazil*, decided in 2004 by the Inter-American Commission, and *Government of Republic of South Africa and others v. Grootboom and others 2000* (11) BCLR decided by the Constitutional Court of South Africa in 2000. For a discussion of the consequences of taking the more limited *Corumbiara* approach to the housing and land issues, rather than a more integrated approach, see Melish,

The Commission has also considered forced evictions and displacements of indigenous populations in situations of armed conflict,[108] and is currently considering the policy of forced deportation/expulsion of persons of Haitian descent in the Dominican Republic,[109] which carries important housing rights implications.

Despite the Commission's limited treatment of the land and housing issues in *Corumbiara*, the Commission has dealt directly with access-to-land claims by the landless and inadequately housed in two other types of cases. The first involves retaliation against members of landless peoples' organisations in an attempt to stifle their activities. The Commission has, for example, found Brazil internationally responsible for violating Articles 4, 5, 8 and 25 of the Convention on account of retaliatory killings of members of a 'landless' workers' organisation by Brazil's military police.[110] It has found a similar case admissible in which nineteen landless rural workers were killed by military ambush, and dozens more wounded, when the military police surrounded their camp on the side of a public roadway in an attempt to dislodge them.[111] The group, consisting of 1,500 rural workers whose families lacked sufficient land to be able to live a life of dignity, were making their way to the capital of Pará to demand respect for an agreement previously made with the state and federal government to expropriate a *hacienda* for their settlement.

The second type of access-to-land claims addressed by the Commission involves the dilatory administrative processing of claims for land or land titling, especially for dispossessed indigenous communities and others with inadequate access to land and housing. The Commission has considered or is considering many such claims from a variety of landless or land-poor communities,[112] but particularly from the indigenous communities of the Enxet People of Paraguay. In the *Yakye Axa* case, for example, the Commission found the State of Paraguay responsible for violating, to the detriment of the members of the Yakye Axa indigenous community, the rights to a dignified life, to communal property and to judicial protection under Articles 4, 21 and 25 of the Convention. During the ten years in which their land claim had formally been in administrative process they lived in deplorable conditions on the edge of a highway adjacent to their ancestral territory. Meanwhile, an injunctive order issued by a local judge prohibited them from entering their ancestral territory to engage in traditional hunting, fishing, and gathering activities or from accessing a nearby water source. The community, prevented by state acts from accessing their subsistence needs on their own, was thereby rendered dependent on state aid for their survival. Based on these facts, the Commission found State responsibility on three intersecting grounds: one, the State's dilatory administrative processing of the community's bid to recover their ancestral lands; two, its prohibition on community members' entry into their ancestral habitat to engage in traditional subsistence economic activities during that administrative processing; and, three, its concurrent failure to provide them with adequate medical and nutritional assistance while prevented from accessing their ancestral territory to provide such goods on their own.[113]

Similar claims have been made by the Sawhoyamaxa and Xakmok Kásek indigenous communities of the Enxet Peoples. Both communities have brought admissible claims against the State of Paraguay for unreasonable administrative delay in processing their land claims. Meanwhile, they argue, the members of their communities, left in

'Rethinking the "Less as More" Thesis' (n. 13 above), pp. 315–23.

[108] See, e.g., *Plan de Sánchez Massacre v. Guatemala*, Report No. 33/99, Case 11.763, Inter-Am. Comm. H.R., OEA/Ser.L/V/II.102, doc. 6 rev. (1999). The Court decided the merits of the case in 2005. For a brief discussion, see the following Chapter in this volume.

[109] *Benito Tide Méndes et al. v. Dominican Republic*, Report No. 68/05, Petition 12.271, Inter-Am. Comm. H.R., OEA/Ser.L/V/II.124, doc. 5 (2006).

[110] *Diniz Bento da Silva v. Brazil*, Case 11.517, Report No. 23/02, Inter-Am. C.H.R., OEA/Ser.L/V/II.117, doc. 1 rev. 1 (2003).

[111] *El Dorado Dos Carajas v. Brazil*, Case 11.820, Report No. 4/03, Inter-Am. C.H.R., OEA/Ser.L/V/II.118, doc. 5 rev. 2 (2003).

[112] See, e.g., *'Ojo de Agua' Cooperative v. Mexico*, Report No. 73/99, Case 11.701, Inter-Am. Comm. H.R., OEA/Ser.L/V/II.106, doc. 6 rev. (2000). The case, involving the refusal by Mexican agrarian authorities to comply with a presidential order that established 4,494 hectares as common land in favour of 132 peasants, was nonetheless found inadmissible for failure to exhaust domestic remedies.

[113] *Yakye Axa Indigenous Community of the Enxet-Lengua People v. Paraguay*, Case 12.313, Report No. 2/02, Inter-Am. C.H.R., OEA/Ser.L/V/II.117, doc. 1 rev. 1 (2003). The Commission's report on the merits was not published as the case was sent to the Court for final resolution.

limbo, are living in sub-human conditions, which, due to lack of adequate food and medical care, has led to the death of several indigenous community members, including minors.[114]

Finally, the Commission has considered a wide variety of cases involving allegedly illegal housing, land, and property confiscations, mostly under Article 21 of the Convention, which protects the right to property. Most of these cases have involved individual property-holders whose houses or lands were expropriated by the State without just compensation or without respecting the 'forms established by law', as required by the American Convention.[115] For these case-specific persons, the housing and land at issue was largely fungible and thus the dispute centred primarily on issues of just compensation.

This is not always the case, however, particularly where the State engages in unjustified 'takings' or expropriation of the ancestral lands and habitat of indigenous communities. In the Americas, this most commonly occurs through the granting of government concessions to extractive industries for the exploitation of natural resources in ancestral territories, without the free and informed prior consent of the affected community. Because of the close tie between ancestral territory and the cultural integrity, economic survival, and even physical existence of indigenous peoples, ancestral territory is rarely if ever fungible for indigenous communities and hence the respective weights in any property-based balancing test must be carefully assessed under fact-specific considerations

that take group-specific threats to life and culture expressly into account. The Commission has decided one such case under the Declaration and is currently considering two under the Convention, having sent the landmark *Awas Tingni* case (discussed in the following Chapter) to the Court in 1998.[116]

In the former, *Maya Indigenous Communities of the Toledo District v. Belize*, the State of Belize granted logging and oil concessions to a foreign extraction company on lands traditionally used and occupied by the Maya people, without their consent and without any process of prior consultation. The Commission found Belize internationally responsible for violating the rights of the affected Maya to property and to equality under Articles XXIII and II of the Declaration. According to the Commission, responsibility arose from the State's failure:

> [T]o take effective measures to delimit, demarcate, and officially recognize their communal property right to the lands that they have traditionally occupied and used, and by granting logging and oil concessions to third parties to utilize the property and resources that could fall within the lands which must be delimited, demarcated and titled, without consultations with and the informed consent of the Maya people.[117]

Based on these findings, the Commission recommended that the State recognise, without detriment to other indigenous communities, the Maya people's communal property right to the lands they have traditionally occupied and used, and to delimit, demarcate and title the territory in which this communal property right exists, in accordance with the customary land use practices of the Maya people. The Commission also recommended that, until the Maya's territory is properly delimited, demarcated and titled, the State abstain

---

[114] *See Sawhoyamaxa Indigenous Community of the Enxet People v. Paraguay*, Case 322/2001, Report No. 12/03, Inter-Am. Comm. H.R., OEA/Ser.L/V/II.118, doc. 5 rev. 2 (2003); *Xakmok Kásek Indigenous Community of the Enxet People v. Paraguay*, Case 326/01, Report No. 11/03, Inter-Am. Comm. H.R., OEA/Ser.L/V/II.118, doc. 5 rev. 2 (2003).

[115] See, e.g., *Maria Chiriboga and Guillermo Chiriboga v. Ecuador*, Case 12.054, Report No. 76/03, Inter-Am. Comm. H.R., OEA/Ser.L/V/II.118, doc. 5 rev. 2 (2003) (finding claim involving expropriation of property for public park without just and prior compensation admissible under Convention Articles 21, 8 and 25); *Benjamin Guerra Duarte v. Nicaragua*, Case 11.433, Report No. 37/05, Inter-Am. Comm. H.R., OEA/Ser.L/V/II.124, doc. 5 (2006) (finding claim involving expropriation of housing property without just compensation admissible for failure to exhaust domestic remedies); *Oscar Siri Suniga v. Honduras*, Case 12.006, Report No. 87/03, Inter-Am. Comm. H.R., OEA/Ser.L/V/II.118, doc. 5 rev. 2 (2003) (same, illegal occupation of land by U.S. Military Group).

[116] An additional case, not discussed here, that involves indigenous property rights and state confiscation is *Mary and Carrie Dann v. United States*, Case 11.140, Report No. 75/02, Inter-Am. C.H.R., OEA/Ser.L/V/II.117, doc. 1 rev. 1 (2003).

[117] *Maya Indigenous Communities of the Toledo District v. Belize* (n. 22 above), para. 5. The Commission also concluded that the State violated the right to judicial protection (Declaration Article XVIII) to the detriment of the Maya people, by rendering judicial proceedings brought by them ineffective through unreasonable delay. Ibid.

from any acts that might lead its agents, or third parties acting with the State's acquiescence or tolerance, to affect the existence, value, use or enjoyment of the property located in the geographic area occupied and used by the Maya people.[118]

Similar property-rights issues arise in *12 Saramaka Clans v. Suriname*, decided by the Court in November 2007 (see the following chapter in this volume), and *Kichwa Peoples of the Sarayaku Community and its Members v. Ecuador*. In the latter case, an oil exploration and extraction concession covering the legally recognised territory of the Sarayaku was granted by the State to a foreign extraction company.[119] This was done without the prior consent or even knowledge of the Sarayaku people, and without any process of prior consultation. The case takes an important step beyond *Maya Toledo* in the sense that legal title to the previously demarcated land was firmly held by the Sarayaku *prior* to the concession. Accordingly, the Commission should address its merits-based conclusions and recommendations directly to the critical issues of free and informed consent, prior consultation, and the conditions, if any, under which oil extraction on the lands of indigenous communities who oppose it may proceed consistent with the Convention. The Commission found the case admissible in 2004 with respect to Articles 4, 5, 7, 8, 12, 13, 16, 19, 21, 22, 23, 24, 25, and 26 of the American Convention, in conjunction with Articles 1.1 and 2.[120]

5.5 Labour Rights

The rights to unionisation, to work, and to just conditions of work have received significant case-based attention as well by the Commission. These cases, most of which have been brought under the guarantees on freedom of association, due process, and judicial protection contained in the American Convention, have tended to fall into two broad and frequently overlapping categories: (1) retaliation for labour union organising or activity, and (2) arbitrary or unjustified job dismissals.

The former set of cases have tended to be framed under either Article 26 or 16 of the Convention, together with Articles 8 and 25 on judicial

guarantees and judicial protection. In addition to the Court-adjudicated cases of *Baena Ricardo v. Panama* and *Pedro Huilca Tecsey v. Peru* (see following chapter in this volume for discussion), the Commission has decided two additional union retaliation cases in 2001 and 2003, respectively: *Milton García Fajardo v. Nicaragua* and *Finca 'La Exacta' v. Guatemala*. The first involved the dismissal of 142 customs workers who went on strike after unsuccessfully trying to negotiate a number of petitions related to wage indexing and job stability with the Nicaraguan Ministry of Labour. The following day the Ministry declared the strike illegal and summarily dismissed all of the striking workers, most of whom were union members.[121] The Commission found the State responsible for violating the workers 'economic rights', including the right to unionise, under Article 26 of the Convention:

> The Commission finds that the economic rights of the customs workers fall within the framework of protection of the economic, social and cultural rights shielded by the American Convention in Article 26. The violations of the workers' rights are plain in terms of the principles of legality and retroactivity, and of protection of judicial guarantees. The violations on the part of the State of Nicaragua caused economic harm to, and infringed the social rights of, the petitioners.[122]

In coming to this conclusion, the Commission noted that the dismissed workers had 600 financial dependents, more than half of them children. It also recalled, for purposes of interpretation, that the American Declaration 'provides that every person has the right to work, leisure time and to social security', and that Nicaragua had signed the Protocol of San Salvador prior to the events in controversy. It therefore determined that by arbitrarily curtailing the workers' right to work, the State had caused 'grave injury to their economic and social rights'.[123]

Interestingly, the Commission held that 'the right to unionize is a substantive labor right'.[124] As such, it was protected by Article 26 of the Convention,

---

[118] Ibid. para. 6.
[119] *Sarayaku Case* (n. 76 above).
[120] Ibid. para. 77.1.

[121] *Milton García Fajardo et al. v. Nicaragua*, Case 11.281, Report No. 100/01, Inter-Am. Comm. H.R., OEA/Ser./ L/V/II.114, doc. 5 rev. (2002).
[122] Ibid. para. 95.
[123] Ibid. para. 101.
[124] Ibid. para. 106.

rather than, as the petitioners had argued, by Article 16 (freedom of association). According to the Commission, 'regardless of any intrinsic link that the right to freedom of association may have with the right to strike, it is not sufficient to prove violation of the right of association of the customs workers under the terms set forth in the Convention'.[125] This position was in many ways superseded by the Court's 2001 decision in *Baena Ricardo*, the holding of which was based on Convention Article 16, together with Articles 8 and 25, rather than Article 26. The Commission adopted the Article 16 approach to union rights in its next significant union retaliation case in 2003: *Finca 'La Exacta'*.

The *Finca 'La Exacta'* case involved a labour dispute between workers on a Guatemalan farm and the farm's owners and administrators. Failure to resolve the dispute prompted the workers to organise themselves, in accordance with the Guatemalan Labour Code, into a union and to institute labour court proceedings. In response, the owners and administrators began to dismiss *en masse* the workers who had signed the petition to initiate the legally prescribed collective bargaining procedure. Though the workers immediately instituted domestic judicial proceedings for their reinstatement, the owners of the estate refused to engage in any negotiations or judicial proceedings. The Guatemalan labour courts took no responsive action. As a result, after four months of efforts to resolve the dispute, the workers occupied the estate. The occupation was followed by an illegal eviction in which excessive force was employed. In assessing that force, the Commission concluded that 'the way in which the raid was planned and executed show[s] that the purpose was to suppress the labor movement and its activities on Finca "La Exacta"'.[126] It decidedly affirmed that:

> In coming together in a trade union to carry out union activities, the workers had embarked on an initiative protected by Article 16 of the Convention.... [Consequently, the] reprisals taken against the union activities and the suppression of the trade union movement constitutes a violation of Article 16.[127]

The Commission also affirmed that the failure of the Guatemalan State to ensure access to justice with respect to the labour claims filed in the domestic court system – both with respect to the initial labour dispute involving working conditions on the *finca* and, later, with respect to the dismissal of the workers – constituted a violation of Articles 8 and 25 of the American Convention. It concluded that 'the dismissed workers were not given an opportunity to be heard nor were they given access to a prompt and effective remedy against the violations of the law that adversely affected their *right to work and their right to freedom of association*, rights recognised both in the Guatemalan Constitution and in the American Convention'.[128] Noting that Guatemalan authorities had admitted that the case formed part of a general tendency of the Guatemalan courts to fail to provide protection in labour-related matters, the Commission urged the State to 'take the necessary measures to ensure that violations of the type that took place in this case do not recur in the future'.[129]

Two similar cases were found admissible by the Commission in 2006, one involving union retaliation by a private company in Costa Rica,[130] the other failure to legally recognise a union of public sector education workers in El Salvador.[131] While the former relies principally on Article 16 of the Convention, which protects the right to freely associate for labour purposes, the latter relies on Article 8.1.a of the Protocol of San Salvador, guaranteeing the right to unionisation. Both concurrently allege violations of the rights to due process and judicial protection, under Convention Articles 8 and 25, with respect to the labour rights abuses.

The Commission has addressed unjustified job dismissals in many other cases as well, although a large number of these have been dismissed for failure to exhaust domestic remedies or for other basic admissibility errors.[132] Of those found

---

[125] Ibid.

[126] *Finca 'La Exacta' v. Guatemala*, Case 11.382, Report No. 57/02, Inter-Am. Comm. H.R., OEA/Ser.L/V/II.117, doc. 1 rev. 1 (2003), para. 75.

[127] Ibid. para. 80.

[128] Ibid. para. 90 (emphasis added).

[129] Ibid. paras. 92 and 134.4.

[130] *Workers Belonging to the 'Association of Fertilizer Workers' (FERTICA) Union v. Costa Rica*, Petition 2893–02, Report No. 21/06, OEA/Ser.L/V/II.127, doc. 4 rev. 1 (2007).

[131] *Union of Ministry of Educational Workers (ATRAMEC) v. El Salvador*, Petition 71–03, Report No. 23/06, Inter-Am. Comm. H.R., OEA/Ser.L/V/II.127, doc. 4 rev. 1 (2007).

[132] Ten cases involved alleged arbitrary or unlawful job dismissals were formally found inadmissible between 2003 and 2005.

admissible, the majority have fallen into two groups. The first involves arbitrary or irregular job dismissals, suspensions, or other retaliatory conduct against judges or magistrates in the region.[133] The second involves similar abuses against members of the police. Of the latter, the grounds for job dismissal have tended to rest either on sex discrimination[134] or on retaliation for protest activities challenging inadequate pay and social security benefits.[135]

5.6 Right to Culture

Finally, although no merits reports have yet been issued on claims involving the autonomous right to culture, the Commission has recognised the admissibility of such claims in two contentious cases: one in 2003 under Article XIII of the American Declaration, the other in 2004 under Article 26 of the American Convention.

In the first, *Grand Chief Michael Mitchell v. Canada*, petitioners have claimed that their right to culture, as indigenous people, has been violated by the imposition of customs duties on the cross-border trade of traditional goods among the First Nations, whose ancestral territory straddles the Canadian/United States border. They assert that trade is an essential distinguishing element of the Iroquois Confederacy and has historically played a central role in the traditional culture of the Mohawk people. The imposition of Canadian customs duties, they contend, impedes trade among the First Nations. That trade is based on historic practices and customs of the indigenous people of Canada that predates the arrival of European settlers. Canada vigorously contests the claim, arguing that the right to take part in the cultural life of the community does not encompass trade as an aspect of culture and that Article XIII does not protect duty-free trade. The Commission found the Article XIII claim admissible on the facts and, given the 'first impression' nature of the case, specifically instructed the parties to include in their final merits-based allegations substantive briefing on the content of the 'right to culture' under the American Declaration, and why the facts of the case are or are not covered by it.[136]

In the 2004 admissibility decision in the *Sarayaku* Case, the Commission again found a potential breach of the right to culture, this time as consecrated in Article 26 of the American Convention.[137] The case involves the government grant to a foreign petroleum company of a concession to explore and exploit the natural resources in the legal territory of the Sarayaku Community, without their knowledge or consent and without any process of prior consultation. Despite the active resistance of the Sarayaku, the company entered their territory, opening trenches, constructing encampments, interring seismic explosives, and felling sacred forests, causing grave cultural impacts on the life of the community. For the Sarayaku, the natural resources of their habitat, both in the soil and subsoil, constitute the core of their cosmovision, providing coherent meaning to their lives, as individuals and as a collective. The lack of consultation with and participation of indigenous peoples in decisions that affect their traditional forms of life, subsistence, and interactions with their ancestral habitat constitutes a classic violation of the right to culture. A merits-based decision is expected in 2008.

6. FRIENDLY SETTLEMENTS

Some of the most interesting regional developments in the area of social rights have emerged as a result of Commission-mediated 'friendly settlements'. Friendly settlements are mutual agreements approved by the Commission or the Court, akin to consent decrees, between the parties to a case as to the consensual measures that will be taken to resolve the controversy. They are generally

---

[133] See *Ana María Ruggeri Cova et al. v. Venezuela*, Petition 282/04, Report No. 24/05, Inter-Am. Comm. H.R., OEA/Ser.L/V/II.124, doc. 5 (2006); *Former Employees of the Judiciary v. Guatemala*, Case 0453/00, Report No. 78/03, Inter-Am. Comm. H.R., OEA/Ser.L/V/II.118, doc. 5 rev. 2 (2003); *Carlos A. Mojoli v. Paraguay*, Case 379/01, Report No. 84/03, Inter-Am. Comm. H.R., OEA/Ser.L/V/II.118, doc. 5 rev. 2 (2003); *Roger Gamboa v. Peru*, Case 185/2002, Report No. 14/03, Inter-Am. Comm. H.R., OEA/Ser.L/V/II.118, doc. 5 rev. 2 (2003).

[134] See *Marcela Andrea Valdes Diaz v. Chile*, Case 12.337, Report No. 57/03, Inter-Am. Comm. H.R., OEA/Ser.L/V/II.118, doc. 5 rev. 2 (2003).

[135] See *Mario Alberto Jara Onate et al. v. Chile*, Case 12.195, Report No. 31/03, Inter-Am. Comm. H.R., OEA/Ser.L/V/II.118, doc. 5 rev. 2 (2003).

[136] *Grand Chief Michael Mitchell v. Canada*, Case 790/01, Report No. 74/03, Inter-Am. Comm. H.R., OEA/Ser.L/V/II.118, doc. 5 rev. 2 (2003), para. 38.

[137] See *Sarayaku Case* (n. 76 above).

entered into before the Commission takes a decision on the merits of a case, although they may be entered into at any stage of proceedings, including during the compliance phase or after a case is submitted to the Court.[138] A friendly settlement will be approved, however, only if certified by the Commission or Court as 'based on respect for human rights'. This means that it must contemplate full reparation for the harm caused, in accordance with Convention Article 63.1, including restitution of the right violated, compensation for actual damages, rehabilitation, measures of satisfaction and guarantees of non-repetition.[139]

Based on these principles, the Commission has approved friendly settlements involving the rights to health, to education, to work, to freedom from slave labour, to housing and land resources, and to women's political participation, among others. Although these settlements do not set formal legal precedents that may be cited in future litigation or jurisprudence, they have often led to important changes on the ground. To ensure due compliance with friendly-settlement undertakings, the Commission continues to play a supervisory role once settlements are approved, monitoring compliance with every point of the agreement and requiring the parties to report to it every three months on the progress achieved. Where friendly settlements are not adequately implemented, the parties may at any point opt to leave the settlement process and return to the contentious processing of their claim.[140]

6.1 Right to Health

The Commission has approved friendly settlements directly involving the right to health in at least two cases, both involving negligent, arbitrary, and/or abusive treatment in public health facilities. One such case, *María Mamérita Mestanza Cháves v. Peru*, involved the forced sterilisa-

tion by doctors in a Peruvian public hospital of a thirty-three year-old mother of seven.[141] Petitioners claimed that the case was representative of a massive, compulsory, and systematic government policy to stress sterilisation as a means of rapidly altering the reproductive behaviour of the population, especially of poor, indigenous and rural women. According to petitioners, the woman and her husband were repeatedly visited and harassed by health personnel, who threatened to report them to the police under a new law allegedly imposing fines and prison time on anyone who had more than five children. When Ms. Mestanza, under threat of criminal penalties, finally agreed to undergo the tubal ligation surgery, she was given negligent and inadequate medical assistance and, despite clear signs of distress, no follow-up care. She died days later from surgery-related causes. The health personnel responsible for the coercive and negligent treatment were administratively exonerated and criminal charges were dismissed.

In a 2003 friendly settlement, the Peruvian State recognised its international responsibility, under both the American Convention and the Inter-American Convention on the Prevention, Punishment and Eradication of Discrimination Against Women, for the harm caused to Ms. Mestanza by its agents. It committed to thoroughly investigate, criminally and administratively, the attacks on the life, body, and health of the victim and to sanction all those found responsible, whether as planners, perpetrators, accessories or in any other capacity. This was to include all those responsible for the 'acts of pressuring the consent' of Ms. Mestanza as well as those who 'ignored the need for urgent care' following her surgery. The State also agreed to pay moral and consequential damages, as well as to make medical, educational and housing payments for each child and the spouse of the victim. These latter payments included psychological rehabilitation (US$7,000 each), permanent health insurance, free primary, secondary and university education for the children, and US$ 20,000 to buy land or a house in the name of the children. To prevent the recurrence of similar violations in the future, the State pledged 'to change

---

[138] See American Convention (n. 3 above), art. 48.1.f; see also Commission Rules of Procedure (n. 5 above), art. 41.1.

[139] See following chapter in this volume, Section 6.

[140] See, e.g., *Maqueda Case*, Resolution of Jan. 17, 1995, Inter-Am. Ct. H.R. (Ser. C) No. 18, para. 27, in which the Court, 'mindful of its responsibility to protect human rights', reserved 'the power to re-open and proceed with consideration of the case, should at any future time a change occur in the circumstances that gave rise to the agreement'. Ibid.

[141] *María Mamérita Mestanza Chaves v. Peru*, Case 12.191, Report No. 66/00, Inter-Am. Comm. H.R., OEA/Ser./L/V/II.111, doc. 20 rev. (2001).

its laws and public policies on reproductive health and family planning, eliminating any discriminatory approach and respecting women's autonomy'. It also agreed to implement continuous training courses for health personnel in reproductive rights and violence against women, to adopt administrative measures to ensure that rules respecting patients' right of free and informed consent are scrupulously followed by health personnel, to take 'drastic action' against any person responsible for forced sterilisation without consent, and to guarantee both that health centres offering sterilisation surgery have proper conditions and that the compulsory reflection period of seventy-two hours is faithfully honoured. The State also committed to implementing a mechanism for the efficient receipt and processing of complaints of human rights violations in health establishments in order to prevent and redress any injury caused therein.[142]

In the earlier case of *MM v. Peru*, a nineteen-year-old Peruvian woman was drugged and then raped by a public health doctor when she came in for medical services. After filing a criminal report, the woman was subjected to mistreatment and discrimination by the criminal justice system. The accused was acquitted of the crime. In 2000, the Peruvian government entered into a friendly settlement with the petitioners in which it admitted international responsibility for the violation of the woman's human rights and agreed to pay her compensation, to professionally sanction the doctor, and to improve legal and administrative measures involving sexual violence claims.[143]

6.2 Right to Education

The right to education was the subject of a significant friendly settlement agreement approved by the Commission in 2003. In the case of *Mónica Carabantes Galleguillos v. Chile*, a teenage girl was expelled from a publicly subsidised private middle school on account of her pregnancy.[144] In friendly settlement proceedings, the Government of Chile

agreed to symbolic and compensatory redress. It officially recognised state responsibility for violating the girl's rights under the American Convention, committed to take steps to disseminate and publicise information about her case, and undertook to publicise recent legislative amendments to the Education Act that recognised the rights of pregnant students or nursing mothers to have access to educational establishments. The Chilean Government also committed to subsidise the petitioner's higher education costs as well as the secondary and higher education of her daughter, basic public education being free.

6.3 Freedom from Slave Labour

In 2003, the Commission approved a far-reaching friendly settlement in an important case involving the practice of slave labour in Brazil. The *José Pereira Case* was pursued on behalf of two rural workers who were injured and killed, respectively, in 1989 while attempting to escape from an estate upon which they and sixty others were held as slave labourers. They argued that the case was illustrative of a more general practice in Brazil in which seasonal agricultural workers (the landless rural poor) are recruited with fraudulent promises, transported to estates far from their places of residence, held against their will through violence and debt peonage, and forced to work in inhuman conditions. Indeed, in the two years immediately prior to the 1994 complaint, the Pastoral Land Commission of Brazil had recorded thirty-seven cases of estates, affecting over 31,000 workers, where slave labour prevailed. Despite the existence of minimum wage laws, laws on minimal working conditions, and criminal laws specifically prohibiting slave labour, no one in the State of Pará had yet, by 1994, been prosecuted under such laws. Petitioners alleged, moreover, that the government had a policy of failing to respond to complaints of slave labour and even of complicity in returning workers who escape from local estates.[145]

In a 2003 friendly settlement, the Brazilian State recognised its international responsibility in relation to the case, paid monetary compensation to the victim, committed to continue its criminal investigation of those responsible, and created

[142] Ibid.
[143] This friendly settlement has not been published. Its terms are available from the parties.
[144] *Mónica Carabantes Galleguillos v. Chile*, Case 12.046, Report No. 33/02, Inter-Am. Comm. H.R., OEA/Ser.L/V/II.117, doc. 1 rev. 1 (2003).

[145] *José Pereira v. Brazil*, Case 11.289, Report No. 95/03, Inter-Am. Comm. H.R., OEA/Ser.L/V/II.118, doc. 5 rev. 2 (2003).

a National Commission for the Eradication of Slave Labour. It also committed to undertake an important series of preventive measures, including federalisation of the crime of 'reduction to conditions analogous to slavery', strengthening its civil and criminal law prohibitions on slave labour, and implementation of the proposed legislative changes contained in the National Plan for the Eradication of Slave Labour. It also committed to strengthen the Ministry of Labour, its Mobile Group, and the Federal Police's Division of Repression of Slave Labour through the allocation of additional human and financial resources, improvements in the collection of administrative and judicial fines, and a renewed focus on investigations and sanctions for perpetrators of the practice of slave labour. Finally, the Brazilian State committed to undertake a national campaign to raise awareness of, and opposition to slave labour, with a particular focus on the State of Pará, including publicity of the terms of the friendly settlement, radio and TV spots, and informative materials geared toward workers.

6.4 Right to Work

The Commission has likewise certified three friendly settlements related to arbitrary or contested deprivations of employment. In all three, the State committed to reinstate the dismissed workers to their previous or similar posts. The first two, approved in 2002 and 2003, respectively, involved arbitrary job dismissals on political grounds in Peru. In *Pablo Ignacio Livia Robles v. Peru*, a public prosecutor was summarily dismissed pursuant to an unappealable decree law following a 1992 military coup. In the friendly settlement agreement, the State acknowledged international responsibility for violating the petitioner's rights under Articles 1, 2, 8, 23, 24 and 25 of the American Convention, paid US$20,000 in compensatory damages, and reinstated the petitioner to his post as Lima's Principal Criminal Prosecutor. It also recognised the years of service the victim was unable to work because he had been arbitrarily removed from his post.[146]

In *Ricardo Manuel Semosa Di Carlo v. Peru*[147] a member of the National Police was arbitrarily dismissed and, despite a judicial ruling in his favour, refused reinstatement. After a complaint was lodged with the Commission, a friendly settlement was reached in which Peru, recognising its international responsibility for violating the victim's rights under Articles 1 and 25 of the American Convention, agreed to the victim's full and immediate reinstatement, including regularisation of his pension rights and recognition of the time that he was arbitrarily separated from the Police Force.

Finally, in the case of *Raúl Savala Málaga y Jorge Pacheco Rondón v. Bolivia*, two high-level public officials in the Ministry of Education, Culture and Sports were administratively dismissed on account of budget cuts and general austerity. Despite judicial orders ordering their reinstatement to their previous posts, the corresponding budgetary allocations were not approved. After Bolivia's Ombudsman presented the case to the Commission alleging violations of the rights to political participation, judicial protection, and to just remuneration, a friendly settlement was entered in 2005 in which the parties mutually recognised that the State could not continue maintaining the salary levels of the officials' previous posts. The State committed to contract the two officials into lower-paying jobs at set monthly wages and to compensate them for back pay during the period of their dismissals.[148]

6.5 Right to Housing and Related Land Resources

The right to housing and to corresponding land resources has also been addressed through friendly settlements, particularly in relation to indigenous populations who have been dispossessed of their homes and land resources due to civil conflict, historic land grabs, and, most recently, extractive industry projects. In *Community of San Vicente Los Cimientos v. Guatemala*,

---

[146] *Pablo Ignacio Livia Robles v. Peru*, Case 12.035, Report No. 75/02, Inter-Am. Comm. H.R., OEA/Ser.L/V/II.117, doc. 1 rev. 1 (2003).

[147] *Ricardo Manuel Semosa Di Carlo v. Peru*, Petition 12.078, Report No. 31/04, Inter-Am. Comm. H.R., OEA/Ser.L/V/II.122, doc. 5 rev. 1 (2005).

[148] *Raúl Savala Málaga y Jorge Pacheco Rondón v. Bolivia*, Petition 241/04, Report N° 98/05, Inter-Am. Comm. H.R., Annual Report 2005.

for example, 672 indigenous families were forced to flee their land in 1982 due to military conflict, abandoning their homes, livestock, and crops. When they returned a month later, their homes had been burned and their belongings stolen. They were once again expelled in 1994 and again in 2001, when their legally titled lands were violently taken from them by neighbours, with Government support.

In 2003, ten years after the original complaint was filed, the parties agreed to a friendly settlement. In it, the State of Guatemala committed to purchase tax-exempt quality land for the resettlement of the entire Los Cimientos Quiché Community, representing at least 233 families who were affected by the violent dispossession, and to 'make all efforts to raise the[ir] living standards'. To this end, and '[a]s a part of the comprehensive, fair, and final solution of this conflict', the parties agreed to jointly identify and negotiate, within sixty days of resettlement, 'urgent projects to reactivate [the Community's] productive, economic, and social capacities, with a view to fostering the community's development and well-being'. For the Community's location and resettlement, the Government committed to 'provide humanitarian assistance, minimal housing, and basic services through the appropriate official agencies'. In so doing, it assumed the responsibility for the physical relocation of the families and their property, as well as the provision of food resources and emergency health care until the beneficiaries were established in their new homes and a formal health facility was established in their settlement. The Government was also to request that UN and OAS verification missions monitor the situation.

Land and other housing-related resources were likewise committed to a dispossessed indigenous community through a 1998 Commission-approved friendly settlement involving Paraguay. In *Enxet-Lamenxay and other Indigenous Communities ('Riachito') v. Paraguay*, the affected Communities had been dispossessed by government sale of their ancestral lands to foreigners between 1885 and 1950. Despite having initiated legal action in 1991 to regain ownership of, and prevent modifications to, their ancestral lands, no action had been taken on their petition by 1996.

The Communities thus presented their case to the Commission alleging State responsibility for violating their rights to due process, judicial protection, property, residence, and the benefits of culture.

In 1998, the Paraguayan State formally recognised the communities' right to land, agreeing to acquire a 21,884.44-hectare tract of land and to register the title deed in their names. The Paraguayan State also agreed to provide the Communities with the necessary assistance for their relocation: foodstuffs, medicines, tools, and transportation to move the families and their belongings from their current residences to their new homes. A similar guarantee ensured that the Enxet-Lamenxay and Kayleyphapopyet (Riachito) Communities would be given sanitary, medical, and educational assistance in their new settlements, and that the access roads leading to their property would be kept in good repair.[149] The State likewise guaranteed that the people then working the purchased land would be removed, together with their belongings and those of the former landowners, and that it would prepare an inventory of all property, electrical and mechanical installations, and other accessories in place on the land. In July 1999, the title deeds were in fact presented to the beneficiary communities by the President of Paraguay, in the presence of the Commission.

Similarly, in *Mercedes Julia Huenteao Beroiza et al. v. Chile*, the government of Chile agreed to purchase 1,220 hectares of land to be transferred free of charge to the Mapuche Pehuenche indigenous families affected by a hydroelectric power plant project constructed without their consent on their lands. The Chilean State committed to provide technical assistance for projects aimed at ensuring the land's continued habitability and development as well as housing subsidies for the construction of homes for the indigenous families who agreed to land swaps. It also agreed to grant eight *ex gratia* pensions and twenty-two study scholarships to the Pehuenche property holders.[150]

---

[149] *Enxet-Lamenxay et al. Indigenous Communities ('Riachito') v. Paraguay*, Case 11.713, Report No. 90/99, Inter-Am. Comm. H.R., OEA/Ser.L/V/II.106, doc. 6 rev. (2000).

[150] *Mercedes Julia Huenteao Beroiza et al. v. Chile*, Petition 4617/02, Report N° 30/04, Inter-Am. Comm. H.R., OEA/Ser.L/V/II.122, doc. 5 rev. 1 (2005).

7. PRECAUTIONARY MEASURES

Finally, a full appraisal of the Commission's case-based jurisprudence on economic, social and cultural rights must take account of the organ's increasing grant of precautionary measures with respect to such rights. Precautionary measures are urgent requests, directed to an OAS Member State, for the taking of immediate injunctive measures in 'serious and urgent cases, and whenever necessary . . . to prevent irreparable harm to persons'.[151] They serve dual preventive and protective purposes and, because of their urgent nature, do not require the exhaustion of domestic remedies. Procedurally, then, they are easy to invoke, and allow the system to respond rapidly to potential human rights violations, without implying any prejudgment on the merits of the claim.[152] When granted, however, they often serve as an important lever for involving the system's organs, in a supervisory or monitoring role, in the substantive dispute on the ground. In this way, they can also act as a catalyst for involving the Commission and Court in new substantive areas of human rights law.

Though interim measures have traditionally been granted in a narrow set of circumstances involving grave and urgent threats to a person's physical integrity or life, they are not substantively bounded and may be granted with respect to any protected right. Over the last six or seven years, the inter-American organs have granted precautionary measures in response to an ever-widening array of human rights abuses in the area of economic, social and cultural rights. In fact, largely because of their urgent nature and the fact that they do not imply prejudgment on the merits of a case, the advances in the system have in many ways been boldest, and most extensive, in the use of urgent interim measures.

7.1. Right to Adequate Housing

The Commission has recently begun to respond, through the issuance of precautionary measures, to credible information on housing rights violations, particularly to prevent forced evictions and removals of people from their homes and lands. In 2001, for example, the Commission urgently responded to credible information that a Paraguayan criminal judge had ordered the removal of dwellings on the side of a highway, built by an impoverished indigenous community after being forced off their ancestral lands.[153] The Commission ordered the Paraguayan State to 'suspend enforcement of any court or administrative order involving the eviction and/or removal of homes of the Yakye Axa indigenous community and its members' and to 'refrain from all other actions and undertakings affecting the[ir] right to property, free transit, and residence'.[154]

In 2003, the Commission intervened again to protect housing rights during a dispute between Chile and members of an indigenous community inhabiting lands on which a hydroelectric plant and dam were being constructed without the community's consent. The petitioners requested precautionary measures to urgently prevent the flooding of their lands as part of the dam construction. When Chile failed to respond to the Commission's initial request to maintain the status quo while the community's merits-based petition was being processed, the Commission formally granted the precautionary measures, requesting the Chilean State to:

> Refrain from taking any steps that might alter the *status quo* in the matter, until the organs of the inter-American system of human rights have adopted a final decision on the case, in particular, *avoiding or suspending any judicial or administrative action that entails eviction of the petitioners from their ancestral lands.*[155]

---

[151] Commission Rules of Procedure (n. 5 above), art. 25.1 ('In serious and urgent cases, and whenever necessary according to the information available, the Commission may, on its own initiative or at the request of a party, request that the State concerned adopt precautionary measures to prevent irreparable harm to persons'.). The Court, by contrast, may issue 'provisional measures' in 'cases of extreme gravity and urgency, and when necessary to avoid irreparable damage to persons'. American Convention (n. 3), art. 63.

[152] Commission Rules of Procedure (n. 5 above), art. 25.4 ('The granting of such measures and their adoption by the State shall not constitute a prejudgment on the merits of a case'.).

[153] Given their inadequate access to food supplies, potable water and health care, they were living in an extremely needy situation, one ultimately declared a 'State of Emergency' by the Paraguayan State itself.

[154] OEA/Ser./L/V/II.114, doc. 5 rev. (2002), Ch. III.C.1 (precautionary measures), para. 49; *Yakye Axa Indigenous Community* (n. 113 above), paras. 11–12.

[155] *Mercedes Julia Huenteao Beroiza* (n. 150 above), para. 15 (emphasis added). A friendly settlement was ultimately reached between the parties.

Another forced eviction in Colombia in 2004 drew the Commission's urgent attention. Upon receiving credible information that a forced eviction involving sixty-three children and more than fifty adults, all victims of intra-city displacement, had been undertaken by Colombian officials 'under conditions that jeopardised [the victims'] health and personal safety', the Commission granted urgent measures of protection. In particular, the Commission requested the Colombian Government to 'adopt the necessary measures to guarantee adequate accommodations and the necessary conditions for the subsistence of the [persons] identified and to report on the actions adopted to clarify the abuse of force that may have been exercised against the beneficiaries'.[156]

7.2. Right to Education

The Commission has interceded with precautionary measures to protect the right to education from arbitrary infringement as well. In 1999, it responded to an unjustified dismissal of a young girl from primary school. Specifically, it required the State to 'adopt measures necessary to prevent [the girl] from being deprived of her right to attend school and to receive the education provided to other children of Dominican nationality'.[157]

7.3. Right to Health

Precautionary measures have been used with particular frequency to protect the right to health. In the most classic application of such measures, the Commission has stepped in on repeated instances to protect health care workers and patients from irreparable harm to their rights due to direct threats to their physical integrity. Often, those threats constitute immediate retaliation for the victim's health-related work[158] or an effort to pre-vent a patient's access to health-related services. While such measures protect the rights to health, life, and integrity of the workers and patients themselves, they also protect the right of access to heath care of the broader population and thus have served multiple roles in protecting the right to health in grave and urgent circumstances.

The Commission, for example, has often granted precautionary measures to protect the right to health of assault survivors who are threatened with further attack while trying to access health treatments. This generally entails guaranteeing their free movement between their homes and health clinics.[159] Such measures have often proved very effective. In one case, within two weeks of the grant of measures, Mexico reported that it was providing each of the beneficiaries access to health centres, and had, in consultation with them, agreed on issues related to medical attention, patients' travelling and accommodation expenses, specialised treatment, and the drugs and medical equipment necessary to meet their health needs.[160]

A second category of health-related precautionary measures, granted regularly by the Commission, has sought to respond urgently to the inadequate provision of health care in custodial settings. Such measures are most frequently granted in prison contexts, but have also been granted in other custodial settings such as state-run psychiatric hospitals, often with important health and rehabilitation consequences for the beneficiaries. By 2003, for example, the Commission had granted nine sets of precautionary measures on behalf of prison inmates in need of specialised medical treatment in Cuba, Jamaica, Peru, and Guatemala. Faced with credible information that sick patients were being refused treatment, the Commission has asked States to transfer the respective inmate to a hospital specialising in the kind of physical ailments suffered and to grant specialised

---

[156] OEA/Ser.L/V/II.122, doc. 5 rev. 1 (2005), Ch. III.C.1 (precautionary measures), para. 16. A number of other rulings of the Commission have protected the housing-related rights of residence and movement, while not specifically discussing housing.

[157] OEA/Ser.L/V/II.106, doc. 6 rev. (2000), Ch. III.C.1 (precautionary measures), para. 27.

[158] In Colombia, for example, the Commission granted precautionary measures to protect forty-six health workers at a hospital in Puerto Lleras, OEA/Ser.L/V/II.117, doc. 1 rev. 1 (2003), Ch. III.C.1 (precautionary measures),

para. 35, and, later that year, another twenty-two health workers at three other hospitals in conflict zones. Ibid. para. 47. In both cases, the health workers had received death threats on account of their health-related activities, interpreted by their attackers as aiding the insurgency.

[159] OEA/Ser./L/V/II.114, doc. 5 rev. (2002), Ch. III.C.1 (precautionary measures), para. 41 (protecting free movement of assault survivor who had traveled to Mexico City to receive medical treatment); ibid. para. 40 (ensuring massacre survivors' access to medical attention, as they still bore physical and psychological scars from it).

[160] Ibid. para 40.

medical attention, to be administered in collaboration with a physician selected by the beneficiary's family.[161] In another case, upon learning that the inmate's health treatment had been terminated upon his transfer to another prison, where his health status worsened, the Commission requested that the State provide the inmate a medical exam, including a diagnosis, prognosis, and recommended treatment for his illness, as well as the treatment prescribed as a result of that exam.[162] As a result of the intervention, the State transferred the prisoner to a facility that facilitated both medical care and family visits. In a series of similar cases, the Commission requested the State to immediately provide the medical examinations necessary to protect the inmates' health, which the State reportedly did.[163]

In other cases, the Commission has requested not only that individual detainees be provided treatment and medical exams, but also that unhealthy detention conditions and facilities that cause or exacerbate ill health be remedied.[164] In *Mendoza Prison Inmates v. Argentina*, for example, the petitioners alleged violation of the inmates' right to health given the sub-human conditions in which they were housed, including lack of bathrooms, showers, sufficient food and adequate medical attention. The conditions of overcrowding were such that, with a maximum allowed capacity of 600, the prison housed approximately 2400 inmates, with 4 to 5 people in each single 3×2 square meter cell. The Commission responded by urgently granting precautionary measures, requesting the State to guarantee, inter

alia, 'adequate conditions of health and hygiene, including access to sanitary services and showers'.[165] When the State did not adequately comply, the Commission requested provisional measures from the Inter-American Court, which were promptly granted.[166]

Another important milestone was achieved in December 2003, when the Commission ordered precautionary measures on behalf of 460 patients at the Neuro-Psychiatric Hospital of Paraguay who were living in grossly inhuman and degrading conditions. The Commission requested that, given the information received describing the inhuman and degrading sanitary conditions in the hospital, which put the health of the hospital internees in grave risk, the State urgently adopt measures to protect the life and physical, mental, and moral integrity of internees. In so doing, it requested the State to elaborate a medical diagnostic of each of the patients and to restrict the use of isolation cells to the situations and under the conditions established in the relevant international standards.[167]

Finally, a third health-related area in which precautionary measures have increasingly been granted by the Commission involves the direct provision of medical services in *non-custodial settings*, where individuals are faced with serious and urgent threats of irreparable harm to their rights to life, integrity, and health. Of the three categories, this has been the most controversial, especially when it involves the ordered provision of antiretroviral drugs. Between 2000 and 2002, the Commission granted precautionary measures on behalf of over 400 persons carrying HIV/AIDS in ten Member States of the OAS. In almost all of these cases it requested the State to provide the beneficiaries with the 'medical examination and treatment indispensable for their survival'. In some cases it specified that this should include comprehensive treatment and the antiretroviral medications necessary to prevent death, as well as the necessary hospital, pharmacological, and nutritional care needed to strengthen their immune systems and

---

[161] See, e.g., ibid. para. 28 (inmate suffering from lung cancer and refused medical attention); OEA/Ser.L/V/II.117, doc. 1 rev. 1 (2003), Ch. III.C.1 (precautionary measures), para. 50 (inmate suffering from back tumours, respiratory difficulties, a chronic ear infection, and a peptic ulcer).

[162] OEA/Ser.L/V/II.117, doc. 1 rev. 1 (2003), Ch. III.C.1 (precautionary measures), para. 73 (suffering prostate condition).

[163] OEA/Ser./L/V/II.114, doc. 5 rev. (2002), Ch. III.C.1 (precautionary measures), para. 50 (suffering mobile breast lumps); see also OEA/Ser.L/V/II.106, doc. 6 rev. (2000), Ch. III.C.1 (precautionary measures), para. 48; OEA/Ser.L/V/II.102, doc. 6 rev. (1999), Ch. III.2.A (precautionary measures), para. 49 (Peru); OEA/Ser.L/V/II.98, doc. 6 rev. (1998), Ch. III.2.A (precautionary measures) (Peru, Nov. 27, 1996).

[164] OEA/Ser.L/V/II.102, doc. 6 rev. (1999), Ch. III.2.A (precautionary measures), para. 24 (preventive detention in Guatemala); OEA/Ser.L/V/II.117, doc. 1 rev. 1 (2003), Ch. III.C.1 (precautionary measures), para. 66 (Jamaica).

[165] *Mendoza Prison Inmates v. Argentina*, Petition 1231/04, Report No. 70/05, Inter-Am. Comm. H.R., OEA/Ser.L/V/II.124, doc. 5 (2006), para. 23.

[166] *Mendoza Prison Case* (Arg.), Order of the Court of Nov. 22, 2004, Inter-Am. Ct. H.R. (Ser. E) (2004).

[167] OEA/Ser.L/V/II.118, doc. 5 rev. 2 (2003), Ch. III.C.1 (precautionary measures), para. 60.

prevent the development of infections.[168] Since the end of 2002, it has nonetheless cut back substantially on the number of precautionary measures granted for the provision of antiretroviral drugs and HIV/AIDS testing by requiring additional information on the medical histories and current health status, including CD4 counts, of potential beneficiaries. In 2004, it granted precautionary measures to thirty-nine additional persons in Guatemala, given that they would not be receiving adequate medication through the Guatemalan public health system.[169]

7.4. Labour Rights

The Commission has used its extensive powers to issue precautionary measures to protect labour and union rights as well. To date, most of these measures have involved the protection of union leaders and their relatives from threats of violence or physical attack. Such measures have been particularly forthcoming for trade unionists in Colombia,[170] but have extended as well to union leaders and their family members in Ecuador and Brazil.[171] In one case, precautionary measures were granted to protect the daughter of an assassinated agricultural labour union leader by preventing her from being transferred up-country to teach in an area especially dangerous to her.[172] Precautionary measures have also been extended to workers involved in labour and land disputes.[173]

7.5. Indigenous Rights to Territory, Culture and Life

The system's organs have also regularly granted interim measures to protect indigenous peoples from threats of irreparable harm to the life, in-

tegrity, and culture of their members, especially in the context of government concessions to extractive industries to explore and exploit natural resources on their ancestral territories. Faced with such situations, both the Commission and Court have requested the *suspension of extraction-related concessions and permissions* until a merits decision on the case is reached. The Commission has viewed such situations as particularly grave and urgent, given the close ties that exist between ancestral territory and the very physical existence and cultural survival of indigenous peoples.

In *Awas Tingni v. Nicaragua*, for example, the Commission requested the Nicaraguan State to adopt precautionary measures 'for the purpose of suspending the concession given by the government to the SOLCARSA Company to carry out forestry work on the lands of the Awas Tingni Indigenous Community'.[174] When the Government failed to comply with the precautionary measures, the Commission requested provisional measures from the Inter-American Court of Human Rights, which were granted to protect the use and enjoyment of the Community's ancestral lands and resources.[175]

The Commission similarly granted precautionary measures in 2000 in *Maya Indigenous Communities v. Belize*, ordering the State 'to take the necessary steps to suspend all permits, licenses, and concessions allowing for the drilling of oil and any other tapping of natural resources on lands used and occupied by the Maya Communities in the District of Toledo'.[176] These concessions had caused environmental damage and threatened to create irreversible long-term harm to the

---

[168] OEA/Ser.L/V/II.106, doc. 6 rev. (2000), Ch. III.C.1, (precautionary measures), para. 32.

[169] *Cuscul Pivaral* (n. 57 above), para. 1.

[170] See, e.g., OEA/Ser.L/V/II.117, doc. 1 rev. 1 (2003), Ch. III.C.1 (precautionary measures), para. 31; OEA/Ser./L/V/II.114, doc. 5 rev. (2002), Ch. III.C.1 (precautionary measures), para. 18; ibid. para. 22.

[171] OEA/Ser.L/V/II.122, doc. 5 rev 1 (2005), Ch. III.C.1 (precautionary measures), para. 26 (Ecuador); OEA/Ser.L/V/II.102, doc. 6 rev. (1999), Ch. III.2.A (precautionary measures), para. 12 (Brazil).

[172] OEA/Ser.L/V/II.102, doc. 6 rev. (1999), Ch. III.2.A (precautionary measures), para. 12.

[173] See, e.g., OEA/Ser.L/V/II.98, doc. 6 rev. (1998), Ch. III.2.A (precautionary measures) (Guatemala, Oct. 2, 1997).

[174] Ibid. (Nicaragua, Oct. 30, 1997).

[175] *Mayagna (Sumo) Awas Tingni Community Case*, Order of the Court of Sept. 6, 2002, Inter-Am. Ct. H.R. (Ser. E) (2002). The Court ordered the State of Nicaragua 'to adopt, without delay, whatever measures are necessary to protect the use and enjoyment of property of lands belonging to the Mayagna Awas Tingni Community, and of natural resources existing on those lands, specifically those measures geared toward avoiding immediate and irreparable damage resulting from activities of third parties who have established themselves inside the territory of the Community or who exploit the natural resources that exist within it, until the definitive delimitation, demarcation and titling ordered by the Court are carried out'.

[176] OEA/Ser./L/V/II.111, doc. 20 rev. (2001), Ch. III.C.1 (precautionary measures), para. 11.

environment, upon which the Community depended for its subsistence.

In 2002, the Commission again granted precautionary measures in the context of government and private activities within the lands and territory of indigenous populations. In *12 Saramaka Clans v. Suriname*, the petitioners claimed that the State of Suriname had granted numerous logging, road-building and mining concessions in Saramaka territory, without consulting the clans and that this constituted an immediate, substantial and irreparable threat to the physical and cultural integrity of the Saramaka people. Indeed, they claimed an estimated 30,000 Brazilian gold miners operated in the Saramaka territory and that, consequently, twenty to thirty tons of mercury had been released into the environment, contaminating the water sources and fish upon which they survived. The Commission responded by granting precautionary measures, requesting the State of Suriname to:

> [T]ake the appropriate measures to suspend all concessions, including permits and licenses for logging and mine exploration and other natural resource development activity on lands used and occupied by these clans, until the substantive claims raised in by the petitioner were examined in Case 12.338, still pending before the [Commission].[177]

The Commission did so again in 2003 in *Kichwa Indigenous Peoples of the Sarayaku Community v. Ecuador*,[178] a case involving the granting of an oil concession to a foreign company over the ancestral territory of the Sarayaku People without their knowledge or consent, and without any process of prior consultation. When the State failed to comply adequately with the requested measures, the Commission requested provisional measures from the Court, which were granted in 2004.[179] Interim measures have been granted in other cases involving the rights of indigenous peoples. In 1999, for example, the Commission ordered precautionary measures in favour of the members of the Western Shoshone people, requesting the United States to suspend ongoing procedures of expropriation of their possessions and cattle.[180]

7.6 Rights of the Child and Special Protection of the Family

Finally, the Commission has regularly issued interim measures to protect the rights of the child and the family in ways that impact their enjoyment of economic, social and cultural rights. It has done so in the context of child protection from familial rape, child adoption against the will of the biological parents, and family reunification. It has also used precautionary measures to protect the rights of children in detention facilities. Such measures have been issued to ensure proper separation of children from adults, relocation of minors to permit regular family visits, and minimum standards of living for children detainees.

8. REMEDIES FOR VIOLATIONS AND SUPERVISORY JURISDICTION

Perhaps because the Commission plays a more hands-on role than the Court in the litigation process and because its final orders constitute 'recommendations', the Commission's final orders tend to be more generalised and more limited than the Court's final binding remedial orders (see following chapter in this volume). They generally include four central aspects, each phrased in broad, non-specific language that is deferential to internal domestic processes: (1) adequate compensation for the victim; (2) effective investigation of the facts giving rise to human rights abuse; (3) sanction for those responsible; and; (4) guarantees of non-repetition. Unlike the Court, the Commission does not assess dollar figures for compensation, nor does it generally specify precise measures for the State to take to prevent the recurrence of particular abuses. These are generally left to the discretion of the State in the first instance, prompted, prodded, and leveraged by the victims, their representatives, the media, and civil society more generally.

---

[177] OEA/Ser.L/V/II.117, doc. 1 rev. 1 (2003), Ch. III.C.1 (precautionary measures), para. 75.

[178] OEA/Ser.L/V/II.118, doc. 5 rev. 2 (2003), Ch. III.C.1 (precautionary measures), para. 34.

[179] *Sarayaku Indigenous People Case*, Order of the Court of July 6, 2004, Inter-Am. Ct. H.R. (Ser. E) (2003). The measures were extended and amplified by Court order on June 17, 2005 and remain in effect as of 2008.

[180] *Dann Case* (n. 116 above), para. 22.

In this regard, it is imperative for users of the regional system to appreciate from the start that final resolution of a case by the Commission is merely the first step in a much larger political process of ensuring compliance with its remedial recommendations. As the cases that come before it have become increasingly complex, the Commission has aided this process through two important and interrelated mechanisms. First, it has increasingly required that the respondent State ensure the participation of the victim and her legal representatives in the crafting of the concrete measures the State will adopt to comply with the Commission's more generalised recommendations. This opens a space for continued interaction and leverage between the parties, which the Commission can encourage and support in an intermediary or facilitative role. Second, the Commission has made increasing use of its supervisory jurisdiction over the compliance stage of litigation. In this regard, the Commission regularly grants working meetings at its ordinary sessions in which a Commissioner meets personally with the parties to a case to discuss on-the-ground progress in implementing the Commission's formal recommendations. It also regularly reviews compliance reports by the parties to ensure that progress in implementation is continually being made. In these ways, the Commission supports a dynamic process of local-level reform that continues at the domestic level, long after its final report is issued.

9. CONCLUSION

The Commission has an undoubtedly vital role to play in ensuring the effective protection of economic, social and cultural rights throughout the American region at the domestic level, where it counts. It has the jurisdictional tools to do so and the growing understanding that its involvement in the field of economic, social and cultural rights is not only important, but indispensable. The main impediment to the further advance of the Commission's work rests in its continuing vacillation around the legal obligations attaching to economic, social and cultural rights under Article 26 of the Convention. Once accepted that the legal obligations attaching to human rights claims do not differ according to subjective classifications of rights as civil, cultural, economic, political or social, the effective regional protection of social rights in the Americas will have a broad and steadfast horizon.

19

The Inter-American Court of Human Rights

Beyond Progressivity

Tara J. Melish*

1. INTRODUCTION AND BACKGROUND

The Inter-American Court of Human Rights was established in 1979 as 'an autonomous judicial institution' of the Organization of American States ('OAS'), charged with applying and interpreting the American Convention on Human Rights, the principal human rights treaty of the region.[1] With its seat in San José, Costa Rica, it is composed of seven part-time, independent judges nominated in their individual capacity by the States parties to the Convention and elected by secret ballot for a renewable six-year term by an absolute majority vote in the OAS General Assembly. The Court's elected judges must be jurists of the 'highest moral authority', of recognised competence in the field of human rights, and possess the qualifications required for the exercise of the highest judicial functions in conformity with the law of the State of which they are nationals or that proposes them as candidates.

As a 'judicial institution', the Inter-American Court has both contentious and advisory functions, the jurisdictional boundaries of which it closely guards. Since its inception, the Court has used both functions broadly. It has adopted nineteen advisory opinions since 1982, and adjudicated the various procedural stages (admissibility, merits, reparations, interpretation, compliance) of over seventy individual cases since its first, the renowned *Velásquez Rodríguez* case, was decided in 1987.[2] Under its contentious function, the Court's judgments on liability and reparations, as well as its issuance of provisional measures,[3] are final and not subject to appeal.[4] OAS Member States commit to comply with those judgments in all cases or matters in which they are parties,[5] a commitment whose compliance record is mixed, but tends toward good.[6]

In recent years, the workload of the Court has increased rapidly. This is principally due to a set of amendments adopted in 2000 to the Rules of Procedure of both the Court and the Inter-American Commission on Human Rights, the second principal organ of the regional human rights system and the only non-State actor authorised to refer cases to the Court.[7] While the Commission previously referred cases to the Court quite

---

* Tara J. Melish is a human rights attorney and legal specialist in the field of comparative systems of social rights protections. J.D., Yale Law School; B.A., Brown University. The author thanks the John D. and Catherine T. MacArthur Foundation for a research and writing grant that made this work possible. All views expressed herein are those of the author alone.

[1] Statute of the Inter-American Court on Human Rights, art. 1, Oct. 1979, O.A.S. Res. 448 (IX-0/79), O.A.S. Off. Rec. OEA/Ser.P/IX.0.2/80, vol. 1, at 98, entered into force Jan. 1, 1989; see also American Convention on Human Rights, art. 62.3, Nov. 22, 1969, 1144 U.N.T.S. 123, O.A.S.T.S. No. 36, at 1, OEA/Ser.L/V/II.23 doc. rev. 2, entered into force July 18, 1978 ('American Convention') (defining the Court's jurisdiction as comprising 'all cases concerning the interpretation and application of the provisions of this Convention that are submitted to it').

[2] As of November 2007, the Court has issued 174 judgments in contentious cases.

[3] Provisional measures are extraordinary measures of interim protection aimed at avoiding the consummation of imminent, grave and irreparable harm to individuals. See American Convention (n. 1 above), art. 63.2.

[4] Ibid. art. 67.

[5] Ibid. art. 68.

[6] More specifically, compliance rates with Court-ordered compensatory awards tend to be quite good; with Court orders involving legislative or regulatory modifications, good to fair; and with Court orders to undertake serious investigations and to impose sanctions on those found responsible for human rights abuse, notably poor.

[7] Technically, State parties to the Convention may also submit a case to the Court, although this competence has never, of yet, been exercised. For more on the Inter-American Commission on Human Rights, see preceding Chapter in this volume.

sparingly,[8] its new Rules of Procedure require referral in all cases examined in which the respondent State has accepted the Court's jurisdiction and has not, within a prescribed period, complied with the Commission's final merits-based recommendations. Only where 'a reasoned decision' against referral is provided by an absolute majority of the Commission's members may referral be avoided.[9] The workload of the Court has further increased with reforms to its own Rules of Procedure, which now authorise the direct participation of victims and their representatives in all procedural stages of litigation. This has added voluminously to the quantity of requests, arguments, and information to which the Court must attend. Taken together, these positive developments have led commentators both on and off the Court to increasingly question the part-time status of the organ and to urge that the Court become a permanent organ of the system.[10]

Given its broad jurisdictional mandate and regional prestige, and in light of the social and economic reality it interfaces, the Inter-American Court of Human Rights has a powerful role to play in the effective protection of economic, social and cultural rights in the Americas. This potential is evident in its small, though growing, social rights jurisprudence, especially in the areas of labour rights, children's rights, the rights of detainees, and the rights of indigenous peoples to their ancestral territories. It is nourished by the Court's reiterated insistence on the individual titularity of rights, its special attention to the most vulnerable, its emphasis on ensuring full and effective reparation for human rights violations, and its insistence on its 'inherent and non-discretional' jurisdiction to supervise and monitor full compliance with its decisions.

These intrinsic attributes are, in turn, made fertile by the contemporary demands of the regional human rights movement, which has undergone a marked transformation in the last decade. From a focus on torture, disappearances, and extrajudicial executions, issues that dominated the human rights agenda in the 1980s and 1990s, the regional movement has adopted a more comprehensive agenda encompassing, as central demands, the rights of access to essential medicines and health care, education, labour protections, social security, housing and land. These concerns, increasingly recognised and vindicated in the region's domestic legislation and internal jurisprudence, are slowly making their way up to the region's international protective organs, the Inter-American Commission and Court of Human Rights, which are beginning to embrace them, if ever slowly and hesitantly.

This chapter assesses the emerging social rights jurisprudence of the Inter-American Court as it has developed to date. It describes the normative framework over which the Court exercises jurisdiction, the complaints procedure it oversees, and the legal obligations that States assume with respect to the protected rights enshrined in the region's instruments. It then assesses four of the normative axes on which the Court has jurisprudentially relied in protecting social rights, and looks to the Court's rich jurisprudence on reparation and supervision of compliance with its decisions. The chapter concludes that the Court's social rights jurisprudence is commendable and requires expansion, but that doing so will require the reversal of two troubling, closely-related trends that currently limit the vast potential of the Court to provide full and effective protection for all economic, social and cultural rights.

2. SOCIAL RIGHTS OVER WHICH THE COURT EXERCISES JURISDICTION

The Inter-American Court is presently competent to apply, under its contentious complaints procedure, some or all of the provisions of four human rights treaties, two of which expressly cover autonomous social rights.[11] These latter

---

[8] See n. 43 below for numbers of cases submitted to Court over years.
[9] Rules of Procedure of the Inter-American Commission on Human Rights, art. 44.1.
[10] See, e.g., M. E. Ventura Robles, 'La Corte Interamericana de Derechos Humanos: la necesidad inmediata de convertirse en un tribunal permanente' ['The Inter-American Court of Human Rights: the immediate necessity of conversion into a permanent tribunal'], *CEJIL Revista: Debates Sobre Derechos Humanos y el Sistema Interamericano*, Vol. 1, No. 1 (2005), pp. 12–22.

[11] The other regional treaties over which the Inter-American Court enjoys contentious jurisdiction include those on torture and forced disappearance. See Inter-American Convention to Prevent and Punish Torture, Dec. 9, 1985, O.A.S.T.S. No. 67, *entered into force* Feb. 28, 1987, art. 8; Inter-American Convention on the Forced

instruments include the American Convention on Human Rights of 1969 ('American Convention') and its Additional Protocol in the Area of Economic, Social and Cultural Rights of 1988 ('Protocol of San Salvador'). Both protect a wide range of economic, social and cultural rights and apply to all persons within a State's jurisdiction, regardless of citizenship or residency status.[12]

While the Court's contentious case-based jurisprudence is the subject of this chapter, it is useful to note that the Court's ratione materiae competence vis-à-vis economic, social and cultural rights extends still further under its advisory jurisdiction. Under that competence, the Court is empowered to interpret *any* treaty that deals with the protection of human rights and is applicable to the American States, including assessing the compatibility of domestic legislation or trade agreements with human rights treaty obligations. The Court may thus pronounce, in an advisory fashion, on the commitments assumed by OAS member states under the International Covenant on Economic, Social and Cultural Rights ('ICESCR'), the Convention on the Elimination of Discrimination Against Women ('CEDAW'), the full range of ILO conventions on labour and indigenous rights, and a host of other bilateral or multilateral treaties entered into by American States that affect or concern human rights.[13] Indeed, the Court has stated

that it's advisory jurisdiction is 'more extensive than that enjoyed by any international tribunal in existence today'.[14] This competence, the Court recognises, ensures that it has 'an important role to play in the promotion and protection of economic, social and cultural rights'.[15]

2.1   The American Convention on Human Rights

Despite commentators' frequent characterisation of the American Convention on Human Rights as a 'civil and political rights' instrument, the American Convention protects a wide range of economic, social and cultural rights, both directly and indirectly. Indeed, the Convention's twenty-three articles identified as 'protected rights' provide the Court with ample tools for the jurisdictional protection of the full range of civil, cultural, economic, political, and social rights. The treaty's preamble, in turn, recognises the imperative of protecting all rights, and recalls the broader incorporation of social rights into the regional human rights regime in 1967. The Court itself has affirmed that '[e]conomic, social and cultural rights are the same in substance as political and civil rights. All derive from the essential dignity of man, all are inalienable right[s] of the individual, and all must be promoted, guaranteed and protected nationally, regionally and globally'.[16] Nonetheless, reflecting the ideologically-divided epoch in which it was drafted – and not, as one former judge of the Court has put it, because of 'juridical differences among [rights]'[17] – these chapters are formally divided, infelicitously, under headings entitled 'Civil and Political Rights' (Chapter II) and 'Economic, Social and Cultural Rights' (Chapter III), respectively, with twenty-two of the twenty-three 'protected rights' articles placed under the former.

The Court has repeatedly insisted that 'mere formalities' should never stand in the way of the

Disappearance of Persons, June 9, 1994, OEA/Ser.P AG/doc.3114/94 rev. 1, *entered into force* Mar. 29, 1996, 33 I.L.M. 1529 (1994), art XIII. The Court has not yet had to opportunity to determine whether it's contentious competence extends to the Inter-American Convention to Prevent, Sanction and Eradicate Violence against Women, June, 1994, entered into force 5 March 1995, which grants express competence over individual complaints only to the Inter-American Commission on Human Rights. Ibid. art. 12.

[12] This principle was most recently reaffirmed in the Court's 2003 advisory opinion, *Juridical Condition and Rights of Undocumented Migrants*, Advisory Opinion OC-18, Sept. 17, 2003, Inter-Am. Ct. H.R. (Ser. A) No. 18/03 (2003).

[13] See American Convention (n. 1 above), art. 64.1. The Court has stated that it's advisory jurisdiction 'can be exercised, in general, with regard to any provision dealing with the protection of human rights set forth in *any international treaty applicable to the American States*, regardless of whether it be bilateral or multilateral, whatever be the principal purpose of such a treaty, and whether or not non-Member States of the inter-American system are or have the right to become parties thereto'. '*Other Treaties' Subject to the Advisory Jurisdiction of the Court (Art. 64 of the American Convention on Human Rights)*, Advisory Opinion OC-1/82 of Sept. 24, 1982, Inter-Am. Ct. H.R. (Ser. A) No. 1, paras. 14, 52 (emphasis added).

[14] Ibid. para. 14.

[15] Inter-Am. Ct. H.R., *Annual Report of the Inter-American Court of Human Rights 1986*, OEA/Ser.L/III.15 Doc. 13 (1986), pp. 44–45, para. 14.

[16] Ibid. p. 42, para. 2.

[17] *Separate Vote of Judge Rodolfo E. Piza Escalante, Proposed Amendments to the Naturalization Provisions of the Constitution of Costa Rica*, Advisory Opinion OC-4/84 of Jan. 19, 1984, Inter-Am. Ct. H.R. (Ser. A) No. 4, para. 6.

primary goal of protecting human rights. Accordingly, the formal chapter headings have, properly, not inhibited the Court from using the rights enshrined in Chapter II of the Convention to protect a broad spectrum of classically-recognised economic, social and cultural rights, including the rights to unionisation, social security, ancestral territory, cultural heritage, health, and education. These 'Chapter II rights', all of which have important economic, social and cultural dimensions, include the rights to life, legal personality, personal integrity, personal liberty, personal security, privacy, inviolability of the home, and special protection for children and the family. They also include the rights to equal protection, due process and judicial protection, political participation, property, a name, and nationality, as well as freedom from forced labour and freedom of conscience, religion, expression, assembly, association, movement and residence.[18]

Chapter III, by contrast, contains only Article 26, a single incongruously-titled provision[19] of broad substantive scope that has to date remained largely neglected in the Court's work. Its recent re-emergence in the Court's jurisprudence has exposed continuing theoretical difficulties with social rights concepts that must be overcome by both the Court and litigants if social rights are to be given full and meaningful effect in the regional system. By its terms, Article 26 guarantees a set of discretely-identified 'protected rights' defined as those 'derived from'[20] or 'implicit in the economic, social, educational, scientific, and cultural standards set forth in the [OAS Charter]', a regional treaty ratified by all OAS Member States. These rights, drawn principally from Articles 34 and 45 to 52 of the Charter, and, once identified, given further substantive content by reference to the economic, social and cultural rights in the American Declaration on the Rights and Duties of Man,[21] include the rights to education, unionisation, strike, employment, adequate food, health, social security, housing, culture, and just labour conditions.[22]

Despite the Court's express jurisdictional competence to apply these autonomous social rights in the individual petitions process,[23] the Court has nonetheless tended to shy from pronouncing upon Article 26 of the Convention, preferring instead to use Chapter II rights, read broadly or used as procedural devices, to protect social rights. It is critical to underscore that this approach does not reflect any judicial antipathy by the Court to the protection of economic, social and cultural rights. Rather, it reflects a particular reading of the text of Article 26, one currently ascendant in the system, that conflates its formal title, 'progressive development', with the autonomous rights it protects and, concurrently, their corresponding obligations. This misreading has led

---

[18] For an analysis of how each of these Chapter II rights may be used to protect classically-understood economic, social and cultural rights, see T. Melish, *Protecting Economic, Social and Cultural Rights in the Inter-American Human Rights System: A Manual on Presenting Claims* (Quito: Orville H. Schell, Jr. Center for International Human Rights at Yale Law School and CDES, 2002), especially pp. 193–332.

[19] Although the trend in international treaty-making is to omit titles for individual treaty provisions, given the interpretative confusion they often create for broadly-framed or multidimensional rights, the formal title for Article 26 ('Progressive Development') has led interpreters, both on and off the Court, to radically misconstrue the nature of the provision by equating its formal title with the substantive rights-based guarantees textually enshrined in the provision itself.

[20] 'Derived from' ('*se derivan de*') is the term used in the Spanish text, which is the official OAS text for purposes of treaty interpretation.

[21] The Court has stated: 'For the member states of the Organization, the [American] Declaration is the text that defines the human rights referred to in the [OAS] Charter'; thus, the Charter 'cannot be interpreted and applied as far as human rights are concerned without relating its norms ... to the corresponding provisions of the Declaration', the instrument which 'contains and defines the fundamental human rights referred to in the Charter'. *Interpretation of the American Declaration of the Rights and Duties of Man Within the Framework of Article 64 of the American Convention on Human Rights*, Advisory Opinion OC-10/89 of July 14, 1989, Inter-Am. Ct. H.R. (Ser. A) No. 10, paras. 43, 45.

[22] The Charter's text refers expressly to the 'right to education', the 'right to material well-being', the 'right to collective bargaining', the 'right to strike', and the 'right to work'. Additional rights are derived from the commitments States parties make with respect to 'adequate housing', 'proper nutrition', 'fair wages, employment opportunities, and acceptable working conditions', the 'protection of [individuals'] potential through the extension and application of modern medical science', and the 'benefits of culture'. See Charter of the Organization of American States, arts. 34, 45, 49, 50.

[23] See American Convention (n. 1 above), arts. 62.3 and 63.1, which grant the Court jurisdiction over 'all cases concerning the interpretation and application of the provisions of this Convention that are submitted to it' and the power to order reparation for the injured party whenever it finds a 'violation of a right or freedom protected by this Convention'.

litigants to advance arguments before the Court that urge the application of *different* standards of adjudication to claims based on Chapter II and Chapter III rights, applying a justiciable set of obligations to the former, a non-justiciable set to the latter.[24] The nature of this differential treatment, not the nature of the rights themselves, explains the Court's preference for adjudicating social rights claims under Chapter II rather than Chapter III norms.[25] Rational social rights litigation under the American Convention requires that this differential treatment be discarded, and that the standard set of 'general duties' identified in Chapter I of the Convention be applied, in their properly justiciable dimensions, to all 'protected rights' enshrined in the Convention, whether formally placed under Chapter II or III.

2.2   Protocol of San Salvador

The Court also has jurisdictional competence to apply the Additional Protocol to the American Convention on Human Rights in the Area of Economic, Social and Cultural Rights ('Protocol of San Salvador')[26] a treaty expressly incorporating an impressive set of detailed, specifically-defined social rights guarantees: the rights to health, a

healthy environment, food, education, work, just and equitable conditions of work, trade unionisation, social security, the benefits of culture, and special protection for the family, children, the elderly, and persons with disabilities.[27]

The Protocol, however, grants ratione materiae jurisdiction to the Court in the individual petitions process over 'direct violations' of only two provisions: Articles 8.1.a and 13. These provisions protect, respectively, the right to unionise and the right to education. The vast majority of the Protocol's substantive protections cannot be invoked directly in contentious proceedings before the Court.[28] The primary function of the Protocol in the individual petitions process (as distinct from the periodic reporting process[29]) at present, therefore, lies not in direct adjudication, but rather in assisting the Court in its evolving interpretation of the scope and content of the Chapter II and Chapter III provisions of the American Convention, pursuant to the interpretive mandate of Convention Article 29.b.[30] While this is true with respect to all substantive rights recognised in Articles 3 through 26 of the Convention, all of which have important social rights dimensions of an adjudicable nature, it is particularly applicable to the social rights recognised autonomously in Article 26.

The Protocol's direct applicability in the individual petitions process is further limited at present by the fact that the Protocol did not enter into force until November 1999 and has been ratified by only thirteen of thirty-five American States. Given the ratione temporis requirement that the facts giving rise to a violation must take place *after* the date on which a given instrument takes effect for a given State, together with other case-based jurisdictional limitations – such as the requirements of

---

[24] For an example, see *Five Pensioners' Case v. Peru*, Judgment of Feb. 28, 2003, Inter-Am. Ct. H.R. (Ser. C) No. 98 (2003), in which litigants urged the Court to 'rule on the progressive development of economic, social and cultural rights in Peru' with respect to a Chapter III claim related to the right to social security, but on the duties to 'respect' and 'ensure' the right to a pension, when framed under Chapter II norms. For a direct critique of this decision, see Tara J. Melish, 'A Pyrrhic Victory for Peru's Pensioners: Pensions, Property and the Perversion of Progressivity', *CEJIL Revista: Debates sobre Derechos Humanos y el Sistema Interamericano*, Vol. 1, No. 1 (2005), pp. 51–66.

[25] For a detailed discussion, see Tara J. Melish, 'Rethinking the "Less as More" Thesis: Supranational Litigation of Economic, Social and Cultural Rights in the Americas', *New York University Journal of International Law and Politics*, Vol. 39, No. 2 (2006), pp. 171–343, which lays out a quadrant-based framework for understanding the litigation-appropriate and litigation-inappropriate dimensions of human rights obligations in the inter-American system, demonstrating that litigants, scholars, and adjudicators often err by applying the former to formally-classified civil–political rights, the latter to formally-classified economic, social and cultural rights.

[26] Additional Protocol to the American Convention on Human Rights in the Area of Economic, Social and Cultural Rights, Nov. 17, 1988, O.A.S.T.S. No. 69 (1988), 28 I.L.M. 156 (1989), *entered into force* Nov. 16, 1999 ('Protocol of San Salvador').

[27] Ibid. arts. 6–18.

[28] See ibid. art. 19.6.

[29] The primary function of the Protocol *in general* may most usefully be seen as lying in the periodic reporting procedure it envisions under Article 19, intended to reinvigorate the similar, but never fully institutionalised procedure under Convention Article 42 and to thereby give progressive content and localised meaning to the social rights guaranteed, in largely parallel and overlapping terms, in both the Protocol's own rights-based provisions and Article 26 of the Convention.

[30] American Convention (n. 1 above), art. 29.b ('No provision of this Convention shall be interpreted as:... restricting the enjoyment or exercise of any right or freedom recognized by virtue of ... another convention to which one of the said states is a party.').

exhaustion of domestic remedies and prior examination by the Commission[31] – a significant mass of cases in which the Protocol may properly be applied will not, in practice, reach the Court for another several years. Fortunately, until that time, the same claims that might have been argued under Articles 8.1.a and 13 of the Protocol may be brought under congruent norms of the American Convention. There does not in fact appear to be any right in the Protocol that is not already subject to the Court's case-based adjudicatory jurisdiction under analogous norms of the American Convention.[32]

2.3 Indirect Application of Other International Instruments

The Court lacks subject-matter jurisdiction to apply directly, under its contentious complaints procedure, other treaties or instruments protecting economic, social and cultural rights, such as the ICESCR, the Convention on the Rights of the Child ('CRC'), and the respective ILO Conventions protecting labour and indigenous rights. Nonetheless, it is competent to consider such treaties *indirectly* in determining the substantive scope and content of the provisions of the American Convention. Indeed, Article 29.b of the Convention prohibits the Court from interpreting any provision of the American Convention in such a way as to restrict the exercise of any right recognised by virtue of the domestic laws of any State party or any treaty ratified by that State party. Finding Article 29's 'innovating breadth ... unmatched in any other international document', a former Inter-American Court Judge has described the provision as incorporating into the Convention, to some degree, the 'principles in other international instruments, in the country's own internal regulations and in the trends in effect in the matter of human rights'.[33] This means, in practice, that, in determining the substantive scope of Convention provisions in concrete national contexts, the domestic laws of a State party and the treaty law applicable to it are regularly brought into play.[34]

In the Court's evolving jurisprudence it has, for example, repeatedly turned to the Protocol of San Salvador and the CRC to 'determine the content and scope' of the general provision established in Convention Article 19 on special measures of protection for the child. In the Court's words, as these instruments 'form part of a very comprehensive *corpus juris* of protection of children that the Court must respect'.[35] Accordingly, it has found that the special measures of protection to which Article 19 refers include those necessary to ensure a child's right to education and right to health as part of the obligation to ensure an adequate standard of living and what the Court has termed a 'project of life'.

Similarly, the Court has turned to domestic law, customary law, and a series of ratified ILO conventions, often in conjunction with the Protocol of San Salvador, to determine the content and scope of the Convention's guarantee of both the right to association in labour contexts[36] and the

---

[31] Ibid. art. 61.2 ('In order for the Court to hear a case, it is necessary that the procedures set forth in Articles 48 and 50 shall have been completed.'); see also ibid. arts. 46–47.

[32] See Tara J. Melish, 'The Protocol of San Salvador: Riddle, Redemption or Just Simply Redundant?' unpublished manuscript. There are in fact important social rights, such as the right to adequate housing, that are not autonomously protected under the Protocol, but which may be adjudicated under a variety of Convention-based norms, such as those in Articles 8, 11, 21, 25 and, especially, 26.

[33] Separate Opinion of Judge Rodolfo E. Piza Escalante, *Proposed Amendments to the Naturalization Provisions of the Constitution of Costa Rica*, Advisory Opinion OC-4/84 of Jan. 19, 1984, Inter-Am. Ct. H.R. (Ser. A) No. 4, para. 2. Articles 60 and 61 of the African Charter on Human and Peoples' Rights enshrine interpretive principles of an equal or even more expansive scope. See chapter 17 in this volume.

[34] As the Court has recognised, '[Article 29] was designed specifically to ensure that [the Convention] would in no case be interpreted to permit the denial or restriction of fundamental human rights and liberties, particularly those that have *already been recognized by the State*'. *Proposed Amendments to the Naturalization Provisions of the Constitution of Costa Rica*, Advisory Opinion OC-4/84 of Jan. 19, 1984, Inter-Am. Ct. H.R. (Ser. A) No. 4, para. 20 (emphasis added).

[35] *Case of Children's Rehabilitation v. Paraguay*, Judgment of Sept. 2, 2004, Inter-Am. Ct. H.R. (Ser. C) No. 112, para. 148 ['*Panchito López Case*']; '*Gómez-Paquiyauri Brothers' Case v. Peru*, Judgment of July 8, 2004, Inter-Am. Ct. H.R. (Ser. C) No. 110, para. 166; *Villagrán Morales et al. v. Guatemala (the 'Street Children' Case)*, Judgment of Nov. 19, 1999, Inter-Am. Ct. H.R. (Ser. C) No. 63, paras. 194–95; *Legal Status and Human Rights of the Child*, Advisory Opinion OC-17/02 of Aug. 28, 2002, Inter-Am. Ct. H.R. (Ser. A) No. 17, para. 24.

[36] *Baena Ricardo et al. v. Panama*, Judgment of Feb. 2, 2001, Inter-Am. Ct. H.R. (Ser. C) No. 72, para. 159; *Pedro Huilca*

right to property for indigenous peoples.[37] Significantly, in addition to the jurisprudence of the UN Human Rights Committee and the European Court of Human Rights, to which it frequently turns, the Court has also looked to the interpretive jurisprudence of the ILO Committee on Freedom of Association, the ILO Committee of Experts, and the UN Committee on Economic, Social and Cultural Rights, including its General Comments, to assist it in interpreting the content and scope of the rights-based norms of the American Convention.[38]

This integrative practice stems from the Court's expansive view of the Convention as a 'living instrument', for which 'dynamic interpretation' is needed, corresponding not to the circumstances that existed at the time of its drafting, but rather to the new juridical and factual circumstances in which a controversy arises.[39] This important interpretive characteristic of the Court's constant jurisprudence is vital for the progressive inclusion in the regional human rights system of more detailed and nuanced guidelines on economic, social and cultural rights, such as those developed in relation to the critical guideposts of availability, accessibility, adequacy and acceptability in the General Comments of the UN Committee on Economic, Social and Cultural Rights. In incorporating such standards into its case-based jurisprudence, the Court must nevertheless be careful to respect the jurisdictional limits of its contentious competence.

3. COMPLAINT PROCEDURES, LEGAL STANDING, AND ACCESS TO LEGAL SERVICES

3.1 Submission of a Case to the Court

Unlike its contemporary European counterpart, the inter-American system is based on a two-tiered approach to contentious cases: before reaching the Court, all cases must first be examined by the Inter-American Commission on Human Rights (see preceding chapter in this volume), which has its own lengthy process for the examination of petitions. After such examination, the Commission 'shall' refer to the Court all cases that meet four conditions: (1) the respondent State has not reasonably complied with the Commission's final, confidential recommendations on the merits; (2) the case involves alleged violations of the American Convention or other treaty over which the Court exercises contentious jurisdiction with respect to the respondent State; (3) the impugned facts occurred *after* the treaty took effect for that State[40]; and (4) the State has made a declaration recognising the Court's jurisdiction as binding, either ipso facto or in the case sub judice.[41] If the case does not meet these conditions, or there is otherwise a reasoned decision by a majority of the Commission's members not to refer the case to the Court,[42] the Commission will publish its final

---

Tecse v. Peru, Judgment of Mar. 2005, Inter-Am. Ct. H.R. (Ser. C) No. 121, paras. 74–75.

[37] See e.g., *The Mayagna (Sumo) Indigenous Community of Awas Tingni v. Nicaragua*, Judgment of Aug. 31, 2001, Inter-Am. Ct. H.R. (Ser. C) No. 79.

[38] See, e.g., *Baena Ricardo et al. Case* (n. 36 above), paras. 162–65; *'Five Pensioners' Case* (n. 24 above), para. 147; *Plan de Sánchez Massacre Case v. Guatemala, Reparations*, Judgment of April 29, 2004, Inter-Am. Ct. H.R. (Ser. C) No. 105, para. 105; *Yakye Axa Indigenous Community v. Paraguay*, Judgment of June 17, 2005, Inter-Am. Ct. H.R. (Ser. C) No. 125, paras. 72–73; *Ximenes Lopes v. Brazil*, Judgment of July 4, 2006, Inter-Am. Ct. H.R. (Ser. C) No. 149, paras. 128–36.

[39] See, e.g., *Legal Status and Human Rights of the Child* (n. 35 above), para. 28; *'Street Children' Case* (n. 35 above), para. 193; *The Right to Information on Consular Assistance in the Framework of the Guarantees of Due Process of Law*, Advisory Opinion OC-16/99 of Oct. 1, 1999, Inter-Am. Ct. H.R. (Ser. A) No. 16, para. 114.

[40] The Court has tended to interpret its *ratione temporis* jurisdiction quite rigorously. See, e.g., *'Serrano Cruz Sisters' Case v. El Salvador*, Preliminary Objections, Judgment of Nov. 23, 2004, Inter-Am. Ct. H.R. (Ser. C) No. 118; *Case of Alfonso Martín del Campo Dodd v. Mexico*, Preliminary Objections, Judgment of Sept. 3, 2004, Inter-Am. Ct. H.R. (Ser. C) No. 113. It has, however, taken an increasingly broad view of 'continuing' or 'permanent' violations, and used 'ongoing denial of justice,' under Articles 1, 8 and 25, as a basis for asserting jurisdiction over the effects of events occurring before the Convention entered into force for a given State. See, e.g., *Case of Moiwana Village v. Suriname*, Judgment of June 15, 2005, Inter-Am. Ct. H.R. (Ser. C) No. 124, paras. 39–44.

[41] Twenty-two of the twenty-five States that have at one time ratified the Convention have formally recognised the competence of the Court to receive individual complaints. In 1998, Trinidad and Tobago denounced the Convention, in accordance with Article 78 of the treaty, thereby removing the Court's jurisdiction over it.

[42] While a presumption exists that a case meeting the above conditions will be referred to the Court, the Commission may by majority vote decide not to refer a case, having given fundamental consideration to obtaining justice in

report on the merits of the case and, where appropriate, continue supervising compliance with its own final recommendations. Given these limitations, the Court's jurisprudence represents but a tiny fraction of the cases submitted to the Commission each year by human rights victims and their representatives.[43]

In order to avoid a procedural time-bar, the Commission must file an application meeting the above conditions with the Court within three months of transmitting to the respondent State its own final, and confidential, conclusions and recommendations on the merits of the case.[44] The alleged victims or their duly-accredited representatives are then given thirty days to present autonomously to the Court their own requests, arguments and evidence, although these must remain within the factual boundaries set forth in the application.[45] This procedure represents a significant and important change in the Court's practice. Prior to the November 2000 reform of the Court's Rules of Procedure, which granted locus standi in judicio to victims and their representatives in all stages of contentious procedure before the Court, victims and their representatives could participate autonomously in Court proceedings only at the reparations stage; otherwise, their interests were purported to be represented by the 'public defender' role of the Commission. The procedural reform is critical for

effective human rights litigation, both for safeguarding self-representation and autonomy interests of victims[46] and because the Commission at times fails to allege violations of autonomous social rights in its application to the Court, even after finding them in its own confidential Article 50 report. Preservation of such claims has been left to the victims and their representatives to assert in their own independent pleadings to the Court.[47] While Court procedure provides for separate hearings at the admissibility, merits, reparations, and compliance stages of a case, the Court can and often does merge stages at its election.

3.2 Legal Standing

The Court has interpreted the conventional rules on legal standing of victims quite restrictively. To have standing before the Court (in contrast to the Commission, which exhibits slightly higher flexibility[48]) all alleged victims must be individualised and duly identified by name in the original application filed with the Court by the Commission. There must, moreover, be *prima facie* evidence that such individuals suffered demonstrable personal harm as a result of acts or omissions that are imputable to the State and in breach of the State's international obligations. Where alleged victims are indicated, but not identified by name and with appropriate identifying documentation in the Commission's application, and the defect is not promptly corrected, the Court will

---

the particular case, based on a series of factors listed in Article 44 of its Rules of Procedure.

[43] The Inter-American Commission currently receives approximately 1,400 contentious petitions per year, and is processing about 1,000 at any given time. Only a handful of these are referred to the Court each year, although this number is growing. As recently reported by a sitting Judge, while the Court received not a single case between 1979 and 1986, the first seven years of its operation, it received seven cases between 1986 and 1993, and thirty-two cases between 1994 and 2001. In the three-year period between 2001 and 2004, the Court received twenty-nine cases, a doubling of the rate immediately prior to the 2000 amendment to the Commission's Rules of Procedure. See Ventura Robles, 'Tribunal permanente' (n. 10 above), p. 14.

[44] If the Commission does not meet this deadline, its final report will be made public and published in its Annual Report. For the elements that must be included in the Commission's application, see Rules of Procedure of the Inter-American Court on Human Rights, art. 33.

[45] Ibid. arts. 23, 35.4. Victims may not allege their own version of the 'facts'; they are limited to those recounted in the Commission's application.

[46] There are now three separate 'parties' to every case before the Court: the alleged victims, the respondent State, and the Commission. Each may present independent evidence, arguments, and requests in all procedural stages.

[47] In the *Yean and Bosico Girls v. Dominican Republic Case*, for example, the Commission found an independent violation of the right to education in its own confidential report, then failed to raise the claim in its application to the Court, leaving it to the petitioners to make it under Article 26. See Judgment of Sept. 8, 2005, Inter-Am. Ct. H.R. (Ser. C) No. 130, para. 29. By contrast, in the *Panchito López Case*, the petitioners raised an Article 26 claim for the first time in their independent arguments to the Court. *Panchito Lopez Case* (n. 35 above), para. 116.

[48] For the Commission it is only necessary that alleged victims are individually determinable. Powers of attorney are not required in Commission proceedings, as they are for the Court.

proceed in considering the case only with respect to the named victims.[49]

This requirement of individualisation and precise identification is rigidly enforced, with only one potential exception: indigenous communities. The Court has required only that their members be 'determinable' before exercising jurisdiction over the self-defined collective.[50] The narrowness of the exception is noteworthy given that persons in state custody (whose individual members are equally or even more easily 'determinable' given that their precise names are identifiable, but within the control of the State) are not afforded the exception. The Court has held that they must be individually named to have their situations taken into account in contentious proceedings.[51]

The rule of individualisation and individualised proof of harm, which precludes the bringing of actio popularis or even, it would appear at present, most class action suits, is based on a narrow reading of the word 'indicate' in the Court's Rules of Procedure[52] together with classic notions of case-based legal standing in which individualised harm, proximately caused by identified acts or omissions, must be proven before a remedy may properly be ordered by the relevant jurisdictional body in favour of an alleged victim or victims.

According to the Court, if individualised harm is not proved, a remedy in favour of a given individual would exceed the jurisdictional limits of the Court imposed by the 'case' requirement in Article 62 of the Convention,[53] a rule that serves to safeguard the rights of presumed victims.[54]

This rule, however, applies to merits-based cases only. The Court has distinguished it from the preventive character of provisional measures, in which the Court has the authority to order the adoption of special measures of interim protection, in situations of extreme gravity and urgency, to avoid irreparable harm to the rights of individuals. In such circumstances, where the merits of a case are not at issue, it is sufficient that the beneficiaries are 'determinable' in order to grant them provisional measures of protection.[55]

3.3 Access to Legal Services

There is currently no formal mechanism for the provision of free legal services to victims of human rights abuse in the inter-American system, outside the public defender function that the Commission itself plays. The inter-American organs are nonetheless attuned to the problem of access to legal services. In an important 1990 advisory opinion requested by the Commission, the Court held that if a victim who is indigent is unable to obtain legal services in the domestic jurisdiction, or is unable to deposit filing fees, because of his or her indigency, then he or she is not required to exhaust domestic remedies before filing a petition with the Inter-American Commission on Human Rights.[56]

Nevertheless, indigency in proceedings before the regional organs themselves has not been addressed. Court proceedings in particular can be

---

[49] *Panchito Lopez Case* (n. 35 above), para. 109. See also *Plan de Sánchez v. Guatemala*, Reparations, Judgment of Nov. 9, 2004, Inter-Am. Ct. H.R. (Ser C) No. 116, para. 62; *Moiwana Community v. Suriname*, Judgment of June 15, 2005, Inter-Am. Ct. H.R. (Ser. C) No. 124, paras. 177–78. But see *Acevedo Jaramillo et al. v. Perú*, Judgment of Feb. 7, 2006, Inter-Am. Ct. H.R. (Ser C) No. 144, para. 227, which appears to open the door to future class actions.

[50] See *Awas Tingni Case* (n. 37 above) (victims identified as 'all members' of the Awas Tingni Community, without provision of the precise names of every individual). The Court has, however, begun to request lists of all members of indigenous communities. See, e.g., *Yakye Axa Case* (n. 38 above), Annex A, pp. 112–20; *Sawhoyamaxa Indigenous Community v. Paraguay*, Judgment of Mar. 29, 2006, Inter-Am. Ct. H.R. (Ser. A) No. 146, Annex A.

[51] *Panchito Lopez Case* (n. 35 above), paras. 107–09. Unnamed victims may nonetheless benefit indirectly from structural remedies issued in the name of duly-identified victims.

[52] The Court explains its approach by reference to Court Rule 33, which requires that 'the parties to the case' (including the 'victim' or 'alleged victim') be '*indicated*' in the Commission's application. The Court interprets this requirement to include the identification by name, with appropriate supporting documents, of each alleged victim. Ibid. para. 106.

[53] Ibid. para. 107. Article 62.3 of the Convention establishes that the Court's jurisdiction 'shall comprise all *cases* concerning the interpretation and application of the provisions of this Convention'. American Convention (n. 1 above), art. 62.3 (emphasis added).

[54] *Panchito Lopez Case* (n. 35 above), para. 109.

[55] Ibid. para. 108.

[56] *Exceptions to the Exhaustion of Internal Remedies (Art. 46(1), 46(2)(a) and 46(2)(b) American Convention on Human Rights)*, Advisory Opinion OC-11/90 of Aug. 10, 1990, Inter-Am. Ct. H.R. (Ser. A) No.11, paras. 30–31, 42. In practice, however, the exception has never in fact been validated in any contentious case considered by the system's organs.

prohibitively expensive for victims of human rights abuse, given the costs of preparing and arguing a case at the international level. An international coalition of NGOs has thus been lobbying the OAS over the last several years for the establishment of a 'Victim Assistance Fund' to facilitate access to the Inter-American Court.[57] The NGO Coalition has also established a 'Lawyer's Pro-Bono Database' to further facilitate such access by expanding and diversifying options and access to technical and legal expertise for victims of human rights abuse.[58]

4. LEGAL DUTIES CORRESPONDING TO PROTECTED SOCIAL RIGHTS

The most formidable obstacle at present to the effective protection of economic, social and cultural rights in the inter-American system lies in the identification and application of the legal duties that correspond to such rights in adjudicatory contexts, particularly under the American Convention. Specifically, it lies in the tendency of advocates to apply *different* standards of adjudication to those claims that rely on norms located in Chapter II and formally identified as 'civil and political' rights (Articles 3–25) than to those that rely on norms located in Chapter III and formally identified as 'economic, social and cultural' (Article 26). Where social rights claims are adjudicated under the former, the general obligations set out in Chapter I (Articles 1 and 2) are consistently applied. These general duties apply, by their terms, to all rights recognised in the Convention, regardless of subjective characterisation. Constitutively, they embody dimensions of a conduct-based and result-based nature.[59] They also encompass

dimensions oriented toward the individual and those oriented toward the collective. Nonetheless, in light of the system's longstanding jurisdictional rules on party standing and causation-based imputation of state responsibility, the Court applies them in the individual petitions process exclusively in their *conduct-based* and *individual-oriented* dimensions, referred to elsewhere as their 'quadrant 1' dimensions.[60] Under this jurisdictional standard, the Court regularly finds State responsibility for discrete violations of protected social rights to the detriment of duly identified individual victims.[61]

By contrast, where claims of social rights violations are alleged autonomously under Chapter III's Article 26, an obligation of so-called 'progressive development' tends to be asserted. This obligation is understood as a *result-based* duty correlative not to the case-specific victim, but to statistical progress or setbacks over broad population aggregates. As a duty of this nature is not directly cognisable under the Court's 'case-based' jurisdiction

whether or not a given right is, as a factual matter, 'respected' or 'ensured' at a particular moment for a given person or collectivity. While the two dimensions are closely related and largely indivisible, the distinction is conceptually important for isolating the dimensions of state duties that are directly adjudicable in non-strict liability jurisdictions for purposes of imputing causal responsibility to the State for human rights violations. In using this terminology, this author does not purport to reopen debates regarding distinctions between 'obligations of conduct' and 'obligations of result' in international law generally. Because these concepts have been interpreted in different ways under different legal systems and because they may so easily be finessed, the International Law Commission ultimately decided to omit the distinction from its Draft Articles on State Responsibility. They elucidate little when discussed in the abstract. Rather, this author seeks to affirm and recover the conceptually useful distinction between 'conduct-based' and 'result-based' dimensions of human rights obligations, given that adjudicatory procedures that insist on a legal or proximate causation requirement, such as the inter-American system's, may only apply the former as a direct basis for establishing State responsibility for discrete human rights violations in individual complaints procedures. For a fuller discussion of this important conceptual distinction, see Melish, 'Rethinking the "Less as More" Thesis' (n. 25 above), pp. 237-254.

[57] See, e.g., Presentation by the International Coalition of Nongovernmental Organizations on the Topic of Resolution AG/Res. 1895 (XXXII-O/02), 'Study on the Access of Persons to the Inter-American Court of Human Rights', OEA/Ser.G, CP/CAJP-1985/02 (2002).

[58] The Database contains the names, substantive legal specialties, and contact information of lawyers and institutions in the region that have worked before the inter-American organs and are willing to counsel, advise or assist cases on a pro bono basis. See <http://www.cejil.org/probono.cfm>.

[59] The *conduct-based* dimensions of the Convention's general obligations refer to the legal duty of States parties to 'adopt all necessary measures to respect and ensure' (or 'give effect to') the rights of all persons within the State's jurisdiction. The *result-based* dimension refers to

[60] See ibid.; see also Tara J. Melish, 'Counter-rejoinder. Justice vs. Justiciability? Normative Neutrality and Technical Precision, The Role of the Lawyer in Supranational Social Rights Litigation', *New York University Journal of International Law and Politics*, Vol. 39, No. 2 (2006), pp. 385-415.

[61] See discussion in section 5, below, of the Court's growing social rights jurisprudence, the entirety of which has been adjudicated under Chapter II rights.

and corresponding rules on legal standing, which require proof of concrete injury to duly identified individuals and causal conduct imputable to the State,[62] the Court has consistently dismissed or set aside Article 26 claims framed under 'progressive development' standards. It has preferred to adjudicate such claims under Chapter II rights, concretised in discrete contexts by Chapter I 'conduct-based' and 'individual-oriented' obligations.

This tendency stems not from the nature of the distinct rights at issue, nor from any Convention-based textual directive. Rather, it derives from widely-internalised stereotypes that equate civil-political rights with 'immediate enforceability', and economic, social and cultural rights with 'progressive realisation'.[63] Although these norm-based stereotypes do not correspond to the reality of rights realisation in a democratic society – in which *all rights*, regardless of normative characterisation, are subject to resource constraints and competing commitments and contain both immediately-enforceable and non-immediately-enforceable dimensions – they remain stubbornly entrenched in the popular legal mindset and hence continue to form the basis of many litigation strategies, including before the Court. The predictable outcome is that the Court, pressed with arguments urging application of litigation-appropriate duties to claims based on Chapter II norms, and litigation-inappropriate duties to those based on Chapter III guarantees, has necessarily centred its case-based jurisprudence on Chapter II norms.

Rational social rights adjudication in the inter-American system requires that these divergent approaches be reconciled into a single duty-based standard for rights-based adjudication. The Convention, by its terms and without distinction, subjects all 'protected rights' recognised therein to the Court's contentious jurisdiction and to the 'general obligations' clauses in Articles 1 and 2. It is these obligations, interpreted and applied in discrete factual contexts in their *individual-oriented* and *conduct-based dimensions*, that correspond equally to Chapter II and Chapter III rights. The following subsection discusses the Court's constant jurisprudence over the last two decades on the content and scope of these 'general obligations', duties assumed by all States parties to the Convention upon ratification. This jurisprudence is then contradistinguished, in section 4.2, from the dimensions of State legal obligations currently being pressed by advocates with respect to Article 26 norms. As one Judge has correctly noted, this latter approach 'does not appear to find a basis in the Convention'.[64] It should cease being pressed in litigation contexts, reserved instead for the regional system's broader non-contentious promotional mandate, particularly as exercised by the Inter-American Commission on Human Rights (see previous Chapter in this volume).

4.1   Duties to 'Respect' and to 'Ensure', Interpreted in Their Justiciable Dimensions

Articles 1.1 and 2 of the Convention, joined in Chapter I, lay out the 'general obligations' that apply to 'each of the rights' recognised in the treaty.[65] As specified in Article 1.1, these encompass the interrelated duties to 'respect' all recognised rights and freedoms and to 'ensure' their free and full exercise by all persons subject to the ratifying State's jurisdiction, without discrimination.[66] Article 2 gives further flesh to the Article 1.1 'duty to ensure' by underscoring that formal guarantees of rights and freedoms, while necessary, are

---

[62] The Court establishes both of these elements in all cases it considers. See generally Melish, *Protecting Economic, Social and Cultural Rights* (n. 18 above), ch. 3, which emphasises the difference between international procedures whose primary purpose is to *adjudicate* cases involving alleged violation of human rights and those whose primary function is to *monitor* and *promote* general compliance with human rights obligations and notes that, given standing and other jurisdictional requirements, the standards adopted by the latter are not necessarily susceptible to adjudication by the former.

[63] While advocates often focus on the need to overcome the classic negative/positive dichotomy between categories of rights, they frequently perpetuate the same categorical approach by uncritically accepting an immediate/progressive dichotomy between the same sets of rights. For a relevant discussion, see Melish, 'Counter-rejoinder. Justice vs. Justiciability?' (n. 60 above), pp. 390–95.

[64] Reasoned Opinion of Judge de Roux Rengifo, '*Five Pensioners' Case* (n. 24 above).

[65] *Velásquez Rodríguez Case*, Judgment of July 29, 1988, Inter-Am. Ct. H.R. (Ser. C) No. 4, paras. 162, 164 ('[Article 1.1] specifies the obligation assumed by the States Parties in relation to *each of the rights* protected [in the Convention]'.) (emphasis added); *Godínez Cruz Case*, Judgment of Jan. 20, 1989, Inter-Am. Ct. H.R. (Ser. C) No. 5, paras. 171, 173; *Neira Alegría et al. Case*, Judgment of Jan. 19, 1995, Inter-Am. Ct. H.R. (Ser. C) No. 20, para. 85.

[66] American Convention (n. 1 above), art. 1.1.

insufficient. Rather, States parties must ensure that recognised rights and freedoms truly have 'domestic legal effect'.[67] This is understood as effective means of domestic implementation and enforcement, including detailed and accessible legislation, plans of action for the short, medium and long-term that adequately target the most vulnerable, appropriate sanctions for non-compliance or breach, adequate resource assignation, and specialised jurisdictional organs where circumstances so require.[68] It also 'entails the elimination of norms and practices that result in the violation of such rights, as well as the enactment of laws and the development of practices leading to the effective respect for these guarantees'.[69] In the Court's words, Articles 1.1 and 2 obligate States parties *to adopt all necessary and appropriate measures*, of a legislative, administrative, judicial or other variety, 'to organize the governmental apparatus and, in general, all the structures through which public power is exercised, so that they are capable of juridically ensuring the free and full enjoyment of human rights'.[70]

In this sense, State responsibility arises not because a person or group of persons is objectively impaired in his or her factual enjoyment of a protected right (i.e., the 'result-based' dimension of the duty to 'ensure'), but rather because the State failed to *adopt the measures* required of it in the particular circumstances to reasonably prevent the harm or to respond to it appropriately and with 'due diligence' (the 'conduct-based' dimension).[71] As the Court has stated: 'It is not possible to make a detailed list of all such measures, since they vary with the law and the conditions of each State Party'.[72] Nevertheless, the Court insists on its ability to determine, in discrete factual contexts and on a case-by-case basis, when the measures adopted by the State have been 'unreasonable', 'inadequate' or 'insufficiently diligent' to ensure an aggrieved individual's rights appropriately, and hence when such measures (or lack thereof) are generative of state responsibility for the alleged harm.[73] In making this balancing determination, resource constraints and the competing rights and duties of others in a democratic society must always be taken into account.[74]

The Court has, accordingly, interpreted the Article 1.1 'duty to ensure' as including several constitutive components of a conduct-based nature: the duty to *prevent*, the duty to *investigate*, the duty to *sanction*, and the duty to *repair*, each assessed on the basis of 'reasonableness in the circumstances'.[75] Where the State fails to undertake reasonable or appropriate measures in each of these categories it in a sense 'aids' the abusive conduct at issue, 'thereby making the State responsible on the international plane'.[76]

---

67 Ibid. art. 2 ('Where the exercise of any of the rights or freedoms referred to in Article 1 is not already ensured by legislative or other provisions, the States Parties undertake to adopt, in accordance with their constitutional processes and the provisions of this Convention, such legislative or other measures as may be necessary to give effect to those rights or freedoms.').

68 Thus, where measures of internal law are lacking or ineffective – whether for insufficient detail, lack of accessible enforcement or remedial mechanisms, or supervening customs or practices – the State has an obligation to introduce all necessary modifications into its domestic law to assure faithful compliance with its international obligations. See, e.g., *'Panchito Lopez' Case* (n. 35 above), para. 205–06, 316–17, citing additional cases.

69 *Case of Claude Reyes et al. v. Chile*, Judgment of Sept. 19, 2006, Inter-Am. Ct. H.R. (Ser. C) No. 151, para.101.

70 *Velásquez Rodríguez Case* (n. 65 above), para. 166.

71 See *Velásquez Rodríguez Case* (n. 65 above), para. 175, in which the Court underscores that 'the existence of a particular violation does not, in itself, prove the failure to take preventive measures' and hence give rise to state responsibility. See also *Pueblo Bello Massacre v. Colombia*, Judgment of Jan. 31, 2006, Inter-Am. Ct. H.R. (Ser. C), No. 140, para. 123.

72 *Velásquez Rodríguez Case* (n. 65 above), para. 175. What is 'appropriate' or 'reasonable' in the circumstances will also vary with the nature and gravity of the harm, evolving norms of decency, legislative priorities, and resource availabilities, including new technologies.

73 The Court regularly refers to the legal duty to take 'reasonable' steps to ensure rights. See, e.g., ibid. para. 174 ('The State has a legal duty to take reasonable steps'); *Pueblo Bello Case* (n. 71 above), para. 123 (noting that the obligation to adopt measures is conditioned on 'reasonable possibilities' of preventing or avoiding the noted harm).

74 See, e.g., American Convention (n. 1 above), art. 32.2 ('The rights of each person are limited by the rights of others, by the security of all, and by the just demands of the general welfare, in a democratic society'. For a discussion of the Court's failure to take these considerations expressly into account in the context of pension reform and property-rights claims, see Melish, 'A Pyrrhic Victory for Peru's Pensioners' (n. 24 above).

75 See, e.g., *Velásquez Rodríguez Case* (n. 65 above), para. 174 ('The State has a legal duty to take reasonable steps to prevent human rights violations and to use the means at its disposal to carry out a serious investigation of violations committed within its jurisdiction, to identify those responsible, to impose the appropriate punishment and to ensure the victim adequate compensation.').

76 Ibid. para. 177; see also *Pueblo Bello* (n. 71 above), para. 145; *Mapiripán Massacre v. Colombia*, Judgment of Sept. 15, 2005, Inter-Am. Ct. H.R. (Ser. C) No. 134, paras. 137, 233; *'Panchito Lopez' Case* (n. 35 above), para. 158.

Most recently, the Court has expanded its under-standing of the conduct-based dimensions of the duty to 'ensure' to include a duty to *provide* (or '*fulfil*'), also assessed on the basis of reasonable-ness in the circumstances. This duty, based on the State's accepted role as ultimate 'guarantor' of the rights in the Convention, arises where indi-viduals cannot meet minimum needs necessary for the enjoyment of their rights without affirma-tive State assistance. Classically, this duty arises where persons are affirmatively deprived of lib-erty in state-controlled custodial contexts, such as prisons, detention centres, and psychiatric hospi-tals.[77] It also arises, however, in private custodial or care-based contexts[78] and in non-custodial sit-uations of vulnerability that, for whatever reason, impede individuals from meeting, on their own, the basic needs necessary for the full and free exer-cise of their Convention-based rights.[79] The Court has, in this sense, affirmed that special conduct-based obligations derive from the general duties in Article 1.1, based on a particular right-holder's needs of protection in the circumstances, needs which can heighten the duty to respond to situa-tions of particular stress or vulnerability.[80]

All of the above is equally true whether the imme-diate harm or threat of harm to an identified indi-vidual or individuals is imputable to the State by way of an arbitrary *act* of a State agent or through an *omission*, such as where a public agent or authority fails to adopt appropriate measures to respond to the abusive conduct of a private third party.[81] In this latter respect, the Court has repeatedly recognised the 'horizontal' dimension of human rights guarantees and insisted that Arti-cle 1.1 generates extensive positive duties on the State to regulate 'inter-individual relations' in soci-ety that may violate the interests safeguarded by

human rights.[82] The conduct-based duties to 'rea-sonably prevent' and 'appropriately respond' to human rights violations, through the adoption of necessary measures, thus apply as fully to harms caused by private third parties, including private employers, landlords, businesses, and health ser-vice providers, as they do to those caused directly by State agents.

It is useful to highlight in this regard that States have extensive and closely-related conduct-based duties of a 'negative' and 'positive' nature under the Convention, breach of the former generally indicating breach of the latter.[83] The Article 1.1 duty to 'respect' constitutes a 'negative' duty of abstention or restraint in state conduct. It is impli-cated whenever State agents engage in *unreason-able conduct* that directly and unjustifiably harms individuals in the exercise of their rights. Arbitrary dismissals from school or work, discrimination in access to health care, or use of excessive force in detentions or evictions are classic examples.

---

[77] See, e.g., '*Panchito Lopez' Case* (n. 35 above).

[78] See, e.g., *Ximenes Lopes Case* (n. 38 above).

[79] See, e.g., *Yakye Axa Case* (n. 38 above); '*Street Children*' *Case* (n. 35 above).

[80] See, e.g., *Pueblo Bello Case* (n. 71), para. 111.

[81] As the Court has stated, 'Article 1 (1) is essential in deter-mining whether a violation of the human rights rec-ognized by the Convention can be imputed to a State Party....Any impairment of those rights which can be attributed under the rules of international law to the *action or omission* of any public authority constitutes an act imputable to the State, which assumes responsibility in the terms provided by the Convention'. Ibid. para. 164 (emphasis added).

[82] See *Pueblo Bello Case* (n. 71 above), paras. 113–14, citing Court's many cases, opinions, and orders that have affirmed this principle. See, in particular, *Velásquez Rodríguez Case* (n. 65 above), para. 176 ('when the State allows private persons or groups to act freely and with impunity to the detriment of the rights recognized by the Convention . . . the State has failed to comply with its duty to ensure the free and full exercise of those rights to the persons within its jurisdiction.'); ibid. para. 172 ('[Acts of private persons] lead to international responsibility of the State, not because of the act itself, but because of the lack of due diligence to prevent the violation or to respond to it as required by the Convention.'); ibid. para. 173 ('What is decisive is whether a violation of the rights recognized by the Convention has occurred with the support or the acquiescence of the government, or whether the State has allowed the act to take place without taking measures to prevent it or to punish those responsible.').

[83] Because both of these dimensions are 'conduct-based', social rights litigation strategies that focus on the nega-tive/positive dichotomy as a way to overcome traditional stereotypes regarding the relative amenability to adjudi-cation of civil-political and social rights norms often miss the mark and continue to lead to the framing of non-justiciable claims. See, e.g., J. L. Cavallaro & E. J. Schaf-fer, 'Less as More: Rethinking Supranational Litigation of Economic and Social Rights in the Americas,' *Hastings Law Journal*, Vol. 56, pp. 217 (2005) (focusing on nega-tive/positive distinction and recommending hypotheti-cal test cases that are non-cognisable in inter-American system). This is because the negative/positive distinction cannot speak to the more important distinction (from a justiciability perspective) between 'conduct' and 'result-based' dimensions of legal obligations, only the former capable of sustaining a justiciable claim in non–strict-liability jurisdictions. See 'Rethinking the "Less as More" Thesis' (n. 25 above).

By contrast, the duty to 'ensure' constitutes the 'positive' obligation, and requires extensive measures on the part of the State in the broad areas of prevention, response, and fulfilment, all assessed on a case-by-case basis for compatibility with the Convention under the common judicial standards of 'reasonableness in the circumstances', 'proportionality', and/or 'due diligence'.[84]

Hard distinctions between 'negative' and 'positive' dimensions of State obligations have thus never been dispositive in deciding any case in the inter-American human rights system, the Court recognising that, in concrete settings, the two are generally inseparable. States are, accordingly, regularly found in simultaneous and coordinated breach of their international legal obligations to 'respect' and 'ensure' rights as interpreted in their individual-oriented and conduct-based dimensions. This occurs, for example, where State agents engage in direct abuse of children or custodial populations, on the one hand, and, on the other, fail to take the necessary preventive and responsive measures to appropriately train State agents and to tend to the victims' 'project of life'.[85] It also occurs where States grant to private extraction companies concessions to exploit natural resources on lands ancestrally inhabited by indigenous communities (negative obligation), without taking appropriate 'preventive' measures to delimit, demarcate and title those lands[86] or to engage in any prior consultation or consent-giving arrangement (positive obligation).[87]

4.2   Article 26: Muddying the Adjudicatory Waters: The Duty of 'Progressive Development'

While the above principles form part of the constant jurisprudence of the system – having been established in the Court's very first merits case, *Velásquez Rodríguez*, in 1988, and reiterated over the last two decades in every decision of that body – advocates before the Court have tended to

apply them consistently to claims based on Chapter II norms only. This is true regardless of whether those norms are invoked to protect essential dimensions of classic civil-political rights or classic social rights, such as health, education, unionisation, culture or social security. Nonetheless, when these latter rights are invoked *autonomously* under Chapter III, advocates have tended, erroneously, to bypass the conduct-based, individual-oriented dimensions of the Article 1 and 2 duties, focusing instead on the formal title of Article 26, 'Progressive Development'. This title is then reimagined[88] as the exclusive *duty* corresponding to autonomous Article 26 rights displacing application of Articles 1 and 2, or, equally disconcerting, as the very article 26-protected *right* itself (a so-called 'right to progressive development of economic, social and cultural rights').[89]

In both cases, the result is to render Article 26 claims non-justiciable. This is because the 'obligation of progressive development' (or 'progressive realisation'), as developed and understood by

---

[84] See generally T. J. Melish & A. Aliverti, '"Positive Obligations" in the Inter-American Human Rights System', *Interights Bulletin*, Vol. 15, No. 3 (2006), pp. 120–22.

[85] *'Street Children' Case* (n. 35 above); *'Panchito Lopez' Case* (n. 35 above).

[86] *Awas Tingni Case* (n. 37 above).

[87] *Saramaka People v. Suriname*, Judgment of Nov. 28, 2007, Inter-Am. Ct. (Ser. C).

[88] Article 26's title is in fact best understood as a simple shorthand reference to Chapter VII of the OAS Charter, entitled '*Integral Development*', from which article 26 rights are expressly derived. That chapter includes Articles 30-52, the provisions referenced in the Convention's Preamble as having been incorporated through the Protocol of Buenos Aires in 1967 to broaden the Charter's standards 'with respect to economic, social and educational rights'. In the 1969 drafting of the Convention, several Latin American States objected to the Commission's original draft proposal on what is now Article 26 in that it incorporated the standards in only *one* of those OAS Charter articles. Brazil complained that this formulation left out of the Convention's protective scope many of the economic, social and cultural rights that were already widely recognised in the domestic jurisdictions of most American States, including the rights to strike, to education, and to culture. See, e.g., Inter-American Specialized Conference on Human Rights, Acts and Documents, OEA/Ser.K/XVI/1.2 (1969), at 121–128 (Brazil). The drafters accommodated this concern by redrafting Article 26 to include all economic, social and cultural rights derived from the OAS Charter's standards. The formal title of Article 26 is thus best seen not as a duty or right *per se*, but rather as an indication of *where* specifically to look in the Charter to identify Article 26's protected rights and a reminder that these rights, like all rights, are to be achieved 'progressively'. For a discussion of this drafting history, see Melish, 'Rethinking the "Less as More" Thesis' (n. 25 above), pp. 225–230.

[89] Under this latter formulation, State responsibility for an Article 26 violation is said to arise where a State fails to 'ensure', as a factual matter, the 'progressive development of economic, social and cultural rights' over a population or sub-group within it.

international expert bodies, such as the UN Committee on Economic, Social and Cultural Rights,[90] cannot satisfy the two core justiciability requirements mandated by the inter-American system's 'case' requirement: namely, concrete injury to duly-identified individuals and imputation of causal responsibility for that harm to the State through its conduct. Indeed, as the Court recognised in its 2003 decision in *Five Pensioners v. Peru*, the only case to date in which it has expressly spoken to an Article 26 claim,[91] the 'progressive development' of rights cannot be measured 'in function of the circumstances of a very limited group of [persons]',[92] but rather only 'in function of the *growing coverage of [protected rights]...over the entire population*'.[93] That is, 'progressive development' is designed to assess not causal responsi-

bility for *individualised* impairments in the enjoyment or exercise of rights,[94] but rather statistical achievement of rights over the national population or vulnerable subgroups within it, usually through the use of indicators and benchmarks, the nomenclature of 'progress' and 'backsliding' (or retrogressions), and the collection and analysis of relevant demographic, legal, educational, health, and other statistical data. This data is then used to identify problem areas and best practices with a view to encouraging, through constructive dialogue procedures, State and civil society actors to collaborate at the political level in the construction of appropriate and targeted policy responses.

While such monitoring procedures frequently give rise to important synergies with litigation strategies, the result-based, collective-oriented duties that drive them are not, by themselves, transferable into the Court's case-based jurisdiction. This was expressly recognised by one of the Court's judges in his concurring opinion in *Five Pensioners*:

> [T]he reasoning according to which only State actions that affect the entire population could be submitted to the test of Article 26 does not appear to have a basis in the Convention, among other reasons because, contrary to the Commission, the *Inter-American Court cannot monitor the general situation of human rights*, whether they be civil and political, or economic, social and cultural. *The Court can only act when the human rights of specific persons are violated*, and the Convention does not require that there should be a specific number of such persons.[95]

---

[90] Under its competence to review States parties' periodic reports under the ICESCR, the Committee monitors the progress and setbacks achieved in the realisation of the rights recognised in the Covenant. While the Committee reviews both conduct and results, advocates have tended to focus on the Committee's development of the result-based concept of 'progressive realization'. See, e.g., CESCR, *General Comment No. 3, The Nature of States Parties Obligations* (Fifth session, 1990), U.N. Doc. E/1991/23, annex III at 86 (1991), para. 10 ('[A] State party in which any significant number of individuals is deprived of essential foodstuffs, of essential primary health care, of basic shelter and housing, or of the most basic forms of education is, prima facie, failing to discharge its obligations under the Covenant.').

[91] The Court has been presented with Article 26 claims in five subsequent cases. See *'Panchito Lopez' Case* (n. 35 above); *Yakye Axa Case* (n. 38 above), para 163; *Yean and Bosico Case* (n. 47 above); *Acevedo Jaramillo Case* (n. 49 above); *Case of Dismissed Congressional Employees (Aguado - Alfaro et al.) v. Peru*, Judgment of Nov. 24, 2006, Inter-Am. Ct. H.R. (Ser. C) No. 158. Nevertheless, it has declined in each to address the article 26 claims directly, preferring to address them under Chapter II norms, i.e., stripped of the 'progressive development' standard, or exclusively at the reparations stage in setting a just quantum of compensation.

[92] This is true, among other reasons, because the associated harm ('retrogression' or 'lack of progress' in result-based rights achievement at the national level) is *statistical* in nature, not *individual*. Such harm defies concretisation in any single 'victim', as required by the system's legal standing rules. In this respect, the inter-American system does not recognise the cognisability of *actio popularis*, as do many domestic jurisdictions in the region. Accordingly, while 'progressive development' claims may be cognisable within certain *national* jurisdictions in the Americas, they cannot proceed under contentious process at the *supranational* level, which has narrower rules of legal standing.

[93] *'Five Pensioners' Case* (n. 24 above), para. 147.

[94] Attempts to convert the concept of 'progressive realisation' or its corresponding 'prohibition on regressivity' into an individually-enforceable right can in fact have highly perverse consequences. Taken to its logical extreme in a world of finite resources, it could effectively be transformed into an individual veto over government-sponsored redistributive policies in the field of economic, social and cultural rights. Any such redistribution would necessarily alter current entitlement levels of the most privileged and hence would be 'regressive' with respect to them as individuals. Perversely, this would be true even where both the intent and effect of the policy was to increase overall enjoyment of the right over the sum of the population. This was, on some level, what was happening in the *Five Pensioners Case*. See Melish, 'A Pyrrhic Victory for Peru's Pensioners' (n. 24 above), p. 63.

[95] Reasoned Opinion of Judge de Roux Rengifo, *'Five Pensioners' Case* (n. 24 above) (emphasis added).

The inevitable result is that every rights-based claim that bases State responsibility on an alleged breach of the duty of 'progressive development' will necessarily be dismissed by the Court as non-cognisable under its case-based jurisdiction. In *Five Pensioners*, a case involving the right to a pension, the Court thus set aside the Article 26 right-to-social-security claim when framed under 'progressivity/regressivity' arguments, stating that it considered it 'in order to reject the request to rule on the progressive development of economic, social and cultural rights in Peru, in the context of this case'.[96] It then proceeded to adjudicate the very same right-to-a-pension claim under the Chapter II right-to-property norm, to which the litigation-appropriate dimensions of Articles 1 and 2 had properly been applied by litigants.

While the Court in *Five Pensioners* did not expressly affirm the jurisdictional appropriateness of applying Article 1 and 2 duties to claims based on Article 26 rights, it signalled to the effect. This is apparent both through the Court's reference to what it can do *'in the context of [a] case'*, as distinct from through the system's promotional or advisory functions, and, perhaps most importantly, in its express recognition that '[e]conomic, social and cultural rights have *both an individual* and a *collective dimension'.*[97] While 'progressive development', the concept to which the Court devoted the remainder of its terse two-paragraph dictum, reflects the 'collective dimension', the Article 1 and 2 duties to 'respect' and 'ensure' protected rights, through appropriate or reasonable measures and without discrimination, to 'all persons' within a State's jurisdiction represents the 'individual dimension'. In the inter-American system, it is this individual dimension of economic, social and cultural rights, and *only* this dimension that, in the words of Judge Sergio García Ramírez in his own *Five Pensioners* concurring opinion, supports their 'justiciable nature'.[98]

These dual signals from the Court should be understood, moreover, in conjunction with the Court's direct reference to the UN Committee on Economic, Social and Cultural Rights's General Comment No. 3 ('The Nature of States Parties Obligations') as useful guidance in defining the meaning of 'progressive development', as used by litigants in their arguments.[99] Indeed, General Comment No. 3 recognises expressly that the duties attaching to economic, social and cultural rights under Article 2.1 of the ICESCR have dimensions of both a 'result-based' and 'conduct-based' nature. The duty of 'progressive realisation' is defined as the 'principal obligation of *result*' under the Covenant.[100] By contrast, the duty 'to take steps … through all appropriate means' to give legal effect to the ICESCR's protected rights, is identified as the treaty's corresponding 'obligation of *conduct*', one that is 'of immediate effect,'[101] and which is frequently broken down into constituent duties to 'respect,' to 'protect,' and to 'fulfil' protected rights. These conduct-based, individual-oriented duties, found in parallel terms in the respective general obligation clauses of the ICESCR and ICCPR, are indistinguishable from the conduct-based, individual-oriented duties in Articles 1 and 2 of the American Convention. While advocates, seduced and distracted by the formal title of Article 26, have tended to disregard these litigation-appropriate duties in arguments before the Court, focusing instead on the result-based, collective-oriented duty of 'progressive realisation' – the frequent emphasis of *non-contentious* treaty-body procedures, such as periodic reporting[102] – it is the conduct-based, individual-oriented duties of Articles 1 and 2 that,

---

[96] *'Five Pensioners' Case* (n. 24 above), para. 147.

[97] Ibid. (emphasis added).

[98] Reasoned Concurring Opinion of Judge Sergio García Ramírez, *'Five Pensioners' Case* (n. 24 above) ('The Convention is a body of rules on human rights precisely, and not just on general State obligations. The existence of an individual dimension to the rights supports the so-called justiciable nature of the latter, which has advanced at the national level and has a broad horizon at the international level.').

[99] See ibid., para. 147 (citing General Comment No. 3, paragraph 9).

[100] General Comment No. 3 (n. 90 above), para. 9.

[101] Ibid. paras. 1–2. General Comment No. 3 has been significantly updated, particularly in its discussion of conduct-based duties, by CESCR, *General Comment No. 9, Domestic Application of the Covenant* (Nineteenth session 1998), U.N. Doc. E/C.12/1998/24 (1998).

[102] See note 90 above. In fact, every international human rights treaty body, within the context of its periodic reporting and special mandate procedures, addresses the 'progressive realisation' of the rights in the human rights instrument(s) it supervises. That is, despite common stereotypes, the concept of 'progressive realisation' is not exclusive to economic, social and cultural rights under international law.

consistent with system-specific justiciability doctrine, apply to *all* Convention-based contentious claims in the inter-American system. This is true irrespective of whether those claims refer to rights set out in Chapter II or Chapter III.

Indeed, if social rights litigation is to proceed rationally and effectively in the inter-American system, common litigation-appropriate dimensions of State obligations must be applied consistently to *all* Convention-based rights and their underlying claims. The implications of not doing so will be taken up again in concluding remarks.

5. JURISPRUDENCE: ANALYSIS OF SPECIFIC RIGHTS

The Court has addressed economic, social and cultural rights in a number of cases, with findings favourable to the petitioners in each.[103] Within this context, two decisive trends are apparent. First, for the reasons described above, the Court tends to rely primarily on Chapter II rights under the Convention, even where Chapter III rights are alleged, interpreting the former as umbrella provisions covering large areas of economic, social or cultural rights or as procedural devices for ensuring fairness in the enforcement, distribution or coverage of such rights, particularly where guaranteed in domestic law or court judgments. Second, the Court has tended to prefer to find social rights protected by virtue of particular groups' special vulnerability, rather than directly recognise social rights of universal application. Specifically, it has tended to find certain social rights required by States' 'heightened' or 'special obligations' to distinct populations, in light of their right to life and personal integrity.

Four discrete sets of cases, each described below, illustrate these two larger trends. They deal, respectively, with the right to harbour a 'project of life', particularly for groups in vulnerable situations; the right of indigenous peoples to their ancestral habitat; the right of workers to unionise freely and enjoy other labour rights; and the right

of retirees to an acquired pension. Within these categories, the Court's social rights jurisprudence has tended to centre on four sets of rights under the Convention: the right to life and personal integrity (Articles 4 and 5); the right to property (Article 21); the right to due process and judicial protection (Articles 8 and 25); and the right to association (Article 16).

5.1 Right to a Dignified Life: Health, Education, Water, Food, Housing and Land

Rather than recognise the autonomous rights of individuals to health, to education or to adequate housing under Article 26 of the Convention, the Court has preferred, at least to date, to subsume these basic rights into a broadly-understood concept of the 'right to life' and, more specifically, the 'right to harbor a project of life'. Essential aspects of the rights to health, education, food, recreation, sanitation, and adequate housing, all of which are necessary for the development of a dignified life, have thus been addressed under Articles 4 and 5 of the Convention, protecting respectively the rights to life and personal integrity.

The concept of a 'life project' was first recognised by the Court in a 1997 reparations judgment, in which the victim, a school teacher, claimed compensation for the harm to her 'life plan' caused by her illegal deprivation of liberty, inhuman treatment, and involuntary exile. While the Court declined to award monetary damages for this identified harm, given the difficulty of translating it into economic terms,[104] it validated and affirmed the concept of a 'life plan', finding it 'akin to the concept of personal fulfilment', the free pursuit of options that are the 'manifestation and guarantee of freedom'. It was 'obvious', concluded the Court, that the human rights abuse suffered by the victim 'radically alter[ed] the course in which life was on' and 'prevented her from achieving her goals for personal and professional growth',

---

[103] All have been brought under the American Convention, rather than the Protocol of San Salvador, given the latter's limitations and recent entry into force.

[104] *Loayza Tamayo Case*, Reparations (Art. 63(1) American Convention on Human Rights), Judgment of Nov. 27, 1998, Inter-Am. Ct. H.R. (Ser. C) No. 42 (1998), para. 153; see also ibid. para. 154 (noting, however, that judgment itself constituted some measure of satisfaction for damages of this kind).

thereby causing 'irreparable damage to her life'.[105] Articulating an idea that would resurface the following year in an important merits decision on the rights of the child, the Court affirmed that '[a]n individual can hardly be described as truly free if he does not have options to pursue in life and to carry that life to its natural conclusions'.[106]

Precisely one year later, the Court decided the *Street Children* case, in which it held the Guatemalan State responsible for the torture and murder by State agents of several street children. Using the case as a vehicle for enunciating broader principles, the Court signalled that the idea of a 'life project' and 'access to the conditions that guarantee a dignified existence', particularly for at-risk groups, was derived from the guarantees in Articles 4 and 19 of the American Convention, protecting the right to life and special measures of protection for children, respectively. According to the Court, the right to life, for which restrictive approaches are 'impermissible', includes the right not to be prevented from having access to the conditions that guarantee a dignified existence.[107] Violations of this right take on heightened gravity where children, particularly 'at-risk' ones, are involved,[108] given that the State bears obligations under Article 19 to 'prevent them from living in misery' and to provide them with 'the minimum conditions for a dignified life'.[109]

In the Court's understanding, 'every child has the right to harbor a project of life that should be tended and encouraged by the public authorities so that [the child] may develop this project for its personal benefit and that of the society to which it belongs'.[110] In defining the 'special measures' of protection owed to children under Article 19, the Court looked to the Convention on the Rights of the Child and, based on its congruent norms, highlighted the measures necessary to ensure every child's 'survival and development' as well as a

'standard of living adequate for his or her physical, mental, spiritual, moral and social development', particularly with regard to nutrition, clothing and housing.

This incipient jurisprudence was further detailed and enriched, with a more express focus on the rights of the child to education and to health care, three years later in a noteworthy advisory opinion. In *Legal Status and Human Rights of the Child*, the Court affirmed that the right to life enshrined in Convention Article 4 includes, for children, the 'obligation to provide the measures required for life to develop under decent conditions'.[111] The Court highlighted in this regard that 'education and care for the health of children … are the key pillars to ensure enjoyment of a decent life by … children, who in view of their immaturity and vulnerability often lack adequate means to effectively defend their rights'.[112] The Court particularly underscored the right to education, which in its view 'stands out among the special measures of protection for children and among the rights recognized for them in Article 19', given that it 'contributes to the possibility of enjoying a dignified life and to prevent unfavorable situations for the minor and for society itself'.[113] Indeed, 'it is mainly through education that the vulnerability of children is gradually overcome'.[114]

It was not until 2004, however, in the *Panchito López* case, that the rights to education and to health care, as essential attributes of the right to a dignified life under Article 4 (particularly for at-risk children), became solidly part of the Court's case-based jurisprudence. *Panchito López* involved a detention facility for minors in Paraguay characterised by grossly inadequate conditions, including overcrowding, lack of basic hygiene, poor nutrition, lack of adequate medical and psychological attention, serious educational deficiencies, lack of recreational activities, and insufficient beds, blankets, infrastructure and trained guards. The Court concluded that, owing to the State's failure to take necessary and sufficient positive measures to guarantee conditions

---

[105] Ibid. paras. 148–49, 152.
[106] Ibid. para. 148 ('Those options, in themselves, have an important existential value. Hence, their elimination or curtailment objectively abridges freedom and constitutes the loss of a valuable asset, a loss that this Court cannot disregard.').
[107] 'Street Children' Case (n. 35 above), para. 144.
[108] Ibid. para. 146.
[109] Ibid.
[110] Ibid. para. 191.

[111] *Legal Status and Human Rights of the Child* (n. 35 above), para. 80.
[112] Ibid. para. 86.
[113] Ibid. para. 84.
[114] Ibid. para. 88.

of a dignified life to the detainees – by, for example, providing adequate health and educational programs – the State violated the rights to life and personal integrity of all the prison inmates.[115] In focusing its analysis on Articles 4 and 5 with respect to health, education, and recreation, it declined to pronounce on congruent allegations advanced by petitioners under Article 26 of the Convention, finding these subsumed within its treatment of Articles 4 and 5.[116]

Reading Articles 4, 5, and 19 together, the Court specifically focused on the State's obligations to the child detainees with respect to health and education. Doing so, it found the State responsible for violating the child detainees' right to life under Article 4 given the Paraguayan officials' failure to provide to them even the 'adequate health attention that is required for every person deprived of liberty', never mind the 'regular medical supervision that assures a child a normal development, essential for his future'.[117] State responsibility under Article 4 also rested on the prison authorities' failure to offer the children detainees an adequate education, with sufficient teachers and resources. This obligation, according to the Court, derives both from the 'correct interpretation' of the right to life as well as by Article 13 of the Protocol of San Salvador.[118] It is heightened by the special duty to children, particularly those from 'marginal sectors of society', to ensure that detention 'will not destroy their life projects'.[119]

The *Panchito López* case represents a critical jurisprudential juncture for the Court, for two reasons. First, it expressly extends the focus on health and guaranteed conditions of a dignified life to cover *all persons*, not only children, thereby squarely relocating the conventional protection from Article 19 (children) to Article 4 (life). In this sense, the measures of protection required for children in matters of health and education

are recognised as no more than heightened obligations, or specialised accommodations, with respect to those required for all human beings, given children's special vulnerability and crucial stage of development.[120] This is vital since the preceding jurisprudence had appeared, inappropriately, to limit application of the rights to health and education to the status of being a child.[121]

Second, the *Panchito López* Court grounds its 'life project' jurisprudence squarely in recognition of an Article 4 'right' to the social conditions necessary for leading and developing a 'dignified life', including educational, health and vocational opportunities.[122] State exposure of detainees to 'conditions of undignified life that affect their right to life, their development and their life projects', therefore violates Articles 4 and 5 of the Convention to their detriment. While the case was closely tied to the special obligations States have to persons deprived of liberty, given that 'the detainee is impeded from satisfying on his own a series of basic necessities that are essential for the development of a dignified life',[123] the rationale clearly extended beyond custodial situations, to those in which the State fails to take reasonable or appropriate measures to guarantee a dignified life to persons who cannot, absent State assistance, meet their basic health, housing, food, water, and sanitation needs on their own.

This extension, originally reflected in obiter dictum in the *Street Children* case, was made explicit in the Court's 2005 resolution of *Yakye Axa Indigenous Community v. Paraguay*,[124] a case involving members of a displaced indigenous community living in extreme misery and an urgent state of food, housing, health and sanitary vulnerability on the side of a highway adjacent to their ancestral territory. Despite the subhuman conditions in which they lived, and their settlement's proximity to their traditional food sources, a court order from a local judge forbade re-entry into their ancestral

---

[115] State responsibility also arose from the prison authorities' failure to take adequate preventative measures for emergency situations. The Court concluded that 'at no time did the conditions exist in the Institute such that the detainees could develop their life in a dignified manner, rather they were made to permanently live in inhuman and degrading conditions'. '*Panchito Lopez*' *Case* (n. 35 above), para. 170.
[116] Ibid. para. 255.
[117] Ibid. para. 173.
[118] Ibid. para. 174.
[110] Ibid. paras. 161, 174.

[120] Ibid. para. 172.
[121] This focus on Article 19 is far from absent in *Panchito López*.
[122] Thus, the question for decision in the case was expressly 'whether the State . . . adopted the initiatives to guarantee to all the detainees . . . a dignified life with the objective of strengthening their life projects'. '*Panchito Lopez*' *Case* (n. 37), para. 164.
[123] Ibid. para. 152.
[124] *Yakye Axa Case* (n. 38 above). See also *Moiwana Case* (n. 40 above) and *Sawhoyamaxa Case* (n. 50 above).

territory, impeding them from nearby and otherwise accessible traditional sources of potable water, cooking wood, building materials and food. Their situation of extreme impoverishment, growing as the years passed in wait of administrative resolution of their land claim, was so grave that the State itself declared a 'State of Emergency'. The Court held that by failing to take appropriate and necessary positive measures with respect to such conditions, conditions that limited the Community members' possibilities of having a dignified life, the State violated the right to life of the members of the Yakye Axa community under Article 4 of the Convention.[125]

Imputation of State responsibility for this violation stemmed from two grounds, one classically 'negative', the other 'positive'. On the one hand, responsibility arose from the local court order that prohibited Community members from entering their ancestral territory to access, on their own, clean water, food, and traditional medicines. On the other, it arose from the sheer inadequacy of the few 'positive' responsive measures the State did take in terms of the provision of food, medical attention and educational materials while the Community was affirmatively prevented from accessing their ancestral lands.[126] Citing General Comments Nos. 12, 14 and 15 of the UN Committee on Economic, Social and Cultural Rights (on the rights to food, health and water, respectively), the Court underscored the close link between access by indigenous peoples to their ancestral territory and enjoyment of their rights to health, to food, to clean water, to education, and to cultural identity, all of which it views as necessary to ensure 'the right to a dignified existence'.[127] It therefore affirmed that the State, as 'guarantor' of the right to life, has the duty to generate the minimum conditions of life compatible with human dignity, and that this requires the adoption of positive, concrete measures oriented to the satisfaction of the right to a dignified life.[128] This is especially so, said the Court, when persons in vulnerable situations are involved. In this regard, the Court stressed the special obligations of the State to the children and elders in the community, in guaranteeing their '*right* to adequate food, to access to clean

water and to health attention', and underscored the primary role of indigenous elders in the oral transmission of culture from one generation to the next.[129]

The right to physical and mental health, particularly for persons with disabilities, has most recently been recognised as a function of the right to a 'dignified life' under Convention Articles 4 and 5 in *Ximenes Lopes v. Brazil*, a case involving the mental health sector. In that case, the Court affirmed the special obligations States parties hold as 'guarantor' of the right to health of persons subject to the State's general health system, duties that extend to regulating, monitoring and investigating health standards, conditions, practices, and complaints of abuse in private as well as public health institutions.[130] The Court underscored in particular the special duties of care held by States with respect to persons with intellectual, developmental, psychiatric, and psychosocial disabilities when subject to the State's custody or care.[131]

Similar obligations were emphasised in the subsequent case of *Albán-Cornejo et al. v. Ecuador*, in which the Court found violations of Articles 4 and 5 for the medical malpractice death of a patient in a private health care facility. Importantly, State responsibility arose not because the State contributed directly to either the medical malpractice or the death, but rather because it failed to ensure a proper investigation, appropriate sanctions, and other aspects of an effective remedy in response to them. The Court thus reemphasized that 'States are responsible for regulating and supervising the rendering of health services, so that the rights to life and humane treatment may be effectively protected'.[132] State responsibility may, accordingly, arise not only from the commission of affirmative acts by state agents in health care settings, but from an 'omission of the duty to supervise the rendering of ... services of public interest, such as health, by private or public entities (as is the case of a private hospital)'.[133]

Finally, it is worth highlighting that the Court has taken up the regular practice of granting

---

[125] *Yakye Axa Case* (n. 38 above), para. 82.
[126] Ibid. paras. 74–75.
[127] Ibid. paras. 72–73.
[128] Ibid. para. 68.

[129] Ibid. paras. 78, 81 (emphasis added).
[130] *Ximenes Lopes Case* (n. 38 above), paras. 124–50.
[131] Ibid. paras. 138–40.
[132] *Albán-Cornejo et al. v. Ecuador*, Judgment of Nov. 22, 2007, Inter-Am. Ct. H.R. (Ser. C), para. 121.
[133] Ibid. para. 119.

'provisional measures' – i.e., urgent measures of protection to prevent grave, imminent and irreparable injury to rights guaranteed in the Convention[134] – to protect the right to health of persons within a State's jurisdiction. Invoking Articles 4 and 5 of the Convention, it has, for example, ordered a State to urgently provide 'proper medical treatment' to a detainee with heart disease 'with a view to protecting his physical, psychological and moral integrity',[135] and to ensure that such treatment be received 'from a doctor of [the beneficiary's] choosing'.[136] The Court has also ordered provisional measures to urgently protect the life and personal integrity of detainees and employees in an Argentine penitentiary that, in terms of sanitation, overcrowding, and poor nutrition, lacked 'the minimum conditions compatible with their dignity'.[137] Similar measures were ordered in 2005 and 2006 in Brazilian and Venezuelan prisons.[138] The Court has, moreover, granted provisional measures to ensure the right to life and freedom of movement of members of an Ecuadorian indigenous community who, for years and with the direct or tacit support of the Ecuadorian State, were blocked by oil workers from using a river they depend on for access to vital goods and services necessary for their subsistence, safety, well-being and cultural integrity, including health care, food, housing materials, and education.[139]

5.2 Right to Property: Indigenous Territory, Self-Determination and Preservation of Culture

A second jurisprudential footpath the Court has cleared with respect to economic, social and cultural rights concerns indigenous communities and their use and enjoyment of their ancestral territories. Several indigenous rights cases have to date been brought to the Court, most dealing expressly with access to and protection of ancestral habitats.[140] At the heart of these cases are the rights to economic subsistence, cultural survival, and self-determination. To protect these fundamental rights, the Court has relied principally on the rights to property and to judicial protection, under Articles 21 and 25 of the Convention. More recently, however, it has extended beyond these norms to additionally embrace the right to a dignified life and life project under Article 4 of the Convention.[141]

The flagship case on indigenous rights was the 2001 *Awas Tingni Case*, in which the Nicaraguan government granted a concession to a foreign extraction company to exploit timber on undemarcated and untitled land that included the lands ancestrally occupied by the Mayagna (Sumo) Community of Awas Tingi. Consequently, timber extraction commenced on the community's ancestral lands, without their consent and without any process of prior consultation. The Court found the State responsible for violating, to the detriment of the members of the Community, the Article 21 right 'to the use and enjoyment of their property', basing such responsibility on the State's granting of 'concessions to third parties to utilise the property and resources located in an area which could correspond, fully or in part, to the lands' of the Awas Tingi Community.[142] Such conduct, said the Court, had created a 'climate of constant uncertainty' among the members of the Awas Tingni, 'insofar as they do not know for certain how far their communal property extends geographically and, therefore, they do not know until where they can freely use and enjoy their respective property'.[143]

---

[134] American Convention (n. 1 above), art. 63.2.
[135] *Cesti Hurtado Case*, Order of the Court of September 11, 1997, Inter-Am. Ct. H.R. (Ser. E), considering 6 (ratifying the President of the Court's order of July 29, 1997, requiring provision of adequate medical treatment in reference to the detainee's state of health, and maintaining measures).
[136] *Cesti Hurtado Case*, Order of the Court of January 21, 1998, Inter-Am. Ct. H.R. (Ser. E), Resolution 2.
[137] *Mendoza Prison Case* (Arg.), Order of the Court of Nov. 22, 2004, Inter-Am. Ct. H.R. (Ser. E).
[138] '*Febem' Prison Case* (Brazil), Resolution of the Court of Nov. 30, 2005, Inter-Am. Ct. H.R. (Ser. E); '*La Pica' Prison Case* (Venezuela), Resolution of the Court of Feb. 9, 2006, Inter-Am. Ct. H.R. (Ser. E).
[139] *Sarayaku Indigenous Community* (Ecuador), Resolution of the Court of July 6, 2004 and June 17, 2005, Inter-Am. Ct. H.R. (Ser. E).

[140] *Yatama v. Nicaragua*, Judgment of June 23, 2005, Inter-Am. Ct. H.R. (Ser. C) No. 127, is an important case not dealt with in this chapter. It involves the right to political participation under Article 23 of the Convention.
[141] In *Awas Tingni*, the Commission sought to raise additional claims in proceedings before the Court, including an Article 4 violation, but the Court considered that it had presented insufficient probative evidence to support them. *Awas Tingni Case* (n. 38 above), paras. 156–57.
[142] Ibid, para. 153.
[143] Ibid.

Consequently, to ensure the Article 21 property rights of the members of the Awas Tingi Community, the Court ordered that the State:

> [C]arry out the delimitation, demarcation, and titling of the territory belonging to the Community; and ... abstain from carrying out, until that delimitation, demarcation, and titling have been done, actions that might lead the agents of the State itself, or third parties acting with its acquiescence or its tolerance, to affect the existence, value, use or enjoyment of the property located in the geographical area where the members of the Community live and carry out their activities.[144]

This holding was critical for a number of reasons. First, it recognised that the right to property protected under Article 21 includes the right to collective or communal property and that, with respect to indigenous communities, the concept of property cannot be understood in a purely individual or economic sense. Rather, it is intimately tied to the group members' collective identity, subsistence, culture, spiritual life, integrity, and economic survival – in short, to their very existence.[145] While the Court did not go on to tie the right to ancestral territory directly to the right to life or a 'community life project', as it would a few years later, it clearly indicated the multi-dimensional importance of ancestral territory to such groups' lives, and thus the special, heightened obligations of the State to protect it.

Second, addressing a problem of hemispheric proportions, it implicitly recognised the property-based right of indigenous communities to free and informed prior consent and prior consultation, before extractive industry concessions are granted to their lands. While the Court did not have to reach this particular question directly, given that the territorial boundaries at issue were not yet established (and thus the basis for con-

sent not yet drawn), the right to consent, subject to the limitations recognised in the Convention, is implicit in the Court's understanding of 'property' and of the right to the full 'use and enjoyment' of the geographic extension in which indigenous communities inhabit. *Awas Tingni* thus set the stage for a new set of emerging cases in which indigenous communities who *do* have legal title to their demarcated land challenge, under Convention Article 21, unilateral state-granted concessions to extractive companies for the exploitation of oil, gas, mineral and timber resources on and in their ancestral territory. This follows where they were not consulted about nor did they give their consent to the illegal entry, and/or other formal legal procedures required in the circumstances were not carried out.

Two such cases have been winding their way through the system since 2000 and 2003, respectively, with the first, *The Saramaka People v. Suriname*, resolved in 2007.[146] In that case, the Court made express what *Awas Tingni* had implied: that indigenous peoples have a right to both prior consultation before extraction concessions are granted on their lands and, where profound impacts may result, to free, prior, and informed consent. In explaining the reasoning behind this principle, the Court recognised that, in accordance with Article 21 of the Convention, a State may restrict the use and enjoyment of the right to property where four specified conditions are met.[147] Where indigenous communities are involved, however, an additional fifth requirement, derived from the interplay between Articles 1, 4 and 21, applies: the restriction cannot 'amount to a denial of their survival as a tribal people.'[148] In order to ensure this last requirement, the State must abide by three critical safeguards:

> First, the State must ensure the *effective participation* of the members of the [indigenous] people, in conformity with their customs

---

144 Ibid. paras. 153, 173.4.

145 Ibid. para. 149 ('Indigenous groups, by the fact of their very existence, have the right to live freely in their own territory; the close ties of indigenous people with the land must be recognized and understood as the fundamental basis of their cultures, their spiritual life, their integrity, and their economic survival. For indigenous communities, relations to the land are not merely a matter of possession and production but a material and spiritual element which they must fully enjoy, even to preserve their cultural legacy and transmit it to future generations'.).

146 The second case is *Kichwa Indigenous People of Sarayaku v. Ecuador*. The Sarayaku enjoy formal title to their territory, a status not in dispute by the State. Referral to the Court is expected in February 2009.

147 These include that the restrictions are: 1) previously established by law; ii) necessary; iii) proportional; and iv) have the aim of achieving a legitimate objective in a democratic society. *Saramaka People v. Suriname*, Judgment of Nov. 28, 2007, Inter-Am. Ct. (Ser. C), para. 127 (citing previous caselaw).

148 Ibid. paras. 128, 129.

and traditions, regarding any development, investment, exploration or extraction plan … within [their] territory. Second, the State must guarantee that the [indigenous people] will receive a *reasonable benefit* from any such plan within their territory. Thirdly, the State must ensure that no concession will be issued … unless and until independent and technically capable entities, with the State's supervision, perform a *prior environmental and social impact assessment*.[149]

According to the Court, 'These safeguards are intended to preserve, protect and guarantee the special relationship that the members of the [indigenous] community have with their territory, which in turn ensures their survival as a tribal people.'[150]

It is from the first of these safeguards – effective participation – that the duties of active consultation and free, prior and informed consent derive. With respect to the former, the Court explained that fulfilment of the duty of active consultation requires that States ensure that consultation processes adhere to at least five constitutive principles. First, the State must 'both accept and disseminate information', ensuring 'constant communication between the parties.'[151] Second, the 'consultations must be in good faith, through culturally appropriate procedures and with the objective of reaching agreement.'[152] Third, to allow time for 'internal discussion within communities and for proper feedback to the State', consultations must take place '*at the early stages of a development plan*, not only when the need arises to obtain approval [consent] from the community, if such is the case.'[153] Fourth, to ensure that the proposed development or investment plan is accepted knowingly and voluntarily, the State must 'ensure that members of the 'indigenous people] are aware of possible risks, including environmental and health risks.'[154] Finally, 'consultations should take account of the [indigenous] people's traditional methods of decisionmaking.'[155]

Where a State neglects any of these constitutive elements of adequate consultation in undertaking development or investment plans that directly impact indigenous territories, it breaches its Convention-based obligations, under Article 1, to respect and ensure the rights of the affected indigenous populations to life and property, as guaranteed under Articles 4 and 21.

The Court went on to affirm that while prior consultation 'is *always* required when planning development or investment projects within traditional [indigenous] territory,' 'free, prior, and informed consent' is *additionally required* when such plans may have a profound impact on the property rights of the members of the indigenous community, such as where large-scale development or investment projects are involved.[156] Thus, 'the safeguard of effective participation that is necessary when dealing with major development or investment plans that may have a profound impact on the property rights of the members of the [indigenous] people to a large part of their territory must be understood to additionally require the free, prior, and informed consent of the [indigenous people], in accordance with their traditions and customs.'[157]

In this way, the *Saramaka* case explicitly develops the duties implied in *Awas Tingni*, and long recognised by indigenous communities throughout the region. It does so while affirming that the right to property, like all rights, is not absolute and can potentially be restricted, yet only under limited and clearly-established conditions under which a core set of procedural and substantive safeguards are strictly adhered to and the rights of affected communities are fully taken into account.

The Court's decision in *Awas Tingni* was critical for a third reason. Based on the State's failure to legislate and put into operation a well-functioning, accessible and effective procedure for demarcation and titling of lands, the Court recognised that the State had violated the right to judicial protection under Article 25 of the Convention. That is, although Nicaraguan legislation did formally recognise the right of indigenous peoples to communal property, that recognition was

---

[149] Ibid. para. 129.
[150] Ibid.
[151] Ibid. para. 133.
[152] Ibid.
[153] Ibid. (emphasis added).
[154] Ibid.
[155] Ibid.

[156] Ibid. paras. 137, 134.
[157] Ibid. para. 137.

limited to an abstract legal norm, without effective implementation machinery. In the absence of a clear legislated procedure for giving legal effect to guaranteed rights, said the Court, there was no 'effective legal remedy against acts that violate...fundamental rights'. Recognition of this enforcement principle has vital implications for social rights protection, given that many economic, social and cultural rights lack effective implementation procedures and machinery at the domestic level, even where formally recognised in legislative or constitutional instruments. The Court's understanding of Article 25 thus has significant implications for a wide variety of social rights cases.

The *Awas Tingni* case has also opened the door to restitution claims by indigenous communities for the legal return of ancestral lands from which they have been dispossessed or uprooted by more powerful groups, and for which administrative land claims procedures have proven ineffective. In 2005 and 2006, the Court resolved three such cases, the *Yakye Axa*, *Moiwana*, and *Sawhoyamaxa* cases, in favour of the displaced indigenous communities at issue. In all three, the Court ordered the State to adopt all measures necessary to ensure restitution of the communities' ancestral lands at no cost to them and to guarantee their use and enjoyment of those lands, through territorial delimitation, demarcation and titling.[158] According to the Court, where such lands from which indigenous communities have been displaced are held in private hands, purchase or expropriation from the private landowners is the expected appropriate response. Provision of alternative lands is permissible only where purchase is opposed and expropriation is found, for concrete and justified reasons, impossible in the circumstances of the particular case, taking into account the principles of legality, necessity, and proportionality in a democratic society.[159] In every case, however, the lands provided must be determined consensually with the indigenous community at issue. This must be done, through processes undertaken in conformity with their values, uses, customs, and internal forms of consul-

tation and decisionmaking. Such lands must also be of sufficient extension and quality to guarantee the maintenance and development of the community's own form of life.[160] Importantly, given the close links between the respective communities' access to their ancestral habitat and their ability to meet their subsistence, survival and existential needs, each case was predicated on State violation not only of the Article 21 right to property, but also of the right to a dignified life under Articles 4 and 5 of the Convention.

The Court's jurisprudential insistence in these cases on the irreducible tie between the right of access to ancestral territory by indigenous peoples and the survival, identity, and existence of those very groups now lies at the heart of the Court's evolving jurisprudence on the rights of indigenous people to their ancestral territory. It will continue to play a central role, as the *Saramaka* case makes clear, in determining when, and with what precise procedural guarantees, Article 21.2 may ever legitimately be invoked to authorise use of indigenous lands without the free and informed prior consent of the communities that inhabit them.

5.3   Right to Association: Freedom of Labour Unionisation

A third component of the Court's emerging social rights jurisprudence involves the right of workers to unionise freely, without intervention by government agents or private actors. The Court, in two important cases, has found this right protected under Article 16 of the Convention, which consecrates the right to freedom of association. That is, the right to unionise freely is but the labour dimension of the broader 'right to associate freely for ideological, religious, political, economic, labor, social, cultural, sports, or other purposes', enjoyed by 'everyone' under Article 16 of the Convention.[161] Significantly, although Article 8 of the Protocol of San Salvador, which directly protects the right of workers to organise and join trade unions, could not be applied in either case given that the facts giving rise to the violations occurred before the Protocol's entry into force, the

---

[158] See *Yakye Axa Case* (n. 38 above), paras. 217–18; *Moiwana Case* (n. 40 above), paras. 209, 233; *Sawhoyamaxa Case* (n. 50 above), paras. 210, 215, 248.

[159] *Sawhoyamaxa Case* (n. 50 above), paras. 138, 212; *Yakye Axa Case* (n. 38 above), paras. 148–49, 217.

[160] *Sawhoyamaxa Case* (n. 50 above), para. 212; *Yakye Axa Case* (n. 38 above), para. 217.

[161] American Convention (n. 1 above), art. 16.1.

Court expressly pointed out that Convention Article 16 'contains the same idea' as the Protocol's Article 8.[162]

The first of these cases, decided in 2001, was *Baena Ricardo et al. v. Panama*. In that case, unionised public workers had been engaged in labour negotiations with the Government to improve working conditions in State institutions. When those negotiations failed, the workers carried out a demonstration and work stoppage aimed at forcing the Government to renew negotiations. The Government responded by summarily firing 270 workers who had participated in the labour demonstration, relying on a hastily passed law with retroactive effect to do so. According to testimony by the State's Attorney General, the law was effectively an attempt to make the powerful unions 'disappear'. The Government thereafter refused to comply with internal judicial rulings that declared the law unconstitutional and ordered the immediate reinstatement of the dismissed workers.

The Inter-American Court responded by finding Panama responsible for violations of the right to association under Article 16 of the Convention, as well as those to due process, non-retroactivity of law, and judicial protection under Articles 8, 9 and 25. As reparation, it ordered Panama to reinstate all 270 named workers to their former positions or, if not possible, to positions of equal salary, remuneration, and conditions. It also ordered full back pay, including pension or retirement payments.

In finding a violation of Convention Article 16, the Court defined the right to 'freedom of trade union association' broadly, finding that it 'consists basically of the ability to constitute labor union organisations, and to set into motion their internal structure, activities and action program, without any intervention by the public authorities that could limit or impair the exercise of the respective right'.[163] Citing the Preamble of the ILO Constitution, which recognises 'freedom of association' as an indispensable requirement for universal and lasting peace, the Court affirmed: 'This Court feels that, in trade union matters, freedom

of association is of the utmost importance for the defense of the legitimate interests of the workers, and falls under the *corpus juris* of human rights'.[164]

Applying these principles to the facts of the case, the Court found that the 'entirety of the evidence' proved that the intention of making Law 25 retroactive 'was to provide a basis for the massive dismissal of public sector trade union leaders and workers, such actions doubtlessly limiting the possibilities for action of the trade union organizations in the cited sector'.[165] In this sense, the right to unionise was affected 'not so much as to any denial of its existence, but as to its general practice'.[166] In coming to this finding, the Court cited the similar conclusions of the ILO Committee of Experts and Committee on Freedom of Association and concluded that the dismissal of a large number of trade union leaders 'affected seriously the organization and the activity of the labor unions that held the workers together, and [thus] violated the freedom of trade union association'.[167]

Two additional points bear mention. The first is that the Court, after finding a presumed violation of Article 16, went on to apply the provision on legitimate restrictions to the right to association found in Article 16.2, asserting decisively that the State bears the burden of demonstrating that the restriction at issue was 'necessary in a democratic society' and 'proportional'. As the State did not meet its burden through the production of persuasive evidence, a violation of 'freedom of trade union association' was found. Second, beyond the Article 16 violation, the Court also found violations of Articles 8 (due process), 9 (non-retroactivity) and 25 (judicial protection) due to lapses in domestic enforcement of the labour rights at issue. These findings underscore the critical importance of Convention-based procedural guarantees for the effective protection of economic, social and cultural rights, guarantees that apply to domestically-guaranteed social rights even when these extend beyond the minimum

---

[162] *Baena Ricardo et al. Case* (n. 36 above), para. 159; *Pedro Huilca Tecse* (n. 36 above), para. 74.
[163] *Baena Ricardo et al. Case* (n. 36 above), para. 156.

[164] Ibid. paras. 157–58.
[165] Ibid. para. 160.
[166] Ibid. para. 161.
[167] Ibid. para. 166.

floor of protection offered by the American Convention.[168]

This was most recently reflected in the February 2006 *Acevedo Jaramillo* case, a labour rights case involving the right to judicial protection under Convention Article 25.[169] In that case, Peruvian authorities fired over a thousand public workers for various union-related activities and for a strike that was declared illegal. When those dismissals were judicially declared unlawful, the State nonetheless refused to execute the final court judgments in the workers' favour, judgments which ordered the workers' immediate reinstatement to their previous posts and the payment of lost wages. While the Inter-American Court found insufficient evidence of an Article 16 violation, it made a clarion statement on the nonconditionality of the State's duty, under Article 25 of the Convention, to comply with all final judicial decisions related to rights guarantees at the domestic level. In particular, the Court made clear that budgetary considerations cannot excuse unreasonable delays in the execution of final judicial decrees.[170]

The second major union-rights case resolved by the Court, *Pedro Huilca Tecse v. Peru*, was decided in March 2005 and involved the extrajudicial execution of one of Peru's most prominent labour leaders in the early 1990s. In that case, one in which the Court repeated and expanded its findings on the right to trade unionisation, Peru in fact accepted its international responsibility under Articles 4 and 16 of the Convention for the union-related killing. Having done so, the factual controversy giving rise to the case ceased. The Court nonetheless felt compelled to make certain statements, in *dicta*, regarding the scope and significance of the right to association in the labour union context, specifically, on the collective or social dimensions of the freedom of association.

The Court found that in failing to take appropriate measures to prevent and respond to the extrajudicial execution, Peru violated both the 'individual' and 'social' dimension of the right to union freedom under Article 16, to Pedro Huilca's detriment.[171] First, by executing him, it restricted his right, in its individual dimension, to utilise any means appropriate to exercise his freedom and to reach, collectively, the licit ends to which that exercise was directed. Second, the execution had a 'frightening effect' on the workers of the Peruvian labour movement and, as such, diminished the freedom of a determined group in the exercise of the right to freedom of association.[172] In this sense, the execution violated the 'social dimension' of the right to freedom of association, in that it represented a limit on the right of the collectivity to reach the ends that it proposes. In so finding, the Court underscored that '[t]he State must guarantee that individuals can freely exercise their freedom to unionize without fear of being subject to any violence; otherwise, the capacity of groups to organize for the protection of their interests could be diminished'.[173]

These holdings make clear that the right to unionise finds solid protection under the American Convention as an expansive and fundamental right. This fact, however, draws into question the San Salvador Protocol's limitations on the Court's contentious jurisdiction to *paragraph (a)* of Article 8.1.[174] The apparent purpose of this jurisdictional limitation is to exclude *paragraph (b)*, which protects the right to strike. Yet, it also excludes Articles 8.2 and 8.3, covering lawful restrictions on unionisation as well as the 'negative' freedom that '[n]o one may be compelled to belong to a trade union'. The Court's jurisprudence on Convention Article 16, however, makes clear that the 'negative' freedom protected in Article 8.3 is an essential and integral part of the right to freedom of association in union matters.[175] It also makes clear

---

[168] For a discussion of this 'indirect' approach to the protection of social rights, see Melish, *Protecting Economic, Social and Cultural Rights* (n. 18 above), ch. 6.

[169] *Acevedo Jaramillo Case* (n. 49 above). See also *Case of Dismissed Congressional Employees* (n. 91 above).

[170] *Acevedo Jaramillo Case* (n. 49 above), para. 225. The Court cited analogous decisions of the European Court of Human Rights.

[171] *Pedro Huilca Tecse Case* (n. 36 above), para. 69 ('The execution of a union leader [when the assassination is motivated by the victim's position as union leader] does not restrict only the freedom of association of an individual, but rather also the right and liberty of a determined group to associate freely, without fear.').

[172] Ibid. para. 78.

[173] Ibid. para. 77. The Court cited analogous decisions of the European Court of Human Rights.

[174] Protocol of San Salvador, (n. 26 above), art. 19.6.

[175] See *Baena Ricardo et al. Case* (n. 36 above), para. 156, in which the Court recognised that freedom of labour unionisation assumes that 'each person may determine, without any pressure, whether or not she or he wishes to form part of the association'.

that the lawful restrictions on the right in Article 8.2 must be read in conjunction with the right to unionise.[176] Most significantly, however, the right to strike, protected in Article 8.1.b of the Protocol, is unquestionably an 'appropriate means to exercise' freedom of association in union matters. As the Court concluded, '[i]n its individual dimension, the freedom of association, in labor matters, is not exhausted with the theoretical recognition of the right to form labor unions, but rather also includes, inseparably, the right to utilize *any means appropriate to exercise that freedom*'.[177]

Subject to accepted limitations, the right to strike should thus be viewed as solidly protected under Article 16 of the American Convention, as a legitimate and appropriate means to exercise freedom of trade union association, with which the State is prohibited from unreasonably interfering or acting to undermine. Significantly, it is also protected under Article 26 of the Convention. Indeed, recurring to the express text of Article 45 of the OAS Charter, Convention Article 26 is appropriately read as including not only the 'right [of workers] to associate themselves freely for the defense and promotion of their interests, including the right to collective bargaining' but also, directly, the 'right to strike'.[178]

5.4 Pensions as Property: The Right to Social Security

Finally, the right to a pension or, more broadly, the right to social security has received recent, though tentative, protection from the Court. In February 2003, the Court decided the *Five Pensioners Case*, unanimously ruling in favour of five Peruvian pensioners, whose generous monthly pension entitlements had been significantly reduced by the Peruvian State pursuant to a 1992 decree law aimed at rationalising distortions in the Peruvian pension regime. Relying on domestic law and inter-

nal judicial rulings in the pensioners' favour, the Court unanimously declared that such recalculations infringed the pensioners' 'acquired right to a pension', finding the State responsible for violating their rights to property and to judicial protection under articles 21 and 25 of the Convention.

While the Court's ruling was decisively in favour of the five alleged victims, all high-level civil service retirees entitled to generous monthly pension benefits under the pre-reform law, the case failed to set any clear or useful standards in the area of pension rights,[179] with one notable exception: The Court reaffirmed that the right to judicial protection of domestically-guaranteed social rights, including the right to a pension, will be enforced rigorously by the inter-American human rights organs, irrespective of the minimum floor of protection afforded to those rights by the regional human rights instruments themselves. That important principle – firmly grounded in the Court's 2003 *Baena Ricardo* case and reaffirmed in its 2006 *Acevedo Jaramillo* decision – is vital for effective social rights protection in the region, particularly where domestic laws provide higher levels of protection than exist at the international level.[180]

Nonetheless, the heart of the parties' dispute went well beyond the Article 25 violation. Indeed, it dealt with a wholly preliminary question: What margin of discretion is available to the State, *under the American Convention*, to modify the parameters for determining a retiree's pension benefits *after* his or her right to a pension has vested under a previous, more-favourable pension regime?[181] Does the State have any discretion? If so, under what conditions? Or, does the vesting of a right to a pension under a given legal regime freeze

---

[176] See ibid. para. 172.
[177] *Pedro Huilca Tecse Case* (n. 36 above), para. 70 (emphasis added).
[178] See American Convention, Article 26, read with OAS Charter Article 45.b. This latter provision refers expressly to both of the noted rights. For more on these apparent contradictions, see Melish, 'Protocol of San Salvador' (n. 32 above).

[179] For a fuller analysis, see Melish, 'A Pyrrhic Victory for Peru's Pensioners' (n. 24 above), pp. 55–57.
[180] Notably, however, Peru responded to the Court's decision by amending its Constitution to remove the pension guarantee at issue in the case.
[181] The Court recognises that this is the central question while limiting its consideration of it to the alleged violation of the right to property. Indeed, noting that 'there is no dispute between the parties about whether the alleged victims have the right to a pension', the Court observes that '[t]he dispute between the parties relates to whether the parameters used by the State to reduce or recalculate the amounts of the pensions of the alleged victims as of 1992 represented a violation of their right to property'. '*Five Pensioners' Case* (n. 24 above), para. 94.

that benefit package in place, preventing modification – at least in a downward direction – as legal, political, economic, social or cultural factors change?

In dealing with these crucial questions, the Court had the choice of addressing them in terms of Article 26, which guarantees the right to social security, or Article 21, which protects the right to property. Either of these norms, interpreted under common standards, would have provided a solid conventional basis for addressing the merits of the pension claim, all parties agreeing that the pensioners' in fact enjoyed a 'right to a pension'.[182] Unfortunately, the petitioners, amici curiae, and the Commission all urged the application of different duty-based standards to the respective rights, insisting that the duties to 'respect and ensure' applied to the claim when framed under the right-to-property norm, while a 'prohibition on regressivity' applied to it when framed under the right-to-social-security norm. Declining to interrogate critically and correct the approach, the Court proceeded to issue perplexing analyses of both rights.

In terms of the right to property, the Court found Peru internationally responsible for violating Article 21 of the Convention. This finding was based on the fact that the Peruvian Constitution recognised the pensions at issue as 'acquired rights', that is, rights 'incorporated into the patrimony of the persons'.[183] The Court thus concluded that, irrespective of the larger social aims motivating the pension reform, the pensioners had 'acquired a right to property related to the patrimonial effects of the right to a pension'.[184] From a jurisprudential and 'social rights' perspective, this decision was unsatisfying on several levels. Most notably, the Court appeared to disregard not only the nature and social function of a pension in a democratic society, but the very text of Article 21 (as well as that of Articles 30 and 32.2), which makes plain that the right to property is not absolute and can legitimately be restricted by the State under defined conditions and in accordance with law,

particularly for purposes of social reform.[185] Had the Court applied those legitimate restrictions in the concrete context of the case at issue, it is unlikely that it would have found a violation of the particular pensioners' right to property, as protected under the American Convention.[186]

If the Court's analysis of Article 21 was normatively deficient in being insufficiently attentive to larger social policy concerns that States may legitimately take into account in limiting or restricting a particular individual's rights, its failure to clarify the jurisdictional inappropriateness, of petitioners' application of the collective-oriented, result-based standard of 'progressive development' to the Article 26 claim appeared to discount any role for the individual in social rights enjoyment vis-à-vis broader society. While the Court did note that '[e]conomic, social and cultural rights have both an *individual* and a *collective* dimension,'[187] it proceeded to comment only on the 'collective dimension', declining to elaborate on what the 'individual dimension' meant with respect to the duties applicable to Article 26 claims in the individual petitions process.[188]

Consequently, with the exception of the firmly grounded Article 25 ruling, the *Five Pensioners Case* stands as a notable stain on the otherwise positive social rights record of the Court. The

---

[182] Ibid.

[183] Ibid. para. 101–02.

[184] Ibid. paras. 103–04. Of course, the Peruvian government promptly responded to the ruling by amending the Constitution so that it no longer recognises pensions as 'acquired rights'.

[185] The Court did formally recognise, in paragraph 116, that property rights under Article 21 may be restricted for reasons of public utility or social interest. It, however, then failed to apply the law on Article 21 to the particular facts of this case. Had it done so, it likely would have come to a different result. It is also troubling that rather than refer directly to Convention Article 21 for permissible restrictions on the right to the patrimonial effects of a pension, the Court referred to Article 5 of the Protocol of San Salvador. *'Five Pensioners' Case* (n. 24 above), para. 116.

[186] The particular pensioners at issue were receiving peculiarly inequitable pensions, constitutionally secured through their favoured political status as high-level civil service employees. A finding that the *Convention-based* right to property was not, in light of legitimate restrictions in a democratic society, violated under the circumstances of the case would not mean that those pensioners' rights to property or to a pension were not violated in the domestic jurisdiction.

[187] *'Five Pensioners' Case* (n. 24 above), para. 147 (emphasis added).

[188] In his concurring opinion, Judge Sergio García Ramírez did, however, underscore that the justiciability of rights-based claims in the inter-American system is limited to their individual dimensions. Ibid.

standards it implies for social rights adjudication under both Articles 21 and 26 – one absolute and unappeasing of larger social needs, the other subordinated entirely to the collective – are in critical need of reassessment and reconciliation into a common equity-based standard of adjudication in the regional system's individual complaints procedure.

6. REMEDIES FOR VIOLATIONS AND SUPERVISORY JURISDICTION

Given the gravity, extension, and scale of human rights abuses in the inter-American region, a major concern of the current Court is ensuring that its decisions have an impact that transcends the individual case under consideration. As such, the Court has invested increasing attention in recent years to the reparations and compliance stages of its proceedings, attempting to ensure remedial effects of more structural and enduring scope.

It is worth noting that this heightened focus on reparations and compliance has been counterbalanced by a more restrictive interpretation of who may access the Court's jurisdiction and on what grounds. Thus, just as the rules of legal standing and temporal jurisdiction have been jurisprudentially limited of late,[189] the Court's remedial orders have been broadened, made more explicit in their details, and have privileged legislative and structural solutions that affect all persons, not just those named in the application. Accordingly, even when the Court rests its admissibility and merits determinations on narrow grounds, without substantively and frontally addressing the social, economic and cultural violations at issue, it increasingly takes those concerns into partial account in the reparations stage, based on its full understanding of restitutio in integrum.[190]

While this reparations approach to social rights litigation is decidedly problematic, particularly in light of the instrumental and expressive value of right-specific merits findings as an organising and mobilising tool for domestic constituencies, the expansion of the Court's remedial orders is generally a salutary development. Indeed, the Court's early reparations judgments were conservatively drawn, limited in large part to monetary compensation for the named victims and their immediate successors.[191] While States tended to comply with such monetary orders, thereby appearing responsive to the Court and hence avoiding further international censure, structural changes in their domestic legal orders did not necessarily follow. At the same time, large individual monetary orders, when issued to the exclusion of other reparative measures of more general scope, may be seen as unjust, privileging the privileged few with cases before the system, while ignoring the multitude of similarly-situated persons who have fallen, or may fall, victim to the same abuses. In this line, some advocates have called for the strategic use of class actions to reach more victims. A wider use of the remedial and monitoring stages for the implementation of structural remedies would, however, appear to address the same concerns in a way that is consistent with the Court's understanding of its limited ratione personae competence. This appears to be the direction in which the Court is heading.

6.1 Reparation for Socio-Economic Harm

The Court's recent reparations jurisprudence is striking and far-reaching. For the Court, the obligation to make reparation, established in Article 63.1 of the Convention,[192] 'is governed by international law in all of its aspects, such as its scope,

---

189 See 'Panchito Lopez' Case (n. 35 above) (personal jurisdiction); 'Serrano Cruz Sisters' Case (n. 40 above) (temporal jurisdiction); Alfonso Martín del Campo Dodd Case (n. 40 above) (temporal jurisdiction).

190 This trend, in which the Court specifically declines to deal with alleged violations of Article 26 rights on the ground that their 'particularly grave effects' on victims will be addressed at the reparations stage, has become increasingly explicit in the Court's jurisprudence. See, e.g., Acevedo Jaramillo Case (n. 49 above), para. 285; see

also Case of Dismissed Congressional Employees (n. 91 above), para. 136.

191 See Melish, Protecting Economic, Social and Cultural Rights (n. 18 above), at 388–91.

192 American Convention (n. 1 above), art. 63.1 ('If the Court finds that there has been a violation of a right or freedom protected by this Convention, the Court shall rule that the injured party be ensured the enjoyment of his right or freedom that was violated ... [and], if appropriate, that the consequences of the measure or situation that constituted the breach of such right or freedom be remedied and that fair compensation be paid to the injured party.').

characteristics, beneficiaries, etc.',[193] and includes five distinct elements: (1) restoration of the legal condition enjoyed before the violation (restitutio in integrum); (2) fair compensation, including material and moral damages; (3) rehabilitation; (4) satisfaction; and (5) guarantees of non-repetition.[194] These five elements are intended to meet the main object of reparations: 'to repair the violated legal condition of the human victim or his[/her] family members'.[195]

Prior to 1998, the Court largely ignored these latter elements of reparation, preferring to issue only monetary compensation. In the one pre-1998 case in which broader reparation was granted – including the reopening and staffing of a school and medical dispensary in a single village – it was not perceived as general 'satisfaction' or 'guarantee of non-repetition', but rather as part of an individual compensatory package for the child successors of the victims to enable them to continue their education:

> The compensation fixed for the victims' heirs includes an amount that will enable the minor children to continue their education until they reach a certain age. Nevertheless, these goals will not be met merely by granting compensatory damages; it is also essential that the children be offered a school where they can receive adequate education and basic medical attention.[196]

Since 1998, however, the Court has, with fair consistency, ruled on reparative measures in most of the five separate categories. Because of their central importance for economic, social and cultural rights, two of these categories are highlighted below: restitution and guarantees of non-repetition.[197]

6.2 Restitution

The Court has insisted that restitution is not limited to restoring the immediate right that was violated. Rather, it extends to restoring the legal condition of the victim before the violation occurred, placing the victim, as far as possible in the position she would have been in had the violations not occurred, without either enriching or impoverishing her. In the 1998 *Loayza Tamayo* case, the first in which broader reparation was granted, the victim was a schoolteacher arrested on charges of subversion and unlawfully held incommunicado. Rather than merely order her release from prison, the Court unanimously ordered 'as measures of restitution': (1) her reinstatement to the teaching service in public institutions, (2) at a remuneration level equal to the pay she was receiving for her teaching services at the time of her detention, appreciated to reflect its value as of the date of judgment, and (3) with a guarantee of full retirement benefits, including time accrued during her detention.[198] This was necessary to restore her to the situation she was in prior to the violation of her Convention rights.

The same occurred in *Baena Ricardo*, where the 270 workers arbitrarily dismissed from their public sector jobs were ordered to be reinstated to their previously held positions with full back pay within a maximum term of twelve months. If reinstatement to their previous positions was not possible, the State was ordered to provide employment alternatives with the same conditions, salaries and remunerations enjoyed previously. Only if that were not possible, would an indemnity corresponding to termination of employment, in conformity with internal labour law, have to be paid. At the same time, the State was ordered to provide full pension or retirement payments to the

---

[193] *El Amparo Case, Reparations*, Judgment of Sept. 14, 1996, Inter-Am. Ct. H.R. (Ser. C) No. 28, para. 15; see also *Aloeboetoe et al. Case, Reparations*, Judgment of Sept. 10, 1993, Inter-Am. Ct. H.R. (Ser. C) No. 15, para. 44 (same); *Loayza Tamayo Case, Reparations*, Judgment of Nov. 27, 1998, Inter-Am. Ct. H.R. (Ser. C) No. 42, para. 86 (same); and *Neira Alegría et al. Case, Reparations*, Judgment of Sept. 19, 1996, Inter-Am. Ct. H.R. (Ser. C) No. 29, para. 37 (same).

[194] See *Loayza Tamayo Case, Reparations*, ibid. para. 85, and the *Joint Concurring Vote of Judges A.A. Cançado Trindade and A. Abreu Burelli*, para. 5 in that case; see also *El Amparo Case, Dissenting Opinion of Judge A.A. Cançado Trindade*, Judgment on Reparations of Sept. 14, 1996, Inter-Am. H.R. (Ser. C) No. 28, para. 6.

[195] *Tomas Porfirio Rondin v. Mexico*, Report No. 49/97, Case 11.520, Inter-Am. Comm. H.R., OEA/Ser.L/V/II.98, Doc. 7 rev. (1998), para. 98.

[196] *Aloeboetoe et al. Case*, Reparations (Art. 63(1) American Convention on Human Rights), Judgment of September 10, 1993, Inter-Am. Ct. H.R. (Ser. C) No. 15, para. 96.

[197] For fuller discussion of other categories of reparation, see Melish, *Protecting Economic, Social and Cultural Rights* (n. 18 above), at 376–91.

[198] *Loayza Tamayo Case, Reparations*, Judgment of Nov. 27, 1998, Inter-Am. Ct. H.R. (Ser. C) No. 42, dec. paras. 1, 2.

beneficiaries.[199] A virtually identical restitution order was granted in the recently-decided *Acevedo Jaramillo et al.* case, involving the dismissal of over a thousand union workers in Peru, and the State's refusal to comply with domestic judicial orders to reinstate them.[200]

In *Awas Tingni*, to put the indigenous community in the position it would have been in 'but for' the violation of their rights to property and to judicial protection, the State was ordered to 'carry out the delimitation, demarcation, and titling of the corresponding lands of the members of the Awas Tingni Community, within a maximum term of fifteen months, with full participation by the Community and taking into account its customary law, values, customs and mores'.[201] In the meantime, until that delimitation, demarcation and titling took place, it was ordered to 'abstain from any acts that might lead the agents of the State itself, or third parties acting with its acquiescence or its tolerance, to affect the existence, value, use or enjoyment of the property located in the geographic area where the members of the Mayagna (Sumo) Awas Tingni Community live and carry out their activities'.[202] In the *Moiwana*, *Yakye Axa*, and *Sawhoyamaxa* cases, in which the respective indigenous communities had been displaced from their ancestral lands, the Court similarly ordered the respondent States to adopt all measures necessary to ensure restitution of the Communities' ancestral lands at no cost to them, including delimitation, demarcation and titling of those lands, to guarantee the Communities' use and enjoyment thereof.[203] Such territory, said the Court, must be of sufficient extension as to guarantee the maintenance and development of each Community's own form of life.[204]

In *Yakye Axa*, the Court ordered that this be done within three years and that, within one year, a specific fund should be set up exclusively for the acquisition of such territory, either through purchase or expropriation with just compensation. Meanwhile, the Court ordered that the members

of the Community be provided 'immediately' and 'periodically' with sufficient potable water to meet their consumption and personal hygiene needs; the medical attention and medicines (including for parasites) required to conserve their health, especially for children, older persons, and pregnant women; food of sufficient quantity, variety and quality to ensure minimum conditions of a dignified life; latrines or other adequate sanitary services to deal effectively with the Community's biological waste; and the provision of a school located in the Community's current settlement, with sufficient bilingual materials for the due education of the students.[205] The State was ordered to provide these measures until the Community was effectively relocated, at which time new health and education programs would commence.

6.3 Guarantees of Non-Repetition

To ensure that violations, once repaired, do not recur – either for the same victim or for similarly-situated persons – the Court also orders 'guarantees of non-repetition'. These often appear under the heading 'Other Forms of Reparation', which also includes measures of satisfaction. Under this broad heading, the Court regularly orders States to implement new legislation, issue clear administrative rules, elaborate national plans of action, and define new State policies in terms consistent with international human rights law. It has also, most recently, ordered the State to develop integral development programs for affected communities, including a housing program for all those in need, as well as vocational, bilingual education, and health programs.[206] Each of these measures is designed to recognise the violations committed and to prevent similar violations from recurring in the future. These broad-scale structural remedies are vital for addressing the core of economic, social and cultural rights violations, even when they are not dealt with explicitly in the Court's judgment on the merits.

In the 2001 *Street Children Case*, for example, in addition to ordering individual compensation to the families of the child victims of police abuse, the Court ordered the State, in accordance with

---

[199] *Baena Ricardo Case* (n. 36 above), para. 214.6 and 214.7.
[200] See *Acevedo Jaramillo Case* (n. 49 above), para. 330.
[201] *Awas Tingni Case* (n. 37 above), paras. 164, 173.4.
[202] Ibid.
[203] See *Yakye Axa Case* (n. 38 above), paras. 217–18; *Moiwana Case* (n. 40 above), paras. 209, 233; *Sawhoyamaxa Case* (n. 50 above), paras. 210, 215, 248.
[204] *Sawhoyamaxa Case* (n. 50 above), para. 212; *Yakye Axa Case* (n. 38 above), para. 217.

[205] *Yakye Axa Case* (n. 38 above), para. 221; see also *Sawhoyamaxa Case* (n. 50 above), para. 230.
[206] *Plan de Sánchez, Reparations* (n. 38 above).

Convention Article 2, to 'adopt in its domestic legislation, the legislative, administrative and any other measures that are necessary in order to adapt Guatemalan legislation to Article 19 of the Convention',[207] which enshrines the rights of the child. Likewise, in the 2001 *Awas Tingni* case, the Court ordered the State, again pursuant to Article 2, to 'adopt the legislative, administrative and any other measures required to create an effective mechanism for delimitation, demarcation, and titling of the property of indigenous communities, in accordance with their customary law, values, customs and mores'.[208] The same structurally-minded order, granted in addition to land restitution for the specific victim communities at issue,[209] was included in the 2005 reparation judgments in the *Moiwana* and *Yakye Axa* cases. Such reparation orders, designed to prevent similar abuses from recurring in the future, tend to be kept broad in their prescriptive scope to enable maximum flexibility in implementation at the internal level. They have, however, been getting progressively more detailed in pointing to specific areas in which reforms must take place.

In the 2004 *Panchito López* case, for example, the Court took the important step forward of requiring not only that Paraguay 'adopt its domestic legislation', but that it do so specifically by elaborating, within six months and in collaboration with civil society, 'a State policy of short, medium and long-term related to children in conflict with the law that is fully consistent with Paraguay's international commitments'. Furthermore, according to the Court's order, the new State policy must contemplate 'strategies, appropriate actions and the assignation of those resources indispensable for ensuring children deprived of liberty are separated from adults... and that integral educational, medical and psychological programs are created for children deprived of liberty'.[210] These mea-

sures, broad and structural in scope, were ordered in addition to the restitution and compensatory damages required for the specifically-named victims, which included State provision of medical and psychological treatment, vocational assistance, and a program of special education.[211]

In addition to legislative and policy changes, the Court has also ordered the implementation of specific housing and 'development' programs in affected communities, particularly where the harm caused was 'extremely grave' and of 'collective character'. Thus, in the 2004 reparations judgment in *Plan de Sánchez v. Guatemala*, the Court ordered the State to 'implement a housing program, through which adequate housing is provided to the surviving victims that reside in said village and need it', within a period not exceeding five years.[212]

Significantly, in specifying a program of 'adequate housing', the Court cited General Comment No. 4 of the CESCR, which defines the 'adequacy' requirement for housing resources. In line with this integral understanding, the Court simultaneously ordered the State to develop an integrated development program of health, education, production and infrastructure in the affected communities. This program, which was to be undertaken independently of public works destined to the region in the national budget, was required to include the provision of potable water, a sewer/drainage system, and the maintenance and improvement of the system of road communication between the affected communities and the municipal centre. It was also required to include the provision of intercultural and bilingual teaching staff in the primary, secondary and diversified schools of the communities and the establishment of a health centre, with adequate staff and conditions, in the village of Plan de Sánchez. Finally, to ensure medical and psychological treatment to all affected persons, not just those in Plan de Sánchez, the State was also required to

---

[207] *'Street Children' Case*, (n. 35 above), para. 123.5.
[208] *Awas Tingni Case* (n. 37 above), para. 164.
[209] One Judge has expressed that the definitive return of ancestral land to a victim community constitutes not only restitution, in the sense of returning it to the *status quo ante*, but also a guarantee of non-repetition of the facts giving rise to the violation (i.e., displacement). See *Concurring opinion of Judge A.A. Cancado, Yakye Axa Indigenous Community v. Paraguay, Interpretation of the Judgment on Merits and Reparation*, Judgment of Feb. 6, 2006 (Ser. C) No. 142.
[210] *'Panchito Lopez' Case* (n. 35 above), paras. 316–17.

[211] Ibid. para. 318–21.
[212] *Plan de Sánchez, Reparations* (n. 38 above), para. 105. This case concerned a 1982 massacre in a Guatemalan indigenous community, part of the government's genocidal military policy in the 1980s. The massacre and related abuses involved the loss and destruction of housing, food, animals and personal effects of all the victims, as well as forced displacement of survivors.

provide appropriate training to the personnel in the municipal health centre.[213]

In a similarly structured order in the case of *Moiwana*, which also involved a massacre and violent uprooting of an indigenous community, the Court ordered the creation of a US$ 1,200,000 development fund, to be administered by a three-person implementation committee. The fund was to finance health, housing and education programs for the members of the affected community.[214] In *Yakye Axa*, the Court similarly ordered the implementation of a community development program and committee-administered fund. The community development program would consist in the provision of potable water and sanitation infrastructure in Yakye Axa territory. The community development fund, publicly financed with US$ 950,000, would consist in the implementation, within two years, of educational, housing, agricultural and health projects to benefit the members of the community.[215]

While measures of this detail and scope are likely to be reserved for cases of broad collective harm that are of overriding gravity, it is important to highlight the movement of the Court toward looking at ways to ensure the underlying determinants of conflict and human rights abuse are themselves remedied.[216] Only in this way can guarantees of non-repetition truly serve their protective and preventive function under international law. In fulfilling this role, however, the Court will need to ensure that reparations ordered truly 'maintain a relationship with the violations previously declared'.[217] If

not, it may face growing resistance from States who view the extensiveness of Court orders as ultra vires.

6.4 Supervisory Jurisdiction and Compliance Orders

The increased detail and complexity of the Court's recent reparations orders has led, necessarily, to an increased focus on monitoring State compliance with Court judgments. From its earliest case, the Court has insisted on maintaining supervisory jurisdiction over its reparation orders, requiring States to submit periodic reports, usually every six months or year, on the compliance measures undertaken.[218] In light of the 'collective enforcement' principle in the inter-American system, the Court then submits to the OAS General Assembly annual reports on State compliance with its judgments and orders.[219] It will close a case file only when convinced that its respective orders have been complied with in full.

In the one and only case in which a State has ever questioned the Court's authority to monitor compliance, the Court responded with an emphatic assertion of its supervisory jurisdiction. Distinguishing itself from other international jurisdictional bodies such as the European Court of Human Rights and the International Court of Justice, which lack this function, it declared unanimously that it had the 'inherent and

---

[213] Ibid. paras. 110–11.

[214] *Moiwana Case* (n. 40 above), paras. 214–15.

[215] *Yakye Axa Case* (n. 38 above), paras. 205–06.

[216] See, for example, *Plan de Sánchez, Reparations* (n. 38 above), in which the Court repeatedly cited the Report of the Guatemalan Commission on Historical Clarification with respect to general effects of armed conflict on indigenous communities.

[217] *'Panchito Lopez' Case* (n. 35 above), para. 261 (citing other cases). The Court may have surpassed these self-described limits in one recent case. In the *Serrano Cruz Sisters* case, involving the forced disappearance of two girls in El Salvador, the Court ruled that it lacked jurisdiction over the actual disappearances, as they had occurred prior to El Salvador's recognition of the Court's jurisdiction. As such, it would exercise jurisdiction only over the alleged violation of Articles 8 and 25 involving irregularities in the continuing judicial proceedings. *'Serrano Cruz Sisters' Case, Preliminary Objections* (n. 40 above), paras. 77–80. Notwithstanding, at the reparations stage, the Court ordered the State to adopt specific and exten-

sive measures directly related to the forced disappearances, designed to determine the location of the girls and others who might be similarly-situated. Among others, these measures included the creation of (1) a national search commission for disappeared children during the armed conflict; (2) a web page for locating the disappeared; and (3) a national genetic information bank. *'Serrano Cruz Sisters' v. Mexico, Merits and Reparations*, Judgment of Mar. 1, 2005, Inter-Am. Ct. H.R. (Ser. C) No. 120, paras. 166–93.

[218] See *Velásquez Rodríguez Case, Compensatory Damages*, Judgment of July 21, 1989, Inter-Am. Ct. H.R. (Ser. C) No. 7 (1989), para. 60. While the Court's first two reparation judgments ordered 'compensatory damages' only, post-1993 decisions referred to 'reparations'. Currently, the standard statement at the end of each reparations judgment provides that the Court, 'Decides that it will monitor compliance with this judgment and will consider the case closed when the State has complied fully with its provisions. Within one year from notification of the judgment, the State must provide the Court with a report on the measures taken to comply with this judgment'.

[219] American Convention (n. 1 above), art. 65.

non-discretional' 'competence to monitor compliance with its decisions'.[220] In the exercise of that competence, said the Court, it 'is authorized to request the responsible States to submit reports on the steps they have taken to implement the measures of reparation ordered by the Court, to assess the said reports, and to issue instructions and orders on compliance with its judgments'.[221] These orders, which provide clarifications, compliance parameters, and instructional guidelines, can get progressively more detailed with lack of compliance by a State. They also tend to include requests for increasingly detailed information on the measures taken in problem areas, with shortened time-lines for reporting. While precise methods of implementation of Court orders are left to the State's discretion, the Court insists on its ability to determine when full compliance has been achieved and to instruct a State on the pace and manner of its implementation. Anything less, says the Court, would imperil 'the *raison d'etre* for the functioning of the Court'; it would 'mean affirming that the judgments of this Court are merely declaratory and not effective'.[222]

To date, the Court has carried out its monitoring function exclusively through a written procedure. This consists in the State presentation of a written report on the measures it has taken to comply with the Court's final judgment, followed by the submission of written observations on the adequacy of the State's compliance measures, or lack thereof, by the representatives of the victims, followed by those of the Commission. The Court considers the three sets of written submissions before issuing its order[223] and before determining whether it should report the State's lack of compliance to the OAS General Assembly. Though the Court has found this practice satisfactory to date, it may in the future decide to order the parties to a hearing in which oral arguments are presented. In either case, the Court's supervisory jurisdiction has proved vital not only for ensuring the fullest possible State compliance with Court orders – 'the materialization of justice for the specific case'[224] – but also for giving victims and their representatives a direct voice in holding their governments accountable for responding effectively to human rights violations.

7. CONCLUSION: BEYOND PROGRESSIVITY

Given the contemporary demands of the regional human rights movement, the rise of national court decisions protecting social rights in Latin America, and the normative structure of the inter-American human rights system, the Inter-American Court is well-positioned to play a leading role in the legal protection of economic, social and cultural rights. Taken as a whole, the Court's social rights jurisprudence is quite positive. Nevertheless, significant concerns remain, particularly as one looks toward the future. These concerns derive principally from the Court's continuing reluctance to consider autonomous social rights norms as the immediate basis for finding State responsibility in the individual petitions process, preferring to frame violations diffusely or indirectly under classic civil-political rights norms. As described above, this reluctance does not reflect any judicial antipathy to social rights claims, but rather responds to the still dominant trend in the region of applying *different* standards of State responsibility to claims framed under Chapter II norms than to those framed under Chapter III norms, with the litigation-*appropriate* dimensions of State legal obligations applied to the former, the litigation-*inappropriate* dimensions to the latter.

Given the indivisibility and interdependence of all human rights, the consequences of this approach tend to be relatively unproblematic in the

---

[220] *Baena Ricardo et al. Case*, Supervisory Jurisdiction, Judgment of Nov. 28, 2003, Inter-Am. Ct. H.R. (Ser. C) No. 104, para. 133.

[221] Ibid. para. 139.2. 'Likewise, with regard to the stage of monitoring compliance with judgments, the Court has adopted the constant practice of issuing orders or sending communications to the responsible State in order, *inter alia*, to express its concern in relation to aspects of the judgment pending compliance, to urge the State to comply with the Court's decisions, to request detailed information on the measures taken to comply with specific measures of reparation, and to provide instructions for compliance, as well as to clarify aspects relating to execution and implementation of the reparations about which there is a dispute between the parties'. Ibid. para. 105.

[222] Ibid. para. 72; see also ibid. para. 95 ('run counter to the goal and purpose of this treaty'); para. 100 (decisions would otherwise be illusory); para. 130 ('If the responsible State does not execute the measures of reparation ordered by the Court at the national level, this would deny the right of access to international justice.').

[223] Ibid. paras. 105, 107.
[224] Ibid. para. 72.

spectrum of cases in which important dimensions of the rights to adequate health, education, housing and social security can be vindicated – and given similar expressive force – through either 'neutral' procedural norms, such as judicial protection, due process or non-discrimination, or the substantively overlapping rights to life, integrity, political participation, privacy and property.[225] Nonetheless, significant problems arise in the more nuanced, but equally important cases in which these latter rights are insufficiently refined to interrogate effectively all aspects of economic, social and cultural rights violations. It is particularly problematic in litigating the crucial elements of adequacy, availability, accessibility and quality as core components of the rights to health, to education and to housing. These concepts often cannot be captured by the broadness of 'life', 'integrity', 'property' or 'participation' – at least not without serious norm dilution or underbreadth of coverage.[226]

These two dangers – dilution and underbreadth – will become increasingly problematic as more social rights cases reach the Court. The problem of underbreadth has already materialised in several cases where Chapter II and Chapter III rights did not sufficiently overlap. Self-constrained to Chapter II norms, the Court has thus consciously bypassed core human rights violations in individual cases that would otherwise have required it to adjudicate social rights claims directly under Article 26. In the 2005 *Yean and Bosico Girls* case, for example, the Court ignored entirely the extensive briefing and testimonial evidence presented to it on the State's direct breach of its obligation to respect and ensure a young girl's 'right to education', the core issue in the case, and a right incontestably protected under Article 26 of the Convention.[227]

The *Yean and Bosico Girls* case involved the arbitrary dismissal from public school of a young, disadvantaged Dominican child for failure to present a birth certificate, a document discriminatorily denied the girl on account of her Haitian ancestry. Consequently, the thirteen-year old, impeded from accessing appropriate public schooling, was left with no educational recourse other than attendance at night literacy classes for adults. Violation of her right to education was incontrovertible on these facts: the school dismissal could not be justified on any non-discriminatory or non-arbitrary ground. Nonetheless, the Court bypassed the parties' right-to-education arguments under Article 26, failing even to cite them in its merits decision.[228] Instead, it found violations, to the girls' detriment, of Chapter II norms only: the rights to nationality, to equal protection, to a name, and to legal personality.

The real world difficulty of the case is that without a clear merits-based finding of state responsibility for violating the young girl's right to education, that core violation was left without a substantive remedy. Indeed, while the Court's final and binding order required the State to adopt all necessary measures to reform its procedures for the *granting of birth certificates*, it was silent on the necessary reforms to the regulatory norms governing *public school registration*. That is, it required no changes to the deficient regulatory framework that had initially authorised and permitted the direct violation by State agents of the girl's nationally- and internationally-protected right to education.

Given the concrete issues raised in the case, a proper response from the Court would have included a strong, decisive statement on the State's Convention-based obligation to adopt all

---

[225] Such an approach is indispensable in those jurisdictions that, unlike the inter-American system, do not autonomously protect economic, social and cultural rights.

[226] The right to health, for example, has distinct dimensions that cannot sufficiently be targeted or addressed under a broad undifferentiating 'right to life' analysis, including physical accessibility, cultural adequacy and quality goods and services. The same is true of the right to culture for indigenous populations. That right goes beyond ties to property; it must be dealt with on its own terms, as both an autonomous and transversal right.

[227] The social rights norms in the OAS Charter, to which Article 26 refers for the derivation of the rights it protects,

refers expressly to the 'right to education'. See OAS Charter, art. 49 ('The Member States will exert the greatest efforts, in accordance with their constitutional processes, to ensure the effective exercise of the *right to education*, on the following bases: a) Elementary education, compulsory for children of school age, shall also be offered to all others who can benefit from it. When provided by the State it shall be free of charge; b) Middle-level education ... c) Higher education ...'.) (emphasis added). The right to education is also guaranteed in express terms under the Constitution of the Dominican Republic, as it is in virtually all political constitutions in the hemisphere.

[228] The Court considered her denial of education exclusively at the stage of reparations for purposes of fixing appropriate compensation. See *Yean and Bosico Girls Case* (n. 47 above), para. 244.

necessary and appropriate measures to ensure the right to education to all persons within its jurisdiction, regardless of nationality, descent or any other discriminatory ground. This should have been accompanied by an appropriate corresponding remedial order, one directly aimed not only at repairing the concrete injury caused the young girl by the State's arbitrary conduct in dismissing her from school but also at preventing recurrence of the same or similar violations in the future. Critical opportunities for human rights enforcement are thus needlessly being neglected through the Court's unnecessary avoidance of direct reliance on Article 26 claims.

The Court's hesitancy around Article 26 also carries the threat of serious norm dilution with respect to Chapter II rights, norms currently forced to absorb the full impact of social rights litigation in the system. The consequences are particularly weighty for Article 4's protection of the right to life, a norm the Court interprets in its most expansive sense as a right to a '*dignified life*' or to '*a life project*'. These concepts are of potentially illimitable scope, capable of subsuming into their protective embrace all nationally and internationally recognised human rights. Indeed, Article 4 has already been interpreted to encompass, in some way, virtually all economic, social and cultural rights, including decent health care, education, access to potable water, and adequate food. Caution must be exercised in going too far with these expansive interpretations. That is, care must be taken to ensure that rights and obligations in the system have predictable consequences for States and that Article 4 does not become a free-for-all provision, implicated by default in all human rights abuses that affect a person's 'dignity' or 'life prospects'. The Court has to date enunciated no limiting principle for Article 4's expanse.

The jurisprudential dangers attendant to the Court's 'life project' approach have not yet fully materialised in the Court's work.[229] This is due to the limited number and complex nature of the social rights cases the Court has considered to date. Indeed, from *Panchito López* (children's

detention facility), to *Plan de Sánchez* (annihilation of indigenous community), to *Yakye Axa* (subhuman living conditions of displaced indigenous community), the violation of rights in these cases have been so sweeping and diffuse as to, in many ways, transcend individualised treatment of each discrete rights-based violation. In these exceptional circumstances, in which the totality of conditions necessary for a dignified existence is lacking and untangling specific violations unduly problematic, the Court's 'life project' jurisprudence constitutes, in many ways, an appropriate and effective jurisprudential response. In such cases the heft of the Court's response must be directed to the remedial order.

Most social rights cases, however, do not fit within this exceptional rubric. As such, the Court's 'life project' jurisprudence, as a methodology, is inadequate for dealing with the vast majority of economic, social and cultural rights claims that arise in the American continent on a daily basis, and that are increasingly making their way up to the regional human rights system. These claims need to be addressed for what they are: claims for protection against arbitrary or unreasonable conduct, imputable to the State, that concretely harms persons' enjoyment of their individually-held rights to health, education, housing, employment or culture.

That is, these claims need to be addressed under the same legal standards used by the Court in its two decades of case-based jurisprudence on the law of State responsibility for human rights violations. This jurisprudence, well developed under Articles 1.1 and 2 and applicable to all human rights recognised in the Convention, must be extended to claims based on Chapter III – derived rights.[230]

For this to occur, the Court – and, most importantly, the litigants who urge arguments upon

---

[229] They have, however, begun to have negative impacts on the Commission's more extensive social rights jurisprudence, particularly in the area of the right to health. For more on this, see preceding Chapter in this volume.

[230] Indeed, the problems of dilution and underbreadth will not effectively be addressed until the Court begins to adjudicate the autonomous social rights in Article 26 directly under appropriate *conduct-based* and *individual-oriented* standards. By taking some of the pressure off of Article 4, this will assist in staving off the problem of its potentially unlimited growth – reserving that norm for the most direct and extreme violations of that right – while also attending to the vital contours of autonomous social rights as they are affected in discrete and diverse factual contexts by conduct to the State.

it – must take a moment to critically reassess the derivation of their understanding of 'progressive development', whether it is in fact the litigation-appropriate standard to apply to claims based on Article 26 rights in the inter-American system's individual petitions process, and whether concepts developed in non-congruent, non-contentious monitoring contexts – such as the UN Committee on Economic, Social and Cultural Rights' periodic reporting process – have simply been transferred unreflectively into the regional system's adjudicatory procedures. A close look will likely indicate to the Court that this is precisely what has occurred. Rational human rights litigation in the inter-American system requires that this course be corrected. Specifically, it requires that the Court clearly articulate that the cognisability of any particular rights-based claim that comes before it depends not on its exterior guise as 'civil-political' or 'economic-social', but rather on how that claim is framed to conform with the Court's claim-based justiciability rules on legal standing and proper litigant access to the adjudicatory function.

20

European Court of Human Rights

Sympathetic Unease

Luke Clements* and Alan Simmons**

1. INTRODUCTION

In analysing the approach of the European Court of Human Rights to socio-economic rights, it is necessary to commence with a rejection of an overly simplistic taxonomy: the categorisation of rights as either social and economic or civil and political is an entirely artificial construct. It is simply not possible to differentiate (save in the loosest possible terms) between such assorted rights. There is no bright line that separates rights into two distinct categories – no rational, and precious little pragmatic, justification for such a divide.

The Strasbourg Court has, to its credit, rejected the argument that the European Convention on Human Rights is a treaty solely concerned with civil and political rights. As long ago as 1979, in one of its most significant judgments, *Airey v. Ireland* the Court held that:

> [T]he mere fact that an interpretation of the Convention may extend into the sphere of social and economic rights should not be a decisive factor against such an interpretation; there is no water-tight division separating that sphere from the field covered by the Convention.

It follows that the 'mere fact' that a human rights violation is capable of being articulated in the language of socio-economic rights does not of itself mean that the Strasbourg Court will cede jurisdiction to the Executive. The Court nevertheless recognises that questions that concern the distribution of scarce resources are often bet-ter addressed by individual governments. The acknowledgment by the Court of its limitations does not however translate into 'doctrine of defer-ence' (as the court/legislature relationship is often described in the highly idiosyncratic UK system). In Strasbourg parlance, the verb 'to defer' is a bet-ter descriptor of the relationship. That the Stras-bourg Court defers to the expertise of legislatures is not a uniquely socio-economic phenomenon. It has also developed the doctrine of 'margin of appreciation' in relation to difficult issues con-cerning state regulation of many civil and political rights.[1]

2. SOCIO-ECONOMIC RIGHTS WITHIN THE CONTEXT OF THE TREATY

2.1 Overview of Relevant Provisions

The Convention contains no unqualified state-ment concerning entitlement to core socio-economic rights. There are no references to health or social care or social security rights. It provides protection for one's (existing) home but contains no reference to 'housing'. The first protocol speaks of education – but not (as drafted) in terms of the State being obliged to provide this.[2]

The traditional argument runs therefore, that the Convention is a classic example of a civil and political rights treaty: not only does it not pro-tect core socio-economic rights, it is also framed in essentially negative terms: that the State should refrain from torturing people (Article 3), arbitrar-ily detaining them (Article 5), interfering with their private lives (Article 8) and so on. Attractive as this

* Professor in Law, Cardiff Law School, United Kingdom. The jurisprudence in this Chapter is updated as to March 2006 except for *D.H. and Others v. Czech Republic.*
** Solicitor of the Supreme Court of England and Wales.

[1] See Sections 2.1 and 2.3 of this chapter.
[2] See Section 5.5 of this chapter.

argument is, it is not an analysis coherent. The negative spin associated with the Convention has more to do with the way it has been interpreted by the Court than the actual text of the treaty. Article 3 is in many ways a particularly positive statement: 'no one shall be subjected to torture or to inhuman or degrading treatment or punishment'. Article 5 commences with a ringing affirmation that 'everyone has the right to liberty and security of person'. Article 8 does not require the State to refrain from interfering in private and family life, but rather obliges it to show 'respect for' individual privacy: respect is not something that can generally be done negatively – it connotes a positive demonstration.

Initially, it is for individual States to assess whether an interference with a particular right is compatible with the Convention: that (for instance) in relation to Article 8, interference with private life or home corresponds to a legitimate aim and is necessary in a democratic society. When it exercises its supervisory jurisdiction, the European Court is reluctant to substitute its own assessment for that of the domestic authorities. Instead it gives the individual States a certain discretion or margin of appreciation because they are deemed better at making the assessment in question than the international judge 'by reason of their direct and continuous contact with the vital forces of their countries'.[3] Thus, according to the European Court, 'the domestic margin of appreciation goes hand in hand with European supervision'.[4] The Court had held that States enjoy a relatively wide margin of appreciation in relation to issues such as planning policy (even in relation to rights of Gypsies)[5] and the right to health care, where priorities need to be made in the context of limited resources.[6]

Where a general consensus exists in Europe about how particular issues are to be dealt with, the margin of appreciation is narrower, because in such cases there is less scope for national differ-

ences. In *Chapman v. United Kingdom*,[7] the Court acknowledged that by virtue of the Framework Convention for the Protection of National Minorities, there was an 'emerging international consensus recognizing the special needs of minorities' (para. 93). However, it concluded that this consensus was not, at that time, sufficiently 'concrete' and therefore it did not affect the relatively wide margin of appreciation enjoyed by the domestic authorities, which had refused to grant the applicant planning permission to station her caravan on her land. However, it is clear that the Court would be prepared to reach a different conclusion in such a case when these standards have become sufficiently concrete.[8]

In analysing the extent to which the Convention has been interpreted to require States to protect socio-economic rights, it is possible to discern two very general and overlapping categories, namely:

Category 1: gross socio-economic deficits directly or indirectly attributable to State action.

Where the complaint discloses direct or indirect state responsibility for a severe socio-economic deprivation which has had (or threatens) gross consequences for the victim. In such cases the State's responsibility under the Convention is generally engaged by reference to its obligations under Articles 3 and/or 8.

Category 2: gross socio-economic destitution for which the state has no direct or obviously indirect responsibility.

Where the complaint is suffering from (or threatened with) severe socio-economic deprivation for which there is no direct or obvious indirect state responsibility. In such cases the State's responsibility under the Convention is generally engaged by

---

[3] See *Chapman v. United Kingdom* (2001), judgment dated 18 January 2001; (2001) 33 EHRR 18, para. 91.
[4] *Handyside v. United Kingdom* (1976), application no: 5493/72, judgment dated 7 December 1976; [1976] ECHR 5, para. 49.
[5] See *Chapman v. United Kingdom* (n. 3 above), para. 92.
[6] See *Sentges v. the Netherlands*, application n. 27677/02, admissibility decision dated 8 July 2003.

[7] *Chapman v. United Kingdom* (n. 3 above).
[8] Recent measures of importance in this context include (1) the widening of article 14 via Protocol 12 to the European Convention on Human Rights and Fundamental Freedoms, European Treaty Series No.177, which entered into force on 1 April 2005; (2) the EU Race Equality Directive 2000/43/EC, 'Implementing the principle of equal treatment between persons irrespective of racial or ethnic origin', Brussels, 20 June 2000; and (3) recent Council of Europe recommendations concerning social rights of Roma and Travellers (e.g. Committee of Ministers Recommendation on improving the housing conditions of Roma and Travellers in Europe, Recommendation Rec(2005)4 adopted on 23 February 2005).

reference to its obligations under Article 1 in combination with Articles 3 and 8.

2.2 Beneficiaries of the Rights and Complaint Procedures

The protection of the Convention extends to everyone within the jurisdiction of any contracting State and accordingly complaints can be brought by 'any person, non-governmental organisation or group of individuals claiming to be the victim of a violation'.[9]

This can include physical persons – that is, human beings, including children and other incapacitated persons,[10] whether or not represented by their parents, or groups of human beings, legal persons such as companies[11] and non-governmental organisations.[12] Neither individuals nor legal persons have to be citizens of the State concerned,[13] nor of any State of the Council of Europe, though this may be relevant to their substantive rights under Article 1 of Protocol 1.[14] They do not have to be established or a resident or physically present on its territory in fact they need never even have visited it. If they are present, they do not have to be lawfully present under national law.[15]

The Convention's complaint and enforcement procedures are without parallel in any other international human rights treaty. Any individual within the jurisdiction of any of the contracting States is entitled to make a complaint to the Court in person – provided he or she (1) claims to be a victim of a violation of the Convention, (2) has exhausted all reasonable domestic remedies and (3) brings the complaint within six months of the date of the final domestic court hearing (or if there is no domestic remedy then within six months of the incident).[16] If the complaint is ruled admissible and no 'friendly settlement' is reached between complainant and the State, then he or she is entitled to a court judgment. If the judgment is favourable, the Court may award compensation to the applicant.[17] States parties are obliged to respect the final judgment of the Court of any action in which they are a party. The Committee of Ministers then supervises its execution.[18]

2.3 Use of Other Instruments by Courts

The Strasbourg Court has developed a unique and in many ways unparalleled international human rights jurisprudence. In doing so, many of the rights protected by the Convention have been given autonomous meanings[19] – distinct from interpretations given to the same or similar rights under analogous treaties – most obviously the International Covenant on Civil and Political Rights.

This does not, however, mean that the Court is indifferent to the content of other instruments. All States that have ratified the Convention have also signed up to many other international human rights treaties and as a consequence are unable to deny the acceptability of their norms. This situation is reinforced by Article 53 of the Convention, which states that:

> Nothing in this Convention shall be construed as limiting or derogating from any of the human rights and fundamental freedoms which may be ensured under the laws of any High Contracting Party or under any other agreement to which it is a party.

The Convention cannot therefore be invoked in a way which would offer a narrower protection than that which is guaranteed under other instruments:

---

[9] Article 34.

[10] *X & Y v. Netherlands* (1986), application no. 8978/80, judgment dated 26 March 1985; (1986) 8 EHRR 235.

[11] E.g., *The Sunday Times v. UK* (1991), application no. 13166/87, judgment dated 26 November 1991; (1992) EHRRR 272.

[12] *Open Door Counselling Ltd & Dublin Well Woman Centre Ltd v. Ireland*, application nos. 14234/88 and 14235/88, judgment dated 29 October 1992; (1993) 15 EHRR 244.

[13] *Ahmed v. Austria*, application no. 25964/94, judgment dated 17 December 1996; (1996) 24 EHRR 278.

[14] *Gasus Dosier-und Fördertechnik v. Netherlands*, application no.15375/89, judgment dated 23 February 1995; (1995) 20 EHRR 403.

[15] *D v. United Kingdom*, application no. 30240/96, judgment dated 2 May 1997; (1997) 24 EHRR423.

[16] See P. Leach, *Taking a Case to the European Court of Human Rights*, 2nd Edition (Oxford: Oxford University Press, 2005).

[17] See Section 5 below on remedies for violations.

[18] See Section 5 below on the impact of judgments of the Court.

[19] For example, 'civil rights and obligations' and 'criminal charge' under Article 6.

it can only augment or enhance the protection offered by national law or other international agreements.

3. THE COURT'S APPROACH TO PROTECTION OF SOCIO-ECONOMIC RIGHTS

It is traditional for Convention commentators to divide its broad impact into two categories – negative and positive – State action that it proscribes and State action that it demands. Such an analysis is of limited value when seeking to describe the extent to which the Convention protects socio-economic rights. As indicated above, it is more appropriate (although still artificial) to categorise the Convention's impact according to context: to what degree can it be said that the State is culpable and just how severe is the destitution in issue?

Category 1: gross socio-economic deficits directly or indirectly attributable to State failure

Where a complaint discloses severe and straightforward socio-economic deprivation that is directly or indirectly attributable to State action (or inaction) and which has had (or threatens) gross consequences for the victim, then the Court is prepared to examine the State's responsibility – primarily in terms of its obligations under Articles 3 and 8. This category can crudely be subdivided into three subgroups.

At the more severe end of the scale, the factual context may consist of clear and deliberate State action directly causing the socio-economic destitution. In such cases, the Court's response may be comprehended in terms of imposing a socio-economic remedy for a gross civil and political violation. An example of this situation might be that described below in the *Hadareni* complaint[20] – where it is alleged that the State was directly culpable for the complainants' homelessness.

A second subgroup of cases demonstrates a substantial socio-economic disadvantage that is only indirectly the responsibility of the State. The situation may arise where legitimate State action has a disproportionate (albeit unintended) socio-economic impact on an individual or group. Most

obviously, this arises where the State is discharging a regulatory function. For example, the exercise of development control over the use of land may cause accommodation shortages – which if severe could interfere with the enjoyment of private life (i.e. Article 8). If the system additionally discriminates against particular groups then it would be a legitimate exercise of the Court's role to scrutinise the proportionality of the scheme. This is precisely the approach that the Strasbourg institutions have adopted in such cases as *G and E v. Norway*[21] and *Buckley v. UK*.[22]

The third subgroup of complaints concerns States that have specifically recognised a particular socio-economic right in their legal system and then failed to uphold the right to a degree that causes or threatens severe consequences for the complainant. *Passannante v. Italy*[23] and *Van Kück v. Germany*[24] are examples of this situation (considered below). A not uncommon variant of this situation concerns individual cases where the State has decided to make available a socio-economic benefit – for instance health care – and then takes action that would terminate the service with dire consequences. Since such action is capable of being characterised as a positive intervention by the State interfering with the status quo, the Court has been willing to review its compatibility with the Convention. *D v. United Kingdom*[25] is an example of a complaint of this type.

Category 2: severe socio-economic deficits neither directly nor (obviously) indirectly attributable to State failure

Cases of this kind are characterised by very severe socio-economic destitution for which responsibility cannot directly or (obviously) indirectly be laid at the door of the State. In such situations, the Convention may nevertheless compel state provision of socio-economic assistance by virtue of the positive obligation contained in Article 1 in conjunction with the requirements of Articles 3 and 8.

---

[20] *Moldovan and others v. Romania (no.2)*; application no. 41138/98 and 64320/01, judgment dated 12 July 2005. See section 4.1.

[21] (1983) DR 35/30.
[22] Application no. 20348/9223, judgment dated 25 September 1996; (1996) 23 EHRR 101.
[23] Application no. 32647/96, admissibility decision dated 1 July 1998; (1998) 26 EHRR CD 153.
[24] Application no., 35968/9, judgment dated 26 December 2003.
[25] *D v. United Kingdom* (n. 15 above).

Lester and O'Cinneide[26] describe the role of courts in this situation as arising when:

> [T]here exists a sufficiently gross failure to uphold basic socio-economic rights. Where the [legislature and the executive] have comprehensively failed to fulfil their responsibilities.

Article 1 contains what is in effect a promise by the contracting State to ensure that Convention rights are protected for all people within its jurisdiction. This means (for instance) that a State must not only ensure that individuals are not subjected to degrading treatment by state officers (contrary to Article 3), but it must also take reasonable measures to ensure that no-one within its jurisdiction is subjected to such treatment.

Accordingly in *A v. UK*,[27] a case where a child had been very severely beaten by his stepfather, the court held that States must have effective laws to prohibit and punish such behaviour. In its view, the existence of an overly wide defence of 'reasonable parental chastisement', which resulted in the stepparent's acquittal of a charge of causing actual bodily harm, meant that the UK had not taken adequate 'positive measure' to safeguard the Article 3 right:

> [T]he obligation … under Article 1 of the Convention to secure to everyone within their jurisdiction the rights and freedoms defined in the Convention, taken together with Article 3, requires States to take measures designed to ensure that individuals within their jurisdiction are not subjected to torture or inhuman or degrading treatment or punishment, including such ill-treatment administered by private individuals. … Children and other vulnerable individuals, in particular, are entitled to State protection, in the form of effective deterrence, against such serious breaches of personal integrity.[28]

It follows that the Convention must protect a set of irreducible socio-economic rights. In effect, at some point of destitution the Court will interpret the Convention as demanding the provision by the State of a minimum level of these fundamentals: in essence, the 'core obligation', identified by the International Covenant on Economic, Social and Cultural Rights Committee, that States ensure no one is deprived of 'essential foodstuffs, of essential primary health care, of basic shelter and housing, or of the most basic forms of education'.[29] This obligation has been described by Lord Hoffman of the United Kingdom's House of Lords as:

> [A] positive obligation upon the State to provide every citizen with certain basic necessities which he requires in order to be able to function as a human being.[30]

4. SELECTED JURISPRUDENCE

4.1 Housing

The Convention may impose a positive duty to provide housing where it is established that the State is directly culpable for the homelessness. In such situations the Convention obligation to provide accommodation may be more accurately characterised as remedial – to *compensate for a deprivation of housing.*

The Court has considered a number of cases in which complaints have been made about the burning of houses by security forces in southeast Turkey, leaving villagers homeless and destitute.[31] The Court has found that the destruction of the applicants' homes and property constituted particularly grave and unjustified interferences with the applicants' rights to respect for their private and family lives and homes under Article 8, and to the peaceful enjoyment of their possessions under Article 1 of Protocol 1. In addition, the Court has considered that the manner in which the home was destroyed and the personal circumstances of the applicant can cause suffering of sufficient severity to be inhuman treatment within

---

[26] Lord Lester of Herne Hill QC and Colm O'Cinneide, 'The Effective Protection of Socio-economic Rights', in Y. Ghai and J. Cottrell (eds.), *Economic & Cultural Rights in Practice* (London: Interights, 2004), p. 21.

[27] Application no. 35373/97, judgment dated 23 September 1998.

[28] Ibid. para. 22.

[29] Committee on Economic, Social and Cultural Rights, *General Comment No. 3, The nature of States parties' obligations,* (Fifth session, 1990), U.N. Doc. E/1991/23, annex III at 86 (1991), para. 10.

[30] Lord Hoffman, 'The 'Separation of Powers', Annual Commercial Bar Lecture, unpublished transcript, COMBAR, London, 2001.

[31] See inter alia *Selcuk and Asker* (1998), application no. 23184/94 and 23185/94, judgment dated 24 April 1998; (1998) 26 EHRR 477.

the meaning of Article 3. For example, in *Dulas v. Turkey,* it noted that:

> The applicant in the present case was aged over 70 at the time of the events. Her home and property were destroyed before her eyes, depriving her of means of shelter and support, and obliging her to leave the village and community, where she had lived all her life. No steps were taken by the authorities to give assistance to her in her plight.[32]

A series of complaints against Romania, collectively known as the *Hadareni* complaint,[33] provides a further stark example of this extreme situation. The case arose from a pogrom in the village of Hadareni in 1993, which resulted in the violent deaths of three young Roma men and the destruction of fourteen Roma family homes. This caused the applicants to have to leave their village and live in dire conditions for over ten years in hen houses and pig sties, sleeping on mud or concrete floors in the cold in grossly overcrowded conditions.

The Court found that the police were complicit in the atrocity and tried to cover up the incident.[34] However, since the incident occurred before Romania's accession to the Council of Europe, the Court could not examine the substantive complaints concerning the destruction of the applicants' houses. Nevertheless, the Court found that the Government's responsibility was engaged regarding the applicants' subsequent living conditions, bearing in mind the direct repercussions of the acts of State agents on the applicants' rights.

The Court found that the Romanian authorities had repeatedly failed to put a stop to the breaches of the applicants' rights, which constituted a serious continuing violation of Article 8. In reaching this conclusion, it noted inter alia that some houses were not rebuilt and those rebuilt were uninhabitable; it took ten years for the domestic courts to award compensation for the destruction

of the houses; no criminal proceedings had been instituted against the police officers involved in the burning of the applicants' houses; and most of the applicants had not returned to their village and lived scattered throughout Romania and Europe.

Moreover, the Court also found a violation of Article 3, as the living conditions of the applicants for ten years had had a detrimental effect on their health and well-being. In conjunction with the racial discrimination to which they had been publicly subjected by the authorities,[35] this constituted an interference with the applicants' human dignity and amounted to degrading treatment.

Other cases concern a situation in which legitimate State action has a disproportionate socio-impact on an individual or group, which amounts to a form of indirect socio-economic discrimination. In a series of complaints made against the United Kingdom, it has been alleged that land development controls in that country have unfairly discriminated against Gypsies, with the result that almost 30 per cent of them are technically homeless. The controls make it particularly difficult to obtain permission for the stationing of a caravan on land – the form of accommodation favoured by the majority of UK Gypsies.

The complainants accept the need for the regulation of land use – but assert that this legitimate State action has had a disproportionate (albeit unintended) socio-economic impact upon them – and accordingly that either (a) the scheme be reconfigured to enable them to accommodate themselves, or (b) that the Convention obliges the State to provide them with accommodation. Since the first such complaint in *Buckley v. United Kingdom,*[36] the Court has gradually refined its position, albeit that its review is still essentially two-dimensional, primarily dictated by the formalities of a proportionality review and a consideration of the extent of the State's margin of appreciation. In *Chapman v. United Kingdom,*[37] a third strand

---

[32] Application no. 25801/94, judgment dated 30 January 2001 at paragraph 54.

[33] *Moldovan and others v. Romania* (N0.2) (n. 20 above).

[34] In *Moldovan and others v. Romania (no. 1)* applications nos. 411138/96 and 64320/01, judgment dated 5 July 2005, some of the applicants reached a friendly settlement with the Romanian government, whereby the latter undertook to pay compensation and undertake a range of measures, including programs to eliminate prejudice against the Roma community and to rehabilitate housing and the environment in the Hadareni community.

[35] The Court found a violation of Article 14 in conjunction with Articles 6 and 8 as the applicants' ethnicity was decisive for the length and outcome of their civil proceedings and there had been repeated discriminatory remarks made by the authorities throughout the case determining their rights under Article 8; *Moldovan and others v. Romania* (No. 2) (n. 20 above).

[36] *Buckley v. United Kingdom,* application no. 20348/92, judgment dated 25 September 1996; (1996) FCHR 39

[37] *Chapman v. United Kingdom* (n. 3 above), para. 96.

began to emerge – namely, the need in such cases for special consideration be given to the needs (in this case of Gypsies) and their different lifestyle both in the relevant regulatory planning framework and in arriving at the decisions in particular cases.[38] In addition, the Court considered that the extent of the available margin of appreciation was being measured by reference to:

> [A]n emerging international consensus amongst the Contracting States of the Council of Europe recognising the special needs of minorities and an obligation to protect their security, identity and lifestyle [para. 93].

In *Connors v. United Kingdom*,[39] the applicant and his family had lived on a local authority caravan site almost continuously for thirteen years. Following alleged incidents of nuisance caused by inter alia his adult children and their visitors, the local authority took summary proceedings to evict the applicant and his family. Thereafter, the family were forced to move on continuously and the stress and uncertainty led to the breakdown of the applicant's marriage. In finding a violation of Article 8, the European Court placed particular emphasis on the lack of procedural protection to Gypsies on local authority sites. It noted that where anti-social behaviour took place on private caravan sites or on local authority housing estates, evictions were subject to independent review by the courts, whereby the landlord had to demonstrate the existence of the nuisance. However, in this case, the applicant denied the allegations but had had no opportunity challenge the reasons for the eviction before the courts.

Category 2 cases (see Section 3 above) test the point at which the Convention requires the State to provide accommodation – even where it bears no obvious responsibility for the homelessness.

In a case before an English Court of Appeal,[40] it has been suggested (in the context of a discussion concerning the scope of Article 3) that it was difficult 'not to regard shelter of some form from the

elements at night . . . as a "basic amenity" at least in winter and bad weather'. Although the European Court has not, as yet, so determined, *Marzari v. Italy*[41] illustrates the type of situation in which such a finding might be made. It concerned a complicated and long-running dispute between the applicant and his local authority relating to his need for specially adapted housing (arising out of his seriously disabling illness). He had been evicted from his apartment for refusal to pay his rent and he had refused alternative accommodation, which he considered inadequate.

Whilst the Court declared the complaint inadmissible, it did however make the following important point:

> [A]lthough Article 8 does not guarantee the right to have one's housing problem solved by the authorities, a refusal of the authorities to provide assistance in this respect to an individual suffering from a severe disease might in certain circumstances raise an issue under Article 8 of the Convention because of the impact of such a refusal on the private life of the individual (p. 8).

A not dissimilar observation was made by the Court in *O'Rourke v. United Kingdom*[42] – a case concerning a homeless person who suffered from an asthmatic condition and chest infection. In rejecting the application, the Court held that any positive obligation to house the applicant was discharged by the local authority's advice that he 'should attend a night shelter pending a decision on permanent housing, and by its continued efforts to find suitable temporary or permanent accommodation' for him.

In *Burton v. United Kingdom*,[43] the applicant, who was suffering from cancer, complained that the authorities failed in its obligations under Article 8 by not providing her with a place where she could live out the remainder of her life in a caravan according to her Romany Gypsy background. The European Commission, in finding the complaint inadmissible, noted that Article 8 could not be interpreted in such a way to extend a positive

---

[38] Nevertheless, in *Chapman* the Court concluded that this 'consensus' was at that time (2001) insufficiently concrete to dictate any specific outcome.

[39] Application no. 66746/2001, judgment dated 27 May 2004; 40 EHRR 189.

[40] Per Carnwarth LJ in *SS Home Dept v. Limbuela, Tesema & Adam* [2004] EWCA Civ. 540, para. 119; 7 CCLR 267; Times, May 26, 2004.

[41] Application no. 36448/97, admissibility decision dated 4 May 1999; 28 EHRR CD 175.

[42] Application no. 39022/97, admissibility decision dated 26 June 2001.

[43] Application no. 31600/96, admissibility decision dated 10 September 1996.

obligation to provide accommodation of an applicant's choosing.[44]

In several cases, the European Court has had to reconcile the competing interests of the right to housing and the right to property. This invariably arises in the relationship between landlord and tenant where the State has adopted rent control legislation. Such a measure will constitute an interference with the right to respect for property and must satisfy two conditions to comply with Article 1 of Protocol 1. First, it must pursue a legitimate aim in the general interest of the community. This has been held to be satisfied where the rent-control legislation aimed to make more housing available to less affluent tenants, while also providing incentives for landlords to improve the conditions of substandard properties.[45] Second, there must be a fair balance struck between the demands of the general interest of the community and the requirements of the protection of the individual's fundamental rights.

In *Hutten-Czapska v. Poland*,[46] the legislation in question did not allow the applicant to receive a level of rent from her properties sufficient to cover the maintenance costs that she was required to incur. The Court concluded that the authorities had imposed a disproportionate and excessive burden on the applicant in violation of the Protocol 1 right. The Court referred to its judgment in *Mellacher and others v. Austria*,[47] in which it found that the applicants did not suffer a disproportionate burden, even where the effect of the legislation had been to reduce the rent receivable by 82 per cent. However, whereas in the Austrian case the landlords were allowed to recover maintenance costs from tenants, the Polish legislation did not provide for balancing the costs of maintaining the property and the income from the controlled rent.[48]

It is clear from the above case law that contracting States have a wide margin of appreciation, both regarding the existence of a problem of public concern that warrants measures of control, and

regarding the choice of the detailed rules for the implementation of such measures. It follows that measures to promote the right to housing of the less affluent in society will generally take precedence over the economic rights of property owners to secure the market rent for their properties, provided that the payments received are sufficient to cover the latter's costs in relation to the maintenance of the properties.

The Court has also had to resolve conflicts between housing rights of different groups. *Blečić v. Croatia*[49] involved the termination of the occupancy/tenancy rights of the applicant in relation to her flat. Whilst visiting her daughter in Italy, the armed conflict had escalated in Croatia, including in the town of Zadar in which the flat was situated. The applicant unsuccessfully argued before the domestic courts that because of the armed conflict, ill health and the fact that the flat had been occupied by third parties during her absence, she had been unable to return to it. The European Court found that the termination pursued a legitimate aim, namely satisfaction of the housing needs of citizens and that it was intended to promote the economic well-being of the country and the protection of the rights of others. The Court stressed that:

> [W]here State authorities reconcile the competing interests of different groups in society, they must inevitably draw a line marking where a particular interest prevails and another one yields, without knowing its precise location. Making a reasonable assessment as to where the line is most properly drawn, especially if that assessment involves balancing conflicting interest and allocating scare resources fall within the State's margin of appreciation.[50]

In finding no violation of Article 8, the Court considered that the authorities had acted within the wide margin of appreciation available to them in implementing social and economic policies. The Court found it significant that the applicant was able to present her arguments orally and in writing

---

[44] Ibid.

[45] *Mellacher and others v. Austria*, application nos. 10522/82, 11011/84 and 11070/84, judgment dated 19 December 1989; (1989) 12 EHRR 391, at paragraph 47.

[46] Application no. 35014/97, judgment dated 22 February 2005.

[47] *Mellacher and others v. Austria* (n. 45 above).

[48] *Hutten–Czapska v. Poland* (n. 46 above), para. 176.

[49] Application no. 59532/00, judgment dated 29 July 2004. On 8 March 2006, the majority of the Grand Chamber declined to consider the merits of the case as the judgment of the Supreme Court which definitively ended the applicant's tenancy was rendered before the date on which Croatia ratified the Convention

[50] Ibid. para. 64.

against the decision in question, thereby ensuring compliance with the procedural requirements implicit in Article 8.

The decision in this case is a disappointing one, particularly bearing in mind that the applicant was sixty-six years old when the decision was taken to terminate her tenancy in relation to a flat that she had occupied since 1953, and she had no other home or place to live.[51] In addition, the case is an example of nearly 2000 terminations of occupancy/tenancy rights in Zadar where the Serb population decreased from 10 per cent in 1991 to 3 percent in 2001[52] and lost tenancy rights continue to prevent Serb refugees from returning to Croatia. The judgment is an example of the timidity and jurisprudential immaturity of the Court in relation to such highly controversial socio-economic questions: essentially ducking a difficult issue by a ritual incantation of 'margin of appreciation' which, as Lord Lester has observed, is not infrequently used 'as a substitute for coherent legal analysis'.[53]

It is important to note that the Court rejected the argument that the authorities could have adopted a less draconian solution to terminating the applicant's tenancy rights by merely allocating the flat temporarily to another person who needed housing. The Court considered that the availability of alternative solutions did not in itself make the termination of the tenancy unjustified.[54] If the Croatian authorities had been found wanting for not having adopted such a solution, one might have drawn from the judgment an obligation for the State to take positive measures to accommodate as much as possible the competing needs of Mrs Blecic to have a permanent home for the rest of her life and those of homeless persons to have temporary shelter until a more lasting solution could be found.

It is arguable that Article 3 of the Convention would require States to provide basic shelter to individuals if the alternative was utter destitution, in which the physical or mental suffering reached the minimum level of severity – bearing in mind the duration and the age or state of health of the victim – and nothing in *O'Rourke* or *Marzari* conflicts with this.[55] Such an interpretation of the Convention would be in line with the judgment in *Grootboom*[56] in which the Constitutional Court of South Africa held that the comprehensive housing programme required under section 26(2) of the South African Constitution must include measures 'to provide relief for people who have no access to land, no roof over their heads and who are living in intolerable conditions or crisis situations' (para. 52).

4.2 Health Care

There are few, if any, reported examples of Strasbourg complaints where the applicant has claimed the right to health care services, because the State has directly or indirectly caused illness. Such cases as there have been generally flesh out the nature and extent of a contracting State's core irreducible health care obligations. In *Osman v. United Kingdom* the Commission, in its preliminary opinion, speculated as to the extent of this obligation in the following terms:

Whether risk to life derives from disease, environmental factors or from the intentional activities of those acting outside the law, there will be a range of policy decisions, relating, inter alia, to the use of State resources, which it will be for Contracting States to assess on the basis of their aims and priorities, subject to these being compatible with the values of democratic societies and the fundamental rights guaranteed in the Convention . . . the

---

[51] Contrast with *Gillow v. United Kingdom* (1986), application no. 9063/80, judgment dated 24 November 1986; (1986) 11 EHRR 335, where in addition to their house in Guernsey, the applicants owned another property in England.

[52] OSCE Mission to Croatia, 'Ruling by the European Court of Human Rights on the *Blecic v. Croatia case*', Background Report dated 19 August 2004.

[53] Lord Lester of Herne Hill, 'Universality versus Subsidiarity: A Reply', *European Human Rights Law Review*, No. 1 (1998), pp. 73–81.

[54] It constitutes one factor, among others, that is relevant for determining whether the means chosen may be regarded as reasonable and suited to achieving the legitimate aim being pursued, *Blecic v. Croatia* (n. 49 above), para. 67.

[55] This is supported by Carnwarth LJ's comments in the English Court of Appeal judgment in the case of *Home Dept v. Limbuela, Tesema & Adam*, in which he said that he did 'not regard *O'Rourke* (where the facts were very different, and the applicant's plight was largely self-inflicted) as establishing the contrary' [2004] EWCA Civ. 540 at para 119; 7 CCLR 267; Times, May 26, 2004.

[56] *Government of the Republic of South Africa v. Grootboom and Others* 2000 (11) BCLR 1169 (CC).

extent of the obligation to take preventive steps may however increase in relation to the immediacy of the risk to life. Where there is a real and imminent risk to life to an identified person or group of persons, a failure by State authorities to take appropriate steps may disclose a violation of the right to protection of life by law.[57]

The effect of this approach is to place on the State the burden of justifying its failure to act where that failure presents a 'real and imminent risk to life'. In this respect it could be argued that the starting point under the Convention is not dramatically different from that in jurisdictions such as India or South Africa with explicit constitutional protection for such socio-economic rights,[58] including the right to emergency treatment. Indeed it is not radically different (given the very limited body of Strasbourg case law in this field) from the situation in countries with unashamedly negative constitutions, such as the United States, where in *Estelle v. Gamble*[59] it was held that deliberate indifference to serious medical needs' would violate the 'evolving standards of decency' protected by the Eighth Amendment (that forbids cruel and unusual punishments). It is possible therefore that the Convention does no more than reflect these emerging common standards of decency.

An example of where the European Court might find a violation of the Convention is where there has been a failure to provide basic medical care, leading to death or serious injury. The European Roma Rights Centre has reported on a case in Croatia in which a local hospital refused to send an emergency medical team to care for a pregnant woman living in a Romani settlement who had gone into labour. The family had no transport to bring her to hospital, and the child when delivered was stillborn.[60]

Beyond this core obligation it is clear that the Court will prove extremely hesitant about reading into the Convention a positive obligation to provide health care. In a series of cases the Court has adopted a reasonably consistent approach, that of accepting the theoretical possibility of the Convention embracing such wider obligations, but in practice, finding no actual violation.

Nitecki v. Poland[61] concerned the system in Poland whereby the State only provided for a 70 per cent contribution towards the cost of a drug used to treat the applicant's chronic and life-threatening condition. The applicant was unable to afford the balance with the result that his condition had deteriorated and he argued the inevitable consequence would be his untimely death. The Court accepted that the positive obligation under Article 2 could be engaged in such cases, but after reviewing the facts, ruled the application inadmissible:

> Bearing in mind the medical treatment and facilities provided to the applicant, including a refund of the greater part of the cost of the required drug, the Court considers that the respondent State cannot be said, in the special circumstances of the present case, to have failed to discharge its obligations under Article 2 by not paying the remaining 30% of the drug price (p. 5).

A similar outcome occurred in *Scialacqua v. Italy*[62] in which the applicant was diagnosed as requiring a liver transplant. Instead he sought help from an herbalist whose treatment proved successful. The applicant's request for a refund from the Italian health service was refused since the herbal medicines were not listed in the official 'medicines list'. In holding the complaint inadmissible, the Commission stated:

> Even assuming that Article 2 ... can be interpreted as imposing on states the obligation to cover the costs of certain medical treatments of medicines that are essential in order to save lives, the Commission considers that this provision cannot be interpreted as requiring states to provide financial covering for

---

[57] Application no. 23452/95, report of the Commission dated 1 July 1997, p. 91.

[58] See for instance *Soobramoney v. Minister of Health (Kwa-Zulu-Natal)* Constitutional Court of South Africa CCT 32/97 (26 November 1997); 50 BMLR 224 and *Paschim Banga Khet Mazdoor Samity v. State of West Bengal* 1996 AIR SC 2426 at 2429. For discussion on these cases, see Chapters 4 and 5 of this volume.

[59] 429 U.S. 97 (1976).

[60] See the European Roma Rights Centre web site at <http://www.errc.org>. See *also Calvelli and Ciglio v. Italy* (2002), application no. 32967/9, judgment dated 17 January 2002.

[61] Application no. 65653/01, admissibility decision dated 21 March 2002.

[62] Application no. 34151/96, admissibility decision dated 1 July 1998; (1998) 26 EHRR CD 162.

medicines which are not listed as officially recognised medicines.

In *Passannante v. Italy*,[63] it held that where a State scheme for the provision of health care based upon compulsory contributions exists, any excessive delay in providing a medical service to which the patient is entitled may raise an issue under Article 8 if the delay is likely to have a serious impact on the patient's health. Such a principle will in fact have general application in almost all contracting States, since the majority have health care systems based upon compulsory contributions. This situation can be contrasted with that disclosed in *Van Kück v. Germany*.[64] This concerned the relatively generous health care entitlement to the reimbursement of the costs of 'necessary medical treatment'. Given this situation, the Court held that both Article 6 and 8 demanded that this phrase be capable of including gender reassignment surgery.

In *Valentina Pentiacova and others v. Moldova* (2005),[65] the applicants, who suffered from chronic renal failure, complained about the failure of the State to provide comprehensive haemodialysis treatment. The Court acknowledged that the Convention does not provide a right to free medical health care but was prepared to accept that Article 8 was applicable to the particular facts of the case. In doing so it stressed that the State enjoyed a particularly wide margin of appreciation, and that:

> In view of their familiarity with the demands made on the health care system as well as with the funds available to meet these demands, the national authorities are in a better position to carry out an assessment than an international court.... While it is clearly desirable that everyone has access to a full range of medical services and drugs, the lack of resources means that there are, unfortunately in the Contracting States many individuals who do not enjoy them, especially in the case of permanent and expensive treatment (p. 131).

The Court noted that the applicant's claims constituted 'a call on public funds which, in view of the scarce resources, would have to be directed from other worthy needs funded by the taxpayer'. In dismissing the complaint under Article 8, the Court underscored the great improvement that comprehensive haemodialysis would bring for the applicants' private and family lives. However, it found that Moldova had struck a fair balance between the competing interests of the applicants and the community as a whole.

The Court will carefully scrutinise any case in which a State decides to withdraw medical or care services which it has previously provided. Thus in *D v. United Kingdom*,[66] the Court held that it was a violation of Article 3 to deport the applicant (who was suffering from AIDS and only had a short time to live) to his state of origin, the island of St Kitts, where he would not have access to appropriate medical treatment and would die in complete destitution, without a hospital bed or any nursing care.[67] In similar terms in *Bensaid v. United Kingdom*,[68] the Court held that where a deportation would subject the applicant to a severe deterioration in his mental health, then Article 8 might, in appropriate situations, restrain the State from removing him. It has however been suggested that the threshold of successful reliance on this principle is high.[69]

These decisions are partially explicable in terms of the negative obligations under the Convention; namely that the State's obligation is to refrain from action that violates Convention rights – such as Articles 3 and 8. This requires refraining from action that will change the status quo but does not in general compel the de novo provision of health care.

Whilst the Convention does not impose any obligation to provide health care, the authorities of contracting States are under an obligation to

---

[63] Application no. 32647/96, admissibility decision dated 1 July 1998.
[64] *Van Kück v. Germany* (n. 24 above).
[65] Application no. 14462/03, admissibility decision dated 4 January 2005.

[66] *D v. United Kingdom* (n. 15 above).
[67] However in *Kossi Archil Amegnigan v. Netherlands* (2004), application no. 25629/94, admissibility decision dated 24 November 2004, the Court found no violation of Article 3 concerning the return of a person with HIV to Togo. In distinguishing the case from that of *D v. United Kingdom*, (ibid.) the Court pointed out that the applicant was not in the advanced or terminal stage of the illness, would have access to medical care in Togo (albeit at a considerable cost) and had family support in that country.
[68] Application no. 44599/98, judgment dated 6 February 2001; (2001) 33 EHRR 205.
[69] *R (Razgar) v. SS Home Department* [2004] UKHL 27.

protect the health of persons deprived of liberty.[70] In *McGlinchey and others v. United Kingdom*,[71] the Court found a violation of Article 3 as a result of the failure of prison authorities to properly monitor the state of health of a woman prisoner who was vomiting repeatedly due to heroin withdrawal symptoms and was severely dehydrated, and to ensure that she was promptly admitted to hospital.

Failure to provide suitable psychological care to mentally disturbed prisoners will also raise issues both under Article 3 and 5 of the Convention. In *Keenan v. United Kingdom*,[72] the applicant's son, who was mentally ill, committed suicide while serving a disciplinary punishment in a segregation unit. In finding a violation of Article 3, the Court considered that the prison authorities had failed to carry out a psychological examination to ensure that the prisoner was able to cope with the segregation and to properly monitor him. In *Aerts v. Belgium*,[73] the Court was critical of the standards in the psychiatric wing of the prison in which the applicant was held. However, there was no evidence that the failure to provide psychiatric care had an adverse effect on his mental health in violation of Article 3. It did, however, find a violation of Article 5, as the psychiatric wing was not an appropriate place for a person suffering from mental illness.

4.3   Social Security

The European Convention does not expressly provide for any right to receive welfare benefits and entitlements such as social security payments and industrial accident payments.[74] However, numerous cases considered by the Court have concerned the right to a fair hearing under Article 6(1) in relation to disputes concerning social security.[75]

In order for Article 6 to apply, the Court initially took the view that proceedings must be decisive for private rights and obligations. In *Feldbrugge v. Netherlands*,[76] the applicant, whose statutory sickness benefit was stopped on the basis that she was fit for work, argued that the appeal procedures did not comply with Article 6. In finding that Article 6 applied, the Court noted that the public law features of the scheme were outweighed by the private law features including the fact that the availability of sickness benefits was determined by reference to the applicant's contract of employment and the personal nature of the rights as they related to her means of subsidence. Since that case, Article 6(1) has been applied to inter alia disability pensions from industrial accidents,[77] disability allowances[78] and annuities in respect of war injuries.[79]

In *Salesi v. Italy*,[80] the applicant had been refused a monthly disability allowance. The benefit in question was a statutory form of social assistance aimed at implementing Article 38 of the Italian Constitution, according to which 'all citizens who are unfit for work and lack the basic wherewithal to live shall be entitled to means of subsistence and welfare assistance'. The benefit was derived from statute and not from a contract of employment and the State was responsible for the financing of the scheme. In that case, the European Court held that the general rule is that Article 6(1) applies in the field of social insurance. However, in *Machatova v. Slovakia*,[81] the Court stressed that Article 6(1) does not apply where the payment of benefits is discretionary.

In the above cases, the Court has found a violation of the right to a fair trial because of a failure to disclose relevant documents to the applicant, to hold

---

[70] *Keenan v. United Kingdom*, application no. 27229/95, judgment of 3 April 2001; (2001) 33 EHRR 913.

[71] Application no. 50390/9, judgment dated 29 April 2003.

[72] *Keenan v. United Kingdom* (n. 70 above).

[73] Application no. 25357/94, judgment dated 30 July 1998; (1998) 29 EHRR 50.

[74] Articles 16 and 17 of the European Social Charter guarantees certain forms of social security; namely family benefits (Article 16) and services for mothers and children (Article 17).

[75] See M. Scheinin, 'Economic and Social Rights As Legal Rights' in A. Eide, C. Krause and A. Rosas (eds.), *Economic*

Social and Cultural Rights: A Textbook, 2nd Edition (Dordrecht: Martinus Nijhoff Publishers, 2001), pp. 29–54 at 35–38.

[76] Application no. 8562/79, judgment dated 29 May 1986; (1986) 8 EHRR 425.

[77] *Schuler-Zraggen v. Switzerland*, application no. 14518/89, judgment dated 24 June 1993; (1993) 16 EHRR 405.

[78] *Salesi v. Italy* (1993), application no. 13023/87, judgment dated 26 February 1993; (1993) 26 EHRR 187.

[79] *Kerojavi v. Finland* (1996), application no. 17506/90, judgment dated 19 July 1997.

[80] *Salesi v. Italy* (n. 78 above).

[81] Application no. 27552/95; admissibility decision dated 2 July 1997.

a public hearing[82] and the unreasonable length of proceedings.[83]

In several cases the Court has further held that welfare benefits and entitlements may constitute 'possessions' or 'property' for the purposes of Article 1 of Protocol 1.[84] In *Gaugusuz v. Austria*,[85] the applicant, who had worked in Austria for a number of years, was refused an 'emergency assistance' payment in the form of an advance on his pension, because he was not an Austrian national. As entitlement to this payment was linked to the payment of contributions to an unemployment insurance fund, the Court concluded that the right to emergence assistance under Austrian legislation was a pecuniary right for the purposes of Article 1 of Protocol 1. There was a violation of Article 14 taken in conjunction with Article 1 of Protocol 1, as discrimination on the basis of nationality as regards such an entitlement could not be justified.

In *Koua Pourriez v. France*,[86] the applicant was a disabled person of Ivorian nationality. His application for adult disability allowance was rejected on the grounds that he was neither a French national nor a national of a country that had entered into a reciprocity agreement with France in respect of the allowance. The Court considered that although it was a non-contributory benefit, the allowance could give rise to a pecuniary interest for the purposes of Article 1 of Protocol 1. It then found a violation of Article 14 in conjunction with Article 1 of Protocol 1, as the difference in treatment regarding entitlement to social benefits between French nationals or nationals of a country having signed a reciprocity agreement and other foreign nationals was not based on any 'objective and reasonable justification'.

It is arguable that a State may, in certain circumstances, be under an obligation to provide social security support where a person cannot work and would be destitute without support. In *Francine*

Van Volsem v. Belgium,[87] the applicant was unable to work, suffering from near-chronic respiratory problems, and lived for the most part on social security payments. She claimed that the action by an electricity company in reducing the power and cutting off the supply as a reaction to her arrears violated, inter alia, Article 3. A committee of the Commission in a cursory decision, devoid of reasoning, merely stated that the disconnection of the electricity supply of the applicant did not reach the requisite level of severity to constitute inhuman or degrading treatment under Article 3.[88] In *Larioshina v. Russia*,[89] the applicant complained, inter alia, that the amount of her pension and other social benefits she received was insufficient to maintain a proper standard of living. The Court emphasised that such a complaint may, in principle, raise an issue under Article 3. However, there was no indication that the amount of the pension and benefits had caused such damage to her physical or mental health that it had attained the minimum level of severity to fall within the ambit of Article 3.

The English High Court case of *R (Q and others) v. Secretary of State Home Department*[90] concerned the issue of destitute asylum seekers who were prohibited from working and denied social security support, including accommodation. The question considered by the Court was whether the withdrawal of support from such people, who by definition lacked the means of obtaining adequate accommodation or meeting their essential living needs, could violate Article 3. The judge (Collins J.) considered that:

It may even be that there is no duty [under the Convention] to provide any form of social security. But the situation here is different since asylum seekers are forbidden to work and so cannot provide for themselves. Unless they can find friends or charitable bodies or

---

[82] See *Feldbrugge v. the Netherlands* (1986), (n.76 above) and *Kerojavi v. Finland* (1996) (n. 79 above).

[83] See *Salesi v. Italy* (1993) (n. 78 above), in which the proceedings lasted for more than eight years and ten months.

[84] *Gaygusuz v. Austria* (1996), application no. 17371/90, judgment dated 16 September 1996; (1997) 23 EHRR 364.

[85] Ibid.

[86] Application no. 40892/98, judgment dated 30 September 2003.

[87] Application no. 14641/89, admissibility decision of the European Commission of Human Rights dated 9 May 1990.

[88] For a critical commentary on this case, see Antonio Cassese, 'Can the notion of inhuman and degrading treatment apply to socio-economic conditions?', *European Journal of International Law*, Vol. 2, No. 2 (1991), pp. 141–145.

[89] Application no. 56869/00, admissibility decision dated 23 April 2002.

[90] [2003] EWHC 195 (Admin), para. 67.

persons, they will indeed be destitute. They will suffer at least damage to their health. I therefore agree [that the withdrawal of support could violate Article 3]. [Para. 67.]

4.4   Social Care

Social care generally consists of support services that protect vulnerable groups such as children, the frail and the elderly and disabled. This may require measures to be taken even where the harm derives from the acts or omissions of other individuals. The Court has held that 'children and other vulnerable individuals, in particular are entitled to State proceedings, in the form of effective deterrence, against such serious breaches of personal integrity'.[91]

In several cases, the Court has stressed that the 'form of effective deterrence' will involve taking effective criminal proceedings against persons who cause harm to vulnerable persons. In *X and Y v. Netherlands*,[92] the perpetrator of a sexual attack against one of the applicants was not prosecuted because the victim, a 16-year-old woman with a mental disorder, was not allowed to bring a criminal complaint under Dutch law. The Court rejected the Dutch government's argument that it had complied with its obligations under Article 8, as it was possible to bring civil proceedings for compensation. The Court stated that:

> [T]he protection afforded by civil law in the case of the wrongdoing of the kind inflicted on Miss Y is insufficient. This is a case where fundamental values and essential aspects of private life are at stake. Effective deterrence is indispensable in this area and can be achieved only by criminal-law provisions; indeed it is by such provisions that the matter is normally regulated.[93]

In addition to effective criminal sanctions, States will also have an obligation to take into care vulnerable persons if they face abuse or neglect at home. *Z and others v. United Kingdom*[94] con-

cerned a number of children who suffered severe neglect at the hands of their parents. The Court noted that the local authority was under a statutory duty to protect the children and found a violation of Article 3, as there had been a gross failure to safeguard the children from long-term neglect and abuse.

On the basis of the above jurisprudence, States may be obliged to protect vulnerable persons from neglect by providing a wide range of community care services including domiciliary and community-based services and care home accommodation. A thorny issue is whether the authorities may compel an elderly person who is unable to look after himself to live in a care home. This matter was addressed in *HM v. Switzerland*,[95] in which the authorities ordered, against the will of the applicant, an eighty-four year old woman, that she be placed for an unlimited time in a nursing home. The applicant claimed that she had been deprived of her liberty under Article 5(1). The Court noted that the applicant had had an opportunity to receive care in her own home but she and her son (with whom she lived) had refused to cooperate with authorities. In its view, the applicant's placement in the nursing home was a responsible measure taken by the authorities in the applicants' own interests in order to provide her with the necessary medical care and adequate living conditions. Thus there was no deprivation of liberty within the meaning of Article 5.

Price v. United Kingdom[96] concerned the conditions of detention suffered by a thalidomide-impaired complainant, who in the course of debt recovery proceedings refused to answer questions put to her and was committed to prison. She alleged that she had suffered inhuman and degrading treatment because the prison had inadequate facilities to deal with her disabilities. The Court found that to detain a severely disabled person in conditions where she was dangerously cold, risked developing sores because her bed was too hard or unreachable and was unable to go to the toilet or keep clean without the greatest of difficulty, violated her Article 3 rights.

---

[91] *A v. United Kingdom* (n. 27 above), para. 22.
[92] Application no. 8978/80, judgment dated 26 March 1985.
[93] Ibid. para. 27.
[94] Application no. 29392/95, judgment dated 10 May 2001.
[95] Application no. 39187/98, judgment dated 26 February 2002. *H.L. v. UK* Application no. 45508/99, judgment dated 5 October 2004.
[96] Application no. 33394/96, judgment dated 10 July 2001.

Of particular interest was the concurring opinion of Judge Greve, in which he stated that:

> In a civilised country like the United Kingdom, society considers it not only appropriate but a basic humane concern to try to ameliorate and compensate for the disabilities faced by a person in the applicant's situation. In my opinion, these compensatory measures come to form part of the disabled person's bodily integrity (p. 12).

A series of cases before the Court have explored uncharted territory regarding the extent to which Article 8 requires a State to take positive measures to permit disabled people to enjoy more autonomy and lead more independent lives, thereby preventing unnecessary institutionalisation.

In *Botta v. Italy*[97] the applicant, who was physically disabled, complained of a lack of access to the beach and lack of accessible toilets in the resort town where he had gone on vacation. In violation of Italian law, the owner of the beach had not provided ramps or other access, and Botta was refused permission to drive onto the beach. He claimed that the State's failure to ensure that he and others in his position had access to the beach was a violation of his right to respect for private life under Article 8. The European Court rejected his claim on the ground that Article 8 did not extend so far as to protect this sort of access. It concluded:

> [T]he right asserted by Mr Botta, namely the right to gain access to the beach and the sea at a place distant from his normal place of residence during his holidays, concerns interpersonal relations of such broad and indeterminate scope that there can be no conceivable direct link between the measures the State was urged to take in order to make good the omissions of the private bathing establishments and the applicant's private life. [Para. 36.]

In *Botta* the Court emphasised the fact that the applicant was on holiday and at a place far from his home. In *Zehnalová and Zehnal v. the Czech Republic*,[98] however, the applicant couple (one of whom was disabled) complained about the inac-

cessibility of a large number of public buildings in their hometown[99] that accordingly impaired their mobility contrary to Czech law. They argued that their case could be distinguished from *Botta*, as they were complaining about their lack of access to facilities providing for their everyday needs in the town in which they were permanently resident.

The Court however stressed that:

> Article 8 cannot be considered applicable each time an individual's everyday life is disrupted, but only in the exceptional cases where the State's failure to adopt measures interferes with that individual's right to personal development and his right to establish and maintain relations with other human beings and the outside world (p. 12).

The Court doubted that the applicant needed to use the inaccessible buildings on a daily basis and considered that there was no direct and immediate link between the measures that the State was being urged to take and the applicants' private lives. It concluded that Article 8 was not applicable to the case and the complaint was inadmissible.

The ability of severely disabled persons to gain more autonomy in their lives was again considered by the Court in *Sentges v. the Netherlands*.[100] The applicant suffered from a form of muscular dystrophy, which made it impossible for him to stand, walk or lift his arms. The authorities rejected his request to be supplied with a robotic arm to be attached to his electronic car on the basis that the regulation governing the supply of medical devices did not provide for such an item. The applicant claimed that this constituted a violation of his right to respect to private life, as the robotic arm would have allowed him immeasurably greater autonomy.[101] The Court held that even assuming that a special link existed between the situation complained of and the needs of the applicant's private life, 'regard must be had to the fair balance that has to be struck between the competing interests of the individual and the community as a

---

[97] Application no. 21439/93, judgment dated 24 February 1998; (1998) 26 EHRR 241.

[98] Application no. 38621/97, admissibility decision dated 14 May 2002.

[99] Including the post office, the police stations, the customs office, the District Office, the district social-security office, cinemas, the District Court, various lawyers' offices, most specialist doctors' surgeries and the town swimming pool.

[100] *Sentges v. Netherlands* (n.6 above).

[101] Allowing him inter alia to make phone calls, pick up objects from the floor, play games, press door bells and lift buttons.

whole'. The Court concluded that in refusing to supply the robotic arm, the Dutch authorities had not exceeded their margin of appreciation, particularly since the case concerned priorities in the context of limited state resources.

4.5 Education

Article 2 of Protocol No.1 provides:

> No person shall be denied the right to education. In the exercise of any functions which it assumes in relation to education and teaching, the State shall respect the right of parents to ensure such education and teaching in conformity with their religious and philosophical convictions.

In the *Belgian Linguistics Case (No. 2)*,[102] the Court stated that despite its negative formulation, the first sentence of Article 2 of Protocol 1 guarantees a right. However, it did not bestow a right to require the authorities to establish a particular type or level of education. Instead it granted the right of access to education facilities that already exist.[103] The Commission has held that the right to education is concerned primarily with elementary education and not necessarily advanced studies.[104] It seems that Article 2 of Protocol 1 now requires universal access to elementary education.[105] However, the Commission has held that States may restrict access to higher education to those students who have attained the required academic level.[106]

Some applicants have claimed that the State has denied them the right to education by not providing special education facilities for their disabled children. In *Simpson v. United Kingdom*,[107] the authorities refused to fund the applicant child – who was dyslexic – to attend a special school, as it considered that he could be adequately educated in a normal State school. In finding no violation of Article 2 of Protocol 1, the Commission considered that:

> [T]here must be a wide measure of discretion left to the appropriate authorities as to how to make the best use possible of the resources available to them in the interests of disabled children generally. [para. 2]

The second sentence of Article 1 of Protocol 1 requires the State to respect parents' religious and philosophical convictions. These have related to, inter alia, objections to compulsory sex education in the school curriculum[108] and to corporal punishment.[109] In *Graeme v. United Kingdom*,[110] the applicant complained that the authorities' insistence that their disabled children be educated in special schools was contrary to their deeply held views regarding integrated schooling for disabled children. The Commission recognised that 'there is a growing body of opinion that, whenever possible, disabled children be brought up with normal children of their own age'. However, it considered that this policy cannot apply to all handicapped children. While the authorities had to take into account the convictions of parents, Article 2 of Protocol 1 does not require the placing of a child with severe development delay in a private school for able children rather than in a special school for disabled children. Nor does this provision grant a right to education in the preferred language of the parents.[111]

The issue of discrimination regarding the right to education was first considered in the *Belgian Linguistics Case (No. 2)*,[112] where certain French speaking children were prevented, solely on the basis of the residence of their parents, from having access to French-language schools (situated

---

[102] *Belgian Linguistics Case (No 2)* 1 EHRR 252; Application nos. 1474/62; 1677/62; 1769/63; 1994/63; 2126/64.

[103] This must at least include elementary education as all member states of the Council of Europe had such a system of state education when the Protocol was adopted.

[104] See, *inter alia, Sulak v. Turkey* (2001), application no. 24515/94; admissibility decision dated 17 January 1996.

[105] See L. Wildhaber, 'The Right to Education and Parental Rights', in R.St.J. MacDonald, F. Matscher and H. Petzold (eds.), *The European System for the Protection of Human Rights* (Dordrecht: Martinus Nijhoff, 1993), pp. 532–551, at 533.

[106] See *Eren v. Turkey*, application no. 60856/00, admissibility decision dated 6 June 2002.

[107] Application no. 14688/89, admissibility decision dated 4 December 1989.

[108] *Kjeldsen, Busk Madsen and Pedersen v. Denmark* (1976), application nos. 5095/71, 5920/72, 5926/72, judgment dated 7 December 1976.

[109] *Campbell and Cosans v. United Kingdom* (1982), application nos. 7511/76, 7743/76, judgment dated 25 February 1982.

[110] Application no. 1887/88; admissibility decision dated 5 February 1990.

[111] *Skender v. Former Yugoslav. Republic of Macedonia*, application no. 62059/00, admissibility decision dated 22 November 2001.

[112] *Belgian Linguistics Case (No. 2)* (n. 102 above).

in the six communes on the Brussels periphery which were subject to a special status as regards the use of languages). The Court held that there had been a violation of Article 14 together with Article 2 of Protocol 1, as a similar impediment would not have applied to Dutch-speaking children.

Applicants to the European Court of Human Rights encounter a particular difficulty in that the Court requires allegations to be proved beyond reasonable doubt. In relation to complaints concerning the discriminatory provision of socio-economic benefits, this has inevitably caused significant problems. *D.H. and Others v. Czech Republic*[113] concerned the practice of segregating Roma children in schools for mentally disabled children. The Grand Chamber (in reversing the Chamber judgment[114]) accepted that in cases involving allegations of indirect racial discrimination, it was necessary for the Court to adapt its previous case law on evidence. It held that where an applicant had established (by advancing statistical evidence if necessary) that a practice had a disparate racial impact, then the burden shifted to the state to demonstrate a just cause for the difference in treatment. In finding a violation, it held that (1) the relevant legislation as applied in practice had a disproportionately prejudicial effect on the Roma community; (2) that the difference in treatment had not been objectively and reasonably justified; and (3) that there did not exist a reasonable relationship of proportionality between the means used and the aim pursued.

5. REMEDIES AND ENFORCEMENT

Where the Court finds that a violation of the Convention has taken place, it is required by Article 41 to consider whether the applicant is entitled to any 'just satisfaction' consisting of compensation and/or costs. The aim of compensation is to place the applicant, as far as possible, in the position that he would have been in if the violation had not occurred. The Court has complete discretion whether or not to make an award and will only do so where the applicant has made a specific claim for such.

In many instances, the Court decides that the finding that a violation has occurred is in itself sufficient 'just satisfaction'. Where it awards compensation, it can be in relation to pecuniary and non-pecuniary loss. Pecuniary loss includes such items as loss of earnings, out-of-pocket expenses and the lost value of an asset resulting from government action. In *Selcuk and Asker v. Turkey*,[115] the applicants claimed compensation in relation to their houses and possessions, which were destroyed by the security forces, and the resulting loss of income from farming. As they did not provide independent evidence on the value of the assets destroyed, the Court made an award for pecuniary losses in relation to each of these items on an equitable basis.

Compensation for non-pecuniary loss concerns matters such as 'stress and anxiety', 'feelings of frustration' caused by the violation of the Convention and damages for ill-treatment or other pain and suffering. In *Price v. United Kingdom*,[116] the applicant claimed to suffer continuing emotional and psychological consequences from her ill-treatment in detention. The Court noted that she had only been detained for a short time and that the authorities had not intended to humiliate her, and accordingly made an award of GBP 4,500 for non-pecuniary damages. In *Van Kück v. Germany*,[117] the Court found that the applicant sustained non-pecuniary damage as a result of the unfairness of the court proceedings and the lack of respect for her private life. It awarded compensation under this head in the mount of EUR 15,000. In *Connors v. United Kingdom*, the Court found that the applicant had suffered non-pecuniary damage through feelings of frustration and injustice, having been denied the opportunity to obtain a ruling on he merits of his claims that his eviction was unjustified or unreasonable. The Court awarded him EUR 14,000 as compensation. The Court has been asked to award exemplary or punitive or aggravated damages in a number of cases, but so far has not done so.[118]

---

113 Application no. 57325/00 13 November 2007.
114 Application no. 57325/00 7 February 2006.

115 *Selcuk and Asker* (n. 31 above), paras. 104–115.
116 *Price v. United Kingdom* (n. 96 above), para. 34.
117 *Van Kück v. Germany* (n. 24 above), para. 96.
118 For example in *Aydin v. Turkey* (1998), application no. 23178/94, judgment dated 25 September 1997 at paragraph 127. Bearing in mind the seriousness of this case concerning the rape and ill-treatment of the applicant by state official while she was held in a police station, it is

As a general rule, the Court will not award anything other than compensation and costs. In *Selcuk and Asker v. Turkey*,[119] it rejected the applicants' request to be re-established in their village, which had been destroyed. However, the Court is now reviewing this approach. In *Hutten-Czapska v. Poland*,[120] it held that a large number of people had suffered violations of their property rights because of restrictive rent control legislation. Before dealing with just satisfaction, the Court referred to Article 46, which requires States to abide by any judgment in case in which they are a party. In this context it ruled that Poland was obliged (*inter alia*) to take appropriate legal and/or other measures to secure a reasonable level of rent to the applicant and those similarly affected.

With respect to the impact of judgments, it is almost certainly the case that Strasbourg judgments have had their most profound impact in the proactive measures states take to ensure that their laws are Convention compliant – the so-called process of 'Strasbourg proofing'. In relation to the specific impact of judgments, however, in accordance with Article 46(1), all States undertake to comply with the Court's judgments. Under Article 46(2) the Court's judgment is transmitted to the Committee of Ministers whose role is to supervise their execution.

There are few cases in which there have been substantial changes made to the law of contracting States following a finding by the Court of a violation of socio-economic rights in the Convention. In most cases, the Committee will merely be concerned with ensuring that compensation has been paid to the complainant within three months of the date of the Court's judgment. However, in some cases, the judgment will identify a specific defect within the State's legal system. This may be a structural failing, e.g. giving rise to complaints about the inordinate length of domestic proceed-

ings[121] or defects in the domestic legislation that have to be amended.[122]

6. CONCLUSION

The European Court of Human Rights, in common with all other courts, is hesitant when asked to determine socio-economic questions: they are frequently controversial, politically charged and above all are generally very difficult.

With the dramatic growth in the number of applications, it is perhaps unsurprising that challenging complaints involving socio-economic rights are becoming more frequent. This requires an intellectually more rigorous response from the Court, which is to be welcomed when compared to the cursory approach adopted by the Commission in the past.[123]

Applicants too, play a vital role in this process – above all by ensuring that complaints are framed in very specific terms. In *Zehnalová and Zehnal v. the Czech Republic*,[124] it is arguable that the applicants should have focused their complaint in detail on how their private lives were affected by the inability to gain access to a small number of public buildings that they used on a regular basis. Even if the outcome of the case had remained unchanged, the Court would have been forced to scrutinise the scope of the social care obligations of States towards disabled persons in greater detail.

In relation to complaints that disclose gross failures of the most basic socio-economic support, the Court's starting point is now an unequivocal acceptance of the view that the Convention protects a core irreducible set of such rights. However, as this case law develops challenging questions arise concerning the boundaries of this 'core'

---

perhaps unlikely that the Court would ever order punitive or exemplary damages.

[119] *Selcuk and Asker v. Turkey* (n.31 above), paras. 123–125.

[120] Application No. 35014/97, judgment dated 22 February 2005 at paragraphs 189–192; See also P. Leach, 'Beyond the Bug River – A New Dawn for Redress Before the European Court of Human Rights?', *European Human Rights Law Review*, No. 2 (2005), pp. 148–164.

[121] See for example *Salesi v. Italy* (1993) (n. 78 above) and Resolution of the Committee of Ministers dated 11 September 1995.

[122] See for example *Feldbrugge v. the Netherlands* (1986) (n. 76 above), Appendix to Committee of Ministers Resolution DH (92)8, 20 February 1992 and *A v. United Kingdom* (n. 27 above); Interim Resolution ResDH (2004)39 of the Committee of Ministers dated 2 June 2004.

[123] See for instance *Francine Van Volsem v. Belgium* (n. 87 above).

[124] *Zehnalová and Zehnal v. the Czech Republic* (n. 98 above).

domain – about those extremely difficult shadowlands where the destitution may not be gross, but conditions nevertheless are unquestionably dreadful. A glaring example is in *Sentges v. the Netherlands*,[125] where by not being provided with the robotic arm, the profoundly disabled applicant was denied the possibility of immeasurably increasing the reach of his otherwise severely limited level of self-determination. It is arguable that one factor which influenced the Court in dismissing the application, was its concern about not establishing a precedent concerning the scope of State obligations to provide health care. However, in cases such as *D v. United Kingdom*,[126] the Court has demonstrated that it is prepared to take bold steps in developing its jurisprudence, which may radically extend the boundaries of State obligations under the Convention, when to do otherwise will have tragic consequences for the applicant. There is a strong case for arguing that the Court should not routinely use the 'precedent justification' for not finding a violation of socio-economic rights. Instead, as it did in its judgment in *D v. United Kingdom*, a violation of the Convention could be found in those cases which have truly exceptional circumstances.

The Parliamentary Assembly of the Council of Europe has recently recommended that the Committee of Ministers examine whether any of the social rights guaranteed by the constitutions of Member States and the European Social Charter may be added to the European Convention on Human Rights[127] in the form of an additional Protocol. It recommended that the rights relate to the protection of basic needs (the right to housing, the right to social and medical assistance and the right to a minimum income) and protection in the work environment.[128] The adoption of such an instrument would indubitably strengthen the protection of economic and social rights under the Convention system. However, in view of the recent substantial changes to the Convention under Protocols 12[129] and 14,[130] and the growing jurisprudence of the European Committee of Social Rights in relation to collective complaints under the European Social Charter, it is uncertain whether this ambitious project will be realised in near future.

Moreover, there are signs that the Court is, very slowly, beginning to be more coherent and surefooted in its human rights analysis of these 'hard cases'. In both *Sentges v. the Netherlands*[131] and *Valentina Pentiacova and others v. Moldova*,[132] the Court placed a great deal of emphasis on the wide margin of appreciation enjoyed by States, where the matter concerned priorities in the context of limited State resources. However, in other cases, crude tools such as the 'margin of appreciation' are no longer being deployed quite so shamelessly.[133] Instead the Court is prepared to look to emerging international norms for inspiration as to the course it should follow, and allying this approach with a more sophisticated application of the principles of proportionality. These are interesting times in one of the most interesting areas of human rights jurisprudence.

---

[125] *Sentges v. the Netherlands* (n. 6 above).

[126] *D v. United Kingdom* (n.15 above).

[127] Recommendation 1415 (1999) Additional protocol to the European Convention on Human Rights concerning fundamental social rights. See also the opinion of the Committee on Legal Affairs and Human Rights dated 3 June 1999, Rapporteur – Mr Erik Jurgens.

[128] The Committee of Ministers has asked the Steering Committee for Human Rights to give its views on the advisability and feasibility of the proposed Additional Protocol Decision of the Committee of Ministers, 750th Meeting, 8 and 13 April 2001, CM/Del/Dec(98)645/4.4 and (99)677b/3.1, Recommendations 1354 (1998) and 1415(1999).

[129] Protocol 12 (n. 9 above).

[130] European Treaty Series no.194, adopted on 13 May 2004.

[131] *Sentges v. the Netherlands* (n.6 above).

[132] *Valentina Pentiacova and others v. Moldova* (n. 65 above).

[133] *Hirst v. UK (No. 2)* (2004), application no. 74025/01, judgment dated 30 March 2004, para. 41.

21

The European Committee of Social Rights

Putting Flesh on the Bare Bones of the European Social Charter

Urfan Khaliq* and Robin Churchill**

1. INTRODUCTION

The European Social Charter is the counterpart, in the field of economic and social rights, of the Council of Europe's much better known European Convention on Human Rights.[1] The original version of the Charter was adopted in 1961.[2] A number of further rights were added by a protocol in 1988.[3] In 1996, a more thoroughgoing revision of the Charter was undertaken, when many of the existing rights were substantially amended and updated and a number of new rights added and included in a new treaty, the Revised European Social Charter.[4] Nine States are parties to the European Social Charter only in its original form. A further seven States are parties to the Charter as amended by the 1988 Additional Protocol, while twenty-three States are parties to the Revised Charter.[5] Thus, of the forty-six members of the Council of Europe, thirty-nine are parties to the Charter in one or other of its versions. The Charter provides two forms of machinery for seeking to ensure that its parties comply with their obligations under it. The first is a system of reporting, which has been in existence since the adoption of the Charter in 1961 and is obligatory for all parties to both versions of the Charter. The second compliance mechanism is a system of collective complaints that was introduced in 1995 and is optional. The two compliance systems are examined in more detail in Section 3 below.

The European Committee of Social Rights ('ECSR'), a body of independent experts in social policy and law, plays a major role in both the reporting and the collective complaint procedures of the Charter, although in both procedures it is subordinate to the Committee of Ministers of the Council of Europe, a political organ, which is the only body that may address recommendations to States parties. Nevertheless, it is recognised, at least in theory if not always in practice, that the ECSR is the only body that is competent to give an authoritative interpretation of the Charter. Such interpretation is often necessary because many of the provisions of the Charter are drafted in broad and imprecise language. It is the ECSR's interpretation of the Charter, together with its views on how the Charter is to be applied in the context of a national report or collective complaint, that constitute its 'jurisprudence'. Unlike UN human rights monitoring bodies such as the Human Rights Committee, the ECSR does not produce General Comments that set out the views of the monitoring body concerned relating to the treaty in question. However, in December 2006

* Senior Lecturer in Law, Cardiff Law School, United Kingdom.
** Professor of Law, School of Law, University of Dundee, United Kingdom.

[1] UN Treaty Series, Vol. 213, p. 221; European Treaty Series ('ETS') No. 5; I. Brownlie and G. Goodwin-Gill, *Basic Documents on Human Rights*, 4th ed. (Oxford: Oxford University Press, 2002), p. 398.
[2] UN Treaty Series, Vol. 529, p. 89; ETS No. 35; Brownlie and Goodwin-Gill, *Basic Documents* (n. 1 above), p. 423. The Charter came into force in 1965.
[3] Additional Protocol to the Charter, ETS No. 128; Brownlie and Goodwin-Gill, *Basic Documents* (n. 1 above), p. 439. The Protocol came into force in 1992.
[4] ETS No. 163; Brownlie and Goodwin-Gill, *Basic Documents* (n. 1 above), p. 455. The Revised Charter came into force in 1999. In this Chapter, the term 'Original Charter' will be used to refer to the version of the European Social Charter adopted in 1961, 'Revised Charter' to refer to the Revised European Social Charter adopted in 1996, and the term 'Charter' or 'European Social Charter' to refer to both versions of the Charter.
[5] The number of ratifications in each case is at 3 April 2007.

the ECSR published a Digest of its case law relating to the Revised Charter.[6] In the case of the original Charter (and in fact also to some extent for the Revised Charter), the jurisprudence of the ECSR has to be gleaned from its conclusions on individual national reports and its findings on collective complaints. Fortunately for the researcher, the ECSR is conscious of the need regularly and clearly to articulate in its conclusions and findings its 'constant' jurisprudence on each right in the Charter.

The aim of this chapter is to examine the ECSR's jurisprudence relating to the socio-economic rights of the Charter. Given the limitations of space and the large number of rights contained in the Charter, it is only possible to examine the jurisprudence relating to a selected number of rights in the Charter. The rights that have been chosen for examination are some of those designed to protect the most vulnerable members of society, namely the rights to health, social security, social and medical assistance, protection for the disabled, protection against poverty and social exclusion, and housing. Before examining the ECSR's jurisprudence relating to the selected rights in Section 5 below, it is necessary first to say a few words about the nature of the rights in the Charter (section 2), to give some more details about the reporting and collective complaints systems (section 3), and to outline the approach of the ECSR to interpreting Charter rights (section 4).

2. THE NATURE OF THE RIGHTS PROTECTED BY THE CHARTER

Both the original and Revised Charters make a distinction between 'core' and 'non-core' rights. In the original Charter there are seven core rights: the right to work; to form trade unions and employers' associations; to bargain collectively; to social security; to social and medical assistance; to social, legal and economic protection for the family; and

to protection for migrant workers.[7] The Revised Charter adds two further core rights – the right of children to protection and the right to equal opportunities and treatment in employment. The second category of rights comprises the non-core rights. In the original Charter these are the rights to just conditions of work; safe and healthy working conditions; fair remuneration; vocational guidance and training; special protection for children, women, the handicapped and migrants; health; social welfare services; and special protection for mothers and children, families, the handicapped and the elderly. The 1988 Additional Protocol to the Charter adds a further four rights – the rights to equal opportunities and equal treatment in employment; of workers to be informed and consulted in the workplace; of workers to take part in the determination and improvement of their working conditions and environment; and of the elderly to social protection. The Revised Charter adds eight more non-core rights – the rights to protection in cases of termination of employment; protection of workers' claims in the event of their employer's insolvency; dignity at work; equal opportunities and treatment for workers with family responsibilities; protection of workers' representatives in the workplace; information and consultation in collective redundancy procedures; protection against poverty and social exclusion; and housing.

The European Social Charter appears to be unique among human rights treaties in permitting its parties not to accept all the rights it contains. The reason for this is because of the considerable differences in the level of economic and social progress among members of the Council of Europe at the time when the original Charter was being drafted.[8] Parties to the original Charter must accept at least five out of the seven core rights, and in total either 10 of the 19 Articles or 45 out of 72 numbered paragraphs, while parties to the Revised Charter must accept at least six of the nine core rights, as well as

---

[6] Council of Europe, *Digest of the Case Law of the ECSR* (Strasbourg: Council of Europe, 2006), available at <http://www.coe.int/t/e/human_rights/esc/7_resources/Digest_en.pdf>.

[7] The seven core rights were selected, not necessarily because they were the most important, but in order to achieve a balance between different groups of rights: see D. Gomien, D. Harris and L. Zwaak, *Law and Practice of the European Convention on Human Rights and the European Social Charter* (Strasbourg: Council of Europe, 1996), p. 380.

[8] Ibid. p. 379.

at least 16 of the 31 Articles or 63 out of 98 numbered paragraphs.[9]

Unlike, say, the International Covenant on Economic, Social and Cultural Rights, the rights found in the European Social Charter are in general not progressive in nature, i.e. they are not to be implemented gradually as a State party's resources and level of development permit, but are of immediate effect. The Charter does share a characteristic of most treaties concerned with economic and social rights, namely that a number of its rights are framed in vague and hortatory language. On the other hand, many of its provisions, particularly those concerned with employment rights, are drafted in sufficiently precise terms to be judicially enforceable.

The rights contained in the Charter apply only to the nationals of the State concerned and to the nationals of other States parties lawfully resident or working regularly in that State,[10] not to all within the jurisdiction of the State concerned, as is the case with the European Convention on Human Rights, for example. Unlike the original Charter, the Revised Charter contains a general clause prohibiting discrimination on various grounds in the application of any of the rights in the Charter.[11] Finally, it is worth noting that some rights contained in the Charter (for example those concerned with social security) have been amplified in later conventions adopted under the auspices of the Council of Europe.

---

[9] States that are parties to the 1988 Protocol must accept at least one of the four rights it contains.

[10] See the Appendix to each version of the Charter. In its general introduction to its 2004 Conclusions on the Charter, the ECSR, after noting that parties to the Charter, by ratifying certain human rights treaties or by domestic legislation, had guaranteed to foreigners not covered by the Charter rights identical to those in the Charter, concluded that as a result 'the implementation of certain provisions of the Charter could in certain specific situations require complete equality of treatment between nationals and foreigners, whether or not they are nationals of member States, party to the Charter'. See Conclusions XVII-1 (2004), p. 10. See also the discussion in section 5.3 below.

[11] Art. E. In Complaint No. 13/2002, the ECSR held that Art. E prohibits both direct and indirect discrimination, and that it covers discrimination on grounds of disability, even though this ground is not explicitly mentioned in Art. E. Complaint No. 13/2002, *Autism-Europe v. France*, Decision on the Merits, paras. 51 and 52. For the texts of Collective Complaint decisions, see the Council of Europe's web site, <http://www.coe.int/T/E/Human_Rights/Esc/4_Collective_complaints/>.

3. COMPLIANCE MECHANISMS

3.1 The Reporting Procedure[12]

Under this procedure parties to the Charter are required to submit a report every two years concerning the application of the core rights of the Charter they have accepted, a report every four years on the non-core rights that they have accepted, and reports 'at appropriate intervals as requested by the Committee of Ministers' on those provisions that they have not accepted.[13] The procedures and bodies by which the reports of States parties are examined have changed over time. Since the early 1990s the system has been as follows.[14] The reports, together with the observations

---

[12] For a fuller discussion of the reporting system than that which follows, see D. Harris, 'Lessons from the Reporting System of the European Social Charter' in P. Alston and J. Crawford (eds.), *The Future of UN Human Rights Treaty Monitoring* (Cambridge: Cambridge University Press, 2000), pp. 347–360; and D. Harris and J. Darcy, *The European Social Charter*, 2nd ed. (New York: Transnational Publishers, 2001), pp. 293–354. For more general discussion of the Charter's supervisory system, see R. Brillat, 'The Supervisory Machinery of the European Social Charter: Recent Developments and their Impact' and P. Alston, 'Assessing the Strengths and Weaknesses of the European Social Charter's Supervisory System' in G. de Búrca and B. de Witte (eds.), *Social Rights in Europe* (Oxford: Oxford University Press, 2005), pp. 31–43 and 45–67, respectively.

[13] Arts. 21 and 22 of the original Charter; Art. C of the Revised Charter. In practice, the last type of reporting has been used infrequently. Its purpose is to try to discover the reasons why States parties to the Charter have not accepted such provisions and to encourage them to accept them: see T. Jaspers and L. Betten (eds.), *25 Years European Social Charter* (Deventer: Kluwer Law Publishers, 1988), p. 14.

[14] In 1991, as part of the revitalisation of the Charter decided on at the Council of Europe's Informal Ministerial Conference on Human Rights held the previous year, a protocol was adopted to amend and streamline the original procedures set out in Arts. 23–29 of the original Charter: see Protocol amending the European Social Charter, ETS No. 142; Brownlie and Goodwin-Gill, *Basic Documents* (n. 1 above), p. 447. The Protocol has not formally entered into force, because it has not (as is required) been ratified by all States parties to the Charter. Nevertheless, nearly all the changes that it makes have already in practice been put into effect. As a consequence of the adoption of Res CM (2006) 53 by the Committee of Ministers, from November 2007 a new reporting procedure will take effect. Under the new system States shall present a report annually on a part of the provisions of the Charter (whether it is the 1961 Charter or the 1996 revised Charter), the provisions having been divided into four thematic groups. Each provision of the Charter will be reported on once every four years.

on them of national trade unions and employers' associations, are examined by a body originally known as the Committee of Experts (later renamed the Committee of Independent Experts), consisting of independent experts of recognised competence in international social questions, together with an ILO representative participating in a consultative capacity. In 1998, the Committee was renamed the European Committee of Social Rights (ECSR) and enlarged from its original seven members first to nine members, then (in 2001) to twelve members and subsequently to its current fifteen members. In examining the reports, the ECSR is to assess from a legal standpoint compliance of national law and practice with the Charter. After being examined by the ECSR, the reports, together with the ECSR's conclusions,[15] are forwarded to the Governmental Committee of the Council of Europe, which consists of one representative of each State party to the Charter (usually a civil servant), together with representatives from up to two international organisations of employers and up to two international trade union organisations sitting as observers in a consultative capacity. The Governmental Committee then sends a report containing its conclusions on the national reports, to which are appended the conclusions of the ECSR, to the Committee of Ministers of the Council of Europe, which comprises a minister, or more commonly a senior diplomat, of each member State of the Council of Europe. In its report the Governmental Committee is to 'select, giving reasons for its choice, on the basis of social, economic and other policy considerations, the situations which should, in its view, be the subject of recommendations' by the Committee of Ministers to each State party.[16] Based on the report of the Governmental Committee, the members of the Committee of Ministers that are parties to the Charter may decide, by a two-thirds majority vote, to address 'any necessary recommendations' to a State party to the Charter. Such recommendations are not legally binding. Until the mid-1990s, the Committee's practice was to adopt general recommendations drawing the collective attention of States parties to the Charter to the comments made by the Committee of Independent Experts and the

Governmental Committee. However, since 1993 the Committee of Ministers has addressed specific recommendations to non-complying States parties, although according to the Council of Europe's web site (assuming it is up to date – and there is no reason to suppose that it is not), the Committee of Ministers has only addressed one such specific recommendation since January 2002 (although it has addressed a number of 'old style' general recommendations during this period).[17]

A fundamental and continuing weakness of the reporting system is that it is not sufficiently independent of the States parties to the Charter – there is too much governmental involvement through the Governmental Committee and the Committee of Ministers. Nevertheless, in spite of past and continuing weaknesses in the reporting procedure, a number of changes to national legislation and practices have been made as a result of the procedure. As Harris and Darcy note, 'a large number of changes that bring the law and practice of contracting parties into line with the Charter are recorded in the Reports of the Governmental Committee as parties argue in that Committee that it should not propose a Committee of Minister's recommendation against them'.[18] However, there have also been a number of cases where States have not changed their law despite a finding of non-compliance with the Charter.[19]

Up to 2006 there had been eighteen cycles of reporting under the original Charter. In the case of the Revised Charter, on the other hand, because it only came into force in 1999 and more than half its parties have ratified it since 2001, there has

---

[15] Some of the more recent Conclusions adopted by the Committee and national reports are available at <http://www.coe.int/T/E/Human_Rights/Esc/>.

[16] 1991 Protocol, Art. 4.

[17] For the Committee's recommendations, see the Council of Europe's web site, <http://www.coe.int/>.

[18] Harris and Darcy, *The European Social Charter* (n. 12 above), p. 402. For practical examples, see A.H. Robertson and J.G. Merrills, *Human Rights in the World*, 4th ed. (Manchester: Manchester University Press, 1996), pp. 175–176; Council of Europe, *Human Rights Information Bulletin*, No. 54 (2001), p. 22; Jaspers and Betten, *25 Years* (n. 13 above), pp. 20–22 and 27–181 *passim*; and the annual *Survey*, published by the Charter Secretariat.

[19] Harris, 'Lessons from the Reporting System' (n. 12 above), pp. 359–360. See, for example, the situation in Greece as examined in Complaint No. 7/2000, *International Federation of Human Rights Leagues* v. *Greece* and the discussion of this case in R. R. Churchill and U. Khaliq, 'The Collective Complaints System of the European Social Charter: An Effective Mechanism for Ensuring Compliance with Economic and Social Rights?', *European Journal of International Law*, Vol. 15, No. 3 (2004), pp. 417–456.

so far been only a limited number of reports that have been examined by the ECSR and thus limited opportunities for it to develop its jurisprudence on the Revised Charter's provisions, especially those that have no equivalent in the original Charter or the 1988 Protocol. This is significant for this chapter, as some of the rights that are discussed below are found only in the Revised Charter.

3.2   The Collective Complaints System[20]

As part of the process of revitalising the Charter decided on in 1990, a system of collective complaints was introduced in 1995.[21] According to the preamble of the 1995 Protocol, the aim of this new mechanism is to 'improve the effective enforcement of the social rights guaranteed by the Charter' and to 'strengthen the participation of management and labour and of nongovernmental organisations'. Under this system, complaints of non-compliance with the Charter by a State party may be made by four types of organisation: international organisations of employers and trade unions which are observers at meetings of the Governmental Committee under the reporting system; other international non-governmental organisations (NGOs) which have consultative status with the Council of Europe and have been put on a list for the purpose of making complaints; representative national organisations of employers and trade unions; and other representative national NGOs with particular competence in matters governed by the Charter (provided that a State has made a declaration allowing such bodies to make complaints. Finland is the only State so far to have done so). Once a complaint has been lodged, the ECSR decides whether it is admissible; and, if it is, the ECSR then draws up a report with its conclusions on the merits of the case, which it forwards to the Committee of Ministers for consideration. If the ECSR finds that the Charter has been complied with, the Committee of

Ministers is to adopt a resolution to this effect by a simple majority. If, on the other hand, the ECSR concludes that the Charter has not been observed in a satisfactory manner, the Committee of Ministers 'shall adopt' by a two-thirds majority a recommendation addressed to the defendant State.

Acceptance by States parties to the Charter of the collective complaints system (and thus to be a defendant to a complaint) is optional. So far only fourteen out of the thirty-nine parties to the Charter have accepted the system. The latter has thus far not been widely used: as of 3 April 2007 no more than thirty-nine complaints had been made, of which thirty had been disposed of. The majority of complaints concern rights that are not considered in this chapter. Apart from its limited acceptance and use, a further weakness of the collective complaints system is the fact that so far the Committee of Ministers has rarely been willing to endorse the findings of the ECSR that a State party is not complying with the Charter and address an appropriate recommendation to it.[22]

3.3   Position of the Charter in Domestic Legal Systems

The Appendix to the Charter provides that it contains obligations of an international character 'the application of which is subject solely to the supervision' procedures described above. Thus, the intention is that in those State parties to the Charter that adopt a monist position as regards the relationship between international law and domestic law (for example, France and the Netherlands), the

---

[20] For a fuller discussion of the procedure, see Churchill and Khaliq, 'The Collective Complaints System', ibid.; and Harris and Darcy, *The European Social Charter* (n. 12 above), pp. 354–370.

[21] By means of the Additional Protocol to the European Social Charter providing for a System of Collective Complaints, 1995, ETS No. 158; Brownlie and Goodwin-Gill, *Basic Documents* (n. 1 above), p. 451. The Protocol came into force in 1998.

[22] See, for example, ResChS(2001)6 and ResChS(2002)3, 10 *IHRR* 583 (2003), adopted in the light of Complaint No. 7/2000, *International Federation of Human Rights Leagues* v. *Greece* and Complaint No. 8/2000, *Quaker Council for European Affairs* v. *Greece*, respectively. See further on this point Churchill and Khaliq, 'The Collective Complaints System' (n. 19 above), pp. 442–5 and 446–7. Brillat, on the contrary, has argued that a resolution by the Committee of Ministers is not intended to be a finding of a violation of the Charter (thus by implication indicating that the Committee neither disagrees with the ECSR's decision nor that it declines to endorse it). Rather, a resolution is designed to remind States of their obligations to comply with a treaty that they have ratified and to take account of the conclusions of the ECSR. See Brillat, ''The Supervisory Machinery of the European Social Charter' (n. 12 above), p. 33.

provisions of the Charter are not intended to be self-executing and thus capable of being invoked by individuals before national courts.[23] Nevertheless, there are a number of reported instances of the Charter being applied by national courts,[24] but there is no central record of such national court decisions nor any indication of how far national courts have taken the jurisprudence of the ECSR into account in arriving at their decisions.

4. THE APPROACH OF THE EUROPEAN COMMITTEE OF SOCIAL RIGHTS TO INTERPRETING THE RIGHTS IN THE CHARTER[25]

Every legal text is likely at some stage to require interpretation. The European Social Charter, like many other human rights treaties, is in particular need of interpretation and presents special challenges to an authorised interpreter because of the breadth and generality of many of its provisions. Examples of such provisions include the right of workers to 'remuneration such as will give them and their families a decent standard of living'[26] and the obligation on States parties 'to prevent as far as possible epidemic, endemic and other diseases'.[27] As pointed out in Section 1 above, the authorised interpreter of the Charter is primarily, and arguably exclusively, the ECSR. The introduction of the collective complaints procedure has allowed the ECSR to articulate its approach to interpretation of the Charter in a way that was and is not possible under the reporting procedure. Thus, much of what is said below about interpretation draws on the emerging jurisprudence of the collective complaints system.

The ECSR has recently set out its general approach and philosophy when interpreting the Charter. In its decision on the merits in Complaint No. 14/2003, the ECSR stated that when it had to interpret the Charter, it did so on the basis of the provisions on interpretation set out in the Vienna Convention on the Law of Treaties. It went on to note that the Charter:

> [W]as envisaged as a human rights instrument to complement the European Convention on Human Rights. It is a living instrument dedicated to certain values which inspired it: dignity, autonomy, equality and solidarity. The rights guaranteed are not ends in themselves but they complete the rights enshrined in the European Convention on Human Rights... Thus, the Charter must be interpreted so as to give life and meaning to fundamental social rights. It follows inter alia that restrictions on rights are to be read restrictively, i.e. understood in such a manner as to preserve intact the essence of the right and to achieve the overall purpose of the Charter.[28]

In a later complaint the ECSR repeated its description of the Charter as a 'living instrument' and stated that it was therefore to be interpreted 'in light of developments in the national law of member states of the Council of Europe, as well as relevant international instruments'.[29]

It follows from this approach that the ECSR does not feel constrained by the literal meaning of provisions of the Charter. Thus, for example, it has included disability as a ground of discrimination, in the non-discrimination provision of the Revised Charter, Article E, even though it is not explicitly mentioned there,[30] and has disregarded the plain wording of Article 13(4), which provides that medical assistance is to be provided to legal immigrants, to extend such assistance to illegal immigrants.[31] The ECSR therefore frequently adopts a teleological approach. Thus, in a case concerned with the protection of children and young persons from violence, the ECSR considered that

---

[23] For discussion of the status of the Charter in the contracting parties, see Gisella Gori, 'Domestic Enforcement of the European Social Charter: The Way Forward' in Gráinne de Búrca and Bruno de Witte (eds.), *Social Rights in Europe* (n. 12 above), pp. 69–88.

[24] See, for example, the Dutch Supreme Court (*Hoge Raad*) 30 May 1986, NJ 1986/688 and the Belgian decision in *Conseil d'Etat* (VI ch.), 22 March 1995, *Henry*, No. 52424, A.P.T. (1995), at 228, both discussed with other national jurisprudence by Gori, ''Domestic Enforcement of the European Social Charter' (n. 12 above), pp. 75–80. See also Harris and Darcy, *The European Social Charter* (n. 12 above), pp. 395–396.

[25] For a fuller discussion, see Harris and Darcy, *The European Social Charter* (n. 23 above), pp. 24–31.

[26] Art. 4(1) of both the original and revised Charters.

[27] Art. 11(3) of both versions of the Charter.

[28] Complaint No. 14/2003, *International Federation of Human Rights Leagues (FIDH)* v. *France*, Decision on the Merits, paras. 26–29.

[29] Complaint No. 18/2003, *World Organisation against Torture v. Ireland*, Decision on the Merits, para. 63.

[30] See further at n. 11 above.

[31] See further the discussion at the end of section 5.3 below, at notes 118–125 and accompanying text.

'a teleological approach should be adopted when interpreting the Revised Charter, i.e. it is necessary to seek the interpretation of the treaty that is most appropriate in order to realize the aim and achieve the object of the treaty, not that which would restrict to the greatest possible degree the obligations undertaken by the Parties'.[32] In doing so, the ECSR frequently refers to the case law of the European Court of Human Rights and other Council of Europe instruments.[33]

One of the notable features of the ECSR's interpretation of the Charter, resulting from its approach and philosophy outlined above, is that it has managed to concretise such broadly drafted rights and obligations as those referred to above. For example, in relation to the right to remuneration sufficient for a decent standard of living, the ECSR has established a 'decency threshold' of 60 per cent of the average national wage: where wages are above this level there will be no breach of the right, provided that this level is also above the poverty line; where wages are below it, there will normally be a breach of the right.[34]

Another important feature of the ECSR's interpretation of the Charter is the way in which it has clarified the general obligations of States when giving effect to the rights contained in the Charter. It has emphasised that rights need to be secured in legislation, not merely reflected in administrative practice.[35] At the same time, legislation is not of itself sufficient: the way in which the legislation is applied in practice must also secure the Charter rights in question. As the ECSR has put it, 'the aim and purpose of the Charter, being a human rights instrument, is to protect rights not merely

theoretically, but also in fact'.[36] The ECSR accepts that the nature of some rights may be such that a State cannot be expected to give full effect to them immediately. In Complaint No. 13/2002, *Autism-Europe v. France*, which concerned Article 15 of the Revised Charter dealing with the rights of the disabled, the ECSR held that 'when the achievement of one of the rights in question is exceptionally complex and particularly expensive to resolve, a State party must take measures that allow it to achieve the objectives of the Charter within a reasonable time, with measurable progress and to an extent consistent with the maximum use of available resources. States parties must be particularly mindful of the impact their choices will have for groups with heightened vulnerabilities as well as for other persons affected including, especially, their families on whom falls the heaviest burden in the event of institutional shortcomings'.[37] In this case France had failed to achieve sufficient progress in advancing the provision of education for the autistic. In the past the ECSR has generally applied a common standard for all States parties, regardless of their relative economic wealth[38] (an approach that is of particular significance with the accession of many poor States from Eastern Europe to the Charter since the late 1990s). The decision in *Autism-Europe* suggests that this will no longer be the case, at least in the case of provisions which the ECSR accepts are subject to progressive implementation. In such cases the fact that a State will be judged in part on the basis of the resources available suggests that different rates of progress by States parties to the Charter towards the realisation of such provisions will be accepted. Related to this is the fact that in the past the ECSR has not allowed States parties a 'margin of appreciation' in respect of their application of the Charter, unlike the European Court of Human Rights, which has adopted such a doctrine for the European Convention on Human Rights.[39] However, in

---

[32] Complaint No. 18/2003, *World Organisation against Torture v. Ireland*, Decision on the Merits, para. 60.

[33] See, for example, Complaint No. 18/2003, ibid. paras. 61–62; Complaint No. 13/2002, *Autism-Europe v. France*, Decision on the Merits, paras. 51–52; and Conclusions XVII-2, Vol. 1 (2005), p. 10.

[34] Council of Europe, *Digest of the Case Law* (n. 6 above), p. 23; Harris and Darcy, *The European Social Charter* (n. 12 above), pp. 74–77; L. Samuel, *Fundamental Social Rights: Case Law of the European Social Charter*, 2nd ed. (Strasbourg; Council of Europe, 2002), pp. 73–81.

[35] See, for example, Complaint No. 18/2003, *World Organisation against Torture v. Ireland*, Decision on the Merits, para. 64; and Complaint No. 16/2003, *Confédération Francaise de l'Encadrement v. France*, Decision on the Merits, paras. 35–38.

[36] Complaint No. 1/1998, *International Commission of Jurists v. Portugal*, Decision on the Merits, para. 32. See also Complaint No. 6/1999, *Syndicat National des Professions du Tourisme v. France*, Decision on the Merits, para. 26.

[37] Complaint No. 13/2002, *Autism-Europe v. France*, Decision on the Merits, para. 53.

[38] Harris and Darcy, *The European Social Charter* (n. 12 above), pp. 26–27.

[39] Ibid. pp. 30–31.

Complaint No. 8/2000 the ECSR accepted that, at least in respect of certain Charter provisions, parties to the Charter do 'indeed enjoy a certain margin of appreciation'.[40]

Other aspects of the ECSRs interpretation of the Charter that are worthy of noting here are that it reads in a remedy for an alleged breach of a right where this is possible (for example, in relation to the right to equal pay and the right of migrant workers not to be deported);[41] and that in the case of the original Charter it has read the principle of non-discrimination that is contained only in the Preamble to the Charter (unlike the Revised Charter, where it is a substantive provision) into many of the Charter rights.[42]

Finally, in interpreting the Charter, the ECSR plays close attention to other human rights treaties, notably the European Convention on Human Rights. It frequently refers to the jurisprudence of the European Court of Human Rights and quotes it in support of its interpretation of the Charter.[43] Where there is a Charter right that has an equivalent in the Convention, the ECSR will interpret the Charter so as to be in harmony with the Convention.[44] The same is true, although not to the same degree, in the case of other human rights treaties.[45] However, the ECSR does not automatically accept that where a State party to the Charter is a party to another treaty that contains a provision similar to one in the Charter, that State party will automatically be in compliance with the Charter.[46]

---

[40] Complaint No. 8/2000, *Quaker Council for European Affairs v. Greece*, Decision on the Merits, para. 24.
[41] Harris and Darcy, *The European Social Charter* (n. 12 above), p. 30.
[42] See, for example, Conclusions XVII-2, Vol. 1 (2005), p. 10.
[43] See, for example, Complaint No. 13/2002, *Autism-Europe v. France*, Decision on the Merits, para. 52; and Complaint No. 15/2003, *European Roma Rights Center v. Greece*, Decision on the Merits, paras. 20 and 25.
[44] See, for example, Complaint No. 8/2000, *Quaker Council for European Affairs v. Greece*, Decision on the Merits, para. 22 (concerning the prohibition on forced labour).
[45] See, for example, Complaint No. 18/2003, *World Organisation against Torture v. Ireland*, Decision on the Merits, para. 63, where the ECSR refers to the Convention on the Rights of the Child.
[46] See, for example, Complaint No. 10/2000, *STTK ry and Tehy ry v. Finland*, Decision on the Merits, para. 25 (regarding an ILO Convention); and Complaint No. 16/2003, *Confédération Française de l'Encadrement v. France*, Decision on the Merits, para. 30 (regarding an EU directive).

5. SELECTED RIGHTS

5.1 Right to Health

Article 11, which is virtually the same in both the original and Revised Charters and is a non-core right, imposes three basic obligations upon States. In the revised version of the Charter these obligations are stated as follows:

> With a view to ensuring the effective exercise of the right to protection of health, the Contracting Parties undertake, either directly or in co-operation with public or private organisations, to take appropriate measures designed inter alia:
>
> 1. to remove as far as possible the causes of ill-health;
>
> 2. to provide advisory and educational facilities for the promotion of health and the encouragement of individual responsibility in matters of health;
>
> 3. to prevent as far as possible epidemic, endemic and other diseases, as well as accidents.

The original Charter does not refer to accidents in Article 11(3).

In the introduction to its Conclusions on the Charter in 2005, the ECSR set out its general approach to the interpretation and application of Article 11. It began by noting that:

> [T]he right to protection of health in Article 11 of the Charter complements Articles 2 and 3 of the European Convention on Human Rights – as interpreted by the European Court of Human Rights – by imposing a range of positive obligations designed to secure its effective exercise. The normative relationship between the two instruments is underscored by the Committee's emphasis on human dignity.[47]

In assessing whether the right to protection of health can be effectively exercised, the ESCR 'pays particular attention to the situation of disadvantaged and vulnerable groups. Hence it considers that any restrictions on this right must not be interpreted in such a way as to impede the

---

[47] Conclusions XVII-2, Vol. 1 (2005), p.10; Conclusions on the Revised Charter 2005, Vol. 1, p. 10.

effective exercise by these groups to the right of protection of health'.[48] Such an interpretation followed from the non-discrimination requirement of Article E of the Revised Charter and the preamble of the original Charter.

The obligations in each of the three paragraphs of Article 11 are appreciably broad and the Committee[49] has interpreted them accordingly. In its first cycle of conclusions on Article 11(1), the obligation to remove causes of ill-health, the Committee listed a number of elements in national health services (which must substantially be paid for by the State) that need to be present to ensure compliance. These include public health arrangements that make available medical practitioners and adequate equipment which can extend medical care to the entire population and prevent and diagnose disease; special measures for the health of the young, the elderly and mothers; and general measures to tackle various forms of pollution and the control of alcoholism and drug abuse.[50] The Committee's usual approach is to look at general indicators to assess the overall state of the population's health. In its 2003 assessment of Sweden's compliance with Article 11(1), for example, the Committee scrutinised the situation in Sweden with regard to: life expectancy and the main causes of death; rates of infant and maternal mortality; access to health care; spending on health care as a percentage of GDP compared to other States; and the number of hospital beds in relation to the population.[51] The situation in Poland, for example, has been found not to be in compliance with Article 11(1) because of the excessive waiting time for some specialised medical services and because of the lack of appropriate waiting lists.[52]

With regard to Article 11(2), the Committee has, since 2001, provided a clearer indication of the requirements of this provision. Firstly, it has

emphasised that Contracting States must encourage individual responsibility through awareness campaigns which target the general population and health education as part of the school curriculum.[53] As Samuel notes, the Committee has focused mainly on the prevention of pathogenic lifestyles, to which the encouragement of responsibility may directly contribute.[54] The Committee has thus sought information from Contracting States on, for example, smoking, alcohol consumption, drug abuse, sexual education and healthy nutrition. Secondly, Contracting States are obliged to have in place what may be described as consultation and screening facilities.[55] In terms of screening, the Committee has stressed the need for frequent medical checks to be carried out in schools and for the screening of illnesses responsible for premature mortality rates to be organised. In terms of consultation, the Committee has recently focused upon antenatal and postnatal consultations. The Committee has also referred to the need for Contracting States to have in place paediatric care for young children. The costs of such care, as well as antenatal and postnatal consultations, must be borne by the State.[56] Since 2001 there has been a very noticeable trend in the Committee's approach to compliance with Article 11(2), to defer its conclusions pending the receipt of further information.[57] Previously, Contracting States were, on the whole, found to comply with their obligations under Article 11(2). The Committee's more recent approach seems to be imposing a greater obligation upon Contracting States.

Article 11(3) requires States to 'prevent as far as possible epidemic, endemic and other diseases'. In assessing compliance with this provision, the Committee mainly considers the healthiness of the environment; measures against ill-health caused by smoking, alcohol or drug abuse; and general prophylactic measures such as immunisation and epidemiological monitoring. In assessing the healthiness of the environment, the Committee

---

[48] Ibid.

[49] The term 'Committee' is used henceforth for the sake of simplicity and refers both to the Committee of Independent Experts (as the ECSR was named until 1998) and the ECSR.

[50] Conclusions I, p. 59, cited by Harris and Darcy, *The European Social Charter* (n. 12 above), p. 150.

[51] Conclusions 2003, Sweden, pp. 31–33.

[52] Conclusions XVI-2, Poland, p. 49. The management of waiting lists and waiting times is assessed in the light of the Committee of Ministers Recommendation No. R (99) 21 on Criteria for the Management for Waiting Lists and Waiting Times in Health Care.

[53] See, for example, Addendum to Conclusions, Slovakia, XV-2, p. 199 and Conclusions XV-2, Belgium, p. 98.

[54] Samuel, *Fundamental Social Rights* (n. 34 above), p. 273.

[55] Ibid. p. 274.

[56] See, for example, Conclusions XV-2, France, p. 208 *et seq.* and further Samuel, *Fundamental Social Rights* (n. 34 above), p. 273 *et seq.*

[57] For recent examples see Conclusions XVI-2, Czech Republic, p. 41 and Conclusions XVI-2, Hungary, p. 52.

routinely refers to a number of different indicators such as air and water pollution, ionising radiation, and exposure to asbestos. In general in determining whether a Contracting State complies with Article 11(3), the Committee has made extensive reference to national statistics and the relevant policies and objectives of the World Health Organisation (WHO). The Committee has found that a number of Contracting Parties are not complying with various aspects of their obligations under Article 11(3).[58] Belgium, for example, was found by the ECSR not to be in compliance with its obligations under Article 11(3) as the immunisation coverage levels for some diseases were not considered sufficient.[59] Notwithstanding the existence of some weaknesses, particularly concerning environmental issues, the situation in Poland, however, has been found to be in conformity with Article 11(3) of the Charter due to the effort made by the Polish authorities in that respect.[60]

5.2 Right to Social Security

Article 12 of both the original and Revised Charters, which are substantively identical, grant a right to social security. This core right is of necessity very broad and unspecific in nature.[61] Under Article 12(1) Contracting Parties undertake to establish or maintain a social security system. Once established, this system must be maintained at a satisfactory level (Article 12(2)). Under the original Charter this level is considered to be at least equal to that required to ratify ILO Convention No. 102 Concerning Minimum Standards of Social Security. Under the Revised Charter, the level must be at least equal to that necessary for ratification of the European Code of Social Security.[62] Article 12(3) requires Contracting Parties

to endeavour progressively to raise the system to higher levels. Finally, under Article 12(4), Contracting Parties are obliged to take steps to extend the benefits granted under their national social security schemes to the nationals of other Contracting Parties.

There is clearly an overlap between Article 12 and other provisions of the Charter, most importantly for our purposes with Article 13, the right to social assistance (discussed below).[63] The Committee has noted on a number of occasions that it is not always possible to distinguish social assistance from social security and that reforms in a number of Contracting Parties have increasingly merged the two.[64] The Committee, however, needs to be able to distinguish between them so as to be able to determine whether national programmes should be assessed under Article 12 or 13.[65] The Committee has stated that social assistance is a set of benefits where needs are the main criterion for eligibility.[66] There does not need to be any affiliation to a social security scheme aimed to cover a particular risk or any requirement of professional activity or payment of contributions. Social security is not defined in the Charter but the Committee has stated that it is a socially more advanced means of social protection and has thus taken over certain areas, which traditionally belonged to social assistance.[67] The Committee

to the minimum requirements as to how many parts must be accepted for the ratification of these instruments (three for the Convention; six for the Code) and the standard of social security protection, with the European Code requiring a higher standard. See Council of Europe, *Explanatory Report on the Revised European Social Charter* (1996), para. 58. (hereinafter the 'Explanatory Report'). Available at: <http://conventions.coe.int/treaty/en/Reports/HTML/163.htm>. For further discussion see Harris and Darcy, *The European Social Charter* (n. 12 above), p. 154.

[63] For some discussion of the relationship between the two Articles, see J. Tooze, 'Social Security and Social Assistance' in T. Harvey and J. Kenner (eds.), *Economic and Social Rights Under the EU Charter of Fundamental Rights: A Legal Perspective*, (Oxford: Hart Publishing, 2003), pp. 160–192.

[64] See, for example, Conclusions XIII-4, pp. 35–37.

[65] Ibid.

[66] Ibid.

[67] See Conclusions VII, France, p. 74 and Conclusions XII-2, p. 29. Art. 9 of the International Covenant on Economic, Social and Cultural Rights, 1966 (UN Treaty Series, Vol. 993, p. 3; Brownlie and Goodwin-Gill, *Basic Documents* (n. 1 above), p. 172) obliges States parties to the Covenant to recognise the right of everyone to the social security, including social insurance. The Committee does

---

[58] Conclusions XV-2, Belgium, p. 104, Conclusions XV-2, Greece, p. 253 and Addendum to Conclusions XV-2, Turkey, p. 265. In a number of States (for example Conclusions XVI-2, Hungary, p. 56), the Committee has recently asked for further information before determining whether the situation is in accordance with the Charter.

[59] Conclusions XV-2, Belgium, p. 104.

[60] Conclusions XVI-2, Poland, p. 647.

[61] See Conclusions I, p. 62. As Harris and Darcy note, there was a clear choice made by the drafters of the Charter to adopt a general provision and to leave more detailed stipulations to specialist instruments: see *The European Social Charter* (n. 12 above), p. 154.

[62] ETS No. 48. The differences between ILO Convention No. 102 and the European Code of Social Security relate

has further stated that social security refers to universal schemes as well as professional ones and includes contributory, non-contributory and combined allowances related to certain risks (sickness, disablement, maternity, family, unemployment, old age, death, widowhood, vocational accidents and illnesses).[68] Social security is seen as 'benefits granted in the event of risks which arise but they are not intended to compensate for a potential state of need which could result from the risk itself'.[69]

In assessing compliance with Article 12(1), the basic approach of the Committee is to consider whether the social security system in Contracting Parties covers certain major risks and whether the level of social security provision is adequate. In its 2003 assessment of Bulgaria, for example, it considered that in terms of scope the social security system was satisfactory as it addressed the nine traditional branches of social security, namely health care, sickness and maternity benefits, unemployment benefits, old-age, disability and survivor's pensions, occupational accident or disease benefits, and family allowances.[70] So long as most of the nine traditional branches of social security are addressed by a national scheme, the situation will be in conformity with the Charter.[71] Any scheme, however, must also cover a 'significant percentage of the population and at least offer effective benefits in several areas'.[72] Income-substituting benefits should not fall below 50 per cent of the median income in the country concerned. The situation in a number of Contracting Parties has been found not to be in compliance with Article 12(1) as the level of allowances have not been considered adequate.[73] Although one might consider that this issue should be determined under Article 12(2), which refers to established social security schemes being maintained at

a satisfactory level, the Committee in fact assesses the issue under Article 12(1).

Article 12(2) has been interpreted in a relatively straightforward manner, with the Committee, on the whole, simply assessing whether the Contracting Party in question has ratified the relevant aspects of either the European Code of Social Security or ILO Convention No. 102. As Samuel notes in the context of States which are party to ILO Convention No. 102, a Contracting Party to the original Charter which has a social security system at least equal to that required to ratify that Convention and which has been found by the ILO Committee of Experts on the Application of Conventions and Recommendations to comply with it, fulfils its obligations under Article 12(2).[74] The approach of the Committee is also the same under Article 12(2) of the Revised Charter, which refers to the European Code of Social Security.[75]

It is not always necessary, however, for a Contracting Party to have ratified ILO Convention No. 102 or the European Code of Social Security in order to comply with Article 12(2). Finland had not ratified ILO Convention No. 102 but was still considered to be in compliance with the Charter as it had ratified a significant number of other overlapping ILO Conventions, which imposed more extensive obligations than Convention No. 102.[76] In the Committee's 2004 assessment of the situation in Romania, the outcome was somewhat different. Romania had signed the European Code of Social Security but had not ratified it. In its report, Romania claimed to have fulfilled the conditions necessary for ratifying the relevant parts of the Code, but the Committee, in the light of its assessment under Article 12(1) of the Charter, preferred to reserve its position as to whether this was the case.[77]

The most dynamic and progressive undertaking on social security in the Charter is that contained

---

not tend to use the term 'social insurance' although its approach to Art. 12 of the Charter is broad enough to encompass that term.

[68] Conclusions XIII-4, pp. 35–37.

[69] Ibid.

[70] Conclusions 2003, Bulgaria, p. 59.

[71] Council of Europe, *Digest of the Case Law* (n. 6 above), p. 97.

[72] Conclusions XIII-4, p. 37. The schemes must provide adequate benefits in relation to the cost of living and income levels in question.

[73] Conclusions 2003, Bulgaria, p. 65, and Conclusions 2003, Estonia p. 131. Also see Conclusions 2004–1, Romania, p. 316 and Conclusions XVII-1, Poland, p. 16.

[74] Samuel, *Fundamental Social Rights* (n. 34 above), p. 287.

[75] See, for example, Conclusions 2004–1, France, p. 232 and Conclusions 2004–2, Norway, p. 420 and Sweden, pp. 578–9, where the Committee simply referred to the relevant resolutions of the Committee of Ministers of the Council of Europe determining the conformity of these States with the Code, and found that therefore these States complied with Art. 12(2) of the Revised Charter.

[76] Conclusions XIII-4, p. 38.

[77] Conclusions 2004–1, Romania, p. 316.

in Article 12(3).[78] It requires a Contracting Party to continually strive to improve and extend the system in terms of coverage and the standard of protection. Harris and Darcy argue that the 'dynamic nature of this provision, allied with the Committee's determination to operate a genuine review of State action in relation to social security, will no doubt give States pause for thought in future when revising their social security arrangements'.[79] It is important to note, however, that Article 12(3) refers to Parties undertaking 'to endeavour to raise progressively the system of social security to a higher level'. This may mean that even if the situation has not in fact improved, as long as a Contracting Party is making efforts to improve the standard of protection that will be sufficient to be in compliance with Article 12(3). This is only likely, however, in the light of the Committee coming to a positive conclusion under Article 12(1).[80]

In the light of the increasing cost of national social security systems, almost all Contracting Parties have sought to review and amend their domestic schemes.[81] The Committee has made it clear that any modifications should not reduce the effective social protection of all members of society against social and economic risks and transform the social security system into a basic social assistance system.[82] The Committee has also been aware and careful to ensure that such reforms have not further marginalised the vulnerable.[83] It has stated that it will keep a close eye on reforms, as social security is vital in protecting the most vulnerable in society.[84] The Committee has particularly identified the disabled, the elderly and migrant workers as groups, which must not be further disadvantaged by reforms.[85]

Reforms of social security schemes which do not respect the dignity of those in receipt of benefits may fail to conform to Article 12(3). The benefits system in Denmark following reform was considered by the Committee to be very stringent and

'virtually compelling unemployed persons on pain of loss of benefits to accept a job regardless of the occupational field from the first day of unemployment'.[86] The Committee held that

> one of the aims of an unemployment benefit system is to offer unemployed persons adequate protection during at least an initial period of unemployment from the obligation to take up any job irrespective of occupational field, precisely with a view to giving them the opportunity of finding a job which is suitable taking into account their individual preferences, skills and qualifications.... [U]nemployed persons should be treated with due respect for their professional, social and family status and not as ordinary labourers, physically and mentally fit for any job.[87]

The Committee reserved its position as to whether the situation was in compliance with Article 12(3). Finland has found itself in a similar position.[88] Poland has argued that it has a right to introduce increasingly narrowly defined social security measures on the grounds that this will help to increase economic growth. The ECSR has not rejected this argument out of hand but has sought further information on the consequences of the measures so as to allow it to evaluate the appropriateness of the measures taken in relation to the objective pursued.[89]

As noted above, Article 12(4) deals with the obligations of Contracting Parties towards certain nonnationals.[90] Each party undertakes, either by concluding agreements with third States or by other means, to treat the nationals of all other Parties (and not simply those that have accepted Article 12(4)) equally with its own nationals in respect of social security rights, including the retention of benefits, whatever movements the protected person may undertake between the territories of the parties.[91] Under paragraph (b) Contracting Parties are required to enable migrants, who have been recognised as having attainments qualifying them

---

[78] This was first recognised by the Committee in Conclusions I, p. 62.
[79] Harris and Darcy, *The European Social Charter* (n. 12 above), p. 161.
[80] For an example of this approach, see Conclusions XVII-1, Belgium, p. 15.
[81] Conclusions XII-2, p. 29.
[82] Council of Europe, *Digest of the Case Law*, p. 62.
[83] See Conclusions XII-1, p. 33 and Conclusions XII-2, p. 29.
[84] Conclusions XII-2, p. 29.
[85] Conclusions XII-1, p. 34.

[86] Conclusions XVII-1, Denmark, p. 17.
[87] Ibid.
[88] Conclusions XVII-1, Finland, p. 13.
[89] Conclusions XVI-2, Poland, p. 542.
[90] See Conclusions XIII-4, p. 42 *et seq.* where the Committee gave a detailed account of the scope of the provision. The following draws heavily from these conclusions. See further Samuel, *Fundamental Social Rights* (n. 34 above), p. 295 *et seq.*
[91] Art. 12(4)(a).

for social security rights under the legal system of another Party to the Charter, to retain and exercise their rights.

Although Article 12(4) envisages that Contracting Parties will fulfil its requirements primarily through the conclusion of treaties with third States, the Committee has concluded that it is not necessary for such treaties to have been agreed for a Contracting Party to comply with this provision. If States have no migration exchanges, such agreements are not required. States may instead take unilateral action. The latter would clearly come within the scope of 'other means' referred to in Article 12(4). The ultimate issue under paragraph (a) of Article 12(4) is whether non-nationals are treated equally, including the avoidance of both direct and indirect discrimination, in terms of all social security rights that exist in that State, and that those rights are effectively protected. The Committee has recognised that as the Appendix to the Charter allows Contracting Parties to require non-nationals to complete a prescribed period of residence before they receive non-contributory benefits, in some circumstances some differentiation in treatment will be permissible. The Committee has, however, reserved the right to assess the proportionality of any residence requirement that may be imposed. In its assessment of the situation in Estonia in 2004, for example, the payment of old-age benefits required a length of residence of at least five years. The Committee considered that this was not unreasonable.[92] The Committee has generally had far less to say about Article 12(4)(b), although it has emphasised its importance for persons who change their country of residence as it allows them to meet the qualifying conditions imposed under the Contracting Parties' national legislation and not to sustain any financial loss. The Committee has concluded that those States, such as Austria, Italy, Luxembourg and Spain, which have ratified the European Convention on Social Security,[93] have taken sufficient steps to comply with Article 12(4)(b).

Almost all national social security schemes have been found by the Committee in some respect to be either directly or indirectly discriminatory against non-nationals.[94] In almost all cases involving EU Member States, their treatment of non-EU nationals has been one of the main reasons for this. They have, on the whole, however, treated other EU nationals equally, as is also required by EU law.

5.3   Right to Social and Medical Assistance

Article 13, which is a core right and identical in both versions of the Charter, ensures the right of social and medical assistance to persons without adequate resources. Article 13(1) requires that any person without access to adequate resources (including social security provision) be granted adequate assistance, and, in the case of sickness, the care necessitated by their condition. Article 13(2) obliges Contracting Parties to ensure that persons receiving such assistance do not, for that reason, suffer a diminution of their political or social rights. Harris and Darcy note that this paragraph reflects an attempt on the part of the drafters of the Charter to break away from an idea of assistance that was bound up with the dispensing of charity.[95] Article 13(3) requires that all persons receive such advice and personal help as required to prevent, remove or alleviate either personal or family needs. Article 13(4) extends the application of paragraphs (1) through (3) under certain circumstances to non-nationals.

The potential scope and importance of Article 13 are directly related to the Committee's definition of the term 'adequate resources'. The broader the approach to that term, the larger the section of the population for which Contracting Parties will have to provide social and medical assistance. The Committee in its jurisprudence has never generally defined the term. It requests Contracting States to inform it of the domestic procedures used to determine whether a person is deemed to have such resources, but that is not conclusive. In practice, the Committee further considers whether persons who lack sufficient resources to provide for the necessities of life as determined by reference to the prevailing cost and standard of living within the Contracting Party concerned are considered to be without 'adequate resources'

---

[92] Conclusions, 2004–1, Estonia, p. 133.
[93] ETS No. 78.
[94] See, for example, the Committee's Conclusions in 2004.

[95] Harris and Darcy, *The European Social Charter* (n. 12 above), p. 165, quoting Conclusions I, p. 64. See also Samuel, *Fundamental Social Rights* (n. 34 above), p. 305.

under the domestic procedure.[96] The Committee's long-standing practice in determining whether or not Contracting Parties provide 'adequate assistance' under Article 13(1) is to refer to the cost of living in the Contracting State in question and the minimum levels of subsistence which have been set in that State.[97] This is due to the vast disparity in levels of social assistance and the cost of living in Contracting States. The Committee assesses all types of assistance and not simply those of the monetary kind. To allow it to draw comparisons between Contracting States, the Committee asks States routinely to inform it of the amount of funds devoted to social assistance and the percentage of the social welfare budget that it represents.[98] It is on the basis of such considerations that the Committee makes its assessment.[99] The Committee has repeatedly stressed that Article 13(1) grants a legal right to assistance, that the awarding of such assistance must not be discretionary,[100] and that there must be a right of appeal to 'an independent body' if applications for assistance are refused.[101] Where Contracting Parties link social assistance to an individual's willingness to seek employment or to undergo vocational training, this is in conformity with the Charter provided that such conditions are reasonable. For example, any reduction or suspension of benefits will only be in conformity with Article 13 if the individual in need is not deprived of their sources of subsistence. Furthermore, the conditions imposed upon the receipt of benefits must contribute to finding a lasting solution to the individual's needs.[102]

The Committee has read the different paragraphs of Article 13 together and stressed that there must be an integrated approach to the alleviation of poverty, so as to allow individuals to regain their places as full members of society.[103] Article 13(1) is, in particular, closely linked to Article 13(3).[104] Article 13(3), as noted above, requires States to assist those threatened with deprivation. Compliance with both paragraphs (1) and (3) of Article 13, therefore, requires an effective social assistance system to be in place.[105] Article 13(3) is also connected to and to some extent overlaps with Article 14, which provides a right to benefit from social welfare services.[106]

Article 13(3), which is more generally worded than Article 13(1), has been interpreted by the Committee as applying to those actually or liable to be without adequate resources and not simply any person threatened with deprivation.[107] One of the essential objectives of Article 13(3) is to enable persons without adequate resources to be given

---

[96] See further Samuel, *Fundamental Social Rights* (n. 34 above), p. 308.

[97] Conclusions 2004–1, p. 71.

[98] Conclusions XIII-4, p. 56.

[99] See, for recent examples, the assessment of the situation in Bulgaria and Estonia where the Committee considered that the levels of social assistance were manifestly inadequate: Conclusions 2004–1, Bulgaria, p. 70 and ibid., Estonia, p. 179 respectively. The Committee, referring to Eurostat information that defines the poverty threshold as 50 percent of median income for the State concerned, decided that where the level of social assistance was significantly below that threshold, this would constitute non-compliance with Art. 13(1).

[100] See Samuel, *Fundamental Social Rights* (n. 34 above), p. 307 and Harris and Darcy, *The European Social Charter* (n. 12 above), p. 167. Greece, for example, has consistently been found not to be in compliance with Art. 13(1) for this reason. See Conclusions XIII-4, Greece, p. 178 and Conclusions XVII-1, Greece, p. 15. The situation in France has also been found not to be in conformity with Art. 13(1) because persons under the age of 25 are not entitled to social assistance as of right: Conclusions 2004, France, p. 204.

[101] For discussion of the Committee's assessment of this aspect, see Samuel, *Fundamental Social Rights* (n. 34 above), p. 308.

[102] Council of Europe, *Digest of the Case Law* (n. 6 above), p. 64.

[103] See Conclusions XIV-1, p. 52.

[104] Ibid.

[105] Samuel, *Fundamental Social Rights* (n. 34 above), p. 311.

[106] The reference in Art. 13(3) to 'family want' also means that there is an overlap with Art. 16, which deals with the right of the family to social, legal and economic protection. In terms of the relationship between Articles 13(3) and 14, the Committee has consistently held that Art. 14 is much broader in its application than Article 13(3). Article 14 applies to any actions taken by the State which aim to assist the development and welfare of individuals and groups and in adjusting to society. It applies to action taken with a view to assisting all persons. Article 13(3) is much narrower in applying only to those in need. Furthermore, Article 13(3) is concerned with a specific form of assistance, 'advice and personal help', whereas Article 14 is concerned with the provision or promotion of services addressing what can be described as social welfare issues. See Conclusions I, p. 64; Samuel, *Fundamental Social Rights* (n. 34 above), p. 321, and Harris and Darcy, *The European Social Charter* (n. 12 above), p. 177. The relationship between Article 13(3) and 16 is similar. Articles 14 and 16, among a number of other provisions, seek 'to give scope to the individual' in highly developed societies, rather than to remedy a need, which is the general objective of Article 13. See Conclusions I, p. 75, cited by Harris and Darcy, *The European Social Charter* (n. 12 above), p. 185.

[107] Conclusions 1, p. 64.

advice about the existence of various forms of assistance, which will help in alleviating their situation. The determination of whether a Contracting Party is in compliance with this aspect of the Charter should *prima facie* depend primarily upon the existence and extent of the advice available and not the nature and quality of the actual assistance itself, which is more a question under Article 13(1). Due to the Committee's integrated approach to the provisions in question, however, the extent of the assistance is also relevant under Article 13(3).[108] To assess whether the situation in Contracting Parties is in accordance with Article 13(3), the Committee requests that national reports regularly provide updated information on the relevant social welfare services and the way in which they are operated and organised; the number, duties and qualifications of the staff employed in the provision of these services; the funding provided for these services; and the methodology utilised to evaluate the adequacy of these services.[109]

Under Article 13(4), Contracting Parties undertake to apply paragraphs 1, 2 and 3 of Article 13 'on an equal footing with their nationals to nationals of other Contracting Parties lawfully within their territories, in accordance with their obligations under the European Convention on Social and Medical Assistance'. This is different from, and broader in ambit than, the general scope of the Charter ratione personae, as the Charter applies only to foreigners who are 'nationals of other Contracting Parties lawfully resident or working regularly' within the territory of the Contracting Party concerned.[110] The original approach of the Committee to Article 13(4) was to consider it in isolation from paragraphs (1) to (3) of Article 13. The Committee's examination of the latter was concerned solely with the situation of the nationals of the Contracting Party whose compliance with the Charter was being assessed, and did not consider the treatment of non-nationals at all: the latter were considered only under Article 13(4).[111] In recent years the Committee has revised its

approach.[112] It now applies the Appendix's criterion of the nationals of other Contracting Parties 'lawfully resident or working regularly' in another Contracting Party in its assessment of compliance with Article 13(1–3), such persons now being considered to be within the application of these provisions. Thus, a number of Contracting Parties, for example, Germany[113] and the United Kingdom,[114] have been considered not to be in compliance with the Charter because their respective national schemes draw distinctions between their nationals and the nationals of other Contracting Parties. In the majority of instances where the Committee has considered that a Contracting Party is not in compliance with Article 13(1) and (3), it has been due to the inequality of treatment of the nationals of other Contracting Parties.

Article 13(4) is considered under the Committee's revised approach to apply to those nationals of other Contracting Parties who are lawfully present but are not resident or regularly working in the Contracting Party in question. As the issue is one of lawful presence, the undertaking essentially extends to those who are temporarily present in the State in question. The Committee has stressed that in these circumstances the 'most appropriate form of assistance would be emergency aid to enable them to cope with an immediate state of need'.[115] Harris and Darcy have criticised the Committee's revised approach, which they consider difficult to reconcile with the actual text of Article 13(4), and they feel that the reference to the 1953 Convention on Social and Medical Assistance is harder to grasp as the personal and material scope of Article 13(4) and the 1953 Convention are different.[116] Article 1 of the 1953 Convention refers to nationals of other Contracting Parties 'who are lawfully present in any part of its territory' and this clearly also applies to resident non-nationals who have been removed, under the Committee's revised approach, from the ambit of Article 13(4). It is also the case that the 1953 Convention applies to all forms of assistance,

---

[108] Harris and Darcy, *The European Social Charter* (n. 12 above), p. 173.

[109] See Conclusion XIII-4, p. 59 and XIV-1, p. 88. In Conclusions 2004–1, p. 261, Norway conformed to Article 13(3) as it spent an amount equivalent to 0.5% of its GDP on such assistance.

[110] Para. 1, Appendix to both versions of the Charter.

[111] Harris and Darcy, *The European Social Charter* (n. 12 above), p. 174.

[112] The Committee changed its approach in Conclusions XIII-4, p. 60 *et seq.*

[113] Conclusions XVII-1, Germany, p. 17.

[114] Conclusions XVII-1, United Kingdom, p. 19.

[115] See Conclusions XIII-4, p. 62 and Conclusions XIV-1, p. 55.

[116] Harris and Darcy, *The European Social Charter*, pp. 175–176 (n. 12 above). For the Committee's assessment of the relationship between the two texts, see Conclusions XIV-1 p. 53 *et seq.*

whereas Article 13(4) is now considered to apply to emergency assistance only.[117] The Committee has concluded, under both its original and revised approaches, that a substantial number of Contracting Parties do not comply with Article 13(4).

In 2004, the Committee took its revised approach a substantial step further, when it held in Complaint No. 14/2003 that 'legislation or practice which denies entitlement to medical assistance to foreign nationals, within the territory of a State party, even if they are there illegally, is contrary to the Charter'.[118] The International Federation of Human Rights Leagues (FIDH), which submitted the complaint, argued that the French 2002 Finance (Amendment) Act[119] violated the right to medical assistance under Article 13 of the Revised Charter as it ended the exemption of illegal immigrants with very low incomes from all charges.[120] The French Government submitted that illegal immigrants did not fall within the scope of the definition of protected persons given in the Appendix to the Charter and were not, therefore, covered by any of the rights guaranteed by the Charter.[121] Although the situation in France was found not to be in violation of Article 13 of the Charter, the Committee disregarded the plain wording of the Charter to extend medical assistance to illegal immigrants by arguing that such assistance 'treads on a right of fundamental importance to the individual since it is connected to the right to life itself and goes to the very dignity of the human being'.[122] The Committee here adopted a teleological approach to Article 13 of the Charter.[123] In applying its finding to the facts in Complaint No. 14/2003, however, it is notable that the Committee did not go as far as its reasoning allowed. It is, for example, unclear whether the Committee's holding is limited to illegal immigrants from other Contracting Parties or applies to all illegal immigrants. Furthermore, the Committee's reference to the right to life as part of its reasoning may mean

that it will only take this approach when interpreting provisions which it considers go 'to the very dignity of the human being'.[124] In its resolution on the outcome of the Complaint, the Committee of Ministers simply took 'note' of the measures subsequently adopted by France to try to implement the ECSRs findings.[125]

5.4 Protection of Persons with Disabilities

Article 15, which is a non-core provision, deals with the rights of persons with disabilities. There are a number of substantive differences between the two versions of the Charter, with the Revised Charter being broader and more comprehensive in the obligations that it imposes upon States. Article 15(1) of the original Charter requires States Parties to take 'adequate measures' for the provision of vocational training for the physically or mentally disabled and their placement in employment. The scope of Article 15 in the original Charter is relatively narrow and is aimed at the social integration of disabled persons.[126] Article 15 of the Revised Charter is not only much broader but also takes a different approach, reflecting the evolution in mentality towards persons with physical and mental disabilities.[127] Nevertheless, Article 15

---

[117] Harris and Darcy, *The European Social Charter*, ibid. p. 176.
[118] Complaint No. 14/2003, *International Federation of Human Rights Leagues (FIDH) v. France*, Decision on the Merits, para. 32.
[119] 2002 Finance (Amendment) Act, No. 2002–1576 of 30 December 2002.
[120] Complaint No. 14/2003 (n. 118 above), para. 16.
[121] Ibid. para. 18.
[122] Ibid. para. 30. The situation in France was not, however, in conformity with Article 17 of the Charter, see para. 37.
[123] Cf. the discussion in section 4 above.

[124] Complaint No. 14/2003, Decision on the Merits, para. 30.
[125] Resolution ResChS(2005)6. The Resolution simply 'takes note of the circular DHOS/DSS/DGAS No. 141 of 16 March 2005 on the implementation of urgent care delivered to foreigners resident in France in an illegal manner and non beneficiaries of State Medical Assistance'.
[126] See Conclusions XIV-2, p. 63.
[127] Cf. the observations of the Committee in Complaint No. 13/2002 that Article 15 of the Revised Charter reflects and advances 'a profound shift in values in all European countries over the past decade away from treating [the disabled] as objects of pity and towards respecting them as equal citizens … The underlying vision of Article 15 is one of equal citizenship for persons with disabilities and, fittingly, the primary rights are those of "independence, social integration and participation in the life of the community."' See Complaint No. 13/2003, *Autism-Europe v. France*, Decision on the Merits, para. 48. For further discussion of this complaint, see Gerard Quinn, 'The European Social Charter and EU Anti-Discrimination Law in the Field of Disability: Two Gravitational Fields with One Common Purpose' in De Búrca and De Witte (eds.), *Social Rights in Europe* (n. 12 above), pp. 278–304, at pp. 293–299. Note also the observations of the Committee in the general introduction to its Conclusions on the Revised Charter in 2003 that Article 15 of the Revised Charter 'reflects and advances the change in disability policy that has occurred over the last decade or more away from welfare and segregation and towards inclusion and choice. In

of the Revised Charter can be considered to have absorbed and evolved all of the obligations in Article 15 of the original Charter as well as adding a number of others. This is reflected in the approach of the Committee to the undertakings in both versions of the Charter, as it routinely refers to its jurisprudence under the original Charter when defining the undertakings of Article 15 of the Revised Charter.[128]

Contracting Parties to the Revised Charter undertake to adopt measures to ensure that disabled persons can effectively exercise their right to independence, social integration and participation in the life of the community. To this end they must in particular adopt measures to provide such persons, in the framework of general schemes where possible, with guidance, education and vocational training. The approach is to try to integrate disabled persons, where possible, into existing general schemes and not to segregate them, as is the case under the original Charter. This difference of approach is also evident in Article 15(2) of both versions of the Charter, which the Committee has stated is inextricably linked to Article 15(1).[129] In the original version of the Charter, Contracting Parties agree to take adequate measures to place disabled persons in employment, such as specialised placing services or sheltered employment, and to encourage employers to admit them. In the Revised Charter Contracting Parties undertake to promote the access of disabled persons, where possible, to the ordinary working environment by encouraging employers to hire them and making appropriate adjustments to working conditions.[130] Where, due to the nature of the dis-

ability, this is not possible, the Contracting Party should arrange or create sheltered employment and in certain cases have recourse to specialised placement and support services.

The strong emphasis on the full social integration of disabled persons is most clearly evident in Article 15(3) of the Revised Charter, which has no equivalent in the original Charter. Contracting Parties undertake to promote such integration and participation in the life of the community by adopting measures, including technical aids, aiming to overcome barriers to communication and mobility, and enabling access to, among other things, transport and housing.

Neither version of the Charter provides a definition of disability. In the case of the original Charter the Committee's practice, in line with ILO Convention No. 159,[131] had been to refer to the criteria recognised by domestic law.[132] However, under both the original and Revised Charters the Committee has now changed its approach to one of asking Contracting Parties to provide information as to what steps, if any, have been taken to move away from a medical definition of disability and towards a more social definition, such as that endorsed by the WHO in its International Classification of Functioning.[133] It seems clear that the Committee is now adopting a definition, which, as Quinn states, places an emphasis on how people are treated rather than on their medical conditions as such.[134] This was also the approach of the Committee in Complaint No. 13/2003 where France was criticised for using a more restricted definition of autism than that adopted by the WHO.[135] In the light of this change in approach, it seems unlikely

---

light of this, the Committee emphasises the importance of the non-discrimination norm in the disability context and finds that this forms an integral part of Article 15'. See Conclusions 2003, p. 10.

[128] See, for example, Conclusions 2003-2, Sweden, p. 608; Conclusions 2003-2, Slovenia, p. 498; and Conclusions 2003-2, Romania, p. 398. In interpreting Article 15 of the original Charter, the Committee has more recently adopted a rights-based approach and, in the words of Gerard Quinn, a Committee member, began to 'reinvigorate' it with the 'newer rights-based approach to disability'. See Quinn, 'The European Social Charter and EU Anti-Discrimination' (n. 127 above), p. 286. This change in approach is borne out, for example, by Conclusions XVI-2, Vol. 1 (2003), p. 224.

[129] Under the original Charter see, among others, Conclusions XIV-2, p. 63.

[130] The *Explanatory Report* (n. 62 above), para. 64 notes that this corresponds to the approach adopted in Recommen-

dation No. R (92) 6 of the Committee of Ministers of the Council of Europe. Nevertheless, since the very first reporting cycle the Committee has emphasised that disabled persons should be fully integrated into society and be independent and that measures such as vocational training and education are a means to that end. See Conclusions I, p. 72, and more recently Conclusions XIV-2, p. 62.

[131] ILO Vocational Rehabilitation and Employment (Disabled Persons) Convention No. 159.

[132] Conclusions XIV-2, p. 64.

[133] See Conclusions XVI-2, Vol.1 (2003), p. 224 on the 1961 Charter and Conclusions 2003-1, France, p. 62; and Conclusions 2003-2, Romania, p. 398 on the Revised Charter.

[134] See Quinn, 'The European Social Charter and EU Anti-Discrimination Law' (n. 127 above), at p. 287.

[135] Complaint No. 13/2003, *Autism-Europe v. France*, Decision on the Merits, paras. 54 and 55.

that the Committee will in future defer to the definition of disability found in domestic laws.

In assessing compliance with Article 15(1) of the Revised Charter, the Committee has made it clear that the explicit reference to 'education' brings important aspects of the right to education for children with disabilities within the remit of that sub-paragraph. Under the original Charter, the Committee assesses general education schemes to test them for their level of inclusiveness and has held that States are required to make tangible progress towards the development of inclusive education systems.[136] Under the Revised Charter the Committee considers that the existence of non-discrimination legislation (in relation to disability in the field of education) is essential.[137] The Committee considers that such legislation should, as a minimum, require a compelling justification for special or segregated educational systems and confer an effective remedy on those who are found to have been unlawfully excluded or segregated or otherwise denied an effective right to education.[138]

In its assessment of the right to an effective education in the mainstream which does not discriminate against the disabled, the Committee has repeatedly asked Contracting Parties for information on: whether and how the normal curriculum has been adjusted to take account of disability; whether and how individualised educational plans are crafted for students with disabilities; whether and how resources follow the child (including support staff and other technical assistance) to enable such plans to be implemented; whether and how testing or examining modalities are adjusted to take account of disability; and whether the qualifications that are obtained are the same for all or whether different qualifications ensue.[139]

Under Article 15(2) of the original Charter, the Committee has decided that non-discrimination

legislation is required in order to create genuine equality of opportunity in the labour market. It has held that this also applies a fortiori to Article 15(2) of the Revised Charter.[140] The Committee has noted that there are a number of different steps Contracting Parties can adopt to integrate those with disabilities into the ordinary labour market. These include: different forms of wage subsidies; grants for adapting the workplace and for workplace assistive devices; grants towards the cost of a work assistant; and business assistance towards setting up a business.[141]

The manner in which paragraphs (1) and (2) of Article 15 of the Revised Charter have been interpreted illustrates, as noted above, that they are a natural evolution of the corresponding provisions in the original Charter and the manner in which they have been interpreted by the Committee. Article 15(3) of the Revised Charter, however, provides the Committee with its greatest potential to make an impact on Contracting Parties with regard to the rights of persons with disabilities. This provision describes the positive action Contracting Parties are obliged to implement in order to achieve the goals of social integration and participation of disabled persons, focusing on the measures needed to achieve these goals in fields such as housing and transport. Such undertakings are important in helping disabled persons exercise their right to an independent existence.[142] The positive measures which Contracting Parties are obliged to adopt must be part of a coherent policy for persons with disabilities.[143] The Committee has also made clear that such measures should be programmed to complement each other on a clear legislative basis.[144]

The Committee has stressed that Article 15(3) requires that persons with disabilities and their representative organisations should be consulted in the design, and ongoing review, of positive action measures and that an appropriate forum should exist to enable this to happen.[145] Although neither Article 15(3) nor the Explanatory Report

---

[136] Conclusions XIV-2, p. 64.

[137] This was one of the reasons for Romania not being in compliance with Article 15(1) of the Revised Charter: Conclusions 2003–2, Romania, p. 402. The Committee deferred its conclusions on Sweden in this regard, despite the non-existence of such legislation, as an ombudsman scheme, pending further information, might be considered to have effectively secured the rights in question: Conclusions 2003–2, Sweden, p. 610.

[138] Conclusions 2003–2, Sweden, p. 608.

[139] See, for example, ibid. p. 609.

[140] Ibid. p. 610.

[141] Ibid. p. 611.

[142] This is confirmed at para. 64 of the *Explanatory Report* (n. 62 above).

[143] Ibid. The Committee has confirmed this: see, for example, Conclusions 2003–2, Sweden, p. 612 *et seq.*

[144] Ibid.

[145] Ibid.

refers to such an undertaking, the Committee would seem to consider that this will more effectively address the actual needs and concerns of disabled persons as well as ensuring that they are participating in society and hence being further integrated into it. The Committee has also stated that the provision of such positive measures must be pursued through a mix of public provision and by the regulation of private actors, for example those in the housing market, and that there must be comprehensive non-discrimination legislation covering both the public and the private spheres.[146]

5.5 Right to Protection against Poverty and Social Exclusion

Article 30 of the Revised Charter, which is a non-core right, provides protection against poverty and social exclusion. There is no equivalent provision in the original Charter. By introducing such a provision into the Revised Charter, it is clear that the Member States of the Council of Europe considered that living in a situation of poverty and social exclusion violates human dignity.[147] Under Article 30, Contracting Parties undertake to 'take measures within the framework of an overall and coordinated approach to promote the effective access of persons who live or risk living in a situation of social exclusion or poverty, as well as their families, to, in particular, employment, housing, training, education, culture and social and medical assistance'. Parties are further obliged to 'review these measures with a view to their adaptation if necessary'. This review is of a general character, the organisation of which is within the discretion of each Party.[148]

Article 30 overlaps with a number of other provisions in the Charter, for example Articles 13 (on social assistance, discussed above) and 31 (the right to housing, discussed below). The purpose of Article 30 is not to repeat the juridical aspects of the protection covered by these other Articles.[149] The Article explicitly aims to relieve poverty and social exclusion by obliging States to have a comprehensive approach towards them. In the

Explanatory Report, 'poverty' is broadly defined and is seen to cover persons who find themselves in situations ranging from severe poverty, which has been ongoing for a number of generations, to those who are temporarily exposed to the risk of it.[150] The term 'social exclusion' is also broadly defined and refers to persons 'who find themselves in a position of extreme poverty through an accumulation of disadvantages, who suffer from degrading situations or events or from exclusion, whose rights to benefit may have expired a long time ago or for reasons of concurring circumstances'.[151] Social exclusion is also seen to apply to those who – without being poor – either are, or are at risk of being, 'denied access to certain rights or services as a result of long periods of illness, the breakdown of their families, violence, release from prison or marginal behaviour as a result for example of alcoholism or drug addiction'.[152] Unlike Article 13, Article 30 does not refer to those without adequate resources. This is presumably because those who come within the scope of this provision will by definition need assistance and be without adequate resources. Nor does Article 30 expressly guarantee a minimum level of resources. In this case, however, the Explanatory Report makes clear that such guarantees are provided for by Article 13 of the Charter and are covered by the reference in Article 30 to 'effective access to … social assistance'.[153]

The Committee does not appear (yet) to have explicitly endorsed the views expressed in the Explanatory Report as to the scope of Article 30. In its first assessment of this provision in 2003, it stated that an overall and coordinated approach against poverty and social exclusion required Contracting Parties to have an analytical framework; a set of priorities and corresponding measures to prevent and remove obstacles of access to social rights; and monitoring mechanisms involving all relevant actors, including civil society and persons affected by poverty and exclusion.[154] States must link and integrate policies in a consistent manner and must not simply adopt a purely sectoral or target group approach.[155] The policies in question

---

[146] Ibid. p. 614.
[147] Conclusions 2003–1, France p. 215.
[148] *Explanatory Report* (n. 62 above), para. 117.
[149] Ibid. para. 113.

[150] Ibid. para. 114.
[151] Ibid.
[152] Ibid.
[153] Ibid. para. 115.
[154] Conclusions, 2003–1, France, p. 214.
[155] Ibid.

must distinguish between poverty and social exclusion and address the specific problems raised by the latter.[156] The Committee has further stated that assessing whether the situation in a Contracting Party is in compliance with the Charter will depend on whether the measures that have been adopted are adequate in their quality and quantity, bearing in mind the nature and extent of poverty and social exclusion in the country concerned.[157] In this respect, the Committee has to date systematically reviewed the definitions and measuring methodologies applied at the national level and has asked States to provide further information on the methods applied to measure social exclusion.[158]

Article 30 is, as noted above, related to Article 31. The Committee considers that the provision of adequate housing is critical in fighting poverty.[159] By raising this issue and making Contracting Parties aware of it, the Committee is seeking to ensure that they adopt a coordinated approach to poverty reduction that is fully integrated with other obligations and policies. The Committee has asked Italy, for example, for further information on the measures it has taken to ensure an appropriate location of (social) housing so as to avoid 'ghettoising' poverty and social exclusion.[160]

5.6 Right to Housing

There are three provisions of the European Social Charter that deal with housing rights.[161] The broadest and most comprehensive provision is Article 31 of the Revised Charter which contains three distinct obligations: to promote access to housing of an adequate standard; to prevent and reduce homelessness with a view to its gradual elimination; and to make the price of housing accessible to those without adequate resources. Article 23 of the Revised Charter, which deals with the rights of elderly persons to social protection, requires States to provide such persons either with housing suited to their needs or adequate support

to adapt their housing.[162] The least specific of the three provisions is Article 16 of the original and Revised Charters, which are substantively identical. This provision obliges States to promote the right of the family, a fundamental unit of society, to social, legal and economic protection by such means as the provision of family housing.[163] Article 16 is a core right, Articles 23 and 31 non-core rights. In Complaint No. 15/2003, *European Roma Rights Center v. Greece*,[164] it was Article 16 of the original Charter, the least specific of the various 'housing' provisions, which was the basis for the submitted complaint. The European Roma Rights Center argued that Greece had failed to apply in a satisfactory manner Article 16 of the Charter, in the light of the latter's Preamble,[165] on the grounds that the Roma were denied an effective right to housing, in that legislation discriminated against the Roma in housing matters, and that in practice there was widespread discrimination against them and they were often the subject of forced evictions.[166] The Committee considered that the substance of the complaint related to the right of Roma to housing in three respects: the insufficient number of permanent dwellings of an acceptable quality to meet the needs of the settled Roma; the insufficient number of stopping places for Roma who choose to follow an itinerant lifestyle or who are forced to do so; and the systematic eviction of Roma from sites or dwellings unlawfully occupied by them.[167] The Committee considered the scope of Article 16 and emphasised that one of the

---

[156] Ibid., p. 217.
[157] Ibid., p. 214.
[158] Conclusions 2003–1, France, pp. 214 and 216.
[159] Conclusions 2003–1, France, p. 218 and ibid., Italy, p. 339.
[160] Conclusions 2003–1, Italy, p. 339.
[161] There are also a number of other provisions which deal with housing in the context of other rights, such as those of migrant workers.

[162] This obligation is substantively identical to that in Article 4 of the Additional Protocol of 1988.
[163] Article 16 of the 1961 and Revised Charter states: 'With a view to ensuring the necessary conditions for the full development of the family, which is a fundamental unit of society, the Contracting Parties undertake to promote the economic, legal and social protection of family life by such means as social and family benefits, fiscal arrangements, provision of family housing, benefits for the newly married, and other appropriate means'.
[164] Complaint No. 15/2003, *European Roma Rights Center v. Greece*, Decision on the Merits, 8 December 2004.
[165] The relevant paragraph of the Preamble states that, 'the enjoyment of social rights should be secured without discrimination on grounds of race, colour, sex, religion, political opinion, national extraction or social origin'. Under the Revised Charter, recourse could have also been had to Art. E. It has been the ECSR's standard practice to read the non-discrimination clause of the Preamble into Article 16: see for example, Conclusions XII I-2, p. 27.
[166] Complaint No. 15/2003, *European Roma Rights Center v. Greece*, para. 11.
[167] Ibid., para. 17.

underlying purposes of the social rights protected by the Charter was to express solidarity and promote social inclusion.[168] With regard specifically to Article 16 and the right to housing that it contains, the Committee, after noting that this right permitted the exercise of many other civil, political, economic and social rights, recalled that in order to satisfy their obligations under it, States had to promote the provision of an adequate supply of housing for families, take their needs into account in housing policies, and ensure that existing housing was of an adequate standard and included essential services, such as heating and electricity.[169] Referring to the Article 8 jurisprudence of the European Court of Human Rights in *Connors v. United Kingdom*[170] and *Buckley v. United Kingdom*[171], the Committee considered that Article 16 also required that itinerant Roma be provided with adequate stopping places.[172] In the light of these observations, the Committee found Greece to be violating Article 16 in the three different respects with which it considered the complaint was essentially concerned.

Article 16 was also considered by the Committee in Complaint No. 31/2005, *European Roma Rights Center v. Bulgaria*.[173] The alleged violation in this complaint was of Article 16 taken together with Article E of the Revised Charter. The issue of discrimination against Roma in the allocation of adequate housing with proper amenities was central to the complaint. The Committee in its assessment stressed that equal treatment required measures appropriate to the 'Roma's particular circumstances to safeguard their right to housing to prevent them as a vulnerable group from becoming homeless'.[174] The Committee also stressed that Articles 16 and E, read in conjunction, further developed a positive obligation with respect to access to social housing and thus a failure to take into 'consideration the different situation of Roma

or to introduce measures specifically aimed at improving their housing conditions, including the possibility for an effective access to social housing' would lead to a violation of Bulgaria's obligations.[175] The Committee found that the absence of positive measures, which did not take into account the relevant differences of the Roma and accordingly prevented them from integrating into mainstream society, meant that the situation in Bulgaria was in violation of Article 16 taken together with Article E.[176] The other substantive issue raised in this complaint concerned a lack of legal security of tenure and the forced eviction of Roma families from sites or dwellings that they had unlawfully occupied. Reiterating its finding in Complaint No. 15/2003, *European Roma Rights Center v. Greece*, the ECSR stressed that while 'illegal occupation of a site or dwelling may justify the eviction of the illegal occupants ... the criteria of illegal occupation must not be unduly wide, the eviction should take place in accordance with the applicable rules of procedure and these should be sufficiently protective of the rights of the persons concerned'.[177] The Committee considered that Roma families are disproportionately affected by the legislation limiting the possibility of legalising illegal dwellings and the evictions carried out did not satisfy the conditions required by the Charter, in particular that of ensuring that evicted persons are not rendered homeless. Consequently the situation in this respect was also in violation of Article 16 read in combination with Article E.[178]

The use of Article 16 to protect Roma housing rights in these collective complaints highlights that the ECSR has, notwithstanding the almost peripheral nature of the housing obligation in this provision, relied upon it to impose obligations upon States parties.[179] The decisions and reasoning in Complaint Nos. 15/2003 and 31/2005 further consolidated and developed the Committee's

---

[168] Ibid. para. 19.
[169] Ibid. para. 24.
[170] *Connors v. United Kingdom*, (2005) 40 E.H.R.R. 9.
[171] *Buckley v. United Kingdom* (1997) 23 E.H.R.R. 101.
[172] Complaint No. 15/2003, *European Roma Rights Center v. Greece*, para. 25.
[173] Complaint No. 31/2005, *European Roma Rights Center v. Bulgaria*, Decision on the Merits, 18 October 2006.
[174] Ibid. para. 41. The Committee was here quoting from its decision in Complaint No. 27/2004, *European Roma Rights Center v. Italy*, Decision on the Merits, 7 December 2005, para. 21, which concerned Article 31. See further n. 207 below and accompanying text.

[175] Complaint No. 31/2005, *European Roma Rights Center v. Bulgaria*, para. 41. The Committee again quoted from its decision in Complaint No. 27/2004, *European Roma Rights Center v. Italy*, para. 46.
[176] Complaint No. 31/2005, *European Roma Rights Center v. Bulgaria*, para. 43.
[177] Ibid. para. 51.
[178] Ibid. para. 57.
[179] It should also be noted that in Complaint No. 31/2005, paras. 13–17, the Committee rejected an argument by Bulgaria that complaints about housing could only be brought under Article 31 and not under Article 16.

established approach to issues that it had established under the reporting procedure.[180]

In comparison to Article 16 of the Charter, Article 31 of the Revised Charter provides a clearer basis for imposing housing right obligations upon the States parties, which have accepted it. Harris and Darcy have noted that due to the reticence among States in agreeing to a right to housing, Article 31 is worded in a rather general way.[181] This provision nevertheless expressly addresses a number of important issues in relation to housing rights which Article 16 does not. Furthermore, Article E of the Revised Charter contains an equality clause, requiring States to ensure that the rights they have accepted are secured without discrimination on any of the listed grounds.[182] In 2003, the Committee, in assessing France's compliance with Article 31, referred to Article E and stated unequivocally that the equal treatment obligation under that provision must be assured to different groups of 'vulnerable persons'.[183] Low-income persons; unemployed persons; single parent households; young persons; persons with physical and mental disabilities or health problems; and persons internally displaced due to wars or natural disasters were all considered by the Committee to be vulnerable persons. They must not, therefore, be discriminated against in the provision of housing, even though Article E refers only to non-discrimination on standard grounds such as race, colour, sex, religion, language and political or other opinion.[184] The Committee's reference to vulnerable groups in the context of Articles E and 31 of the Revised Charter illustrates the progres-

sive manner in which it has already been prepared to interpret aspects of the right to housing.

The obligations under Article 31 are, as noted above, threefold. Under Article 31(1), States must promote access 'to housing of an adequate standard'. The Explanatory Report to the Revised Charter states that this refers to housing 'of an acceptable standard with regard to health requirements' and that it is for the relevant national authorities of each State to determine what the appropriate standards are.[185] However, the Committee, in its first analysis of Article 31, made clear that adequate housing means 'a dwelling which is structurally secure, safe from a sanitary and health point of view and not overcrowded'.[186] It elaborated by stating that 'a dwelling is safe from a sanitary and health point of view if it possesses all basic amenities, such as water, heating, waste disposal; sanitation facilities; electricity; etc'.[187] This implies that rights of access to certain utilities such as water, sewerage, and electricity for lighting and heating are included in the obligation and, at the very least, should be provided by the State to those who cannot afford them. The Committee has so far expressly stated in this respect that public authorities have an obligation 'to guard against the interruption of essential services such as water, electricity and telephone',[188] which entails a less onerous obligation than that just suggested. Overcrowding is a relative concept and refers to the size of a dwelling in the light of the number of persons living there.[189] The Committee has not yet determined minimum specifications in this regard but it may well do so in the future.

The obligations under Article 31(1) are applicable to both rented and owner-occupied housing.[190] Furthermore, these obligations apply not only to new constructions but are also to be gradually applied when existing housing stock is being renovated.[191] The manner in which the Committee applies the latter obligation will be of the utmost importance. Under domestic legislation it is usually

---

[180] For discussion of the approach of the Committee to housing rights under Article 16, see Harris and Darcy, *The European Social Charter* (n. 12 above), pp. 190–192.

[181] Ibid. p. 282.

[182] See further n. 11 above and accompanying text. As noted above, where, as is the case with Bulgaria, a State is party to the Revised Charter but has not accepted Article 31, then the ECSR will read Article 16 in conjunction with Article E of the Charter.

[183] Conclusions 2003–1, France, p. 221.

[184] Ibid. Article E of the Revised Charter has no counterpart in the original Charter. The Committee has, however, read an obligation not to discriminate into some of the substantive rights in the original Charter, for example, Article 1(2) (the right of a worker to earn his living in an occupation freely entered upon) and Article 16. See further on this issue Harris and Darcy, *The European Social Charter* (n.12 above), p. 47 and further n. 174 above and n. 207 below and accompanying text.

[185] *Explanatory Report* (n. 62 above), paras. 118–119.

[186] Conclusions 2003–1, France, p. 221. The Committee has repeated each of its general understandings of Article 31 each time that it has assessed it.

[187] Ibid.

[188] Ibid. p. 224.

[189] Ibid. p. 221.

[190] Ibid.

[191] Ibid.

the case that each new building must comply with current building regulations as specified in that State. To be in compliance with Article 31, States will have to ensure that these domestic regulations comply with the standards set by the Committee in terms of, for example, sanitation and structural safety. Article 31(1) is potentially very dynamic and could have a substantial impact in its application to existing housing stock (which typically has greater problems in terms of sanitation and structural safety[192]), as opposed to new stock. The Committee has stated that Article 31(1) will apply 'gradually, in the case of renovation' to existing housing stock.[193] If the Committee leaves discretion to States as to when existing residences are to be renovated, the impact of the measure will be less than if the Committee starts to define certain minimum standards and a timeframe for existing residences. If the Committee were to do this and adopt a dynamic approach, the impact of the provision would be significant. However, the manner in which the Committee has so far interpreted this obligation suggests that it probably will not adopt such an approach.[194]

The Committee has specified that States must define in law the notion of 'adequate housing' and that there must be some system of supervision by public authorities to ensure compliance with the standards defined.[195] Such definitions are essential in order to allow the Committee to evaluate State compliance with Article 31(1). In its conclusions on France's compliance in 2003, for example, the Committee sought to determine whether there was an adequate definition of 'decent housing' in French legislation which, despite some shortcomings, there was.[196]

Article 31(2) imposes an obligation upon States to reduce homelessness. The Committee has defined homeless persons as those individuals who do not legally have at their disposal 'a dwelling or other forms of adequate shelter'.[197] The supply of a shelter to such individuals, even if adequate, is not sufficient to comply with the obligation if it is tem-

porary.[198] Furthermore, States are obliged to provide homeless persons with adequate housing, if they so request it, within a reasonable period of time.[199] The obligation, which is clearly progressive, entails both reactive and preventative measures.[200] As the Committee noted in its assessment of France, reducing homelessness requires 'the introduction of measures, such as provision of immediate shelter and care for the homeless and measures to help such people overcome their difficulties and prevent a return to homelessness'.[201] The Committee's detailed assessment of homelessness in Contracting States has, as predicted by Harris and Darcy, made it clear that the Committee will be analysing the progress made by States in this regard from cycle to cycle with a view to seeing whether homelessness has been reduced and what measures have been taken to this end.[202] Statistics providing details about the demand for social housing, the average waiting-time for being allocated such housing, and the measures adopted to reduce the waiting-time for disadvantaged households, for example, will all be important in this regard.

The Committee has also placed emphasis upon vulnerable persons and prevention of homelessness. As it has noted, States are required to implement a housing policy 'for all disadvantaged groups of people to ensure access to social housing and housing allowances'. They are also required to put in place procedures 'to limit the risk of evictions and to ensure that when these do take place, they are carried out under conditions which respect the dignity of the persons concerned'.[203]

Article 31(3), as noted above, requires States to make the price of housing accessible to those without adequate resources. The Committee considers housing to be affordable when the household 'can afford to pay the initial costs (deposit, advance rent), the current rent and/or other costs (utility, maintenance and management charges) on a long-term basis and still be able to maintain a minimum standard of living, as defined by the society

---

[192] See, for example, the Committee's analysis of the situation in France, Conclusions 2003–1, France, p. 221 *et seq.*
[193] Conclusions 2003–1, France, p. 221.
[194] Ibid. pp. 223–4.
[195] Ibid. pp. 221–224.
[196] Ibid. pp. 222–223.
[197] Ibid. p. 225.

[198] Ibid.
[199] Ibid.
[200] Ibid.
[201] Ibid. p. 226.
[202] Harris and Darcy, *The European Social Charter* (n. 12 above), p. 283. Conclusions 2003–1, France, pp. 225–232 and Conclusions 2003–2, Sweden, pp. 653–655.
[203] Conclusions 2003–1, France, pp. 228–229.

in which the household is located'.[204] States parties are thus obliged to ensure that there is an adequate supply of affordable housing to those who lack 'adequate resources'. The Explanatory Report makes clear that the term 'adequate resources' is to be defined by reference to the Committee's jurisprudence under Article 13 of the Charter.[205] The Committee has stated in this regard that States are required to increase the supply of social housing and to make it financially accessible by engaging in the construction of housing, in particular social housing, and to introduce housing benefits for low-income and disadvantaged sectors of the population.[206]

Article 31 has so far been considered by the Committee in one complaint, Complaint No. 27/2004, *European Roma Rights Center v. Italy* although two others are pending.[207] In this complaint against Italy a number of the allegations were similar to those raised in Complaint No. 15/2003, *European Roma Rights Center v. Greece,* although in the complaint against Greece the alleged violations were of Article 16 of the Charter, not Article 31. The Committee considered that the substance of the complaint against Italy related to the right of Roma to housing in three respects: the insufficient capacity of and inadequate living conditions in camping sites for Roma who choose to follow an itinerant life style or who are forced to do so;[208] the systematic eviction of Roma from sites or dwellings unlawfully occupied by them; and the lack of permanent dwellings of an acceptable quality to meet the needs of the settled Roma. The latter two issues are in substance identical to the allegations which the European Roma Rights Center raised in Complaint No. 15/2003 against Greece. In Complaint 27/2004 against Italy, however, the European Roma Rights Center also relied upon Article E read in conjunction with Article 31. The Committee unanimously found that Italy had failed to comply

with its obligations and was in violation in all three respects. The Committee in its decision emphasised the notion of equal treatment and the State's positive obligations. In particular, with regard to the allegation concerning the lack of permanent dwellings, the Committee placed the burden of proof on the State to show how its commitment to the principle of equal treatment for Roma as regards their access to social housing was effective in practice, or that the criteria regulating access to social housing were non-discriminatory.[209] This is noteworthy as it will make it more difficult for States to rebut allegations of discriminatory treatment with regard to housing in future complaints.

As with Article 16 of the Charter, the Committee has adopted a broad and progressive approach to Article 31. Despite the fact that the right to housing in Article 31 is worded in a rather general way the Committee has through both the reporting and complaints procedure given it real meaning. It is to be hoped that this is an approach it will persevere with.

6. CONCLUSIONS

For reasons of space, it has been possible to examine in this chapter only a small selection of the rights found in the European Social Charter (seven out of thirty-one). Although quite a number of the rights in the Charter are drafted in fairly precise and concrete language (particularly those concerned with employment rights), most of the rights examined in this chapter are couched in broad and relatively imprecise terms. In its jurisprudence, the Committee has made notable efforts to identify, concretise and clarify the scope of the obligations of the Contracting Parties in relation to these rights. One's initial reaction is that the Committee's efforts are warmly to be welcomed since they clearly promote the interests of the intended beneficiaries of these rights. However, this response must be tempered by two reservations. The first is that as the Committee has read more, and more concretely, into what is required of Contracting Parties in order to fulfil their obligations to realise the rights concerned, so the greater is the amount of information the Committee requires the parties

---

[204] Ibid., p. 232.
[205] *Explanatory Report* (n. 62 above), para. 118. See further the discussion in section 5.3 above.
[206] Conclusions 2003–1, France, pp. 232–233.
[207] Complaint No. 39/2006, *European Federation of National Organisations Working with the Homeless (FEANTSA)* v. *France,* declared admissible 19 March 2007 is also concerned with Article 31. Complaint No. 33/2006, *International Movement ATD Fourth World* v. *France,* declared admissible 12 June 2006, alleges violations of Articles 16, 30, 31 and E of the Revised Social Charter.
[208] In Complaint No. 15/2003, this issue was not raised.

[209] Complaint No. 27/2004, *European Roma Rights Center* v. *Italy,* para. 46.

to provide in order for it to be able to make a judgment about their compliance with their obligations, and the more difficult it becomes for the Committee to make a definitive judgment about such compliance, as is evident from the more recent conclusions of the Committee on national reports. In contrast, the collective complaints system requires the Committee not only to apply its interpretation of the Charter to a set of specific circumstances, but also to reach a definite conclusion about how the Charter applies to those circumstances. The system may thus act as a counter-balance to the risk of failure by the Committee to reach conclusions in the reporting procedure. However, the ability of the system to fulfil this function depends on the degree to which it is used. There are, regrettably, some significant limitations on its possible use, in particular the relatively small number of parties to the Charter that have accepted the system and the fact that only one of those parties at present permits national organisations concerned with the social rights with which this chapter deals to make complaints.

The second reservation that must be expressed is that the Committee's efforts risk becoming simply an academic exercise unless they are followed up by the Committee of Ministers (the only body competent to do so) addressing appropriate recommendations to States found by the Committee to be in non-compliance. As was pointed out in the earlier part of this chapter, the Committee of Ministers has in general been reluctant to address recommendations to non-complying States in both the reporting and collective complaints procedures. In relation to the rights examined in this chapter, although the Committee has found numerous cases of non-compliance in the reporting procedure (as indicated in Section 5

above), the Committee of Ministers has made only a limited number of recommendations to Contracting Parties, in particular to Greece and Italy in respect of Article 13 and to Turkey in respect of Article 11.[210] In the case of the two collective complaints where the Committee found non-compliance in relation to the rights examined in this chapter, the Committee of Ministers failed to endorse these findings: in the first case (concerning Article 15 and the treatment of the autistic in France) it simply took note of an undertaking by France to bring the situation into conformity with the Charter and the measures being taken in this respect,[211] while in the second (concerning Article 16 and the housing rights of the Roma in Greece) it noted various steps being taken by Greece concerning housing and the social integration of Greek Roma.[212] The end result is that in the absence of any coercive mechanism in the Charter and the reluctance of the Committee of Ministers to apply peer political pressure to non-complying States, the intended beneficiaries of the rights surveyed here are largely dependent for the realisation of those rights on the degree to which States are prepared to respond positively to findings by the Committee that they are not in compliance with the Charter. Although there are a number of instances of States amending their legislation and practice in order to comply with findings of the Committee (as pointed out above), there are, regrettably, also examples of States failing to do so.

---

[210] See Recommendations RecChS (93)1, 94(4) and (2002)1, respectively, texts in Council of Europe, *European Social Charter: Collected Texts*, 4th ed. (Strasbourg: Council of Europe, 2003), pp. 421, 438 and 475.

[211] See Resolution ResChS(2004)1, Collective Complaint No. 13/2002, *Autism-Europe v. France*.

[212] See Resolution ResChS(2005)11, Collective Complaint No. 15/2003, *European Roma Rights Centre v. Greece*.

22

European Court of Justice

Creative Responses in Uncharted Territory

Philippa Watson*

1. INTRODUCTION[1]

Although not always readily admitted, the reality is that the European Community ('EC'),[2] is primarily concerned with economic rights. It is this body of rights that is given the greatest degree of protection within the Community legal order. Social rights depend, for the most part, on either the exercise of an economic activity, which brings

entitlement to those rights, or are an integral part of that economic activity, in the sense that they regulate the conditions under which that economic activity may be exercised. It is rare to find purely social rights – that is, rights that are unconnected to any economic activity on the part of the beneficiary – which are justiciable under EC law. The most notable exception to this general rule is the directive on racial equality which grants the right to equal treatment in many spheres of life unconnected with, and not contingent upon, the exercise of an economic activity, such as housing, social protection, health care and education.[3] Moreover, the European Court of Justice ('ECJ') has confirmed in a number of recent cases that the European citizen who moves within the Community, but who is not necessarily economically active, may enjoy some entitlement to social rights which was previously believed to be confined to those who were economically active or who were dependants of economically active persons. This development is discussed more fully below at Section 5.5.

2. SOCIO-ECONOMIC RIGHTS IN EUROPEAN ECONOMIC LAW: SOURCES

Socio-economic rights within European Community law are derived from sources operating at a different level within the Community legal order.

The primary source of law and policy is the EC Treaty itself. In addition, and complementary to, the provisions of the Treaty, are the general principles of law which form an essential part of the constitutional framework of the Community. Subordinate to, and dependent upon these, is secondary

---

* Barrister, Essex Court Chambers; Visiting Professor City Law School, London.

[1] This subject has been previously addressed by the author some twelve years ago: 'The Role of the European Court of Justice in the Development of Community Labour Law', in K. Ewing, C. Gearty and B. Hepple (eds.), *Human Rights and Labour Law: Essays for Paul O'Higgins* (London: Mansell, 1994). Readers may like to compare this paper with the earlier one if only to note the extent to which the corpus of social economic rights within the Community legal order has been expanded in the intervening years and how much the European Court of Justice has contributed to that expansion. See also T. Tridimas, 'The Court of Justice and Judicial Activism', *European Law Review*, Vol. 21 (1996), pp. 199–210; D. Keeling, 'In praise of Judicial Activism. But what does it mean? And has the European Court of Justice ever practised it?', *Scritti in onore di Giuseppe Federico Mancini*, Vol. II (Milano: Diritto dell'Unione Europea, 1998), pp. 505–536; P. Davies, 'The European Court of Justice, National Courts and the Member States', in P. Davies *et al.*, (eds.), *European Community Labour Law: Principle and Perspectives. Liber Amicorum Lord Wedderburn of Charlton* (Oxford: Clarendon Press, 1996), pp. 95–138; V. Hatzopoulos, 'A (more) Social Europe: A Political Crossroad or a Legal One Way? Dialogues between Luxembourg and Lisbon', *Common Market Law Review*, Vol. 42 (2005), pp. 1599–1635; S. Simitis, 'Dismantling or Strengthening Labour Law: The Case of the European Court of Justice', *European Law Journal*, Vol. 2 (1996), pp. 156–176.

[2] The European Economic Community was re-named the European Community by the Maastricht Treaty. That same treaty also established the European Union, which has a wider competence than the Community. It created two pillars of activity to be pursued by the Union but not the European Community, namely Justice and Home Affairs and Common Foreign and Security policy.

[3] Directive 2000/43 OJ [2000] L180/22.

legislation and more indirectly – but not to be underestimated – soft law. To these sources must be added the case law of the ECJ. This body of jurisprudence should not strictly speaking be regarded as a source of rights in itself since the task of the Court as set out in Article 220 EC is to 'ensure that in the interpretation and application of this Treaty the law is observed'. But given the active role of the Court in the development of socio-economic rights, which at times assumes a role beyond the mere articulation of instruments granting those rights, it can be said that case law is a source of rights in itself since without it the corpus of socio-economic rights would be quite meagre indeed. Proof that the case law of the Court is a source of rights lies in the fact that quite frequently we see legislation being amended or introduced to reflect that case law.[4] The legislator is therefore seen to be reacting to, and implementing into, legislation rights articulated by the Court. Its case law has thus been the foundation of rights, which are subsequently enshrined by legislation, and can therefore be properly described as a source of rights.

This judicial activism has been born out of necessity. Traditionally such socio-economic rights as were bestowed upon the Community citizen were few and were generally poorly articulated, thus forcing the Court to take a more activist role than perhaps would otherwise have been the case had provisions been somewhat less vaguely and confusingly drafted.

The original provisions of the EC Treaty contained few justiciable socio-economic rights.[5] No specific legislative power was conferred on the Community institutions until the Maastricht Treaty. That is not to say the Community institutions were without legislative power in the socio-economic field. They could, and did, resort to the general law making provisions of the Treaty in what are now Article 94 and 308 of the EC Treaty.

Article 94 provides for the adoption of directives for the approximation of the laws, regulations and administrative provisions of the Member States that directly affect the establishing or functioning of the common market. Article 308 provides that if action by the Community should prove necessary to attain one of the objectives of the Community, and the Treaty has not provided specific powers for that purpose, the Council, acting unanimously and after consulting the European Parliament, shall take appropriate measures. Most of the earlier social and employment legislation was adopted on the basis of Articles 94 or 308.[6]

The necessity of ensuring unanimity within the Council made the legislative process difficult and had a prejudicial effect on the quality of the instruments ultimately adopted. Legislation often came into being following protracted intensive negotiation and compromise. Frequently this resulted in instruments of less than optimal clarity and precision. Key concepts were either not defined at all or set out in overly broad terms, which proved difficult to apply to concrete cases. This opacity made the application of many Community measures difficult on a national level and led to numerous preliminary rulings from national courts and tribunals seeking guidance from the ECJ on what the law meant and how it should be applied.

Two characteristics which lie at the heart of the Community legal order also merit mention here as they have contributed considerably to both the substance and the effective enforcement of socio-economic rights before the ECJ: (i) the supremacy of Community law and (ii) the doctrine of direct effect. Community law is superior to national law,

---

[4] For example Directive 98/70 OJ [1998] OJ L201/88.

[5] See R. Goebel, 'Employee Rights in the European Community: A Panorama from the 1974 Social Action Program to the Social Charter of 1989', *Hastings International and Comparative Law Review*, Vol. 17 (1993), pp. 2–95, at 4–10; D. O'Keeffe, 'The Uneasy Progress of European Social Policy', *Columbia Journal of European Law*, Vol. 2 (19970, pp. 241–263, at 241–243; P. Watson, 'The Community Social Charter', *Common Market Law* Review, Vol. 28 (1991), pp. 37–68, at 39–41.

[6] Examples of measures which were adopted on the basis of Article 94 include Directive 75/117 on the approximation of the laws of the Member States relating to the approximation of the principle of equal pay for men and women [1975] OJ L 48; Directive 77/129 on the approximation of the laws of the Member States relating to the safeguarding of employees' rights in the event of transfers of undertakings, businesses or parts of businesses [1977] OJ L61. Directives which have as their legal basis Article 308 include Directive 76/207 on the implementation of the principle of equal treatment for men and women as regards access to employment, vocational training and promotion and working conditions [1976] OJ L39; Directive 79/7 on the principle of equal treatment for men and women in matters of social security [1979] OJ L6.

that is it takes precedence over national law.[7] In cases of conflict between the two legal systems, Community law prevails. The superior nature of EC law has been a vital factor in ensuring the protection of socio-economic rights as will become apparent from the discussion of the case law of the ECJ at Section 5 below. Equally important is the quality of direct effect whereby citizens can rely on Community law as a source of rights, which national courts must safeguard. A striking example of this is the *Defrenne*[8] case in which the Court held that Article 141 of the EC Treaty, which laid down the principle of equal pay for men and women, was directly applicable.

2.1 Overview of EC Treaty Provisions

Social and employment rights figure prominently in the statement of principles set out in Part I of the EC Treaty. Article 2 enumerates the social principles upon which the Treaty is based:

(i) A high level of employment and social protection;

(ii) equality between men and women;

(iii) the raising of the standard of living and equality of life within the Community;

(iv) social cohesion and solidarity among the Member States.

Title VIII of the treaty entitled 'Employment' acknowledges the Community's role in the development of a skilled labour force responsive to economic change and the fostering of the alignment of the employment policies of the Member States with the Community's economic objectives. The title consists of six provisions (Articles 125–130). Whilst the primary responsibility for employment policy rests with the Member States themselves, the Community assumes the complementary role of co-ordinating the efforts of the Member States in the development of their employment policies so as to ensure a commonality of objectives between them, which reflect Community economic policy.

Title XI is headed 'Social Policy, Education, Vocational Training and Youth'. Article 136–137 set out the Community's competence in social policy. Article 136 states that the Community and the Member States:

[S]hall have as their objectives the promotion of employment, improved living and working conditions, as to make possible their harmonisation whilst the improvement is being maintained, proper social protection, dialogue between management and labour and the development of human resources with a view to lasting employment and the combating of exclusion.

These objectives are to be achieved by measures which take account of 'diverse national practices' and which maintain competitiveness of the Community economy. Inspiration for these objectives is stated to be drawn from the European Social Charter signed in Turin on 18 October 1961 and the Community Charter on the Fundamental Social Rights of Workers.

Article 137(1) sets out how the objectives listed in Article 136 are to be attained. The principle of subsidiarity is respected – the Community is to support and complement the activities of the Member States in 11 specified fields: (a) the improvement of the working environment, in particular health and safety; (b) working conditions; (c) social security and social protection at work; (d) the protection of workers following termination of a contract of employment; (e) the information and consultation of workers; (f) the representation and collective defence of the interests of workers and employees including co-determination; (g) conditions of employment for third country nationals legally resident in Community territory; (h) the integration of persons excluded from the labour market; (i) equality of treatment between men and women with regard to labour market opportunities and treatment at work; (j) the combating of social exclusion; and, (k) the modernisation of social protection schemes.

Objectives (a) to (i) may be achieved by means of directives. However the power of the Council to adopt directives is subject to five principles: directives must be in support of, and complementary to, activities of the Member States; directives must have regard to the conditions and technical rules obtaining in each Member State;

---

[7] Case 26/62 *Van Gend en Loos* [1963] ECR 1; Case 6/64 *Costa v. ENEL* [1964] ECR 585; Case 106/77 *Simmenthal* [1978] ECR 692.

[8] Case 43/75 [1976] ECR 455.

directives must not impose administrative, financial and technical constraints in a way which would hold back the creation and development of small and medium sized enterprises; directives must maintain the competitiveness of the European economy; and, directives must consist of minimum requirements for the gradual implementation.[9] The Community has no legislative competence with respect to a number of collective labour rights including the right to strike, the right of association and the imposition of lock-outs or pay levels.[10] Measures concerning social security and the social protection of workers; the protection of workers after termination of employment; the representation of workers and employers including co-determination; conditions of employment for third country nationals legally resident in Community territory and certain financial contributions to the Social Fund require a unanimous vote[11] in the Council; other measures may be adopted on the basis of a qualified majority.

Article 140 enables the Commission with a view to achieving the objectives of Article 136 and without prejudice to other provisions of the Treaty, to encourage co-operation between the Member States and to facilitate the coordination of their actions in all social policy fields particularly in matters relating to: (a) employment; labour law and working conditions; (b) basic and advanced vocational training; (c) social security; (d) prevention of occupational accidents and diseases; (e) occupational hygiene; (f) the right of association and collective bargaining between employers and workers.

For these purposes, the Commission can act in close contact with the Member States by producing studies, delivering opinions and arranging consultations.

2.2 General Principles

Finally, mention must be made of the general principles of Community law[12] that may also be a source of socio-economic rights. The function of these principles is to control the use by the Community institutions of the many powers granted to them and the actions of the Member States in implementing Community legislation. The general principles derive from the laws common to the Member States, more particularly the constitutional traditions of the Member States and international conventions to which they are a party, the most notable examples being the European Convention of Human Rights and the European Social Charter. Of all the general principles, two are most relevant to socio-economic rights in the context of the ECJ: the principle of equality and the principle of proportionality. The principle of equality finds specific expression in both the Treaty itself and in secondary legislation. The principle of proportionality has most often been invoked to ensure that exceptions or derogations from Community law rights are interpreted strictly. For example, indirect discrimination between men and women in the matter of pay can be objectively justified if pay differences are necessary to attain a particular objective and provided the discriminatory measures are no more than what is necessary to achieve that objective.[13]

2.3 Secondary Legislation

There are five types of legal instrument prescribed by Article 249 of the EC Treaty for the realisation of its objectives: regulations, directives, decisions and recommendations and opinions. *Regulations* are of general application; they are binding in their entirety and are directly applicable. Whilst some Regulations may require – and provide for – the adoption of national implementing measures, the Regulations themselves enter directly in to national law without any need for implementing measures.[14] *Directives* – by far the commonest

---

[9] This is not to be interpreted as limiting Community competence to the lowest level of protection within the Member States. Article 137(2) means that the standards set in directives are to be regarded as a floor rather than as a ceiling, leaving Member States free to provide a level of protection more stringent than that resulting from Community law: Case C-94/84 *United Kingdom v. Council* [1996] ECR I-5755 Judgment para. 17; Case C-2/97 *IP v. Borsana* [1998] ECR I-8597 Judgment para. 35.

[10] Article 137 (5).

[11] Article 137 (2).

[12] See in general T. Takis, *The General Principles of EC Law*, 2nd Ed. (Oxford: Oxford University Press, 2006).

[13] Case 170/84 *Bilka Kaufhaus* [1986] ECR 1607.

[14] Case 230/78 *Eridania* [1978] ECR 2749 Judgment, at para. 25.

form of legislative measure dealing with socio-economic rights – are binding, as to the result to be achieved, on each Member State to which they are addressed.[15] National authorities can choose the form and method by which to implement directives. Directives, in contrast to regulations, are not directly applicable. They require transposition into national law. They can however have direct effect. This will be the case if their provisions are clear and unconditional. Directives have vertical direct effect only; they can create rights enforceable against the State or emanations of the State. In contrast to EC Treaty provisions and regulations, they do not create rights as between private parties (horizontal direct effect).[16] *Recommendations* are not binding but they may have interpretative value.[17] *Opinions* have no binding legal effect but by analogy with recommendations they may be of interpretative value.

As mentioned above, socio-economic rights are normally expressed in directives, the exception being rights arising out of the exercise of free movement. Article 40 of the EC Treaty empowers the Council to adopt Regulations to bring about the free movement of workers and many of the social and economic rights given to workers and their families are found in these Regulations, notably Regulation 1612/68[18] which gives workers the right to 'social advantages' on the same terms as nationals of the host Member State. Article 12 of the same regulations gives the children of migrant workers the right of equality of access to educational facilities in the host Member States, a right which has been interpreted as including the right to scholarships and grants.

2.4 Soft Law

Additionally, and importantly in this area, given the paucity of legislative power, extensive use had been made of non-binding acts such as Resolutions, Action Programmes and Charters. Such instruments are generally of programmatic nature, setting out objectives to be achieved. Given the political sensitivity arising from the tension between the Member States as to the extent to which they alone should remain responsible for such matters, which has traditionally surrounded the sphere of socio-economic rights, soft law has often been the only means to mark a commitment to such rights. Over time such sensitivities may abate and soft law norms may translate into legislation and even achieve the ultimate accolade and unimpeachable status, which comes with enshrinement within the EC Treaty itself.

The Court has bolstered the status of a number of soft law instruments by decreeing them to be of interpretative value, thereby allocating them a role within the Community legal order: Although not a source of justiciable rights, they influence the content and extent of those rights which must be interpreted in a way which reflect the will of the Member States as expressed in soft law instruments.[19]

3. THE EUROPEAN COURT OF JUSTICE

It is the responsibility of the Court to ensure that the law is observed in the interpretation and the application of the Treaties establishing the European Communities.[20] Various types of actions are possible. The Court is competent to rule on actions for annulment of Community legal acts; actions for failure of the Community Institutions to act; actions against Member States for failure to fulfil their obligations under EC law; references for preliminary rulings and appeals against decisions of the Court of First Instance. Proceedings are, for the large part conducted in writing. A short oral hearing follows the completion of the written procedure in each case. Parties are not required to appear at the oral hearing although most inevitably do.

Issues relating to socio-economic rights arise mainly in the context of preliminary ruling proceedings, but they may also be the subject of other types of proceedings, notably actions brought by the EC Commission against Member States for failure to fulfil their implement, or implement

---

[15] Article 149 EC.
[16] Case 152/84 *Marshall* [1986] ECR723 Judgment, at paras. 15 and 16.
[17] Case 322/88 *Grimaldi* [1988] ECR 4407.
[18] OJ 1968 Eng. Sp. Ed. (II) 475.

[19] For a recent example, see C-540/03 *Parliament v. Council* [2006] ECR I-5049.
[20] Article 220 EC.

correctly, directives. These actions are brought directly before the Court. In the case of references for preliminary rulings, proceedings are commenced in national courts, by individuals asserting their rights under EC law. Where these rights are unclear or where the national court is uncertain as to the meaning or extent of the EC law provisions upon which the litigant relies, they can (and indeed must if they are a court of final instance) suspend proceedings and refer a question for interpretation to the ECJ.[21] Once the ECJ has given judgment on the matter, the case reverts to the national court, which then applies the law as interpreted to the particular facts of the case in front of him. It is in the context of preliminary rulings that the ECJ has contributed to a broad and functional interpretation of socio-economic rights.

4. THE COURT'S APPROACH TO PROTECTION OF SOCIO-ECONOMIC RIGHTS

In protecting socio-economic rights, the Court has adopted an approach that is essentially functional. It has looked at the objective of the rules which are in issue before it and has interpreted them according to what they are designed to achieve and the wider objectives of the Community. The specific objective of a particular rule has often been held to be subject to the broader general objectives of the Community thus rendering at times either invalid, or as is more frequently the case, requiring an interpretation that will fulfil the wider objectives of the Treaty. This approach is well illustrated in the case law on the right to cross border health care services discussed below at Section 5.2. The Court has equally adopted a liberal approach in determining the limits of rights or restrictions to be placed upon their exercise. Where rights have been conferred upon a particular class of persons, that class has been interpreted broadly to include a wide rather than a narrow range of persons. The case-law on movement and residence is illustrative (see Section 5.1 below). Permissible restrictions on the exercise of rights have been required to be proportionate to the objective which they seek to attain. Provisions prohibiting discrimination have been held to include both direct and indirect discrimina-

tion, which is where apparently neutral provisions applicable equally to two groups have in reality a disparate impact with one group being more disadvantaged than another due to circumstances particular to them.[22] In short, the Court seeks to give the fullest effect to socio-economic rights.

5. SELECTED CASE LAW OF THE EUROPEAN COURT OF JUSTICE

This Section discusses a number of judgments of the ECJ, which illustrate its approach to socio-economic rights. The cases have been loosely grouped into five categories dealing with the right to move and reside, health care, education and employment, the European citizen and sex discrimination.

5.1   The Right to Move and Reside

In the early years of the Community, only the right of the economically active, that is the employed and the self-employed, and their dependants, to move freely throughout the Community, was clearly articulated in the EC Treaty[23] and secondary legislation.[24] It was left to the ECJ to elaborate the rights of others who did not fit neatly into any of these categories. For example, whilst the Treaty provided for the movement of suppliers of services and their right to supply services under the same terms and conditions as nationals of the Member States in which the services were to be provided, it was silent on the rights of recipients of services. Likewise the right to move to another Member State to work was set out in Article 39, but no mention was made of the right to enter a Member State to seek work. Nor was there any definition either in the Treaty or secondary legislation of what was worker or who was a worker. What level of economic activity endowed a person with the status of worker? And what of the family of the worker? Whilst legislation granted spouses the right to enter and reside with the worker, what was the position if the marriage broke down? Could children in the middle of their schooling be

---

[21] Article 234 EC.

[22] Case 41/84 *Pinna* [1986] ECR 1.
[23] Articles 39 and 43 EC.
[24] Regulation 1612/68 on the Free movement of Workers OJ Sp Ed 1968 L275/2.

required to leave the host country when the parent upon whom they depended for their right to be in the host country was no longer economically active in the host country? And what of motive? Did a person have to be genuinely seeking employment in the host Member State or could ulterior motives drive their apparent exercise of Community law rights? The creation by the Treaty of Maastricht of the status of citizen of the European Union has raised numerous issues: Can citizens of the Union take up residence in a Member State and if so, under what conditions?

In short, whilst the EC Treaty and, to a certain extent, secondary legislation, set out the basic right to move in the case of those engaged in economic activity, and created the status of citizen of the Union, it was left to the Court to set out the parameters and content of those rights which was mainly done in the context of requests for preliminary rulings from courts and tribunals across the Community framed against a given factual and national legal background.

Luisi and Carbone[25] established the right of nationals to move freely to receive services; *Cowan*[26] and *Bickel and Franz*[27] established the principle that recipients of services had to be treated in the same manner as citizens of the country in which the services were provided. Thus Mr Cowan was entitled to compensation under the French criminal injury compensation for injuries received as a result of an attack outside a Paris metro station whilst he was in Paris as a tourist. Bickel and Franz were held to have the same linguistic rights with respect to court proceedings arising out of certain criminal offences committed whilst they were recipients of services in the Province of Bolzano in Italy. They had a right to have proceedings conducted in German in the same way the German-speaking people of that region had. In short, the ECJ has held that persons receiving services on the territory of another Member State must be treated in the same way as citizens of the area in which those services are provided, even if the rights being claimed were unconnected to the services being provided. Since discrimination on the basis of nationality was prohibited by Article 12 EC, any person in a situation governed by Community law must be placed on an equal footing with national of the Member State in which he seeks to exercise his Community law rights.

The right to enter and remain in a Member State for a reasonable period of time for the purposes of seeking work was established in *Antonissen*.[28] The Court reasoned that the chances of finding employment would be prejudiced if a work seeker could not go to another Member State to search for work and this could render Article 39 ineffective. A reasonable period should be allowed to find employment and the Court found that six months was not an unreasonable period. After that point in time a worker could be required to leave the Member State in question unless he could prove that he was continuing to seek employment and had a genuine chance of finding work if he remained in the territory.[29] Thus work seekers cannot be required to leave automatically after the expiry of the 'reasonable period'.[30]

On the issue of what constitutes work[31] or who is a worker, the Court has refused to lay down specific criteria such as hours worked,[32] income levels[33] or methods of payment,[34] preferring instead to require the pursuit of genuine economic activity as a pre-requisite for the attainment of the status of worker.[35] The Court has also emphasised that these are Community concepts: national law has no relevance[36] since otherwise Member States would be in a position to define the applicability of Article 39 with no possibility of control by the Community institutions.

---

[25] Joined Cases 286/82 and 26/83 [1984] ECR 377.
[26] Case 186/87 [1989] ECR 195.
[27] Case C-274/96 [1998] ECR I-7637.

[28] Case C-292/89 [1991] ECR I-745.
[29] Subsequent legislation laid down the specific periods of time allowed to work seekers to be present in a Member State.
[30] Case C-344/95 *Commission v. Belgium* [1997] ECR I-1035; Case C-171/91 *Tsiotras* [1993] ECR I-2925.
[31] Joined Cases 115 and 116/81 *Adoui and Cornaille* [1982] ECR 1665; Case C-357/89 *Raulin* [1992] ECR I – 1027; Case C-337/97 *Meeusen* [1999] ECR I-3289.
[32] Case 139/85 *Kempf* [1986] ECR 1741.
[33] Case C-53/81 *Levin* [1982] ECR 1035.
[34] Case 344/87 *Bettray* [1989] ECR 1621.
[35] Case 66/85 *Lawrie-Blum* [1986] ECR 2121; *Kempf* (n. 32 above; Case 344/87 *Bettray* [1989] ECR 1621.
[36] Case C-27/91 *Le Manoir* [1991] ECR I-5531; G. F. Mancini, 'The Free Movement of Workers in the Case Law of the European Court of Justice, in D. Curtin and D. O'Keeffe (eds.), *Constitutional Adjudication in European Community and National Law. Essays for the Hon. Mr. Justice T.F. O'Higgins* (Dublin: Butterworths Law, 1992), pp. 67–77.

Baumbast and Chen

These two cases raised the delicate issue of the rights of children and the parent who cares for them to enter and remain on the territory of a Member State. Both cases were referred to the ECJ from the United Kingdom.

The Baumbast sisters came to the United Kingdom with their parents in 1990. From 1990–1993, Mr Baumbast pursued an economic activity first as an employed person and then as a self-employed person. After that he worked for a number of German companies in China and Lesotho. The family was financially self-sufficient: They were not reliant in any way on the social welfare system of the United Kingdom. In 1996, the United Kingdom authorities refused to renew the residence permit of Mr Baumbast and the residence documents of Mrs Baumbast and her daughters, one of who was a Colombian national, while the other held dual Colombian and German nationality.

R was a citizen of the United States who came to the United Kingdom with her husband, a French national. Her two children had dual French and American nationality. She divorced her husband in 1992 but continued to remain in the United Kingdom, sharing the care of her two children with their father. The family was not in any way dependant upon United Kingdom social welfare benefits or services.

Baumbast differed from R in that Mr Baumbast, although he had entered the United Kingdom as a worker, was no longer economically active there.[37]

On the question of the rights of the children of these two families, the Court held that they could have the right to reside and attend educational courses in the Member State to which they had been brought by a parent exercising the right to free movement. In reaching this conclusion, the Court followed its judgment in *Echternach and Moritz*,[38] reasoning that the integration of the family into the society of the host Member State required that children must have the possibility of completing their education successfully in that State. The possibility that a child might not be able to continue his education in the host Member State might dissuade his parent from exercising the right to free movement. The Court in that case refused to accept the argument of the German government that the right to remain in the host Member State should be conditional upon the child's inability to continue education in his Member State of origin.

The Court in *Baumbast and R* found the marital status of the parents of the children and the nationality of the children to be irrelevant:

> The fact that the parents of the children concerned have meanwhile divorced, the fact that only one parent is a citizen of the Union and that parent has ceased to be a migrant worker in the host Member State and the fact that the children are not themselves citizens of the Union are irrelevant...[39]

Not only did the children have the right to remain in the host Member State for educational purposes, the parent who is their primary carer also has the right to reside with them in order to facilitate the exercise of their right to attend general educational courses.

Chen[40] went further than *Baumbast*. Mr and Mrs Chen were Chinese nationals who worked for a Chinese undertaking established in China. Mr Chen was the majority shareholder in this company and he travelled frequently to a number of Member States, particularly the United Kingdom, for his work. The Chens had a child born in China in 1998. They wanted another child but this was impossible in China under the Chinese one-child policy. Mrs Chen therefore came to England in May 2000 when she was six months pregnant. She gave birth to a daughter, Catherine, in Belfast on 16 September 2000. By virtue of Irish law, as it stood at that time, any person born on the island of Ireland had a right to Irish nationality. Catherine Chen was issued with an Irish passport and she and Mrs Chen proceeded to settle in Cardiff, claiming the right to do so by virtue of Catherine's European citizenship, Catherine having a right to take up residence as a result of that status and Mrs Chen had the right to reside with her as her primary carer and mother.

[37] Case C-413/99 *R* Baumbast and R [2002] ECR I-7091.
[38] Joined cases 389 and 390/87 [1989] ECR 723.
[39] See Note 37 para. 63.
[40] Case C-200/02 [2004] ECR I-9925.

The Chen family were well-off; they were not dependent on public funds in the United Kingdom and there was no realistic prospect of them becoming so. They could provide for all their needs.

The Secretary of State for the Home Department refused to grant a long-term residence permit to Mrs Chen and Catherine. They appealed this decision to the Immigration Appellate Authority, which referred a series of questions to the ECJ, which held:

> Article 18 EC and Council Directive 90/364/EEC of 28 June 1990 on the right of residence confers on a young minor who is a national of a Member State, is covered by the appropriate sickness insurance and is in the care of a parent who is a third country national having sufficient resources for that minor not to become a burden on the public finances of the host Member State, a right to reside for an indefinite period in that State. In such circumstances, those same provisions allow a parent who is the child's primary carer to reside with the child in the host Member State.[41]

5.2   Health Care (and Social Security)[42]

The Community's role in the sphere of public health is confined to complementary and incentive measures. These may not involve harmonisation measures.[43] Public health care systems, along with their organisation and financing, are matters which remain exclusively within the competence of the Member States[44] but when exercising that

power the Member States must comply with the provisions of the Community legal order.

Some of the most controversial judgments of the ECJ in recent years have concerned the right of citizens to procure health care outside their home territory, and to be reimbursed for the cost of such care by the social security system to which they are affiliated. The extent of this right has been set out in Article 22 of Regulation 1408/71 on the application of social security schemes to employed persons, to self-employed persons and to members of their families moving within the Community[45] which provides that an employed or self-employed person who is entitled to sickness benefits under the social security system to which he is affiliated in his home State, receives health care in another member State if he has been authorised to go to that State to receive treatment. In such circumstances the cost of the treatment is borne by the health care system with which he is insured in his home State.

Until the *Kohll*[46] and *Decker*[47] judgments of April 1998, it was generally believed that Article 22 of Regulation 1408/71 was the only provision under which citizens could claim the right to receive health care in another Member State. And the exercise of that right was subject to a number of substantive and procedural conditions, notably the requirement that prior authorisation from the social security institution of affiliation was necessary. Public care systems thus had a wide margin of discretion to determine who should get health care outside the national territory. *Kohll* and *Decker* challenged this perception. Both plaintiffs were subject to the Luxembourg social security system. Mr Decker bought a pair of glasses in Arlon for which he sought reimbursement; Mr Kohll got orthodontic treatment for his daughter in Trier for

---

[41] Ibid. para. 47.

[42] D. Wyatt, 'Community competence to Regulate Medical Services', in M. Dougan and E. Spaventa (eds.) *Social Welfare and EU Law* (Oxford: Hart Publishing, 2005), at pp. 131–144; M. Fuchs, 'Free Movement of Services and Social Security – Quo Vadis?', *European Law Journal*, Vol. 8, No. 4 (2002), pp. 536–555; A. Dawes, 'Bonjour Herr Doctor? National Healthcare Systems: The Internal Market and Cross-Border Medical Care within the European Union', *Legal Issues of European Integration*, Vol. 33 (2006), pp. 167–182.

[43] Article 152 EC.

[44] Article 152 (5) EC provides that 'Community action in the field of public health shall fully respect the responsibilities of the Member States for the organization and delivery of health services and medical care'. Case C-239/82 *Duphar* [1984] ECR 523; Case 110/79 *Coonan* [1980] ECR

1445; Joined Cases C-4/95 and C-5/95 *Stoeber and Pereira* [1997] ECR I-511.

[45] OJ 1971 L 149/2.

[46] Case C-158/96 [1998] ECR I-1931.

[47] Case C-120/95 [1998] ECR I-1831. R. Giesen, 'Comments to ECJ's judgements in C-120/95, *Nicolas Decker* v. *caisse de maladie des employés privés* and C-158/96, *Raymond Kohll* v. *Union des caisses des maladie*', *Common Market Law Review*, Vol. 36 (1999), pp. 841–850. A. P. van der Mei, 'Cross-Border Access to Medical care within the European Union – Some Reflections on the Judgments Decker and Kohll', *Maastricht Journal of European and Comparative Law*, Vol. 5, No. 3 (1998), pp. 277–297.

which he too wished to be reimbursed. Neither had received authorisation for the procurement of such goods and services outside the national territory, from the Luxembourg authorities. Both claimed reimbursement within the limits of Luxembourg social security system. Neither sought to claim any more than would have reimbursed had the services been provided within Luxembourg. The Luxembourg authorities refused their claims. Before the ECJ, both plaintiffs argued that the right to provide and receive cross-border services set out in Article 49 of the EC Treaty gave them the right to get medical equipment and dental services in another Member State without seeking the prior authorisation of the Luxembourg authorities. The Court agreed. In the case of *Decker* the Court held:

> Articles 30 and 36 of the Treaty preclude national rules under which a social security institution of a Member State refuses to reimburse to an insured person on a flat rate basis the cost of a pair of spectacles with corrective lenses purchased from an optician established in another Member State on the ground that prior authorization is required for the purchase of any medical product ... [48]

In *Kohll*, the Court held that the requirement to obtain prior authorisation from the relevant competent authorities to receive dental treatment provided by an orthodontist established in another Member State as a condition for reimbursement for that treatment according to the rules of that health care system was incompatible with Article 49 and 50 EC Treaty.

Neither *Kohll* nor *Decker* involved hospital treatment. In its subsequent case law, the Court held that no distinction should be made between care provided in a hospital environment and care outside such an environment, but the prior authorisation of the insuring social security authority may be required in order to ensure the financial equilibrium of health care systems. This is reasonable: Member States must have an indication of what their liabilities for health care treatment abroad are likely to be and if necessary, they must be able to limit their exposure to such costs to secure the viability of the national health care system and the rights of their citizens to adequate and appropriate services from that system. However, the right

of citizens to exercise their right to obtain health care services abroad requires that such authorisation may not be withheld unreasonably and the Court had laid down a number of principles which must govern the grant and refusal of authorisations. The treatment in question must be 'normal' in the sense that it must be sufficiently recognised in the professional circles concerned[49] and it must be necessary to the patient's condition and not capable of being provided without 'due delay' within the health care system of the Member State in which the patient is insured.[50]

As to the amounts which may be claimed for non-hospital treatment received in another Member States without the prior authorisation of the responsible social security authority, the Court has held in *Muller Faure and Van Riet*[51] that reimbursement can be claimed only within the limits of the cover provided under the social security system under which the claimant is insured. Any amounts over and above those amounts must be borne by the recipient of the medical services or goods.

Muller Faure and Van Riet raised the issues of how reimbursement is to be organised where a health care system provides benefits in kind but no cash exchanges hands. In such a case a Member State can establish a scale at which costs paid for treatment in another Member State will be reimbursed but these rates of reimbursement must be based on criteria that are objective, non-discriminatory and transparent.

A more recent judgment, pronounced on 16 May 2006, on the right to cross-border health care services is *Watts*.[52] In that case, the Court was asked whether and in what circumstances a patient insured under the United Kingdom National Health Service ('NHS') scheme is entitled under Article 49 EC, to receive hospital treatment in another Member State and to be reimbursed for that treatment.[53] Two characteristics of the NHS were brought to the Court's attention:

---

[40] *Decker*, ibid. para. 46.

[49] Case C-157/99 *Geraerts-Smits and Peerbooms* [2001] ECR I-5473; Case C-385/99 *Muller-Faure and Van Riet* [2003] ECR I-4509.
[50] Ibid. para. 103.
[51] *Muller-Faure and Van Riet* (n. 49 above).
[52] Case C-372/04 [2006] ECR I-4325.
[53] There were seven questions referred to the ECJ by the Court of Appeal. It is beyond the scope of this paper to deal with all of them.

(i) there is no fund available to NHS bodies out of which the cost of treatment abroad may be paid for and (ii) there is no duty on the NHS to pay for hospital treatment received by an NHS patient in a private hospital in England or Wales. With respect to the last point the Court held that the conditions for the NHS assuming responsibility for the cost of hospital treatment obtained in another Member State should not be compared to the situation under national law of hospital treatment received by patients in local private hospitals. The proper point of comparison is the conditions under which the NHS provides such services in its hospitals. Confirming its previous rulings, the Court held that Article 49 EC does not preclude the right of a patient to receive hospital treatment in another Member State at the expense of the system with which he is insured from being subject to prior authorisation, but the conditions attaching to such authorisation must conform to the principle of proportionality. An authorisation system must be substantively and procedurally transparent so as to circumscribe the exercise of the discretion of national authority's discretion. It must be based on objective, non-discriminatory criteria that are known in advance and the procedural system for obtaining such authorisation must be easily accessible and capable of ensuring that such requests are dealt with objectively, impartially and within a reasonable period of time. Refusals must be capable of being challenged in judicial or quasi-judicial proceedings.

5.3 Education[54]

Responsibility for education lies primarily in the hands of the Member States. Article 149(1) stipulates that the Community shall fully respect the responsibility of the Member States for the content of teaching and the organisation of education systems and their cultural and linguistic diversity. Article 149(4) expressly provides that the Community institutions are not empowered to harmonise national rules and regulations. These provisions

were inserted into the EC Treaty by the Treaty of Amsterdam.

The original EEC Treaty of 1957 made no mention of education, but Article 128 thereof provides that the Council is to lay down general principles for the establishment of a common vocational policy. Regulation 1612/68[55] gave Community workers the right of equality of access to training in vocational schools in the Member State in which they were employed[56] and the children of such workers the right to be admitted to the host Member State's 'general educational, apprenticeship and vocational training courses under the same conditions as nationals of that State' provided they were residing on the territory of the host State. The right of access to education granted in Article 12 was held by the ECJ to include entitlement to grants and scholarships.[57] Although migrant workers were only expressly granted equal treatment to vocational training courses, their right to receive social advantages on the same terms as nationals would have included the right of access to all educational facilities and any measures intended to facilitate such access, including grants and scholarships.[58] On the basis of the Treaty provisions and legislation, education thus remained territorial in scope.

This was the position at the time of the *Gravier*[59] case, which came before the ECJ in 1983. Francoise Gravier was a French national who moved to Liege in Belgium to study the art of strip cartoon, a talent for which the Belgians are well known. As a non-national, she was required to pay a fee (minerval), which was not chargeable to Belgian students. She contested this requirement before the Belgian courts arguing that it was contrary to Community law. The ECJ held that the imposition of a fee as a condition of access to a vocational training course where the same fee was not imposed on nationals constituted discrimination on the grounds of nationality contrary to what was then Article 7, now Article 12 of the EC Treaty. Article 12 prohibits any discrimination on the grounds of nationality 'within the scope of application of this Treaty'.

---

[54] M. Dougan, 'Fees, Grants, Loans and Dole Cheques: Who covers the cost of migrant education within the EU?', *Common Market Law Review*, Vol. 42, No. 4 (2005), pp. 943–986; P. Watson: 'Wandering Students: Their Rights under Community Law', in D. Curtin and D. O'Keeffe (eds.), *Constitutional Adjudication* (n. 36 above) pp. 79–88.

[55] N. 24 above.
[56] Article 7(3).
[57] Case 9/74 *Casagrande* [1974] ECR 773; Case 68/74 *Alaimo* [1975] ECR 109; Joined Cases 389 and 390/89 *Echternach* [1989] ECR 723.
[58] Case 39/86 *Lair* [1988] ECR 3161.
[59] Case 293/83 [1985] ECR 593.

Pointing to Article 128 of the EEC Treaty and Articles 7 and 12 of Regulation 1612/68, the Court held that conditions of access to vocational training fell within the scope of the Treaty and must be made available to nationals and non-nationals on the same terms by virtue of Article 12.

The *Gravier* case established the principle of free movement for students within the Community – at least for those pursuing vocational training courses. The concept of vocational training, initially defined by the Court as preparation for a qualification in a particular profession, trade or employment was subsequently held in *Blaizot*[60] to extend to most university studies with the exception of those courses which were intended to increase general knowledge rather than to prepare for a particular occupation. In *Humbel*,[61] the Court not unsurprisingly held that primary and secondary schooling could not constitute vocational training. However, since the expansion of the Community's powers in the sphere of education resulting from the Treaty of Amsterdam, it is now probable that access to primary and secondary education must be granted to nonnationals on the same terms as nationals.

Where *Gravier* and *Blaizot* established the right of equality of access vocational training courses with the result that fees and other access criteria had to be equally applicable to both nationals and non-nationals, *Lair* and *Brown* raised the question of entitlement to maintenance grants. Were non-nationals entitled to maintenance grants on the same terms as nationals? This, the Court held, depended on their status.

Brown[62] was a student of electrical engineering. He had dual French and British citizenship but had completed all his schooling in France. He came to Scotland eight months before he commenced his university studies. There he worked at a job described as 'pre-university electrical training'. He was refused a student allowance by the Scottish Educational Department. This allowance comprised two elements: (i) payment of tuition fees and (ii) a maintenance grant. The Court found that whilst assistance with tuition fees charged for access to vocational education courses fell

within the scope of the Treaty and had therefore to be made available to non-nationals on the same terms as nationals, maintenance grants, being a matter of general educational and social policy, fell outside the scope of the spheres of competence of the Community institutions and were not subject to the principle of non-discrimination and could therefore be denied to non-nationals.

Lair[63] differed from *Brown* in that Sylvie Lair, a French national had worked in Germany prior to commencing a course of studies in Romance languages. As a worker therefore she was entitled to a maintenance grant since this fell to be regarded as a 'social advantage' within the meaning of Article 7(3) of Regulation 1612/68.[64] Lair was therefore entitled to the maintenance grant in her own right. Brown was not. The Court found that although he was employed, his employment relationship was merely ancillary to the studies to be funded by the grant and could not therefore found a basis from which rights could derive.

The position thus immediately following the judgments in *Brown* and *Lair* was that university fees, since they pertained to access to vocational training courses, were a matter which fell within the scope of the Treaty and had to be levied in accordance with the principle of equal treatment. 'Vocational training' was interpreted by the Court broadly as any course of studies, which prepared for or led to employment. The categorisation of courses was to be done by looking at the course as a whole: the Court refused to entertain the splitting of course into 'vocational' and 'non-vocational' years. Maintenance grants were not deemed to be sufficiently related to access to education to fall within the treaty and hence were not subject to the principle of equality. Where the claimant was a migrant worker or the child of a worker, entitlement to all types of grants or scholarships for all types of educational courses, both vocational and non-vocational could be grounded on the basis of either Article 7(3) or Article 12 of Regulation 1612/68.

The Maastricht Treaty created the concept of the citizen of the European Union and added a new Chapter 3 devoted to educational and vocational training to Title VIII Part 3. This led the Court in

---

[60] Case 24/86 [1988] ECR 375.
[61] Case 263/88 [1988] ECR 5356.
[62] Case 197/86 [1988] ECR 3205.

[63] Case 39/86 [1988] ECR 3161.
[64] N. 24 above.

Grezelczyk[65] to rule that Rudy Grezelczyk, a French national who had pursued a course of university studies in physical education in Belgium for three years, was entitled to claim the minimex, a minimum income benefit, on the same terms as Belgian nationals. By virtue of his French nationality, Grezelczyk held Union citizenship, described by the Court as 'destined to be the fundamental status of nationals of Member States'.[66] As such he could rely on the prohibition against discrimination on the basis of nationality in all situations, which fell within the scope ratione materiae of Community law. Education and vocational training fell within the scope of the Treaty. Consequently, Mr Grezelczyk had a right to the minimex if he fulfilled the conditions of entitlement laid down for Belgian nationals. However the right of enjoyment of the minimex was not absolute: in order to prevent beneficiaries, having the right of residence in the host Member State, becoming an unreasonable burden on the public finances of the host Member State, a Member State can take the view that a student who can no longer support himself, no longer fulfils the conditions of residence and hence cannot claim the right to continue to reside on the territory.

In 2005, the Court was again faced with the issue of student support.[67] A French national, *Dany Bidar*, had come to the United Kingdom with his mother in 1998. He completed his secondary school education and went to study economics at the University College, London. His application for a student loan was turned down on the ground that he had not settled in the United Kingdom within the meaning of the Immigration Act 1971. This was one of the conditions of entitlement he was required to fulfil. He was neither a migrant worker nor the child of a migrant worker. The Court, following *Grezelczyk*, found that he was entitled to a student loan but modified its ruling by stating that it was legitimate for a Member State to grant such assistance only to students who have demonstrated a certain degree of integration in to the society of that State. In adopting this position of qualified entitlement to financial support from public funds, the Court followed its position previously adopted in *D'Hoop*[68] and *Collins*,[69] discussed below in Section 5.5. There is thus little possibility of a student arriving in a Member State with which he has had no previous link being entitled to either social assistance or other financial assistance in the shape of student grants or loans. *Grezelczyk* referred to 'solidarity' between citizens of the host Member State and foreign students, *Bidar* to 'integration' with the host society. There must be a substantial link with the host Member State prior to any claim for student support.

5.4 Employment

Community employment legislation deals with both collective employment rights (i.e. rights given to the collectivity of the workforce) and individual employment rights (rights attached to individual workers themselves).

Collective employment rights fall into the first phase of Community legislation on socio-economic rights. They implement the objectives of the Social Action Programme drawn up by the Commission and adopted in January 1974 by a Resolution of the Council.[70]

Collective employment rights to date comprise measures dealing with collective redundancies, rights of employees upon the transfer of the operation and control of an employing undertaking to another undertaking carrying on the same business, rights of employees upon the insolvency of their employer and information and consultation rights. The objective of this legislation is to protect employees in the face of the major restructuring of industry that was envisaged as a result of the operation of the internal market and to introduce some commonality of costs to industry.

Legislation adopted in the immediate aftermath of the Social Action Programme tends to be clear as to its objectives but somewhat cloudy on the details of how these should be achieved. This resulted in numerous references for preliminary rulings to the Court, notably with respect the Transfer of Undertakings Directive.[71] The Directive was amended in 1998 to take account of this

---

[65] Case C-184/99 [2001] ECR I-6193.
[66] Ibid. para. 31.
[67] Case C-209/03 [2005] ECR I-2119.

[68] Case C-224/98 [2002] ECR I-6191.
[69] Case C-138/02 [2004] ECR I-2703.
[70] OJ 1974 C13/1.
[71] Directive 2001/23 OJ 2001 L82/16.

extensive case law.[72] Meanwhile fundamental questions such as the date on which a transfer is deemed to have taken place continue to be referred to the Court.[73] It can be fairly said that the rights which employees have today, upon the transfer of their employing undertakings, are in a large measure due to the efforts of the Court to breathe life into a confused legislative measure.

The Transfer of Undertakings Directive has as its objective the protection of employees in the event of a change in employer by safeguarding their rights that have been acquired or are in the process of being acquired. In brief, the rights conferred on employees who fall within its scope of application can be divided into three categories: Employees have the right upon the transfer of their employer undertaking to be taken over by the new owner of the undertaking without any change to their existing terms and conditions of employment (Article 3); dismissals by reason of the transfer alone are prohibited but dismissals for 'economic, technical or organizational reasons entailing change in the work force' are permitted (Article 4); and employees must be informed and consulted when a transfer is about to take place (Article 7).

The Directive applies to any transfer of an undertaking, business or part of a business to another employer as a result of a legal transfer or merger (Article 1 (1)). Three concepts determine the scope of the Directive. None of these is given any precise definition in the Directive. This has lead to a vast number of references for preliminary ruling to the Court, the flow of which does not abate as ways and means of doing business change. Developments such as the rise in outsourcing of aspects of a business and its counterpart, in-sourcing, have raised issues which the original Directive did not address and which in fact may not even have been in the minds of the legislators at the time of its adoption. The Court has had to resolve these and in doing so it has focused upon the objectives of the Directive, giving concepts set out therein the meaning best suited to protecting the employee. The Directive was amended in 1998 to reflect this case law Article 1 (b) was inserted:

[T]here is a transfer within the meaning of this Directive where there is a transfer of an eco-

nomic entity which retains its identity, meaning an organized grouping of resources which has the objective of pursuing an economic activity, whether that activity is central or ancillary.

The distillation of principles evolved over decades of case law into a single provision proved difficult. Reference back to the case law itself is necessary, and indeed required by the provision of the Directive itself, for a clear picture.[74]

The approach of the Court has been as follows: given the discrepancies between the linguistic versions of this provision coupled with the divergences between the legal systems of the Member States with respect to what constituted a 'transfer', the Court in *Abels*[75] held that the scope of the Directive could not be determined on the basis of textual interpretation alone. In numerous cases in the twenty years after *Abels*, the Court has given the concept of a legal transfer a flexible interpretation. It has held the Directive to be applicable whenever in the context of contractual relations there is a change in the natural or legal person who is responsible for carrying on the business in question. Beginning with *Spijkers*,[76] the Court has determined the scope of the Directive by reference to a wide variety of factors deemed indicative of the transfer of an on-going business. The Court has therefore favoured a practical and factually based assessment of the concept of a transfer: A transfer was deemed to occur where a business changed owner but retained its identity as a business. In other words, where the economic activity carried on remained the same. For example in *Schmidt*,[77] it held that the transfer of the cleaning activities of a branch of an undertaking which had been performed by a single employee to an outside cleaning contractor would constitute a transfer of an undertaking within the meaning of the Directive. The Court rejected an argument advanced by the German and the United Kingdom governments that the absence of a transfer of tangible assets precluded a finding that a transfer had

---

[74] Preamble Recital 8: 'Considerations of legal security and transparency required that the concept of a transfer be clarified in the light of the case-law of the Court of Justice. Such clarification has not altered the scope of Directive 77/187 as interpreted by the Court of Justice'.

[75] Case 135/83 [1985] ECR 469.

[76] Case 24/85 [1986] ECR 1119.

[77] Case C-392/92 [1994] ECR I 1311.

---

[72] Directive 98/70 OJ [1998] L.

[73] Case C-478/03 *Celtec* [2005] ECR I-4389.

occurred. The transfer of tangible assets was, it held, not decisive in determining whether a transfer had occurred:

> [T]he fact that in its case-law the Court includes the transfer of such assets among the various factors to be taken into account by a national court to enable it, when assessing a complex transaction as a whole, to decide whether an undertaking has in fact been transferred does not support the conclusion that the absence of these factors precludes the existence of a transfer...the decisive criterion for establishing whether there is a transfer for the purposes of the directive is whether the business in question retains its identity. (Paras. 16 and 17.)

In interpreting the Collective Redundancies Directive,[78] the Court has also taken a pragmatic stance aimed at ensuring that the objective of the Directive is fulfilled. The purpose of the Directive is to ensure that employees are informed and consulted about proposed redundancies. In recent years there have been instances where information and consultation has been treated as a mere formality, if not entirely dispensed with. The Court in the *Junk*[79] case made reference to the need to 'negotiate' with the workforce. It is uncertain as to what precisely the Court means by this term. The Directive only imposes an obligation to inform and consult: no mention is made of negotiation with the workforce. The term 'negotiation' implies a process aimed at reaching an agreement and that is certainly not provided for in the Directive. In these circumstances it can be argued that what the Court had in mind was a meaningful consultation and information exercise.

The legislation granting collective employment rights defines many key concepts by reference to national law. In order that these rights may be respected, the Court has insisted that national law may have to be amended or altered. In *Commission v. United Kingdom*,[80] the Court held that the requirement to consult workers' representatives was an obligation which required the United Kingdom to put in place the structure necessary to achieve such consultation. The fact that the Directive referred to national law and practice did not mean that if there was no law or practice regarding the consultation of the workforce, that none need be established.

5.5 Citizens' Rights[81]

The European citizen came into being with the Maastricht Treaty. What was then Article 8 of the EC Treaty, now Article 18 provides:

> Every citizen of the Union shall have the right to move and reside freely within the territory of the Member States, subject to the limitations and conditions laid down in this Treaty and by the measures adopted to give it effect.

No clear indication is given as to the rights of the European citizen: were they more or less than the economically active Member State national exercising his right to free movement? What precisely were the limitations and conditions referred to in Article 18? Were they to be read as the same as those applicable to the free movement of economically active citizens?

It was left to the Court to deal with these fundamental issues, which it did with a degree of zeal that has provoked accusations of judicial activism above and beyond what is the proper sphere of its competence. In a series of cases beginning with *Martinez Sala*,[82] the Court has endowed the European citizen with a substantive body of rights, thereby giving life to what can only be described as a foetus (albeit with constitutional pedigree). Paragraph 63 of that judgment contains a powerful statement:

> It follows that a citizen of the European Union...lawfully resident in the territory of the host Member State can rely on Article 6 of the Treaty in all situations which fall within the scope ratione materiae of Community law.

This ruling appeared to state unconditionally that lawful residence generates entitlement to all socio-economic rights within the scope of the Community legal order. However, it is important

---

[78] Directive 98/59 [1998] OJL 225/16.
[79] Case C-188/03 [2005] ECR I-883.
[80] Case 165/82 [1983] ECR 3431.
[81] G. T. Davies, ' "Any Place I Hang My Hat?" or: Residence is the New Nationality', *European Law Journal*, Vol. 11 (2005), pp. 43–56; J. D. Mather, 'The Court of Justice and the Union Citizen', *European Law Journal*, Vol. 11 (2005), pp. 722–743.
[82] Case C-85/96 [1998] ECR I-2691.

to view this case against its factual background: Mrs Martinez Sala did have a long standing connection with Germany, from whose authorities she sought a child raising allowance, having lived there since the age of twelve years and been employed at substantial intervals. Even if the Court in *Martinez Sala* did intend, as its wording would suggest, to give all persons lawfully on the territory of a Member State entitlement to Community socio-economic rights it has moved away from this stance in subsequent case law, requiring that there is a link between the claimant of benefits and the Member States from which those benefits are claimed.

In *Trojani*,[83] the Court held that the exercise of the right to free movement is not unconditional but is subject to the limitations set out in Community law. A right to reside in a Member State does not flow automatically from Article 18 EC but is dependant upon the fulfilment of the various conditions laid down both in the Treaty itself and secondary legislation. However, once a person was lawfully resident in a Member State, they had the right to be treated equally with nationals of that State and could rely on Article 12 EC to claim a social assistance benefit.

Grezelczyk and *Bidar*, as we have said above, established that entitlement to benefits and loans from a Member State on the same terms as nationals of that State was dependant on the claimant having a link with that State, an issue to be determined in the circumstances of each case.

Collins[84] went further than *Trojani* in that the Court found that although the claimant (who was of dual American-Irish citizenship) was lawfully resident in the United Kingdom and that the job seekers allowance which he claimed was within the scope of the EC Treaty, it was legitimate for the United Kingdom to grant such an allowance only after it was possible to establish that a genuine link existed between the person seeking work and the employment market of that State. Such a link may be determined in particular by establishing that the person concerned has, for a reasonable period, in fact genuinely sought work in the Member State in question.

The position at present thus seems to be that lawful residence alone will not bring entitlement to equal treatment – some further link with the host State is necessary to engender the solidarity that warrants support from the citizens of that State.

5.6 Gender Discrimination

The influence of the ECJ in the development of law and policy on gender discrimination has been considerable. This is an area in which there is abundant evidence of legislation being case-led. It would not be an exaggeration to state that the women of Europe are deeply indebted to the ECJ for what, to date, has been achieved in ensuring their equality of treatment in the workplace and beyond. In short, for all the inequality that still persists,[85] without the Court's judicial activism, the position today probably would be much worse.

Article 141 gives specific expression to the principle of equality of treatment in the EC Treaty. It was inserted into the Treaty by the Treaty of Amsterdam, but its provisions had formed part of the Agreement on Social Policy adopted as a Protocol to the Maastricht Treaty. It replaces Article 119. Whilst retaining some of the wording of Article 119, it expands that provision in three ways: the principle of equality of treatment is extended from its previous confines of pay to 'matters of employment and occupation, including the principle of equal pay for equal work or work of equal value'; the Council is endowed with legislative competence; and the Member States are permitted to engage in positive discrimination, thus embodying the *Kalanke* case law within the EC Treaty:[86]

> With a view to ensuring full equality in practice between men and women in working life, the principle of equal treatment shall not prevent any Member State from maintaining or adopting measures providing for specific advantages in order to make it easier for the underrepresented sex to pursue a vocational

---

[83] Case C-456/02 [2004] ECR I-7573.
[84] Case C-138/02 [2004] ECR I-5547.

[85] And it does persist. See Report on Equality between Men and Women 2006 EC Commission 2006, para. 2.2.
[86] Case C-450/93 *Kalanke* [1997] ECR I-6363; Case C-409/95 *Marschall* [1997] ECR I-6363; Case C-158/97 *Badeck* [2000] ECR I-1875; Case C-407/98 *Abrahamsson and Anderson* [2000] ECR I-5539; Case C-476/99 *Lommers* [2002] ECR I-2891.

activity or to prevent or compensate for dis-advantages in professional careers.[87]

Article 119 of the original EC Treaty was con-cerned with gender discrimination strictly from an economic point of view. The Ohlin Commit-tee,[88] set up in 1956 to examine what the social aspects of the future European Economic Com-munity should be, concluded that there was only one aspect of social policy which should be reg-ulated on a European level and that was the pay levels of the female workforce. At that time, with few exceptions, notably France, women were paid at a lower rate than men. This could, the Commit-tee concluded, lead to a distortion in production costs with consequent imbalances in competition conditions within the common market.[89]

Article 119 thus provided for equal pay for men and women doing equal work. It was designed to ensure free and fair competition and was not viewed in the early years of the Community as hav-ing a social objective;[90] although, with the evolu-tion of the Community from a purely economic entity to a Community concerned with the well being of its citizens and their fundamental rights, the Court placed a broader interpretation on it:

> [T]he economic aim pursued by Article 119 . . . namely the elimination of distortions of com-petition between undertakings established in different Member States, is secondary to the social aim pursued by the same provision, which constitutes the expression of a funda-mental human right.[91]

Article 119 did not provide for the adoption of Community measures to enforce this principle. Instead, it relied on requiring the Member States themselves to bring about equal pay for equal work within their own legal systems by 1 January 1964. This deadline was not respected and so the Commission began drawing up proposals for what ultimately became the Equal Pay Directive.[92] In the meantime, Gabrielle Defrenne, an air stew-ardess with the now defunct national Belgian air-line, SABENA, began a series of actions complain-ing of discrimination with respect to her pay and a number of other working conditions which she claimed were less favourable than those of her male colleagues doing the same work.

In the second of these actions, *Defrenne II*,[93] in support of her claim to parity of pay she relied upon Article 119. In a preliminary ruling referred to the ECJ by the Cour de Travail Brussels, the Court was asked whether Article 119 had direct effect with the result that workers could rely on it before national courts to claim equal pay. The Court held that indeed they could. It began its analysis of the point by stating that Article 119 had a double aim: to avoid a situation in which undertakings in Member States where the princi-ple of equal pay for equal work had been imple-mented from suffering a competitive disadvantage as compared to undertakings established in Mem-ber States where that principle was not respected, and since Article 119 was part of the chapter in the Treaty devoted to social policy it had the social aim of improving working conditions and living stan-dards.

The Court went on to find that Article 119 was 'directly applicable and may therefore give rise to individual rights which the Court must pro-tect'. Article 119 imposed upon Member States a duty to bring about a specific result within a fixed period. It was not a vague declaration nor did it give the Member States any discretion. The Court pronounced the principle of equal pay to be one of the foundations of the Community, which must be attained by raising the lowest salaries rather than lowering the highest. Women's pay was to move up to the level of that of men.[94]

The *Defrenne II* case was, at the time, viewed as being dramatic: far from the Member States

---

[87] Article 141(4).

[88] This was a group of independent experts appointed by the International Labour Organisation chaired by Profes-sor Ohlin.

[89] Social Aspects of European Economic Co-Operation. Report by a Group of Experts, Studies and Reports, New Series, No. 46 (Geneva: ILO, 1956), para. 109. The Report is summarised in *International Labour Review*, Vol. 74 (1956), pp. 99–123.

[90] C. Barnard, 'The Economic Objectives of Article 119', in T. K. Hervey and D. O'Keeffe (eds.), *Sex Equality Law in the European Union* (Chichester: John Wiley & Sons, 1996), pp. 321–334.

[91] Case 50/96 *Deutsche Telecom v. Schroeder* [2000] ECR I – 743, Judgment at para. 57.

[92] Directive 75/117 OJ 1975 L45/19.

[93] Case C-43/75 *Defrenne II* [1976] ECR 455.

[94] Re-iterated in Case C-7/93 *Beune* [1994] ECR I-4471, Judg-ment para. 28, where the Court held that the principle cannot be determined by a formal criterion, which is in itself dependent upon a rule or practice followed in the Member States.

meandering gently on their own terms towards equal pay for men and women, they were faced with the prospect of the Court declaring this to be a directly effective right, the substance of which could not be limited by national legislation. There could have been grave financial consequences for many sectors of industry and it was because of that that the Court bowed to the argument advanced, in particular, by the governments of Ireland and the United Kingdom, to limit the effect in time of its judgment. It held that Article 119 could not be relied upon to support claims for pay periods prior to the date of judgment, 8 April 1976, save with respect to those claimants who had instituted proceedings prior to that date.[95]

In two other sets of proceedings instituted by Miss Defrenne, the Court found that Article 119 related to pay only and did not require equal treatment with respect to working conditions[96] or within state social security systems.[97]

In the thirty years which have elapsed since the judgment in *Defrenne II*, much has occurred. A sizeable body of EC legislation has been enacted. The law relating to gender discrimination is currently found in some six directives all of which, in addition to Articles 119 and 141, have spawned a significant body of case law,[98] some of which has either caused legislative amendment or has actually inspired legislation, which in many cases simply codifies the case law.

Following the Equal Pay Directive of 1975, two directives were respectively adopted in 1976 and 1979: the Equal Opportunities Directive[99] and the Equal Treatment in Social Security Directive.[100] In 1986, the Equality of Treatment in Occupational Welfare Schemes Directive was adopted,[101] in the mistaken belief that the concept of 'pay' did not extend to occupational welfare schemes such as pensions. Shortly after its enactment, the ECJ held in *Barber*[102] that occupational pensions and redundancy payments were 'pay' for the purposes of Article 119, if they derived for employment and were paid under contractual arrangements between the employer and the employee. Whilst not rendering the Directive otiose, it did require it to be amended.[103]

Three further directives complete the corpus of gender discrimination legislation. Directive 97/80,[104] on the burden of proof in cases of discrimination based on sex, codified the Court's case law on balancing the burden of proof between parties in gender discrimination cases.[105] Directive 86/613 extended the principle of equal treatment to the self-employed[106] and Directive 2004/113 implemented the principle of equal treatment between men and women in the access to and supply of goods and services.[107]

In interpreting and applying this complex body of legislation, and Articles 119 and 141 of the EC Treaty, the Court's approach has been to confine the right to equality to the situations where it has been outlawed, refusing, for example, to extend the concept of 'pay' to working conditions or state social security systems and limiting the right of equal treatment in the sphere of social security to those risks and benefits which are specified in the Equal Treatment in Social Security Directive.[108] It has thus refused to be persuaded to elasticise rights beyond the confines laid down in the Treaty or legislation. But at the same time it has insisted that whatever rights have been conferred on individuals must be given full effect.

---

[95] A similar approach was adopted in Case C-262/88 *Barber* [1999] ECR I-1889, in which the Court found to everyone's apparent astonishment that occupational pensions were part of pay.

[96] Case C-148/77 *Defrenne III* [1978] ECR 1365.

[97] Case C-80/70 *Defrenne I* [1971] ECR 445.

[98] See C. Kilpatrick, 'Community or Communities of Courts in European Integration: Sex Equality Dialogues between UK Courts and the ECJ', *European Law Journal*, Vol. 4, No. 2 (1998), pp. 121–147. 'The supremacy and direct effect doctrines give victims of sex discrimination a constitutional sledge hammer to attack national laws that restrict rights conferred by EC law'. This explains why test cases have been deployed to explore how far national discrimination law is compatible with EC law': D. Chalmers, C. Hadjiemmanuil, G. Monti G and A. Tomkins, *European Union Law* (Cambridge: Cambridge University Press, 2006), p. 881.

[99] Directive 76/207 OJ 1976 L39/40.

[100] Directive 79/7 OJ 1979 L6/24.

[101] Directive 86/378 OJ 1986 L225/40.

[102] Case C-262/88 [1980] ECR I-188.

[103] Directive 96/97 OJ 1997 L46/20.

[104] OJ 1998 L14/6.

[105] Ibid. Recital 18.

[106] OJ 1986 L359/56.

[107] OJ 2004 L37/37.

[108] Directive 79/7 on the principle of equal treatment for men and women in matters of social security OJ 1979 L6/24.

A broad view has been taken as from early years to the concept of 'pay', defining it as any consideration that a worker receives directly or indirectly in respect of employment from an employer. This approach has proved to be particularly insightful as remuneration has moved from what it was in the early years of the Community, to more complex arrangements referred to as 'packages'. Pay has been held to include sick leave pay,[109] allowances during maternity leave,[110] Christmas bonuses,[111] family and marriage allowances,[112] special travel concession,[113] compensation for unfair dismissal,[114] redundancy payments and severance payments,[115] supplementary pay for working unsocial hours,[116] benefits paid under an occupational pension scheme (provided they are financed by the employer and form part of the employment contract)[117] and access to an occupational pension scheme.[118]

The essential criterion is that the money or benefit in question must be attributable to employment, and be paid by the employer as a result of a contract of employment. The fact that the obligation to pay the money arises out of legislation, a judicial decision or a collective agreement is irrelevant.

With respect to social security systems the Court has held that where a benefit or a risk covered comes within the ambit of the Equal Treatment in Social Security Directive, the right to equality of treatment should not be prejudiced by the way in which a social security system is organised, which inevitably will be different from State to State. It matters not whether a benefit is paid directly to the person who is suffering the risk or to someone who is caring for that person.[119] Likewise, if the objective of a benefit is to cover a risk specified in the Directive, the nature of that benefit is irrelevant.[120]

Equally, the Court has held that Article 119 and the Equal Opportunities Directive were concerned with differential treatment based on sex only,[121] a concept which excluded sexual orientation. In *Grant*, the Court ruled that Article 119:[122]

[I]s to be determined only by having regard to its wording and purpose, its place in the scheme of the Treaty and its legal context. It follows that Community law as it stands at present does not cover discrimination based on sexual orientation.[123]

This position has changed though with the Treaty of Amsterdam. Article 13 EC enables the Council to adopt measures to combat discrimination based on sexual orientation.

Both direct and indirect discrimination are prohibited. Direct discrimination has been defined by Advocate General Jacobs in *Schnorbus*[124] in the following terms:

[D]iscrimination is direct where the difference in treatment is based on a criterion which is either explicitly that of sex or necessarily linked to a characteristic indissociable from sex.[125]

It is now defined in Article 2 (a) of the Equal Opportunities Directive as occurring:

[W]here one person is treated less favourably, on grounds of sex, than another is, has been or would be treated in a comparable situation.

Indirect discrimination, a concept developed by the Court from the early 1980s, has been more problematic to apply given the Court's insistence that an actual adverse impact on one gender or another of a particular pay regime or term of employment and how that adverse impact had to be proved. Potential adverse impact was not sufficient to ground a claim.[126] Following the approach of the Court, the Burden of Proof Directive[127]

---

[109] Case 171/88 *Rinner Kuhn* [1989]ECR 2743.
[110] Case C-342/93 *Gillespie* [1996] ECR I-475.
[111] Case C-333/97 *Lewen* [1998] ECR I-7243.
[112] Case C-187/98 *Commission v. Greece* [1999] ECR I-7713.
[113] Case C-12/81 *Garland* [1982] ECR 359.
[114] Case C-167/97 *Seymour Smith and Perez* [1999] ECR I-623.
[115] Case C-262/88 *Barber* [1990] ECR I-1889.
[116] Case C-236/98 *Jamo* [2000] ECR I-2189.
[117] Case C-170/84 *Bilka* [1986] ECR 1607.
[118] Case C-256/01 *Allonby* [2004] ECR I-873.
[119] Case 150/85 *Drake* [1986] ECR 1995.
[120] Case C-137/94 *Richardson* [1995] ECR I-3407;Vase C-382/98 *Taylor* [1999] ECR I-8955.

[121] In Case C-13/94 *P v. S and Cornwall County Council* [1996] ECR I-2143, it was held that the Equal Opportunities Directive applied to discrimination against transsexuals: 'Such discrimination is based, essentially if not exclusively on the sex of the person concerned' (para. 21).
[122] Case C-249/96 [1998] ECR I-621.
[123] Ibid. para. 47.
[124] Case C-79/99 [2000] ECRI-10997.
[125] Ibid. at 11008.
[126] See exceptionally Case C-321/98 *Kachelmann* [2000] ECR I-7505.
[127] See n. 104 above.

defined indirect discrimination in the following terms:

> [I]ndirect discrimination shall exist where an apparently neutral provision, criterion or practice disadvantages a substantially higher proportion of the members of one sex unless that provision, criterion or practice is appropriate and necessary and can be justified by objective factors unrelated to sex.[128]

This position appears to have changed with the amendment to the Equal Opportunities Directive introduced in 2002. Article 2(b) of that Directive now defines indirect discrimination as occurring:

> [W]here an apparently neutral provision, criterion or practice would put persons of one sex at a particular disadvantage compared with persons of the other sex, unless that provision, criterion or practice is objectively justified by a legitimate aim and the means of achieving that aim are appropriate and necessary....

This amendment was made to bring the Equal Opportunities Directive into line with the definition of indirect discrimination in the Race Directive[129] and the Equality of Employment Directive[130] both of which gave rights with respect to potential adverse impact.

Disparate impact has been held by the Court to occur when a measure affects 'a considerably smaller percentage of women than men',[131] 'a far greater number of women than men'[132] or 'far more women than men'. Little indication has been given of just how the disparate impact was to be assessed. What constitutes 'considerably smaller' or 'a far greater number' or 'far more'? Advocate General Cosmos in *ex parte Seymour Smith and Perez*[133] gave a number of examples of statistical evidence which the Court had found to be proof of indirect discrimination, concluding:

> [T]he determination of the question of indirect discrimination constitutes a complex assessment which takes account of objective and numerical factors alike. The percentages

per se are not absolute but rather of relative value which follows from their relationship to all other factors to be taken into account. Above all they are an indication, not proof, of discrimination.[134]

In its judgment, the Court held that it was for the national court to assess statistical evidence and issued a caution on the use of such material. The national court should assess whether the statistics concerning the situation of the workforce were valid, that is whether they covered every individual, whether they were purely fortuitous or short-term phenomena and whether in general they appeared to be significant.

The case law of the Court on methods of proving disparate impact is complex and difficult to apply. Statistical evidence can be difficult to assemble and analyse. There appears to be a move away from the approach of the Court in the 2002 amendment of the Equal Opportunities Directive, which provides in Recital 10 that indirect discrimination may be established 'by any means including on the basis of statistical evidence'. It remains to be seen what direction future case law will take on this matter.

5.7 Conclusion

An attempt has been made to illustrate the effect of the case law of the Court on combating gender discrimination. Space permits the consideration of only a sample of the rich jurisprudence. A Directive[135] has been adopted which further integrates this case law into legislation. For example, the principle of a single source of pay – but not necessarily derived from one and the same employer – developed by the Court in *Allonby*[136] and *Lawrence*[137] is included in Article 4 of the Directive. The case law on gender discrimination in occupational pension schemes following *Barber* is also incorporated. Additionally the Directive merges the three Directives on Equal Pay, Equal

---

[128] Ibid. Article 2 (b).
[129] Directive 2000/43 OJ 2000 L180/22.
[130] Directive 2000/78 OJ 2000 L303/16.
[131] Case 96/80 *Jenkins* [1981] ECR 911.
[132] Case 171/88 *Rinner Kuhn* [1989] ECR 2743.
[133] Case 167/97 [1999] ECR I-623.

[134] Ibid. at 658.
[135] Directive 2006/54 of the European Parliament and of the Council on the implementation of the principle of equal opportunities and equal treatment of men and women in matters of employment and occupation, OJ 2006 L204/23.
[136] Case 256/01 [2004] ECR I-873.
[137] Case C-320/00 [2002] ECR I-7325.

Opportunities and Equality of Treatment in Social Security, thereby tidying up the legislative landscape.

6. REMEDIES FOR VIOLATIONS AND IMPACT OF JUDGMENTS

As we have stated above, actions in the social and economic fields may consist either in infringement proceedings brought against a Member States for failure to fulfil its obligations, notably by not implementing directives within the required time frame. Such actions, if successful, result in a declaration by the Court that the Member State in question has failed to fulfil its obligations under Community law. Non-compliance with a judgment of the Court may result in the imposition of a lump sum or penalty payment.[138]

In the case of preliminary rulings, on the other hand, proceedings originate before a court or tribunal of a Member State and the law of the Member State governs the remedies available to the parties. However, the Court has laid down that remedies for a breach of Community Law rights must be effective.[139]

In the case of direct actions, a judgment of the Court will normally find that a Member State has either infringed upon its obligations under the EC Treaty or not as the case may be. As such the judgment binds only the Member State in question but is of general application in so far as it interprets Community law. In the case of preliminary rulings, the judgments of the Court – being interpretative rulings of provisions of Community law over which the Court has exclusive competence – apply erga omnes.

7. CONCLUSIONS

Within the limits of this chapter an attempt has been made to illustrate the considerable contribution the Court has made to the development of socio-economic rights within the Community. From the original arid provisions of the EEC Treaty and, at time, vague and imprecise legislative measures, a corpus of rights has been created which has had a huge impact on the lives of ordinary men, women and children within the Community – a difference in the quality of their lives which, at least in some cases, their own governments were reluctant to sanction. For all the rhetoric from politicians to law makers, it is not from them that social Europe, such as it is, has come. It has come from the citizens themselves, bringing legal proceedings from the length and breadth of the Community, asserting their rights and from a Court that has been willing to put flesh on rather skeletal legal provisions.

But of late the Court has been subject to increasing criticism: it is alleged that it has been overly zealous in the matter of social and economic rights. More seriously the Court is accused of exceeding its jurisdiction: it has not confined itself to interpreting and applying the law, but has assumed the function of legislator.[140] There is in some quarters unease that far from improving the lot of the citizen, the Court's activism may actually threatened the fabric of national social welfare systems which the Member States have sought to protect by limiting the competence of the Community Institutions. Thus although Member States remain responsible for their social security systems, the Court by interpreting conditions of entitlement broadly to include groups of persons who were never envisaged as being within the scope of a national social security system, may actually dilute that system with the result that benefit structures and level may have to be reviewed to cope with increasing and unforeseen demands.

This unease has in particular set in with the case law on the rights of the European citizen with which the Court has had to grapple in the face of little or no guidance in either the Treaty or secondary legislation. In the face of loosely drafted provisions of a constitutional status which presumes the granting of rights and the assumption of obligations what was the Court supposed to do? It did what was reasonable, it assumed that the status of European citizen was meant to be meaningful and in the absence of any articulation of that meaningfulness it feel to it to determine what they

---

[138] See Article 228 EC.

[139] Case C-271/91 *Marshall II* [1993] ECR I-4367.

[140] K. Hailbronner, 'Union citizenship and access to social benefits', *Common Market Law Review*, Vol. 42, No. 5 (2005), pp. 1245–1267; Davies, 'The European Court of Justice' (n. 2 above); Simitis, 'Dismantling or Strengthening Labour Law' (n. 2 above).

might be. It did what it has always done in sphere of socio-economic rights, it dressed the skeleton, and can it be blamed for that? If the Member States are concerned at the extent of judicial activism of the ECJ they have but to articulate the parameters of socio-economic rights in either the Treaty itself or in legislation. Contrary to what was the position in the past, opportunities do arise for Treaty amendment and there is adequate legislative competence, the effective use of which could lessen the Court's influence on the formulation of socio-economic rights.

PART FOUR

International Human Rights Procedures and Jurisprudence

Committee on Economic, Social and Cultural Rights

Past, Present and Future

Malcolm Langford* and Jeff A. King**

1. INTRODUCTION

After the adoption in 1948 of the Universal Declaration of Human Rights ('UDHR'), which included a relatively full catalogue of human rights, the UN General Assembly instructed the Commission on Human Rights to commence the drafting of a single covenant on human rights.[1] While the drafting of a treaty covering civil and political rights was completed in short time, disagreement over whether to include economic, social and cultural rights led the Economic and Social Council ('ECOSOC') to request guidance from the General Assembly.[2] The General Assembly initially ordered the Commission to produce one covenant but later reversed its position[3] due to mediocre drafting progress, further prompting from ECOSOC and opposition of some Western States to economic, social and cultural rights.[4] In 1966, it approved the adoption of two Covenants: the International Covenant on Civil and Political Rights ('ICCPR')[5] and the International Covenant on Economic, Social and Cultural Rights (the 'Covenant' or 'ICESCR'),[6] the latter lacking a complaints mechanism.

Two decades after this schism, the 'renaissance' of economic, social and cultural rights ('ESC rights') is partly attributable to the pioneering work of the UN Committee on Economic, Social and Cultural Rights ('the Committee').[7] Established in 1987, the Committee has developed a 'jurisprudence' through its general comments and State-specific concluding observations. This work has been influential and catalytic in helping develop the conceptual framework of economic, social and cultural rights. This influence has been particularly noticeable in the work of non-governmental organisations and UN actors who have sought to champion economic, social and cultural rights in the fields of development, social justice and traditional human rights advocacy and litigation.[8] At the same time, the Committee's work has attracted criticism from some States and commentators on the grounds that it has been too demanding of

* Research Fellow, Norwegian Centre on Human Rights, University of Oslo. We would like to kindly thank Eibe Riedel, Asbjørne Eide, Matthew Craven and Wouter Vandenhole for comments on an earlier draft.
** Fellow and Tutor in Law, Balliol College, University of Oxford.

[1] GA Resolution 217 E(III) (10 December 1948), 3 UN GAOR, Resolutions Part I, at 71 (1948).
[2] M. Craven, *The International Covenant on Economic, Social and Cultural Rights: A Perspective on Its Development* (Oxford: Oxford University Press, 1995), pp. 16–20.
[3] GA Resolution 543 (VI) (5 February 1952) UN GAOR, Resolutions Supp. (No. 20), at 36 (1952).
[4] See Craven, *The International Covenant on Economic, Social and Cultural Rights* (n. 2 above), p. 9. Though he and others note diverse reasons for the division of the two Covenants. See H. Steiner and P. Alston (eds.), *International Human Rights in Context: Law, Politics and Morals* (New York: Oxford University Press, 1996) 260–263. See also Annotations on the Text of the Draft International Covenants on Human Rights, U.N. Doc. A/2929 (1955), reproduced in Steiner and Alston.

[5] International Covenant on Civil and Political Rights, G.A. res. 2200A (XXI), 21 U.N. GAOR Supp. (No. 16) at 52, U.N. Doc. A/6316 (1966), 999 U.N.T.S. 171, *entered into force* Mar. 23, 1976.
[6] International Covenant on Economic, Social and Cultural Rights, G.A. res. 2200A (XXI), 21 U.N. GAOR Supp. (No. 16) at 49, U.N. Doc. A/6316 (1966), 993 U.N.T.S. 3, *entered into force* Jan. 3, 1976. Currently ratified by 156 States parties.
[7] The former Human Rights Ambassador of Germany singles out the Committee for particular praise in this regard in his Foreword to E. Riedel and P. Rothen (eds.), *The Human Right to Water* (Berlin: Berliner Wissenschafts Verlag, 2006).
[8] In effect, these actors have often been the key messengers of the Committee's work, whether to States, courts, international financial institutions and even social movements.

States, or lacked conceptual rigour. Others have argued the opposite, namely, that the Committee is too conservative, for example in the areas of intellectual property rights and its approach to women's rights.

This chapter reviews the evolution of the ICESCR, as guided chiefly by the work of the Committee. Section 2 traces the history of the Covenant and the development of the Committee's innovative working methods. Sections 3 and 4 analyse the manner in which State obligations have been interpreted and focuses critically on the Committee's more recent jurisprudence. Section 5 examines the Committee's work on two selected rights in order to illustrate its approach to the Covenant rights while the remainder of the piece examines the development of a complaints mechanism.

2. THE COMMITTEE IN CONTEXT

The Covenant is unique among the nine major United Nations human rights conventions in that the text of the treaty does not provide for the creation of a specialist and independent supervisory body. The task of reviewing State party reports was entrusted to ECOSOC,[9] which is composed of State representatives rather than independent experts, and is occupied with a diverse agenda. With the entry of the Covenant into force in 1976, a sessional working group of States parties representatives was created to 'assist' ECOSOC with monitoring the Covenant, which involved a three-stage reporting process over six-year intervals.[10] But its work came under sustained criticism,[11] and in 1985 a standing Committee composed of independent experts was created.[12] The Committee functions under the umbrella of ECOSOC, to which it submits its reports and rules of proce-

dures and so forth,[13] but this latent umbilical cord may be shortly removed. In March 2007, the UN Human Rights Council resolved to initiate a process to 'rectify … the legal status of the Committee on Economic, Social and Cultural Rights, with the aim of placing the Committee on a par with all other treaty monitoring bodies'.[14]

Interestingly, from the 1950s to the 1980s, the mainstay of the opposition to the creation of the Committee was the Socialist states, initially with the support of the United Kingdom and Australia.[15] The United States was a strong supporter, along with Latin American and other European states, until 1985 where it became the sole country

---

[9] See Part IV of the Covenant.

[10] See Economic and Social Council Resolution 1978/10 (3 May 1978) and Economic and Social Council Resolution 1988 (LX) (11 May 1976).

[11] See Economic and Social Council Resolution, 1980/24 (2 May 1983), para. 2 and Craven, *The International Covenant on Economic, Social and Cultural Rights* (n. 4 above), pp. 40–41, for a convenient catalogue of defects. See also Alston, 'Committee on Economic, Social and Cultural Rights', (n. 13 below), pp. 479–487.

[12] Economic and Social Council Resolution 1985/17. Note in this respect that Craven's cornerstone scholarship on the development of the Covenant makes little reference to the pre-Committee discussion of legal standards.

[13] The Committee is able to adjust its terms of reference rather easily through requests to this Council. While this unique genealogy is lauded by some for its flexibility (Craven, *The International Covenant on Economic, Social and Cultural Rights* (n. 2 above), p. 103), it is viewed as a liability by others. P. Alston, 'The Committee on Economic, Social and Cultural Rights', in P. Alston, (ed.) *The United Nations and Human Rights: A Critical Appraisal* (Oxford: Oxford University Press, 1992) pp. 473–508, at p. 488, notes that the Committee exists 'entirely at the pleasure' of ECOSOC.

[14] U.N. Doc. A/HRC/4/L.17. Text Taken from UN Press Release, 'Human Rights Council Adopts Seven Resolutions and Two Decisions, Including Text on Darfur', 30 March 2007.

[15] Indeed, the constant ebb and flow of approval over half a century shows that various countries supported or opposed at different times and for various reasons the creation of a more effective system of supervision for economic, social and cultural rights. The socialist/capitalist ideological divide does not always appear to be the guiding consideration in the matter. Lebanon, an ally of the West in the 1950s, proposed the establishment of an independent committee but it was opposed by numerous states, including China. In 1954, France suggested that the Human Rights Committee (to be established under the draft ICCPR) consider State party reports concerning the ICESCR but objections were made again by China, the UK and Australia. In a last minute attempt to amend the draft Covenant in 1966, Italy proposed the creation of an ad hoc body of experts, and the United States proposed the creation of an expert body composed of independent experts with recognised competence in the field. Several Western states, including Canada, the Netherlands, Finland and Norway had also supported a milder Italian proposal to create an ad hoc body of experts, which was also unsuccessful. Alston also points out that of the eighteen respondents on a survey of the ECOSOC working group in the 1970s, the half that expressed dissatisfaction and endorsed the creation of a new independent Committee were nearly all Western states, including the United Kingdom, Australia, Canada and the Federal Republic of Germany. See Alston, 'The Committee on Economic, Social and Cultural Rights' (n. 13 above), pp. 476–484. See also Craven, *The International Covenant on Economic, Social and Cultural Rights* (n. 2 above).

to vote against the resolution establishing the Committee.[16]

2.1 Structure of the Committee and Its Sessions

The Committee is composed of eighteen individual experts with 'recognized competence in the field of human rights, serving in their personal capacity'.[17] According to the ECOSOC resolution, the function of the Committee is to 'assist' the Council with its consideration of State party reports. In practice, it has primarily developed this role to include adoption of concluding observations on State party reports or compliance with the Covenant absent reports, and clarification of norms under the Covenant through its days of general discussion and particularly the drafting and adoption of General Comments. As with the other human rights bodies and UN in general, the Committee is required to reflect equitable geographical distribution and representation of various legal systems. Committee members are currently elected by ECOSOC for four-year terms after nominations from States parties to the Covenant. Committee members are frequently re-elected, which, together with its strictly observed policy of consensus decision-making, promotes a certain stability. Some argue that this has led to consistency in the Committee's results,[18] but it is also possible to observe some significant contrasts between the first and second decades of work due to changes in membership and leadership within the Committee.

2.2 Concluding Observations

State party reports often range up to several hundred pages, and the Committee reviews and adopts concluding observations on about five reports in each of its twice-yearly, three-week sessions. The new Committee realised early on that the three-stage reporting process was ineffective, and requested and was subsequently granted a single global report on conformity, to be submitted every five years.[19] The guiding philosophy of the reporting process is that Committee members engage in a 'constructive dialogue' with State party representatives. This facilitates the Committee's recommendation of useful measures to implement the provisions of the Covenant. In respect of each State party's report, the Committee also considers submissions from NGOs and UN specialised agencies, information that the Committee members have as experts in their field, and general information collected by the Secretariat from other UN sources and which is placed in a 'country file'.

To focus its work amid this gigantic flow of paper, the Committee has adopted two principal methods. First, it has issued detailed reporting guidelines to assist States in providing the information it deems most relevant.[20] Second, it created a Pre-Sessional Working Group ('PSWG') composed of five members to review reports and prepare a publicly available 'list of issues' for discussion with the State party at the next session.[21] The Committee also decided to schedule for consideration the situation in countries with significantly overdue reports, and notify the State concerned.[22] For instance, due to long overdue reports, the Committee proceeded to review the compliance of the Solomon Islands (1999) and Congo (Brazzaville) (2000) in the absence of a State party report.[23]

[16] The Republican Party candidate Ronald Reagan became President of the United States in 1981, reversing then President Jimmy Carter's warmer attitude to international human rights, and to the Covenant in particular.

[17] Economic and Social Council Resolution. 1985/17 (28 May 1985), para. b. The Committee's first session was held in 1987. See P. Alston and B. Simma, 'First Session of the UN Committee on Economic, Social and Cultural Rights', *American Journal of International Law*, Vol. 81 (1987), pp. 747–756.

[18] Craven, *The International Covenant on Economic, Social and Cultural Rights* (n. 2 above), p. 43.

[19] *Report on Second Session of the Committee on Economic, Social and Cultural Rights*, ECOSOC Official Records, Supp. No.2 (1988) U.N. Doc. E/1998/14. para. 351.

[20] *Official Records of The Economic and Social Council*, 1991, Supp. No.3 (E/1991/23-E/C.12/1990/8), Annex IV. Note that the guidelines are currently being updated.

[21] See Economic and Social Council Resolution. 1995/39 (25 July 1995) and *Report of the Thirtieth and Thirty-First Sessions*, ECOSOC Official Records, Supp. No.2, (2004) (E/2004/22-) para. 27.

[22] Though if the State party indicates that a report will be provided, the Committee has indicated it will defer consideration of the report for one session: Ibid. paras. 42–44.

[23] See *Concluding Observations of the CESCR: Solomon Islands*, UN Doc. E/C.12/1/Add.33 (1999); *Concluding Observations of the CESCR: Republic of Congo [Brazzaville]*, UN Doc. E/C.12/1/Add.45. (2000). In 2004, the Committee further decided that in such cases of overdue reports, and when the Committee has received

2.3   General Comments

To date, the Committee has adopted eighteen general comments and at the time of writing was considering drafts on social security and non-discrimination. While general comments are in one sense not comparable to an ordinary judgment, as they are not developed in the context of a specific case, their contents are shaped primarily by the Committee's experience of reviewing State-party reports. Thomas Burgenthal has likened the practice of adopting general comments to the advisory jurisdiction of courts.[24] The Committee declares the function of the general comments as being, among other things, to:

> [M]ake the experience gained so far through the examination of these reports available for the benefit of all States parties in order to assist and promote their further implementation of the Covenant; to draw the attention of the States parties to insufficiencies disclosed by a large number of reports; to suggest improvements in the reporting procedures and to stimulate the activities of the States parties, the international organizations and the specialized agencies concerned in achieving progressively and effectively the full realization of the rights recognized in the Covenant.[25]

This suggests in theory a strong relationship between the insight generated by concluding observations and the content of the Committee's general comments. But such a relationship is not always evident in practice. Some authors consider this desirable since the Committee has the opportunity to reflect more deeply, unshackled

by the concluding observations.[26] One Committee member also observed that the quality of concluding observations on a particular right usually increases after it has been the subject of a General Comment.[27] On the other hand, Dowell-Jones claims that the concluding observations are more sensitive to the resource constraints of States in comparison to the general comments,[28] although this argument may only hold true for some general comments (see discussion in Section 3.5 below).

Lawyers from the US State Department, writing in their personal capacity, claim that the Committee's recent general comments can be seen as an example of a 'unilateral alteration in the substantive content of the Covenant'.[29] They claim that the Committee's 'revisionist' views have not been generally accepted by States, pointing to a few international conferences in which the Committee's views have not been accepted by the States present. They have attacked the detailed wording of more General Comments as well as those that are addressing implied rights. For example, General Comment No. 5 found that the catch-all prohibited ground of non-discrimination in Article 2(2) – 'other status' – included 'disability'. In General Comment No. 15, the Committee derived the right to water from the right to an adequate standard of living,

---

information from national and international NGOs, it may either informally or formally bring such information to the attention of the State party and urge it to submit its report. If the request is formal, the Committee may also 'request the State party to provide it with information addressing issues raised in non-governmental organizations' submissions'. *Report of the Thirtieth and Thirty-First Session* (n. 21 above), paras. 605–606.

[24] T. Burgenthal, *International Human Rights in a Nutshell*, 2nd Ed. (St. Paul, MN: West Publishing, 1995), p. 46.

[25] Committee on Economic, Social and Cultural Rights, *Introduction, The purpose of general comments*, U.N. Doc. E/1989/22, annex III at 87 (1989), reprinted in Compilation of General Comments and General Recommendations Adopted by Human Rights Treaty Bodies, U.N. Doc. HRI\GEN\1\Rev.6 at 8 (2003), para. 3, quoting its 1989 report to ECOSOC.

[26] See Craven, *The International Covenant on Economic, Social and Cultural Rights* (n. 2 above), p. 90; and M. Sepúlveda, *The Nature of Obligations under the International Covenant on Economic, Social and Cultural Rights* (Antwerp: Intersentia, 2003), p. 41.

[27] As noted orally to one of the authors by Eibe Riedel, Committee member, in November 2006.

[28] M. Dowell-Jones, *Contextualising the International Covenant on Economic, Social and Cultural Rights: Assessing the Economic Deficit* (Leiden: Martinus Nijhoff Publishers, 2004).

[29] M. Dennis and D. Stewart, 'Justiciability of Economic, Social, and Cultural Rights: Should There Be an International Complaints Mechanism to Adjudicate the Rights to Food, Water, Housing, and Health?' *American Journal of International Law*, Vol. 98 (2004), pp. 462–515. The point being made with that phrase, however, was explicitly rebutted by Craven's more searching analysis in *International Covenant*, p. 301. Nonetheless, at 493, the authors state that 'under the Committee's approach, states and government officials could, for example – with respect to the right to health – be found liable to individual claimants for unlawful water pollution, inappropriate health care services, failure to insure that individual health practitioners meet professional standards, or failure to provide sufficient food or essential drugs'. This is a telling example of the fears the maximalist approach may generate.

including food, housing and clothing and the right to health.[30]

These arguments are overstated and potentially misleading. Despite the Committee requests that ECOSOC bring to its attention any comments by States parties or specialised agencies, there has to date been no formal objection to the Committee's general comments, unlike the Human Rights Committee.[31] The UN Economic and Social Council has instead encouraged the Committee to 'continue using that mechanism'[32] and the former UN Commission on Human Rights regularly urged the Committee to draft 'further general comments to assist and promote the further implementation by States parties of the Covenant'.[33] As will be argued later in the chapter, the Committee also had sufficient justification in international law for articulating implied rights and obligations in General Comments No. 5 and 15.

Nonetheless, there remain practical problems with the general comments. We are partly critical of the way in which the Committee has articulated the normative content of rights, the tripartite obligations of respect/protect/fulfil, and the minimum core obligation, as becomes clearer further below. On a more general level, however, two problems are evident. The first is stylistic. The current structure of the General Comment may need reconsideration.[34] Currently, each General Comment is divided into normative content, special topics of broad application (often concerned with non-discrimination and marginalised groups), State obligations, violations, international obligations, implementation at a national level and relevant obligations of non-State actors. While some NGOs and States have praised the structure for its clarity, others have bemoaned the resulting length and repetition in the General Comments. The second problem is that, even if Dennis and Stewart's

claims are overstated, the general comments do at times tend to be quite ambitious. Some of the more recent general comments, particularly General Comment No. 14 on the Right to Health, suffer from the appearance of a pastiche of observations and comments from many quarters – the Committee received numerous submissions from the health sector. This results in an overload of detail and a possible bewilderment at how a country can achieve all these directives.[35] Some may understand, however wrongly, that the long lists of obligations are all viewed by the Committee to be immediately enforceable entitlements. This would fuel misconceptions and challenges to the legitimacy of both the Covenant and Committee. Increased care and concision would thus be advisable.

2.4 Involvement of NGOs

The Committee, in it's own words, 'attaches great importance to the information provided to it by sources other than the State party in connection with its consideration of a State party's report'[36]

---

[30] See Dennis and Stewart, 'Justiciability of Economic, Social, and Cultural Rights', ibid., and also S. Tully, 'A Human Right to Access Water? A Critique of General Comment No. 15', *Netherlands Quarterly of Human Rights*, Vol. 23, No. 1 (2005), pp. 35–63.

[31] Sepúlveda, *The Nature of Obligations* (n. 26 above), p. 42.

[32] Economic and Social Council Resolution 1991/33, para. 9.

[33] Commission on Human Rights Resolution 2003/18, para. 11(a)(ii).

[34] The current guidelines for the structure of General Comments appear to have been drafted and pushed by the Committee's Secretary during the transition between the first and second Chairperson of the Committee.

[35] Paragraph 17 of *General Comment 14, The right to the highest attainable standard of health* (Twenty-second session, 2000), U.N. Doc. E/C.12/2000/4 (2000) provides a good example:

> The creation of conditions which would assure to all medical service and medical attention in the event of sickness (art. 12.2 (d)), both physical and mental, includes the provision of equal and timely access to basic preventive, curative, rehabilitative health services and health education; regular screening programmes; appropriate treatment of prevalent diseases, illnesses, injuries and disabilities, preferably at community level; the provision of essential drugs; and appropriate mental health treatment and care. A further important aspect is the improvement and furtherance of participation of the population in the provision of preventive and curative health services, such as the organization of the health sector, the insurance system and, in particular, participation in political decisions relating to the right to health taken at both the community and national levels.

Obviously, the Committee cannot be understood to suggest that all of these are entitlements that the Covenant obliges all States to fulfil immediately. Rather, we suggest, passages such as this one describe in a non-exhaustive way the full scope of the right that State parties are required to realize progressively in accordance with the obligation set forth in Article 2(1).

[36] *Report of the Thirtieth and Thirty-First Session*, ECOSOC Official Records, U.N. DOC. E/2004/22 (8 March 2004) para. 602.

and describes them as 'crucial' in following up on measures taken to give effect to the recommendations listed in the Committee's prior concluding observations.[37] In many cases, the Committee will not have the time or resources to conduct this analysis. Only through carefully prepared submissions akin to pleadings can the Committee come to a reasonable conclusion on this issue. Alston writes that the Committee therefore 'broke the mould' in 1988 by being the first UN human rights treaty body to permit the formal submission of written statements by NGOs.[38] The main areas in which the Committee invites the participation of NGOs is assistance with the consideration of State party reports, participation in the preparation of General Comments, and participation in days of general discussion.[39]

3. EVOLUTION OF THE COVENANT'S LEGAL STANDARDS

In Part III of the Covenant, States parties 'recognise' a significant range of social rights, including: the right to work (Article 6); to just and favourable conditions of work (Article 7); to form trade unions and strike (Article 8); to social security (Article 9), to an adequate standard of living (Article 11(1)); freedom from hunger (Article 11(2)); to the highest attainable standard of health (Article 12) and to education (Articles 13 and 14). Article 15 contains a number of 'cultural' rights including the right to take part in cultural life, enjoy the benefits of scientific progress and to protection of authorship interests in scientific, literary and artistic creations, while Article 10 obliges States to provide assistance to families and children.

Parts I and II of the Covenant overlap with the ICCPR with recognition of the right to self-determination and the setting out of States par-

ties obligations in respect of the rights. But the ICESCR and the ICCPR differ in one seemingly crucial manner: the phrasing of the primary State obligation. Article 2(1) of the latter provides that States parties shall 'respect' and 'ensure' the respective civil and political rights, while the equivalent provision of the former is more nuanced. Each State party commits itself to:

> [T]ake steps, individually and through international assistance and co-operation, especially economic and technical, to the maximum of its available resources, with a view to achieving progressively the full realization of the rights recognized in the present Covenant by all appropriate means, including particularly the adoption of legislative measures.

Many have made much ado about this difference, suggesting that the Covenant's obligations are merely aspirational. However, the Committee, drawing on a body of scholarly work developed during the 1980s, put paid to this simplistic view, providing a coherent understanding of terms such as 'maximum of available resources', 'achieving progressively', 'all appropriate means' and 'legislative measures'. Since this has been amply discussed elsewhere,[40] our aim in this section is to critically review the development of the doctrines on these key obligations in the Committee's general comments and concluding observations in the context of the wider scholarship and debate.

3.1   Conduct and Result

In 1977, the International Law Commission cited Article 2(1) of the Covenant as an example of a

---

[37] Ibid. para. 27.

[38] Alston, 'Committee on Economic, Social and Cultural Rights' (n. 13 above), p. 501.

[39] The Committee recently decided that NGOs should not send to it information concerning follow-up measures on the last report unless such information was specifically requested by the Committee in its concluding observations. Instead, it should send the information to the State party directly, which can take it into account in reporting back to the Committee in its next report. NGOs should then monitor the accuracy of the State party's compliance with its obligation to report back on follow-up measures, and report to the Committee at its next review.

[40] See for example, P. Alston and G. Quinn, 'Nature and Scope of States Parties' Obligations under the International Covenant on Economic, Social and Cultural Rights', *Human Rights Quarterly*, Vol. 9 No. 1 (1987), pp. 156–229, at 185; R. E. Robertson, 'Measuring State Compliance with the Obligation to Devote the "Maximum Available Resources" to Realizing Economic, Social, and Cultural Rights', *Human Rights Quarterly*, Vol. 16, No. 4 (1994), pp. 693–714; Craven, *The International Covenant on Economic, Social and Cultural Rights* (n. 2 above); and Sepúlveda, *The Nature of Obligations* (n. 26 above). See also the expert guidelines: 'The Limburg Principles on the Implementation of the International Covenant on Economic, Social and Cultural Rights', UN doc. E/CN.4/1987/17, Annex reprinted in *Human Rights Quarterly*, Vol. 9 (1987), pp. 122–135; and 'Maastricht Guidelines on Violations of Economic, Social and Cultural Rights', January 22–26, 1997, reprinted in *Human Rights Quarterly*, Vol. 20, no. 3 (1998), pp. 691–704.

provision that gives rise to obligations of result, but gives the State party its choice of means to achieve the result.[41] Interestingly, the ICCPR Article 2(2), which requires the State party to ensure the civil and political rights, has been similarly interpreted: 'the obligation leaves the State at least an initial freedom of choice of the means to be used to achieve the result required by the obligation'.[42] It is thus contrasted with obligations of conduct, which are more specific and leave a State no discretion as to the selection of its means of compliance. However, a liability of this view of the Covenant is that it may 'deprive it of any serious content'.[43] If results are only to be achieved progressively over time, giving States an unrestricted choice of means would provide 'little basis upon which to judge whether or not they were acting in good faith'.[44]

The Committee therefore reacted swiftly to this perspective in General Comment No.3, declaring that the Covenant contains legal obligations both of conduct and result. In an earlier article on the nature of obligations under the Covenant, Philip Alston, later to become Chairperson of the Committee, and Gerard Quinn, pointed out that the obligation 'to take steps' in Article 2(1) is an obligation of conduct.[45] They concluded that due to the uniqueness of the 'progressive implementation' character of the Covenant, the obligations are of a hybrid nature. States would be evaluated as to both types of obligations: whether they have appropriately taken (or refrained from) the necessary action under the Covenant, and the extent to which they have progressively realised the rights with the resources at their disposal.

This conclusion would be almost redundant these days, except that it has been revived in a surprising if not bizarre form. An Independent Expert appointed by the Commission on Human Rights to examine the question of a draft optional protocol to the Covenant, Hatem Kotrane, concluded in 2002 that part of the great difficulty in asserting justiciability of Covenant rights is that they are

obligations of *means* (i.e., conduct), not of result, unlike the ICCPR.[46] Despite its inconsistency with both the International Law Commission's and Committee's approach, this was not merely a mistake of terminology, as the point was explained in some, albeit brief, detail. This point was then picked up by critics of the optional protocol, Dennis and Stewart. They endorsed the Expert's views claiming that he 'acknowledged the important differences in the understandings of states parties to the two Covenants'.[47] Later in the same article, while explaining the West's opposition to the idea of 'juridical recognition' of Covenant rights, the authors refer to the comments of René Cassin noting that 'most economic and social rights, however, could only give rise to obligations to take action'.[48]

In addition to missing the ILC's classification, it seems these authors have also missed the point of a long and involved discussion. In 1987, Alston and Quinn were straining to argue that there were some obligations of conduct, which they call 'obligations of a more conventional and tangible nature'.[49] Furthermore, Craven has shown that the ILC's classification was difficult to sustain in practise: '[i]n the face of the indeterminate and conditional nature of the results to be achieved, the Committee has tended to concentrate on obligations of conduct'.[50] Perhaps the lesson from this confusion is to follow Sepúlveda's well-argued recommendation and set aside the conceptual framework altogether.[51] The distinction has proven no less a headache in other areas of international law.[52]

[41] 'Report of the International Law Commission on Its Twenty Ninth Session', *Yearbook of the International Law Commission*, Vol. 2, pp. 20–21 (1977), para. 8.

[42] Ibid.

[43] Craven, *The International Covenant on Economic, Social and Cultural Rights* (n. 2 above), p. 107; see also Sepúlveda, *Nature of Obligations* (n. 26 above), p. 188.

[44] Craven, ibid.

[45] Alston and Quinn, 'Nature and Scope of States Parties' Obligations' (n. 40 above), p. 185.

[46] *Report of the Independent Expert on the Draft Optional Protocol to the International Covenant on Economic, Social and Cultural Rights*, Commission on Human Rights, Fifty-Eighth Session, Item 10 of the Provisional Agenda, UN Doc. E/CN.4/2002/57, 12 February 2002, paras. 16–20.

[47] Dennis and Stewart, 'Justiciability of Economic, Social, and Cultural Rights' (n. 29 above), p. 470.

[48] UN Doc. E/CN.4/SR.270, at 11 (1952); cited in Dennis and Stewart, 'Justiciability of Economic, Social, and Cultural Rights', ibid. p. 484.

[49] Alston and Quinn, 'Nature and Scope of States Parties' Obligations' (n. 40 above), p. 185.

[50] Craven, *The International Covenant on Economic, Social and Cultural Rights* (n. 2 above), p. 108.

[51] Sepúlveda, *Nature of States Parties Obligations* (n. 26 above), pp. 184–196. The author notes at p. 196 that this would require amending the Committee's Outline for Drafting General Comments. In any case, the distinction barely features in the Committee's work.

[52] See P. M. Dupuy, 'Reviewing the Difficulties of Codification: On Ago's Classification of Obligations of Means and

3.2 Respect, Protect and Fulfil

Drawing on the work of Professor Asbørn Eide, which found expression in his UN reports on the right to food under the Covenant,[53] the Committee introduced a typology of obligations known as respect, protect and fulfil in General Comment No. 12 and has continued to use it in all subsequent general comments:

> The obligation to *respect* existing access to adequate food requires States parties not to take any measures that result in preventing such access. The obligation to *protect* requires measures by the State to ensure that enterprises or individuals do not deprive individuals of their access to adequate food. The obligation to *fulfil (facilitate)* means the State must pro-actively engage in activities intended to strengthen people's access to and utilization of resources and means to ensure their livelihood, including food security. Finally, whenever an individual or group is unable, for reasons beyond their control, to enjoy the right to adequate food by the means at their disposal, States have the obligation to *fulfil (provide)* that right directly.[54]

The Committee was not alone in this endeavour. South Africa adopted the model in its 1996 post-apartheid constitution and it is now used by the Committee on the Elimination of Discrimination Against Women.[55] The typology is particularly useful as a pedagogical tool, even with courts, and its original point was to affirm that in certain key respects, ESC rights are similar to civil and political because both types of rights involve three types of duties: respect (refrain from impeding), protect (ensure others do not impede), and fulfil (actually provide) the conditions necessary for realising human rights. The typology also attempts to overcome the positive/negative dichotomy that has been criticised and discredited as a baseline for appropriate judicial intervention.[56]

Since the duties to respect and protect are also familiar attributes of civil and political rights, the Committee may potentially use these two categories to state that prima facie, if the obligation under consideration is one of respect or protect, then there is a presumption that resource constraints are an insufficient reason for failing to implement the obligation. For instance, the Committee has found that forced evictions are 'prima facie incompatible with the requirements of the Covenant'.[57] By contrast, the obligation to protect does require positive action and may on occasion require significant resources. Nonetheless, the Committee has been of the view that such obligations often are of immediate effect and States parties are thus held to a high standard of compliance, as illustrated in Section 5 below. However, in a recent statement it has indicated the obligation often requires 'positive budgetary measures'.[58]

This schema has been highly developed in the Committee's general comments and examples are given of the types of obligations that would apply in practice. It is this ease of communicating the

---

Obligations of Result in Relation to State Responsibility', *European Journal of International Law*, Vol. 10, pp. 371–385 (1990), pp. 374–378.

[53] See A. Eide (UN Special Rapporteur on the Right to Food), *The Right to Food (Final Report)* U.N. Doc. E/CN.4/Sub.2/1987/23 (1987), paras.66–69. A similar typology was developed contemporaneously and for different purposes by the American philosopher Henry Shue: see *Basic Rights: Subsistence, Affluence and US Foreign Policy* (Princeton: Princeton University Press, 1980). For the history of this development, see A. Eide, 'State obligations revisited' in W.B. Eide and U. Kracht (eds.) *Food and Human Rights in Development, Vol. II: Evolving issues and emerging applications* (Antwerp: Intersentia, 2007), pp. 137–160.

[54] *General Comment No. 12, Right to adequate food* (Twentieth session, 1999), U.N. Doc. E/C.12/1999/5 (1999), para. 15.

[55] Constitution of the Republic of South Africa, Section 7(2); *General Recommendation No. 24* (20th session, 1999) U.N. Doc. A/54/38 at 5 (1999), paras. 14–17.

[56] For judicial treatments, see *Dunmore v. Ontario (Attorney General)*, [2001] 3 SCR 10, para. 20ff (majority) and para. 71ff (L'Heureux-Dubé J). (Supreme Court of Canada); *R v. Secretary of State for the Home Department, ex p Limbuela* [2005] UKHL 66, para. 92 (Lord Brown) (UK House of Lords): 'I repeat, it seems to me generally unhelpful to attempt to analyse obligations arising under article 3 as negative or positive, and the state's conduct as active or passive. Time and again these are shown to be false dichotomies. The real issue in all these cases is whether the state is properly to be regarded as responsible for the harm inflicted (or threatened) upon the victim'. Positive obligations are now an entrenched aspect of international human rights law, including civil and political rights. See e.g. A. Mowbray, *The Development of Positive Obligations under the European Convention on Human Rights by the European Court of Human Rights* (Oxford: Hart Publishing, 2004).

[57] *General Comment No. 7, Forced evictions, and the right to adequate housing,* (Sixteenth session, 1997), U.N. Doc. E/1998/22, annex IV at 113 (1997), para. 2.

[58] An evaluation of the obligation to take steps to the 'maximum of available resources' under an Optional Protocol, Statement, U.N. Doc. E/C.12/2007/1 (2007), para. 7.

wide-ranging obligations of States in a straightforward format that has appealed to both advocates and many States alike. The obligation to respect and protect Covenant rights has received considerable treatment by the Committee. Examples include forced evictions, arbitrary restrictions on trade union organisers or discriminatory refusal of access to health care services. The first example was the subject of an entire General Comment.[59] For any proposed eviction, the Committee required there be substantial justification, due process, including consideration of alternatives, and provision of legal remedies. If an eviction proceeded, remedies were to include provision of adequate alternative housing within maximum available resources with the minimum proviso that no one would be rendered homeless as a result of an eviction. Similar conditions were laid down with respect to interferences with the right to water. Examples also crop up in the Committee's concluding observations, though it appears to largely depend on the amount and quality of information provided by non/governmental sources. For instance, the Committee found that planned evictions by the Dominican Republic were not justified,[60] called on Israel to stop land confiscations and housing demolitions,[61] requested Norway to 'ensure that asylum seekers are not restricted in their access to education while their claim for asylum is being processed'[62] and called on Belarus to 'eliminate the restrictive legislation governing trade unions'.[63]

However, the typology is ripe for a more critical conceptual review.[64] The first problem is that no legal reasoning was given for the introduction of the typology in General Comment No. 12, whilst all previous categorisations introduced by the Committee were at least given some measure of justification. Furthermore, it is still not clear how the obligation to respect relates to the duty

of non-retrogression (examined further in Section 3.3 below). In the view of the Committee, the obligation to respect includes not only interference with 'self-help measures', as the Committee originally termed them, and freedom to self-organise access to the Covenant right, but access to government provided schemes.[65] Perhaps it is the individual or discriminatory aspect of the denial that is in focus, while non-retrogression refers to collective changes that affect all persons. But the Committee does not make this clear. Yet another complicating factor is that the obligation to respect in the context of the European Court of Human Rights is deemed to have positive duties, and the Committee should have perhaps indicated that its more circumscribed view of the obligation to respect was being made in a very different context, lest it be watered down at the regional level.

Most problematic, however, is that the conceptual scheme might be considered unworkable or an oversimplification of the interconnected nature of certain problems. A particular State action (e.g., a severe cut in welfare allowances) could potentially constitute a breach of the duty to respect, protect or fulfil. Certainly the decision and legal machinations invoke the first notion. The stakeholders may well assume that they have some property or vested interest in the government programme, backed by their tax payments, that is being taken from them.[66] And the alteration of legislation suggests that the duty to protect is under threat, particularly when putting homeless people at the mercy of private actors in the job and housing markets. It will doubtless also be characterised by the State as an issue concerning the government's duty to fulfil, and it will plead resource constraints and the need to choose between various priorities under the Covenant. The government will also argue that the duty to respect begins and ends in the state of nature, so to speak, and does not vest a property-like interest in every public privilege extended. What of the decision to privatise a water system? Is the positive act of contracting the services of a corporation an issue of respecting the right to

---

[59] *General Comment No. 7* (n. 57 above).

[60] *Concluding observations of CESCR: Dominican Republic*, U.N. Doc. CESCR E/1991/23, para. 326.

[61] *Concluding observations of CESCR: Israel*, 12 April 1998, U.N. Doc. E/C.12/1/Add.27, paras. 41.

[62] *Conclusions and recommendations of CESCR: Norway*, U.N. Doc. E/C.12/1/Add.109 (2005) para 93.

[63] *Conclusions and recommendations of CESCR: Belarus*, U.N. Doc. E/C.12/1/Add.7/Rev.1 (1996), para. 25.

[64] For another critique, see I.E. Koch, 'Dichotomies, Trichotomies or Waves of Duties?', *Human Rights Law Review*, Vol. 5, (2005), pp. 81–103.

[65] For instance, the first example given in *General Comment No. 14* (n. 35 above), concerns denial or limitation of equal access to 'preventive, curative and palliative health services'.

[66] See in this vein, C. Reich, 'The New Property', *Yale Law Journal*, Vol. 73, (1963–64), pp. 732–787.

water, or is the contentious view that private management is more efficient while equally universal an issue of fulfilling the right to water? The same issues arise concerning labour market reforms, rolling back subsidies on key commodities (e.g., cooking gas, rice, milk), and signature of foreign trade and investment treaties.[67] In other words, some of the most pressing contemporary issues under the Covenant defy clear classification under this typology.[68] Indeed, the typology does not feature particularly in the Committee's concluding observations, even though Sepúlveda has done excellent work in reviewing the Committee's concluding observations and classifying situations post-facto as falling into the duties to respect, protect and fulfil.[69]

As Shue originally noted in a separate article in 1979:

> There is considerable danger that all the difficulties that haunt the dichotomy of positive rights and negative rights will simply move across the rights/duties line and continue to rattle around in the more spacious trichotomy of forbearance duties, protection duties, and assistance duties. One might suspect that forbearance duties are largely 'negative', assistance duties are largely 'positive', and protection duties are intermediate, and one might wonder whether the 'new' conceptualization, even if marginally more adequate, were not fairly superficial.[70]

---

[67] Sepúlveda, *Nature of Obligations* (n. 26 above), pp. 218–222. The author puts the implementation of IMF sponsored Structural Adjustment Programmes as examples of violations of the duty to respect, while noting the caution the Committee itself has taken in treating this issue in its concluding observations.

[68] These points are not to suggest that the concepts are somehow conflated, since many concepts involve similar problems when applied to social facts, but rather that in actual practice, there will be obstinate viewpoints about classification and this may give rise to two practical problems. The first is that if the Committee devotes itself to mainstreaming this classification in its concluding observations, it may find itself arguing with States over classification rather than the nature of steps it must take. Second, it may open lines for academic criticism that would undermine the project of ratifying an optional protocol creating an individual complaints system.

[69] Sepúlveda, *Nature of Obligations* (n. 26 above), pp. 209–246.

[70] H. Shue, 'Rights in Light of Duties', in P. Brown and D. Maclean (eds.), *Human Rights and US Foreign Policy* (Lexington: Lexington Books, 1979), pp. 65–82, at p. 76 (note 64), quoted in Mary Dowell-Jones, *Contextualising the*

The lesson of these considerations is, perhaps, that the application of the concept should be clear. General comments on other rights or obligations could take the time to address some of the above questions. They should also clarify how the obligations to respect and protect are linked with processes that the Committee demands in the case of interference, which has only been done for housing and water so far, though it is also included in the draft general comment on the right to social security (see section 5.1 below). It may also be possible to argue for more expansive notions of the obligation to protect, particularly in the context of privatisation as discussed in Section 5.2 in the case of the right to water. General Comment No. 15 on the right to water was clear but an earlier draft had proposed that the Committee call for deferral of privatisation until a human rights-based regulatory framework was in place (see Section 5.2 below). Since critics might exploit such findings, careful wording would be necessary.

3.3 Taking Steps: Obligations with Immediate Effect

The most persistent myth about the Covenant is that it does not give rise to the obligation to act in a particular way immediately. This persistence is likely because of the formulation of Article 2(1), which requires the obligation to realise the rights *progressively*, to the maximum of available resources. The peculiar challenge posed by Article 2(1) is to know what a State must do today to realise a particular individual's right to, for example, the highest attainable standard of health. The task at first seems to defy comprehension, but the Committee gave a fairly clear roadmap in General Comment No. 3:

> [W]hile the Covenant provides for a progressive realisation and acknowledges the constraints due to the limits of available resources, it also imposes various obligations which are of immediate effect...the fact that realization over time, or in other words progressively, is foreseen under the Covenant should not be misinterpreted as depriving the obligation of all meaningful content. It is on the one hand a necessary flexibility device,

International Covenant on Economic, Social and Cultural Rights (n. 28 above), p. 33.

reflecting the realities of the real world and the difficulties involved for any country in ensuring full realization of economic, social and cultural rights. On the other hand, the phrase must be read in the light of the overall objective, indeed the raison d'être, of the Covenant, which is to establish clear obligations for States Parties in respect of the full realization of the rights in question. It thus imposes an obligation to move as expeditiously and effectively as possible toward that goal.[71]

This obligation to take steps is comparable in some respects to the 'reasonableness' standard employed by the South African Constitutional Court in a case[72] that has been the subject of warm reception by former social rights sceptics.[73]

However, this original idea of obligations of immediate effect has been gradually massaged by the committee into a dichotomy between so-called progressive and immediate obligations, which may have the unintended effect of watering down the strength of the Covenant obligations. In General Comment No. 12, the Committee writes somewhat ambiguously that 'some *measures*.... are of a more immediate nature, while other measures are of a more long-term character'.[74] It is not until General Comments Nos. 13, 14, and 15 that the Committee uses the expression 'immediate obligations', though in these cases, it reiterates the same obligations as discussed in General Comment No. 3. Yet, it should be clear that it is the right, or the entitlement or any sub-entitlement,

that is the object of either progressive or immediate *implementation*. That is, the State is required to realise the *full entitlement* either over time (e.g., the obligation to provide access to safe sanitation to everyone) or right away (e.g., equal treatment under the law), but in neither case is it entitled to not act at all. The danger of the dichotomy is that once one manages to classify something as a progressive rather than immediate *obligation*, it might lead a State to believe that it does not need to act in any specific way immediately.

The Committee has given several examples of obligations of immediate effect. Generally speaking, measures that normally implicate the duties to respect and protect, discussed in Sections 3.1 and 3.2 above, are often viewed as generating obligations of immediate effect.[75] As discussed, obligations to protect might not always be immediately feasible if it requires extra resources that might not be immediately available (e.g., additional police forces to protect certain social interests).

Adoption of *legislation* should be viewed as being an obligation of immediate effect notwithstanding the somewhat delicate task of ensuring the passage of legislation. With regard to housing, for example, the Committee has been very specific. It requires the State party to 'take immediate measures' to ensure security tenure of housing for all,[76] and specifically adopt legislation 'against forced evictions'.[77] This legislation on forced evictions should provide the 'greatest possible security of tenure to occupiers of houses and land', control 'strictly the circumstances under which evictions may be carried out' and applies to both State and non-State actors. Sepúlveda notes that the duty to adopt legislation to protect the right to join unions and strike, and to adopt anti-discrimination legislation in respect of women were identified in the Committee as obligations of immediate effect.[78] General Comment No. 12 contains a call, somewhat indirectly, for legislation on the right to adequate food for infants and young children through maternal and child protection, namely 'legislation

---

[71] *General Comment No. 3, The nature of States parties' obligations*, (Fifth session, 1990), U.N. Doc. E/1991/23, annex III at 86 (1991), para. 9. In *General Comment No. 9*, the Committee considered 'many of the provisions in the Covenant to be capable of immediate implementation'. *General Comment 9, The domestic application of the Covenant* (Nineteenth session, 1998), U.N. Doc. E/C.12/1998/24 (1998), para. 10.

[72] See *Government of the Republic of South Africa v. Grootboom and Others* 2000 (11) BCLR 1169 (CC). These criteria are listed by Sandra Liebenberg in Chapter 4 in this volume in Section 3.2.

[73] See C. Sunstein, *Designing Democracy: What Constitutions Do* (Oxford: Oxford University Press, 2003), Ch.10. *Cf.* C. Sunstein, 'Against Positive Rights', in A. Sajó (ed.) *Western Rights? Post-Communist Application* (The Hague: Kluwer, 1996), p. 225; see also *Report of the Joint Committee on Human Rights of the House of Lords and House of Commons: The International Covenant on Economic, Social and Cultural Rights, Twenty-First Report of Session 2003–2004* (London: HMSO, 2004), para. 73

[74] *General Comment No. 12* (n. 54 above), para. 16.

[75] Sepúlveda, *Nature of Obligations* (n. 26 above), suggests that negative obligations must always be considered 'of immediate application' (p. 184).

[76] *General Comment No. 4, The right to adequate housing*, (Sixth session, 1991), U.N. Doc. E/1992/23, annex III at 114 (1991), para. 8.

[77] *General Comment No. 7* (n. 57 above), para. 10.

[78] Sepúlveda, *Nature of Obligations* (n. 26 above), p. 180.

to enable breast-feeding' and regulate the 'marketing of breast milk substitutes'.[79]

Within its concluding observations, the Committee does however raise the need for specific legislation recommending that Australia 'consider enacting legislation on paid maternity leave',[80] Austria 'enact legislation to strengthen the protection of persons working under atypical employment contracts',[81] and Nepal 'enact or enforce legislation prohibiting customary practices, such as polygamy, dowry, Deuki and prostitution among the Bedi caste'.[82] In Cameroon, it regretted the absence of legislation 'which provides for free primary education'[83] and in Ireland legislation that deals with the rights of the physically disabled.[84] In addition, the Committee has generally required a review of existing legislation to ensure conformity with the Covenant rights (though it rarely appears to ask States parties whether they have actually done so).[85] It has increasingly called, somewhat gently, for framework legislation to guide the realisation of each right.[86]

Similarly, the Committee has, from its inception, highlighted that all States should immediately develop a *plan of action or strategy* and take steps to *implement* it.[87] Recent general comments provide significant detail in the manner in which these are to be developed through a human rights approach, which is to include the setting of targets or goals to be achieved and the time-frame for their achievement, establishment of institutional responsibility for the process, identification of resources available and establishment of accountability mechanisms to ensure implementation. They also call for recognition of the 'the right of individuals and groups to participate in decision-making processes' whether it be a policy, programme or strategy.[88] While it may appear somewhat obvious that plans of action could be developed by States, it is clear that many States have not sufficiently developed a comprehensive vision for addressing the social rights. Indeed, the best-known domestic case on ESC rights, *Grootboom*,[89] turned on this issue of defective planning. The Governments housing programme was found wanting since it failed 'to provide relief for people who have no access to land, no roof over their heads, and who are living in intolerable conditions or crisis situations'.[90]

During its review of States parties, the issue of plans of action has often been manifest. Morocco was criticised for not adopting 'a national strategy and action plan on health' when their State-provided health care did not reach more than 20 per cent of the population.[91] Serbia was commended for devising 'a strategy to address the HIV/AIDS pandemic' but the Committee noted 'the absence of national benchmarks upon which the State party's achievements in this or other areas of health could be assessed'.[92] Ireland was encouraged to revisit its 'National Health Strategy with a view to embracing a human rights

---

[79] *General Comment No. 12* (n. 54 above), para. 30.

[80] *Conclusions and recommendations of CESCR: Australia*, E/C.12/1/Add.50 (2000), para. 28.

[81] *Conclusions and recommendations of CESCR: Austria*, U.N. Doc. E/C.12/AUT/CO/3 (2006), para. 22.

[82] *Conclusions and recommendations of CESCR: Nepal*, U.N. Doc. E/C.12/1/Add.66 (2001), para. 43.

[83] *Conclusions and recommendations of CESCR: Cameroon*, U.N. Doc. E/C.12/1/Add.40 (1999), para. 27.

[84] *Conclusions and recommendations of CESCR: Ireland*, U.N. Doc. E/C.12/1/Add.35 (1999), para. 15. The Irish delegation asserted though 'that the State party is committed to redressing this situation through existing administrative policies and measures'.

[85] This is certainly an important exercise. For instance, one study estimated that seventeen Kenyan laws are 'outrightly hostile and unaccommodating' in relation to residents of informal settlements, which account for up to 60 per cent of the population in some Kenya urban centres. See W. Mitullah and K. Kibwana, 'A Tale of Two Cities: Policy, Law and Illegal Settlements in Kenya', in E. Fernandes and A. Varley (eds.), *Illegal Cities: Law and Urban Change in Developing Countries* (London: Zed Books, 1998), pp. 191–212, at 207.

[86] See for instance, *General Comment No. 12* (n. 54 above), para. 30; *General Comment No. 14* (n. 35 above), para. 53; and *General Comment No. 15, The right to water* (Twenty-ninth session, 2002), U.N. Doc. E/C.12/2002/11 (2003), paras. 46, 50.

[87] For housing, see *General Comment No. 4* (n. 76 above), para. 12; for food, see *General Comment No. 12* (n. 54 above), para. 21; for health, see *General Comment No. 14* (n. 35 above), para. 53; for education, see *General Comment No. 13, The right to education* (Twenty-first session, 1999), U.N. Doc. E/C.12/1999/10 (1999), para. 52.

[88] See for instance, *General Comment No. 15*, (n. 86 above), paras. 47–49. See also *General Comment No. 14* (n. 35 above), paras. 53–62.

[89] See *Grootboom* (n. 72 above).

[90] Ibid., para. 99.

[91] *Conclusions and recommendations of CESCR, Morocco*, U.N. Doc. E/C.12/1/Add.55 (2000), para. 28.

[92] *Conclusions and recommendations of the CESCR: Serbia and Montenegro*, U.N. Doc. E/C.12/1/Add.108 (2005), para. 35.

framework' which would include a 'common waiting list for treatment in publicly funded hospitals for privately or publicly insured patients'.[93]

Recently, the Committee has devoted more attention to indicators/benchmarks as part of international (and national) monitoring and reporting to the Committee,[94] calling on States to develop them in consultation with the Committee.[95] For instance it invited Serbia to 'identify disaggregated indicators and appropriate national benchmarks in relation to the right to water, in line with the Committee's General Comment No. 15, and to include information on the process of identifying such indicators and benchmarks in its next report'.[96] However, the process of so-called scoping,[97] where the Committee and the State party agree on benchmarks for the next reporting period, has yet to become embedded in the Committee's practice. Moreover, some debate still exists over the correct way to develop indicators to measure the realisation of the rights in the Covenant.[98]

The clear existence of obligations to develop and adopt national plans of action in consultation with civil society groups is a significant justiciable aspect of the Covenant. The failure to adopt a plan of action gives rise to an identifiable breach. The failure to include important provisions would be an identifiable breach. The failure to consult civil society would be an identifiable breach. Similarly, the failure to take steps to *implement* a plan in good faith would also be an identifiable breach. Most importantly, the issue of resource constraints begins to fade. Once a State has set its own goals

and given its own estimate of the availability of its resources, it becomes more difficult to justify inaction on resource grounds (though of course there will remain scope for a state to reassess its resource availability). The role for a reviewing body in such cases becomes familiar.

This discussion of obligations of immediate effect is not exhaustive and other similar obligations are examined below. These include duties to guarantee all of the rights on a non-discriminatory basis and gender equality between men and women,[99] to ensure a minimum essential level for each right and, at a minimum, monitor the realisation of the Covenant rights as part of a duty to provide domestic remedies and accountability mechanisms.

3.4 Non-Discrimination and Equality

Some have suggested that non-discrimination and equality 'constitute the single dominant theme of the Covenant'[100] and this is partly borne out by its text and the Committee's practice. The sister obligations to 'taking steps' in the Covenant are found in Articles 2(2) and 3, which respectively require States to guarantee the rights will be exercised without discrimination on certain prohibited grounds and to ensure the equal rights of men and women to enjoyment of the right. Article 7 also refers to 'equal remuneration for work of equal value' and Article 13 to ensuring higher education is 'equally accessible to all'.

This explicit and implicit approach to nondiscrimination and equality is evident in the Committee's general comments but less so in practice. After an extensive review of non-discrimination and equality in the work of the UN human rights treaty bodies, Vandenhole concludes that the Committee 'has paid strikingly little attention to issues of discrimination in its concluding observations', with the exception of gender discrimination.[101] Farha in this book disputes even this saving grace in relation to gender. She claims that the Committee has failed to focus sufficiently on women's equality rights and that any concerns

---

[93] *Conclusions and recommendations of the CESCR: Ireland,* U.N. Doc. E/C.12/1/Add.77 (2002), para. 35.

[94] Although, General Comment No. 1 also lays down the basic reporting obligations. See Committee on Economic, Social and Cultural Rights, *General Comment No. 1, Reporting by States parties* (Third session, 1989), U.N. Doc. E/1989/22, annex III at 87 (1989).

[95] See generally, E. Riedel, 'New Bearings to the State Reporting Procedure', in S. von Schorlemer (ed.), *Praxishandbuch UNO* (Berlin: Springer Verlag, 2003), pp. 345–358.

[96] *Conclusions: Serbia* (n. 91 above), para. 59

[97] *General Comment No. 14* (n. 35 above), paras. 57–58; *General Comment No.15* (n. 86 above), para. 54.

[98] *Cf.* V. Roaf, A. Khalfan and M. Langford, *Indicators for the Right to Water. Concept Paper* (Berlin: Heinrich Boell Foundation, Bread for the World and Centre on Housing Rights and Evictions, 2005); and *Report on Indicators for Monitoring Compliance with International Human Rights Instruments,* U.N. Doc HRI/MC//2006/7 (2006).

[99] *General Comment No. 3* (n. 71 above), para. 1.

[100] See Craven *The International Covenant on Economic, Social and Cultural Rights* (n. 2 above), pp. 154–5.

[101] W. Vandenhole, *Non-discrimination and Equality in the View of the UN Human Rights Treaty Bodies* (Anterwepen-Oxford: Intersentia, 2005), p. 135.

over usurping the mandate of CEDAW are unwarranted.[102] Indeed, Alston, a former Chairperson of the Committee, acknowledges this, as follows:

> While there is a very significant degree of overlap in the range of issues addressed by each of these three committees [CESCR, CEDAW and CRC], there is in practice some degree of specialization and a division of labour, even if this is unlikely to be formalized or even officially acknowledged in such terms. The CESCR would reasonably be expected to focus on more policy initiatives.... [103]

It may be arguable that since the Committee is one of the few committees with a specific mandate to look at ESC rights in general, it should defer to more focused UN committees on race discrimination and the rights of women, people with disabilities, children and migrants. But this argument does not necessarily hold when it is considered that violations of economic, social and cultural rights are concentrated amongst women and excluded groups. Further, while the Human Rights Committee (HRC) monitors a free-standing right to equality and non-discrimination in Article 26 ICCPR,[104] the HRC is not systematic in monitoring its application in the area of economic, social and cultural rights. Since the Committee has now adopted a general comment on gender equality and is moving to conclude a specific general comment on non-discrimination in Article 2(2), this focus may potentially intensify. This trend is partly discernible already as the review of right to water and social security indicates in Section 5 of this Chapter.

Although the Committee can be critiqued for the unevenness in its coverage of equality and non-discrimination in its concluding observations, it has perhaps made a more theoretical contribution, albeit not always with finesse, concerning the prohibited grounds of non-discrimination. Article 2 lists the prohibited grounds of discrimination

as 'race, colour, sex, language, religion, political or other opinion, national or social origin, property, birth or other status'. In 1994, the Committee issued a comprehensive General Comment No. 5 on Persons with Disabilities, on the basis that disability was covered by the term 'other status'.[105] Katarina Tomaševski criticised this reading-in as undermining the 'principle of legal security' since this group is not specifically mentioned in the Covenant. But this claim has little force. The General Assembly and the UN Commission on Human Rights earlier invited the Committee 'to monitor the compliance of States with their commitments under the relevant human rights instruments in order to ensure the full enjoyment of those rights by disabled persons'.[106] There is also a multitude of other supportive international standards and the Committee's position has been essentially confirmed by the recently adopted Convention on the Rights of Persons with Disabilities.[107]

In 1999, the Committee in General Comments specifically expanded this category to include further grounds: 'age', 'health status (including HIV/AIDS)', 'sexual orientation' and 'civil, political, social status', and indirectly, 'nationality'.[108] In 2005, in its gender comment on gender equality (No. 16), this was expanded to include 'ethnicity',[109] 'marital status' and 'refugee or migrant status'. 'Place of residence' has also been suggested as a possible ground of discrimination by the Committee in its general comment on education, and geographical disparities are regularly analysed by the Committee.[110] The Committee has also examined the plight of a range of other groups, but has refrained from placing them within a discrimination lens, such as 'victims of natural

---

[102] See Farha, Chapter 26, Section 2.1 and 2.2.

[103] P. Alston, 'Ships Passing in the Night: The Current State of the Human Rights and Development Debate Seen Through the Lens of the Millennium Development Goals', *Human Rights Quarterly*, Vol. 27, No. 3 (2005), pp. 755–829, at 822.

[104] *General Comment No. 18 (27)*, reproduced in U.N. Doc. HRI/GEN/1/Rev.8/Add.1 (2006). See commentary by Scheinin in Chapter 25.2 of this volume.

[105] *General Comment No. 5, Persons with disabilities,* (Eleventh session, 1994), U.N. Doc E/1995/22 at 19 (1995), para. 2.

[106] See, e.g., the World Programme of Action concerning Disabled Persons, adopted by the General Assembly by its resolution 37/52 of 3 December 1982 (para.165) and Commission on Human Rights in resolutions 1992/48 (3 March 1992), para. 4 and 1993/29 (5 March 1993), para. 7.

[107] UN General Assembly, U.N. Doc. A/61/611, 6 December 2006. Within eight months, the Convention had 102 signatories and three parties.

[108] See *General Comment No. 12* (n. 54 above), para. 18.

[109] Vandenhole notes that this was unnecessary and could have been included under 'national or social origin': *Non-discrimination and Equality* (n. 100 above), pp. 144–145.

[110] Ibid. p. 144.

disasters' and 'people living in disaster-prone areas' amongst others.[111]

But these 'other status' grounds are not consistently included. Sexual orientation and health status are not included in General Comment No. 16, while age, ethnicity, marital status, refugee or migrant status are absent from General Comment 18 on Right to Work issued six months later.[112] While these startling inconsistencies can be explained by simultaneous drafting by different members of the Committee, it indicates that the Committee has given insufficient time to properly considering and consolidating the prohibited grounds. It also indicates that the Committee's habit of adopting the final text without sufficient room for a proper final legal view should be altered.

More importantly, there is a lack of justification for these implications from the Covenant. The Committee needlessly leaves itself open to criticism.[113] These developments are important but they should have been properly legally justified, as it was in General Comment No 5. This is particularly so in the case of age, since the Committee had declined in its General Comment No. 6 on Older Persons to view age as a prohibited ground of discrimination, though it left the door open to a different interpretation in the future.[114] The ground of 'nationality' also requires careful thought as Craven argues, particularly the objec-

tive criteria that can be used to defend distinctions on this basis, including the method for determining whether discrimination is based on economic reasons or prejudice.[115]

The Committee's construction of the States obligations is largely consistent with other human rights committees. Borrowing from the Convention on Elimination of Racial Discrimination, it sent a clear message that a State's intention to discriminate was irrelevant and that its focus was on distinctions or exclusions that 'have the effect of nullifying or impairing'.[116] This reading is consistent with the wording of Article 2(2) and 3 of the Covenant. States must respectively 'guarantee' that the Covenant rights 'will be exercised without discrimination of any kind' and 'ensure the equal rights of men and women'. In its General Comment on the latter article, the Committee also appears to be more careful in it wording of the obligation. It indicates that distinctions with the 'purpose' of discrimination are also discriminatory but are clearly not necessary to show discrimination.[117] Equally, it was only in General Comment No. 16 that the Committee explicitly clarified that distinctions which could be objectively justified were not to be considered discriminatory.[118] This is the position of other UN human rights committees and while Sepúlveda argues it was always implicit in the Committee's practice,[119] Vandenhole notes some seemingly contradictory statements.[120]

The Committee's focus has been on both de jure and de facto discrimination, or formal and substantive equality. This vision of substantive equality was fully articulated in General Comment No. 16 in the context of Article 3:

> Substantive equality is concerned, in addition, with the effects of laws, policies and practices and with ensuring that they do not maintain, but rather alleviate, the inherent

---

[111] See for example, *General Comment No. 12* (n. 54 above), para. 13.

[112] Cf. *General Comment No. 16, The equal right of men and women to the enjoyment of all economic, social and cultural rights (Article 3 of the International Covenant on Economic, Social and Cultural Rights* (Thirty-fourth session 2005) U.N. Doc. E/C.12/2005/4 (2005), para. 5 and *General Comment 18, Article 6: the equal right of men and women to the enjoyment of all economic, social and cultural rights* (Thirty-fifth session, 2006), U.N. Doc. E/C.12/GC/18 (2006), para. 12(b)(i)

[113] Cf. Human Rights Committee, *Toonen v. Australia*, Communication No. 488/1992, U.N. Doc CCPR/C/50/D/488/1992 (1994).

[114] 'The Committee notes that while it may not yet be possible to conclude that discrimination on the grounds of age is comprehensively prohibited by the Covenant, the range of matters in relation to which such discrimination can be accepted is very limited'. *General Comment No. 6, The economic, social and cultural rights of older persons,* (Thirteenth session, 1995), U.N. Doc. E/1996/22 at 20 (1996), para. 12.

[115] Craven, *The International Covenant on Economic, Social and Cultural Rights* (n. 2 above), pp. 172–174.

[116] See for instance, *General Comment No. 15* (n. 86 above), paras. 13–14.

[117] *General Comment No. 16,* (n. 12 above), para. 11.

[118] Ibid. para. 12. Although, oddly, this statement only comes in the context of the discussion on direct discrimination.

[119] Sepúlveda, *The Nature of Obligations* (n. 26 above), p. 385.

[120] Vandenhole, *Non-discrimination and Equality* (n. 100 above), pp. 63–4.

disadvantage that particular groups experience....Substantive equality for men and women will not be achieved simply through the enactment of laws or the adoption of policies that are, prima facie, gender-neutral. In implementing article 3, States parties should take into account that such laws, policies and practice can fail to address or even perpetuate inequality between men and women because they do not take account of existing economic, social and cultural inequalities, particularly those experienced by women.

For instance in the case of China, it criticised the formal *hukou* registration system that discriminated against internal migrants as well as discrimination in practice that affected women, particularly in employment and participation in decision-making.[121]

According to General Comment No. 16, discrimination can be direct: a difference in treatment is based on explicitly made distinctions on prohibited grounds. It can also be indirect: a law, policy or program does not appear to be discriminatory but has such an effect when implemented. But concluding observations on the latter are rare.

It is also notable that the Committee draws no conceptual distinction between non-discrimination and equality. Both require positive measures, which may be temporary or permanent as long it is intended to ensure non-discrimination or gender equality.[122] The Committee has also focused on systematic discrimination for some groups (often using the term pervasive or persistent) and its recent General Comment No. 16 is notable for its wide-reaching recommendations on the types of mechanisms States parties need to adopt. However, the Committee could consider developing further a framework for systemic discrimination since its concluding observations indicate that the situation for women and some minorities (particularly that of Roma and Palestinians) has barely changed since it began monitoring.

3.5   Minimum Core Obligations

Building on scholarly views,[123] the Committee introduced in General Comment No. 3 the idea of minimum core obligations to address the dire situation in which the minimum essential level[124] of a given right was being denied:

> [T]he Committee is of the view that a minimum core obligation to ensure the satisfaction of, at the very least, minimum essential levels of each of the rights is incumbent upon every State Party. Thus, for example, a State Party in which any significant number of individuals is deprived of essential foodstuffs, of essential primary health care, of basic shelter and housing, or of the most basic forms of education is, prima facie, failing to discharge its obligations under the Covenant....In order for a State Party to be able to attribute its failure to meet at least its minimum core obligations to a lack of available resources it must demonstrate that every effort has been made to use all resources that are at its disposition in an effort to satisfy, as a matter of priority, those minimum obligations.[125]

Thus the effect created by the denial of a minimum core obligation is to create (1) a prima facie violation,[126] and (2) an obligation to use every effort to (3) make the satisfaction of the need in question a matter of priority. This requirement has been consistently included in each general comment on

---

[123] P. Alston, 'Out of the Abyss: The Challenges Confronting the New U. N. Committee on Economic, Social and Cultural Rights', *Human Rights Quarterly*, Vol. 9, No. 3 (1987), pp. 332–381, at 352–3: ('A logical implication of the use of the terminology of rights. In other words, there would be no justification for elevating a claim to the status of a right (with all the connotations that concept is generally assumed to have) if its normative content could be so indeterminate as to allow for the possibility that the right holders possess non minimum entitlement, in the absence of which a State Party is to be considered to be in violation of its obligations'.)

See also A. Eide, 'Realization of Social and Economic Rights and the Minimum Threshold Approach', *Human Rights Law Journal*, Vol. 10 (1989), pp. 35–51, at 43–47.

[124] For a history of the development this idea, see K. Arambulo, *Strengthening the Supervision of the International Convenant on Economic, Social and Cultural Rights: Theoretical and Practical Aspects* (Antwerp: Intersentia, 1999), pp. 136–141.

[125] *General Comment No. 3* (n. 71 above), para. 10.

[126] See Craven's nuanced discussion of what he calls 'the presumption of guilt' in *The International Covenant on Economic, Social and Cultural Rights* (n. 2 above), p. 143.

---

[121] *Conclusions and recommendations of CESCR: People's Republic of China*, U.N. Doc. E/C.12/1/Add.107 (2005), paras. 15, 17.

[122] See *General Comment No. 16* (n. 112 above), para. 35.

a specific Covenant right. However, the Committee is not always rigorous in its concluding observations. With regard to Suriname, the Committee was quite specific in its criticism of the country's social assistance programme, including the level of the 'official subsistence minimum', but does not situate its criticism within its understanding of 'minimum core obligations'.[127]

Despite addressing what appeared to be a pressing issue, the doctrine has been subject to the criticism that some level of 'mission creep' is occurring over time. In General Comment No. 3, the Committee was clear that it would consider the unavailability of resources as a defence against failure to fulfil the minimum core obligation. However, from 2002, a shift is evident. In General Comment No. 13 on the Right to Education the obligation is stated without any qualification[128] while in General Comment No. 14, after a detailed statement of core obligations, the Committee takes an entirely new approach. It addresses the resources issues by simply noting that wealthier States should assist developing ones in accordance with Article 2(1), and then stresses that 'a State party cannot, under any circumstances whatsoever, justify its non-compliance with the core obligations . . . which are non-derogable'.[129] This sentence has provoked charges of maximalism where States parties may be held liable for denials of the rights that are beyond their control.[130] The critics are right. But the finger should be perhaps equally pointed at the 1997 Maastricht Guidelines on Violations of Economic, Social and Cultural Rights,

prepared by a group of experts, which states: 'Such minimum core obligations apply irrespective of the availability of resources of the country concerned or any other factors and difficulties'.[131] The guidelines then state that this is based on the 'developing jurisprudence of the Committee' and the 1987 Limburg expert principles. The first claim is incorrect and the claim concerning the Limburg principles is not necessarily borne out since they only refer to 'minimum subsistence rights for all'.[132] Dowell-Jones argues that this is complicated further by the partial retreat in General Comment No. 15 on the Right to Water, which refers to nonderogability but also reintroduces the qualification from General Comment No. 3, that a State party is permitted to argue that the resources are unavailable.[133]

In any case, the circle is perhaps now complete. The Committee's 2007 Statement on Maximum Available Resources restates the original position in General Comment No. 3, as does the 2006 draft of the General Comment on Right to Social Security. There is no mention of non-derogabilty in either. We would commend this development. The idea of non-derogability was introduced haphazardly and is arguably inconsistent with the limitations provision of the Covenant.[134] In our view, the Committee can achieve the goal of prioritising minimum core obligations without the manifold theoretical, legal, and practical problems that the doctrine of non-derogability may engender in its present form.

The second area of potential trouble has been the gradual bundling of some 'immediate obligations' under the heading of minimum core obligations, such as the duty to adopt a plan of action or ensure non-discrimination. The source of such an approach is perhaps found in the 'minimum

---

[127] The Committee was 'concerned that social assistance to the poor (FB) is administered on a discretionary basis and hence opens the possibility of unequal protection of the poor. Moreover, the Committee is concerned that even provided with social assistance, many disadvantaged persons receive inadequate amounts of assistance or, when their incomes fall slightly above the official subsistence minimum, do not receive any assistance at all from the FB programmes. The Committee considers that the subsistence minimum requires revision and that, as it presently stands, it excludes many persons genuinely in need of assistance'. See *Conclusions and recommendations of the CESCR*, Suriname, U.N. Doc. E/C.12/1995/6 (1995), para. 12.

[128] *General Comment No. 12* (n. 54 above), para. 14.

[129] *General Comment No. 14* (n. 35 above), para. 47.

[130] Dennis and Stewart, 'Justiciability of Economic, Social, and Cultural Rights' (n. 29 above), pp. 492–3. See also criticisms by Dowell-Jones, *Contextualising the International Covenant on Economic, Social and Cultural Rights* (n. 28 above), pp. 23–25.

[131] Maastricht Guidelines (n. 40 above), para. 9.

[132] Limburg Principles (n. 40 above).

[133] *General Comment No. 15* (n. 86 above), paras. 40 and 41.

[134] In some ways, the 'minimum core content' as referred to by Committee members is reminiscent of the 'core content' in German jurisprudence. But there seems to be no consideration of the important textual differences between the German constitution and the ICESCR. Cf. the Constitutional Rights Provisions of the German Basic Law, Article 19(2): 'In no case may the core content of a constitutional right be infringed'. See also R. Alexy, *Theory of Constitutional Rights* (trans. J. Rivers) (Oxford: Oxford University Press, 2002) pp. 192–196 ('On the Guarantee of an Inalienable Core as a Limit to Limits').

core obligations' school of thought which has not only championed an expansive reading of the minimum core, but the identification of a clear set of minimum standards which are applicable to each State.[135] The result in the General Comments is a degree of arbitrariness, with some immediate obligations included and others not, such as obligations of respect or obligations to protect. This process of bundling may be symptomatic of a deeper source of potential confusion, namely, whether the original idea of minimum core obligations, concerned as it was with 'minimum essential levels of each right', fits well conceptually with items such as national action plans. It may suggest that there are two distinct concepts rolled into one, namely, (1) the idea of minimum essential resources needed for an individual's survival or basic dignity, and (2) the idea of a heightened obligation to take certain crucial steps, from which derogation is allowed only in the rarest of circumstances. The latter subset may include the former, but it may also be, as the process of bundling noted in this paragraph may illustrate, much larger. Despite these concerns, it is important to note that non-lawyer activists have often expressed appreciation at finding the key obligations in one section in simple bullet-point form. This suggests that it is useful to its most important readership at present. Nonetheless, it may unravel in difficult ways if and when any complaints system might be introduced.

Even if we remain only with the original conception of minimum core obligations, two challenges remain. Craven notes the concern that the Committee 'will primarily direct its attention to the actions of developing States'.[136] Such a prophesied trend is difficult to discern in the Committee's practice but some advocates from more developed countries have noted its unhelpful influence at the domestic level. Porter in particular points out the somewhat shaky philosophical foundations of the approach, noting the dangers of what he terms the 'misguided search for universal, transcendental components of ESC rights',[137] arguing it is incon-

sistent with more modern notions of grounding human rights, including civil and political rights, in their historical context where citizens, particularly rights claimants, can argue for the interpretation that is most consistent with their 'dignity related interests'. The Millennium Development Goals have been similarly criticised for their one-size-fits-all approach to reaching a set of universal minimum levels of development.[138]

The second challenge is more practical and that is the identification of the minimum essential level of each right. Craven questioned whether the Committee could establish 'minimum thresholds' at the international level.[139] The subsequent General Comments do give some degree of specificity (e.g., access to a particular medicine or service), but they generally refrain from attempting to quantify it, preferring to leave it to an evaluation of the specific context, which can be seen in its concluding observations. The Committee is often focused on whether the country has set a minimum (e.g., a poverty line or level of adequacy for benefits) which they can interrogate for its reasonableness and how it applies in the country. At the national level, Porter argues though that this problematic dimension of the minimum core obligation is actually used as a weapon against ESC rights as 'governments have routinely argued that the inability of experts to agree on a clearly defined poverty line of universal application is proof that courts should not wade into this area of policy'.[140] Indeed, the South African Constitutional Court rejected the minimum core obligation on the basis that in the case of the right to housing it could not determine the minimum due to the diversity of the needs and groups, noting that 'there are those who need land; others need both land and houses; yet others need financial assistance'.[141] It also raised concerns about whether the minimum could be realised immediately in the South African context. However, Sandra Liebenberg argues that

135 See A. Chapman and S. Russell, (eds.), *Core Obligations: Building a Framework for Economic, Social and Cultural Rights* (Antwerp/Oxford: Intersentia, 2002).
136 Craven, *The International Covenant on Economic, Social and Cultural Rights* (n. 2 above), pp. 145–6.
137 B. Porter, 'The Crisis of ESC Rights and Strategies for Addressing It', in J. Squires, M. Langford, and B. Thiele (eds.), *Road to a Remedy: Current Issues in Litigation of*

Economic, Social and Cultural Rights (Sydney: Australian Human Rights Centre and University of NSW Press, Sydney, 2005), pp. 48–55.
138 See generally, A. Saith, 'From Universal Values to Millennium Development Goals: Lost in Translation', *Development and Change*, Vol. 37, No. 6 (2006), pp. 1167–1199.
139 Craven, *The International Covenant on Economic, Social and Cultural Rights* (n. 2 above), p. 143.
140 Porter, 'The Crisis of ESC Rights and Strategies for Addressing It' (n. 137 above), p. 51.
141 Grootboom (n. 72 above), para. 33.

the Court's reasonableness test, which it applies to the progressive realisation of the right, could also be adapted to cover 'survival interests'. There could be a presumption that government programs do not meet the test of reasonableness if certain minimums are not met.[142] David Bilchitz develops this argument further, illustrating why a minimum core approach matters both for South Africa and more generally.[143]

For our part, while we see certain problems with the minimum core approach, and in particular with the idea of non-derogability, we believe that a cautious continuation of the doctrine is warranted at the present time. However, it must be understood in context. A country that has more ample resources must be held to a higher level of realisation of the Covenant rights. Alternatively, the minimum essential level could be seen as rising upwards as resources permit. For instance, while addressing starvation may represent a minimum core obligation in one country, eliminating chronic malnutrition might be the core in another; while direct exposure to the elements may breach the core in one country, absence of structurally sound accommodation might do so in another.

This nuanced approach to country context can generally be seen in the Committee's concluding observations. For countries in transition, such as Russia, the Committee required 'the raising of minimum pension levels' and it criticised Georgia for failing to meet the minimum.[144] To Canada it recommended that the State 'establish social assistance at levels which ensure the realization of an adequate standard of living for all' and interrogated very closely its existing social security schemes.[145] In Senegal it only urged the country 'to allocate more funds for its 20/20 Initiative, designed as a basic social safety net for the disad-

vantaged and marginalized groups of society',[146] though it is arguable that it could have required much more of Senegal given ILO research.[147] Thus, the Committee expected a more sophisticated form of social security from the developed State (a social assistance scheme not just an 'initiative') and a safety net that would provide an *adequate* standard of living not a bare *minimum* like in Senegal. Nonetheless, the Committee fails to link its conclusions to its minimum obligation doctrine. It is not clear whether these concerns are expressed on the basis of a failure to progressively realise the rights or reach a contextualised minimum core obligation. This should be rectified particularly as it would give States parties a deeper understanding of their precise obligations.

3.6   Domestic Remedies and Accountability for Violations

All States are expected to develop the necessary *monitoring and accountability* systems to ensure the observance of rights and that implementing measures are effective. The Committee has given significant emphasis to national level monitoring, particularly the role of national human rights commissions and ombudspersons. In a general comment on the subject, it noted that one of the roles of commissions should be 'Monitoring compliance with specific rights recognized under the Covenant and providing reports thereon to the public authorities and civil society'.[148] In the case of El Salvador, the Committee noted 'with satisfaction' the creation in 1991 of the post of Procurator for the Defence of Human Rights under the constitution, which had the competence to conduct inspections and investigations, file complaints and draft recommendations, and also welcomed the creation of local units of this office.[149]

[142] See S. Liebenberg, 'Enforcing Positive Social and Economic Rights Claims: The South African Model of Reasonableness Review', in Squires, Langford and Thiele, *Road to a Remedy* (n. 137 above), pp. 73–88.

[143] D. Bilchitz, *Poverty and Fundamental Rights: The Justification and Enforcement of Socio-economic Rights* (Oxford: Oxford University Press, 2007).

[144] *Conclusions and recommendations of CESCR: Russian Federation*, U.N. Doc. E/C.12/1/Add.94 (2003), para. 50; *Conclusions and recommendations of CESCR: Georgia*, U.N. Doc E/C.12/1/Add.83 (2002), para. 17.

[145] See further Section 5.1 below.

[146] *Conclusions and recommendations of CESCR: Senegal*, U.N. Doc. E/C.12/1/Add.62 (2001).

[147] *Cash benefits in low-income countries: Simulating the effects on poverty reduction for Senegal and Tanzania*, Issues in Social Protection, Discussion Paper 15, ILO, 2006.

[148] *General Comment 10, The role of national human rights institutions in the protection of economic, social and cultural rights* (Nineteenth session, 1998), U.N. Doc. E/1999/22 at 18 (1998), para. 3(f).

[149] *Concluding observations of the CESCR: El Salvador*, UN Doc. E/C.12/1/Add.4 (1996), para. 6.

It tentatively made its foray into the field of judicial remedies and justiciability of the Covenant rights in 1991. It noted that appropriate measures under Article 2(1) might include provision of judicial remedies and singled out some provisions that it believed were capable of immediate application by the judiciary, e.g., non-discrimination and equality, right to fair wages and equal remuneration for work of equal value, trade union rights, special measures to protect children, provision of compulsory and free primary education to all, rights of parents to choose alternative schooling to fit religious and oral beliefs, non/interference with educational institutions and the freedom for scientific research and creative activity.[150] Six years later, the Committee was rather more emboldened, perhaps after its call to receive information on actual jurisprudence.[151] In General Comment No. 9, the Committee placed the burden upon States to justify the absence of legal remedies, called for the incorporation of the Covenant in the domestic legal order, and stated that 'there is no Covenant right which could not, in the great majority of systems, be considered to possess at least some significant justiciable dimensions'.[152] They explicitly indicated that Courts could make orders affecting resource allocation while noting 'the respective competences of the various branches of government must be respected'.[153] The Committee emphasised that the principles of indivisibility and interdependence of human rights together with the judiciary's role in protecting 'the rights of the most vulnerable and disadvantaged groups in society', presumably on the basis that their voices might not be heard in a majoritarian democracy.[154]

This enhanced sensitivity on justiciability has meant that States without constitutional and justiciable ESC rights have been subjected to greater scrutiny. The Committee stated with some exasperation that 'the Covenant has still not been incorporated in the domestic legal order' of the United Kingdom, and it reiterated its 'concern

about the State party's position that the provisions of the Covenant, with minor exceptions, constitute principles and programmatic objectives rather than legal obligations that are justiciable'.[155] Likewise, in the case of Canada, in 1998, the Committee placed more emphasis on anti-discrimination legislation being applied to economic and social rights[156] but in 2006, the Committee was more straightforward asking for 'immediate steps … to create and ensure effective domestic remedies for all Covenant rights in all relevant jurisdictions'.[157]

What is notable in the case of Canada is the attention of the Committee to the manner in which national litigation was playing out in the country and the need to ensure that remedies would be available to all and effectively used. In both 1998 and 2006, the Committee called on federal, provincial and territorial governments to promote interpretations of the Canadian Charter and other domestic law in a way consistent with the Covenant, to provide civil legal aid and to extend the Court Challenges Programme to include 'challenges to provincial legislation and policies which may violate the provisions of the Covenant'.[158]

Recent general comments have also asked States to encourage 'Judges, adjudicators and members of the legal profession to pay greater attention to violations of Covenant rights'.[159] In 2006, the Committee appeared to address the courts of Canada directly, noting that they should 'take account of Covenant rights where this is necessary to ensure that the State party's conduct is consistent with its obligations under the Covenant, in line with the Committee's General Comment No. 9 (1998)' and referred to a particular case of concern, *Chaoulli v. Quebec – Attorney General*.[160] The Committee

---

[150] *General Comment No. 3* (n. 71 above), para. 5.
[151] See *General Comment No. 4* (n. 76 above), para 16.
[152] *General Comment No. 9, The domestic application of the Covenant* (Nineteenth session, 1998), U.N. Doc. E/C.12/1998/24 (1998), para. 10.
[153] Ibid.
[154] Ibid.

[155] *Conclusions and recommendations of CESCR: United Kingdom of Great Britain and Northern Ireland – Dependent Territories*, U.N. Doc. E/C.12/1/Add.79 (2002), para. 10.
[156] *Conclusions and recommendations of CESCR: Canada*, U.N. Doc. E/C.12/1/Add.31 (1998), para. 46.
[157] *Concluding Observations of CESCR: Canada* UN Doc. E/C.12/CAN/CO/4-E/C.12/CAN/CO/5 (2006), para. 40.
[158] See *Conclusions and recommendations of CESCR: Canada* (1998) (n. 156 above), para. 59; and *Concluding Observations of CESCR: Canada* (2006) (n. 157 above), para. 42.
[159] *General Comment No. 15* (n. 86 above), para. 58.
[160] *Concluding Observations of CESCR: Canada (2006)* (n. 157 above), para. 36. This case is discussed in Chapter 11 of this book. See also J.A. King, 'Constitutional Rights and Social Welfare: A Comment on the Canadian *Chaoulli*

clearly benefited from detailed information provided by non-governmental organisations in this case, but such close scrutiny should be extended to all States parties. The Committee has also paid some attention to the health of other actors in society who play a role in ensuring accountability. For instance, 'States parties should respect, protect, facilitate and promote the work of human rights advocates and other members of civil society with a view to assisting vulnerable or marginalized groups in the realization of their right to health'.[161]

3.7   Limitations of Covenant Rights (Article 4)

Article 4 of the Covenant is a somewhat familiar form of limitations provision, allowing limitations only where determined by law, when compatible with the nature of the right, and when solely for the purpose of promoting the general welfare in a democratic society. Given that many have interpreted the Covenant as giving rise to obligations that only must realised over time, relatively little attention has been paid to the question of limitations of Covenant rights. A notable exception is the thorough examination of the travaux préparatoires carried out by Alston and Quinn.[162] They demonstrate that it was generally accepted in the drafting of the Covenant that Article 4 was introduced to deal with situations involving limitation of Covenant rights that were not justified on the basis of resource constraints.[163] Arguments concerning resource constraints were thought to fall mainly if not exclusively for consideration under Article 2(1).

The requirement that limitations be 'compatible with the nature of [the] rights' is a somewhat more unusual aspect of Article 4. A briefly stated finding by Alson and Quinn suggest this phrase may mean that 'some rights, by virtue of their very nature, might be considered not to be subject to any limitations (other than those relating to resource

availability in accordance not with Article 4 but with Article 2(1))'.[164] They offer the freedom from hunger as part of the right to adequate food as a potential example.

It was foreseen by the drafting body that infringements of Covenant rights would be justified on other grounds, particularly when relating to the rights to non-discrimination and the duties to respect. The International Court of Justice addressed such a situation in its advisory opinion on the legality of the wall constructed in the Occupied Palestinian Territories.[165] However, it unfortunately did not devote much consideration to the issue and instead concluded without much explanation that the limitations imposed by Israel simply failed to promote the general welfare in a democratic society.[166]

A related issue as to the relationship between the obligation to realise social rights progressively and the limitation of social rights was discussed in the *Khosa* decision of Constitutional Court of South Africa.[167] The Court observed in passing that in a social rights case, the limitations provision in section 36 of the Constitution would only be relevant if its reasonable requirements differed from those in sections 26 and 27 (which requires States to take reasonable steps to realise various social rights).[168] In that case, the Court simply found that 'the exclusion of permanent residents from the scheme for social assistance is neither reasonable nor justifiable within the meaning of [s]ection 36' as well as section 27.[169] In the subsequent Constitutional Court case of *Jaftha*, it was assumed without any particular discussion of the

---

[164] Ibid. p. 201.
[165] *Legal Consequences of the Construction of a Wall in the Israeli Occupied Territories*, (2004) ICJ Reports 136, at p. 193.
[166] Ibid. 'The Court would further observe that the restrictions on the enjoyment by the Palestinians living in the territory occupied by Israel of their economic, social and cultural rights, resulting from Israel's construction of the wall, fail to meet a condition laid down by Article 4 of the International Covenant on Economic, Social and Cultural Rights, that is to say that their implementation must be "solely for the purpose of promoting the general welfare in a democratic society"'.
[167] *Khosa and Others v. Minister of Social Development and Others; Mahlaule and Another v. Minister of Social Development and Others*, 2004 (6) BCLR 569 (CC).
[168] Ibid. para. 83.
[169] Ibid. para. 84.

Health Care Decision', *Modern Law Review*, Vol. 69, (2006) pp. 631–643.
[161] *General Comment No. 14* (n. 35 above), para. 62.
[162] Alston and Quinn, 'Nature and Scope of States parties Obligations' (n. 40 above), pp. 192–203.
[163] Ibid. pp. 194, 197, 205–206.

point that infringements of negative obligations arising under section 26 may potentially be justified under section 36.[170] Any principle to emerge from the Constitutional Court's approach is that, at the very least, infringements to the negative obligations in the South African constitution must comply with the generally accepted requirements of proportionality. If such reasoning were adopted for the Covenant, a State would also need to show that such a limitation is both proportionate and compatible with the right. Support for this view is found in General Comment No.14, in which the Committee found that limitations of the right to health must be proportional in the sense that the least restrictive means is adopted to achieve the goal.[171]

3.8   International Obligations

The term 'international obligations' is employed by the Committee to refer to what scholars often call 'extra-territorial' obligations.[172] International obligations concern what duties States parties may owe to persons located in places other than their own territory. The textual departure point for such an obligation is Article 2(1), which requires States to take steps, individually and through international cooperation, to progressively realise the rights, which is supported and complemented by other articles in the Covenant such as Articles 11, 15, 22 and 23.

In its General Comment No. 3 the Committee noted that the 'phrase "to the maximum of its available resources" in Article 2(1) was intended by the drafters of the Covenant to refer to both the resources existing within a State and those available from the international community through international cooperation and assistance'. It went on to highlight the role of international cooperation in helping facilitate the realisation of the Covenant rights which it saw as both an opportunity and a responsibility of States. In General Comment No. 4, it noted that 'less than 5 per cent of all international assistance has been directed towards housing or human settlements' and that which is provided 'does little to address the housing needs of disadvantaged groups'.[173] It called on States parties, both recipients and providers, to reverse this.

The Committee has also specifically addressed the role of the UN, UN agencies and other specialised agencies such as World Bank and IMF under Article 22 of the Covenant. In General Comment No. 2 (1990), it called on the UN to adequately promote ESC rights in its work, including prioritising projects and objectives that enhanced enjoyment of all human rights, not just economic growth[174] and to avoid projects that would involve contravening the Covenant, citing projects that may use child labour, involve discrimination or result in large-scale displacement without appropriate protection and compensation. A later General Comment was also devoted to adopting a human rights approach to sanctions regimes by the UN Security Council, with the need to ensure Covenant rights are taken into account in their design, the effect of the sanctions are monitored, and appropriate responses are made.[175]

---

[170] *Jaftha v. Schoeman and others,Van Rooyen v. Stoltz and others*, 2005 (1) BCLR 78 (CC), para. 34, 35ff.

[171] *General Comment No. 14* (n 35 above), para. 29. Cf. *General Comment No. 13* (n. 87 above), para. 42 (no reference to proportionality).

[172] There is a considerable recent interest on this point: M. Craven, 'The Violence of Disposession: Extra-territoriality and Economic, Social and Cultural Rights', in M. Baderin and R. McCorquodale, *Economic, Social and Cultural Rights in Action* (Oxford: Oxford University Press, 2007), pp. 71–88; R. Künnemann, 'Extraterritorial Application of the International Covenant on Economic, Social and Cultural Rights', in F. Coomans and M. Kamminga, (eds.), *Extraterritorial Application of Human Rights Treaties* (Antwerp: Intersentia, 2004), pp. 201–231; M. Sepúlveda, 'Obligations of "International Assistance and Cooperation" in an Optional Protocol to the International Covenant on Economic, Social and Cultural Rights', *Netherlands Quarterly of Human Rights*, Vol. 24, (2006), pp. 271–303; see also W. Vandenhole, 'Economic, Social and Cultural Rights in the CRC: Is There a Legal Obligation to Cooperate Internationally for Development?', *International Journal for Children's Rights*, Vol. 15, (2007) (forthcoming).

[173] *General Comment No. 4* (n. 86 above), para. 19.

[174] *General Comment No. 2, International technical assistance measures* (Fourth session, 1990), U.N. Doc. E/1990/23, annex III at 86 (1990), para. 6. In a harbinger of the human rights approach to development that was to come much later to the UN system, the Committee articulated many of its essential elements for UN agencies. The need to recognise the relationship between human rights and development, prepare human right impact assessments before major activities are commenced, train UN personnel and ensure the Covenant rights are taken into account in the design and implementation of projects (ibid. para. 8).

[175] *General Comment 8, The relationship between economic sanctions and respect for economic, social and cultural rights*, (Seventeenth session, 1997), U.N. Doc. E/C.12/1997/8 (1997), paras. 12–14.

The Committee later created a special section of the general comments devoted to these 'international obligations' (see General Comments Nos. 14 and 15). Generally, the Committee calls upon States to refrain from actions that interfere directly or indirectly with the enjoyment of the rights in other countries. Examples would include harmful embargoes[176] and conclusion of damaging international trade agreements or debt service conditions (whether bilateral or through a multilateral agency).[177] States also have the duty to protect people in other countries from the harmful activities of transnational private actors based in their jurisdiction. This may include raids by paramilitary or guerrilla squads, or the more widespread concern of transnational corporate activity.[178] States are further called upon to ensure that their actions as members of international organisations respect, protect and fulfil Covenant rights.[179] Finally, it is 'particularly incumbent' upon States to give the highest priority to minimum core obligations when seeking or providing international cooperation and assistance.[180]

The more difficult issue is whether there is an obligation to provide aid. In General Comment No.15, the Committee says that where resources are available, States 'should facilitate realisation of the right to water in other countries'.[181] In General Comment No.14, it writes that States must cooperate to provide disaster relief.[182] Craven points out that during the drafting of Article 2(1), the idea that States could claim assistance from others as a legal right was rejected by general consensus,[183] and the

Committee has not yet gone this far. However, it is clear from the above that the committee certainly recognises an extra territorial legal obligation even if the nature of the obligation is not as demanding as the obligation on States to realise the rights for residents within their own jurisdiction.

4. ASSESSING COMPLIANCE

Turning to the question of how States must approach their obligations, the Committee has articulated a number of general and specific standards as well as applied them, to some extent, in its concluding observations.

In its General Comment No. 3, the Committee focused on the key obligation of *taking of steps* under Article 2(1), noting that they must 'be taken within a reasonably short time after the Covenant's entry into force for the States concerned... [and] should be deliberate, concrete and targeted as clearly as possible towards meeting the obligations recognized in the Covenant'.[184] To formulate this information as a more definitive legal standard, one may consider the following. First, the State is obligated to take steps as discussed above and only in the rarest of circumstances can a State justify not taking steps, such as times of war or national emergency, and even in those cases some action to protect Covenant rights is necessary. A State may be able to demonstrate, however, that a certain type of step (e.g., promotion of preventative health care) may have been temporarily out of reach. Second, if the State has taken steps, such steps must be (a) effective and not of negligible impact, (b) expeditious (i.e., not taking an unreasonable amount of time to create effects), and (c) targeted such that they are (i) rationally connected with clearly identified ends, (ii) are not based on improper or irrelevant considerations, and (iii) the ends are identified in reference to implementing progressively the *full* scope of the right in question. The full entitlement in question is elaborated by the Committee in its individual general comments.

Moreover, the Committee could amend its reporting guidelines to ask States, in particular, how

---

[176] *General Comment No. 14* (n. 35 above), para. 41; and *General Comment No. 15* (n. 86 above), at para. 32.

[177] See *General Comment No. 14*, ibid. para. 39; *General Comment No. 15*, ibid. para. 35. For e.g., 'Agreements concerning trade liberalization should not curtail or inhibit a country's capacity to ensure the full realization of the right to water'.

[178] See *General Comment No. 14*, ibid., para. 39, for an oblique reference, and *General Comment No.15*, ibid., at para. 33, where companies are singled out as a concern.

[179] *Statement of the Committee on Economic, Social and Cultural Rights to the Third Ministerial Conference of the World Trade Organization*, (1999), UN Doc: E/C.12/1999/9.

[180] *General Comment No. 14* (n. 35 above), para. 45; *General Comment No. 15* (n. 86 above), para. 38.

[181] *General Comment No. 15*, ibid., para. 34; see too *General Comment No.14*, ibid., para. 40.

[182] *General Comment No.14*, ibid.

[183] Craven, *The International Covenant on Economic, Social and Cultural Rights* (n. 2 above), pp. 147, 144–150.

[184] See *General Comment No. 3* (n. 71 above), para. 2.

it has taken effective, expeditious and targeted steps under each substantive right, a more useful data-set for helping both the State and Committee assess compliance. There are several advantages to using this test. It holds the State to performance standards, and ones that are familiar and appropriate for courts and quasi-adjudicative tribunals. They are useful standards for assessing efforts that evidence bad faith, and facts will demonstrate this as they do under administrative law concepts of reasonableness and irrelevance, civil and labour law notions of good and bad faith, and US securities law and public international law notions of due diligence. Second, it magically dispenses with the issue of resource constraints, or at least puts it in the background. In asking whether steps *actually taken* are effective, expeditious and targeted, one does not need to look at resources. The real issue of resource constraints will rear its head when the State pleads that it could *not take steps* because it had no resources. Third, it focuses the Committee, State party and NGOs more carefully on the steps taken, rather than focusing on general social conditions, a problem that seems to be the Achilles heel of the reporting process under the Covenant.

4.1 Appropriate Measures

In General Comment No. 3, the Committee simply indicated that: 'While each State party must decide for itself which means are the most appropriate under the circumstances…the ultimate determination as to whether all appropriate measures have been taken remains one for the Committee to make'.[185] Craven notes that in determining whether measures are 'appropriate' under Article 2(1), the Committee employs a type of 'margin of discretion' doctrine similar to the European Court of Human Rights[186] and in General Comment No. 12 this became explicit: 'Every State will have a margin of discretion in choosing its own approaches' but that each 'State party take whatever steps are necessary to ensure that everyone is free from hunger and as soon as possible can enjoy the right to adequate food'.[187] Similar phras-

ing is found in later general comments on rights to health and water. The Committee has then proceeded to outline the types of steps to be taken (e.g., plans of action, reviewing legislation etc.). In some cases it has outlined some criteria for these measures (e.g., a human rights based approach for plans of action) but they still lack the coherency of that developed by the South African Constitutional Court.

In May 2007, the Committee explicitly signalled that it would use the 'margin of appreciation' approach: 'In line with the practice of other treaty bodies, the Committee will respect the margin of appreciation of the State party to determine the optimum use of its resources and to adopt national policies and prioritize certain resource demands over others'.[188] This statement is partly incorrect. The Human Rights Committee has rejected this methodology: 'The scope of [Finland's] freedom to do so is not to be assessed by reference to a margin of appreciation, but by reference to the obligations it has undertaken in [A]rticle 27 [of the ICCPR]'.[189] The ICESCR Committee should be wary of exploiting this doctrine as the European Court on Human Rights has done on occasion.[190] The European Court has often applied the margin of appreciation doctrine to rule out consideration of social policy issues, issues that lie at the heart of the Committee's mandate. Moreover, the Covenant was drafted to account for the need for state flexibility. The margin of appreciation doctrine thus risks further unnecessary dilution of what are to some already diluted provisions. The term 'appropriate' in our view allows for enough State latitude. Any of the potential advantages of employing a margin of appreciation doctrine (the only one of which seems to be the placation of States worried about a complaints mechanism) appear insignificant by comparison with the disadvantages.

The Committee has, until recently, been less forthcoming on what is the 'maximum available resources' that must be devoted to these 'steps'. This is despite arguments from scholars such as Robert Robertson that it is the 'heart of the

---

[185] *General Comment No. 3* (n. 71 above), para. 4.
[186] Craven, *The International Covenant on Economic, Social and Cultural Rights* (n. 2 above), p. 116.
[187] *General Comment No. 12* (n. 54 above), para. 21.

[188] See CESCR, *Statement on Maximum Available Resources* (n. 58 above), para. 12.
[189] See *Länsman v. Finland (No. 2)* (Communication No. 671/1995), Views of 30 October 1996, para. 10.5.
[190] See E. Ebnvenisti, 'Margin of Appreciation, Consensus and Universal Standards', *International Law and Politics*, Vol. 31 (1999), pp. 843–854.

problem' in realising ESC rights and that the Committee should develop standards and indicators to measure the extent to which resources (which he categorises as financial, natural, human, technological and informational) are being used for ESC rights.[191] The Committee, however, and for possibly good reason, has tended to treat the question as a secondary issue and one where the State has the burden of indicating where there are resource constraints. For instance, in the case of not meeting the minimum core obligation or the institution of deliberative retrogressive measures, States must demonstrate that the necessary resources are not available. In the concluding observations, the Committee does occasionally use indicators of resource usage, partly in the way proposed by Robertson, as a way of highlighting that the obligation to use the maximum is not being met. In the case of South Korea, the Committee noted in 2001 that it was 'disturbed' by the budgetary allocation for health, which was low (less than under 1 per cent of the total budget) and declining.[192] In the case of Uzbekistan, it used the arguably more objective measure of spending (spending per capita per GDP)[193] to mark a similar concern concerning devotion of resources to the health sector.[194]

Under pressure from States to provide more guidance in the context of the Human Rights Council's moves to develop a complaints mechanism for the ICESCR (see Section 6 below), the Committee has set out in its Statement on Maximum Available Resources how it would measure compliance in that context. It repeats its earlier standards (particularly on minimum core and retrogressive measures) but in relation to the positive devotion of resources it is cautious in being prescriptive. In wording similar to the South African Constitu-

tional Court it had highlighted that the devotion of resources must be 'adequate', 'reasonable' and, more vaguely, in accordance with 'international human rights standards'.[195] The omission of discussion of general indicators on resource allocation in this Statement may be justifiable since it is of less relevance in the context of a focused case, although it may be relevant if a government claims sufficient resources are unavailable or a collective complaint is submitted: see Section 6 below.

4.2   Retrogressive Measures

Due to the obligation to take steps towards progressive realisation, retrogressive measures are examined with particularly heightened scrutiny by the Committee. Amartya Sen has highlighted the importance of reviewing roll-backs of positive government interventions:

> The need for trade-offs is often exaggerated and is typically based on very rudimentary reasoning. Further, even when trade-offs have to be faced, they can be more reasonably – and more justly – addressed by taking an inclusive approach, which balances competing concerns, than by simply giving full priority to just one group over another.[196]

The Committee has articulated its principle of non-retrogression with some sparseness though carefulness: 'any deliberately retrogressive measures...would require the most careful consideration and would need to be fully justified by reference to the totality of the rights provided for in the Covenant and in the context of the full use of the maximum available resources'.[197] Dowell-Jones is less flattering, arguing that the 'principle of non-retrogression is an extremely crude and unsatisfactory yardstick' and 'fails to capture the complexity and fluidity of the task of realising socio-economic rights', particularly in what she sees as the current post-Keynesian paradigm where States can no longer sustain the levels of welfare spending and budget deficits that may

[191] R. E. Robertson, 'Measuring State Compliance with the Obligation to Devote the "Maximum Available Resources" to Realizing Economic, Social, and Cultural Rights', *Human Rights Quarterly*, Vol. 16, No.4 (1994), pp. 693–714.
[192] *Conclusions and recommendations of CESCR: Republic of Korea*, U.N. Doc. E/C.12/1/Add.59 (2001), para. 26.
[193] Robertson, 'Measuring State Compliance' (n. 191 above), argues that this measure is more objective since it adjusts for the fact that governments budgets per capita vary widely and 'available resources' extends to all possibly available societal resources not just presently available fiscal resources.
[194] *Conclusions and recommendations of CESCR: Uzbekistan*, U.N. Doc. E/C.12/UZB/CO/1 (2006), para. 30.

[195] CESCR, *Maximum Available Resources Statement* (n. 58 above), para. 8.
[196] A. Sen, 'Work and Rights', *International Labour Review*, vol. 139, No. 2 (2000), pp. 119–128 at 120–121.
[197] *General Comment No. 3* (n. 71 above), para. 9.

have been possible in the 1960s and 1970s.[198] Although she concedes that the Committee's concluding observations on the subject have not been always crude or dogmatic.[199]

Her criticism is only partially warranted, particularly given the Committee's limited mandate and the variance in the amount of critical and useful information it receives. In the case of Argentina in 1999, which Dowell-Jones subjects to some analysis, the Committee is not specific on the specific 'disadvantaged groups' – something she is particularly concerned with, although it conflicts with her more conservative macro-economic outlook. But the committee does require that minimum pensions should be paid,[200] and not deferred or reduced, something that Dowell-Jones omits in her analysis. The minimum core obligations are clearly red lines for the Committee, which it is anxious to protect in economic and other crises. Dowell-Jones also dismisses the Committee's concern with the effect of privatisation in the crisis, arguing that although it may increase poverty it was necessary due to the large numbers of loss-making public enterprises. She is equally critical of its suggestion that Argentina request greater leeway from the International Monetary Fund given the impotence of the Government and its shared responsibility for the crisis. Without delving into the issue at great length, it is interesting to observe that in the next economic crisis, Argentina's response was seemingly consistent with the Committee's recommendations. The Government froze tariffs charged by private utilities, for instance water and electricity,[201] and took a more robust stance with the IMF as well as private creditors on the repayment of debt.[202] Argentina's growth rate and currency largely recovered. While there is a debate as to whether it should have done more to protect the poorest,[203] it is certainly arguable that this approach was not economically suicidal.

In any case, the Committee may be slowly moving towards articulating a clearer framework for evaluating the justification for 'deliberately retrogressive measures'. In its draft General Comment on the right to social security it states that the Committee will:

> [L]ook carefully at whether (1) alternatives were comprehensively examined; (2) there was genuine participation of affected groups in examining proposed measures and alternatives that threaten their existing human right to social security protections; (3) the measures were directly or indirectly discriminatory; (4) the measures will have a sustained impact on the realization of the right to social security; (5) the individual is deprived of access to the minimum essential level of social security unless all maximum available resources have been used, including domestic and international; (6) review procedures at the national level have examined the reforms.[204]

Another set of criteria concerning the resource dimension of retrogressivity has also been enunciated in a recent statement.[205] The Committee will examine the country's level of development, the severity of the alleged breach, in particular whether it impinges upon 'the minimum core content of the Covenant', the country's current economic situation and whether it was experiencing a recession, the existence of other serious claims on the State party's limited resources, whether the State party had sought to identify low-cost options, and whether the State party had sought international cooperation and assistance or rejected offers of resources without sufficient reason. It is thus clear that while deliberate retrogressive measures are not automatically non-compliant with the Covenant, they engage a particularly strict form of scrutiny or high level of justification. In this sense, the standards for non-retrogression are not dissimilar to those with which it measures interferences with the rights, for example under the obligations to respect and protect, as discussed above in Section 3.2.

---

[198] Dowell-Jones, Contextualising the International Covenant on Economic, Social and Cultural Rights (n. 28 above), pp. 52–54.

[199] Ibid. pp. 71–81.

[200] *Conclusions and recommendations of CESCR: Argentina*, U.N. Doc. E/C.12/1/Add.38 (1999), para. 33.

[201] See C. Fairstein, 'Legal Strategies and the Right to Water in Argentina', in Riedel and Rothen (n. 7 above) pp. 93–112. It is arguable that the Government erred though by overly protecting middle classes.

[202] A. Ciblis, 'Argentina's IMF Agreement: The Dawn of a New Era?', *Foreign Policy in Focus*, 10 October 2003.

[203] Ibid.

[204] *General Comment 20: The Right to Social Security (Article 9)*, (Thirty-sixth session, 2006), E/C. 12/GC/20/CRP. 1, 16 February 2006, para. 31 ('Draft General Comment No. 20').

[205] The CESCR opines in its Statement on Maximum Available Resources (n. 58 above).

4.3   Declaring Violations in the Concluding Observations: Naming and Shaming

From General Comment No. 12 onwards, the Committee has also included in its general comments a specific section on violations under the Covenant. While the language slightly varies,[206] the Committee emphasises that failure to implement the obligations in good faith amounts to a breach of the Covenant in accordance with international law and that it will therefore distinguish between inability and unwillingness to act.[207] The Committee then lists various examples of violations which are largely either conceptual in nature (drawn from the Limburg principles) or are the inverse of the various examples it gives with respect to obligations to respect, protect and fulfil.

An obvious question is whether the Committee has applied these standards in its concluding observations. In 1993, the Committee decided to organise its concluding observations into five categories, as did the other treaty bodies: introduction, positive steps, factors and difficulties impeding the implementation of the covenant, principal subjects and concerns, and suggestions and recommendations.[208] Sepúlveda says that notwithstanding this 'diplomatic structure', the Committee is quite often making formal declarations of compliance or non-compliance. Although the language is typical of international quasi-judicial bodies, referring to 'non-compatibility' for example. In its 1995 observations on the Philippines, the Committee stated that if the number of evictees substantially exceeded the number of resettlement sites, as alleged by NGOs, then '[s]uch a situation would not be compatible with respect for the right to housing'.[209] It also criticised the use of a criminal law and a presidential decree to authorise evictions and convict squatters on the basis that it did not comply with its requirement that 'forced evictions are not carried out except in truly exceptional circumstances, following consideration of all possible alternatives and in full respect of the

rights of all persons affected'.[210] The decree was repealed shortly after the concluding observations were publicised in the Philippines.[211]

Scott Leckie, who regularly attended the Committee's sessions, has charged, however, that many recent concluding observations are 'so general as to lose any hope of being taken seriously'.[212] A survey of the Committee's jurisprudence in recent years only partially supports this observation. In some concluding observations one does find rather vague calls (e.g. Croatia was called on to 'reinforce its efforts to address the high level of unemployment'[213]). One suspects that this variance is largely due to the quality and quantity of information received from NGOs. Indeed, Craven notes that: 'Perhaps the most crucial factor in the success of any reporting procedure is the extent to which the supervisory body has access to information other than that provided by the State concerned'.[214] In addition, the expertise and concentration of the relevant Committee rapporteur who is appointed to draft the relevant concluding observations may be relevant. There is also a partial discord between the maximalist approach taken in recent general comments and the curiously timid nature of some concluding observations. Some of this is understandable. As Bruno Simma has noted, there would have been 'fierce opposition' in the mid-1980s if the Committee were to declare something a violation, while nowadays it is becoming increasingly common.[215] Yet even faced with these constraints, the problem is not just with the Committee's reluctance to declare conduct violative, but with its use of vague language and reference to general conditions rather than to particular state actions or omissions.

---

[210] Ibid. para. 31. (See also para. 15).
[211] See interview with S. Leckie in M. Langford, *Litigating Economic, Social and Cultural Rights: Achievements, Challenges and Strategies* (Centre on Housing Rights & Evictions, 2003), pp. 161, 163.
[212] S. Leckie, 'The Committee on Economic, Social and Cultural Rights: A Catalyst for Change in a System Needing Reform', in P. Alston and J. Crawford, *The Future of the UN Human Rights Treaty Monitoring System* (Cambridge: Cambridge University Press, 2000) p. 132.
[213] *Conclusions and recommendations of CESCR: Croatia*, U.N. Doc. E/C.12/1/Add.73 (2001), para. 32.
[214] Craven, *The International Covenant on Economic, Social and Cultural Rights* (n. 2 above), p. 75.
[215] Sepúlveda, *The Nature of Obligations* (n. 26 above), pp. 36–40 for analysis and examples.

---

[206] *General Comment No. 14* (n. 35 above), overly eulogises the process, When the normative content of article 12 (Part I) is applied to the obligations of States parties (Part II), a dynamic process is set in motion which facilitates identification of violations of the right to health.
[207] See *General Comment No. 15* (n. 86 above), Section IV.
[208] E/1993/22, para. 265.
[209] *Conclusions and recommendations of CESCR: Philippines*, U.N. Doc. E/C.12/1995/7 (1995).

We would suggest the following to improve the quality of concluding observations. First, there should be a direct connection between the 'concerns' and the 'recommendations'. The Human Rights Committee ('HRC') and the Committee on the Rights of the Child ('CRC') have combined these two sections and set off the recommendation in bold face under the concern. Second, the Committee can indicate in the concluding observations what Article is at issue (as the Human Rights Committee does), and, where useful, refer to a standard set out in one of its general comments. While the Committee is now referring to its general comments in its concluding observations with regularity, it rarely directs the State to the relevant part. The CRC deals with each right systematically. Third, the Committee should give serious consideration to the idea of creating, as Leckie suggests,[216] a new category entitled 'Violations of the Covenant' or 'Non-Compliance with the Covenant'. While it would be a bold step forward, it is the common practice of the European Committee on Social Rights. Lastly, it should consider, as the HRC and CRC have done, creating a section of the observations that notes the success of follow-up measures in the State party, and perhaps a note on particular follow-up required at the end of the report.[217]

5. SELECTED RIGHTS

In this section, we analyse two specific rights, social security and water, to examine how the Committee's doctrine have more fully played out

in practice. This selection is slightly arbitrary, though other Covenant rights have perhaps been more fully analysed elsewhere.[218]

5.1 Right to Social Security

The right to social security is widely recognised in international and regional treaty law though its precise content has received somewhat limited attention,[219] the European Committee of Social Rights notwithstanding.[220] However, the right has enjoyed more attention in recent times, partly due to the acknowledgment of glaringly low levels of social security in many countries, the ramifications of two-decade reductions in 'welfare spending' (whether under structural adjustment programmes or the greater endorsement of neo-liberal economics amongst policy and decision-makers) and the push for privatisation of social security systems.[221] For instance, in 2001, the International Labour Organisation ('ILO'), composed of governments, employers and worker representatives, reaffirmed the right to social security and emphasised that social security models should focus on providing access to the excluded and address discrimination against women.[222]

---

[216] Leckie, 'Catalyst for Change' (n. 205 above), p. 144.

[217] At its twenty-first session, the Committee decided to strengthen generally its follow up procedures and that it could either request information on follow-up in the State's next periodic report or prior to the date if there is a specific pressing issue. *Report of the Twentieth and Twenty-First Sessions*, ECOSOC Official Records, Supp. No.2 (2000) para. 38. The Pre-sessional working group is to consider the State's response at the next meeting, and may recommend that the Committee simply take note of the information, adopt additional concluding observations in response to that information, request further information or authorise the Chairperson to inform the State party that the Committee will take up the issue at its next session and that, for that purpose, welcome the participation of a representative. For an exhaustive examination of the Committee's follow up procedures see Arambulo, *Strengthening the Supervision of the International Convenant on Economic, Social and Cultural Rights* (n. 123 above).

[218] For example, Craven's foundational work only examines Articles 6–8 and 11 – rights to work, work conditions, trade union rights and general right to adequate standard of living: see *The International Covenant on Economic, Social and Cultural Rights* (n. 2 above), Chs. 5, 6, 7 and 8. See also B. Toebes, 'The Right to Health as a Human Right in International Law' (Amsterdam: Hart/Intersentia, 1999). Alhough, both studies were prepared in the 1990s.

[219] There has been some academic attention: see, for example, M. Scheinin, 'The Right to Social Security' in A. Eide, C. Krause and A. Rosas (eds.), *Economic, Social and Cultural Rights* (Dordrecht: Martinus Nijhoff Publishers, 2001), pp. 211–219; L. Lamarche, 'The Right to Social Security in the International Covenant on Economic, Social and Cultural Rights', in Chapman and Russell, *Core Obligations* (n. 32 above), pp. 87–114. As regards the Convention on the Rights of the Child, see W. Vandenhole, 'Article 26: The Right to Benefit from Social Security', *A Commentary on the United Nations Convention on the Rights of the Child* (Leiden: Martinus Nijhoff, 2007).

[220] See Chapter 21 in this volume.

[221] The level and coverage of benefits has declined significantly in developed and developing countries alike. Governments frequently cite fiscal constraints, but a preference for smaller government appears to be the dominating factor. See, for example, K. Duffy, *Opportunity and Risk: Trends of Social Exclusion in Europe* (Strasbourg: Council of Europe, 1998), chap. 4.

[222] ILO, Social Security: A New Consensus (Geneva, 2001).

In 2004, the Committee embarked on drafting a General Comment on the subject. A draft was made public for discussion in May 2006[223] but changes will surely be made in the final version, currently being discussed by the Committee, in light of some of the comments made during the Day of General Discussion.[224] The Committee defines the right to social security stating that it encompasses a right to 'access benefits, through a system of social security' in order to address 'income insecurity', economic 'access to health care' and 'family support'.[225] The Committee also notes that social security may be provided in different ways – whether through social insurance, social assistance or even through private mechanisms – but they 'must conform to the essential elements of the right to social security'.[226]

The content of the right to social security in the Committee's practice has largely and traditionally been determined with reference to ILO standards. The different forms of social security set out in ILO Convention 102 are repeated, for example, in the reporting guidelines of the CESCR:[227] These are benefits for medical care, sickness, unemployment, old-age, employment injury, family, maternity, invalidity, and death of family members. In its draft general comment, the Committee opened up the possibility of coverage for other risks, such as housing, water, food for specific groups, or protection from natural disasters and emergencies,[228] but this was opposed by the ILO representative and it seems unlikely to survive in the revised draft.[229]

In defining the content of the right and State obligations, the Committee's approach is only partially consistent with ILO Convention 102.[230] The ILO conventions require States to establish a system for providing social security (see Articles 71 and 72). This requirement is not always apparent in the Committee's concluding observations, which tend to focus more on the result: providing minimum or adequate social security. Canada was requested, however, to establish national programmes that supply specific cash transfers for social assistance and social services that provide universal entitlements.[231] The current draft General Comment would bring the Committee into line with the ILO by requiring that there must be 'a *system*, whether composed of a single or variety of schemes' to ensure that 'benefits can be accessed for the relevant categories of social security' and which 'should be established under national law' and where 'public authorities must take responsibility for the effective administration or supervision of the system'.[232] Both approaches focus on the *adequacy* of benefits though the method of calculation diverges. The ILO Convention links the level of benefits to a percentage of previous earnings or the average wage of specified workers.[233] The Committee is concerned that individuals will have sufficient income in order to secure the goods and services necessary to realise their Covenant rights,[234] an approach comparable to its views on affordability in other general comments.

The divergence is most apparent though with respect to coverage in terms of benefits and accessibility. ILO Convention 102 allows countries to select a minimum number of benefits to be provided while the Committee requires in theory all benefits to be provided but adjusts its expectations

---

[223] Draft *General Comment No. 20* (n. 204 above), para. 16.
[224] See the report available at <http://www.ohchr.org/english/bodies/cescr/discussion.htm>.
[225] According to Liebenberg, social security systems should aim to cover all those risks that impinge upon a person's ability to generate income and maintain an adequate standard of living. See S. Liebenberg, 'Social Security as a Human Right' in Human Rights Resource Centre, University of Minnesota, *Circle of Rights: Economic, Social and Cultural Rights Activism, a Training Resource* (Minneapolis, 2000), Module 11.
[226] Draft *General Comment 20* (n. 204 above), 11(a)(i).
[227] Revised General Guidelines (n. 20 above), sub-section 2.
[228] Scheinin for example argues that other risks associated with the inability to realise ESC rights must also be included. See Scheinin, 'The Right to Social Security' (n. 219 above), p. 215.
[229] See Day of General Discussion: The Right to Social Security (Article 9 of the Covenant), available at <http://www.ohchr.org/english/bodies/cescr/docs/discussion/report_dogd.doc>

[230] For a discussion of the consequences of a human rights approach to social security, see: M. Langford, 'The Right to Social Security and Implications for Law, Policy and Practice', in E. Riedel (ed.) *Social Security as a Human Right: Drafting a General comment on Article 9 ICESCR – Some challenges* (Berlin: SpringerVerlag, 2006), pp. 29–53.
[231] *Conclusions: Canada (1998)* (n. 152 above), para. 40.
[232] Draft *General Comment No. 20* (n. 204 above), para. 11(a)(i). This is defensible if we understand that social security is ordinarily defined as some form of collective, and not purely individual, arrangement to guarantee protection against risks and contingencies. See further the arguments in Lamarche, 'The Right to Social Security' (n. 211 above), p. 103.
[233] *See* Articles 65–67, ILO Convention 102.
[234] Draft *General Comment No. 20* (n. 204 above), para. 11(a)(ii).

according to the level of the country's development and other circumstances such as armed
conflict or economic crisis.[235] The Committee's
concluding observations on more developed
countries tend to focus on access to each of the
benefits, with criticism, for example of the lack
of unemployment benefits in Hong Kong and
maternity benefits in Australia. With poorer countries, the focus is more on the general absence
of social security schemes that extend beyond a
small part of the formal labour force. Of Zambia,
for instance, it required that 'the State party
undertake all necessary measures to guarantee an
adequate standard of living, including through the
provision of social safety nets to the most disadvantaged and marginalised groups'.[236] It is fair to
say though that the Committee in its concluding
observations has mostly focused on six particular
benefits: pensions,[237] access to health care, maternity leave, disability benefits,[238] unemployment
benefits and children and family benefits – and
less on sickness benefits, employment injury and
survivor's benefits.[239]

ILO Convention 102 contains a target-based
approach to coverage of persons. In the case of
medical benefits, this is 50 per cent of all employees and their families, 20 per cent of all economically active residents and their families or
50 per cent of all residents.[240] However, the Committee is more concerned with 'universal coverage', a theme that is consistent in its concluding observations. The Dominican Republic, for
instance, was urged to 'continue its review of
the Social Security Law' and the Committee laid
emphasis on the 'obligation for universal coverage
under [A]rticle 9 of the Covenant'.[241] However, the
Committee is not yet clear of what the minimum
requires. In its draft General Comment, it requires
that it ensures 'access to the minimum essential
level of social security that is essential for acquiring water and sanitation, foodstuffs, essential primary health care and basic shelter and housing,
and the most basic forms of education'. But it has
refrained from indicating whether this minimum
applies to all benefits or whether it will accept a
State demonstrating that it has ensured universal
access to a core group of benefits. The ILO has
indicated for example that all States could immediately provide a package of basic benefits for all
persons, including those in the informal sector,
particularly old-age pensions, invalidity benefits,
basic health care and child benefits.[242] It would
then be up to the State to presumably justify this
selection of benefits to the Committee.

In its draft General Comment, the Committee also
requires States to make sure that any contributions
to a social insurance scheme are affordable, that
there is information about the schemes, particularly in remote and deprived areas, and there is
adequate participation in the design and operation of the schemes.[243] The question of information has arisen in the context of concluding observations, with the Committee finding it 'disturbing
that approximately 1 million persons do not apply
for benefits to which they are entitled' in the
United Kingdom.[244] In addition, conditions of

---

[235] See for *example Conclusions and recommendations of the Committee on Economic, Social and Cultural Rights: Australia*, E/C.12/1/Add.50 (2000), para. 28.

[236] *Conclusions and recommendations of CESCR: Zambia*, U.N. Doc. E/C.12/1/Add.106 (2005), para. 48.

[237] The CESCR, in *General Comment No. 6* (n. 114 above), also stated that Article 9 implicitly recognises the right to old-age benefits and that States Parties should, within the lim-its of available resources, provide non-contributory old-age benefits and other assistance for all older persons who are not entitled to an old-age pension or social secu-rity benefit or assistance under a contributory scheme and have no other source of income.

[238] In *General Comment No. 5* (n. 105 above), the CESCR also stated that social security and income-maintenance schemes are of particular importance for persons with disabilities. Support provided by States should 'reflect the special needs for assistance and other expenses often associated with disability and, as far as possible, such support should also cover carers of people with disabili-ties' (para. 28).

[239] In General Comment No. 6 (n. 114 above) though, the CESCR directs that, in order to give effect to the provisions of Article 9 of the Covenant, States Parties must guaran-tee the provision of survivors and orphans benefits on the death of breadwinners who were covered by social secu-rity or who were receiving pensions, para. 29.

[240] Article 9.

[241] *Conclusions and recommendations of CESCR: Dominican Republic*, U.N. Doc. E/C.12/1/Add.16 (1997).

[242] See 'Costing of basic social protection benefits for selected Asian countries: First results of a modelling exer-cise', Issues in Social Protection, Discussion Paper 17, ILO, 2006 and 'Cash benefits in low-income countries: Sim-ulating the effects on poverty reduction for Senegal and Tanzania', Issues in Social Protection, Discussion Paper 15, ILO, 2006.

[243] Draft *General Comment No. 20* (n. 204 above), para. 11(c)(ii) and (iii).

[244] *Conclusions and recommendations of CESCR: United Kingdom of Great Britain and Northern Ireland*, U.N. Doc. E/C.12/1/Add.19 (1997). This problem is not confined to

eligibility have been raised with States. Ireland was criticised for removing the right to free medical care from persons with disabilities who received the minimum wage for work done in 'sheltered workshops',[245] South Korea for having 'eligibility criteria [that] are apparently so rigid as to exclude many of the poor',[246] and Serbia and Montenegro for legislation that permitted suspension of social security rights of essential services workers who went on strike.[247]

The rights to non-discrimination and equality are of particular importance in the context of the right to social security since certain social risks only arise among certain groups (for example, pregnancy only among women), and marginalised groups are most likely to be the groups in need of social protection. Discrimination in terms of social security is specifically prohibited on the grounds of race, colour, sex, language, religion, political or other opinion, national or social origin, property, birth or other status[248] and the Committee specifically addressed the rights of older persons and persons with disabilities, under other status, in General Comments Nos. 5 and 6. The exclusion of certain groups from the social security system has been raised with States parties, particularly the rights of women,[249] non-nationals (whether migrant workers,[250] refugees or asylum

seekers[251]), minorities such as the Roma who are often denied the documents needed to secure social security,[252] and indigenous peoples.[253]

With regard to women's rights to social security, the Committee has closely examined in social insurance schemes the degree of equality in outcomes for women. This issue is highlighted in the draft General Comment on Right to Social Security.[254] In the case of Austria in 1994, the Committee noted that 'despite the considerable legislative efforts' that sometimes 'inequality persists in practice' in the provision of social security benefits and that authorities 'should continue their efforts to ensure de facto equality between men and women'.[255] In 2006, it noted a new Law on the Harmonization of Pensions which took 'the entire professional career as the basis for calculating old-age pension benefits' and pressed Austria to provide it with data on the levels of old-age pensions, disaggregated by sex, number of children, income groups and other relevant criteria, so as to enable an assessment of the law's impact on the pension benefits of women and other marginalised groups who were often exposed to career interruptions.[256] With Belgium, it instead welcomed a process to ensure greater equality in pension outcomes.[257]

The Committee has also focused on particular groups who don't ordinarily attract the explicit

developed countries. The Indian Supreme Court ordered authorities to publicise the right to grain among families living below the poverty line: *People's Union for Civil Liberties* v. *Union of India* as discussed in chapter 5 of this book.

[245] *Conclusions and recommendations of CESCR: Ireland*, U.N. Doc. E/C.12/1/Add.77 (2002), para. 15.

[246] *Conclusions on Republic of Korea* (n. 192 above), para. 23.

[247] *Conclusions: Serbia and Montenegro* (n. 92 above), para. 19.

[248] *See* Article 2(2) of ICESCR and Article 2(1) of ICCPR.

[249] In Jordan, the Committee criticised the exclusion of foreign workers from the social security system: *Conclusions and recommendations of CESCR: Jordan*, U.N. Doc. E/C.12/1/Add.46 (2000), para. 19.

[250] In relation to Hong Kong: 'The Committee expresses its concern about the particularly precarious situation of foreign domestic workers, a majority of whom are from Southeast Asia, who are unpaid and are not entitled to social security'. (*Conclusions and recommendations of CESCR: People's Republic of China*, U.N. Doc. E/C.12/1/Add.107 (2005), para. 83. In the case of Norway, the Committee expressed particular satisfaction that social security rights were based on residence: *Conclusions and recommendations of CESCR: Norway*, U.N. Doc. E/C.12/1995/18, paras. 203–227 (1997).

[251] *Conclusions and recommendations of CESCR: Azerbaijan*, U.N. Doc. E/C.12/1/Add.104 (2004), para. 48.

[252] See for example, *Conclusions on Serbia and Montenegro* (n. 92 above).

[253] 'The Committee is deeply concerned about the poor working conditions of indigenous workers, who are frequently underpaid or not paid at all, receive no social security benefits or paid vacations, and often work on daily contracts or as unpaid family members'. *Conclusions and recommendations of CESCR: Mexico*, U.N. Doc. E/C.12/MEX/CO/4 (2006), para. 14.

[254] 'In order to ensure that women receive the equal benefit from social security schemes that link benefits with contributions, States parties will need to take steps to redress the factors that prevent women from making equal contributions (for example, intermittent participation by women in the workforce on account of family responsibilities and unequal wage outcomes). These factors could be addressed through the design of the benefit formulas in such schemes'. Draft General Comment No. 20 (n. 204 above), para. 17.

[255] *Conclusions and recommendations of CESCR: Austria*, U.N. Doc.E/C.12/1994/16 (1994), paras. 12, 16.

[256] *Conclusions and recommendations of CESCR: Austria*, U.N. Doc. E/C.12/AUT/CO/3 (2006), para. 25.

[257] *Conclusions and recommendations of CESCR: Belgium*, U.N. Doc. E/C.12/1994/7 (1994), para. 7.

protection of non-discrimination clauses, such as those who are working under atypical working contracts or in the informal economy, but who are likely to struggle to access social security. The Committee has expressed a growing unease with the lack of coverage in the growing informal economies of many developing countries and the fact that 'social security protection is limited to public, administration, State–controlled entities and large enterprises'.[258] This also raises questions of indirect discrimination. Many of those working under atypical contracts or in the informal economy are often predominantly women, as the Committee has pointed out in the case of Austria and Korea.[259]

The obligation to respect requires that States 'refrain from interfering directly or indirectly with the enjoyment of the right to social security',[260] and the draft General Comment appears to apply this duty to schemes developed outside of the official system (such as traditional or communal arrangements or mutual schemes) as well as arbitrary or unreasonable exclusion from State-sanctioned schemes. This aspect has not received significant attention by the Committee in its concluding observations. One exception was the recommendation to Mexico, which was asked to 'supervise and regulate' the military (and paramilitary forces) in the state of Chiapas 'in order to guarantee that development and social assistance programmes are implemented with the active participation of the populations concerned and without the interference of armed forces'.[261]

The Committee has paid more attention to the obligation to protect. It has occasionally reprimanded States for failing to regulate the activities of employers in social insurance schemes. In the case of Saint Vincent and the Grenadines, concern was expressed that 'employers do not comply with their legal obligation to send information and contributions for their employees to the National Insurance Scheme (NIS)' and that there was a 'high incidence of failure of employers to register domestic workers under the scheme'.[262] More attention has been paid to the growing trend of privatisation of social security within States parties.[263] Such particular concern is justified given that the right has a more collective nature than some other rights by definition, given the need for pooling of funds and the requirement that the State provide for an overarching system. The need for social security has been largely motivated by 'market failure'.[264] Moreover, it is difficult in theory, let alone practice, for the private sector to respond effectively to the needs of women and marginalised and poorer groups since it is difficult to achieve cross-subsidisation within a private individual-based system and where administrative costs are often passed onto the insured. Many of these arguments can, of course, be made for other Covenant rights.

As early as 1994, the Committee expressed concern over the Argentinean government's plan to shift to a 'capitalization scheme', largely following the Chilean model being advocated by the World Bank, raising concerns that benefits would be dependent on contributions with the likely possibility that pensions would not be adequate for lower-paid workers, and unemployed and underemployed persons.[265] This was followed up in 1999 by calls for a minimum pension and concerns that

---

[258] *Conclusions and recommendations of CESCR: Guinea*, U.N. Doc. E/C.12/1/Add.5 (1996), para. 17. In the case of Panama, the concern was that rural areas were largely excluded from social security: *Conclusions and recommendations of CESCR: Panama*, U.N. Doc. E/C.12/1/Add.64 (2001), para. 18.

[259] In the case of Austria, the Committee recommended that the country 'adopt measures to enforce the principle of equal pay for equal work, as well as enact legislation to strengthen the protection of persons working under atypical employment contracts, and that it intensify its efforts in the field of qualification programmes for women working in low-paid jobs and unemployed women'. *Conclusions: Austria* (2006) (n. 256 above), para. 22. See also *Conclusions on Republic of Korea* (n. 192 above), para. 17.

[260] Ibid. para. 33.

[261] *Conclusions: Mexico* (n. 253 above).

[262] Furthermore, it notes the absence of provision for registration of self-employed persons under the NIS, and that, although the NIS provides for benefits to be paid in case of sickness, invalidity, retirement and death, no provision is made for compensation in case of workplace accidents.

[263] For an excellent overview of this origins and impact of this trend, see K. Müller, *Privatising Old-Age Security: Latin America and Eastern Europe Compared* (Cheltenham: Edward Elgar Publishing, 2003).

[264] On this issue, see generally M. Gilman, 'Legal Accountability in an Era of Privatized Welfare' *California Law Review*, Vol. 89 (2001) pp. 569–642; J. Freeman 'Extending Public Law Norms Through Privatization' *Harvard Law Review*, Vol. 116 (2002–2003) pp. 1285–1352; D.J. Kennedy, 'Due Process in a Privatized Welfare System' *Brooklyn Law Review*, Vol. 64 (1998), pp. 231–306; J. Freeman, 'Private Parties, Public Functions and the New Administrative Law', *Administrative Law Review*, Vol. 52 (2000) pp. 813–858.

[265] *Conclusions and recommendations of CESCR: Argentina*, U.N. Doc. E/C.12/1994/14; E/1995/22, paras. 221–242 (1994).

the Government could reduce and even not pay pensions by 'invoking economic constraints'.[266] In 2004, the Committee addressed Chile's privatised system and its inability to meet the right to social security of women and marginalised workers:

> The Committee is deeply concerned that the private pension system, based on individual contributions, does not guarantee adequate social security for a large segment of the population who do not work in the formal economy or are unable to contribute sufficiently to the system, such as the large group of seasonal and temporary workers. The Committee notes that women are particularly affected in this regard: "housewives" and about 40 per cent of working women do not contribute to the social security scheme and are consequently not entitled to old age benefits. Moreover, the Committee is concerned at the fact that working women are left with a much lower average pensions than men as their retirement age is five years earlier than that of men.[267]

The Committee raised similar concerns with the Czech Republic, Peru, Mexico and Zambia,[268] but in the case of Bulgaria noted positively that privatisation of health services had not resulted in medicines no longer being distributed free of charge to disadvantaged groups.[269]

With regard to the duty to fulfil, the Committee has consistently placed a strong emphasis on all countries putting in place non-contributory schemes.[270] The principle was first outlined in

General Comment No. 6 with regard to older persons. States parties were obliged, within the maximum of available resources, to provide non-contributory old-age benefits and related assistance for all older persons and not entitled to an old-age pension or other social security benefit or assistance and who have no other source of income. In the draft General Comment on Right to Social Security, the Committee justifies this requirement on the basis that 'it is unlikely that every person could be adequately covered through an insurance-based system'.[271] It has been consistent in requiring this of all States, though as noted in Section 3.2, the level required of developing, transitional and developed States varies. In the case of Canada in 2006, the Committee was perhaps the most comprehensive, urging the State to 'establish officially a poverty line and to establish social assistance at levels' consistent with an adequate standard of living, amend the National Child Benefit Scheme 'so as to prohibit provinces from deducting the benefit from social assistance entitlements', reform Canada's Employment Insurance Programme 'so as to provide adequate coverage for all unemployed workers in an amount and for a duration which fully guarantees their right to social security', and address homelessness and inadequate housing partly through 'increasing shelter allowances and social assistance rates to realistic levels'.[272]

5.2   Right to Water

Water is not specifically mentioned in the Covenant, but the Committee's recent attention to the right to water has been the catalyst for significant momentum in the area. The Committee initially addressed water (and sanitation) in its general comments on housing, health and education[273] and the Committee's reporting guidelines asked States to provide information on access to both under the right to housing and health.[274] Many of the concluding observations therefore simply addressed the lack of access to a basic water supply

---

266 *Conclusions: Argentina* (n. 200 above), paras. 18 and 33.
267 *Conclusions and recommendations of CESCR: Chile*, U.N. Doc. E/C.12/1/Add.105 (2004), para. 20. Chile was asked to 'take effective measures to ensure that all workers are entitled to adequate social security benefits, including special measures to assist those groups who are currently not able to pay into the private social security system, paying special attention to the disadvantaged position of women and the large number of temporary and seasonal workers and workers in the informal economy'. Ibid. para. 43.
268 See *Conclusions and recommendations of CESCR: Czech Republic*, U.N. Doc. E/C.12/1/Add.76 (2002), para. 10; *Conclusions: Mexico* (n. 253 above), para. 24; *Conclusions and recommendations of CESCR: Peru*, U.N. Doc. E/C.12/1/Add.14 (1997), para. 32; *Conclusions: Zambia* (n. 236 above), paras. 22 and 48.
269 See *Conclusions and recommendations of CESCR: Bulgaria*, U.N. Doc. E/C.12/1/Add.37 (1999), para. 6.
270 See for example, *General Comment No. 6* (n. 114 above),

271 Draft *General Comment No. 20* (n. 204 above), para. 3.
272 *Conclusions: Canada* (n. 160 above), paras. 60,55, 54 and 62.
273 *General Comment No. 4* (n. 76 above); *General Comment No. 13* (n. 87 above); *General Comment No. 14* (n. 35 above).
274 Revised *General Guidelines* (n. 20 above), paras. 3(b) 9(iii) and 4(b).

and recommended improvement. For instance, in the case of Cameroon, the Committee states:

> The Committee regrets the lack of access to potable water for large sectors of society, especially in rural areas where only 27 per cent of the population have access to safe water (within reasonable reach), while 47 per cent of the urban population have such access. . . . The Committee calls upon the State party to make safe drinking water accessible to the entire population.[275]

The Committee has on other occasions been more specific and also addressed water in the context of obligations to respect, protect and not discriminate. In its 1995 conclusions on Russia, the Committee raised the problem of pollution of water and its impact on health and food contamination[276] and in its 1998 concluding observations on the report of Israel, the Committee stated:

> Excessive emphasis upon the State as a "Jewish State" encourages discrimination and accords a second-class status to its non-Jewish citizens. This discriminatory attitude is apparent in the lower standard of living of Israeli Arabs as a result, *inter alia*, of lack of access to housing, water... while the Government annually diverts millions of cubic metres of water from the West Bank's Eastern Aquifer Basin, the annual per capita consumption allocation for Palestinians is only 125 cubic metres while settlers are allocated 1,000 cubic metres per capita. . . . That a significant proportion of Palestinian Arab citizens of Israel continue to live in unrecognized villages without access to water, electricity, sanitation and roads. . . . Bedouin Palestinians settled in Israel. . . . have no access to water, electricity and sanitation. . . .[277]

The Committee made a number of recommendations and it is notable that they specifically include the *right to water*. They called on Israel 'to cease the practices of . . . expropriating land, water and

resources, demolishing houses and arbitrary evictions' and urged the State to 'recognize the existing Arab Bedouin villages, the land rights of the inhabitants and their *right to basic services, including water*' (emphasis added). Lastly, in 2001, they made recommendations concerning the privatisation of water in Nepal recommending that the State 'ensure that projects involving privatization of water supply provide for continued, assured and affordable access to water by local communities, indigenous people, and the most disadvantaged and marginalized'.[278]

In 2002, the Committee proceeded to adopt a General Comment on the right to water under Articles 11 and 12.[279] Article 11 states that everyone has the 'right to an adequate standard of living, including food, clothing and housing' and the Committee argued that the 'use of the word "including" indicates that this catalogue of rights was not intended to be exhaustive'.[280] The Committee found that the right to water 'clearly falls within the category of guarantees essential for securing an adequate standard of living, particularly since it is one of the most fundamental conditions for survival'.[281] The Committee also stated that the right can be derived from the right to health in Article 12, though it devotes less attention to this argument.

While the majority of the literature has recommended or applauded the Committee's recognition of the right,[282] this 'reading-in' of the right

---

[278] Ibid. paras. 41 and 42.
[279] *General Comment No. 15* (n. 86 above).
[280] Ibid. para. 2.
[281] Ibid.
[282] See S. McCaffrey, 'A Human Right to Water: Domestic and International Implications' (1992) 5 *Georgetown International Environmental Law Review* 1, 1–24; P. Gleick, 'The Human Right to Water', (1999) 1 *Water Policy* 487, 478–503; H. Smets, 'Le Droit de chacun a l'eau' *Revue europeene de droit de l'environnement* Vol. 2 (2002), pp. 123–170; M. Vidar and M. Mekouar, *Water, Health and Human Rights* (2001) WHO <www.who.int> accessed 15 February 2007; S. Salman and S. McInerney-Lankford, *The Human Right to Water: Legal and Policy Dimensions* (Washington D.C.: World Bank 2004); S. McCaffrey, 'The Human Right to Water' in E. Brown Weiss, L. Boisson De Charzounes and N. Bernasconi-Osterwalder (eds.), *Fresh Water and International Economic Law* (Oxford: Oxford University Press 2005); T. Kiefer and C. Brolmann, 'Beyond State Sovereignty: The Human Right to Water' (2005) 5 *Non-State Actors and International Law* Vol. 5 (2005) pp. 183–208; A. Cahill, 'The Human Right to Water – A Right of Unique Status: The Legal Status and Normative Content of the Right to Water' (2005) 9 *International*

---

[275] *Conclusion: Cameroon* (n. 83 above), para. 27.
[276] 'It is also very concerned that there has been a curtailment of funds to modernize an out-of-date water delivery system which adversely affects the access of the population to clean water'. *Concluding observations of the Committee on Economic, Social and Cultural Rights: Russian Federation.* 20/05/97. E/C.12/1/Add.13, para. 25. See also para. 38
[277] *Conclusions: Israel* (n. 61 above), paras. 10, 24, 26 and 28.

to water has provoked some scholarly controversy.[283] Tully has levelled a number of arguments at the General Comment, particularly that Article 11 offers no interpretive space for 'new' rights, an amendment to the Covenant was necessary for incorporation of the right to water in the treaty, and that deference must be given to the States' omission of water in the drafting of the Covenant.[284] He alleges that the General Comment has received only a lukewarm or negative reaction from States and contends that the topic of access to water would be better placed within other social rights, such as food, housing and health.

However, the Committee's approach is fairly defensible and amendment was clearly not needed.[285] The Committee limits the expansion of the number of rights by requiring that they be comparable to food, clothing and housing and of a serious and fundamental nature.[286] Moreover, the right to water is recognised in a significant number of international declarations[287] such as the 1977 Declaration from the UN Water Conference,[288] and States have generally been significantly supportive of the General Comment.[289] Indeed, the Committee has been bold enough to publicly regret the opposition to the right by Canada and strongly recommended the State review its position.[290] Moreover, water should be carved out as a separate human right for both conceptual and instrumental reasons – the relevant UN human rights mechanisms on other social rights for instance have not been able to keep a steady focus on the issue.

The General Comment provides significant detail on the content of the right, and addresses what is perhaps the most difficult issue: what is the inalienable entitlement? The Committee resolves this question by largely following a universalistic approach, reducing the right to its household water uses (personal consumption, cooking, hygiene and, where necessary, sanitation) and noting that other uses may be covered by other rights: for example, the Committee indicates that marginalised farmers should be able to access sufficient water to secure their right to food.[291] The Committee follows its standard recipe of availability, quality and accessibility[292] in further breaking down the content of the right though it doesn't give a magic number for an adequate or minimum amount, though it references WHO documents indicating it should be fifty litres of water per day, with twenty litres as a minimum.[293] According to the Committee, water must also be of adequate

Journal of Human Rights 389, 389–410; 'The UN Concept of the Right to Water: New Paradigm for Old Problems?' (2005) 21 *International Journal of Water Resources Development* 273, 273–282; Riedel and Rothen, *The Human Right to Water* (n. 7 above).

[283] See S. Tully, 'A Human Right to Access Water? A Critique of General Comment No. 15', *Netherlands Quarterly of Human Rights*, Vol. 23 (2005), pp. 35–63; Dennis and Stewart, 'Justiciability of Economic, Social, and Cultural Rights' (n. 29 above).

[284] He makes a number of other arguments such as the absence of a UN agency for water which is somewhat absurd given the late creation of an agency for housing and the absence of one for clothing. In any case, UN Water was recently established as an initiative of 23 UN agencies.

[285] The arguments are fully set out in M. Langford, 'Ambition that overleaps itself? A Response to Stephen Tully's 'Critique' of the General Comment on the Right to Water', *Netherlands Quarterly of Human Rights* Vol. 26 (2006) pp. 433–459. See also S. Tully, 'Flighty Purposes and Deeds: a Rejoinder to Malcolm Langford' (2006) 26 *Netherlands Quarterly of Human Rights* 461, 461–472; M. Langford, 'Expectation of Plenty: response to Stephen Tully' (2006) 26 *Netherlands Quarterly of Human Rights* 473, 473–479.

[286] General Comment No. 15 (n. 86 above), para. 3.

[287] See generally M. Langford, A. Khalfan, C. Fairstein and H. Jones, *The Right to Water: National and International Standards* (Geneva: Centre on Housing Rights & Evictions, 2003).

[288] Mar del Plata Declaration: 'all peoples, whatever their stage of development and their social and economic conditions, have the right to have access to drinking water in quantities and of a quality to their basic needs'.

[289] For instance, in 2003, the European Parliament declared that water was a human right, the former UN Commission on Human Rights, in its annual omnibus resolution on economic, social and cultural rights has regularly taken note of the General Comment on the Right to Water; *and* its 2004 resolution on toxic wastes, strongly supported by developing states, referred to a range of rights, including the right to water; the Group of seventy-seven nations endorsed the right to water in a May 2006 resolution and in November 2006, the United Kingdom reversed its position and unequivocally supported the right to water. In April 2006, Spain and Germany commenced a process within the newly named Human Rights Council that aims to have an authoritative resolution and Special Rapporteur on the right to water in 2007. For progress on the latter, see Decision 2/104 (1996) which authorises the preparation of a study.

[290] *Conclusions: Canada* (n. 153 above), para. 30 and 64.

[291] Ibid. para 7.

[292] Ibid [12]. For a comprehensive analysis of rights-based implementation for each of these five elements, see COHRE, WHO and AAAS, *Right to Water Manual* (2007).

[293] See for example, P. Gleick, 'Basic water requirements for human activities: meeting basic needs', *Water International* Vol. 24 (1996), 83–92.

quality (WHO Guidelines are noted), safely accessible to people within or in close proximity to their homes, accessed without non-discrimination, and must be affordable, though free in some circumstances.

The Committee refers to the duty of government to confront the obstacles faced by an extensive range of groups in accessing water, including women, people with disabilities, children, refugees, prisoners and nomadic communities as part of the requirement of guaranteeing non-discrimination and equality under Articles 2(2) and 3. Importantly, the General Comment covers the situation of residents of informal settlements, where it stresses their right to receive water irrespective of the legal status of their occupation of the land or housing. This concern with non-discrimination and right to water has become more apparent since the General Comment, with the Committee recommending that Libya 'implement the right of the Amazigh population to access safe water in the regions of Nefoussa and Zouara, and to report back to the Committee on this issue in its next report' given that other regions in the country had greatly improved access.[294] The Committee also expresses concern with the right to water of prisoners in Yemen and Zambia,[295] particularly women in the case of Yemen, Roma in European countries,[296] Travellers in Ireland, Indigenous peoples in Canada,[297] internally displaced and a range of other marginalised groups in Georgia,[298] refugees and internally displaced in Azerbaijan,[299] though the specificity of the recommendations differs between the concluding observations. The Committee also seemed to have moved on from just comparing urban and rural disparity, and not-

ing the denial of right to water in deprived urban areas, particularly informal settlements.

In relation to the duty to respect, the Committee gives examples of required State action such as refraining from interference with customary or traditional arrangements consistent with human rights, polluting water or destroying water facilities in times of armed conflict. Returning to the approach of General Comment No. 7, the Committee is also more rigorous in setting out the steps a Government must take before removing existing access to water. Disconnection should only proceed if there is sufficient justification, due process and an alternative adequate and appropriate water source.[300] The Committee took up these particular issues a year later in its concluding observations on Israel, expressing concern at the impact on security fence on access to water resources for Palestinians and the 'inequitable management, extraction and distribution of shared water resources' by the Israeli government which limited 'access to, distribution and availability of water for Palestinians in the occupied territories'.[301] It also made a number of recommendations with reference to the General Comment.

With regard to the duty to protect, General Comment No. 15 is more precise than earlier general comments.[302] After providing examples of State duties to legislate, ensure private actors do not deny equal access and to prevent pollution and inequitable extraction by third parties, the General Comment addresses private actors who provide water services. It specifically requires the State to ensure that the private sector will act consistently with *democratic principles*, such as participation, create a sufficient regulatory framework, including penalties for non-compliance, and ensure that private actors ultimately must take the *necessary steps* to assist in the realisation of the right to water, or at least not frustrate the objective. An earlier draft was stronger – calling for the deferral of privatisation until a regulatory framework was in place – though this was ultimately removed. At the same time, the General Comment opens with the

---

[294] *Concluding Observations of CESCR: Libyan Arab Jamahiriya*, 25 January 2006, UN Doc. E/C.12/LYB/CO/2, paras. 18 and 35. See also comments on Amazigh population and right to water in *Concluding Observations of CESCR: Morocco* UN Doc. E/C.12/MAR/CO/3 (2006) and access to water in Republika Srpska in *Concluding observations of CESCR: Bosnia and Herzegovina*. 24/01/2006. E/C.12/BIH/CO/1, paras. 27 and 49.

[295] *Concluding observations of CESCR: Yemen* E/C.12/1/Add.92 (2003), para. 18; *Concluding Observations of CESCR: Zambia* UN Doc. E/C.12/1/Add.106 (2005).

[296] See *Concluding Observations of CESCR: The former Yugoslav Republic of Macedonia* 24/11/2006. E/C.12/MKD/CO/1; and *Conclusions: Serbia* (n. 92 above).

[297] See *Conclusions: Canada* (n. 160 above), para. 16.

[298] *Conclusions: Georgia* (n. 144 above).

[299] *Concluding observations of CESCR: Azerbaijan* E/C.12/1/Add.20 (1997), para. 52.

[300] *General Comment No. 15* (n. 86 above), para. 56. It concludes its prescriptions on due process by noting that '[u]nder no circumstances shall an individual be deprived of the minimum essential level of water'.

[301] *Concluding Observations of CESCR: Israel* UN Doc. E/C.12/1/Add.90 (2003), para. 25.

[302] Ibid. paras. 23–24.

phrase that water is a 'public good', which has been interpreted by some as showing the Committee's unease with private solutions. But some authors such as Craven have criticised the Committee for not going far enough on the question of privatisation: 'one may sense that the Committee may be legislating for its own absence – or excluding its own competence – in the very area in which the discussion of water rights is most acute and in which the Committee's voice is perhaps most needed'.[303] Nonetheless, the Committee has been perhaps more stringent in its concluding observations: in the case of Morocco, it expressed concern over 'privatization of public services such as water and electricity in urban centres in Morocco, the effect of which is to impose an additional economic burden on families living in shantytowns and thus aggravate their poverty'.[304]

The final domestically oriented obligation is the duty to fulfil. In setting out the other obligations of States, the Committee strove to emphasise in General Comment No. 15 that the realisation of the right was practical despite the assumption that water scarcity and resources constraints for *some* States was a limiting factor: 'Realization of the right should be feasible and practicable, since all States parties exercise control over a broad range of resources, including water, technology, financial resources and international assistance, as with all other rights in the Covenant' (para 18). According to the Committee, this requires that governments use all available resources to implement progressively the right to water. The right to water does not have to be realised overnight, the Committee maintained, but the government must immediately take steps in the direction of ensuring universal access. According to the General Comment, this includes developing a plan and strategy on expanding affordable access as well as protecting the quality of the water supply; actively searching for the available resources, nationally and locally; implementing the plan and monitoring its implementation over time; and providing systems of accountability so that citizens, NGOs and others can bring information or complaints about failures in the system. The General Comment also refers to the need for States to ensure

that regional governments and local authorities have sufficient resources to ensure the right to water and do not discriminate.[305]

In concluding observations, the Committee has been growing slightly more specific on the steps needed to improve access. In the case of Georgia, the Committee recommended that it:[306]

[T]ake effective measures, in consultation with relevant civil society organizations, to improve the situation of internally displaced persons, including the adoption of a comprehensive programme of action aiming at ensuring more effectively their rights to adequate housing, food and water, health services and sanitation, employment and education, and the regularization of their status in the State party....[and] continue its efforts to improve the living conditions of its population, in particular by ensuring that the infrastructure for water, energy provision and heating is improved....

In the case of Yemen, a water-stressed State, the Committee importantly addressed the human rights dimension of water allocations and the need to take preventive action to protect and improve water resources.[307]

The General Comment also sets out the 'international' obligations to respect, protect and fulfil under Article 2 (1), and they quite specific in this General Comment. States are required to respect the right in other countries, prevent their nationals and registered corporations from harming the rights of others overseas, take steps to provide financial and in-kind support to poorer countries struggling to assist their residents, ensure that the international financial institutions, of which they

---

[303] M. Craven, 'Some Thoughts on the Emergent Right to Water', in Riedel and Rothen, *The Human Right to Water* (n. 7 above), pp. 35–46, at 45–46.

[304] *Conclusions: Morocco* (n. 294 above).

[305] *General Comment No. 15* (n. 86 above), para. 51.

[306] *Conclusions: Georgia* (n. 144 above), para. 31.

[307] 'The Committee is concerned about the persisting water crisis which constitutes an alarming environmental emergency in the State party, and which prevents access to safe and affordable drinking water, particularly for the disadvantaged and marginalized groups of society, and for rural areas....The Committee urges the State party to introduce strategies, plans of action, and legislative or other measures to address the scarcity of water problems, in particular the sustainable management of the available water resources. The Committee recommends that effective water management strategies and measures be undertaken in urban setting, exploring possibilities for alternative water treatment and developing ecological dry sanitation methods in rural settings'. *Conclusions: Yemen* (n. 295 above), paras. 19, 37, 38.

are members, do not violate the right,[308] and that sanctions regimes should provide for repairs to infrastructure essential to provide clean water and not disrupt access to water.

6. CONCLUSION: TOWARDS A COMPLAINTS MECHANISM

One of the key and lingering differences between the Committee on Economic, Social and Cultural Rights and other international and regional human rights treaty bodies is the lack of a complaints mechanism. As this Chapter has demonstrated, the Committee has demonstrated an ability to construe the ICESCR in a manner that provides concrete legal obligations. Together with the burgeoning jurisprudence as the national level, the absence of a complaints mechanism for the ICESCR increasingly looks like a historical hangover. The renaissance of economic, social and cultural rights has therefore been accompanied by growing demands for an optional protocol. At a seminal international conference on the right to food in 1984, Westereveen concluded that 'it is not to be expected that States will readily submit to a complaints procedure' for the ICESCR.[309] But FIAN, an international NGO that was to emerge from that conference, together with Habitat International Coalition, commenced a nascent campaign and drafted the text of a possible complaint.[310]

In 1990, the Committee began discussing the possibility of an optional protocol,[311] which culminated in a report to the then UN Commission of Human Rights in 1996.[312] A draft optional protocol was annexed to the report. The report strongly

argued for an optional protocol on the grounds that it would better highlight 'concreter and tangible issues', provide a focused 'framework for inquiry', 'encourage governments to ensure more effective remedies are available' at the national level, spur individuals and groups to formulate their demands for ESC rights more concretely and help realise ESC rights since the decisions would carry some weight with governments even though they would be 'non-binding'.[313] In this latter regard, the Committee points to the results of the complaints mechanism for the ICCPR. Indeed, the mere existence of an optional protocol for the ICCPR was a pivotal argument by the Australian High Court in holding that the common law of the country, in this case concerning land title of indigenous peoples, should be interpreted in accordance with international law.[314]

It was not until a decade later that the UN Human Rights Council officially created a working group to draft an optional protocol.[315] The intervening years witnessed an ever growing and influential NGO campaign,[316] strong leadership by Portugal on the issue within the Commission, the commissioning of a report by an independent expert by the Commission[317] and the creation of the wonderfully titled 'Open-ended working group to consider options regarding the elaboration of an Optional Protocol'.[318] The key issue that dogged these debates was whether ESC rights were justiciable but the first working group provided an ideal forum for the presentation of national

---

[308] See further, A. Khalfan, *Implementing General Comment No. 15 on the Right to Water in National and International Law and Policy* (2005) available at <www.Rcohre.org/water>.

[309] G. Westerveen, 'Towards a System for Supervising States' Compliance with the Right to Food', in P. Alston, and K. Tomaševski, *The Right to Food* (The Hague: Martinus Nijhoff, 1984), pp. 119–134, at 127.

[310] As told to one of the authors by Scott Leckie.

[311] U.N. Doc. E/C.12/1991/Wp.2. See generally, Arambulo, *Strengthening the Supervision of the International Convenant on Economic, Social and Cultural Rights* (n. 123 above).

[312] UN Doc. E/C.12/1996/CRP.2/Add.1. The report was distributed widely by the Commission for comments which are consolidated in U.N. Doc. E/CN.4/1998/84.

[313] U.N. Doc. A/CONF.157/PC/62/Add. 5, paras. 32–38.

[314] 'The opening up of international remedies to individuals pursuant to Australia's accession to the Optional Protocol to the International Covenant on Civil and Political Rights (68). See Communication 78/1980 in *Selected Decisions of the Human Rights Committee under the Optional Protocol*, vol. 2, p. 23 brings to bear on the common law powerful influence of the Covenant and the international standards it imports'. *Mabo & Ors v. Queensland* (No. 2) [1992] HCA 23; (1992) 175 CLR 1, per Brennan J, para. 42.

[315] Resolution 1/3.

[316] The campaign was initially a loose and changing grouping of international and national NGOs which has since grown to become a major actor in the negotiations: See <http://www.opicescr-coalition.org/>.

[317] See *Report of the Independent Expert* (n. 46 above); *and Report of the Independent Expert on the Draft Optional Protocol to the International Covenant on Economic, Social and Cultural Rights*, Commission on Human Rights, Fifty-Ninth Session, Item 10 of the provisional Agenda U.N. Doc. E/CN.4/2003/53.

[318] Commission on Human Rights Resolution 2002/24, (14 August 2002) para. 9(F).

and international experiences that largely helped largely lay this issue to rest.[319] Although the related and more technical issue of whether States should be able to select which rights in ICESCR are made subject to an optional protocol has been slightly more intractable. Other issues included whether the Committee should be the appropriate forum to hear complaints, concerns over duplication with other international bodies and what consideration should be given to the resource situation of developing countries.

In July 2007, a draft optional protocol was presented to the newly mandated working group by the Portuguese Chairperson Catarina de Albuquerque.[320] The draft draws heavily on the proposal by the Committee with some exceptions, including bracketed text for discussion. The draft explicitly recognises the competence of the Committee to hear complaints (Article 1) and that communications may be submitted by individuals or groups (Article 2). However, the scope of the complaints is heavily bracketed reflecting ongoing disagreements over the comprehensive approach, particularly over whether the complaints procedures should apply to Article 1 on self-determination and should permit States to opt-in or out of selected rights in Part III. A slight majority of States seemed to favour a comprehensive approach, which is indeed preferable since it is consistent with the optional protocol to ICCPR and does not establish a hierarchy of rights.[321] However, there did not appear to be sustained debate on including Part 1. The NGO international coalition has strongly argued for its inclusion on the grounds to exclude it would undermine the value of the complaints mechanism for indigenous groups and that in any case, the Human Rights Committee has adopted a restrictive approach in considering individual complaints since the right is a collective right.[322]

This attempt to divide the rights has been consistently present in the discussions of the obligations, for instance to 'respect and protect' or to 'non-discrimination'. The Chairperson appears to have tried to allay States fears by explicitly introducing the concept of reasonableness in her draft for the stage in a complaint when the Committee assesses compliance.[323] Such a step is questionable since one could argue that the optional protocol is essentially changing, without precedent, the text of the substantive treaty. Indeed, Lichtsenstein proposed just deleting the word 'reasonableness' and was supported by Ecaudor.[324] However, the Committee has also indicated it will use the 'reasonableness' concept anyway, as discussed in Section 3.8 above. In the most recent discussion, some States tried to re-introduce the idea of limiting the obligations, though with less force this time. The African group proposed that the 'focus' of the Committee be on the 'respect and protect' dimensions of the obligation and that the Committee, secondly, 'address, where and as required the reasonable of steps taken by the States parties, but it attracted little support'.[325] A similar proposal by the USA to use the term 'unreasonable' also found little favour.

While the draft Optional Protocol for ICESCR has similar admissibility criteria and procedures to that for the ICCPR, it introduces procedural innovations that have been developed in more recent international and regional treaties. Similar to the regional human rights systems, the draft allows for collective communications by groups with UN consultative status. This proposal faced some stiff opposition and calls for further study which the Chairperson tried to defuse by noting that certain rights under the Covenant can only be exercised collectively.[326] However, other governments actually saw the necessity for U.N. ECOSOC

---

[319] See Report of first session (U.N. Doc. E/CN.4/2004/44); Report of second session; (U.N. Doc. E/CN.4/2005/52); Report of third session (U.N. Doc. E/CN.4/2006/47).

[320] See *Draft Optional Protocol to the International Covenant on Economic, Social and Cultural Rights*, Prepared by Chairperson-Rapporteur, Catarina de Albuquerque, Human Rights Council, Sixth Session, Open-Ended Working Group on an Optional Protocol to the International Covenant on Economic, Social and Cultural Rights, Fourth Session, Geneva, 16–27 July, U.N. Doc. A/HRC/6/WG.4/2.

[321] See Report of fourth session (U.N. Doc. A/HRC/6/8).

[322] However, inclusion of the collective complaints procedure in Article 3 of the proposed ICESCR Optional Protocol may provide Indigenous and other groups with more possibilities to press the right to self-determination through the complaints system.

[323] *Draft Optional Protocol to the International Covenant on Economic, Social and Cultural Rights* (n. 320 above).

[324] See *Report of the Open-Ended Working Group on an Optional Protocol* (n. 321 above), para. 96.

[325] Ibid. paras. 88–91.

[326] Ibid. paras. 46, 50 and 54.

consultative status for complainant organisations as too restrictive and called for the standing provision for NGOs to be widened.[327] There was also division over an inquiry procedure for grave and systematic violations. Opponents cited concerns that it would overlap with the work of Special Rapporteurs but it was clear that the concern was the possibility for the Committee to take a more proactive approach to identifying violations. However, an inquiry procedure would be well suited to the Covenant given the intractable and systemic violations uncovered during the current reporting procedure. The procedure would allow the Committee to make better and focused recommendations. Proposals for the Committee to order interim measures (Article 5), assist with friendly settlements (Article 7) and a special fund for States that lack the 'financial means to implement effective remedies' (Articles 13 and 14) tended to have more support. However, some developed States expressed concerns over the proposed fund on the basis that would 'duplicate existing funds' and that it would 'send a wrong signal that non-compliance with the Covenant rights could be justified by a lack of international assistance'.[328]

In conclusion, the rapid pace at which the drafting of the optional protocol is proceeding indicates that the Committee has been able to develop a robust enough jurisprudence to garner sufficient respect from States and simultaneously convince non-governmental organisations that it is an international body worth taking seriously. At the same time, this article has pointed out a number of areas where the Committee can improve the coherency and quality of both its concluding observations and general comments, a process that will of course be assisted by the adoption of an optional protocol.

Postscript: On 4 April 2008, the Chairperson of the optional protocol working group submitted a draft optional protocol to the Human Rights Council, which approved it after some amendment. The optional protocol draft will be considered by the General Assembly with a vote expected on 10 December 2008. It is pertinent to note that collective complaints are not possible under the revised draft but that economic, social and cultural rights inherent in the right to self-determination are included after a compromise was reached in the Human Rights. The U.N. Committee has also adopted the final text of the General Comment on Right to Social Security (see U.N. Doc. E/C.12/GC/19(2008)).

---

[327] Ibid. para. 53.
[328] Ibid. para. 125.

24

Committee on the Elimination of Racial Discrimination

Confronting Racial Discrimination and Inequality in the Enjoyment of Economic, Social and Cultural Rights

Nathalie Prouvez*

1. INTRODUCTION

The Committee on the Elimination of Racial Discrimination ('CERD' or 'the Committee'),[1] a body of eighteen independent experts,[2] monitors the implementation of the International Convention on the Elimination of All Forms Racial Discrimination ('the Convention')[3] by States parties. Article 9 of the Convention provides for a system of reporting,[4] which requires the submission of an initial report within one year after the entry into force of the Convention for the State concerned and thereafter every two years. The second compliance mechanism is an optional system of individual and group complaints[5] provided for in Article 14 of the Convention. Bearing in mind the number of States that do not comply regularly with their reporting obligations, the Committee has also introduced a so-called review procedure[6] through which it reviews the implementation of the Convention without a report by States that are at least five years late in the submission of their reports. Additionally, the Committee adopted in 1993 a working paper providing for early warning and urgent action procedures.[7]

The Committee views the 'Convention, as a living instrument, [to] be interpreted and applied taking into account the circumstances of contemporary society'.[8] The general approach of the Committee to the interpretation of the Convention has been increasingly creative, as can be seen through the thirty-one General Recommendations which it has adopted between 1972 and 2005.[9] Furthermore, the Committee also provides its interpretation of the Convention in the concluding observations

---

* Former Secretary of the Committee on the Elimination of Racial Discrimination. The opinions expressed in this paper are the author's and do not reflect those of the United Nations.

[1] Hereafter 'CERD' or 'the Committee'.

[2] The experts, following nomination by States parties, are elected by secret ballot in a meeting of States parties (See article 8 of the Convention). Nine members are elected every two years for renewable terms of four years.

[3] Hereafter 'the Convention'. As at 1 February 2007, 173 States were party to the Convention (for the text of the Convention, see the website of the Office of the High Commissioner for Human Rights, <http://www.ohchr.org/english/law/cerd.htm>).

[4] See section 4.1 below.

[5] See section 4.3 below.

[6] See section 4.2 below.

[7] See section 4.4 below.

[8] See, for example, Communication No. 26/2002, *S. Hagan v. Australia*, opinion adopted on 20 March 2003, U.N. Doc. CERD/C/62/D/26/2002, para 7.3. All documents of the Committee mentioned in this chapter can be found on the website of the Office of the High Commissioner for Human Rights at the following address: <http://www.unhchr.ch/tbs/doc.nsf>.

[9] For the text of CERD General Recommendations, see <http://ohchr.org/english/bodies/cerd/comments.htm, or chapter III in HRI/GEN/1/Rev.7> (except for General Recommendations XXX and XXXI that can be found in the annual reports of the Committee to the General Assembly, respectively UN Doc. A/59/18 (2004) (available at: <http://daccessdds.un.org/doc/UNDOC/GEN/G04/437/35/PDF/G0443735.pdf?OpenElement>), Chapter VIII and A/60/18, Chapter VIII). Several of these General Recommendations were adopted as a response to calls for further protection from victims and groups representing victims. For instance, *General Recommendation XXVII on discrimination against Roma*, *General Recommendation XXIX on descent-based discrimination* and *General Recommendation XXX on non-citizens* were adopted following thematic discussions organised by the Committee on these issues during which it organised a hearing of civil society representatives, including testimonies of victims of discrimination. For a summary of these thematic discussions, see U.N. Docs. CERD/C/SR. 1422 and 1423; CERD/C/SR. 1531 and 1532; CERD/C/SR. 1624 and 1625.

adopted under its reporting and review procedures as well as in decisions adopted under the early warning and urgent action procedures and opinions on individual and group communications. The jurisprudence[10] of CERD on racial discrimination regarding social, economic and cultural rights is quite abundant, as racial discrimination primarily affects the most vulnerable members of society in the sphere of these rights. This chapter will first provide a general outline of the scope of the Convention (Section 2) and will identify the main beneficiaries of the protection which it offers (Section 3). After a presentation of the various compliance mechanisms used by the Committee (Section 4), Section 5 will assess its approach to protection against racial discrimination in the enjoyment of selected economic, social and cultural rights, in particular labour, housing and land rights, but also the right to health, education, cultural and linguistic rights. Concluding remarks will focus on the impact of the recommendations, decisions and opinions of the Committee (Section 6).

underlined that Article 5 'implies the existence and recognition of civil, political, economic, social and cultural rights' and that 'full respect for human rights is the necessary framework for the efficiency of measures adopted to combat racial discrimination'.[12] General Recommendation XX stresses that 'the rights and freedoms mentioned in article 5 do not constitute an exhaustive list'.[13] This list includes a broad range of economic, social and cultural rights, such as labour rights,[14] the right to housing, to public health, medical care, social security and social services, education and training, and equal participation in cultural activities. The States parties are recommended to report on the non-discriminatory implementation of each of these rights one by one.[15] The Committee ordinarily seeks to ascertain to what extent all persons within the State's jurisdiction, and particularly members of vulnerable groups, enjoy these rights in practice, free from racial discrimination. If States cannot provide quantitative data relevant to the enjoyment of these rights, they are advised to report the opinions of representatives of disadvantaged groups.[16]

2. SCOPE OF THE CONVENTION

2.1 Obligation to Ensure Equal Enjoyment of all Human Rights

Article 5 of the Convention, apart from requiring a guarantee that the exercise of human rights shall be free from racial discrimination, does not of itself create rights.[11] The Committee, however, has

2.2 Obligation to Intervene in Relations Between Private Actors

Whilst Article 1(1) of the Convention defines racial discrimination in terms of discriminatory acts performed in 'field[s] of public life', Article 2(1)(d) requires States parties to bring to an end 'racial discrimination by *any persons, group or organization*'.[17] To the extent that private institutions influence the exercise of rights or the availability of opportunities, States parties must ensure that the result has neither the purpose nor the effect of

---

[10] The term 'jurisprudence' refers to the interpretation of the Convention as elaborated by the Committee not only in opinions adopted under its individual and groups communications procedure, but also in its general recommendations, concluding observations and decisions.

[11] See *General Recommendation XX, the guarantee of human rights free from racial discrimination* (48th session), U.N. Doc. A/51/18, annex VIII at 124 (1996) and in particular para. 1. In 1990, the Committee had already stated in an opinion adopted on an individual complaint: 'It is not within the Committee's mandate to see to it that these rights are established; rather, it is the Committee's task to monitor the implementation of these rights, once they have been granted on equal terms'. The Committee also added in this opinion that 'the rights protected by article 5 (e) of the Convention are of programmatic character, subject to progressive implementation'. (Communication No. 2/1989, *Demba Talibe Diop v. France*, para. 6.4 in CERD/C/390, p. 8).

[12] See *Concluding observations on Malawi*, UN Doc. A/58/18 (2003) para. 557.

[13] *General Recommendation XX* (n. 11 above), para. 1.

[14] Article 5 (e) (i) refers to 'the right to work, to free choice of employment, to just and favourable conditions of work, to protection against unemployment, to equal pay for equal work, to just and favourable remuneration, to form and join trade unions and to bargain collectively'.

[15] *General Recommendation XX* (n. 11 above), para. 4.

[16] See the general guidelines regarding the form and contents of reports to be submitted by States parties under Article 9, Paragraph 1 of the Convention, U.N. Doc. CERD/C/70/Rev.5, p. 5.

[17] Ibid. Emphasis added.

creating or perpetuating racial discrimination.[18] Article 3 of the Convention protects individuals and groups against de facto segregation frequently encountered, in particular in the sphere of housing and education, which may arise as an 'unintended by-product of the actions of private persons'.[19]

Some States parties have stated that the prohibition and punishment of purely private conduct lies beyond the scope of governmental regulation, even in situations where the personal freedom is exercised in a discriminatory manner.[20] In such cases, the Committee has recommended that 'the State party review its legislation so as to render liable to criminal sanctions the largest possible sphere of private conduct which is discriminatory on racial or ethnic grounds'.[21]

2.3 Obligation to Adopt Special Measures

Article 2(2) of the Convention prescribes the adoption of 'special and concrete measures by States to ensure the adequate development and protection of certain racial groups or individuals belonging to them, for the purpose of guaranteeing them the full and equal enjoyment of human rights'. One example of such measures would be the adoption of a bill reserving a 10 per cent quota for members of a descent-based group in the civil service.[22] Special measures, however, should not be continued after the objectives for which they were taken have been achieved and should not lead to the maintenance of separate rights for different racial groups.[23]

Some States have argued that the provisions of the Convention permit but do not require them to adopt affirmative action measures to ensure the adequate development and protection of certain racial, ethnic or national groups.[24] The Committee has not accepted this position and has underlined that 'the adoption of special measures by States parties when the circumstances so warrant, such as in the case of persistent disparities, is an obligation stemming from Article 2, Paragraph 2, of the Convention'.[25]

2.4 Punishment of Discriminatory Acts and Adequate Remedies for Victims

Article 4 is often considered as the backbone of the Convention. It provides for the obligation to adopt legislation punishing acts of racial discrimination, including incitement to racial hatred,[26] and prohibiting participation in racist organisations, which should also be banned.[27] This article is to be read in conjunction with Article 6, which concerns the availability of adequate remedies for victims of racial discrimination. The Committee expects States parties to include in their periodic reports statistical information on prosecutions launched and penalties imposed in cases

---

[18] General Recommendation XX (n. 11 above), para. 5.
[19] General Recommendation XIX, the prevention, prohibition and eradication of racial segregation and apartheid (47th session, 1995), U.N. Doc. A/50/18 at 140 (1995), para. 3.
[20] Concluding observations on the United States of America, U.N. Doc. A/56/18, para 392 (All concluding observations that will be referred to in this chapter can be found in the UN treaty body database at the following website address: <http://www.unhchr.ch/tbs/doc.nsf>).
[21] Ibid.
[22] This measure was welcomed by Morten Kjaerum, member of the Committee acting as country Rapporteur, during the dialogue of CERD with Nepal in 2004. See U.N. Doc. CERD/C/SR. 1630, para. 21.
[23] See Articles 1 (4) and 2 (2) of the Convention. It should be stressed, however, that minority rights and indigenous peoples' rights must be distinguished from special measures. These rights, to the extent that they are endorsed by the Committee, will not be temporary.

[24] See Concluding observations on the United States of America (n. 20 above), para. 399.
[25] Ibid.
[26] Article 4 (1) of the Convention.
[27] Article 4 (2) of the Convention. Article 4 has been the subject of discussion with many States. Some have made reservations when ratifying the Convention, as they consider that Article 4 contradicts the protection of individual freedom of speech, expression and association enshrined in their constitution (see for instance the reservation entered by the United States of America at <http://www.ohchr.org/english/countries/ratification/2.htm#reservations>). Other States have argued that the obligation to criminalise certain expressions and statements must be balanced against the right to freedom of expression, as protected by other international human rights instruments. In the opinion of the Committee, however, the prohibition of the dissemination of all ideas based upon racial superiority or hatred is compatible with the right to freedom of opinion and expression, given that a citizen's exercise of this right carries special duties and responsibilities, among which is the obligation not to disseminate racist ideas (see General Recommendation XV, Measures to eradicate incitement to or acts of discrimination U.N. Doc. A/48/18 at 114 (1994) para. 4; see also the opinion of the Committee on Communication 30/2003, Jewish Community of Oslo et al. v. Norway, CERD/C/67/D/30/2003, para. 10.5).

of offences that concern racial discrimination.[28] In response to the argument of some governmental delegations, which had not provided such information because of the absence of cases, the Committee responded that:

> The mere absence of complaints and legal action by victims of racial discrimination may be mainly an indication of the absence of relevant specific legislation, or of a lack of awareness of the availability of legal remedies, or of insufficient will on the part of the authorities to prosecute.[29]

In such cases, the Committee requests States to ensure that appropriate provisions are available in national legislation, and to inform the public about all legal remedies in the field of racial discrimination.[30]

3. BENEFICIARIES OF THE PROTECTION AGAINST DISCRIMINATION

Article 1 of the Convention prohibits discrimination on the grounds of race, colour, descent and national or ethnic origin. These terms are not further defined by the Convention, nor does Article 1 of the Convention specify the groups that fall under its protection. Through its General Recommendations and concluding observations, CERD has elaborated upon the scope of protection of the Convention and demonstrated its continuing relevance and application to contemporary forms of racism suffered by specific groups.

3.1 Minorities, Indigenous Peoples and Descent-Based Groups

General Recommendation XXIII affirms that discrimination against indigenous peoples falls

under the scope of the Convention and States are urged to take all appropriate means to combat and eliminate such discrimination.[31] While the Committee has yet to adopt an equivalent General Recommendation on minorities,[32] it has consistently interpreted the Convention so as to ensure protection of these groups and persons belonging to them and has addressed this issue on numerous occasions when considering reports and individual communications.[33] Furthermore, in 2000, the Committee organised a thematic discussion[34] on discrimination against Roma, which culminated in the adoption of General Recommendation XXVII[35] on the same issue. The second thematic discussion[36] ever organised by the Committee was on descent-based discrimination. It also led to the adoption by the Committee of a General Recommendation on the same question, which clarifies that the term 'descent' in Article 1, Paragraph 1 of the Convention 'does not solely refer to "race" and has a meaning and application which complement the other prohibited grounds of discrimination'.[37] The Committee 'strongly reaffirms that discrimination based on "descent" includes discrimination against members of communities based on forms of social stratification, such as caste and analogous systems of inherited status which nullify or impair their equal enjoyment of human rights'.[38] CERD recommends to States parties the adoption of legislative measures to outlaw all forms of discrimination against indigenous peoples, Roma and descent-based groups. Furthermore, States should ensure equal enjoyment of, *inter alia*, economic, social and cultural rights by these groups and all their members.[39]

---

[28] See the general guidelines regarding the form and contents of reports to be submitted by States parties under article 9, paragraph 1 of the Convention, U.N. Doc. CERD/C/70/Rev. 5, p. 7.

[29] See for instance, the *Concluding Observations on Tunisia*. U.N. Doc. CERD/C/62/CO/10(2003).

[30] Ibid. See also General Recommendation XXXI adopted by the Committee in August 2005 on the prevention of racial discrimination in the administration and functioning of the criminal justice system (U.N. Doc. CERD/C/GC/31/Rev. 4 (2005), pp. 98–108) in particular pp. 102–104.

[31] General Recommendation XXIII, (n. 9 above), para. 4(a).

[32] General Recommendation VIII, however, provides guidance to States on ways to identify which individuals are part of a particular racial or ethnic group. It recommends that States respect the principle of self-identification (see n. 9 above, p. 203).

[33] See the numerous examples given in Section 5 below.

[34] See n. 9 above.

[35] See General Recommendation XXVII (n. 9 above), pp. 219–224.

[36] See n. 9 above.

[37] General Recommendation XXIX (n. 9 above), p. 227, preamble.

[38] Ibid.

[39] See General Recommendation XXIII (n. 9 above), pp. 215–216; General Recommendation XXVII (n. 9 above), pp. 221–222 and; General Recommendation XXIX (n. 9 above), pp. 231–232.

3.2 Non-Citizens

CERD originally found itself restricted by the provisions of Article 1 (2) of CERD according to which the Convention 'shall not apply to distinctions, exclusions, restrictions or preferences made by a State Party to this Convention between citizens and non-citizens'. This Article is to be read, however, in conjunction with Article 1(3), which provides that:

[N]othing in this Convention may be interpreted as affecting in any way the legal provisions of States Parties concerning nationality, citizenship or naturalization, *provided that such provisions do not discriminate against any particular nationality.* [Emphasis added]

Over the years, it became increasingly evident for CERD, when examining the reports of States parties to the Convention, that a key concern regarding the implementation of the Convention was racial discrimination against migrants, refugees and asylum-seekers, undocumented non-citizens and stateless persons.[40] This growing preoccupation led the Committee to identify the need for further clarification of the responsibilities of States parties in this regard. Therefore, it requested the Sub-Commission on the Promotion and Protection of Human Rights to undertake a study on the rights of non-citizens. The Special Rapporteur appointed for this purpose by the Sub-Commission submitted his final report in 2003.[41] CERD also held a thematic discussion during its sixty-fourth session (March 2004), so that it could hear the views of various stakeholders.[42] This dis-

cussion led to the adoption of a new General Recommendation[43] in which CERD elaborated upon the brief General Recommendation XI, which it had adopted on the issue in 1993.[44] General Recommendation XXX makes clear that:

Article 1, paragraph 2, must be construed so as to avoid undermining the basic prohibition of discrimination; hence, it should not be interpreted to detract in any way from the rights and freedoms recognized and enunciated in particular in the Universal Declaration of Human Rights, the International Covenant on Economic, Social and Cultural Rights and the International Covenant on Civil and Political Rights.[45]

The Committee further clarified that human rights are, in principle, to be enjoyed by all persons[46] and that States parties are under an obligation to guarantee equality between citizens and non-citizens in the enjoyment of these rights 'to the extent recognized under international law'.[47] It concluded that:

Under the Convention, differential treatment based on citizenship or immigration status will constitute discrimination if the criteria for such differentiation, judged in the light of the objectives and purposes of the Convention, are not applied pursuant to a legitimate aim, and are not proportional to the achievement of this aim.[48]

General Recommendation XXX prescribes the adoption of a series of measures of a general nature, as well as more specific measures in various

---

[40] In 2001, the issue was also given due consideration during the Durban World Conference against Racism, Racial Discrimination, Xenophobia and Related Intolerance, and participating States recognised through their final declaration that 'xenophobia against non-nationals, particularly migrants, refugees and asylum-seekers, constitutes one of the main sources of contemporary racism and that human rights violations against members of such groups occur widely in the context of discriminatory, xenophobic and racist practices'. See United Nations, *World Conference Against Racism, Racial Discrimination, Xenophobia and Related Intolerance*, Declaration, para. 16, available at <http://www.un.org/WCAR/durban.pdf>.

[41] D. Weissbrodt, *Final report on the rights of non-citizens*, U.N. Doc. E/CN.4/Sub.2/2003/23, available at <http://ap.ohchr.org/documents/mainec.aspx>.

[42] During half a day, international and national non-governmental organisations (NGOs), the Special Rapporteur on the rights of non-citizens, two Special Rappor-

teurs of the Commission on Human Rights, representatives of the United Nations High Commissioner for Refugees and the International Labour Organisation, as well as States parties, put forward their views before the Committee. For summary records of the hearing and the discussion that ensued between members of the Committee, see U.N. Docs. CERD/C/SR.1624 and CERD/C/SR, p. 1625.

[43] See, for the text of *General Recommendation XXX* (n. 9 above), U.N. Doc. A/ 59/18, pp. 99–103.

[44] *See General Recommendation XI* (n. 9 above), p. 205.

[45] *General Recommendation XXX* (n. 43 above), para. 2.

[46] CERD had already expressed this view in its *General Recommendation XX* (n. 11 above).

[47] Ibid. para. 3.

[48] Ibid. para. 4.

fields, including economic, social and cultural rights to which it devotes particular attention.[49]

3.3 Gender-Related Dimensions of Racial Discrimination

General Recommendation XXV[50] adopted by the Committee in 2000, notes that 'racial discrimination does not always affect women and men equally or in the same way' (para. 1) and that 'certain forms of racial discrimination may be directed towards women specifically because of their gender' (para. 2) such as, for example, 'abuse of women workers in the informal sector or domestic workers employed abroad by their employers' (para. 2). The General Recommendation acknowledges the detrimental impact of double discrimination on grounds of race and sex on women's enjoyment of their civil, political, economic, social and cultural rights[51] and requests States parties to describe, in quantitative and qualitative terms, the difficulties experienced by women in enjoying their rights under the Convention.[52] Data which has been categorised by race or ethnic origin should also be disaggregated by gender.[53] Furthermore, the Committee declared in the General Recommendation that when examining forms of racial discrimination ' [it will] enhance its efforts to integrate gender perspectives and incorporate gender analysis'[54] in all its activities and to 'include in its sessional working methods an analysis of the relationship between gender and racial discrimination'.[55] Although such an analysis was never undertaken,[56] several general recommendations and the concluding observations of the Committee contain numerous expressions of concern and recommendations regarding discrimination against women belonging to ethnic minorities or indigenous groups[57] as well as women refugees[58] or female migrant workers.[59]

4. COMPLIANCE MECHANISMS

4.1 The Reporting Procedure

States parties to the Convention are required to submit every two years a report that will allow the Committee to assess not only compliance of national law with the Convention, but also the practical situation regarding racial discrimination in the State concerned.[60] After the consideration of the reports[61] in the presence of a governmental delegation that answers the questions raised by its members, the Committee adopts concluding observations in which it makes recommendations on ways to address the concerns expressed regarding inadequacies in the implementation of the Convention at the national level.

4.2 The Review Procedure

The delays in reporting by States parties severely hamper the Committee in monitoring implementation of the Convention.[62] In 1991, the

---

[49] Ibid. paras. 29–38. See section 5 for numerous references to this part of the General Recommendation.

[50] See *General Recommendation XXV, Gender Related Dimensions of Racial Discrimination* (50th Session, 2000) U.N. Doc. A/55/18, annex V at 152 (2000).

[51] Ibid. para 3.

[52] Ibid. para 6.

[53] Ibid.

[54] Ibid para. 4

[55] Ibid. para. 5.

[56] One can also deplore the fact that gender balance is not respected in the membership of the Committee. As at 1 October 2005, there were only two women on the Committee, both from the African region. Between 2002 and 2004, the Committee included only one female member.

[57] For instance, in its concluding observations on Ecuador, the Committee, 'notes that women belonging to ethnic minorities are subject to double discrimination, based on their ethnic origin as well as their gender' and requests 'Information relating to gender-related discrimination against indigenous and Afro-Ecuadorian women and on action taken by the State Party in this regard'. Furthermore, it recommends to the State party 'in formulating the action plan on the rights of women ... [to] address the problem of double discrimination against women belonging to ethnic minorities as well as their lack of political representation in Ecuador, in line with the Committee's General Recommendation XXV on gender-related dimensions of racial discrimination' (see A/58/18, para. 61).

[58] See *Concluding observations on Tanzania* in which the Committee expresses concern in relation to acts of violence particularly affecting women refugees and the lack of access to adequate remedies (U.N. Doc. A/60/18, para. 353).

[59] See numerous references to the relevant parts of these general recommendations and concluding observations in section 5 below.

[60] See reporting guidelines of the Committee (CERD/C/70/Rev.5, para. 5).

[61] In two, three-hour-long public meetings.

[62] The periodicity of two years for CERD reports provided in Article 9 of the Convention is much shorter than that requested for the other treaty bodies (four to five

Committee decided that it would proceed with the review of the implementation of the Convention by States parties that were excessively late in the submission of periodic reports.[63] This review was to be based upon the last reports submitted by the State party concerned and their consideration by the Committee.[64] In 1996, this practice was extended to States that were at least five years late in the submission of their initial report and the review was to be made on the basis of all information submitted by the State party to other organs of the United Nations or, in the absence of such material, on the basis of reports and information prepared by these organs.[65] In practice, the Committee also takes into consideration all relevant information from other sources, in particular national human rights institutions and non-governmental organisations.[66] Most States which are informed that they have been scheduled for consideration without a report respond by a commitment to submit the overdue reports[67] within the next few months. This reaction is the best possible outcome of the procedure, as States are far more likely to implement recommendations of the Committee if they are adopted on the basis of a State report and at the end of a dialogue with a governmental delegation. If the State party does not commit to send a report, the Committee adopts concluding observations on the basis of this review and in most cases in the absence of any dialogue with the State party concerned. At its sixty-fourth session, the Committee decided that the concluding observations adopted under the review procedure would be considered as provisional and would be communicated confidentially to the State party concerned. In the absence

of any response of the State party, including a commitment to submit a report within the next few months, these concluding observations are adopted as a final document and made public at the following session. At its sixty-sixth and sixty-seventh sessions held in 2005, the Committee adopted another approach with States for which the main cause of non-reporting was thought to be a lack of capacity to draft a report.[68] A letter is first sent by the Chairman reminding the State party of its reporting obligations, together with a list of issues to which the Government concerned is requested to respond before the next session of the Committee. In the absence of such a response, the Committee will proceed with the adoption of concluding observations.[69]

4.3   The Early Warning and Urgent Action Procedures

In 1993, the Committee adopted a working paper[70] to guide it in its future work concerning possible measures to prevent, as well as more effectively respond to, violations of the Convention. This working paper provided that both early warning measures and urgent procedures could be used to try and prevent serious violations of the Convention. Early warning measures are to be directed at preventing existing problems from escalating into conflicts. Criteria for early warning measures include, inter alia, a significant pattern of racial discrimination evidenced in social and economic indicators, or encroachment on the lands of minority communities.[71] Urgent procedures are to respond to problems requiring immediate attention to prevent or limit the scale or number of serious violations of the Convention. Criteria for initiating an urgent procedure could include

---

years), and is seldom respected by States parties. In 2005, sixteen States were more than ten years late in the submission of their reports, and twenty-five were more than five years late. A majority of States tend to report every three to four years. For the reporting status at 19 August 2005, see CERD/C/502.

[63] U.N. Doc. A/46/18, para. 27.

[64] Ibid.

[65] U.N. Doc. A/51/18, para. 608.

[66] On the Committee's relations with national human rights institutions and non-governmental organizations, see the working paper adopted by the Committee in 2002 on its working methods, A/58/18, Annex IV.

[67] The overdue reports are to be submitted in one single combined document which in fact focuses on the current implementation of the Convention, thus in practical terms exonerating States of their reporting obligation irrespective of the number of overdue reports.

[68] This approach was adopted in relation to Papua New Guinea which has failed to react to the numerous concluding observations previously adopted under the review procedure and to several decisions adopted by the Committee under its early warning and urgent action procedures since 1984, as well as for Saint-Lucia and Malawi, which have never submitted any report since, respectively, 1991 and 1997, and for Seychelles which interrupted its dialogue with the Committee in 1986. See A/60/18, paras. 431–434.

[69] As this approach was adopted for the first time in 2005, it is too early to assess its success in reinstating a dialogue with these States.

[70] See A/48/18, Annex III.

[71] For the full list of criteria, ibid. para. 9.

the presence of a serious, massive or persistent pattern of racial discrimination or a serious situation where there is a risk of further racial discrimination.[72] These procedures have been used since 1993 in relation to more than twenty States parties.[73] Several decisions adopted by the Committee have concerned indigenous peoples' land rights and have followed calls for urgent action from non-governmental organisations representing the peoples concerned.[74]

4.4 The Individual and Group Complaints Procedure

Under Article 14 of the Convention, individuals or groups of individuals who claim that any of their rights enumerated in the Convention have been violated by a State party and who have exhausted all available domestic remedies may submit written communications to the Committee for consideration. This procedure is optional, and as at 1 February 2007, only fifty-one out of the one hundred and seventy-three States parties to the Convention had recognised the competence of the Committee to consider such communications. The Committee began its work under Article 14 of the Convention in 1984 and since then has only examined thirty-five complaints. Thirteen petitions were considered inadmissible, and nineteen opinions were adopted on the merits. Violations were established in only twelve cases.[75] As pointed out by van Boven, it appears from these statistics that '[A]rticle 14 is one of the most under-utilized provisions' of the Convention.[76] Several notable aspects of the procedure, however, are worth high-

lighting. First of all, in a majority of cases, the complainants have alleged a violation of Article 5(e) of the Convention providing for the principle of equality and non-discrimination in the area of economic, social and cultural rights.[77] Furthermore, Article 14 of the Convention provides the possibility for groups to make complaints,[78] which can be particularly useful regarding violations of economic, social and cultural rights of national or ethnic minority groups or indigenous peoples.[79] The Committee shall not consider any communication from a petitioner unless it has ascertained that the petitioner has exhausted all domestic remedies. However, this shall not be the rule where the application of remedies is unreasonably prolonged.[80] Finally, CERD may forward to the State party concerned its 'suggestions and recommendations'[81] and has used this possibility to go beyond the question of the violation of the Convention in the individual case concerned and make suggestions with broader policy implications. The Committee frequently makes such suggestions even though it has found the complaint

---

[72] Ibid.

[73] See N. Prouvez, 'The Prevention of Racial Discrimination through Early Warning and Urgent Procedures', in B. G. Ramcharan (ed.), *Conflict Prevention in Practice* (Leiden/Boston: Martinus Nijhoff Publishers, 2005), pp. 265–269.

[74] See section 5 below for further detail.

[75] Furthermore, complaints have originated from only eight States parties. This under-utilisation of the procedure may be explained partly by the lack of awareness by victims of racial discrimination of the availability of this international remedy and by a preference for a recourse to the Human Rights Committee, which also has a mandate to examine cases of racial discrimination on the basis of Article 26 and 27 of the International Covenant on Civil and Political Rights, the articles respectively concerning discrimination and the rights of minorities.

[76] T. van Boven, 'CERD and Article 14: the unfulfilled promise', in G. Alfredsson et al. (eds.), *International Human*

Rights Mechanisms (Dordrecht Kluwer Law International, 2001), pp. 153–166, at 155.

[77] See the jurisprudence of the Committee at: <http://www.unhchr.ch/tbs/doc.nsf/FramePage/TypeJurisprudence>. See also Section 5 below for numerous references to cases concerning economic, social and cultural rights.

[78] See the opinion of the Committee on Communication 30/2003, *Jewish Community of Oslo et al. v. Norway*, in which the Committee considered that organisations, bearing in mind the nature of their activities and the classes of person they represent, can satisfy the 'victim' requirement in Article 14. In the same opinion, the Committee also decided that individuals can be considered as 'victims' solely on the basis of their membership of a particular group of potential victims (CERD/C/67/D/30/2003, paras. 7.3 and 7.4).

[79] See for instance the recent complaint made by a group of Roma concerning the violation of their housing rights by a municipal council in Slovakia (CERD/C/66/D/31/2003). The petitioners argued that they were victims as they were directly targeted by the resolutions of the municipal council.

[80] Article 14(7)(a) of the Convention.

[81] Ibid. para. 7 (b). See for an example of such a situation, Communication N0 6/1995, *Z.U.B.S. v. Australia*, in which the Committee considered that even if the petitioner could have availed himself of the possibility to appeal to the Supreme Court of New South Wales, it was necessary to take into account the length of the appeal process. As the consideration of the author's grievances had already taken in excess of two years before the previous instances, the circumstances of the present case justified that the application of domestic remedies would be unreasonably prolonged (CERD/C/390, p. 36, para. 6.4).

inadmissible or when it has not found any violation.[82]

5. RACIAL DISCRIMINATION AND ECONOMIC, SOCIAL AND CULTURAL RIGHTS

Racial discrimination all too often leads to marginalisation and social exclusion. Those most vulnerable to economic and social deprivation are members of marginalised groups that fall within the scope of Article 1 of the Convention, whether they are members of minorities such as Roma or indigenous people, people of African descent or victims of descent-based discrimination. Ghanea argues that 'there are serious shortcomings in the international protection of ESCRs[83] as it extends to minority groups' and that 'present standards and mechanisms are inadequate in the face of this multi-faceted challenge'.[84] CERD itself has been criticised by Felice in 2002 for 'a glaring meekness in [its] approach to the economic and social rights of minority racial groups'.[85] In particular, criticisms have been expressed towards the lack of specificity of the recommendations addressed to States parties. This Section examines the recent practice of the Committee in order to assess whether such remarks are justified.

5.1 Labour Rights

High levels of unemployment, discrimination in relation to access to work and bad working conditions constitute a major problem for members of

particularly vulnerable groups. This issue is raised by the Committee on a regular basis during its dialogue with States parties and has been mentioned in various General Recommendations. It has also been the cause for several individual and group complaints examined by the Committee.

Bearing in mind the severe difficulties encountered by Roma in the field of employment, the Committee has paid specific attention to this issue in its General Recommendation XXVII[86] as well as in the concluding observations made following the examination of reports from States including large Roma communities on their territory. CERD has emphasised the need for these States to increase the effectiveness of legislation prohibiting discrimination in employment and all discriminatory practices in the labour market affecting members of Roma communities.[87] States should also 'take special measures to promote the employment of Roma in the public administration and institutions, as well as in private companies'. Furthermore, CERD suggests that they 'adopt and implement, whenever possible, at the central or local level, special measures in favour of Roma in public employment such as public contracting and other activities undertaken or funded by the Government, or training Roma in various skills and professions'.[88]

The Committee has also acknowledged the need to 'develop or refine legislation and practice specifically prohibiting all discriminatory practices based on descent in the labour market'.[89] In General Recommendation XXIX, it draws particular attention to the need to take measures against public bodies, private companies and other associations that investigate the descent background of applicants for employment.[90] The Committee considers that the situation in some States parties may require the adoption of special measures to promote the employment of members

---

[82] See for instance Communication No. 3/1991, *Michel L. Narrainen v. Norway*, in which the Committee did not find any violation of the Convention. However, this did not prevent it from recommending to the State party to ensure that 'every effort should be made to prevent any form of racial bias from entering into judicial proceedings which might result in adversely affecting the administration of justice on the basis of equality and non-discrimination' (para. 10).

[83] Economic, social and cultural rights.

[84] N. Ghanea, 'Repressing Minorities and getting away with it? A consideration of Economic, Social and Cultural Rights', in N. Ghanea and A. Xanthaki (eds.) *Minorities, Peoples and Self-Determination* (Leiden: Martinus Nijhoff Publishers, 2005), pp. 193–209, at 194.

[85] William F. Felice, 'The UN Committee on the Elimination of All Forms of Racial Discrimination: Race and Economic and Social Human Rights', *Human Rights Quarterly*, Vol. 24, No. 1 (2002), pp. 205–236, at 217.

[86] See paras. 27–29 of General Recommendation XXVII (n. 9 above), pp. 221 and 222.

[87] *Concluding observations on Slovakia*, A/59/18, para. 386. See also for similar recommendations the concluding observations adopted by the Committee on Spain (A/59/18, para. 174), the Czech Republic (A/58/18, para. 384), Slovenia (Ibid, para. 237) and the United Kingdom (Ibid. para. 542).

[88] General Recommendation XXVII (n. 9 above), paras. 27–29.

[89] General Recommendation XXIX (n. 9 above), para. 7 (kk).

[90] Ibid. para. 7 (ll).

of descent-based communities in both the public and private sectors.[91] General Recommendation XXIX also raises the attention of States parties to the special vulnerability of children of descent-based communities to exploitative child labour and the need to take measures addressing this problem.[92] Finally, the Committee urges States to 'take resolute measures to eliminate debt bondage and degrading conditions of labour associated with descent-based discrimination'.[93]

When examining the report of a State party in 2004, the Committee expressed concern about the system of agricultural bonded labour and recommended that the concerned State ensure effective enforcement of a law prohibiting bonded labour and of programmes adopted to put an end to such practice affecting descent-based communities. More generally, it expressed concern about the persisting restriction to certain types of employment for Dalits and recommended that the State party, as a matter of priority, take measures to prevent, prohibit and eliminate private and public practices that constitute segregation of any kind, and make determined efforts to ensure the practical and effective implementation of these measures.[94]

Some concluding observations may be considered too general, as the Committee limits itself to expressing concern about high unemployment rates and recommending the adoption of national strategies and programmes to improve the situation of a minority group.[95] Others, however, are more precise and address complex and sensitive issues that impact negatively on the economic survival of some minorities or indigenous peoples. For instance, while stating that it understood the need for policies aimed at eradicating the production and trafficking of coca, the Committee requested a State party to:

Provide in its next periodic report additional and more specific information on the amount of land withdrawn from coca production, the alternative ways of cultivating or utilizing this land, the amount of land continuing to produce coca, the numbers of persons affected and the ethnic origin of those persons, as well as the impact of the State party's policies on their living standards.[96]

Non-citizens are also particularly affected by discrimination in employment. An issue of double discrimination on the ground of national origin and sex in relation to employment was tackled by the Committee in the first individual communication ever considered in 1987.[97] A Turkish national had been dismissed by her employer after informing him of her pregnancy. Both the Director of the Labour Exchange and the Cantonal Court had endorsed the termination of the employment contract despite the discriminatory statement made by the employer to justify the dismissal. The employer raised the issue of differences in absenteeism owing to childbirth and illness between foreign female workers and female workers who were nationals of the State. Furthermore, the complainant was unable to have the discriminatory termination of her contract reviewed by a higher court. The State party argued that the decision of the Cantonal court did not in any way justify the conclusion that the Court accepted the reasons put forth by the employer and had merely considered the case in the light of the relevant rules of civil law and civil procedure. The Committee found that there had been a 'failure to take

---

[91] Ibid, para. 7 (jj).

[92] Ibid. para. 7 (pp).

[93] Ibid. para. 7 (qq).

[94] See *Concluding observations on Nepal*, A/59/18, paras. 127 and 133.

[95] See for instance the rather general recommendation of the Committee to the United Kingdom (A/58/18, para. 542), following an expression of concern regarding high unemployment rates, to 'adopt national strategies and programmes with a view to improving the situation of the Roma/Gypsies/travellers against discrimination by State bodies, persons or organisations'.

[96] *Concluding observations on Bolivia.* A/58/18, para. 342. For discrimination against ethnic groups and in particular indigenous peoples in the sphere of employment, see also the concluding observations of CERD on Ecuador, (n. 57 above) para. 59.

[97] *Yilmaz-Dogan v. the Netherlands* (Communication No. 1/1984). Three subsequent complaints that were declared inadmissible, because of the non-exhaustion of domestic remedies, also concerned labour rights: Communication No. 7/1995, *Paul Barbaro v. Australia*; Communication No. 9/1997, *D.S. v. Sweden* and Communication No. 28/2003, *Documentation and Advisory Centre on Racial Discrimination v. Denmark.* Five other complaints regarding labour rights were considered admissible but led to a finding of non-violation: Communication No. 2/1989, *Demba Talibe Diop v. France*; Communication No. 6/1995, Z.U.B.S. v. Australia; Communication No. 8/1996, B.M.S. v. Australia; Communication No. 15/1999, *E.I.F. v. The Netherlands*; Communication No. 14/1998, *D.S. v. Sweden* and Communication No. 21/2001, *D.S. v. Sweden.*

into account all the circumstances of the case' and that the petitioner had not been afforded adequate protection in respect of her right to work. It recommended, therefore, that 'the State party ascertain whether she was again gainfully employed and provide her with such relief as may be considered equitable'.[98]

Other individual complaints concerning discrimination in employment for non-nationals have led the Committee to declare that no breach of the Convention had occurred. CERD, however, seized the opportunity to make some policy recommendations to States parties. It stressed in particular the need to 'simplify the procedures to deal with complaints of racial discrimination, in particular those in which more than one recourse measure is available, and avoid any delay in the consideration of such complaints'.[99] In another case ruled upon in 1999, the Committee stressed that measures related to employment do not violate Article 5(e)(i) if they affect all non-nationals in a similar way.[100]

The examination of State party reports has given the Committee the opportunity to reflect further on the issue of discrimination against non-citizens in the sphere of employment. In the course of its dialogue with one State party in 2002, CERD stressed that, although the State was not obliged to provide work permits to foreign residents, it was bound to 'guarantee that foreigners who are entitled to a work permit are not discriminated against in their access to employment'.[101] The Committee confirmed this position in General Recommendation XXX which provides that, while States parties may refuse to offer jobs to non-citizens without a work permit, 'all individuals are entitled to the enjoyment of labour and employment rights, including the freedom of assembly and association, once an employment relationship has been initiated until it is terminated'.[102] More generally, General Recommendation XXX requests from States that they 'take measures to eliminate discrimination against non-citizens in relation to working conditions and work requirements, including employment rules and practices with discriminatory purposes or effects'.[103] The General Recommendation addresses in particular the plight of many non-citizen domestic workers, and recommends that States 'take effective measures to combat such practices as debt bondage, passport retention, illegal confinement, rape and physical assault'.[104] This issue has been raised by the Committee during its dialogue with several States parties to which it has expressed concern about allegations of substantial prejudice against these workers.[105]

5.2 Housing Rights

Over the years, the Committee has repeatedly requested States to monitor more closely the housing situation of marginalised racial and ethnic groups and to enact or strengthen legislative measures prohibiting racial discrimination in housing policies. It has also stressed the link between the

---

[98] In accordance with Rule 95, Para. 5 of the Committee's Rules of Procedure, States parties are invited to inform the Committee in due course of the action they take in conformity with the Committee's opinion. The State party informed the Committee in its ninth periodic report that, after her dismissal, the petitioner had been either employed or received social security benefits, with the exception of a brief period. In respect of the period of unemployment, the Government of the Netherlands had agreed to provide for ex gratia payment See CERD/C/182/Add, 4, para. 37, ninth periodic report of the Netherlands.

[99] Communication No. 6/1995, *ZUBS v. Australia*, para. 11.

[100] Therefore, CERD determined that an examination and quota system for foreign trained doctors did not violate Article 5(e)(i) of the Convention as the system applied to all overseas trained doctors irrespective of race or national origin. The Committee, however, recommended to the State party that it 'take all necessary measures and give transparency to the procedure and curriculum established and conducted by the Australian Medical Council, so that the system is in no way discriminatory towards foreign candidates irrespective of their race or national or ethnic origin'. Furthermore, it also recommended that 'every effort be made to avoid any delay in the consideration of all complaints by the Human Rights and Equal Opportunity Commission': Communication No. 8/1996, *B.M.S. v. Australia*, Opinion adopted on 12 March 1999, paras. 9.2, 10, 11.1 and 11.2.

[101] The Committee made this recommendation to Denmark after having noted the difficulties in access to employment among groups of immigrants of non-European and non-North American descent. CERD/C/60/CO/5, § 15.

[102] General Recommendation XXX, para. 35 (n. 43 above).

[103] Ibid. para. 33.

[104] Ibid. para. 34. As mentioned in Section 3.3 above, this issue had already been raised by the Committee in General Recommendation XXV (n. 50 above) on gender-related dimensions of racial discrimination, which refers to 'abuse of women workers in the informal sector or domestic workers employed abroad by their employers'.

[105] See the recommendations on this issue addressed to Saudi Arabia, U.N. Doc. A/58/18, para. 217, and Bahrain, U.N. Doc. A/60/18, para. 85.

enjoyment of the right to housing and that of other economic, social and cultural rights. For instance, it encouraged a State party to:

> Take all possible measures to further improve housing conditions for Roma, taking also into account that for families, and particularly children, living in a proper environment is an essential prerequisite for access to education and employment on an equal footing.[106]

Access to housing and housing conditions remain a central preoccupation for CERD, as members of ethnic minorities, in particular Roma communities, often live in sub–standard conditions, their settlements often lacking access to running water, electricity, sanitation and other essential services. The Committee also stresses that States should 'refrain from placing Roma in camps outside populated areas that are isolated and without access to health care and other facilities'.[107] Necessary measures should be taken 'as appropriate, for offering Roma nomadic groups or Travellers camping places for their caravans, with all necessary facilities'.[108] The Committee is also concerned about eviction or threats of eviction reportedly faced by the most vulnerable groups and recommends to States that 'they devise measures to prevent [such] evictions or mitigate their negative effects'.[109] Similarly, General Recommendation XXVII requests that States parties 'act firmly against local measures denying residence to and unlawful expulsion of Roma'.[110]

The Committee raised the issue of segregation in housing in its General Recommendation XIX on Article 3, which provides that:

> In many cities, residential patterns are influenced by group differences in income, which are sometimes combined with differences of race, colour, descent, national or ethnic origin, so that inhabitants can be stigmatized

and individuals suffer a form of discrimination in which racial grounds are mixed with other grounds.[111]

The Committee has highlighted that such segregation limits access to many kinds of services, both public and private, distorts participation in political processes, affects the formation and maintenance of social groups, can lead to segregation in education, and influences the sense of moral worth, or the lack of it, which children acquire as they grow up in favoured or in stigmatised neighbourhoods.[112]

General Recommendations on Roma, descent-based discrimination and non-citizens all make reference to this issue of segregation. CERD recommends to States that they develop and implement policies and projects aimed at avoiding segregation of these communities in housing.[113] In recent concluding observations, the Committee welcomed the information on housing projects for Roma implemented by the State party and noted 'the significant efforts invested in seeking optimal solutions to improve their deteriorating housing conditions'.[114] While noting that 'in the short term, construction of housing units … occupied predominantly by Roma may be successful', the Committee was concerned, however, that, 'in the long term, such solutions may perpetuate segregation'. It therefore urged the State party to 'seek solutions that *promote the social integration* of the Roma'.[115] This reference to social integration must be read in conjunction with the recommendation to States that they 'develop educational and media campaigns to educate the public about Roma life, society and culture, and the importance of building an inclusive society *while respecting the human rights and the identity of the Roma*'.[116] Furthermore, the Committee has highlighted the importance of 'involv[ing] Roma communities and

---

[106] *Concluding observations on Slovakia*, A/59/18, para. 387.
[107] General Recommendation XXVII (n. 9 above), para. 31.
[108] Ibid. para. 32. See also *Concluding observations on France*, A/60/18, para. 110, in which the Committee recommends that the State party 'step up its efforts to provide travellers with more parking areas equipped with the necessary facilities and infrastructures and located in clean environments'.
[109] *Concluding observations of CERD on the Czech Republic*, A/58/18, para. 385.
[110] *General Recommendation XXVII* (n. 9 above), p. 222, para. 31.

[111] Ibid. p. 211, para. 3.
[112] See the Statement made by CERD in 1996 to the second United Nations Conference on Human Settlements (Habitat II). A/51/18, Annex. II, para. 4.
[113] See *General Recommendation XXVII* (n. 9 above), p. 222, para. 30, *General Recommendation XXIX* (n. 9 above), p. 229, para. (o)) and *General Recommendation XXX* (n. 43 above), p. 97, para. 32.
[114] *Concluding observations on the Czech Republic*, A/58/18, para. 385.
[115] A/58/18, para. 385. Emphasis added.
[116] *General Recommendation XXVII* (n. 9 above), p. 223, para. 38. Emphasis added.

associations as partners together with other persons in housing project construction, rehabilitation and maintenance'.[117]

Despite measures taken by States, the unfavourable situation faced in practice by immigrants and population groups of immigrant origin is also of particular concern to the Committee. In recent concluding observations, it recommended to a State party, while taking note of legislation concerning general principles and planning for cities and urban renewal, to 'strengthen its policy for the integration of immigrants and population groups of immigrant origin, especially in the field of housing'.[118]

The Committee has emphasised the need for measures against discriminatory practices of local authorities or private owners with regard to residence and access to adequate housing in its General Recommendations on Roma, descent-based communities[119] and non-citizens.[120] This question had already been raised in a decision adopted in 2001[121] regarding the complaint of an individual who had been provided by an agency with lists of vacant accommodation for which landlords indicated that persons from certain groups were not desired as tenants. Although the Committee found the complaint inadmissible,[122] it took 'the opportunity to urge the State party to take effective measures to ensure that housing agencies refrain from engaging in discriminatory practices and do not accept submissions from private landlords which would discriminate on racial grounds'.[123]

Local authorities have a major role to play in remedying the situation of vulnerable groups such as Roma that often live in appalling conditions. In a case which the Committee ruled upon in March 2005,[124] the petitioners were a group of twenty-seven Roma complaining about discriminatory denial of the right to housing by a municipal council, coupled with denial of the right to an effective remedy by judicial authorities. A municipal council had drawn up and approved a plan to develop low-cost housing, principally benefiting Roma. The decision had given rise to a petition by local inhabitants, referring disparagingly to the Roma that were to benefit from the plan, and seeking cancellation of the municipal decision. The council, citing the petition, had annulled its original decision without any substitution of an alternative. Criminal and constitutional complaints up to the level of the Constitutional Court were unsuccessful. At the admissibility stage, the Committee recalled its jurisprudence according to which acts of municipal councils amount to acts of public authorities and are sufficient to invoke the State party's international responsibility and, further, that domestic remedies had been properly pursued.[125] On the merits, the Committee considered that the circumstances disclosed a case of indirect discrimination against Roma in the form of the second council resolution. The State party had argued that the resolution of the municipal council did not confer a direct and enforceable right to housing but rather amounted to but one step in a complex process of policy development in the field of housing. The Committee stressed that the first resolution, a necessary first step in policy-making, was an important and practical component for the realisation of the right to housing. That stage was thus covered by the Convention, even though the resolution did not itself confer a directly enforceable right to housing. As a result, the Committee concluded that the petitioners were victims of racial discrimination in breach of Articles 2 and 5 (e) of the Convention.[126] The failure of the national judicial system to remedy this discrimination represented a separate violation of Article 6. By way of remedy, the Committee

---

[117] Ibid. p. 222, para 30. See also *Concluding observations on Slovakia*, A /59/18, para. 387.

[118] *Concluding observations on France*, A/60/18, para. 106.

[119] See *General Recommendation XXVII* (n. 9 above), p. 222, para. 31 and *General Recommendation XXIX* (n. 9 above) p. 231, para. mm.

[120] See *General Recommendation XXX* (n. 43 above), p. 97, para. 32.

[121] Communication No. 18/2000, *F.A. v. Norway*.

[122] The author had submitted the communication more than six months after the exhaustion of domestic remedies, thereby not meeting the requisite of Rule 91 (f) of its rules of procedure.

[123] The Committee recalled in this respect 'its concluding observations on the consideration of the fifteenth periodic report of Norway, in which it expressed concern that persons seeking to rent or purchase apartments and houses were not adequately protected against racial discrimination on the part of vendors. In this connection, the Committee recommended that Norway give full effect to its obligations under Article 5(e)(iii) of the Convention' (Communication No. 18/2000. *F.A. v. Norway*, para. 8).

[124] Communication No. 31/2003, *L.R. v. Slovakia*.

[125] Ibid. para. 6.3.

[126] Ibid. para. 10.9.

indicated that the petitioners should be returned to the situation in which they were when the first resolution was adopted.

In its follow-up observations, the Slovak Government informed the Committee that the Opinion had been translated and distributed to relevant governmental offices and State authorities, including municipalities and the National Centre for Human Rights. The municipal council concerned, taking into consideration the Committee's Opinion, decided to cancel both resolutions and reached an agreement stating that it would become engaged in proposals related to low-cost housing. In that context, the council would pay serious attention to the housing problems of the Roma community with a view to the practical realisation of the right to housing. Regarding the alleged discriminatory petition of the inhabitants, the Slovak Government informed the Committee that legal proceedings had been initiated against the five-member 'petition committee'.[127]

5.3   Land Rights

The claim by indigenous peoples of their land rights has been one of the most contentious questions for States in their relationship with these peoples. The importance of this issue was fully acknowledged by CERD in its General Recommendation XXIII, in which it:

> [E]specially calls upon States parties to recognize and protect the rights of indigenous peoples to own, develop, control and use their communal lands, territories and resources and, where they have been deprived of lands and territories traditionally owned or otherwise inhabited or used without their free and informed consent, to take steps to return these lands and territories.[128]

Over the past few years, the Committee has addressed this issue on numerous occasions in its concluding observations as well as in decisions adopted under its early warning and urgent action procedures[129] and its follow-up procedure.[130]

Despite clear calls made by CERD in its concluding observations, many States parties are still to adopt an adequate legislative and policy framework

---

[127] U.N. Doc. A/60/18, para. 449.

[128] *General Recommendation XXIII* (n. 9 above), p. 216, para. 5. See also for comparison and further detail ILO Convention No. 169 on Indigenous and Tribal Peoples, which devotes a whole section to issues related to land (Articles 13 to 19). The issue of indigenous land rights has also frequently been pressed by the Human Rights Committee which, in its *General Comment No. 23*, recognises that culture as mentioned in Article 27 of the International Covenant on Civil and Political Rights 'manifests itself in many forms, including a particular way of life associated with the use of land resources' (HRI/GEN/1/Rev.7, p. 158). Land rights of indigenous peoples also consti-

tute a major concern for the Committee on Economic, Social and Cultural Rights, which deals with this question under Article 11 of the International Covenant on Economic, Social and Cultural Rights. For further developments, see P. Thornberry, *Indigenous Peoples and Human Rights*, (Manchester: Manchester University Press, 2002), pp. 163–172 and pp. 187–190.

[129] See for instance the decision adopted by the Committee in March 2005 on the New Zealand Foreshore and Seabed Act (Decision 1 (66), A/60/18, para. 18). Reports from Maori organisations had alerted the Committee to a bill to be adopted by New Zealand governing the ownership rights over the country's foreshore and seabed (the so-called 'Foreshore and Seabed Bill'), which they claimed would impact very negatively on Maori traditional land rights. The law was passed before the Committee could consider the matter. Shortly after the enactment of the law and following a dialogue with a governmental delegation, the Committee adopted decision 1(66). The Committee expressed its concern 'at the apparent haste with which the law had been passed'. Furthermore, it stated its fear that 'insufficient consideration may have been given to alternative responses, which might have accommodated Maori rights within a framework more acceptable both to the Maori and to all other New Zealanders'. In this regard, the Committee regretted that 'the processes of consultation did not appreciably narrow the differences between the various States Parties on this issue'. See also the two decisions on Suriname concerning indigenous peoples' land rights adopted respectively in 2003 and 2005 (A/58/18, para. 15 and A/60/18, para. 19). The first decision was adopted by the Committee following receipt of NGO information concerning the alarming situation of indigenous peoples and concerning, inter alia, their land rights. It led to the submission by the Government of Suriname of its initial report, which had been overdue since 1986. The second decision was adopted following information received from the same NGO according to which Suriname was considering the adoption of a new Mining Act, which would affect the rights of indigenous peoples, despite the recommendation made in this regard by the Committee in its concluding observations (A/59/18, para. 193).

[130] For further detail on the follow-up procedure, see concluding remarks, p.23. See also the decision on Suriname (A/60/18, para. 417) and the letters addressed to the United States of America and Ukraine, requesting a response to detailed questions concerning, respectively, land rights of the Western Shoshone Tribe and Crimean Tatars (ibid. paras. 418–424). These three decisions were adopted by the Committee following receipt of information from NGOs representing the indigenous peoples concerned.

recognising the rights of indigenous and tribal peoples over their lands, territories and communal resources. For instance, the Committee has repeatedly raised the issue of Sámi land rights during its dialogue with the concerned States[131] and has expressed regret at their continuing failure to find an appropriate solution. The Committee has also addressed in several sets of concluding observations the reasons given by States to justify the appropriation of land traditionally occupied and used by indigenous peoples. A frequent justification is that the constitution of the State sets forth the principle that natural resources are the property of the nation and must be used to promote economic, social and cultural development. The Committee has responded that this principle 'must be exercised consistently with the rights of indigenous and tribal peoples' and that States need to 'ensure ways of guaranteeing effective protection for indigenous peoples' rights of ownership and possession'.[132] Similarly, in a case of allegations of forced relocation and violations of the rights of indigenous peoples over their traditional homelands and resources in the name of wildlife preservation, the Committee has recommended that the State make 'efforts to reconcile indigenous people's land rights with the preservation of wildlife'.[133] The Committee, however, is not oblivious to the need to bear in mind the interests and rights of non-indigenous communities. In one State party, Fiji, it expressed concern about the alleged eviction of numerous farmers following the expiry of many leases of Native land as well as about the apparent insufficiency of the resettlement programme for farmers concerned. It under-

lined the State's responsibility to provide assistance to evicted tenants, and recommended that it increase its efforts to compensate and resettle affected families. It also urged the State party to develop measures of conciliation between indigenous people and the rest of the population over the land issue, with a view to obtaining a solution acceptable to both communities.[134]

The Committee insists during its dialogue with States not only on the need to adopt adequate legislation recognising indigenous land rights, but also on their obligation to ensure that this legislation is duly applied. In one instance, legal provisions aimed at recognising the title to and ownership of land of indigenous groups and individuals as well as the right to exclusive benefit of renewable natural resources situated on their lands had not prevented the allotment of indigenous lands to private companies.[135] The Committee therefore 'invite[d] the State party to implement consistently in practice the commendable legislation it adopted in order to recognize the fundamental rights of indigenous peoples and to improve their living conditions'.[136]

Indigenous peoples should be granted a right of appeal to courts or to any independent body created for the purpose of allowing them to claim their rights over their lands. Failure to recognise the legal personality of indigenous peoples can constitute an obstacle to judicial claim of their land rights. The Committee has stressed that this difficulty needs to be remedied so that indigenous and tribal peoples can, as such, seek recognition of their traditional rights before the courts.[137] Financial obstacles to judicial claims by indigenous peoples as well as discriminatory attitudes should also be eliminated.[138] Furthermore,

---

[131] For the Committee's reiterated expressions of concern over the lack of solution to this issue, see the *Concluding observations on Finland* adopted in 1996 (CERD/C/304/Add.7, paras. 11 and 23), 1999 (CERD/C/304/Add.66, paras. 10 and 14), 2001 (CERD/C/304/Add.107, para. 11), 2003 (U.N. Doc. A/58/18, paras. 405), the *Concluding observations on Norway* adopted in 2003 (ibid. para. 481) and the *Concluding observations on Sweden* adopted in 2004 (A/59/18, para. 222). See also the concluding observations on Suriname, in which CERD regretted that 'more than 10 years after the 1992 Peace Accord, the State party [had] not adopted an adequate legislative framework to govern the recognition of the rights of indigenous peoples (Amerindian and Maroons) over their lands, territories and communal resources' (U.N. Doc. A/59/18, para 191).

[132] Ibid. para. 190.

[133] *Concluding observations on Nepal*, U.N. Doc. A/59/18, para. 128.

[134] *Concluding observations on Fiji*, ibid. paras. 88 and 89. For further detail on this issue, see M. Salomon, 'Masking Inequality in the Name of Rights: The Examination of Fiji's State Report under the International Convention on the Elimination of All Forms of Racial Discrimination', *Asia-Pacific Journal on Human Rights and the Law*, Vol. 1 (2003), pp. 86–129.

[135] *Concluding observations on Bolivia*, A/58/18, para. 335.

[136] Ibid. para. 339.

[137] *Concluding observations on Suriname* and *Argentina*. A/59/18, paras. 193 and 246.

[138] In concluding observations addressed to Sweden, the Committee noted 'the allegations that in cases of land disputes between Sámi and non-Sámi in courts of law, the interests of the non-Sámi frequently override those of the Sámi, and that the latter are allegedly not provided

General Recommendation XXIII provides that 'only when this is for factual reasons not possible, the right to restitution should be substituted by the right to just, fair and prompt compensation' and that 'such compensation should as far as possible take the form of lands and territories'.[139]

The extent to which States should go beyond consultation and specifically require and obtain consent of the indigenous peoples concerned for any decisions affecting them, thus conferring on them a right of veto, remains a subject for debate.[140] General Recommendation XXIII requests States parties to ensure that 'no decisions directly relating to the rights and interests of indigenous peoples are taken *without their informed consent*'.[141] In concluding observations adopted in 2003,[142] the Committee applied this principle to the question of resource exploitation and stressed that '*merely consulting* [indigenous] communities prior to exploiting the resources falls short

of meeting the requirements set out in...General Recommendation XXIII'. The Committee therefore recommended 'that the prior informed consent of these communities be sought, and that the equitable sharing of benefits to be derived from such exploitation be ensured'. The formulation adopted by CERD in more recent concluding observations is, however, more nuanced. In 2004, the Committee invited the authorities of a State party to 'check that the established mechanisms for notifying and consulting the indigenous and tribal peoples are working', and recommended that the State party '*strive to reach agreements* with the peoples concerned, *as far as possible*, before awarding any concessions'.[143] Similarly, in concluding observations adopted in March 2005, the Committee recommended that the State party refrain from adopting measures that withdraw existing guarantees of indigenous rights and 'that *it make every effort to seek the informed consent* of indigenous peoples before adopting decisions relating to their rights to land'.[144]

---

with financial means to support litigation in respect of their rights to land. The Committee request[ed] that the State Party provide information on this issue, as well as information on the outcome of cases related to these claims' (U.N. Doc. A/59/18, para. 224).

[139] General Recommendation XXIII (n. 9 above), p 216, para.5. See also for an example of concluding observations on this issue the concluding observations on Suriname in which highlighted the need to ensure that fair compensation be granted in the case of judicial claims relating to damage suffered by indigenous peoples following the exploitation of natural resources on their traditional lands (U.N. Doc. A/59/18, para. 193).

[140] This issue is also under discussion in the Working Group on Indigenous Populations of the former Sub-Commission on the Promotion and Protection of Human Rights. See the preliminary working paper and the expanded working paper prepared respectively in 2004 and 2005 on the principle of free, prior and informed consent of indigenous peoples in relation to development affecting their lands and natural resources submitted by Antoanella-Iulia Motoc and the Tebtebba Foundation (E/CN.4/Sub.2/AC.4/2004/4 and E/CN.4/Sub.2/AC.4/2005/WP.1).

[141] General Recommendation XXIII (n. 9 above), p. 213, para. (d). Emphasis added. The position of CERD should be compared with ILO Convention No. 169 which merely requires States to undertake consultations. Article 15 provides that 'governments shall establish or maintain procedures through which they consult [indigenous] peoples, with a view to ascertaining whether and to what degree their interests would be prejudiced, before undertaking or permitting any programmes for the exploration of...resources pertaining to their lands'. For a discussion of the possible right a veto granted by CERD to indigenous peoples, see Thornberry, *Indigenous Peoples and Human Rights* (n. 127 above), p. 217.

[142] *Concluding observations on Ecuador*, U.N. Doc. A/58/18, para. 62.

5.4   Right to Health

Article 5(e)(iv) of the Convention refers broadly to the obligation of States parties to ensure the enjoyment without discrimination by all of the right to public health, medical care, social security and social services. This obligation has been reiterated by the Committee in General Recommendations regarding specific groups. CERD requests from States that they ensure equal access to health care and social security services and eliminate any discriminatory practices in this field against Roma and persons belonging to descent-based communities.[145] The Committee has also stressed the need to 'initiate and implement programmes and projects in the field of health for Roma, mainly women and children, having in mind their disadvantaged situation due to extreme poverty and low level of education, as well as to cultural differences'.[146] Furthermore, it has emphasised the importance of the involvement of the concerned

---

[143] *Concluding observations on Suriname*, A/59/18, para. 192. Emphasis added.

[144] *Concluding observations on Australia*, A/60/18, para. 36. Emphasis added.

[145] *General Recommendation XXVII* ((n. 9 above), p. 222, para. 33) and *General Recommendation* XXIX (n. 9 above) p. 231, para. nn.

[146] *General Recommendation XXVII*, ibid. p. 222. para. 34.

communities and their representatives, 'mainly women, in designing and implementing health programmes and projects'.[147]

When considering specific country situations, the Committee has expressed concern in relation not only to limited access to health care but also to higher child mortality, high maternal mortality rates and shorter life expectancy for Roma.[148] Some recent concluding observations are more detailed; for instance, in concluding observations adopted in 2004, the Committtee devoted an entire paragraph to the critical health situation of Roma in a State party, which the Committee interprets as 'largely a consequence of their poor living conditions'. The Committee specifically requested that the State party 'take further measures to address the issues of drinking water supplies and sewage disposal systems in Roma settlements'.[149]

The deleterious effects of natural resource exploitation on the health of indigenous people is of concern to CERD. It has stressed that 'development objectives are no justification for encroachments on human rights, and that along with the right to exploit natural resources, there are specific, concomitant obligations towards the local population'.[150] The State party concerned was urged to adopt a legislative framework that clearly sets forth the broad principles governing the exploitation of the land, 'including the obligation to abide by strict environmental standards'.[151] The Committee also recommended that the State party 'set up an independent body to conduct environmental impact surveys before any operating licenses are issued, and to conduct health and safety checks on small-scale and industrial gold-mining'.[152] The spread of sexually transmitted diseases such as HIV/AIDS amongst indigenous and tribal people, in connection with the expansion of mining and forestry operations, is also a cause for concern for the Committee, which has emphasised the need for the introduction of national plans of action to combat AIDS.[153] The Committee

has also recommended that national social security systems take into account the specific needs of minorities and indigenous peoples.[154]

The provision of health and social security services to non-citizens is a particularly contentious issue. During its dialogue with States parties, the Committee has recommended to them that they ensure the rights of migrant workers to social security and social services[155] and has also expressed concern at the situation of refugees[156] in this respect. General Recommendation XXX requires from States that they 'respect the right of non-citizens to an adequate standard of physical and mental health by, inter alia, refraining from denying or limiting their access to preventive, curative and palliative health services'.[157]

Issues relating specifically to the health of women are regularly raised by the Committee. During its recent dialogue with a State party, the Committee addressed the question of forced sterilisation of Roma women. It welcomed the assurances given by the delegation that a draft law on health care, which would address shortcomings in the system by specifying the requirement of free and informed consent for medical procedures and guarantee patients' access to medical files, had been approved by the Government and should shortly be adopted by the Parliament. Furthermore, CERD 'strongly recommend[ed] that the State party take all necessary measures to put an end to this regrettable practice, including the speedy adoption of the above-mentioned draft law on health care'. It added that 'the State Party should also ensure that just and effective remedies, including compensation and apology, are granted to the victims'.[158]

The harmful impact on the health of women and children of traditional practices has also been addressed by the Committee. During its dialogue with a State party, CERD expressed concern about the high prevalence of female genital mutilation among some ethnic groups and recommended that the State party 'take all necessary measures to

---

[147] Ibid. For descent-based communities, see *General Recommendation* XXIX, (n. 9 above) p. 231, para. (oo).
[148] *Concluding observations on the United Kingdom*, U.N. Doc. A/58/ 18, para. 542.
[149] *Concluding observations on Slovakia*, U.N. Doc. A/59/18, para. 388.
[150] *Concluding observations on Suriname*, U.N. Doc. A/59/ 18, para. 194.
[151] Ibid.
[152] Ibid.
[153] Ibid. para. 196.

[154] *Concluding observations on Argentina*, U.N. Doc. A/59/ 18, para. 250.
[155] *Concluding observations on the Republic of Korea*, U.N. Doc. A/58/ 18, para. 495.
[156] *Concluding observations on Uzbekistan*, CERD/C/304/ Add.87, paras. 13 and 14.
[157] U.N. Doc. A/59/18, p. 97. para. 36.
[158] *Concluding observations on Slovakia*, U.N. Doc. A/59/18, para. 389.

put a stop to such practices'. Furthermore, it added that 'information and awareness-raising measures aimed specifically at, and designed for, relevant population groups should be adopted'.[159]

5.5   Education, Language and Culture

The Committee pays great attention to the equal enjoyment of the right to education by all without discrimination.[160] Furthermore, it regularly stresses during its dialogue with States parties the need to ensure that members of minority and indigenous groups can exercise their right to their culture, the use of their language and the preservation and development of their identity.[161]

Combating discrimination in education and promoting the education of children belonging to vulnerable groups, in particular Roma,[162] people of African descent,[163] caste-based communities[164] and non-citizens, including children of undocumented migrants,[165] has been identified as a major priority by the Committee. This entails taking measures to eliminate any discrimination and racial harassment of these children,[166] to support their inclusion in the school system, and to act to reduce drop out rates.[167] Segregation has been

identified as an issue of continuing concern not only in relation to children of descent-based communities,[168] and children of non-citizens,[169] but also for Roma children placed in so-called special schools, including in special remedial classes for mentally disabled children.[170] The Committee has discussed this issue at length with several States parties and has acknowledged the complexity of the problem of special schooling, which some States attempt to justify by the specific educational needs of Roma children.[171] CERD has nevertheless stressed its concern regarding the lower standard of education in segregated classes.[172] It has recommended to the concerned States the 'enrolment [of Roma children] in mainstream schools, the recruitment of school personnel from among members of Roma communities, and the sensitization of teachers and other education professionals to the social fabric and world views of Roma children and those with apparent learning difficulties'.[173] The issue of separate classes for foreign pupils[174] or children of immigrant origin,[175] whether it be a policy or a case of de facto segregation, has also been raised by the Committee.

More generally, CERD insists on the need to make further efforts for the provision of *quality* education to indigenous and minority children.[176] The lack of teachers from the concerned minorities or indigenous groups is often a problem. These teachers should be provided with adequate training and measures taken to combat all forms of

---

[159] *Concluding observations on Mauritania*, ibid. para. 346.

[160] Article 5 (e)(v) of the Convention refers to the equal enjoyment by all of the right to education and training, whereas Article 7 of the Convention requests from States that they undertake to adopt immediate and effective measures, inter alia, in the field of teaching and education with a view to combating prejudices with leads to racial discrimination. See also on this issue other relevant international instruments such as the UNESCO Convention against Discrimination in Education, Article 4, Paras 3 and 4 of the UN Declaration on the Rights of Persons Belonging to National or Ethnic, Religious and Linguistic Minorities, Articles 26–31 of ILO Convention No. 169, and Articles 29 (1)(c) and 30 of the Convention on the Rights of the Child.

[161] *Concluding observations on Morocco*, U.N. Doc. A/58/18, para. 142.

[162] General Recommendation XXVII (n. 9 above), p. 221, paras. 17–26.

[163] See *Concluding observations on Ecuador* (U.N. Doc. A/58/18, para. 60), *Concluding observations on Bolivia* (n. 96 above), para. 341.

[164] General Recommendation XXIX (n. 9 above), pp. 231–232, paras. rr-vv.

[165] *General Recommendation XXX*, paras. 30–31 (A/59/18, p. 96).

[166] *General Recommendation XXVII*, para. 20 and General Recommendation XXIX, para. (tt).

[167] *General Recommendation XXVII* (n. 9 above), para. 17 and *General Recommendation XXIX* (n. 9 above), paras. (rr). and (ss).

[168] *General Recommendation XXIX*, ibid. para. 0.

[169] A/59/18, p. 96, para. 31. *General Recommendation XXX* refers not only to segregated schooling but also to 'different standards of treatment being applied to non-citizens on grounds of race, colour descent, national or ethnic origin in elementary and secondary school and with respect to access to higher education'.

[170] See *Concluding observations on Slovakia*, U.N. Doc. A/59/18, para. 385.

[171] See *Concluding observations on Poland*, U.N. Doc. A/58/18, para. 163.

[172] Ibid.

[173] *Concluding observations on the Czech Republic*, U.N. Doc. A/58/18, para. 386. See also the *concluding observations on Slovenia*, (n. 87 above) para. 238.

[174] See *Concluding observations on Switzerland*, U.N. Doc. A/58/18, para. 252.

[175] See *Concluding observations on the Netherlands*, U.N. Doc. A/59/18, para. 152.

[176] See *Concluding observations on Tajikistan* (U.N. Doc. A/59/18, para. 412). Emphasis added.

discrimination against them.[177] CERD has also stressed that the consultation of the population groups concerned is crucial when studying the question of discrimination in education and identifying adequate solutions to current difficulties and shortcomings. It has identified as urgent the need to improve dialogue and communication between the teaching personnel, the children, their parents and more generally the communities concerned.[178]

The Committee has also underlined that the particularly disadvantaged situation of girls and women requires specific attention and needs to be taken into account in programmes, projects and campaigns in the field of education.[179] Concerning children of travelling Roma communities, CERD recommends to States that they take 'necessary measures to ensure a process of basic education [for these children], including admitting them temporarily to local schools, by establishing temporary classes in their places of encampment, or by using new technologies for distance education'.[180] Furthermore, the Committee has acknowledged the need for measures promoting adult education among Roma communities through adequate forms and schemes of education in order to improve literacy.[181]

Combating racial discrimination requires efforts to educate the population as a whole in a spirit of non-discrimination[182] and respect for the communities subject to such discrimination. General Recommendation XXIX therefore prescribes the 'review [of] all language in textbooks which conveys stereotyped or demeaning images, references, names or opinions concerning descent-based communities and [its replacement] by

images, references, names and opinions which convey the message of the inherent dignity of all human beings and their equality of human rights'.[183] Similarly, General Recommendation XXVII requests the inclusion in textbooks, at all appropriate levels, of chapters about the history and culture of Roma. States should also 'encourage and support the publication and distribution of books and other print materials as well as the broadcasting of television and radio programmes, as appropriate, about [Roma] history and culture, including in languages spoken by them'.[184] CERD frequently recommends to States parties that they take adequate measures to promote intercultural education. For instance, in concluding observations adopted in 2004, CERD stressed the need to take measures so as to ensure that indigenous peoples benefit from 'a bilingual and intercultural education in full respect of their cultural identity, languages, history and culture, bearing also in mind the wider importance of intercultural education for the general population'.[185]

The Committee recommends that States parties ensure that school curricula foster understanding, tolerance, and friendship among nations and ethnic groups.[186] It has also noted that State control over school curricula may have a negative impact for minorities. In one instance, CERD warned that, although state policies ensuring that the curricula in private and public schools are identical can be justified by a desire to monitor the quality of private education, such control over private schools may not be 'conducive to the teaching of the languages and cultures of minority groups'.[187] States should 'respect parents'' freedom to choose the type of education they wish for their children and to choose private schools that offer programmes meeting their expectations in terms of culture and language'.[188]

---

[177] See *Concluding observations on Argentina* (n. 137 above), para. 249, and on *Slovakia* (n. 170 above), para 385.
[178] General Recommendation XXVII (n. 9 above), p. 221, paras. 17 and 24.
[179] Ibid. p. 221, para. 22 and p. 231, para. ss.
[180] Ibid. p. 221, para. 21.
[181] Ibid. para. 25.
[182] See footnote 169 referring to Article 7 of the Convention, which constitutes the legal basis for such requirements. This provision of the Convention is too often neglected by States parties which do not provide sufficient information on its implementation in their periodic reports despite the suggestions made in the reporting guidelines of the Committee (see requirements regarding information to be provided on measures to implement Article 7 under the heading of education and teaching, HRI/GEN/2/Rev.1, p. 38).

[183] General Recommendation XXIX (n. 9 above), para. uu.
[184] General Recommendation XXVII (n. 9 above), para. 26.
[185] See *Concluding observations on Argentina*, A/59/18, para. 249. See also the *Concluding observations on Suriname* for an emphasis on the need to encourage the learning of mother tongues of indigenous and tribal people with a view to preserve the cultural and linguistic identity of the various ethnic groups (ibid, para. 201). See also concluding observations on Tajikistan, ibid. para. 417.
[186] *Concluding observations on Turkmenistan*, U.N. Doc. A/60/18, para. 326.
[187] *Concluding observations on Mauritania*, U.N. Doc. A/59/18, para. 348.
[188] Ibid.

States parties' obligations go beyond mere respect for indigenous and minority cultural rights. In concluding observations adopted in 2004,[189] CERD noted that 'the authorities appear to limit themselves to not hampering the exercise by the various ethnic groups and their members of their cultural rights'. The Committee recommended that the State party not only 'respect' but also 'promote' the indigenous and tribal peoples' cultures, languages and distinctive ways of life. States are also encouraged to carry out a survey, in collaboration with the groups concerned, of the impact of economic development in the indigenous and tribal peoples' lands on their collective and individual cultural rights. When looking at the situation of indigenous peoples in another State party, the Committee expressed concern at 'the inadequate protection in practice of indigenous peoples' ownership and possession of ancestral lands and the consequential impairment of indigenous peoples' ability to practise their religious beliefs'. Measures were required to safeguard indigenous rights over ancestral lands, especially sacred sites, and to ensure respect the special importance for the culture and spiritual values of indigenous peoples of their relationship with the land.[190]

The Committee pays great attention to the question of linguistic rights. The lack of provision in the educational curriculum for the teaching of, or education in, minority or indigenous languages has been frequently identified as a concern.[191]

States should remedy this situation while ensuring that 'education in national languages [does] not lead to the exclusion of the group concerned'.[192] The question of resource allocation may become quite sensitive, in particular in poorer countries that argue the need to strike a balance between the minorities' interests and those of the nation as whole. In one instance, a State party declared to the Committee that it was only able to grant a right to study and to be taught in the mother tongue in areas including a sufficient number of members of a minority. While understanding the financial difficulties encountered by the concerned State, CERD nevertheless recommended that it 'ensure that the rights of members of minorities are not unduly restricted outside areas where the minorities are concentrated'.[193] In concluding observations addressed to another State party, the Committee expressed concern about the reported closure of minority cultural institutions and of numerous schools teaching in minority languages, and recommended that the State party consider re-opening these schools. This recommendation was combined with the requirement to abolish the rule according to which students belonging to national or ethnic minorities had to wear the national dress of the dominant ethnic group in the country.[194]

CERD has also stressed that minorities should have the right to express themselves in their own language when communicating with the relevant authorities through provision, if necessary, of translation services.[195] Access for persons belonging to minorities to public media in their language is also an issue to which the Committee attaches great importance.[196] Sufficient time should be devoted to programmes in minority languages on public radio and television and States should take

---

[189] *Concluding observations on Suriname*, U.N. Doc. A/59/18, para. 201.

[190] *Concluding observations on Argentina*, U.N. Doc. A/58/19, para. 246.

[191] See for instance concluding observations on Mauritania concerning the absence of provision in the curriculum for the inclusion of several national languages, A/59/18, para. 347; see also *concluding observations on Ecuador* (U.N. Doc. A/58/18, para. 60), and *Argentina* (A/59/18, para. 249). CERD has paid particular attention to the specific situation of the Baltic States and the impact on Russian speakers and other minorities of the move to bilingual education in a short time frame. For instance, in its concluding observations on Latvia (A/58/18, para. 452), without contesting the move as such, CERD has encouraged the State party 'to remain attentive and flexible to the needs and abilities of the persons primarily affected' and stressed 'the importance of maintaining a close dialogue with the schools and local communities, including both parents and children'. CERD has further urged the States parties to 'monitor the reform process closely in order to ensure that a high quality of education is maintained by, inter alia, considering an extension of the tran-

sition period to bilingual education and preventing any negative effects that might otherwise arise'.

[192] *Concluding observations on Mauritania*, (U.N. Doc.) A/59/18, para. 347.

[193] See *Concluding observations on Albania*, (U.N. Doc. A/58/18, para. 310): CERD had noted the complaint of the Greek and Macedonian-Slav minorities 'about the lack of mother-tongue education system outside the regions in which these minorities are traditionally concentrated'.

[194] *Concluding observations on Turkmenistan*, U.N. Doc. A/60/18, para. 321.

[195] See *Concluding observations on Latvia*, U.N. Doc. A/58/18, para. 445.

[196] See *Concluding observations on Morocco* (n. 161 above), para. 145 and on *Albania* (n. 193 above), para. 317.

steps to facilitate the publication of newspapers in minority languages.[197] Members of minorities or indigenous groups should be able to use first names that only exist in their own language. When considering the situation of a State party with a large Amazigh community, CERD therefore recommended that an end be put to the prohibition to enter Amazigh first names in the civil register.[198]

6. CONCLUDING REMARKS

The present review of the practice of CERD shows that the equal enjoyment of economic, social and cultural rights has been a matter of continuing and major concern for the Committee, which has fully acknowledged the importance of these rights in the context of racial discrimination. Contrary to the views of some authors,[199] the deplorable socio-economic situation in which many members of these vulnerable groups live, together with the lack of effectiveness of measures taken to remedy the violations of their economic social and cultural rights, has been relentlessly stressed by the Committee. These issues have been dealt with extensively in concluding observations and decisions as well as in several General Recommendations and opinions on individual and group complaints adopted by the Committee. The dialogues organised by the Committee with two Special Rapporteurs of the Commission on Human Rights dealing with economic, social and cultural rights[200] are further evidence of the particular interest of the Committee in furthering its assessment of the equal enjoyment of these rights without racial

discrimination. However, discrimination in the sphere of economic, social and cultural rights still remains a major problem, despite the repeated recommendations of the Committee in this area. This situation may lead at times to questioning the effectiveness of the action of the Committee. The main priority of CERD, as of other UN treaty bodies, has increasingly focused on devising new ways to ensure that their recommendations have more practical impact in the countries concerned. Some governments have pointed out that treaty body recommendations are difficult to implement because of their general nature. CERD and other treaty bodies are aware of this criticism and have made efforts to make their recommendations more concrete and specific, so as to facilitate follow-up.

As pointed out in Section 5 of this chapter, many concluding observations adopted by CERD during the past few years have identified specific defects within the State's legislative and policy frameworks or in the practical implementation of national measures. CERD requests States parties to provide information on the implementation of the recommendations contained in previous concluding observations in their subsequent report as well as during the oral dialogue with government delegations. It has a long-standing procedure whereby it may request further information or an additional report concerning, inter alia, action taken by States parties to implement recommendations.[201] This procedure was supplemented in 2004 with the appointment of a coordinator on follow-up, who works in cooperation with the country rapporteurs.[202] Furthermore, the Committee now selects in its concluding observations up to four recommendations that should be considered as priorities. States are requested to report

---

[197] *Concluding observations on Tajikistan*, A/59/18, para. 413.

[198] *Concluding observations on Morocco*, A/58/18, paras. 142 and 143.

[199] Such as Felice, 'The UN Committee on the Elimination of All Forms of Racial Discrimination' (n. 85 above).

[200] Mr. Miloon Kothari, Special Rapporteur on adequate housing as a component of the right to an adequate standard of living, met with the Committee in 2002 and in 2004 (see summary records of the Committee CERD/C/SR. 1533 and CERD/C/SR/1666). Mr. Paul Hunt, Special Rapporteur on Health as a Component of the Right of Everyone to the Highest Attainable Standard of Mental and Physical Health, met with the Committee in 2004 (see summary records of the Committee, CERD/C/SR.1698). The only other Special Rapporteur regularly meeting with the Committee is Mr. Doudou Diène, Special Rapporteur on Contemporary Forms of Racism, Racial Discrimination, Xenophobia and Related Intolerance.

[201] CERD Rules of procedure, Rule 65, para. (a) (HRI/GEN/3/Rev.2, p. 79).

[202] Rule 65, para (b) (ibid. p, 80). See also the terms of reference of the mandate of the co-ordinator in A/60/18, Annex IV. This procedure was adopted on the model of similar procedures adopted by the Human Rights Committee and by the Committee against Torture whereby these Committees identify a number of specific recommendations in its concluding observations as requiring immediate attention and request the State party to provide additional information on their implementation within a set period. See the decisions adopted by HRC on 21 March 2002, U.N. Doc. A/57/40, vol. 1, Annex III. See also Annex X to the Annual Report submitted by CAT/C to the General Assembly in 2002 (U.N. Doc. A/57/44).

within a year on the measures taken to implement these recommendations, some of which concern economic, social and cultural rights.[203]

Apart from the Committee itself, all other stakeholders should play a more active role in ensuring that CERD recommendations are implemented. Coordination between the various branches of government, national human rights institutions and civil society organisations, while each maintaining their independent and autonomous role, should be strengthened in order to achieve better follow-up. Concluding observations should be systematically translated into local languages and duly disseminated among state authorities and civil society. Government agencies should draw up a plan with specific deadlines in order to ensure the implementation of the recommendations, and national human rights institutions and civil society organisations should lobby for, and monitor this implementation process.

In line with the report of the United Nations Secretary-General, 'Strengthening the United Nations: an agenda for further change',[204] and particularly with its emphasis on helping countries to advance the protection of human rights, the Office of the High Commissioner for Human Rights ('OHCHR') is constantly striving to increase its activities regarding capacity building at the national level for the implementation of human rights obligations of States as provided in the seven core human rights treaties, including the Convention. In this context, OHCHR has started a programme which includes training of national human rights institutions, non-governmental organisations and media representatives prior to the consideration of their State reports by treaty bodies, including CERD. These training sessions held in Geneva prior to treaty body sessions are designed to encourage participants to adopt a plan of action on their contribution to the implementation of the recommendations adopted once the State report has been examined.[205] They

have been supplemented by sub-regional workshops[206] on follow-up to concluding observations organised in various parts of the world involving government officials as well as civil society representatives.

In addition to implementation of recommendations adopted at the end of the reporting procedure, follow-up to the opinions adopted by the Committee on individual and group communications is also a cause of concern. As is the case for recommendations included in concluding observations, these opinions are not legally binding.[207] When it finds that the Convention has been violated, the Committee merely requests that States send information, within six months, about the measures taken in the light of its opinion. The Committee has therefore recently decided to increase its efforts to ensure that its individual opinions have an impact on the ground. At its sixty-seventh session held in August 2005, it decided to appoint rapporteurs on follow-up for the purpose of ascertaining the measures taken by States parties to give effect to the Committee's suggestions and recommendations for action included in its individual opinions.[208]

As these new follow-up procedures had only just started operating at the time of writing, it is not yet possible to assess their effectiveness. It is hoped, however, that the conjunction of these various efforts will contribute to a higher level of implementation by States of the recommendations addressed to them by the Committee. As noted in the Durban Declaration, 'the obstacles to overcoming racial discrimination and achieving

---

[203] CERD has for instance requested Australia to report within a year on its recommendations made in March 2005 concerning indigenous peoples' land rights. See U.N. Doc. A/60/18, para. 48.

[204] A/57/387. See also the emphasis placed on country engagement and on implementation in the Plan of Action adopted by the High Commissioner in May 2005 (U.N. Doc. A/59/2005/Add.3, in particular pp. 28 and 30).

[205] These training sessions are organised twice a year and include a preliminary session held at the national level, followed by a training session in Geneva involving par-

ticipants from several countries. Participants are also granted funding so that they can attend the sessions of the treaty bodies during which their national report is examined.

[206] A first pilot workshop, which focused on the implementation of the concluding observations adopted by HRC, was held in Quito in 2002. It was followed by two workshops on the implementation of the concluding observations of CRC/C, held in Damascus (2003) and Bangkok (2004). A similar workshop, which focused on all treaty bodies, was held in Guatemala (2004), another one in Sri Lanka in May 2005. In December 2005, the first workshop on follow-up to concluding observations of CERD and CEDAW will be held in Cairo (Egypt) for six States of the sub-region.

[207] Article 14 of the Convention only refers to the fact that 'the Committee shall forward its suggestions and recommendations, if any, to the State party concerned' but does not include any provisions concerning the action to be taken by the State.

[208] For the text of the amendment to Rule 95 of the Rules of Procedure, see U.N. Doc. A/60/18, Annex IV.

racial equality mainly lie in the lack of political will, weak legislation and lack of implementation strategies and concrete action by States'.[209] In the views which it conveyed in 2004 on the implementation and effectiveness of the Convention to the third session of the Intergovernmental Working Group on the Effective Implementation of the Durban Declaration and Programme of Action, CERD fully agreed with this observation and stressed that:

> As is the case with all international normative standards, the Convention is very useful and effective for States that genuinely wish to abide by it. The Convention has helped to improve the situation in many countries. Where it has failed, it is because the necessary political will is lacking in the State concerned.[210]

[209] Durban Declaration, adopted at the end of the World Conference against Racial Discrimination, Racism, Xenophobia and Related Intolerance, para. 79.

[210] U.N. Doc. E/CN.4/2004/WG.21/10, para. 2.

25

Human Rights Committee

Not Only a Committee on Civil and Political Rights
Martin Scheinin*

1. INTRODUCTION

There is no water-tight division between different categories of human rights. In particular, it is important to note that although the project of transforming the 1948 Universal Declaration of Human Rights into treaty form culminated in separate Covenants including, on the one hand, civil and political Rights and, on the other hand, economic, social and cultural Rights, it did not result in complete compartmentalisation of those two categories of human rights. On the contrary, there is both interdependence between different human rights and direct overlap between the two Covenants.[1]

The operation of the Human Rights Committee, the expert body established under the Covenant on Civil and Political Rights ('ICCPR'),[2] has provided ample evidence of such interdependence and overlap. The International Covenant on Civil and Political Rights is not a treaty on economic, social and cultural rights but neither is it a treaty solely on civil and political rights. There is considerable similarity between the two Covenants of 1966, so that for instance ICCPR Articles 1 (self-determination), 18 (freedom of thought, conscience and religion, including in the domain of education), 22 (freedom of association, including the right to join and form trade unions) and 27 (minority rights, including the right to enjoy one's own culture) even textually refer to economic, social or cultural rights. In addition, the freestanding non-discrimination provision in Article 26 opens up possibilities for claims related to social security benefits and many other economic, social and cultural rights. Furthermore, important dimensions of economic, social or cultural rights have been articulated and adjudicated through other provisions of the ICCPR, such as Article 6 on the right to life, Article 7 on the prohibition against torture and other inhuman treatment, Article 10 on the treatment of detainees and Article 17 on the right to privacy, family and home.

This chapter provides an overview of the jurisprudence of the Human Rights Committee through which it has, under the provisions of the ICCPR, in substance addressed issues pertaining to economic, social and cultural rights, particularly through its individual complaints procedure.[3]

---

* Professor of Public International Law at the European University Institute in Florence.

[1] For a deeper conceptual analysis of justiciability in the context of the indivisibility of human rights, see M. Scheinin, 'Justiciability and the Indivisibility of Human Rights', in J. Squires, M. Langford and B. Thiele (eds.), *The Road to a Remedy: Current Issues in the Litigation of Economic, Social and Cultural Rights* (Australian Human Rights Centre, The University of New South Wales with Centre on Housing Rights and Eviction, Distributed by UNSW Press, 2005), pp. 17–26.

[2] The Committee is entrusted with the oversight of the ICCPR and is composed of 18 independent experts who are elected on the basis of expertise, not their nationality. The Committee has four main functions: (a) to review implementation of the rights contained in the ICCPR by considering periodic reports from States parties; (b) to issue General Comments that give guidance in the interpretation of the rights; (c) to consider inter-State complaints, i.e., complaints lodged by one State party against another State party (there have been none to date); and (d) to consider communications (i.e., complaints) from individuals submitted under the first Optional Protocol procedure.

[3] Individual communications to the Committee can be made against those States parties to the ICCPR which have ratified the Optional Protocol to the International Covenant on Civil and Political Rights (1966). As at 6 December 2006, 109 of the 160 States parties to the Covenant had accepted the complaint procedure. However, there are strict admissibility criteria for making a complaint, including exhaustion of domestic remedies (see articles 1–5 of the Optional Protocol, available at <http://www.ohchr.org/english/law/ccpr-one.htm>). For commentary on the operation of the mechanism, see Manfred Nowak, *U.N. Covenant on Civil and Political*

2. A SURVEY OF THE COMMITTEE'S JURISPRUDENCE ON ECONOMIC, SOCIAL AND CULTURAL RIGHTS

2.1 The Right to Social Security

The freestanding provision on equality and non-discrimination in Article 26 of the ICCPR is generally known as the principal opening for economic and social rights claims within the ICCPR framework:

> All persons are equal before the law and are entitled without any discrimination to the equal protection of the law. In this respect, the law shall prohibit any discrimination and guarantee to all persons equal and effective protection against discrimination on any ground such as race, colour, sex, language, religion, political or other opinion, national or social origin, property, birth or other status.

In contrast to many other human rights treaties, the provision does not prohibit discrimination merely in the enjoyment of rights otherwise protected under the treaty but *any* discrimination. In more recent jurisprudence, the right to equality has also obtained independent meaning beyond situations of discrimination.

In 1987, the Human Rights Committee decided three cases from the Netherlands, addressing claims about discrimination in the application of certain social security schemes. In two of the cases, *Zwaan – de Vries*[4] and *Broeks*,[5] the Committee found a violation of Article 26, when a married woman was entitled to unemployment benefits only if she proved that she was the breadwinner of the family, while neither unmarried women nor married or unmarried men had to meet such a condition. Before assessing whether the denial of unemployment benefits to Mrs Zwaan – de Vries amounted to discrimination[6] on the basis of sex, the Committee confirmed the freestanding nature of Article 26 and hence its applicability to discrimination in the field of social and economic rights. In

addressing the State party's argument to the contrary, the Committee reasoned:

> 12.2 The Committee has also examined the contention of the State party that article 26 of the International Covenant on Civil and Political Rights cannot be invoked in respect of a right which is specifically provided for under article 9 of the International Covenant on Economic, Social and Cultural Rights (social security, including social insurance). In so doing, the Committee has perused the relevant *travaux preparatoires* of the International Covenant on Civil and Political Rights.... The discussions, at the time of drafting, concerning the question whether the scope of article 26 extended to rights not otherwise guaranteed by the Covenant, were inconclusive and cannot alter the conclusion arrived at by the ordinary means of interpretation referred to in paragraph 12.3 below.

> 12.3 For the purpose of determining the scope of article 26, the Committee has taken into account the 'ordinary meaning' of each element of the article in its context and in the light of its object and purpose (art. 31 of the Vienna Convention on the Law of Treaties). The Committee begins by noting that article 26 does not merely duplicate the guarantees already provided for in article 2. It derives from the principle of equal protection of the law without discrimination, as contained in article 7 of the Universal Declaration of Human Rights, which prohibits discrimination in law or in practice in any field regulated and protected by public authorities. Article 26 is thus concerned with the obligations imposed on States in regard to their legislation and the application thereof.

> 12.4 Although article 26 requires that legislation should prohibit discrimination, it does not of itself contain any obligation with respect to the matters that may be provided for by legislation. Thus it does not, for example, require any State to enact legislation to provide for social security. However, when such legislation is adopted in the exercise of a State's sovereign power, then such legislation must comply with article 26 of the Covenant.

> 12.5 The Committee observes in this connection that what is at issue is not whether or not social security should be progressively established in the Netherlands but whether the

---

Rights, *CCPR Commentary,* 2nd edition (Kehl: N.P. Engel, 2005).

[4] *Zwaan – de Vries v. the Netherlands* (Communication No. 182/1984), Views of 9 April 1987.

[5] *Broeks v. the Netherlands* (Communication No. 172/1984), Views of 9 April 1987.

[6] *Zwaan – de Vries* (n. 4 above), para. 15.

legislation providing for social security violates the prohibition against discrimination contained in article 26 of the International Covenant on Civil and Political Rights and the guarantee given therein to all persons regarding equal and effective protection against discrimination.

These carefully formulated arguments built a position that the Committee has since maintained. Article 26 of the ICCPR does not establish any obligation to provide social security, or in respect of the level of social security. However, if and when States establish schemes of social security, any allegations of discrimination within them can be addressed by the Committee under Article 26.

The Committee's position on Article 26, that it constitutes a freestanding right to non-discrimination, was later affirmed in a general form in its 1989 General Comment No. 18 on non-discrimination:

> In the view of the Committee, article 26 does not merely duplicate the guarantee already provided for in article 2 but provides in itself an autonomous right. It prohibits discrimination in law or in fact in any field regulated and protected by public authorities. Article 26 is therefore concerned with the obligations imposed on States parties in regard to their legislation and the application thereof. Thus, when legislation is adopted by a State party, it must comply with the requirement of article 26 that its content should not be discriminatory. In other words, the application of the principle of non-discrimination contained in article 26 is not limited to those rights which are provided for in the Covenant.[7]

A third Dutch case was also decided at the time of *Zwaan – de Vries* and *Broeks*. In *Danning*,[8] a different social security benefit and a different alleged ground of discrimination were considered. Mr Danning, a person using a wheelchair, was cohabiting with a woman and had been denied cer-

tain social security entitlements that were available to married couples. The Committee took the view that a differentiation between married and unmarried couples did not constitute discrimination because the decision to marry or not to marry, with all benefits and responsibilities that follow, lies entirely with the cohabiting persons:

> 14...In the light of the explanations given by the State party with respect to the differences made by Netherlands legislation between married and unmarried couples..., the Committee is persuaded that the differentiation complained of by Mr. Danning is based on objective and reasonable criteria. The Committee observes, in this connection, that the decision to enter into a legal status by marriage, which provides, in Netherlands law, both for certain benefits and for certain duties and responsibilities, lies entirely with the cohabiting persons. By choosing not to enter into marriage, Mr. Danning and his cohabitant have not, in law, assumed the full extent of the duties and responsibilities incumbent on married couples. Consequently, Mr. Danning does not receive the full benefits provided for in Netherlands law for married couples. The Committee concludes that the differentiation complained of by Mr. Danning does not constitute discrimination, in the sense of article 26 of the Covenant.

In the subsequent case of *Gueye at al.*,[9] which involved 743 retired soldiers of Senegalese nationality as complainants, the Human Rights Committee established that Article 26 had extraterritorial applicability in the sense that persons affected by the laws of a State party could claim protection under the provision although physically situated abroad. Holding that nationality fell under 'other status' as a prohibited ground of discrimination under Article 26,[10] the Committee concluded that

---

[7] Human Rights Committee, *General Comment No. 18 (27)*, reproduced in UN document HRI/GEN/1/Rev.8/Add.1 (2006). See, para. 12.

[8] *L.G. Danning v. the Netherlands* (Communication No. 180/1984), Views adopted 9 April 1987, Report of the Human Rights Committee, GAOR, Forty-second Session, Suppl. No. 40 (A/42/40), pp. 151–159. See, in particular, para. 14 of the Views.

[9] *Gueye et al. v. France* (Communication No. 196/1985), Views of 3 April 1989.

[10] 'The Committee recalls that the authors are not generally subject to French jurisdiction, except that they rely on French legislation in relation to the amount of their pension rights. It notes that nationality as such does not figure among the prohibited grounds of discrimination listed in Article 26, and that the Covenant does not protect the right to a pension, as such. Under Article 26, discrimination in the equal protection of the law is prohibited on any grounds such as race, colour, sex, language, religion, political or other opinion, national or

France had violated Article 26 by providing different pension benefits for retired soldiers of its armed forces, depending on whether they were French citizens or not:

> In determining whether the treatment of the authors is based on reasonable and objective criteria, the Committee notes that it was not the question of nationality which determined the granting of pensions to the authors but the services rendered by them in the past. They had served in the French Armed Forces under the same conditions as French citizens; for 14 years subsequent to the independence of Senegal they were treated in the same way as their French counterparts for the purpose of pension rights, although their nationality was not French but Senegalese. A subsequent change in nationality cannot by itself be considered as a sufficient justification for different treatment, since the basis for the grant of the pension was the same service which both they and the soldiers who remained French had provided. Nor can differences in the economic, financial and social conditions as between France and Senegal be invoked as a legitimate justification. If one compared the case of retired soldiers of Senegalese nationality living in Senegal with that of retired soldiers of French nationality in Senegal, it would appear that they enjoy the same economic and social conditions. Yet, their treatment for the purpose of pension entitlements would differ. Finally, the fact that the State party claims that it can no longer carry out checks of identity and family situation, so as to prevent abuses in the administration of pension schemes cannot justify a difference in treatment. In the Committee's opinion, mere administrative inconvenience or the possibility of some abuse of pension rights cannot be invoked to justify unequal treatment. The Committee concludes that the difference in treatment of the authors is not based on reasonable and objective criteria and constituted discrimination prohibited by the Covenant. [Para 9.5]

social origin, property, birth or other status. There has been a differentiation by reference to nationality acquired upon independence. In the Committee's opinion, this falls within the reference to "other status" in the second sentence of Article 26. Ibid. para. 9.4

The *Gueye* case remains important, as it established the principle that States parties are not allowed to discriminate against non-nationals in social security arrangements. However, the later case of *van Oord*, related to differences in bilateral social security agreements concluded by the Netherlands with other countries, indicates that bilateral treaties based on reciprocity between states may justify certain differences in pension entitlements. The 2002 case of *Karakurt*, which was about the eligibility of non-EU nationals to workers' councils, shows though that the force of the reciprocity argument has its limits as justification for a differentiation based on nationality and the main rule of nationality-based distinctions being prohibited remains valid.[11]

In some of its more recent cases, the Committee has explicitly confirmed that also indirect discrimination is prohibited under Article 26. However, as demonstrated by *Danning* above, the Committee does not treat as discriminatory differentiations that are based on reasonable and objective criteria and do not have disproportionate effects.

In *Althammer*, the claim was that a change in a pension scheme to provide better benefits for employees with children while abolishing a household benefit related to the existence of a dependent spouse amounted to discrimination against retired persons, as compared to active employees who were more likely to have children of relevant age (under twenty-seven years). The Committee stated that a violation of Article 26 can also result from indirect discrimination, i.e., 'the discriminatory effect of a rule or measure that is neutral at face value or without intent to discriminate'. Prohibited indirect discrimination would be at issue if 'the detrimental effects of a rule or decision exclusively or disproportionately affect persons having a particular race, colour, sex, language, religion, political or other opinion, national or social origin, property, birth or other status' and was not based

---

[11] *Jacob and Jantina Hendrika van Oord v. The Netherlands* (Communication No. 658/1995), Decision on admissibility adopted 23 July 1997, Report of the Human Rights Committee, Vol. II, GAOR, Fifty-second Session, Suppl. No. 40 (A/52/40), pp. 311–316. *Mümtaz Karakurt v. Austria* (Communication No. 965/2000), Views adopted 4 April 2002, Report of the Human Rights Committee, Vol. II, GAOR, Fifty-seventh Session, Suppl. No. 40 (A/57/40 (Vol. II)), pp. 304–311.

on objective and reasonable grounds.[12] In the view of the Committee, these conditions were not met and there was no violation of Article 26.

In the case of *Derksen and Bakker*, however, a violation of Article 26 was found through a similar characterisation of indirect discrimination.[13] Ms Derksen had been cohabiting with Mr Bakker but was after the latter's death denied a survivor's pension for their daughter Katja Bakker. Although the Netherlands had through legislation remedied the unequal treatment of children born within and outside marriage in respect of pension benefits, the change affected only children who were born after the entry into force of the new law. The Committee concluded:

> The Committee recalls that article 26 prohibits both direct and indirect discrimination, the latter notion being related to a rule or measure that may be neutral on its face without any intent to discriminate but which nevertheless results in discrimination because of its exclusive or disproportionate adverse effect on a certain category of persons. Yet, a distinction only constitutes prohibited discrimination in the meaning of article 26 of the Covenant if it is not based on objective and reasonable criteria.... The Committee considers that the distinction between children born, on the one hand, either in wedlock or after 1 July 1996 out of wedlock, and, on the other hand, out of wedlock prior to 1 July 1996, is not based on reasonable grounds...[14]

In another, more recent stream of jurisprudence, the Human Rights Committee has held that Article 23 of the ICCPR does not require the recognition of same-sex unions as marriage,[15] but has nevertheless found a violation of Article 26 in *Young* v. *Australia*, a case involving the denial of a survivor's pension to a same-sex partner of a war veteran.[16] This conclusion in the case of *Young* was based on the following factors, which demonstrate the Committee's quest for consistency in

its jurisprudence. First, in the earlier *Toonen* case concerning severe criminal penalties for homosexual conduct between consenting adults, the Committee had stated that distinctions based on sexual orientation fall under the notion of 'sex' in the ICCPR.[17] Second, in *Danning*, the Committee had argued that differential social security entitlements for married and unmarried heterosexual couples were justified on the basis that the latter have freedom of choice when deciding whether or not to marry. Third, under Australian law, *same-sex* partners such as Mr. Young and his partner who was a war veteran, did not have the possibility to formalise their relationship as marriage, and the Committee had, in the case of *Joslin* involving New Zealand, held that such recognition is not required by the Covenant. Fourthly and finally, Australia had extended survivor's pension benefits to unmarried partners of war veterans but only if they were of the opposite sex than that of the veteran. The Veteran's Entitlement Act provided that individuals who are part of a married couple or of a heterosexual cohabiting couple (who can prove that they are in a 'marriage-like' relationship) fulfil the definition of 'member of a couple' under the legislation, and are therefore a 'dependent' who is entitled to receive pension benefits.

Against this background of factual elements and earlier case law, it flows logically that the Committee concluded in *Young* (footnotes omitted):

> 10.4 The Committee recalls its earlier jurisprudence that the prohibition against discrimination under article 26 comprises also discrimination based on sexual orientation. It recalls that in previous communications the Committee found that differences in the receipt of benefits between married couples and heterosexual unmarried couples were reasonable and objective, as the couples in question had the choice to marry with all the entailing consequences. It transpires from the contested sections of the VEA that individuals who are part of a married couple or of a heterosexual cohabiting couple (who can prove that they are in a "marriage-like" relationship) fulfill the definition of "member of a couple" and therefore of a "dependent", for the purpose of receiving pension

---

[12] *Rupert Althammer et al. v. Austria* (Communication No. 998/2001), Views of 8 August 2003, paragraph 10.2.

[13] *Derksen and Bakker v. the Netherlands* (Communication No. 976/2001), Views of 1 April 2004.

[14] *Derksen and Bakker v. the Netherlands* (n. 13 above), para. 9.3.

[15] *Juliet Joslin et al. v. New Zealand* (Communication No. 902/1999), Views of 17 July 2002, para. 8.2.

[16] *Edward Young v. Australia* (Communication No. 941/2000), Views of 6 August 2003.

[17] *Nicholas Toonen v. Australia* (Communication No. 488/1992), Views adopted on 31 March 1994.

benefits. In the instant case, it is clear that the author, as a same sex partner, did not have the possibility of entering into marriage. Neither was he recognized as a cohabiting partner of Mr. C, for the purpose of receiving pension benefits, because of his sex or sexual orientation. The Committee recalls its constant jurisprudence that not every distinction amounts to prohibited discrimination under the Covenant, as long as it is based on reasonable and objective criteria. The State party provides no arguments on how this distinction between same-sex partners, who are excluded from pension benefits under law, and unmarried heterosexual partners, who are granted such benefits, is reasonable and objective, and no evidence which would point to the existence of factors justifying such a distinction has been advanced. In this context, the Committee finds that the State party has violated article 26 of the Covenant by denying the author a pension on the basis of his sex or sexual orientation.

2.2   The Right to Work

In the case of *Love et al.* the Committee addressed the question whether distinctions based on age – a characteristic not explicitly mentioned in the non-exhaustive list of prohibited grounds of discrimination in Article 26 – may amount to prohibited discrimination under Article 26. Answering in principle in the affirmative, the Committee held that sufficient objective and reasonable grounds existed for upholding the mandatory retirement age of sixty for airline pilots. In arriving at this conclusion the Committee did not exclude age discrimination from the scope of Article 26 or generally declare mandatory retirement age as non-discriminatory:

8.2 ... While age as such is not mentioned as one of the enumerated grounds of prohibited discrimination in the second sentence of article 26, the Committee takes the view that a distinction related to age which is not based on reasonable and objective criteria may amount to discrimination on the ground of "other status" under the clause in question, or to a denial of the equal protection of the law within the meaning of the first sentence of article 26. How-

ever, it is by no means clear that mandatory retirement age would generally constitute age discrimination. The Committee takes note of the fact that systems of mandatory retirement age may include a dimension of workers' protection by limiting the life-long working time, in particular when there are comprehensive social security schemes that secure the subsistence of persons who have reached such an age. Furthermore, reasons related to employment policy may be behind legislation or policy on mandatory retirement age. The Committee notes that while the International Labour Organisation has built up an elaborate regime of protection against discrimination in employment, mandatory retirement age does not appear to be prohibited in any of the ILO Conventions. These considerations will of course not absolve the Committee's task of assessing under article 26 of the Covenant whether any particular arrangement for mandatory retirement age is discriminatory.

8.3   In the present case, as the State party notes, the aim of maximising safety to passengers, crew and persons otherwise affected by flight travel was a legitimate aim under the Covenant. As to the reasonable and objective nature of the distinction made on the basis of age, the Committee takes into account the widespread national and international practice, at the time of the author's dismissals, of imposing a mandatory retirement age of 60. In order to justify the practice of dismissals maintained at the relevant time, the State party has referred to the ICAO regime which was aimed at, and understood as, maximising flight safety. In the circumstances, the Committee cannot conclude that the distinction made was not, at the time of Mr Love's dismissal, based on objective and reasonable considerations. Consequently, the Committee is of the view that it cannot establish a violation of article 26.[18]

As the right to work also includes the liberty to choose one's work or occupation, it is relevant for the protection of this right that the ICCPR includes in Article 8 a prohibition against forced labour. So far, the case law by the Committee has remained

[18] *John K. Love, William L. Bone, William J. Craig, and Peter B. Ivanoff v. Australia* (Communication No. 983/2001), Views of 25 March 2003.

very limited. In *Faure*, the Committee addressed the issue of whether the requirement of performing labour in exchange for unemployment benefits was contrary to Article 8. In the absence of a degrading or dehumanising aspect of the specific labour performed, the Committee held that the labour in question did not fall under the scope of the proscriptions set out in Article 8. However, as the Committee considered that the author had presented an arguable claim of a breach of Article 8 and there was no domestic remedy available to pursue that claim, there had been a violation of the right to an effective remedy under Article 2(3), read in conjunction with Article 8.[19]

Reference can also be made to one inadmissibility decision concerning a claim that the taxation imposed on legal aid lawyers recruited from abroad turned their work into prohibited forced labour.[20]

2.3   The Right to Form and Join Trade Unions, Including the Right to Strike

Article 22 of the ICCPR represents considerable overlap with Article 8 of the twin International Covenant on Economic, Social and Cultural Rights, as the ICCPR provision on freedom of assembly explicitly includes 'the right to form and join trade unions for the protection of his interests' and as paragraph 3 of the provision makes reference to International Labour Organisation Convention No. 87 of 1948 concerning Freedom of Association and Protection of the Right to Organize.

Despite this overlap, the Human Rights Committee in the fairly early case of *J.B. et al. v. Canada* interpreted that Article 22 does not afford protection to the right to strike. Basing itself on the fact that Article 8 of the ICESCR explicitly refers to the right to strike as an element of trade union rights, the Committee held that such a right could not

be inferred from the right to form and join trade unions as protected by Article 22 of the ICCPR.[21]

Five Committee members dissented, and the Committee's subsequent practice under the reporting procedure indicates that the *J.B.* case may not be authoritative. For instance, in its Concluding Observations on Chile (1999) the Committee held that a general prohibition imposed on the right of civil servants to organise a trade union and bargain collectively, 'as well as their right to strike', raised serious concerns under Article 22 of the Covenant.[22]

2.4   The Right to Education

Turning to the right to education, while the ICCPR does not include a comprehensive clause on this right, Article 18(4) provides for a right of parents and, when applicable, legal guardians to ensure the religious and moral education of their children in conformity with their own convictions. Also other provisions in Article 18, as well as Article 26 on non-discrimination, have proven applicable in the educational context.

In the *Hartikainen* case, the Committee held that providing instruction in religious matters within the public school curriculum is not in itself incompatible with Article 18(4) if an alternative course of instruction was available for students whose parents or guardians objected to religious instruction and that alternative course was given in a neutral and objective way and respected the convictions of the families in question.[23] Later on, the same approach was applied in the case of *Leirvåg*, resulting in a finding of violation of Article 18(4) since the available scheme of exemptions, as it was implemented in the authors' cases, was not extensive enough to accommodate the convictions of non-religious families.[24]

---

[19] *Bernadette Faure v. Australia* (Communication No. 1036/2001), Views of 31 October 2005.

[20] *Welvidanelage Don Hugh Joseph Francis Silva* (Communication No. 825/1998), *Don Clarence Godwin* (Communication No. 826/1998), *Sunil Randombage de Silva* (Communication No. 827/1998) and *T.J.A. Perera* (Communication No. 828/1998) *v. Zambia*, joint admissibility decision of 25 July 2002.

[21] *J.B. et al. v. Canada* (Communication 118/1982), Decision on admissibility of 18 July 1986. For discussion of ILO Convention No. 87 and the right to strike, see chapter 28 in this volume.

[22] *Concluding Observations on Chile* (CCPR/C/79/Add.104), paragraph 25.

[23] *Erkki Juhani Hartikainen et al. v. Finland* (Communication No. 40/1978), Views of 9 April 1981, paragraph 10.4.

[24] *Unn Leirvåg et al. v. Norway* (Communication No. 1155/2003), Views of 3 November 2004, paragraph 14.7.

In the case of *Blom,* the Committee took the view that when a State party's educational system provides for both private and public education, the State party cannot be deemed to act in a discriminatory fashion if it does not provide the same level of subsidy for the two types of establishments, when the private system is not subject to state supervision.[25] However, in the *Waldman* case it was held to constitute discrimination that a State party funded religious education for one minority but not for other minorities in a comparable situation. The case originated from the province of Ontario where, as a result of a constitutional compromise in the nineteenth century, Roman Catholic schools were maintained and funded as a part of the public education system, parallel to secular schools. No comparable arrangement existed, however, to facilitate or fund religious education to other minorities. In *Waldman,* the Committee found a violation of Article 26 as the complainant, a Jewish father, had to fund the private religious education of his children. The Committee's conclusion of discrimination was based on the following argument:

10.6...In this context, the Committee observes that the Covenant does not oblige States parties to fund schools which are established on a religious basis. However, if a State party chooses to provide public funding to religious schools, it should make this funding available without discrimination. This means that providing funding for the schools of one religious group and not for another must be based on reasonable and objective criteria. In the instant case, the Committee concludes that the material before it does not show that the differential treatment between the Roman Catholic faith and the author's religious denomination is based on such criteria. Consequently, there has been a violation of the author's rights under article 26 of the Covenant to equal and effective protection against discrimination. [26]

Finally, in the *Hudyoberganova* case a violation of Article 18(2) was found as the Committee held that the expulsion of a student from university due to her refusal to take off an Islamic headscarf amounted to prohibited compulsion in the meaning of the provision.[27]

2.5 The Right to Housing

In its concluding observations on periodic reports by States, the Committee has addressed a number of aspects of the right to housing. Article 6 on the right to life gave rise to such a finding when the Committee considered a periodic report by Canada in 1999. The Committee expressed its concern that 'homelessness has led to serious health problems and even to death', and recommended that Canada take 'positive measures required by Article 6 to address this serious problem'.[28] In 2005, the Committee criticised Kenya for the practice of forced evictions, drawing on the right to privacy and protection of the home:

While noting the delegation's explanations on the issue, the Committee remains concerned about reports of the forcible eviction of thousands of inhabitants from so-called informal settlements, both in Nairobi and other parts of the country, without prior consultation with the populations concerned and/or without adequate prior notification. This practice arbitrarily interferes with the Covenant rights of the victims of such evictions, especially their rights under article 17 of the Covenant.

The Committee recommended, in terms not dissimilar to the Committee on Economic, Social and Cultural Rights General Comment No. 7 on Forced Evictions,[29] that:

The State party should develop transparent policies and procedures for dealing with evictions and ensure that evictions from settlements do not occur unless those affected have been consulted and appropriate resettlement arrangements have been made.[30]

[25] *Carl Henrik Blom v. Sweden,* Views of 4 April 1988, (Communication No. 191/1985), paragraph 10.3.

[26] *Arieh Hollis Waldman v. Canada* (Communication No. 694/1996), Views of 3 November 1999.

[27] *Raihon Hudoyberganova v. Uzbekistan* (Communication No. 931/2000), Views of 5 November 2004, paragraph 6.2.

[28] *Concluding Observations on Canada,* U.N. Doc. CCPR/C/79/Add. 105, paragraph 12.

[29] See discussion in M. Langford and J. du Plessis, *Dignity in the Rubble? Forced Evictions and Human Rights Law,* COHRE Working Paper, June 2005, available at <http://www.cohre.org/kenya>.

[30] *Concluding Observations of the Human Rights Committee: Kenya,* 28 March 2005, U.N. Doc. CCPR/CO/83/KEN.

2.6 The Right to Health

The Human Rights Committee has adopted a broad understanding of State obligations under the right to life. Hence, many dimensions of the right to health may be addressed under Article 6 of the ICCPR. For instance, in its first General Comment on Article 6 adopted in 1982, the Committee points out that the right to life should not be understood narrowly. It requires also positive measures, inter alia, 'to reduce infant mortality and to increase life expectancy, especially in adopting measures to eliminate malnutrition and epidemics'.[31]

There is no case law under the Optional Protocol addressing these broad dimensions of the right to health under the right to life provision in the ICCPR. However, in the more specific context of how a State treats persons it keeps deprived of their liberty, health issues have been adjudicated and assessed. For instance, in the case of *Lantsov*, a violation of Article 6 was established when a person died of pneumonia after one month in pre-trial detention under deplorable conditions, and the State party had not taken appropriate measures to provide medical treatment to the person who was held by the authorities.[32] The case has wide ramifications in respect of prison conditions that entail the subjection of inmates to tuberculosis and other contagious diseases.

In the case of *Mukong*, the Committee explicitly addressed the question whether a country's level of economic development provides an excuse for not complying with international standards in respect of the health and well-being of prisoners:

> 9.3 As to the conditions of detention in general, the Committee observes that certain minimum standards regarding the conditions of detention must be observed regardless of a State party's level of development. These include, in accordance with rules 10, 12, 17, 19 and 20 of the Standard Minimum Rules for the Treatment of Prisoners, minimum floor space and cubic content of air for each prisoner, adequate sanitary facilities, clothing which

shall be in no manner degrading or humiliating, provision of a separate bed and provision of food of nutritional value adequate for health and strength. It should be noted that these are minimum requirements which the Committee considers should always be observed, even if economic or budgetary considerations may make compliance with these obligations difficult. It transpires from the file that these requirements were not met during the author's detention in the summer of 1988 and in February/March 1990.[33]

Furthermore, the Committee has addressed as violations of either Article 7 (prohibition against torture or other inhuman treatment) or Article 10 (humane treatment of detainees) measures such as the deliberate denial to a detainee of medically assessed treatment and medication,[34] destroying the prisoner's medication,[35] the denial to a prisoner of his medical records,[36] as well as the removal of a schizophrenic person to a country where he would not get appropriate treatment and medication.[37]

2.7 Reproductive Rights

The Committee's leading case in the field of reproductive rights is *K.N.L.H. v. Peru* which related to the denial of an abortion to a minor whose pregnancy exposed her to a life-threatening risk known to the authorities, and compelled her to go through the pregnancy despite a known lethal disability of the foetus.[38] In the extreme circumstances of the case, the Committee concluded that the denial of abortion to the author amounted to a violation of Article 7 (prohibition against torture and other inhuman treatment). It may be of even broader significance that the Committee also found a violation of Article 17 (right to privacy and family life), albeit with the qualification that the

---

[31] *Human Rights Committee, General Comment No. 6 (16)*, UN doc. HRI/GEN/1/Rev.8, para. 5.

[32] *Yekaterina Pavlovna Lantsova, on behalf of her son, Vladimir Albertovich Lantsov, v. the Russian Federation* (Communication No. 763/1997), Views of 26 March 2002.

[33] *Albert Womah Mukong v. Cameroon* (Communication No. 458/1991), Views of 21 July 1994 (footnote omitted).

[34] *Uton Lewis v. Jamaica* (Communication No. 527/1993), Views of 18 July 1996.

[35] *Christopher Brown v. Jamaica* (Communication 775/1997), Views of 23 March 1999.

[36] *Alexander Zheludkov v. Ukraine* (Communication No. 726/1996), Views of 29 October 2002.

[37] *C. v. Australia* (Communication No. 900/1999), Views of 28 October 2002.

[38] *K.N.L.H. v. Peru*, Communication No. 1153/2003.

abortion would have been lawful under the State party's own law.

2.8 The Right to Property

As is well known, although the Universal Declaration of Human Rights includes a provision on the right to property,[39] in the drafting of the two Covenants during the Cold War era this economic right fell between the cracks and ended up without recognition. It does not come as a surprise that under the ICCPR it has been mainly the non-discrimination clause in Article 26 that has served the function of providing indirect protection to the right to property. Above, reference was already made to the case of *Ato del Avellanal v. Peru* which was about the right of a married woman to appear as a party in a legal dispute before a court in respect of her own property, instead of having to be represented by her husband.

A line of cases relates to property restitution schemes introduced by some of the countries of the former socialist block of Eastern Europe as they moved to a market economy system. Many of the laws, with varying levels of success, have tried to maintain a balance between achieving justice for the victims of Communist confiscation policies and minimising instability, and have therefore contained conditions or qualifications that many have experienced as discriminatory.[40]

In *Simunek*, the Human Rights Committee established that the double requirement of citizenship and permanent residence in the Czech restitution law was a discriminatory provision and amounted to a violation of the ICCPR Article 26.[41] However, in the cases of *Drobek*,[42] *Schlosser*[43] and *Malik*,[44]

the Committee held that the mere fact that a State does not extend the scheme to confiscations by earlier regimes, when legislatively creating property restitution schemes to the benefit of the victims of a past (communist) regime, does not constitute prohibited discrimination.

In some of its later cases related to property restitution, the Committee has broadened its approach in respect of the prohibition against discrimination, not necessarily requiring that the author demonstrate different treatment compared to a comparator. In the case of *Pezoldova*, the Committee established a violation of Article 26 because of the arbitrary way in which Czech authorities had denied the access of the author to documents through which she sought to argue her restitution claim, thus frustrating her access to an effective remedy.[45] The Committee's position can be interpreted as holding arbitrariness as a form of discrimination, even in the absence of a comparator. In the case of *Des Fours Walderode*, a violation of Article 26 was found due to the enactment of a law of with retroactive effect, frustrating the author's ongoing restitution proceedings. In the Committee's words:

> This raises an issue of arbitrariness and, consequently, of a breach of the right to equality before the law, equal protection of the law and non-discrimination under article 26 of the Covenant.[46]

2.9 The Right to Culture

Article 27 on minority rights represents an explicit extension by the ICCPR into the field of economic, social or cultural rights. That clause includes, for members of minorities, a right to 'enjoy their own *culture*' in community with other members of the group. In a line of cases, the Human Rights Committee has applied Article 27 and the notion of culture for the protection of a traditional or otherwise typical way of life of an indigenous people or other distinctive community, including the *material* basis for their lifestyle. Hunting, fishing and semi-nomadic reindeer herding are among such

---

[39] Article 17.
[40] For a comparison of the approaches taken by the Human Rights Committee and the European Court of Human Rights in respect of property restitution claims, see P. Macklem, 'Rybná 9, Praha 1: Restitution and Memory in International Human Rights Law', *European Journal of International Law*, Vol. 16 (2005), pp. 1–23.
[41] *Simunek et al. v. the Czech Republic* (Communication No. 516/1992). Views of 19 July 1995. See, also, *Adam v. the Czech Republic* (Communication No. 586/1994), Views of 23 July 1996.
[42] *Drobek v. Slovakia* (Communication No. 643/1995), Views of 14 July 1997.
[43] *Schlosser v. the Czech Republic* (Communication No. 670/1995), Views of 3 November 1998.
[44] *Malik v. the Czech Republic* (Communication No. 669/1995), Views of 3 November 1998.

[45] *Alzbeta Pezoldova v. the Czech Republic* (Communication No. 757/1997), Views of 25 October 2002.
[46] *Karel Des Fours Walderode v. the Czech Republic* (Communication No. 747/1997), Views of 30 October 2001, paragraph 8.3.

activities that require the use of lands and natural resources of a particular area and have constitutive importance for the preservation of a particular way of life of a community. In its General Comment on article 27, the Committee expressed its position as to what the notion of 'culture' means in the provision:

> With regard to the exercise of the cultural rights protected under article 27, the Committee observes that culture manifests itself in many forms, including a particular way of life associated with the use of land resources, especially in the case of indigenous peoples. That right may include such traditional activities as fishing or hunting and the right to live in reserves protected by law. The enjoyment of those rights may require positive legal measures of protection and measures to ensure the effective participation of members of minority communities in decisions which affect them.[47]

As the present author has extensively discussed the Committee's jurisprudence under Article 27 elsewhere,[48] it suffices here to highlight only some of the most important aspects of that case law.

In the *Ominayak (Lubicon)* case, it was established that a gradual erosion of the hunting and fishing possibilities of the Lubicon Lake Band, through oil and gas drilling, cutting of forests, construction of roads and so forth, amounted to a prohibited 'denial' of the community's right to enjoy their own culture in the meaning of Article 27.[49] The Committee has also consistently taken this position further, holding that although the wording of Article 27 is negative in respect of the right to enjoy one's culture ('...shall not be denied'), the resulting State obligations entail also *positive* measures of protection to ensure that interferences amount-

ing to 'denial' do not result from the activities of the State itself or from the side of third parties, including private corporations.[50]

In the first *Länsman* case, part of a series of cases emanating from Finland,[51] the Committee developed a combined test for assessing what kind of interferences in the unhindered use of natural resources are permissible and when they turn to prohibited 'denial'. This involved assessing whether there was effective consultation of the group and whether the measures affected the sustainability of the indigenous economy.[52] However, in the same case the Committee also confirmed that the protection as 'culture' under Article 27 is not restricted to traditional means of livelihood in their traditional form but extends also to new methods utilizing modern technology, as long as the activity in question is typical for a distinct minority community.[53] Nonetheless, no violation was found because the stone quarry approved

---

[47] Human Rights Committee, *General Comment No. 23 (50)*, reproduced in UN document HRI/GEN/1/Rev.8/Add.1 (2006), para. 7. (Footnote omitted).

[48] See, M. Scheinin, 'Indigenous Peoples' Rights under the International Covenant on Civil and Political Rights', in J. Castellino and N. Walsh (eds.), *International Law and Indigenous Peoples* (Leiden: Martinus Nijhoff Publishers, 2005), pp. 3–15; M. Scheinin, 'The Right to Enjoy a Distinct Culture: Indigenous and Competing Uses of Land', in T. S. Orlin, A. Rosas and M. Scheinin (eds.), *The Jurisprudence of Human Rights Law: A Comparative Interpretive Approach* (Turku: Institute for Human Rights, 2000), pp. 159–222.

[49] *Bernard Ominayak, Chief of the Lubicon Lake Band v. Canada* (Communication No. 167/1984), Views of 26 March 1990.

[50] Human Rights Committee, *General Comment No. 23 (50)*, reproduced in UN document HRI/GEN/1/Rev.8/Add.1 (2006). See paragraph 6.1.

[51] In *Länsman v Finland (No. 2)* (Communication No. 671/1995), Views of 30 October 1996, Sami herdsmen challenged the granting by the Forestry Board of a forestry concession in winter herding lands. These untouched forests were a rich source of lichen, a reindeer food. The Committee noted that the herdsmen were consulted on the logging plans and decided that, in the circumstances, the profitability of reindeer herding would not be affected. But they issued a strong warning to Finland that future large-scale logging and mining may violate Article 27. In 2001, the Sallivara Cooperative of Herdsmen challenged a logging concession. In cases emanating from the Kariselkä area, the herders in *Äärelä and Näkkäläjärvi v Finland* (Communication No. 779/1997), Views of 7 November 2001, had lost a much earlier case before the Committee in 1994 when the Finnish government was able to show, at a very late stage, that the dispute could be brought before national courts. In the new case initiated after unsuccessful proceedings in domestic courts the Committee decided that the domestic courts' conclusion that logging would not significantly impact reindeer herding was tainted by a procedural violation of fair trial and should be reconsidered. Also, it held that the imposition of a large legal costs award by Finland's Court of Appeal against the reindeer herdsmen was a violation of their right to a fair trial under Article 14.

[52] *Ilmari Länsman et al. v. Finland* (Communication No. 511/1992), Views of 26 October 1994.

[53] Ibid. para. 9.3: 'The right to enjoy one's culture cannot be determined in abstracto but has to be placed in context. In this connection, the Committee observes that Article 27 does not only protect traditional means of livelihood of national minorities, as indicated in the State party's submission. Therefore, that the authors may have adapted their methods of reindeer herding over the years and practice it with the help of modern technology does not prevent them from invoking Article 27 of the Covenant'.

by the National Forestry Board was adjudged to have minimum impact on herding practices, but the Committee warned against future large-scale mining and emphasised the importance of pre-consultation with Sami. They also noted that the mountain, which was partially quarried, had spiritual significance for the Sami. This case though, and the related cases from Finland, have had a remarkable impact at the national level with much stricter domestic review of consultation processes for example.[54]

In the case of *Mahuika*, the Committee applied Article 27 and the combined test of effective consultation and economic sustainability in addressing a nationwide settlement on fisheries quota management. The case demonstrated that the role of Article 27 is not restricted to 'exotic' pockets of indigenous economies but may be relevant also in areas that are of major importance for the national economy, provided an indigenous people have a special relationship to the activity in question.[55]

2.10 The Right to Self-Determination

Another area of explicit overlap with rights covered by the Covenant on Economic, Social and Cultural Rights is Article 1 of the ICCPR which is identical to Article 1 of the twin Covenant and provides for the right of all peoples to self-determination. In particular, Paragraph 2 of the provision pertains to the social and economic aspects of self-determination, as it declares for all peoples the right to 'freely dispose of their natural wealth and resources' and prohibits depriving a people 'of its own means of subsistence'.

In practice, Article 1 is often invoked by groups that claim the status of a distinct people within a State where they are in a minority situation. Often complaints submitted to the Human Rights Committee on behalf of indigenous peoples have been presented under Article 1 instead of, or in addition to, Article 27. Although the right of self-determination is a right protected under the ICCPR, the traditional approach of the Human

Rights Committee is that the provision is procedurally in a different position than other rights enshrined in the Covenant. As one of the admissibility conditions under the Optional Protocol is that the complainant is personally a victim of an alleged violation of the Covenant and as the right of self-determination is a truly collective right without individual beneficiaries, cases cannot be adjudicated before the Committee under Article 1 of the Covenant.[56] Nevertheless, Article 1, including its economic and social dimensions, can be addressed in the reporting procedure. For instance, in its consideration in 1999 of a periodic report by Canada, the Committee stated:

> …the Committee emphasizes that the right to self-determination requires, inter alia, that all peoples must be able to freely dispose of their natural wealth and resources and that they may not be deprived of their own means of subsistence (art. 1, para. 2). The Committee recommends that decisive and urgent action be taken towards the full implementation of the [Royal Commission on Aboriginal Peoples] recommendations on land and resource allocation. The Committee also recommends that the practice of extinguishing inherent aboriginal rights be abandoned as incompatible with article 1 of the Covenant.[57]

In its more recent case law the Committee has acknowledged that Article 1 may also have interpretive effect in cases adjudicated under other provisions of the Covenant through the Optional Protocol procedure for individual complaints.[58]

3. CONCLUSION

A number of general conclusions can be drawn from the case law of the Human Rights Committee. Despite its name, the ICCPR is not a treaty merely concerned with civil and political rights. Both textually and in the jurisprudence of the Human Rights Committee, there are several areas of overlap and interdependence between the ICCPR and the category of economic, social and cultural rights. Hence, a disservice is done to

---

[54] See for example, M. Scheinin, 'Covenant on Civil and Political Rights Limits Mining Activities in Sami Homelands. Finnish Supreme Administrative Court Overrules 109 Mining Claims', available at: <http://arkisto.sll.fi/tiedotus/kaivokset+saam/samirights.html>.

[55] *Apirana Mahuika et al. v. New Zealand* (Communication No. 547/1993), Views of 27 October 2000.

[56] See, inter alia, *Ominayak (Lubicon)* (n. 49, above).

[57] *Concluding Observations on Canada*, U.N. Doc. CCPR/C/79/Add.105, para. 8.

[58] See, *Mahuika* (n. 55 above) and *Marie-Hélène Gillot et al. France* (Communication No. 932/2000), Views of 15 July 2002.

the principle of interdependence and indivisibility of human rights if the Human Rights Committee is referred to as the 'committee on civil and political rights'.[59] It is also worth mentioning that Article 28(2), spelling out the required qualifications for membership on the Committee, includes 'recognized competence in the field of human rights' (instead of 'in the field of civil and political rights').

The freestanding right to equality and non-discrimination in ICCPR Article 26 is the best known and most important substantive area of human rights law where the Human Rights Committee has made a contribution in the protection of economic, social and cultural rights. At least until a complaint mechanism is operative under the Covenant on Economic, Social and Cultural Rights, it is likely that the Human Rights Committee will be the most important forum for the further evolution of jurisprudence in respect of equality and non-discrimination in the enjoyment of economic, social and cultural rights. Protocol 12 to the European Convention on Human Rights, although already in force, has been ratified by a relatively small number of European countries, and the refusal of many Western European countries to ratify this instrument is likely to slow down the emergence of substantive jurisprudence by the European Court of Human Rights.

There are many other openings for jurisprudence on economic, social and cultural rights in the practice of the Human Rights Committee. The right of members of minorities to enjoy their own culture (Article 27), trade union rights under the freedom of association (Article 22), economic and social dimensions of the right to life (Article 6) and issues related to education argued in respect of the right to thought, conscience and religion (Article 18) are only a few examples of areas where there is both existing jurisprudence and a wider potential for further evolution in respect of economic, social and cultural rights.

---

[59] Such proposals are curently being made because the replacement of the Commission on Human Rights with the Human Rights Council has created a situation that there are two bodies that use the acronym 'HRC'.

26

Committee on the Elimination of Discrimination Against Women

Women Claiming Economic, Social and Cultural Rights – The CEDAW Potential

Leilani Farha[*]

1. INTRODUCTION

[I]nternational law accords priority to civil and political rights, rights that may have very little to offer women generally. The major forms of oppression of women operate within the economic, social and cultural realms.[1]
Hilary Charlesworth, Christine Chinkin and Shelly Wright

Economic, social and cultural rights have a particular significance for women because as a group, women are disproportionately affected by poverty, and by social and cultural marginalization.[2] *Montreal Principles on Women's Economic, Social and Cultural Rights*

It is now generally recognised that economic, social and cultural rights are of particular significance to women, especially in light of women's historic and ongoing experiences of discrimination and inequality in social, economic and cultural realms.[3] What remains relatively unexplored, however, is the issue of where, within the international human rights system, women's economic, social and cultural rights are best protected and promoted. This chapter argues that while a number of international treaties may be applicable, the Convention on the Elimination of All Forms of Discrimination Against Women ('the CEDAW Convention'), which has been ratified by 182 States,[4] has the potential to be the most effective international human rights instrument for the protection and promotion of economic, social and cultural rights for women.

The chapter unfolds in two main sections. It commences with an analysis of the characteristics of the Convention that make it particularly well placed to advance women's economic, social and cultural rights claims. It highlights, for instance, the Convention's focus on women and women's real living conditions, its equality rights

---

[*] Leilani Farha (BA, MSW, LLB) is the Executive Director (Acting) at CERA – (Centre for Equality Rights in Accommodation) in Ottawa, Canada. Thanks to P. Sweeney who assisted with research for this chapter.

[1] 'Feminist Approaches to International Law', *American Journal of International Law*, Vol. 85, No. 4 (1991), pp. 613–645, at 635.

[2] Reprinted in *Human Rights Quarterly*, Vol. 26, No. 3 (2004), pp. 760–780.

[3] See United Nations Division for the Advancement of Women, Promoting women's enjoyment of their economic and social rights, Report of the Expert Group Meeting, Abo/Turku, Finland, 1–4 December 1997, UN Doc. EGM/WESR/1997/Report, para. 18; S. Day and G. Brodsky, 'Beyond the Social and Economic Rights Debate: Substantive Equality Speaks to Poverty', *Canadian Journal of Women and the Law*, Vol. 14, No. 1 (2002), pp. 185–220; D. Otto, '"Gender Comment": Why Does the UN Committee on Economic, Social and Cultural Rights Need a General Comment on Women?', *Canadian Journal of Women and the Law*, Vol. 14, No. 1 (2002), pp. 158–184; L. Farha, 'Is There a Woman in the House? Re/conceiving the Human Right to Housing', *Canadian Journal of Women and the Law*, Vol. 14, No. 1 (2002), pp. 118–136; K. Frostell and M. Scheinin, 'Women', in A. Eide, C. Krause, A. Rosas (eds.), *Economic, Social and Cultural Rights: A Textbook* (Dordrecht: Martinus Nijhoff, 2001), pp. 331–352.

[4] Division for the Advancement of Women (March 02, 2006), available at <http://www.un.org/womenwatch/daw/cedaw/states.html>. This is one of the most ratified human rights treaties within the UN System. The Convention on the Rights of the Child has been ratified by 189 states, available at <http://www.unhchr.ch/html/menu3/b/k2crc.htm>.

framework and its individual complaints mechanism. This Section is contextualised in the work of the Committee on the Elimination of Discrimination Against Women ('the CEDAW Committee'): its General Recommendations, Concluding Comments and Decisions. In some instances, the work of other treaty monitoring bodies is compared with that of the CEDAW Committee. The second part of the chapter provides an overview of the central weaknesses of the CEDAW Convention and the Committee's work in terms of protecting and promoting women's economic, social and cultural rights. Issues touched upon include the marginalisation of the CEDAW Committee, and the inherent risks in equality rights analysis. The chapter concludes with modest recommendations of how the work of the CEDAW Committee might be improved to ensure the full exercise and enjoyment of economic, social and cultural rights for women, in light of current debates on the reform of the human rights treaty monitoring system.

2. THE ROAD TO CEDAW

Undoubtedly, the covenant with the greatest potential influence is the Convention on the Elimination of All Forms of Discrimination Against Women...It's as though it were the Magna Carta for women. No other convention is quite so powerfully worded. Not only does it aggressively assert equality, but it does so, article by article, in every domain: health, education, justice, social welfare, ad infinitum.[5]

The CEDAW Convention is particularly well-placed to promote and protect women's economic, social and cultural rights. It is women focused, it codifies a broad range of economic, social and cultural rights drawing on women's living conditions, it recognises the indivisibility of all rights, it has an expansive and progressive understanding of equality, it addresses women's inequality in both the private and public spheres, and it includes an individual complaints mechanism. What follows is an overview of these five key strengths.

[5] S. Lewis, *Race Against Time* (Toronto: Anansi Press, 2005), pp. 112–113.

2.1 Women Focused

Unlike the other human rights treaties, the focus of the CEDAW Convention is on women. As a result, the CEDAW Committee is devoted to understanding and addressing the human rights implications of women's experiences in political, economic, social, cultural and civil fields. This focus on women is reflected in the Committee's work: the review of State party compliance with the Convention and the drafting of General Recommendations.[6] This is not the case for other treaty monitoring bodies. As Dianne Otto notes, up until the mid-1990s, little attention was paid by the treaty bodies to women-specific human rights violations.[7] Otto shows that before 1995, the General Comments adopted by the Human Rights Committee ('HRC') make scant reference to specific gender differences.[8] For example, the HRC's General Comment 19 on the family refers to a variety of issues of particular importance to women, such as marriageable age, and family planning policies. And yet, the Comment fails to consider that men and women might be affected differently by these issues.[9] Even since gender mainstreaming became part of the United Nations human rights system,[10] the treaty bodies, with the exception of the CEDAW Committee, have been reluctant to focus their work on women. For example, some members of the Committee on Economic, Social and Cultural Rights ('CESCR') are still of the view that a focus

[6] General recommendations or comments are legal interpretations of treaty provisions.
[7] Otto, 'Gender Comment' (n. 3 above), p. 22. Otto notes that of the treaty monitoring bodies, in the pre-1995 period the CESCR had the best record with several of its General Comments demonstrating a 'nascent understanding of the differences gender can make in the enjoyment of economic, social and cultural rights'. (p. 23).
[8] Ibid.
[9] Ibid. p. 23.
[10] Gender mainstreaming was called for at the World Conference on Human Rights in Vienna. See Vienna Declaration and Programme of Action, World Conference on Human Rights, UN Doc. A/CONF.157/23 (1993) at para.18. The Beijing Platform for Action establishes gender mainstreaming as the 'conceptual approach and strategy for achieving gender equality' (UN Division for the Advancement of Women and Department of Economic and Social Affairs, Promoting Women's Enjoyment of Economic and Social Rights in the Framework of the Platform for Action, prepared for the Expert Group Meeting on Promoting Women's Enjoyment of their Economic and Social Rights, UN Doc. EGM/WESR/1997/BP.2, November 1997, para. 58).

on women in the context of the rights contained in the International Covenant on Economic, Social and Cultural Rights ('ICESCR') is more appropriately handled by the CEDAW Committee.[11] This is not to suggest that the CESCR is disinterested in the economic, social and cultural rights of women. In fact, in some instances – for example during the review of some States parties – the CESCR has demonstrated an interest in and a good understanding of the barriers to women's enjoyment of these rights. Rather, the CESCR appears to be wary of delving *too deeply* into economic, social and cultural rights matters of concern to women for fear of usurping the mandate of CEDAW.[12] To some extent, the CESCR's work has been affected by this reluctance. For example, in its recent General Comment No. 16 on Article 3, the equal right of men and women to the enjoyment of all economic, social and cultural rights,[13] the Committee vacillates between acknowledging that this Article, and equality rights more specifically, are particularly important for women[14] and emphasising that Article 3 is of equal significance and is equally applicable to men and women.[15] During the development of the General Comment, the CESCR often rejected the suggestion that the comment is really about *women's* equality with respect to the rights in the Covenant, insisting instead that it is about the equal right of *men* and *women* to the enjoyment of the rights in the ICESCR.[16]

2.2 Contextualising and Interpreting Rights

In every aspect of society, women experience structural discrimination and inequality. This is particularly so in economic, social and cultural realms – health, education, housing, food, standard of living, and employment. In order for women to exercise and enjoy economic, social and cultural rights, it is imperative that discrimination against women and women's inequality in these areas are addressed. The CEDAW Convention provides an effective legal framework to do this.

At the heart of the CEDAW Convention are economic, social and cultural rights, with the bulk of the protections falling in these areas.[17] Because the Convention focuses on the elimination of discrimination against women in all areas, it does not codify specific economic, social and cultural rights (e.g., the right to health, education, etc.) as does, for example, the ICESCR. Instead, the CEDAW Convention protects women's *right to equality and non-discrimination* in economic, social and cultural realms,[18] including education,[19] employment and labour,[20] social security,[21] health,[22] access to family benefits, bank loans, mortgages and other forms of credit,[23] participation in all aspects of cultural life,[24] housing for rural women,[25] legal capacity, especially with respect to property rights,[26] and marriage and family relations.[27] 'The Convention is the only

---

[11] At least one CESCR Committee member expressed this view as recently as May 2006, during the review of Canada.

[12] This is not an official, 'on the record' position adopted by the CESCR, rather it has been conveyed to the author orally and occasionally by Committee members in session.

[13] (34th session, 2005), U.N. Doc. E/C.12/2005/3.

[14] See, for example, paragraph 5 which notes that women in particular are often denied equal enjoyment of their human rights and paragraph 11 which discusses the meaning of discrimination against women.

[15] For example, in the opening paragraph the Committee makes sure to assert, 'The International Covenant on Economic, Social and Cultural Rights (ICESCR or the Covenant) protects human rights that are fundamental to the dignity of every person'.

[16] This information was shared verbally between Committee members and the author. The CESCR indicated that if the General Comment was too obviously about women, certain members of the CESCR would have some difficulty adopting it. Therefore, it was felt that vascillating between the two positions would be the most effective way to proceed.

[17] F. Acar, 'Promotion and Protection of Women's Economic and Social Rights: Possibilities Offered by CEDAW', [unpublished paper, on file with author], p. 4. Prepared for, Expert Group Meeting, Promoting women's enjoyment of their economic and social rights, Finland, Åbo/Turku, December 1997.

[18] On a practical level, for women to enjoy and exercise their economic, social and cultural rights it makes little difference whether specific rights are codified, as in the ICESCR, or whether the rights entitlement comes through women's right to equality. Regardless of how the rights are articulated, the end goal is the same: women's full and equal enjoyment of economic, social and cultural rights.

[19] Convention on the Elimination of All Forms of Discrimination Against Women, adopted Dec. 18, 1979, GA Res. 34/180 (entered into force Sept. 3, 1981) [hereinafter CEDAW], Article 10.

[20] Ibid. Article 11.

[21] Ibid. Article 11.1.e.

[22] Ibid. Article 12.

[23] Ibid. Article 13.a and 13.b.

[24] Ibid. Article 13.c.

[25] Ibid. Article 14.2.h.

[26] Ibid. Article 15.

[27] Ibid. Article 16.

human rights treaty which affirms the reproductive rights of women and targets culture and tradition as influential forces shaping gender roles and family relations'.[28]

Because the Convention is focused on women, its provisions and their application by the CEDAW Committee are based on women's lived-experiences and tailored to address the specific barriers encountered by women in economic, social and cultural areas of life. Beyond providing detailed, women-specific rights, the Convention also identifies discrimination in economic, social and cultural rights areas that are of unique concern to women, such as social and cultural patterns[29] and the suppression of trafficking in women and exploitation of prostitution of women.[30]

The CEDAW Committee has adopted a number of General Recommendations to assist States parties in their periodic reports. Many of these also address economic and social issues of particular concern to women and that are based in women's experiences. General Recommendations have been adopted on a number of issues, including: equal remuneration for work of equal value,[31] female circumcision,[32] women and AIDS,[33] unpaid women workers in rural and urban family enterprises,[34] and the measurement and quantification of the unremunerated domestic activities of women and their recognition in the GDP.[35] The focus of these General Recommendations on social and economic issues that are of specific concern to women stands in contrast to

the General Comments of the CESCR, for example.[36] The CESCR to date has addressed women's inequality through the adoption of a single general comment on Article 3 of the ICESCR and by incorporating a few paragraphs about women in general comments on broader themes or issues, such as the right to education, and the right to health.[37]

Many of its Concluding Comments demonstrate that the CEDAW Committee examines the economic, social and cultural realities of women closely, and at times, much more closely than other Committees do.[38] For example, in the 2005 review of Ireland,[39] the CEDAW Committee expressed concern with respect to the absence of a detailed definition of discrimination to cover all areas of life in compliance with the CEDAW Convention,[40] the persistence of traditional stereotypical views of the social roles and responsibilities of women and men in the family and society at large,[41] the prevalence of violence against women and girls,[42] the trafficking of women into Ireland,[43] the under-representation of women in certain

---

[28] Division for the Advancement of Women (May 2006), available at: <http://www.un.org/womenwatch/daw/cedaw/states.html>. CEDAW (n. 20 above), Article 10.

[29] Ibid. Article 5.

[30] Ibid. Article 6.

[31] *General Recommendation 13, Equal remuneration for work of equal value* (Eighth session, 1989), U.N. Doc. A/44/38 at 76 (1990).

[32] *General Recommendation 14, Female circumcision* (Ninth session, 1990), U.N. Doc. A/45/38 at 80 (1990).

[33] *General Recommendation 15, Avoidance of discrimination against women in national strategies for the prevention and control of acquired immunodeficiency syndrome (AIDS)*, (Ninth session, 1990), U.N. Doc. A/45/38 at 81 (1990).

[34] *General Recommendation 16, Unpaid women workers in rural and urban family enterprises* (Tenth session, 1991), U.N. Doc. A/46/38 at 1 (1993).

[35] *General Recommendation 17, Measurement and quantification of the unremunerated domestic activities of women and their recognition in the gross national product* (Tenth session 1991), U.N. Doc. A/46/38 at 2 (1993).

[36] Other treaty monitoring bodies have adopted General Comments/Recommendations on discrimination against women and equality. See for example: Human Rights Committee, *General Comment No. 28: Article 3. (Equality of Rights between Men and Women)*, 68th Session, 2000, UN Doc. HRI/GEN/Rev.5, 26 April 2001 (this General Comment updates its 1981 comment on the same article); Committee on the Elimination of Racial Discrimination, *General Recommendation XXV: Gender Related Dimensions of Racial Discrimination*, 56th Session, 2000, UN Doc. HRI/GEN/1/Rev.5, 26 April 2001.

[37] For example, in the CESCR's *General Comment No. 14: The right to the highest attainable standard of health (article 12 of the International Covenant on Economic, Social and Cultural Rights)*, (22nd session, 2000) UN Doc. E/C.12/2000/4, (2000), women are mentioned in a number of paragraphs (e.g., paragraphs 12.b, 21, 34, 35, 51). While these provisions are an important component of the General Comment, they stand in contrast to the General Recommendations adopted by the CEDAW on a number of health matters of specific concern to women such as: AIDS, violence against women, and female circumcision.

[38] It should be noted that it is difficult to do a comparison of Concluding Observations/Comments because a number of factors can influence the content of these documents, for example, NGO materials before the Committee, different government representatives may provide more/less information, the attendance of NGOs during the review of the State party.

[39] CEDAW, *Concluding Comments Ireland*, UN Doc. Supplement No. 38 (A/60/38).

[40] Ibid. para. 22.

[41] Ibid. para. 24.

[42] Ibid. para. 28.

[43] Ibid. para. 30.

jobs,[44] particular groups of women who are at risk of consistent poverty and social exclusion,[45] barriers to education, employment, health care and other social services for marginalised women,[46] the concentration of women in part-time, low-paid work and the significant pay gap between women and men,[47] and restrictions on access to abortions.[48] This stands in stark contrast with the CESCR which, in its 2002 review of Ireland,[49] did not express any concerns regarding the position of women in Ireland in any economic, social or cultural context, though they did note the lack of consistency between the provisions in the Constitution pertaining to equality before the law and Articles 2(2) and 3 of the ICESCR.

In many instances, the CESCR's Concluding Observations do provide a more robust analysis of women's experiences of economic, social and cultural rights than the example above.[50] However, a comparison of Concluding Observations/Comments from both bodies over the last five years reveals that those of the CEDAW Committee generally provide a more complete picture of women's experiences of inequality in economic, social and cultural realms by addressing a greater number of issues. This can, of course, be attributed to the nature of the CEDAW Convention, with its focus on women and with the bulk of its provisions pertaining to the economic, social and cultural spheres.

The CEDAW Convention and Committee are also committed to the concept of the indivisibility of human rights. Because the CEDAW Convention is aimed at eliminating *all forms* of discrimination against women, it recognises that economic, social, cultural, civil and political rights are interrelated and of equal importance.[51] It also recog-

nises that the infringement of one right will invariably lead to the infringement of another right. The CEDAW Convention recognises that de facto equality for women will not be achieved unless the indivisibility of human rights is taken seriously. It demonstrates this by codifying at once women's equality in civil, cultural, economic, social and political realms. For example, the Convention codifies the right to equality in education and health, as well as in legal and civil matters. Similarly in General Recommendation No. 19, Violence Against Women, the CEDAW Committee recognises that violence is as much about women's rights to economic security as it is about women's right to life and liberty of the person.[52]

To better understand how both the Convention and the CEDAW Committee contextualise and interpret women's equality in economic, social and cultural realms, examples of how women's rights to education, health, and employment have been addressed and applied are illustrative and examined below.

EDUCATION

Article 10 of the CEDAW Convention codifies the right to be free from discrimination and to equality in the field of education. Rather than merely providing for a general 'equal right to education', the Convention highlights, in some detail, specific aspects of education where women experience inequality: access to career and vocational guidance;[53] access to studies and for the achievement of diplomas in educational categories in all areas (urban and rural) and at all levels and types of educational institutions;[54] access to the same curricula, examinations, and teaching staff as men;[55] stereotypes about the roles of men and women at all levels and in all forms of education;[56] opportunities to benefit from scholarships and grants;[57] access to continuing education;[58] female drop-out rates;[59] equal access to sports

---

[44] Ibid. para. 32.
[45] Ibid. para. 34.
[46] Ibid. para. 34.
[47] Ibid. para. 36.
[48] Ibid. para. 38.
[49] *Concluding Observations of the Committee on Economic, Social and Cultural Rights: Ireland*, UN Doc. E/C.12/1/Add.77, 5 June 2002.
[50] See for example: *Concluding Observations on Brazil*, UN Doc. E/C.12/1/Add.87, 23 May 2003; *Concluding Observations on Germany*, UN Doc. E/C.12/1/Add. 68, 24 September 2001; *Concluding Observations on Jamaica*, UN Doc. E/C.12/1/Add. 75, November 30, 2001; *Concluding Observations on Canada*, UN Doc. E/C.12/1/Add.31, May 2006.
[51] Partners for Law in Development (PLD), *CEDAW: Restoring Rights to Women* (New Delhi, 2004), p. 12.

[52] CEDAW Committee, *General Recommendation No. 19, Violence Against Women* (11th Session, 1992), UN Doc. HRI/GEN/1/Rev.6, at para 243.
[53] Article 10 (a).
[54] Article 10 (a).
[55] Article 10 (b).
[56] Article 10 (c).
[57] Article 10 (d).
[58] Article 10 (e).
[59] Article 10 (f).

and physical education;[60] and equal access to specific educational information, including information and advice on family planning.[61] With this rather detailed description of the many aspects in which women are denied equal rights to education, the CEDAW Committee consistently has applied this Article in its review of States parties.[62] In so doing, it has expressed concern on a number of issues including: high or disproportionately high female illiteracy rates;[63] high drop-out rates of girls;[64] low enrolment for girls;[65] disproportionately low enrolment of women in post-secondary education;[66] and the marginalisation or segregation of particular groups of women within education systems.[67]

The CEDAW Committee has applied women's right to education in a manner that exposes the indivisibility of human rights in the lives of women. The Committee is concerned, for example, with the direct relationship between women's inequality in education and women's ability to secure opportunities for economic survival.[68] On occasion, the Committee also highlights the relationship between high rates of teenage pregnancies and/or early or forced marriage and high school drop-out rates[69] and between access to non-discriminatory education and family planning.[70] This textured analysis of the implications of the failure to fulfil the right to education for women is in keeping with the women centred indivisibility approach of the Convention and the Committee. The CEDAW Committee also consistently applies Article 10 in a manner that obliges States parties to undertake positive obligations to address women's inequality in education. For instance, in its Concluding Comments on Togo the Committee recommends that the government increase the educational infrastructure available to women by increasing the number of facilities and qualified teachers[71] and commends the State party for having undertaken temporary special measures in the area of women's education.[72] This commitment to requiring States parties to undertake positive obligations is in keeping with the CEDAW Convention and the Committee's substantive equality approach to women's human rights.[73]

HEALTH CARE SERVICES

Article 12 of the Convention addresses women's right to be free from discrimination in access to health care services including those related to family planning, 'pregnancy, confinement and the post-natal period'.[74] Though, on its face, this article is somewhat narrow in scope, it places women at its centre by focusing on a few health issues of particular and unique concern to women. To offer a more expansive understanding of the equality issues of concern to women in the area of health, the CEDAW Committee relies upon its General Recommendations. Beyond recommendations adopted on female circumcision, and HIV/AIDS as well as others that touch

---

[60] Article 10 (g).

[61] Article 10 (h).

[62] The CEDAW Committee has not yet adopted a general recommendation on education.

[63] See for example: *CEDAW Concluding Comments on Congo* (n. 80 below), para. 223; Egypt (2001), UN Doc. A/56/38, para. 338; *Morocco* (n. 83 below) and *Portugal* (2002), UN Doc. A/57/38, para. 339; *Togo* (2006), UN Doc. CEDAW/C/TGO/CO/5, para. 24; *Cambodia* (2006), UN Doc. CEDAW/C/KHM/CO/3, para. 25.

[64] See for example: *CEDAW Concluding Comments on Congo* (n. 63 above), para. 223; *Saint Lucia* (2006), UN Doc. CEDAW/C/LCA/CO/6, para. 27; *Togo* (n. 63 above), para. 24; *Cambodia* (n. 63 above), para. 26.

[65] Ibid.

[66] See for example: *CEDAW Concluding Comments on Austria* (2000), UN Doc. A/55/38, para. 231; New Zealand (2003), UN Doc. A/58/38, para. 409.

[67] See for example: *CEDAW Concluding Comments on Spain* (2004), UN Doc. A/59/38, para. 344, on Roma women; *Uzbekistan* (2001), UN Doc. A/56/38, para. 189 on rural women.

[68] See for example: *CEDAW Concluding Comments on Eritrea* (2006), UN Doc. CEDAW/C/ERI/CO/3, para. 26; and *Cambodia* (n. 63 above), para. 25.

[69] See for example: *CEDAW Concluding Comments on Togo* (n. 63 above), para. 24; *Cambodia* (n. 63 above), para. 26.

[70] See for example: *CEDAW Concluding Comments on Saint Lucia* (n. 64 above), para. 27.

[71] *CEDAW Concluding Comments on Togo* (n. 63 above), paras. 24 and 25.

[72] Ibid.

[73] For more about substantive equality, see section 2.3 ('Equality rights framework') below.

[74] CEDAW (n. 19 above), Article 12. Article 12 states:

> 1. States Parties shall take all appropriate measures to eliminate discrimination against women in the field of health care in order to ensure, on a basis of equality of men and women, access to health care services, including those related to family planning.
> 2. Notwithstanding the provisions of paragraph 1 of this article, States Parties shall ensure to women appropriate services in connection with pregnancy, confinement and the post-natal period, granting free services where necessary, as well as adequate nutrition during pregnancy and lactation.

on health related matters,[75] in 1999 the CEDAW Committee adopted the broad-reaching General Recommendation No. 24 pertaining to women and health.[76] This recommendation lays down over-arching principles regarding women's equality in the area of health. For example, it notes that soci-etal factors, along with biological differences, are determinative of the health status of women and men and that therefore attention needs to be paid to women in disadvantaged groups.[77] The recom-mendation then notes that the full realisation of women's right to health[78] can only be achieved if States parties 'respect, protect, and promote women's fundamental human right to nutritional well-being through their life span by means of a food supply that is safe, nutritious and adapted to local conditions'.[79] The recommendation sug-gests that States parties should report on how their policies and measures on health care address women's specific health needs and interests, out-lining a number of distinctive features that may have health-related ramifications for women such as: biological factors, socio-economic factors such as the unequal power relations between women and men, psycho-social factors such as post-partum depression, and confidentiality issues in relation to the reporting of sexual or physical vio-lence. The recommendation also outlines specific and general actions that States parties must under-take to meet their obligations to respect, protect and fulfil women's right to health. Throughout, the recommendation highlights health issues of par-ticular concern to women, including: the provi-sion of reproductive health services to women; the restriction of women's access to health services on the ground that women do not have the autho-risation of husbands, partners, parents or health authorities; gender-based violence; the criminal-isation of medical procedures required only by women; maternal mortality; HIV/AIDS and other

sexually transmitted diseases; female genital muti-lation; and barriers (e.g., fee for service) to health care services for women.

The CEDAW Committee applies Article 12 and General Recommendation No. 24 in its review of State party compliance with the CEDAW Conven-tion, albeit in a more sparse and general way. For example, in a number of instances the Commit-tee expresses concern about high rates of mater-nal and/or infant mortality[80] and low rates of con-traceptive use.[81] It also expresses concern about the use of abortion as a form of contraception in some countries[82] and the lack of access to health services for women and particular groups of women.[83] Because Concluding Observations are concise documents, often highlighting only the most egregious conditions, the breadth of health issues confronting women in every country and reflected in General Recommendation No. 24 are not always touched upon.

WORK

Article 11 of the CEDAW Convention situates the elimination of discrimination against women in employment in the broader context of the human right to work. The Article also provides a detailed list of obligations of States parties to ensure that women can exercise and enjoy this right. These obligations include: guaranteeing that women and men enjoy the same employment opportunities; the right to free choice of profession and employ-ment (so that women are not relegated to gen-dered work); the right to equal remuneration and pay equity (equal pay for work of equal value); the right to social security; and the right to a violence-free work place. The second part of Arti-cle 11 focuses on the prevention of discrimina-tion against women in employment and labour on

---

[75] For example: *General Recommendation 18, Disabled women* (Tenth session, 1991), U.N. Doc. A/46/38 at 3 (1993); *General Recommendation 19* (n. 52 above); *General Recommendation 21, Equality in marriage and family relations* (Thirteenth session, 1992), U.N. Doc. A/49/38 at 1 (1994).

[76] CEDAW, *General Recommendation No. 24, Women and Health*, (Twentieth session, 1999) UN Doc A/54/38/Rev.1.

[77] Ibid. para. 6.

[78] This General Recommendation suggests that there is little difference between 'women's right to health' and women's right to be free from discrimination with respect to health. On this issue see discussion in n. 18 above.

[79] Ibid. para. 7.

[80] See for example: *CEDAW Committee review of Democratic Republic of Congo* (2000) UN Doc. A/55/38, para. 227; *Brazil* (2003) UN Doc. A/58/38, para. 126; *Ukraine* (2002) UN Doc. A/57/38, para. 289.

[81] See for example: *CEDAW Committee review of Demo-cratic Republic of Congo* (200) UN Doc. A/55/38, para. 227; *Jamaica* (2001) UN Doc. A/56/38, para. 224; *Russian Fed-eration* (2002) UN Doc. A/57/38, para. 399.

[82] See for example: *CEDAW Committee review of Russian Federation* (2002), Ibid. para. 399; *Uzbekistan* (2001) UN Doc. A/56/38, para. 185.

[83] See for example: *CEDAW Committee review of Morocco* (2003) UN Doc. A/58/38, para. 172; *Uzbekistan*, Ibid. para. 189.

the grounds of marriage or maternity. This part requires States parties to prohibit dismissal on these grounds; introduce maternity leave with pay and without loss of former employment; encourage the provision of the necessary social services to allow families to balance family obligations, work and participation in public life; and to provide special protection to women during pregnancy in types of work proved to be harmful to them.

Although Article 11, like Article 10, offers States parties some detail with respect to the content of the right to work, its scope is somewhat slanted toward women in the formal work sector and concern for pregnant and parenting women in the workforce, as opposed to other groups of women (e.g., young women, immigrant and racialised women, older women) who may also be discriminated against for gendered reasons.[84] In this way, the CEDAW Convention may be regarded as protecting the labour rights of more privileged women over more marginalised women.

This critique is answered, at least in part, by the CEDAW Committee's General Recommendations and country specific Concluding Comments. The CEDAW Committee has attempted to elaborate on the meaning of Article 11 by adopting several General Recommendations on issues not covered or fully elaborated upon in the Convention such as: unpaid women workers in family enterprises;[85] equal remuneration for work of equal value;[86] violence against women,[87] which refers to sexual harassment as a form of gender discrimination at the workplace; and the measurement and quantification of unremunerated domestic activities of women and their recognition in the gross national product.[88] Moreover, in the application of women's right to work when reviewing States

parties, the CEDAW Committee is often able to address a broad range of relevant issues, sometimes moving beyond the content areas of the Convention and General Recommendations. For example, in its review of Togo, the Committee expressed concern for women in both the formal and informal sectors.[89] In its review of Saint Lucia, the CEDAW Committee expresses concern about sexual harassment in the labour sector, women migrant workers and their susceptibility to violence, exploitation and trafficking,[90] occupational segregation and the concentration of women in low-wage, low-skill areas of work,[91] and discrimination against ethnic minority women and disabled women in accessing employment.[92] As with its application of other rights, the CEDAW Committee consistently demonstrates the indivisibility of women's right to work with other rights, particularly the right to education and health.

Overall, this brief review of the rights to education, health and employment for women demonstrates that the Convention and its application are tailored to address the specific barriers women encounter in these economic and social areas. The CEDAW Committee's work is clearly focused on ensuring that women's real, everyday conditions of disadvantage and inequality are being addressed, reflecting the often complicated interdependence of rights in the lives of women.

2.3 Equality Rights Framework

The CEDAW Convention, like other treaties, calls for the elimination of discrimination against women. Not only does it require equality between women and men, but it also prohibits practices that may perpetuate women's inequality.[93] For

---

[84] The Committee on Economic, Social and Cultural Rights adopted *General Comment No. 18 on the Right to Work* in 2006 (Thirty-fifth session, 2006), UN Doc. E/C.12/GC18 (2006). This comment includes one paragraph on the right to work and women (para. 13) and adopts a somewhat narrow interpretation of the systemic issues that might impede women's exercise and enjoyment of this right, focusing on equal pay for work of equal value and pregnancy. The CESCR does include reference to cultural practices that might impede the enjoyment of this right as well as the difficulty many young women have in accessing employment opportunities.
[85] *General Recommendation No. 16* (n. 34 above).
[86] *General Recommendation No. 13* (n. 34 above).
[87] *General Recommendation No. 19* (n. 52 above).
[88] *General Recommendation No. 17* (n. 34 above).

[89] *Concluding Comments on Togo* (n. 63 above), para. 26.
[90] *CEDAW Concluding Comments on Cambodia* (n. 63 above), para. 21.
[91] Ibid. para. 27.
[92] Ibid. para. 35.
[93] Association for Women's Rights in Development, 'The Convention on the Elimination of All Forms of Discrimination Against Women and the Optional Protocol', August 2002, p. 2, available at: <http://www.awid.org/publications/primers/factsissues2.pdf.\> Article 3: 'States Parties shall take in all fields, in particular in the political, social, economic and cultural fields, all appropriate measures, including legislation, to ensure the full development and advancement of women for the purpose of guaranteeing them the exercise and enjoyment

the equality provisions in any treaty to have real-world significance for women, the right to non-discrimination and equality must be understood substantively and not just formally.[94]

Discrimination and inequality can occur in different ways. The most obvious form of discrimination that results in inequality is when a law, policy, or practice blatantly excludes or restricts a protected group or prefers and distinguishes between people based on an enumerated ground, for example, laws which prohibit women from owning title to land or voting. To remedy this type of discrimination and inequality, treating everyone the same or de jure equality may be effective. In contemporary times, however, discrimination is not always this blatant. In particular, discriminatory effects are often obscured by the non-discriminatory language of a law, policy, or practice. For example, a government may establish a lending scheme to assist individuals to buy land or housing. The scheme is open to all individuals, but some form of collateral is required to secure the loan. On the face of it the policy is neutral, as it is open to everyone. But the policy may have discriminatory effects, as women are often over-represented amongst the poor and thus they are less likely than men to have the necessary collateral to secure the loan. In turn, the scheme is, in practice, unavailable to most women. In instances such as this, the discrimination arises not because women are treated differently by the rule itself but, rather, because they are situated differently in the world in which the rule operates.

If the different situation of women is not taken into account in defining discrimination and equality, then women enjoy only formal equality – that is, they would be equal only in the sense that they would be treated in the same way that men are treated. To the extent that women and men are situated identically in the world, being treated equally in a formal sense is, of course, important.

However, to the extent that women experience different and often disadvantageous conditions, a merely formal conceptualisation of equality is insufficient. 'Gender-neutral laws and policies can perpetuate sex inequality because they do not take into account the economic and social disadvantage of women; they may therefore simply maintain the status quo'.[95] Rather, 'in those circumstances where women and men are not identically situated, which is most of the time', a substantive conceptualisation of equality is necessary.[96] Substantive equality recognises that equality is not a matter of 'superficial sameness and difference'[97] but, rather, that it is about the 'accommodation of differences'.[98] It understands that women as a group are disadvantaged and that equality must address the economic, social, legal, and political dimensions of that group.[99] Consequently, adopting a substantive conceptualisation of equality means recognising that inequality exists when gender-neutral laws, policies, or practices have differential negative effects on women and also when the differential disadvantage of women is not addressed by laws, policies, or practices. As a result, substantive equality may require positive action by States to address the needs that are related to disadvantage.[100]

The CEDAW Convention and the work of the CEDAW Committee are particularly strong tools for enforcing economic, social and cultural rights for women because they embrace substantive equality. The CEDAW Convention contains several provisions, which indicate that it is premised

---

of human rights and fundamental freedoms on a basis of equality with men'.

[94] S. Day and G. Brodsky, *Women and the Equality Deficit: The Impact of Restructuring Canada's Social Programs* (Ottawa: Status of Women Canada, 1998), p. 43. For a discussion of the need for substantive equality (rather than formal equality) in the context of housing rights, see L. Farha, 'Is There a Woman in the House?' (n. 3 above). This section of the chapter has been adapted from that publication.

[95] Montreal Principles (n. 2 above), para. 9
[96] Day and Brodsky, *Women and the Equality Deficit* (n. 94 above), p. 43.
[97] G. Brodsky and S. Day, 'Women's Economic Inequality and the Canadian Human Rights Act', in *Women and the Canadian Human Rights Act: A Collection of Policy Research Reports* (Ottawa: Status of Women Canada, 1999), pp. 113–176, at 135.
[98] *Andrews* v. *Law Society of British Columbia*, [1989] 1 S.C.R. 143. See discussion in M. Jackman and B. Porter, 'Women's Substantive Equality and the Protection of Social and Economic Rights under the Canadian Human Rights Act', in *Women and the Canadian Human Rights Act: A Collection of Policy Research Reports* (Ottawa: Status of Women Canada, 1999), pp. 43–113, at 56.
[99] Day and Brodsky, *Women and the Equality Deficit* (n. 94 above), p. 45.
[100] Jackman and Porter, 'Substantive Equality' (n. 98 above), p. 56.

on the principle of substantive equality.[101] For example, it includes the following definition of discrimination: '"discrimination against women" shall mean any distinction, exclusion or restriction made on the basis of sex which has the *effect* or purpose of impairing or nullifying the recognition, enjoyment or exercise by women ... of human rights and fundamental freedoms in the political, economic, social, cultural, civil or any other field'.[102] And then, Article 3 of the Convention requires States parties to take 'all appropriate measures, including legislation, to ensure the full development and advancement of women, for the purpose of guaranteeing them the exercise and enjoyment of human rights and fundamental freedoms on a basis of equality with men'.[103] These Articles impugn laws and practices, which are detrimental in their effect, even if they are expressed in gender-neutral terms.[104] In this way, the Convention acknowledges that gender neutrality – or de jure equality – may not achieve de facto equality – because gender-neutral laws may still have discriminatory effects.

Article 4 of the Convention on temporary special measures, and General Recommendation No. 25,[105] which explores the meaning and application of Article 4, underscore the Convention's commitment to substantive equality. Temporary special measures are used by governments to accelerate the improvement of the position of women in recognition of the fact that even if de jure equality exists, women may not experience de facto equality.[106] The General Recommendation asserts that 'a purely formal legal or programmatic approach is not sufficient to achieve women's de facto equality with men, which the Committee interprets as substantive equality'.[107] Temporary special measures require governments to assess the particular disadvantage experienced by women 'in a contextual way'[108] and to take positive steps to achieve a 'real transformation of opportunities, institutions and systems so that they are no longer grounded in historically determined male paradigms of power and life patterns'.[109] This stands in stark contrast with a formal equality approach that requires gender neutral laws only and does not necessitate an examination of the historic and real conditions of women, nor the undertaking of positive obligations by the State.

This commitment to substantive equality is also reflected in the Concluding Comments issued by the CEDAW Committee. For example, in its 2003 review of Canada, the Committee urged the State party to 'take additional measures to increase the representation of women in political and public life' and to introduce 'temporary special measures with numerical goals and timetables'.[110] In its review of Cuba, the Committee called on the Government to implement temporary special measures to address the high levels of unemployment found amongst women.[111] And in its review of Romania, the Committee called on the Government to 'improve the availability, acceptability, and use of modern means of birth control to avoid the use of abortion as a method of family planning. It encourages the Government to include sex education systematically in schools'.[112]

The inclusion of substantive equality within the CEDAW Convention along with the understanding and application of substantive equality by the CEDAW Committee is somewhat unique within the treaty monitoring body system. No other treaty includes an explicit understanding of substantive equality within its provisions. Furthermore, the CEDAW Committee itself has embraced substantive equality unequivocally, as reflected

---

[101] See A. Lewis-Landsberg, *Bringing Equality Home* (New York: UNIFEM, 1998), p. 12.

[102] CEDAW Convention, Article 1. Emphasis added.

[103] Ibid. Article 3.

[104] R. Cook, 'State Accountability Under the CEDAW Convention' in Rebecca Cook (ed.), *Human Rights of Women* (Philadelphia: University of Pennsylvania Press, 1994), pp. 437–461, at para. 236.

[105] CEDAW, *General Recommendation No. 25, on Article 4, Paragraph 1, of the Convention on the Elimination of All Forms of Discrimination against Women, on temporary special measures*, (Thirtieth session, 2004). UN Doc. No.CEDAW/C/2004/I/WP.1/Rev.1.

[106] *General Recommendation No. 25* (n. 105 above), para. 15 and UNHCHR, 'Fact Sheet No. 22, Discrimination Against Women: The Convention and the Committee', Geneva (1994), p. 11.

[107] *General Recommendation No. 25* (n. 105 above), para. 8.

[108] Ibid. para. 10.

[109] Ibid.

[110] *CEDAW, Concluding Comments on Canada*, UN Doc. Supplement No. A/58/38, para. 372 (1997).

[111] *CEDAW, Concluding Comments on Cuba*, UN Doc. Supplement No. A/55/38, para. 270. (2000).

[112] *CEDAW, Concluding Comments on Romania*, UN Doc. Supplement No. A/55/38, para. 315, (2000).

in the definitive manner in which they invoke substantive equality in General Recommendation No. 25. While other Committees have also embraced substantive equality in their General Comments[113] and Concluding Observations, some uncertainty has been expressed about its meaning and application.[114]

2.4   Private Realm Violations

The CEDAW Convention is regarded as a particularly useful legal tool for women because it is the only international human rights treaty that explicitly prohibits discrimination in the private sector.[115] Article 2 obliges States parties to:

[C]ondemn discrimination against women ... and, to this end, undertake: ... (e) To take all appropriate measures to eliminate discrimination against women by *any person, organization or enterprise* ...[116]

Article 5 obliges States parties to 'modify the social and cultural patterns of conduct of men and women' to eliminate customary and other practices which are discriminatory and based in stereotypes.[117]

The Convention extends the ambit of State party accountability to preventing and deterring *private acts* of discrimination.[118] This is not to suggest that the State is directly responsible for the actions of private persons. Rather, it means that States are bound to:

[U]ndertake means to eliminate or reduce and mitigate the incidence of private discrimination, and to achieve the result that such private discrimination should not recur ... A state will not be directly accountable for the behavior of private individuals or agencies, but their behavior indirectly implicates the state through its lack of due diligence in awareness of the risk of violation of human rights, or the failure of its punitive and/or compensatory responses to such violations.[119]

The CEDAW's commitment to having discrimination in the private realm addressed is reflected in several General Recommendations. For example, General Recommendation No. 17 recommends that States focus on quantifying the unremunerated domestic activities of women and include their labour in the gross national product.[120] General Recommendation No. 24 on women and health discusses the relationship between HIV/AIDS and unequal power relations within a household that make it difficult for women to refuse sex or insist on safe and responsible sex.[121] And, the General Recommendation on violence against women includes a focus on family violence, recommending that States parties ensure that 'laws against family violence and abuse, rape, sexual assault and other gender-based violence give adequate protection to all women'.[122]

As these General Recommendations expose, women's economic and social disadvantage often takes place within the private sector (the home) or at the hands of non-State actors (landlords, employers, family members). In turn, the explicit extension of the ambit of State party accountability to private acts of discrimination is essential if women are to exercise and enjoy equality in all

---

[113] See Human Rights Committee, *General Comment No. 18, Non-discrimination* (Thirty-seventh session, 1989), *Compilation of General Comments and General Recommendations Adopted by Human Rights Treaty Bodies*, U.N. Doc. HRI/GEN/1/Rev.6 at 146 (2003) and CESCR, *General Comment No. 16* (n. 13 above).

[114] The meaning and applicability of substantive equality in the context of the ICESCR was one of the most fraught issues during the drafting process of General Comment No. 16 on Article 3 of the ICESCR.

[115] Otto, 'Gender Comment' (n. 3 above), p. 43.

[116] CEDAW, Article 2(e). Emphasis added.

[117] CEDAW, Article 5.

[118] Cook, 'State Accountability' (n. 104 above), p. 236. It should be noted that the CESCR has also recognised that States parties are responsible for the violations of ICESCR rights by private actors such as landlords and employers. See for example, Committee on Economic, Social and Cultural Rights, *General Comment No. 4, The right to adequate housing*, (Sixth session, 1991), U.N. Doc. E/1992/23, annex III at 114 (1991).

[119] Cook, ibid. p. 237; CEDAW, General Recommendation No. 19 (n. 52 above), para. 9.

[120] *General Recommendation No. 17* (n. 88 above).

[121] *General Recommendation No. 24* (n. 76 above), para. 18.

[122] *General Recommendation No. 19* (n. 52 above), paras. 23, 24 (b).

realms, including economic, social and cultural realms.

2.5   Optional Protocol

There are two principal ways in which the CEDAW Convention can be enforced. States parties are required to submit a national report every four years on measures they have taken to comply with their obligations under the Convention. The Committee reviews these reports and has an opportunity to ask the State party questions. Based on this review, the Committee issues Concluding Comments, which include recommendations as to how the State party could improve its performance. The CEDAW Committee also makes General Recommendations on issues of relevance to women, upon which States should focus. General Recommendations provide further guidance to States regarding their obligations under the Convention. And now, the CEDAW Convention can be enforced through the Optional Protocol.

In October 1999, the UN General Assembly adopted the Option Protocol to CEDAW,[123] which came into force in December 2000 after it had been ratified by ten States.[124] The Optional Protocol provides two special procedures: a communications procedure for individual complaints[125] and an investigation procedure regarding grave or systemic violations of women's rights. To date the CEDAW Committee has heard four communica-

tions and has issued three decisions.[126] Each of the decisions raises equality rights concerns in social, economic, and cultural contexts. *B.J. v. Germany*, concerned gender based discrimination in equalisation payments in the context of divorce; *A.T. v. Hungary*, concerned domestic violence by a common law partner and raised a number of housing issues; and *Rahime Kayhan v. Turkey*, concerned the dismissal of a female public school teacher because of the headscarf she wore to work. The Committee has also undertaken one country visit to investigate the abduction, rape and murder of women in Juarez, Mexico.[127]

While two of the three cases failed to meet admissibility criteria and thus decisions on the merits were not rendered,[128] as a whole, the cases expose the potential that the Optional Protocol to CEDAW offers in the enforcement of economic, social and cultural rights of women. Each raises economic and social rights claims that are gender specific. In *Rahime Kayhan v. Turkey*, the complainant was dismissed from her employment as a public school teacher because she wore a headscarf to work. She alleged that her dismissal and termination as a civil servant for wearing a headscarf, 'a piece of clothing unique to women',[129] was in violation of Article 11 of the CEDAW Convention. In *A.T. v. Hungary*, the complainant alleged that the

---

[123] Resolution Adopted by the General Assembly, 54/4. Optional Protocol to the Convention on the Elimination of All Forms of Discrimination Against Women, UN Doc. A/RES/54/4, 15 October 1999.

[124] As of 13 March 2006, 78 countries have acceded to or ratified the Optional Protocol to CEDAW. See: Division for the Advancement of Women, available at <www.un.org/womenwatch/daw/cedaw/states.html>.

[125] In order to make a valid communication, the following conditions must be met: exhaustion of all domestic legal remedies; the country against which they are complaining is a party to CEDAW and the Optional Protocol; the violation occurred after the date that the Optional Protocol came into effect; the right they are claiming is found in the CEDAW Convention; another international procedure has not been engaged to address the same complaint; if the communication is being submitted on behalf of someone else, that person must provide consent (AWID, 'The Convention on the Elimination of All Forms of Discrimination Against Women and the Optional Protocol', August 2002).

[126] *B.-J. v. Germany*, 1/2003 (concerning gender based discrimination in equalisation payments in the context of divorce in Germany); *A.T. v. Hungary*, 2/2003 (concerning domestic violence by a common law partner and raises a number of housing issues – access to a shelter for abused women that will also accommodate her disabled child); *Rahime Kayhan v. Turkey*, 8/2005 (concerning the dismissal of a female public school teacher because of the headscarf she wore to work).

[127] CEDAW Committee, *Report on Mexico Produced by the Committee on the Elimination of Discrimination Against Women Under Article 8 of the Optional Protocol*, UN Doc. CEDAW/C/2005/OP.8/MEXICO, 22 January 2005.

[128] In *Rahime Kayhan v. Turkey*, the CEDAW Committee found that the complainant had failed to exhaust domestic legal remedies (see para. 7.9) and thus did not consider the merits of the case. In *B.-J. v. Germany*, the CEDAW Committee also found that the complainant had failed to exhaust domestic legal remedies, see para. 8.8. In the latter case, two Committee members issued a dissenting opinion, stating that the issues of spousal maintenance and accrued gains were in accordance with the admissibility criterion that domestic remedies are unreasonably prolonged may be considered exhausted for the purposes of engaging the Optional Protocol.

[129] *Rahime Kayhan v. Turkey* (n. 126 above), para. 7.7.

State party had failed to provide her with effective protection (e.g., safe housing) from her abusive common law husband.[130] In *B.-J. v. Germany*, the complainant – a fifty-seven year old woman who sacrificed her career and education by staying at home to raise the children to allow her husband to pursue his career – alleged that the State regulations regarding the law on the legal consequences of divorce systematically discriminate against older women who are divorced after long marriages. Moreover, two of the cases, *A.T. v. Hungary* and *B.-J. v. Germany*, required the Committee to address State responsibility with respect to economic and social rights violations that occurred in the private realm (the home), where women most often experience economic and social disadvantage. In this way, the CEDAW Committee underscores the principle that States may be responsible for private acts if they fail to act with due diligence to prevent violations of rights.[131]

A.T. v. Hungary – the sole decision on its merits under the Optional Protocol – sets a good example for subsequent cases by demonstrating the CEDAW Committee's unequivocal commitment to the realisation of substantive equality for women in economic and social realms. The Committee's analysis recognises the particularity of the complainant's case and situates it within the broader context of women's position in Hungarian society. For example, in its decision the Committee considers the specific recourse taken by A.T. to try to escape the abuse and concludes that the legal and social protections available were grossly inadequate.[132] At the same time, the Committee expresses concern regarding the entrenched stereotypes regarding the roles and responsibilities of men and women within families, drawing on its own concluding comments on Hungary from August 2002.[133]

Complementarily, the Committee fashions a remedy that addresses the complainant's particular situation while simultaneously instructing the State party on actions it must take to respect, protect, promote and fulfil women's human right to be free from all forms of domestic violence. To this end, and in keeping with the principle of substantive equality, the CEDAW Committee requires the State party to undertake positive obligations to remedy the complainant's situation and to ensure better protections for women more generally. In this regard, the State is required to ensure that the complainant is given a safe home in which to live with her children, and that she receives child support, legal assistance and reparations for the violations of her rights.[134] More generally, the State is required to introduce a 'specific law which prohibits domestic violence against women, which would provide for protection and exclusion orders as well as support services, including shelters'.[135] Under a formal equality approach, the Committee could have concluded that A.T. and other women in Hungary were no worse off than men because safe shelters were unavailable to the entire population, not just women. Clearly, this formal analysis would be nothing more than 'equality with a vengeance'[136], and an unsatisfactory answer to the violation of A.T.'s rights.

In order for rights to be meaningful, individuals must be able to claim and enforce them. As these cases indicate, the Optional Protocol to CEDAW is positioned to play an important role in the realisation of women's economic, social and cultural rights, in light of the fact that in many jurisdictions, these rights cannot always be claimed in domestic courts and tribunals, and in light of the fact that as of yet there is no individual complaints mechanism associated with the ICESCR.

3. THE ROAD BLOCKS TO CEDAW

In order to accurately assess whether the CEDAW Convention and Committee can truly be effective tools in the struggle to enforce women's economic,

---

[130] In this case, the State's failure to provide the complainant with safe housing and her economic dependence on her spouse were key factors in her ongoing experiences of violence and in the deprivation of her human rights. For this reason, this case can be understood as being about the complainant's equal right to an adequate standard of living, including adequate housing in conjunction with her right to be free from all forms of discrimination and violence.

[131] *A.T. v. Hungary* (n. 126 above), para. 9.2.
[132] Ibid. para. 9.4.
[133] Ibid.

[134] Ibid.
[135] Ibid.
[136] This term was coined by the Canadian based Women's Legal Education and Action Fund (LEAF) and was referred to in a Supreme Court of Canada case: *Schachter v. Canada* [1992] 2 S.C.R. 679 at 701–702.

social and cultural rights, it is imperative to discuss the weaknesses of both the Convention and the Committee's work.

3.1 Marginalisation

The marginalisation of the CEDAW Committee in relation to other treaty monitoring bodies is well documented.[137] Of course, over time this is changing. The CEDAW Committee now meets, like other treaty bodies, for two three-week sessions each year. The Convention has influenced constitutional reform in a number of instances,[138] has been used in many domestic legal challenges,[139] and has influenced national legislation.[140] Also, over time its General Recommendations have become more detailed and in many respects pioneering. That being said, there is some concern that the CEDAW Committee still does not garner the same respect as other human rights treaty bodies, such as the Human Rights Committee and the Committee Against Torture. This concern is underscored by the number of reservations that have been made to the CEDAW Convention.

3.2 Reservations

It is well documented that the CEDAW Convention is subject to a large number of reservations.[141] These reservations often go to the very core of the document, attached to Article 2 (pertaining to the obligations of States parties) and/or Article 16 (pertaining to marriage and family). The common perception is that it is mostly countries in the Middle East that have registered reservations. While it is true that some countries in the Middle East have done so, they do not stand alone. As Katarina Tomaševski notes,

> Some reservations reflect the exclusively male heritage in the exercise of royal powers (Belgium, Luxembourg, Spain), others exclude women from employment in the armed forces or from the access to combat duties (Germany, New Zealand, Thailand), yet others restrict employment of women in night work or at jobs deemed hazardous to their health (Malta, the United Kingdom). Most, however, retain restrictions on equal rights regarding women's personal status, namely marriage, family, citizenship and the legal personality and capacity of women in general.

Australia has a reservation with respect to Article 11(2)(b) to exempt itself from having to provide women with paid maternity leave.

Reservations such as these suggest a lack of genuine commitment to the realisation of women's equality in all fields, as mandated by the Convention. There is no doubt that the sheer number as well as the content of the reservations casts a long shadow over the CEDAW Convention.

3.3 Equality and Non-Discrimination

Some have argued that one of the central weaknesses of the CEDAW Convention is that it is focused on non-discrimination and equality. In particular, it is argued that the paradigm of 'equality with men' is insufficient as it only allows women to argue that they have a right to enjoy the same opportunities, results and outcomes as men who are similarly situated. This is regarded as insufficient because women are uniquely situated in the world and an effective rights strategy must be able to respond to and address women's particular disadvantage. Of course, this is only a problem if equality is understood formally. If, however, a substantive understanding of equality is employed, this critique is moot. Substantive equality is an expansive principle that is based on

---

[137] D. Otto (n. 3 above), p. 21. See also A. Byrnes, *Advancing the Human Rights of Women: Using International Human Rights Standards in Domestic Litigation*, (London: Centre for Comparative and Public Law, 1997).

[138] I. Landsberg-Lewis, *Bringing Equality Home: Implementing the Convention on the Elimination of All Forms of Discrimination Against Women* (New York: UNIFEM, 1998), pp. 11–19. Landsberg-Lewis cites a number of examples: the CEDAW Convention influenced constitutional debates in Colombia, in particular by having substantive equality included within the new Colombian constitution. Similar results were achieved in South Africa and Brazil.

[139] H. Shin, 'CEDAW and Women's Human Rights: Achievements and Obstacles', paper presented at the Annual Conference of the Castan Center for Human Rights Law, 3 December 2004. See also Landsberg-Lewis ibid. pp. 19–27, where examples from India, Botswana, Nepal, and Australia, among others, are highlighted.

[140] Landsberg-Lewis, ibid. pp. 28–32. Examples from Hong Kong, Costa Rica, China, Japan and the United States are provided.

[141] Division for the Advancement of Women (n. 124 above).

women's real conditions and experiences. It allows women to achieve what men have achieved, but it also recognises that women are differently situated as a result of historic, institutional and systemic discrimination. That being said, the CEDAW Convention is vulnerable – like all laws that codify discrimination and equality – to a narrow or formal interpretation, one that does not guarantee women's de facto equality. This is where, particularly for women, the strength of the ICESCR may lie. In that treaty, women do not necessarily have to invoke rights to equality and non-discrimination to claim their economic, social and cultural rights, because the ICESCR codifies distinct rights (the right to health, education, food, etc.), which can be claimed directly by women and men.

4. CONCLUSIONS

The international human rights community is at a crossroads. The treaty monitoring bodies are being critiqued as ineffective, with States parties filing reports so late that they become irrelevant and with backlogs that make the timely review of States parties impossible. A number of suggestions have been put forward for the reform of treaty monitoring bodies, including the suggestion that States parties submit a single report to the UN detailing their progress with respect to all the treaties to which they are a party.[142] It has also been suggested that this single report would be submitted to a single body responsible for monitoring compliance with all treaties. What does this type of reform mean for the realisation of women's equality in economic, social and cultural realms? While there is no doubt that the protection and promotion of economic, social and cultural rights for women have suffered from the limits of the treaty monitoring body system, there is little doubt that under a 'single report' system, women's equal rights will not be better protected.[143]

This chapter has exposed that the CEDAW Committee has particular expertise in the analysis of women's economic, social and cultural disadvantage. They are the only body that is unequivocally concerned with women's equality in all realms. There is a real concern that under the proposed reporting system, women's particular disadvantage and inequality will not receive the same attention that it currently receives through this specialised body.[144] Women's inequality in economic, social and cultural realms can only be detected, understood and addressed if the details of women's particular experiences are exposed, analysed and assessed. It is the details, the particularity of women's experiences, which substantive equality aims to address. And so, any reform to the treaty monitoring system must leave intact a mechanism that requires States parties to report, in depth, on women's equal enjoyment of economic, social and cultural rights and that allows a specialised body, with expertise on the application of substantive equality in all realms, to review State party compliance with the CEDAW Convention.

That being said, it cannot be denied that the current treaty monitoring body system is not as effective as it could be. There are a number of reforms

[142] See: *Report of the Secretary-General, Strengthening of the United Nations: an agenda for change*, UN Doc. A/57/387, 9 September 2002, paras. 52–54, available at: <http://daccessdds.un.org/doc/UNDOC/GEN/N02/583/26/PDF/N0258326.pdf>.

[143] It should be noted that a 'single report approach' to treaty reform was not supported by a meeting of international experts on treaty body reform in Malbun, Liechtenstein. See UN General Assembly, Letter from the UN Permanent Representative of Liechtenstein to the United Nations

Addressed to the Secretary-General, Annex: Report of a meeting on reform of the UN human rights treaty body system, Malbun, Liechtenstein, 4–7 May, 2003, UN Doc. A/58/123, paras. 20–28.

[144] This cause for concern has been expressed in other areas of United Nations reform. For example, Stephen Lewis, UN Special Envoy for HIV/AIDS in Africa, in a speech at Harvard University for a conference on UN reform, critiqued the new High-Level Panel on UN System-Wide coherence in areas of development, humanitarian assistance and environment on the basis that it is not promoting women's rights. The panel, comprised of fifteen experts, includes just three women and calls for gender mainstreaming within the three identified areas. Lewis states:

> [I]t's darn near criminal to believe, as so many nation states apparently believe, that mainstreaming gender through those three operational activities will lead to improvement in the human rights of women. It never has; in fact, mainstreaming, with its pathetic illusion of transformation, leads to a cul de sac for women. What is needed – I've said it before, and I shall say it ad nauseam – is an international women's agency, within the United Nations, to do for women what UNICEF does for children. It's as simple and straightforward as that.

See Speech by Stephen Lewis to Harvard University Rights Journal Conference on UN Reform and Human Rights, 25 February 2006.

that could be implemented that would ensure a focus on women's rights is not lost, while rendering the CEDAW Committee more effective in terms of enforcement. For example, the CEDAW Committee could try to create a real dialogue between States parties and NGOs. This could assist in the establishment of more constructive relationships between NGOs and governments. The CEDAW Committee could require States parties to file frequent periodic updates on progress made on particular issues of concern, to ensure that the State party is taking concrete action on the issue. The CEDAW Committee could ensure that its Concluding Comments are concrete and specific, rather than overarching and general. This would make it very clear to States parties what actions are required of them to be in compliance with the CEDAW Convention.

Ultimately, the efficacy of the CEDAW Committee may be determined by the political will of States parties. And so, perhaps the most important work to be done to ensure States parties meet their human rights obligations to women is to continue to pressure, shame and embarrass governments by reminding them of their commitments made and their commitments broken.[145]

---

[145] A good starting point for exerting this type of pressure would be to draw on the 'pledges' made by those countries appointed to the newly established Human Rights Council. Many of these pledges refer broadly to commitments within the treaty monitoring body system.

27

Committee on the Rights of the Child

Overcoming Inertia in This Age of No Alternatives

Geraldine Van Bueren*

1. INTRODUCTION: OVERCOMING INERTIA IN THIS AGE OF NO ALTERNATIVES

It is ironic that an economic right, the right of the unborn to inherit property, is recognised and well protected by many countries. Yet, the economic and social rights of children, whilst alive, are rarely as well protected.[1] This is despite the recognition by the Inter-American Court of Human Rights', amongst others,[2] that the true and full protection of children requires their enjoyment of all rights, including their economic, social and cultural rights enshrined in treaty law, such as those in the UN Convention on the Rights of the Child.

The UN Convention on the Rights of the Child was, at its adoption, a pioneering global treaty embracing the full range of human rights – civil, political, economic, social and cultural – in one treaty with a unified monitoring body. At the time of drafting, some cynicism was expressed about the wisdom of this 'alternative' approach but time has shown that the holistic approach of the Convention on the Rights of the Child has served to challenge the concept that child poverty only concerns economic and social rights and that in order to eradicate child poverty the full range of rights needs to

be considered. The importance of civil and political rights in combating child poverty ought not to be overlooked. The Committee on the Rights of the Child, for example, recommended to South Africa that there ought to be the full participation of youth (defined as those below the age of 25) in the development of strategies to respond to HIV/AIDs.[3]

The Convention's unitary approach has since been followed in the African Charter on the Rights and Welfare of the Child, which focuses not only on the implementation of economic and social rights in peace but also armed conflict and which has created its own Committee of Experts on the Rights and Welfare of the Child.[4] The Charter may serve in the future as a catalyst to assist African states to incorporate expressly children's economic and social rights provisions into their national constitutions as some have done,

---

* Geraldine Van Bueren, a barrister, is Professor of International Human Rights Law in Queen Mary, University of London and Visiting Fellow at Kellogg College, Oxford.

[1] See for example the decision by the European Commission on Human Rights in *Paton v. United Kingdom*, 'certain rights are attributed to the conceived but unborn child, in particular the right to inherit'. Application number 6959/75. *Cf.* Islamic states and children born outside of marriage in G. Van Bueren, 'The International Protection of Family Members' Rights as the 21st Century Approaches', *Human Rights Quarterly*, Vol. 17, No. 4 (1995), pp. 732–766.

[2] *Juridical Condition and Human Rights of the Child*, Advisory Opinion OC-17/2002 of August 28 2002, Inter-Am. Ct. H. R. (Ser. A) No. 17 (2002).

[3] UN Doc CRC/A/55/41. See also the discussion of participation of children and families in the policy development of non-governmental organisations in Uganda in J. Boyden, 'Childhood and the Policy Makers: A Comparative Perspective on the Globalisation of Childhood', in A. James and A. Prout (eds.), *Constructing and Reconstructing Childhood: Contemporary Issues in the Sociological Study of Childhood* (London: Routledge Falmer, 1997), pp. 184–201 . This has also been the approach of the Supreme Court of the Philippines in *Minors Oposa v. Secretary of the Department of the Environment and National Resources* (DENR) 1994, Vol. 33 International Legal Materials 173; see also T. Allen, 'The Philippine Children's Case: Recognising Legal Standing for Future Generations', *Georgetown International Environmental Law Review*, Vol. 6 (1994), pp. 713–741.

[4] A. Lloyd, 'How to guarantee credence? Recommendations and Proposals for the African Committee of Experts on the Rights and Welfare of the Child', *International Journal of Children's Rights*, Vol. 12, No. 1 (2004), pp. 21–40 and B. Mezmur, 'The African Committee of Experts on the Rights and Welfare of the Child: An Update', *African Human Rights Law Journal*, Vol. 6, No. 2 (2006), pp. 549–571. See further chapter 17.

including Algeria,[5] Angola[6] and South Africa.[7] Enshrining such rights for children in treaties also means that they become 'politically enforceable' in the sense that they carry a more persuasive force in political debates on the budget and other questions of resource.[8]

Such a holistic approach is important as it creates the necessary space to include cultural rights as an equal partner in the combating of poverty. The dangerous tendency to omit cultural in the consideration of 'economic and social rights' appears to be more than an attempt to reduce lengthy titles and descriptions. There is almost a silent and unpublished assumption that culture represents the forces of conservatism and could be used to obstruct the implementation of economic and social rights. Yet the recognition and implementation of cultural rights is essential for combating all forms of poverty including child poverty. It is for this reason that the term social justice will be used interchangeably in this chapter to refer to all economic, social and cultural rights.

The deeply embedded nature of child poverty persists for a number of reasons. Children suffer from a double disadvantage caused by the operation of two distinct ideologies: the role and capacity of the family to provide for the economic and social entitlements of the children and resistance of the law to take its capacity for the strategic alleviation of poverty as a legal cause of action seriously. Economic and social entitlements are frequently and erroneously regarded as exclusively adult. This common but erroneous perception fails to consider that economic, social and cultural rights are not only commodities, but also essential for the right to live in security and dignity, a right which is as pertinent for children as for adults.

There has also been a lack of focus on the implications of the best interests of the child principle and children's social justice rights. Consequentially it is only a minority, albeit a growing minority, of States, which have enshrined general economic, social and cultural rights applicable to both adults and children in their bills of rights, and fewer expressly for children.[9] However, even in States which do not enshrine specific economic, social and cultural rights in their national constitutions, binding international law, in a variety of forms, is still applicable to both monist and dualist States, as this Chapter will demonstrate.

Finally, children who live in jurisdictions where social justice rights have not been legally enshrined at the domestic level can only legally rely upon those rights recognised at the international level, particularly the 1989 United Nations Convention on the Rights of the Child. However, this Convention has still not been used to its full potential or fully enforced, as the child poverty statistics shamefully bear witness. This under-enforcement is not because efficacy is measured by the number of decisions that courts or other bodies may find against government. It is because, unacceptably, child poverty has risen in many states since the coming into force of the Convention on the Rights of the Child in 1990, including, for example, in most of the wealthier industrialised states: in seventeen of the twenty-four surveyed member states of the Organisation for Economic Cooperation and Development (OECD).[10]

This prompts the question of whether, despite the successes in the reduction of child mortality discussed above, there is an effective role for international law, and particularly the UN Convention on the Rights of the Child, in combating child poverty. The answer is that there is a role, but it requires new and innovative constructive approaches. Such fundamental changes in realising the potential of law is difficult to obtain as lawyers in most of the world's jurisdictions have been educated in law schools to accept that law cannot play a strategic role in poverty reduction. This in turn prolongs the jurisprudence which

---

[5] Article 59, Constitution of the People's Democratic Republic of Algeria.

[6] Article 31, Constitutional Law of the Republic of Angola.

[7] Section 28, Constitution of South Africa.

[8] H. Schwartz, 'Social Welfare Rights Should be Constitutional Rights', in H. J Cremer et al. (eds.), *Tradition und Weltoffenheit des Rechts Festschrift fur Helmut Steinberger*, (Berlin, Springer-Verlag Berlin and Heidelberg GmbH & Co. K, 2002), pp. 989-1000. This argument was made in relation to Bills of Rights but is also applicable in relation to international legislative forms, see further below.

[9] For States which have incorporated the Convention, both generally and specifically, see G. Van Bueren, 'Combating Child Poverty – Human Rights Approaches', *Human Rights Quarterly*, Vol. 21, No. 3 (1990), pp. 680–706.

[10] UNICEF, 'Child Poverty in Rich Countries', *Innocenti Report Card* No. 6 (Florence: UNICEF Innocenti Research Centre, 2005).

does not create sufficient space to allow in alternative views of law.[11]

The first step is to accept that in our twenty-first century 'age of no alternatives', the Convention on the Rights of the Child provides a different path in establishing a new juridical order for children. Consequently, the UN Committee on the Rights of the Child is duty bound, as a matter of international law, to try all approaches, including innovative ones, to combat child poverty. Because of the position of children in international law, these may be different from actions taken under other treaties.[12]

The second step is to accept that there ought to be, as a matter of international law, much greater analysis of the international legal status of the principle of the best interests of the child as it applies to children's economic, social and cultural rights. This is not only important for children living in the States parties to the Convention, but also has significant implications for children living in the two non-States parties: Somalia and the United States of America.

Finally, because States either have a scarcity of resources or plead that their resources are scarce, the UN Committee on the Rights of the Child needs to provide guidance and reasons, not just on the content of children's social justice rights, but also on how States balance the concepts of 'progressive' and 'available resources' with other priorities. This is the most challenging of the tasks, but also potentially the most fruitful, as it would provide practical and reasoned guidance, which States could include in their budgetary planning.

The challenge is urgent because, as the Committee on the Rights of the Child itself has recognised, '[g]rowing up in relative poverty undermines children's well-being, social inclusion and self-esteem and reduces opportunities for learning and development. Growing up in conditions of absolute poverty has even more serious consequences, threatening children's survival and their health, as well as undermining the basic quality of life'.[13]

2. THE COMMITTEE ON THE RIGHTS OF THE CHILD

The Committee on the Rights of the Child was established pursuant to Article 43 of the Convention on the Rights of the Child to supervise the implementation of the Convention. It meets annually for three sessions. The States Parties to the Convention are required by Article 44 to submit an initial report on measures adopted which give effect to the rights recognised therein and on the progress made on the enjoyment of those rights within two years of its entry into force for the State party concerned and thereafter every five years.

The non-discrimination duty enshrined in Article 2 is unusual as it not only applies the duty not to discriminate in relation to the subject of the treaty i.e. children, but Article 2(1) places a duty on States parties to respect and ensure the rights in the Convention 'irrespective of the child's or his or her parent's or legal guardian's race, colour, sex, language, religion, political or other opinion, national, ethnic or social origin, property, disability, birth or other status'. Hence the principle of equality in implementing the economic and social rights of children extends to all children regardless of the status of the child's parents or legal guardians and in this way family members indirectly benefit from the economic and social entitlements of the child.

Article 4 of the Convention on the Rights of the Child appears on the face of the treaty to contain an extraordinary omission, the omission of the word and concept 'progressive' as Article 4 only provides that, '[w]ith regard to economic, social and cultural rights, States parties shall undertake such measures to the maximum extent of their available resources and, where needed, within the framework of international co-operation'. In contrast to Article 2(1) of the International Covenant on Economic, Social and Cultural Rights Article 4 of the Convention on the Rights of the Child omits

---

[11] This pertains even thought principle 4 of the UN Basic Principles of the Role of Lawyers 1990 emphasises the role of lawyers in assisting the poor: 'Governments and professional associations of lawyers shall promote programmes to inform the public about their rights and duties under the law and the important role of lawyers in protecting their fundamental freedoms. Special attention should be given to assisting the poor and other disadvantaged persons so as to enable them to assert their rights and where necessary call upon the assistance of lawyers'.

[12] See the analysis of customary international law and jus cogens below in Section 2.

[13] General Comment No. 7 (n. 25 below), para. 26.

any express reference to achieving progressively the full realisation of the rights. However, the Committee, in its General Comment on General Measures of Implementation does refer to the General Comments of the Committee on Economic, Social and Cultural Rights, which 'should be seen as complementary'.[14] The Committee also notes that Article 4 is 'similar' to Article 2(1) of the Covenant and the omission has not appeared to have made any negative impact on the approach of the Committee on the Rights of the Child particularly as the Committee observes, however without producing any evidence, that Article 4 'introduces the concept of "progressive realization" of such rights'.[15] It is also arguable that as progressive appears in the Covenant which applies to 'everyone' and all States parties to the Covenant are also party to the Convention then the concept of progressive is applicable to the States parties of both treaties. Nevertheless it is a regrettable omission.

The Committee has observed that the duty enshrined in Article 4 includes ensuring that all domestic legislation is fully compatible with the economic and social rights of the Convention and that these provisions 'can be directly applied'.[16] The Committee on the Rights of the Child has consistently emphasised that economic, social and cultural rights, as well as civil and political rights, must be regarded as justiciable and that domestic law sets out children's entitlements in sufficient detail to enable remedies for non-compliance to be effective.[17]

A 'satisfying' consequence of the almost universal ratification of the Convention has been the development at the national level of a wide variety of new child-focused and child-sensitive bodies including children's rights units at the heart of Government, ministers for children, inter-ministerial committees on children, parliamen-

tary committees, child impact analysis, children's budgets and 'state of children's rights' reports, NGO coalitions on children's rights, children's ombudspersons and children's rights commissioners.[18] Whilst the Committee on the Rights of the Child acknowledges that 'some of these developments may seem largely cosmetic', their emergence at the least indicates that good governance includes good child governance.

Although the Committee on the Rights of the Child has striven generally successfully to use its mandate to the fullest, the protection of children's economic, social and cultural rights is significantly weakened by the inability of the Committee to receive individual and group complaints from children on violations of these rights. This is in striking contrast to the Committee under the African Charter on the Rights and Welfare of the Child, which has been given the jurisdiction by the African Union to receive such complaints. The fact that children living in one region of the world are entitled to petition on violations of their social justice rights trumps any arguments about justiciability and children's competence as the institutional competence, as distinct from the constitutional competence, is a universal.[19] If a regional tribunal is able to accept petitions from children alleging violations of their economic and social rights so are all regional and international tribunals focusing on children's rights. It is only the artificial restraints placed by national State interests which prevent them from so doing rather than any inherent disability in the powers and structures of the tribunal. There is an urgent need for States to adopt an optional protocol to the UN Convention on the Rights of the Child on implementation in general and petitioning in particular.[20]

Instead, the UN Committee on the Rights of the Child principal powers are focused on monitoring the States parties' reports and providing technical advice and assistance, adopting the same holistic method for both civil and political rights and

---

[14] Committee on the Rights of the Child, *General Comment No. 5, General measures of implementation of the Convention on the Rights of the Child* (arts. 4, 42 and 44, para. 6), U.N. Doc. CRC/GC/2003/5 (2003).

[15] Ibid. at para. 7.

[16] In 1999, the Committee on the Rights of the Child held a two-day workshop to commemorate the tenth anniversary of adoption of the Convention on the Rights of the Child by the United Nations General Assembly. The workshop focused on general measures of implementation following which the Committee adopted detailed conclusions and recommendations, see U.N. Doc CRC/C/90, para. 291.

[17] *General Comment No. 5* (n. 14 above), para. 25.

[18] Ibid. at para. 9.

[19] G. Van Bueren, 'Including the Excluded: The Case for an Economic, Social and Cultural Human Rights Act', *Public Law* (2002), p. 456.

[20] See further below. The need for a petitioning mechanism for the UN Convention on the Rights of the Child was first raised by the author when she represented Amnesty International during the drafting of the UN Convention itself. In this she was supported by the International Commission of Jurists.

economic, social and cultural rights. The provision of technical advice and assistance is central to implementation of the Convention but does not reduce a State party's responsibility in the field of child poverty eradication. The Convention does incorporate useful innovations and refinements. Article 42 recognises that although frequently disparaged, a 'trickle down' effect can be effective and important to children. Children's rights are to be made known to children and adults alike through 'appropriate and active means', which provides an opportunity to involve children in social justice policy and political considerations and once fully informed, to help improve and implement them. The Convention intends that both children and adults should participate in the ongoing dialogue which is the theoretical justification of the reporting process.

To assist it in reaching a better understanding of the issues, the Committee has adopted the constructive approach of arranging thematic discussions and these have included implementing child rights in early childhood[21], the private sector,[22] HIV/AIDS[23] and economic exploitation.[24] Following on from the discussions, the Committee adopts recommendations, taking into account the issues raised. Representatives of governments, United Nations human rights mechanisms, United Nations bodies and specialized agencies, non-governmental organizations, national human rights institutions as well as individual children and experts are invited to participate.

In addition, the Committee has followed the practice of other human rights treaty bodies in adopting General Comments on the ambits of the Convention's rights. Although the Committee was initially slow to produce its General Comments they are now, cumulatively, beginning to develop into a valuable resource and dovetail, reinforce and expand upon those of the Committee on Economic, Social and Cultural Rights. They have issued ten General Comments of which those most pertinent to removing the causes of child poverty are: implementing child rights in early child-

hood;[25] treatment of unaccompanied and separated children outside their country of origin;[26] general measures of implementation for the Convention on the Rights of the Child;[27] adolescent health and development in the context of the Convention on the Rights of the Child;[28] and HIV/AIDS and the rights of the children.[29] Other General Comments also have a bearing on the denial of children's economic, social and cultural rights including children's rights in juvenile justice,[30] the first General Comment on the aims of education[31] and the rights of children living with disabilities.[32]

The General Comments have particular significance in contributing to the 'jurisprudence' of the Convent due to the lack of a petitioning system. General Comment No. 5 interprets 'to the maximum extent of their available resources' to include extra-territorial obligations.[33] According to the Committee on the Rights of the Child, when States ratify the Convention they take upon themselves obligations not only to implement it within their jurisdiction, but also to contribute, through international cooperation, to global implementation, thus seeking to develop the concept of an international responsibility for child poverty alleviation, beyond state borders;[34] such an approach being consistent with the best interests of the

---

[21] *United Nations Committee on the Rights of the Child Day of Discussion: Implementing Child Rights in Early Childhood* (17 September 2004), UN Doc SR 979, Palais Wilson.

[22] U.N. Doc. CRC/C/121, 31st Session, 20 September 2002.

[23] U.N. Doc. CRC/C/79, Annex VI, 19th Session, 5 October 1998.

[24] U.N. Doc. CRC/C/20, 4th Session, 4 October 1993.

[25] Committee on the Rights of the Child, *General Comment No. 7, Implementing child rights in early childhood*, Fortieth session (2005), U.N. Doc. CRC/C/GC/7/Rev.1.

[26] Committee on the Rights of the Child, *General Comment No. 6, Treatment of Unaccompanied and Separated Children Outside their Country of Origin*, Thirty-ninth session (2005), U.N. Doc. CRC/GC/2005/6.

[27] Committee on the Rights of the Child, *General Comment No. 5, General measures of implementation of the Convention on the Rights of the Child* (Thirty-fourth session, 2003), U.N. Doc. CRC/GC/2003/5.

[28] Committee on the Rights of the Child, *General Comment No. 4, Adolescent health and development in the context of the Convention on the Rights of the Child* (Thirty-third session, 2003), U.N. Doc. CRC/GC/2003/4.

[29] Committee on the Rights of the Child, *General Comment No. 3, HIV/AIDS and the right of the child* (Thirty-second session, 2003), U.N. Doc. CRC/GC/2003/3.

[30] *Children's rights in juvenile justice* (Fortieth session, 2007) U.N. Doc. CRC/C/GC/10. 9 February 2007

[31] *General Comment No. 1, The aims of education.* U.N. Doc CRC/GC/2001/1. (2001).

[32] Committee on the Rights of the Child, *General Comment No. 9, The rights of children with disabilities*, Forty-third session (2007), U.N. Doc. CRC/C/GC/9.

[33] *General Comment No 5* (n. 17 above), para. 7.

[34] The articles of the Convention which relate to international cooperation explicitly are: Articles 7 (2); 11 (2); 17 (b); 21 (e); 22 (2); 23 (4); 24 (4); 27 (4); 28 (3); 34 and 35.

child. The Committee seeks to trace the historical source of the international obligation to combat global child poverty by arguing that Articles 55 and 56 of the Charter of the United Nations identifies the overall purposes of international economic and social cooperation and that members pledge themselves under the Charter 'to take joint and separate action in cooperation with the Organization' to achieve these purposes.[35] Consistent with this the United Nations General Assembly special session on children, in 2002, also committed States not only 'to develop or strengthen as a matter of urgency if possible by the end of 2003 national...action plans with a set of specific time-bound and measurable goals and targets based on this plan of action...', but also regional plans with similar time goals and measurable targets.[36]

The Committee has emphasised that particular attention needs to be given to identifying and giving priority to marginalised and disadvantaged groups of children,[37] including children living with disabilities. The General Comment on the rights of children with disabilities is critical for the rights of 150 million children living with disabilities,[38] and was drafted prior to the adoption of the Convention on the Protection and Promotion of the Rights and Dignity of Persons with Disabilities. Since the draft of the convention had been concluded, the General Comment was able to take into account the philosophy of the new treaty. They both begin from the assumption that the barrier is not the disability itself but rather a combination of social, cultural, attitudinal and physical obstacles which children with disabilities encounter in their daily lives. The Convention on the Rights of the Child was also the first human rights treaty that contained a specific reference to disability as a prohibited ground for discrimination[39] and a specific article was dedicated to the rights of children with disabilities, namely Article 23. The social jus-

tice facets of this article are strengthened by the absence of any reservations or declarations to it by any of States parties to the Convention's and it is particularly valuable to children with disabilities living in poverty as the treaty concerning persons with disabilities has not yet entered into force.

The goal of this General Comment is therefore to promote the necessary action to remove those barriers, which is particularly relevant to the more than 80 per cent of children with disabilities living in developing countries with little or no access to services, schooling and literacy skills. The Committee endorses the recognition that most of the causes of disabilities, such as war, illness and poverty, are preventable and these in turn also prevent and reduce the secondary impacts of disabilities, often caused by the lack of early and timely intervention. However, the implementation of Article 4 of the Convention on the Rights of the Child[40] in relation to children living with disabilities has been a concern, as many States parties do not allocate sufficient resources and have even reduced the budget allocated to children over the years.[41] This has particularly grave consequences for children with disabilities as where State parties fail to allocate sufficient funds to ensure compulsory and free quality education for all children, they are unlikely to allocate funds to train teachers for children with disabilities or to provide for the necessary teaching aids and transportation for children with disabilities. The increasing emphasis on decentralisation and privatisation of services do not reduce the ultimate legal responsibility of the State parties to ensure that adequate funds are allocated to children with disabilities along with strict guidelines for service delivery.

The General Comment also notes that funding must also be ensured for other programmes aimed at including children with disabilities into mainstream education, inter alia by renovating schools

---

[35] *General Comment No 5* (n. 17 above), para. 60. In the United Nations Millennium Declaration and at the United Nations General Assembly special session on children, States have pledged themselves, in particular, to international cooperation to eliminate poverty.

[36] Ibid., para. 35.

[37] Ibid., para. 30.

[38] Ibid.

[39] See Article 2. The other treaty bodies have considered disability under the 'other status' provision. See W. Vandenhole, *Non-Discrimination and Equality in the View of the UN Human Rights Treaty Bodies*, (Antwerpen/Oxford: Intersentia, 2005), pp. 170–172.

[40] Article 4 provides that, 'States Parties shall undertake all appropriate legislative, administrative, and other measures for the implementation of the rights recognized in the present Convention. With regard to economic, social and cultural rights, States Parties shall undertake such measures to the maximum extent of their available resources and, where needed, within the framework of international co-operation'.

[41] *General Comment No. 9* (n. 28 above), para. 20.

to render them physically accessible to children with disabilities.[42]

3. REASONS FOR PRIORITISING CHILDREN'S ECONOMIC AND SOCIAL RIGHTS

The Convention on the Rights of the Child does not contain a specific recommendation regarding the most appropriate percentage of a State party's budget which should be dedicated to services and programmes for children. It is, however, clearly not only economic resources which are needed to end child poverty; those who seek to argue that children must take priority in the allocation of resources to end poverty need to substantiate such claims. There needs to be argument to convince governments and courts that such prioritisation is required by law. So far such a justification has been lacking. In order to justify prioritising children's social justice rights enshrined in the Convention over other vulnerable groups, attention ought to be paid to the status of a particular international legal rule, in this case, the principle of best interests of the child. These reasons depend upon arguments concerning the uniqueness of childhood.

Firstly, children differ from other vulnerable groups because their disempowerment is socially constructed and so is largely capable of being reduced, whereas childhood is a biological and psychological irreducible fact.[43] Secondly, the human rights specific to childhood are 'essential to their cognitive, physical, cultural, emotional and social development, particularly as children are disproportionately vulnerable to the negative effects of adequate and insecure living conditions'.[44] This is based on the recognition that a higher standard is required, because childhood cannot wait, cannot be placed on hold, and failure to realise their rights now will have long-lasting consequences. This is not to defend the inadequacy of some international human rights law standards as they apply to other vulnerable groups, particularly

in relation to adults living with disabilities. However, the solution is to raise the standards of entitlement of other sections of the community and not to ignore the priority status that children have in relation to economic, social and cultural rights.

4. THE STATUS OF THE BEST INTERESTS OF CHILD AS ENSHRINED IN THE CONVENTION

There are a number of rights in the Convention on the Rights of the Child whose full implementation would have a direct impact on child poverty, including the right to an adequate standard of living, education rights, and health rights. However, before discussing these rights, it is necessary to examine the legal status of the principle of the best interests of the child. It is tempting but erroneous to conclude that because the Convention on the Rights of the Child has acquired almost universal ratification[45] it has evolved in its entirety, albeit rapidly, into customary international law. The number and range of reservations makes such a claim implausible.[46] Yet without acclaim some of the provisions of the Convention have quietly attained the status of customary international law.[47]

The best interests of the child is sometimes casually dismissed as sentimental, but the principle offers much unexplored potential for eradicating child poverty even though there still remains vestiges of the belief that the standard of best interests applies only to what were traditionally described as private law and not to public law.

The Convention on the Rights of the Child did not create the principle of best interests but rather transformed it through clearly placing it in a more holistic context. The principal regional and global children's rights treaties enshrine the clear recognition of the symbiotic relationship between civil and political rights and economic, social and cultural rights, or what Scott describes as an 'organic

---

[42] Ibid.

[43] O. O'Neill, *Constructions of Reason – Explorations of Kant's Practical Philosophy* (Cambridge: Cambridge University Press, 1989), pp. 202–203.

[44] *Report of the Special Rapporteur on adequate housing as a component of the right to an adequate standard of living, Mr. Miloon Kothari*, U.N. Doc E/CN.4/2001/51, para. 69.

[45] One hundred ninety-two states parties are party to the Convention, with only Somalia and the United States as non-parties.

[46] The full list of reservations available at <http://www.ohchr.org>.

[47] Article 38(1)(b) Statute of the International Court of Justice, 'international custom as evidence of a general practice accepted as law' available at <http://www.icj-cij.org/documents/index.php?p1=4&p2=2&p3=0>.

interdependence'.[48] In particular, the Convention through the application of the best interests of the child to 'all actions' highlights the symbiotic relationship between civil and political rights and economic, social and cultural rights for children and it is beyond dispute that the words 'all actions' clearly include social justice, particularly as from the earliest child rights instrument, the 1924 Declaration of the Rights of the Child, social justice rights have been a strong component of children's rights.[49] However, the impact of the best interests of the child in relation to children's economic and social rights has yet to have a significant systematic impact at the national level. This is also partly because in the *discourse* on children's rights, best interests has been used principally to redress the consequences of violations of *civil* rights, and has not been effectively developed as a strategic legal instrument of child poverty reduction. At one level this is surprising, as the application of best interests to children's social justice rights, such as the right to clean water, is in some ways easier to implement, because the right to clean water does not concern the complex issues of weighing different cultural and religious values or of investigating the sometimes hidden dynamics of family life.

Importantly, the Convention demonstrates that children as a group, rightfully or wrongfully, as a matter of international law stand in a different position to other groups in democratic societies, as they are the only vulnerable group to whom the best interests principle applies. In international law the best interests' principle does not apply to adults living with disabilities or to other vulnerable groups. Although this may be a reason for extending the application of the principle in international law, such shortcomings should not be used to undermine the principle as applied to children as the Constitutional Court of South Africa appeared to do in *Grootboom*, ironically at the urging of the

counsel for Grootboom.[50] The judgment of the Constitutional Court in this case deservedly attracted plaudits for setting out the requirements of a housing policy towards the general population[51] and highlighting the entitlements of impoverished adults, and also children without families,[52] but its judgement in relation to homeless families[53] laid down a significantly lower standard of protection for many children than international law requires. This may have been because no arguments were presented to the Court on the Court's international legal duty to consider the best interests of the child, even though South Africa is party to the Convention on the Rights of the Child.

As a general overriding principle, the best interests of the child are enshrined in Article 3(1) of the UN Convention on the Rights of the Child as, 'in all actions concerning children...the best interests of the child shall be a primary consideration'. The reference to all actions is sufficiently broad to encompass all actions and inaction. Article 3(1) therefore has the advantage, unlike most other provisions in the Convention on the Rights of the Child, as a principle to be considered in relation not only to all the rights in the treaty but residually to all economic and social actions concerning children, whether expressly protected by the Convention or not.

Two approaches offer themselves. Firstly, the identification of any provisions which have not attracted reservations and which may amount to facets of existing norms of customary international law, such as forms of sexual exploitation violating the prohibitions on inhuman or

---

[48] See C. Scott, 'The Interdependence and Permeability of Human Rights Norms: Towards a Partial Fusion of the International Covenants on Human Rights', *Osgoode Hall Law Journal* Vol. 27 (1989), pp. 769–878, at 779–781.

[49] In the Preamble, 'mankind owes to the child the best it has to give'. See Articles. 1,2,3 and 4 of the five article Declaration reproduced in G. Van Bueren, *International Documents on Children*, 2nd Edition (Amsterdam: Kluwer, 1998).

[50] Conversation of the author with Geoff Budlender, one of the lawyers acting in *Grootboom*. For case, see *Government of the Republic of South Africa v. Grootboom and Others* 2000 (11) BCLR 1169 (CC).

[51] C. R. Sunstein, 'Social and Economic Rights, Lessons from South Africa' (May 2001), *University of Chicago, Public Law Working Paper No. 12*.

[52] J. Sloth-Nielsen, 'Child's Right to Social Services, the Right to Social Security, and Primary Prevention of Child Abuse: Some Conclusions in the Aftermath of Grootboom', *South African Journal of Human Rights*, Vol. 17 (2001), p. 210; G. Van Bueren, 'No Turning Back – The Right to Housing is Justiciable', in M. Cheadle, D. Davis and N. Haysom (eds.), *South African Constitutional Law: The Bill of Rights*, (Durban: Butterworths 2002), pp. 473–490.

[53] For a critical approach towards the Court's approach to reasonableness and the homeless see D. Bilchitz, 'Towards a Reasonable Approach to the Minimum Core', *South African Journal of Human Rights*, Vol. 19 (2003), p. 1–26.

degrading treatment.[54] Secondly, the identification of provisions which are without reservation and which are also reflected universally in national, regional and global legislation and jurisprudence and are 'a clear and continuous habit of doing certain actions which has grown up under the conviction that these actions are, according to international law, obligatory or right'.[55] It is this second approach which is applicable in establishing the normative status of the best interests of the child.

Article 3(1) has been accepted by 192 states. Although the making of reservations is by no means a conclusive test, as States are able to opt out of customary rules by persistent and consistent objection, the few reservations to Article 3(1) which have been made are of such a nature that that they endorse the principle rather than reject it.[56] The author has argued elsewhere that in every economic and social action concerning a child, the best interests of the child as a primary although not the sole consideration, is a principle that has attained the status of international customary law.[57] In this, the customary principle reflects the language of the Convention on the Rights of the Child.

The author has also argued that the status of best interests as enshrined in Article 3(1), as well as attaining international customary law status, has evolved into the enhanced status of jus cogens or a peremptory norm of general international law.[58] Under the Vienna Convention on the Law of Treaties 1969, such a norm is of considerable significance, as it means that it is a norm recognised and accepted by the entire international community, from which no derogation is permitted, and which can only be modified by a subsequent norm

of general international law having the same character.[59] Thus, the attainment of the jus cogens status of the principle that the best interests of the child applies as a primary consideration in all actions concerning children, including economic and social actions by the State, opens up significant alternative approaches in which to explore the potential of the Convention on the Rights of the Child in combating child poverty in both State and non-State parties.

However, the impact of the best interests of the child in relation to children's economic and social rights has yet to have a significant systematic impact on child poverty. This is partly because in the discourse of children's rights, best interests has been used principally to redress the consequences of violations of children's civil rights in the context of family law, even though the Committee on the Rights of the Child has emphasised that the principle requires 'active measures throughout government, parliament and the judiciary' and that every legislative, administrative and judicial body or institution, including in the economic and social rights sphere is required to apply the best interests principle systematically.[60]

5. CHILD POVERTY AND THE PRIMARY AND CAUSATIVE RIGHTS ENSHRINED IN THE CONVENTION

The Convention on the Rights of the Child[61] has raised the visibility of violations of children's within the work of the Committee on Economic, Social and Cultural Right.[62] Unlike the differences in jurisprudence between the UN Committee on the Rights of the Child and the regional human rights courts,[63] there appears so far to be

---

[54] See further G. Van Bueren, 'Protection against Child Sexual Abuse and Exploitation – A Suggested Human Rights Approach', *Int. Journal of Children's Rights*, Vol. 2 (1994), pp. 45–61.

[55] R. Jennings and A. Watts, *Oppenheim's International Law*, Vol. 1: Peace, parts 1 to 4, 9th Edition (London: Longman Publishing, 1992), p. 27.

[56] See the study of reservations to the best interests principle in G. Van Bueren, *The Separation of Powers and the International Legal Status of the Best Interests of the Child in Assisting Domestic Courts Protect Children's Economic and Social Rights*, Proceedings of the International Conference on the Rights of the Child, (Montreal, Canada: Wilson Lafleur 2007).

[57] Ibid.

[58] Ibid.

[59] Article 53.

[60] *General Comment No. 5* (n. 17 above), para.12.

[61] At the time of writing only Somalia and the United States have not ratified this Convention.

[62] See for example: Committee on Economic, Social and Cultural Rights, *General Comment 11, Plans of action for primary education* (Twentieth session, 1999), U.N. Doc. E/C.12/1999/4 (1999); Committee on Economic, Social and Cultural Rights, *General Comment 15, The right to water* (Twenty-ninth session, 2003), U.N. Doc. E/C.12/2002/11 (2002), para. 16.

[63] See for example the differences between the European Court of Human Rights and the UN Committee on the Rights of the Child in relation to child physical punishment discussed in G. Van Bueren, *Child Rights in*

a welcome mutual reinforcement of raised standards between the Committee on the Rights of the Child and the Committee on Economic, Social and Cultural Rights.

As the Convention on the Rights of the Child and the two Protocols are holistic instruments, each and every right in these three treaties may, in specific circumstances, be relevant to combating child poverty, not only those classically described as being economic, social and cultural rights. The most relevant right in this regard includes the umbrella right to non-discrimination, both as an obstacle to access to resources and as a consequence of living in relative or absolute poverty.[64] The Convention on the Rights of the Child adds ethnic origin and disability to the prohibited grounds found in the International Covenant on Economic and Social Rights. These groups also include children of other nationalities and children who are born stateless and are particularly vulnerable to violations of their economic and social rights. The Committee on Economic, Social and Cultural Rights has expressed concern over the discrimination against aliens by Spain, particularly amongst Romani and North African children and over the nationality of Haitian children born in the Dominican Republic; this is consistent with Article 2 (2), which also prohibits discrimination and punishment not only on the basis of the child's parentage, but also the status, activities, expressed opinions or beliefs of the child's parents, legal guardians, or family members. Such grounds also form part of the minimum core of States' obligations of equality and non-discrimination to children under the Covenant.[65]

The economic, social and cultural rights provisions of the Convention on the Rights of the Child include the following: the right to life and to survival and development and to birth registration;[66] the right not to be separated from parents because of poverty;[67] the right of access to information and material aimed at reducing poverty and improving the chances of individual child and group

claims;[68] the right to be protected from all forms of abuse and neglect;[69] the right of those temporarily separated to special protection and assistance;[70] the rights of children with disabilities;[71] the right to health;[72] the right to social security, including social insurance;[73] the right to an adequate standard of living;[74] the right to education and leisure;[75] the right to be protected from economic and sexual exploitation and abuse, and from illicit use of narcotic drugs;[76] the right to be protected from abduction, sale and trafficking as well as torture or other cruel, inhuman or degrading treatment or punishment;[77] and, depending upon the consequences of the abuse arising or resulting from poverty, the right to physical and psychological recovery and social reintegration.[78]

These rights build upon the '[s]pecial measures of protection and assistance' to be taken 'on behalf of all children and young persons' enshrined in Article 10(3) of the International Covenant on Economic, Social and Cultural Rights. In this regard it is interesting to note the observation of the Committee on Economic, Social and Cultural Rights that any suggestion that Article 10(3) is inherently non-self executing 'would seem difficult to sustain'.[79] Unless it is found that any of the specific economic, social and cultural rights of the Convention on the Rights of the Child fall outside of the broad ambit of Article 10(3) then the same self-executing capacity must logically apply to each of the Convention on the Rights of the Child's social justice rights.

The provisions enshrining children's economic, social and cultural rights in the Convention can helpfully be divided[80] into primary rights and causative rights, although they are not always mutually exclusive. Primary rights include the rights to an adequate standard of living, health, education,

---

Europe, Convergence and Divergence in Judicial Protection, (Council of Europe, 2007).

[64] Article 2.

[65] G. Van Bueren, 'Of floors and ceilings – minimum core obligations and children', in D. Brand and S. Russell (eds.), *Exploring the Core Content of Socio-Economic Right: South African and International Perspectives,* (Pretoria: Protea, 2002), pp. 183–200.

[66] Articles 6 and 7.

[67] Article 9.

[68] Articles. 12 and 17.

[69] Article 19.

[70] Article 20.

[71] Article 23.

[72] Article 24.

[73] Article 26.

[74] Article 27.

[75] Articles 28 and 31.

[76] Articles 32, 33, 34 and 36.

[77] Articles 35 and 37.

[78] Article 39.

[79] Committee on Economic, Social and Cultural Rights, *General Comment No. 3, The nature of States parties' obligations* (Fifth session, 1990) U.N. Doc E/1991/23 (1990).

[80] This is a taxonomical division and not one indicating any form of hierarchy.

and social insurance, and violations of these rights directly cause poverty. It is rare that children suffer from a violation of one primary right in isolation from the other rights,[81] so that a lack of adequate housing makes children 'twice as likely as others to suffer from such chronic diseases as respiratory or ear infections, gastrointestinal disorders and sexually transmitted diseases including HIV/AIDS'.[82]

The causative rights are rights such as the right to protection from sexual exploitation and the right to be protected from economic exploitation, to which children living in poverty are more likely to be vulnerable. In Guatemala, violence against children is increasing and, as the Committee on the Rights of the Child noted, children live in fear because they are 'continually threatened and are victims of violence, notably when they are living and/or working in the street'.[83] The division into primary rights and causative rights is helpful, as it both highlights the need to remedy violations to sexually exploited children, and simultaneously focuses attention on the necessary sustained action required in relation to primary rights, to ensure that the root cause, child poverty, is also addressed.

It also highlights the interdependence of children's civil rights in protecting against violations of children's economic and social rights. The obligation on States parties to establish an accessible register of birth (Article 7(1)) is essential, as without a verifiable record of numbers and ages it is impossible for States to plan effectively economic and social rights policies and programmes. In addition, an absence of birth documents make minimum age legislation preventing the economic, social and sexual exploitation of child labour impossible to enforce effectively.[84] It is, inter alia, for

these reasons that the Committee on the Rights of the Child has urged Ethiopia to create institutional structures that are accessible and free to implement effective birth registration including by using mobile birth registration facilities.[85] Similarly for the effective prevention of the trafficking of children for the purposes of adoption or sexual exploitation, an effective legal regime for controlling inter-country adoption is required.[86]

Although extradition is not frequently associated with violations of social justice rights, the Optional Protocol to the Convention on the Rights of the Child on the Sale of Children, Child Prostitution and Child Pornography which covers essentially the same ground as Articles 32 to 36 of the main Convention,[87] makes significant improvements in the enforcement of law and the creation of child-focused proceedings. The Protocol importantly clarifies that States may need to exercise extraterritorial jurisdiction and that offences concerning the sale of children, child prostitution and child pornography are deemed extraditable. When a request for extradition is received from a State with no extradition treaty, the requested State may usefully consider the Protocol as the legal basis for such extradition thus adding an additional layer of protection to violations of children's economic, social and cultural rights.

5.1   Right to an Adequate Standard of Living

Article 27 of the Convention is a keystone article for eliminating child poverty and creates a tripartite responsibility, of which the primary role is placed on the family, the secondary supportive role on the State and the tertiary role is undertaken by the international community. Article 27(1)

---

[81] The Committee on the Rights of the Child recommended that Germany should give greater priority to an analysis of the linkages between housing conditions, family support to the child at home and in school and the risk of dropping out of school. It also recommended that such an analysis could serve as the basis for a well-informed national debate about responding to child poverty. See U.N. Doc A/51/41, paras. 714–749.

[82] P. Alston, 'Homelessness: Hardship in the Midst of Plenty', *UNICEF, The Progress of Nations* (New York, UNICEF, 1998),

[83] U.N. Doc CRC/C/15/Ad paras. 228–287

[84] The Committee urges States parties to take all necessary measures to abolish all forms of child labour, starting with the worst forms. It is estimated that 8.4 million children are still exploited in the worst forms of child labour, to continuously review national regulations

on minimum ages for employment with a view to making them compatible with international standards, and to regulate the working environment and conditions for adolescents who are working (in accordance with Article 32 of the Convention, as well as ILO Conventions Nos. 138 and 182), so as to ensure that they are fully protected and have access to legal redress mechanisms.

[85] See Committee on the Rights of the Child, *Concluding Observations in relation to Ethiopia*, Report of the Forty-Third Session, (2006) UN Doc CRC/C/43/3, para. 157.

[86] See the concern expressed by the Committee on the Rights of the Child to Azerbaijan, *Concluding Observations on Azerbaijan*, U.N. Doc. CRC/C/AZE/CD/2 (2006).

[87] See also International Labour Organisation Convention No. 182 Concerning the Prohibition and Immediate Action for the Elimination of the Worst Forms of Child Labour l999.

recognises the right of every child to a standard of living that is adequate for the child's development and this includes eliminating the different standards of living between children living in urban and in rural areas.[88] Adequacy may not at first sight appear a sufficiently high standard, differing as it does from sufficiency, but the concept of adequacy is drawn from the International Covenant on Economic, Social and Cultural Rights[89] and includes the duty on States to 'the continuous improvement of living conditions', which is also found in Article 11(1) of the Covenant.[90] In addition, for children the principle of best interests is also applicable.[91]

Parents and others responsible for the child have the primary responsibility 'within their abilities and financial capacities'. The Convention does not restrict the primary duty or the duty of State support to any specific family structure such as supporting only the nuclear family. The 'others responsible for the child' includes extended family members and members of the community, as provided by local custom, as well as legal guardians and others legally responsible for the child.[92] It also includes the children themselves; thus the Committee found there was a duty on the Philippine government to support the efforts 'of street children to organise themselves in order to enhance their self-esteem'.[93] Hence, the holistic nature of the Convention on the Rights of the Child strengthens the combating of child poverty by combining the child's right to freedom of expression with the right to an adequate standard of living. In this way, the Convention can be developed to improve the lives of children living and working on the streets, even though the Convention itself does not expressly include children living and working on the streets amongst its groups of most vulnerable children.[94]

Homelessness also increases the vulnerability to abuse by corrupt institutional agencies, such as the State Civil Police in Guatemala.[95] The necessity of fully implementing children's rights is highlighted by the United Nations Special Rapporteur on Housing, who argues that, '[T]hese human rights are essential to their cognitive, physical, cultural, emotional and social development, particularly as children are disproportionately vulnerable to the negative effects of adequate and insecure living conditions'.[96]

Times of economic recession do not lessen the duty on States parties with regard to a child's entitlement to an adequate standard of living. The approach of the UN Committee on the Rights of the Child to France confirms that it is during times of economic recession that the situation of the most vulnerable of children, including children of migrant workers and socially marginalised children, requires particularly careful monitoring to ensure that they continue to benefit from their housing rights.[97]

Article 27(3) is silent as to the measures that States are obligated to undertake to assist parents and caregivers. The article only provides that this should be done in accordance 'with national conditions and within their means'. At first sight there is a risk that the phrase 'national conditions' could be interpreted as a limiting clause. However, the overriding duty in Article 4 of the Convention to undertake such measures to the maximum extent of their available resources would rule out such an approach. Therefore, rather than being a hollow phrase and referring to economic conditions, 'national conditions' must refer to conditions other than the economic. Thus the 'national conditions' refer to the 'conditions of living' necessary for the child's development, which is incorporated into Article 27(2). In India, for example, the high percentage of children living in inadequate housing, including slums, impacts directly on their

---

[88] See the *Concluding observations in relation to Samoa*, (Report of the Forty-Third Session, 2006) U.N. Doc. CRC/C/43/3 (2060) para. 1122.

[89] See discussion in chapter 18 in this volume.

[90] For further discussion on Article 11 of the International Covenant on Economic, Social and Cultural Rights, see chapter 23 in this volume.

[91] See Section 3 in this Chapter.

[92] See further G. Van Bueren, *The International Law on the Rights of the Child* (The Hague, Boston, London: Martinus Nijhoff, 1995).

[93] *Concluding Observations in relation to Philippines* (Report of 39th session, 2005), U.N. Doc. CRC/C/150, para. 187.

[94] For a criticism of this exclusion see Pare, *Street Children's Right to Education. The Failure of International Law in*

Protecting the Rights of A Vulnerable Group, unpublished PhD thesis on file with PIRCH (the Programme on International Rights of the Child), Queen Mary, University of London.

[95] (Report of the Twenty-seventh session, 2001), U.N. Doc. CRC/C/108 paras. 228–287. This is not to deny the vulnerability of some children to violence in the home.

[96] U.N. Doc. E/CN.4/2001/51 para. 69.

[97] *Concluding Observations in relation to France* (Report of the sixth session, 1994) U.N. Doc. A/51/41, paras. 64–91.

inadequate access to drinking water and sanitation. Such national conditions would include environmental and other conditions.

'National conditions' must also take into account the level and types of discrimination existing in different States. The UN Committee on the Rights of the Child noted with concern the disparity of access to housing for children in the travelling community in Ireland, and recommended that the children benefit from positive measures aimed at facilitating their access to housing.[98]

Article 27(3) also envisages a seamless transfer of housing and shelter support from parental responsibility to State responsibility if needed. However, older children may be particularly vulnerable when making the transition to adulthood and taking on increased responsibilities both for themselves and sometimes for others. Many older homeless children's situations owe much to past neglect accompanied by a lack of community or State support.[99] Social assistance is available in some States to children under the age of majority and who are living without adults, but often legislation and programme conditionality require parental consent before granting such assistance. This is a problem found in both poorer and wealthier states for different reasons. In industrialised states residential tenancy legislation may require adult guarantors or references. In developing states where the impact of HIV/AIDS is forcing a rethink of family structures and an increase in child-headed households, identity documents may be required before granting access to social assistance.[100]

The third level of legal responsibility lies with *all* the States parties to the Convention on the Rights of the Child in relation to all the economic, social and cultural rights in the treaty. Responsibility is placed at this tertiary role through international cooperation. The UN Committee on the Rights of the Child, reiterating the recommendations made by the UN Committee on Economic, Social and

Cultural Rights,[101] recommends, for example, that Ecuador ensures that free trade agreements do not negatively impact on the right of the child to access to affordable medicines, including generic ones. Because of the duty enshrined in the final sentence of Article 4,[102] this duty is also shared by all States parties negotiating such free trade treaties. In this way the economic, social and cultural rights of the child operate as a shield, placing limits on the effects of globalisation.

5.2 Right to Life, Survival and Development to the Highest Attainable Standard of Health, and to Education

Contemporary data gathered by the United Nations Children's Fund (UNICEF) provides evidence that for the first time in modern history, the number of children dying before the age of five has fallen below 10.8 million per year.[103] This is not a cause for celebration but the fall in child mortality, despite the very long way to go, demonstrates that the right to life, survival and development and the right to health of the child incorporated in the almost universally-ratified UN Convention on the Rights of the Child has arguably contributed to the reduction in the numbers of newborn and child deaths, although unfortunately it is not a universally distributed reduction, due to malaria and HIV/AIDS in Sub-Saharan Africa. Although it is difficult to quantify precisely how much any treaty contributes to the attainment of a specific human rights goal, it is clear that the Convention's provisions gives legal strength to governments, intergovernmental and non-governmental programmes by transforming what for some States had been only a matter of political discretion[104] into a legal responsibility with budgetary consequences.

In interpreting and monitoring States parties' legal obligations under the Convention, the Committee

---

[98] U.N. Doc. CRC/C/IRC/CD(2)(1996), para. 45.

[99] *Special Rapporteur on Adequate Housing as a component of the right to an adequate standard of living. Miloon Kothari,* Regard to commission on Human Rights, Sixty Second Session. UN Doc E/CN.4/2005/48, para. 53.

[100] See in relation to South Africa J. Sloth-Nielson, 'Child's Right to Social Services, the Right to Social Security, and Primary Prevention of Child Abuse' (n. 52 above).

[101] *Concluding Observations of CESCR: Ecuador,* U.N. Doc. E/C.12/1/Add.100 (2004), para. 55.

[102] 'With regard to economic, social and cultural rights, States Parties shall undertake such measures to the maximum extent of their available resources and, where needed, within the framework of international cooperation'.

[103] Available at <http://www.unicef.org/childsurvival/index_40850.html>.

[104] For States that were not party to the International Covenant on Economic, Social and Cultural Rights 1966.

also utilises the Millennium Development Goals as a floor.[105] As the Committee observes in relation to Bhutan, the health sector is at the centre of the fulfilling of the government commitment to fulfil the Millennium Development Goals including the reduction by 2015 of the under-five mortality rate by two-thirds.[106] Yet when Bhutan already achieved this Goal in 2005, the Committee urged that the Conventions goals in this area, which arguably in ensuring 'to the maximum extent possible the survival and development of the child' set higher standards than the Millennium Development Goals, are fulfilled and that the mortality rate of 40.1 per 1000 live births is further reduced.[107]

There has also been a reinforcement of the goals of Article 24 through the mechanism of the UN Special Rapporteur on the Right of Everyone to the Highest Attainable Standard of Physical and Mental Health who, in reiterating the recommendations of the Committee on the Rights of the Child to Mozambique, for example, creates greater international legal pressure for States parties to the Convention to takes steps to diminish infant and child mortality, ensure medical assistance to children and to combat child diseases and child malnutrition.[108]

The ambit of Article 24 of the Convention on the Rights of the Child expressly obliges States parties to 'promote and encourage international cooperation' taking into account 'the needs' of developing States.[109] Although the Convention refers to 'the needs' of developing States as distinct from the entitlements of developing States, the provision is important as the international cooperation includes a legal responsibility to progressively achieve the full right of the child to the enjoyment of the highest attainable standard of health.[110] Although the legal responsibility still lies

with the State, in some States such as Liberia, it is non-governmental organisations, which provide approximately three quarters of all health services.[111]

The inherent right to life, survival and development are rights which the Committee has recognised as warranting particular attention for children with disabilities.[112] The right to the highest attainable standard of health for children living with disabilities includes the legal obligation on States to adopt and implement comprehensive health policies addressing early detection of disabilities, early intervention, including psychological and physical treatment, rehabilitation including physical aids, for example limb prosthesis, mobility devices, hearing aids and visual aids. The Committee on the Rights of the Child emphasises that these health services should be provided within the same public health system which provides for children without disabilities, free of charge, whenever possible, and as updated and modernised as possible and based on a child-centred approach. In some States, children with disabilities are subject to a variety of practices that nullify or partially compromise these rights.[113] In addition to being more vulnerable to infanticide, some cultures view a child with any form of disability as a bad omen which may 'tarnish the family pedigree' and in some communities designated individuals systematically kill children with disabilities. These crimes may be unpunished or subject to reduced sentences.[114] Violations of the child's social right to health sometimes fall within the jurisdiction of national criminal law.

The Committee on the Rights of the Child has also considered adolescent health for adolescents up to the age of 18.[115] This is a welcome approach as too often in the past United Nations bodies focused on early child health to the detriment of older

[105] In relation to the health goals see generally A. Wagstaff, and M. Claeson, *The Millennium Development Goals for Health: Rising to the Challenges,* (Washington, DC: World Bank, 2004).

[106] Consideration of Committee on the Rights of the Child, *Reports Submitted by States Parties Under Article 44 of the Convention Bhutan* U.N. Doc. CRC/C/BTN/2, para. 88.

[107] Ibid.

[108] *Report submitted by the Special Rapporteur on the right of everyone to the highest attainable standard of physical and mental health, Mission to Mozambique* U.N. Doc. GEN/GO 5/101/ 64. para. 25 April 2002

[109] Article 24(4).

[110] Reading Article 24(1) and (4) together.

[111] See, Save the Children UK, *Annual Report 2006/7,* available at <http://www.savethechildren.org.uk/en/54_3249.htm> at 6.

[112] See Section 2 above.

[113] *General Comment No. 9* (n. 32 above) para. 13. See also G. Quinn, T. Degener, and A. Bruce *Human Rights and Disability: The Current Use and Future Potential of United Nations Human Rights,* (Geneva OHCHR, 2002).

[114] Ibid.

[115] Convention on the Rights of the Child, *General Comment No. 4, Adolescent health and development in the context of the Convention on the Rights of the Child* (Thirty-Third session, 2003), U.N. Doc. CRC/GC/2003/4.

children. According to the Committee States parties ought to ensure that for sexual consent, marriage and the possibility of medical treatment without parental consent. Applying Article 2 of the Convention means that these minimum ages should be the same for boys and girls.

The Committee defines both child health and child development more broadly than the strict application of Articles 6 and 24 of the Convention. It has observed that the General Comment on Adolescent Health should be read together with the Convention and its two Optional Protocols on the Sale of Children, Child Prostitution and Child Pornography, and on the Involvement of Children in Armed Conflict, as well as other relevant international human rights norms and standards.[116] This creates the legal space for the Committee to consider all effective measures to eliminate acts and activities which threaten the right to life of adolescents, including honour killings.

One facet of the right to health is the duty on States to prohibit traditional practices prejudicial to the health of children.[117] The Committee strongly urges States parties to develop and implement awareness-raising campaigns, education programmes and legislation aimed at changing prevailing attitudes, and address gender roles and stereotypes which contribute to harmful traditional practices. The Committee recommends that States parties should facilitate the establishment of multidisciplinary information and advice centres regarding the harmful aspects of some traditional practices, including early marriage and female genital mutilation.[118] Early marriages occur more frequently in the poorest 20 per cent of society thus involving the most vulnerable children and access to primary education has been demonstrated to have a preventative effect upon the rates of early marriage.[119]

The Convention places a legal obligation on States to recognise the reinforcing relationship between the child's right to health and education. Article 29(1) of the Convention provides that education must be directed to 'the development of the

child's personality, talents and mental and physical abilities to their fullest potential' and in its first General Comment on the aims of education, the Committee observes that:

> Education must also be aimed at ensuring that ... no child leaves school without being equipped to face the challenges that he or she can expect to be confronted with in life. Basic skills should include ... the ability to make well-balanced decisions; to resolve conflicts in a non-violent manner; and to develop a healthy lifestyle [and] good social relationships ...[120]

The Committee urges in its General Comment on Adolescent Health that the State parties provide well-functioning school and recreational facilities that will not pose health risks to students. This includes the provision of clean drinking water and sanitation and safe journeys to school and that necessary action is undertaken to prevent and prohibit all forms of violence and abuse, including sexual abuse by school personnel as well as among students and to initiate and support measures, attitudes and activities which promote healthy behaviour by including relevant topics in school curricula. The implementation of this recommendation, however, has to be balanced with the findings of the UN Special Rapporteur that in 2006 only three African states, Mauritius, Sao Toami and Seychelles, provided a 'proper' free and compulsory primary education.[121]

Regrettably, the child health entitlements of the Convention on the Rights of the Child were drafted before the full impact that HIV/AIDS had on children was realised.[122] However, the General Comment by the Committee on the Rights of the Child on HIV/AIDS and the Rights of the Child recognises that children of all ages are at the core of the pandemic: there are high numbers of children who are themselves HIV-infected; they are affected by the loss of a parental caregiver or teacher and/or because their families or communities are severely strained by its consequences; and they are most prone to be infected or affected. Over 2 million children under the age of 15 are

---

[116] In light of Articles 3, 6, 12, 19 and 24 (3) of the Convention.
[117] Article 24(3).
[118] *General Comment No. 4* (n. 115 above).
[119] UNICEF, *Early Marriage – A Harmful Traditional Practice: A Statistical Exploration*, 2005, available at <http://www.unicef.org/publications/files/Early_Marriage_12.lo.pdf>.

[120] *General Comment No.4* (n. 28 above).
[121] K. Tomasevski *The State of the Right to Education Worldwide Free or Fee* (Copenhagen: Global Report, 2006), p. 15.
[122] No drafts were presented concerning the specific entitlements of children affected by HIV/AIDS.

living with HIV/AIDS[123] and in Southern Africa alone 3.2 million children have been orphaned due to HIV/AIDS.[124] More focus is needed both on children's entitlements and the specific needs of child-headed households.

Of particular concern is gender-based discrimination combined with taboos or negative or judgemental attitudes towards the sexual activity of girls, and often as a consequence, limiting their access to preventive measures and other services. The same is also true of discrimination based on sexual orientation, which the Committee acknowledges but pays insufficient attention to in its observations on country reports. In the design of HIV/AIDS-related strategies, States parties must give careful consideration to prescribed gender and social norms within their communities with a view to eliminating discrimination as they directly impact on the vulnerability of both girls and boys to HIV/AIDS. The Committee on the Rights of the Child observes that United Nations agencies have recommended that where replacement feeding is affordable, feasible, acceptable, sustainable and safe, avoidance of all breastfeeding by HIV-infected mothers is recommended; otherwise, exclusive breastfeeding is recommended during the first months of life, which should be discontinued as soon as it is feasible.[125]

The acknowledgement of progress in human rights, and particularly in the field of economic, social and cultural rights, is essential but it is also undervalued. Such acknowledgement encourages and empowers those working in the field. Hence the approach of the Committee on the Rights of the Child in welcoming positive developments such as the free anti-retroviral programme established in Ethiopia in 2005[126] is welcome. The fear that such acknowledgement risks inducing complacency or blinds the Committee to other problems is not borne out by the evidence. In relation to Ethiopia, the Committee has expressed concern

that the provision of anti-retroviral drugs has not reached all those who need it and that Ethiopia lacks a strategy to support and counteract discrimination against children who have HIV/AIDS infection.

6. FUDGING INDIVISIBILITY: CRITICAL PERSPECTIVES ON THE STRUCTURE OF THE COMMITTEE'S CONCLUDING OBSERVATIONS

On grounds of equitable treatment the UN Committee on the Rights of the Child adopts the same formula in its Concluding Observations for each State party. The Committee considers 'General Measures of Implementation', 'Definition of the Child and General Principles' and also 'Civil Rights and Freedoms'. This latter category is the commonly accepted human rights law classification for all the rights ranging from privacy to freedom of expression, and thus this nomenclature correctly conveys an understanding of the extent of State accountability and the legal duties of implementation. However, in striking contrast the Committee does not utilise the complementary and universally accepted classification of economic, social and cultural rights.[127] What ought to be classified as the economic, social and cultural entitlements of children in the Convention is only classified by the UN Committee as 'Basic Health and Welfare'. This appears to be a backward step recognising only welfarism rather than entitlement and is also inconsistent with the Committee's statement that it 'believes that economic, social and cultural rights, as well as civil and political rights, should be regarded as justiciable'.[128] The approach of the Committee is also questionable as increasingly modern constitutions and bills of rights are embracing the economic, social and cultural rights of children and amongst these states are Brazil,[129] Colombia,[130] Croatia,[131] Malawi,[132]

---

[123] Annual Report (n.111 above), p. 14.
[124] These are the figures for 2001 cited in UNICEF, Africa's Orphaned Generations, 2003.
[125] New data on the prevention of Mother-to-Child Transmission of HIV, and their policy implications Technical consultation, UNFPA/UNICEF/WHO/UNAIDS Inter-Agency Team – Conclusions and recommendations 2001.
[126] See Committee on the Rights of the Child, *Concluding observations in relation to Ethiopia*, (Report of the Forty-Third Session, 2006) UN Doc CRC/C/43/3, para. 128.

[127] The categories of Education, Leisure and Culture Activities, and of Special Protection Measures in the concluding observations cover both civil and political rights, and economic, social and cultural rights.
[128] UN CRC/GC/2003/5 para. 6.
[129] Constitution of Brazil, Article 7, para. 25
[130] Constitution of Columbia, Article 44(1).
[131] Constitution of Croatia, Article 62.
[132] Constitution of Malawi, para. 13(h). See above for other African states.

South Africa[133] and Turkey.[134] Courts from other jurisdictions including India and the Philippines have also made significant rulings concerning children's social justice rights.[135]

Maintaining the nomenclature of rights is not pedantry but is of fundamental importance, because the notion of children's economic, social and cultural rights has been hard fought. The theoretical underpinnings of international human rights law that all human rights, civil, political, economic, social and cultural are equal and indivisible[136] requires such an approach and it is almost as if the Committee believes it can achieve more by using a less powerful vocabulary in its dialogue with States parties. There is also some truth in Evan's suggestion that in relation to general human rights, legal regimes reject rights that are 'regarded as contrary to market interests'.[137]

The risk is that it places children's social justice rights on a less than equal footing with children's civil and political rights. Indeed it is partly for this reason that the United States has not become party to the Convention on the Rights of the Child, preferring the more outdated concept of welfare which encompasses much more political discretion and far less direct legal accountability. Welfare focuses on the setting of targeted reductions in child poverty by the legislature, which rarely carries with it legal accountability. The failure to meet domestic government-set targets does not create any opportunity for children, who in most countries of the world are disenfranchised, to hold their governments accountable. The UN Committee expressed concern over the failure by Nepal to meet its own target date of 2000 to achieve universal primary education and the targeted period has now been set back to 2015.[138] This prompts the question: What happens to those children who have now been deprived of primary education in Nepal as there is not any domestic legal mechanism by which they can challenge such a failure? Although the Committee has been concerned about the lack of national child-friendly procedures to address legitimate grievances from children including their social justice entitlements,[139] relying solely on such political target-setting risks treating children as the means to a fairer society in the future, rather than entitled to a socially just society to be enjoyed whilst they are still children. Whether a child will grow up living in poverty is dependent upon whether the child is fortunate to be included within the prioritised targeted group of children, and although the aims of such targets are laudable the effect is playing dice with many children's lives.

As a first and relatively simple stage, is the adoption of the universally accepted international human rights classifications. It is within the control of the UN Committee on the Rights of the Child to restore the correct nomenclature and request States to report on the implementation of children's economic, social and cultural rights. The grouping of rights by implementing bodies is important as it often sets boundaries, and in this case inappropriate boundaries, on possible solutions.

7. THE NEED FOR A GENERAL COMMENT ON PRIORITISING RESOURCES FOR CHILDREN AND AN INTERNATIONAL COMPLAINTS MECHANISM

There is also an urgent need for both a 'General Comment on the Prioritising of Resources for Children' and the creation of an international complaints mechanism. In its conclusions on the report of Saint Lucia, the UN Committee on the Rights of the Child welcomed the increases

---

[133] Constitution of South Africa section 28(1). See also Sunstein (n. 51 above) on the nature of the South African constitution, which he describes as transformative. Sunstein draws a distinction between 'preservative' constitutions, which 'seek to maintain existing practices', and 'transformative' constitutions, which 'set out certain aspirations that are emphatically understood as a challenge to longstanding practices'. See C. R. Sunstein, 'Social and economic rights? Lessons from South Africa', *Constitutional Forum* Vol. 11, No. 4 (2001) pp. 123–; T. Roux, 'Understanding Grootboom – a reply to Cass R. Sunstein', *Constitutional Forum* Vol. 12, No. 2 (2002) pp. 41–51.

[134] Constitution of Turkey Article 58.

[135] See for example *Mehta v. State of Tamil Nadu* (1996) 6 SCC 756; *Minors Oposa et al. v. Fulgencio S. Factoran, Jr. et al.* (G.R. No. 101083) judgment of 30 July 1993.

[136] See *World Conference on Human Rights*, Vienna Declaration and Programme of Action (12 July 1993) A/CONF.157/23

[137] T. Evans, 'International Human Rights Law as Power/Knowledge', *Human Rights Quarterly*, Vol. 27, No. 3 (2005), pp. 1046–1068.

[138] UN Doc CRC/C/150.

[139] See for example the comments of the Committee on the Rights of the Child in relation to South Africa at UN Doc CRC/A/55/41, para. 144.

during the decade in budget allocation for social services but, as acknowledged by Saint Lucia itself, the Committee was concerned at the lack of sufficient financial resources for the implementation of the Convention. Saint Lucia conceded the lack of sufficiency, thus implying that the Government of Saint Lucia was seeking advice and technical assistance, beyond the wording of the treaty, on how to deal with the seeming shortfall. The response of the UN Committee was:

> [T]hat the State Party makes a systematic increase of budgetary allocations to 'the maximum of extent of the State Party's available resources and where needed within the framework of national cooperation' as provided for by article 4 of the Convention and using the rights based approach. In relation to this the Committee recommends that the State Party establishes firm priorities for addressing the rights of the child in its national strategic plan for poverty reduction.[140]

The recommended solution, according to the Committee, was to cite the relevant provisions back at the State party and simply recommend that it prioritise. This, however, States parties already know, and what is required is guidance within the ambit of international human rights law on the complex question as to how a State should prioritise the relevant provisions. The Committee on the Rights of the Child appears to accept that there is a need for prioritisation. In its concluding observations on the Philippines it recommends that the Philippines strengthen its existing mechanisms for data collection, and that these are disaggregated by gender, urban and rural, and by children in need of special protection.[141]

If it is accepted that some States regard apportioning greater resources as impossible, the Committee has to consider that within the duty of the State progressively to implement all of the social justice rights of children, there are some aspects of the rights, which require urgent and immediate implementation. Although there is the risk that governments may perceive the minimum core as the maximum of a State party's duty, the Committee needs to consider whether there is a minimum core to children's economic, social and cultural

rights provisions,[142] and, further, what is the content of the minimum core.[143]

To assist it in this complex task the Committee on the Rights of the Child may wish to utilise the interpretation of the relevant provisions in General Comment No. 3 of the Committee on Economic, Social and Cultural Rights and parts of other General Comments focussing on the content of the minimum core.

The Committee must progress its jurisprudence on child poverty, and in such a way that it does not interfere with national sovereignty. The Committee has made a start in stating that it requires 'to know what steps are taken at all levels of Government to ensure that economic and social planning and decision-making and budgetary decisions are made with the best interests of children as a primary consideration and that children, including in particular marginalized and disadvantaged groups of children, are protected from the adverse effects of economic policies or financial downturns'.[144] However, it would be valuable if the Committee on the Rights of the Child were to develop this and consider which areas are to be prioritised and how, aside from international cooperation, the State party is able to garner the resources necessary to implement the right.

The importance of child rights budgeting in this task cannot be overstated. Child rights budgeting assesses how much is being currently spent on specific rights; the retained data provides a pattern over a number of years, which makes it possible to assess whether the rights are being implemented progressively introducing a degree of accurate accountability and child rights budgeting also helps assess whether the State party is using resources to the maximum extent of its available resources. If it is not, then simply restating the duty, as it did in relation to Saint Lucia, is insufficient.

Complementary to this is the importance of persuading States to incorporate children's economic, social and cultural rights into domestic legislation

---

[140] UN Doc CRC/C/15/Add.258 21/09/2005.
[141] UN Doc CRC/C/150, para. 120.
[142] See A. Chapman and S. Russell (eds.), *Exploring the Minimum Core Content of Economic, Social and Cultural Rights* (Antwerp: Intersentia, 2002).
[143] In relation to children and the minimum core, see G. Van Bueren, 'The Minimum Core of Article 10(3)' in Chapman and Russell, ibid. pp. 147–161,
[144] See *General Comment No. 5* (n. 27 above).

as national social justice remedies may provide a more accessible and effective remedy for children. It has to be accepted that these arguments are unlikely to be a catalyst for instant law reform but the Convention has already operated as a successful catalyst for the incorporation of children's civil rights.

These are complex issues, which cannot simply be responded to in the very short time that the Committee has to consider each report. Their responses also need to be as focused and constructive as the General Comments on Early Childhood and also HIV/AIDS.[145] Since many of children's civil rights are already enshrined in bills of rights, albeit in frequently general terms along with adults, it would be helpful for the Committee on the Rights of the Child to strategise on methods within its mandate to persuade States of the importance of incorporating domestic child economic, social and cultural rights into national bills of rights.[146] This would be helpful particularly as the Committee in its General Comment on General Measures of Implementation 'emphasizes that economic, social and cultural rights, as well as civil and political rights, must be regarded as justiciable'.[147]

The lack of any effective remedy for most of the world's children for violations to their economic, social and cultural rights also highlights the consequences of the lack of any petitioning mechanism in the Convention on the Rights of the Child with which they could challenge such violations.

The Convention on the Rights of the Child has too few tools at its disposal and a new Protocol ought belatedly to be negotiated implementing a child-friendly procedure to address complaints from children including violations to their economic, social and cultural rights. Now that the 1990 African Charter on the Rights and Welfare of the Child incorporates a petitioning mechanism, it is simply indefensible that the Convention on the Rights of the Child lacks any opportunity for children directly to attempt to prevent and remedy violations of their social justice rights. For girls there is a clear chain between the Convention on the Rights of the Child and the Convention on Elimination of All Forms of Discrimination Against Women. If national conditions, for example, are depriving girls living in rural areas of adequate living conditions, then a State may also be in violation of Article 14(2)(h), opening up the possibility of girls being able to petition under the Women's Convention where there is a pattern of inadequate housing or sanitation or water supply based on gender discrimination. Because of a lack of a treaty on the rights of men, (although many would quip that all other treaties protect men!) there is no possibility at present of boys petitioning a United Nations tribunal on violations of any of their economic and social rights beyond the piecemeal protection offered by the International Covenant on Civil and Political Rights.[148]

In this age of seemingly no alternatives it is, to paraphrase Galbraith, important to realise that 'reality and truth, lie not with what was believed in the past but with what is compelled by the present'.[149]

---

[145] See, *General Comment No. 3 HIV/AIDS and the rights of the child*. U.N. Doc. CRC/GC/2003/3 (2003).

[146] Some states, such as Norway in 2003, have incorporated the Convention into their domestic law.

[147] UN Doc CRC/GC/2003/5 27, November 2003.

[148] See for example Articles 6, 17 and 26.

[149] J. K. Galbraith, *The Affluent Society* (Boston/New York: Houghton Mifflin Company, 1998), Afterword at p. 262.

PART FIVE

Special Topics

28

The International Labour Organisation

An Integrated Approach to Economic and Social Rights

Colin Fenwick*

1. INTRODUCTION

This chapter concerns the socio-economic rights jurisprudence of the International Labour Organisation ('ILO'). Founded in 1919, the ILO's primary focus is the promotion of labour rights, or rights at work.[1] Since its creation, the ILO has promulgated 185 Conventions and 195 Recommendations dealing with a wide array of matters pertaining to labour relations.[2] ILO Conventions and Recommendations cover (among other things) workers' human rights, wages, working time, social security, and the working conditions in particular economic sectors, including migrant workers, seafarers and home-workers. There is a clear relationship between these instruments and the broader field of socio-economic rights: ILO conventions provide in detail for the implementation of many of the principles contained in Articles 6 to 9 of the International Covenant on Economic, Social and Cultural Rights ('ICESCR').[3] The ILO has

also promulgated a variety of other standards, and its supervisory bodies have generated a significant volume of material relating to the application of these instruments.

The long history of the ILO and the scale of its activities have been widely studied; indeed they are the subject of numerous books and countless journal articles.[4] In the space available therefore I will focus on two things: first, the ILO's Core Labour Standards ('CLS'). These deal with: (1) freedom of association and the right to bargain collectively; (2) freedom from forced labour; (3) freedom from discrimination in employment; and (4) freedom from harmful child labour. As will appear presently, the identification of the 'core' is contested. Notwithstanding the significant questions in the debate over core labour standards and their impact, I have chosen to highlight CLS because they represent a key area of the ILO's activity and current focus. And, if the arguments

---

* Centre for Employment and Labour Relations Law, University of Melbourne.

[1] In recent years the ILO has somewhat reduced its emphasis on the creation and promotion of standards and their associated jurisprudence, in favour of seeking to help member states achieve the goal of 'Decent Work'. See ILO, *Decent Work – Report of the Director General to the ILO Conference* (Geneva: ILO, 1999); ILO, *Reducing the Decent Work Deficit – A Global Challenge – Report of the Director General to the ILO Conference* (Geneva: ILO, 2001), and ILO, *Working Out of Poverty – Report of the Director General to the ILO Conference* (Geneva: ILO, 2003). Compare the former emphasis on standard setting in a globalising world: ILO, *The ILO, Standard-Setting and Globalization – Report of the Director General to the ILO Conference* (Geneva: ILO, 1997).

[2] To the time of writing.

[3] N. Valticos, 'International Labour Standards and Human Rights: Approaching the Year 2000', *International Labour Review* Vol. 137, No. 2 (1998), pp. 135–147, at 140; H. Bartolomei de la Cruz, G. von Potobsky and L. Swepston, *The International Labor Organization – The International Standard Setting System and Basic Human Rights* (Boul-

der, Colorado: Westview Press, 1996) p. 128. See further ICESCR Articles 6 (right to work), 7 (right to just and favourable conditions of work), 8 (right to form and join trade unions) and 9 (right to social security). As an illustration of this point, see General Comment No. 18 of the Committee on Economic, Social and Cultural Rights on The Right to Work, which is replete with references to ILO standards: UN Doc. E/C.12/GC/18, 6 February 2006.

[4] In recent years a number of books have been written that compare the ILO and its standards to other organisations, particularly those in Europe: see, e.g., J. Murray, *Transnational Labour Regulation: The ILO and the EC Compared* (The Hague: Kluwer Law International, 2001), and T. Novitz, *International and European Protection of the Right to Strike* (Oxford: Oxford University Press, 2003). For earlier works focused only on the ILO see, e.g., A. Alcock, *History of the International Labour Organisation* (London: MacMillan Press, 1971), C. W. Jenks, *Social Justice in the Law of Nations* (London: Oxford University Press, 1970) and D. Morse, *The Origin and Evolution of the International Labour Organization and its Role in the World Community* (New York: New York State School of Industrial and Labor Relations, Cornell University, 1969).

in favour of the emergence and promotion of CLS are accepted, then it is only right to do so.

Secondly, by way of comparison and contrast, I will consider the ILO's work in two other areas: the socio-economic rights of indigenous and tribal peoples, and the right to social security. These examples help to illustrate several key themes that I wish to explore in this chapter. One is the ILO's insistence on the inter-relationship of labour rights with other economic and social rights (as we will see below, the ILO instruments on indigenous and tribal peoples have very few provisions that deal with work or labour at all). This in turn is related to a broader theme of the ILO's work, which is its effective insistence on the interdependence of all human rights. Another is the continuing importance of even some of the oldest ILO instruments, especially as a basis for engaging in dialogue with states about their efforts to implement economic and social rights.

In Section Two, I outline the structure of the ILO, including its systems for setting and for supervising international labour standards, and I divert (briefly) to the CLS debate. In Section Three, I give an outline of key aspects of ILO jurisprudence on its core labour standards. In Section Four, I deal with ILO work relating to indigenous and tribal peoples, and in Section Five with the ILO's work on the right to social security, using as a case study its consideration of the case of Chile's privatised pension system. Throughout Sections Three, Four and Five, I emphasize four points. First, that the ILO has developed expansive understandings of the norms it has developed. Secondly, that the ILO does not limit itself to 'mere' labour rights: rather, it frequently ranges across many inter-related areas of social and economic policy. Thirdly, that the ILO emphasises participation and consultation between states and their citizens, particularly (but not only) in the form of representative organisations of workers and employers. And fourthly, that ratified ILO conventions can be significant as a means of pressing states to do better to implement economic and social rights, even where they are among its oldest instruments. In the Conclusion, I venture some thoughts about what can be learned from the ILO's mechanisms when considering how to promote and protect social and economic rights.

I argue that the ILO has significant institutional strengths and experience in dealing with social

and economic rights, in particular because it gives workers a voice in the institutions of the organisation itself. Thus, civil society representatives are more closely integrated into the development of the jurisprudence on socio-economic rights than in many other contexts. Nevertheless, as others have noted,[5] the ILO faces significant challenges to ensure that its systems remain effective in a globalising economy. A key issue for the ILO in the future will be the extent to which it is able to accommodate the interests of workers and other groups who are not (able to be) represented by a trade union. I suggest, however, that its work with indigenous and tribal peoples offers some reason for hope. Both this work and its CLS jurisprudence also offer important models of how to develop and promote all human rights in a way that emphasises their fundamental interconnections.

2. THE ILO AND ITS SYSTEM FOR SETTING AND SUPERVISING INTERNATIONAL LABOUR STANDARDS

2.1 The Constitution and the Principal Organs

KEY CONSTITUTIONAL PRINCIPLES

The original Constitution of the ILO, which formed part of the Treaty of Versailles, contains a number of key guiding principles. These were reaffirmed (and somewhat expanded) with the adoption in 1944 of the Declaration of Philadelphia, which was later annexed to the ILO's Constitution. Among the ILO's key constitutional principles are the notion that labour is not an article of commerce, and protection of freedom of association to organise, for both workers and employers.[6] In the Declaration of Philadelphia the organisation reaffirmed its mission to pursue social justice,[7]

---

[5] S. Cooney, 'Testing Times for the ILO: Institutional Reforms for the New International Political Economy', *Comparative Labor Law and Policy Journal*, Vol. 20 (1999), pp. 365–399.

[6] Others include: an adequate wage by local standards, abolition of child labour, equal remuneration for work of equal value, and non-discrimination in the application of standards.

[7] Novitz, *Protection of the Right to Strike* (n. 4 above), p. 99; see also B. Langille, 'The ILO and the New Economy: Recent Developments', *International Journal of Comparative Labour Law and Industrial Relations*, Vol. 15 (1999), pp. 229–257, at 232.

declaring (among other things) that 'poverty anywhere is a danger to prosperity everywhere'.

The ILO Constitution (the 'Constitution') creates a tripartite organisation: that is, workers, governments and employers are each represented in its main organs. This makes the ILO unique among international organisations, and enables it to develop and implement social and economic rights that reflect the needs of the communities they are intended to benefit and protect. There are, however, some limitations to the involvement of employers and workers in the organisation's activities, which have been created in part by the impact of globalisation on methods of production.[8] A related problem is that trade union movements throughout much of the developed world have suffered declining membership in recent years. Thus, it is legitimate to consider whether the employer and trade union participants in ILO structures are representative of *all* workers. This question is all the more pertinent for the vast majority of workers in the developing world, who are in the informal economy, and rarely have full-time employment with an identified employer.[9] While the ILO has for many years allowed representative international membership-based NGOs to be present as observers at its Conference, no moves have been made to offer an institutional role to groups other than employers and trade unions. The ILO's work with indigenous and tribal peoples does show, however, that its structures can be adapted to consider the interests of groups who are neither employers nor trade unions.

The Organs of the ILO

The ILO Constitution creates three key institutions: the International Labour Office, the Governing Body and the International Labour Conference. The Office is the administrative secretariat, employing some 2,000 staff stationed in offices around the world, the majority of whom serve in the ILO headquarters in Geneva. The ILO Governing Body is the organisation's executive and has fifty-six members, of whom twenty-eight represent governments. Of these, ten places are reserved for the States of chief industrial importance.[10]

Workers and employers each have fourteen representatives. The ILO Governing Body oversees the Office in the performance of its duties, sets policy for the organisation, and determines the agenda for the International Labour Conference (the 'Conference').

The Conference is the ILO's annual meeting: it has many functions including, as I explain below, a role in the supervision of ratified Conventions. It is the ILO Conference that adopts its Conventions and Recommendations. Obviously there is some tension in the roles of worker, employer and government representatives in adopting binding Conventions. While workers and employers are represented at the Conference and therefore have important roles in determining the texts of instruments, it still remains for Member States to decide whether to ratify them, and then how to implement them. On occasion the Conference also adopts other instruments, commonly in the form of Declarations. It has adopted Declarations on the independence of trade unions (1952), on trade unions and civil liberties (1970), and on social policy and multinational enterprises (1977, revised 2000).[11] In 1998, the ILO adopted a Declaration on Fundamental Principles and Rights at Work (the 1998 Declaration), to which I will return in the context of CLS.

2.2   Setting ILO Standards

If the Governing Body places an item on the Conference agenda for standard-setting, it is usually discussed at two consecutive sessions of the Conference. The International Labour Office plays a key role in standard-setting, in accordance with established procedures. It develops and distributes preparatory material including comparative studies of existing law and practice, questionnaires about matters to be included in the text of any instrument, compilations of replies from Members, and proposed texts of any standards. Together these form the basis of the standard-setting discussion at the Conference, which will designate a specific committee to examine the issue.

Experience in the field of economic and social rights shows that States are frequently unable or

---

[8] The issues I outline here are dealt with in some detail in Cooney, 'Testing Times' (n. 5 above).

[9] Ibid.

[10] At present they are Germany, Brazil, China, USA, France, India, Japan, UK, Italy, and the Russian Federation.

[11] ILO Doc. GB279/12 (November 2000).

unwilling to implement their obligations; in part this is a product of the idea (referred to expressly in the ICESCR) that economic and social rights are to be implemented progressively. ILO standards offer an interesting model. They are intended to be minimum universal standards;[12] to this end, the Constitution requires the Conference to take into account, where relevant, 'the imperfect development of industrial organisation'.[13] ILO instruments therefore often include 'measures of flexibility' concerning the application. States may have discretion in how to apply a broadly expressed standard; they may be obliged only to accept a minimum number of parts within a Convention (an approach also taken by the European Social Charter); or, they may have the option to elect to be bound by a slightly more lenient standard (as we will see below in the case of child labour).[14]

In the ILO's view, it is precisely because it takes these issues into account when adopting a standard that member States may not lodge a reservation or declaration concerning a Convention: any appropriate measure of flexibility will already have been identified.[15] Obviously this is an unusual situation in international law, and in international human rights law in particular, where many States frequently lodge reservations and/or declarations to aspects of treaties.

2.3   Supervision of ILO Standards

The ILO's supervision machinery is sophisticated and complex. Like other human rights institutions it includes State reporting to a committee of independent experts. Unique features of ILO supervision include the role of the Conference (which provides political supervision), special procedures on freedom of association, and constitutional procedures for complaints. A key feature of many of these is that workers' and employers' organisations are able to play an active role.

REPORTING MECHANISMS

States must submit regular reports on ratified Conventions (Constitution, Article 22); under procedures adopted by the Governing Body, States must submit reports on the core conventions every two years and on the others every five. The reports are examined by the Committee of Experts on the Application of Conventions and Recommendations ('CEACR'), which meets in closed session. First established in 1927,[16] the CEACR is composed of senior jurists who serve in their independent capacity. They are appointed by the Governing Body on the recommendation of the Director General. At the time of writing, the chair of the CEACR is Justice Robyn Layton, a member of the Supreme Court of the Australian state of South Australia.

The CEACR reports to the Conference. The report is largely a record of 'individual observations': that is, the CEACR's views on cases where there are issues of non-compliance. The CEACR also engages in dialogue with governments, sending them 'direct requests'. It does not publish the content of direct requests, although it does indicate that they have been sent. The CEACR is resolute in its use of diplomatic language and methods, although it is also persistent. On occasion it requests a country to submit a report more frequently than otherwise required by the reporting cycle.

The CEACR also considers reports from Member States on instruments that they *have not ratified* (Constitution, Article 19). This is obviously a most unusual mechanism in international law. The procedure is used, among other things, to enable the CEACR to prepare each year a 'General Survey' on a particular topic, usually dealing with more than one instrument. In this way the CEACR is able to develop a global picture on a set of issues, regardless of whether Members have ratified relevant ILO instruments.

The full CEACR report is considered by the Conference Committee on the Application of Standards ('CCAS'). It also gives individual consideration to special cases, selected by the officers of the committee. In these cases the country in question is invited to send a representative to the CCAS to participate in a public discussion.[17] At the end of each discussion, the CCAS adopts a conclusion on the

---

12 ILO Constitution, Article 19(8).
13 ILO Constitution, Article 19(3).
14 Bartolomei de la Cruz et al., *ILO Standards* (n. 152 above) pp. 42–43.
15 Ibid. p. 42.

16 Ibid. p. 75.
17 The discussion is public in the sense that it takes place in open session, unlike the closed sessions of the CEACR; it is not possible however for persons other than committee members and invited representative of governments to participate in the discussion.

case, which, if it is particularly serious, may result in the country being mentioned in a 'special paragraph' of the Committee's report. In most cases, whether or not a special paragraph is adopted, the CCAS urges the country in question to continue to report to the CEACR, and in many cases, to avail itself of the facilities of the Office for advice and technical cooperation.

SPECIAL PROCEDURES FOR FREEDOM OF ASSOCIATION

The ILO has established special mechanisms to oversee Member States' compliance with the principles of freedom of association. The cardinal feature of these procedures is that they do not depend upon a Member State having ratified the relevant ILO instruments: on the contrary, the juridical basis for the supervisory mechanisms lies in the fact that the importance of freedom of association is referred to in the ILO's Constitution. Thus, it is by virtue of the very fact of membership that States must comply with the relevant principles.

Initially, the ILO established a Fact-Finding and Conciliation Commission on Freedom of Association ('FFCC'). It has had little use, however, principally because Member States must consent to it being established in any given case.[18] The limitations of the FFCC led the Governing Body in November 1951 to establish its own (tripartite) Committee on Freedom of Association ('CFA'). The CFA meets in closed session and reports at each Governing Body session. It considers complaints that Member States have failed to comply with the constitutional principle of freedom of association. In practice, the content of this principle is virtually identical to the content given by the CEACR to the relevant Conventions. The CFA has developed a significant body of principles and jurisprudence over the more than fifty years of its operation, having dealt now with in excess of 2,300 cases.

CONSTITUTIONAL COMPLAINT PROCEDURES

The ILO Constitution establishes two complaint procedures. Under Article 24 a workers' or employ-

ers' organisation may lodge a 'representation' alleging that a State has 'failed to secure...the effective observance' of a Convention to which it is a party. If the representation is considered receivable, it will be referred to an ad hoc tripartite committee appointed by the Governing Body. The committee has a relatively free hand procedurally: it may seek a response from the government concerned, and/or further information from either the body submitting the representation or the government (or both); it may ask a government representative to attend. The committee reports to the Governing Body and its report is therefore part of the public record. The representation procedure has been used more frequently since the end of the 1970s. Whereas only fourteen representations were submitted before 1978, a further forty-five were submitted between 1978 and 1994.[19]

Article 26 of the Constitution provides for the lodgement of a 'complaint'. A Member may file a complaint against any other Member (Article 26(1)), or the Governing Body may initiate the procedure, either of its own motion, or on receipt of a complaint from a delegate to the Conference (Article 26(4)). Once formed, a Commission of Inquiry is constituted by three independent members, who swear an oath based on that administered to members of the International Court of Justice. They then proceed on an inquiry that is not guided by any strict rules of procedure and which is in form quasi-administrative and quasi-inquisitorial: the procedure is sui generis in international human rights law. There have been no more than a dozen Commissions of Inquiry in the ILO's history.[20] The two most recent commissions of inquiry reported on freedom of association in Belarus (2004)[21] and on forced labour in Burma (1998).[22]

---

[18] One of its more recent uses was in the case of South Africa in the years immediately before its transition to democracy: ILO, *Prelude to Change: Industrial Relations Reform in South Africa – Report of Fact-Finding and Conciliation Commission on Freedom of Association Concerning the Republic of South Africa* (Geneva: ILO, 1992).

[19] Bartolomei de la Cruz et al, *ILO Standards* (n. 3 above), pp. 80 (fn. 1), and 89.

[20] Ibid. pp. 93–4.

[21] ILO, *Trade Union Rights in Belarus. Report of the Commission of Inquiry appointed under Article 26 of the Constitution of the International Labour Organization to examine the observance by the Government of the Republic of Belarus of the Freedom of Association and Protection of the Right to Organise Convention, 1948 (No. 87), and the Right to Organise and Collective Bargaining Convention, 1949 (No. 98)* (Geneva: ILO, 2004).

[22] ILO, *Report of the Commission of Inquiry Appointed under Article 26 of the Constitution of the International Labour Organization to Examine the Observance by Myanmar of the Forced Labour Convention, 1930 (No. 29)* (Geneva: ILO, 1998).

A key feature of these procedures is the role that they give the social partners. It is *only* an employers' or workers' organisation that can lodge a representation under Article 24 of the Constitution. A single workers' delegate to the Conference may initiate the Article 26 procedure that leads to the establishment of a Commission of Inquiry. There is no formal role for others who might seek to represent the interests of workers in cases of noncompliance. As we will see, however, indigenous people's groups have been involved in a number of Article 24 representations concerning the application of Convention 169, which suggests that the constitutional structures are neither so rigid nor as exclusionary as might at first be thought.

2.3   Core Labour Standards

CLS have become a key focus of ILO activity in recent years; their origins are generally traced to the final Declaration of the Social Summit in Copenhagen.[23] The content of the core is largely replicated in the 1998 Declaration, although this is a promotional instrument, not a binding standard. There is considerable scope – and good reason – to argue that the identification of a core of standards is not a positive development for the ILO, for workers, or for economic and social rights. To take the last matter first, there are very many matters that might be thought essential to the protection of workers' social and economic interests that are protected not only in ILO instruments, but also in the broader corpus of international human rights law. These include in particular working time, wages, and occupational health and safety. Moreover, broader lists of 'essential' or 'core' standards might be identified in a number of other places, including under certain US Trade Laws.[24] Yet these rights have been excluded by the

ILO from the 'core'. On the other hand, it may be argued that that the rights protected by CLS are essential processes by which workers might be enabled to pursue other economic and social goals.[25]

Leaving these issues aside, it is necessary to outline the nature and function of the 1998 Declaration.[26] It is (expressly) not a standard that might be ratified and by which a Member State might be bound; on the contrary, it is 'strictly promotional'.[27] The 1998 Declaration does, however, identify obligations that bind all ILO Member States, *by virtue of membership* 'to respect, to promote and to realize ... the principles concerning the fundamental rights'[28] that are the subject of the core labour standards. Thus it has a similar juridical basis to the freedom of association procedures: the obligations flow from membership of the ILO and the fact of being bound by its Constitution. A major difference from the freedom of association machinery, however, is that there is no complaint mechanism associated with the 1998 Declaration. Under its follow-up procedures, ILO Members must submit reports about any of the core conventions that they have not yet ratified (pursuant to Article 19 of the Constitution).

Deakin and G. Morris (eds.), *The Future of Labour Law – Liber Amicorum Bob Hepple QC* (Oxford: Hart Publishing, 2004), p. 268.

[25] These issues have been traversed at length elsewhere: Alston, 'Transformation' (n. 23 above); and P. Alston and J. Heenan, 'Shrinking the International Labour Code: An Unintended consequence of the 1998 ILO Declaration on Fundamental Principles and Rights at Work?', *New York University Journal of International Law and Politics*, Vol. 36 (2004), pp. 221–264. These articles drew two replies: B. Langille, 'Core Labour Rights – The True Story (Reply to Alston)', *European Journal of International Law*, Vol. 16 (2005), pp. 409–437, and F. Maupain, 'Revitalization Not Retreat: The Real Potential of the 1998 ILO Declaration for the Universal Protection of Workers' Rights', *European Journal of International Law*, Vol. 16 (2005), pp. 439–465. Alston in turn responded: 'Facing up to the Complexities of the ILO's Core Labour Standards Agenda', *European Journal of International Law*, Vol. 16 (2005), pp. 467–480.

[26] For commentary on the Declaration see: J. Bellace, 'The ILO Declaration on Fundamental Principles and Rights at Work', *International Journal of Comparative Labour Law and Industrial Relations*, Vol. 17 (2001), pp. 269–287; Trebilcock, 'A New Tool' (n. 24 above); H. Kellerson, 'The ILO Declaration of 1998 on Fundamental Principles and Rights: A Challenge for the Future', *International Labour Review*, Vol. 137 (1998), pp. 223–235; and Langille, 'New Economy' (n. 7 above).

[27] Annex, Follow-up to the 1998 Declaration, Article 2.

[28] 1998 Declaration, Article 2.

[23] See, e.g., A. Trebilcock, 'The ILO Declaration on Fundamental Principles and Rights at Work: A New Tool', in R. Blanpain and C. Engels (eds.), *The ILO and the Challenges of the 21st Century – The Geneva Lectures* (The Hague: Kluwer Law International, 2001), pp. 105–116; Novitz, *Protection of the Right to Strike* (n. 4 above), p. 104; Langille, 'New Economy' (n. 7 above). Philip Alston contests this view: '"Core Labour Standards" and the Transformation of the International Labour Rights Regime', *European Journal of International Law*, Vol. 15 (2004), pp. 457–521, at 464–466.

[24] B. Creighton, 'The Future of Labour Law: Is There a Role for International Labour Standards?', in C. Barnard, S.

These reports are considered by a separate committee of Expert Advisors, whose members are not jurists, but have expertise in development, economics and other fields. Separate from this reporting process, the Office prepares a 'global report' each year on the theme of one of the pairs of core labour standards, which is considered at the Conference.[29]

3. ILO JURISPRUDENCE ON ITS CORE LABOUR STANDARDS

3.1 Freedom of Association

The ILO has developed a vast array of principles on freedom of association, particularly through the work of the CFA.[30] I will give a short overview of the normative content of the main instruments – Conventions 87 and 98[31] – and then consider two of the key issues that commonly arise concerning their application in practice.[32] The first is the exercise of the right to strike, which I have selected

because it illustrates how the ILO has developed an expansive interpretation of its norms. The second is the ILO's insistence on the importance of maintaining a climate of civil liberties as a prerequisite to the exercise of freedom of association. This illustrates how the ILO's work emphasises that all human rights are interconnected.[33]

CONVENTIONS 87 AND 98

The Freedom of Association and Protection of the Right to Organize Convention, 1948 (No. 87) protects the right of workers and employers to form and to join, without prior authorisation, organisations of their own choosing (Article 2), for the defence of their occupational and industrial interests (Article 10). The organisations they form may join federations and confederations, which are entitled to exercise all the rights that Convention 87 confers on first level organisations (Articles 5 and 6). These include the right to control their internal administration and programmes of activity free of interference (Article 3), and to operate without being subject to administrative suspension or dissolution (Article 4), provided they comply with the law of the land (Article 8). The only limitations permitted on the exercise of the right of freedom of association apply to those workers in the armed forces and the police (Article 9).

The Right to Organize and Collective Bargaining Convention, 1949 (No. 98) requires that workers be protected from acts of anti-union discrimination (Article 1). Workers' organisations must also be protected from discriminatory action and from acts liable to bring them under the control of employers' organisations (Article 2). States parties to Convention 98 must take measures to 'encourage and promote' the full realisation of the right to voluntary collective bargaining (Article 4). States may determine at the national level the extent to which these rights apply to members of the armed forces and the police (Article 5); the Convention

---

[29] ILO, *Your Voice at Work* (Geneva: ILO, 2000); ILO, *Stopping Forced Labour* (Geneva: ILO, 2001); ILO, *A Future Without Child Labour* (Geneva: ILO, 2002); ILO, *Time for Equality at Work* (Geneva: ILO, 2003); ILO, *Organising for Social Justice* (Geneva: ILO, 2004); ILO, *A Global Alliance Against Forced Labour* (Geneva: ILO, 2005); ILO, *The End of Child Labour: Within Reach* (Geneva: ILO, 2006).

[30] The principles of the CFA are consolidated and published from time to time: ILO, *Freedom of Association – Digest of decisions and principles of the Freedom of Association Committee of the Governing Body of the ILO*, 5th (revised) edition (Geneva: ILO, 1996).

[31] Other ILO instruments on freedom of association include the Right of Association (Agriculture) Convention, 1921 (No. 11), the Workers' Representatives Convention, 1971 (No. 135), the Rural Workers' Organisations Convention, 1975 (No. 149), and the Labour Relations (Public Service) Convention, 1978 (No. 151).

[32] For fuller treatments of Freedom of Association see, e.g., ILO, *Digest* (n. 30 above); ILO, *Freedom of Association and Collective Bargaining* (Geneva: ILO, 1994); B. Creighton, 'Freedom of Association', in R. Blanpain and C. Engels, *Comparative Labour Law and Industrial Relations in Industrialized Market Economies*, 7th (revised) edition, (The Hague: Kluwer Law International, 2001); Bartolomei de la Cruz et al, *ILO Standards* (n. 3 above), chs. 12 and 20 to 23; L. Betten, *International Labour Law – Selected Issues* (Deventer: Kluwer, 1993), ch. 3; S. Leader, *Freedom of Association: A Study in Labor Law and Political Theory* (New Haven: Yale University Press, 1992); F. von Prondzynski, *Freedom of Association and Industrial Relations: A Comparative Study* (London: Mansell Publishing Ltd, 1987); Lord Wedderburn, 'Freedom of Association and Philosophies of Labour Law' *Industrial Law Journal* ,Vol. 18 (1989), pp. 1–38.

[33] Other issues that commonly arise include matters of trade union structure (monopoly vs multiplicity); the extent to which States may limit the exercise of certain rights only to the most representative organisations; the permissibility and scope of union security clauses; the right of organizations to determine their own rules; and the question whether workers have a right to engage in collective bargaining. See, e.g., ILO, *Digest* (n. 30 above), and ILO, *Freedom of Association* (n. 32 above).

does not deal with 'public servants engaged in the administration of the State' (Article 6).

THE EXERCISE OF THE RIGHT TO STRIKE

The ILO's jurisprudence in this area alone is considerable, and this is reflected in the significant body of academic work on the topic.[34] My goal here is simply to show how the ILO has developed the normative content of its instruments: neither Convention 87 nor Convention 98 refers to the right to strike.[35] The ILO has nevertheless developed an extensive body of principles concerning the right to strike, determining that it derives from the right of workers' organisations to pursue their own programmes of activities to defend workers' economic and social interests (C. 87, Articles 3, 8 and 10). The CEACR has referred to the right to strike as an 'intrinsic corollary' of freedom of association,[36] and as 'one of the essential means available to workers and to their organizations for furthering and defending their interests'.[37]

ILO principles on the right to strike deal in particular with the extent to which States may limit or control the exercise of the right. Among other things, they stress that any procedural requirements that are prerequisites to the lawful exercise of the right (as for example secret ballots, or advance notice to employers) should not be so onerous as to amount to a limitation or restriction on the exercise of the right. At the same time, however, it may be permissible to limit or even totally abrogate the right for workers engaged in services properly identified as essential. This means 'only those the interruption of which would endanger the life, personal safety or health of the whole or part of the population'.[38] The ILO also insists that States guarantee rapid dispute resolution where they limit the exercise of the right. Other important issues covered by ILO jurisprudence include the legality of so-called 'political' strikes, and the importance of the right to picket.

Another issue that arises is whether public servants might exercise the right to strike. Convention 98 'does not deal with the position of public servants engaged in the administration of the state' (Article 6). The ILO's supervisory bodies have held, however, that any limitation that this permits on public servants' right to strike must be narrowly construed. This appears to mean that only senior officials in ministries and comparable bodies may be denied the right to strike. In the case of Germany, for example, the CFA observed that teachers in particular do not fall within the exception, as they do not perform tasks that are peculiar to the public administration.[39]

A CLIMATE OF CIVIL LIBERTIES

Here the ILO shows itself to be aware of the important connections between labour rights and other human rights. Both the CFA and the CEACR insist that a State must maintain a general climate in which it is possible to exercise one's civil liberties, without which it would be impossible to exercise the freedom of association. This is not surprising when around half of all complaints to the CFA have involved cases of violence against trade unionists.[40] A country in which these principles and issues have frequently arisen in recent years is Colombia, where thousands of trade unionists have been killed during the course of civil insurrection.[41] The ILO's insistence on the necessity for a general climate of civil liberties shows it reaching beyond 'mere' labour rights and into broader matters of economic and social rights. Indeed, in this area it plays a role in the broader realm of civil and political rights, thus showing its acceptance (even if only implicitly) of the principle of the indivisibility of all human rights.

3.2 Freedom from Forced Labour

The Forced Labour Convention, 1930 (No. 29) was adopted following the adoption of the Slavery

---

[34] Of the many works on the topic see, e.g., Novitz, *Protection of the Right to Strike* (n. 4 above); K. Ewing, *The Right to Strike* (Oxford: Clarendon Press, 1991); R. Ben-Israel, *International Labour Standards: The Case of the Freedom to Strike* (Deventer: Kluwer, 1988).

[35] ILO, *Freedom of Association* (n. 32 above), p. 62; Novitz, *Protection of the Right to Strike* (n. 4 above), pp. 114–120.

[36] ILO, *Freedom of Association* (n. 32 above), p. 77.

[37] Ibid. p. 67.

[38] Ibid. p. 70.

[39] Novitz, *Protection of the Right to Strike* (n. 4 above), p. 305.

[40] Creighton, 'Freedom of Association' (n. 32 above), p. 244.

[41] As a result, worker delegates to the Conference lodged a complaint under article 26 of the Constitution in June 1998; in June 2001 the Governing Body put its consideration of the issue 'in abeyance'. The ILO has since continued to employ diplomatic means and technical cooperation to attempt to address the situation.

Convention in 1926: the League of Nations specifically referred the matter to the ILO. Convention 29 was aimed principally at the practice of exacting forced labour from the populations of territories ruled as colonies. The most widely ratified of all ILO Conventions, it requires States parties to suppress all forms of forced labour 'within the shortest possible period' (Article 1(1)). States may, however, resort to forced labour in certain cases in which there is a perceived public benefit, including in cases of national emergency, under laws for compulsory military service, and in the case of convicted prisoners (Article 2(2)). States must impose criminal penalties on those who illegally exact forced labour (Article 25).[42] The Abolition of Forced Labour Convention, 1957 (No. 105) was adopted much later, in light of the practices in several countries, including those of the Stalin regime.[43] It provides that forced labour must not be used for political coercion or education, for economic development, for discipline, to punish strikers, or as a means of discrimination (Article 1).

The ILO's jurisprudence on Convention 29 again illustrates how it has developed extensive principles from limited normative beginnings and its insistence on the interconnectedness of human rights. In recent years, the ILO has frequently considered the application of Convention 29 to the work done by prisoners held in privately run facilities.[44] At issue are the elements of Article 2(2)(c), which provides that States may exact forced labour from prisoners, subject to three conditions: that the prisoners have been properly convicted; that

they work under the supervision and control of the public authorities; and that they are not 'hired to or placed at the disposal of private individuals, companies or associations'. The CEACR has determined that virtually all forms of private operation of prison facilities are inconsistent with Article 2(2)(c) because they lead to a private benefit.[45] At the same time, Convention 29 does not prohibit a prisoner working *voluntarily* for private interests. From this proposition, the CEACR has developed extensive principles to be satisfied that the work is voluntary, including whether the conditions of work are roughly equivalent to those available for similar work in the free labour market.

In considering the case of prisoners, the CEACR has located the right not to be subject to forced labour within the broader context of international human rights law. Indeed the ILO has more than once referred to Convention 29 as a source of a 'peremptory norm'. The CEACR did so in 2002, in response to the argument that there is an *inevitable* commercial benefit from private operation of prisons (and from the use of prisoners' labour), flowing from 'universal acceptance of the free market principle'. The CEACR remarked that such an approach,

> [M]ight make obsolete legal requirements of a basic human rights Convention, in a field where an even older international instrument first interfered with the then free trade in human beings. Such suggestion disregards the peremptory character of basic human rights standards in international law, and is unacceptable.[46]

The Commission of Inquiry concerning forced labour in Burma used similar language. After surveying the state of international law on forced labour generally, the Commission remarked that 'there exists now in international law a peremptory norm prohibiting any recourse to forced labour and . . . the right not to perform forced or compulsory labour is one of the basic human rights'.[47]

---

[42] Many provisions of Convention 29 regulate the terms under which forced labour might be exacted. These provisions are not relevant to the exaction of forced labour pursuant to the exceptions in article 2(2). Rather, they reflect the fact that during a 'transitional period' after the Convention came into force, States might continue to exact forced labour.

[43] Bartolomei de la Cruz et al., *ILO Standards* (n. 3 above), p. 151.

[44] The CEACR recently concluded a general survey on forced labour and reiterated its previous positions on these issues: ILO, *Eradication of Forced Labour* (Geneva: ILO, 2007), pp. 24–33, 58–67. In this area the CEACR has proved itself most willing to engage at length with both governments and employers, concerning the effects of the privatisation of formerly public services. In so doing, it has been engaged at the heart of one aspect of economic globalisation, and so with some of the more significant challenges facing the realisation of economic and social rights. See further C. Fenwick, 'Private Use of Prisoners' Labour: Paradoxes of International Human Rights Law', *Human Rights Quarterly*, Vol. 27. (2005), pp. 249–293.

[45] ILO, *Report of the Committee of Experts on the Application of Conventions and Recommendations* (Geneva: ILO, 1995), (individual observation concerning France).

[46] ILO, *Report of the Committee of Experts on the Application of Conventions and Recommendations* (Geneva: ILO, 2002), p. 96.

[47] *Report of the Burma Commission of Inquiry* (n. 22 above), p. 66.

3.3 Freedom from Discrimination in Employment

The principles of non-discrimination in employment and of equal pay for men and women for work of equal value were first recognised by the ILO in its Constitution, and have since been addressed in specific instruments. The Equal Remuneration Convention, 1951 (No. 100), obliges States to promote and to ensure the application wherever possible of the principle of equal remuneration for work of equal value (Article 2(1)). It also requires objective assessment of work value (Article 3), and cooperation with organisations of workers and employers (Article 4).[48] The other main ILO instrument relating to equality in employment is the Discrimination (Employment and Occupation) Convention, 1958 (No. 111). Its principal obligation is 'to declare and pursue a national policy designed to promote ... equality of opportunity and treatment in respect of employment and occupation' (Article 2). There are two quite distinctly different qualifications to this obligation. One is that States are not prevented from taking measures against individuals 'justifiably suspected of, or engaged in, activities prejudicial to the security of the State' (Article 3). The other is that '[s]pecial measures of protection' are not inconsistent with the general obligation to prohibit discrimination (Article 5).

Here I will briefly consider the ILO's consideration of the application of Convention 111 in Romania, which illustrates its willingness to range widely across social and economic policy. The ILO has repeatedly emphasised the need to develop a broad approach to social and economic policy in order to overcome discrimination against the Roma and also against Hungarian and German-speaking minorities. Worker delegates to the Conference lodged a complaint about the situation in 1989. Notwithstanding the fall of the Ceaucescu regime, the ILO established a Commission of Inquiry, which reported in 1991.[49] Since then the CEACR has continued to follow the case and to publish individual observations from time to time. The CCAS considered the case in 1989, 1993 and 1994.

The Commission of Inquiry found that the Roma suffered both direct and indirect discrimination in employment. Direct discrimination resulted in the Roma being allocated the most arduous jobs with low social status, or wage differentiation, or difficulties in promotion. Indirect discrimination was identified in training and access to employment. Tellingly, the Commission noted that certain Roma suffered discrimination because of their low incomes, which meant that their children had insufficient access to vocational education and training; this in turn prevented those children in time from getting access to skilled (and more highly paid) jobs.[50]

The Commission made many recommendations, ranging across all areas of social and economic policy: while the Commission did not refer to these in terms of socio-economic rights, it plainly saw the critical interconnections between civil and political rights, and economic and social rights, and also the interconnections between labour rights, narrowly conceived, and the wider framework of economic and social rights. The Commission recommended, for example, the adoption of a language policy to meet the 'cultural and economic needs of minorities'. It also recommended efforts to improve the social situation of the Roma by adopting 'an integrated programme drawn up in collaboration with their representatives, covering education, employment, housing and the other elements necessary to their progress'.[51]

The CEACR has offered similarly broad views. In 2000, for example, it observed that Romania should adopt 'measures aimed at ... promoting a climate of tolerance through awareness raising and education in the entire field of employment and education and beyond'.[52] In 2003, the CEACR urged the Government 'to reinforce its efforts to promote a climate of respect and tolerance towards the Roma [being] a precondition to make substantial progress in fighting economic

---

[48] More guidance on how to comply with these obligations can be found in the accompanying Equal Remuneration Recommendation, 1951 (No. 90).

[49] ILO, *Report of the Commission of Inquiry Appointed under Article 26 of the Constitution of the International Labour Organisation to examine the observance by Romania of the Discrimination (Employment and Occupation) Convention, 1958 (No. 111)* (Geneva: ILO, 1991).

[50] Ibid. para. 592.

[51] Ibid, para. 617, recommendations 9 and 14.

[52] ILO, *Report of the Committee of Experts on the Application of Conventions and Recommendations,* (Geneva: ILO, 2000), p. 350 (individual observation, Romania).

marginalization and exclusion'.[53] From a normative point of view, the ILO has perhaps been able to take this broad approach because Convention 111 defines 'employment' and 'occupation' as including access to vocational training and access to employment (Article 1(3)). This implicates the broader issues of education, language and culture. The approach is consistent, however, with its general insistence on the importance of its human rights protections and their links to other human rights.[54]

3.4 Freedom from Harmful Child Labour

There are two main ILO instruments in this area: the Minimum Age Convention, 1973 (No. 138) and the Worst Forms of Child Labour Convention, 1999 (No. 182). Convention 138 is an instrument that consolidates the requirements of a number of earlier instruments that regulated the minimum age for admission to employment in particular economic sectors. Reflecting the fact that some of those earlier instruments had been adopted at the very first session of the Conference, in 1919, the approach to the regulation of child labour is somewhat rigid.

Convention 138 sets quite prescriptive rules about the age at which children might enter different types of employment, although it does include some flexibility.[55] States parties' primary obliga-

tion is to commit to abolish child labour, by progressively increasing the minimum age for entry to employment (Article 1), which should be fifteen years (or fourteen for developing countries), *provided* that the minimum age should not be lower than the minimum age for attendance at compulsory schooling (Article 2). The minimum age for hazardous work should be eighteen, or sixteen, with provision for instruction and vocational training (Article 3). Convention 138 allows work below the required minimum ages for vocational education and training (Article 6), for light work that is not harmful to the child (Article 7), and for work in artistic performances (Article 8).

Convention 138 includes certain 'measures of flexibility': as noted, developing countries may specify a lower minimum age for employment than developed countries (Article 2). All States may also exclude certain categories of work, in particular where there are 'special and substantial problems of application' (Article 4). States may exclude the application of the Convention to certain sectors of the economy (Article 5). While Convention 138 does identify a number of economic sectors that *cannot* be excluded from its operation, it does permit states to exclude its operation in noncommercial agricultural work, described as 'family and small-scale holdings producing for local consumption and not regularly employing hired workers'. The limitations inherent in such a provision can immediately be seen when considering the figures produced by the ILO on the number of child workers in the world today, and the types of work that they do: in 2002, the ILO reported that 70 per cent of the world's 245 million child workers were engaged in agriculture, fishing, hunting or forestry.[56] Four years later, the ILO reported that of the 317 million economically active children in the world, 218 million could be considered to be involved in child labour. Of these, 69 per cent were still engaged in agriculture, fishing, hunting or forestry.[57]

---

[53] ILO, *Report of the Committee of Experts on the Application of Conventions and Recommendations*, (Geneva: ILO, 2003), p. 517 (individual observation, Romania).

[54] It is of some note that the breadth of areas in which the ILO Commission of Inquiry made recommendations in 1991 was later largely replicated by the Committee on the Elimination of Racial Discrimination in its General Recommendation No. 27: Discrimination against Roma. Here too we see States being urged to take measures in the areas of law, politics, education, employment, the media and public life. Committee on the Elimination of Racial Discrimination, *General Recommendation No. 27: Discrimination against Roma*, UN Doc. A/55/18, annex V (2000).

[55] On Convention 138, see B. Creighton, 'Combating child labour: the role of international labour standards', *Comparative Labor Law and Policy Journal*, Vol. 18 (1997), pp. 362–396; and D. Smolin, 'Conflict and Ideology in the International Campaign Against Child Labour', *Hofstra Labor & Employment Law Journal*, Vol. 16 (1999), pp. 383–451, at 413–419. On the shift from Convention 138 to Convention 182 see, e.g., D. Smolin, 'A Tale of Two Treaties: Furthering Social Justice Through the Redemptive Myths of Childhood', *Emory International Law Review*, Vol. 17

(2003), pp. 967–1000. For comment on Convention 182 see, e.g., C. Corlett, 'Impact of the 2000 [sic] Child Labor Treaty on United States Child Laborers', *Arizona Journal of International and Comparative Law*, Vol. 19 (2002), pp. 713–739, at 725–728.

[56] ILO, *A Future Without Child Labour* (n. 29 above), pp. 22–27.

[57] ILO, *The End of Child Labour*, (n. 29 above), pp. 6–8.

More recent experience in the ILO under the auspices of its International Programme for the Elimination of Child Labour (IPEC) led to the adoption of Convention 182, which takes a very different approach. Its principal obligation is to take 'immediate and effective measures to secure the prohibition and elimination of the worst forms of child labour as a matter of urgency' (Article 1). The 'worst forms of child labour' are defined to include slavery, prostitution, and illicit activities (including drug trafficking) (Article 3). States must define these types of labour in national laws (Article 4(1)), and 'design and implement programmes to eliminate as a priority the worst forms of child labour' (Article 6(1)). Convention 182 also requires specific measures to ensure the availability of education, the removal of children from the worst forms of child labour and their rehabilitation, and particular attention to the situation of girls (Article 7).

As Convention 182 has only recently come into force, the ILO has as yet developed little jurisprudence in this area. At the time of writing, the CEACR has published individual observations in many cases, but no case has been considered in the CCAS, and the constitutional procedures have not been invoked. In its individual observations, the CEACR has emphasised the need for governments to take immediate and effective action, and has sought very detailed information on States parties' efforts to comply. In the case of the United States, it has sought 'copies of or extracts from official documents...and information on the nature, extent and trends of the worst forms of child labour, the number of children covered by the measures giving effect to the Convention, the number and nature of infringements reported, investigations, prosecutions, convictions and penal sanctions applied'.[58] In the case of Sri Lanka, the CEACR drew on information from the UN program on HIV/AIDS to develop an observation about the extent to which children infected with or affected by the virus might be more vulnerable to exploitation in the worst forms of child labour.[59] In the case of Turkey, we see the impact of IPEC: the CEACR drew on IPEC reports,

and also remarked favourably on Turkey's participation in IPEC projects.[60] In each of these cases then we see again (at least in a protean way) the willingness of the ILO to address a wide range of areas of economic and social policy, as they relate to its particular concern with (child) labour.

4. THE ILO AND INDIGENOUS AND TRIBAL PEOPLES' RIGHTS

In this section I briefly consider the ILO's work in the area of indigenous and tribal peoples, as a comparison with its work on core labour standards. We see, however, very similar themes that emerge, in particular, that the ILO insists on the interconnection of rights at work with other economic and social rights. Moreover, in considering the representations that have been lodged under Article 24 of the Constitution, we see that the ILO has been able to incorporate and respond to the interests of groups other than workers represented by trade unions, and indeed to do so in relation to rights other than rights at work.

4.1. ILO Conventions 107 and 169

The ILO has long been active regarding rights of indigenous and tribal peoples. It carried out a study on the situation of indigenous workers in 1921. Convention 29 (adopted in 1930) was also important: many of those it sought to protect from forced labour were indigenous or 'native' populations. During the 1930s the ILO adopted a number of instruments specifically concerned with indigenous workers.[61] A Committee on Indigenous Labour met twice in the early 1950s,

---

[58] ILO, *Report of the Committee of Experts on the Application of Conventions and Recommendations* (Geneva: ILO, 2005), p. 259 (individual observation, USA).

[59] ILO, *Report of the Committee of Experts on the Application of Conventions and Recommendations* (Geneva: ILO, 2005), pp. 248–249 (individual observation, Sri Lanka).

[60] ILO, *Report of the Committee of Experts on the Application of Conventions and Recommendations* (Geneva: ILO, 2005), p. 250 (individual observation, Turkey).

[61] These were the Recruiting of Indigenous Workers Convention, 1936 (No. 50), the Contracts of Employment (Indigenous Workers) Convention, 1939 (No. 64), and the Penal Sanctions (Indigenous Workers) Convention, 1939 (No. 65). See further L. Swepston and R. Plant, 'International standards and the protection of the land rights of indigenous and tribal populations', *International Labour Review*, Vol. 124 (1985), pp. 91–106, at 92. See also S. Pritchard and C. Heindow-Dolman, 'Indigenous Peoples and International Law: A Critical Overview', *Australian Indigenous Law Review*, Vol. 3 (1998), pp. 473–509, at 477; and S. Anaya, *Indigenous Peoples in International Law*, 2nd edition (Oxford: Oxford University Press, 2004), p. 54.

and in 1953, the ILO published 'Indigenous Peoples: Living and Working Conditions of Aboriginal Populations in Independent Countries'.[62] At the same time the ILO took the lead within a consortium of international agencies responsible for delivering the United Nations' Andean Indian Programme.[63]

These experiences led the ILO to adopt its Convention Concerning the Protection and Integration of Indigenous and Other Tribal and Semi-Tribal Populations in Independent Countries 1957 (No. 107). Although it was not widely ratified,[64] Convention 107 is significant as the first binding international instrument in the area. It was the first to use human rights concepts specifically for indigenous populations,[65] creating a place in the international system for 'the subject of people identified by their indigenousness'.[66] Convention 107 urged States to ensure that indigenous populations benefited from national economic development projects and to include them in education and other public benefits.[67] Particularly from the early 1970s,[68] Convention 107 was seen as outdated as it was overwhelmingly influenced by a philosophy of integration, or assimilation. This is starkly illustrated by the terms of Article 2(1) of the Convention, which provides that '[g]overnments shall have the primary responsibility for developing co-ordinated and systematic action for the protection of the populations concerned *and their progressive integration into the life of their respective countries*' (emphasis added).

Following the recommendation of a meeting of experts in September 1986,[69] the ILO Conference discussed the matter and adopted the Indigenous and Tribal Peoples Convention, 1989 (No. 169). Commentators have differed in their views of the legitimacy and effectiveness of the ILO's efforts to involve parties representing tribal and indigenous peoples in the process of adopting Convention 169.[70] My point is not to try to resolve these differences, but simply to emphasise that (contestation aside) all parties agree that the ILO made some efforts to adapt its structures to the involvement of representatives of indigenous and tribal peoples: it was willing to move beyond its strict tripartite framework. Although it has since attracted only seventeen ratifications (of which thirteen are Latin American countries, and none is from Africa or Asia),[71] Convention 169 is important (at least) because it remains the only binding international instrument that deals with policy relating to indigenous and tribal peoples. It is 'a central feature of international law's contemporary treatment of indigenous peoples' demands'.[72]

The normative content of Convention 169 is starkly different from Convention 107, both in detail and in philosophical approach.[73] Its

---

[62] Referred to in H. Hannum, 'New Developments in Indigenous Rights', *Virginia Journal of International Law*, Vol. 28 (1988), pp. 649–678, at 653.

[63] L. Swepston, 'A New Step in the International Law on Indigenous and Tribal Peoples: ILO Convention No. 169 of 1989', *Oklahoma City University Law Review*, Vol. 15 (1990), pp. 677–714, at p. 679.

[64] Predominantly from the Americas, the 27 parties to Convention 107 were Angola, Argentina, Bangladesh, Belgium, Bolivia, Brazil, Colombia, Cost Rica, Cuba, the Dominican Republic, Ecuador, Egypt, El Salvador, Ghana, Guinea-Bissau, Haiti, India, Iraq, Malawi, Mexico, Pakistan, Panama, Paraguay, Peru, Portugal, the Syrian Arab Republic, and Tunisia. See further R. Barsh, 'Revision of ILO Convention No. 107', *American Journal of International Law*, Vol. 81 (1987), pp. 756–762, at 757.

[65] Anaya, *Indigenous Peoples* (n. 61 above), p. 54.

[66] Ibid., p. 56.

[67] Barsh, 'Convention No. 107' (n. 64 above), p. 757.

[68] The UN appointed a Special Rapporteur on Discrimination Against Indigenous Populations in 1972: Swepston, 'New Step' (n. 63 above), p. 687.

[69] Ibid., p. 688; Barsh, 'Convention No. 107' (n. 64 above), Anaya, *Indigenous Peoples* (n. 61 above), p. 58.

[70] Barsh refers to the 'low level of indigenous representation': 'Convention No. 107', (n. 64 above), p. 758, (at n. 13), while Pritchard and Heindow-Dolman assert that 'indigenous people were largely excluded' from the process: 'Critical Overview' (n. 61 above), p. 478, referring to H. Berman, 'The International labour Organisation and indigenous peoples: revision of ILO Convention 107 at the 75th session of the International Labour Conference 1988', in J. Ferguson (ed.), *Aboriginal Peoples and Treaties*, (Hunters Hill: Conventions Coverage International, 1989). Anaya and Swepston are more positive: *Indigenous Peoples* (n. 61 above), p. 59; 'New Step' (n. 63 above), pp. 686–7.

[71] As at 1 July 2005, the parties to Convention 169 were: the Netherlands, Fiji, Ecuador, Colombia, Mexico, Norway, Bolivia, Costa Rica, Peru, Honduras, Denmark, Guatemala, Argentina, Paraguay, Venezuela, Dominica, and Brazil.

[72] Anaya, *Indigenous Peoples* (n. 61 above), p. 58.

[73] It should be noted that Convention 169 revises Convention 107 (Convention 169, art. 36). Thus states may no longer ratify Convention 107 (Convention 107, art. 36(1)(b)). States parties to Convention 107 that ratify Convention 169 are taken as a matter of law to have denounced Convention 107 (Convention 107, Article 36(1)(a)). Nine States that were parties to Convention 107 have ratified Convention 169, and therefore,

underlying theme is 'respect for the cultures and ways of life of indigenous and tribal peoples'.[74] This is clear from Article 2(1), which provides that:

> Governments shall have the responsibility for developing, *with the participation of the peoples concerned*, co-ordinated and systematic action to protect the rights of these peoples and to guarantee respect for their integrity.[75] (Emphasis added).

Part I of Convention 169 deals with general social policy toward indigenous and tribal peoples (Articles 1–12). It deals with non-discrimination and full enjoyment of human rights (Article 3); special measures to protect indigenous peoples' property, culture and environment (Article 4); respect for their 'social, cultural, religious and spiritual values' (Article 5); the obligation to consult (Article 6); a right to decide their own development priorities and to exercise control (to the extent possible) over their own economic, social and cultural development (Article 7(1)); a requirement that governments pay due regard to indigenous people's customary laws, including their traditional criminal punishments (Articles 8 and 9); another concerning punishments that might be imposed on indigenous persons under general criminal law (Article 10); and protection from abuse of rights, and in particular from the imposition of forced labour (Articles 11 and 12).

Part II of Convention 169 deals with land rights, among other things requiring governments to 'respect the special importance for the cultures and spiritual values of the peoples concerned of their relationship with the lands or territories ... which they occupy' (Article 13(1)). The ILO has emphasised the importance of the relationship that indigenous and tribal people have to land, noting in one case involving Peru that 'the loss of communal land often damages the cohesion and viability of the people concerned'.[76]

Convention 169 creates specific obligations to respect traditional rights of ownership and possession, including methods for transferring land-use rights (Articles 14 and 17); and to safeguard indigenous peoples' rights with respect to natural resources (Article 15). Generally speaking, indigenous peoples should not be removed from their lands (Article 16). Part III of Convention 169 creates an obligation to take special measures in relation to the recruitment and employment conditions of indigenous peoples; Part IV concerns vocational training, handicrafts and rural industries; Part V deals with social security and health, and Part VI with education and means of communication.

4.2 ILO Jurisprudence on Convention 169

Trade unions, often on behalf of indigenous peoples, have lodged twelve representations under Article 24 of the Constitution concerning Convention 169. They have concerned, among other things, the rights of the former inhabitants of Thule, Greenland, to compensation for removal from the area in the early 1950s;[77] the implementation of legislation to facilitate the alienation of coastal peasant farmers' lands in Peru;[78] and the extent to which the government of Colombia consulted the Embera Katío people of Alto Sinú concerning the construction and operation of the Urrá hydroelectric dam.[79] The CEACR has also published individual observations on many occasions, and the CCAS has twice examined the case of Mexico. I will focus on the reports of the committees considering Article 24 representations: as they arise from contentious proceedings they reveal a

---

denounced Convention 107: Argentina, Bolivia, Brazil, Colombia, Costa Rica, Ecuador, Paraguay and Peru. It remains binding, however, on 18 States: Angola, Bangladesh, Belgium, Cuba, Dominican Republic, Egypt, El Salvador, Ghana, Guinea-Bissau, Haiti, India, Iraq, Malawi, Pakistan, Panama, Portugal, Syria and Tunisia.

[74] Swepston, 'New Step' (n. 63 above), p. 690.

[75] Convention No. 169, Article 2(1).

[76] ILO, *Report of the Committee set up to examine the representation alleging non-observance by Peru of the Indigenous and Tribal Peoples Convention, 1989 (No. 169), made under article 24 of the ILO Constitution by the General*

Confederation of Workers of Peru (Geneva: ILO, 1998), para. 30.

[77] ILO, *Report of the Committee set up to examine the representation alleging non-observance by Denmark of the Indigenous and Tribal Peoples Convention, 1989 (No. 169), made under article 24 of the ILO Constitution by the National Confederation of Trade Unions of Greenland (Sulinermik Inuussutissarsiuteqartut Kattuffiat-SIK) (SIK)* (Geneva: ILO, 2001).

[78] ILO, *Peru Representation* (n. 76 above).

[79] ILO, *Report of the Committee set up to examine the representation alleging non-observance by Colombia of the Indigenous and Tribal People's Convention, 1989 (No. 169), made under article 24 of the ILO Constitution by the Central Unitary Workers' union (CUT) and the Colombian Medical Trade Union Association* (Geneva: ILO, 2001).

little more of the parties' opposing positions than do the CEACR reports, which involve dialogue principally with governments.

There are three interesting procedural points arising from the Article 24 representations. One is that it is not necessary to exhaust domestic remedies before lodging one.[80] A second is that parties other than workers, governments or employers have gained access to ILO supervisory mechanisms. Indeed, one of the committees pointed out that the standing orders for examining a representation under Article 24 of the ILO Constitution 'do not require the complainant organization to have a direct connection with the events that constitute the basis of the complaint'.[81] Thirdly, the ILO committees have received and addressed representations about events that occurred long before Convention 169 came into force for the country in question. Here the committees have emphasised that while Convention 169 does not apply retrospectively, its consultation requirements do apply to the ongoing consequences of the actions complained of.[82]

Indeed, the ILO has focused on the requirement of indigenous consultation and participation,[83] which are described variously as 'the hallmark',[84] and the 'cornerstone' of Convention 169.[85] The committees have emphasised that consultation does not require consensus, but a good faith effort to engage.[86] While consultation should be prompt

and adequate,[87] it is not enough just to provide 'information sessions' to indigenous peoples about the impact upon them of decisions that have already been reached.[88] Moreover, consultation should be sensitive to, and give enough time for, indigenous modes of consultation and decision-making. In the case of a representation against Colombia, the committee remarked:

> The adoption of rapid decisions should not be to the detriment of effective consultation for which sufficient time must be given to allow the country's indigenous people to engage their own decision-making processes and participate effectively in decisions taken in a manner consistent with their cultural and social traditions.[89]

Similarly, the ILO has emphasised that consultation depends upon the groups 'representing' indigenous and tribal peoples actually being representative.[90] In that respect, the committees have noted that the Convention does not impose any particular model of representative institution – 'the important thing is that they should be the result of a process carried out by the indigenous people themselves'.[91]

4.3   The Significance of Convention 169

According to Anaya, Convention 169 has had significant influence in other places. Its adoption helped to accelerate and focus international discussion on the adoption of a normative instrument in other forums,[92] including the

---

[80] Anaya, *Indigenous Peoples* (n. 61 above), p. 250. See also ILO, *Denmark Representation* (n. 77 above), para. 30; ILO, *Report of the Committee set up to examine the representation alleging non-observance by Mexico of the Indigenous and Tribal Peoples Convention, 1989 (No. 169), made under article 24 of the ILO Constitution by the Trade Union Delegation, D-111–57, section XI of the National Trade Union of Education Workers (SNTE), Radio Education* (Geneva: ILO, 1997), para. 31.

[81] ILO, *Report of the Committee set up to examine the representation alleging non-observance by Ecuador of the Indigenous and Tribal Peoples Convention, 1989 (No. 169), made under article 24 of the ILO Constitution by the Confederación Ecuatoriana de Organizaciones Sindicales Libres (CEOSL)* (Geneva: ILO, 2001), para. 29.

[82] See, e.g., ILO, *Denmark Representation* (n. 77 above): the action in question occurred in 1953, the Convention came into force in February 1997, and the complaint was submitted in 2000.

[83] Anaya, *Indigenous Peoples* (n. 61 above), 250.

[84] ILO, *Denmark Representation* (n. 226 above), para. 43.

[85] Ibid. para. 31.

[86] See, e.g., ILO, *Report of the Committee set up to examine the representation alleging non-observance by Mexico of the Indigenous and Tribal Peoples Convention, 1989 (No.*

[89] 169), made under article 24 of the ILO Constitution by the Authentic Workers' Front (FAT)* (Geneva: ILO, 2004), para. 106.

[87] ILO, *Report of the Committee set up to examine the representation alleging non-observance by Bolivia of the Indigenous and Tribal Peoples Convention, 1989 (No. 169), made under article 24 of the ILO Constitution by the Bolivian Central of Workers (COB)* (Geneva: ILO, 1999), para. 38.

[88] See, e.g., ILO, *Ecuador Representation* (n. 81 above), para. 38.

[89] ILO, *Report of the Committee set up to examine the representation alleging non-observance by Colombia of the Indigenous and Tribal Peoples Convention, 1989 (No. 169), made under article 24 of the ILO Constitution by the Central Unitary Workers' Union (CUT)* (Geneva: ILO, 2001), para. 79.

[90] ILO, *Ecuador Representation* (n. 81 above), para. 44.

[91] ILO, *Mexico Represenation (FAT)* (n. 86 above), para. 102.

[92] Anaya, *Indigenous Peoples* (n. 61 above), p. 64.

Organisation of American States,[93] and the Working Group at the UN Sub-Commission.[94] Convention 169 has been influential in the inter-American human rights system. Its Commission on Human Rights has affirmed the benchmark role of Convention 169 in its approach to land rights for indigenous peoples.[95] At least one judge of the Inter-American Court has identified Convention 169 as a possible aid to the interpretation of the American Convention on Human Rights.[96]

My point here is that again we see the ILO engaged in economic and social issues well beyond 'work'. The content of Convention 169 is all closely related to the ILO's core concerns,[97] but there are some striking examples of how ILO action for indigenous and tribal peoples transcends 'mere' labour issues, perhaps none more so than the emphasis that the ILO has placed on land rights. While there are different opinions on the strength of the land rights protections contained in both Convention 107[98] and Convention 169,[99] it remains true that the ILO has attempted to recognise 'the fundamental importance of respect for indigenous land rights as a prerequisite for the effective enjoyment of other rights and the protection of vulnerable groups'.[100]

A second point I wish to emphasise is that the ILO has managed to involve representatives of indigenous and tribal peoples in both the development of Convention 169, and to some extent in its supervision. In playing a role in the adoption of Convention 169, NGOs were accommodated by an institutional process that is designed for, part of, and constrained by, ILO processes and habits.[101] Thus, their views were considered more or less directly in the adoption of the text of the instrument. Since then, they have proved adept at prosecuting their concerns through the ILO's supervisory system, which has again emphasised the relationships between all economic and social rights, and their interconnection with other fundamental human rights.

5. THE ILO AND THE RIGHT TO SOCIAL SECURITY

The ILO has been concerned with social security since its inception: the preamble to the original Constitution mentioned, among other things, the significance of action against unemployment, workplace illness and injury, and the importance of disability and pension benefits. The Declaration of Philadelphia later reiterated the need for social security measures, including, where necessary, provision of a basic income and comprehensive medical care.[102] The number and longevity of ILO instruments on social security show the importance of its normative work in the area, which has significantly influenced other human rights instruments. Some ILO instruments are also notable for the specificity with which they articulate States' obligations to take steps to implement economic rights. In turn, the continuing impact of even very old ILO instruments on social security is illustrated by how the ILO's supervisory bodies have used them to engage in dialogue with Chile

[93] Ibid. p. 66 and p. 146.
[94] Ibid. p. 65.
[95] Ibid. pp. 146–147, referring to *Dann v. United States*, Inter-Am. Ct. H.R. (Ser. C) No. 75/02 (merits decision of Dec. 27, 2002).
[96] Anaya, *Indigenous Peoples* (n. 61 above), p. 70.
[97] Swepston, 'New Step' (n. 63 above), p. 681.
[98] According to Barsh it 'did relatively little to restrict state power': 'Convention No. 107' (n. 62 above), p. 747. Compare A. Lawrey, who refers to Article 11 of Convention 107, which provides that '[t]he right of ownership ... shall be recognized' as a 'strong provision on indigenous land rights': 'Contemporary Efforts to Guarantee Indigenous Rights Under International Law', *Vanderbilt Journal of Transnational Law*, Vol. 23 (1990), pp. 703–777, at 717.
[99] Articles 13–19 of Convention 169 deal with land rights issues. The concept underlying them is that the State must recognise indigenous land rights even where they are not in the same form as those provided by the national legal system. 'At the same time, the national legal system is the framework within which these rights must be realized': Swepston, 'New Step' (n. 63 above), p. 696. Some indigenous groups expressed the view that this approach itself obstructs their fundamental claim to self-determination: ibid. at n. 90.
[100] Swepston and Plant, 'Protection of Land Rights' (n. 61 above), p. 93.

[101] Anaya, *Indigenous Peoples* (n. 61 above), p. 64; Swepston, 'New Step' (n. 63 above), p. 686.
[102] Declaration of Philadelphia, paragraphs I(d) and III(f). See J. M. Servais, *International Labour Law* (The Hague: Kluwer Law International, 2005) p. 256; and L. Lamarche, 'The Right to Social Security in the International Covenant on Economic, Social and Cultural Rights', in A. Chapman and S. Russell (eds.), *Core Obligations: Building a Framework for Economic, Social and Cultural Rights* (Antwerp: Intersentia, 2002), pp. 87–114, at 90.

over its shift in 1981 from a public pension scheme to one based on private sector funds.

5.1 ILO Conventions on Social Security

To date, the ILO has adopted twenty-two conventions relating to social security, of which fifteen were adopted by 1935;[103] that is, more than ten years before the adoption of the Universal Declaration of Human Rights, which includes a right to social security (Article 25). The early ILO instruments identify nine different categories of 'social risk': sickness and medical care, unemployment, old age benefits, workers' compensation, family and maternity benefits, disability, and survivors' benefits.[104] The ILO adopted a further three conventions on social security in 1952, 1962 and 1964 respectively;[105] that is, in sufficient time to influence the content of both the European Social Charter and the International Covenant on Economic, Social and Cultural Rights (ICESCR).[106] One of these was the Social Security (Minimum Standards) Convention, 1952 (No. 102), the most important of all ILO instruments in the field.[107] Convention 102 brings together the nine specific branches of social security into different parts of the one instrument; they are reflected in turn in the reporting guidelines for Article 9 of the ICESCR.[108]

Convention 102 offers more comprehensive protection than earlier ILO instruments, which defined the persons to be protected in legal terms, such as type of contract, or category of economic activity. Convention 102 simply specifies a percentage of the population that must be covered; in most cases a State must cover either 50 per cent of employees, or 20 per cent of all residents.[109] At the same time, however, it adopts a 'menu-type' approach.[110] Convention 102 allows a State party to confine its ratification to three of the nine branches of social security, provided that among these is at least one of the following: unemployment, employment injury, old age, invalidity or survivor's benefit (Article 2). This sort of approach was later adopted in the European Social Charter. Convention 102 allows States whose 'economy and medical facilities are insufficiently developed' a particular measure of flexibility in its application (Article 3). It is also more flexible than earlier ILO instruments as to how a State might achieve the social security ends that it promotes.[111]

Convention 102 is also however very specific in certain cases about the minimum level of benefit that must be provided. The benefit of medical care identified in Article 10, for example, may be limited to a duration of twenty-six weeks in the case of a morbid condition (Article 12(1)). The level of unemployment benefit required by Article 19 must, by virtue of article 22(1), be calculated

---

[103] *Workmen's Compensation (Agriculture) Convention, 1921 (No. 12), Workmen's Compensation (Accidents) Conventions, 1925 (No. 17), Workmen's Compensation (Occupational Diseases Convention, 1925 (No. 18), Equality of Treatment (Accident Compensation) Convention, 1925 (No. 19), Sickness Insurance (Industry) Convention, 1927 (No. 24), Sickness Insurance (Agriculture) Convention 1925 (No. 25), Old-Age Insurance (Industry, etc.) Convention, 1933 (No. 35), Old-Age Insurance (Agriculture) Convention, 1933 (No. 36), Invalidity Insurance (Industry, etc) Convention, 1933 (No. 37), Invalidity Insurance (Agriculture) Convention, 1933 (No. 38), Survivors' Insurance (Industry, etc.) Convention, 1933 (No. 39), Survivors' Insurance (Agriculture) Convention, 1933 (No. 40), Workmen's Compensation (Occupational Diseases) Convention (Revised), 1934 (No. 42), Unemployment Provision Convention, 1934 (No. 44), and Maintenance of Migrants' Pension Rights Convention, 1935 (No. 48).*

[104] Lamarche, (n. 102 above), p. 90; see also A. Otting, 'International labour standards: A framework for social security', *International Labour Review*, Vol. 132, No. 2 (1993), pp. 163–171, at 164.

[105] *Social Security (Minimum Standards) Convention 1952 (No. 102), Equality of Treatment (Social Security) Convention, 1962 (No. 118),* and *Employment Injury Benefits Convention, 1964 (No. 121).*

[106] It follows that a further four were adopted after the mid 1960s: *Invalidity, Old-Age and Survivors' Benefits Convention, 1969 (No. 128), Medical Care and Sickness Benefits Convention, 1969 (No. 130), Maintenance of Social Security Rights Convention, 1982 (No. 157),* and *Employment Promotion and Protection against Unemployment Convention, 1988 (No. 168).*

[107] It has been referred to as 'the basic reference in the field of social security': Lamarche, 'Right to Social Security' (n. 102 above), p. 90; and the 'principal ILO instrument in the field of social security': M. Scheinin, 'The Right to Social Security', in A. Eide, C. Krause and A. Rosas (eds.), *Economic, Cultural and Social Rights: A Textbook*, 2nd revised ed. (Dordrecht: Martinus Nijhoff Publishers, 2001), pp. xxx–xxx, at 162.

[108] Scheinin, 'Right to Social Security' (n. 107 above), p. 162.

[109] Otting, 'International labour standards' (n. 104 above), p. 167.

[110] Scheinin, 'Right to Social Security' (n. 107 above), p. 162. The revised European Code of Social Security also adopts the nine-part model of ILO Convention 102: ibid. p. 165.

[111] Otting, 'International labour standards' (n. 104 above), p. 167.

consistently with either Article 65 or Article 66. Those provisions in turn contain much detail about the level of payment required in order to support a worker and perhaps their family. Each also refers to an item in a Schedule to Part XI of the Convention, which provides that unemployment benefit should be equal to at least 45 per cent of a worker's former earnings.

This level of detail makes ILO conventions on social security especially important for the realisation of the human right to social security, which is often more generally expressed in other human rights instruments. ILO instruments are important because they identify specific normative requirements that give concrete expression to the extent of States' obligations in relation to the right to social security. This makes them unique among international instruments on economic and social rights: 'only social security conventions incorporate technical benchmarks aimed at guaranteeing the content of an economic right (level and duration of benefit)'.[112] They therefore help to ensure that States adopt strategies to fight poverty and exclusion that contribute positively to realisation of the right to social security.[113]

5.2   The ILO and the Case of Chile

CHILE'S PRIVATE PENSION SYSTEM

In the late 1970s, Chile had one of the best social security systems in its region. The publicly funded scheme ensured generous, defined benefits for almost all risks for virtually the whole population.[114] Chile replaced that system from 1981 with a privately operated, defined-contribution scheme.[115] Under the new system, all wage and salary earners contribute a sum of money equal to 10 per cent of their salary directly to a privately run *Administradora de Fondos de Pensiones* (Pension Fund Administrator, or AFP). They also pay an administration fee that can be as much as a further

3 to 4 per cent of their salary.[116] Neither employers nor the government contribute directly: any and all contributions come directly from the employees themselves. The possibility of inequity arising from this has been to some extent addressed by Government-mandated increases in wage levels.

The Chilean State plays an important ongoing role as both regulator and guarantor. It continues to run the public pension fund for workers who elected not to join the new scheme, which is only compulsory for those employed after its introduction. Secondly, it guarantees a legislated minimum pension. Thirdly, it guarantees the money invested on behalf of those who elected to transfer accumulated sums into the new scheme. What it does not guarantee, however, is that workers will contribute as required, and that their contributions will be sufficient to meet their needs. Several analyses have suggested that a large proportion of low-income workers, in particular, do not make sufficient contributions and therefore fall back to the minimal State pension. The same problem does not afflict higher-income workers, who apparently contribute with greater alacrity.

Presumably the shift to a defined-contribution scheme is integrally related to the involvement of the private sector, on the assumption that it is better placed than the State to make necessary investment decisions.[117] In any event, the new scheme exposes individual beneficiaries to many risks that were previously borne by the public scheme. Contributors now bear all the risks that arise from personal misfortune (sickness, invalidity or unemployment); mismanagement or bankruptcy of the pension fund; general economic developments; uncertainties arising from their own longevity; and in the case of low-income workers, the risk that their income level will not have been enough to

---

[112] Lamarche, 'Right to Social Security' (n. 102 above), p. 95.
[113] Ibid.
[114] C. Gillion and A. Bonilla, 'Analysis of a National Private Pension Scheme: The Case of Chile', *International Labour Review*, Vol. 131 (1992), pp. 171–185, at 178.
[115] The outline of the scheme presented here is based on Lamarche, (n. 102 above), pp. 105–106, and Gillion and Bonilla, 'National Private Pension Scheme' (n. 114 above).

[116] Lamarche, (n. 102 above), p. 106. According to Gillion and Bonilla, the fee is calculated as 0.3 per cent of the annual contributions that are made (although it is deducted when the contribution is made), and it is broadly equivalent to 2.5 to 3.5 per cent of the worker's salary: Gillion and Bonilla, 'National Private Pension Scheme' (n. 114 above), pp. 173, 177.
[117] However Gillion and Bonilla observe that there are restrictions on where the funds may be invested, especially as to the proportion in equities and in Central Bank bonds: Gillion and Bonilla, 'National Private Pension Scheme' (n. 114 above), p. 177; cf. Lamarche, who suggests that the extent of regulation invites criticism from the financial markets: Lamarche, 'Right to Social Security' (n. 102 above), p. 106.

support a satisfactory pension payment.[118] It is therefore not really a pension scheme at all, but a state-imposed system of compulsory savings.[119] Given its allocation of risk, as a system of social security, it is evidently not particularly secure. Neither is it especially social:

> It contains no element of mutual insurance between members of the workforce; there are no links of solidarity between social groups; there are no inter-generational transfers, explicit nor implicit; neither the Government nor employers contribute to the individual's retirement account.[120]

Not surprisingly, soon after the introduction of this scheme the trade union movement drew it to the attention of the ILO.

THE APPLICATION OF ILO STANDARDS TO CHILE'S PRIVATE PENSION SYSTEM

Chile is a party to more than ten ILO Conventions concerning social security.[121] Of these, six that date from the 1920s and 1930s have been considered repeatedly by the ILO supervision system in relation to Chile's private pension system: Conventions 24 and 25 (ratified by Chile in 1931) and Conventions 35 to 38 (ratified by Chile in 1935). The CEACR has published numerous individual observations concerning these Conventions, as well as Conventions 3 (Maternity Protection), and 121 (Employment Injury Benefits). Trade unions have also lodged a number of representations under Article 24 of the ILO Constitution.

In a representation lodged in 1985, the National Trade Union Co-ordinating Council (CNS) of Chile alleged that Chile had contravened nine Conventions, including Conventions 35, 37 and 38.[122] The CNS argued that under Legislative Decree No. 3500 of 1980, the State and employers were effectively

absolved of any duty to contribute to the maintenance and continuance of pension funds (apart from the State's role in guaranteeing minimum pensions).[123] This was said to be inconsistent with Articles 9(1) and (4) of Convention 35, and also with Articles 10(1) and (4) of Conventions 37 and 38, which each require that employers and governments contribute to pension funds. The Chilean Government argued that employers contributed to the pension system, even if indirectly, because of the 'compulsory increase of a worker's gross remuneration'.[124] As to this, the Committee considering the representation concluded that Chile had failed to give effect to the relevant provisions,[125] and recommended that the Government take appropriate steps to ensure that employers do in fact contribute directly to the pension funds.[126]

The Chilean government argued that its role as guarantor in the event of an AFP collapsing, and as provider of a minimum pension, satisfied the requirement of State contribution. As to this, the Committee considering the representation expressed the view that the role of the State as a provider of a guarantee was 'conditional and thereby exceptional', and that the State's role did not therefore amount to a regular financial contribution as required.[127] Not surprisingly, it recommended that Chile take appropriate measures to ensure 'the contribution of the public authorities to the financial resources of . . . the insurance scheme'.[128]

The CNS also challenged the private management of the AFPs. It complained in particular of them being profit-making entities, and of workers being excluded from their management. These features were said to contravene Articles 10 (1) and (2) of Convention 35, and Articles 11 (1) and (2) of Conventions 37 and 38.[129] Those provisions

---

[118] Gillion and Bonilla, 'National Private Pension Scheme' (n. 114 above), p. 176.

[119] Ibid. p. 175.

[120] Ibid. p. 185.

[121] For complete information, see the ILOLEX database: <http://www.ilo.org/ilolex/english/index.htm>.

[122] ILO, *Report of the Committee set up to examine the representation submitted by the National Trade Union Co-ordinating Council (CNS) of Chile under article 24 of the ILO Constitution, alleging non-observance by Chile of International Labour Conventions Nos. 1, 2, 24, 29, 30, 35, 37, 38 and 111* (Geneva: ILO, 1988).

[123] Ibid. paras. 105 and 121. In 1992, the CEACR observed that before the enactment of Legislative Decree No. 3500 of 1980, employers and/or the State made the *largest* contributions to the pension scheme: ILO, *CEACR: Individual Observation Concerning Convention No. 24, Sickness Insurance (Industry), 1927 Chile (ratification: 1931) and Convention No. 25, Sickness Insurance (Agriculture), 1927 Chile (ratification: 1931)* (Geneva: ILO, 1992).

[124] ILO, *CNS Representation*, (n. 122 above), para 116.

[125] Ibid. paras. 164–167.

[126] Ibid. para. 185 (vii).

[127] Ibid. para. 170.

[128] Ibid. para. 185(viii).

[129] Ibid. para. 111.

require, among other things, that pension funds not be conducted with a view to profit, unless they are established on this basis on the initiative of the parties concerned. The committee considering the representation concluded the AFPs were essentially 'private bodies operating on a profit-making basis'.[130] It recommended that Chile take appropriate measures to ensure that the pension funds were not administered by institutions conducted with a view to profit, and that representatives of the insured persons participate in the management of all insurance institutions.[131]

The CEACR has taken a similar position in examining Chile's report on its compliance with various social security conventions. It has reiterated its views in individual observations issued in subsequent years, in relation to Chile's failure to give effect to Article 7 of Conventions 24 and 25, which requires that employers 'share in providing the financial resources in the sickness insurance system'.[132] The CEACR has persisted in requesting that the Chilean Government adopt measures to enable employers to 'share directly in providing the financial resources of the sickness insurance system in favour of the wage-earners'.[133] The CEACR has rejected the idea that a salary increase in a worker's gross wage could be regarded as amounting to an employer contribution to the pension fund system for these purposes.[134]

The CEACR has also urged Chile to upgrade its ratification of relevant ILO Conventions, noting that in 1998 the ILO Governing Body called on States parties to Conventions 35 to 40 to consider ratifying Convention 128, and, as appropriate, denouncing Conventions 35 to 40.[135] The CEACR specifically recommended that Chile follow this course as a means of remedying its non-compliance with Conventions 35 to 38. The Government of Chile, however, has apparently concluded that Convention 128's provisions on administration and funding of pensions are not different from those of Conventions 35 to 38.[136]

Another representation under Article 24 of the ILO Constitution has led to a dialogue between Chile and the ILO that shows again how the ILO supervisory system will delve deep into a State's administration of its social and economic policy. It also illustrates the ILO's insistence on the role and responsibility of the State in securing social and economic rights for those under its jurisdiction. The College of Teachers of Chile A.G. submitted a representation in 1998 alleging non-compliance with Conventions 35 and 37.[137] The representation

[130] Ibid. para. 173.

[131] Ibid. para. 185 (ix) and (x).

[132] ILO, *CEACR: Individual Observation Concerning Convention No. 24, Sickness Insurance (Industry), 1927 Chile (ratification: 1931) and Convention No. 25, Sickness Insurance (Agriculture), 1927 Chile (ratification: 1931)* (Geneva: ILO, 1992). See also, ILO, *CEACR: Individual Observation Concerning Convention No. 35, Old-Age Insurance (Industry, etc.), 1933 Chile (ratification: 1935)* (Geneva: ILO, 1990); *CEACR: Individual Observation Concerning Convention No. 36, Old-Age Insurance (Agriculture), 1933 Chile (ratification: 1935)* (Geneva: ILO, 1989); *CEACR: Individual Observation Concerning Convention No. 37, Invalidity Insurance (Industry, etc.), 1933 Chile (ratification: 1935)* (Geneva: ILO, 1990) and *CEACR: Individual Observation Concerning Convention No. 38, Invalidity Insurance (Agriculture), 1933 Chile (ratification: 1935)* (Geneva: ILO, 1990).

[133] ILO, *CEACR: Individual Observation Concerning Convention No. 24, Sickness Insurance (Industry), 1927 Chile (ratification: 1931) and Convention No. 25, Sickness Insurance (Agriculture), 1927 Chile (ratification: 1931)* (Geneva: ILO, 1993, 1996 and 2002).

[134] ILO, *CEACR: Individual Observation Concerning Convention No. 24, Sickness Insurance (Industry), 1927 Chile (ratification: 1931) and Convention No. 25, Sickness Insurance*

[135] ILO, *CEACR: Individual Observation Concerning Convention No. 35, Old-Age Insurance (Industry, etc.), 1933 Chile (ratification: 1935)* (Geneva: ILO, 1998).

[136] ILO, *CEACR: Individual Observation Concerning Convention No. 35, Old-Age Insurance (Industry, etc.), 1933 Chile (ratification: 1935)* (Geneva: ILO, 2001). Gillion and Bonilla reached a similar conclusion, noting that 'a pension is *not always* paid on a permanent basis...the replacement rate of the pensions granted is indeterminate...workers have to pay 100 per cent of the contributions...[and] neither workers nor employers participate in the administration of the scheme': Gillion and Bonilla, 'National Private Pension Scheme' (n. 114 above), p. 193.

[137] ILO, *Report of the Committee set up to examine the representation alleging non-observance by Chile of the Old Age Insurance (Industry, etc.) Convention, 1933 (No. 35) and the Invalidity Insurance (Industry, etc.) Convention, 1933 (No. 37) submitted under article 24 of the ILO Constitution by the College of Teachers of Chile A.G.* (Geneva: ILO, 1999). Other representations have since been made: see ILO, *Report of the Committee set up to examine the representation alleging non-observance by Chile of the Old-Age Insurance (Industry, etc.) Convention, 1933 (No. 35), the Old-Age Insurance (Agriculture) Convention, 1933 (No. 36), the Invalidity Insurance (Industry, etc.) Convention, 1933 (No. 37) and the Invalidity Insurance (Agriculture) Convention, 1933 (No. 38), made under article 24 of the ILO Constitution by a number of national trade unions of workers of the Private Sector Pension Funds (AFP)* (Geneva: ILO, 1999); and ILO, *Representation alleging non-observance by Chile of the Old-Age Insurance*

concerned failures to make necessary payments for teachers' social security contributions, failures to use available powers to oversee and enforce the operation of the system, and the consequent liability of the public authorities.[138]

The Committee that considered the representation noted the obvious importance of these matters, given their adverse effects on workers.[139] In its recommendations, the Committee asked that Chile provide a full report to the CEACR, covering issues about both the enforcement of its legislation and proposed amendments to it. The Committee sought information, for example, on the number of checks carried out by the Ministry of Education, the number of violations, the penalties imposed for non-compliance, and the number of municipalities continuing to be in arrears.[140] In a subsequent individual observation on Convention 35, the CEACR followed up these requests by considering the Government's response, and by seeking further information about the penalties that might be applied to any municipality in arrears and whether any penalties had been applied. It also sought information to enable it to better assess compliance with Article 19 of the Convention, which requires that the rate of any pension paid be sufficient to cover the pensioner's 'essential needs'. In particular the CEACR sought 'statistical information . . . on the evolution of the cost of living and the evolution of benefits, including the amount of minimum pensions'.[141]

In the face of Chile's privatisation of its pension system, the ILO's supervisory bodies have emphasised its own continuing obligations: '[b]y ratifying these Conventions, the State recognises its responsibility for the protection of workers in the sphere of social security'.[142] Here then the ILO has used concepts familiar to international human rights law, focusing on the responsibility of the State under a ratified legal instrument to ensure that a particular outcome is achieved. The ILO's position is therefore of interest for the implementation of economic and social rights generally, particularly in light of the trends to privatisation and State restructuring in the context of globalisation, which are generally thought to be likely to have adverse effects on the protection and promotion of human rights, and in particular on economic, social and cultural rights.[143]

The ILO's persistence in its dialogue with Chile over its private pension system illustrates its important role in defending and promoting economic and social rights, and the continuing relevance of some of its older instruments. It is of some note that Conventions 35 to 38 have been 'shelved',[144] given that they have been revised in particular by Convention 128. So long as they remain in force, however, they evidently have important potential as a bulwark to protect economic and social rights against some of the harsher effects of globalisation and state restructuring.

6. CONCLUSION: WHAT CAN BE LEARNED FROM THE ILO?

Virginia Leary argued in 1991 that the ILO has significant advantages as an institution for the protection of socio-economic rights. Her views may have altered since then, given the changes in the UN system with which she compared the ILO. The UN's resource base, for example, may be much improved since the advent of the Office of the High Commissioner for Human Rights. Leary also referred to the ILO's 'institutional' characteristics, including the legitimacy that it derives from its tripartite structure. Among other things, Leary was positive about the independence and the working methods of the CEACR, particularly its willingness and ability to work in diplomatic dialogue with member states.[145]

(Industry, etc.) Convention, 1933 (No. 35), and the Invalidity Insurance (Industry, etc.) Convention, 1933 (No. 37), made under article 24 of the ILO Constitution by the Colegio de Profesores de Chile A.G. (Geneva: ILO, 2005). The latter has been received, and a decision is pending.
[138] ILO, *Teachers' Representation* (n. 137 above), para. 25.
[139] Ibid. para. 31.
[140] Ibid. para. 33(b).
[141] ILO, *CEACR: Individual Observation Concerning Convention No. 35, Old-Age Insurance (Industry, etc.), 1933 Chile (ratification: 1935)* (Geneva: ILO, 2000).
[142] ILO, *Teachers' Representation* (n. 137 above), para. 26.

[143] Fenwick, 'Private Use of Prisoners' Labour' (n. 44 above), pp. 252–255.
[144] As part of its process of prioritising those instruments that remain most relevant, the ILO has 'shelved' some Conventions. States are no longer required to submit detailed reports on these Conventions. The representation and complaint procedures remain available, and the CEACR may still request a detailed report.
[145] V. Leary, 'Lessons from the Experience of the International Labour Organisation' in P. Alston (ed.), *The United*

By comparison Cooney,[146] and more recently Creighton,[147] have been far more critical. One of their concerns has been the over-production of standards, many of which are neither ratified nor implemented. This means naturally that they don't have as much force and, by association, detract from the force of those instruments and processes, which are otherwise valuable. They are also critical of the structure of the ILO, with its insistence upon tripartism, which, they argue, no longer enables appropriate representation of either workers or employers. Other critics have fixed on the more recent developments of CLS and the (associated) 1998 Declaration. In that debate there has been some frank assessment of some of the weaknesses and difficulties identified by Cooney and by Creighton.

Nations and Human Rights: A Critical Appraisal (Oxford: Clarendon Press, 1991), pp. 580–619.

[146] Cooney, 'Testing Times' (n. 5 above).

[147] Creighton, 'The Future of Labour Law' (n. 24 above).

What I suggest is that we can still draw positive lessons from the institutional structure of the ILO, and its approach to the protection of social and economic rights. It has proved remarkably adept at developing significant bodies of important principle from its Conventions, and at making continuing use of some of its very oldest instruments as a means to protect workers' economic and social interests. It has found ways to accommodate the interests of groups that have no privileged place in its Constitutional structure, without the trouble of embarking upon constitutional amendment. Perhaps most importantly, it has rigorously promoted the view that labour rights are interconnected with other economic and social rights, and that economic and social rights are interconnected with civil and political rights. Although it has rarely used the express language of human rights in doing so, it has nevertheless developed an extensive and important body of principles, from which other systems might usefully learn and draw.

29

Liability of Multinational Corporations

Sarah Joseph[*]

1. INTRODUCTION

The activities of multinational corporations ('MNCs') often have a positive effect on economic, social and cultural rights. They provide employment, thus facilitating the right to work. Their innovations can lead to the creation of new products, such as new medicines and computers, which facilitate the enjoyment of the rights to health or the right to education. Corporate employers may voluntarily provide for certain economic and social benefits for their workers, such as the provision of antiretroviral drugs for HIV-positive workers in the developing world, or the provision of education for younger workers. Corporate philanthropy can of course assist millions outside a corporation's direct sphere of influence. Their investment activities may be assumed to increase wealth, thus increasing the level of affluence in societies, and the ability of people to afford satisfactory levels of economic and social prosperity.[1]

However, the picture is not all rosy. MNCs are capable of committing acts that detrimentally impact on the enjoyment of economic, social and cultural ('ESC') rights. MNCs have been accused of adopting exploitative labour practices, breach-

ing rights to just conditions of work. MNCs are also accused of practices that are antipathetic to trade unions. Poor occupational health and safety ('OHS') standards can harm the rights to health of workers, and people in the vicinity of a corporation's operations. Corporate negligence and/or subsequent cover-ups can unacceptably expose consumers to dangerous goods, such as unsafe automobiles or asbestos products. Poor environmental practices can contaminate food sources, which can harm rights to food and health. Corporate ownership of vital commodities, such as water or the patents in life-saving drugs, may drive the price of essential commodities so high as to price them out of the reach of poor people. This is not to say that MNCs, on the whole, are detrimental for the enjoyment of ESC rights.[2] It is to say that MNCs are capable of harming ESC rights in a multitude of ways.

When MNCs perpetrate abuses of human rights, it is to be hoped that they will be held responsible for those abuses. The most obvious source of such corporate accountability is regulation by the government of the territory in which those abuses take place, such as laws regulating labour, OHS, and environmental practices. For example, one might expect liability for the Bhopal disaster in India in 1984, when a Union Carbide plant leaked poison gas and killed and maimed tens of

[*] Sarah Joseph is a Professor of Human Rights Law at Monash University, Melbourne, and the Director of the Castan Centre for Human Rights Law. This chapter is part of the outcomes of an Australian Research Council Linkage grant on 'Multinational Corporations and Human Rights'. The author would like to thank Joanna Kyriakakis, who assisted with the footnotes in this chapter, and the editor for inviting my contribution.

[1] However, while the increase in MNC activity across the world may have contributed to an increase in world wealth, it has not contributed to a more equal distribution of that wealth. It seems that the benefits of MNC investment flow disproportionately to the richest people, while the very poor receive little to no benefit.

[2] For debate on the positive and negative effects on MNC activity, W. H. Meyer, 'Human Rights and MNCs: Theory versus Quantitative Analysis', *Human Rights Quarterly*, Vol. 18 (1996), pp. 368–397 (arguing that the 'net' effect of MNC activity is beneficial for human rights), J. Smith, M. Bolyard and A. Ippolito, 'Human Rights and the Global Economy: A Response to Meyer', *Human Rights Quarterly*, Vol. 21 (1999), pp. 207–219, and subsequently, W. H. Meyer, 'Confirming, Infirming and "Falsifying" Theories of Human Rights: Reflections on Smith, Bolyard and Ippolito Through the Lens of Lakatos', *Human Rights Quarterly*, Vol. 21 (1999), pp. 220–228.

thousands, to be imposed upon Union Carbide by an Indian court enforcing Indian law. It is beyond the scope of this chapter to outline the many examples of MNCs being held liable in domestic litigation for ESC violations that occur within the territory of the State where the litigation takes place.[3] Domestic cases concerning transnational violations, that is those that takes place overseas, are discussed in Section 3, below.

Unique problems can arise in holding MNCs accountable for abuses of ESC rights. First, it is trite to note that some MNCs are very powerful economic entities. In some cases, MNCs may be more powerful than the countries in which they operate. Certainly, some individual MNCs are more economically wealthy than individual countries.[4] Some developing nations may perceive that they need corporate investment to attain a satisfactory level of economic development. In such situations, a developing nation may be reluctant to punish corporate malfeasance, fearing that such punishment may repel corporate investment. Indeed, local laws may not prescribe adequate regulations. It is feared that developing countries may be competing with each other to offer attractive labour and environmental regimes to corporate investors, generating a 'race to the bottom', which is seriously prejudicing labour rights and those rights prejudiced by environmental degradation.[5] Essentially, the first problem in holding MNCs account-

able for abuses of ESC rights is that accountability is expected to flow from host governments, which may be in a subordinate power relationship with the MNC. It is always problematic for accountability and the rule of law for a less powerful entity to be required to regulate a more powerful entity.

Second, the corporate form of MNCs may facilitate the avoidance of responsibility. Each corporate component of an MNC is a separate legal person, insulating the broader group from liability for the actions of one of its parts. An MNC can allocate its resources and legal responsibilities so as to minimise risk, even if, as is often the case, it in fact operates as a single commercial unit.[6] Therefore, a vigilant host country may not be able to exercise effective jurisdiction in regard to an abuse perpetrated by an MNC, as it may only have jurisdiction over a local subsidiary that does not have sufficient assets to adequately compensate for its human rights abuses. For example, Indian courts clearly had jurisdiction over Union Carbide's subsidiary in Bhopal. However, that Indian subsidiary did not have enough money to provide adequate compensation for the disaster. On the other hand, the parent company in New York probably did have sufficient assets. Any Indian judgment against the New York company would have required an Indian court to pierce the corporate veil between the Indian and US companies. If the US company did not comply with the judgment, the Indian court would have had to rely on a US court to enforce the judgment.[7]

Therefore, it is possibly unsatisfactory to rely solely on host States to provide adequate measures of

[3] Examples of relevant cases include the string of litigation against James Hardie in Australia regarding its production and sale of asbestos products, resulting in asbestos-related diseases in Australia. Such litigation will often take place outside an explicit human rights context. For example, any action against a company regarding its product safety or OHS practices has implications for the ESC rights to health and work. However, the legal arguments made in such a case will focus on the words of the applicable product safety or OHS standards, which might not be drafted in 'rights' language.

[4] See, for example, the influential study by S. Anderson and J. Cavanagh, 'Top 200: The Rise of Global Corporate Power', *Institute for Policy Studies*, 4 December 2000, <www.ips-dc.org/reports/top200.htm> (accessed 27 March 2007).

[5] See M. J. Rogge, 'Towards Transnational Corporate Liability in the Global Economy: Challenging the Doctrine of Forum Non Conveniens in Re: Union Carbide, Alfaro, Sequihua, and Aguinda', *Texas International Law Journal*, Vol. 26 (2001), pp. 299–317, at 314–7, H. Ward, 'Towards a New Convention on Corporate Accountability? Some Lessons from the Thor Chemicals and Cape Plc cases', *Yearbook of International Environmental Law*, Vol. 12 (2001), pp. 105–143, at 109.

[6] See P. Blumberg, 'Accountability of Multinational Corporations: The Barriers Presented by Concepts of the Corporate Juridical Entity', *Hastings International and Comparative Law Review*, Vol. 24 (2001), pp. 297–320, at 303.

[7] See U. Baxi, 'Geographies of Injustice: Human Rights at the Altar of Convenience', in C. Scott (ed.), *Torture as Tort* (Oxford: Hart, 2001), pp. 197–212 at 209. See also detailed discussion of the Bhopal care in chapter 5 of this volume. Note, for example, that a judgment against Shell, Dow Chemicals, and Dole Food in the sum of US$ 489 million by a Nicaraguan court was found to be unenforceable by a Californian court on the grounds that the companies were not properly named or legally notified in the originating action. The award of damages was for injuries caused by pesticides that have been linked to cancer and sterility. The pesticide, dibromochloropropane, has been removed from the US market. 'World Business Briefing Americas: Nicaragua: Pesticide Claim Dismissed', *New York Times*, 25 October 2003, p. C.4.

accountability for MNCs when they perpetrate abuses of ESC rights. I now turn to examine alternative potential sources of accountability.

2. INTERNATIONAL LAW

2.1 Human Rights Treaties

States have duties to respect, protect and fulfil human rights under international human rights law. The duty to protect human rights entails an obligation to protect people from abuse of their rights by other people, including artificial entities like MNCs. For example, the UN Committee on Economic Social and Cultural Rights, the body established to monitor the International Covenant on Economic Social and Cultural Rights ('ICE-SCR'), stated in its General Comment 14 on the Right to Health:[8]

> Violations of the obligation to protect follow from the failure of a State to take all necessary measures to safeguard persons within their jurisdiction from infringements of the right to health by third parties. This category includes such omissions as the failure to regulate the activities of individuals, groups or corporations so as to prevent them from violating the right to health of others ...

Though the contours of the State's duties regarding human rights in the private sphere are underdeveloped in international jurisprudence, it is clear that States can be held to have violated their human rights obligations if they fail to exercise due diligence in preventing or punishing human rights abuses in that sphere.[9] Thus, States are required, under international law, to prohibit, prevent and punish actions by MNCs that violate ESC rights.

There have been a number of international cases where States have been found to have breached their international ESC rights obligations by

unduly favouring corporate interests over those of the complainants. For example, Nigeria has been held to be in breach of the African Charter of Human and Peoples' Rights by the African Commission on Human and Peoples' Rights in *SERAC & CESR v. Nigeria*,[10] entailed in its failure to prevent human rights abuses by a consortium conducting oil exploration operations in Ogoniland; the consortium included the Nigerian government, the Nigerian National Petroleum Company (NNPC), and the Shell Petroleum Development Corporation (SPDC), a subsidiary corporation within the global Shell group. The Commission found breaches of the rights to health and a general satisfactory environment, the right to property, the right to housing, the right to food, and the right to be free from the forced deprivation of one's wealth and resources.[11]

Nicaragua has been held to be in breach of the American Convention on Human Rights, in particular the right to property in Article 21 thereof, in *Awas Tingni Community v. Nicaragua*,[12] in granting a South Korean company a concession to conduct logging operations on the lands of the indigenous Awas Tingni community. In *Lubicon Lake Band v. Canada*, the Human Rights Committee, the monitoring body established under the International Covenant on Civil and Political Rights ('ICCPR'), found that the Canadian government had breached the rights of the Lubicon Lake Band indigenous minority to enjoy their own culture by allowing the state of Alberta to expropriate some of their lands for the benefit of private corporate interests (e.g. leases for energy exploration, wood pulping).[13] In October 2004, the Inter-American Court found a similar complaint against Ecuador, regarding its failure to protect indigenous rights from the activities of an oil company, to be

---

[8] Committee on Economic, Social and Cultural Rights, *General Comment No. 14, The right to the highest attainable standard of health* (Twenty-second session, 2000), U.N. Doc. E/C.12/2000/4 (2000), para 51.

[9] See, for example, *Velasquez-Rodriguez v. Honduras* (decision of the Inter-American Court of Human Rights), *Human Rights Law Journal*, Vol. 9 (1988), 212, para 172, and *A v. UK* (decision of the European Court of Human Rights), *Butterworths Human Rights Cases*, Vol. 5 (1998), 137.

[10] Communication No. 155/96, African Commission on Human and Peoples' Rights, 27 May 2002, ('*SERAC v. Nigeria*'). See detailed discussion in chapter 23 of this book.

[11] See also *Concluding Observations of the Committee on the Elimination of Racial Discrimination on Nigeria*, UN doc. A/48/18, para 309, 15 September 1993.

[12] Inter-American Court of Human Rights, *Case of the Mayagna (Sumo) Awas Tingni Community v. Nicaragua*, Judgment of 31 August 2001 ('*Awas Tingni*'), available via <http://www.corteidh.or.cr/docs/casos/articulos/seriec_79_ing.pdf> (accessed 27 March 2007). See also chapter 29.5.2 of this book.

[13] Communication No. 167/1984 (26 March 1994), UN Doc. Supp. No. 40 (A/45/40) at 1 (1990).

admissible in *The Kichwa Peoples of the Sarayaku Community and its Members v. Ecuador*.[14]

There have also been a number of relevant cases before the European Court of Human Rights. For example, in *Lopez Ostra v. Spain*,[15] the Court held that the severe pollution caused by a privately owned waste treatment plant, which constituted a health hazard, breached the rights of persons who lived in the plant's vicinity to enjoy their private and family life, contrary to Article 8 of the European Convention on Human Rights and Fundamental Freedoms. The State, in that case, had failed to take sufficient measures to control the relevant pollution. The *Lopez Ostra* decision ostensibly concerned civil rights regarding family life and privacy rather than ESC rights such as the right to health, which was clearly relevant on the facts of the case.

Of course, a problem with the above jurisprudence regarding human rights abuses by private actors is that the locus of responsibility remains with the host State. The dissatisfying consequences of that situation were discussed in Section 1. Indeed, it may be noted that the Awas Tingni peoples have filed an *amparo* action against the Nicaraguan government in Nicaraguan courts for its apparent failure to implement the decision of the Inter-American Court of Human Rights.[16] On 27 May 2003, the Lubicon Lake Band released a press statement detailing its disappointment at the Canadian government's apparent failure to implement the Human Rights Committee's decision of thirteen years earlier.[17] These developments demonstrate the weakness of the enforcement mechanisms in international human rights law. On the other hand, States may at least be held liable for their failure to appropriately regulate MNCs; a State cannot argue that its inadequate regulation of MNCs is a matter of domestic concern if that inadequacy permits human rights violations by MNCs. The shining of an international spotlight on a State for its failure to regulate MNCs may shame that State into a change of behaviour.

It may also have significant consequences for the reputations of the relevant MNCs. It also must be noted that there are only a few international cases on this issue. If States were more regularly held liable in this way, it could potentially make a real difference to the perceived accountability of MNCs for human rights abuses.

It is doubtful that international human rights law has evolved so as to hold States responsible for the activities of their citizens abroad, including corporate citizens.[18] However, such a duty was definitely implied by the Committee on Economic Social and Cultural Rights in its General Comment 15 on the Right to Water in 2002:[19]

> Steps should be taken by States parties to prevent their own citizens and companies from violating the right to water of individuals and communities in other countries. Where States parties can take steps to influence other third parties to respect the right, through legal or political means, such steps should be taken in accordance with the Charter of the United Nations and applicable international law.

This author is not however aware of any instance where a State has been rebuked by the Committee or any other international body for its failure to constrain the human rights behaviour overseas of a corporate citizen. Such duties regarding the extraterritorial behaviour of private bodies are not however unprecedented.[20] The OECD

---

[14] Petition no. 167/03, Report no. 64/04, 13 October 2004. See Chapters 18 and 19 of this book.

[15] (1995) 20 EHRR 277. See also *Guerra v. Italy*, judgement of 19 February 1998 (1998) 26 EHRR 357.

[16] See <http://www.indianlaw.org/PR_2003-01-16_AT_sue_President_.pdf> (accessed 27 March 2007).

[17] See <http://www.lubicon.ca/27MayPress_statement.html> (accessed 27 March 2007).

[18] See S. Joseph, 'Taming the Leviathans: Multinational Enterprises and Human Rights', *Netherlands International Law Review*, Vol. 46 (1999), 171–203, at 181. See also 'Report of the Special Representative of the Secretary General on the issue of human rights and transnational corporations and other business enterprises: Business Human Rights: Mapping International Standards of Responsibility and Accountability for Corporate Acts' ('SRGS report'), UN Doc. A/HRC/4/035, para. 15. *Cf.* M. Sornarajah, 'Linking State Responsibility for Certain Harms caused by Corporate Nationals Abroad to Civil Recourse in the Legal Systems of Home States' in C. Scott (ed.), (n. 7 above), pp. 491–512.

[19] Committee on Economic, Social and Cultural Rights, General Comment No. 15, The right to water (Twenty-ninth session, 2002), U.N. Doc. E/C.12/2002/11 (2003), para. 33.

[20] States clearly have some duties regarding the extraterritorial behaviour, or impacts, of their public officials. See, e.g., S. Joseph, J. Schultz and M. Castan, *The International Covenant on Civil and Political Rights: Cases, Materials and Commentary*, 2nd edition (Oxford: Oxford University Press, 2004), pp. 87–91. See also Concluding Observations

Bribery Convention of 1977 requires States parties to exercise jurisdiction over acts of bribery by their nationals, wherever they may occur.[21] Furthermore, UN human rights treaty bodies are increasingly 'encouraging' home States to regulate the overseas activity of their companies in the area of human rights.[22] Perhaps such duties are evolving.

Under international human rights law, including the main treaties regarding ESC rights, private entities like MNCs do not have direct duties under international treaties, as they are not parties to them.[23] The continued State-based focus of international human rights law is arguably inappropriate, as State bodies do not have a monopoly on power yet the public/private dichotomy in international law persists. Private parties have few direct duties in international human rights law, excepting those few duties imposed by customary international law, such as the prohibitions on genocide, the most grievous war crimes and crimes against humanity, piracy and slavery. It is doubtful whether any fully fledged ESC rights per se are accepted as being within this very limited category of rights.[24] In any case, no international tribunal currently has jurisdiction to hold MNCs liable for breaches of ESC rights.

2.2 Guidelines and Other International Standards

Voluntary guidelines for MNC behaviour have been formulated by a number of international organisations. For example, the UN Global Compact requires MNCs to commit to ten core principles, which relate to human rights, labour rights, environmental protection, and anti-corruption. The Global Compact provides a useful forum for dialogue and information transfer on these issues. However, there is no monitoring of the human rights record of signatory corporations, so no accountability is built into the mechanism beyond some reporting requirements.[25]

The International Labour Organization (ILO) adopted the Tripartite Declaration of Principles Concerning Multinational Enterprises and Social Policy in 1977,[26] which provides clarification of appropriate MNC behaviour regarding labour rights. As with the Global Compact, it is not envisaged that MNCs can be held to account for failure to abide by the ILO Declaration. An ILO procedure for providing interpretations of the Declaration to help resolve disputes over their meaning in the context of actual situations has been established, but is thus far underutilised.[27]

The Organization of Economic Cooperation and Development ('OECD') originally adopted its Guidelines for Multinational Enterprises in 1976, and they were revised in 2000.[28] The Guidelines

---

of the Committee against Torture on the USA, confirming the US's responsibility for the treatment of prisoners in offshore prisons, such as that in Guantánamo Bay, UN doc. CAT/C.USA/CO/2, 18 May 2006, paras. 15–16 and 22.

[21] See Convention on Combating Bribery of Foreign Public Officials in International Business Transactions ('OECD Bribery Convention'), 17 December 1997 (text available at <http://www.oecd.org>), Articles 2 and 4. The OECD Bribery Convention entered into force on 15 February 1999.

[22] See *Report of the Special Representative of the Secretary General on the issue of human rights and transnational corporations and other business enterprises: 'Protect, Respect, and Remedy: a Framework for Business and Human Rights'*, U.N. Doc. A/HRC/8/5, 7 April 2008, para 19. See, e.g., UN doc. CERD/C/CAN/CO/18, para. 17.

[23] International criminal law treaties are exceptional in this regard, but do not, as yet, impose liabilities on MNCs as opposed to natural persons. For example, the International Criminal Court only has jurisdiction over natural persons. Of course, proceedings could commence against corporate directors or executives in their individual capacities.

[24] See B. Simma and P. Alston, 'The Sources of Human Rights Law: Custom, Jus Cogens, and General Principles', *Australian Year Book of International Law*, Vol. 12 (1992), pp. 82–108, on the tendency amongst many scholars, particularly US scholars, to classify a wide range of rights as part of customary international law (though not necessarily in the context of non-State action). *Cf.* chapter 27 of this volume.

[25] See generally, <www.unglobalcompact.org> (accessed 27 March 2007). UN Global Compact companies are required to publicly communicate with the Global Compact office on their progress in implementing Global Compact norms. If they do not communicate, they are listed on the Global Compact website as non-communicating or inactive companies.

[26] Reprinted in *International Legal Materials*, Vol. 17 (1978), pp. 422–431.

[27] Procedure for the Examination of Disputes (Multinational Enterprises: Tripartite Declaration of Principles), ILO Doc. OB Vol. LXIX, 1986, Series A, No. 3, available at <http://training.itcilo.org/ils/foa/library/tridecl/procedure_en.htm> (accessed 27 March 2007). See also C. Scott, 'Multinational Enterprises and Emergent Jurisdiction on Violations of Economic, Social and Cultural Rights', in A. Eide, C. Krause and A. Rosas (eds.), *Economic, Cultural and Social Rights: A Textbook*, 2nd revised ed. (Dordrecht: Martinus Nijhoff Publishers, 2001), pp. 563–595.

[28] Available at <http://www.oecd.org/dataoecd/56/36/1922428.pdf> (accessed 27 March 2007).

cover some issues of relevance to human rights, though many of its provisions relate to essentially commercial matters; again, the Guidelines are not enforceable. The Guidelines do provide for the establishment by member States[29] of national contact points ('NCPs') to promote the Guidelines nationally, and to deal with complaints that may arise in respect of the Guidelines. The effectiveness of an NCP depends upon the powers conferred by the relevant government, and the type of personnel within it. For example, the setting up of NCPs within economic ministries might risk 'capture' by corporate interests.[30] Non-governmental organisations are increasingly raising complaints with NCPs regarding the behaviour of MNCs,[31] including complaints relating to ESC rights.[32] In dealing with such cases, NCPs generally attempt to facilitate agreement between the parties. The NCPs have no power to enforce the Guidelines. Nevertheless, NGOs may make use of NCP proceedings to publicise and mobilise campaigns against companies, to enter into meaningful dialogue with companies, and to conciliate settlements with companies. NCPs have the capacity to become, and indeed are, an important part of the developing matrix of corporate accountability.

In August 2003, the UN Sub-Commission on the Promotion and Protection of Human Rights adopted the UN Norms on the Responsibilities of Transnational Corporations and other Business Enterprises with regard to Human Rights ('the Norms').[33] Paragraph 1 of the Norms suggests that, while State retain the primary obligations with regard to human rights, companies have human rights obligations within 'their respective spheres of activity and influence'.

Paragraph 12 makes clear that these duties include ESC rights obligations:

> Transnational corporations and other business enterprises shall respect economic, social and cultural rights as well as civil and political rights and contribute to their realization, in particular the rights to development, adequate food and drinking water, the highest attainable standard of physical and mental health, adequate housing, privacy, education, freedom of thought, conscience, and religion and freedom of opinion and expression, and shall refrain from actions which obstruct or impede the realization of those rights.[34]

It is envisaged in Part H of the Norms that these duties will be enforceable in a variety of ways, including, in Paragraph 18, enforcement by national courts and international tribunals.

Therefore, an MNC's enforceable duties with regard to ESC rights, according to the Norms, extend to their 'spheres of activity and influence'. This key term is not comprehensively defined in the Norms. Some guidance is given in Paragraph (b) of the Commentary on Paragraph 1 of the Norms:

> Transnational corporations and other business enterprises shall have the responsibility to use due diligence in ensuring that their activities do not contribute directly or indirectly to human rights abuses, and that they do not directly or indirectly benefit from abuses of which they were aware or ought to have been aware. Transnational corporations and other business enterprises shall further refrain from activities that would undermine the rule of law as well as governmental and other efforts to promote and ensure respect for human rights, and shall use their influence in order to help promote and ensure respect for human rights. Transnational corporations and other business enterprises shall inform themselves of the human rights impact of their principal activities and major proposed activities so that they can further avoid complicity in human rights abuses. The Norms may not be used by States as an excuse for

---

[29] The Guidelines have been adopted by OECD nations as well as some non-OECD nations, namely Argentina, Brazil, Chile, Estonia, Israel, Latvia, Lithuania, Romania and Slovenia.

[30] O. Perez, 'Reflections on an Environmental Struggle: P&O, Dahanu, and the Regulation of Multinational Enterprises', *Georgetown International Environmental Law Review*, Vol. 15 (2002), pp. 1–27, at 20.

[31] See, e.g., 'Table of Cases Raised by NGOs at National Contact Points', January 2005, at <http://www.oecdwatch.org/docs/Update%20cases.pdf> (accessed 27 March 2007). See also <http://www.oecd.org/dataoecd/15/43/33914891.pdf> (accessed 27 March 2007).

[32] For example, one complaint against Adidas related to labour issues in the Indian football industry. Another complaint against three mining companies related to resettlement in Zambia. See 'Table of Cases', ibid.

[33] UN Doc. E/CN.4/Sub.2/2003/12/Rev.2 (2003), approved 13 August 2003 by resolution 2003/16, UN Doc. E/CN.4/Sub.2/2003/L.11 at 52 (2003).

[34] See also ibid. paras. 5–9 (rights of workers), 10, 13, and 14.

failing to take action to protect human rights, for example, through the enforcement of existing laws.

Therefore, it was clearly envisaged in the Norms that an MNC's human rights obligations, including its obligations regarding ESC rights, will extend beyond merely negative duties (the duty to refrain from abuses) and will also encompass positive duties (the duty to take actions to prevent rights violations and, on occasion, enhance the enjoyment of human rights).

In April 2005, the UN Commission on Human Rights resolved to appoint a Special Representative, Harvard Professor John Ruggie, to investigate and clarify various aspects of the relationship between MNCs and human rights, including identification of appropriate human rights standards, including of course ESC standards.[35]

In the Special Representative's interim report, issued in February 2006, the Special Rapporteur was very critical of the Norms in two respects.[36] First, the Special Representative argues that the Norms suffer from doctrinal excesses in presuming to identify direct obligations for MNCs, which simply do not exist. With respect, it is submitted that this first criticism entails a misreading of the Norms: the Norms are not a binding document and therefore cannot, despite their language, impose direct obligations. They are more an expression of the obligations that MNCs *should* have, and which might come to be accepted under international human rights law, according to the authors of the Norms. The second criticism is that the Norms are unhelpfully vague with regard to the split of responsibilities between States and MNCs. In that respect, it must be noted that part of the Special Representative's mandate was to undertake such clarification.

Whilst it is premature to say that the Special Representative has 'killed' the Norms, his subsequent reports have certainly diverted the spotlight from them. His 2008 report[37] refocuses attention on the need to strengthen and clarify the duty of States to protect people from corporate human rights abuses, a clear retreat from the idea of international direct regulation of companies envisaged in the Norms. The report also acknowledges the possible development of home State duties, and is neutral on that issue. Certainly, there is scope for cooperation between home States and a host State when the latter lacks the financial and technical resources to regulate MNCs.[38]

The report goes on to outline the appropriate content of legally enforceable corporate duties that should be imposed by States, namely the 'duty to respect' human rights: corporations should be expected to refrain from harming human rights, or remedy abuses that they perpetrate. The Special Representative does not envisage that corporations should have binding duties to improve a human rights situation, but their operations should at least be human rights neutral. The duty to respect does not merely entail negative duties, as fulfilment of such duties will not realistically result in the non-occurrence of harm; companies therefore have to exercise due diligence to prevent human rights harm.

The Special Representative adds that a corporation's 'duties to respect' will be enforced by 'social expectations', rather than only by legally imposed obligations. Therefore, he prompts corporations to respect human rights even in the absence of legal obligations, a situation which arises when a State fails in its duties to appropriately regulate a company, or in numerous grey or ambiguous zones which will inevitably continue to exist at the margins of a 'duty ro respect'. "Social expectations" help to prevent legal obligations from becoming a ceiling as opposed to a floor for corporate human rights impacts.[39]

---

[35] The Special Representative's mandate is found at UN Doc. E/CN.4/2005/L.87 (15 April 2005).

[36] UN Doc. E/CN.4/2006/97 (22 February 2006), at paras 56–69.

[37] UN doc. A/HRC/8/5, 7 April 2008.

[38] Ibid. para 45.

[39] Ibid. para 55. The power of 'social expectations' in the MNC/human rights debate should not be underestimated, and may impact beyond the duty to respect human rights. Many MNCs are highly dependent on their reputations for their success and therefore are susceptible to moral arguments. For example, it is unlikely that charitable contributions by MNCs to disaster relief (unless an MNC causes the disaster) would be part of an MNC's duties to 'respect' human rights. Yet Australian companies were undoubtedly 'shamed' into making or increasing their charitable contributions to tsunami aid appeals. See, e.g., S. Creedy, 'Lonely Planet Challenges the Big End', *The Australian*, 31 December 2004, p. 6; G. Elliot, 'PM Urges Big Business to Dig Deeper', *The Australian*, 3 January 2005, p. 6; A. McDonald, 'Call for Companies to Give', *The Australian*, 5 January 2005, p. 9; G. Elliot, 'Big

Finally, the Special Representative focuses on the need for remedies to be devised to redress corporate breaches of the duty to respect human rights. Such remedies should essentially be provided by States, including in judicial and appropriate non-judicial forums. Less formal mechanisms, such as internal company grievance procedures and multi-stakeholder initiatives (e.g., initiatives adopted between companies, NGOs, and States) can help to fill accountability gaps, but they cannot be used to thwart the development of legal accountability. They can however help to give effect to the above-mentioned 'social expectations'.

The rejection by the Special Representative of the development of directly binding international norms for companies is probably a disappointment to many human rights activists worldwide. However, his approach of seeking clarification of the duties that States are required to impose on companies may yield a similar result to the clarification of directly binding duties for companies which had been envisaged in the Norms. The ultimate source of corporate accountability remains international law: indirect in the first instance and direct in the second. The practical difference between the two approaches is diminished by the fact that enforcement, at least in the short to mid-term, can only emanate from State institutions, due to a lack of appropriate international forums. Of course, a major difference between the two approaches is that only the State is directly responsible in international law if breaches arise with Ruggie's approach, whereas shared responsibility between State and corporation was anticipated in the Norms. However, if States are vigorously pursued in international forums, such as existing human rights institutions, for their failure to regulate a particular company, that circumstance could hardly reflect well on the relevant company. Indeed, that company could expect to face global condemnation.

Interestingly, the Special Representative leaves open the possibility of an 'international ombudsman' which could act as a backstop to receive complaints.[40] Such a body could play an important enforcement role if it had the power to make decisions that a company has in fact violated (or has not violated) human rights. Whilst international enforcement would likely be lacking, the decisions of such a body, so long as it commanded sufficient respect from States, business and civil society, could have an important shaming (or exonerating) effect. Shame could have a significant galvanising effect on a company, particularly one which relies on its brand to attract customers.

2.3 International Trade and Investment Mechanisms: MNC Rights

The flipside of the absence of direct duties for MNCs in international law is that they are conferred significant benefits or rights under certain international trade and investment mechanisms. MNCs, as the main engines of global trade, are the indirect beneficiaries of the World Trade Organisation's drive to break down free trade barriers, though it is reliant upon States to enforce those rights.[41] MNCs do have standing to directly enforce their rights under certain regional (such as Chapter 11 of the North American Free Trade Agreement [NAFTA]) and bilateral investment treaties [BITs]. For example, an Italian company has challenged South Africa's 'black economic empowerment' laws, designed to provide economic advantages to South Africa's historically disadvantaged black community, under a BIT between Italy and South Africa. The case will be heard by the International Centre for the Settlement of Investment Disputes [ICSID].[42]

A previous case before ICSID, in which corporations sued a State over actions that may have in fact protected ESC rights, was brought by water companies against Bolivia for breach of contract under a bilateral investment treaty ('BIT') between

Business Slammed over Aid Response', *The Australian*, 5 January 2005, p. 9; F. Carruthers, 'Give and Take of Corporate Donations', *Financial Review*, 8 January 2005, p. 18; N. O'Malley, 'It's All About the Dividends', *The Sydney Morning Herald*, 29 March 2005, p. 11.

[40] UN doc. A/HRC/8/5, 7 April 2008, para 103.
[41] A number of cases have clearly been brought by States on behalf of their companies, such as the so-called Kodak/Fuji case: see J. L. Dunoff; 'The Misguided Debate over NGO Participation at the WTO', *Journal of International Economic Law*, Vol. 1 (1998), pp. 433-456, 441–448. The official name of the case is *Japan-Measures Affecting Consumer Photographic Film and Paper* WT/DS44/R, 31 March 1998.
[42] *Piero Foresti, Lauro de Carli and others v. Republic of South Africa*, ICSID Case no. ARB(AF)/07/1.

the Netherlands and Bolivia for US\$ 25 million. The case arose out of a disastrous attempt to privatise water supply in Cochabamba, Bolivia. The privatisation tender was awarded to Aguas del Tunari, a company owned by International Water (a Dutch company) and Bechtel. Subsequent massive price increases in water resulted in riots. Staff at Aguas del Tunari abandoned the operations, as their safety could not be guaranteed. The Bolivian government eventually cancelled the contract, and the companies commenced the suit under the BIT. The suit was dropped on 19 January 2006, when the water companies abandoned their claims. The Democracy Center, NGO which ran a strong campaign against Bechtel throughout the currency of the ICSID case, claimed:

> This is the first time that a major corporation has ever dropped a major international trade case such as this one as a direct result of global public pressure, and it sets an important precedent for the politics of future trade cases like it.[43]

For its part, Bechtel claimed that the suit was dropped as soon as it received an unambiguous admission that the concession failed due to civil unrest, rather than any fault of the companies.

It is uncertain whether States have yet submitted explicit human rights arguments in relevant cases, given that most relevant cases, such as that mentioned above regarding South Africa, are pending. NGOs have submitted amicus briefs in a number of international trade and investment cases in which they use human rights arguments to defend the actions of the respondent states.[44] Indeed, an ICSID tribunal has affirmed its power to accept amicus briefs from NGOs in the Suez/Vivendi case, despite an objection from one of the parties.[45] Human rights arguments have thus been used as a shield in international cases involving MNCs, but not yet as a sword. It is uncertain whether they will

operate as an effective shield in the face of international investment rights. On the other hand, the harsh spotlight of civil society pressure may have the potential to be a substitute shield, as arguably demonstrated in the Bechtel case.

3. TRANSNATIONAL LITIGATION

If it is unsatisfactory for legal accountability for MNC activity to arise solely from the government with territorial jurisdiction over that activity, an alternative source of MNC accountability arises from extraterritorial regulation by other governments. In the last decade, there has been a marked growth in the instances of transnational litigation against companies regarding their offshore activities.[46] Such litigation has normally occurred in the MNC's home State.[47] While home States may not have an international legal duty to regulate the overseas activities of their companies, they may nevertheless choose to do so.[48]

3.1 Alien Tort Claims Act (US)

A notable source of such 'transnational accountability' is the ancient US statute, the Alien Tort Claims Act 1789 ('ATCA'), which grants aliens rights to sue people in US federal courts for breaches of the 'law of nations'.[49] Almost all ATCA cases have involved allegations of human rights abuse. Numerous MNCs are currently being sued under ATCA with regard to allegations about their behaviour in developing countries. Clearly, a key to this statute is the interpretation by courts of the concept of 'the law of nations'. Generally, US courts have found that a breach of the law of nations entails a breach of customary international law.[50] An alternative formulation

---

[43] See generally, http://www.democracyctr.org/bolivia/investigations/water/ (accessed 23 May 2008).

[44] See H. Mann, *International Investment Agreements, Business and Human Rights: Key Issues and Opportunities* (International Institute for Sustainable Development, February 2008), pp. 25–29.

[45] See <http://www.ciel.org/Tae/ICSID_AmicusCuriae_1Jun05.html> (24 May 2008). The case concerns a dispute regarding a contract for water privatization in Argentina. The relevant foreign investor unsuccessfully objected to the acceptance of the NGO briefs.

[46] See generally, S. Joseph, *Corporations and Transnational Human Rights Litigation* (Oxford: Hart, 2004).

[47] Some cases in the US have concerned the overseas actions of non-US companies; see, e.g., *Wiwa v. Royal Dutch Petroleum* No. 96 Civ. 8386, 2002 US; Dist LEXIS 3293 (SDNY 2002, Unreported), regarding the actions of Shell, an Anglo-Dutch company.

[48] Nationality is a commonly accepted basis for the exercise of jurisdiction over a defendant. Cf. R. M. M. Wallace, *International Law*, 4th ed. (Sweet & Maxwell, London, 2002), p. 112.

[49] *Filartiga v. Pena-Irala* 630 F 2d 876 (2d Cir 1980).

[50] See Joseph, 'Corporations' (n. 46 above), p. 23, n. 16. The customary law standard was confirmed by the US

is that the relevant breach of international law must be 'definable, obligatory and universally condemned'.[51] It seems that this latter formula is simply a method by which US courts 'have attempted to translate the test for identifying customary international law into a domestic context'.[52]

In ATCA jurisprudence to date, only a small group of the most egregious civil and political rights violations have been found to breach 'the law of nations'.[53] In contrast, allegations regarding egregious environmental damage and breaches of ESC rights have been found to fall outside the ATCA. For example, in *Flores v. Southern Peru Copper*,[54] the Court of Appeals for the Second Circuit stated, with regard to the customary international law status of the right to health:

> As noted above, in order to state a claim under the ATCA, we have required that a plaintiff allege a violation of a "clear and unambiguous" rule of customary international law.... Far from being "clear and unambiguous," the statements relied on by plaintiffs to define the rights to life and health are vague and amorphous.... These principles are boundless and indeterminate. They express virtuous goals understandably expressed at a level of abstraction needed to secure the adherence of States that disagree on many of the particulars regarding how actually to achieve them. But in the words of a sister circuit, they "state abstract rights and liberties devoid of articulable or discernable standards and regulations."[55] The precept that "[h]uman beings are ... entitled to a healthy and productive life in harmony with nature," [Rio Decla-

ration, Principle 1] for example, utterly fails to specify what conduct would fall within or outside of the law. Similarly, the exhortation that all people are entitled to the "highest attainable standard of physical and mental health," [ICESCR, article 12] proclaims only nebulous notions that are infinitely malleable.

By concentrating on the bare words of international treaties, the *Flores* decision fails to recognise the enormous amount of work that has been done to clarify the meaning of the rights in those treaties, such as the adoption by the Committee on Economic Social and Cultural Rights of a detailed General Comment on the Right to Health.[56] However, given the history of US scepticism over the validity of ESC rights as 'rights',[57] and that country's failure to ratify the ICESCR, it is not surprising that US courts have failed to classify ESC rights as falling within the inner core of human rights protected by custom.

Furthermore, the relevant breach of the law of nations under ATCA normally must include an element of 'State action'. That is, breaches of the law of nations are normally only found if a government is somehow involved in the breach. This requirement arises from the fact that international law, including the law of nations, has generally evolved as a system that binds governments rather than non-governmental actors. Therefore, in the cases against MNCs, an element of State complicity in a violation perpetrated by an MNC, or MNC complicity in a violation by a State, must normally be present on the facts. This requirement again narrows the range of human rights abuses for which a corporation can be held liable under ATCA.[58]

It therefore seems that ATCA does not offer a remedy to victims of ESC violations by MNCs. However, ATCA is relevant where an ESC violation can be simultaneously characterised as a breach of a civil and political right that forms part of the law of nations. For example, the rights to be free from

---

Supreme Court in *Sosa v. Alvarez-Machain* at 124 S. Ct 2739 (2004), 2766–9. See also *Vietnam Association for Victims of Agent Orange v. Dow Chemical Co* 517 F 3d 104, 116 (2d cir, 2008).

[51] *Forti v. Suarez-Mason* 672 F Supp 1531 (ND Cal 1987) 1539–40; see also *Sosa v. Alvarez-Machain* 542 US 692 (2004).

[52] Joseph, 'Corporations' (n. 46 above), p. 24.

[53] See Joseph, ibid. pp. 26–7. The exception is that breaches of the UN Convention on the Law of the Sea have been found to violate the law of nations: see *Sarei v. Rio Tinto* 221 F Supp 2d 1116 (CD Cal, 2002), 1162 and 487 F 3d 1193, 1210 (9th cir, 2007). *Cf.* chapter 12 of this book.

[54] 406 F 3d 65, 86 (2d Cir 2003). The case concerned allegations of environmental damage that was so extreme as to amount to violations of the rights to life, health and sustainable development.

[55] *Beanal v. Freeport-McMoran Inc* 197 F 3d 161 (5th Cir 1999), at 167.

[56] UN doc. E/C.12/2002/1, 20 January 2003.

[57] See H. Steiner and P. Alston, *International Human Rights in Context*, 3rd ed. (Oxford: Oxford University Press, 2008), pp. 280–282.

[58] There are a few exceptional violations of the law of nations that, according to US courts, can arise in the absence of State action. Thus far, those violations are: the right to be free from genocide, certain war crimes, piracy, slavery, forced labour, and aircraft hijacking. See Joseph, *Corporations* (n. 46 above), p. 48, ns. 206–208.

slavery and forced labour have been classified as being protected under 'the law of nations'.[59] These violations constitute breaches of Article 8 of the ICCPR, but are also particularly egregious violations of Article 7 of the ICESCR, the right to just and favourable conditions of work. On the other hand, the court in *In re Agent Orange Product Liability Litigation* found that the deliberate use of a herbicide in the Vietnam war for military purposes, which had grave and long-term effects on the health of affected Vietnamese people, was not recognised as a war crime or any other type of breach of customary international law at the time of its use (which finished in April 1975).[60]

3.2   General Tort Law

There are other bases for transnational causes of action that have not attracted the same publicity as ATCA. MNCs can be sued under ordinary tort law for their overseas activities in the US and other common law countries.[61] Human rights abuses will often equate with a tort, even if the language of tort may not reflect the egregiousness of the human rights violation. Tort law formed the basis for actions against Texaco,[62] Freeport McMoran[63]

and Southern Peru Copper[64] for alleged egregious environmental harm in, respectively, Ecuador, West Papua, and Peru, resulting in deprivation of ESC rights such as the rights to health and food. A similar action commenced against BHP in Australia in *Dagi v. BHP*[65] regarding environmental damage in the Ok Tedi river basin in Papua New Guinea.

Apart from the above-mentioned environmental cases, tort law has also formed the basis of cases regarding OHS, with plaintiffs alleging that the defendant company has negligently, or even knowingly, adopted substandard OHS regimes in its offshore operations, leading to consequent health problems for workers and/or people in the vicinity of those operations. For example, tort has formed the basis of complaints against Shell Oil and Dow Chemicals for their continued production and use of a pesticide, dibromochloropropane ('DBCP'), on banana plantations in the developing world, despite their knowledge that DBCP had been banned in the US for causing sterilisation to those exposed.[66] A claim was brought in the US against Union Carbide regarding the Bhopal industrial accident.[67] Finally, a number of actions have been brought against MNCs in the UK, alleging severe harm to the health of workers caused by deficient OHS standards in the operations of their African subsidiaries.[68]

3.3   Procedural Obstacles to Transnational Litigation

None of the above-mentioned cases against MNCs, including the ATCA cases, have been finally

[59] *Doe v. Unocal* 2002 US App LEXIS 19263 (9th Cirt. 2002) 14208.

[60] 2005 U.S. Dist. LEXIS 3644, Judgment 10 March 2005, (United States District Court for the Eastern District of New York). See also *Vietnam Association for Victims of Agent Orange v. Dow Chemical Co* 517 F 3d 104, 119-123 (2d cir, 2008). The case was brought against the manufacturers of 'agent orange', a herbicide used during the Vietnam War to clear forests and mangroves for military purposes. The plaintiffs claimed that the defoliation was a war crime or another breach of customary international law, and the manufacturers aided and abetted the perpetration of those breaches.

[61] See generally, Joseph, 'Corporations' (n. 46 above), Ch. 3. This author is unaware of any transnational civil cases against corporations in civil law jurisdictions. The civil legal tradition is not as reliant on litigation as the common law tradition as a means of resolving disputes. Furthermore, there is less scope for judges to influence and develop the law. See Joseph, 'Corporations' (n. 46 above), p. 16. See also J. G. Apple and R. P. Deyling, *A Primer on the Civil Law System*, Federal Judicial Center, at <http://www.fjc.gov/public/pdf.nsf/lookup/CivilLaw.pdf/$file/CivilLaw.pdf> (7 January 2003), p. 37 (accessed 24 May 2008).

[62] *Aguinda v. Texaco, Inc* 142 F Supp 2d 534 (SDNY 2001). The plaintiffs, as in many of these transnational tort cases, also raised an unsuccessful ATCA argument.

[63] *Beanal v. Freeport-McMoran Inc* 197 F 3d 161 (5th Cir 1999).

[64] *Flores v. Southern Peru Copper* 406 F 3d 65 (2d Cir 2003).

[65] [1995] 1 VR 428.

[66] See, e.g., *Martinez v. Dow Chemical Co* 219 F Supp 2d 719 (ED La 2002). See also note 7 above, regarding a DBCP case in Nicaragua.

[67] *In re Union Carbide Corp Gas Plant Disaster at Bhopal* 634 F Supp 842 (SDNY 1986); *In re Union Carbide Corp Gas Plant Disaster at Bhopal* 809 F 2d 195 (2d Cir 1987); *Bano v. Union Carbide* 273 F 3d 120 (2d Cir 2001); *Bano v. Union Carbide* 361 F 3d 696 (2d cir, 2004).

[68] See below, discussion in text at notes 81-85. For a detailed discussion of the litigation and impact of these cases, see R. Meeran, 'Multinational Litigation as a Weapon in Protecting Economic and Social Rights', in J. Squires, M. Langford and B. Thiele (eds.), *Road to a Remedy: Current Issues in Litigation of Economic, Social and Cultural Rights* (Sydney: Australian Human Rights Centre and University of NSW Press, 2006), pp. 183–211.

decided on the merits. The cases have largely stalled due to the numerous preliminary challenges raised by the corporate defendants, which have taken some time to resolve, and have often led to dismissal of the case. So far, cases have tended to settle if plaintiffs make it through the minefield of preliminary hearings. I will discuss two bases for such preliminary challenges: forum non conveniens and the corporate veil.

In almost every transnational human rights case against a company, the corporate defendant has sought to have the case dismissed on the basis of the common law doctrine of forum non conveniens ('FNC'). This doctrine may be applied at a judge's discretion to dismiss a case on the basis that the case should properly be heard in another jurisdiction. Given that transnational human rights cases against companies involve allegations regarding actions or consequences in another country, there is clearly scope to argue that the case should properly be heard in that other country.

In the US, a defendant must establish that there exists an adequate alternative forum for the litigation, and that the balance of private and public interests favours litigation in the alternative forum rather than in the US, in order to persuade a court to dismiss a case on the basis of FNC. FNC arguments are becoming less successful in ATCA cases, as judges are increasingly willing to recognise that the alternative jurisdiction in an ATCA case, which necessarily involves allegations of extreme human rights abuses and normally involves allegations that the relevant foreign government is involved in that abuse (due to the State action requirement), may be too corrupt or dangerous for a plaintiff to proceed in.[69] In ATCA cases, judges are also willing to recognise the US policy interests in providing a forum to avail plaintiffs of human rights remedies under ATCA.[70] However, most of the above-named US cases based on ordinary tort law have been dismissed on the basis of FNC.[71] As state action is not necessarily present in the ordinary tort cases, there is less scope to argue that the alternative forum is

too dangerous or corrupt to provide an adequate forum for the purposes of FNC arguments.

An encouraging sign for non-ATCA plaintiffs is the decision in *Martinez v. Dow Chemicals*, one of the more recent cases in the DBCP litigation.[72] In *Martinez*, Barbier J decided not to dismiss the case on the grounds of FNC for two reasons. The relevant alternative forums were Costa Rica, Honduras and the Philippines. First, Barbier J found that the courts in the latter two jurisdictions were too corrupt and beset by inefficiency to constitute an adequate alternative forum.[73] Second, Barbier J found that none of the three countries was an available alternative forum. All three countries had enacted legislation, that prohibited the commencement of a suit if that suit had already been commenced in an alternative jurisdiction.[74] By definition, a suit that has been dismissed for FNC has been previously commenced elsewhere. Indeed, it seems that such legislation is designed to thwart FNC arguments and prevent the US from dumping mass tort cases on lesser developed legal systems.[75] Such legislation, which is common in Latin America, may effectively trump FNC arguments. Note however that an argument regarding a similar law in Ecuador failed to fend off an FNC dismissal in *Aguinda v. Texaco*.[76] In his decision, Rakoff J doubted the validity of the Ecuadorian law, Law 55, under Ecuador's Constitution.[77] However, Rakoff J conceded that the court could reconsider the issue of FNC if the case should be dismissed in Ecuador on the basis of Law 55.[78] At the time of writing, a parallel suit had indeed commenced in Ecuador.[79]

---

[69] See Joseph, 'Corporations' (n. 46 above), pp. 89–92.

[70] Ibid. pp. 92–96.

[71] See P. Blumberg, 'Asserting Human Rights against Multinational Corporations under United States Law – Conceptual and Procedural Problems', *American Journal of Comparative Law*, Vol. 50 (2002), pp. 493–529, at 505.

[72] 219 F Supp 2d 719 (ED La 2002). In this case, Costa Rican, Honduran and Filipino workers sued a chemical company for producing a fertiliser that caused sterility on banana plantations.

[73] Ibid. pp. 737 and p. 740.

[74] Ibid. pp. 728, p. 735, and p. 741.

[75] See L. W. Newman, 'Latin America and *Forum non Conveniens* Dismissals', *New York Law Journal*, Vol. 221, Issue 23 (1999), pp. 3–4; and W. Anderson, '*Forum non Conveniens* Checkmated? The Emergence of Retaliatory Legislation', *Journal of Transnational Law and Policy*, Vol. 10 (2001), pp. 183–216, at 186.

[76] In *Aguinda v. Texaco, Inc* 142 F Supp 2d 534 (SDNY 2001), Peruvian and Ecuadorian nationals sued a parent oil company for property damage, personal injury and risk of disease from alleged negligent pipeline management by Texaco subsidiaries in Peru and Ecuador.

[77] Ibid. p. 547.

[78] Ibid. p. 547.

[79] See D. R. Baker, 'ChevronTexaco on the defensive: Suit in Ecuador alleges drilling by Texaco caused environmental damage in Amazon', *San Francisco Chronicle*, 3 March 2005.

Therefore, the status quo in the US is that FNC poses a formidable hurdle for plaintiffs in transnational human rights cases against MNCs, especially if the jurisdictional basis for the case is not ATCA, which will normally be the case in suits involving ESC rights violations. However, the emergence of 'retaliatory legislation' in a number of developing countries may stave off FNC dismissals.

In Australia, FNC is less of a problem for plaintiffs. The test for FNC dismissal is significantly stricter: an Australian court must be a 'clearly inappropriate forum' for the litigation. This is a more difficult test to satisfy than in other common law countries, where there simply must exist a 'more appropriate' alternative forum. The strictness of the Australian test may explain why FNC was not rigorously argued by the defendant in the only transnational human rights case against an MNC launched to date in Australia, *Dagi v. BHP*.[80]

In the UK, the test for FNC used to be closer to the US than to that of Australia. Nevertheless, defendants' FNC arguments were dismissed in the three significant cases to date. In *Connelly v. RTZ*[81] and *Lubbe v. Cape Plc*,[82] the House of Lords kept both cases within jurisdiction on the basis that substantive justice could not be achieved in the putative alternative forums in Namibia and South Africa, respectively. In particular, the plaintiffs in both cases were felt to be in need of free legal counsel in order to run their cases. Legal aid, or free legal counsel on some other basis such as contingency, was available in the UK but not in the respective African jurisdictions. The UK courts have therefore paid greater attention to whether it is likely or even possible that proceedings will go ahead in the alternative jurisdiction than their US counterparts.[83]

In both *Connelly* and *Lubbe*, the plaintiffs had tried to get around the FNC argument by suing the parent companies for their alleged negligent failure to adequately supervise the OHS policies of their African subsidiaries. On that analysis, the true sites of the torts in both cases were the boardrooms in the UK rather than the subsidiary operations in Africa. It seems that the argument was not accepted in *Lubbe*, as in that case South Africa was found to be a more appropriate forum from a purely geographic point of view. It is unlikely to have been deemed a more appropriate geographic forum if the court had accepted that the UK was the true site of the relevant tort.[84] In *Ngcobo v. Thor Chemical Holdings Ltd*, an unreported case again concerning poor OHS standards in Africa by a UK-based MNC, a similar argument appears to have been accepted by the Court, thus leading to rejection of an argument that South Africa was a more appropriate forum for the litigation.[85]

The arguments regarding FNC in the UK have now become largely moot. *Owusu v. Jackson*,[86] a 2005 decision of the European Court of Justice ('ECJ'), concerned the application of Article 2 of the Brussels Convention,[87] to which all members of the EU are party. Article 2 prescribes that defendants domiciled within the EU may be sued in their domicile State. In *Owusu*, the ECJ confirmed that it does not matter if the case has a strong connection with another jurisdiction, including a State that is not party to the Brussels Convention. Thus, FNC, a common law doctrine that never applied in

Hague: Kluwer Law International, 2000), pp 241–250, at p. 246.

[84] In *Connelly*, the arguments located the torts in both the UK and Namibia, so the Court was not called upon to decide whether the UK was the 'true' site of the tort.

[85] Mr. James Stewart QC, sitting as a Deputy Judge of the High Court, in *Ngcobo v. Thor Chemicals Holdings Ltd*, unreported judgment of 11 April 1995, implicitly accepted that the alleged tort arose in England with the decisions of the parent company rather than in South Africa with the implementation of those decisions (transcript at 20).

[86] Case C-281/02, (1 March 2005) (Grand Chamber of the European Court of Justice).

[87] Convention of 27 September 1968 on Jurisdiction and the Enforcement of Judgments in Civil and Commercial Matters (OJ 1978 L304, p. 36), as amended by the Convention of 9 October 1978 on the Accession of the Kingdom of Denmark, Ireland and the United Kingdom of Great Britain and Northern Ireland (OJ 1978 L 304, p. 1, and – amended version – p. 77), by the Convention of 25 October 1982 on the Accession of the Hellenic Republic (OJ 1982 L 388, p. 1) and by the Convention of 26 May 1989 on the Accession of the Kingdom of Spain and the Portuguese Republic (OJ 1989 L285, p. 1).

[80] See P. Prince, 'Bhopal, Bougainville and Ok Tedi: Why Australia's *Forum Non Conveniens* Approach Is Better', *International and Comparative Law Quarterly*, Vol. 47 (1998), pp. 573–598. See also *Renault v. Zhang* (2002) 210 CLR 491 (High Court of Australia).

[81] [1998] AC 854 (HL). In this case, RTZ was sued in tort regarding workplace injuries sustained in a uranium mine operated by a Nigerian subsidiary.

[82] [2000] 4 All ER 268 (HL). In this case, Cape Plc was sued by employees at its South African subsidiary regarding asbestos-related injuries.

[83] See M. Byers, 'English Courts and Serious Human Rights Violations Abroad: A Preliminary Assessment' in M. Kamminga and S. Zia-Zarif (eds.), *Liability of Multinational Corporations under International Law* (The

most of the EU, can no longer apply in the UK to dismiss cases against defendants domiciled in the UK, regardless of the strength (or weakness) of the connection between the case and the UK.[88] The UK has therefore become a more attractive forum for transnational human rights litigation.

In most of these cases, the parent company is being sued in its home state with regard to the alleged actions of an offshore subsidiary. The parent company will naturally argue that it is a separate legal entity from its subsidiary, and is therefore not involved in the alleged human rights abuse. Such an argument led to the dismissal of a case against Freeport McMoran in *Alomang v. Freeport McMoran*,[89] where the Louisiana Court of Appeal found that the New Orleans–based parent could not be held liable for the alleged actions of its Indonesian subsidiary. Arguments regarding the corporate veil probably also influenced the decision by Rakoff J in *Aguinda v. Texaco*, where the judge found, in a decision to dismiss the case on the basis of FNC (see above), that there was not 'a meaningful nexus between the US and the decisions and practices' in Ecuador that were the subject of the suit.[90]

As noted above with regard to the UK cases, plaintiffs have occasionally directly targeted the actions and omissions of parent companies in an attempt to get around the corporate veil, and also to thwart FNC arguments. Such issues can only be resolved on the merits, and no salient case has yet been decided on the merits. Most courts in these cases have been prepared to assume that the subsidiary company is an alter ego of the defendant parent for preliminary purposes. However, the issue of separate corporate personality is likely to be reopened on the merits in most of the salient cases. It may be that the corporate veil will prove to be a greater obstacle for plaintiffs than FNC.

Transnational human rights litigation is in its formative stages, and potentially provides an important avenue of redress for the victims of ESC abuses by MNCs. This avenue however is littered with preliminary obstacles, such as arguments regarding FNC and the corporate veil. Nevertheless, such litigation provides an important alternative to international legal processes, which lack efficient enforcement mechanisms, and host state processes, which may be neither adequate nor realistically available in some circumstances. The potential effectiveness of transnational litigation is evinced by the concern that MNCs have over such litigation. For example, business groups have lobbied the US government to repeal the ATCA.[91] Furthermore, several high profile cases have been settled.[92] Settlement has prevented merits decisions which could set broad precedents binding on all MNCs, but have at least provided the relevant plaintiffs with some measure of redress for their suffering.

On the other hand, merits decisions have also been thwarted by numerous dismissals on procedural grounds. At the time of writing, no merits decision had been delivered in a transnational human rights case against a company.

4. CONCLUSION

MNCs are not inherently antagonistic to ESC rights. Indeed, many MNCs are taking the concept of 'corporate social responsibility' seriously by voluntarily performing above and beyond that required by law to assist in the enhancement of the enjoyment of ESC rights. Of course, the record of MNCs in this regard is not perfect. When 'things go wrong' and ESC rights are violated due to MNC operations, those MNCs should be accountable for those violations. Violations will proliferate if there are no consequences for them.

At present, the most likely source of accountability is the laws of the host state in which the violations

---

[88] See G. Cuniberti, 'Forum non Conveniens and the Brussels Convention', *International and Comparative Law Quarterly*, Vol. 54, (2005), pp. 973–981.

[89] 811 So 2d 98 (La App 2002). In this case, Indonesian nationals unsuccessfully sued a parent mining company for its subsidiary's activities, which allegedly constituted cultural genocide, environmental damage and human rights abuses, under the Louisiana equivalent of the ATCA.

[90] *Aguinda v. Texaco*, 142 F Supp 2d 534 (SDNY 2001), pp. 548–550.

[91] See, e.g., the campaign waged by USA-Engage, which operates under the auspices of the National Foreign Trade Council in the US: <http://www.usaengage.org/legislative/2003/alientort/index.html> (accessed 27 March 2007).

[92] The cases in *Lubbe v. Cape Plc*, *Dagi v. BHP*, and *Doe v. Unocal* have now been settled. For example, see <http://www.earthrights.org/legal/unocal/> (accessed 24 May 2008) for details of the *Unocal* settlement.

occur. In many situations, those laws will suffice to appropriately punish a delinquent MNC. However, given the unique power and mobility of MNCs, and their ability to manipulate risks and liabilities within their corporate structures, it is important that alternative sources of accountability beyond the borders of host states be developed.

With the adoption of the Norms in 2003, momentum seemed to be building for the adoption of enforceable international human rights duties for MNCs. However, the UN Special Representative seems to have abandoned that route for now. Instead, he recommends clarification and strengthening of the duties of States, possibly including home States, to provide for and enforce human rights duties for corporations.

Victims of ESC rights violations have increasingly sought to hold MNCs accountable in transnational litigation. While plaintiffs have had to withstand a barrage of preliminary challenges in the salient transnational cases, some cases have been settled leading to the delivery of a measure of redress to victims, and other cases are ongoing, with possibilities for further redress and vindication.

Of course, litigation, whether it takes place in host states, home states, third party states, or international forums, only represents 'the tip of the iceberg'[93] of ESC abuses by MNCs. Many victims lack the resources or ability to bring such cases. It is therefore important that legal sources of accountability continue to be supplemented by informal non-legal sources of pressure, such as that exercised by NGOs, consumers, the media, investors, employees, and shareholders.

---

[93] Joseph, 'Corporations' (n. 46 above), p. 153.

30

The World Bank Inspection Panel

Dana Clark*

1. ORIGINS OF THE INSPECTION PANEL

In the 1980s and early 1990s, the World Bank (or the 'Bank') came under increasing public criticism and scrutiny for helping to catalyse projects with immense negative environmental and social impacts. In response to public and internal critiques, the World Bank adopted a series of social and environmental policies to try to minimise, mitigate and compensate for these negative impacts, thereby aiming to improve decision making, project quality and development effectiveness. These policies became known as the 'safeguard' policies, reflecting the assumption that they would help to prevent harm from occurring. Although many of these original policies were considered strong when they were first adopted, controversial projects were still approved and constructed despite violations of those policies.

The Sardar Sarovar dam project on the Narmada River in India is a classic example of the World Bank's involvement in, and promotion of, high-impact projects. Resistance to the project at the local level was joined by national and international civil society organisations. This coordinated pressure led to the first ever independent review of a World Bank project. The review, authorised by the World Bank, was led by Bradford Morse, and the report of the investigation became known as the Morse Commission report.[1]

The Morse Commission documented numerous instances in which World Bank staff had knowingly violated the Bank's environmental and social policies. The report also showed that the Bank had tolerated violations of the loan covenants by the borrowing governments. The report linked these failures to significant adverse impacts, particularly on the hundreds of thousands of local people who would be displaced, including indigenous *adivasi* people living in the flood zone. To make a long story short, when the Bank and the governments failed to implement an effective plan for bringing the Sardar Sarovar project into compliance with Bank policy and Indian law, the World Bank withdrew from the project.[2]

Building on the lessons learned from the Sardar Sarovar investigation experience, civil society advocates and some member governments of the World Bank called for the establishment of a permanent, independent inspection mechanism and accountability system, which would serve as a forum to respond to the concerns of affected people and help address some of the governance lapses at the Bank. In 1993, the World Bank's Board of Executive Directors[3] passed a resolution

---

* Dana Clark is a human rights and environmental lawyer working with Rainforest Action Network's Global Finance Campaign; she also serves as President of the International Accountability Project. She is a co-author and co-editor of *Demanding Accountability: Civil Society Claims and the World Bank Inspection Panel* (Rowman & Littlefield, 2003), which analysed the first ten years of the Inspection Panel's case history.

[1] B. Morse and T. Berger, 'Sardar Sarovar: Report of the Independent Review' (Ottawa: Resources Future Int'l, Inc., 1992).

[2] To minimise embarrassment and save face, the Bank's withdrawal from the Sardar Sarovar project was effectuated by the Indian government telling the Bank that it did not wish to receive any further disbursements under the loan. The Bank's withdrawal was seen as a victory by local activists. They then switched to a domestic legal strategy, which succeeded in preventing any increase in the height of the dam for many years. However, in October 2002, the Indian Supreme Court authorised further increases in the height of the dam, conditioned in theory on prior resettlement and rehabilitation of affected people. See further chapter 6.5 in this book for a detailed discussion.

[3] The Board of Executive Directors is the day-to-day decision-making body at the Bank, approving all loans and projects financed by the Bank, and with considerable oversight over Bank policies. There are 24 executive directors, or board members, representing 184 member governments of the World Bank Group.

authorising the development of the Inspection Panel (the 'Panel').

Although the Panel was created by and reports to the board, it was primarily designed to be responsive to people who are affected by a World Bank-financed project. The citizen-driven nature of the process is reminiscent of citizen suit provisions in some national environmental laws, whereby concerned citizens can help ensure better enforcement of the law.

The World Bank Inspection Panel was an innovative experiment in global governance when it began operations in 1994. It was the first attempt by an international financial institution to implement an accountability system to improve compliance with a binding policy framework. The development of the Inspection Panel was noteworthy in terms of international law, in that it is an international forum that is available to local people, even in situations where the national government may be unsympathetic, or hostile,[4] to their concerns.[5]

The Bank's Board of Executive Directors, which approved the Panel process, hoped that the new mechanism would improve the development effectiveness of World Bank projects, and help the Bank avoid future involvement in high-profile 'development disasters'. The Operating Procedures of the Inspection Panel state its objectives:

> The Panel has been established for the purpose of providing people directly and adversely affected by a Bank-financed project with an independent forum through which they can request the Bank to act in accordance with its own policies and procedures. It follows that this forum is available when adversely affected people believe that the

Bank itself has failed, or has failed to require others, to comply with its policies and procedures, and only after efforts have been made to ask the Bank Management itself to deal with the problem.

The role of the Panel is to carry out independent investigations. Its function, which is triggered when it receives a request for inspection, is to inquire and recommend: it will make a preliminary review of a request for inspection and the response of Management; it will independently assess the information and then recommend to the Board of Executive Directors whether or not the matters complained of should be investigated. If the Board decides that a request should be investigated, the Panel will collect information and provide its findings, independent assessment and conclusions to the Board. On the basis of the Panel's findings and Management's recommendations, the Executive Directors will consider the actions, if any, to be taken by the Bank.[6]

The Panel process also helps to effectuate a shift in the balance of power between the Bank and affected people, promoting greater respect for, and in some circumstances better responsiveness to, people who are affected by the World Bank's lending decisions. This, in turn, helps to diminish the culture of impunity at the world's most powerful development bank, and helps increase Bank staff's sensitivity to the environmental and social impacts and risks of particular projects.

The World Bank Inspection Panel also fuelled greater awareness of, and public demand for, systems of accountability in international project finance, and many other international financial institutions are developing or have implemented (and in some cases have reviewed and revised) similar citizen-based accountability systems.[7] The fact that the inspection panel model is being replicated at other international financial institutions is a reflection of the increased demand by civil society and member governments that international financial institutions ('IFIs') conform to

---

[4] Claimants can request that the Inspection Panel keep their identities confidential, which has been done in situations where there is fear of retaliation for having filed the claim.

[5] I. Shihata, 'The World Bank Inspection Panel: Its Historical, Legal and Operational Aspects', in G. Alfredson and R. Ring, (eds.) *The Inspection Panel of the World Bank: A Different Complaints Procedure* (The Hague: Kluwer Law International, 2001). When the Panel was created, then World Bank General Counsel Ibrahim Shihata recognised that providing affected citizens with access to an international forum 'where they can submit their complaints and see them addressed' constituted 'a progressive step in the development of both the law of international organizations and the international law of human rights'. Ibid. p. 25.

[6] World Bank Inspection Panel, Operating Procedures (1994), p. 3.

[7] Professor Daniel Bradlow has recently done a comparative overview of various inspection mechanisms. *See* D. Bradlow, 'Private Complaints and International Organizations: A Comparative Study of the Independent Inspection Mechanisms in International Financial Institutions', *Geo. J. Int'l L.*, Vol. 36 (2005), pp. 403–491.

sustainable development standards and that they submit to public accountability for violations of those standards. In addition, the demand for IFIs to operate within environmental and social policy framework has rippled out to private financial institutions as well. More than forty private banks have signed onto the 'Equator Principles', which are closely linked to the Performance Standards of the International Finance Corporation, the arm of the World Bank Group that supports private sector investors.[8]

The existence of the Panel appears to have some deterrent effect, as there has to some extent been increased emphasis on compliance with the safeguard policies. While discussing the after-effects of an Inspection Panel claim that challenged and ultimately brought a halt to the World Bank's controversial plan to help finance China's population transfer into Tibet, the Bank's Vice President for Environmentally and Socially Sustainable Development (a department that has since been dissolved) noted that:

> People are recognizing that the costs of non-compliance are higher than the costs of compliance at the end of the day. An ounce of prevention is worth a pound of cure. It has made quite a big difference ... I think there is a genuine desire to do the right thing. If you don't do due diligence, and you get caught, you pay a price.[9]

2. ELIGIBILITY REQUIREMENTS OF THE WORLD BANK INSPECTION PANEL

The Inspection Panel process can be initiated by, first and foremost, any two or more people with common interests or concerns, living in an area affected by a World Bank project, who believe that

they have been, or are likely to be, harmed as a result of the Bank's violation of its operational policies and procedures, or a breach of the terms of the loan agreement. A local representative can also file a claim on behalf of project-affected people, so long as that representative provides the Panel with written authorisation from affected people to act as a representative on their behalf. In exceptional circumstances, where local representation is not available (which could include countries where local non-governmental organisations are not allowed to operate or where there is a risk of retaliation), a non-local representative (with the same proof of authorisation described above) can file a claim on behalf of local affected parties.

Furthermore, the Bank's Board of Executive Directors has recourse to the Panel.[10] Any single executive director of the World Bank may, 'in special cases of serious alleged violations of such policies and procedures, ask the Panel for an investigation'. In addition, the executive directors, acting collectively as a full board, may also 'instruct the panel to conduct an investigation'.

Most of the requests for inspection have been initiated by local affected people and/or their local representatives. There has been only one claim filed by a non-local representative, and only one that was requested by the board. Ironically, both of these unusual instances occurred in the same Inspection Panel case, in the claim filed against the China Western Poverty Reduction Project.

In that case, the claim was filed with the Panel by the Washington, DC-based International Campaign for Tibet ('ICT'), based on written authorisation from Tibetans living in the project area, who asked for ICT's assistance in raising their concerns and fears with the World Bank. Local Tibetans were afraid that the population transfer project would endanger the environment, threaten their way of life, and undermine their cultural survival. Prior to filing the claim, ICT and others documented violations of policies on information disclosure, indigenous peoples, involuntary resettlement, and environmental assessment, among others. This analysis was shared in meetings and correspondence with bank staff, senior management including then-President Wolfensohn, the

---

[8] The Equator Principles can be found at <www.equator principles.com>. One problem that has been noted with the Equator Principles is that they lack an accountability or enforcement mechanism. See <www.banktrack.org>. The IFC policy and performance standards can be found at <www.ifc.org>; a critique can be found at Halifax Initiative, *One Step Forward, One Step Back* (May 2006), available at <www.halifaxinitiative.org/index.php/ Reports_Analysis/683>

[9] Ian Johnson, quoted in K. Treakle, J. Fox and D. Clark, 'Lessons Learned' in D. Clark, J. Fox and K. Treakle (eds.), *Demanding Accountability: Civil Society Claims and the World Bank Inspection Panel* (Lanham, Md.: Rowman & Littlefield Publishers, Inc., 2003), pp. 247–277, at p. 270.

[10] World Bank, IBRD Resolution No. 93–10 (22 September 1993), para. 12.

Board of Executive Directors, and various government officials who were monitoring the case. In the week leading up to the Board vote to approve the project, eleven out of twenty-four Board members wrote to Wolfensohn asking that he withdraw the project from consideration. However, with intense pressure from China, the project remained on the board's agenda for approval on 24 June 2000.

The claim was filed with the Inspection Panel by International Campaign for Tibet on 18 June, one week before the board meeting. At the board meeting that gave conditional approval of the project (subject to subsequent board review of the findings of the Inspection Panel investigation), the Chinese Government agreed to allow the Panel to investigate the claim. However, it subsequently voiced displeasure with ICT as a claimant because of links the organisation has with the Dalai Lama, Tibet's exiled leader. In order to bypass China's objection, and to get the board off the hook from having to evaluate whether or not there could be appropriate local representation in China, the Italian executive director requested the Inspection Panel to investigate the exact policy violations that had been alleged in ICT's claim. Because that request formally came from a board member, rather than ICT, China did not object to this method of filing the claim, and the Panel investigation proceeded.[11]

The Inspection Panel is tasked with investigating the extent to which the Bank has, or has not, acted in compliance with its own policies and procedures. A request for inspection essentially asks the Inspection Panel to impartially evaluate whether or not the World Bank has acted (or failed to act) in violation of its own policies and procedures, and/or whether it has violated (or knowingly tolerated the violation of) the terms of a loan agreement between the Bank and a borrowing government. The Panel conducts an impartial investigation, evaluating the submissions of the claimants and the responses of Bank Management

and developing a report of its findings which ultimately is delivered to the Board and the President of the Bank.

There are several limitations on the use of the Inspection Panel. One limitation on the scope of the Panel's investigation is that it cannot investigate the actions or omissions of actors other than the Bank (such as borrowing governments or corporations), except to the extent that those actions reflect a failure of the World Bank to follow its own policies and procedures. Furthermore, the claim (also known as a 'request for inspection') needs to draw a link between actions or omissions on the part of the Bank and harm or threat of harm to the claimants.

In addition, there is an 'exhaustion of remedies' type of provision, which requires that before seeking recourse from the Panel, claimants must first try to raise their concerns with the Bank, so that the Bank has an opportunity to respond to and potentially correct the problems. Concerns can be raised through meetings, phone calls or correspondence. If the Bank fails to respond, or if the response is considered unsatisfactory, affected people, or their representatives, can then take their concerns to the Panel.[12]

One of the major limitations on access to the Inspection Panel is that a claim can only be filed up until the point when the loan has been 95 per cent disbursed by the Bank to the borrower. In other words, if the loan funds have been fully disbursed or are between 95–100 per cent disbursed, it is too late to file a claim to the Panel. One problem with this 95 per cent cut-off rule is that the loan funds are often disbursed relatively early in the life cycle of the project and are then repaid over time, often twenty years. Many of the project impacts, such as involuntary displacement, can occur during the time after disbursement and before repayment. Although the Bank's policies technically should apply to projects until the time when the loan is repaid, there is effectively no system of public accountability for projects that are in the post-disbursement phase, and no guarantee that the World Bank's policies, or

---

[11] The Panel report confirmed the policy violations alleged in the claim, and documented a 'climate of fear' in the project area. For a more complete description of the case, see D. Clark and K. Treakle, 'The China Western Poverty Reduction Project', in D. Clark, J. Fox and K. Treakle (eds.), *Demanding Accountability: Civil Society Claims and the World Bank Inspection Panel* (Lanham, Md.: Rowman & Littlefield Publishers, Inc., 2003), pp. 211–245.

[12] For more information about the claim process, see D. L. Clark, *A Citizen's Guide to the World Bank Inspection Panel* (Washington, DC: CIEL, 1999), available at <http://www.ciel.org/Publications/citizensguide.pdf>

the terms of the loan agreement, will be complied with throughout project implementation.

The designers of the revamped accountability mechanism at the Asian Development Bank (ADB) learned from this shortcoming in the World Bank's approach, and empowered the Compliance Review Panel at the ADB to monitor progress on obtaining compliance for a period of years after the review is complete.[13] It is encouraging that the Asian Development Bank has taken such an approach and taken steps to improve the crucial remedial measures phase. An important contrast with the World Bank process and the revised ADB accountability mechanism is that the latter has also done away with the 95 per cent disbursement cut-off, and the ADB Compliance Review Panel (CRP) can address projects through 'project completion', although that is also defined rather narrowly.[14]

3. OBTAINING REDRESS THROUGH THE WORLD BANK INSPECTION PANEL

Among other things, claimants to the Panel have 'sought to receive adequate compensation for being forcibly displaced; to demand implementation of environmental protection and mitigation measures; to have their livelihoods restored; to receive support for social programs; to prevent threatened harm by stopping or delaying potentially destructive projects; and to hold the Bank accountable for its role in causing their problems'.[15] However, it is important to recognise that the Panel by itself does not have the authority to stop a project, nor can it award damages to claimants who are found to have suffered

harm. Rather, its role is limited to conducting an impartial investigation and producing a public report documenting the findings of its investigation, which is delivered to the Board of Executive Directors and Bank Management, and, after consideration by the Board, is released to the public.

Bank Management is provided with an opportunity to review the Panel's findings and to make recommendations to the Board prior to the Board meeting to discuss the report. The claimants do not have a similar opportunity to respond; indeed, they are not allowed to even see the report before the Board of Directors meets to discuss it. Note that this imbalance in access to the process was also changed in the revised Asian Development Bank inspection mechanism, such that a draft report is released to both the Bank and the claimants, and both are provided an opportunity to comment before a final report is sent by the Compliance Review Panel to the Board.

After reviewing the Panel's report, Management is supposed to outline the steps, if any, that it is taking, or proposes to take, to bring the project into compliance. After discussing the Panel report and reviewing Management's recommendations, it is then up to the Board to announce what, if any, remedial measures will be undertaken in response to the Panel's findings. In some cases, this leads to an 'action plan' approach, in which Bank Management and the borrower make commitments to improve the project.

The Board tends to adopt action plans proposed by Management, which is also responsible for their implementation. This contributes to one of the troubling elements in the panel process, which is that the remedial measures are often designed by Bank Management, without necessarily engaging in meaningful consultation with the claimants or other affected people. Such action plans or remedial measures should theoretically be designed to bring the project back into compliance with applicable policies and remedy the harm caused by policy violations. However, with a few exceptions, oversight of their implementation has not been a high priority for the Bank; this is something that needs to be addressed if the Panel process is to lead to true accountability and problem solving. The Board has explicitly prevented the Inspection

---

[13] Email correspondence from Richard Bissell to author (22 November 2005) (copy on file with author).

[14] The CRP cannot accept requests regarding a project for which a 'project completion report' has been issued. Project completion reports are issued 1–2 years after the project is physically completed and in operation. For private sector projects in which no project completion report is issued, the CRP can no longer take requests once the project is physically completed and in operation. Where physical completion has been waived, or is irrelevant, the CRP can take requests for one year after the final disbursement or termination of ADB's involvement in the project, whichever occurs earlier. See Asian Development Bank, Operating Procedures of the Compliance Review Panel, Section G (5 June 2004).

[13] Clark, Fox and Treakle, 'Lessons Learned', p. 257.

Panel from overseeing action plans,[16] while at the same time the Board itself lacks a standing committee or other formal structure for ensuring that the actions called for under the action plan actually take place. There is no post-hoc system for evaluating whether the action plan actually brought the project into compliance with the Bank's policies and procedures.

Combined with the fact that executive directors have a fairly frequent turnover rate, this lack of institutional oversight also results in a loss of institutional memory with respect to the Panel investigations. This can mean that individual cases drop off the radar screens of the Board, and it also means that fundamental policy lessons are not effectively internalised.[17]

4. JURISDICTION AND JURISPRUDENCE

The jurisdiction of the Inspection Panel is bounded by the World Bank's policy framework, including the safeguard environmental and social policies, and others that are relevant, such as the policy on project supervision. As noted above, the Panel can investigate the extent to which the Bank has or has not complied with these policy requirements, and with the terms of the loan agreement. As of this writing, the World Bank Inspection Panel had registered thirty-five requests for inspection, most of which have focused to some extent on economic and social rights. The World Bank policies and procedures that have most frequently been the subject of a complaint include those on environmental assessment, indigenous peoples, involuntary resettlement, and project supervision.[18]

Since the Inspection Panel was created, the World Bank has revised all of its safeguard policies, in many cases instituting language changes that make the policies more discretionary and less rigorous for bank staff and borrowers. The policy framework for the International Bank for Reconstruction and Development ('IBRD') and International Development Association ('IDA'), the public sector arms of the World Bank Group ('WBG'), is now reflected in a system of Operational Policies ('OPs'), Bank Procedures ('BPs') and Good Practice ('GP') documents. In most cases, the OP/BP/GP framework replaced a series of Operational Directives (or 'ODs') that had been issued earlier. Compliance with the OP and BPs can be evaluated by the Inspection Panel, but the GPs are not binding, and not subject to review by the Panel.

The WBG's private sector arms, the International Finance Corporation ('IFC') and Multilateral Investment Guarantee Agency ('MIGA') – which provide loans and guarantees for private sector investors – are covered by a different set of policies and by a different accountability system. The accountability mechanism for the IFC and MIGA is the Compliance Advisor/Ombudsman ('CAO'), which reports to the President of the WBG.[19] The IFC revised its policy framework as of 30 April 2006, and adopted a new environmental and social policy and 'performance standards'. The IFC's performance standards provide some new protections (for example, by including core labor standards), but in some instances they are weaker than the policies that they are replacing.[20] The new IFC approach was explicitly designed to be more flexible and discretionary; it depends heavily on self-reporting and self-monitoring by clients/borrowers, which include powerful international and national corporations. For the sake of clarity, it bears repeating that the World Bank Inspection Panel can only register

---

[16] In a 1999 resolution issued by the Board of Directors to clarify the role of the Inspection Panel, the Board deliberately excluded the Inspection Panel from having oversight over these corrective action plans. Again, this problem has been corrected at the ADB, where the Board has requested the Management to report to the CRP on the progress and timeline for corrective action, with the corrective actions based on recommendations made by the CRP and mandated by the Board.

[17] For an argument for systemic change at the World Bank to address the lack of institutional capacity for implementation of effective remedial measures in panel cases, see Dana L. Clark, 'The World Bank and Human Rights: The Need for Greater Accountability', *Harvard Human Rights Journal*, Vol. 15 (Spring 2002), pp. 205–226.

[18] A review of the Inspection Panel website (<www.inspectionpanel.org>) shows that of 35 registered claims at the time of writing this chapter, 26 (74 per cent of the

claims) alleged violations of the Environmental Assessment policy, 24 (68 per cent of the claims) alleged violations of the Project Supervision policy, 18 (51 per cent of the claims) alleged violations of the Indigenous Peoples policy, and 18 (51 per cent of the claims) alleged violations of the Involuntary Resettlement policy.

[19] For more information about the CAO, see <www.cao.org>.

[20] For an analysis of the IFC's new policies, see 'One Step Forward, One Step Back', Halifax Initiative (May 2006); see also <www.grrr-now.org>. The policy and performance standards are at <www.ifc.org>

claims brought against IBRD and IDA projects. Complaints against IFC and MIGA projects can be lodged with the CAO.

The evaluation of jurisprudence in the context of the Inspection Panel must be done in a more loose way than for more legalistic fora, as the Panel is not a legal proceeding, it does not formally decide cases, and it has not relied on principles of stare decisis in its decision-making. Claimants do not have an opportunity to appeal if they disagree with the Panel's findings, and, furthermore, the Panel's findings do not necessarily have binding effect. Rather, they are advisory to the Board of Directors, which has the responsibility for announcing what actions, if any, will be taken by the Bank in response to the Panel's findings and recommendations. Oversight and implementation of effective remedial measures remains ad hoc and elusive. The Panel's case history does, however, provide a window into the implementation of the environmental and social policy framework at the Bank. The remainder of this section will look at selected Panel jurisprudence relating to some of the key social and environmental policies – Environmental Assessment, Indigenous Peoples, and Involuntary Resettlement.

4.1 Environmental Assessment

The World Bank's policy on environmental assessment ('EA'), reflected in Operational Policy/Bank Procedure 4.01, has an overall objective of helping to ensure that projects proposed for Bank financing are environmentally sound and sustainable.[21] The EA policy covers the natural environment, human health and safety, transboundary and global impacts, and also social aspects such as involuntary resettlement and indigenous peoples. An environmental assessment process should include: evaluating the project's potential environmental risks and impacts; examining project alternatives; and identifying ways to improve project selection, siting, planning and implementation. The goal is to prevent, minimize, mitigate and compensate for any adverse environ-

mental impacts, and to enhance positive impacts, preferring prevention over mitigation whenever feasible.

The World Bank's EA policy also says that the Bank should take into account, among other things, 'the country's overall policy framework, national legislation, and institutional capabilities related to the environmental and social aspects; and obligations of the country, pertaining to project activities, under relevant international environmental treaties and agreements. The Bank does not finance project activities that would contravene such country obligations, as identified during the EA'.[22] An example of the Panel's application of the EA policy is contained in the Chad/Cameroon case study below.[23]

4.2 Indigenous Peoples

The World Bank Indigenous Peoples' policy, now OP 4.10, seeks to avoid or mitigate adverse effects of the project on indigenous peoples, and to ensure that they share in the development benefits associated with a project.[24] It articulates various characteristics that can help identify indigenous peoples, including:

(a) self-identification as members of a distinct indigenous cultural group and recognition of this identity by others;

---

[21] Operational Directive (OD) 4.01 on Environmental Assessment was replaced by Operational Policy/Bank Procedure (OP/BP) 4.01, which applies to projects reviewed on or after 1 March 1999.

[22] World Bank, OP 4.01 (1999), para. 3.
[23] Some of the other Inspection Panel cases alleging violations of the Environmental Assessment policy include: the Arun III hydroelectric project in Nepal; Jamuna Bridge project in Bangladesh; the Yacyretá hydroelectric project in Argentina and Paraguay (subject of two claims); the Itaparica Resettlement and Irrigation Project in Brazil; the NTPC Power Generation Project in Singrauli, India; the Lagos Drainage and Sanitation project in Nigeria; the China Western Poverty Alleviation Project, in Tibet; the Lake Victoria Environmental Management Project in Kenya; the Mining Development and Environmental Control Technical Assistance Project in Ecuador; the Coal Sector Environmental and Social Mitigation Project in India; Bujagali power project in Uganda; the Governance Promotion Adjustment loan in Papua New Guinea; the Cartagena water supply project in Colombia; the Mumbai Urban Transportation Project in India; and the Forest Management project in Cambodia. For copies of these claims, visit the Inspection Panel website at <www.inspectionpanel.org>.
[24] Operational Directive 4.20 on Indigenous Peoples was replaced by Operational Policy 4.10 in July 2005.

(b) collective attachment to geographically distinct habitats or ancestral territories in the project area and to the natural resources in the habitats and territories;

(c) customary cultural, economic, social or political institutions that are separate from those of the dominant society and culture; and

(d) an indigenous language, often different from the official language of the country or region.[25]

The policy requires that the Bank conduct a screening early on, to determine whether indigenous peoples are present in, or have a collective attachment to, the project area. This screening must include the technical judgment of qualified social scientists with expertise on the social and cultural groups in the area.

Operational Directive 4.20 also requires a process of free, prior, informed consultation with affected indigenous peoples, at each stage of the project, to identify their views and ascertain whether they have provided their broad community support for the project.[26] In the absence of broad community support, the World Bank will not proceed with a project.[27] If indigenous peoples will be affected by a project, the Bank requires the borrower to prepare an Indigenous Peoples Plan, to ensure that they receive culturally appropriate social and economic benefits and that any adverse effects are avoided, minimised, mitigated or compensated for.[28]

4.2.1. CHAD/CAMEROON PROJECT AND INSPECTION PANEL CLAIMS

Background on the Project

The Chad-Cameroon Oil Pipeline Project is the largest energy infrastructure project in Africa, composed of 300 oil wells in southern Chad and a 1,100 km export pipeline that traverses rainforests in Cameroon, inhabited by indigenous peoples, before leading offshore to feed into tanker ships that take the oil to Europe and North America for consumption.

The IBRD (public sector side) of the WBG provided $39.5 million in loans to the governments of Chad and Cameroon, to support their minority investments in the project, and the IFC (private sector side) provided $100 million to a multinational consortium of oil companies, ExxonMobil, Chevron and Petronas. The WBG's involvement in the Chad-Cameroon project provided not just a financial infusion, but also the political capital that cemented the $3.7 billion deal. At the time, the US State Department listed 'both Chad and Cameroon as major abusers of human rights and countries where citizens do not have the power to change their government via the electoral process',[29] and both countries ranked among the most corrupt in the world in Transparency International's index of corruption. The oil companies insisted on WBG participation to provide 'political risk insurance in a volatile region', to increase the legitimacy and stability of the project, and to help attract additional financing, which included 144 million Euro from the European Investment Bank, and investment by private commercial banks.[30]

Local groups in Chad and Cameroon, concerned about the dangers associated with an infusion of oil money to their governments, urged the World Bank to sequence its lending. They asked the Bank to focus first on building capacity in the countries to manage environmental risks, control revenues, provide for the equitable distribution of development benefits, strengthen the rule of law and good governance, and improve systems of accountability – to provide for the conditions for sustainable

---

[25] World Bank, Operational Policy on Indigenous Peoples, OP 4.10 (July 2005), para. 4.

[26] Ibid. paras. 6 (c), 10.

[27] Ibid. para. 11.

[28] Some of the cases alleging violations of the Indigenous Peoples policy include: the Arun III hydroelectric project in Nepal; the Rondonia Natural Resources Management Project in Brazil; the Yacyretá hydroelectric project in Argentina and Paraguay (the first of the two claims); the Itaparica resettlement project in Brazil; the NTPC Power Generation Project in Singrauli, India; the Ecodevelopment project in India; the China Western Poverty Alleviation Project in Tibet; the Ecuador Mining Development and Environmental Control Technical Assistance Project; the Chad/Cameroon claims; the Coal Sector Environmental and Social Mitigation Project in India; the Bujagali dam in Uganda; the COINBIO project in Mexico; the Cartagena water supply project in Colombia; the National Drainage Program Project in Pakistan; and the Cambodia Forestry project. <www.inspectionpanel.org>.

[29] K. Horta, 'Rhetoric and Reality: Human Rights and the World Bank', *Harvard Human Rights Journal*, Vol. 15 (Spring 2002), pp. 227–243, at p. 233.

[30] Ibid.

development before proceeding with financing of the pipeline.

While the Bank disregarded the civil society request for the sequencing of initiatives related to governance and capacity building prior to the oil investment, the project was modified in response to concerns raised by local and international civil society organisations. Capacity building was included as an objective of the Bank loans, and some changes were made to address some of the environmental risks. To help address the governance risks involved, the Bank required the Chadian government to adopt a new revenue management law, with some of the oil proceeds to be put aside for future generations.

Although there was armed conflict in the North, and a rebellion developing in the South of Chad at the time of the Board's consideration of the project, the Bank's Project Appraisal Document failed to mention or evaluate the risks to an oil pipeline of armed conflict, or the risk that the struggle for control of oil revenues could escalate the conflict.[31]

In fact, the diversion of oil revenues for arms purchases has been an ongoing source of tension in the project. Shortly after the oil started to flow, the Bank was embarrassed when the oil companies' very first payment to the Chadian Government bypassed the revenue management fund, and instead was used to purchase weapons. Then, in December 2005, the Government of Chad revised the revenue management law, abolishing the set-aside for future generations, allowing itself to divert the flow of oil funds to purchase weapons, and changing the oversight body. These actions were justified by assertions of national sovereignty over how to spend resources in light of a deteriorating security climate for the regime, including attacks from rebels backed by Sudan, and the regime's desire to maintain political survival. The Bank responded to the Chadian Government's change to the revenue management law by suspending all World Bank loans to Chad.[32]

The World Bank Inspection Panel Claims

There were two inspection panel claims filed on the Chad/Cameroon project, one from Chad in 2001, and one from Cameroon in 2002. In March 2001, Ngarlejy Yorongar, a representative of the oil fields region in Chad's National Assembly, filed a request for inspection on behalf of about 120 residents in the area.[33] The request alleged that the Bank had violated its Environmental Assessment, Indigenous Peoples, Cultural Heritage, Disclosure of Information, Involuntary Resettlement, Natural Habitats, Evaluation of Economic Investment Alternatives, Project Supervision, and Forests policies, among others. Environmental concerns included inadequate planning and management for oil spill contingencies; concerns about potential water pollution, including the contamination of Lake Chad; contamination, disruption or loss of local water supplies; and contamination of surface and groundwater from drilling operations. The requesters alleged that the Bank failed to notify and meaningfully consult indigenous people and their representatives.

In response to this first claim, the Panel found that the environmental assessment was too narrow, failing to properly evaluate the full impacts of the project.[34] The Panel found violations of OD 4.01, noting that the EA failed to include assessments of the regional, sectoral and cumulative impacts, particularly considering that 'it is very likely that the Project will lead to other energy development projects in the future' and that one of the major objectives was to assist the Government of Chad 'in developing the energy sector in a sustainable

---

officials still hope for a settlement that preserves the government's promise to use its oil money to build schools, clinics and roads rather than to support an army that has recently experienced a rash of defections among rebellious officers'.

[33] Mr. Yorongar was also a candidate for president and just before presidential elections in May 2001, he and five other opposition candidates were arrested. Mr. Yorongar was detained and tortured, until World Bank President James Wolfensohn personally intervened with a phone call to Chadian President Idriss Deby to secure the release of the opposition candidates. See J. Useem, 'Exxon's African Adventure', *Fortune Magazine*, 15 April 2002, p. 102. See also K. Horta, 'Rhetoric and Reality' (n. 29 above), p. 236.

[31] See Center for International Environmental Law, *Association Tchadienne pour la Promotion et la Defense des Droits de L'homme* (ATDPH), Environmental Defense, Chad-Cameroon Project Fact Sheet, 15 May 2000, p. 1–2.

[32] See 'Chad's Oil Riches, Meant for Poor, Are Diverted', *The New York Times*, 18 February 2006, which notes that: 'High level talks in Paris to resolve the crisis with Chad ended inconclusively this month, though World Bank

[34] World Bank Inspection Panel, 'Investigation Report, Chad-Cameroon Petroleum and Pipeline Project; Petroleum Sector Management Capacity Building Project; and Management of the Petroleum Economy' (July 2002) ('Investigation Report Chad').

manner'.[35] The Panel found that particularly in the early stages of the project, some consultations had taken place in the presence of security forces, and stated that 'full and informed consultation is impossible if those consulted perceive that they could be penalized for expressing their opposition to, or honest opinions about, a Bank financed project'.[36] However, the Panel found OD 4.20 to be inapplicable, having determined that the people in the project area in southern Chad did not fit the definition of indigenous peoples.[37] In response to the Panel's findings, Bank management presented an action plan, approved by the Board in September 2002.

Also in September 2002, the Center for the Environment and Development, based in Cameroon, filed a request for inspection on behalf of people affected by the export component of the project. In Cameroon, the pipeline traverses forest areas inhabited by Bakola/Bagyeli pygmies. The pygmies, famously small in stature, are marginalised and vulnerable to mistreatment and physical abuse by the more dominant Bantu population living in the same area. They have low literacy rates, poor access to health care and social services, and higher mortality rates than the population at large, and have little influence in the community. For these reasons, the Panel considered the Bakola/Bagyeli pygmies a 'vulnerable population' subject to the requirements of OD 4.20.

The requesters alleged that the Indigenous Peoples Plan was not in compliance with Bank policy and that due to delays in launching mitigation efforts, the Bakola were deprived of the benefits of that mitigation. The Panel report in May 2003 found that OD 4.20 had been violated because the Bank failed to conduct a regional assessment, taking into account resources used by the Bakola/Bagyeli outside of the immediate project area. It also found that environmental and social capacity building was lacking, in violation of the environmental assessment policy. With regards to mitigation delays, the Panel found no policy violation, citing the 'in process' nature of the Indigenous Peoples Plan.[38]

In December 2005, the Chadian National Assembly revised the revenue management law. The World Bank, noting that these changes amounted to a breach of contract, suspended new loans to Chad and disbursements under eight other World Bank loans. This also triggered a freeze on oil revenues that passed through a Citibank account in London.[39] On 6 January 2006, the World Bank suspended all loans to Chad. The coincidence between World Bank President Paul Wolfowitz freezing loans to Chad a few months before freezing loans to India in the context of the Mumbai Urban Transit Project, described below, is interesting and in need of further exploration.

Shortly after the suspension of loans, Delphine Djiraibe of the Chadian Association for the Promotion and Defense of Human Rights stated:

> We agree with the World Bank's decision to suspend funding for Chad because new money would mainly be used for military purposes and increased repression of the Chadian people. But we regret that the Bank did not listen to the warnings of civil society organizations earlier because now we face greater poverty and severe environmental problems as a result of this mega-project.[40]

Shortly thereafter, President Deby of Chad threatened to freeze all oil exports. In late April, the Bank entered into an interim agreement with Chad to resume lending on certain loans, with a promise from the regime that 70 per cent of oil revenues would be used for poverty alleviation efforts.

The Chad/Cameroon situation provides a rare example of heightened Bank supervision, leading to enforcement of loan conditions that had been insisted upon by local and international civil society organisations. However, the Inspection Panel's role in the case was fairly limited, and demonstrates that a Panel claim is often just one element in a broader civil society toolkit of engagement around problem projects and their various sponsors. In this case, ongoing vigilance by civil

---

[35] Ibid. p. 13–14.
[36] Ibid. p. xiv–xv.
[37] Ibid. p. xvi.
[38] World Bank Inspection Panel, 'Investigation Report, Cameroon: Petroleum Development and Pipeline Project and Petroleum Environment Capacity Enhancement

Project', (2 May 2003) ('Investigation Report Cameroon'), pp. xxii–xxiii.
[39] World Bank website, FAQ on the Chad-Cameroon Pipeline Project, <www.worldbank.org> (accessed 23 June 2006).
[40] Press Release, 'World Bank Suspension of Loans to Chad: What Comes Next?', 9 January 2006 (copy on file with author).

society, holding the Bank accountable to commitments made in the course of the project, made a critical difference in the terms of the deal, and in the way the project has been monitored and enforced.

4.3   Involuntary Resettlement

The objective of the IBRD and IDA's Involuntary Resettlement policy is to ensure that people who are displaced by a World Bank-financed project – who face the risks of losing their homes, their lands and/or their livelihoods – should also see benefits from the project, and should have their standards of living improved, and their livelihoods at least restored.[41] The policy calls for avoiding and minimising displacement through the exploration of alternative project designs, and, if displacement is unavoidable, it requires the reduction and mitigation of impacts. Valuation of and compensation for lost assets, provision of a choice of acceptable alternative sites, community participation in project planning, integration with the host/receiving population, and environmental protection are among the things that should be addressed in resettlement plans, which must also include a timetable and budget.

Accomplishment of the policy's objectives has been challenging, and many reviews have shown that, in the vast majority of cases, people displaced by World Bank-financed projects have seen their livelihoods and standards of living decline, rather than improve.[42] Inspection Panel cases have frequently been brought by people who have suffered from the impacts of involuntary resettlement.[43]

In some cases, the claims have triggered action plans or revised compensation programs that have sought to address some of the shortcomings.

4.3.1. THE SINGRAULI INSPECTION PANEL CASE

Three hundred thousand people have been displaced in the Singrauli region of India, initially by the Rihand dam, and subsequently by the development and expansion of coal mines and power plants. The World Bank has been a key player in the industrialisation of Singrauli, beginning with its first loan to the National Thermal Power Corporation (NTPC) in 1976. In 1993, the World Bank provided $400 million, intended to be the first of three loans totaling $1.2 billion, to expand the capacity of two coal-fired power plants operated by NTPC in Singrauli. This expansion necessitated the acquisition of more land, including for the disposal of fly ash. The ash is a waste by-product of combustion of the coal in the power plants; the ash is then mixed with water to form a slurry. Ever-expanding waste disposal pits, known as ash dikes, are carved out of prime agricultural and residential land, and filled with grey sludge. To address the new wave of involuntary resettlement, and to also address the negative environmental and social impacts of earlier NTPC and World Bank projects in Singrauli, the 1993 World Bank loan included an Environmental Action Plan, two Resettlement Action Plans and three Remedial Action Plans.

In May 1997, families who would be displaced by ash dikes from the Rihand power plant submitted a request for inspection to the Panel, focusing primarily on the harm caused by violations of the Bank's involuntary resettlement policy, among others. In June 1997, the Panel briefly visited the project area to evaluate the eligibility of the complaint, and in July 1997 it reported to the Board that it found the claim eligible, having found prima facie evidence of harm caused by serious violations of OD 4.30 and recommended a full inspection.

---

[41] Operational Policy/Bank Procedure 4.12 applies to projects reviewed after 1 January 2002 and replaced Operational Directive 4.30.

[42] The most comprehensive review of resettlement projects in the Bank's portfolio was the 1994–1995 review of resettlement, 'Resettlement and Development: The Report of the Bankwide Resettlement Review', which evaluated all of the projects in the bank portfolio with resettlement components. It has been more than a decade since such an effort was undertaken, and there is no systematic record-keeping or reporting on the number of people displaced by Bank-financed projects each year, nor their rehabilitation status over time.

[43] Inspection Panel cases alleging violations of the Involuntary Resettlement Policy have included: the Arun III dam in Nepal; the Jamuna Bridge Project in Bangladesh; the Yacyretá hydroelectric project in Argentina and Paraguay (both claims); the Itaparica resettlement project in Brazil; the NTPC Power Generation project in Singrauli, India;

the Ecodevelopment project in India; the Lagos Drainage and Sanitation project in Nigeria; the China Western Poverty Alleviation project in Tibet; the Chad/Cameroon pipeline project; the Coal Sector Environmental and Social Mitigation project in India; the Bujagali power project in Uganda; the Mumbai Urban Transportation project in India; and the National Drainage Program Project in Pakistan.

Due to opposition from the Indian government, the Board would authorise only a desk review; the Panel could not return to India for a thorough investigation. Nonetheless, after conducting its Washington-based investigation, the Panel found serious violations of the involuntary resettlement policy. These violations were attributed in part to pressure from World Bank management to accelerate approval of the NTPC loan before to the end of the Bank's fiscal year. As a result, the Bank failed to ensure that the NTPC had sufficient commitment and capacity to appropriately handle the complex resettlement and rehabilitation aspects of the project.[44]

In response to the Inspection Panel claim, the Indian government implemented an improved compensation package for about 1,200 families. While this revision to the compensation package was not enough to bring the project into compliance with the requirements of the resettlement policy, it was seen as a critically important step for those families that did receive the package.[45]

4.3.2. MUMBAI URBAN TRANSPORT PROJECT

More recently, Operational Policy 4.12 on involuntary resettlement was the subject of several claims brought on behalf of persons being displaced by the Mumbai Urban Transportation Project (MUTP) in India, including shop owners and slum dwellers. The MUTP was designed to revamp Mumbai's overcrowded railways and road-based transportation systems. The project included the resettlement and rehabilitation of more than 100,000 people from urban households and business. The World Bank provided US $542 million in loans for the US $942 million project.

The claims, considered jointly by the Inspection Panel,[46] alleged that in failing to provide for the restoration of living standards for project affected persons, the Bank had violated its involuntary resettlement policy, which expressly requires the

standards of living of displaced persons to be improved or at least restored to pre-displacement levels. One request, filed by the United Shop Owners Association, also objected to the arbitrary allocation of 225 square feet to each displaced business, regardless of the size of the area taken for the project. The request further complained that shop owners were instructed, without consultation or consent, to move their shops to distant locations, destroying their livelihoods and causing dispersal of supportive kinship groups.[47] Another request, filed on behalf of residents in the Gazi Nagar area of the city, raised similar allegations and also included claims involving sanitation problems and the environmental contamination and unsuitability of one proposed resettlement site, located in one of the most polluted areas in Mumbai.

After investigating these claims, the Inspection Panel issued a report in January 2005, documenting serious violations of the Bank's policy on involuntary resettlement. One finding concerned problems relating to environmental and living conditions at resettlement sites, including the fact that many displaced persons were not receiving adequate access to water and sewage. The report also documented inadequate income restoration, found that the needs of the low- and middle-income shopkeepers had been overlooked, and found flaws in the consultation and grievance procedures.

On 1 March 2006, the World Bank temporarily suspended financial support for the road and resettlement components of the project, until concerns about the treatment of project affected persons are resolved. In a press release, World Bank President Paul Wolfowitz said: '[T]he flaws identified by the Inspection Panel need to be addressed with urgency now. The Report proves the worth of the Inspection Panel'.[48] The Bank's suspension was apparently acceptable to Maharashtra, the state government that borrowed from the Bank, which

---

[44] World Bank Inspection Panel, 'Report on Desk Investigation, India: NTPC Power Generation Project', (22 December 1997).

[45] For a longer discussion of Singrauli, see D. Clark, 'Singrauli: An Unfulfilled Struggle for Justice', in D. Clark, J. Fox and K. Treakle, (eds.) *Demanding Accountability* (Lanham, Md: Rowman & Littlefield Publishers, Inc., 2003), p. 233.

[46] World Bank Inspection Panel, 'Investigation Report, India: Mumbai Urban Transport Project', (9 January 2006), p. 12–13.

[47] The secretary of the United Shop Owners Association was subsequently arrested and jailed by the State government, on grounds of drug dealing and extortion; his allies maintain that the charges are baseless and the arrest was an attempt to silence a vocal critic of the project. See 'Medha Slams Mumbai Urban Transport Project', *The Hindu*, available at <www.thehindu.com/2006/02/16/stories/2006021604421300.htm>.

[48] World Bank, News Release: Inspection Panel: MUTP (29 March 2006).

was not interested in meeting World Bank policy requirements on resettlement. The newspaper DNA reported that:

> World Bank will no longer be the state government's 'most preferred bank.' Upset with the bank's 'illogical' policies on resettlement and rehabilitation, the government has decided not to borrow money from the bank. The state's next preferred partner is Japan, along with some Indian financial institutions.... the Mumbai Urban Transportation Project (MUTP) will be the last big project with the World Bank's involvement. 'It was our oversight that we signed an agreement, which said those displaced can't be worst off. Technically, we are safe as the policy is not applicable to shopkeepers, something which the bank is not willing to accept,' said a senior bureaucrat. The government is miffed over the bank's policy of sending inspection teams to rehabilitated areas.[49]

5. USING THE INSPECTION PANEL TO ADVANCE SOCIO-ECONOMIC RIGHTS

The creation of the World Bank Inspection Panel constituted an important innovation in citizen-based access to systems of accountability. The Panel has had dramatic institutional impacts and has succeeded in raising the awareness amongst Bank staff of the importance of complying with safeguard policies, including those that have direct impacts on the socio-economic rights of affected people. There are, however, aspects of the process that limit its accessibility and its effectiveness as an instrument of accountability.

The 95 per cent cut-off on eligibility was likely included for a number of reasons – not least of which was to avoid retroactive claims against closed projects, such as Sardar Sarovar. The rule also reflects the Bank's concern that it loses influence over government implementation once the funds are disbursed, and that it is harder to rec-

[49] S. Deshmukh, 'State Spurns World Bank, Looks for Love in Tokyo', DNA Mumbai (18 May 2006), p. 5.

tify problems if there are no longer loan proceeds available. Note, however, that this constraint argues not so much for limiting access to an accountability function, but rather for the need to include additional checks and balances in project financing, including the use of environmental and social contingency funds which can be available if and when problems arise during project implementation.

Also needed is the establishment of improved systems of accountability at the Board level, to ensure that there is appropriate monitoring and follow-up on the action plans in all Inspection Panel cases, including implementation of action plans that will actually strive to bring projects back into compliance. This will require developing the Bank's capacity to design and implement effective remedial measures. First and foremost, remedial action planning should be developed in consultation with affected people, including claimants, and the action plans must reflect their priorities for mitigation and development. Furthermore, the Bank and the Panel need to evaluate the means for leverage and persuasion in their relationship with the borrowers, both to ensure the policies are committed to and complied with from the beginning, as well as ensure that corrective measures are implemented if problems arise and/or policies are violated.

One way of moving towards this goal would be for the Bank to take at least partial responsibility for the additional costs associated with bringing flawed or failed projects into compliance. The Panel process, by definition, works to establish that the Bank has or has not acted in violation of its own policies and procedures. In situations where it is established that the Bank did violate its policies, and local people were harmed as a result, it is reasonable to expect the Bank to bear some financial and institutional responsibility for at least part of the mitigation of and reparation needed to address that harm. This lack of capacity to rectify the harm done and develop effective remedial measures has turned out to be a fundamental flaw in the effectiveness of the World Bank Inspection Panel as a tool for true accountability.

Notes on Contributors

Cathy Albisa is the Executive Director of the National Economic and Social Rights Initiative (NESRI). Ms. Albisa has significant experience working in partnership with community organisers in the use of human rights standards to strengthen advocacy in the United States, and co-founded NESRI along with Sharda Sekaran and Liz Sullivan in order to build legitimacy for human rights in general, and economic and social rights in particular, in the United States. She is committed to a community centred and participatory human rights approach that is locally anchored but universal and global in its vision. Ms. Albisa also formerly directed the U.S. program at the Center for Economic and Social Rights, was the Associate Director at the Human Rights Institute at Columbia Law School, co-taught the International Women's Human Rights Clinic at CUNY Law School and litigated constitutional cases at the American Civil Liberties Union and the Center for Reproductive Rights. Ms. Albisa is a graduate of Columbia Law School.

Iain Byrne is a Senior Lawyer for the Commonwealth with additional responsibility for leading litigation work on economic and social rights at INTERIGHTS. He has litigated widely in domestic fora across the Commonwealth and beyond and before the UN Human Rights Committee and the European Committee of Social Rights. Recent European Social Charter cases include sexual and reproductive health rights education in Croatia; health rights of prisoners in Bulgaria and the housing rights of the Roma in Greece addressing systematic and ongoing forced evictions. Since 2000 he has been a Fellow of the Human Rights Centre, University of Essex. He has taught for many years on both the LLM and MA Human Rights courses at the University of Essex focusing on economic, social and cultural rights. He has conducted training courses for the United Nations,

Amnesty International and the British Council in Europe, Latin America, Africa, South Asia and the Pacific. In April 2007 he was Visiting Professor at the Human Rights Centre, UN University of Peace, Costa Rica. He was previously Research Officer and then an Associate of the University's Democratic Audit project, carrying out British Council consultancy projects in Palestine and Zimbabwe and currently sits on the Advisory Board. He has authored numerous articles, papers and books on human rights and democracy including *Unequal Britain: an ESR Audit of the UK* with Stuart Weir et al. He is currently co-authoring *The Judicial Protection of ESR in South Asia* which is due to be published by OUP in 2008.

Danwood Mzikenge Chirwa is a Associate Professor in the Law Faculty at the University of Cape Town (UCT), where he lectures in human rights law and administrative law. He was admitted to practise law in Malawi in January 2001. He is a holder of degrees from the Universities of Malawi, Pretoria, and the Western Cape. Before he joined UCT, he worked as a doctoral researcher in the Socio-Economic Rights Project of the Community Law Centre between 2002 and 2004. He also practised law with the firm of Savjani & Company of Malawi from March 2000 to April 2002. Dr. Chirwa has published more than twenty articles in international journals and chapters in books in the fields of socio-economic rights, the horizontal application of human rights, children's rights, privatisation, women's rights, and the protection of human rights under the Malawian Constitution.

Robin Churchill is Professor of International Law at the University of Dundee (United Kingdom). He was formerly professor of law at Cardiff University and has also worked at the University of Tromsö (Norway) and the British Institute of International and Comparative Law. He has also been a visiting fellow at the University of Wollongong (Australia) and the European University Institute. His principal research interests are the international law of the sea, international environmental law and human rights. In the field of human rights he has written on the European Social Charter, the EU and human rights and the impact of the European Convention of Human Rights on British law.

Dana Clark is the Corporate Accountability Director at Rainforest Action Network and is President of the International Accountability Project. From 1994–2000, Ms. Clark worked with the Center for International Environmental Law, where she served as Director of the International Financial Institutions program. She is a co-author and co-editor of *Demanding Accountability: Civil Society Claims and the World Bank Inspection Panel* (Rowman & Littlefield, 2003), and has written numerous other publications about accountability of international financial institutions (IFIs) and development-induced displacement. In 2003, she founded the International Accountability Project, an organisation that supports people seeking to hold IFIs accountable for violations of environmental and human rights, and that helps defend the rights of communities threatened with displacement by international development projects. In 2006, Ms. Clark joined the Global Finance Campaign at the Rainforest Action Network, where she brings her expertise on accountability and implementation of environmental and social policies to bear on the private sector banks. Ms. Clark is a 1992 graduate of the University of Virginia School of Law.

Luke Clements is a solicitor, a Professor in Law at Cardiff University and Associate Fellow of the Department of Social Policy and Applied Social Studies at the University of Warwick. He has taken many cases to the European Commission and Court of Human Rights on behalf of socially excluded people and written widely on social exclusion, particularly the rights of disabled people and Roma.

Christian Courtis is the Legal Officer for Economic, Social and Cultural Right at the International Commission of Jurists, Geneva. He is also a law professor at the University of Buenos Aires Law School, and invited professor at ITAM Law School, Mexico City. He was a visiting/invited scholar in several universities including the Universities of Toulouse-Le Mirail (France), Castilla-La Mancha,

Deusto, Pablo de Olavide (Valencia), Carlos III (Madrid), University of California (Berkeley), the European Masters Program on Human Rights and Democratization (Venice), the International Institute of Sociology of Law, Oñati Diego Portales, Nacional Autónoma de Honduras, amongst others. He has acted as consultant for the World/Panamerican Health Organisation, UNESCO and the UN Division for Social Development and was a lawyer for Centro de Estudios Legales y Sociales (CELS), legal counsel for the Argentine Senate, and legal clerk for the Buenos Aires Supreme Court. He has worked in legal reform issues in Latin American, Caribbean and African countries and has published books and articles on human rights, constitutional law, legal theory and sociology of law.

Andrea Durbach is Associate Professor at the Faculty of Law, University of New South Wales and Director of UNSW's Australian Human Rights Centre. Born and educated in South Africa, she practised as a political trial lawyer and human rights advocate, representing victims and opponents of apartheid laws. After leaving South Africa in 1989, she worked as a solicitor at Freehills in Sydney and in 1991, she joined the Public Interest Advocacy Centre (PIAC), and was its Director between 1997 and 2004. Her teaching and research has a distinct focus on public interest litigation, legal ethics, access to justice, and economic, social and cultural rights. She is member of various boards, including the Advisory Council of Jurists, Asia Pacific Forum of National Human Rights Institutions and the New South Wales Legal Aid Board.

Leilani Farha is the Director of the Women's Program at CERA – Centre for Equality Rights in Accommodation. CERA is a non-profit human rights organization based in Canada that uses both domestic and international human rights law to address issues of homelessness and poverty. Leilani Farha has been working to promote and protect women's economic and social rights both domestically and internationally for almost 15 years. Much of her work has focused on exposing the relationship between women's everyday experiences of poverty, homelessness, and housing disadvantage, and human rights norms and practice. To this end, she has engaged in pioneering litigation, advocacy, legal standard setting and research internationally and in Canada. Leilani helped to spearhead and author the Montreal Principles on the meaning and application of economic and social rights for women, and has published widely on a variety of economic and social rights issues.

Colin Fenwick is the Director of the Centre for Employment and Labour Relations Law at the University of Melbourne, where he is a Senior Lecturer in the Faculty of Law. He is also one of the editors of the *Australian Journal of Labour Law*. Mr. Fenwick's research interests lie predominantly in comparative and international labour law, particularly labour law in Southern Africa, and the effectiveness of human rights law as a means of promoting workers' interests.

Enrique González is a human rights and social activist and researcher. He was born in Spain but has been based in Venezuela for the past 11 years. He worked for Provea, a leading national NGO promoting economic, social and cultural rights (ESCR) (1995–98), ACCSI (human rights and HIV/AIDs) and Cecodap (children's rights). He took part in the Circle of Rights Project (1999–2002), organised by Forum Asia and the International Human Rights Internship Programme (IHIRP), which was aimed at developing global ESCR training tools for activists. He was co-facilitator of two global ESCR training courses, organised by Dignity International and IHRIP in Portugal (2002–03), and in 2004 he took part in the Analyzing Budgets from a Rights Perspective Project (IHRIP, Fundar, International Budget Project). He has also been human rights advisor to the Ombudsperson office, and has recently done research for the National Commission for Police Reform. He is the author of several human rights training manuals and research articles.

Sara Hossain is a barrister at the law firm of Dr. Kamal Hossain and Associates, and has practiced as an advocate in the Supreme Court of Bangladesh since 1992, in the areas of constitutional law, human rights and public interest litigation. She is a member of Ain o Salish Kendra (ASK), a national human rights organisation. She has been engaged in litigation, research and advocacy on the rights to livelihood and shelter, access to water, health and safety in the workplace; choice in marriage; and freedom of association of non-governmental organisations. While serving as Legal Officer for South Asia at INTERIGHTS, London she worked on amicus briefs for the European

Court of Human Rights and for superior courts in South Asia on among others cases challenging laws regarding the prosecution of rape and the non-criminalisation of marital rape, and also conducted a multi-country research project on 'honour-based' crimes of violence against women which included policy and casework on forced marriage. She was educated at Oxford University and called to the Bar of England and Wales from Middle Temple. She writes and speaks on access to justice, domestic application of human rights norms, public interest litigation and women's rights. Her most recent publication is *'Honour': Crimes, Paradigms and Violence against Women* (ed.), with Lynn Welchman, Zed Books, London 2005.

Martha Jackman, B.A. (Queen's), LL.B. (Toronto), LL.M. (Yale), is a Professor of constitutional law at the University of Ottawa. She has published and lectured extensively on socio-economic rights, equality and the *Canadian Charter*, and is regularly involved in lobbying, litigation and continuing judicial and legal education in these areas, most recently as counsel for the Charter Committee on Poverty Issues in the *Chaoulli* case. She is the academic director of the Social Rights Accountability Project; a former member of the Equality Rights Panel of the Court Challenges Program of Canada; and a recipient of the Augusta Stowe-Gullen Affirmative Action Medal for her work in advancing women's equality.

Sarah Joseph is a Professor of Law at Monash University, Melbourne, and the Director of the Castan Centre for Human Rights Law. She has written numerous publications in various areas of human rights, including business and human rights, the World Trade Organization (WTO) and human rights, terrorism and human rights, freedom from torture, and the right of self-determination. Her books include the co-authored *The International Covenant on Civil and Political Rights: Cases Commentary and Materials* (OUP, 2004), *Seeking Remedies for Torture Victims* (OMCT, 2006) and the sole authored *Corporations and Transnational Human Rights Litigation* (Hart, 2004). She is also an expert in Australian constitutional law, is a lead investigator on two Australian Research Council funded grants, and has acted as a human rights consultant on numerous occasions to government and intergovernmental bodies, NGOs and businesses.

Urfan Khaliq is a senior lecturer in European Union, Public International and Human Rights Law at Cardiff Law School, Cardiff University in the United Kingdom and was a Visiting Research Scholar at the University of Michigan, Ann Arbor, in 2005. He is currently a member of the Research Consultant's Panel at Matrix Chambers in Gray's Inn London. He was formerly a researcher in international law at the Faculty of Law, Southampton University also in the United Kingdom. He is the author of a number of articles on international, European Union and human rights law and *Ethical Dimensions of the Foreign Policy of the European Union: A Legal Appraisal* (Cambridge: Cambridge University Press, 2008), which examines the international legal issues which arise when international organisations, such as the European Union, decide to integrate an 'ethical dimension' into their foreign policy formulation.

Jeff A. King is a Fellow and Tutor in Law at Balliol College, University of Oxford, and a member of the Bar of New York. He previously held posts as a Research Fellow and Tutor in Public Law at Keble College, Oxford, a Legal Officer at the Centre on Housing Rights and Evictions, a Legal Research Fellow at the Centre for International Sustainable Development Law, and as an attorney at Sullivan and Cromwell LLP. His research focuses on social rights, administrative law, constitutional law, jurisprudence, comparative and international human rights law, international law of sovereign debt, and empirical legal studies. His primary concern is the role and competence of courts in welfare rights adjudication, and more generally with how law can be used to improve the situation of the socio-economically marginalised.

Malcolm Langford is a Research Fellow at the Norwegian Centre on Human Rights University of Oslo. Between 2001 and 2006, he worked as a Senior Legal Officer at the Centre on Housing Rights and Eviction (COHRE), an international housing rights organisation based in Geneva. He is also a Research Associate with the Australian Human Rights Centre University of NSW and was previously a Visiting Fellow at the University of Mannheim. He has been at the forefront at the development of new international human rights standards and regularly advises various UN agencies and NGOs on human rights and development issues. He lectures and teaches on economic, social and cultural rights and has published widely in human rights, economics and law. He continues to assist with social rights litigation and advocacy projects in many regions of the world in collaboration with local and international organisations.

Sandra Liebenberg currently holds the H.F. Oppenheimer Chair in Human Rights Law in the Law Faculty of the University of Stellenbosch, where she teaches constitutional and human rights law. She previously served as a member of the Technical Committee advising the Constitutional Assembly on the Bill of Rights in the 1996 Constitution of South Africa. She founded and directed the Socio-Economic Rights Project based at the Community Law Centre (University of the Western Cape) where she was involved in research, advocacy and supporting litigation in the area of socio-economic rights. In this capacity she was involved in the Centre's *amicus curiae* interventions in the groundbreaking cases of *Government of South Africa v Grootboom, Minister of Health & Ors v Treatment Action Campaign & Ors*, and *President of the RSA and Another v Modderklip Boerdery (Pty) Ltd*, and other cases. She has published widely in the field of socio-economic rights and her board memberships includes the *South African Journal on Human Rights* and the *African Human Rights Law Journal*.

Tara J. Melish is a human rights attorney and legal specialist in comparative social rights protections. She has taught on the law faculties of the Universities of Notre Dame, Oxford, George Washington, Virginia, Georgia, St. Thomas, and Åbo Akademi. She has likewise served as staff attorney and legal advisor to the Center for Justice and International Law; as United Nations representative of Mental Disability Rights International in the drafting negotiations of the UN Convention on the Rights of Persons with Disabilities and its Optional Protocol; and as Associate Social Affairs Officer in the UN Department of Economic and Social Affairs. Active in reporting procedures and litigation initiatives before UN and OAS bodies, she serves as consultant or counsel to a range of domestic and international organizations, has published and lectured widely on social rights protections, and has conducted human rights trainings in over a dozen countries on social rights, women's rights, disability rights, indigenous rights, and the use of regional and UN human rights systems to effect domestic rights protections. She has degrees from Brown University and the Yale Law School.

S. Muralidhar was appointed judge of the Delhi High Court in May 2006. Since 1987 he practised as an advocate in the Supreme Court of India, with cases concerning constitutional law, election law, criminal law, human rights, legal aid and public interest litigation. He was previously the lawyer for the victims of the Bhopal Gas Tragedy, pursuing their cases in the Supreme Court for monetary compensation, medical relief and rehabilitation. He served as a member of the Supreme Court Legal Services Committee from 2000 to 2004 and is a visiting faculty at the National Judicial Academy in Bhopal. He has written and spoken widely on access to justice, public interest litigation, economic, social and cultural rights and the death penalty. His book titled *Law, Poverty and Legal Aid: Access to Criminal Justice* was released in August 2004. Dr. Muralidhar earned his doctorate from the University of Delhi and was a part-time Member of the Law Commission of India between 2002 and 2006.

Aoife Nolan is Assistant Director of the Human Rights Centre and Law Lecturer at Queen's University Belfast. She has previously worked as a Senior Legal Officer with the Economic, Social and Cultural Rights Litigation Programme at the Centre on Housing Rights and Evictions, where she has conducted research and participated in litigation in the area of socio-economic rights. Her primary areas of research and teaching are economic and social rights, children's rights and constitutional law. She has written and been published on these topics. Amongst other activities, she is Coordinating Editor of the Housing & ESC Rights Law Quarterly and has served as a Council of Europe Expert on economic and social rights. In 2007–2008, she was Legal Adviser to the Working Group on Economic and Social Rights, including Relevant Equality Issues, of the Northern Ireland Bill of Rights Forum. In early 2008, she provided legal advice to members of the NGO Coalition for an OP-ICESCR. She is co-investigator on a research project on 'Budget Analysis and the Advancement of Social and Economic Rights in Northern Ireland', which is based at the Human Rights Centre, Queen's University Belfast. She is currently working on a monograph on children's socio-economic rights, democracy and the courts, which will be published by Hart Publishing in 2009.

Laurent Pech is *Jean Monnet* Lecturer in EU Public Law at the National University of Ireland, Galway (NUIG). He holds a Doctorate in Law and a master's degree in Public Law from the Faculty of Law of Aix-en-Provence (France). He currently teaches Constitutional Law of the EU, the Law of the European Internal Market and EC Competition Law. Before joining NUIG in 2004, he was a Postdoctoral Research Fellow at the Canada Research Chair on Globalization, Citizenship and Democracy. He has published a book on the right to free speech in the United States and in Europe and several articles in the field of fundamental rights. He is now working on a book that explores the current juridical status of the European Union and addresses a number of assumptions about its constitutional status.

Flávia Piovesan is a professor of Constitutional Law and Human Rights at the Catholic University of São Paulo. She also teaches human rights at the Catholic University of Paraná and Pablo de Olavide University (Spain). In 2005, she was a human rights fellow at the Centre for Brazilian Studies, University of Oxford, and in 2007–2008 she was a visiting fellow at the Max-Planck Institute for Comparative Public Law and International Law. She was previously a São Paulo State Attorney, and the coordinator of the São Paulo State Attorney-General's Office Working Group on Human Rights from 1996 to 2001. She has written many books on human rights, including *Direitos Humanos e o Direito Constitucional Internacional* (10th edition), *Temas de Direitos Humanos* (3rd edition), *Proteção Judicial contra Omissões Legislativas* (2nd edition) and *Direitos Humanos e Justiça Internacional: estudo comparado dos sistemas regionais interamericano, europeu e africano*. She is the co-author of *A Figura/Personagem Mulher em Processos de Família*.

Bruce Porter is a human rights researcher and advocate. He is the Director of the Social Rights Advocacy Centre, the Co-ordinator of the Charter Committee on Poverty Issues (CCPI) and Community Director of the Social Rights Accountability Project. He has been active internationally in advocating for ESC rights and promoting reform of UN treaty monitoring procedures in this area. He is serving currently as a member of the Steering Committee of the NGO Coalition for an OP-ICESCR. He has published widely on social and economic rights and poverty issues, has been involved in judicial education both in Canada and internationally, and has provided expert evidence in a number of test cases in Canada dealing with the rights of poor people.

Nathalie Prouvez, now Secretary of the Human Rights Committee, Secretary of the Committee on the Elimination of Racial Discrimination at the United Nations Office of the High Commissioner for Human Rights (OHCHR) from 2002 to mid 2008. From 1995 to 2001, she was Legal Officer at the International Commission of Jurists (ICJ) in Geneva. She was responsible for ICJ activities in Europe and Central Asia and programmes relating to economic, social and cultural rights and racial discrimination. She lectured in public international law, international human rights law and European Union law at the Universities of Warwick (1987–1989), Lancaster (1989–1991) and Cambridge (1991–1995), where she was Assistant Director of the Centre for European Legal Studies at the Law Faculty and Fellow of Newham College.

Kent Roach is a Professor of Law at the University of Toronto in Canada, where he holds the Prichard-Wilson Chair in Law and Public Policy, and is a graduate of the University of Toronto and Yale Law Schools. He is the author of eight books including *Constitutional Remedies in Canada* (winner of the 1997 Owen Prize) and *The Supreme Court on Trial: Judicial Activism or Democratic Dialogue* (short listed for the 2001 Donner Prize). He is the co-author of the *Charter of Rights and Freedoms* (3rd edition, 2005) and the co-editor of *Global Anti-Terrorism Law and Policy* published by Cambridge University Press in 2005. In 2002, he was elected a Fellow of the Royal Society of Canada. In addition to his academic work in Canada and abroad, Professor Roach has frequently appeared as counsel for civil society groups before the Supreme Court of Canada.

Martin Scheinin is Professor of Public International Law at the European University Institute in Florence and currently he serves also as UN Special Rapporteur on Human Rights and Counter-Terrorism. Until August 2008 he was Professor of Constitutional and International Law at Åbo Akademi University where he also served as Director of the Institute for Human Rights. Prof. Scheinin has held a number of human-rights-related positions. Between 1997 and 2004, he was a member of the UN Human Rights Committee.

He has authored or edited a number of books, including *International Human Rights Norms in the Nordic and Baltic Countries, The Jurisprudence of Human Rights Law – A Comparative Interpretative Approach, Constitutionalism and the Welfare State in the Nordic Countries* and *Leading Cases of the Human Rights Committee.* He is also the author of some 200 articles, some dealing with the legal nature and justiciability of economic, social and cultural rights.

Jessica Schultz is a lawyer with a specialization in international human rights and refugee law. After a two-year position with the Ford Foundation in New York focused on humanitarian protection, transitional justice, and social and economic rights, she moved to Africa to work with both UNHCR and Oxfam GB as a protection officer for refugees and internally displaced populations. Jessica now coordinates the Bergen-based U4 Anti-Corruption Resource Centre, which supports bilateral donor agencies in their efforts to reduce corruption as an obstacle to the enjoyment of basic rights.

Magdalena Sepúlveda is a Chilean lawyer who holds a Ph.D. in International Law from Utrecht University and an LL.M. in Human Rights from University of Essex. She is Research Director at the International Council on Human Rights Policy in Geneva. She serves also as UN Independent Expert on the question of human rights and extreme poverty. Before joining the Council, Ms. Sepulveda was the Co-Director of the Department of International Law and Human Rights of the United Nations–affiliated University for Peace in Costa Rica. She has also worked as a researcher at the Netherlands Institute for Human Rights, staff attorney at the Inter-American Court of Human Rights, consultant to UNHCR and to the Norwegian Refugee Council in Colombia. She has worked with numerous NGOs, notably as a member of the Steering Committee of the NGO Coalition for an Optional Protocol to the ICESCR. Magdalena has written extensively on ESCR and published a major work in the field entitled *The Nature of the Obligations under the International Covenant on Economic, Social and Cultural Rights.*

Alan Simmons is a solicitor and holds an LL.M. in International Human Rights Law from the University of Essex. He is experienced in taking cases to the European Commission and Court of Human

Rights and has given lectures on the European Convention on Human Rights in Central and Eastern Europe for the Council of Europe and the Raoul Wallenberg Institute.

Geraldine Van Bueren, a barrister, is Professor of International Human Rights Law at Queen Mary, University of London and Visiting Fellow, Kellogg College, Oxford. She was awarded the UNICEF Child Rights Lawyer Award honouring outstanding work in the field of children's rights. She is one of the original drafters of the UN Convention on the Rights of the Child and helped draft the United Nations Rules for the Protection of Juveniles Deprived of their Liberty, the UNHCR Guidelines on Refugee Children and the United Nations Programme of Action on Children in the Criminal Justice System. Professor Van Bueren's writings have been cited in courts around the world including in the House of Lords, the Constitutional Court of South Africa and the European Court of Human Rights. She is currently working on a project for UNESCO on how law can be used constructively to help combat poverty.

Philippa Watson is a barrister practising from Essex Court Chambers, London. She specialises in EU law, making regular appearances before the European Court of Justice in Luxembourg and the superior courts of England and Ireland. Additionally she advises large undertakings, governments and international organizations. She has written extensively on a number of aspects of EU, including social and employment law. Her latest work *Social and Employment Law and Policy in an Enlarged Europe* will be published by Oxford University Press in 2008. She holds a Visiting Chair at City Law School London.

Table of Authorities

Index

For EU product safety concerns, contact us at Calle de José Abascal, 56–1°, 28003 Madrid, Spain or eugpsr@cambridge.org.

www.ingramcontent.com/pod-product-compliance
Ingram Content Group UK Ltd.
Pitfield, Milton Keynes, MK11 3LW, UK
UKHW030658060825
461487UK00010B/923